S0-BNY-366

FORM AND SUBSTANCE

AN ADVANCED RHETORIC

RICHARD M. COE
Simon Fraser University

JOHN WILEY & SONS
New York Chichester Brisbane Toronto

To

Samuel Coe,
my first and most important writing teacher,

Kenneth Burke,
the great North American rhetorical theorist,

and all the writing students
in interaction with whom
I have learned
whatever I know about teaching writing.

Library of Congress Cataloging in Publication Data:

Coe, Richard M.
Form and substance, an advanced rhetoric.

Includes index.
1. English language—Rhetoric. I. title.
PE1408. C5425 808'.042 81-630
ISBN 0-471-04585-3 AACR2

Printed in the United States of America

10 9 8 7 6 5 4 3 2 1

HOW TO USE THIS BOOK

This study is theoretical only that it may become practical.
I. A. Richards

What makes for successful writing cannot be summed up in two dozen simple rules, or divided into twenty lessons.
Hans Guth

PRESUMPTIONS

This is a presumptuous book. It is designed to challenge you. In my teaching, I have found that the less I expect of students, the less they learn. So I teach to the *highest* common denominator. Teaching—or learning—to the lowest common denominator is defeatist; it runs contrary to that essential faith in the ability of human beings to learn and understand which is the cornerstone of humanism. It also runs against my stubborn streak.

This is a highly practical book. It will help you develop your confidence and general ability as a writer. It will also help you learn to produce whatever special types of writing you may want or need to produce. As many experts—from Dionysius of Halicarnassus to Hans Guth of California—have insisted, however, the ability to write well cannot be reduced to a short list of simple rules, lessons, or "sub-skills." Writing is a creative, communicative process. To write with any degree of sophistication, you must do more than mechanically follow rules and formulas. There are short cuts. There are formulas that allow people to perform particular writing tasks without thinking much. But, as Kenneth Burke wisely says, the trouble with short cuts is that they prevent you from taking the long way round. And the long way round is often the better way.

This is an *advanced* textbook, even though some instructors may find it appropriate for less than advanced students. It does not start from scratch. It does not assume that you know nothing. On the contrary, it presumes that, although you probably still make some mechanical errors, you already know most of the so-called "basics." It presumes that you can write more or less clear, correct sentences and coherent paragraphs most of the time. It presumes that you can already write 500-word essays well enough to pass an ordinary first-year college English course. It also assumes you have moderately competent, college-level reading and thinking abilities. This is not a simplified or remedial presentation.

Because it makes these assumptions and does not start from scratch, *Form and Substance* can go beyond ordinary college composition textbooks. Because it assumes that you can handle, at least minimally, the immediate demands placed on your writing, it can take the time to go the long way round and thus to get to the real basics—the basic principles of good writing. Because it assumes that you start with some degree of competence, it can move from simple to more sophisticated forms and techniques, which ordinary composition textbooks never reach.

This book is both "state of the art" and traditional. It is based on the most recent composition theory and research (e.g., Professor Nancy Sommers' investigations of revision processes). But, since it makes no sense to ignore centuries of accumulated study and insight, this book is based also on two venerable, intertwined traditions: humanism and rhetoric. *Form and Substance* does *not* formally discuss the theory of composition, rhetoric or humanism, although it does make reference to them where useful. It is, however, based on a distillation of all we know about effective verbal communication. And it does insist, for pedagogically sound reasons, on treating writing as a humanistic discipline, not as a technical skill. Since the relationship among humanism, rhetoric, and the development of writing abilities has not always been clear, and since that relationship has a great deal to do with the nature of this book, I will summarize it briefly here. Those readers who want to get on to practicalities may skip the next five paragraphs.

The tradition of humanistic education stretches back to the humanism of the fourteenth-century European renaissance, and beyond that to the *paideia* of classical Greece. Rhetorical theory began among the ancient Greeks and became the core of classical "higher education," the center of the liberal arts. What the Romans called *humanitas*, what the Greeks called *paideia*, were the classical equivalents of a liberal arts education. That meant—and means—the education of the whole person, not just the professional training of a specialist (although it may include that).

Historically, humanism was a revolt against both intellectual and political authoritarianism. It was founded on the belief that people both can and should understand the world and control their own lives. Thus, in the context of its own time, it was an exaltation of human freedom and an assertion of confidence in human abilities. That confidence was the beginning of modern science, but it was also more than that.

The humanists of the European renaissance looked back, past the narrow interpretations of medieval scholastics, to the classical culture of Greece and Rome. Like those who study anthropology in our time, they came to appreciate how different peoples in different contexts develop distinctive modes of perception and distant insights. Thus they discovered the basis of intellectual tolerance and empathy.

Rhetoric, too, was founded on a faith in human freedom and abilities. Rhetorical study arose in classical Greece—and nowhere else in the entire ancient world—*because* political democracy and a legal system based on advocacy made formal speaking abilities important. Given the diversity of ancient Greece, the practical experiences of speaking to particular audiences in particular contexts made rhetoricians intensely aware that not all people are the same or have the same responses.

Rhetoric became the core of advanced education because it was the means by which Greek students could develop and demonstrate their understanding. Writing and speaking remain central to humanistic education today for the same reason: it is only by actively using concepts you have studied that you make those concepts your own. Writing a term paper is a way of exercising your mind, a way of developing the ability to use—not just to regurgitate—what you have learned.

Not only is writing crucial to any modern humanistic education, but a humanistic approach to writing is crucial to the full and proper development of writing abilities. The most basic pedagogical principle of humanism is that students should rely primarily on their own intellectual powers, and only secondarily on authority. This coincides with the well-established educational principle that active learning is far more effective than passive learning: the human mind is neither a blank slate to be written on nor a container to be filled; the human mind is an active intelligence that develops when engaged. Any approach that pretends to be humanistic and effective should give students that knowledge of basic principles which allows them to make their own critical decisions, to depend on themselves even while accepting guidance from their instructors. That is why this book occasionally takes the long way round: to establish the basic principles of composition from which particular rules can be intelligently derived.

This book is designed to help you formulate—and reformulate—questions as you read, to help you decide specifically what you want to learn, and to help you set your own goals. Approach this text looking for questions and answers, for ways to achieve what you want to achieve, and you will learn much more than if you sit back and wait to be told what to do. Use this book; do not let it use you.

STRUCTURE AND ORDER

Form and Substance contains more than any one writer needs, certainly more than can be covered in one university course. To use this book efficiently, you will have to make choices.

Not all writers—or teachers of writing—work the same way. Although we *can* make generalizations about how to write effectively, different techniques and approaches will work best for different, individuals and types of writing. Chapter 1, for example, presents six techniques for getting a piece of writing started. Which is best depends in part on your personality, in part on the nature of the particular writing task. What you must do is to select. Read about all six techniques, experiment with several, adapt them, and choose one or two that meet your needs. Do not feel compelled to master all six.

This book moves up and down levels of generality, from basic principles to practical hints. Some sections are more difficult than others. Remember that you do not need to understand everything easily on first reading. Read through the difficult sections. Go on to the practical applications. Then look or think back to see if the more general discussions or difficult citations make sense.

Chapter 0. This book begins with a Chapter 0, so numbered because it is preliminary to the rest of the book and also optional. Few other writing textbooks contain the equivalent of this chapter. It is not about writing, but about learning to write. It is an introduction, designed to help you use the rest of this book more effectively and to adapt this textbook to your particular purposes. If you are using this book on your own, outside of an instructed course, I strongly recommend that you begin with this chapter. But instructors and students who wish to skip over Chapter 0 will find the book complete without it.*

The process approach. Within the rhetorical tradition, there are basically two ways to develop writing abilities. *Form and Substance* uses both. Part One takes a process approach. In Chapter 1, the emphasis is on writing as a creative process. The focus is on how writers discover and shape meanings. In Chapter 2, the emphasis is on writing as a communicative process. The focus is on how writers consider and are responsive to their readers. In Chapter 3, the emphasis is on style. The focus is on how writers use style to create voice and *persona*.

The formal approach. Part Two approaches writing through the study of forms and models, which students can practice and imitate. Chapters 4 and 5 discuss basic forms, one or more of which underlie virtually any piece of writing. Chapter 4 covers description, comparison/contrast, classification and division, definition, analogy and exemplification. Chapter 5 covers narration, process-analysis, and causal explanation. The discussion of these forms is more thorough, and builds to much more sophisticated applications, than similar discussions in other textbooks. Chapter 6 focuses on persuasion, with treatment of logical argumentation, classical and Rogerian persuasion, and constructive criticism. Chapter 7 emphasizes certain special forms likely to be useful to advanced students and professionals: term papers, literary criticism, proposals, letters, and résumés. Perhaps more

*Instructors who do wish to use this chapter may find it helpful to read an article, "Using Problem-Solving and Process-Analysis to Help Students Solve Writing Problems," coauthored by Kris Gutierrez and myself, published in 1981 *College Composition and Communications*. They may also find useful Ellen Nold's, as yet only self-published, *Managing Writing* and Mary Beavin's 'Individualized Goal Setting, Self-Evaluation, and Peer Evaluation,' in Charles Cooper and Lee Odell, eds., *Evaluating Writing* (Urbana, Ill.: NCTE, 1977).

importantly, it presents a heuristic and a model that you can use to teach yourself how to do *any* specialized type of writing. The book ends with a brief discussion of publication because the act of writing is ultimately incomplete unless it reaches readers.

Order of presentation. This book is designed to allow flexibility to instructors and students. There is a clear logic to the order in which material is presented, but other orders are possible. Just as you can decide which sections are most pertinent to you or your students, so you can choose an order of presentation that supports your emphases.

One could go through the book as written. One would begin with Chapter 0, using it to define problems and set goals. One would follow the process approach through Part One, using the various concepts and techniques presented in those chapters to intervene in students' writing processes and resolve problems. The movement from Chapter 1 through Chapter 3 creates an increasingly sophisticated sense of process. Having resolved students' most basic problems, one would then turn to the study and imitation of forms in Part Two, using those models to encourage increasingly complex and sophisticated writings. One could use *Form and Substance* in this order with or without Chapter 0. Parts One and Two could even be used separately in two consecutive courses. Alternatively, one could use Chapter 0 to define goals and then move to whatever sections of the text deal most directly with the particular problems of your group of student writers.

Many other orders are possible. I, myself, when teaching this material, begin with description and narration (the first two sections of Chapter 4 and the first section of Chapter 5). I begin there because description and narration are what my students do best, and I want to start from their strengths. For a writing assignment, I usually allow students to choose between Exercise 1 and Exercise 2 at the end of the section on description. Once they have done this writing, I move back to Chapter 0 to help them analyze that writing experience and define their own strengths and weaknesses as writers. We then work through Chapter 0. But working through Chapter 0 means considering one's own writing process, doing a process-analysis, and writing a proposal. So we look ahead to the first section of Chapter 1 (on the creative process and time management), the second section of Chapter 5 (on process-analysis), and the fourth section of Chapter 7 (on proposal writing).

Once students have defined their weaknesses and set their goals, we move on to Part One, treating writing as a creative, cognitive, expressive, and communicative process. For assignments, however, I turn to Part Two, asking students to practice one major form from Chapter 4 (usually definition), Chapter 5 (usually causal explanation), and Chapter 6 (usually Rogerian persuasion). Finally, we move to Chapter 7, where students focus on whatever special forms are important to themselves. Usually each student writes a "mini-manual" on how to do that particular type of writing. Sometimes several students with similar interests work together. Either way, they not only learn how to do a particular type of writing, but they also learn how to learn. Since most of my students will never receive any more formal writing instruction, I think this last achievement is especially important.

That order works very well, for my students and myself. But I can easily imagine other students and other instructors using very different orders. With students who are under immediate pressure to do university writing assignments, for instance, one might start with the second section of Chapter 7. Having started with something so specific, one would then move back to more general forms and processes as they became pertinent.

Other texts. In recent years, writing has typically been taught by using the following:

a dictionary (and perhaps a thesaurus),
a handbook of grammar and usage,
a rhetoric (i.e., a book like this one), and
an anthology of readings.

This textbook does assume that you have a dictionary and a handbook, probably left over from a previous writing course. The function of the dictionary is to help you choose, use and spell words accurately. If you are at a level to be using this textbook, you will want a fairly good dictionary, not a little paperback. A thesaurus, used carefully and *in conjunction with a good dictionary*, can also help you find the words you need to represent your meanings accurately and precisely. You will want a handbook to look up those proprieties of usage, grammar, and punctuation about which you may not be certain. The principles behind such proprieties and certain exemplary rules are discussed in this textbook (especially in Chapter 2), but *Form and Substance* is a rhetoric and does not contain a complete handbook.

Form and Substance can be used either with or without an anthology of readings. The function of such a reader is twofold: to provide models of good writing, which you can analyze and imitate, and to provide intellectual stimuli, which can help get you started on your own writing. There are many writing samples in this textbook, most of them by writers who are probably at approximately your own level of ability. Together with pieces of writing produced in your own class or workshop, these can provide models of good, adequate, and poor writing. There are also, integrated into the text, what I call "mini-essays" on subjects related to writing. These—together with the writing samples, other courses you may be taking, and your life experiences—can provide the stimuli to get you writing. *Form and Substance* is substantial enough to be used without a reader. On the other hand, I myself have occasionally used a reader when teaching this material.

SPECIAL FEATURES

Student writing. This textbook contains many writing samples. Some are short pieces by published writers. Most were written by the students who took my two most recent advanced composition courses. These writings are reproduced here essentially as the students handed them in for grading. Aside from the regularization of spelling and, sometimes, punctuation, they have not been specially revised or cleaned up. They have their strong points and their weak points. None of them is perfect, although each does illustrate something effective. Some are quite impressive; others are less so. You should read and imitate them critically. How are they effective? How could they be improved? Before doing a particular type of writing yourself, read the samples. Discuss them. Develop a sense of how that particular type of writing works. Try to list the qualities of a good piece of writing of that type. Thus you will get a clearer sense of what you are trying to do and of what pitfalls you are trying to avoid.

Headnote quotations. There are quotations from writers and rhetoricians at the head of each chapter and section, as well as occasionally within the text. There are also reproductions of manuscript pages from famous writers. Some of the quotations are difficult, more difficult than the material in the chapter or section that follows. You may not understand them on first reading. Do not worry about that. After you read the chapter or section, however, you should go back to them. Ask yourself what they mean, how they relate to the material below them, how they can help you understand what writers do. Look at the reproductions of manuscript pages and read the quotations from writers about how they work to learn whatever you can about the creative process that produces successful writing.

Mini-essays. There is a specific information about writing and related matters that writers should know. This information is not absolutely necessary; people have assuredly written successfully without it. But it will help you understand what you are doing, and thus it will enable you to think about and resolve problems that may arise. There are sections and subsections of this textbook that discuss subjects like creativity, the psychology of reading, how people perceive and conceive, constructive criticism, approaches to literature, and so forth. If you are eager to get immediately to the practical applications, you can skip over these sections—but I believe you will be a better writer sooner if you digest this information. It is important background to understanding what you are doing as a writer, and it also raises basic intellectual issues that can be subject matter for your own writings.

Cross-references. This book contains significant new material, as well as traditional material that may be unfamiliar. Since you may not be reading the entire book or may not be reading it in order, you may run into concepts or terms that are unfamiliar even though they have been explained elsewhere in the text. Consequently, I have included many cross-references to help you find the pages where these concepts and terms are discussed. There is also an index, which serves a similar function. If you understand the passage you are reading, you can ignore the cross-references and get on with your reading.

Additional reading. For most readers, *Form and Substance* will contain more than enough information on almost all the subjects it discusses. Nonetheless, I have listed additional reading at the end of most sections. My main motive for doing so is to make a point: this is an informed textbook, based not just on my own expertise and experience, but also on the cumulative insights of a community of scholars, teachers, theorists, and researchers. The lists of additional reading connect this book with its intellectual basis. My more practical motive, of course, is that you probably will occasionally want to find out more about some concept or technique that is particularly important to you—be that by reading more about human creativity or skimming a book on how to conduct an effective interview.

Exercise. Having assignments and exercises at the ends of sections of a textbook is certainly not unusual. I have titled them "Exercise" to revitalize a dead metaphor and remind you of their function: they are there to help you exercise your mind and develop your ability to use what you have learned from reading that section. Some of them are quite the ordinary sort of exercise that you will find in most composition textbooks. Some of them are different, as befits an advanced textbook. Many ask you to investigate something about writing, to find something out for yourself instead of taking my word for it. Many ask you to investigate how a general principle applies to some particular type of writing that is of special interest to you. This last set of exercises, which begins in Chapter 1, leads up to the section on specialized writing in Chapter 7.

Chapter introductions. People read more efficiently and with better comprehension if they can anticipate, at least in a general way, what they will be reading. Consequently, each chapter is preceded by an introduction. That introduction both tells you what the chapter will discuss and suggests how you should approach it. It indicates both what you should know and what you should be able to do by the time you have finished working through that chapter. Reading these introductions will help you use these chapters more effectively.

RULES AND PRINCIPLES

Would-be writers often want a set of simple, hard-and-fast rules for good writing. Such rules can be useful, especially if taken with a grain or two of salt. But such rules also have their dangers, and their place in any humanistic education must be clearly delimited. Rules are useful shorthand so long as the people applying them understand the principles on which they are based.

You may, for example, have been given this rule: "Every paragraph should begin with a topic sentence," that is, with a sentence that states the main point of the paragraph. To what extent is this rule valid? Do good writers generally begin paragraphs with topic sentences? What is the principle behind the rule?

According to one study of essays published in the "better" magazines—for example, *Harper's, The Atlantic Monthly*—13% of paragraphs begin with topic sentences. Actually, the percentage seems to vary considerably from one type of writing to another. Some paragraphs begin with topic sentences, some have topic sentences in the middle or at the end, and many have no topic sentence at all.

Does this mean that the rule should be discarded, that we should forget about topic sentences? No, it means that we should be clear about the principle behind the rule. Then we will know when to honor the rule.

In this case, the underlying principle is that a paragraph should be focused, and that focus is usually built around a main point or controlling idea. The easiest way to be certain that each of your paragraphs has such a main point is to state it in your first sentence.

And why should a paragraph have this kind of focus? Because it helps readers to get the point. Just as each chapter in this book begins with an introduction that helps you to read by helping you anticipate what will be in that chapter, so a topic sentence can help your readers. A paragraph that begins with a topic sentence is the easiest kind of paragraph to read—which is why such paragraphs predominate in elementary textbooks and scientific reports.

So if you have trouble keeping your paragraphs focused or if you are writing for readers likely to have trouble grasping your points, then the rule about beginning paragraphs with topic sentences, probably is for you. But it is also important that you understand the principle underlying the rule so that you can make intelligent decisions about when and how to obey it. Knowing the principle behind the rule is the difference between being educated and being just "trained," the difference between being able to make decisions yourself and having to depend on "experts" to make decisions for you.

The point is that rules can be useful, but they should not be learned dogmatically—should not be memorized and obeyed without being understood—not even if they are only the rules of conventional punctuation.

As I wrote some years ago in an extended essay called "Rhetoric 2001,"

> *The survival of Homo sapiens has always been based on superior adaptability, on the ability to distinguish different contexts and choose the appropriate behavior. Having no fur, we choose clothing appropriate to various contexts; thus we can live everywhere from the tropics to the arctic. There are absolutes (e.g., the high value attached to survival), but those absolutes take various forms relative to various contexts or environments. For an inland Inuit (i.e., Eskimo) survival means a diet that is at least 25% fat; that same diet could mean heart attack to a professor in California.*
>
> *This principle applies equally to the biological ecosystem and to the ecosystem of ideas. The Boy Scout who twenty years ago memorized the rule that one should always bury cans and other nonburnable garbage has had the environmental context shift out from under him. Most North American backpacking areas are so crowded these days that people would be burying cans faster than the earth could decompose them. Although the higher-level value of preserving for other hikers an undamaged natural environment has remained the same, the specific rule has now been inverted—now a good Scout carries out her or his unburnable garbage. What this example illustrates is the tendency to memorize low-level rules instead of understanding higher-level principles. This tendency leads to inappropriate behavior when the context shifts.*

In other words, principles must be general and flexible enough to be broadly applicable—otherwise they are not properly called principles. Although the principle remains the same, its application varies somewhat from context to context, so it takes a certain intelligence and experience to use a principle correctly. Rules, by contrast, are more particular and rigid, but they are appropriately applied only in certain limited contexts. ("Honesty is the best policy" is a principle because the word *honesty* is abstract enough to take on somewhat different implications in different contexts; "Always tell the truth, the whole truth, and nothing but the truth" is a rule—and one that will get you into a lot of trouble in certain contexts.) A fully explicit statement of a principle stipulates how it will vary with changing contexts. A fully explicit statement of a rule indicates the limited set of contexts to which it applies.

This distinction between rules and principles is heady stuff, the sort educational philosophies are made of. (*Rule:* "Never end a sentence with a preposition."*) What should matter to students of writing is the realization that any rule is a particular application of some more general principle. This remains true even if the underlying principle is not known to the person using the rule. Genuine mastery of the craft of writing—or any other craft—requires an understanding of principles, not memorization of rules alone. Humanism, moreover, is founded on the egalitarian belief that people should understand the principles behind what they do, even if they can acquire enough skill to satisfy their employers without that knowledge. Both from a practical and from a humanistic point of view, therefore, it is important that you use this book in such a way as to grasp the basic principles of composition. That will make you a better writer—and, probably, a better person. It will take a bit more work, but the results will be worth the effort.

ACKNOWLEDGEMENTS

I wish not only to thank those people without whom this book would be less than it is, but also to make an assertion about the nature of the knowledge I am thus acknowledging. I take full responsibility for this text; the errors, as the saying goes, are mine. But knowledge is not individual: insofar as I stand high that is not, to paraphrase Isaac Newton, because my legs are long; the credit belongs to those whose shoulders support my feet—those who established the basis from which I started, those who taught me, and those who cared enough to criticize

**Response:* "That is something up with which I will not put"—Winston Churchill.

me and my work. The knowledge represented in this textbook is a synthesis of many people's work and insights, as is all knowledge. Along just one tradition, the knowledge presented here can be traced back more than two millennia to Corax of Syracuse, Gorgias of Leotini, and, especially, to Isocrates.

I owe great thanks to a community of dedicated teachers, researchers, and scholars who are drawn together by the Conference on College Composition and Communication (and, more recently, by the Association of Teachers of Advanced Composition). The list of those to whom I and most immediately indebted resembles a directory or those active in the CCCC. But some people must be singled out. First among them is Edward P. J. Corbett, a gentleman in the full Chaucerian sense of *gentilesse*, whose suggestion was the seed out of which this book grew, and who waded throught the entire manuscript twice while it was taking form. Many other friends, colleagues, and strangers—some of whom remain anonymous—read the manuscript. Among those whose encouragement and criticism was most useful are Ann Berthoff, Ed White, Lil Brandon, Lee Odell, Kris Gutierrez, Wally Douglas, Dori Wagner, Andrea Lunsford, Ellen Nold, Doug Buttruff, Nancy Sommers, and Keltie McCall. Less direct, but not less important support came from Dave Bartholomae, Frank D'Angelo, Lou Kelly, Erika Lindemann, Richard Larson, and Susan Miller. Special thanks go to Diana Zacharia Worby and Anthony Wilden, who not only criticized the manuscript generally but also saved me from certain sexist errors.

Another set of thanks must go to the composition faculty at Central Michigan University, who created in the early 1970s what was probably the most advanced composition/rhetoric program in North America—among them Dean Memering, Ray Kytle, Regina Hoover, Bob Kline, Dave Hay, Jim Howell, and Dave Higgins. Together with others in Mount Pleasant, Michigan—notably Norm Rasulas, Alice Littlefield, Ron Williams, and Sharon Dowe—they formed a community in which I mastered the craft of teaching writing.

Equally important in a similar respect is another community, in San Diego, California, which did most to educate me, which provided criticism, love, and sometimes even a sense of belonging to an intellectual communality—most especially I would like to thank Carol Becker, Ran Mitra, Susan Orlofsky, Judy Rosenthal, Barry Shapiro, Evelyn Shapiro, Carla Wayne, Don Wayne, Mathilde Villas, and Peter Zelin.

I am also grateful to the following groups for copyright permissions: to the Association for the Study of Afro-American Life and History (and especially J. Rupert Picott) for Ossie Davis' words; to the Anti-Defamation League of B'nai B'rith for an image from the "Rumor Clinic"; to Viking-Penguin (and especially Shelley Slater) for facsimile manuscript pages from *Writers at Work*, copyright 1957, 1958, 1963, and 1967 by The Paris Review, Inc.; to the National Council of Teachers of English (and especially April Snyder and Marsha Castellon) for a chart from Janet Emig's *The Composing Processes of Twelfth Graders*, copyright 1971, reprinted by permission of the publisher and the author; to Oxford University Press for two paragraphs from Edward P. J. Corbett's *Classical Rhetoric* for the *Modern Student*; to McGraw-Hill for an image from R. L. Gregory's *The Intelligent Eye*; and to the University of Illinois press for a puzzle picture from the *American Journal of Psychology*.

This textbook could not have been written without the gracious permission of many writing students, most of whose names appear in the text beneath their writing, to reproduce their work. Virtually without exception, they can now write much better than these samples indicate, but they have allowed these reproductions so that other students might learn more easily. In the same vein I must thank those who, formally and informally, taught me to write: in addition to my father, Sandra Heit, Barbara Schwartzbaum, Irwin Stark, and Brewster Ghiselin, among many others.

For their confidence, creative support, and constructive criticism, I am grateful to many people at John Wiley & Sons, especially Tom Gay, Cliff Mills, and Joan Knizeski.

Reading back over this long list of names, and remembering also the many unnamed, I realize how fortunate I have been in my life, my education, and my work. These people have my gratitude, my love, and my apologies for not yet being more than I am.

There is another tradition that must be mentioned to bring this preface round full circle. This text is an affirmation that begins in a nay-saying. While recognizing that genuine teaching begins where the learners are and proceeds at their pace, I have tried in this book to say nay to all those who underestimate the potential of the human mind and spirit—and thus underestimate the power of people to learn and understand. Given enough time and care, any ordinary person can learn to write effectively in a full and humanistic way. The strength—and stubbornness—for this nay-saying and the affirmation it makes possible come from all those who were strong enough, often in more perilous contexts, to say, "No! This will not do. This is not enough for a human being"—among them my grandfather, Charles Diamond, and Rachel's grandfather, Zachy Zacharia. It is from them that I inherit whatever it takes to write a presumptuous book.

Vancouver, British Columbia
Thanksgiving Day *1980*

CONTENTS

FORM AND SUBSTANCE

Matter × *Form* ⟶ ***Substance***
(Aristotle)

For the rules in textbooks of rhetoric cannot by themselves make expert those who are eager to dispense with study and practice.

Dionysius of Halicarnassus

When we speak of improving the mind *we are usually referring to the acquisition of information or knowledge, or to the* type of *thoughts one* should *have and not to the actual* functioning *of the mind. We spend little time monitoring our own thinking and comparing it with a more sophisticated ideal.*

James L. Adams

True, just, and well-ordered discourse is the outward image of a good and faithful soul.

Isocrates

Of all those arts in which the wise excel,
Nature's chief masterpiece is writing well.

John Sheffield

CHAPTER 0

LEARNING TO WRITE

This is called Chapter 0 because it is not so much about writing as about *learning to write*. People learn better when they participate actively in their own learning processes, when they set their own goals and help monitor their own progress. People also learn better when they have specific strategies for achieving those goals instead of vague intentions like, "I want to learn to write better."

This chapter is designed to help you assess your present writing abilities and to define the tasks before you as a writing student. It should provide both a platform from which you can grow and a basis for evaluating that growth later. By the time you have worked your way through this chapter, you will have

(a) Analyzed your own writing process.
(b) Identified your own strengths and weaknesses as a writer.
(c) Defined your writing problems and established an order of priority for dealing with them.
(d) Determined the relationship between your writing process and writing problems.
(e) Set writing goals and devised plans for achieving those goals.

Because learning begins with motivation, this chapter begins with a discussion of motives—both practical and humanistic. Briefly, but seriously, it attempts to convince you that you should develop not only your writing abilities but also your understanding of writing, that you have much to gain by treating writing not as a technical skill but as a humanistic discipline. Next, comes a section called "How People Write"—because the best way to improve the quality of your written products is to improve the *process* which produces them. The last section—"Setting Goals"—

should help you define problems and establish individual goals for yourself.

This chapter has two basic purposes. One is to help you focus your attention so that you can take maximum advantage of the rest of the book and learn what you as an individual most need to learn about writing. The other is to help you take control of your own learning processes. People who *learn how to learn* acquire a special kind of power and independence. This chapter should help you learn to write better now and also give you the ability to continue learning in the future.

WHY WRITE?

Put writing in your heart . . . . The scribe is released from manual tasks; it is he who commands.
Ancient Egyptian

Where there is much desire to learn, there of necessity will be much arguing, much writing, many opinions; for opinion in good men is but knowledge in the making.
John Milton

Lucidity . . . is unquestionably one of the surest tests of mental precision.
David Lloyd George

Learn your ABC's, it is not enough, but learn them! . . . begin! You must know everything! You must take over the leadership!
Bertolt Brecht

PRACTICAL MOTIVES

Writing matters. Writing began in ancient times as a way of keeping records—a kind of social memory—and soon developed into an important means of communication. In spite of computers, televisions, tape recorders, and various other new means of recording and communicating information, there is now more writing than ever. The ability to write is now more important to more people than ever in human history.

In a modern industrial society, the ability to write with some degree of competence is one of the qualities that generally distinguishes professionals from other workers. To get a professional job, you usually must write—if only an application letter and a résumé. To do the job, you ordinarily must write: records, reports, proposals, recommendations, instructions, memoranda, and letters of various sorts. And, of course, you usually have to write in university classes just to qualify for a professional job.

The technology of writing is changing. Word processors are beginning to replace typewriters. Inexpensive photocopying and computer storage have changed our relationship to the written word. For all the changes, however, technological advances have made writing more common and more important than ever.

This importance follows from the nature of our society. In a modern, specialized, computer-based, industrial society like ours, the division of labor is complex and hierarchial. The people who make important decisions are often far from the decision points: their awareness of options and consequences usually depends on written reports and on recommendations from specialists and experts. To make their decisions known and to get them implemented, moreover, the decision makers usually depend on written instructions and guidelines. In a complex and centralized society, this kind of information flow is necessarily crucial.

Much of this information is communicated in writing because writing has certain advantages over other means of communication. Unlike a conversation, writing is easily preserved. Unlike a recording, writing is easily edited and updated. Since writing is so important, a person who can write effectively gains a significant degree of power and respect.

The power of the written word extends to arenas beyond your job. As a consumer in an economy where manufacturers, suppliers, and even sources of credit may be hundreds or thousands of miles away from users, your ability to write an effective letter of complaint may be crucial to your getting what you paid for—or even a response. A letter to the editor, a local union leaflet, a grant proposal for a community project—there are many uses to which you can put your ability to write. As a citizen in a large democratic society, your ability to write persuasively can make the difference between your opinion having some impact or having none at all.

HUMANISTIC MOTIVES

Beyond these practical applications, writing also has personal and humanistic virtues. To write cogently, you must think cogently. To write effectively, you must understand people—both your readers and yourself. Learning to write well is, therefore, part and parcel of developing your most human potentials, both rational and intuitive.

Writing is a discovery process as well as a communicative process. The act of writing usually forces you to explore, clarify, and sharpen your ideas. Often you must verify information and resolve contradictions. You must also organize ideas and perceive interrelationships. By the time you have your thoughts down on paper and revised, you usually have emerged with a deeper understanding. That is why term papers and essay tests are such important parts of a university education. That is why keeping a diary or journal can help you understand your own life.

Academically, personally, and in many other ways writing promotes insight.

To write effectively, moreover, you need a sense of audience. The ability to write is the ability to communicate with readers. Since not all readers are alike, the same message may have to be written somewhat differently for distinct groups of readers. To write effectively for readers who are not like yourself, you need to develop the sensitivity and empathy that will allow you to understand them.

To write honestly, you must also understand yourself. The tone of your writing, like the tone of your speaking voice, inevitably projects an image of who you are. To make this tone accurately and honestly reflect your motives and personality, you must have some sense of yourself.

Thus learning to write well means developing insights into your subject matter, your readers, and yourself. That is why writing is such a crucial part of a humanistic education.

You can achieve minimal competency at some particular, specialized type of writing—such as business writing, technical report writing, or news reporting—by just memorizing rules, practicing techniques, and following formulas. But the ability to write perceptively, thoughtfully, critically, and sensitively is more than a technical skill. To develop your ability to write excellently in any area, or to write even competently as a generalist, you must also develop your understanding.

At its highest development, writing is the creation and communication of insight. When Percy Bysshe Shelley wrote, "poets are the unacknowledged legislators of the world," he was asserting the creative power of writing to shape the perceptions—and hence to influence the behavior—of readers as well as writers. This is the ultimate power of writing. Here the practical and humanistic reasons for learning to write well merge.

HOW PEOPLE WRITE

[O]ne must understand . . . the process of writing in order to conceive of a basis from which to intervene in the process. . . . [O]ne must have a conception of the process in which he is intervening.

Ellen Nold

The great use of studying our predecessors is to open *the mind.*

Joshua Reynolds

PROCESS AND PRODUCT

The best way to improve the quality of your writing is to improve the process by which you create it. To be sure, the writing process is a means to an end: once the process of creation is completed, it is the written text that must communicate. Whether the goal is to evoke a feeling or to provoke a bureaucracy into taking action, it is the written text that must get the job done. It is the written text that will be praised and blamed, criticized and rewarded. But the quality of the written product depends on the quality of the creative process. A person who is having trouble writing or who wants to learn to write better should focus on the writing process.

Writing, unlike mechanistic processes, cannot be reduced to a standard procedure. That is why we say *writing is a craft*. Like any craft, it has a basis in technique. But it is also more than just a set of technical skills—although we may sometimes focus on those skills because they are the most teachable and measureable aspects of writing.

On the other hand, writing is ordinarily something less than a full-fledged art. There are, of course, certain genres of writing that may fairly be called arts (e.g., poetry), and people commonly call anything art if it is extraordinarily well done. But, unlike true arts, most types of writing can be mastered by most anyone who is willing to put in the necessary apprenticeship. We do not know how to teach anyone to write as well as Shakespeare, or even Hemingway; but most people can become competent writers.

To say that in writing, unlike in manufacturing, there is no rigid standard procedure is not an invitation to anarchy. Human creativity has been well-studied in both ancient and recent times, by both scientists and practitioners—and writing, of any type, is a creative process. The writing process itself has also been much studied—recently with considerable rigor.

We can make certain useful generalizations about the kinds of cognitive acts that are usually necessary to successful writing and about the kinds of procedures that usually work. We cannot prescribe exactly how or in what order they must take place, but we can make useful generalizations.

Many would-be writers want formulas. There are textbooks that offer such formulas. Standard writing procedure, according to most traditional textbooks, is a follows: find (or be assigned) a topic; narrow and focus the topic; collect information and arguments; formulate a thesis statement; make a sentence outline; write a rough draft from the outline; revise for clarity, coherence, and correctness; recopy and proofread. This is not a bad procedure—for certain writers and certain types of writing. It seems to be particularly suitable for writing research reports, theses, and dissertations.

Consider, for example, the outline. Students have often objected to it or found ways around it. When required to hand in an outline, many students write the paper first and make the outline second. Even among academic writers, our research indicates that it is only a minority who actually write out more than a rough list of potential topics before starting their drafts. Professor Janet Emig's classic study of student writers indicated that only a minority use even informal outlines (see table below). Those students in her study who did use outlines, incidentally, did not get better grades (nor, it must be added did they get worse grades).

TABLE 0.1 **Types of Outlines Accompanying 109 Expository Themes Written by 25 Eleventh Grade Students**

THEME ASSIGNMENT	TOTAL NUMBER OF EXPOSITORY THEMES WRITTEN	TOTAL NUMBER OF OUTLINES	NUMBER OF INFORMAL OUTLINES	NUMBER OF FORMAL OUTLINES
1.	25	15	9	6
2.	14	6	6	0
3.	23	6	5	1
4.	22	4	3	1
5.	25	9	8	1
Total	109	40	31	9

The point here is not about outlines, which (as will be shown below) have a number of potential uses beyond those usually claimed. The point is about how real people write, and the first thing to remember is that *different people write differently*. Not only that, but the same writer may use distinct procedures for distinct types of writing. John Ciardi, for instance, uses outlines when he writes essays but not when he writes short stories. You can help your own writing process immensely by learning how other people write. But slavishly following a formula may actually interfere with successful writing.

Much of the guilt people feel about writing, moreover, is centered not on the written product itself, but on the writing process. ("I don't usually know what my thesis statement is until after I've written my draft. There must be something wrong with me.") As Professor Donald Murray insists, the writer, as artisan, ultimately asks only one question: Does it work? You should do what works best for you.

CASE HISTORIES

ASSIGNMENT: *Think of something you wrote recently. Narrate everything you did from the time you first got started on the topic (or received the assignment) to the time the written product was complete and ready for its readers. As you narrate (or if that does not work, after you narrate), explain how this particular writing was typical or atypical of the way you usually write.*

Be careful: many people have a tendency to idealize the way they usually write and to think their processes are closer to the "standard" textbook procedure than it actually is. Note: what you are doing here is a process analysis—a form of which is discussed in Chapter 5—using the narrative as exemplification.

After you have done this assignment—or if you do not do it, after you have thought about how you write—it may be useful to compare writing processes with other writers who are more or less your peers.

Here are two advanced composition students' analyses of their own writing processes. Although they started the course as relatively good writers, both lacked confidence in their writing abilities and felt guilty about the difficulties they had getting started.

PICKING MY OWN BRAIN: THE MASOCHISM OF WRITING

The writing process for me nearly always includes pressures that I create. I seldom begin assignments well ahead of time and have broken this pattern only in rare instances. I am also a formula writer, using as a guide what I can recall of my somewhat patchy high school composition courses. My procedure in writing the first assignment in English 304 this term was typical of my approach.

The day before the assignment was due, I had nothing but free time; however, true-to-form, I filled up the available hours with finding things to do around the house. That afternoon I decided to try using my daily meditation as a source of inspiration. This worked well, I thought, and having observed the scenarios that my subconscious unfolded before my inner eye, I settled upon a topic—"The English Class." Thereafter I discussed my choice with my husband and finally at 5:30 in the afternoon I sat down to write.

Once I have a vague idea of what I want to express in an essay, I jot down a rough outline. Usually I do not have an ending in mind. My outlines are little more than lists of words, each word or couple of words representing the main point in a paragraph. The word order corresponds to the order I intend to follow in arranging my paragraphs. Beginning with the first line on the list, I start work on the introductory paragraph. I may get as far as writing one or two sentences and then the revision begins. The rest of the exercise continues in similar fashion—I write, revising as I go, until I'm satisfied with the result. As the crossed-out and scratched-over streaks thicken and begin to obscure my vision, I write out a corrected copy on a clean page. For as long as the fresh page and neat writing remain free of marks and arrows, they help to clarify the form of the composition. In writing "The English Class." I revised the opening paragraphs about half a dozen times and in doing so ended up with a very different viewpoint from the original. This in turn altered the direction of the rest of the essay.

Closing paragraphs are not one of my strong points. I tend to deal with them when I get there. Then, in accordance with my formula, I attempt to sum up. My closing paragraphs are usually too brief and consequently do not adequately cover the overall theme of the writing. My formula requires organizing paragraphs in a logical sequence and concluding with an appropriate summary. In the case of "The English Class," this meant going from a general description of a room and a group of people to a description of a specific individual and ending with my subjective opinion of the whole lot put together.

. . .

Vicki Workman

What follows is excerpted from a piece entitled, "Why I Cannot Write This Paper." (No less a writer than the journalist, Tom Wolfe, incidentally, testifies that such explanations can be good ways to get a difficult assignment started.)

The process by which I construct my essays may be divided into four main stages: a gathering stage, a kernel stage, a general overhaul stage and a fine tuning stage (pardon the mixed metaphor). The gathering stage is prior to any actual writing, aside from note-taking, and is mainly the period during which I gather thoughts and information pertinent to the general topic which my paper will be dealing with. I then organize the information within my mind and draw a conclusion which in turn becomes the central idea or theme of my essay.

Converting this central idea into a kernel sentence initiates the second stage of my writing process. I build my first draft about this kernel sentence, selectively incorporating the information gathered in stage one, i.e., quotes and paraphrased material. I then conclude the first draft with a summation of the general points of the essay.

During stage two I pay little or no attention to sentence structure, paragraph formation or transitions, and the organization is very loose; the overhaul of structural and stylistic defects is attempted in stages three and four. At stage three I try to structure my ideas according to a coherent pattern, which I have been formulating in my mind since stage one; this usually entails a degree of reorganization at every level from sentence structure through to whole sections. Also, it is at this stage that I reappraise the amount of information and expand or edit as deemed necessary.

Fine tuning is the fourth or final stage. In essence this stage is a continuation of stage three but on a more superficial level, my main concern being with the mechanical aspects of the paper, i.e., grammar and spelling.

Tom Longridge

The writing process logically begins with having or discovering something to say. That is what Vicki was doing as she found things to do around the house, meditated, and spoke with her husband. That is what Tom's gathering stage is about, whether he does it in the library or in his mind. That is what I did most of yesterday afternoon as I read over some students' writing process analyses, watered the garden, wandered around the porch talking to the puppies in Spanish, and finally drafted one page just before I had to stop writing and start cooking dinner.

Many writing students, quite correctly, conceive of their writing problems as starting here: "But I don't have anything to say about that topic," or even more basically, "What should I write about?" These students are right. Unless a piece of writing is just an exercise, no one is likely to care how well it is written if the substance is not interesting, useful, or otherwise valuable. The main distinction between these students and myself is that I have come to accept this difficulty getting started as an inevitable part of my writing process and no longer feel guilty about it. Instead, I allow time for it by starting well before my deadline. Like other experienced writers, I have also learned certain techniques for discovering what I am trying to say. (The first sections of Chapter 1 deal with these matters.)

But having something significant to say is not enough. The word *composition* comes from the Latin verb *componere*, "to put together." In a sense, the central aspect of writing is the literal composing, the "putting together," of a pattern of meaning. Much of the meaningfulness of a piece of writing (as of any conception or communication) comes from the way information is organized. Information is not really information until it has been put *in formation* or *in-formed*.

This is what Tom is doing during stages two and three. This is what Vicki is doing as she jots down a rough outline and works and reworks her opening paragraphs. Many writers find the beginning hardest to write because they use the beginning to structure the rest of the piece. Tom's "kernel sentence" (i.e., the first sentence of the excerpt) structures the whole writing. It is not just another sentence, so it is not surprising that it takes him a long time to come up with it.

Other writers find it easier not to worry about structure (or make an outline) until after a draft has been completed. Sometimes they do not write an opening paragraph until the rest of the draft is done. Not surprisingly, such writers usually have an easier time getting started. That is because they have postponed problems of organization. Often they make outlines after the draft is written.

The difference is largely a matter of timing. Either way, the shaping—the giving of form to substance—is a basic to any creative or communicative process, and especially to writing. The process of ordering exposes the gaps and imbalances in the material being presented (and thus contributes to the discovery of more substance). The need to supply readers with transitions forces the discovery of interrelationships.

Similarly, some writers worry about language and style right from the beginning. Like Vicki, they revise as they go. Other writers, like Tom, try to postpone such matters until questions of substance and structure have been settled.

There would seem to be—and, up to a point, is—a certain efficiency in dealing with substance first, structure second, and style third. But real people's composing processes rarely divide so neatly into lineal stages. Organization, or structure, often creates the basis for further discovery; likewise, Tom's "coherent pattern" has been taking form in his mind "since stage one." And the search for "the right word" is often an attempt to hone the idea represented by that word.

The common notion that we first collect information, second think about it, and third write it down is reductive and erroneous. To be sure, in the early phases "gathering" often predominates, but not to the exclusion of thinking or "wording." In intermediate phases, "thinking" or organizing tends to become primary. And "actual writing" may come later. But the tendency to separate thinking from writing is both misleading and inaccurate. The implication is that one thinks about a subject first and then, after one's thoughts are totally in order, "just" writes it out. Writing is then conceived as merely a matter of style and diction, reduced to little more than a technical skill.

Real writers rarely work that way. Tom, who is in this sense typical, is forming his thesis sentence between stages one and two; he is still developing and organizing information through his stage three. Rare, indeed, is the writer for whom composing sentences and paragraphs is not part of the process of forming and interrelating concepts. Most writers are playing with potential sentences, perhaps even revising syntax, during the earliest phases of composition. Trying to "think and *then* write" gets many would-be writers in trouble. In fact, it seems to contribute to writer's block (see pages 36-38). More typically, writers—from E. M. Forster to Erica Jong—assert that they do not know what they think until they read what they have written.

All writers have to deal with matters of substance, structure, and style; but the appropriate process for doing so varies considerably from individual to individual. For other case histories, see pages 287-288 and 294-295.

THE DEPARTMENTS OF CLASSICAL RHETORIC

One intriguing observation about the writing processes of real people is that they match the teachings of the classical rhetoricians more closely than they match the "standard" textbook procedure. In part this is because the classical rhetoricians were more flexible than most modern textbook writers. They recognized that different individuals and different circumstances called for different strategies.

In the rhetorical tradition which goes back to classical Greece, composition is conceived as beginning with the discovery or invention of arguments (Latin, *inventio*; Greek, *heuresis*), roughly equivalent to Tom's "gathering stage." In this "department," the rhetoricians taught their students techniques for discovering what to say (see pages 36-73, and especially pages 71-73).

The second department of classical rhetoric is concerned with the literal composing, the "putting together," of the invented "arguments" into an effective pattern (Latin, *dispositio*; Greek, *taxis*). This is roughly equivalent to what Tom does in stages two and three. Although they emphasized the importance of remaining flexible and adapting to particular audiences and occasions, in this department the classical rhetoricians taught particular formulas to help their students arrange their compositions (see especially pages 331-332).

The choosing and combining of words and phrases, correctly and with style—what most people think of as "actual writing"—is the third department of classical rhetoric (Latin, *elocutio*; Greek, *lexis* or *hermeneia* or *phrasis*). This is what Tom leaves mostly to his stage four. (see especially pages 148-198). It is here that the emphasis of many modern English composition classes and textbooks has fallen, especially on correctness.

Make no mistake: although it is sometimes overemphasized, this aspect of writing is important. A poorly chosen word may not convey the intended concept. Awkward syntax may confuse readers. "Bad grammar," moreover, conveys a significant message about the social background of the writer (which is why the upwardly mobile lower-middle class is typically most concerned about correctness).

It is unfortunate that an overemphasis on correctness has contributed to the belief that this is what writing is *all* about. But the reaction against that mis-emphasis should not lead us to disregard this aspect of writing. Style and correctness not only facilitate communication; they are also part of the message.

For the classical rhetoricians, who were primarily concerned with formal speech, not with writing or ordinary talking, there were two more aspects to the composing process: memory (Latin, *memoria*; Greek, *mnēmē*) and delivery (Latin, *pronuntiatio*; Greek, *hypokrisis*). The ancient rhetoricians did not say a great deal about either of these aspects. Memory, at least, does not have much importance in respect to writing because permanence is in the very nature of the medium.

Delivery as related to writing might well refer to such matters as format, neatness, and so forth. It is important that you use the proper format, achieve good penmanship or neat typing (including clean keys and a good ribbon), proofread carefully, and so forth. Several studies have demonstrated that such matters have a significant effect on grades in school writing. In one study, typewritten papers averaged a full letter grade higher than handwritten papers, and these matters make a similarly important impression in other writing situations. The classical rhetoricians did not consider the process complete until the message was successfully *delivered* to its audience. A lot more will be said about that in Chapter 2.

In this section, the main point has been about process and product. If you want to improve the quality of what you write, you should pay some attention to how you write. The process produces the product. Empirical research and theory, both ancient and modern, can help you examine and improve your own writing process. The next step will be to figure out the relationship between your process and the strengths and weaknesses of the writing it produces. This is the subject of the next section of this chapter.

SETTING GOALS

Thought is like all behavior. The child does not adapt himself right away to the new realities he is discovering and gradually constructing for himself. He must start by laboriously incorporating them within himself and into his own activity.

Jean Piaget

The "creative problem solving" we develop as we learn to compose is called thinking . . . .

Ann Berthoff

DEFINING PROBLEMS

Most writing students have been told for years what their writing problems are. Nonetheless, because of how they were told, and because of their usually passive attitude toward learning, most writing students cannot state in any precise way just what those problems are. No wonder they have difficulty solving them.

One of the truisms of problem-solving is that a precise problem definition is often the key to solution. A well-defined problem often suggests the appropriate means of solution. Until a problem is so defined, however, all the hard work you can muster may be wasted to no avail.

Many people find this hard to believe. The work ethic is so strong in industrialized countries that we have difficulty accepting what should be obvious: hard work misapplied often gets you nowhere (or even into a worse fix than you were in to begin with). You can work on a piece of writing and work on it and work on it, but if you are working the wrong way, it may just get worse and worse. Morally, you are then to be applauded for your dedicated effort; practically, you ought to be criticized for being wasteful.

Most writing students have had their "errors" pointed out to them innumerable times, but not defined on the proper level of generalization. They have seen that such and such a comma in some particular sentence is wrong, and they have some sense that they do not punctuate well. They know that some particular word does not say quite what they wanted, and they have been told that they often use "wrong words." They feel that some particular draft is not well organized, and they know that they have a "problem" with organization. But all this knowledge is either too particular or too general.

The level of problem definition that is often the prerequisite to solution has not been achieved. Most people who are trying to learn to write cannot say, "I do not know how to use commas with conjunctions." They have even greater difficulty, moreover, with problems beyond the sentence level. Only atypically can they say, "I tend to choose oversimplified theses" or "My writings are organized but not coherent because I don't give the reader adequate transitions to follow that organization."

Yet it is these precise, middle-level generalizations that are the key to devising solutions. The person who does not know how to use commas with conjunctions can be referred to a particular rule, which can be mastered in half an hour or less by doing a few exercises and writing a few sentences. The person who does not know how to use commas is referred to a dozen or more rules and often learns nothing.

ASSIGNMENT: *Describe as specifically as possible the strong and weak points of your writings. Give concrete examples whenever you can.*

One good way to approach this assignment is to collect ten or twelve fairly recent writings (papers from a number of different courses you took in the past year or two, with comments from several different instructors, would be particularly useful). Reread these old writings, and then generalize any feedback you received and any insights you now have about the strong points and flaws of those writings.

The success of this assignment depends on your ability to generalize from concrete "errors" while still remaining fairly specific. (See page 165 for the distinction between "concrete" and "specific.")

Be sure to consider strengths and weaknesses in such areas as finding a good topic, organization, coherence, and so forth, as well as sentence-level strengths and weaknesses.

Do this writing to the best of your ability, and be prepared to discuss it in order to define your "problems" more precisely.

Here are some excerpts from papers written in response to an earlier version of this assignment. (The assignment has been revised in response to the way these papers exposed its flaws.)

My major writing handicap is an inability to express my thoughts concisely in a direct, penetrating fashion. My tendency is to enlarge sentences to include often redundant information. Such excessive verbosity is for show rather than effect and results in bulky, awkwardly structured sentences. For example, one sentence in my definition essay reads, "The problem with scientific explanations for supernatural activity is that all truths, and the knowledge that follows are not dependent on a state of consciousness because there are many things one knows that he is unaware of such as the knowledge that the ceiling will not cave in while sitting under it." This sentence re-written reads, "Scientific explanations for supernatural activity create a problem. Knowledge does not depend on a state of consciousness. For example, someone sitting under a ceiling unconsciously realizes it will not cave in." This tapered version uses "knowledge" to replace "all truths and the knowledge that follows" because truths necessarily precede knowledge and therefore have the same relationship to a "state of consciousness" as knowledge.

Ann Morrison

Notice how Ann's "excessive verbosity" led to several grammatical problems as well as stylistic difficulties. More importantly, note that, from her very first sentence, her style here denies her thesis: she does have the ability to express her thoughts "concisely in a direct, penetrating fashion." In cases like this, mere statement of the problem focuses the writer's attention in such a way as to solve the problem.

Here is an excerpt from another student's paper.

A major fault that runs consistently through my essays is the problem of fully developing themes and ideas. The problem is usually due to laziness in elaborating rather than a lack of knowledge. A comment that I got on a second-year English essay said:

> The conclusion is "cruel" in that it holds a promise it does not fulfill. . . . How tantalizing to raise these questions and then leave your reader without a clue to the answer.

I make false assumptions that the reader clearly understands my ideas and can read between the lines. The answer is to assume that the reader is not knowledgeable in your area and, consequently, needs a great deal of elaboration in order to understand.

Janice Carroll

Note that once again the problem being described does not exist in the particular passage where the writer's attention is focused on it. Once you have located a problem, therefore, you should restate it positively as a goal. *Preliminary goal-statement* is simply an inversion of the problem statement in positive terms. Thus Ann's goal should be to tighten her style in order to express herself with more penetrating directness. Janice's goal should be to provide more fully explicated and supported statements of her ideas.

The following excerpt describes some more difficult problems.

In most formal research papers I have a tendency to switch my tenses back and forth from past to present and vice versa. This shows most readily in history essays. I find difficulty in keeping my tense consistent when writing in the present but constantly referring to historical events taking place many years ago. This is not only evident in history papers as it occurs in English papers as well. For example, my tense was extremely inconsistent when writing a paper on Hagar in Margaret Lawrence's *The Stone Angel.* The difficulty became apparent when I was writing in the present tense and constantly referring to events of Hagar's past. In addition, the recollections of her life were in the past tense, and therefore my quotations were also. A suggestion once given to me that I should keep in mind is "The book is here; therefore it is *present* not past." This problem not only occurs in these two genres of papers but also in informal ones like this.

Another detriment to my style that I frequently make use of is padding. In many cases I find myself using two words to describe something which, in most cases, is unnecessary, and in actual fact both words mean relatively the same thing. The same problem occurs in sentence form. Often I will repeat the same information in a sentence that was stated in the previous one. Therefore my attempt to sound more knowledgeable backfires.

Many professors find my sentence structure to be somewhat elementary for a fourth-year student. I use two short sentences when a longer more complex amalgamation of the two results in a more sophisticated version. Many attempts at doing this put an end to the short choppy ones, but give rise to longer sentences that tend to flow with irregularity. It is here that comments such as "awkward" appear.

Kaye Hetherington

Here definition of the problem and statement of the goal are not enough. Kaye's first problem requires both attention and information: she should find (or be directed to) an English handbook that has a good section on tense sequence; once she has learned the principles of tense sequencing, awareness of the problem will lead to its resolution. Her second problem is easier: she need only watch for "padding" during revision. Her third and double problem is instructive, because it demonstrates how attempting to solve a problem can sometimes (at least temporarily) produce the problem's antithesis. The solution is a combination of tightening and sentence combining (see pages 177-179 and 187-191).

One lesson to be learned from this case is that a *developed goal statement* should include a plan. It should state the means by which the goal will be achieved. It may be necessary to revise the plan later, but it should be stated as soon as possible.

PROCESS AND PRODUCT

Figuring out *how* to solve one's writing problems—or, to put it positively, figuring out how to achieve one's goals in writing—means looking at one's writing process. The process produces the product (including the problem). One student put it this way:

> If a professional tennis player were having trouble with his serve, there would be a number of procedures he could follow that might aid him in correcting it. However, before any correction could begin the tennis player would need to know specifically when and where the error took place, not just how the ball missed. This would require a detailed analysis of his actual serve. Perhaps the most effective procedure, therefore, would be to break down his serve by having a sequential series of photographs taken of it. Because the actual serve is dependent upon a vast number of different stages, ranging from backswing to follow-through, it might then be possible to analyze each photograph and thus pinpoint the error directly responsible for the 'bad' serve.
>
> While tennis service and the essay writing process may initially seem totally different, there is a quality to them that makes them similar: both involve a series of stages that lead to a final and definite result, whether it be the serve itself or the final draft of a paper. Yet, although both work on a similar principle, the procedures and focus of attention used for analysis are far different. Where the service analysis focuses on the stages leading up to the delivery of the ball, the essay analysis centralizes primarily on the final result.
>
> Andrew Crosse

Writing is a far more complex type of process than serving a tennis ball, but Andrew's point is well-taken. To improve your writing, you should try to pinpoint the place in your writing process where the problem arises or a place where it can readily be corrected. Consider the following case.

> The problem of organization is foremost in my writing of class essays. I go about writing this type of paper by studying as many facts as I possibly can, which usually ends up being a vast array of facts which are spilled out during the exam in a confused order. The facts are down on the paper but are not clear; instead of focusing in on the central theme, I cover a number of areas surrounding the main issue. The issues I do raise are not well enough developed. A comment on a first year in-class history paper states, "Your paper really needs to be more clearly organized. Also, you might have been much clearer in your discussion of the Gregorian Reform Movement. Furthermore, you needed to cite more specific examples throughout your paper. You raised a number of interesting points, but you have failed to develop them."
>
> Janice Moulton

A preliminary goal statement for Janice would say that she should organize her in-class papers more clearly and provide more support for her generalizations. The central problem here is the relationship between generalizations and particulars (see Chapter 1). But the problem really begins with Janice's study habits. Instead of studying as many facts as she possibly can, Janice should organize those facts under more general statements *during her study process*. In general, one should structure one's studying to match the structure of what one will be asked to produce on an examination, and this case is no exception. There are also several changes Janice could make in how she writes examinations that would probably improve her grades significantly. A specific technique Janice could use would be to ask herself after each generalization, "How do I know this is true?" and "What is a good example of this?" The answers to these questions would provide the logical support and examples that her professors find lacking.

Another student writes this about his writing.

> . . . Very often when I don't express myself well at the start, the rest of my ideas suffer for it. I feel that sometimes I'm playing with a conceptual puzzle which has too many pieces and has more which can't be used until a later stage. This is my first writing dilemma.
>
> Whether it is due to subject matter or to my rigid conceptual boundaries, my writing tends to be blatant and choppy. Once my initial thinking process is completed, my conceptual field is narrowed so that I do not always see all facts of subject matter. Sometimes I cut pieces to fit the puzzle for the time being. Later I pay for it because a struggle arises between my conceptual boundaries and those of the reader. My ideas often become more blatant when put on paper.
>
> Colin Grady

Colin's problem in one sense is not a problem at all. If one does not sometimes feel as if one is "playing with a puzzle which has too many pieces," one is not doing the sort of writing from which people learn. Specifically, one is not doing the sort of writing that is basic to a humanistic education—which should expand your conceptual boundaries.

In another sense, Colin's problem is that he tries to think first and write second. As he himself suggests later in the paper, he needs to do more exploratory writing before locking onto a thesis. He could also try to correct the problem by compensating for it during revision. One way to do that is discussed on pages 58-61.

To sum up the implications of these excerpts, one could say:

(a) Sometimes just defining a problem focuses the writer's attention in such a way as to resolve it.

(b) Sometimes defining a problem points to specific information (e.g., a punctuation rule) that the writer should learn.

(c) Sometimes there are specific exercises for specific problems (e.g., sentence combining for a choppy style).

(d) Sometimes the juxtaposition of a problem with a narrative of the writer's process suggests the means for resolving the problem.

GOAL STATEMENT

As was said above, to turn a preliminary goal statement into a developed goal statement, you must indicate the means by which you intend to achieve that goal. Two more items should be added also. The first is a time limit or schedule. The second—crucial and too often ignored by planners of all sorts—is a verification procedure (i.e., a way of knowing later whether you have, indeed, achieved your goal). Thus a problem like "I don't know how to use commas with conjunctions" becomes "By a week from Friday I will read pages 103-105 in Corbett's *Little English Handbook* and write out at least twenty sentences that use commas correctly with conjunctions; there will be no more than three errors of this type in my next three writings." A problem like "I make too many unsupported generalizations" becomes "From now on I will underline every generalization in my drafts and make certain that I explain how I know each is true (i.e., supply logical support) and give an example; by next month I will no longer receive complaints about unsupported generalizations and by the end of the year I will no longer need to use this underlining procedure."

ASSIGNMENT: *List your major strengths as a writer. List your main problems (in rough order of priority). Rephrase those problems as goals, including: (a) means for achieving each without undermining your strengths, (b) a time limit or schedule, and (c) criteria by which you will be able to judge whether you have reached each goal. Remember that successful goal statement depends on precise problem definition (because that leads to the specification of achievable goals).*

ASSIGNMENT: *Combine your paper analyzing your own writing process (revised) and your paper analyzing your own writing problems (revised) with the immediately preceding assignment. Try to create one coherent essay because the process of making these three assignments cohere will give a balanced assessment of both your present writing abilities and the tasks before you as a writing student. It will provide both a platform from which you can grow and a way to evaluate that growth later.*

Here is a student essay written in response to these assignments.

THE GUY SAID "TRY IT, YOU'LL LIKE IT," SO HERE GOES

Imagine you are standing near the edge of the high diving board at your neighborhood pool. You are ready to jump, until you look down and realize how high you are above the water. You hesitate. The longer you wait, the higher the board becomes in your imagination. Time passes. Fright and uncertainty freeze any forward motion. It is only when someone threatens to push you off and moves toward the ladder that you discover your fear of heights is not as great as your fear of being pushed. At the last minute, you hold your nose and jump, landing with a somewhat awkward splash. No matter, you have survived.

After being assigned an essay, I find myself suffering from the same sort of predicament. Instead of jumping right in and starting my essay, I hesistate. I actively search for excuses to avoid writing it. The instant I get a pen in my hand and see the empty sheet of paper in front of me, I discover that the room is too hot. Or it is too cold. Suddenly, I get an uncontrollable urge to consume an entire bowl of popcorn. Since my hands are now too greasy to hold the pen, I take a jaunt to the bathroom to wash up. While there I notice, for the first time, how incredibly tempting an empty bathtub can be. I abandon the empty sheet of paper for the empty tub, convinced that there will always be a tomorrow to write the essay. As each day passes, the essay becomes larger and more impossible to write. So, I do nothing. In effect, I freeze. The due date creeps nearer and soon a stronger fear, the fear of the deadline, takes hold of me. At the last minute, I hold my nose and jump right into my essay. I write hurriedly in an effort to get finished as quickly as possible. I write with little imagination and even less sophistication. Simple phrases and ideas are my emblems. In other words, I do the least amount of work I can to get a "B-." This results in feelings of intense dissatisfaction and mediocrity on my part, but at least I have survived.

However, the time has now come to change. Fortunately, this problem, as well as other, related, writing problems have solutions. Once these problems are stated positively, complete with a definite set of goals, their solutions can be readily seen. The following is a proposal which will outline my major writing problems, point to their solutions, and state my goals for the year.

Obviously, my biggest problem is that of time-mismanagement. I have to start the writing process much sooner. I need to have the time to think about my essay, the time to develop it, and the time to revise it. Let's face it, there is not much time for any of this when writing the entire essay in one night.

So, with the help of a schedule, I am going to try time-*management.* This schedule will set a series of mini-deadlines. By a certain date, I will have written a preliminary draft of ideas, outlines, and sketches for my essay. Another deadline will be set for writing the first draft. I will then set two more deadlines, the first for major revisions, and the second for final revisions. By the assigned due date, I will have typed the paper. An example of such a schedule follows:

Subject 400: Essay due Dec. 6

assigned Nov. 1, 8-10 pages
due Nov. 5—preliminary draft
due Nov. 12—first draft
due Nov. 19—revisions
due Nov. 26—final revisions
due Dec. 6—typed and completed paper

Not only will this schedule help me break my psychological block by forcing me to start writing earlier, it will also give me the time to do my essays justice.

Instead of my writing the essay all in one night, the writing process will be broken up, giving me more time for thought, development, and revision.

Another writing problem can also be linked to time-mismanagement. In my rush to finish the essay, I do not think through my ideas. My thoughts are not as well developed as they could be. This problem is best solved by using a heuristic. Since a heuristic is a set of questions designed to focus attention on various aspects of a subject, it should enable me to investigate my topic more fully. Burke's Pentad should prove helpful to my English essays since it is designed to explain human behavior. I will use this heuristic to delve more deeply into the characters' motives and psyches. Not only will a heuristic help me in developing my essay, it can also help me to start it. I used a visual diagram [see figure on page 66] to help me organize my ideas for this essay. With the use of the right heuristics, the development of ideas and themes in my essays as well as their organization should improve noticeably.

Another problem that should be discussed is my tendency to write simple, single-level papers. I need to practice varying the levels of generality in my papers. First, I am going to obtain a journal containing prize-winning student essays. I will then make diagrams of the different patterns of complexity and generality. I will apply these to some of my old essays to see where mine differ from those in the journal. Noting these differences, I will make up a heuristic as a guideline for future use.

The success of my proposal will be measured by my own personal feelings and by my professor's responses. I will be more satisfied with my writing. Physically, I will feel better—I will not have to stay up until 4:00 A.M. typing—and my papers will be the better for it. It is surely an achievement to be proud of one's own papers. Professors' responses are harder to predict. If I write a more complex essay well, my marks should improve. On the other hand, if I botch it, my marks may very well be worse than before. Still, I will be comforted by the fact that I have finally broken the bounds of my "mediocre" rut and stepped forward towards writing more sophisticated essays.

Margaret Coe*

---

*No relation to the author of this textbook.

ADDITIONAL READING

Writers at Work: The Paris Review Interviews. Ed. Malcolm Cowley. New York: Viking, 1958. This is the first of four volumes of interviews with famous writers about their work. All four are valuable sources of information about how successful writers write.

Corbett, Edward P.J. *Classical Rhetoric for the Modern Student.* 2nd ed. New York: Oxford, 1971. See especially pages 594-630 for a survey of rhetorical theory from the fifth century B.C. to the twentieth century.

EXERCISE

1. Write a short essay explaining why writing matters (or will matter) in your life. Use that essay to help focus your goals as a student of writing.

2. Together with three or four other people, choose an essay anthology. After you have practiced identifying topic sentences, have each person in your group count topic sentences in a sample from the anthology. Compare results. Make tentative generalizations.

3. Collect a sample of the type of writing with which you are most concerned. Analyze the sample for frequency and placement of topic sentences. Make tentative generalizations.

4. Do the assignment on page 10 of this chapter. Compare your writing processes with other writers (e.g., other students in a writing class).

5. Interview some good writers to find out how they think they write. (See page 45 on interviewing.) Interview some average and below-average writers. Can you detect any pattern of differences.

6. Watch somebody write (preferably one of the people you interviewed). If possible, get that person to "think out loud" while being watched.

7. Compare your ideal writing process with your typical writing process. Consider any implications.

8. Consider the divisions of classical rhetoric. What, if anything, can you learn from them that might help you as a writer?

PART ONE

THE WRITING PROCESS

For the one point in which we have our greatest advantage over the brute creation is that we hold converse one with another and can reproduce our thought in words.

Cicero

For in the other powers which we possess . . . we are in no respect superior to other living creatures . . . . Through [language] we educate the ignorant and appraise the wise; for the power to speak well is taken as the surest index of a sound understanding, and discourse which is true and lawful and just is the outward image of a good and faithful soul. With this faculty we both contend against others on matters which are open to dispute and seek light for ourselves on things which are unknown; for the same arguments which we use in persuading others when we speak in public, we employ also when we deliberate in our own thoughts . . . . [N]one of the things which are done with intelligence take place without the help of speech.

Isocrates

Perhaps the most important thing to remember about your writing process is that writing involves a number of activities of the mind. Writing includes almost all of the mental activities that you engage in during the course of a day, and learning to write well means that you will be working to improve all of these separate activites as well as to focus them . . . .

Susan Miller

CHAPTER 1

THE CREATIVE PROCESS

To create is both to generate and to form substance. In the creative process of writing,

1. We must generate or discover material (both ideas and words).
2. We must critically select and modify, arrange and rearrange that material.

This chapter begins with a short discussion of human creativity and then moves to the importance of managing one's writing time effectively. The next section presents a variety of techniques for getting started: talk-then-write, freewriting, brainstorming, meditation, keeping a journal, and research (interviewing, experimenting, reading). The third section begins by discussing two techniques for focusing a piece of writing without trivializing it and goes on to consider ways to overcome the perceptual, conceptual, and attitudinal blocks that can interfere with the creative process. The fourth section presents several techniques that can be used to guide discovery processes in predictably fruitful directions. The fifth section introduces selection and revision, with an emphasis on truth as the first criterion by which a statement should be judged. The last section moves to a consideration of the second type of revision—arrangment and rearrangement—with an emphasis on structure and unity. Two techniques and a series of questions are presented to help guide revision processes.

As you read this chapter, you should be doing two things. First, you want to develop your general understanding of writing as a creative process, so you will be better able to guide your own writing process. Second, you want to experiment with the various techniques offered, to choose those which best meet your needs, modifying them to serve your own purposes as a writer.

MAKING PLANS

Nil posse creari
De nilo.
[*Nothing can be created out of nothing.*]
Lucretius

Writing depends on both strategy and intuition . . . .
William Irmscher

He that sings a lasting song
Thinks in a marrow bone.
William Butler Yeats

HOW PEOPLE CREATE

To start with a blank page and finish with a piece of writing is to create. As a writer, you should know a bit about the human creative process. That knowledge can help you to tolerate the chaos out of which inspiration so often arises. It can also help you figure out what to do when your creativity seems to be blocked.

In one of the more interesting little books on the subject, *The Creative Process*, Brewster Ghiselin, himself a poet as well as a scholar, has collected the testimony of "thirty-eight brilliant men and women" about how they create. He includes Einstein, Mozart, van Gogh, Yasuo Kuniyoshi, D. H. Lawrence, Katherine Ann Porter, Jean Cocteau, Henry Moore, Gertrude Stein, Nietzsche, Jung, and others. He argues that human creation typically follows a certain general pattern:

1. A period of hard work (which sets the mind to the topic or problem and gathers necessary information).
2. A period of doing "nothing," of incubation.
3. Inspiration (which often occurs at some unexpected moment when one's conscious attention is focused elsewhere).
4. And another period of hard work during which the inspiration is developed in detail, criticized, verified, and so forth.

This basic pattern is confirmed in essence by other researchers and theorizers, such as Jerome Bruner and Arthur Koestler.

The mathematician, Henri Poincaré, for example, tells the following tale.

> *For fifteen days I tried to prove that there could not be any functions like those I have since called Fuchsian functions. I was then very ignorant; every day I seated myself at my work table, stayed an hour or two, tried a great number of combinations and reached no results. One evening, contrary to my custom, I drank black coffee and could not sleep. Ideas rose in crowds; I felt them collide until pairs interlocked, so to speak, making a stable combination. By the next morning I had established the existence of a class of Fuchsian functions, those which come from the hypergeometric series; I had only to write out the results, which took but a few hours.*
>
> *Then I wanted to represent these functions by the quotient of two series; this idea was perfectly conscious and deliberate, the analogy with elliptic functions guided me. I asked myself what properties these series must have if they existed, and I succeeded without difficulty in forming the series I have called theta-Fuchsian.*
>
> *Just at this time I left Caen, where I was then living, to go on a geologic excursion under the auspices of the school of mines. The changes of travel made me forget my mathematical work. Having reached Coutances, we entered an omnibus to go some place or other. At the moment when I put my foot on the step the idea came to me, without anything in my former thoughts seeming to have paved the way for it, that the transformations I had used to define Fuchsian functions were identical with those of non-Euclidean geometry. I did not verify the idea; I should not have had time, as upon taking my seat in the omnibus, I went on with a conversation already commenced, but I felt a perfect certainty. On my return to Caen, for conscience's sake I verified the result at my leisure.*

Even readers who know nothing about Fuchsian functions, hypergeometric series, or non-Euclidean geometry can recognize the underlying structure of the creative process. On one level or another, most of us have had comparable experiences, if only the experience of trying hard to remember a familiar name, giving up, and having it "pop" into mind later when our attention was elsewhere.

Ghiselin's theory, shared by Poincaré among others, is that inspiration is the result of an unconscious process of selection. The initial, preparatory stage of hard work serves to collect necessary information and to focus our unconscious attention on the topic or problem. This is followed by a period of incubation, when we may do nothing consciously, but when our unconscious processes are surveying myriad potential combinations and permutations (probably more than we would have time to consciously review). Inspiration, then, is a kind of creative recognition, which Poincare compares with an aesthetic sense; the "solution," in some respect more aesthetic than the other possibilities, "pops" from the unconscious into consciousness.

Gertrude Stein compares this process to having a baby.

> *You cannot go into the womb to form the child; it is there and makes itself and comes forth whole—and there is it and you have made it and have felt it, but it has come itself—and that is creative recognition. Of course you have a little more control over your writing than that; you have to know what you want to get; but when you know that, let it take you and if it seems to take you off the track don't hold back, because that is perhaps where instinctively you want to be and if you hold back and try to be always where you have been before, you will go dry.*

That part of the creative process which is most quintessentially creative—the moment of inspiration—is not subject to will power or rationality. It cannot be directly controlled or forced. But it does not arise out of nothingness, and it can be constrained; one can learn how to create space for it, to encourage it. One can develop ways of working and habits of mind that are conducive to creativity.

TIME MANAGEMENT

Creativity requires time. It can be accelerated, but there is no formula for instant inspiration. Sometimes inspiration comes in the nick of time, perhaps the night before a paper is due, and sometimes just *after* the nick of time, for example, five minutes after the examination is over.

One of the more important subsidiary skills for a writer to develop is the ability to manage time. Managing your time effectively is one of the quickest ways to improve your written product—because it allows you to take full advantage of the writing abilities you already have.

Time management is doubly important for writing students. Too often students hand in writing that is not their best work, that is filled with typographical and mechanical errors, is awkwardly organized and sloppily thought out—papers the students themselves are perfectly capable of improving. Late the night before the paper was due, however, eyes were too bleary to see the errors; reorganization was clearly in order, but it meant recopying the whole paper; and there certainly was no time to refine the concepts. Then the instructor, concentrating on what seems most basic or most elementary, marks a set of problems of which the students were well aware and *from which the students have little to learn*. The whole purpose of the writing class is undermined and everyone feels bad.

Here is what two writing students have to say about time. (See also the student essay on pages 22-24.)

For me, essay writing is a painful chore which I am unwillingly forced to carry out. If something is painful, you try to avoid it; therefore, when faced with an essay assignment, my first response is to put it out of my mind for as long as possible. As a result of this procrastination, my essays are handed in either late or in a semi-completed form. Even when I decide that I can no longer procrastinate but must now sit down and get on with it, this désire to escape persists; suddenly, in mid-sentence of course, I get the urge to make coffee, read the newspaper, clean up the apartment or take out the garbage. Escaping into this other activity disrupts my writing process; for each time I get up and sit down again I have to regain my train of thought, and in order to do so I must reread what I have previously written. Not only does this stalling ritual take up even more of what little time I have left before the deadline, but it also contributes to a lack of coherence in my essays.

Another form of escapism which effects my writing process occurs once I have begun to write. Because of my desire to "get this painful process over with," I rush through the actual writing. It is this tendency to rush which accounts for the remarks made on my essays, such as "should have made this point clearer" or "expand," which reflect that I have not fully expressed my ideas. It is also for this reason that most of my papers are under length. Furthermore, a great many surface errors and awkward sentences are a direct result of too much haste, for example, unnecessary punctuation errors such as leaving out apostrophes which show possession or placing commas in the wrong place, and careless spelling mistakes caused by leaving out letters or running words together. Also, since this need to "get the chore over with" extends to the revision process as well, most of these errors are carried intact into the final draft.

Finally, my negative attitude toward essay writing affects the manner in which I approach each essay: rather than viewing each paper as being part of a continually evolving process, I view each as a separate task. When my essays are returned, although I look over the comments, I make no conscious effort to analyze the errors I make or what I could do to prevent the same type of error from recurring in my next assignment; therefore any improvement in my writing is incidental.

[Author's name withheld]

When I am given a topic for assignment, I am usually eager to get my thoughts onto paper. I mull the assignment over in my mind, loosely organizing the essay there. Certain phrases and sentences are seen as effective, and these are jotted down. After a day of two of this process, I sit down and write until I feel that I have written a general overview of the topic. It is at this point that I hit a snag. No matter how much time I have in which to complete the assignment, the actual draft is not written until the night before the essay is due. Until the pressure of the deadline finally forces me to, I just don't want to write.

> Margaret Atwood once spoke of finding her nerve to write. That is how I feel. Words which sound perfectly splendid rolling around in my mind sound like lead when they are written down. Perhaps it is fear of failure which has caused my recent aversion to writing, but the result of this aversion is always a hurriedly written paper which is written for a deadline rather than for my own enjoyment. These papers usually lack any revision, and so are rife with simple errors of grammar and speech. Any proofreading that is done is too superficial to correct major errors in sentence construction and organization.
>
> Most of the faults in my writing could be corrected through careful rereading and revision. However, revision is difficult at five o'clock on the morning that an essay is due. For most people, a solution to this problem would be to manage time more effectively so that the essay would not be rushed. However, my problem is not one of time-management. My essays are not ready in time because I really dread writing them. I put off the task of applying pen to paper for so long that I cannot possibly do the topic justice.
>
> [Author's name withheld]

As these examples indicate, managing one's time effectively is not necessarily a cut-and-dried affair. Often problems of attitude and motivation underlie the misuse of available time. But that only makes effective time management even more important.

The writing process should be started early enough to allow for proper incubation (not to be confused with stalling). Your draft should ordinarily be completed in plenty of time, so that it can be put aside for a while, thus permitting you to see it afresh during revision. A final copy should be completed early enough so that it can be proofread carefully and alertly.

Start the preparation phase as early as possible. Gather your information, jot down notes, and perhaps do some very rough writing. That will start the incubator. As ideas "pop" up, jot them down. Try to do at least a rough draft well before the deadline. Get the drafting completed and start revising soon enough so that you can make major changes, such as modifying ideas, reordering paragraphs, or writing a new introduction.

Most people are incapable of following the advice of the preceding paragraph without a schedule. So as soon as you know you are going to write something, *make a schedule*, a plan for how and when you will write. Do not worry about sticking to it too rigidly—inspiration may not come when you scheduled it (perhaps it will even come early)—but make a schedule.

Starting early and managing your time effectively does not mean expending much more time on a given piece of writing; it just means dividing that time over a longer span. You will probably save some time during the early phases, perhaps by doing some thinking on the bus or getting an inspiration in the shower. If the writing involves library research, you may actually be able to obtain the materials that contain the information you really need. You will probably save some time while drafting, too, because you may be a little more organized or have a few key phrases ready. And you will probably find yourself putting more time into revision because you will have the time to do so.

The extra time you put into revision may be more than what you save earlier. Instead of spending twelve hours on a paper by staying up all night just before it must be finished, you may put fourteen hours into it during the course of a week. But those hours will be less strained, and you will probably get a lot more satisfaction out of the final product. In a writing class, moreover, the criticisms you receive later will much more likely be criticisms you can learn from instead of just feeling bad about.

ADDITIONAL READING

Koestler, Arthur. *The Act of Creation.* New York: Dell, 1967. This is an ambitious, transdisciplinary attempt to produce a unified theory of creativity. It is well-researched and contains an excellent bibliography.

The Creative Process. Ed. Brewster Ghiselin. Berkeley: University of California, 1952. Also available as a New American Library (Mentor) paperback. Ghiselin, himself a poet and critic of some note, presents his theory of creativity in a succinct introduction and then includes accounts from a symposium of writers, nonliterary artists, creative scientists, and thinkers.

EXERCISE

1. Consider the material just presented on human creativity (and perhaps do some outside reading). List implications for yourself as a writer. Consider how these implications might vary somewhat for the different types of writing you do.

2. The next time you have to write, make yourself a schedule as soon as possible. Keep track of how you manage your time. What effect, if any, does this have on your writing process or on the quality of the final written product? What do you learn from it about writing?

GETTING STARTED

... [I]f you wish the first part of the speech to have a close agreement and connection with the main statement of the case, you must derive it from the matters which are to be discussed afterward.

Cicero

How can you write the beginning of something till you know what it's the beginning of? Till you know what it's leading up to? But how can you know that till you get your beginnings?

Peter Elbow

Writing and rewriting are a constant search for what one is saying.

John Updike

GENERATING THE FIRST WORDS

Getting a piece of writing started can be most difficult. The very first problem a would-be writer may encounter is called *writer's block*, the inability to get anything written at all.

Actually a certain difficulty getting started is typical. Most writers experience it. There are a number of well-established techniques for overcoming this difficulty and generating the first words.

TECHNIQUE 1: TALK-THEN-WRITE

One reason for writer's block follows from the very nature of writing. In ordinary verbal communication, one gets feedback from listeners. Even if the listeners say not a word, the speaker knows from facial expression, body position, breathing patterns, and so forth how well the communication is proceeding. As a speaker, you are probably not much aware of this because your conscious attention is focused on what you are saying (as it should be). Nonetheless, unconsciously you depend on this nonverbal feedback.

It has been demonstrated, for example, that head nods give speakers significant feedback (to which almost all of us respond, although most of us are not consciously aware of it). Short nods (less than 0.4 seconds) seem to indicate understanding and agreement; they encourage the speaker to continue. But long or repeated nods seem to indicate lack of understanding or disagreement. Long nods (more than 0.8 seconds) are often followed by the speaker's returning to the last main point and reexplaining it. Repeated nods (at least three) are usually followed by vocal hesitation, changing of the subject, and so forth.

Writers do not have the advantage of immediate feedback. Writing is, in this respect, very much like speaking into a radio microphone without the presence of a studio audience; and writer's block is much like *mike fright*. When feedback is delayed, it is hard to continue verbalizing. But delayed feedback is in the very nature of writing: you write a sentence; then, before receiving any indication of whether that sentence has been understood, you have to write the next.

This problem, once it has been thus carefully defined, suggests one of the techniques commonly used to overcome writer's block and to generate the raw material for a piece of writing. It is called simply *talk-then-write*. It involves nothing more difficult than finding a listener or two and talking about what you want to write about. In the process, you will discover more about what you want to say, partly as a result of having verbalized and partly because of the feedback from your listeners. Questions they may ask about the substance of what you say are likely to be particularly good indicators; it can also be useful to ask what they think your main points are.

If you leave a tape recorder on as you talk, you will be able to listen to yourself afterwards and take notes on whatever was useful. Or you can take notes from memory after you finish. If the note taking does not interfere with the flow of your talking, you can jot down thoughts as you talk. But even if you keep no record at all, the process of talking it out is a good way to generate your material without having to "actually write."

TECHNIQUE 2: FREEWRITING

A second reason for writer's block, which also suggests its own solution, follows from the contradictory nature of the writing process. Like any creative process, writing has two contrary aspects. In the first place, writers need to generate material (or, even before that, to discover topics). But much of what is generated will not be usable: images and concepts that are not quite accurate or correct; malformed sentences and sentences that do not fit with what has gone before or what is to follow; nonstandard usage in standard contexts; idiosyncratic punctuation that would confuse readers to no purpose; misspelled words; and so on.

Thus, in the second place, writers must criticize and select, censor and correct. Dissatisfied with a sentence, a writer rephrases it several distinct ways and then selects the version that seems to work best. Uncertain about an argument, a writer tries it out on a friend and, in the process of receiving criticism, modifies it. Uncomfortable with the way a word looks, a writer turns to the dictionary and finds the correct spelling.

Any creative process—from biological evolution to musical composition—must involve both of these aspects. The problem for the writer is that sometimes the second aspect becomes so dominant that everything is censored, and the would-be writer is left with a blank page.

If your critical side is so strong that it totally censors all starting points, you have writer's block. The solution is to give it your word of honor that it will have its turn, but insist that it must go off and take a nap first. One excellent way to do this is called *freewriting*. Freewriting is very effective, partly because it forces you to write from the very start, and it is probably the most commonly taught technique for generating material. It follows the advice of Gertrude Stein, who said to

> *think of writing in terms of discovery, which is to say that creation must take place between the pen and the paper, not before in a thought or afterwards in a recasting. Yes, before in a thought, but not in careful thinking. It will come if it is there and if you will let it come, and if you have anything you will get a sudden creative recognition.*

Freewriting works like this. You set a time limit, usually ten or fifteen minutes for beginners but eventually as long as forty-five minutes. You sit down with pen and paper (or at a typewriter if you are adept). You think of your topic if you have one (or of whatever comes to mind if you do not), and you start writing. The only rule is that you must keep writing constantly, without censoring. If you cannot think of anything to write, you write "Nothing comes to mind" or (better) you recopy the preceding sentence until something does come to mind. You do *not* worry about spelling, punctuation, grammar, or usage. (You are allowed to misspell, mispunctuate, and violate the rules of grammar and usage.) You do *not* worry about style. You do *not* worry about whether one idea or sentence has any connection with another. You do *not* even worry about making sense—yet.

Most people soon find that they can fill a handwritten page in less than fifteen minutes. Occasionally, a writer gets lucky and has a page of good writing—or at least a draft that can be revised to suit her or his purposes. Not surprisingly, freewriting also produces a considerable quantity of garbage. That is no problem, however, if you have access to a wastebasket. Think of the garbage as compost. Among it you will usually find at least one well-phrased sentence, one good idea, one provoking image which the rest of the page helped to fertilize.

Here are two examples of freewriting which worked. Neither is a finished piece of writing, but both are very good starts. Each is good, honest self-expression. In each the writer's voice is clear and the feelings come across. Each writer has generated good contrasts and good particulars. Neither is written in Standard English or adapted to other demands many readers might make. The first begins with little sense of purpose. The second seems to be written more to express and clarify strong emotions than to communicate with readers. However, whatever faults they might seem to have if judged as finished pieces of writing, both are successful freewritings with excellent potential.

> Fifteen minutes at the library. The steam is streaming out of the thermos of that girl. No, . . . out of the girl's thermos. She is pretty. Should I say something to her? She has no rings on her left hand. Why is she sitting at this table in front of me and not some other seat, there are plenty around. I should get on with my home work. What time is it? Plenty of time till 2:30 class. I should be thinking about science. Not girls. What makes her so beautiful? No, not that kind of science. Let light trigger a sort of chemicals like CO_2 and H_2O, to simulate photosynthesis. Why did she turn sideways? What is she thinking. How beautiful she is. Should I ask her to read this? May be she'll like it. She has a nice profile. Would the professor laugh at this? Great! Ten seconds to go.
>
> [Author's name withheld]

> & today riding back from the grocery store on my bike, going past men working on the sidewalk—stares, one whistle & one man repeating hi there til i turned the corner. i can't describe the leering look on his face or the tone of his voice, but i know it so well, i've seen it heard it, countless times & it makes me ashamed—less ashamed now & more angry, but still ashamed.
>
> we've a mirror in the bedroom, attached to the dresser—i liked the way i looked in it this morning. i liked the sunshine around me—our room is on the south side—i liked my clothes which were clean, functional & recycled & i liked me—clean, no more makeup, glasses instead of contacts, hair that does what it wants—clean.
>
> & those men made me feel dirty
>
> converted me to an object for their pleasure. i could tell them i'm intelligent, i have consciousness, mostly i wanted to tell them they have their heads up their asses—but i didn't cuz i was scared—around the corner & i was home.
>
> Sharon Dowe

After you have done one or more freewritings, take a short break. Then look for that good idea, provoking image, or well-phrased sentence. Copy it at the top of a blank page, and use it to start another freewriting. Let it take your mind and your pen where they will.

Probably this second freewriting will be more fertile (and possibly even more organized) than the first. Again, after a short break, look for another starting point. Very likely, you will find several potential starting points. Use at least one to do yet another freewriting. Do not feel committed to your starting point, and do not yet aim for organization.

By now you have "wasted" almost an hour on these freewritings—but you probably have enough material to form the basis of a five-hundred word paper. If you are lucky (and people who do relatively longer freewritings are more likely to be lucky), a "center of gravity" has started to emerge. That is, you may have found something that you can use as the center or main point of a paper. If it has not emerged, look for it; make it emerge. Reread what you have written, and ask yourself what "it" is trying to say. Attempt to sum it up, or at least most of it. That center of gravity may be a rough version of the thesis statement of your final paper (or the main event of your short story, the central image of your poem). You may be able to use it to organize the rest of the material you have salvaged from your freewritings. You may now be ready to start drafting your paper in a more conventional manner.

At first you may feel silly doing freewritings. After all, you are intentionally producing "bad" writing. Or perhaps you may have trouble identifying those kernels of usable material in the sea of compost, so you may well need a little help from your friends or from a teacher. Also at first, especially if you do not let yourself really loose, you may not be very fertile. (Even experienced freewriters occasionally produce several in a row with no apparent value.)

Freewriting is hard for many people because it requires that the writer tolerate chaos. Chaos is a necessary phase of any creative process: order (what the Greeks called *cosmos*) can be formed only out of chaos; even the transition from one order to another requires at least a brief period of chaos. Unfortunately, most of us are so strongly socialized to believe in order that we have difficulty tolerating even that chaos which is a necessary phase of creativity.

Freewriting liberates writers from several contradictions: How can I write the beginning until I have written the middle and know what I am introducing? How can I start writing when my mind is still in chaos? How can I think of everything—ideas, transitions, logical support, examples, diction, spelling, punctuation—at once? Freewritings can start anywhere, they are supposed to be chaotic, and you are supposed to ignore transitions, diction, and mechanics—the logical support can be found later.

The underlying principle and point to be remembered is that freewriting helps you generate both material and focus by allowing you to postpone the criticizing, selecting, and editing until later. In the extreme case, you can start writing even before you know what you are writing about. You can use freewriting to develop and sharpen a vague conception, to discover your focus. You can use it to explore the implications of a key term or proposition. Freewriting allows you to start with whatever you have and to develop from there.

TECHNIQUE 3: BRAINSTORMING

Brainstorming is well-established group technique, in some ways similar to talk-then-write, in some ways similar to freewriting. Like talk-then-write, it is oral and based on interaction among people. Like freewriting, it is a way of generating chaos in the hope that somewhere among the chaos will be a germ of inspiration.

Brainstorming works like this. You need a small group of people—perhaps students starting on the same assignment or several people doing a collaborative writing, perhaps you and several friends who have agreed to help you start your paper. Members of the group think of the topic, problem, or assignment and then free associate. Each person calls out any idea or image that comes to mind. Nobody does any evaluating, but one person's idea may suggest another idea to some other person. Meanwhile, there is either a tape recorder on or one person has been assigned to take notes. The group collects as many ideas as possible in whatever order they come off the tops of everyone's heads. Later the ideas are evaluated, and the wheat separated from the chaff.

Although originally devised as a group problem-solving technique, brainstorming can be applied to topics that are still too vaguely defined to be called problems in the proper scientific sense. This method can also be used by an individual, who simply jots down as many ideas as possible as quickly as possible. Individual brainstorming may be less fertile than group brainstorming, but it is still valuable discovery technique. It is to ideas what freewriting is to words.

TECHNIQUE 4: MEDITATION

Professor Edward Corbett suggests *meditation* as a discovery process. At first that may strike you as a bit odd. Given the nature of the human creative process, however, it actually makes a great deal of sense. Inspiration cannot be forced, but we can "make space" for it, and meditation is a good way to make that space.

In the Eastern traditions, meditation is often described as an *emptying* of the mind. Inspiration comes to those who wait, provided they wait properly; and the relaxed yet disciplined "wide focus" of the meditator is a proper state in which to wait for enlightenment or any other form of inspiration. In the Christian tradition, to use Corbett's words, "the technique consists in taking a short passage from the Scriptures or from the text of the day's Mass and, in an atmosphere of silence and freedom from distraction, thinking about it in a serious persistent way, trying to see the relevance of the passage to one's own life and spiritual growth."

Even without taking up meditation in the full spiritual sense, you can apply the underlying principle to writing and to learning. You simply take the central idea or topic of the potential writing and use it instead of the mantra or Scriptural passage.

Inspiration literally means *inhalation* and is derived from the image of breathing in the divine breath of the gods. The basic principle that underlies meditation is a good basis for opening yourself to the divine breath of inspiration.

TECHNIQUE 5: KEEPING A JOURNAL

Many serious writers use another technique: *keeping a journal.* A writing journal is not the same as a diary, although it can be combined with one. A writing journal is a lot like a basket in which you can collect bits and pieces which may later be useful in one way or another.

Given the nature of the creative process, a writer may find a usable image or a potentially meaningful bit of information at any time. Often it is not clear just when, where, or how that image or information will be usable. Inspiration, moreover, can strike at any time. The writer's journal is a place to collect these images, bits of information, and inspirations. It can also be the place to do short freewritings when the impulse strikes. Its virtue is that it is bound, so what is collected is not likely to be lost (as it often is if left in the mind, told to a friend, or jotted on a scrap of paper). The notebook in which you keep the journal, incidentally, should be large enough to work in but small enough so that you will actually carry it around with you—after all, it has to be there when you discover an interesting item in the newspaper or are struck by that unscheduled inspiration. (*Note:* You can paste things into journals as well as write in them.)

A journal is especially useful for academic and other types of intellectual writers because it has a useful function in any high-level learning process. If you are learning just information which fits neatly into concepts you already have, it is easy to take organized notes and to incorporate the information quickly into your image of the world. But if you are learning new concepts, which may require you to reorganize information you already know or even to reject beliefs you already have, then it is more difficult to make them your own. You have to play with them and discover their implications if you are to develop the ability to use them. This sort of high-level learning is exactly what a broad or humanistic education is all about. Using the new concept in a written paper is one of the best ways to get a hold on it (which is why writing—usually in the form of essay examinations and term papers—is basic to a humanistic education).

If a concept is genuinely new to you, then you probably do not have enough control over it to use it in a paper immediately. That is where the journal comes in. A journal entry, since it is essentially for your own edification and future use, is like a freewriting in the sense that it does not have to be "good" and certainly does not have to be correct. A journal entry is a place to play with ideas and images.

It is sometimes useful to structure journal entries, especially if you are starting your first journal. Make the first part of the entry a report: restate an idea, describe an image, narrate a potentially significant event (even if you do not yet understand how it may be significant); the first part of the entry might even be a quote or a statistic. Then make the second part of the entry deal with the implications of the report section: argue with it, give an example of it, relate it to your own life or to some other concept.

Used in this way, a journal becomes a source book. When you are about to start writing, you turn to your journal for a topic, for material, or for concepts that can suggest how to organize your writing. (*Note*: If you are about to keep a journal for the first time, you will be wise to make a rule about the minimum number of times a week you must write in it—perhaps three. Once the habit is established, you can drop the rule.)

Here are some sample journal entries.

> Definition: I listened to Carly Simon's first album for a long time before I realized what was bothering me: *all* the songs were about men. Does that say anything about how Carly defines herself (as a person? as an artist?)

> Pirsig does not balance his philosophizing with his story-telling. I'm taking a British drama course, and I think Pirsig should have used George Bernard Shaw as an example. Shaw had ideas which were far ahead of his time, but managed to put them across in conjunction with highly entertaining literature. Pirsig's *Zen and the Art of Motorcycle Maintenance* is a textbook masquerading as a novel.

> A sign can be divided (for analysis) into signifier/signified; and one signifier can simultaneously represent more than one signified. I want to cut down on my smoking (because cigarettes signify cancer), but I realize I have a problem. Last year a psychologist friend of mine showed me a picture an eight-year-old

> boy had drawn of his father: the man was smoking a cigarette; the boy felt that was an important aspect of his father. In my self-image I see a "cancer stick"; I think it is from a Marlboro commercial. I want to give up smoking, but I need a replacement for this signifier of masculinity.

Journal entries can also be structured in other ways. For example, you can create dialogues real or imagined, among people or among points of view; you can write letters, often the sort you know you will never mail; you can record dreams and fantasies, perhaps together with interpretations; you can make lists, perhaps of goals or fears or things to do; you can write character sketches, real or imaginary. What you collect in your journal and how you structure it should depend on what you are trying to understand and what types of writing you plan to do. The virtue of the journal is that it allows you to write a little about something one day, then return to it another day, and perhaps another, as your understanding deepens. When you are finally ready to attempt a fuller and more formal writing, you have some material to start with. You also have a record of how your understanding developed, which can be useful when you are thinking about how to make that understanding clear to your readers.

It is often helpful for writers and writing students to make journal entries *about their writing*. You can use your journal to get started on a piece of writing and also to keep track of how you write it. Thus you use the journal to develop an understanding of your own writing processes. Later you can look back to see what sorts of approaches seem to lead to your most successful writings, which problems you have put behind you, what works and what does not work, and so on. A writer's journal can help you develop an understanding of whatever you are writing about, and it can also help you to understand and develop yourself as a writer.

TECHNIQUE 6: RESEARCH

Research (literally, *re-search*, to search again) is a most respectable technique for getting started and is of unquestionable value as a way of gathering information and making connections. Most people interpret the word *research* much too narrowly, thinking of it only as a process that takes place in libraries and laboratories.

In a sense, any form of observation that is structured as a search should be considered research. For instance, to go see a hockey game (or three) prior to writing a paper on violence in hockey is research. Usually, however, we reserve the word *research* for somewhat more structured forms of observation.

Interviewing is a good research technique. Prior to writing an article on the "literacy crisis" in the schools of North America, one might interview teachers, pupils, and parents. When you interview, the "interviewees" present your material to you—which makes interviewing a relatively painless way to gather material.

On the other hand, conducting an effective interview is itself a craft. You must create an atmosphere and ask the right questions to get the person you are interviewing talking, and talking to your point. At the same time, you must give that person enough room to say things you would never have thought to ask about and even things with which that person may well expect you to disagree. A good interviewer is open and perspicacious, sensitive and perceptive. (Learning to be a good interviewer, like learning to be a good writer, is good for your character.)

The key to a successful interview is good preparation. It helps to know something about the topic—not necessarily a great deal, but something—so you can know what questions to ask. It also helps to know something about the person you will be interviewing, so you can know *how* best to ask those questions. And it helps to have a strategy—not just a list of questions, but a plan about the order in which you will ask them.

You may start with a general question and use the answer to focus on particulars. Or you may start with particulars and build toward more general implications. In either case, you want to establish rapport, so the person you are interviewing opens up and speaks freely.

Once the person is talking, be sure you are getting specifics. Do not be embarrassed to admit you do not understand something. Do push for specifics, dates, names, anecdotes, details, supportive evidence. Do not interrupt—you want the person to keep talking—but remember to come back to key points. Always remember the purpose of the interview, which is for you to get information; express your own point of view only enough to get responses. And, since you may not have asked all the right questions, a good closing question is, "Is there anything important I haven't asked?"

Experiments, although most common in the sciences, are good for gathering all sorts of material. One student at Central Michigan University, for example, turned a question into an experiment by giving three versions of it to students in his dormitory. The question was simple: "Should a girl [sic] ask a guy out?" The variants were ". . . if she has known him for over two years?" and ". . . if she just met him within the last two weeks?" The responses were not surprising (for 1973), but the student was not centrally concerned with the responses as such. His hypothesis was that the results of polls and other questionnaires are influenced by the ways the questions are worded. Indeed, the answers to the first question seemed to indicate that there was considerable disagreement on the campus. However, the two follow-up questions revealed that the apparent disagreement was the result of interviewees making distinct assumptions about what the question did not stipulate: Central Michigan students in those days apparently thought that women should ask men out only if they had known them a long time.

In the same writing class, an assignment on nonverbal communication led to a number of papers based on informal experiments. What these students each did was to pick an unspoken rule of behavior and violate it. For instance, one writer went to a party and made a practice of standing about six inches closer than usual to other people. These papers, perhaps because the students used concrete, structured experiences instead of writing "out of their heads," were among the best in the batch.

Such experiments are not conclusive. They are similar to the preliminary experiments that scientists (and educators) do prior to designing the serious experiments that are supposed to produce reliable results. But even an informal experiment, especially when combined with other forms of research, is an excellent technique for getting started on a piece of writing. It may not prove anything, but it is very likely to suggest a lot.

Last, and certainly not least (in this incomplete list of discovery techniques which can be called research), is **reading**. The details of research we will leave to Chapter 7 because most of those details have to do with the selection process, not with the generation of material; the library is filled with information, the writer's main problem is to find the relevant sources.

Reading is not usually listed in textbooks among the other discovery techniques. But reading about your topic is a way of consulting other people (in this sense like interviewing or group brainstorming). Reading is a way of gathering information and a way of setting your mind to work, of preparing the incubation process, which will result in inspiration and insights. When done properly, reading is one of the best ways to start writing.

ADDITIONAL READING

Brady, John. *The Craft of Interviewing*. Cincinnati: Writer's Digest, 1976. A very useful book on interviewing, which includes both practical advice and fascinating examples from the experiences of well-known journalists and famous interviewees. Although slanted toward the journalistic interview, this text will be useful for any interviewer.

Corbett, Edward P. J. *The Little Rhetoric & Handbook*. New York: Wiley, 1977. See pages 20-22 on the use of meditation as an informal discovery technique.

Elbow, Peter. *Writing Without Teachers*. New York: Oxford, 1973. An excellent guide for anyone who wishes to take a freewriting approach. Designed for use in a teacherless writing group, this text has also been widely influential among writing instructors and composition theorists. An exceptionally honest and useful book.

EXERCISE

1. Do a ten- or fifteen-minute freewriting that is totally free (no topic). Do two more, either totally free or following from the first. Reread them. Share one with a small group. Let people in the group ask questions, pick out good points, and offer compliments (no negative responses allowed at this stage).

2. Keep a journal. Record what happens as you write papers. Record ideas from this book; play with those ideas and relate them to other experiences and ideas you have had. Record ideas and happenings from your writing class or workshop and speculate about their implications. Carry your journal with you always. Jot down notes for writings as they occur to you. Jot down intriguing quotations and statistics. Do freewritings. Write in this journal at least three times a week.

3. Try at least two of the following techniques: talk-then-write, freewriting, meditation, journal writing, and brainstorming. Compare your experiences with those of other writers. Consider ways in which you might adapt one or more of these techniques to your own writing needs.

4. Try using a research technique as a way of getting started on a piece of writing. Compare your experience with those of other writers. Consider various ways you might use research in the kinds of writing you are likely to be doing in the near future.

5. Peter Elbow, whose *Writing Without Teachers* is probably the best book on a freewriting approach to composition, suggests the following four-hour procedure (here rephrased) for producing a short paper:

   1. Do a forty-five minute freewriting in which you try to write down everything which comes to mind about your subject. Spend fifteen minutes reading it over and looking for an emerging center of gravity.

   2. Start from that center of gravity, and do another forty-five minutes of freewriting. Sum it up again.

   3. Start from that summation, and do another forty-five minutes of writing. This time make it semi-free. Try to develop that emerging center of gravity. Aim for a bit of coherence, but still let new ideas or images flow.

   4. Spend fifteen minutes making your meaning clear to yourself.

Perhaps make an outline. Definitely focus on a single assertion that can serve as a thesis.

5. Now spend forty-five minutes writing the paper and fifteen minutes editing it.

(*Note*: These time lengths may be "stretched or squeezed"; the clock is being used because most of us need it to discipline ourselves.)

Use this procedure to write a short paper. How well does it work for you? Could you modify it to make it work better for you? If you know other people who are trying this procedure, compare your results with theirs. Are there particular types of writing for which it seems to be most appropriate?

FOCUSING AND NEGATIVE INVENTION

May God us keep
From Single vison & Newton's sleep.
William Blake

There are many notable aspects of language, such as classification, specification, abstraction, which have their analogues in purely nonverbal behavior. But the negative is a peculiarly linguistic resource. And because it is so peculiarly linguistic, the study of man as the specifically word-using animal requires special attention to this distinctive marvel, the negative.
Kenneth Burke

HOW TO FOCUS A TOPIC

Good writing almost always is, in one sense or another, focused writing. In the standard textbook procedure for writing a paper, the second step—after finding (or being assigned) a topic—is to limit or "narrow and focus."

Narrowing or limiting reduces a large topic to one that can be covered in a relatively short paper. Supppose, for example, that your topic is "The Literacy 'Crisis' in North America." Clearly, you cannot say all there is to say on that topic in five hundred words or eight to ten pages (or even 80 to 100 pages) without being very general. So you narrow to one separable *part* of the topic—for example, "The Literacy 'Crisis' in New York City."

Simultaneously, you focus on a particular *aspect* of the topic, like "What are the dimensions of the 'crisis?'" or "What should be done about the 'crisis?'" The combination of this narrowing and focusing results in a topic like "What should be done about the literacy 'crisis' in New York City?"

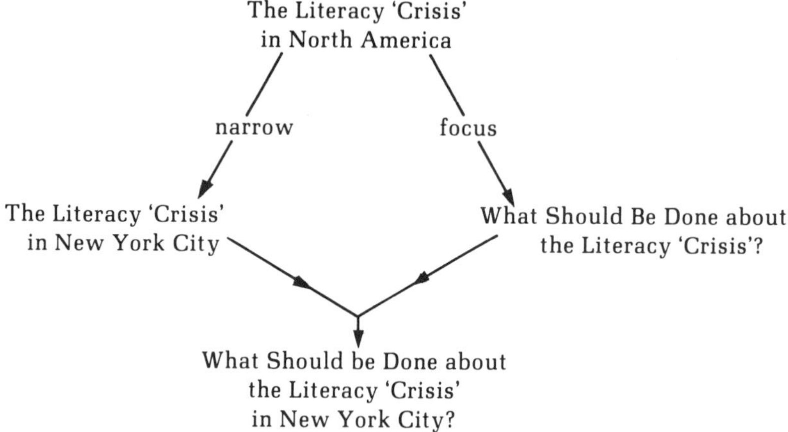

Good start, says the textbook; now keep narrowing. The final topic for a short paper eventually becomes "One remedy for increasingly poor punctuation among first-year students at Stuyvesant High School." This topic—which was reached by carefully following the instructions of one widely used handbook—has several virtues. It is likely to make the writer deal with the concrete realities of the problem instead of writing a paper filled with vague generalizations. It is specific and easily manageable.

On the other hand, it is in grave danger of becoming trivial. Thus, even as an exercise, it is not likely to inspire your best performance. Nor is it likely to interest many readers. Even in the hands of an experienced professional, it is likely to lead the writer to consider the narrowed topic out of context. Thus it serves as a reminder that there is a second aspect to the narrowing-and-focusing method: *make certain that you narrow-and-focus on a topic that is not only specific, but has broad implications.* Make certain that your solution to the punctuation problems of first-year students at Stuyvesant High School is not one that will interfere with other, more important, aspects of their writing. Make certain that you discuss this very narrow topic in such a way as to clearly imply (or explicitly state) its broader implications for responding to problems of literacy in general.

It must also be remembered that a writer who has just started on a topic might not be ready to narrow or to focus. As the preceding discussion of human creativity suggests, it may sometimes be better to delay trying to focus until you are a little further along in the writing process. Perhaps you may let the writing "find its own focus," for example, after a few freewritings. Perhaps you may use the technique of narrow-and-focus but only after you have done a considerable amount of preliminary writing and even drafting.

PROBLEM-SOLVING FOR FOCUS

As a casual survey of most any anthology of "great essays" will demonstrate, it is often acceptable to write a short essay on a very general topic. The master essayists, of course, were capable of various feats which should not be lightly attempted by the ordinary writer. Still, their example raises the question: How else may one focus a piece of writing?

One other way to focus, although it does have ancient antecedents, has recently been derived from research on problem-solving methods. Here is how it works.

As you gather material on your chosen (or assigned) general topic, you look for a "problem." That is, among the various statements you collect or generate, look for two or more that seem to contradict each other (or for one that seems to be self-contradictory).

The contradiction should be specific and, ordinarily, should involve statements (although contradictory images will also work well, especially for certain types of writing). Thus you do not look for traditional debating topics like "University Education—For the Many or for the Few?" Instead, look for statements like these.

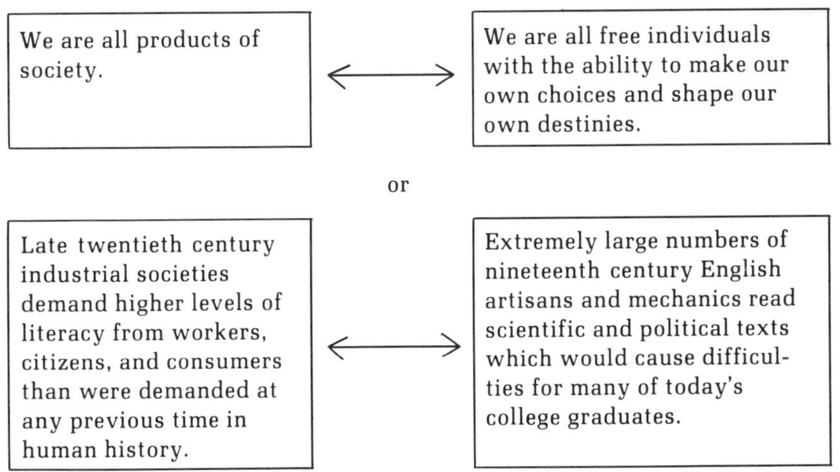

An apparent contradiction between two statements may be dissolved by disproving one of the statements: perhaps we are not free individuals; perhaps late twentieth century industrial societies do not demand such high levels of literacy as is ordinarily believed. A genuine contradiction is resolved by generating a statement that combines the two originals and demonstrates the extent or sense in which each contains some truth. It is this sort of contradiction that constitutes the sort of "problem" which can focus a piece of writing.

In the real world, it is very often the awareness of such a problem that motivates the writing. In many situations, however, writers discover the "problem" as they write. The resolution of the "problem," which often occurs during some middle phase of the writing process, generates the thesis of the piece of writing. You might, for example, discover that nineteenth and late twentieth century industrial societies demand distinct *types* of literacy. (If you do discover that and can identify the types, you will have the thesis statement for a ten-to-twenty page article, which could easily be published in a variety of fine magazines and journals.) You might decide to argue that human beings are *in a certain sense* products of society but *in another sense* free individuals—or that people have freedom to choose *within certain constraints*.

Finding a contradiction focuses the problem for you. It may also focus your attention on one aspect of the original general topic. Resolving the contradiction also complicates your viewpoint: to argue that we are in one sense products of society but in another sense free individuals is more complicated than to argue *either* that we are just products of society *or* that we are simply free individuals. Thus one reaches a more complex (or, it you will, a more sophisticated) thesis.

The complex thesis is harder to think about and may also be harder to write about. Initially, it forces you to look at your topic from at least two perspectives and to develop a representation that more closely approximates the complexity of the real world. Thus it is consistent with the values of a broad or humanistic education, and the technique that generates such theses is especially appropriate for writing which forms part of such an education. It is from wrestling with complex theses that one learns how to think.

By contrast, the narrow-and-focus technique is appropriate to a specialist's education and is suitable for the empirical investigation of specifics. Yet that specific paper on the poor punctuation of first-year students at Stuyvesant High School might provide information and insights that could then help you to think and write more broadly about the literacy crisis. Thus there is a role for each technique.

Notice that this section on problem-solving as a way to focus a topic has just exemplified itself. The opposition between *narrow*-and-*focus* and *problem-solving to focus* has just been resolved: each has its assigned role, and the relationship between them has been defined. Narrow-and-focus is a narrower technique. It should be subordinate to problem-solving in the same sense that "facts" are subordinate to the "opinions" they support. But both techniques are useful, and sometimes both can be used to tightly focus one topic.

If you search and research a topic until you find a contradiction which interests you, that contradiction will focus your attention and your writing. It will lead you to theses that are both specific and complex. It will encourage what John Dewey called "an attitude of suspended conclusion" and help you avoid simplistic conclusions that can become overly simple thesis statements. Such an attitude of suspended conclusion typifies the mature writing process and helps produce first-class writing. (In university classes, incidentally, the sort of thesis and tone likely to follow from such an attitude generally secure excellent, as opposed to merely good, grades.)

ON CONTRADICTIONS

Contradictions take various forms that can be useful to you as a writer. As stated above, the technique of focusing through contradictions, although most recently derived from the problem-solving method, has venerable antecedents. In classical Greece, it was the method of Socrates and of the early Sophists. Truth was to be discovered through discussion, with one speaker representing (literally, *re-presenting*) each perspective on the subject. Through discussion, the group of speakers and listeners would approach a fuller and more accurate truth than any of those represented by any of the original viewpoints.

According to Aristotle, certain truths could be known definitely. Other types of truth could be only approached and were best reached by the method of discussion—more generally called *dialectic*. Rhetoric, then conceived as the craft of persuasive public speaking, could be seen as a servant of truth because truth was to be reached through the discussion of contradictions and made known to the citizenry through convincing presentations.

Thus, in the Socratic discussion, as in the talk-then-write technique (pages 36-37), the form of the contradiction is *interaction among people*. Two or more minds are better than one, and two or more minds interacting are better than the same number of minds operating in isolation. When you focus and develop your topic by the problem-solving method, the form of contradiction is *interaction among ideas*. Often the contradiction is between an apparent "fact" and a previously held belief, theory, or opinion. Karl von Frisch, for example, describes the beginning of forty years of research in this way:

> *About 1910 a famous ophthalmologist, Professor C. von Hess asserted that . . . fishes and invertebrates, and in particular bees, are totally color-blind. If this were true, the colors of flowers would have no biological significance. But I could not believe it, and my skepticism was the first motive which led me to begin my studies of bees about forty years ago. I tried to find out whether bees have a color sense.*

Certain types of contradiction are generated by writing. For this reason—because the writing process concretizes various types of contradiction—writing is a learning process. For example, writers often run into a contradiction *between words and ideas,* as when semiformed ideas seem not to "fit" into the available words or sentence structures. This is a problem, and it often leads to better or fuller development of the words, the ideas, or both. Once ideas are in words, moreover, writers often feel "distanced" from them and, therefore, better able to criticize and evaluate what is being said.

Another form of contradiction is *the mixed metaphor.* Broadly conceived, a mixed metaphor occurs whenever a writer makes two comparisons which contradict each other.

Now that Ronnie's back in the saddle, we will have smooth sailing.

The two images—of Ronnie on horseback and Ronnie in a sailboat—clash, with results that can be stylistically disastrous. Mixed metaphors sometimes represent not only stylistic problems but substantive contradictions. The classic example of such a contradiction comes from physics, where light was usefully conceived both as a stream of particles and as a wave in space; the resolution of this mixed metaphor, or contradiction, took decades, but it led to a better understanding of subatomic physics.

It may seem that contradiction is negative, not in any way positive. Logically, a contradiction *is a negation* of one statement by another. We all know that it is "not nice to contradict." Logical contradiction, however, is not negative in any moral of judgmental sense. Logical contradiction can be a positive process, which can lead to the discovery of positively new ideas.

CONCEPTUAL BLOCKBUSTING

Having achieved focus—whether by locating a "problem" or a contradiction, or by narrowing-and-focusing—what you want next is a solution, resolution, or thesis statement. Having decided what you are going to write about it, you need to decide what you are going to say about it, what your main point is going to be.

But you may not be ready. Having just defined the problem or narrowed the topic, you may not yet be ready to make a judgment about it. A "rush to judgment" can interfere with the creative process, can destroy that "attitude of suspended conclusion" which typifies the mature writing process and often leads to academic success.

The "rush to judgment" can also cut off or diminish inspiration and insight. Often it can lead you to reach conclusions based on a stereotyped image or idea. It can interfere with your ability to approach a subject from several perspectives; it can interfere with your ability to develop a new conception—to see the contradictions.

In order to develop a new conception, one must destroy—or at least, temporarily set aside—old concepts and perspectives. This process has been called *conceptual blockbusting* by James L. Adams, a humanistic professor of engineering. It is a form of what we will call *negative invention* in that it negates the old conception in order to create the new one. Like a contradiction, it is formally negative but creatively positive. Conceptual blockbusting can explode a stereotypical conception that may be blocking a more useful view of the subject or problem.

Consider, for example, the following story-riddle:

> *A father and son were in an automobile accident. The father was instantly killed. The son, seriously injured, was rushed to a nearby hospital for emergency surgery. The surgeon entered, apparently ready to operate, and then declared, "I can't operate. This boy is my son!" What is the relationship between the boy and the surgeon?*

The answer, which *ought* to be obvious, is that the surgeon is the boy's mother. But when a writer, using experiment as a discovery technique to prepare an article for an early issue of *Ms.*, asked this riddle of 51 people at a cocktail party, only two could answer correctly. Their view of the obvious was blocked by a conceptual stereotype of surgeons as men. Nowadays that stereotype has been significantly undermined, so in most North American contexts a much higher percentage of people can solve the riddle quickly.

Stereotyping—that is, perceiving what one expects to perceive instead of what is really there—is an example of *perceptual block*. A person who is "blocked" by a stereotype literally does not "see what you mean" if your meaning contradicts the stereotype.

Closely related to stereotyping is the failure to look at a topic or problem from various perspectives. The ability to switch viewpoints is often crucial to successful rhetorical invention (i.e., to generating the material and devising the stategy for a successful communication). The ability to perceive from various relevant perspectives is often crucial to scientific discovery, to technical design, and to almost any sort of humanistic vision. That is why William Blake prayed to be saved from "Single vision." It is also why much of the rest of this chapter is devoted to a series of rhetorical techniques for generating a variety of perspectives.

Other perceptual blocks (e.g., the tendency to overly narrow a topic and the failure to adequately limit a problem) have already been discussed. Several more, which follow from the tendency not to notice the familiar, will be discussed in Chapter 4. Here the point is not so much to catalog types of perceptual blocks but to emphasize their existence.

The surgeon riddle exemplifies the sense in which *attitudes* may underlie perceptual stereotypes and thus block creative discovery. In that example a sexist stereotype is allowed to exist because a sexist attitude has not been eradicated. Consider the following paper, very much like a freewriting, which was written by a basic writing student at Boston University. Notice how it circles round and round an attitudinal block, getting ever closer to a conceptual breakthrough it does not quite reach.

> I really don't know what to make of today, Liz trying to give me the money for her prom ticket. I really don't see why she even thought I would take it. I mean if I wanted her to pay for her ticket I would have said so when I asked her.
>
> But this really put me to thinking, she's said things about when we go out, yet I never really paid much attention to them. I guess it's because I feel that the guy should be responsible for the date, after all he's the one who did the asking. Ah, but that brings up a good point I've never thought of before, what if the girl should do the asking. I guess I'll worry about that if the situation ever comes up. Meanwhile I should worry about the situation at hand, sooner or later Liz is going to say something since I don't take her out as often now that I don't have a job. But there isn't too much you can do with little or no money, even less on weekend nights. Another point is transportation, since I don't always have a car it gets to be a pain, because then we either have to walk or get a ride with someone else. That can be a hassle especially since you're then limited to where you can go and what you can do. I've often wondered about that, I always decide what and where we go to. But occasionally I've heard girls say they don't always want to go where their date is taking them. Yet they never say anything, or if you ask them where they'd like to go they say, you decide. That's sort of a pain because generally if the guy has asked his date where she'd like to go it's probably because he doesn't want to resort to the old standby movie or bowling and can't think of something different to do.
>
> So I guess I'm saying that when asked out on a date the girl shouldn't have to pay for any of it, or worry about where to go unless the guy asks her where she'd like to go. I also believe the guy should be responsible for the transportation and definitely should be the one to ask. Furthermore if the girl has a curfew the guy should see that she's home on time.
>
> This is all quite interesting because I've just decided I really don't know if Liz agrees with these views. As a matter of fact I know she doesn't agree that the guy should have to pay for the entire date. She probably wouldn't hesitate to suggest something if I asked her, although it would more likely than not be the movies. She's also said she doesn't think the guy should always be responsible for the ride. However I know she agrees that the guy should see to it that the girl gets home on time, although her parents would do nothing more than ask if she wasn't out kind of late last night.
>
> That's weird because I never realized just how much people disagree on certain issues of this nature. Why I'd probably bet that no two people have the exact same image-model of anything. I guess this all just goes to show that no man is like any other.
>
> Edward Scanlon

In this case, the block is specific to a cultural attitude men have about women and so causes difficulty only for this paper. There are also more general cultural blocks, which can interfere with problem-solving and creativity. Quite commonly among North Americans, for example, there is a need to be always rational, orderly, and "in control." These personality traits can prevent a writer from tolerating the period of unconscious incubation and conscious chaos, which so often precedes inspiration and insight.

To what extent do you share common attitudes that may be interfering with your development as a writer? Do you believe that playfulness and humor should always be kept apart from "serious" work, that fantasy and reflection are often signs of laziness (if not craziness)? Do you share the common Anglo-American anti-intellectualism that rejects any theoretical knowledge unless it has *immediate* practical applications? Putting some effort into overcoming such blocks may be a very important part of improving your writing abilities.

A writer may also suffer from an *emotional block*. To what extent does the fear of failure interfere with your development as a writer? Although we say, "Nothing ventured, nothing gained," some students and even some professional writers will stick with one formula they have mastered (e.g., for a five-paragraph essay, a term paper, a newspaper report) rather than experiment with other forms and develop their writing abilities more broadly. Even in a writing class, where the main point is to develop one's writing abilities, many people are tempted to play it safe.

We are all human; we are all more comfortable with our old conceptions, just as we are with our old slippers. But a writer who is too comfortable with old conceptions is not likely to have anything new to say, nor even a significantly fresh way to say something old. To be competent at negative invention one must be open, able to tolerate contradictions and new ideas—even new *ways* of thinking—at least long enough to genuinely comprehend and consider them.

Problems do not exist autonomously. A problem is a problem only *for some person or group of people*. Difficulty resolving a problem or contradiction is sometimes best overcome by changing the person or people. This may mean you. An apparently intractable problem may be quickly solved if a change is effected *in the problem-solver*—that is, you.

Interestingly, this assertion has its roots in antiquity. Quintilian and Cicero both asserted that the good orator (or writer) must be the good person! To be good at negative invention, beyond narrow and specialized bounds, the writer must display certain personality traits which we ordinarily consider "mature" or "good." Such traits include openness, tolerance, and empathy, as well as a balanced development of emotional, intuitive, and rational faculties—traits that are also among the goals of a genuinely humanistic education. Since negative invention is crucial to the development of writing abilities beyond a certain level and certain narrow bounds, it is in this sense true that the good writer must be a good person.

THE POWER OF NEGATIVE THINKING

One of the mottos of our culture is "Think positively!" Positive thinking certainly has its uses, as when we insist on believing something can be done and therefore persevere until we discover a way to do it, or when we insist on defining a concept in positive terms (see page 263). A less-than-positive thinker might have given up before the task was accomplished or accepted a definition that did not really expose the nature of the concept.

But negative or critical thinking, as may be clear by now, is often the basis from which positive concepts are developed. Thus what is *logically* negative thinking can be more positive in its effects than so-called positive thinking. In truth, each type of thinking has it uses.

The epitome of negative thinking is the *law of the interpenetration of contraries* (sometimes called the *law of the unity of contradictions*). It is as old as Taoism, Buddhism, and pre-Socratic Greek philosophy. It is as new as relativity and quantum physics or modern dialectics. It is basic to thinking about change and process—because any process involves change, and any change involves the replacement of the old with the new, the development of the new from its contrary, the "not-new."

The implications of this law, as it is applied in various disciplines from theology to physics (often by people who do not even realize they are applying it), are diverse and complex. Here we need be concerned only with one particular application. As a discovery technique, this law asserts that *if any statement is true, there must be some sense or some context in which its contraries are true.* (A corollary is that if any statement is true there must be some sense or some context in which it is false.)

On the face of it, the law seems to fly in the face of common sense, which asserts that a statement is either true or false. That particular common sense, however, is common mostly in Western logics, so let us suspend judgment for a bit and consider how the law works as a discovery technique.

Just at the point when you have reached your conclusion, when you have decided that a certain generalization is true, this discovery technique forces you to pause and rethink that statement. It forces you to

look from other perspectives in order to see other sides. It forces you to search for contexts in which your generalization might not apply, for exceptions to your rule. It turns any statement into a potential "problem" or contradiction by juxtaposing it with its contraries. It demands, as least provisionally, that you *blockbust* each conception.

After you have applied this law, you often decide that your original generalization was and still is basically correct. Having considered the exceptions, you decide that they "prove the rule." But your understanding is fuller and deeper for having turned full circle, even if you have in a sense returned to your starting point. And very often you end up qualifying your original generalization, thus making it more correct (and more defensible).

Take, for instance, a proposition that seems obvious:

> The best place to begin is at the beginning.

Clearly, this is correct, at least in some senses. Consider nonetheless, some contrary propositions:

> The best place to begin is in the middle.
>
> The best place to begin is at the end.

Are there senses of contexts in which these statements are also true?

When you start a piece of writing with a thesis statement, in a sense you are starting at the end. That is, you are starting with your *conclusion*, with a generalization that sums up your thinking on the subject, with the end result of your thought process. It might sometimes make more sense to lead up to your conclusion and to put it at the end, as Socrates does (to cite just one example). Often, however, the most effective place to state your thesis is at the beginning of a piece of writing (see pages 137-142). When you do that you are, in a sense, beginning at the end.

As for beginning in the middle, that is precisely where many good fictional narratives do begin. There is even a common Latin term, *en medias res*, for beginning in the middle. The *Illiad* begins in the middle. So does *Oedipus Rex*. So does much modern literature. The importance of earlier events is often clear only in the context of the crisis, which precedes the climax. So it often makes narrative sense to begin in the midst of that crisis and introduce earlier events (including the beginning of the story) as flashbacks. (Some modern literature seems to go one step further: Samuel Beckett's *Waiting for Godot*, for example, is in a sense all middle; essentially it has neither a beginning nor an ending, so it could not possibly begin at the beginning.)

Of course, there is a sense in which one always begins at the beginning. Literally, the fact that a text begins there makes it the beginning. And if we understand "beginning" to mean the rhetorically effective place to begin (as opposed to what-happened-first or what-is-logically-prior), then the beginning is where one should begin. So the original proposition is in several senses correct. But one's understanding is much more full for having considered the ways in which it is not so.

The great American rhetorician Kenneth Burke, a consumate dialectician, seems to apply this discovery technique almost constantly. Reading his essays, one gets the feeling that he almost never makes an assertion without also considering the senses in which its contraries are correct. Much of the admirable fullness of his conceptions seems to come from his application of this law. He explicitly bases an entire essay, for example, on the ideas generated by applying this discovery technique to the proposition, "Words are signs for things":

> *There is so much that is substantially correct in this commonsense view (summed up in the proposition that "Words are the signs of things"), we tinker with it at our peril. But we would here ask, if only as a tour de force, if only as an experiment tentatively tried for heuristic purposes, what might be said for the reverse proposition, "Resolved: That things are the signs of words." And even if we didn't dare assert that it should flatly replace the traditional view, we still might hope that it could supply a needed modification of that view, like adding an adjective to a noun.*

And, indeed, Burke goes on to reach many important insights about language and communication from this starting point. [The full essay, "What are the Signs of What?" (A Theory of 'Entitlement')" may be found in Burke's *Language as Symbolic Action*, a collection of essays to be recommended to writing students both as a methodological model and for what it says.]

This discovery technique can be applied to images as well as to propositions (although, in a sense we do so by converting the image into a statement). Imagine the stereotypic image of "the writer," for example, in its Romantic extreme: a gaunt young man, lonely and suffering, dressed in his only suit of threadbare black clothes, starving and unappreciated in some dark garret, torturing his soul over each line of lyric poetry. There are many potentially contrary images we can think of (the idea that each term, image, or statement has one-and-only-one opposite is a conceptual block that also needs to be "busted"). One will serve. Imagine, "the writer" now as a *group* of people, male and female, of various ages, adequately fed and clothed, excitedly creating an extended argument. In what senses or contexts is this second image accurate or useful?

In fact, this image is in several ways accurate: much of the writing in North America these days *is* done by groups, is explanatory or persuasive (rather than literary or expressive), pays quite adequately, and involves somewhat less suffering than our Romantic images of "the writer" suggest. Writings are produced by groups of people in various ways, with various degrees and types of division of labor, but the fact remains that much of the writing you read is produced by more than one person. Most newspaper and newsmagazine articles are group productions, either because they combine the work of several reporters or because one person discovered, organized, and drafted the report and then another person revised, edited, titled, and perhaps reorganized it. Certainly most corporate reports are produced corporately. The same is true of government reports and press releases. Academic reports usually come out of committees (and are typically drafted by subcommittees). Scientific papers are often co-authored. Political and union leaflets are often written collectively. Even many novels are written by teams of writers, though only one name appears on the cover (in deference to the public stereotype). There are even "factories" where large numbers of writers, editors, and typists produce many books simultaneously under the direction of one or two people who approve the ideas and control the publishing contracts.

It remains true that certain types of writing, such as poetry, are still written predominantly by individuals. And the actual drafting of a given passage of prose is almost always done by a single person. But if the substance of that passage was invented by a group interaction, if the draft was reorganized and revised by a group or by anyone other than the person who drafted it, if it was combined into a single written product with other passages drafted by other writers—then the final written product is in several significant senses a group production.

The point of this example, as of the two preceding examples, is that the law of the interpenetration of contraries can be a powerful discovery technique. It can help you open yourself to perspectives that you had not considered. It can help you improve the content of your writings, the strategies you devise for communicating that content, and even your writing processes. There is much more to be said about this law as a rule of logic or dialectic, but that goes beyond the purposes of this book. What has been presented here is difficult enough. Play with it, work with it, learn how to use it. It may lead you to more sophisticated, more correct, and more effective writings.

ADDITIONAL READING

Adams, James L. *Conceptual Blockbusting*. San Francisco: W. H. Freeman, 1974. A slim, wide-ranging, and popular guide to creative problem-solving.

Burke, Kenneth. "What Are the Signs of What? (A Theory of Entitlement)". In Burke's *Language as Symbolic Action*. Berkeley: University of California, 1966. In that same volume, see pages 3-23, 419-436, and 457-464 for discussion of the importance of the negative as a defining characteristic of human language and thought.

Elbow, Peter. *Writing Without Teachers*. New York: Oxford, 1973. See pages 48-60 on the various types of contradictions that can be useful to writers.

EXERCISE

1. Pick several general topics. Focus each by narrowing-and-focusing. Then focus each by finding a contradiction or "problem." Compare and contrast your results. Imagine contexts (purposes, audiences, and occasions) for which each focused topic might be appropriate.
2. Explain the statement (on page 52), "Notice that this section on problem-solving as a way to focus a topic has just exemplified itself." Consider whether having the form of a piece of writing exemplify its content is ordinarily useful.
3. Pick several propositions which matter to you. Apply the law of interpenetration of contraries. What type of insights, if any, do you get?
4. Read Burke's essay, "What Are the Signs of What? (A Theory of Entitlement)," in his *Language as Symbolic Action*. What does he mean by "entitlement," and what relevance does that concept have for writers? Mark the points at which Burke seems to be using the law of the interpenetration of contraries. What effect does it have on his writing? In what ways does it seem useful? In what ways is it bothersome?
5. Consider the prospect of group-writing? How do you think you would go about it?

POSITIVE INVENTION

For excellence in speaking cannot be made manifest unless the speaker fully comprehends the matters he speaks about.

Cicero

Every writer confronts the task of making sense of events in the world around him or within him . . . and of making what he wants to say understandable and believable to particular readers. He uses a method of invention when these processes are guided deliberately by heuristic procedures, that is explicit plans for analyzing and searching which focus attention, guide reason, stimulate memory and encourage intuition.

Richard Young

QUESTION HEURISTICS

If your find yourself encountering the same type of problem regularly, it makes sense to devise a procedure for approaching it. Otherwise you have to start from scratch each time.

In the more mathematical and precise disciplines, a problem, after it is well-defined and reduced to some recognizable pattern, can often be solved mechanically by applying a standard procedure. Such procedures are called *algorithms* (after the ninth-century Arab mathematician, Muhammad ibn-Musa *al-Khwarizmi*). Writing "problems" are not often so easily handled.

In rhetoric, too, there are standard procedures for discovery, called *heuristics* (from the Greek, *heuresis*, to discover or invent). A heuristic differs from an algorithm in that it only increases the probability of discovery, whereas an algorithm leads mechanically and infallibly to a correct solution. A heuristic is merely a guide that increases the likelihood of your discovering the information you need and decreases the likelihood of your overlooking relevant material. A heuristic replaces neither thought nor intuition. Instead, it makes both thought and intuition more effective and comprehensive.

Heuristics often come in the form of questions. Even when a heuristic comes in some other form, it can usually be translated into a set of questions. Probably the most well-known question-heuristic is *the journalist's five W's*: *who? what? where? when? why?* (and, sometimes, *how?*). By answering these questions, a reporter discovers the information needed to begin a straight news report.

The formula is not automatic. The questions can be answered in various ways, and reporters use a combination of experience and intuition to pick answers that will be considered appropriate at their particular newspapers. It is, moreover, not always appropriate to answer all the questions (*why?* and *how?* are those most often left out). The writer must also decide how to order the answers. Nonetheless, an experienced reporter usually can quickly generate the opening of a news report with these questions.

> Protesting U.S. military occupation of their land [*why*], fishers from the Puerto Rican island of Vieques [*who*] last week (*when*) stymied military maneuvers [*what*] in the area [*where*] for more than five hours.

Since a newspaper report usually tries to catch readers' attention by putting the most important or dynamic bit of information first, the reporter could have begun, "Military maneuvers were stymied for five hours last week . . ." In this case, however, she decided to avoid the passive sentence and put the emphasis on the protest. She also decided that *how?* was not an important question to answer in the first sentence (and that using the unfamiliar "fishers" was better than implying that all the protesters were fisher*men*). Although she used the heuristic, she still had a lot of decisions to make.

The journalist's five W's (with or without the *how?*) is useful for generating narrative reports of various types. It is one of a large number of question-heuristics that are available to writers for various purposes. Some of them are rather broadly applicable to a wide variety of writing tasks. Others are quite specific. (Grade-school teachers, for example, often make up a specific question-heuristic to guide pupils through a particular writing assignment.)

You can make up question-heuristics to meet your own special needs. For any particular type of writing task you face regularly, you can devise a set of questions that will help you generate the substance of such a writing and help you avoid leaving out anything important. This set of questions can also help you choose an effective rhetorical strategy for communicating that substance. If your writings tend to have a particular shortcoming, you can devise a heuristic to help you overcome it.

One advanced writing student at the University of British Columbia, for example, had a problem with under-, over-, and mis-developed paragraphs. She always chose good topics, generated clear and complex theses, wrote detailed sentence outlines which contained topic sentences for her main paragraphs, and organized the writing effectively. But some of her paragraphs had inadequate support, some concepts were supported more than necessary, and much of the detail in her papers did not seem clearly attached to anything. In her university courses, her papers generally received B's and B-minuses, grades which did not satisfy her. But even when the flaws in a particular paper were marked, she did not seem able to correct them. Finally, after doing the self-analyses of her writing process assigned in the preceding chapter, she devised for herself the following heuristic, which she applied to each topic sentence in her outline:

1. What do you mean?
2. Explain that!
3. Give details!
4. Give an example!
5. This means that . . .
6. Why do you believe that?

This heuristic may sound like a bit of overkill, and it does sound as if she is yelling at herself; but it produced an immediate qualitative leap in her writing (and A's on term papers in several courses just weeks later).

This heuristic worked because it matched the particular individual's problem and personality: it suited her purpose. There are simpler heuristics for turning a topic sentence into a developed paragraph with logical and exemplary support, for example,

1. To what extent is this true?
2. How do I know it is true?
3. What is a good example of it?
4. So what?

You can devise heuristics to focus your attention on whatever aspects of your writing are weakest, from discovering a topic to revising punctuation. There is no guarantee of an immediate leap in the quality of your writing. But *if you insert the heuristic at the right point in your writing process*, you should see significant improvement soon. Various types of heuristics will be discussed in this and the following chapter, so you may even be able to find some ready-made heuristics that suit your needs.

But a heuristic is a means to an end. Whatever works for you will do. Some writers may actually find it useful to prepare a specific heuristic for each particular writing task. Figure 1.1 is one student's personal heuristic for doing the final assignment from Chapter 0; the essay she wrote using this heuristic is reproduced on pages 22-24.

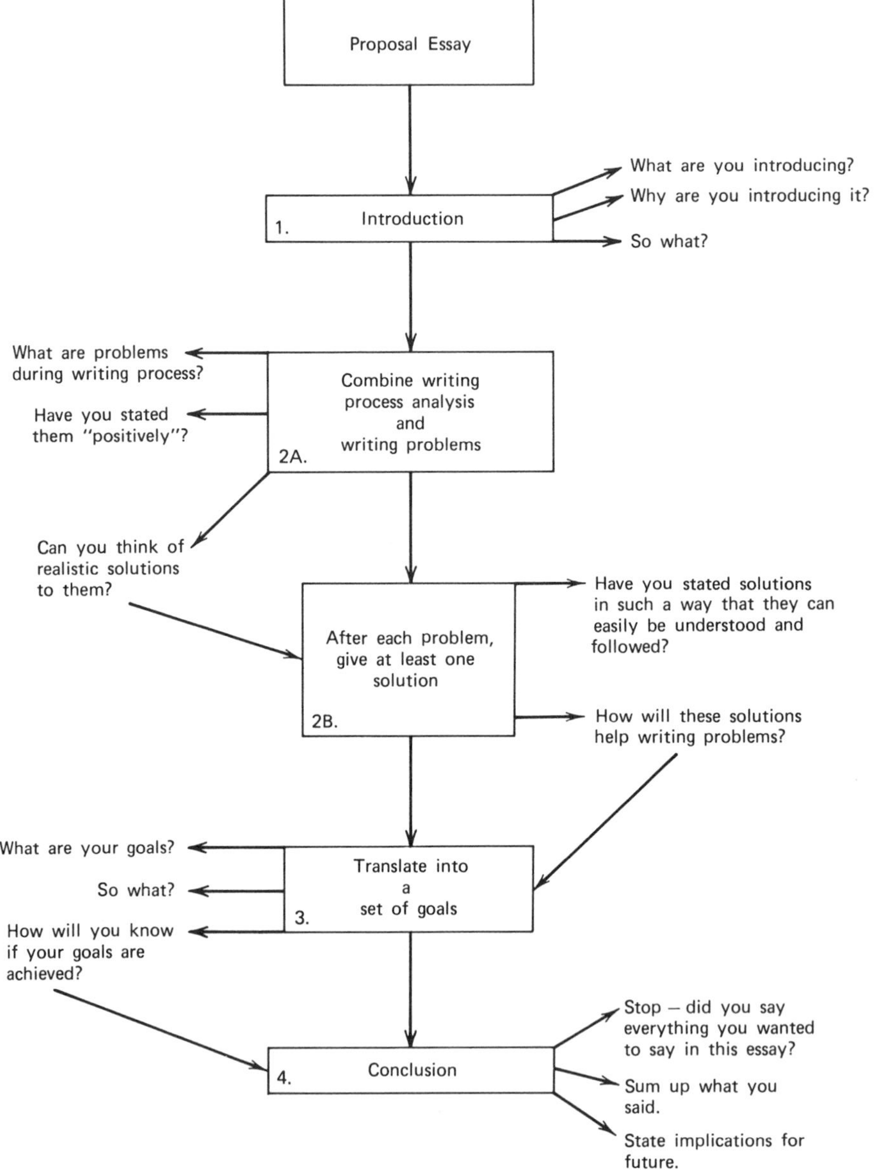

FIGURE 1.1 One Student's Personal Heuristic for Doing the Assignment on Page 22 Above

THE PENTAD

One of the better-known heuristics, superficially similar to the journalist's five W's, is Burke's Pentad. It was designed for investigating motivation. It is particularly useful for writing about human behavior, either as it actually occurs or as it is represented in literature, cinema, and so forth. Thus the Pentad could help you write a sociological case history or a critical analysis of a novel. It is less likely to help you if you are writing about nonhuman matters (unless you are writing about them as they relate to human beings).

This heuristic was derived from the metaphor "human drama" and is sometimes called the Dramatistic Pentad. Here is Burke's own introduction to the Pentad.

> *What is involved, when we say what people are doing and why they are doing it? . . .*
>
> *We shall use five terms as generating principle of our investigation. They are: Act, Scene, Agent, Agency, Purpose. In a rounded statement about motives, you must have some word that names the* act *(names what took place, in thought or deed), and another that names the scene (the background of the act, the situation in which it occurred); also you must indicate what person or kind of person* (agent) *performed the act, what means or instruments he used* (agency), *and the* purpose. . . . *[A]ny complete statement about motives will offer* some kind *of answer to these five questions: what was done (act), when or where it was done (scene), who did it (agent), how he did it (agency), and why (purpose).*

The terms of the Pentad should be understood rather broadly. Anything a human being does, has done, or might do can be considered an **act**, according to Burke's formulation. Thus a thought, a decision, or a statement is an act. A piece of writing was an act when it was written and continues to be an act whenever anyone reads it. A poem, when it is read, is a communicative act, which Burke would call a "symbolic action." So is the body posture of an excessively proud person. Identifying an act involves not only discovering the facts (what happened, is happening, or might happen) and making inferences from them, but also *naming* the act. Attaching a name to an act (is it love?) means making a judgment, putting it in a catgegory.

The **scene** or context of an act can be narrowly interpreted as equivalent to the journalist's *where* and *when*. In Burke's usage, however, it also includes other sorts of contexts—historical, social, and psychological. The scene in which a novel exists might include the literary traditions in which it was written and is read. The scene in which a person chooses a vocation might include the economic situation, social trends, and personality traits of that individual. The question—what is the background of this act?—should be explored on various levels.

The term **agent** also can be considered on several levels. In the case of a drama, for example, a character in the story could be considered an agent. In another sense, the playwright or the actor is the agent. The term, agent, can be subdivided: a person's act might be modified by friends (co-agents) or by enemies (counter-agents). Aspects of a person's character could, by extension, be represented as agents. One might say, for instance, "Her stubbornness made her hold out for a better contract," or "It is his good looks that cause him to act so uppity."

Agency raises the question *how.* What means were used to perform the act? How was it done? If a judge made a decision, agency might refer to the logical "tools" used in thinking it through. On another level, it might refer to the means by which the decision was made known to others. When the act is communicative, agency can refer to the medium: thus the agencies by which world news is made known include newspapers, radio, and television.

Purpose raises questions about intention and function. What purposes were served by the act? What did the agent intend to accomplish? The agent's intentions and the actual function need not, of course, be the same. All of the terms in the Pentad are ultimately aimed at discovering motivation, at answering the question *why?* Purpose refers to a narrower version of the same question. The distinction is best made clear by explaining how Burke uses all five terms together to explore motivation.

As stated thus far, the Pentad adds little to the journalists' formula. Burke, however, is primarily concerned with the predictable relationships among the five terms, not with the terms themselves. He calls these relationships "ratios." The "ratios" are the ten pairs that can be made from the terms. Burke begins by discussing the "scene-act ratio." By that he means the predictable ways in which the *scene* or context can motivate the *act* (and *vice versa*, the ways in which the act can modify the scene). The influence of the social context on the development of an individual is an example of the scene-act ratio in action. That ratio is particularly clear in the novels of Thomas Hardy and other regionalist authors, where much of what happens must be explained in terms of the geographical and cultural environment.

The use of the scene-act ratio can be observed in Senator Edward Kennedy's explanation of the death of Mary Jo Kopechne in 1969 at Chappaquiddick. Kennedy stated,

> Little over a mile away the car that I was driving on an *unlit road* went off a *narrow bridge* which had *no guard rails* and was built on a *left angle* to the

road. The car overturned into a *deep pond* and immediately filled with water. [Italics added.]

Although elsewhere in his statement Kennedy formally accepted responsibility for Kopechne's death, here he piles up *scenic references* in such a way as to imply that the *scene* was to some degree responsible for the *act*. As David Ling pointed out at the time, the implicit argument is that, considering the darkness of the road, the narrowness of the bridge, the absence of guard rails, and the angle of the bridge to the road, it is not surprising that the car ended up in the pond. Furthermore, considering the depth of the pond and how immediately the car filled up with water, it is not surprising that Kennedy failed to rescue Kopechne. Thus isolated and made explicit, the argument starts to sound like an excuse. But in the context of the speech and left implicit, it successfully deflects some responsibility from Kennedy as agent.

Any pair of terms from the Pentad can form a *ratio* and thereby suggest an explanation or argument. The Pentad is, of course, only a guide. The writer remains responsible for judging the validity of each argument in a given case. Consider, for instance, the five ratios that can be used to explain an act. In the following table, the ratios are exemplified by tentative answers to the question, "Why can so few university students write well enough to satisfy their professors?"—that is, the act to be explained is *unsatisfactory writing*.

Like many heuristics, the Pentad may seem awkward at first. Once mastered, however, it can be used to generate quickly a complex set of explanations from which a writer may pick and choose. As will be seen in Chapter 2, it can also be used to analyze an audience. That is, a writer can use the Pentad to discover which sorts of arguments are likely to be effective with a particular group of potential readers. It can also be used to analyze arguments that a writer might want to refute and thereby to suggest effective refutations.

The Pentad is *not* designed to produce simple explanations. People act as they do for reasons that are typically complex, ambiguous, and multiple; and the Pentad is designed to explain human motivations. Rarely, if ever, is a single, simple reason adequate to explain any human action. Burke takes it for granted that

> *there must remain something essentially enigmatic about the problem of motives, and that this underlying enigma will manifest itself in inevitable ambiguities and inconsistencies among the terms for motives. Accordingly, what we want is not terms that avoid ambiguity,* but *terms that clearly reveal the strategic spots at which ambiguities necessarily arise.*

TABLE 1.1 The Pentadic Act Ratios

RATIO	DEFINITION	EXAMPLE: "Unsatisfactory Writing"
Scene-Act:	The act follows from the nature of the circumstances.	Since employers are demanding more and more years of schooling for all sorts of jobs, an ever-larger percentage of the population has to attend college including many "underprepared" students.
Agent-Act:	The act follows from the nature of the person.	Many students are unintelligent, untalented, "underprepared," "culturally deprived," or whatever.
Agency-Act:	The act follows from the nature of the available means (or tools).	Schools are underfunded and understaffed. Professors judge writing by unrealistically high standards. Many English teachers and most English professors, having been trained primarily as literary critics, do not know much about teaching writing.
Purpose-Act:	In order to achieve the desired act, such-and-such needs to be done.	In order to develop all students' writing abilities to the desired level of competency, we would need to make a financial and intellectual commitment which would not be cost-effective (according to current standards of social accounting).
Act-Act:	The act in question follows from another act.	Students can't write well because they have not been taught "the basics."

Such a perspective, although quintessentially humanistic, is not likely to be popular among those who demand simple explanations. But writers who want to write for and about human beings must be prepared to deal with ambiguities and complexities if they are not to oversimplify their subject matter.

A particular entity, for example, may be classified in various ways, depending on the points of view. Thus a person's body might be seen by a coach as a means to a winning season (i.e., as an agency), by a doctor as an object (i.e., as scenic), by a novelist as an expression of personality (i.e., as a property of the agent), by a nutritionist as the result of an unbalanced diet (i.e., as the result of an act), and by a deodorant manufacturer as a potential customer and hence as a potential profit (i.e., as defined by the manufacturer's purpose). A single individual, moreover, might view that same body from more than one perspective, even in a single moment. Such is the complexity of human affairs.

To master the Pentad requires a certain amount of study and practice. It is, however, a particularly seminal heuristic, and mastering it is well worth the effort.

THE CLASSICAL *TOPOI* AND THE FORMS OF DISCOURSE

The English word *topic* comes from the Greek *topos* (plural, *topoi*), meaning *place*. In classical rhetoric, the *topoi* were "places" one could "go" in search of substance or strategies for a speech. There were special *topoi* for particular types of speeches (e.g., for arguments to be presented in law courts). There were also common *topoi*, based on the essential tendencies of human minds, for more general use.

The common *topoi* can be summarized by five basic questions:

1. What is it?
2. What is it like and unlike?
3. What caused it?
4. What can come of it?
5. What has been said about it?

Even by themselves, these five general questions make a useful heuristic. Asked about almost any subject, they generate a broad range of information. Whatever you may be writing about, the first question can lead you to describe it, define it, classify it, and divide it into its parts or aspects. The second question can lead you to compare and constrast, make analogies and give examples. The third and fourth can lead you to consider it as part of a process, analyze its functions, explain why it exists, perhaps tell a story in which it plays a part. The fifth can lead you to quote authorities, cite statistics and precedents, and refer to proverbs, parables, and other common wisdom.

The classifical rhetoricians enumerated the common *topoi* in great detail. A Greek or Roman teacher of rhetoric provided his students with a list of *topoi* and examples of each. Aristotle, for instance, lists twenty-eight valid and nine fallacious *topoi* in his *Rhetoric*. His first *topos* is based on opposites (a variant of "what is it unlike?"), and he cites among his examples this argument, attributed to Alcidamas, "If war is the cause of our present troubles, peace is what we need to put things right." Following the pattern of the examples, his students could use the list of *topoi* to invent supporting arguments for whatever they might want to prove.

Much of the suggestiveness of the common *topoi* follows from their having been developed in such detail. The classical rhetoricians were primarily concerned with formal argumentation, such as speeches to be delivered in law courts or political assemblies. If you are interested in that type of discourse, it might well be worth your while to investigate the classical texts, beginning with Aristotle's *Rhetoric*, Book II, Chapter 23.

If there is some other type of writing you will be doing regularly, perhaps as part of your profession, it would be useful to have a set of *topoi* that would help you invent the substance of your writings. Such a heuristic or set of *topoi* may exist in your area of special interest (although it will probably be called neither a heuristic nor a set of special *topoi*). If it does not exist, it would probably be useful for you to invent it. In the long run, it could save you a lot of time and effort.

The modern equivalents of the common *topoi*—known as forms of discourse or patterns of development—are presented in Chapters 4 and 5 of this textbook. Although they are discussed there primarily as ways to structure and develop writings (i.e., as patterns of arrangement, of *dispositio*), they are also *topoi*. They can help you discover both substance and structure. These chapters discuss description, comparison-/contrast, definition, classification and division, analogy and exemplification, narration, process analysis, causal analysis, and logical progression. If you use them and describe something, say what it is like and unlike, define it, classify it, divide it into its parts or aspects, make some analogies, give some examples, tell a story in which it figures, analyze it as a process, explain why it exists and what its functions are, discuss its implications, and so forth—you will have generated a great deal of material, probably more than you could use in a short paper.

You may detect a similarity between the modern patterns of development and the classical *topoi*. That is because both are based on the workings of the human mind. And, although there is considerable variation in how the human mind works from culture to culture, there is also a basic structure of human thought.

The basic structures that give *form* to our speech and writing reflect the processes of the human mind (as it has evolved on this planet). Thus *the form of a piece of writing can function as a heuristic for the discovery of its substance.* As the law of the interpenetration of contraries might lead you to expect, form and substance are a unity as well as an opposition. Indeed, Aristotle himself argued that substance does not exist except as given shape by form. Hence the title of this textbook: *Form and Substance.* The patterns of development discussed in Part Two are both structures that can give shape to your writings and also ways to develop the substance of those same writings. Chapters 4 and 5 deal with very general patterns, the equivalents of the common *topoi*. Chapters 6 and 7 deal with more specific patterns, the equivalents of the special *topoi*. Use these forms and you will discover that your attempt to follow a particular pattern helps (and even forces) you to discover appropriate substance. In fact, you will find that form helps you to shape not only your communication, but also your perceptions, thoughts, and feelings. Form can generate substance.

ADDITIONAL READING

Burke, Kenneth. *A Grammar of Motives*. Berkeley: University of California, 1969. (First published by Prentice-Hall in 1945.) Burke introduces the Pentad here. See especially pages xv-20.

Corbett, Edward P. J. *Classical Rhetoric for the Modern Student*. 2nd ed. New York: Oxford, 1971. See pages 107-155 on the classical *topoi*.

D'Angelo, Frank. *A Conceptual Theory of Rhetoric*. Cambridge, Mass.: Winthrop, 1975. See pages 38-59 on the interrelationship between invention and arrangement, which are discussed in terms of the classical *topoi* and patterns of arrangement.

Readings in Classical Rhetoric. Eds. Thomas Benson and Michael Prosser. Bloomington: Indiana University, 1972. See pages 141-188 for selections on invention from Aristotle, Cicero, Quintilian, and Augustine.

The Rhetoric of Aristotle. Trans. Lane Cooper. New Jersey: Prentice-Hall, 1932. See Book II, Chapter 23 (pages 159-172) for Aristotle's *topoi*.

Young, Richard, Alton Becker, and Kenneth Pike. *Rhetoric: Discovery and Change*. New York: Harcourt, Brace & World, 1970. Young, Becker, and Pike offer a heuristic called *the tagmemic grid*, which guides writers through nine different perspectives on any subject. See especially Chapter Six, pages 119-136, and also Chapter Three, pages 53-60.

EXERCISE

1. Devise a question-heuristic which meets one or more of your own needs. Perhaps one that will focus your attention on a particular writing problem you have. Perhaps one to generate a particular type of writing you need to produce regularly (be that something for your field of special interest or a letter to your parents). Then use this heuristic to generate a piece of writing. Submit the heuristic and the piece of writing together.

2. Research and study a formal heuristic. This could be one from the discipline of rhetoric, such as the Pentad, the tagmemic grid of Young, Becker, and Pike, or the common *topoi* of Aristotle. Or it could be one from your field of specialization. (*Remember:* Any set of questions designed to generate information needed in your field is a heuristic, even if it is not so titled.) Whichever formal heuristic you choose, use it, to generate a piece of writing. Submit the heuristic and the piece of writing together.

MEAN WHAT YOU WRITE

The only justification for our concepts and system of concepts is that they serve to represent the complex of our experience.

Albert Einstein

The compelling job of all teaching of language . . . is to get at truth, reality, the world as we know it and believe it to be, through words. It is the specific and special job of language teaching to establish the methods by which this can be done and the conviction that it is worth doing.

Louis Zahner

GENERATION AND SELECTION

Thus far this chapter has emphasized getting started, generating words and meanings. Like any creative process, writing begins by generating potentials. Like any creative process, also, it is brought to fruition by a process of critical selection and arrangment. For a variety of reasons, much that has been generated may not serve a writer's purposes. After careful thought, it may even appear to the writer that some of what has been generated is not entirely true. Or perhaps the words do not accurately represent what they were intended to mean.

The basic principle to be grasped is this: writing is brought to fruition by a process of *selection*. Material must be generated, perhaps by using the discovery techniques discussed above, and then it must be culled. Like a gardener whose seeds have sprouted and whose young fruit trees are starting to branch, a writer must cut, thin, transplant, graft, prune, and even refertilize.

Of course, the two processes—generation and selection—interpenetrate: writers do not first uncritically generate a complete set of potential words and meanings, and second select the ones that serve their purposes. The two contraries coexist within the composing process. Very often it is precisely the rejection of a phrase that leads to the generation of an alternative.

Many of the discovery techniques discussed earlier in this chapter actually embody principles of selection. To focus a topic, for instance, is to rule out material that does not fit within that focus. To constrain a set of freewritings toward an emerging "center of gravity" is to select. Any research process requires the researcher to select information. Certainly any heuristic for positive invention embodies a principle of selection which constrains the writer toward discovering relevant information.

Even if we cannot treat them as two distinct stages, however, the distinction between generation and selection is useful for thinking about writing. The generation or discovery of material does usually predominate in the early phases of writing, and the critical selection and arrangement does usually predominate in the later phases. Inexperienced writers, or writers who are blocked, often find it useful to separate the two because, as contraries, they can impede each other.

Consider this analogy. As the wolves cull the caribou herds, they have a clear principle of selection. They select the aged, the deformed, the weak, the slow, and the poorly protected young. Their principle of selection constrains them to take those caribou that are unfit for survival. They remove certain genes from the genetic pool of the herd and create space for caribou that are more fit. Thus, by selecting out those few caribou who are genuinely unfit, they serve *the natural purpose* of strengthening the caribou species. The Inuit who hunt the caribou therefore say, "The wolf and the caribou are one."

Just so, generation and selection are one within the creative process. What, then, in the writing process is the equivalent of "the natural purpose"? On what principle or principles should writers select? The rest of our discussion of the writing process will be concerned with answering this question.

REVISION MEANS TO RE-ENVISION

For most inexperienced writers, revision is largely a matter of (1) attempting to eliminate errors of usage, grammar, spelling, and punctuation, and (2) trying to find more accurate words to substitute for the "wrong words" in their drafts. But revision is really much more than that. Experienced writers spend much more time on revision—because they can see so much more to revise. Learning to see potential revisions is one of the most important abilities for a writer to develop. The rest of this chapter, and the two which follow, are focused on developing this ability.

Revision is a combination of the root *vision* with the prefix *re-*, meaning "again." So *re-vision* is literally "to see again," "to obtain a new vision." A new vision implies a changed written representation, so the word *revision* has come to refer to the process of changing that written representation. But if we forget that the change is, on one level or another, based on a new vision, we lose the meaning of the process. Even

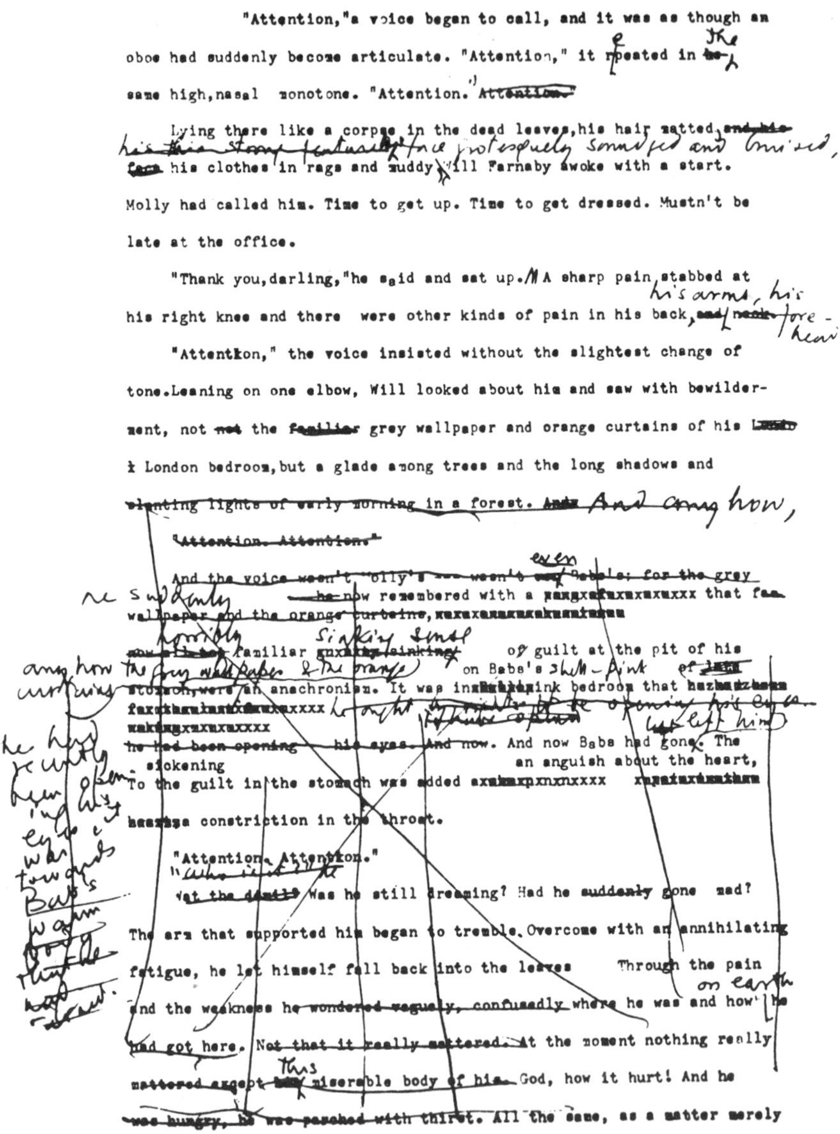

"Attention," a voice began to call, and it was as though an oboe had suddenly become articulate. "Attention," it repeated in the same high, nasal monotone. "Attention."

Lying there like a corpse in the dead leaves, his hair matted, his clothes in rags and muddy, Will Farnaby awoke with a start. Molly had called him. Time to get up. Time to get dressed. Mustn't be late at the office.

"Thank you, darling," he said and sat up. A sharp pain stabbed at his right knee and there were other kinds of pain in his back,

"Attention," the voice insisted without the slightest change of tone. Leaning on one elbow, Will looked about him and saw with bewilderment, not the grey wallpaper and orange curtains of his London bedroom, but a glade among trees and the long shadows and slanting lights of early morning in a forest.

"Attention. Attention."

And the voice wasn't Molly's ... wasn't Babs's; for the grey he now remembered with a ... that ... wallpaper and the orange curtains, ... familiar ... of guilt at the pit of his stomach, were an anachronism. It was in ... on Babs's ... pink bedroom that ... he had been opening his eyes. And now. And now Babs had gone. The sickening guilt in the stomach was added ... an anguish about the heart, ... a constriction in the throat.

"Attention. Attention."

Was he still dreaming? Had he suddenly gone mad? The arm that supported him began to tremble. Overcome with an annihilating fatigue, he let himself fall back into the leaves. Through the pain and the weakness he wondered vaguely, confusedly where he was and how he had got here. Not that it really mattered. At the moment nothing really mattered except this miserable body of his. God, how it hurt! And he was hungry, he was parched with thirst. All the same, as a matter merely

FIGURE 1.2 Aldous Huxley Manuscript Page

on the level of language, as Professor Gary Tate has said, "A search for a better word is a search for a better vision."

That search is often arduous. When we read it, a polished piece of writing often flows so naturally that we assume it must have flowed just as naturally when the writer wrote it. But the writers who produce such writing generally spend much more time on revision than do less experienced writers who produce less polished writing.

Whoever said writing is not hard work was either lying or befuddled by some Romantic myth. Inspiration is real and wonderful and sometimes even easy, but it is not the whole story. Although there have been a few well-publicized exceptions, the revision of that inspiration generally takes a lot of time and effort. The more you know about writing, the more potentials you see, the more changes you consider. That is very exciting, both in the process itself and because of the quality of the resulting product. But it is also hard work.

Good writers can, of course, generally turn out a given quality of writing with less effort than poorer writers need to produce the same quality. But as your writing abilities improve, you are not likely to be satisfied with that same quality. For any given writer, producing good writing is usually more work than producing bad writing—whether we measure that work in intensity of labor or simply in number of hours per page.

Here is what some people who have produced excellent writing say about revision.

Rewriting is the difference between the dilettante and the artist, the amateur and the professional, the unpublished and the published. William Gass testifies, "I work not by writing but rewriting." Dylan Thomas states, "Almost any poem is fifty to a hundred revisions—and that's after it's well along. Archibald McLeish talks of "the endless discipline of writing and rewriting and rerewriting." Novelist Theodore Weesner tells his students at the University of New Hampshire his course title is not "Fiction Writing" but "Fiction Rewriting."

Donald Murray

. . . [T]here are days when the result is so bad that no fewer than five revisions are required. In contrast, when I'm greatly inspired, only four revisions are needed.

John Kenneth Galbraith

Oh, bother the MSS., mark them as much as you like: what else are they for? Mark everything that strikes you. I may consider a thing fortynine times; but if you consider it, it will be considered 50 times; and a line 50 times considered is 2 per cent better than a line 49 times considered. And it is the final 2 per cent that makes the difference between excellence and mediocrity.

George Bernard Shaw

Each book is completely written three times and then given a polish and overhaul. . . . I start by combing the first draft through and listing every alteration. Then I rewrite, chapter by chapter. It takes about six months. Then I leave it aside for at least three weeks without looking at it . . . . This is where the book is cut, shaped, tightened up, discrepancies ironed out. . . .

Mary Stewart

After writing about twenty pages, I go over them and over them and over them, cutting and changing words to bring out the meaning more clearly. Sometimes I destroy the pages entirely. Or, at best, I rewrite them several times.

Taylor Caldwell

To rewrite ten times is not unusual.

Saul Bellow

I do a great deal of rewriting. Almost never is a paragraph right the first time or the sixth or seventh time either.

Peg Bracken

Life is the elimination of what is dead.

Wallace Stevens

I always try to write on the principle of the iceberg. There is seven-eighths of it underwater for every part that shows. Anything you know, you can eliminate and it only strengthens your iceberg. It is the part that doesn't show. If a writer omits something because he does not know it there is a hole in the story.

Ernest Hemingway

A young author is tempted to leave anything he has written through fear of not having enough to say if he goes cutting out too freely. But it is easier to be long than short. . . . Think of and look at your work as though it were done by your enemy. If you look at it to admire it you are lost. . . . If we look at it to see where it is wrong, we shall see this and make it righter. If we look at it to see where it is right, we shall see this and shall not make it righter. . . . I always intend to read, and generally do read, what I write aloud to some one. . . . I feel weak places at once when I read aloud. . . .

Samuel Butler

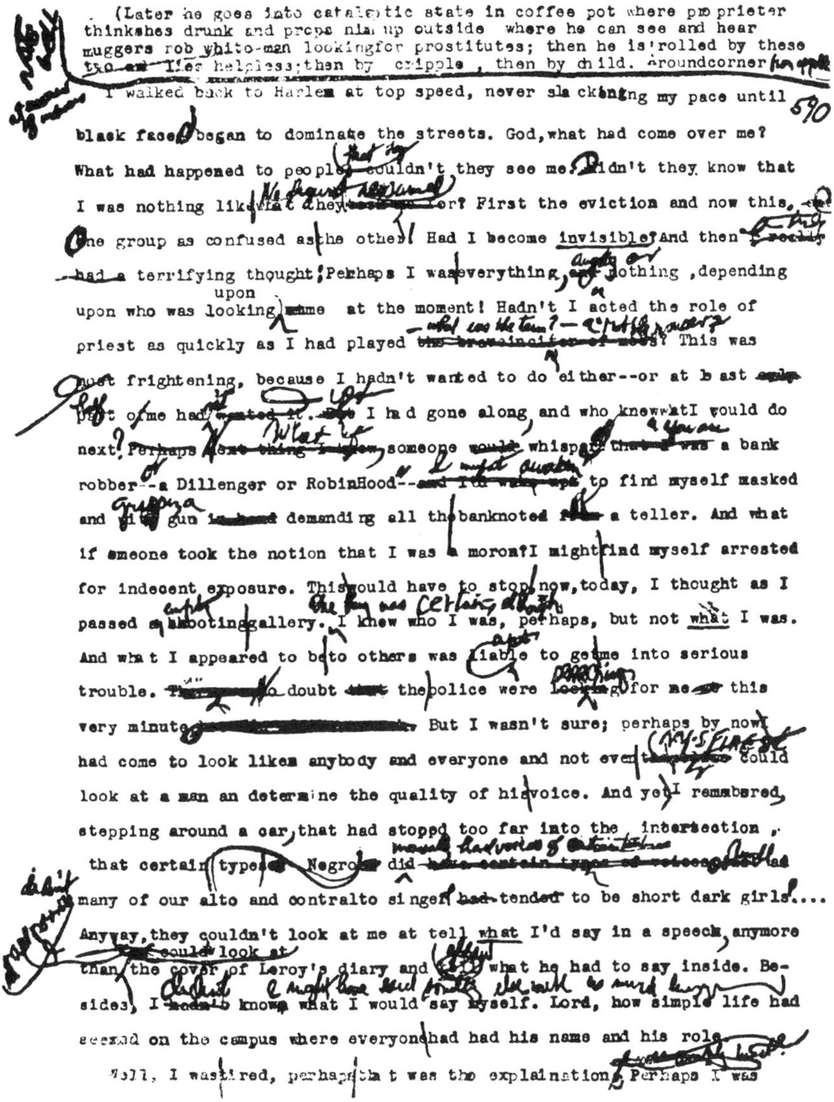

. (Later he goes into catalaptic state in coffee pot where proprieter thinkshes drunk and props him up outside where he can see and hear muggers rob white-man lookingfor prostitutes; then he is rolled by these two as lies helpless; then by cripple , then by child. Aroundcorner

I walked back to Harlem at top speed, never slackening my pace until black faces began to dominate the streets. God, what had come over me? What had happened to people couldn't they see me? Didn't they know that I was nothing like what they took me for? First the eviction and now this, one group as confused as the other! Had I become invisible? And then I suddenly had a terrifying thought! Perhaps I was everything, or nothing ,depending upon who was looking upon me at the moment! Hadn't I acted the role of priest as quickly as I had played the rabble-inciter of mobs? This was most frightening, because I hadn't wanted to do either--or at least only part of me had wanted it. Yet I had gone along and who knew what I would do next? Perhaps next thing I knew someone would whisper that I was a bank robber--a Dillenger or RobinHood--and I'd wake up to find myself masked and with gun in hand demanding all the banknotes from a teller. And what if someone took the notion that I was a moron? I might find myself arrested for indecent exposure. This would have to stop now, today, I thought as I passed a shootinggallery. I knew who I was, perhaps, but not what I was. And what I appeared to be to others was liable to get me into serious trouble. There was no doubt that the police were looking for me at this very minute. But I wasn't sure; perhaps by now I had come to look like anybody and everyone and not even the police could look at a man an determine the quality of his voice. And yet I remembered, stepping around a car that had stopped too far into the intersection , that certain types of Negroes did have certain types of voices, that as many of our alto and contralto singers had tended to be short dark girls.... Anyway, they couldn't look at me at tell what I'd say in a speech, anymore than they could look at the cover of Leroy's diary and tell what he had to say inside. Besides, I hadn't known what I would say myself. Lord, how simple life had seemed on the campus where everyone had had his name and his role.

Well, I was tired, perhaps that was the explaination. Perhaps I was

FIGURE 1.3 Ralph Ellison Manuscript Page

After the first draft is finished, I put it aside temporarily and work on other things. Then when I feel the time has come for me to really formalize it, I begin a second and final draft—and this part of the process is strangely the most enjoyable of all. I cut each chapter drastically, seeing as objectively as possible what can be eliminated or shortened (my manuscripts would be very long, sometimes twice as long, if I didn't cut so severely), trying to read the work as if from another part of myself, or from the point of view of another person. Though the original, spontaneous part of writing can be very exciting, the real reward for me at least is this third and most conscious, most "intellectual" organization of material.

Joyce Carol Oates

After I've written two to three thousand words I go through the penciled copy and correct it and mark it up. Sometimes it looks pretty terrible. Then, when I can't read it any more myself because it is so marked up, I have it typed. I then go over the typed copy once; I may take out some material or put more in.

Norman Vincent Peale

I write my first version in longhand (pencil). Then I do a complete revision, also in longhand. . . . Then I type a third draft on yellow paper. . . . Well, when the yellow draft is finished I put the manuscript away for a while, a week, a month, sometimes longer. When I take it out again, I read it as coldly as possible, then read it aloud to a friend or two, and decide what changes I want to make and whether or not I want to publish it. I've thrown away a few short stories, an entire novel, and half of another. But if all goes well, I type the final version on white paper and that's that.

Truman Capote

In baseball you only get three swings and you're out. In rewriting, you get almost as many swings as you want and you know, sooner or later, you'll hit the ball.

Neil Simon

As you continue writing and rewriting, you begin to see possibilities you hadn't seen before.

Robert Hayden

Revision is all there is.

Nancy Sommers

THE FIRST PRINCIPLE OF SELECTION

The writing process has its own rhythms and its own internal logic. Very often it generates statements with which the writer, upon careful consideration, cannot fully agree. It is quite amazing what can happen to a draft if one stops at each assertion to ask, "Is this really true?"

The answer is usually "yes." But it often takes the form of "yes, but . . . ." Thus the real question is "To what extent is this true? How true is it?" Very often the statement is true in the context the writer originally had in mind, but not generally true. Then the correct response is to modify or qualify the original statement. And sometimes—especially in opening passages, for some reason—writers have to admit to themselves that they have drafted statements that are simply not true.

As rhetorical theorists from Plato to Richard Weaver have insisted, the first principle of selection is *truth*. Most generalizations contain at least some degree of truth; hardly any generalization is totally true. Concrete and specific statements can often be classified simply as true or false. But abstract and generalized statements usually need to be qualified. Next time you are about to start an essay with a statement like,

> Throughout history, human societies have always been characterized by competition.

ask yourself to what extent it is true—or even if you know enough to know how true it may be. Probably you will end up qualifying the generalization—or perhaps even deciding that it is not necessary to the point you are trying to make in that essay. Especially in explanatory writing, and most especially when the rhetorical context is academic, scientific, or professional, *one of the most important and common revision operations is the qualification of propositions.*

Excessive qualification can reflect an excessive (and even paranoid) need to avoid responsibility for one's statements. But considerable qualification is often necessary if the meanings received by readers are to match those intended by writers. Consider the qualifications in the first two paragraphs on this page. The cues of the level of language include these: "Very often . . . upon careful consideration . . . fully . . . quite . . . usually . . . often. . . . Very often . . . sometimes. . . ." Delete those qualifiers and you reduce the validity of the passage.

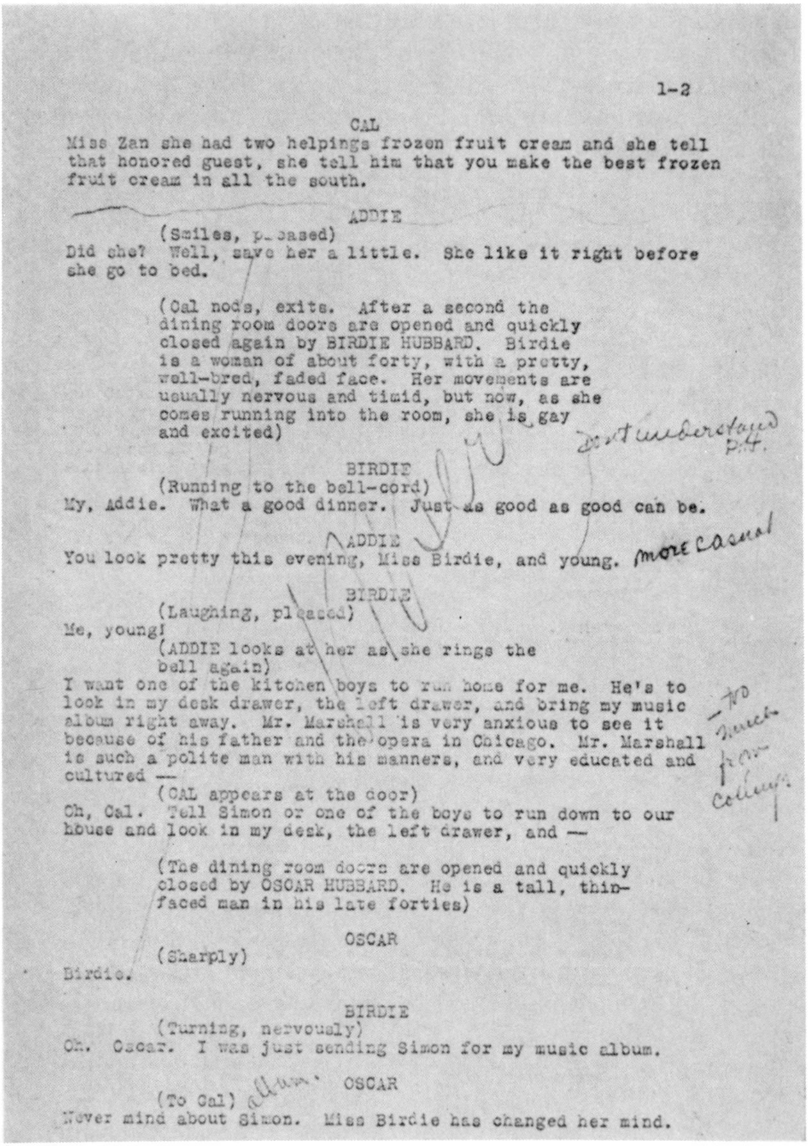

1-2

CAL

Miss Zan she had two helpings frozen fruit cream and she tell that honored guest, she tell him that you make the best frozen fruit cream in all the south.

ADDIE

(Smiles, pleased)

Did she? Well, save her a little. She like it right before she go to bed.

(Cal nods, exits. After a second the dining room doors are opened and quickly closed again by BIRDIE HUBBARD. Birdie is a woman of about forty, with a pretty, well-bred, faded face. Her movements are usually nervous and timid, but now, as she comes running into the room, she is gay and excited)

BIRDIE

(Running to the bell-cord)

My, Addie. What a good dinner. Just as good as good can be.

ADDIE

You look pretty this evening, Miss Birdie, and young.

BIRDIE

(Laughing, pleased)

Me, young!

(ADDIE looks at her as she rings the bell again)

I want one of the kitchen boys to run home for me. He's to look in my desk drawer, the left drawer, and bring my music album right away. Mr. Marshall is very anxious to see it because of his father and the opera in Chicago. Mr. Marshall is such a polite man with his manners, and very educated and cultured —

(CAL appears at the door)

Oh, Cal. Tell Simon or one of the boys to run down to our house and look in my desk, the left drawer, and —

(The dining room doors are opened and quickly closed by OSCAR HUBBARD. He is a tall, thin-faced man in his late forties)

OSCAR

(Sharply)

Birdie.

BIRDIE

(Turning, nervously)

Oh. Oscar. I was just sending Simon for my music album.

OSCAR

(To Cal)

Never mind about Simon. Miss Birdie has changed her mind.

FIGURE 1.4 Lillian Hellman Manuscript Page

THE FIRST TYPE OF REVISION

From the first principle of selection follows the first type of revision. *One can approach truth*—or correctness or effectiveness—*by adding, deleting, or substituting*. This may mean no more than adding a qualifier to an excessive generalization or substituting a more accurate word for one that does not really represent the intended meaning. Sometimes, however, the reconceiving becomes so substantial that the statement should be radically modified or redrafted. Sometimes an untrue statement which is tangential to the point of the writing should be totally deleted.

The following sentences, written by advanced composition students, are easily fixed:

> During the time that it was spoken, however, Latin gave root to new languages, such as Italian and English.

> I often have to interrupt the flow of the narrative when I find myself at a loss for the exact word to express a certain emotion or convey a feeling, etc.

There are two problems with the first sentence. First, although many modern European languages did evolve from Latin, English is not one of them; English is basically a Germanic language which was strongly influenced by Latin (through French) after the Norman conquest of England in A.D. 1066. One solution would be to substitute "Rumanian" or "French" for "English." Second, although the modern languages contain many words with Latin roots, "gave root" does not accurately describe the relationship. One solution would be to substitute "gave rise."

There are two problems also with the second sentence. First, "narrative" is not the right word because the writer is clearly referring to the flow of the writing process, not of the written product. (In context, moreover, it was clear that the writer was referring to any sort of writing, not just to narratives.) A solution would be to substitute "writing process" for "narrative." Secondly, "convey a feeling" is redundant after "express a certain emotion," and "etc." is vague. It seems probable that the writer really meant "express a certain idea or convey a feeling." But one would have to ask the writer just what he meant before fixing the end of that sentence.

Often one can detect an inaccurate expression only in context. In such cases, the problem is that the phrase or sentence or passage seems to contradict the gist of the whole piece of writing. In a persuasive essay, reproduced in full on pages 349-350, for example, a writer asserts,

> Even at the seventh grade level, many children are not mature enough to be told about sex. It is something they may not be concerned with personally for a good many years.

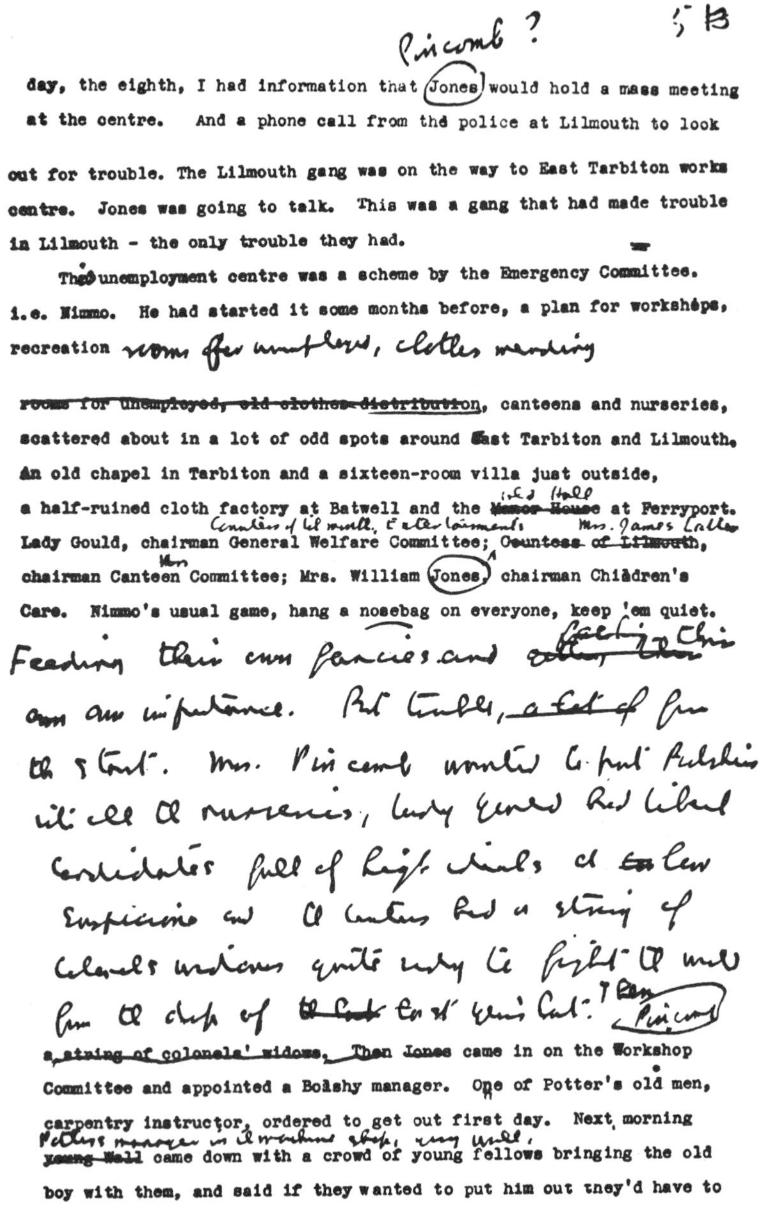

Pincomb ? 5 B

day, the eighth, I had information that Jones would hold a mass meeting at the centre. And a phone call from thd police at Lilmouth to look

out for trouble. The Lilmouth gang was on the way to East Tarbiton works centre. Jones was going to talk. This was a gang that had made trouble in Lilmouth - the only trouble they had.

The unemployment centre was a scheme by the Emergency Committee. i.e. Nimmo. He had started it some months before, a plan for workshops, recreation rooms for unemployed, clothes mending

~~rooms for unemployed, old clothes distribution~~, canteens and nurseries, scattered about in a lot of odd spots around East Tarbiton and Lilmouth. An old chapel in Tarbiton and a sixteen-room villa just outside, a half-ruined cloth factory at Batwell and the ~~Manor House~~ Old Hall at Ferryport. Lady Gould, chairman General Welfare Committee; ~~Countess of Lilmouth~~, chairman Canteen Committee; Mrs. William Jones, chairman Children's Care. Nimmo's usual game, hang a nosebag on everyone, keep 'em quiet.

Feeding their own fancies and [illegible] their own importance. But trouble, [illegible] from the start. Mrs. Pincomb wanted to put [illegible] in all the nurseries, Lady Gould had Liberal candidates full of [illegible] [illegible] suspicions and the canteens had a string of colonels widows quite ready to fight [illegible] [illegible] Pincomb

~~a string of colonels' widows.~~ Then Jones came in on the Workshop Committee and appointed a Bolshy manager. One of Potter's old men, carpentry instructor, ordered to get out first day. Next morning ~~young Wall~~ came down with a crowd of young fellows bringing the old boy with them, and said if they wanted to put him out they'd have to

FIGURE 1.5 Joyce Cary Manuscript Page

Since the writer goes on to urge parents to support sex education classes for seventh graders, it would seem that these sentences do not accurately represent her intended meaning. In context it seems clear that what she really wishes to concede is considerably less than what the sentences say. What she probably wishes to admit is that many of the children will not be engaging in sexual activity for some years, that they may not have reached puberty, and that they may not be thinking very much about sex yet. But she ends up inadvertently undercutting (and even, in effect, contradicting) some of the arguments she will make later.

Similarly, to return to the example used on page 81—"Throughout history, human societies have always been characterized by competition"—the solution is to narrow and qualify. Any of the following could be substituted, depending on the writer's knowledge and the point to be made.

> Our society is characterized by competition.
>
> Although not all human societies are dominated by it, they all do contain some degree of competitiveness.
>
> At least since the industrial revolution, those nations which have dominated the world have been characterized by competition.

Sometimes the qualifications and modifications become so substantial that the statement should be reexamined and redrafted. Take, for example, the following statement.

> Writing consists of pre-writing, writing, and re-writing.

This proposition, which from the late-1960s through the 1970s was a commonplace among professional writing teachers, contains a considerable degree of correctness. Certainly, it is more correct than the propositions it tended to replace: "writing consists of finding the right words to represent one's thoughts"; "writing is what happens while a pen (or other writing implement) is moving on paper (or other writing surface)." But the proposition can still stand considerable revision.

The statement is in conventionally acceptable form, so it need not be revised on that level. "Pre-writing" is a bit of jargon, which is familiar to most professional writing teachers. It refers to the discovery or generation of material, to the *inventio* of classical rhetoric (see page 14), and also to any plans about how to present the material generated. Most of what has been discussed in the preceding sections of this chapter could be considered instructions on "pre-writing." If we can assume that readers will know the term, the bit of jargon is acceptable.

On the level of language, however, the repetition of "writing" stands out. It suggests an ambiguity: how can "writing" be a stage of writing unless the word is being used in two distinct senses? And even if the ambiguity were acceptable, the repetition inevitably suggests that "writing" is the most important stage of writing. Let us try, therefore, to substitute "drafting" for the second "writing":

> Writing consists of pre-writing, drafting, and re-writing.

A problem still remains. The prefix *pre-* (meaning "before") clearly implies that "pre-writing" is a preliminary. Juxtaposed with the suffix *re-* in "re-writing," it connotes three distinct stages. But we know that discovery actually continues, on one level or another, throughout the entire writing process; and we know that selection or revision ("re-writing") begins very early on, certainly before the start of "drafting." We know that drafting is itself a discovery process and that good writers typically do some revising while they are still drafting. So the proposition needs to be revised substantially for accuracy.

Note what has happened in the two preceding paragraphs because it represents one typical revision process of effective writers: problems on the level of language (the repetition of "writing" and the implications of *pre-* and *re-*) have suggested problems on the level of meaning and lead toward revision of the underlying *concepts*. Rewriting here leads to rethinking (and redrafting):

> Writing consists of two contradictory subprocesses: on the one hand, we must generate or discover material; on the other, we must select and order that material. The first subprocess usually predominates in the early phases, the second in the late phases of writing. Both are typically active during drafting (which is an important writing technique, not a subprocess).

This is quite far from the original statement. The revision process which took us from the one statement to the other is certainly not trivial—and nothing one would want to attempt at 5 a.m. on the night before a deadline. (In a sense, it took this writer five years to get from one to the other.)

USE A SUMMARY STATEMENT

"Writing and rewriting are a constant search for what one is saying," asserts John Updike. "I don't know what I think until I see what I've said," declares E. M. Forster.

What one has written is often not what one meant to write. It is important to look back over each draft to see what *it* says. But that is very difficult because we tend to read into our own drafts what we meant to say. One way to find out what you have said is to write a brief **summary statement**, which states your main point or points.

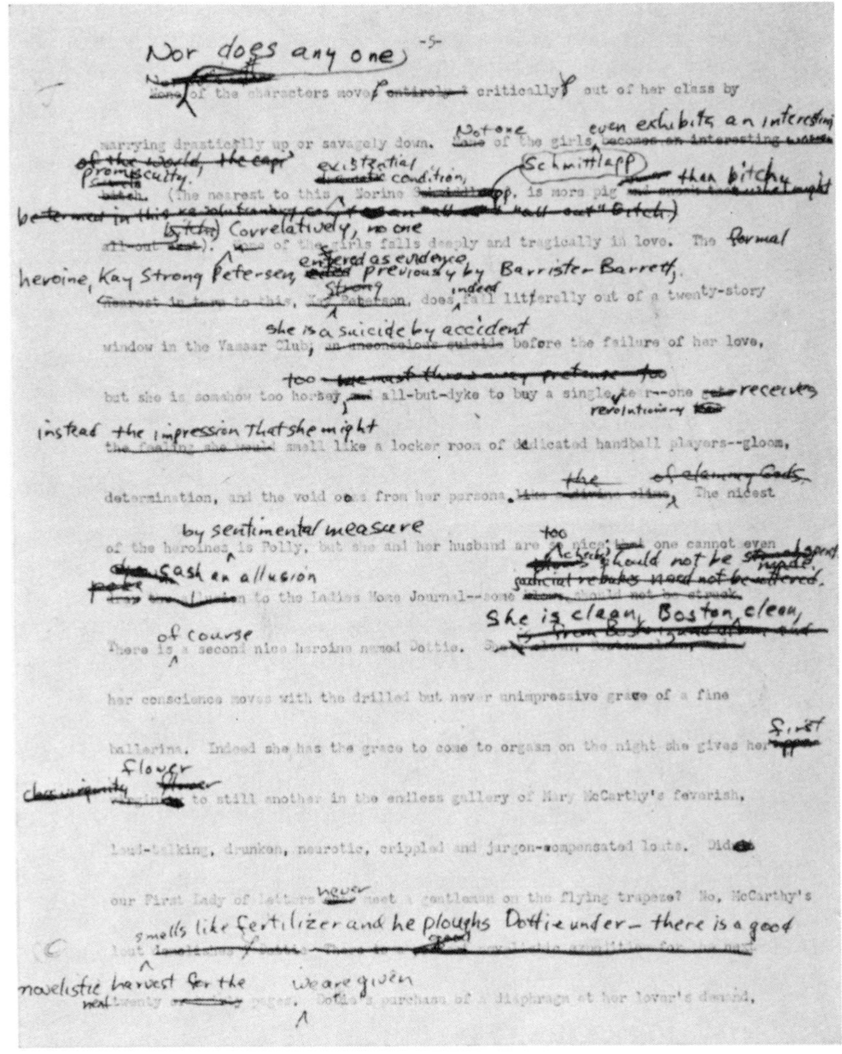

-5-

Nor does any one

of the characters move critically out of her class by

Not one even exhibits an interesting

marrying drastically up or savagely down. of the girls

existential

promiscuity.

condition,

Schmittlapp

than bitchy

(The nearest to this, Norine pp. is more pig

Correlatively, no one

). of the girls falls deeply and tragically in love. The formal

heroine, Kay Strong Petersen, entered as evidence previously by Barrister Barrett,

Strong

indeed

, does fall literally out of a twenty-story

she is a suicide by accident

window in the Vassar Club; before the failure of her love,

too

but she is somehow too horsey, all-but-dyke to buy a single tear--one receives

revolutionary

instead the impression that she might

smell like a locker room of dedicated handball players--gloom,

the

determination, and the void ooze from her persons. The nicest

by sentimental measure

too

of the heroines is Polly, but she and her husband are so nice one cannot even

should not be made.

cash an allusion

n to the Ladies Home Journal--some

She is clean, Boston clean,

of course

There is a second nice heroine named Dottie.

her conscience moves with the drilled but never unimpressive grace of a fine

first

ballerina. Indeed she has the grace to come to orgasm on the night she gives her

flower

to still another in the endless gallery of Mary McCarthy's feverish,

loud-talking, drunken, neurotic, crippled and jargon-compensated louts. Did

never

our First Lady of Letters meet a gentleman on the flying trapeze? No, McCarthy's

smells like fertilizer and he ploughs Dottie under—there is a good

lout

novelistic harvest for the

we are given

next twenty pages. Dottie's purchase of a diaphragm at her lover's demand,

FIGURE 1.6 Norman Mailer Manuscript Page

Such a statement should be short: for a 10 to 20 page paper, aim at 100 to 200 words. A summary of this length is harder to produce than one of twenty or one of a thousand words. It requires more than a simple thesis statement, but it still forces you to pick out only what is most important. And the more difficult it is to produce such a summary statement, the more important it is to do so—because the difficulty indicates the extent to which you cannot articulate precisely what your main points are. (If you are writing collaboratively, or if you have a really devoted friend or colleague, you might try having someone else produce a summary statement of your draft. Such a summary is more likely to be faithful to what the draft actually says.)

Having created the short summary statement, you should then ask yourself certain questions about it. You might ask other people, too. Someone else is more likely to see flaws and exceptions than you are. If you are writing a term paper for a univerity course, you might show the summary statement to the professor. If you are writing an article for a magazine or journal, you might show it to the editor. Key questions to ask include the following.

To what extent is this true? Does it need to be qualified or modified? Have I considered important exceptions?

What has been left out? Have I considered all important and relevant aspects of the subject?

How do I know this is true? What are some good examples of it?

It is worth noticing that the last two questions begin to take us beyond the simple consideration of truth and raise the consideration of *proof.* These two questions begin to imply a logical *order* by generating support, which is logically subordinate to the main points. They lead toward the second type of revision—reordering—which is the subject of the next section.

ADDITIONAL READING

Murray, Donald. "Internal Revision: A Process of Discovery." Gabriel M. Della-Piana. "Research Strategies for the Study of Revision Processes in Writing Poetry." Both in *Research on Composing:* Points of Departure. Eds. Charles R. Cooper and Lee Odell. Urbana, Ill. National Council of Teachers of English, 1978. Although both of these articles are theoretical, they are suggestive and can help writers to reconceptualize revision as a process of re-envisioning. Murray cites much testimony from practicing writers.

EXERCISE

1. Consider what *you* do when you revise. Write a narrative of how you revised a piece of writing you wrote recently. Expand that narrative into a process-analysis by adding information about how you typically and ideally revise. Share this information with other writers (e.g., other people in your writing class or group) to see what you can learn.

2. Tape record yourself in conversation. Listen to the tape of discover how you revise while talking. Listen for overt corrections and also for sentences that seem to change midstream. Listen also for ideas that get restated—some of them will be restated for emphasis, others will actually be revisions.

3. Find out how other writers revise. Listen to your peers. Interview a writer about revision. If possible, watch a writer revise (preferably that same writer you interviewed). Find some manuscript pages from successful writers; what can you infer about their revision processes? Contrast a draft with a final version of a piece of writing (e.g., James Joyce's *Stephen Hero* with his *Portrait of the Artist as a Young Man*).

4. Check some writing textbooks to see what specific types of revision and rewrite techniques they recommend. See if any of that is useful to you. Read Gabriel Della-Piana's article on revision in writing poetry and Donald Murray's article on "internal revision" —both in *Research on Composing: Points of Departure*, edited by Charles R. Cooper and Lee Odell (Urbana, Ill. National Council of Teachers of English, 1978). Do you think distinct types of writing demand distinct types of revision?

5. Working in a group of, say, four people, have each person bring in a short draft. Pass them around, and have *every* person do a quick revision of *every* draft. What can you learn from the ways other people revised your drafts?

6. As you continue working with this textbook, record your revision processes in your writing journal. See if they change. Try to figure out what effects any changes have on the quality of your final products.

GET ORGANIZED

The recognition of structure gives the mind its ability to find meaning.

Susanne Langer

[T]he mature writer is recognized not so much by the quality of his individual sentences as by his ability to relate sentences in such a way as to create a flow of sentences, a pattern of thought that is produced, one suspects, according to the principles of yet another kind of grammar—a grammar, let us say, of passages. . . . [T]he quality of an idea is not to be found in a nucleus or thesis statement but in the sentences that follow or lead up to that statement. An idea in this sense, is not a "point" so much as a branching tree of elaboration and demonstration.

Mina Shaughnessy

THE SECOND TYPE OF REVISION

Contrary to popular opinion, what makes us call a piece "well written" generally has as much, or more, to do with structure as it does with substance or style. Structure is often discussed in terms of "support." In many contexts, including academia, you are allowed to express any opinion you like—so long as you support it properly. In other words, it is not so much *what* you say but *how* you say it. And, although style does matter, structure is crucial. This is as it should be because the logic of the way you have arranged your ideas reflects the quality of your thought.

It is not enough that an idea or phrasing be accurate. It must also be properly combined with other ideas or phrasings. Certain problems can be resolved by adding, deleting, or substituting. Other problems have to do not so much with selection as with *arrangement*. This suggests a second type of change that writers should make in their drafts.

If a piece of writing is criticized as illogical, badly organized, or improperly developed, the problem is structure. If the problem is structure, then the solution is not to change what you are saying, nor to change how you have phrased it, but to change the arrangement. In other words, you have to get organized—or reorganized. This is the second type of revision: *reordering*.

One of the clearest distinctions between experienced and inexperienced writers is that *inexperienced writers rarely reorder*. Inexperienced writers add, delete, and substitute, but they rarely reorder. Thus there is a whole type of revision that inexperienced writers typically do not even consider. That type of revision is concerned with structure—logic, organization, development—and is often the key to successful writing, especially in academic and professional contexts.

Reordering an entire writing, a passage, or even a sentence is often the quickest and easiest way to radically improve a draft. Whole sections or paragraphs can be moved—often literally, with a scissors and stapler—and suddenly a seemingly incoherent writing reveals its true unity. The parts of a sentence can be reordered, and suddenly a whole passage flows. The reordered parts usually need to be re-cemented with new transitions (see pages 142-144 below), but the logic that mandated the reordering often suggests the transitions.

(Incidentally, the paragraph you just read used to be part of the following subsection, and this entire section was originally drafted as part of Chapter 2.)

OUTLINE LATER

In order to revise the structure of a piece of writing, you must see it. This is often difficult, especially with longer writings. The basic structure can get lost under a mass of details. The solution is to make an outline *of what is already written*. Since the draft already exists, it is easy to create such an outline. And that outline is a representation of the structure of the draft.

First, generate a list of points you have made. One good way to do this is to go through the draft and try to find a sentence to represent each paragraph, either a summary sentence you make up or one which already exists in the draft. You will probably also need to make up or find more general summary sentences to represent larger sections of the draft.

Second, to transform this list of points into an outline, you need to classify statements according to importance (or level of generality). Mark the most important (i.e., the most general) statements, the ones which seem to encompass the others. The traditional way to mark them, of course, is with roman numerals. The remaining statements may need to be subclassified. Try indenting and using capital letters, arabic numerals and lowercase letters—tradition is often useful. What matters is not the particular format but that the outline allows you to see the *relationships* among the statements.

It is wise to try to keep the outline on a single sheet of paper. This may mean using a very large sheet. For very long writings, it may even mean

2-[illegible]

pity, when I beheld a poster that mercifully [illegible] set me off on quite another tangent. "Win a fabulous week for two at the Stardust in Las Vegas plus $2500. in cash!" it trumpeted. "Play Eagle Pencil Company's Quality Control Game!" I never ascertained whether I was to watch for some magic serial number or to hawk the pencils from door to door. In the next breath, I was ejected to the platform, and there superimposed itself on my mind a memory of this self-same Stardust, fabulous indeed, as I saw it during a short enforced visit to Las Vegas a year ago.

My trip to the [illegible] it [illegible] I flew there from Rome, a [illegible], and I undertook the journey with the direst misgivings. The circumstances were [illegible] as follows. Several months before, an Italian film producer [illegible] had engaged me to devise a vehicle for a meteoric tenor [illegible] it might be prudent to call [illegible] success in the United States and Europe; his presence in a picture, it was universally felt, would make it a bonanza; and Signor Bombasti, from the moment I began work in Rome, declared himself ready to go to any lengths to win Fauntleroy's approval of our story. I soon found out what he meant. Shortly after finishing the treatment, which is to say the narrative outline of the scenario, I was [illegible] hailed as a composite of Congreve, Pirandello, and [illegible], and affirmed [illegible] to convey the [illegible] in person to Fauntleroy. Nobody else could adequately interpret its gusto and sparkle, its rippling mirth and delicious nuances.* My expostulations, my protests that I was anathema to performers, went for naught; in a supplication that would have reduced Ralph Henry Barbour to tears, Bombasti entreated me, for the sake of the team if not my own future, to comply. Seven hours later, I [illegible] Ciampino West Airdrome.

* (And nobody else in the [illegible] organization spoke even rudimentary English, he might well have added.)

FIGURE 1.7 S.J. Perelman Manuscript Page

making one general outline and then detailed outlines of each chapter or section. What matters is that you are able to see the pattern of the whole writing (or of whatever section you are considering).

The "outline later" revision technique is directed toward problems of order. The key question is, "Does the pattern of meaning make sense as it stands? Would it make more sense if reordered?" It is certainly useful to ask of each point on your outline the same questions you asked about your summary statement (pages 86-88). You certainly want to make sure that each individual point is true. But the most important question which the outline helps you to answer is whether each point is where it belongs in relation to all the others. Negative answers are resolved relatively painlessly by reordering.

Thus, the "outline later" technique reveals the structure of your draft and allows you to revise it. It allows you to see if your various points fit together into a *meaningful* pattern (see pages 95-99).

The "outline later" technique also has other uses. For example, the outline can be made before the draft is complete, perhaps just before the conclusion is drafted, or at any point during the drafting when you are blocked and do not know what to say next. Looking at the outline, you can see the pattern of what you have drafted up to that point. If you are blocked in mid-draft, the emerging pattern often suggests what else needs to be said. If your conclusion is to be a summary, the main points of the outline often represent the substance of the conclusion.

The "outline later" technique also allows you to evaluate the development of the piece of writing. Are some points left unsupported or supported less than they need to be? Are some points supported beyond their actual importance. Is the development balanced? Sometimes the answers to these questions are obvious as soon as you look over the outline. But if the development is problematic, you should apply a question-heuristic to each main point, perhaps this one:

To what extent is this true?

How do I know it is true?

What is a good example of it?

So what?

If the writing is well developed, the answers will be in the draft and will be located in the immediate vicinity of the point. If they are not in the draft, you probably should add them. If they are in the draft but not near the point they support, you probably should move them.

You may also discover the some points are supported more than they need be or that some of what you have written is actually irrelevant to the point of the whole writing. You may then need to substitute (e.g., an appropriate example for an inappropriate one) or to delete. Deleting can

96——
HERZOG 10|12|24 TR-OS (VIKING) 4591

"We're all right."

"Comfortably settled? Liking Chicago? Little Ephraim still in the Lab School?"

"Yes."

"And the Temple? I see that Val taped a program with Rabbi Itzkowitz—Hasidic Judaism, Martin Buber, *I and Thou*. He's very thick with these rabbis. Maybe he wants to swap wives with a rabbi. He'll work his way round from 'I and Thou' to 'Me and You'—'You and Me, Kid!' I suppose you wouldn't go along with everything."

Phoebe made no answer and remained standing.

"Maybe you think I'll leave sooner if you don't sit. Come, Phoebe, sit down. I promise you I haven't come to make scenes. I have only one purpose here, in addition to wanting to see an old friend. . . ."

"We're not really old friends."

"Not by calendar years. But we were so close out in Ludeyville. That is true. You have to think of duration—Bergsonian duration. We have known each other in duration. Some people are *sentenced* to certain relationships."

"You earned your own sentence, if that's how you want to think about it. We had a quiet life till you and Madeleine descended on Ludeyville and forced yourself on me." Phoebe, her face thin but hot, eyelids unmoving, sat down on the edge of the chair Herzog had drawn forward for her.

"Good. Sit back. Don't be afraid. I'm not looking for trouble. We've got a problem in common."

Phoebe denied this. She shook her head, with a stubborn look, all too vigorously. "I'm a plain woman. Valentine is from upstate New York."

"Just a rube. Yes. Knows nothing about fancy vices from the big city. Had to be led step by step into degeneracy by me—Moses E. Herzog."

Stiff and hesitant, she turned her body aside in her abrupt way, then, her decision reached, turned just as abruptly to him again. "You never understood a thing about him. He fell for you. Adored you. Tried to become an intellectual because he wanted to help you—saw what a terrible thing you had done in giving up your respectable university position and how reckless you were, rushing out to the country with Madeleine. He thought she was ruining you and tried to set you on the right track again. He read all those books so you'd have somebody to talk to, out in the sticks, Moses. Because you needed help, praise, flattery, support, affection. It never was enough. You wore him out."

"Yes . ? What else? Go on," said Herzog.

"It's still not enough. What do you want from him now? What are you here for? More excitement? Are you still greedy for it?"

Herzog no longer smiled. "Some of what you say is right enough, Phoebe. I was certainly floundering in Ludeyville. But you take the wind out of me when you say you were leading a perfectly

FIGURE 1.8 Saul Bellow's Revisions on Printer's Galleys

be painful, especially if a lot of work has gone into what should be deleted, but it can be a crucially important revision process. The blue pencil, used for deleting, was certainly a key to Ernest Hemingway's success as a writer (see page 78).

Used together with the short summary statement and the reconsideration of individual points, the "outline later" technique helps writers to revise their drafts to accurately represent the intended pattern of meanings. Since the pattern of meanings is often more important then individual propositions, the "outline later" technique is particularly important.

It is not, however, the techniques that are crucial. What matters is that the revision processes they represent be performed. Writers who already perform these operations "naturally" and satisfactorily need not adopt these techniques. But writers who do not perform these operations satisfactorily—and that includes virtually all less experienced writers—have a lot to gain from adopting these techniques. Inexpert writers typically look at a first draft and—aside from changing a word here or there and looking for mechanical errors—cannot see what else to do. The "outline later" technique is particularly useful for breaking this block. It also directs attention to the crucial, but often neglected, questions of structure.

THE GENERAL AND THE PARTICULAR

One of the most important characteristics of a unified piece of writing is the proper relationship between generalities and particulars—or, to put it a bit more precisely, the proper relationships among various levels of generality. The proper relationship seems to vary somewhat according to genre and type of discourse. It may be very different for an expressive poem, a piece of explanatory prose, or a persuasive political statement. But it is always very important.

Not enough research has yet been done to make definitive statements about the precise nature of these "proper relationships," especially beyond the level of single sentences. It is clear, however, that the propriety of the relationships is often crucial to the acceptance of a piece of writing—be that writing a fictional narrative or a scientific report. What has traditionally been called unity and coherence in writing is created not only by making certain that all particulars are relevant to the general propositions with which they appear, but also by observing proper relationships among various levels of generality.

There are certain exceptions. Within a personal relationship, as Professor Mina Shaughnessy has pointed out, a speaker or writer may make a series of rather general, unsupported statements which will be accepted (or rejected) because the other person trusts (or distrusts) the first person's judgment on the matter. Likewise, people who have lived or worked together may understand the implications of a simple statement of fact so similarly that they do not need to state the implications. In fact-to-face communication, moreover, people often can ask questions if they feel a gap in the message.

But aside from these exceptions, you will find that the proper relationship among levels of generality is crucial to the success of your writing.

There are two rules of thumb that address this point:

"Generalizations should be inferred from particulars."

"Opinions should be supported by facts."

These rules derive from empirical scientific thinking, but they are generally enforced in modern Western discourse (e.g., in literary criticism, in popular magazine writing, and often even at dinner-table discussions).*

Here we will confine ourselves to the first rule (leaving the second for Chapter 4). The rule is simple enough, but its application often is not. In the first place, one is rarely dealing with just "the general" and "the particular." More typically, writers are faced with various levels of generality (which may never get down to absolute particulars).

This is more easily illustrated than explained. A table or list is a convenient illustration here because, with the exception of headings and totals, the items on a chart or list are by definition of the same level of generality.

In Table 1.2, the numbers obviously represent generalizations from much more specific information. The level of generality is still fairly low—one could even refer to these numbers as "facts." Yet the real particulars behind this chart would be found on a list of individual investments. The makers of this chart presumably started out with that list and considered the totals on the chart to be, relatively, a high level of generality.

On the other hand, the information in this table is certainly particular enough for someone writing a short paper on control of the Canadian economy. For this topic, these numbers would probably be the lowest level of generality. *The distinction among levels of generality is relative to the function of statements in a particular piece of writing.*

*This textbook does not necessarily endorse these rules (certainly not without qualifications). They are common to certain cultures—particularly modern Western cultures—and they reflect the dominance of empirical science. Medieval Western culture was dominated by discourse rules quite antithetical to these (i.e., "Particulars should be deduced from generalizations," and "Opinions should be supported by authorities.") Almost anyone trying to learn from this textbook, however, is presumably operating in a modern Western culture and so should be aware of the rules.

TABLE 1.2 Who Controls the Canadian Economy?

SECTOR OF THE ECONOMY	PERCENTAGE OF CAPITAL CONTROLLED BY: (IN BILLIONS) CANADIAN GOVERNMENT		CANADIAN PRIVATE		U.S. PRIVATE		ALL OTHERS	
Manufacturing (including forest products)	$ 0.4	2%	$ 9.4	37%	$11.7	47%	$ 3.4	14%
Railways	4.3	73	1.5	25	0.1	2	—	—
Other utilities	14.7	69	5.3	24	0.8	4	0.6	3
Merchandising and construction	0.1	1	17.2	87	1.5	8	0.9	4
Mining and smelting	0.1	1	1.9	29	3.9	59	0.7	11
Oil and natural gas	0.3	2	2.7	22	7.5	61	1.9	15
Total	$20.0	22%	$37.9	42%	$25.5	28%	$ 7.5	8%

Source: Canadian International Investment Position, 1968-70.

Here we will use Table 1.2 as our lowest level of generality (i.e., as our "particulars") and attempt some further generalizations.

Assuming that size of investment in some general way correlates with control, from this table students have made the following tentative generalizations about the Canadian economy:

> Railways and utilities are generally controlled by the Canadian governments (federal or provincial).
>
> Merchandising and construction are controlled by private Canadian capital.
>
> Mining, smelting, oil, and natural gas are largely controlled by U.S. capital.
>
> Control of manufacturing seems to be shared between private Canadian and U.S. capital, although U.S. capital seems to have the larger share.

Before actually writing the proposed article, one would be wise to find out what type of manufacturing is U.S.-controlled and what type Canadian-controlled.

The generalization which might form the thesis statement of an article based on this information would probably need to be even more general than these points, possibly something like this:

> U.S. capital controls most of the natural resources and much of the manufacturing in Canada, whereas Canadian capital (public and private) controls secondary industries and some manufacturing.

If one were to pass **judgment, then** one would have created a fourth level of generality. Canadian students, for example, usually assert that

U.S. capital control of most basic Canadian industry is undesirable because it is likely to interfere with Canadian political independence.

A unified piece of writing based on this information should present these four levels of generality in some meaningful relationship. It might proceed inductively from the lowest level (the numbers from the table) to the highest (the judgment). Or it might start with the potential thesis statement, work down to the numbers from the table, and use the judgment for a conclusion. There are other possibilities, and the choice should be determined largely by rhetorical context. But any arrangement should be based on an underlying *conceptual* pattern in which the judgment is ultimately supported by the "facts," the highest level of generalization by the lowest.

In this light, reconsider the first extended piece of writing cited in Chapter 0, Tom Longridge's "Why I Cannot Write This Paper." For purposes of analysis, each sentence (or where two "sentences" are connected by a semicolon or coordinating conjunction, each independent clause + attachments) will be treated as a unit.

1 The process by which I construct my essays may be divided into four main stages: a gathering stage, a kernel stage, a general overhaul stage and a fine tuning stage (pardon the mixed metaphor).

  3 The gathering stage is prior to any actual writing, aside from note-taking, and is mainly the period during which I gather thoughts and information pertinent to the general topic my paper will be dealing with.

    4 I then organize the information within my mind and draw a conclusion which in turn becomes the central idea of theme of my essay.

  3 Converting this central idea into a kernel sentence initiates the second stage of my writing process.

    4 I build my first draft about this kernel sentence, selectively incorporating the information gathered in stage one, i.e., quotes and paraphrased material.

    4 I then conclude the first draft with a summation of the general points of the essay.

    4 During stage two I pay little or no attention to sentence structure, paragraph formation or transitions,

    4 and the organization is very loose;

 2 the overhaul of structural and stylistic defects is attempted in stages three and four.

  3 At stage three I try to structure my ideas according to a coherent pattern, which I have been formulating in my mind since stage one;

    4 this usually entails a degree of reorganization at every level from sentence structure though to whole sections.

    4 Also, it is at this stage that I reappraise the amount of information and expand or edit as deemed necessary.

3 Fine tuning is the fourth and final stage.
 4 In essence this stage is a continuation of stage three but on a more superficial level, my main concern being with the mechanical aspects of the paper, i.e., grammar and spelling.

On the level of meaning, this is a clearly patterned piece of writing. The number of level 4 statements varies from section to section according to how much meaning Tom has to communicate. The generalization (level 2) linking "stages three and four" suggests the possibility of a parallel generalization linking stages one and two, which could be inserted after the opening sentence—although that degree of parallelism is hardly mandatory. This quibble aside, the analysis of levels of generality demonstrates the underlying unity of the piece of writing. There is no irrelevant material, and all statements are appropriately ordered.

On the other hand, this underlying unity is not represented in the paragraphing or sentence breaks, as you can see by referring to the unanalyzed version on pages 11-12. The level 2 generalization, which one might expect to begin a paragraph, actually occurs in mid-sentence, immediately after a semicolon. Perhaps this is because Tom titled the paper "Why I Cannot Write This Paper" and handed it in after his stage two, still having paid "little or no attention to sentence structure, paragraph formation or transitions."

Although it is not *always* necessary that the structure of a piece match the structure of its meaning, such a match does make it easier for readers to grasp that meaning. This congruity between structure and meaning may also help writers more clearly perceive their own meanings.

The more serious problem is when some logically necessary level of generality is simply left out. Then the reader must fill in the gap; if the reader fails to do so, the meaning is not communicated.

DEVELOP YOUR OWN REVISION-HEURISTIC

One good way to improve the quality of your writings is to improve your revision processes. Especially if you are not a very experienced writer, you probably do not take advantage of all the possibilities available to you.

From other textbooks and writing courses, you have probably learned to do the first type of revision—adding, deleting, and substituting—in an attempt to obey the conventions of Standard English and to avoid "wrong words" and "awkward" sentences. That is all to the good, but there is much more you can do to improve your drafts. Revision does aim for good style and correctness, but there is more to it than just that.

Inexperienced writers typically do not revise very much because they do not see the potentials for revision. One way to help yourself see those potentials is to develop your own *revision-heuristic* and revision process. That means to develop a set of questions to focus your attention and a procedure for using them. The questions should pinpoint your weaknesses and focus your attention on flaws likely to appear in your drafts. Since your attention is limited, your questions should be grouped, thereby allowing you to concentrate on one type of question at a time.

In this chapter we have been considering the level of *meaning* and its relationship to structure. The revision-heuristic which follows suggests some questions on this level. The next two chapters will raise other considerations, on the levels of rhetorical context and language. Many of these questions may not be relevant to your individual needs; and there is no point in focusing your attention on your areas of strength. If you have too many questions in your revision-heuristic, moreover, it will grow overwhelming and useless. Choose only those questions which match your own weak points, particularly those weaknesses you want to

TABLE 1.3 Revision-Heuristic, Level 1: Meaning[a]

SELECTION	ARRANGEMENT
To what extent is this true? Does it need to be qualified or modified? Has anything been left out? Are there any important aspects of the subject which have not been considered? What does this writing exclude? Is there anything included which does not belong here? How do I know this is true? What is a good example of this? Are there any exceptions which have not been considered? Are the implications clear?	Do the various ideas in this writing fit together into a meaningful pattern? (Do they, for example, all support a main thesis or theme?) Are they presented in an order which represents their real relationships? Would this writing make more sense if it were reordered? If some section of it were reordered? Are all high-level generalities supported? Are any points supported less than they need to be? Are any points supported beyond their actual importance? If you make (or imagine) an outline of this writing, does the structure look logical? Do the examples exemplify what they are intended to exemplify?

[a]*Remember*: This is only a list of suggested questions. Choose from it only those questions which match your individual needs. Rephrase them more specifically, if possible, to focus your attention on your own particular weak points. Add any questions you need to. Use this list to develop your own revision-heuristic. And do not rely on this list alone: read the sections of the text which explain the concepts behind these questions.

concentrate on now. If there is no suggested question for one of the weaknesses you need to work on, make up your own.

Many of the suggested questions are, of necessity, phrased in rather general terms. If you have read and understood the sections of the text which discuss the matters to which those questions refer, the questions should make sense. Otherwise, they may well not be useful. If you can make a question more specific so that it points more particularly at one of your individual problems, do so. Remember these are just suggestions. What are you trying to do is to develop your own individual revision-heuristic.

Most of my students have derived their revision-heuristics from the models in this text. A few, however, have produced their own revision-heuristics from scratch. The point is to direct your attention effectively during revision. Use whatever form works for you. Here are two examples of highly individualized revision-heuristics. Note that each includes not only a set of questions but also a procedure for inserting them into the individual's writing process.

REVISION HEURISTIC:

1. What is the purpose of this exercise?
2. To what extent have you fulfilled this purpose?
3. Can you title the piece of writing?
4. Who are you writing this piece for? Would the piece work for this intended audience?
5. Have you said everything that you wanted to say? Have you said more than you wanted to say?
6. Is the style obvious, repetitive, predictable?
7. Is the piece too sentimental, too dry, too vague, etc.?
8. Is there a consistency in tone? (Does it jump from a formal use of words to overly simple phrases? Does it try to be funny where humor is inappropriate?)
9. Can this piece be published while the characters are still living?
10. Do you feel good about this piece of writing. Do you feel good about showing it to another person?

The above heuristic is used after the first draft of the story has been completely written. A process of revision is going on while the first draft is being generated. This process involves removing words, sentences and whole paragraphs. It also involves changing words, rearranging the order of sentences and paragraphs, and adding to the body of what has already been written. This process takes anywhere from several hours to several days. No heuristic is used for the process, nor will it be.

After the first draft is completed I use the revision heuristic. In the case of 'Jude' it resulted in a complete re-write. This is not always the case.

Sometimes I cannot answer the questions in the heuristic to my satisfaction, but choose to leave something in or take something out anyway because I like the sound of it. However, I feel that the questions are very beneficial and generally serve as an effective set of guidelines.

Ginny Fortin

REVISION HEURISTIC AND CHECKLIST

After writing the first draft—put it away for anywhere from 5 hours to a day. Now read it over keeping in mind the following questions.

Does this essay fulfill the assignment?

How does it fulfill the assignment?

Is its purpose shown clearly?

Does it communicate effectively to its chosen audience?

Now, outline the ideas and arguments in the essay.

Could your organization be improved?

Are your arguments reasonable and proven by facts?

Is your conclusion weak or indecisive?

Outline the levels of generality and complexity in your paper.

Is your essay too simple?

Is there another side to your viewpoint?

What idea or ideas could be added to improve the quality of your paper?

Did you use Burke's Pentad if your paper deals with human motivation?

If not, why not?

Wait for another short period—then read the essay closely and ask these questions:

Are there meaningful transitions between paragraphs?

Does each sentence flow smoothly into the other?

Are the rhythms and structures of the sentences varied and interesting?

Finally—check for mispelling and punctuation errors.

Margaret Coe*

*No relation to author of this textbook.

ADDITIONAL READING

Christensen, Francis, "A Generative Rhetoric of the Paragraph." *College Composition and Communication*, Volume 16 (October 1965), pages 144-156. D'Angelo, Frank, *A Conceptual Theory of Rhetoric*. Cambridge, Mass.: Winthrop, 1975, pages 60-72. Shaughnessy, Mina. *Errors and Expectations*. New York: Oxford 1977, pages 226-257. Taken together, these three authors provide both a theoretical justification and practical advice about levels of generality analyses. See the quotation from Shaughnessy at the beginning of this section.

Wilson, John. *Thinking with Concepts*. London: Cambridge, 1966. See especially pages 1-59 for "how to" advice on critical thinking.

EXERCISE

1. Analyze the following writings, done by inexperienced basic writers, by numbering the levels of generality. Contrast your results with the analysis done on Tom Longridge's writing (pages 98-99 above). What distinctions can you make? How can those distinctions help you understand what you need to do when revising your own writings? (*Note:* The third passage turns out to be two paragraphs scrambled together.)

I started reading before I started school. My mother was the main reason why I did so. When I was young she would take the time to read to me and also try and teach me to read. I can remember the first volume of *The Nancy Drew Mystery Stories* that my mother bought for me, and my faithfully reading and buying the other volumes until I had completed the set. In the fourth grade, my mother made a big fuss with the principal of my school because my teacher would not let me read if I finished my work early. In the fifth and sixth grades I won first place in the school library contest.

The point that I'm trying to make is that I've been brought up with the idea that reading is full of pleasure, not tedious as some people think and say it is. Reading also expands vocabulary by implementing new words that you can either understand from context or by looking them up in a dictionary. Books expand your knowledge by going into detail and initiating new subject matter.

DeAnne Paulis

WHEELING & DEALING

Two individuals approach the drive-in window of a bank. One is driving a late-model, shiny silver Rolls-Royce with a black top and white-wall tires. The other person is driving a 1963 Volkswagen sedan with three different colors of paint on it. What images immediately come to mind? The person in the Rolls-

Royce lives in a twenty-room house with maids and butlers and talks with that certain air of extravagance. He's always had an abundance of money right at his fingertips. The guy in the beat-up little Volkswagen wears jeans, knows the value of a dollar because he's had to sweat for everything he's got and the biggest extravagance he can afford is to take his family to McDonald's for dinner. Right? This is an example of signifier/signified—the automobile being the signifier and the image of status being the signified.

Cathy Stine

To the poor man (lower class) living in the slums of the city, money signifies the comforts and luxuries he will never know but can only dream of because he can't even afford the necessities of food, medical care and clothing his family needs. The American population consists of immigrants from many countries. (The American Indian is becoming more and more non-existent.) I asked my grandmother why she came to America, and her response was a common one which I learned in school, "America is the land of opportunity." My French grand-uncle wants his son and daughter to move to America so that they and their children can flourish in the land of plenty. The Irish, Italian, Armenian, Bulgarian, Chinese, Russian, German, Moslem, Hungarian, Japanese and the most recent example, the Vietnamese, (and etc. . .) flowed and still flow into the dream land of prosperity. Although for the majority America turns out to be a better place to live compared to what they've left behind, the factory worker and unemployed worker can see but only dream of having the boy next door wash his Cadillac.

Peter Sahagian

2. Analyze some piece of writing you admire from your own area of special interest by numbering levels of generality. Then analyze one of your own more recent writings in the same way. Compare and contrast both results with the results of the previous exercise.

3. Take any extensive list or table and use it to generate a hierarchy of generalizations (as done on pages 96-98).

4. Apply the "Level 1: Meaning" questions (see Table 1.3) to the writings you did while working on Chapter 0 (or if you did not do those writings, to any other recent writings). Generate a summary statement and use the outline later technique to help yourself do so. Then evaluate the usefulness of this part of the revision-heuristic and change it to meet your individual needs.

5. The following activity, devised by Professor Peter Elbow, is somewhat similar to the "Level 1: Meaning" questions. Try it in a group of four or five writers. See if you can use it to improve the questions of the heuristic (or the questions to improve it). Read a piece one of the writers has written and then do the following:

a. *First tell very quickly what you found to be the main points, main feelings, or centers of gravity. Just sort of say what comes to mind for fifteen seconds, for example, "Let's see, very sad; the death seemed to be the main event; um . . . but the joke she told was very prominent; lots of clothes."*

b. *Then summarize it into a single sentence.*

c. *Then choose one word from the writing which best summarizes it.*

d. *Then choose a word that isn't in the writing which best summarizes it.*

The point is to show the writer what things he or she made stand out most . . . , what shape the thing takes in your consciousness.

6. One way to describe the relationships among levels of generality is in terms of patterns of inference. (Not surprisingly, moreover, the ability to recognize and evaluate inferences has been found to correlate significantly with college grade point averages.) Do the following exercise on inferences. Assume the statements in each reading passage to be true. Then mark each suggested inference as correct (C), probably correct (PC), impossible to determine from the reading (ID), probably false (PF), or false (F). Worry less about getting the answers right than about grasping principles of inference.

Rhetoric has been defined as the study of the symbols which we manipulate and which manipulate us. Rhetoricians are often more concerned with the effects of communications, with the meanings which reach an audience, than with the objective content of statements. First-year university and college rhetoric courses often focus on the communications abilities needed by students in their academic work.

__1. Nine out of ten rhetoricians teach first-year university students.

__2. A rhetorician might study advertising.

__3. First-year rhetoric courses have a different focus than graduate rhetoric courses.

__4. Many rhetoricians believe that our behavior can be manipulated by the symbols we use.

NORTH AMERICANS ALL LOOK ALIKE

HAMILTON, Ont., June 27 1973 (AP).—A visiting Chinese said today that all North Americans look alike. "We can't tell them apart from the faces," said Chu Muchih, director of the New China News Agency.

(Note: *In proper international usage, "American" signifies anyone from North or South America; "North American" signifies someone from Canada or the United States.*)

__1. The facial features of the Chinese are more diverse than those of North Americans.
__2. Chu Muchih is a woman.
__3. Chu visited Canada in June 1973.
__4. Chu had not spent much time in North America.

Unlike cattle, sheep or goats, pigs do not eat grasses. They live, instead, on roots and grains—foods which are in short supply in the desert and which are eaten also by Homo sapiens. *Pigs, therefore, are in ecological competition with people in a way which is significant in the desert. The cultures which became dominant in the Middle East were not burdened with pigs.*

Insofar as why? *is a question about psychological motives, the reason neither Moslems nor Jews eat pork is because they believe Allah and Yahweh told them not to (and because those beliefs were enforced by social pressures within certain communities). But when* why? *is a question about survival or dominance, the taboo on pork must be explained as an adaptation to the environment.*

__1. Pigs will eat wheat.
__2. Sheep will not eat wheat.
__3. Roots and grains are important in the diet of human beings.
__4. The Hindu taboo on beef can be explained as an adaptation to the Indian environment.

Form *in literature is an arousing and fulfillment of desires. A work has form in so far as one part of it leads a reader to anticipate another part, to be gratified by the sequence.*

Kenneth Burke

The author's whole art is bent on obliging me to create what he discloses, . . . so both of us bear the responsibility for the universe. . . . In order for the works to have any effect it is necessary for the public to adopt them.

Jean-Paul Sartre

CHAPTER 2

THE COMMUNICATIVE PROCESS

Writing is a communicative process. We write not just for the pleasure of self-expression, nor just to clarify our own understandings, but also to communicate with readers. On this level, a piece of writing can be judged objectively by asking to what extent it achieves the writer's purposes with the intended readers.

A writer's first responsibility should be to truth. A writer's second responsibility is to readers. To meet this responsibility, you should develop a general understanding of how people read and also an understanding of your particular readers. Many of the qualities of "good writing" can be explained objectively in terms of the needs and expectations of readers.

The first section of this chapter should help you to evaluate readers and to understand the reading process. The second and third sections deal with particular structures—paragraphs, titles, openings, transitions, and endings—that give coherence to a piece of writing and help readers comprehend it accurately. The last section emphasizes the importance of conventions, which ordinarily form part of the expectations of readers. Certain punctuation rules that are particularly important to advanced writers are used to illustrate that importance, but it is assumed that writing students using this book also have access to a handbook of standard usage and a dictionary. (Certain conventions of format are discussed in Chapter 7.)

As you read this chapter, you should try to grasp the interrelationship between writing and reading. You want to master the effective use of those devices that function as signals to readers about the structure of your writing—and of the ideas it represents.

WRITING TO BE READ

Indeed, an idea, or a notion, like the physicist's ultimate particles and rays, is known only by what it does.

I. A. Richards

Although ambiguous sentences seldom seem ambiguous to the writer (who knows what he means), . . . [t]he effective writer learns to predict his reader's reactions to his words and to act accordingly.

R. Young, A. Becker, and K. Pike

WHAT IS RHETORICAL CONTEXT?

Certain writing tasks—such as journal entries written to clarify inchoate feelings or most school exercises—allow writers to focus almost entirely on meanings, on the substance of what they are trying to say. Tom Longridge's "Why I cannot write this paper" (pages 11-12 and 98-99) is a case in point: the main purpose of the exercise was to clarify Tom's understanding of his own writing process.

But writers generally have other purposes as well. In addition to being a creative process by which writers discover, select, and arrange meetings, writing is also *a communicative process*. Most writing is written to be read. The written text is a means to an end. It represents a message the writer desires to communicate. In a sense, the writing process is not complete until the writer's meanings have been understood by readers. In some cases, the writing process in not really complete until those meanings have also been believed and perhaps even acted upon.

As soon as the writing task includes among its goals that *readers* should *understand* its meanings, it becomes an interpersonal transaction. When writers want their readers to go beyond simple understanding and to *empathize, believe*, or *do* something—to be convinced—then writing becomes a rhetorical act. Its successes and failures can be judged objectively according to how readers respond to it.

In all honesty, the first principle of selection should be truth, as the writer understands it. A writer's first concern should be whether the writing accurately represents the intended meanings and whether those meanings are true. But most meanings may be represented and supported in various ways. So the second principle of selection should be effective communication. As rhetorician Richard Weaver asserts, the writer's second responsibility is to consider "the special circumstances" of his or her readers.

The juxtaposition of writers' purposes with "the special circumstances" of readers constitutes *the rhetorical context* of a piece of writing. Writers should ask themselves these questions:

What am I trying to accomplish with this writing?

With whom am I trying to accomplish it?

In what situation am I trying to accomplish it?

In the terms of classical rhetoric, this means that the decisions writers make about *how* to express their meanings should depend on *purpose, audience,* and *occasion.* Especially during revision, writers' decisions should not be based on meaning alone; they should be based also on what the writer is trying to accomplish (purpose), with whom (audience), and in what situation (occasion). This is because writing is generally not just self-expression but also communication.

For a certain type of writing, usually called explanatory or expository, the purpose may be no more than that certain readers understand the intended meanings. A team of geophysicists publishing their results in a specialized geophysical journal will have succeeded as writers if other geophysicists read and understand those results. The same geophysicists writing for a more general scientific journal (e.g., *Science*) could better fulfill their purpose if they gave fuller explanations and used less specialized jargon. Writing for an even more general audience (e.g., in *Scientific American*), the same writers would be wise to choose yet a third representation of the same meanings, perhaps providing more analogies and examples, because some readers would be coming to the article with even less scientific knowledge and expertise.

In persuasive writing, where the purpose is to convince readers to believe or do something, it is even more necessary to consider audience and occasion. In expressive writing, where the purpose is usually to give readers a sense of some experience and to have them empathize, the relationship is sometimes more subtle and complicated; but for the writing to succeed, writers must provide images, analogies, or other structures to which the readers can relate.

HOW TO EVALUATE RHETORICAL CONTEXTS

Most inexperienced writers are insufficiently aware of rhetorical contexts. When asked about the purpose, audience, and occasion of a particular piece of writing, they often do not have much to say. Experienced writers, by contrast, are usually highly conscious of rhetorical contexts, especially of audiences. This distinction may well explain some of the difficulty inexperienced writers often have with revision. A writer who does not consider rhetorical contexts does not have much of a basis for making certain types of decisions.

Student writers often have special difficulty identifying rhetorical contexts. To some extent that may be because they have not been taught to do so. To some extent it is because of the special nature of most school writing. Most such writing is explanatory; the explicit purpose is just to make meanings clear. Moreover, most school writing is done as exercise: the implicit purpose is not so much to communicate information (which the teacher-reader usually knows better than the student-writer) as to demonstrate the student-writer's knowledge and abilities and usually to convince the teacher-reader to award the desired grade or credit.

Yet the conventions of most school writing demand that students make believe they are writing not for the teacher, but for the "rest of the class" or for "a general educated reader." Thus a double rhetorical context is created: a conventional one (often vague) and a real one (in which the student tries to obtain a grade or credit).

Double rhetorical contexts are not unusual. A magazine or journal article must be adapted to the readers of that magazine or journal; but it must also convince the editors to publish it, or it will not reach those readers. A textbook must be adapted to the students who will use it; but it must also convince instructors to adopt it, or it will not reach those students.

In writing courses, as in other school writing, the solution is often to make the conventional rhetorical context explicit. The instructor may assign a specific purpose, audience, and occasion. Or the student may imagine a rhetorical context that will constrain the writing toward an appropriate form.

In general, inexperienced writers should try to make themselves more aware of rhetorical contexts. Just as you can make yourself more aware of what you are trying to say by writing out a short summary statement (pages 86-88), so you can make yourself more aware of rhetorical contexts by writing down the purpose, audience, and occasion for each piece of writing. Then you will have an explicit and objective basis for deciding what should be emphasized, what can be deemphasized, and what can be left out altogether. You will also have an explicit and objective basis for deciding how to structure and phrase what you decide to say.

Your statement of rhetorical context should be brief. Here is an example:

> My main point [meaning] is that dolphins are a wonderful and endangered species. My *purpose* is to convince readers to support political action to protect

dolphins. Most of my readers [primary *audience*] will be residents of British Columbia. They will read what I have written on the *occasion* of a visit to the Vancouver Aquarium, where it will be handed to them as a leaflet.

The nature of one's purpose is usually clear enough as soon as one takes the trouble to make it explicit. Problems concerning purpose usually have to do with there being several distinct purposes for a single piece of writing. For example, two of those purposes may turn out to be, to some degree, contradictory—a writer wants to communicate clearly about dolphins but also to impress readers with technical terms and "big words." An explicit statement of purpose thus can help one choose between primary and secondary purposes.

The nature of one's audience, on the other hand, may require a bit of thought or even investigation. What about those people who will be visiting the Vancouver Aquarium? What does one have to know about those people in order to communicate effectively with them about dolphins and to convince them to support political action to protect dolphins?

First, the people who visit the Vancouver Aquarium are not all alike. If you had time to talk with each of them individually, you would probably take a slightly different tack with each one, sizing up each individual as the discussion continued and choosing arguments likely to reach that individual.

As a writer producing a single piece of writing for a mass of individuals, you are less flexible. Like a politician, you have to think about the majority—about the *typical* reader. Even that can be problematic if the people you are addressing fall into several distinct groups. In a case like this, a writing aimed at the *average* reader might fall between the groups and end up convincing nobody at all.

In such a case, you should identify *primary and secondary audiences.* For the piece on dolphins, the primary audience will be residents of British Columbia who visit the Vancouver Aquarium. Most of them will be Canadian-born and speak English as their first language. Most will be adults, but a goodly number will be teenagers. Many will have friends or relatives involved in the fishing industry, and most will know how important that industry is to the economy of British Columbia. Many will be rather knowledgeable and sophisticated about ecological issues.

However, some readers will be immigrants to Canada, including a fair number of Asian-born Chinese. There will also be tourists from elsewhere in Canada, including some Quebecois, whose first language is French. And there will be tourists from other countries, largely from the United States, Japan, and Western Europe.

Generally, one should write to the primary audience and then make adjustments, additions, or deletions to appeal to various secondary audiences—insofar as one can without undermining the appeal to the primary audience. What are those people like?

> What can one say, in general, about British Columbians who visit the Aquarium?
>
> More specifically, what do they *know* about dolphins and related subjects? (Do they think dolphins are fish?)
>
> What *beliefs* and *attitudes* do they have toward dolphins, toward animals in general, toward ecological issues? (Do they believe animals have rights or do they believe animals should be treated in the ways that best serve human beings?)
>
> What *vested interests* do they have in how dolphins are treated? (Will the protection of dolphins interfere with the fishing industry?)
>
> Does the survival and well-being of dolphins in any way affect the quality of life in British Columbia?

An estimate of your primary readers' knowledge about the subject, their relevant attitudes and beliefs, and their vested interests will enable you to make rhetorical choices more appropriately. Certainly there is a sense in which each reader is a unique individual, but it is possible to make generalizations about what they have in common.

You should also ask which of all the potential appeals you could make are likely to work *on this occasion*? The occasion in this case consists of the medium (a leaflet) and the situation in which it will be read. Since people tend not to read long leaflets or leaflets with a lot of small print, this occasion makes it particularly necessary to choose only the most salient of the potential appeals and to make them as succinctly as possible.

It might be worthwhile to investigate your primary audience, to go to the Aquarium and talk to some visitors. Perhaps your stereotype of British Columbians who visit the Aquarium is inaccurate. Or perhaps it is just not specific enough. Perhaps you have not thought enough about how many of them speak Chinese, Japanese, or French as a native language.

Few modern politicians prepare speeches without consulting polls, talking to important constituents, and so forth. While one should not sell one's soul and allow readers totally to determine the nature of what one writes, neither should anyone who wishes to communicate effectively ignore the nature of the audience. There is something to be learned from successful politicians and advertisers about how to consider "the special circumstances" of one's readers—so long as one remembers the first responsibility of Weaver's "honest rhetorician," to write the truth.

USE THE PENTAD TO DISCOVER MUTUAL PURPOSES

Not only writers but readers have purposes. Readers read for reasons. They have motives. Skilled readers especially read with focus, with a sense of purpose. As a writer you will do well to find the areas where your purposes overlap with your readers' purposes and to emphasize those areas. That is, you should try to locate *mutual purposes* that you share with your readers. Sometimes a mutual purpose may be nothing more than your desire to convey information they wish to acquire. Other times you may find that your readers have an objective vested interest in your subject, perhaps one of which they are not even aware. Perhaps the survival and well-being of dolphins is more important to them than they realize. In such a case, it would be good rhetorical strategy to make them aware of their objective self-interests, probably near the beginning of the piece of writing.

Burke's Pentad was discussed in Chapter 1 as a heuristic for generating subject matter. As a heuristic for the investigation of human motives, the Pentad can also be used *to discover how to motivate readers*. That is, it can be used to discover how best to motivate your readers to fulfill your purpose.

With what sorts of appeals do they most easily identify?

What motives (i.e., purposes) do they already have?

How can you establish mutual purposes?

Burke himself argues that certain types of people respond to certain types of appeals. He suggests that liberals tend to argue from *scene* (e.g., crime is caused by poverty), conservatives from *agent* (e.g., crime is cused by immoral and degenerate people), pragmatists from *agency* (e.g., crime is caused by the availability of weapons), mystics and idealists from *purpose* (e.g., crime is part of the divine plan), and philosophical realists from *act* (e.g., crime is caused by permissive upbringing, or by the experience of injustice). And, in general, people are most easily motivated by the same sorts of appeals they themselves use.

Professor Charles Kneupper has applied this supposition to the problem of choosing appeals that will match the purposes particular groups of readers bring to a piece of writing. He presents the following example of how he uses the Pentad to choose appropriate appeals when addressing various groups within the university. His purpose is to get a new course approved. His problem is to discover how that purpose matches up with purposes his readers already have. Here is his solution.

I tend to find my faculty colleagues liberal and idealistic on educational issues. They seem most receptive to scene and purpose ratios. In contrast, administrators seem dominantly realist and pragmatist and

> *are correspondingly more attuned to act and agency ratios. Finally, students seem conservative and idealistic and are moved by agent and purpose ratios. Put in more concrete terms, in proposing a new course the faculty is most moved by justifications concerning educational* purpose *and responsiveness to the social* scene. *Administrators are most moved by demonstrations of feasibility of the* act *within the constraints of* agency. *In other words, I need to show the course is staffable with minimal cost and will probably generate substantial FTE. Finally, students are attracted to courses partially by their nature* [purpose], *but also by whom they are taught* [agent]. . . .
>
> . . . *Faculty tend to be uninterested in the details of administration. Administration has some interest in* purpose, *but wants to get to the nitty-gritty questions of* agency. . . . *In a well thought-out proposal, a rounded statement of motive will include appeals to each respective decision-making group.* [*Emphasis added.*]

In other words, Kneupper appeals to the purposes and concerns of each of the three groups of readers. His decisions about which arguments to use are based on his analysis of his readers.

ROOT METAPHORS

There is another Burkean concept which writers can use to evaluate audiences. This concept has other uses as well and is discussed more fully in Chapter 4 (pages 273-275). Here it will be presented briefly as it applies to analyzing potential readers.

The basic idea is that peoples' assumptions, beliefs, and attitudes are often reflected in certain metaphors or analogies. These *root metaphors* are so commonly used that people tend to accept them without thinking about them, perhaps even without realizing they are metaphorical. Root metaphors often live in cliché, for example. When we speak of "*falling* in love," we make an analogy between a physical event and an emotional event. The comparison has implications: that "falling in love" is something that happens to you rather than something you go out and do purposively, that there is an element of danger involved, that it can be your "downfall" in one sense or another.

What matters is not the analogy but its implications. Thus, I. A. Richards criticizes the assertion that language is "a dress which thought puts on" because he is worried about assumptions being made by people who use or accept that metaphor. What he is really criticizing is the assumption that one thinks first and verbalizes second. When he argues that we should instead conceive of meaning "as though it were a plant that has grown," he is arguing for the assumption that we discover our thoughts in the process of articulating them.

The point here is that you can discover what assumptions your readers bring to a topic by thinking about the root metaphors they bring to it. Their clichés and standard analogies may be important clues to their attitudes and beliefs. Thus Richards tries to counter assumptions built into the root metaphor about thought and language which his audience brought to his lectures. Thus psychiatrist Erich Fromm begins his book on loving by discussing the implications of the notion that we "fall into" love (see page 276).

Investigating your readers' root metaphors helps you to communicate with them. If you think the assumptions built into those metaphors are valid, you can use the metaphors. They will help establish a frame of reference you share with your readers.

Insofar as you may decide the assumptions are invalid, you have located specific beliefs and attitudes of your readers that you must try to change. Depending on the circumstances, you can try to finesse the situation by unobtrusively substituting your own analogies (and thus your own assumptions), or you can argue explicitly against the assumptions you consider invalid. Generally, the latter strategy is more honest, but it involves a sort of intellectualizing for which not all readers will sit still.

WRITE READER-BASED PROSE

For many writers, learning to be considerate of "the special circumstances" of their readers requires a significant change of perspective. These writers believe that the goal of the writing process is a perfect piece of writing. They think of what they are doing in terms of "writing an essay," not in terms of "writing to communicate." Much of their effort during revision is devoted to polishing. (Consider the assumptions implicit in the root metaphor, "revision is polishing.")

With the probable exception of literary composition, aiming for "a perfect piece of writing" will usually focus your attention in the wrong place. The ultimate aim is not a perfect piece of writing, but a piece of writing that communicates perfectly. Perfection is a relationship between a piece of writing and its readers. Only a written product that accomplishes all your purposes with your intended readers is "perfect."

Your purposes can be accomplished only with the cooperation of your readers. It is impossible to create a text that no reader can manage to misinterpret. What you want to produce is a piece of writing that induces the cooperation of your readers, facilitates the communication of your meanings, and achieves your purposes as well as can be done with those readers.

Writing that does this is *reader-based* prose. To produce it, you should be aware of the significant differences between you and your readers. Although you decide *what* to say largely in terms of your purposes, you should decide *how* to say it largely in terms of their purposes. Reader-based writings present the information the readers need or want—which may not be entirely the same information that interests the writers. It is focused and organized according to the needs or desires of the readers. It is structured to facilitate the readers' discovery processes, not as a narrative of the writers' discovery processes.

Chapter 1 focused on your discovering and articulating the substance of what you want to say. Chapter 2 is focused on communicating that substance to readers.

HOW PEOPLE READ

To understand what makes for good writing, you should know how people read. The principles of effective writing can all be derived from an understanding of how people read.

Fluent readers are always anticipating. They have a book in context, often before they pick it up. By the time they get to the first word on page one, they have gleaned a lot of information by skimming blurbs, introductions, a table of contents, a title page, even an index—or by talking to others about the text, reading reviews, and so on. Thus they have narrowed their expectations. Because they are anticipating types of meanings that are likely, they can understand the text more quickly (and usually more accurately) than can beginning readers who start with the first word on page one and read word by word. As fluent readers move through a text, they continue to focus their attention ever more sharply.

You may think that you read word by word, that you grasp the meaning of the whole text by adding up the meanings of individual words. Most people think that. But if you really did read like that, your reading speed would be lower than forty words per minute, and you would not be reading a book as complex as this one.

The principle of anticipatory reading can be illustrated even on the level of the sentence. Suppose a sentence begins, "Is . . . ." As a fluent reader of English, you have already anticipated that the sentence will be a question—and not only that, but a particular type of question which can be answered by "yes" or "no." You have also anticipated that the next word or phrase will name the grammatical subject of the question. (You have done so even if you do not know what a grammatical subject is.)

Suppose the sentence continues, "Is the book . . . ." You now anticipate a word or phrase that will ask something about the book. You can accept a variety of completions: "Is the book here?" "Is the book worth reading?" "Is the book available in paperback?" "Is the book green?" But there is a much larger set of potential completions which, for a variety of reasons, you will not readily accept: "Is the book elephant?" "Is the book cat?" "Is the book ill?" "Is the book para mí?" "Is the book schmab?" "Is the book nicely?" All these potential completions fall outside the range of your anticipations.

If while reading you run into something that falls outside the range of your anticipations, it immediately throws you back—how far back depending on the nature of whatever does not fit. Your assumption is that either the writer erred or you anticipated falsely, and you look back to check the basis of your anticipation. Perhaps you are reading a science fiction story in which books are animate and can become ill. Perhaps you are reading a bilingual Chicano poem in which sentences can contain both English and Spanish words.

Except in special cases, such as writing intended to violate readers' stereotypes, writers should avoid throwing readers back like that. On the contrary, writers should help readers read by helping them to anticipate accurately.

Writers should also remember that readers read by creating clusters of meaning. As ten individual letters, "t-h-o-u-g-h-t-f-u-l" overloads your short-term memory. So you perceive it as two syllables, "thought-ful," or as one word, "thoughtful." Similarly, to read a sentence, you group words into phrases. To comprehend a paragraph, you group sentences conceptually. Ultimately, successful reading involves the comprehension not of individual meanings but of a pattern of meaning.

Effective writing contains cues that help readers to cluster meanings into the patterns intended by the writer. Without such cues, readers could correctly read each sentence you wrote but still get the wrong *pattern of meaning*. The way you use generalizations, transitions, paragraph indentations, repetitions and redundancies, introductions, conclusions, and so forth, are cues of this sort. They function as signals to readers about how to pattern meanings.

The point to remember is that readers are not sponges: they do not absorb meanings. The written text represents a message or set of messages that readers try to reconstruct. Reading is an active process. Readers do not only extract meanings, they also build them by making generalizations, constructing relationships, drawing inferences, and so on.

Although a piece of writing may well say more than the writer consciously intended, effective writers create texts that guide readers toward intended meanings and constrain them away from mis-readings.

WHAT IS READABILITY?

News reports often contain statements like, "Only 53% of high school graduates in __________ can read at the ninth grade level." In this sentence, "ninth grade level" signifies "the level of difficulty at which some experts decided ninth grade students should be able to read." That rephrasing raises several interesting questions. The one which concerns us here is, How does one determine the "level of difficulty" of a piece of writing?

Reading experts have tried to figure out what makes a text hard to read. They have also tried to figure out what *quantifiable* characteristics correlate with reading difficulty. Then they have classified texts according to those quantifiable characteristics, and they have established norms that define such-and-such a level of difficulty as "ninth grade reading ability." Those norms are based on experience in schools, but they do also represent a social *judgment* about what level of difficulty a person *ought* to be able to handle after a certain number of years of schooling.

A typical U.S. newspaper is written on about a sixth to eighth grade level. *The New York Times* is about eleventh grade reading. Since people's *comfortable reading levels* are lower than their *maximum reading abilities*, many college graduates find *The New York Times* difficult reading. (See Table 2.1).

TABLE 2.1 The Readability Levels of Some Popular Magazines

SCHOOL GRADE READING LEVEL	MAGAZINE
College	No popular magazine is this difficult
12	*Atlantic Monthly*
11	*Harper's*
10	*Time*
9	*Reader's Digest*
8	*Ladies' Home Journal*
7	*True Confessions*

Of the characteristics that make a text hard to read, the two most obvious are *vocabulary difficulty and complexity of sentence structure.* Since these two characteristics correlate roughly with word length and sentence length, they can be easily counted. Most measures of readability are, therefore, based on these two quantifiable characteristics (or on their correlates). Although as a rough measure, that is usually good enough, writers sometimes need to make finer and more qualitative distinctions.

Two other important characteristics are the *familiarity and complexity of concepts*. We learn new ideas by putting them in relationship to familiar ideas. It is sometimes said in the publishing industry that even an innovative book should be 90% old hat. Familiar concepts are relatively easy to grasp no matter what their complexity. New concepts are easier to grasp if they are less complex.

The implications for writers seem clear. When possible, try to use concepts that are familiar to your readers. When you are introducing a new idea, try to relate it to familiar concepts, perhaps through the use of analogies. If the new idea is complex, see if you can break it down into a number of simpler ideas without oversimplifying it. Try also to give concrete examples because readers can often grasp an idea through several concrete examples even if they cannot understand it when it is presented abstractly (see pages 177-179 and 269-273).

As may be apparent, there are potential contradictions here. What if your intended meanings cannot be represented with familiar concepts? What if the pattern of meaning is distorted when the complex concept is broken down into a number of simpler ideas? As is often the case in popular journalism and especially in popular science, writers sometimes make their writing readable by oversimplifying. The correct principle is to *make your writing as readable as you can without oversimplifying your meanings.*

When you write about certain subjects with some degree of sophistication, as-readable-as-possible-without-oversimplifying may be very complex indeed. Sometimes the ideas you wish to communicate are both complex and unfamiliar to your readers. You may need to use unfamiliar and difficult words to represent some of those ideas because commonplace synonyms have the wrong connotations and implications. You may also need to use complex sentences to represent complex relationships. Beyond using analogies and examples, what then should you do?

There are various factors that lower the reading difficulty without affecting meanings. Some of these have to do with format: type size, margin width, illustrations, headings and subheadings, boldface and italic typefaces, and so forth. In a sense, these have more to do with printing than with writing; but, as the classical rhetoricians knew, *delivery* is an important aspect of the communications process. Typewriting is generally easier to read than handwriting, printing generally easier than script. (This may, incidentally explain the clearly established fact that typewritten term papers tend to receive higher grades than handwritten term papers and that neatly handwritten papers tend to receive higher grades than sloppier papers.)

The questions in Table 2.2 summarize the practical implications of this section. Consider whether you need to add any of them to your own revision-heuristic (see pages 99-101). Other important factors that affect readability have to do with structure and style. These will be the focus of the rest of this chapter and Chapter 3 (and, in a somewhat broader sense, the rest of the book).

TABLE 2.2 Revision-Heuristic, Level 2A: Rhetorical Context[a]

SELECTION	ARRANGEMENT
Is this written in a way that will accomplish its purpose(s) with the intended reader(s) on the particular occasion(s) when it will be read?	Will the order of presentation help this writing accomplish its purpose(s) with the intended reader(s) on the particular occasion(s) when it will be read?
Is the presentation appropriate to the knowledge, beliefs, attitudes, and vested interests various readers will bring to it?	Is it ordered in accordance with the knowledge, beliefs, attitudes, and vested interests various readers will bring to it?
Does it appeal to a mutual purpose shared by writer(s) and reader(s)?	Is it focused according to readers' needs? Is it organized to facilitate readers' discovery processes?
Does it present all the information readers will expect and want?	Does the format facilitate readability?
Is the writing within the comfortable reading ability of its intended readers? Or does it demand the maximum reading ability?	Are the concepts presented in an order that the intended readers will find relatively easy to understand?
Are the concepts as familiar and concrete as they can be without oversimplifying the meaning?	

[a]*Remember*: This is only a list of suggested questions. Choose from it only those questions that match your individual needs. Rephrase them more specifically, if possible, to focus your attention on your own particular weak points. Add any questions you need to. Use this list to continue developing your own revision-heuristic (see pages 99-101). And do not rely on this list alone: read the sections of the text that explain the concepts behind these questions.

ADDITIONAL READING

Fry, Edward. "A Readability Formula That Saves Time." *Journal of Reading*, Volume 11 (1968), pages 513-516 and 575-578. A discussion of the Fry readability scale and its uses. This scale combines relative ease of use with relative accuracy.

Smith, Frank. *Understanding Reading*. 2nd ed. New York: Holt, Rinehart and Winston, 1978.

Young, Richard, Alton Becker, and Kenneth Pike. *Rhetoric: Discovery and Change*. New York: Harcourt, Brace & World, 1970. See Chapter Eight, pages 171-180, on utilizing readers' knowledge, values, and social relationships.

EXERCISE

1. Next time you write, generate a statement of rhetorical context (see pages 113-114 for a model), either before you begin or by the time you complete a first draft. State your main point(s) [meaning] and your purpose(s). Describe briefly your readers, perhaps divided into primary and secondary audiences, and the occasion(s) on which you expect them to be reading. After you have a completed draft and have generated this statement of rhetorical context, apply the Level 2A revision-heuristic presented in Table 2.2. After you have completed your writing, evaluate the usefulness of both the statement and heuristic. Is it really useful to *write out* the statement of rhetorical context? Can you modify the revision-heuristic so that it better fits your needs? Compare your evaluations with those of other writers who have tried this activity.

2. Look at a theoretical book or article about reading (e.g., Frank Smith, *Understanding Reading*) and also at a practical manual (of the sort used in college "reading skills" courses). What can you learn from them about how to *write*.

3. Estimate the readability level of your own writing. Take ten 100-word samples of your writing. (If the one hundredth word falls within a sentence, the sample ends at the end of the sentence.) Figure out the number of sentences per hundred words (*not* per sample if your samples are not exactly a hundred words long). Figure out the number of syllables per hundred words. Plot the results on Fry's readability graph (see Figure 2.1). Fry's readability graph is not the easiest way to measure readability, but it is more accurate than the easier methods and its

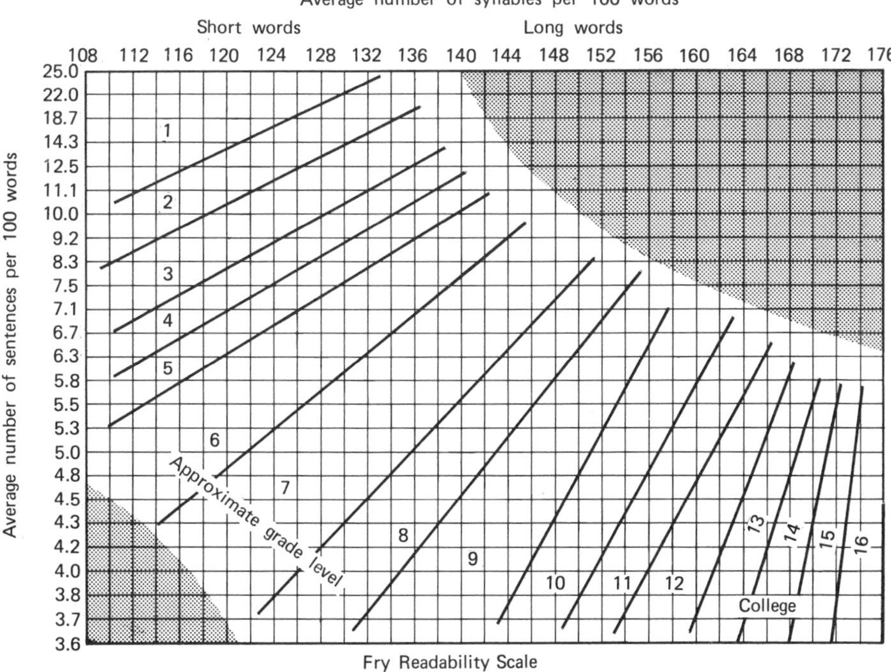

FIGURE 2.1

results correlate well with the results obtained from more complex methods (e.g., Dale-Chall and Flesch). It is accurate from first grade through college senior (16th). Of what potential use is its estimate of the readability of your writing? Does the estimate vary from one piece of your writing to another?

4. Readability estimates are based on sentence length and vocabulary difficulty (usually measured by word length). On the average, these two factors produce fairly reliable estimates. Write some short sentences using short words which would actually be difficult to read (e.g., "The id gyres, the ego mires, and I transpire.") Write some long sentences with long words which would actually be easy to read. (*Hint*: Try long independent clauses coordinated with conjunctions, colons, or semicolons, and long words that are combinations, of shorter words, e.g., "bookkeeper").

5. Take a short piece you have written recently. Imagine a rhetorical context radically distinct from the one for which you wrote it. Rewrite it for that new rhetorical context. Consider what types of changes you made.

PARAGRAPHING

Translated into terms of the composition class, "form" becomes "organization" and brings with it overtones of outlining; orders of paragraph development; beginnings, middles, and endings—in short, the most dismal stuff that students and teachers must deal with. And yet, the concept of form in discourse is utterly fascinating, for it concerns the way in which the mind perceives infinitely complex relationships. The way, indeed, in which the mind constructs discourse.

W. Ross Winterowd

Following a paragraph is more like following a dance than a dash. The topic sentence draws a circle, and the rest of the paragraph is a pirouette within that circle.

Francis Christensen

WHAT IS A PARAGRAPH?

Paragraphing is an ancient custom. Writers have been indenting for centuries. The doctrine of *the* paragraph, however, was first put forth in 1866 by the rhetorician Alexander Bain, in his *English Composition and Rhetoric.* Bain believed that the paragraph should be conceived as "a developed idea" just as the sentence had been conceived as a complete thought. The belief that each paragraph should contain one main proposition and its development is Bain's rule.

In truth, not all paragraphing matches the textbook descriptions of "the paragraph." Some paragraphs serve as introductions, transitions, or conclusions—such paragraphs may not be well "developed," and there is no reason why they must be. Moreover, writers often indent for emphasis or because a paragraph is getting too long. (In newspaper writing, to cite an extreme example, a new paragraph starts every 35 to 70 words or so, almost irrespective of meaning.) A paragraph which is much longer than it is wide seems hard to read (and journalistic paragraphs are so short because newspaper columns are typically only two inches wide). In general, frequent paragraphing enhances readability, but the development of complex meanings often requires long paragraphs.

Paragraphing depends primarily on how writers perceive their messages dividing into subordinate meanings. Not everybody—not even all good writers—will indent a given text in the same places. The same group of words and sentences can deliver somewhat different meanings if the paragraph indentations occur at different points. Let us, therefore, consider the following paper as it was handed in by a basic writing student, with no indentations whatsoever. As or after you read it, decide where you would break it into paragraphs.

DANGER! SHARK!

I have an image-model of sharks that they are very ferocious and vicious. As far as I can remember I always read that sharks were the wolves of the sea. In stories the shark always played the part of evil. Last summer I saw the movie, "Jaws," and was even more convinced of the terribleness of sharks. When I think of sharks I conjure up in my mind a picture of a large black tube with a point for a head and a swooping tail. This shark seems to be made of steel, and the beady gaze of its eyes strikes terror into anything that passes its way. I see a large pearly white smile with rows and rows of dagger-like teeth. I see him cruising through the depths, master of the sea, tearing apart any fish brave enough to cross his path. As he glides through the water there is a mysterious sound about him, like the drone of a great industrial engine. A few times the mystery of the shark has haunted me so much that I was beckoned to the library in search of more information about this curious devilfish. When I saw pictures of sharks I was confirmed in my image of them. I saw pictures of them with their great mouths agape. I saw pictures of sharks hanging from a beam, with fishermen standing beside them. It was easy to see that the shark could have eaten the fishermen. There were also pictures of victims of shark attacks, dead and alive. Some were torn beyond recognition and one man, who is alive, had teeth marks on his belly. The movie, "Jaws," really made an image of sharks in my mind. The movie was about a shark's shark. There were lots of people being mangled by the shark and everyone was terrified. There were lots of scenes of the shark thrashing about in the water and showing off his superiority. Even though "Jaws" was a fictional shark, it had a big impression on me because I had never seen a real shark. In books I have read that sharks are generally very peaceful, except when they are provoked or excited, but after all the other image-models I had of sharks it was kind of hard to believe. When I first got to Boston I heard about the shark exhibit at the New England Aquarium. I was so excited to see them. Now I could really see this monster first hand. I even had a dream about what it would be like. I dreamt of a brave Aquarium employee carefully leaning over the shark tank and throwing large chunks of fish to the snapping mouths of the sharks below. I dreamt I saw a little girl, overzealous in her desire to see a shark, lose her grip and fall into the steaming water. Within seconds the poor child was devoured and the weeping parents just stared into the water where she had fallen. Finally one day I made it to the Aquarium. After paying what I thought was an overwhelming amount to see a shark ($3.50) my girlfriend and I slowly walked in the entrance with anticipation of a most terrifying event. Much to our surprise that first pool we came to was filled with brightly colored sharks. They were very beautiful and handsome. I had expected them to be dark black. As I watched them they seemed to be lethargic. I had expected to see them darting around, causing the water to churn. One shark which was lying in a corner, very casually let two big sea turtles walk right over him. My first reaction was that this wasn't the same kind of shark I had heard or read about. So we proceeded on to the next shark tank, which is a huge cylinder that stands in the center of the Aquarium. Besides sharks, there were many other species and I couldn't understand how they could leave those fish in the same tank with the sharks. There are three levels to the tank and at the bottom level we saw a few sharks, not as big as I imagined, lying lazily on the floor. Not one of those sharks paid the least bit of attention to all the little fish swimming right in front of them. On the second level we saw even smaller sharks. They looked almost lifeless and perpetually swam in circles around the tank. When we finally reached the top floor we were looking at the surface of the water. On the wall was a sign that announced that feeding times would be in just a few minutes. I was really excited because I thought that now I would get to see what I had been waiting for. When time came for feeding I was really surprised to see a man in a wet suit come walking out. I couldn't believe he was actually going to dive into the tank. When he did jump in we rushed down to the second floor to see the fool eaten alive. Much to our disbelief, though, the diver began to take food out of a bag he had and push the fish into the shark's mouth. I was totally confused. Where was the awesome death machine I had imagined for so long? What was this imposter before me? I came to the conclusion that the poor shark had been drugged in order to make it safe for captivity. My image-model of a shark may be partly correct. I'm sure the wild ones are more fierce than those in the aquarium, but my image-model is a far cry from the real thing.

Tom Rindfleisch

Some of the slight discomfort you probably feel while reading this essay comes from the lack of identation. As a practiced reader of English, you subconsciously expect units of meaning to be marked by paragraph indentations. Since this writer did not provide those indentations, you as reader have to figure out for yourself where the essay divides into sections that represent units of meaning. In other words, you as reader must do some of the work that you ordinarily expect the writer to do. And very possibly you did not divide the essay as the writer would have intended.

Probable points for beginning paragraphs in "Danger! Shark!" are in lines 7, 18 or 21, 30, 37 or 41, 53, 64 or 66, 78 or 79, 83, 90, and 94.

The three opening sentences present readers with a framework for the first part of the paper; one expects that the writer will go on to describe his "image-model" of sharks, his reading about sharks (factual and literary), and "Jaws," presumably in that order. The first sentence is on a higher level of generality than the second and third; logically the three together form an introductory paragraph.

"When I think of sharks I conjure up in my mind . . ." begins a group of sentences about Tom's "image-model of sharks." From the word "mind," the level of generality remains very specific through the next four sentences, all of which are about Tom's image of sharks.

Then we come to

> A few times the mystery of the shark has haunted me so much that I was beckoned to the library in search of more information about this curious devilfish.

Clearly we are moving on to what Tom has learned about sharks from books. This sentence functions as a transition out of the last section and into this one, which is controlled by "When I saw pictures of sharks I was confirmed in my image of them." That relatively general topic sentence encompasses the next five sentences, which give the particulars of the "pictures of sharks."

Then come five sentences about "Jaws": a relatively general topic sentence, three specific sentences, and a concluding sentence which restates and amplifies the meaning of the first—a classic textbook paragraph, if only Tom had indented.

If the essay were about to end, as the introductory framework might have led one to expect, the next sentence could stand alone as a concluding paragraph (not that it would be an especially good one). Since the essay continues, however, and since "sharks are generally very peaceful" and "it was kind of hard to believe" foreshadow the second part of the essay, it is better attached to the paragraph immediately following. The second part then turns out to be a narrative, concluding with just a bit of analysis, which refers back to the opening sentence of the essay.

Speaking particularly of literature, Kenneth Burke defines form as "an arousing and fulfullment of desires." He states that "a work has form in so far as one part of it leads a reader to anticipate another part, to be gratified by the sequence." What does that mean in terms of this humble school essay?

What we have called the introductory paragraph leads readers to anticipate three units of meaning, which do in fact follow. Thus the opening three sentences can be said to arouse three "desires." In a sense, those sentences make three promises about what is to follow.

What is sometimes called "responsibility" in writing is the adequate fulfillment of such implicit promises. When a piece of writing adequately fulfills the anticipations it has aroused in its readers, it is said to have achieved *closure.* Of the three specific expectations set up by Tom's introduction, two are brought to closure.

What we have called the second paragraph adequately fulfills the promise to describe Tom's "image-model of sharks"—if anything it could have been improved by being tightened or cut slightly. What we have called the third paragraph is not so adequate: it is entirely about photographs and does not at all fulfill the part of the promise about stories in which "the shark always played the part of evil." The promise about "Jaws," on the other hand, is fulfilled.

A useful way to think about anticipations and closure is to think about questions implicit in a piece of writing. Occasionally, those questions are explicit, as above: "What does that mean in terms of this humble school essay?" Then they are called *rhetorical questions*, because they serve the rhetorical function of setting up readers' anticipation. But that function continues even when the question is not explicit. In revising a piece of writing, you can ask yourself, "What questions does this writing implictly raise? Is each adequately answered?" If a writing achieves closure on all implicit and explicit questions, it can be said to be *complete*.

WHAT MAKES WRITING COHERE?

Thus far, the paragraph has been discussed as a unit of meaning. A paragraph—or any other piece of writing—that achieves complete closure and contains no irrelevant material is said to have *unity*. Unity refers to the level of meaning. "Danger! Shark!" turns out to have fairly good unity.

In rhetorical context, however, meaning must be considered not just as it appears on paper, but also as it is communicated to readers. Although readers share the responsibility for making this communication accurate, there is much that writers can do to facilitate accuracy. *Coherence* is a term that refers to what writers do to make unity visible to readers. Adding paragraph indentations to a piece of writing, for example, does not affect its unity but does improve its coherence. Paragraphing is a *cue* from writers to readers about how to perceive the structure of the writing.

Of what, aside from paragraphing, does this coherence consist? One very important way writers make unity visible is to repeat key words and concepts. Go through Tom's essay again and underline every use of the word "shark" or a synonym for "shark," and you will see this repetition at work.

The way repetition and redundancy work is clearest in cases where it is misused and backfires. Reconsider this sentence:

> In books I have read that sharks are generally very peaceful, except when they are provoked or excited, but after all the other image-models I had of sharks it was kind of hard to believe.

This sentence could be improved by rephrasing and repunctuation; but, in context, the main problem is in the first five words. "In *books* I have *read* . . ." reminds readers of "I always *read* that sharks were the wolves of the sea." "Read" and "books" (which suggest the same concept) raise reader anticipation that the second promise is about to be fulfilled. There is a brief confusion before readers realize that this is not a mislocated development of that unfulfilled promise, but rather a conclusion to the first part of the essay.

The *repetition of key words and concepts*, like paragraph indentations, cues readers to the unity of meaning. A word like "shark" runs through the entire piece and helps the writing cohere. The repetition of "picture" helps hold together what we have called the third paragraph; "Jaws" helps the fourth. This may be hard to accept if your English teachers have spent a lot of red ink writing "repetitive" and "redundant" in the margins of your papers; but your English teachers were (I hope) referring to excessive, unnecessary, or inappropriate repetitions and redundancies. Do an analysis of the verbal repetitions and conceptual redundancies in some good writing, and you should emerge convinced. (*Note*: Pronouns are important for creating conceptual redundancy without verbal repetition.)

"Danger! Shark!" makes extensive use of another important type of *coherency cue*. Look at the sentences that were marked as possibly beginning paragraphs. No fewer than five of them begin with "When." Four more begin with "Last summer . . . ," "A few times . . . ," "Finally, one day . . . ," and "My first reaction . . . ." Aside from the conclusion, only a few of the sentences marked as possible paragraph openings do not begin with a word or phrase indicating progression in time. This particular type of cue (an adverbial cue) is typical of narrative writing (and also of most writing by less advanced writers). Such cues mark *chronological* development either in the event being narrated or in the discovery process of writer or reader.

A similar sort of coherency cue, referring to *logical* rather than chronological patterns, is the use of *transition words* and phrases. Possibly because the essay is predominantly narrrative, only one of the potential paragraph-opening sentences of "Danger! Shark!" is marked with a logical transition word (i.e., "*So* we proceeded . . ."). See Table 2.4 on page 144 for a list of transition words and phrases categorized according to the types of logical relationships they represent.

Interestingly, we are so attuned to these verbal cues that we often imagine some unity of meaning where none exists if enough coherency cues are supplied. Consider the following paragraph.

> Governor Romero advocates statehood for Puerto Rico. However, there are no wild elephants in Colorado. That is why Einstein set off a revolution in epistemology as well as in physics. Therefore you must learn to communicate more clearly in writing.

Now reread it with transition words deleted.

> Governor Romero advocates statehood for Puerto Rico. There are no wild elephants in Colorado. Einstein set off a revolution in epistemology as well as in physics. You must learn to communicate more clearly in writing.

The power of the coherency cues is such that one can start to imagine meaningful connections among these four sentences. That, however, has more to do with the nature of the human mind than the nature of the sentences.

To summarize, then, coherence is the equivalent on the rhetorical level of unity on the level of meaning (i.e., the semantic level). Coherence can be achieved by repetitions of words and phrases concepts, or sentence structures. It can be cued by words and phrases which indicate logical or chronological relationships. The setting up and fulfilling of reader anticipations helps bring about both unity and coherence.

In these terms, consider a more sophisticated piece of writing, an excerpt from Edward P. J. Corbett's "A Survey of Rhetoric." The three paragraphs that precede this passage review "the first hundred years of the Boylston Professorship of Rhetoric at Harvard University" because, Corbett says, that "reveals what happened to rhetorical training during the nineteenth century and early years of the twentieth century."

> Part of the nineteenth-century development in the teaching of rhetoric, though not associated primarily with the Boylston Professorship, was the doctrine of the paragraph, stemming from Alexander Bain's *English Composition and Rhetoric* (1866) and fostered by such teachers as Fred Scott, Joseph Denney, John Genung, George Carpenter, Charles Sears Baldwin and Barrett Wendell. Barrett Wendell's successful rhetoric texts helped to establish the pattern of instruction that moved from the word to the sentence to the paragraph to the whole composition. Henry Seidel Canby reversed that sequence, moving from the paragraph to the sentence to the word. It is to these men that we owe the system of rhetoric that most students were exposed to in the first half of the twentieth century—the topic sentence, the various methods of developing the paragraph (which were really adaptations of the classical "topics"), and the holy trinity of unity, coherence, and emphasis.
>
> But even this kind of rhetorical approach to writing disappeared from our classrooms and our textbooks sometime in the 1930's. With the clamor from parents, businessmen, journalists and administrators for correct grammar, correct usage, and correct spelling, rhetoric books began to be replaced with handbooks. By 1936 the study of rhetoric had sunk to such an estate in our schools that I.A. Richards, in his *The Philosophy of Rhetoric*, could say of it that it was "the dreariest and least profitable part of the waste that the unfortunate travel through in Freshman English," and W. M. Parrish, reviewing the situation in 1947 could say, in an article addressed to teachers of speech, "English teachers . . . have almost abandoned the very name of rhetoric, and the classical tradition is now completely in our hands."

Note that the two opening phrases of Corbett's first sentence repeat the words, "nineteenth-century," "rhetoric," and "Boylston Professor-

TABLE 2.3 Revision-Heuristic, Level 2B: Rhetorical Context[a]

SELECTION	ARRANGEMENT
Does each paragraph represent a unit of meaning or have some other meaningful function?	Does this writing answer all the implicit questions in the order readers will expect?
Is there sufficient—but not excessive—repetition (of words) and redundancy (of concepts) for the intended readers?	Does the paragraphing guide readers through the pattern of meaning?
Does each paragraph answer whatever question(s) it implicitly raises?	Are phrases and concepts repeated at important junctures in the writing?
	Are chronological sequences and logical relationships adequately marked (e.g., with transition words) to meet the needs of intended readers?

[a]*Remember*: This is only a list of suggested questions. Choose from it only those questions that match your individual needs. Rephrase them more specifically, if possible, to focus your attention on your own particular weak points. Add any questions you need to. Use this list to continue developing your own revision-heuristic (see pages 99-101). And do not rely on this list alone: read the sections of the text that explain the concepts behind the questions.

ship," as well as the concepts of *training* ("teaching") and *what happened* ("development"), and thus tie this passage to what preceded it. The phrase, "the doctrine of the paragraph," announces the topic of Corbett's first paragraph, and the rest of the sentence adds particulars. The second sentence begins with a repetition of "Barrett Wendell," repeats the word "rhetoric," and also repeats the concepts of *English composition and rhetoric* ("rhetoric texts") and *teaching* ("instruction).

The third sentence parallels the second in beginning with the name of an influential teacher and repeats "the word," "the sentence," and "the paragraph," but in reversed order. Thus it has *iteration* of sentence structure but *alternation* of word order. It also repeats with variation the verb "to move" and the structure "establish the pattern"/"reversed that sequence."

The fourth sentence begins with a conceptual repetition ("these men"), repeats "rhetoric," refers to *teaching* ("students were exposed"), and moves from the "nineteenth century" to the "first half of the twentieth century." Thus it introduces the new information which follows the dash (new information which does include repetition of "developing" and "paragraph"). The second paragraph then begins with the transition word "But," which indicates *negation* and defines the relationship between the two paragraphs.

It is important to emphasize that *writers do not ordinarily think about these sorts of repetitions, transitions, and other coherency cues.* Corbett will probably be surprised when he reads this and discovers just how much cement be (unconsciously) used to make the passage cohere. It is useful, however, for writers to know what makes for coherence because that knowledge will guide their unconscious processes and will help them to recognize, analyze, and revise incoherent passages in their drafts. We will continue with the subject of coherence as we move on to *frameworks*: titles, openings, transitions, and conclusions.

The questions in Table 2.3 summarize the practical implications of this section. Consider whether you need to add some of them to your own revision-heuristic (see pages 99-101).

ADDITIONAL READING

Shearer, Ned. "Alexander Bain and the Genesis of Paragraph Theory." *Quarterly Journal of Speech* 58 (December 1972), pages 408-417.

Christensen, Francis. "A Generative Rhetoric of the Paragraph." *College Composition and Communication* 16 (October 1965), pages 144-156.

Braddock, Richard. "The Frequency and Placement of Topic Sentences in Expository Prose." *Research in the Teaching of English* 8 (Winter 1974), pages 287-302.

Halliday, Michael, and Rugaiya Hasan. *Cohesion in Spoken and Written English.* London: Longman, 1973.

EXERCISE

1. Select some passages, each two to three paragraphs long, from good writing by several different authors in your area of specialization. Analyze them. See if you can identify the types of repetitions and cues which make them cohere, the basis on which new paragraphs are started, and typical ways the paragraphs are organized. (Do they typically begin by stating the main point? Do they typically make only one point? Do they typically restate that point in closing?) Compare and contrast results with those obtained by others who investigated distinct kinds of writing.

2. Collect short articles from a newspaper, a popular magazine, three academic journals (one from the sciences, one from the social sciences, one from the humanities), a collection of readings anthologized for university students, a cookbook (or other manual), and several other sources. Compare and contrast the principles of paragraphing.

3. Retype a short article from a popular magazine *without making any paragraph indentations.* Ask a number of people to indicate where they would paragraph it. Then ask them to explain why. Analyze the results.

4. Take several paragraphs you have written in the past that you suspect are not very good. Analyze them for unity (Do they achieve closure on all implicit questions? Are they free of irrelevant material? Is there a pattern of levels of generality?) and for coherence (underline repetitions, redundancies, adverbials, transition words, pronouns, demonstratives, etc.) Do the same for several paragraphs you have written that you suspect are fairly good. Compare and contrast the results. Rewrite the paragraph you think is the worst of the lot.

FRAMEWORKS

The Introduction is the beginning of the discourse, and by it the hearer's mind is prepared for attention.
Rhetorica ad Herennium, Anonymous

An exordium is a passage which brings the mind of the auditor into a proper condition to receive the rest of the speech. This is accomplished if he becomes well-disposed, attentive and receptive. . . . A partition correctly made renders the whole speech clear and perspicuous.
Cicero

THE FUNCTION OF FRAMEWORKS

The framework is all the parts of a piece of writing that mark its structure: title and opening, transitions, and conclusion. They frame the writing and give it shape. They allow readers to anticipate, follow, and reaffirm the substance, structure, and tone. Like an external skeleton, the framework supports the piece of writing.

Fluent readers anticipate. The titles and opening allow them to do so. The title and opening are your chance to shape their anticipations and to help them to anticipate accurately. You can set the tone, indicate the substance and structure. As fluent readers read, they focus ever more sharply. Transitions allow you to guide this process, to reaffirm the structure, and to clarify the relationships among the parts of the writing. Fluent readers construe patterns of meaning and draw inferences. Transitions allow you to shape those patterns and guide those inferences. Conclusions allow you to reaffirm and correct, to constrain readers from misreading. A clear framework makes a piece of writing readable. The framework allows readers to perceive the structure of the writing and thus the *pattern* of meaning.

TITLES AND OPENINGS

Titles have two general functions:

1. They make *contact* with readers, open a channel of communication, and encourage readers to read at least the opening passage.
2. They help readers to *anticipate the tone and substance* of the writing to follow, thus providing the beginning of a framework.

Openings perform both these same functions and also a third:

3. They help readers to *anticipate the structure* of the writing to follow, often by indicating its major divisions.

The extent to which the title and opening of a particular piece of writing should perform each of these functions varies, of course, from one rhetorical context to another. From an understanding of these three basic functions, however, you can deduce the right sort of title and opening for any particular writing. (*Reminder*: As was indicated in Chapter 1, it is often easiest to settle on a title and opening *after* the rest of the piece has been drafted, i.e., after you have settled the substance, structure, and tone you are helping readers to anticipate.)

The two functions of a title are not necessarily separate because it is often an anticipation of the substance which attracts readers' attention and convinces them to read on. Thus an apparently unattractive title which announces tone and substance clearly—for example, "The Application of Transformational-Generative Grammar to the Analysis of Similes and Metaphors in Modern English"—will attract exactly the right readers (those interested in an academic treatment of the specialized topic) while dissuading those who would not want to read the article anyhow.

A title is more than a label, but it is a label. Like the label on a can of beans, it functions to inform readers of the contents it represents (literally, re-presents). Thus students who write atop their papers "Rhetoric Assignment, No. 1" or "English Theme" do understand one of the functions of titles. But, again like the label on a can of beans, under certain circumstances a title functions also to *persuade* people to sample its contents.

The ideal title persuades intended readers to read and dissuades any undesired readers, while helping readers to accurately anticipate the tone and substance of the writing. Thus the nature of a good title varies according to the tone and substance of the writing and the nature of the intended readers.

The two functions of a title do sometimes contradict each other. A writer may have to choose between an *attractive* title that somewhat misrepresents the tone or substance of the writing, and an *accurate* but unattractive title. In such a case, remember that the relative importance of the two functions depends on the nature of the writing. An article in a scientific journal, to take one extreme, should have an accurate title; most of those who read it will do so because they are interested in the substance. A short story title, to take another extreme, need not indicate the substance of the story very specifically. With a satire, to take yet another extreme, it may be most important to indicate the tone and genre.

Consider the following list of titles culled from a set of student essays. The assignment was to describe and analyze a situation in which two people (or one person at two distinct times) had radically distinct perceptions of the same phenomenon.

Blind, Blind Date
The Image-Model of a Cantor
A Conflict
How the Greek People Feel about the Americans Before and After the Cyprus Situation
An Age Conflict
Danger! Shark!
Between Image and Reality
Different Strokes for Different Folks
First Appearance
Every Coin Has Two Sides
How to See Something Two Different Ways
Another Side of Ron Hubbard

To what extent does each title allow you to predict the tone and substance of the essay? If this list were the table of contents of the only magazine in a waiting room, which three would you read first?

In one section of the course for which these essays were written, the top three choices were "Danger! Shark", "Between Image and Reality," and "An Age Conflict," followed by "How to See Something Two Different Ways" and "Blind, Blind Date." Those preferences probably had something to do with the nature of the prospective readers: almost all of them were about 18 to 19 years old, almost all of them had recently seen the movie, "Jaws," and all of them had recently been exposed to material about human perception in several university courses.

One can imagine groups of prospective readers who would be more attracted to "How the Greek People Feel about the Americans Before and After the Cyprus Situation" and "Another Side of Ron Hubbard." (In those two cases, it is largely the substance of the writing that would be attractive.) "A Conflict" is the title for which it is hardest to imagine a prospective audience because it is both vague and not intrinsically attractive.

Here are some titles from three magazines. What can you infer *about the readers* of each?

1. Bette Midler: Gutsy, Unique and *Divinely* Talented
   All About Shampoos
   Ways to Tell Somebody You're Mad
   What Every Girl Should Know About Wine
   The Eastern Way of Love
   How to Cope When Your Parents Are Suddenly *Old*
2. Paperback Romance
   Pets and People: Cat Grooming
   Big Tomato Cookbook
   Make Perfect Rice—Every Time
   How To Tell If Your Child Is Gifted
   Short Cuts to Summer Beauty
   How To Save Money on Jeans
3. 12-Meter Duel
   Dehydrated Foods
   Nor'West Passage
   Pacific Shell Collecting
   Pearson-323
   Racing Forum

What can you infer about title writing if you assume that these titles are effective for their respective audiences and occasions?

In addition to appealing to readers and helping them to anticipate tone and substance, the opening passage can also help readers read by helping them to anticipate the structure of what will follow. In classical rhetoric, this was called the *division* or *partition* because it indicates how the piece of writing will be divided in parts.

For some types of writing, the appeal aspect of the opening passage is crucially important. Newspaper and magazine readers typically move on to another article if the opening passage does not "grab" them, one way or another.

To take another extreme, certain pieces of writing will be virtually "assigned reading." Scientists, for instance, are expected to keep up with the latest research in their fields. In these cases, the opening passage should emphasize its other potential functions: to give readers a sense of what is to come and provide them with a framework so that they can efficiently reconstruct the intended meanings.

Consider the following opening passages from student essays. To what extent can you predict the substance and structure of each writing? To what extent does each make you want to read on? Why?

> Although political modernization is currently a popular fundamental concept in the social sciences, it is a malleable term whose definition and application often vary with the needs of its users.

A short time ago the Social Credit government of British Columbia shut down Notre Dame University in Nelson.

On March 17, 1978, Garibaldi Lifts Limited, the controlling voice of Whistler Mountain, officially announced that a new chairlift was to be built in the Alpine region of the mountain in the summer of that year. Their announcement was subsequently met with disapproval from a host of organizations.

There are many approaches to coherence, but some are more effective than others.

Is our prison system a viable means of dealing with "crime"? I say, it is not!

Faith is defined in the *Random House College Dictionary* as "confidence or trust in a person or thing, belief that is not based on proof, belief in God or in the doctrines or teachings of religion, belief in anything."

Now consider the following opening passages of some articles from a popular magazine. To what extent can you predict the substance and structure of each writing? What can you infer about the readers of the magazine?

Everybody's doing it—going to parties, *discos* and new clubs. And the clothes you wear should be as much fun as all that crazy dancing, drinking and God knows what you're up to.

If you've just now come into the market for an audio rig that will turn your wheels into a concert hall, you're in luck; there's a cornucopia of really spectacular sound equipment waiting for you at your neighborhood highway-sound store in a range of prices from the modest budget to the price-is-no-object level.

Now that everyone—except a few gin diehards and the outreachers who are into white rum or tequila—is drinking vodka, whiskey is passé, right? Don't you believe it.

Victor Morrison is that success story uniquely of our times—intellectual, corporate strategist and gambler.

Now, with the same questions in mind, consider the following opening passages of articles from journals published by the National Council of Teachers of English.

We ask students never to judge ideas or events out of context, but fail to see our composition classes in any larger world. That is why they are such astonishing failures. For decades we have been smearing the bloody marks (*sp, awk, gr*) in the margins of what we call "themes." These papers are not meant to be *read*, but *corrected*.

In an age of overpopulation and underachievement, of instant credit and a growing knowledge industry, some processes still take time.

Style is the art of choosing, and one of our tasks, as writers and teachers of writing, is to identify as many compositional choices as possible.

If the new grammar is to be brought to bear on composition, it must be brought to bear on the rhetoric of the sentence.

What can you infer about the relationship between "a good opening" and intended audience? Assuming that many English teachers also read the popular magazine, what can you infer about the relationship between "a good opening" and the *occasion* on which the writing will be read?

To sum up then, both titles and openings are "good" insofar as they serve their functions. The first function can be deduced from a principle of communication theory, which states that communication can occur only when a channel is open. Applied to human beings, that means you must make *contact* to communicate. It also means you must maintain contact, but that has more to do with transitions than with openings.

The second and third functions can be deduced from the nature of the fluent reading process. Since readers anticipate meanings, the opening should help them do so. Since readers retain meanings by relating them to frameworks, the opening should either provide such frameworks or suggest frameworks the readers already know.

However, if your readers are likely to violently disagree with your main points, you might do best to lead up to those points rather gently—even if that means you cannot state those points, or provide much of an accurate framework, until the middle or even the end of the piece of writing. The general principle is that good writing achieves its purposes with its intended readers. If we can generalize about good writing, that is because we can generalize about human beings. If we can be somewhat more particular, that is because we are actually thinking of those particular human beings who are likely to be reading English-language writings in the latter part of the twentieth century. The fact remains, as the philosopher Jean-Paul Sartre points out, "In order for the works to have any effect it is necessary for the public to adopt them." That is why he also says, "The author's whole art is bent on obliging me to *create* what he discloses."

MAKING TRANSITIONS VISIBLE

Broadly defined, whatever establishes coherence among the parts of a writing is a transition. Often this is no more than a phrase in the first sentence of a passage that repeats some concept from the previous passage, as in Corbett's reference to the Boylston Professorship (pages 133-134). Sometimes a standard format functions to make a transition. When readers of a scientific article find the heading "Experimental

Procedure" at the end of a section listing hypotheses, they need no further transition (although there would be no harm in supplying one).

Narrowly defined, a transition is a word, phrase, sentence, or group of sentences that makes visible the chronological or logical relationship between two or more parts of a writing. Transitions make writing coherent. They act as cues. They call readers' attention to the unity of the writing by indicating the chronological or logical relationships which make that writing whole and complete. Ordinarily, we think of transition words or phrases, but any passage that serves this function may properly be called a transition. Even an entire chapter, if its primary function is to connect one part of a book with another, is a transition.

For the most part, writers do not have to think about transitions. Unless you have a problem with transitions, there is no need to devote conscious attention to them. When, however, a draft is criticized (either by the person who drafted it or by other readers) for a lack of coherence, you should be able to add transitions.

One point which often does need to be made about transition words and phrases has to do with their placement. Less mature writers tend to put almost all their transition words and phrases at the beginning of sentences. The beginning of a sentence is relatively emphatic (as contrasted with some point in the middle). The beginning of a sentence is thus a strong position for the transition. It is also a logical position since it is exactly in between the proposition represented by that sentence and the one that preceded it. And it is a "natural" position because that is where transitions usually go in speech.

On the other hand, why fill an emphatic position with a transition when it could be used for the subject of the sentence? Why not put the emphasis on what the sentence is about? In speech, the listeners prefer the transition at the beginning because they immediately get the framework for the sentence or passage to follow. Readers, however, are more flexible because they have the freedom to go back if they miss something. Consider what happens to the preceding sentence if the transition word is moved:

> However, readers are more flexible because they have the freedom to go back if they miss something.

Either version is adequate, but the emphasis shifts slightly. It is of such choices that style is made. In the passage cited above, for example, Corbett puts heavy emphasis on the contrast between the two paragraphs by beginning the second with "But. . . ." Consciously or subconsciously, he chose not to write,

> Even this kind of rhetorical approach to writing disappeared from our classrooms and our textbooks, however, sometime in the 1930's.

TABLE 2.4 Transition Words and Phrases

LOGICAL TYPE	EPITOMIZED BY	EXAMPLES[a]
Sequence	THEN	then, next, finally, afterwards, eventually, later, meanwhile, soon, presently, while, immediately, since, formerly, previously, last, at last, at length, subsequently, simultaneously, in the meantime, first, second
Coordination	FURTHERMORE, IN ADDITION, AND	furthermore, in addition, and, also, besides, likewise, moreover, similarly, again, equally important, too, what is more
Contrast	BUT, HOWEVER	but, however, on the other hand, at another extreme, yet, still, instead, despite this, nonetheless, for all that, on the contrary, conversely, although, notwithstanding
Causation	THEREFORE, BECAUSE	therefore, because, for, as a result, accordingly, because of this, hence, consequently, thus, if . . . then
Inclusion	FOR EXAMPLE, THAT IS	for example, for instance, in particular, specifically, to illustrate, to demonstrate, that is, namely, in other words, as a matter of fact, indeed
Alternation	OR	or, either or, another possibility, as an alternative, neither . . . . . . nor
Conclusion	SO, IN CONCLUSION	so, in conclusion, in short, on the whole, to sum up, in brief, to summarize

[a]Some of the words and phrases cited here actually fit more than one category, depending on how they are used. The words in each category, moreover, vary considerably in their connotations. Like a thesaurus, this list should be used with care, especially if you are not familiar with the normal use of the word or phrase you are considering.

The important point to remember about transitions is that they make visible the structure of meanings in the writing. They are an important aspect of the framework that makes good writing readable.

ENDINGS

A bit of popular wisdom about writing says, "Tell them what you are going to say, say it, and tell them what you said." In terms of efficient reading, this makes a lot of sense. "Tell them what you are going to say" means to give readers a framework which allows them to anticipate effectively. "Tell them what you said" means, at the end, to help readers pick out the points you think are important. As long as you remember that the *telling* should not always be overt and explicit, this is good general advice.

Like openings, conclusions provide a framework. At the end, of course, the purpose of providing a framework is not to help readers anticipate. Instead it is to reemphasize what, out of all that you've written, you want to stick in readers' minds. Thus a conclusion is a final opportunity to indicate emphasis, to instruct readers about what you want them to remember.

Endings also have a psychological function. They serve rhythmically to bring the writing to a close. Directly or indirectly, they announce, "This is the end." A sudden, unmarked stop after the last point usually disrupts readers and leaves them feeling unsatisfied. If a piece has a beginning, this implies formally and rhythmically that it will have an ending. The absence of such an ending is usually a failure to gratify a desire aroused by the writing.

Which of these two functions takes precedence depends, of course, on the genre and purpose of the writing. If the purpose is to instruct, for example, an explicit summary is often a good conclusion. If the purpose is to arouse empathy, on the other hand, an image which reconcretizes the feeling of the piece may better fulfill the rhythm of the whole.

With this in mind, consider the endings of the student essays whose openings you considered above (on pages 140-141).

> As a result, political scientists will continue to use the concept of political modernization in various ways, while hoping that a complete concise definition will crystalize from its transitional foundation.

> Notre Dame added something to the West Kootenays that no mere college could. It gave Nelson the depth, the awareness, and the provincial voice that few communities in the interior of British Columbia share.

> Through analyzing the constraints that limited Garibaldi Lifts' decision it is possible to see that their decision was the best alternative to an Olympic Run lift.

> For, whether we imprison one Joe Badguy or one million like him, we are not affecting any of the constraints which prevent individuals from obeying the law; therefore we are not solving the crime problem.

> Faith then is rested on God and trust put in Him alone. He is described as worthy to have faith placed in. And he is picturesquely expressed as my rock

TABLE 2.5 Revision-Heuristic, Level 2C: Rhetorical Context[a]

SELECTION	ARRANGEMENT
Is the title sufficiently attractive? Does it indicate the subject of the writing?	Does the opening help readers anticipate the substance and structure of the piece? Does it give them a framework?
Will the opening appeal to the intended readers? Does it indicate the subject of the writing?	Are transitions clear? Are transition words and phrases properly placed for intended emphasis. Do they indicate the intended logical or chronological relationships?
Is there an ending? Does it help readers catch the intended emphasis? Does it help them grasp implications?	Does the ending bring the piece of writing rhythmically to a close?

[a]*Remember*: This is only a list of suggested questions. Choose from it only those questions that match your individual needs. Rephrase them more specifically, if possible, to focus your attention on your own particular weak points. Add any questions you need to. Use this list to continue developing your own revision-heuristic (see pages 99-101). And do not rely on this list alone: read the sections of the text that explain the concepts behind these questions.

> and my fortress and my deliverer; my God, my strength, in whom I will trust; my buckler, and the horn of my salvation and my higher tower. Faith may be confidently rested on a God like that.
>
> Finally, coherence should be recognized not only as a quality of writing but also, along with unity and emphasis, as a basic principle of writing because the quality of coherence influences the clarity of meaning in composition.

It is difficult, of course, to evaluate an ending in the absence of the writing which it ends, but these give some sense of the variety possible within the single genre of student essay. All of them serve both functions of a conclusion, although the balance between the two functions varies considerably.

In conclusion, then, we should note that titles and openings, transitions and conclusions, all serve both a logical and a psychological function. They provide a framework that allows readers to anticipate, follow, and remember the pattern of meanings. They open, maintain, and close the channel that allows the communication of those meanings.

The questions in Table 2.5 summarize the practical implications of this section. Consider whether you need to add any of them to your own revision-heuristic (see pages 99-101). The rest of this chapter considers the conventions of Standard English in terms of readers' expectations.

ADDITIONAL READING

Burke, Kenneth. *Counter-Statement.* Los Altos, Calif. Hermes, 1953. See especially pages 124-149.

D'Angelo, Frank. "A Generative Rhetoric of the Essay." *College Composition and Communication* 25 (December 1974), pages 388-396.

Fort, Keith. "Form, Authority, and the Critical Essay." *College English* 32 (March 1971), pages 629-639.

EXERCISE

1. Select an issue of a popular magazine that you read—or one that you strongly dislike. Look at the titles, openings, and endings of all the articles. Make as many probable inferences as you can about the typical readers of the magazine. Write a brief description of those readers. Expand that description into an analytical piece by using evidence from the magazine to justify your description. Try to obtain the magazine's own description of its readers (usually available to advertisers in one form or another); compare and contrast it with the one you inferred.

2. Select several pieces of good writing from your own area of special interest. Analyze them to discover what type of framework they provide for readers and what devices they use to do so.

3. Select several pieces you have written in the past that you suspect are not very good. Analyze them to discover how you used titles, openings, transitions, and endings. See if you can make them more coherent—if you think lack of coherence is what you do not like about them. Then analyze your use of titles, openings, transitions, and endings in some of your better writing.

4. Take some titles from published articles. Imagine the same articles with radically distinct purposes, audiences, and occasions. Rewrite the titles to suit the new rhetorical contexts. Then rewrite the openings and endings.

5. Take some titles, openings, and conclusions that emphasize the logical function of a framework. Rewrite them to emphasize the psychological function.

CONVENTIONS

. . . only what fits is allowed.

Norman Podhoretz

For boys do not need the art of grammar, which teaches correct speech, if they have the opportunity to grow up and live among men who speak correctly. Without knowing any of the names of the errors, they criticize and avoid anything erroneous they hear spoken on the basis of their own habits of speech. . . .

Augustine

The English language is a public code; as such it has rules.

R. Young, A. Becker, and K. Pike

THE IMPORTANCE OF CONVENTIONS

Standard English has many conventions. Some of them seem both to make sense and to be useful. Some of them seem arbitrary but still useful. Some of them seem arbitrary and useless—at least to writers who have not learned them. But all of them matter. They are all signals from writer to reader about how to read the text. They all help readers read.

Some of the arbitrary conventions were imposed on the language, especially during the eighteenth century, by authorities who grossly misunderstood language processes. Several rules, for example, were imposed by analogy from mathematics. For instance, the rule against double negatives (e.g., "I'm *not* going to do *nothing* until he shows up.") is based on the mathematical principle that "two negatives equal a positive." In most languages, two negatives equal an emphatic negative, but the rule against double negatives is now well-established in Standard English. The rule that tells you to say, "It is *I*," also based on a false mathematical analogy, is less well-established but still enforced in certain social contexts.

Other rules were established by analogy with Latin. One such rule says infinitives should not be split: do not write, "to carefully compose" because that "carefully" splits the infinitive, "to compose." (The English infinitive consists of the preposition, *to*, plus the verb.) Latin infinitives are never split for an excellent reason. They cannot be: Latin infinitives are one word (e.g., *componere*).

Whether they make sense or not—and many of them do—conventions matter. In the first place, they create a certain stability in the written language. Language functions as a "tool," a means of production; like other means of production in an industrialized society, it must be to some degree standardized if communication is to be efficient and cooperation maximized.

In the second place, conventions make reading easier by allowing readers to anticipate more accurately. In this sense, *conventions* are *reader expectations*. You violate them at the risk of confusing readers, and a confused reader may misunderstand—or simply stop reading.

Thus the underlying principle about conventions is this: all else being equal, *obey the conventions of format, usage, grammar, punctuation, and spelling that your readers expect you to obey*. Violate those conventions only when the violation positively serves your purposes or helps you to represent your meanings accurately. Try to avoid unintentional violations. Try to use the conventions with which your readers will be comfortable. For example, when writing to a Canadian audience, which prefers such spellings, use "labour" and "tire centre." When writing for a British audience, make that "tyre centre." For a United States audience, "labor" and "tire center."

Since conventions are conventional and only sometimes make intrinsic sense, some people downgrade them: "Oh, you might as well get out your handbook and learn those silly comma rules; you'll have to do it sooner or later, and it will make life easier."

But those comma rules are not just silly; they are signals from you to your reader about how to read your sentences. Like paragraph indentations and transition words, they are cues to your readers about how to divide and to interrelate your meanings. As such, they matter. Once you have mastered the code, punctuation marks help you to read and write more effectively.

We will demonstrate this first with *colons, formal dashes,* and *semicolons,* punctuation marks that are especially important to advanced writers (for reasons we will come to). Then we will reiterate by reviewing some of the more important comma rules. But the same principle could be illustrated with any other conventions, from dangling modifiers, to manuscript format, to footnote form (see pages 383-384).

COLONS, DASHES, AND SEMICOLONS

THE COLON. The colon is often said to be like an equals sign (=). In a sense it is. What follows a colon must be in some way equivalent to what precedes it. But there is more to it than that: what follows a colon should be on a lower level of generality than what precedes it. (Note that, in the preceding sentence, what follows the colon is equivalent to "more to it than that," but more specific.)

Colons are typically used in the following situations: (1) to introduce a series, (2) to introduce a quotation, especially a long one, (3) to add a specific detail after a general description, (4) wherever the second clause restates the meaning of the first but more specifically. (Note that the preceding sentence contained a colon which introduced a series.) Here are four examples to illustrate these four uses:

1. The Andes Mountains run through the following countries: Colombia, Ecuador, Peru, Bolivia, Chile, and Argentina.
2. In "Progressive Insanities of a Pioneer," Margaret Atwood attacks narrow rationalism for its need to control and its failure to comprehend ecological wholeness:

   If he had known unstructured
   space is a deluge
   and stocked his log house-
   boat with all the animals

   even the wolves,

   he might have floated.

3. This applicant lacks one essential quality: literacy.
4. That is the nature of growth, at least among human beings: it is often accompanied by "growing pains."

In all four cases, what follows the colon is more specific than what precedes it. *The colon throws the readers' attention forward* toward the more specific meaning(s).

Something else is true in all four examples, something that illustrates a rule about using colons: the colon is always preceded by an *independent clause.* (To obey that rule, of course, you must know what an independent clause is. Most simply put, an independent clause is a series of words that *could* stand alone as a sentence. There are more technical definitions—for example, an independent clause verbally represents a complete logical proposition, or an independent clause contains both a subject and a predicate—but for writers with "sentence sense" the first definition will serve.)

This rule about preceding a colon with an independent clause is beginning to develop exceptions. Traditionally, if what preceded the colon was not quite an independent clause, one completed the clause with a phrase like "the following":

> Presidents of the United States who died in office after being elected in a year divisible by twenty include the following: John Kennedy, Franklin Roosevelt, Woodrow Wilson, and William McKinley.

In many contexts, it is now becoming permissible to delete "the following." The rule still stands, but this ellipsis is becoming a partial exception.

THE DASH. The formal dash is the opposite of the colon. It too represents a kind of equation, but what follows the dash should be on a *higher* level of generality than what precedes it. It throws readers' attention *back*:

> John Kennedy, Franklin Roosevelt, Woodrow Wilson, and William McKinley—all these Presidents of the United States died in office during the twentieth century after having been elected in a year divisible by twenty.

Dashes have other uses too. They may be used for emphasis, either in place of other punctuation or where no punctuation is needed at all.

> What follows a semicolon and what precedes it are usually on the same level of generality—otherwise the writer probably should have used a colon or a dash.

They may also be used to set off parenthetical elements (i.e., as emphatic parentheses).

> As individuals, we have to communicate—and to a large degree even perceive, think, and feel—with concepts that are provided by the languages of our societies.

And in colloquial writing or representations of speech, they may be used to indicate breaks in the flow of the sentences—especially the sort of breaks which defy any other sort of representation. (That last dash set off a parenthetical element.) On a typewriter, a dash is usually indicated by two hyphens, although it may also indicated by space-hyphen-space; in handwriting, a dash is longer than a hyphen. In the nineteenth century, it was good practice to use a dash and a colon together (:—), but this is no longer standard.

THE SEMICOLON. The general rule about semicolons is that they are used to join what could have been two separate sentences. In general, therefore, a semicolon requires an independent clause on each side of it.

What follows the semicolon and what precedes it are usually on the same level of generality—otherwise the writer probably should have used a colon or a dash. The semicolon indicates that the meanings it connects are so closely related that the writer preferred not to put them in two separate sentences. Usually that is because they are more closely related to each other than to the meanings of other nearby sentences.

> Some people use books; others collect them.
>
> Those carrots cost the farmers only 8 cents a pound to produce; nonetheless, they cost fifty cents a pound in the supermarket.

A secondary rule about semicolons states that they may be used to replace commas whenever a sentence gets too complicated. In this sense a semicolon is a "strong" comma. For instance, if you write a long sentence with a lot of commas, you can arbitrarily make the most important comma(s) into semicolon(s). If the items are long enough or contain commas, a list introduced by a colon is often punctuated with semicolons.

> These punctuation marks are cues to the reader about the relationships among levels of generality: the colon is followed by a more specific meaning; the formal dash by a more general meaning; and the semicolon by a meaning of the same level of generality.

PUNCTUATION IN GENERAL

We have used colons, formal dashes, and semicolons to exemplify the principle that punctuation marks are signals to the readers about how to read sentences because these three marks are important to advanced writers. With certain exceptions, such as the colon used to introduce a series, writers do not usually need these punctuation marks until their sentences reach a certain level of complexity. Their sentences typically reach that level of complexity when their ideas do. In contemporary North American societies, this seems to happen at an intellectual level roughly equivalent to the second or third year of college. So an advanced writing textbook is an appropriate place to learn about colons, formal dashes, and semicolons.

Writers who fail to learn how to use these marks often run into problems. Sometimes they have trouble getting the full complexity and subtlety of their meanings into their sentences. Sometimes they fail to adequately qualify their meanings. Sometimes they write the sentences they need, but try to punctuate them with commas. The result then is a comma-splice.

> The most common error seems to be that I do not use specific enough examples when writing papers, my references need to be better.

> Not much of Old English remains today in active language, in fact, over eighty-five percent of Old English words have been lost.

Both of those sentences become correct as soon as a comma is replaced with a semicolon.

The same principle here exemplified with colons, formal dashes, and semicolons holds for all punctuation and, indeed, for all conventions. For example, one of the most important comma rules says to put a comma in front of a coordinating conjunction that joins independent clauses. Suppose a sentence begins,

> She met his father and . . . .

Whether or not that *and* is preceded by a comma tells readers whether to anticipate an addition to that proposition or a new proposition. Without a comma, the sentence is likely to end something like this:

> She met his father and his mother.

With a comma, it is likely to end something like this:

> She met his father, and then she understood Chu Teh better than she ever had before.

That is why it is important to use a comma when a coordinating conjunction connects two independent clauses and not to use a comma when one clause is dependent (unless another comma rule takes precedence). The comma after an independent clause and before a coordinating conjunction is a signal to readers about what to anticipate. If you can follow this rule—which means being able to recognize independent clauses and coordinating conjunctions—then you can help readers read more fluently. There are seven coordinating conjunctions in English: *and, but, or, nor, for, yet,* and (sometimes) *so.*

Another important rule says to use commas to enclose modifying clauses that do not restrict the meaning of what they modify. Loosely, this means, put commas around modifying clauses that could be deleted without changing the meaning of the sentence. Thus the commas are a signal to readers about the nature of the modifying clause. Suppose a sentence begins,

> The speaker who used sexist language . . .

Without commas, readers will infer that there were a number of speakers and that the modifying clause, *who used sexist language,* is there to identify the particular speaker who is the subject of the sentence. With commas, readers will assume that there was only one speaker and that the modifying clause simply supplies additional information about that speaker. The two versions might end like this:

> The speaker who used sexist language was criticized after the meeting.
>
> The speaker, who used sexist language, was nonetheless applauded by many feminists.

Punctuation is not the most important matter for writers to master. But standard punctuation does help readers read sentences, and sentences are the basic units of language. Remembering that conventions make sense if they are explained as *reader expectations* should help you understand punctuation rules as well as conventions of format, usage, grammar, and spelling. Doing some exercises, which you can find in most handbooks, will also help you understand the rules.

But this understanding is of no use unless you transfer it to your own writing. Educational research indicates that transfer should be expected only if you follow up your abstract understanding by writing sentences *of your own* that utilize the rules. If among your writing problems you have identified problems with particular conventions, you should look up those conventions in a handbook, do some exercises, and also *write sentences that use them.*

The questions in Table 2.6 generally summarize this section. Add to your own revision-heuristic more specific questions that will call your attention to those particular conventions with which you have difficulty.

TABLE 2.6 Revision-Heuristic, Level 2D: Rhetoric Context[a]

SELECTION	ARRANGEMENT
Does your usage, grammar, punctuation, and spelling match the expectations of your readers?	Are you following the format that matches the expectations of your readers?
[Add specific questions to remind yourself of errors you typically make: for example, "Have I used commas correctly with conjunctions?"]	Have you punctuated your sentences so as to give readers accurate cues about the interrelationships among meanings?

[a]*Remember:* This is only a list of suggested questions. You will need to make up questions about format, usage, grammar, punctuation, and spelling, which will call your attention to your own typical problems. Use these questions to continue developing your own revision-heuristic (see pages 99-101). Refer to the preceding section of this text and to a handbook to help yourself understand rules and devise questions.

ADDITIONAL READING

Follett, Wilson. *Modern American Usage*. Ed. Jacques Barzun. New York: Hill and Wang, 1966.

Fowler, H. W. *A Dictionary of Modern English Usage*. Ed. Ernest Gowers. New York: Oxford, 1965.

EXERCISE

1. Choose a rule of English usage, grammar, or punctuation that troubles you. Look it up in one or more handbooks. Rewrite it as a principle about reader expectations. Write three sentences of your own which correctly obey that rule. Write a question for your revision-heuristic that will call your attention to that rule when you are revising your writings.

2. Write ten sentences that use colons correctly: two that use them to introduce a series, two to introduce a quotation, two to add a specific details after a general description, and four in which the second clause restates the meaning of the first but more specifically.

3. Write four sentences that use the formal dash as the opposite of a colon, one for each of the four types of sentences you wrote using colons. Be certain that what follows the dash is always of a higher level of generality than what precedes it.

4. Write two sentences using dashes for emphasis and two using dashes to set off parenthetical elements.

5. Write three sentences using semicolons to connect independent clauses (of the same level of generality) and three using semicolons to avoid confusion in complicated sentences with several commas.

Every style points to a self-interpretation of man [sic], thus answering the question of the ultimate meaning of life. Whatever the subject matter which an artist chooses, however strong or weak his artistic form, he cannot help but betray by his style his own ultimate concern, as well as that of his group, and his period.

Paul Tillich

It is a ridiculous demand which England and America make, that you should speak so that they can understand you . . . . As if Nature could support but one order of understandings, . . . and hush *and* whoa, *which Bright can understand, were the best English. As if there were safety in stupidity alone. I fear chiefly lest my expression may not be extra-vagrant enough . . . so as to be adequate to the truth of which I have become convinced. Extra vagrance!*

Henry David Thoreau

Every man's language has, first, its individualities; *secondly, the common properties of the class to which he belongs; and thirdly, words and phrases of universal use.*

Samuel Taylor Coleridge

CHAPTER 3
STYLE AND VOICE

Style must do for the writer much of what voice tone and body language do for the speaker. In writing, style creates tone and thus gives readers an image of the writer. Your readers' sense of who you are—and thus of whether they ought to trust you, believe what you say, respect your conclusions—depends very much on the stylistic choices you make.

Style should not be your first consideration. Worrying too much about style and self-image can impede the early phases of the creative composing process. Your first concern should be with the substance of what you want to communicate. But although it may not come first, style is a very important consideration. Subtleties of meaning can be misrepresented by an inappropriate style. An inappropriate style can also offend readers, sometimes even cause them to stop reading.

Perhaps the most significant and positive function of style is that it projects an image of the writer—what we call the writer's *persona*—which influences readers' responses to the writing. This chapter begins with a section on *persona* and voice, with special emphasis on that stylistic quality called "honesty" in writing. The second section discusses word choice and connotation, using the issue of sexism in language as an example; the virtue of using specific nouns and verbs is given special attention. The last section is about sentence structure and emphasizes the importance of developing your ability to use a variety of complex structures.

As you read this chapter, try to grasp the relationship between the style you choose for a particular writing and the image readers will form of you. Try to understand the various stylistic qualities that are discussed in terms of the triangular relationship among your subject matter, your readers, and yourself. That understanding should help you make sense of the stylistic choices that you face as a writer.

A competent writer can use a variety of styles as situations demand them. The specifics of this chapter should make you aware of the options available to you. Stylistic revision depends on your ability to perceive and create alternative wordings. To take proper advantage of this chapter, you should practice the kinds of rewordings that are discussed in the first two sections and practice generating and transforming sentences as discussed in the third section.

THE WRITER'S VOICE

The distinction I am working toward should be obvious enough. The writer is not physically present to his reader. He is all words. The writer has no resources at all for dramatizing himself and his message to his reader, except those scratches on paper—he has . . . no way of introducing himself beyond what he can make his reader "see" by means of abstract written words in various arrangements. To these words the reader responds in a social situation—that is, he infers a personality—but he has only words to go on.

Walker Gibson

[I]s it not highly indicative that the word for mask, persona (that-though-which-sound-comes), has given both to the ancients and to us the word for person?

Walter Ong

[S]o much is done by good taste and style in speaking that the speech seems to depict the speaker's character.

Cicero

PROJECTING A PERSONA

In at least one significant sense, a writer's style is the equivalent of a speaker's voice. It creates tone. It creates the image that writer will project. Thus it helps to define the relationship between writer and reader.

We associate style with the personal. Each individual, we say, has her or his own unique style. Ask a number of people to do the same task, and each will do it slightly differently. These differences we take as signs of individual personality, and we call them style.

Of course, style is more than just personal. The style of a piece of writing should be appropriate to its subject matter and its rhetorical context as well as to the individuality of its creator. But, within the constraints imposed by subject, purpose, audience, and occasion, there is room for flexibility. Subject matter and rhetorical context do not absolutely determine the nature of a piece of writing. Writers make choices among the various words that could represent their meanings to their readers. Writers make choices about how to combine those words in sentences. Although there is actually a bit more to it, when we speak of style in writing we generally are referring to these word- and sentence-level choices.

An individual writer will not make these choices the same way every time. In the context of various relationships, an individual person may be a physicist, gardener, surfer, mother, wife, lover, do-it-yourself-er, political activist, homeowner, and so on. Each of these roles requires a somewhat different style. The physicist does not talk to her colleagues in the same way she talks to her youngest child. Just so, a writer will use different styles at different times.

What readers perceive behind a piece of writing is not really the writer, but an image. It is not a person's character, but a facet of that character. It may, moreover, be fictive. But it does help shape how readers will relate to the writing.

To distinguish this image, created by the style of the writing, from the actual human being who wrote the words, we call it a *persona*, from the Greek word for *mask*. Thus when we speak of Shakespeare's sonnets, we distinguish between William Shakespeare, the person who lived between 1564 and 1616, and William Shakespeare, the *persona* projected behind the sonnets. There is a relationship between the two, of course, and the *persona* may be shaped in part by what we know about the historical person; but the distinction is important.

Many writers, especially the less experienced, go wrong here. An honest person honestly trying to communicate may, by his or her style, inadvertently create an evasive *persona*, which readers will distrust. In writing, as in most things, good intentions are not enough. A reader who does not know you personally can judge you only by the *persona* created by your style. Thus the nature of the *persona*, created by stylistic choices, is a good place to begin a discussion of style.

HONESTY

Honesty in writing, as in life, means more than not lying. Honesty means revealing what you actually think and feel, at least insofar as it may be significant and relevant. That may mean telling "the whole truth"; it may even mean getting in touch with thoughts and feelings that have been repressed. Honesty is often frightening and, in the context of certain power relationships, can get one into trouble. Powerful writing, however, is usually honest writing.

Honesty in writing actually refers to a stylistic quality that encourages readers to believe that writers are revealing their thoughts and feelings fully. Honesty can be avoided by lying or simply by totally avoiding certain subjects. A dishonest style, however, is more devious. It allows writers to raise a subject, seem to discuss it (often at considerable length), tell no overt lies—but nonetheless avoid revealing their true thoughts and feelings about the subject.

Dishonest writing is dishonest because it is really an attempt to *avoid* communicating. Since the very act of writing can be taken as an assertion that one is trying to communicate, writing that strives to avoid communicating is intrinsically paradoxical and dishonest.

Dishonest writing is often so abstracted from the realities it describes that readers may hardly notice what it is saying. Such writing avoids making an impact on readers by using generalities, abstractions, clichés, unintelligible jargon, ambiguous assertions, passive constructions, and other techniques that allow writers to "tell the truth" (in some technical sense) while avoiding "the whole truth." Dishonest writing sometimes has so little impact on readers that they barely notice whether it is true or false.

The "ho-hum" opening is often dishonest in this way. A student once began a paper,

> The automobile is a mechanism fascinating to everyone in all its diverse manifestations and in every conceivable kind of situation or circumstance.

That sentence has so little impact that most readers do not consider it carefully enough to notice that it is blatantly false. Concretize the statement by listing some of the less pleasant manifestations of automobiles (e.g., smog, middle-aged people so accustomed to driving that they grow tired if they must walk a quarter mile) or certain situations (e.g., a broken fuel pump on a lonely road late one cold and rainy night)—or simply ask, "Is *everyone* really *always* fascinated by cars?—and the proposition becomes highly improbable. This writer in this instance did not take the trouble to think about what he was writing and whether he actually believed it. In Eudora Welty's words, this is "bad writing" because it "is not serious and does not tell the truth." Writing concretely and honestly, the same writer probably has something to say about cars.

Professor Ken Macrorie contrasts this opening sentence with a short passage by a seventh-grader:

> I'd like to be a car. You get to go all over and get to go through mud puddles without getting yelled at . . . that's what I'd like to be.

For all its stylistic flaws, this passage makes a meaningful comparison and speaks honestly (about getting yelled at, not about cars).

Dishonest writing is characterized by a lack of commitment. For some reason, the writer feels a need to write but does not really want to say anything. The situation is analogous to when your friend asks what you think of his terrible photographs, and you reply, "interesting, very interesting effect," in order to avoid giving your true opinion. The bureaucrat who does not want to make waves, the student forced to write on a subject perceived as irrelevant, the politician trying to avoid any assertion that might alienate a voter, the prude caught in some situation where it is necessary to refer to sex, the schizophrenic who wants to avoid responsibility for any statement—all of these are likely to produce dishonest writing.

Such writing is called bureaucratese, Engfish, doublespeak, euphemism, or schizophrenese—according to the context in which it is found. It varies somewhat: the schizophrenic is more likely to use concrete ambiguity, the student to use abstraction, the technocrat to use unnecessary jargon. But it is always basically the same, an attempt to write or speak without saying anything for which one could be held responsible. Because it so often uses complicated phrasings to make nearly meaningless statements, the generic terms for it is *gobbledygook*.

Dishonest writing, it must be added, is sometimes somewhat justifiable ethically. On the basis of past experience, the schizophrenic probably believes (perhaps accurately) that definite statements will be punished. The bureaucrat's supervisor may demand bureaucratese, as the student's instructor sometimes demands Engfish. Euphemism can serve to avoid unnecessarily offending people. Doublespeak can allow diplomats to communicate without forcing other governments to take offense.

Much as we might wish for a world in which it were never necessary, the point here is not to condemn dishonest writing, but to understand it. Too many writers slip into a dishonest style even when they are honestly trying to communicate what they really believe. And too many readers are too easily fooled by gobbledygook (often because they are insecure about their reading abilities and assume that their failure to make sense of a passage is their fault, not the writer's).

Honest writing, it should be added, calls only for the expression of those perceptions, feelings, opinions, and beliefs that are relevant to the writers' and readers' purposes. The readers of a literary biography of Robert Graves want to know about Robert Graves and probably not about the biographer's feelings. The readers of a scholarly journal of literary criticism do not ordinarily want to know the scholar-author's feelings about *King Lear*. The readers of a scientific article about butterflies are probably interested in butterflies, not in the scientists' feelings about butterflies. (This distinction is especially true in North America; the British literary essay, for example, allows much greater intrusion of the writer's feelings and unsupported opinions than would be tolerated in most North American publications.)

Dishonest writing is defined by what it does *not* say more than by what it does say. Sometimes this is a matter of literal omissions. Often, however, it is a matter of style. Thus an executive might write, "It is imperative to maximize potentials for synchronized managment options," in order to avoid saying whatever that might specifically mean (perhaps, "We should not commit ourselves until we see what other departments are doing.") In either case, dishonest writing omits or obscures objectively relevant information. Typically, it also disguises or mystifies the writer's attitudes and biases.

On the level of style, honesty in writing means being concrete and specific enough so that readers get the full impact and understand the full implications of the statement. Honest writing is literally effective writing: it has an effect on readers. It establishes a *persona* contemporary readers will consider reliable and trustworthy.

CONCRETE AND ABSTRACT

Show—don't tell is one of the basic slogans in most creative writing classes. Behind that slogan is the understanding that concrete words, phrases, and images affect readers in ways that more abstract terms and ideas do not. To *show* means to verbally recreate images that allow readers to re-perceive what you are describing. That usually has more emotional impact and is more convincing than if you *tell* them *about* whatever you are describing.

Suppose, for example, that you write,

> His outrageous remark upset her.

You have told your readers what happened. In the telling you have included your interpretation of what you heard and saw: it is your *judgment* that the remark was outrageous; you have *inferred* from her response that the remark upset her. Even assuming that your inference is valid and your judgment correct, a description that quotes his remark and describes her response will generally be more effective because it will allow readers to interpret and judge for themselves. Not only will the more concrete description create more vivid images, but the readers' active involvement in the interpretative process will make the conclusions more convincing.

> "Mrs. Hennessey has told me of a part-time job I could probably have," she said quietly, her eyes fixed on her knitting. "It would bring in a bit of extra money and give me something to do mornings while the children are in school."
>
> "Woman's place is in the home," he said coldly, picking up his newspaper.

> Her cheeks reddened, her fingers trembled and she missed a stitch, though she still did not raise her eyes from the stocking she was knitting.

This bit of dialogue and description is slanted so as to bias most readers toward the conclusion that "his outrageous remark upset her." But the bias is only in the writer's selection and juxtaposition of "facts." The conclusion is unstated. The readers draw it themselves, almost as if they had heard and seen with their own ears and eyes. The unstated conclusion is more convincing. In Ernest Hemingway's words, "Anything you know, you can eliminate and it only strengthens your iceberg."

The sorts of words and phrases likely to create vivid images in readers' minds are called *concrete*. Concrete language usually refers quite specifically to objects or events that we could experience with our five senses. By contrast, *abstract* language usually refers to intangibles, such as concepts, relationships, and judgments. It usually has less impact on readers (and is often used by writers who wish, for one reason reason or another, to downplay the impact of certain aspects of their reports).

To say that someone was "upset" is more abstract than to say that "her cheeks reddened, her fingers trembled and she missed a stitch." To say that someone is "lonely" is more abstract than to say that "sitting in his rented room, he longed to speak to somebody, anybody . . . even a door-to-door salesperson would have been welcome."

Consider the following series, each of which moves from the relatively abstract to the relatively concrete:

> Fruit . . . apple . . . a mealy, red MacIntosh.
>
> Environmental problem . . . polluted water . . . cancer-causing chemicals in the city's drinking water.
>
> Moved . . . walked . . . strode.
>
> Made . . . built . . . sawed and nailed.
>
> Ten percent of writers . . . some modern novelists . . . Faulkner, Hemingway, and Fitzgerald.

In each series the third term has the most potential as an image. Whether those images will be created depends on the readers' knowledge and experience. For readers with the appropriate knowledge, "Faulkner, Hemingway, and Fitzgerald" is more concrete than "ten percent of writers."

Some textbooks flatly assert, "Use concrete language." Such advice can be useful especially for inexperienced writers, who sometimes tend to confuse abstraction with profundity. An abstract term, however, is less likely than its concrete equivalents to have the same meaning for both writer and reader, so a concrete style tends to make communication more precise. A writer may write "bird" while thinking of a swan; a reader may imagine a magpie—or not imagine any concrete image at all.

What matters is actually the proper relationship between abstract and concrete, and the choice of language that is appropriate to writers' purposes. In this sense, the distinction between abstract and concrete should be used like that between general and particular*—not to eliminate either type of language from your writings, but to choose in each case what will achieve your aims. You might, for example, use a relatively abstract style to present a rational argument and then follow it with a concrete illustration for emotional impact.

Often it is the interplay between abstract and concrete that makes a writing work. Susan-Ann Green's description of North Bend, British Columbia (reproduced in full on pages 230-231), turns abstract when she writes,

> I was troubled by the idea that my world was linked to this other world by a cable. That constituted a connection and I found it hard to see the relationship, for my world seemed not as complicated.

Read out of context, these sentences do not have much effect. In context, the abstraction works because it is well-grounded in the concrete description which preceded it and because the contrast between simplicity and complexity is a predominant theme of the essay.

The point to remember is that concrete terms have greater impact and communicate more vividly. They have *more* effect on readers and that effect is more precisely predictable—in this literal sense they are more *effective*. A concrete style can, moreover, contribute to an honest *persona*. In general, therefore, writers should prefer concrete language.

*The distinction between abstract and concrete is often confused with a somewhat similar distinction between general and particular (or specific). See pages 95-99 for a discussion of general and particular.

But it is possible to be quite specific while remaining abstract. Statistics, for example, are specific and abstract. To report that one-quarter of the world's people go to sleep—not to bed, these people often do not have beds—hungry each night is specific. But readers often remain abstracted from such specifics. As the advertising agencies which run charity campaigns well know, readers will find it harder to ignore a concrete image of one hungry child.

A relatively abstract term may also be more specific than a concrete description. Contrast the following two sentences:

> He had the measles.
>
> His body was covered with a rough, red rash; he was feverish and itched terribly.

The second sentence is more concrete, but it could describe a number of diseases. The first sentence is more specific (though it has less emotional impact) and would be more useful to someone who had to prescribe a treatment.

This advice is especially relevant for less experienced writers, so long as they remember that there are important exceptions.

CLICHÉS

A cliché is a linguistic preconception, the verbal equivalent of a stereotype (see pages 215-220). Indeed, the word *cliché* comes into English from the French, where one of its meanings is "stereotyped." In English, it refers to a phrase that has been used (and overused) to the point of extreme familiarity. Such phrases are similar to abstractions in that, however concrete they may seem to be, they have little impact on readers and do not communicate vivid images.

Clichés are not always and automatically to be shunned. Much common sense and conventional wisdom is stored in clichés. In certain contexts, the very familiarity of a cliché can make it persuasive, or at least reassuring. But clichés must be used self-consciously and with extreme caution.

To a writer the key point about clichés is the effect that they have (or do not have) on readers—and the nature of the *persona* they, therefore, create. The English lover who first compared his true love's lips to a red rose was using a metaphor that brought to her mind a vivid image; he was (we may presume) suitably rewarded, at the very least with a smile from those lips he so admired. A lover who attempted the same comparison today would more likely be rewarded with a grimace or a groan. The comparison is so familiar that it has worn out. It is, therefore, called *trite* (from the Latin, *tritus*, "worn out.") The *persona* it creates is almost embarrassingly inept and unoriginal.

Many clichés are "worn out" metaphors. "The spur of the moment" once brought to mind a vivid image of horse and rider. "To be thrown off the track" once brought to mind a vivid image of a train wreck. "Cash on the barrel-head" once referred to the barrel top in a country store where many a deal was consummated (probably because the store lacked a counter). Such clichés usually do not produce even a grimace or a groan; more often they are so familiar that readers barely respond at all. They are, therefore, called *dead metaphors*.

Many nonmetaphorical phrases which were once powerful because they were fresh and vivid are now powerful only as soporifics. "Tried and true" once suggested that a person had passed tests of loyalty. "The humanities" and "humanistic education" once had specific connotations related to the whole human being (as opposed to the specialist)—as the phrase "humanistic psychology" still does. The power "progressive" once had came from connotations related to "progress" (back when "progress" did not yet suggest "pollution").

Similarly, the instructor who first wrote, "This is basically a good paper, but . . . ," probably communicated the opinion that the paper was basically good. Instructors who use that introductory clause now might just as well save their ink: most students have come to take the remark as a perfunctory and essentially meaningless preliminary (which it often is).

Language evolves as it is used. A word or phrase that once had a certain effect on readers and communicated a particular image or idea may no longer do so. One may argue about whether language change is progressive or regressive, but it is real. It is also, generally, adaptive (although the social context to which it adapts is sometimes less than edifying). The writer who wishes to recreate that certain effect and communicate that image or idea often must verbalize it in a distinctly different way.

One way to do that is to coin a new and fresh phrase. Another is to revivify an old one. Clichés can be very powerful when brought back to life. A writer who can provide a verbal context that revivifies a dead metaphor sometimes creates a doubly effective phrase, as Henry Thoreau did with "the spur of the moment" when he wrote, "I feel the spur of the moment thrust into my side. The present is an inexorable rider." Similarly, one could create a persuasive effect by reminding readers of the "human" in "humanistic education." One can also revive a cliché by inverting it, as in "tried and untrue" or "both gladder and wiser" (which takes its power from each and every time readers have heard or read "both sadder and wiser").

Writers should be concerned with the effect of the phrase. Ordinarily, writers using description and narration are attempting to create vivid and specific images and ideas in their readers' minds. Clichés ordinarily do not do that. So effective writing generally avoids clichés or uses them in an extraordinary way.

There is, it must be noted, an important set of exceptions. These are circumstances in which writers do not wish to communicate specifically and vividly. If you are describing a situation you wish to criticize in order to induce the person who created that situation to change it, you may wish to understate your criticism (i.e., to state it in a way that we would ordinarily call "ineffective"). If you are writing a ceremonial speech for a politician who actually has nothing to say and wishes, more than anything else, to avoid antagonizing anyone, you may find clichés extremely useful. If you are a bureaucrat who needs to hand in a thick report but does not want to step on any toes, you may find "ineffective" clichés extremely effective. Certain types of clichés sometimes work quite well for writers of grant proposals.

As the preceding paragraph may suggest, many of the circumstances in which clichés "work" are morally questionable. This textbook would be negligent if it did not both point out that they do work and raise the question of morality. In general, however, clichés do not work; unless a writer has specific justification, therefore, they are best shunned.

The questions in Table 3.1 should help call your attention to any tendencies toward a dishonest style in your drafts. Add to your own revision-heuristic any that could help you develop a more direct and effective style.

TABLE 3.1 Revision-Heuristic, Level 3A: Language[a]

SELECTION	ARRANGEMENT
Have you left out any relevant information (thereby distorting the accuracy of your representation)?	Have you used examples and images to concretize abstractions or ambiguities you have chosen to use.
Are any passages overly abstract or ambiguous?	If there is any jargon your readers might not understand, has it been defined or explained?
Is there any jargon that is unnecessary? That readers may not understand?	
Are there any clichés or trite passages?	
Have you chosen words that will have the desired impact on your readers?	

[a]*Remember*: This is only a list of suggested questions. Choose from it only those questions that match your individual needs. Rephrase them more specifically, if possible, to focus your attention on your own particular weak points. Add any questions you need to. Use this list to continue developing your own revision-heuristic (see pages 99-101). And do not rely on this list alone: read the sections of the text that explain the concepts behind the questions.

ADDITIONAL READING

Gibson, Walker. *Persona.* New York: Random House, 1969. See also, by the same author, *Tough, Sweet & Stuffy.* Bloomington: Indiana University, 1966. Gibson categorizes and analyzes styles in terms of the ways they project images of the writers who use them.

Macrorie, Ken. *Telling Writing.* New York: Hayden, 1970. Macrorie's first three short chapters are a very clear discussion of stylistic honesty. His fifth chapter gives particularly concrete advice about how to achieve a concrete style. His chapters on "tightening" and "sharpening" are also clear and specific. If "wordiness' is one of your problems, Macrorie can probably help.

EXERCISE

1. Find a piece of dishonest writing produced by a bureaucracy. Rewrite it clearly and concretely. Contrast the two versions.
2. Find a piece of dishonest writing you wrote sometime in the past. Rewrite it, adding details and concretizing to make it more honest. Contrast the two versions.
3. Study the doublespeak produced by a government around some historical event (e.g., U.S. government press releases about the Vietnam War, Chinese government statements about the political conflicts that became overt after the death of Communist Party Chairman Mao Zedung, U.S.S.R. government statements about the invasion of Afghanistan). Try to show a relationship between the style of the doublespeak and the purposes it served in its historical context.
4. Create several series of three or more terms illustrating transitions from highly abstract to highly concrete (e.g., fruit . . . apple . . . mealy, red MacIntosh).
5. Pick an issue about which the facts are in dispute (e.g., nuclear power). Obtain reports written by proponents of distinct positions (e.g., a corporation that owns nuclear power plants, an organization opposed to nuclear power, a scientific commission evaluating nuclear waste disposal for the government). Examine the factual statements in each report to determine which "facts" are in dispute, where writers conveniently exclude facts harmful to their positions, and so forth.

CHOOSING WORDS

Every speech . . . consists at once of that which is expressed and that which expresses, that is to say of matter and words.

Quintilian

By words the mind is winged.

Aristophanes

The ill and unfitting choice of words wonderfully obstructs the understanding.

Francis Bacon

The difference between the right word and the almost right is the difference between lightning and the lightning bug.

Mark Twain

WORDS AND IDEAS

As your ability to perceive, think, and feel grows, you are likely to find yourself needing a greater variety of words to communicate the full subtlety of those perceptions, thoughts, and feelings. Similarly, although to a lesser extent, as your vocabulary grows, you are likely to be able to perceive, think, and feel more precisely and subtly.

As individuals, we have to communicate—and, to a significant extent, perceive, think, and feel—with concepts that are provided by the languages of our societies. Of course, those languages themselves evolved in response to natural and social realities. Thus those concepts, and the words which represent them, roughly reflect the realities that formed them.

The point, as I. A. Richards insists, is that language is not just "a dress which thought puts on." Language and thought interpenetrate; they are mutually interdependent. Our *terms* to some extent de-*term*ine our ideas. The process of "finding words" is also a process of defining and developing ideas. To articulate an idea is usually also to refine it. Your ability to think is to some degree dependent on the quality of your vocabulary. Your ability to think critically is to some degree dependent on your appreciation of the power of words.

If you are a native speaker, words exist in English for most of what you, as a social individual, will want to communicate. Not only was

English part of the environment in which you developed, but the English language continues to evolve in the environment in which you live.

Insofar as words do not exist to represent meanings you wish to communicate, they can be invented. In 1948, for instance, as computers began to enter our social reality, Norbert Wiener coined the word *cybernetic* from the Greek root, *kybernan,* meaning "self-steering." It now refers to computers and other devices that are in a sense self-steering (once they are programmed by human beings). English, like any living language, continually evolves to meet the needs of the people who use it.

DENOTATIONS AND CONNOTATIONS

A language reflects its past as well as its present environments. In a changing world, that sometimes causes problems. The English word *fair*, for example, originally meant "light-colored," as in "fair-skinned" or "fair hair." Metaphorically, it came to mean "lovely," "just and equitable," "consistent with the rules," "favorable," and so on. Gradually, those metaphors ceased to be metaphors, and those meanings now belong to the word. This association between "light-colored" and various admired qualities was not accidental: it reflected the racist biases of the English-speaking people of the time. That bias is now built into the language itself. (See pages 235-236 for further examples and discussion.)

A word has *denotations*, which you can look up in a dictionary. A word also has *connotations*. These are more subtle tones which the word has picked up from the company it habitually keeps, from the contexts in which it is usually found. Connotations have to do primarily with our attitude toward the word, with the relationship between us and the word.

To use a word well, you must know its connotations as well as its denotations. Your choice of a certain word connotes something about you, and thus it helps to shape your *persona*. It also connotes something about your attitude toward your subject matter and thus suggests the attitude you want readers to take.

You learn a word's connotations by seeing how it is used, by seeing and hearing it in contexts. That is why it is best to grow your vocabulary naturally: by reading books and talking with people who use words you do not know (or know but do not use). That way you get the word in context and eventually intuit its connotations. There are also vocabulary-building exercises of various sorts. They are quicker but more dangerous. They build your vocabulary rather than allowing it to grow; thus you may pick up words without learning their connotations.

One of the writing problems frequently listed by university students, and especially by the better writers among them, is a tendency to use "wrong words." In a sense, this is often not a problem but a "growing pain." As you learn new words, you are likely to misuse them for a while; and if you never use them, you may never fully learn them. As your ideas grow, moreover you may not have the words to represent them, so you may fumble around for a while with "wrong words."

Of course, "wrong words" can also result from laziness: often the writer knows that the word is not quite right, but does not want to bother finding a better one. The solution to this kind of "wrong word" is the proper use of the dictionary, thesaurus, or advice from a friend or editor. (The thesaurus, it should be noted, is often a source of "wrong words" if it is used without doublechecking connotations.)

To make matters more complex, word choice involves more than finding (or inventing) words that accurately represent meanings. Words should be appropriate to rhetorical context as well. That means they should match your purpose, audience and occasion, as well as matching your meanings.

It was perhaps Jeremy Bentham who first wrote systematically about what we now call *purr-words* and *snarl-words*, words which have distinctly positive or negative connotions. Thus when you are feeling positively toward the police, they are "police officers"; when you are feeling negatively, they become "cops" (or even "pigs"). The denotation remains the same—you are still referring to the same people—but the connotations shift radically. Betham suggests that tyranny can be called "order," lust for power "love of country," fear of punishment or of a bad reputation a "sense of duty," sexual desire "love," greed "industriousness," and so forth—when we need "fig leaves" to cover "the unseemly part of the human mind." Likewise, courage on the part of your enemy may be called "rashness." My frugality I call "being careful with money" and "knowing the value of a dollar"; but another's is "penny-pinching" if not downright "cheap."

Betham believed that there were neutral words, halfway between the purr-words and the snarl-words, with which reasoned discourse could be conducted. In any particular rhetorical context, there may be. It used to be said, for instance, that "policeman" was a neutral term between the purr-word, "police officer," and the snarl-word, "cop." Then the feminists pointed out that "policeman" has connotations too: it implies that the police are (or should be) male. Those connotations evolved, of course, because the police *were* all male. In the present context, however you may feel about women's right to equal employment opportunities, those connotations can hardly be called neutral.

In reality, *all words have connotations.* Word choices matter precisely because words both reflect and influence attitudes. The *persona* you project through your writing is shaped in large part by your word choices. Readers will perceive the words you choose as a reflection of your attitudes. The exactness with which your writing represents your intended meanings will also depend on the precision with which you choose words. And, if your writings are successful, your choice of words will influence your readers' attitudes.

Since there are no neutral words—no words *without* connotations—the best you can do as a writer is to choose words with connotations that suit your purposes., If you are an "honest rhetorician," you will also choose words with connotations that accurately match the meanings you believe to be true and that project a *persona* which honestly matches your attitudes. To whatever extent the words you use may influence the attitudes of your readers, you also have an ethical responsibility to choose thoughtfully.

The bottom line is that, if you use words offensive to your readers, they may stop reading. As rhetoricians have been aware at least since classical Greece, you should choose words that suit your audiences and the occasions on which you are addressing them. On one level, this is what my mother used to tell me: "You can use that language on the street if you like, but don't use it at home in front of me." Above that bottom line, you should think about the image and attitudes your words will project.

A most interesting manifestation of this rhetorical reality occurred in North America in the 1970s. As a result of the activities of feminists in the early-70s, there came about a renewed awareness of sexism and of sexist bias in language, even among people who would never call themselves feminists. In response to this social awareness, by the mid-70s, many educational organizations, government agencies, and private publishing companies were creating guidelines to help their authors avoid such biased language.

In large part, what is called sexist bias in language is a matter of word choice and connotation. Social attitudes about women are changing and, instead of waiting decades (or even centuries) for the language to catch up, feminists are consciously inventing an anti-sexist vocabulary. What matters, of course, is not the words themselves, but the attitudes they reflect. Although attitudes are primary and words secondary, however, changing the words can help change the attitudes (or at least make people conscious of the attitudes).

For instance, it used to be—and in some circles still is—commonplace to refer to fully mature women as "girls." Intriguingly, the word *girl* originally meant a child or young person of either sex (as the word *man* originally meant an adult person of either sex). The connotation of immaturity, frivolousness, and so forth remains with the word *girl*. The choice to refer to an adult woman as a "girl," therefore, communicates a certain attitude toward either women in general or that woman in particular. The speaker or writer may or may not be consciously intending to communicate that attitude, but there it is in the choice of the word. The speaker or writer may not even agree with that attitude, but the word choice projects a *persona* which does.

Sometimes the anti-sexist vocabulary involves coining new terms: *Miss/Mrs.* becomes *Ms.* to parallel *Mr.* and avoid the connotation that marital status is more important when considering women than when considering men; *chairman* likewise becomes *chairperson*, which some people find hard on their ears but only because it is unfamiliar. (In 1936, I. A. Richards noted that certain authorative people objected to such new words as *psychology*, *tasteful*, and *colorful*—words that are no longer hard on the ears. *Colorful*, apparently, came into the language about 1890.)

More typically, the anti-sexist vocabulary involves using existing words that do not identify people by sex when sex is not relevant. Here are some anti-sexist alternatives.

OLD USAGE	ALTERNATIVES
airline stewardess	flight attendant
bachelor	single person
businessman	business executive, manager
cameraman	camera operator
career woman	doctor, lawyer, secretary, etc.
cleaning woman	housekeeper, office cleaner
coed	student
congressman	member of congress
craftsman	worker, artisan
divorcee	single person, unmarried
fireman	firefighter
foreman	supervisor
housewife	homemaker
layman	layperson
maid	servant, housekeeper
mailman	letter carrier
male nurse	nurse
man and wife	husband and wife

man, mankind	humanity, human beings, human race, humankind, people
manhood	adulthood
man-made	manufactured, synthetic
middleman	intermediary
newsboy	newspaper carrier
policeman	police officer
primitive man*	hunters-and-gathers, pastoral people, subsistence farmers, tribal peoples
salesman	salesperson
spinster	single person
spokesman	spokesperson
statesman	leader, public servant
workman	worker
women's libber	feminist
women's liberation	the feminist movement, feminism, the women's movement

A greater difficulty for those who want to avoid sexist connotations in their writing is pronouns, specifically third-person singular neuter pronouns (*he, him, his*). Some languages have neuter pronouns for cases where the gender is unspecified; English uses the masculine pronouns, thus creating the connotation that unidentified people are male. For example, "Each student must open *his* book," technically denotes nothing about the sex of the students, but the connotation remains (especially since few people say, "Each secretary must get *his* typing finished by 5 p.m.").

There are a number of potential solutions. One can switch to the plural: "Everyone likes his bacon crisp" then becomes "All people like their bacon crisp." One can avoid the pronoun altogether: "Most people like crisp bacon." One can use both pronouns: "Anyone can fail if *he* relies on common sense alone" becomes "Anyone can fail if *he or she* relies on common sense alone." (Some writers then alternate *he or she* with *she or he*.) One can alternate throughout the text: "Students often complain about instructors, saying, '*She's* a hard marker' or *He* requires too much work." One can use *he/she* or *s/he*.

Perhaps the most interesting solution is the one most common in people's speech: *They, them,* and *their* are starting to evolve into singular pronouns! As Ann Bodine has pointed out, in addition to retaining their traditional uses, these pronouns are becoming increasingly com-

*Note that the problem here is not only "man," but the ethnocentric judgment inplicit in "primitive."

mon in sentences like, 'Everyone will get *their* turn," or "Someone took my pen again, and *they're* going to get it." This usage is *not* yet generally acceptable in formal written English, although the National Council of Teachers of English (NCTE) and many major publishers are willing to accept it.

Another approach to the problem is simply to use *she* and *her* whenever a singular neuter pronoun is required—presumably on the grounds that turn-about is fair play—at least until there is no more sexism and no one cares. A small but significant number of published articles do this; reading them, one is constantly reminded of one's linguistic biases.

At present, there is no solution that will be totally acceptable to all contemporary readers. Some guidelines, therefore, suggest avoiding the problem whenever possible: "The editor uses *his* skills, tact, and common sense in making his changes on the manuscript" then becomes "The editor uses skill, tact, and common sense in making changes on a manuscript." An increasing number of apologetic prefaces indicates that many writers wish the problem could always be avoided so easily.

The point here is not primarily about sexism, but about language and, in particular, about word choice. Writers' choices on the level of language should be made in terms of semantic and rhetorical implications. In other words, the levels of meaning and of rhetorical context encompass the level of language and provide contexts for linguistic decisions.

Bentham's point was that purr-words and snarl-words are the equivalent of the logical fallacy called *begging the question*. To beg a question is to somehow assume or take for granted what should be proven. Implicit in purr-words and snarl-words are *judgments* that Bentham thought should be made explicit and validated logically. If you think industrialized people are superior to pastoral people, say so and explain why; but do not hide that moral judgment in the connotations of the snarl-word, "primitive." If you object to feminism, say so and explain why; do not use the derogatory term, "women's libber."

Betham called purr-words and snarl-words "question-begging appellatives." He wrote,

> *Begging the question is one of the fallacies enumerated by Aristotle; but Aristotle has not pointed out . . . the mode of using the fallacy with the greatest effect, and least risk of detection—namely, by the employment of a single appellative.*

Bentham's desire for neutral terms may haved been utopian, but his point is not without merit and should be considered carefully.

WRITING WITH NOUNS

Nouns are most precisely defined in terms of their grammatical function. Loosely, however, we may say that nouns (from the Latin, *nomen*, name) are words that *name* things, people, places, acts, qualities, and concepts. The traditional advice to prefer concrete terms generally emphasizes the choice of concrete nouns.

English, like other Indo-European languages, is noun-based. All the other words in an English sentence are attached to a noun or noun phrase, which names what the sentence is about, and is called the *subject* of the sentence. (Certain other languages, e.g., Hopi, build their sentences around verbs and are therefore called verb-based; such languages tend to produce statements that at least sound more process- and relationship-oriented than do English sentences.)

One can name a particular thing or concept by choosing a somewhat general noun and adding modifiers that limit its meaning. Or one can choose a noun that by itself precisely represents the intended meaning.

false statement	lie
baby dog	puppy
deciduous trees	oaks, maples, and birches
ritual purification	ablution
hired soldier	mercenary
excessive daring	rashness

Where a noun alone can represent either the same meaning or an even more specific meaning than a noun-plus-modifier, the noun alone will generally have more impact.

The principle is this: *when their meanings are functionally equivalent and greater impact is desired, choose the noun alone over the noun-plus-modifier.* This principle must not, however, be interpreted to mean, "Avoid modifiers." (See pages 184-187 on the importance of modifiers.)

Indeed, one reason for preferring specific nouns over nouns-plus-modifiers is that *more* modification can then be added to the specific noun. Suppose the draft sentence reads,

> Deciduous trees grew along the riverbanks.

Substituting "oaks, maples, and birches" allows one to add modifiers and produce a revision which reads,

> Young oaks, sugar maples, and silver birches grew along the riverbanks.

Similarly, changing "baby dog" to "puppy" opens the potential of writing "hungry mongrel puppy." Changing "false statement" to "lie" opens the potential of writing "bald-faced lie." Thus using specific nouns allows writers to reach for more concrete images.

Sometimes, however, writers wish to minimize impact. It will be easier to get someone to admit to a "false statement" than to a "bald-faced lie." It is easier to defend "excessive daring" than "rashness." Specific nouns are likely to have specific connotations, which writers may well choose to avoid in particular rhetorical contexts.

When greater impact is desired, seek the most concrete noun available— and only then consider modifiers. Always remember, however, that other factors may override this principle.

WRITING WITH VERBS

Like nouns, verbs are most precisely defined in terms of their grammatical function. Loosely, however, we may say that verbs are words that express action, occurence, or existence. Not surprisingly, therefore, they are especially important in writings that communicate about processes: narratives, process analyses, and causal analyses (see Chapter 5). Often it is writers' choices of effective verbs that make narratives come alive, that make process and causal analyses precise. And it is difficulty with verbs that often makes narration a difficult mode for writers to whom English is not a native language.

As with nouns, so with verbs the most powerful are likely to be the most specific and concrete. Narratives that lack impact often rely too heavily on the verb *to be (am, is, are, was were,* etc.) Similar verbs to be wary of include *to have, to make, to go, to come, to move,* and *to get*. All of these are, of course, important English verbs, and we could not write very well without them. But inexperienced writers often rely on them where more particular verbs would carry more meaning and have more impact.

Consider, for instance, the following pairs of sentences.

She went up the mountain.
She climbed the mountain.

He was in bed.
He lay in bed.

He had the appearance of an assembly-line worker.
He looked like an assembly-line worker.

In barely a minute, she made her decision: she would handle the matter herself.
In barely a minute, she decided to handle the matter herself.

They went away together.
They eloped.

TABLE 3.2 Revision-Heuristic, Level 3B: Language[a]

SELECTION	ARRANGEMENT
Do the words chosen have the desired connotations to represent your meanings accurately and without unintended implications? Do they have connotations that may be offensive to any of your readers? Is there any misuse of purr-words or snarl-words?	Is the style and tone (and hence the *persona*) of this piece consistent?
Can a specific noun be substituted for a noun-plus modifier?	Do the connotations of words chosen at one point in any way contradict the connotations of words used elsewhere?
Can a specific verb be substituted for a modified verb or verb-plus-object?	

[a]*Remember*: This is only a list of suggested questions. Choose from it only those questions that match your individual needs. Rephrase them more specifically, if possible, to focus your attention on your own particular weak points. Add any questions you need to. Use this list to continue developing your own revision-heuristic (see pages 99-101). And do not rely on this list alone: read the sections of the text that explain the concepts behind the questions.

He came to the conclusion that there should be no taxation without representation.
He concluded that there should be no taxation without representation.

The baby walked across the stage in rhythm to the salsa.
The baby tottered across the stage in rhythm to the salsa.

In a morning's work, he got only two pages written.
In a morning's work, he wrote only two pages.

The prison was situated on a hilltop.
The prison stood on a hilltop.

In each case, the second sentence either substitutes a more specific verb or transforms a verb-plus-object into a verb (*made her decision* becomes *decided; got written* becomes *wrote; was situated* becomes *stood*). In each case, the second sentence carries a more specific meaning or transforms the key word into the verb for greater impact. The underlying principle is well understood by advertisers, for example, whose products will rarely "make hair moist" when they could instead "moisturize hair" (and who make heavy use of verbs and verbals in a variety of other ways).

Out of context, one cannot say definitively which version of each sentence is better. If a writer wanted to put emphasis on the *making* of a decision, "she made her decision" might be better than "she decided." In certain contexts, moreover, one might want a less emphatic version. What can be said is that the second version of each sentence is more specific or emphatic and that it should be chosen when those qualities are desired.

The questions in Table 3.2 should help call your attention to the quality of word choice in your drafts. Add to your own revision-heuristic any questions that can help pinpoint your own weaknesses.

ADDITIONAL READING

Burke, Kenneth. *A Rhetoric of Motives*. New Jersey: Prentice-Hall, 1950. See, in particular, the short section on "Rhetorical Analysis in Bentham."

Lakoff, Robin. *Language and Women's Place*. New York: Harper & Row, 1975.

Richards, I.A. *The Philosophy of Rhetoric*. London: Oxford, 1936. See especially Chapters Three and Four on the "interanimation of words" and criteria for choosing words.

Weaver, Richard. *Language Is Sermonic*. Baton Rouge, La.: Louisiana State University, 1970. See especially "The Power of the Word" and "Ultimate Terms in Contemporary Rhetoric."

EXERCISE

1. For the next day or two, listen for purr-words and snarl-words as you talk with people. The find an official statement that purports to be objective (e.g., a government press release, a "fact-finding" report, a biography of a political figure). Search through it for purr-words and snarl-words. What questions do they beg? Revise a passage by substituting a snarl-word for every purr-word and a purr-word for every snarl-word. (Be certain you do not change any denotations.) What effect does your revision have on the statement?

2. Bertrand Russell made a point similar to Bentham's by offering the following "declensions":

I'm cautious. You're timid. He's chickenhearted.
I'm thrifty. You're a bit of a tightwad. She's a skinflint.
I'm human. You're prone to error. He's a blundering idiot.

Compose a similar "declension" of your own.

3. An anti-sexist vocabulary is prescriptive in somewhat the same sense that traditional grammar is prescriptive: both tell how language *should* be used; neither just describes how it is used. The difference is that traditional grammar is based in the past, whereas the anti-sexist vocabulary is oriented toward the future. Think of some attitude other than sexism that is presently common in North America and that you think is undesirable. How, if at all, does the English language embody that attitude? How could the English language be modified to help counteract that attitude?

4. Go through one of your recent writings and underline all nouns and verbs. In each case, ask yourself if you can substitute a more specific noun or verb and if you can then delete modifiers. If you can make some changes, what effect do they have on the tone of the piece?

CONSTRUCTING SENTENCES

The [meaning] of a [word] can be modified without our changing in any way either its sense or its sounds, but only by the fact that some neighboring term or other has undergone a modification.

Ferdinand de Saussure

When you put one word after another, your statement should be more precise the more you add.... The noun, the verb, and the main clause serve . . . as a base on which the meaning will rise.

John Erskine

SOME WORDS ABOUT SENTENCES

The basic unit of language is neither the word nor the paragraph, but the sentence. Developmentally, human infants begin to talk by uttering sounds that represent whole sentences. The infant may say no more than "Dada" or "Muk Chrissie," but those sounds represent meanings like, "I want my father" or "Give me [Chrissie] some milk." Only later do infants realize that the sounds they have been using can be broken down into smaller units (i.e., phrases, words, syllables, morphemes) and recombined to represent other meanings.

Logically, too, the sentence is the basic unit. An English sentence, like a logical proposition, has two parts. The first, called *the subject*, names what the sentence is about. The second, called *the predicate*, tells something about the subject. A string of words that does not both name a subject and tell something about it is not logically complete. It is not meaningful and not a sentence.

This completeness, it must be added, need not always be verbalized. "Read this" is a sentence with the subject, "You," understood. This device, called *ellipsis*, of not verbally articulating the entire meaning is quite common in speech.

"Read this." [*You* read this.]

"Why?" [Why *should I read this*?]

"Because it will help you understand sentences." [*You should read this* because it will help you understand sentences.]

Used inappropriately in writing, ellipsis can be a problem. An incompletely articulated sentence is a *sentence fragment*. Used appropriately and sparingly in contexts where the meaning is clear, however, ellipsis can be one basis of a forceful style.

A sentence is sometimes defined as "a complete thought." That definition, which refers back to the idea of a sentence as a logically complete proposition, works on the level of meaning. But a sentence is actually a verbal representation of meaning; it must, therefore, be complete on the levels of language and rhetoric. It must be grammatically complete (or, if it uses ellipsis, whatever is not verbalized must be clear in rhetorical context).

There are grammatical signals, which function like coherency cues (see pages 131-135), to show that a sentence is complete. Lewis Carrol's "Jabberwocky" uses many meaningless nonsense words; yet it sounds like a series of English sentences, because it provides all the necessary grammatical signals. Noam Chomsky makes the same point with these two "sentences."

1. Colorless green ideas sleep furiously.
2. Furiously sleep ideas green colorless.

"Any speaker of English," Chomsky declares, will recognize that only the first is "grammatical."

Although both series of words are non-English on the level of meaning, a grammarian could call "Colorless green ideas sleep furiously" a sentence. Even if you do not know grammatical terminology, you know enough grammar to recognize the first series of words as acceptable English word order (i.e., as acceptable English *syntax*) and the second as non-acceptable word order. Since a grammar is a description of the ways words may be combined (within the system of a particular language or dialect), you have recognized the second as ungrammatical. Although, from a writer's perspective, the first is not a sentence because it is not meaningful, it does obey the rules of English syntax.

There are many types of grammar. Traditional English grammar is, in a sense, really Latin grammar. Historically, it began with the application to the English language of terminology taken from Latin grammar. Traditionally, English grammar is also a *prescriptive* grammar. Its study usually begins with the identification of eight "parts of speech": nouns, verbs, pronouns, adjectives, adverbs, conjunctions, articles, and interjections. These terms are then used in rules that *prescribe* how people are supposed to combine words into socially acceptable English sentences. The dominant goal is correctness.

In this chapter, we are trying to go beyond correctness and talk about style. Most writers using this textbook already write socially acceptable English sentences most of the time. You should, moreover, own or have access to a *handbook* that prescribes socially acceptable English usage, grammar, and punctuation. If there are certain errors you still make regularly, you should have a list of them and you should check for them during revision (see page 54). The primary concern here is not with avoiding errors but with developing style. The idea is to build on what you can already do and to go beyond it.

THE CUMULATIVE SENTENCE

The basic English sentence consists of a subject and a predicate, in that order. The subject is a noun or noun phrase or pronoun. The predicate is a verb (with or without an object or complement attached). Reduced to its basics, an ordinary declarative English sentence can be just two words:

> They huddled.

Such a sentence is called a *kernel sentence*. When it forms part of a larger sentence, it is called a *main clause*. However much more there may be in a sentence, the basic information is usually represented by the nouns and verbs of the main clause. That is why nouns and verbs are so important (see pages 177-179).

But from another point of view, this becomes a reason for arguing that the words which *modify* the meanings of nouns and verbs are even more important. Although that may seem paradoxical, it can also be very valid. Consider, for example, what William Faulkner adds to "they huddled":

> Calico-coated, small-bodied, with delicate legs and pink faces in which their mismatched eyes rolled wild and subdued, they huddled, gaudy motionless and alert, wild as deer, deadly as rattlesnakes, quiet as doves.

The basic meaning of this sentence is "they huddled." All the words that precede this clause just describe "they." And all the words that follow just describe how they "huddled."

Looking at Faulkner's sentence, one can understand the sense in which the *basic* or kernel sentence—the main clause—serves as the *base* on which meaning rises. The modifiers which Faulkner has *added* qualify and particularize the basic information of "they huddled." The modifiers *modify* and add to the basic meaning of the sentence, and what they communicate can often be more important than that basic information.

The following sentence comes from an article in *Fortune*:

> Yet another source of instability in the Middle East is the resurgence of Islamic fundamentalism, itself partly a reaction against alien intrusions and the pressures of modernization.
>
> David B. Tinnin

The main clause, which begins the sentence, restates common knowledge. Typical readers of *Fortune* are well-informed corporate managers, and the idea that a resurgence of Islamic fundamentalism was a destabilizing factor in the Middle East had appeared frequently in the daily press at the time. What might be news to *Fortune*'s readers is found in the long modifier which follows. The important information in the sentence is that the resurgence of Islamic fundamentalism is not just a religious phenomenon but also a reaction against sociopolitical and economic changes that have been imposed on the peoples of the Middle East. Grammatically, the sentence could well have ended with "fundamentalism." Had it done so, however, the nature of the resurgence might well have been misunderstood by most readers.

This sort of sentence is called *cumulative*, because of the way in which modifiers are added on, or *accumulate*, after the main clause and refer back to it. The preceding sentence is a cumulative sentence—the last ten words of which clarify and add onto the main clause—as is this sentence.

The relationships among the parts of a cumulative sentence can be analyzed according to level of generality, just as paragraphs were so analyzed in Chapter 1 (pages 95-99). The main clause is the most general. Each modifier is more particular than whatever it modifies. Thus if we label the main clause as level 1, whatever modifies it becomes level 2. Whatever modifies a modifier of the main clause becomes level 3. And so on, like this:

1 The jockies sat bowed and relaxed,
  2 moving a little at the waist with the movement of their horses.

Katherine Anne Porter

1 They regarded me silently,
  2 Brother Jack with a smile that went no deeper than his lips,
    3 his head cocked to one side,
    3 studying me with his penetrating eyes;
  2 the other blank-faced,
    3 looking out of eyes that were meant to reveal nothing and to stir profound uncertainty.

Ralph Ellison

1 He could sail for hours,
  2 searching the blanched grasses below him with his telescopic eyes,
  2 gaining height against the wind,
  2 descending in mile-long, gently declining swoops when he curved and rode back,
  2 never beating a wing.

Walter Van Tilburg Clark

1 Joad's lips stretched tight over his long teeth a moment, and
1 he licked his lips,
  2 like a dog,
    3 two licks,
      4 one in each direction from the middle.

John Steinbeck

Each of these sentences could have ended after the main clause (level 1). Written by inexperienced writers, they probably would have. In Ralph Ellison's place, for example, an inexperienced writer probably would have produced something like this:

> Brother Jack and the other man regarded me silently.

That is not a bad sentence, but it offers the reader so much less than Ellison's.

The cumulative sentence, with modifiers added after the main clause, is important in all kinds of modern prose. It is especially important in description and narration, which is why so many of the cited examples come from works of fiction. The details that accumulate behind the main clause of a cumulative sentence provide readers with much additional information. Thus cumulative sentences allow writers to follow the dictum, "Show, don't tell." Faulkner's "they huddled" tells what they did, but the modifiers show them huddling.

The additions, as Faulkner's sentence indicates, can be added before as well as after the main clause. Thus, in the same *Fortune* article cited above, Tinnin writes, for example,

> Amid war, threats of war, and the drama of peace negotiations, relatively little attention has been paid to Israel's economic problems.

As in the other sentence, Tinnin is turning readers' attention toward the economic basis for events, but here he does so by adding the modifiers *before* the main clause. The preliminary modification throws readers' attention *forward* toward the main clause and explains *why* "relatively little attention has been paid to Israel's economic problems."

Cumulative sentences are easily practiced (see page 198 below), and the practice of cumulative sentences has two potential virtues. One is that, with practice, cumulative sentences will come to seem "natural" (if they do not already); and once they seem "natural" to a writer, they start appearing where appropriate in his or her writing, often quite without conscious effort. The other virtue is that using the cumulative sentence can help writers to discover the details, qualifications, and explanations that have been left out of their drafts.

A writer who has drafted the main clause, "he could sail for hours," might force himself to verbalize the details of "how he sailed" by adding modifiers to create a cumulative sentence. A writer who has drafted the main clause, "he licked his lips," might well discover "like a dog" if required to generate a cumulative sentence.

In other words, a writer can work on the level of meaning and ask, "To what extent is this true?" or "Have I *shown* this in sufficient detail?" The answers to those questions will generate the qualifications and details, which can then be added to the basic sentence. Or a writer can work on the level of grammar and ask, "What would happen if I tried to expand this sentence into a cumulative sentence?" Either way, the writer has a good chance of discovering those additions that can turn ordinary prose into more sophisticated and "meaning-full" writing. Francis Christensen, who initiated and popularized instruction in the cumulative sentence, put it this way.

> *The additions stay with the same idea, probing its bearings and implications, exemplifying it or seeking an analogy or metaphor for it, or reducing it to details. Thus the mere form of the sentence generates ideas. It serves the needs of both the writer and the reader, the writer by compelling him to examine his thought, the reader by letting him into the writer's thought.*

Note that Christensen's first and third sentences are cumulative.

COMBINING SENTENCES

Jane Thomas, the well-known editor, works hard at her chosen profession.

For the seventeenth time, the dedicated writer edited the near-perfect manuscript.

Logically, each of these complex sentences may be seen as a combination of a number of kernel sentences:

Jane Thomas is an editor.
The editor is well-known.
Jane Thomas works hard.
Jane Thomas works at her profession.
Her profession is chosen.

The writer is dedicated.
The writer edited for the seventeenth time.
The writer edited the manuscript.
The manuscript is near-perfect.

The type of grammar that describes how kernel sentences can be transformed into complex sentences is called *transformational grammar*. Although writers do not need to know the rules of transformational grammars, an understanding of the basic principle of such grammars can help you to improve your style and your ability to handle problems of emphasis within sentences. You can use this basic principle—that a complex sentence may be seen as a combination of kernel sentences—for at least three purposes:

1. To create complex sentences which indicate the relationships among ideas and, in particular, to subordinate secondary ideas.
2. To rephrase sentences for emphasis or to avoid awkward structures.
3. To transform passive constructions into active, (and vice versa).

Although they are harder to read, complex sentences are typical of mature writing. They say more than do the equivalent kernel sentences. Each kernel sentence represents a single meaning; but two kernel sentences combined represent two simple meanings and the relationship *between them*. Sometimes the simple juxtaposition of the two meanings makes clear their relationship; other times the juxtaposition forces the writer to insert a transition word indicating the relationship. In either case, the relationship between the two simple meanings can be the most important information in the complex sentence:

John cooked dinner.

\+

Mary left.

John cooked dinner because Mary left.

Mary left because John cooked dinner.

Even where the relationship is fairly evident, the combination helps the readers to grasp it:

> Many professors find my sentence structure to be somewhat elementary for a fourth-year student.
>
> \+
>
> I use two short sentences when a longer, more complex amalgamation of the two would result in a more sophisticated version.
>
> ↓
>
> Many professors find my sentence structure to be somewhat elementary for a fourth-year student because I use two short sentences when a longer, more complex amalgamation of the two would result in a more sophisticated version.

Does Jane Thomas work hard because she got to choose her profession or because she is a well-known editor (or despite the fact that she is a well-known editor)?

Because she works at her chosen profession, the well-known editor, Jane Thomas, works hard.

Because she is a well-known editor, Jane Thomas works hard at her chosen profession.

Although she is a well-known editor, Jane Thomas works hard at her chosen profession.

Consider the following excerpts from student writings in their original versions and as they might be revised by combining sentences. (In some cases the original has been tightened just a bit by deletion or substitution.)

Fort Nelson is a small town that is fairly isolated from other communities. It is surrounded by a beautiful green forest. There are two ways to get to Fort Nelson, one is by plane and the other is by the Alaska Highway. Most people prefer the plane rather than having to drive almost three hundred miles along a winding, dusty, unpaved road to get to Fort Nelson.

There are two ways to get to Fort Nelson, a small, fairly isolated community surrounded by a beautiful green forest: one is by plane and the other is by the Alaska Highway. Most people prefer the plane rather than having to drive almost three hundred miles along a winding, dusty, unpaved road.

I can still remember my first day of school in West Van. I couldn't believe I could pick whatever I wanted to wear. I had gone to a private school the year before and had worn a uniform every day.

I can still remember my first day of school in West Van. Having gone to a private school the year before and having worn a uniform every day, I couldn't believe I could pick whatever I wanted to wear.

The place that I grew up in had no name. It was just a few houses and a gas station that developed along a strip of the island highway between Ladysmith and Nanaimo. It was not a community in any true sense of the word. The people who lived there had little in common except location.

The place where I grew up had no name and was not a community in any true sense of the word. It was jut a few houses and a gas station that developed along a strip of the island highway between Ladysmith and Nanaimo. The people who lived there had little in common except location.

Note how the recombination of the original meanings not only changes the sentence structure and style, but also subordinates certain information and thereby changes the emphasis. In the first example, the isolation of Fort Nelson is emphasized by subordinating "surrounded by a beautiful green forest" and focusing on how hard it is to get there. In the second example, the reason the writer could wear whatever he wanted was subordinated to the fact that he could. In the third example, the statement with the highest level of generality was incorporated into the first sentence to provide a framework for the paragraph. Although the remaining two sentences also could have been combined, this was not done because the separate sentences seem to create a more appropriate tone.

The process by which this type of revision is done has two basic stages: first, one breaks the original passage or sentence down into kernel or near-kernel sentences; second, one recombines these elementary units in various ways until one discovers a version that creates the desired effects. In this way, consider the following sentence:

> It was a small community, mainly French; but it had a bit of international flavor because various ethnic groups had settled in the area.

To generate stylistic alternatives, first break the sentence down into kernel or near-kernel sentences, like this:

> It was a community.
> It was small.
> It was mainly French.
> It had a bit of international flavor.
> Various ethnic groups had settled in the area.

Then recombine the kernels in various ways, and choose the version with the desired emphasis.

In principle, there are three distinct ways to build a complex sentence after one has chosen a main clause: information can be embedded in the middle of that clause, added to the beginning, or added to the end. If the central point of the sentence is to be "it had a bit of international flavor," one could add the rest of the information at either end:

> A small, mainly French community, *it had a bit of international flavor* because various ethnic groups had settled in the area.

Likewise, if the central point is to be "the community was small":

> Although it had a bit of international flavor because various ethnic groups had settled in the area, *the community was small* and mainly French.

Other possibilities include these variants:

> It was a small, mainly French community, which had a bit of international flavor because various ethnic groups had settled in the area.
>
> Although it was mainly French, the small community had a bit of an international flavor because various ethnic groups had settled in the area.

Moving "mainly French" to a position before "community" or coordinate with "small" makes the sentence easier to read. Other recombinations primarily change the emphasis of the sentence. (Note that the grammatical subordination of a clause has an effect similar to reordering; that is because, logically, it changes the *order* of importance.)

Out of context, it is impossible to say which of the four revised versions would be preferable. Choosing the best version means choosing the one which

1. is as readable as possible:
2. indicates the correct relationship among the ideas;
3. provides the desired emphasis;
4. and fits smoothly into the larger passage which contains it.

Consider the first revised version in the following passage.

> I grew up in a town in northern Quebec. Although it had a bit of international flavor because various ethnic groups had settled in the area, the community was small and mainly French. There were immigrants from almost every country in eastern Europe and a few from Asia, too.

The part of the second sentence which repeats meanings from the first is at the end (*community* = *town; Quebec* = *mainly French*). The first part of the second sentence, on the other hand, matches the meanings which are to follow in the third. Thus the passage is a bit awkward and harder to read than it need be. Another variant produces a better fit.

> I grew up in a town in northern Quebec. A small, mainly French community, it had a bit of international flavor because various ethnic groups had settled in the area. There were immigrants from almost every country in eastern Europe and a few from Asia, too.

The term "awkward" is an awkwardly vague concept. Generally, it means that the person who describes a passage as "awkward" knows there is something wrong but does not have the time to, or cannot, figure out just what is wrong with the passage. Simply put, an awkward sentence is hard to read, and sometimes the reason has to do with the structure, with the way words are combined in that sentence. In such a case, reordering the sentence can solve the problem. (In other cases, the problem may be word choice, and the solution is to change the words.)

ACTIVE AND PASSIVE CONSTRUCTION

One very basic English sentence structure is *subject* + *verb* + *object*:

Coleridge wrote the poem.
S + *V* + *O*

This is known as an *active* construction, because the grammatical subject of the sentence ("Coleridge") performed the real action represented by the verb ("wrote"). The sentence can be transformed, however, to read,

> The poem was written by Coleridge.

And it can be further transformed (by deletion) to read simply,

> The poem was written.

In these two versions, the grammatical subject of the sentence ("The poem") is no longer the real actor. Indeed, in the last version, the real actor has been deleted from the sentence altogether. These two versions exhibit what is known as *passive* construction (and the verb is said to be in the *passive voice*).

Traditional wisdom advises writers to prefer active constructions (just as it advises them to prefer concrete nouns and specific verbs). In this case, too, traditional wisdom is right—most of the time.

The underlying principle is one of emphasis. To transform the sentence is to shift the emphasis from "Coleridge" (the real actor) to "the poem." Since the intended emphasis of a sentence is usually on the real actor, active construction ordinarily puts the emphasis where it belongs.

Passive construction can be used to obtain a desired word order, in this case to get "poem" near the beginning of the sentence and "Coleridge" or "wrote" near the end. Passive construction can be used to shift the emphasis away from *who did it* and toward *what was done*.

The passive is commonly used, for example, in journalistic openings to get the key phrase right at the beginning of the first sentence:

> A "state of emergency" was proclaimed in Puerto Rico Sunday by Gov. Romero, who is asking federal officials to declare a disaster zone.

Thus the key phrases, which tell what was done, are in the emphatic positions at the beginning and end of the sentence.

The passive is also commonly used in bureaucratese to avoid responsibility; for example,

The President made a mistake.

↓

A mistake was made.

(In proper bureaucratese, a milder word would also be substituted for "mistake.")

This same passive construction can be put to good use when you have to criticize an action. Suppose your draft reads,

> You made a mistake and you should do something about it.

If you are more concerned with preventing future mistakes than with assigning blame, you might transform that sentence into a passive construction:

> A mistake was made and something should be done about it.

The second version is, in a sense, weaker. The emphasis is now on the mistake, not on the person who made it. As a result, that person is less likely to respond defensively. Thus the purpose is more likely to be achieved. (If your actual purpose is to assign blame, however, the first version is preferable.)

A good rule of thumb is *use active constructions—except when you have a good reason not to.* Or, to put it the other way round, *use the passive when you have a reason to.*

Consider these passive contructions written by students in an advanced writing class.

> In some cases as many as five or six students in one class were found to be involved in this change.

> The businesses in and around a ski area, like those in a one industry town, are dependent upon the ski area as the chief resource for drawing clientelle. It is, therefore, a natural concern among the smaller businesses exactly what the future plans of the ski area involve.

These could be transformed into active constructions, such as the following.

> In some cases this change involved as many as five or six students in one class.

> The smaller businesses are, therefore, concerned about exactly what the future plans of the ski area involve.

There are many situations in which passive constructions are appropriate, effective, and desirable. Nonetheless, your general tendency should be to prefer active constructions in which the real and the grammatical subjects of a sentence are the same.

BALANCE AND PARALLELISM

Common in public oratory and aphorism, the balanced sentence is a special device to be used on special occasions. A balanced sentence has a "ring" that makes it memorable. It stands out. Parallel structures and verbal repetitions are juxtaposed—like weights on a balance scale. Readers feel the stylistic symmetry and anticipate a symmetry of meaning. When you deliver that symmetry—whether with parallel ideas or with antithetical ideas—the sentence has impact.

Politicians often make use of balanced sentences. U.S. President John Kennedy is perhaps best remembered for this one:

> And so my fellow Americans, ask not what your country can do for you; ask what you can do for your country.
>
> John Kennedy

Here the balance point is the semicolon, and the beginning of each of the parallel structures is marked by the repetition of "ask." The symmetry is antithetical: Kennedy was contrasting two attitudes. The antithesis is marked by the "not," and the contrasted elements—"you" and "your country"—exchange positions.

Here are some other balanced sentences from political speeches:

> The test of our progress is not whether we add more to the abundance of those who have much; it is whether we provide enough for those who have too little.
>
> Franklin Roosevelt

> Let us never negotiate out of fear, but let us never fear to negotiate.
>
> John Kennedy

> Extremism in the defense of Liberty is no vice; and . . . moderation in the pursuit of Justice is no virtue.
>
> Barry Goldwater

Balanced sentences have been used for millennia, in verse as well as prose, to serve a variety of purposes. Here are some more examples:

> Many are called but few are chosen.
>
> Matthew XXII.14

> The old pine tree speaks divine wisdom; the secret bird manifests eternal truth.
>
> Zen proverb

> Where there's marriage without love, there will be love without marriage.
>
> Benjamin Franklin

> Parting is all we know of heaven, And all we need of hell.
>
> Emily Dickinson

The effect of a balanced sentence can most easily be understood by rewriting it to express the same ideas without the verbal repetitions or parallel structures. Suppose Franklin had written this:

> Where marriage occurs without love, there will also be extramarital sex.

The underlying concept remains the same, but the balance is gone—and so is the impact. Likewise, Kennedy's statement would not be so well remembered had it been composed thusly:

And so my fellow Americans, do not inquire how your government can serve you; instead ask what you can do to help your country.

A balanced sentence sometimes turns on a semicolon or comma.

The spoken word dies; the written letter remains.

Anonymous

When the going gets tough, the tough get going.

Anonymous

Other times, a coordinating conjunction is the fulcrum.

Hope for the best and prepare for the worst.

Anonymous

Occasionally, like other types of parallelism, balance may be marked by certain pairs of conjunction: *both . . . and, either . . . or, neither . . . nor, as . . . as, not only . . . but, so . . . as.*

As a vessel is known by the sound, whether it be cracked or not, so men are proved by their speeches, whether they be wise or foolish.

Demonsthenes

The general principle of parallelism, which underlies the balanced sentence, may also be used to structure phrases or clauses within a sentence—and it may be reiterated—as in these examples:

There was a time also when in the first fine flush of laundries and bakeries, milk deliveries and canned goods, ready-made clothes and dry-cleaning, it did look as if American life was being enormously simplified.

Margaret Mead

He had come not to make a scandal but to avoid it; not to raise a danger but to make one plain; not to oppose a truth but to offer it.

Giorgio de Santillana

Similarly, the same principle may be applied to larger units, such as sentences within a paragraph.

In your statement you assert that our actions, even though peaceful, must be condemned because they precipitate violence. But is this a logical assertion? Isn't this like condemning a robbed man because his possession of money precipitated the evil act of robbery? Isn't this like condemning Socrates because his unswerving commitment to truth and his philosophical inquiries precipitated the act of a misguided populace in which they made him drink hemlock. Isn't this like condemning Jesus because his unique God-consciousness and never-ceasing devotion to God's will precipitated the evil act of crucifixion? We must come to see that, as the federal courts have consistently affirmed, it is wrong to urge the individual to cease his efforts to gain his basic constitutional rights

> because the quest may precipitate violence. Society must protect the robbed and punish the robber.
>
> Martin Luther King

(For an analysis of this passage from King's "Letter from Birmingham Jail," see page 271).

Parallelism is a powerful device, but it should be used with care. A balanced sentence in the wrong place can overly emphasize a minor point. You may also be tempted to crimp your intended meaning to fit a stylistic mold. The following sentence could be revised for sharper parallelism.

> The view that neurosis is a severe reaction to human trouble is as revolutionary in its implications for social practice as it is daring in formulation.
>
> Jerome Bruner

Deleting the phrase, "for social practice," would improve the parallelism and enhance the impact; it would also delete part of what Bruner wanted to communicate. You should also remember that once you lead readers to expect parallelism—as by using one of the pairs of conjunctions just listed above—you have made a commitment. If you lead readers to anticipate parallelism and then do not deliver, you may distort your intended meaning, disrupt their reading, and project an irresponsible or incompetent *persona*.

When you first study the balanced sentence, parallelism, or any new stylistic device, you may be tempted to overuse it. Remember, however, the reason for studying sentence structure. It is not that certain sentence constructions are intrinsically good or bad. It is that competent writers ought to be able to generate and consider alternative versions of the sentences they draft—and then to chose the ones that best serve their creative and communicative purposes. You should, therefore, develop your ability to expand sentences—for example, along the lines suggested by the model of the cumulative sentence. You should also develop your ability to combine sentences, especially when a passage is choppy because it uses many short sentences or when relationships among ideas are not clearly indicated. You should develop your ability to deconstruct and re-construct sentences in order to generate alternative versions of problematic sentences. You should develop your ability to transform sentences from one construction to another—for example, from passive to active, and *vice versa*. And you should develop your ability to use balanced sentences and other parallel structures when and where they will enhance the effect of your writing.

The questions in Table 3.3 should help call your attention to the sentence structure of your drafts. Add to your own revision-heuristic any questions that pinpoint your own stylistic weaknesses.

As your ability to observe, think, and feel grows, you are likely to find yourself needing not only a better vocabulary, but also a greater variety of complex sentence structures to communicate the full subtlety of those observations, thoughts, and feelings. Similarly, although to a lesser extent, as you internalize a greater variety of complex sentence structures, you may be able to think and feel more subtly. Developing your style will help you communicate. It may also do more than that.

TABLE 3.3 Revision-Heuristic, Level 3C: Language[a]

SELECTION	ARRANGEMENT
Is each sentence as "tight" as possible? Can you shorten any sentences, either by deletion or by substitution, without losing any meaning which matters?	Does each sentence have the emphasis you want? Does any sentence sound "awkward"? Have you dangled any modifiers? Should any sentences be rearranged?
	Are there any undesirable passive constructions? Any undesirable active constructions?
	Is each sentence phrased in such a way as to flow smoothly out of the preceding sentence and into the following sentence?
	Is the style "choppy"? If so, should that be solved by generating cumulative modifiers or by combining sentences?
	Is each sentence phrased in such a way as to accurately indicate the interrelationships among the meanings it contains? Would the relationships among meanings be more clear if certain sentences were combined?
	Have you avoided faulty parallelism? Have you used parallelism effectively for emphasis?

[a]*Remember*: This is only a list of suggested questions. Choose from it only those questions that match your individual needs. Rephrase them more specifically, if possible, to focus your attention on your own particular weak points. Add any questions you need to. Use this list to continue developing your won revision-heuristic (see pages 99-101). And do not rely on this list alone: read the sections of the text that explain the concepts behind the questions.

ADDITIONAL READING

Christensen, Francis. "A Generative Rhetoric of the Sentence." *College Composition and Communication* 14 (October 1963).

Memering, Dean, and Frank O'Hare. *The Writer's Work*. New Jersey: Prentice-Hall, 1980. See Chapter Six on sentences.

EXERCISE

1. Find some choppy passages in your own writings. Generate cumulative modifiers and combine sentences to eliminate the choppiness.

2. Find some awkward sentences in your own writings (perhaps some which have been pointed out to you by writing instructors). Rearrange them to see if you can eliminate the awkwardness. Try this activity in a small group, and see if you can analyze and modify other writers' awkward sentences and passages more easily than your own.

3. Search your writings for unnecessary passive constructions. Try to figure out why you used them. Transform them into active constructions.

4. Choose some good sentences you wrote. Imagine new contexts that require you to change the emphasis of these sentences. Rewrite them to achieve that new emphasis.

5. Here are some rules commonly given to inexperienced writers. Evaluate three in terms of the writer's *personna* and the reader's needs to expectations. Rewrite them in those terms. (See pages xvi-xix on the distinction between rules and principles.)

   a. Avoid the passive.
   b. Put statements in positive form.
   c. Omit needless words.
   d. Keep related words together.
   e. Place the emphatic words at the end of the sentence.
   f. Express coordinate ideas in parallel form.

PART TWO

FORMS

Composing is like an organic process, not an assembly line on which some prefabricated parts are fitted together. However, plants and animals don't just "grow" mystically, developing from seed to flower and fully framed creatures, without plan or guidance or system. All organic processes are forms in action: the task of the composer is to find the forms that find forms; the structures that guide and encourage growth; the limits by means of which development can be shaped. The method of composing that we've been discussing and practicing is a way of making meanings by using the forms provided by language to re-present the relationships we see.

Ann Berthoff

If rhetoric is self-discovery, candor is not merely an incidental virtue in the writer, but a necessary condition of his labor . . . . As Northrop Frye puts it, "genuine speech is the expression of genuine personality."

"Because it takes pain to make itself intelligible," Frye continues, "it assumes that the hearer is a genuine personality too—in other words, wherever it is spoken it creates a community." . . . The community that a piece of genuine writing creates is one not only of ideas and attitudes, but of fundamental modes of perception, thought, and feeling. . . . Experience, subtle shapechanger, is given form only by this or that set of conceptual habits, and each set of habits has its own patterns of linguistic expression, its own community.

Hans Guth

CHAPTER 4

SYNCHRONIC PATTERNS

There are certain basic patterns for organizing information that recur in almost all types of writing. If you master these basic patterns of arrangement, you have a basis for learning quickly how to structure any particular type of writing you may have to do.

This chapter is about a group of rhetorical forms, abstracted from description, that rhetoricians have called the "spatial" or "static" or *synchronic patterns of arrangement*. This is to distinguish them from the progressive patterns, abstracted from narration, which are the subject of Chapter 5. See Table 4.1.

	SYNCHRONIC PATTERNS (Chapter 4)	PROGRESSIVE PATTERNS (Chapter 5)
REPORT PATTERNS	Description	Narration
EXPLANATORY PATTERNS	Comparison/contrast Classification and division Definition Analogy and exemplification	Process-analysis Causal explanation Logical progression (not treated separately, but see pages 296-298 and 328-331.)

TABLE 4.1 Basic Patterns of Arrangement

The word *compose*, as noted in Chapter 1, comes from the Latin *componere*, meaning "to put together, to make up." We use the synchronic patterns when we break a subject into its aspects in order to analyze it (*decomponere*) and also when we recombine and synthesize those separated aspects in order to understand the meaning of the whole (*recomponere*).

The goal of composition is the "putting together" of meaning. We start with questions about the whole, and we should end with an understanding of the whole. In between, we analyze (decompose). Unfortunately, people sometimes resist analysis. Beginning literature students, for example, often complain that they lose the feeling of a poem while analyzing its symbols and structures. In one limited sense, these students are right: analysis serves no human purpose unless it leads to recomposition. Remember, however, it is precisely out of decomposition that life begins; *compost*, too, comes from *componere*. We analyze a poem in order to re-create the feeling more fully later.

Here we will be concerned with description, comparison/contrast, classification and division, definition, and analogy and exemplification primarily as patterns of arrangement for written compositions. But it is important to remember that, even more basically, they are thought structures. Like all cognitive forms, they can be used to discover material as well as to arrange it. If you describe your subject, define your terms, invent analogies, find examples, compare and contrast, classify and divide, you will generate material as well as organize it.

Beneath all the forms discussed in this chapter lies one basic mental process, what I. A. Richards calls "sorting". In all our perceiving, thinking, feeling, and communicating, we categorize. You do not, for instance, simply see this textbook; you see it *as* a textbook. That means you have categorized it, grouped it together with all other textbooks and distinguished it from every other type of thing in the universe.

Good writing begins with perceptive observation. And your purpose in writing is always, in at least one sense, to get readers to "see it your way." This chapter begins with a discussion of human peception, of "seeing and writing." This section on "the grammar of perception," perhaps used together with the discussion of invention in Chapter 1, should enable you to learn techniques and develop understandings that will make you a more perceptive observer and a more sensitive writer. Because it is so important in academic and professional writing, you should also learn what it means to observe and write objectively.

The second section of this chapter is about description, a mode often used for self-expression as well as for reporting information. A report writer's task is to discover, select and arrange information in order to re-create it for readers. This remains the case whether you are writing a literary description to evoke the grandeur of a storm in the mountains, a scientific description of the equipment used in an experiment, or a commercial description of a product you wish to sell. You know something your readers do not, and your immediate purpose is to communicate that knowledge.

From description, the chapter moves to more and more analytic patterns: comparison/contrast, classification and division, and definition. Try to look at these forms as thought processes, as ways to structure information, and as patterns of arrangement.

The chapter closes with a section on analogy and exemplification. These are important techniques for clarifying and convincing—for getting your readers to see your point clearly and to "see it your way." Especially in their extended forms, they are also much more than that. This section brings the chapter around full circle, actualizing the idea that "a search for a better word is a search for a better vision." Learn how to use analogies and examples to make a piece of writing clear and convincing. Use this section also to understand how writing is "a search for a better vision"—because that understanding will enable you to grasp and harness the full power of these forms.

SEEING AND WRITING

Nature hath no outline, but Imagination has.
William Blake

Our world divides into facts because we so divide it.
Susanne Langer

We don't take in the world like a camera or a set of recording devices. The mind is an agent, not a passive receiver; experience isn't poured into it. The active mind is a composer and everything we respond to, we compose.
Ann Berthoff

You can't depend on your eyes when your imagination is out of focus.
Mark Twain

THE GRAMMAR OF PERCEPTION

In order to write about something, you must know about it. The quality of a piece of writing depends to a significant extent on the quality of the information it presents. The good writer is often the perceptive observer.

But observation is not simple, at least not for human beings. We very often look at something and fail to "see" it in any detail, especially if it is familiar. Different people, moreover, can look at (or feel, taste, smell, or hear) the same phenomenon and make quite distinct observations. Indeed, the very purpose of a piece of writing is often to get other people to "see it your way."

Every academic or professional discipline demands the ability to observe rigorously for detail and to distinguish between relevant and irrelevant details. A rule generally applied to the writing done in academic and professional contexts is that you may hold any opinion you like—*if* you support it with facts (see page 96 ff.) These "facts" are observations, whether your own or someone else's. Although the rule is occasionally broken by teachers, editors, and bosses who are biased in favor of their own opinions, it remains a generally accepted rule which will be enforced (especially if your opinions are unpopular).

Because observation is such a crucial aspect of the writing process, because it so greatly constrains what gets written and how, and

FIGURE 4.1 Goblet and Two Faces

because one of the most basic rules of academic and professional writing requires rigorous observation, this section is about how we perceive. Its central thesis is that *we compose our perceptions* (using a process in many ways parallel to that by which we compose our writings). This thesis is doubly relevant, moreover, because it sheds light on the process by which *readers recompose* as they read (see page 119).

To understand human perception one must first realize that reality is much more detailed and complex than our observations of it. At this very instant, your eyes are picking up and transmitting to your brain thousands of "bits" of information. Communication theorists estimate that a person's sense organs transmit about ten thousand "bits" of information every second. Since it would be impossible for a human mind to be conscious of that many "bits" of information, you unconsciously select those which seem most significant, because they form patterns. Then, still preconsciously, you compose those patterns into images, sounds, smells, tastes, and feelings.

This human ability to perceive meaningful patterns instead of individual stimuli is crucially important. It prevents us from being over-

FIGURE 4.2 Owl(s)

whelmed by masses of trivial information. It allows us to focus on what matters (or seems to matter) while ignoring what does not matter.

Because there are many potential patterns in a batch of stimuli, different people will "see" different patterns. Even after a simple traffic accident, bystanders often give contradictory reports. Considering the nature and complexity of our perceptual processes, it is perhaps more amazing that people often agree about "what happened," although our attention gets focused on those instances where there is conflict. Sixty thousand people may leave a baseball game agreeing on what the final score was and who scored the winning run, even if 50,000 think that the runner should have been called out at the plate. Five hundred and sixty-three out of 600 students may agree about what was served for dinner in their dormitory, and 497 of them may even agree that it tasted terrible.

Paradoxically, however, it is when our perceptual processes go awry that we can learn most about how they work. Psychologists, therefore, have often experimented with certain images that are designed to encourage ambiguous or even false perceptions. Perhaps the most famous of the ambiguous figures is called the "Goblet and Two Faces." Some people are tempted to title this image, "Goblet *or* Two Faces," but objectively it is both. Which you perceive depends on how you look at it: if you look at a white figure on a black background, you will see a goblet; if you focus on a black figure on a white background, you will see two symmetrical faces in profile. As you look at the image, you make a perceptual choice about what to emphasize and what to push into the background; and that choice determines what you see.

With this particular image it is easy for most people consciously to control that choice and to switch back-and-forth between seeing the goblet and seeing the two faces. Our consciousness of the double image thus makes this a special case. Usually when we observe reality we perceive only one aspect (and consequently convince ourselves that there is only one aspect to be seen).

Figure 4.2, which may be either one or two owls depending on how you look at it, is yet another illustration of the same principle.

The implications of these trick images may become clearer if we look at another type of picture. Here, instead of two alternate images, we have a seemingly meaningless mass of dark and light shapes.

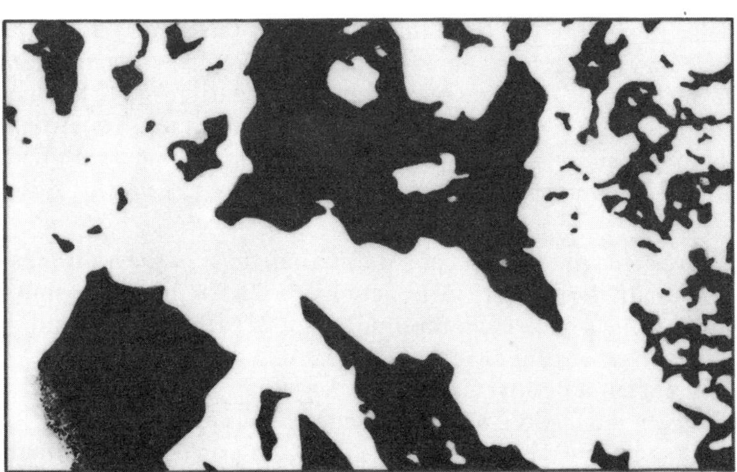

FIGURE 4.3 Christ-in-the-clouds

If you stare at it long enough, perhaps with a little help from your friends, you will probably see the image of a bearded man who resembles a late-medieval representation of Jesus Christ. The top border of the photograph cuts across his brow; his eyes, hair, beard, and the outline of his nose are dark areas; his cheeks, mouth, and lower lip are white. Although a few people see this Christ-figure immediately, most have to study the photograph for some time before the image emerges, and a few people never manage to perceive it.

The differences among these people have nothing whatsoever to do with eyesight. The retinal images and the optic nerve impulses to the brain are effectively the same for everyone with normal (or corrected) eyesight who looks at the photograph. But one cannot see the Christ-figure without *conceptualizing* the proper pattern, and the process of composing that conceptualization takes different people different amounts of time.

One significant fact about the perception of this image is that once you have seen it you will be virtually unable to make it go away: once you have settled this pattern in your mind, you will continually see a bearded man and not a meaningless blotch. Even if you should manage to forget, as you may if you put the photograph away for some months, it will be less difficult to reconstruct the figure than it was to construct it the first time—because you will know where and how to look. In its permanency then, this image is different from the goblet-and-two-faces and the owl(s).

In order to see the Christ-figure, you must push most of the visual stimuli from the photograph into the background while focusing on certain key features. To do so takes conceptualization—or to use another word, *imagination* (image-ination). Yet the concept must be brought to mind *before* the image can be seen. This has paradoxical implications, which can be understood more clearly in terms of the following photograph.

In Figure 4.4, a photograph of a dalmatian, most of the halftones have been lost (as in moonlight). And yet one can distinguish the spots that make up the dog's back from the similar spots in the background. A few of the lines that "outline" the dog do exist objectively in the picture, but most of them must be supplied by the perceiver. And in order to do that, the perceiver must have a mental image (i.e., concept) from which to work. To someone who had never seen a dog or doglike animal, this photograph would be a meaningless blotch of spots (or perhaps something else altogether).

In order to perceive, a human being must make "automatic" (i.e., preconscious) decisions about what to emphasize, what to push into the background, and what to totally ignore. Often, as with the photograph of the dalmatian, the human perceiver must also *fill in* certain aspects of the perception that are not supplied by sensory stimuli. What actually happens is that *the stimuli trigger a preconscious sorting process which*

FIGURE 4.4 Dalmatian as if by moonlight

locates a concept, and then that concept is used to focus a mass of sensations into a meaningful perception.

This understanding of human perception is very close to the one put forth by Samuel Taylor Coleridge, who used the term "Primary Imagination" to describe the human faculty that shapes sensory input into meaningful perceptions. In the twentieth century, this understanding has been confirmed by the work of cognitive psychologists, including investigations into the early perceptions of infants.

We can understand the implications of this kind of perception by asking what would be the visual experiences of a blind person who was suddenly given physically normal vision by surgery. Having been blind from birth, such a person would have no mental images (i.e., no visual concepts) with which to organize visual perceptions. What would such a person see?

Case histories of people born blind but given physically normal vision as adults (by newly developed surgical techniques) dramatically confirm the understanding of human perception presented above. When the bandages are first removed, such a person's initial visions are *disorganized blurs.* In other words, with completely normal sensory input, *but no visual concepts*, the person cannot focus and cannot, in any meaningful sense, *see.*

Over a period of weeks, the previously blind person "translates" concepts based on previous touch experiences into visual forms and learns to see. The development of totally new concepts (and therefore of the ability to see objects with which the person had no previous experience), however, can take a year or more. And when there are "translatable" concepts, they can sometimes overpower objective stimuli (as in the case of a man who drew—and presumably perceived—buses with spoked wheels, like those he had helped wash as a blind child, even though he had never seen such a bus and was trying to draw the modern buses which passed outside his window).

Unlike previously blind adults, infants cannot tell us what they perceive. But insofar as we can make indirect inferences from experimental evidence, it seems that newly born infants also perceive only disorganized blurs. Only as they develop concepts does their vision slowly become more focused and specific.

The same process occurs preconsciously in a split second for every perception a person has—except that instead of having to develop a concept, the person need only locate a preexisting concept based on previous experiences (i.e., literally, a *pre*-conception). What a human being perceives is not determined entirely by sensory stimuli and is therefore not an exact copy of what is really "out there." Neither, however, is it entirely subjective, determined by the perceiver's preconceptions. Instead, a human being's conscious *perception is a synthesis of the interaction of sensory stimuli with mental concepts.*

Since the sensory stimuli come from the real world, and since the mental concepts were formed from previous experiences with that same world, human perceptions are usually fairly accurate reflections of reality. Since the mental concepts are to some degree shaped by a person's socialization, including language experiences, however, human perceptions are not exact copies of reality and vary somewhat according to the person's cultural, linguistic, and personal background. The mental "lenses" that focus human perceptions also refract—thus they may reflect reality much in the same sense that a distorting carnival mirror does. An accurate perception is a reflection of reality, but it is also a selection—and thus inevitably a deflection of whichever aspects of reality are not selected.

PERCEIVING IN CONTEXT

Human perception would be simpler—and report writing easier—if it reflected reality exactly. However, the advantage of a more complex type of perception is that it allows us to perceive *in context*. Although this sometimes creates problems, it is usually highly efficient and sometimes even corrects faulty perceptions. This point can be clarified by considering certain illusions.

These two lines are the same length.

If we draw a bit on context around them, they will still be the same length, but it is almost impossible to see them as equal.

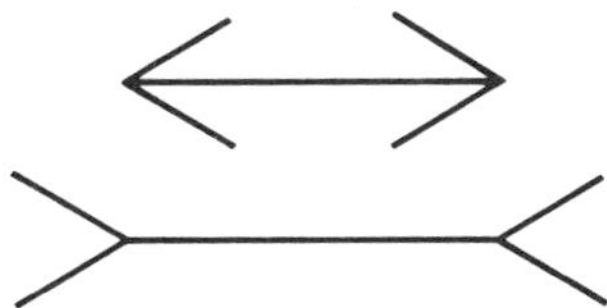

Even if we place them up against a ruler, which proves they are the same length, we still cannot "see" them as equal (see Figure 4.5.).

This influence of context on perception applies to all five senses because it is not "in" the eye but rather a quality of human minds. This can be demonstrated by few simple experiments.

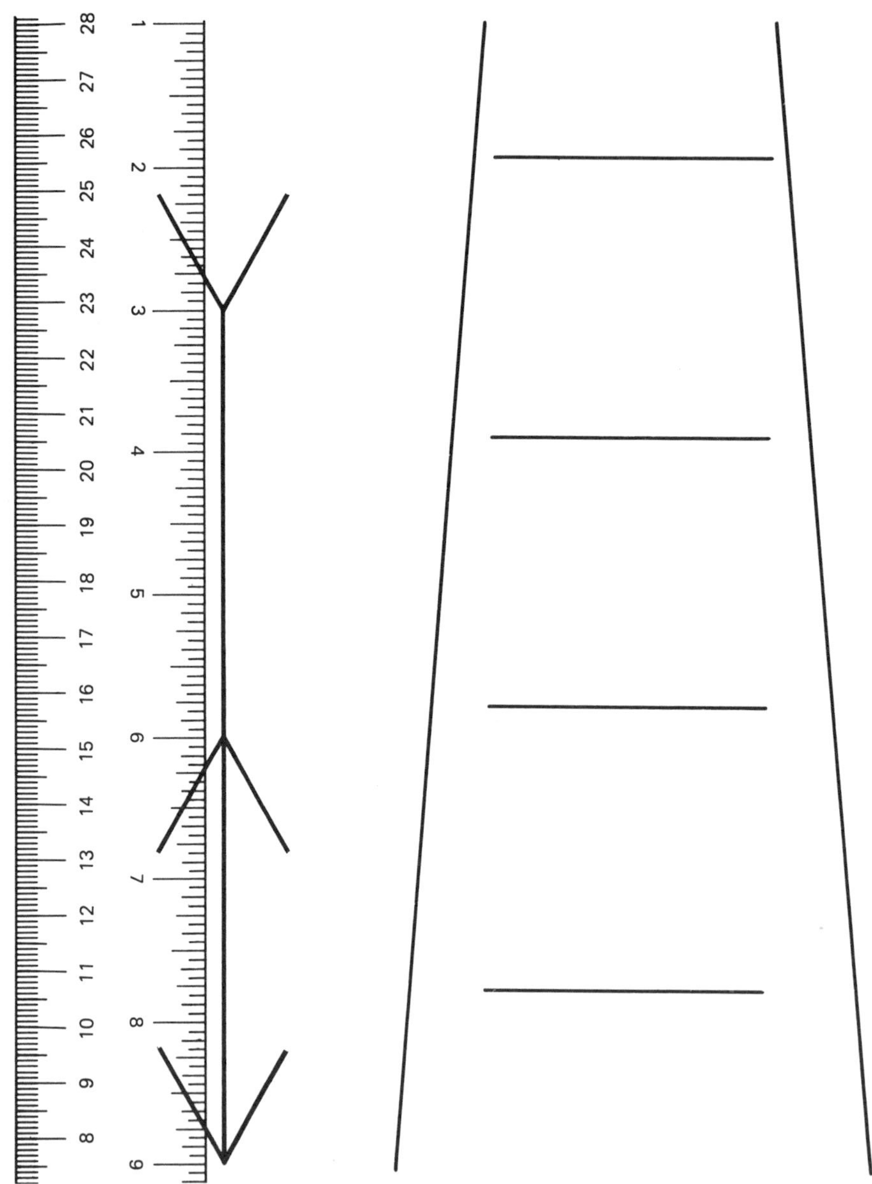

FIGURE 4.5 Muller-Lyer and "Railroad Track" Perspective Illusions

PERCEPTION EXPERIMENT 1: *Prepare three containers of water: one hot, one lukewarm, and one cold. Place one hand in the hot water and the other in the cold water, and keep them immersed until acclimated (about three minutes). Now that you have established two distinct temperature contexts for your two hands, place both hands simultaneously in the lukewarm water.*

If you do this experiment, you will find it difficult (probably impossible) to believe the evidence of your senses. You will have perceived the lukewarm water in two distinct temperature contexts—and your mind will probably overrule the resulting contradictory perceptions.

A similar experiment demonstrates the contextual relativity of taste perception:

PERCEPTION EXPERIMENT 2: *Pour a glass of water and taste a sip. Then eat an ice cream cone or keep a strong solution of sugar-water in your mouth for one minute. Now that you have established a new taste context, immediately taste the glass of water again.*

Similar demonstrations can be done with the loudness or pitch of sound, but they are dangerous and should not be attempted except in a supervised laboratory. Virtually all North Americans have had a parallel experience with velocity: after some hours on a superhighway at 55 miles (or 90 kilometers) per hour, a city speed limit of 30 miles (or 50 kilometers) per hour seems ridiculously slow—even though it ordinarily does not.

STEREOTYPES AND CLICHÉS

PERCEPTION EXPERIMENT 3: *On a circle divided into quadrants (like the one below), draw as accurately as you can the dial of an ordinary dial telephone (of the sort that preceded the pushbutton phones). Do so before reading on.*

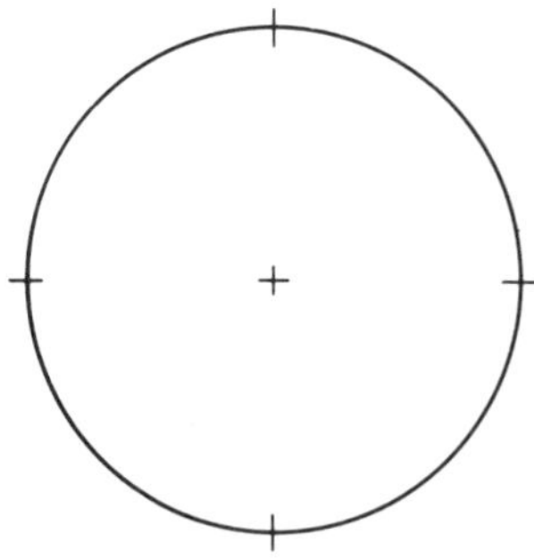

This experiment usually demonstrates two points. The first is that our perception is utilitarian. People who have looked at and touched dial telephones tens of thousands of times often cannot remember many details—details that are of no importance to a person dialing the telephone. For example, most people cannot remember which two letters of the alphabet do not appear. Many people cannot remember the proper orientation of the ten finger-holes or the details of the center disc.

The second, and more interesting point, is that our perception is conceptual. A significant number of people draw the numbers in the finger-holes. Conceptually, those holes do represent those numbers; so conceptually that is an accurate representation. But only on very old-fashioned dial telephones are the numbers actually in the holes. More than two decades ago, on the basis of a quarter-of-a-million-dollar study, the telephone manufacturers moved the numbers out of the holes onto the rim and placed little dots in the holes. (Since the number now remains visible even when the person's finger is in the hole, this has reduced "wrong numbers" and saves the company millions of dollars every year.) Nonetheless, many people continue to perceive the numbers as in the holes because the holes continue to signify the numbers when one is dialing.

The following picture was drawn for a psychological experiment and intentionally violates stereotypes that were current at the time.

In the experiment, people were shown the picture and then asked to describe it from memory. Very often they remembered seeing the stereotype even though the picture explicitly violates it. For example, many *white* observers remembered the knife as being held by the black man in the picture.

The word *stereotype* was originally a printers' term for a block that was used to reproduce the same image time and time again. It has come to refer to *a preconception that constrains people toward the same perception time and time again, even though actual experience often violates that perception.* Usually the word *stereotype* is used only for preconceptions that lead to harmful and erroneous conclusions. Thus the preconception that leads people to draw the numbers in the finger-holes of the telephone dial would not ordinarily be called a stereotype. But the preconception that led observers to perceive the knife in the hand of the black man would be called a stereotype. The use of the word *stereotype* implies a judgment about the preconception.

Both instances demonstrate that, as Mark Twain wrote in *A Connecticut Yankee in King Arthur's Court,* "You can't depend on your eyes when your imagination is out of focus." In the first case, however, the perceptual inaccuracy does not matter; in the second case, it matters very much.

The verbal equivalent of a preconception is a *cliché.* (See pages 166-168 for a discussion of the stylistic implications of clichés.) Here the important point is that sometimes *the context in which we perceive is verbal.* The terms we use to names things and events create conceptual contexts that, to some significant degree, shape our perceptions. A set of lines may mean nothing at all, or have various meanings for various people—until they are placed in context by being described. In such cases to *de*-scribe is also to *circum*-scribe, or at least to constrain, perceptions. The following drawing, for example, usually does not signify much to most people.

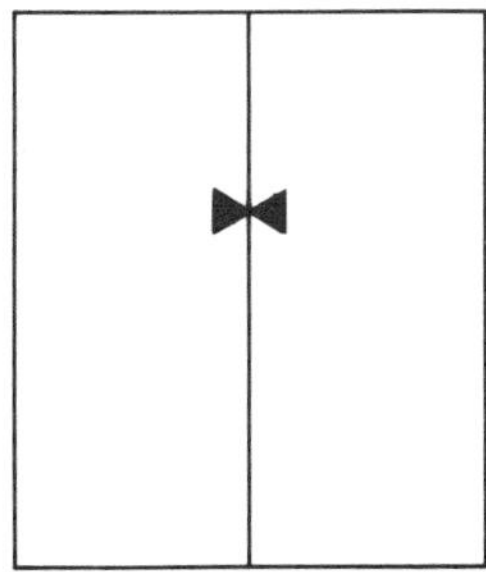

When *described* as a picture of a man wearing a bowtie who stood too close to an elevator door, however, it suddenly focuses into a meaningful perception.

The linguist, Edward Sapir, argued that "we see and hear and otherwise experience very largely as we do because the language habits of our community predispose certain choices of interpretation." Since 1929 when Sapir made that assertion (later known as the Whorf-Sapir hypothesis), it has been much debated. The debate, however, turns not on whether language influences perception, but on *how* "very largely" it does so. There is little question that our perceptions reflect what Sapir called "social reality" and that "language is a guide to 'social reality.' " Language and culture significantly shape our perceptions. Most of our concepts—and especially the abstract concepts we use to understand and contextualize our concrete experiences—are learned, stored, and remembered through words. This is one of the important ways in which we differ from other organisms on this planet. It is also what allows us to adapt flexibly to a variety of environments and situations.

An insect or a fish perceives much more simply and reliably. For example, when a male stickleback fish sees red, he does not consciously or even preconsciously think about what it might mean in the particular context. Controlled by his instincts, he attacks—every time. In his normal environment this response is very efficient because a red object is likely to be another male stickleback he should chase out of his territory. In any event, the stickleback's tiny brain could not handle a more complex concept of redness without impairing his ability to function in other areas.

The honeybee exhibits a similar reaction to red, because most times red in the bee's normal environment indicates flowers. But occasionally certain unfortunate bees spend a great deal of time searching for pollen on other red objects.

Unlike bees and sticklebacks, which have instinctively programmed responses to red, people respond more flexibly. When I am driving and see a red light, I stop (the car). When I am in a radio station and see a red light, I start (talking into the microphone). In a sense, it would be more accurate to say that I do not see red lights—I see signals. That is, I see red lights in contexts, which give them their meanings. Thus a symbolic, contextualized mode of perception gives human beings some degree of freedom from sensory tyranny. We are less predictable (and less reliable) than insects, but we are much more flexible.

Human perception, although it has a basis in our hereditary makeup, is significantly shaped by language, education, and culture. We have evolved from instinctive animals, which respond largely by hereditary reflex, into learning animals, who respond more responsively to varied and variable environments.

The flexible and contextualized nature of human perception has important implications for writers. The first is that you should strive to perceive whatever you are going to write about in various distinct contexts in order to discover as much as possible about it. Remember that your own perceptual habits, concepts, beliefs, and feelings significantly shape and limit your perceptions. Use the techniques discussed in Chapter 1 to broaden—and sharpen—your perceptions.

Second, remember that your readers do not necessarily have the same educational, cultural, or social backgrounds as you do. To communicate effectively with them, you should try to understand how they see things. In order to achieve stability, groups of people establish their more important perceptual values as cultural mores, reinforced by language, education, and other kinds of socialization—and your readers' backgrounds may be quite different than your own. Use the techniques suggested in the first section of Chapter 2 to evaluate your audience.

Third, you should remember that human perceptions are composed in contexts—physical, social, linguistic, and emotional, among others. You have perceived your subject in contexts that make it meaningful for you. Your words should, at least by connotation, re-create enough of these contexts to make your subject meaningful for your readers—to make it *matter* to them.

Fourth, the forms you use to compose your writings also help shape the substance of what you discover and write about your subject. The choice of a form particularly influences the selection and arrangement of material—and thus emphasis. Part Two of this textbook is designed to acquaint you with a variety of patterns of arrangement and other forms, so you can choose and use the most appropriate one in each case.

Fifth, remember that, even if you refrain from overtly expressing your opinions, the decisions you make about how to contextualize, what to emphasize, what to deemphasize, and what to leave out reflect your perspectives and biases. Your perceptions, however socialized, are generally functional; but on occasion they distort. Where objectivity is desired, it can be approached only if writers are clear about the bases for their decisions and honest about biases that may have influenced them.

Recognizing that perceptions are not always accurate, modern scientists and other empirically minded Westerners have devised procedures for verifying observations. Writers should know how to do this.

FOUR WAYS TO VERIFY OBSERVATIONS

Since good writing is usually based on accurate and perceptive observations, would-be writers will do well to develop their abilities as observers. The various techniques for negative invention (pages 51-62 can help develop those abilities. Particular heuristics for positive invention (pages 63-73) can also develop abilities related to observing the particular circumstances for which they were devised—for example, the Pentad can help one to observe human behavior more insightfully. Perceptiveness can be learned.

However, it is not easy to evaluate one's own observations. Whatever preconceptions and carelessnesses may have biased the observations are likely to bias the evaluation as well. Indeed, there is a kind of paradox here. In order to decide if one has observed all that is important and relevant, one must somehow consider that which was not observed. One must somehow see what one is not seeing!

What follows is a heuristic for evaluating the accuracy and fullness of observations. It does not entirely transcend the paradox, but it can help.

1. What preconceptions do I have about whatever I am observing? How do they influence my selection of "facts"? Is my observation consistent with my ideas? If I specifically look for inconsistencies, can I find any? Does what I observe conflict with what I believe? If so, is that because my observations are faulty or because I need to modify my beliefs? (See Perception Experiment 1, page 215.)
2. What have I excluded? To which details have I (consciously or preconsciously) chosen not to pay attention?
3. If I "look again"—perhaps more carefully or more closely (or more widely) or from a distinct perspective or "through" a different heuristic—do I observe anything different? If so, is that difference important?
4. Does my observation give me the information I need? Is it useful? Does it serve my purposes (and the purposes of my perspective readers)?

Thus one checks for (1) *consistency* between particular observations and ideas, beliefs, and theories; one checks for (2) *exclusions*, for what may have been overlooked or left out; one checks for (3) *correspondence* among observations made from various perspectives; and one checks for (4) *usefulness*, for whether the information selected serves the purposes, which motivated the observation in the first place.

No observation will ever be absolutely complete. The trick is not to see everything. The trick is to avoid leaving out information that matters (and to avoid distortion). The ultimate test of observations—and of reports written on the basis of those observations—is the fourth, *usefulness*. Except as an exercise, one observes not randomly, but purposively. Observations are made and reports are written to be used. The question is whether the report is accurate and complete *enough* to fulfill its purposes, to give readers the information they need to achieve insight and understanding, to make decisions and act correctly.

BEING OBJECTIVE

In practical terms, *objectivity* usually means focusing on the "object" or event being described. It means excluding personal feelings, opinions, and beliefs that reveal more about the writer than about the reality being described. The guiding purpose behind an objective report is this: the readers want to know about what is being described, not about the writer's relation to what is being described, not about the writer's feelings, opinions, or beliefs. This notion of objectivity became dominant with the growth of modern science. Its original function, during the European Renaissance, was to exclude Christian religious beliefs and preconceptions from scientific investigations.

Objectivity is often confused with neutrality. In practical terms that makes some sense. If one wants to know the truth about a matter being disputed by two or more interested parties, obviously one wants a chief investigator who is not initially biased toward one of those interested parties. That is what we mean by "open-mindedness."

But absolute, pure neutrality is not humanly possible. As was demonstrated above, perception is not simple for human beings. What we perceive, even on the level of "fact," is not a simple copy of what is "out there." We compose sensory input into meaningful patterns, influenced by our conceptions, stereotypes, and various contexts. Moreover, as David Broder told the U.S. National Press Club in 1979,

> *All of us know as journalists that what we are mainly engaged in deciding is not what to put in [our reports] but what to leave out. . . . [T]he process of selecting what the reader reads involves not just objective facts but subjective judgments, personal values, ideals and, yes, prejudices.*
>
> *[In 1959,] Walter Lippmann said: "It is all very well to say that a reporter collects the news and that the news consists of facts. The truth is that in our world the facts are infinitely many, and that no reporter can collect them all, and that no newspaper could print them all—even if they were fit to print—and nobody could read them all. We have to select some facts rather than others, and in doing that, we are using not only our legs but our selective judgment of what is interesting or important or both."*

Any report must be based on a *selection* of information—which is inevitably a *rejection* of other information that has been excluded from the report. The honesty of a piece of writing cannot be judged simply by asking if each assertion in the writing is true. No written communication can actually tell "the whole truth"—the whole truth includes masses of trivia that would just confuse the issue. Any report, moreover, must be written in words, and all words have connotations: there are no absolutely neutral words to use (see pages 171-176).

What then is objectivity?

First, objectivity means including all important and relevant information. In order to know what is important and relevant to any particular writing, we must know the purposes of both the writer and the intended readers. Only in terms of those mutual purposes can we decide what information matters. In most academic, scientific, and professional contexts, for example, writers' feelings and moral beliefs are not important or relevant to objective reports. (On the other hand, many writers hide behind "objectivity" to exclude or disguise their feelings, opinions, or beliefs in contexts where those feelings, opinions, or beliefs are relevant.) To judge objectivity, we must always consider the purposes of the writing and ask whether any important and relevant information has been left out or expressed only vaguely.

Second, objectivity means not manipulating. It means not manipulating your readers by presenting information favorable to your own conclusions or interests while excluding unfavorable information; it means giving them all the information they need to make their own informed judgments. It means not manipulating your choice of words so as to disguise your value judgments.

Third, being objective means revealing yourself. Since selection and exclusion of information is humanly inevitable, objectivity means revealing the criteria by which you made your selection. It is not dishonest or nonobjective to exclude information from a report or to use words with connotations. An honest, objective writer should exclude all irrelevant information and should choose words with connotations that accurately suggest the implications of whatever is being described. But since human beings inevitably observe from some perspective, being objective means allowing readers to be aware of your perspective and of the prejudices, biases, preconceptions, and interests that might influence it.

Objectivity is not easy. It requires insights not only into your subject but also into yourself. It is based on the Socratic dictum: "Know thyself." Ultimately, if you do not know yourself, you cannot be objective about your subject or fully honest with your readers.

The issue of honesty in writing is complex. Perhaps the most honest policy that writers can follow is to make their purposes and biases explicit so that readers can better judge their selections, exclusions, and emphases. As Gerhart Wiebe asserts,

> *Even the reporting of pure physical research findings, to cite an extreme example, is not unbiased. . . . The question is not whether a communication is biased. The question is:* toward what value system is the communication biased?

Or, in the words of the psychiatrist, Erich Fromm, "Objectivity does not mean detachment, it means respect; that is, the ability not to distort and to falsify things, persons, and oneself."

ADDITIONAL READING

Berger, John. *Ways of Seeing*. Harmondsworth, England: Penguin, 1972. Based on a B.B.C. television series, this book uses art to explain human perception.

Gibson, Walker. *Seeing and Writing*. New York: McKay, 1974. Fifteen exercises are included for composing based on experience.

Neisser, Ulric. *Cognition and Reality*. San Francisco: Freeman, 1976. This is one of the best serious books about human perception, although there are certain problems with the concluding chapter.

Patterson, Freeman. *Photography & The Art of Seeing.* Toronto: Van Nostrand Reinhold, 1979. This book is about photography, but the principles it asserts can be applied to composing in any medium.

Richards, I. A. *The Philosophy of Rhetoric.* London: Oxford, 1936. See Richards' second chapter for a discussion of the relationship between the composition of perceptions and the composition of meanings, and especially for his attack on what he calls "The One and Only One Meaning Superstition."

EXERCISE

1. Sometimes when people disagree they share the same perception but nonetheless have *a difference of opinion* about what it means or what should be done. Often, however, people disagree because of *a difference of perception*: although they are observing the same situation, they do not perceive it the same way. Write a paper about such a difference of perception. Your paper should include a report of each observer's perception and also an analysis explaining how their distinct preconceptions lead them toward distinct perceptions. You may write about a real situation or use characters from literature, cinema, or television. You may also use a situation in which *one* person has two distinct perceptions at two different times.

2. Read Gregory Bateson's "Bali: The Value System of a Steady State" in his *Steps to an Ecology of Mind* and look at *Balinese Character: A Photographic Analysis* (by Bateson and Margaret Mead). Write a paper on the socialization of perception in Bali and in your own culture.

3. Select and read some essays from Benjamin Lee Whorf's *Language, Thought and Reality.* Find and read several critiques of the Whorf-Sapir hypothesis (see page 218). Write your own short essay on the relationship between language and thought. As a touchstone to concretize your discussion, use the following example, one of seven cases reported by Whorf in which he asserts that a fire was caused by language habits.

> *An electric glow heater on the wall was little used and for one workman had the meaning of a convenient coathanger. At night a watchman entered and snapped a switch, which action he verbalized as 'turning on the light.' No light appeared, and this result he verbalized as 'light is burned out.' He could not see the glow of the heater because of the old coat hung on it. Soon the heater ignited the coat, which set fire to the building.*

4. Write a paper describing a stereotype, showing how it leads to distorted perceptions of reality and to socially harmful behaviors. Consider including a section on the virtues of nonstereotypic preconceptions and generalizations.

DESCRIPTION

A town or a countryside, seen from a distance, is a town or a countryside. But as one draws closer, they are houses, trees, tiles, leaves, grasses, plants, weeds, ants, legs of ants, ad infinitum. *All this is enveloped in the name 'countryside.'*

Blaise Pascal

. . . [W]e can never break out of the circle of language and seize the object barehanded, as it were, or without some ideational operation.

Richard Weaver

The 'thing itself'—that of course would be pure, dead-end truth—is wholly incomprehensible even to the creator of language and in no sense worth striving for. He merely describes the relation of things to man and resorts for their expression to the boldest metaphors. A nerve stimulus first translated into an image. First metaphor.

Friedrich Nietzsche

MUTUAL PURPOSE AND SELECTION

Description is a very common mode. Scientists describing the observations made during an experiment, a poet describing emotions felt while watching a child sleep, a mail-order merchant describing an item which is for sale—all of these are descriptions. Since they serve very distinct purposes, they will be written with distinctly different tones; but the mode of discourse remains description.

The descriptive writer's main task is the *selection* and verbal representation of information. You must choose the details that matter—that are important to the purposes you share with your readers—as well as a pattern of arrangement relevant to those mutual purposes. Necessarily, these choices about what to include are also choices about what to exclude. Any description is bound to leave out a lot more than it includes. Writers should be careful that what is excluded is not important to themselves or their readers.

Description can be an engineer describing the terrain where an embankment must be built, a novelist describing a farm where the novel will take place, a realtor describing a house and land for sale, a journalist describing a celebrity's birthplace, or a tourist describing a rural scene to friends back home. That engineer, novelist, realtor, journalist, and tourist may all be describing the very same place. If each is truthful, their descriptions will not contradict each other. But they will certainly include and emphasize different aspects. Because their purposes are widely divergent, they will use distinct principles of selection and patterns of arrangement.

Although the term *description* usually suggests a concrete description of material realities, the descriptive mode can also be used to represent ideas or even other reports. For example, one can write a description of René Descartes' theory of perception (perhaps preliminary to criticizing it in terms of what has since been learned about human perception). Similarly, a scientist or a scholar who summarizes a published article is describing that article. In such a case, the object being observed is in a sense not really an object, but the writer's descriptive tasks remain essentially the same: observation (or, in these instances, reading), selection, arrangement, and verbalization. Even if it summarizes another report, any summary is itself a report. (Whether we call that report description or narrative depends on the nature of what is being summarized. See page 281.)

There is, for example, a form of summary known as an *abstract*. An abstract briefly summarizes the main points of an article (usually in 100 to 200 words) so that other readers (usually scientists or scholars) can decide whether they should read it. In at least one sense, the writer of an abstract is like the writer of a mail-order catalog description: both save prospective users the work of having to examine the item itself in order to decide whether they should acquire it. In the one case, we have an objective description of the main ideas of an article. In the other, we have a suasive description of a material object which is for sale. In both cases, the writer is using the descriptive mode.

Consider for example, the following description of students at Benedict College in South Carolina. It was written by a graduate student who is also a professor at Benedict. Her assigned purpose was to give colleagues from other schools in South Carolina a sense of the students she teaches.

WHOSOEVER WILL, LET HIM COME

During homecoming week, when distinguished alumni of many years past return to the campus of the small private school where I work to reminisce over the "good old days," the conversation inevitably drifts to laments about what they perceive to be Benedict's "going to the dogs," as manifested in students' apparent lack of aspirations toward academic and cultural excellence. Back "then" students were poor just as students are today, and they were largely rural, too, as they are today. The big difference is that for some outsiders present-day students have acquired a new image: instead of being highly motivated, industrious, and respectful, many are viewed as loafing uncultivated, rude, incompetent boors. The insider, like me, sees something else, however—something that has come as a result of the college's redefinition of its mission and purpose and adoption of a policy of open admissions. Like that of the church that has nurtured it, the motto of the school can be interpreted as, "Whosoever will, let him come, without respect for age, race, sex, family background, economics or academic standing," a stance strongly encouraged by easily accessible federal and state funds for the disadvantaged. Against this backdrop, I will give a composite description of the students I teach.

Anyone interested can note the statistics on the academic standing of entering students, the ones assigned to me. Over 70%, according to standardized test scores, read and write below the 8th grade level and at least 15% below the 6th grade. Only about 2% place at 12th grade or above. An alarming situation, a casual observer might conclude. But the truth of the matter is that with conscientious and humane guidance, both in the classroom and out, these students make tremendous strides in their freshman year. The problem is not lack of intelligence but lack of exposure: 90% of these students pursued vocational, not college preparatory, courses in high school. Consequently, they were able to get by with easy, often irrelevant courses, especially in English, thinking that they would never have any need to read anything more than simple directions and possibly the comics section of the newspaper and that, having the increasingly convenient telephone and tape recorder/player, they would never need to write more than a casual letter or fill in a few blanks. "Big words" to these students were for showoffs. But, lo and behold, after 12 years of school and "vocational training," most discovered that few jobs were to be had, and those available paid pitifully little. When they came face to face with the bleak reality and began to cast about for alternatives, the open door college loomed before them as the answer to their prayers: tuition grants and BEOG would provide a place to stay and food to eat. All they had to promise in return was to "play school," as they had often done back home. This brings me to the second characteristic.

Many entering students are accustomed to getting by and "getting over the man." Their main objective is to find out what game is being run down so they can "psych" out those in charge. Knowledge about and appreciation for great ideas and accomplishments of civilization are not top priority. What millions take for granted—museums; music other than gospel, rock and soul; theater (not movies); world literature—is entirely foreign to the majority of them. More than half have never been on a plane or a train and would be frightened half to death of the subway. One student of mine had never ridden an elevator until the summer after she graduated from high school. The Pentagon, the

Smithsonian Institute, Chase Manhattan are as foreign as Olympus. In short, their world view is limited to small towns and school buses. And their social knowledge is equally limited. Most of what they know they learned in home economics classes or experienced at the 4-H banquet, a high school disco, and possibly the prom. They seem unaware of many of the formalities which mark a person of refinement.

Professionally, entering students are pathetically naive: they tend to believe that the possession of a B.S. or B.A. degree, irrespective of how little they may know or be able to do, is the passport to lucrative positions in the business world. (A large percentage major in business related fields.) They overlook competition as something they will have to contend with: some still think that racial and sexual tokenism will get them placed where they want to be. This naivete persists even when their own relatives and friends remain unemployed or underemployed after graduation.

For the entering student, the greatest need is to become worldly-wise, to acquire broader and more nearly accurate perceptions of the way things really are and of what it takes to succeed. Teaching them to write is made especially difficult because so much has to be done in the pre-writing stage to fill the knowledge and experience void which is so characteristic of them. Once the gap—or chasm—is bridged, students such as the ones I have described can and very often do become highly efficient and productive writers.

Willease Sanders

Here the principle of selection is to give teachers the information they would need to understand these students and to design writing curricula for them. Note how carefully all information is put into context so that readers will be able not only to perceive it but to understand its significance. The first paragraph actually declares itself to be "backdrop" (i.e., context). The statistics which open the second paragraph are immediately put into motivational and then socioeconomic contexts. In the second half of the piece, the students' educational goals are similarly put into contexts which make sense of them.

Without all this "backdrop," the report would have been a lot shorter. It would still have been an accurate report—that is, it would have contained no false statements and no glaring omissions. But it would not have achieved its purpose because it would not have given its readers the information they would need to understand these students.

Even with the contexts supplied, this report could have been considerably shorter. The writer says, for example,

One student of mine had never ridden an elevator until the summer after she graduated from high school. The Pentagon, the Smithsonian Institute, Chase Manhattan are as foreign as Olympus. In short, their world view is limited to small towns and school buses.

The first two sentences could be deleted. Indeed, the whole paragraph from which this passage comes could be cut by half. But it is those details which could be cut that make the description vivid and give readers a concrete sense of the students. (See pages 163-166 for a discussion of abstract and concrete.)

ARRANGEMENT AND FOCUS

The arrangement of a description usually follows from the arrangement of reality. "Whosoever Will, Let Him Come," after its introductory paragraph, starts with the present reading and writing abilities of entering students. It then moves outward to the educational contexts which produced those abilities. It shifts to the students' attitudes and motivations and again moves outward to the educational and social contexts. Of course, it could have been arranged the other way around, moving from broad contexts to individual students. Other arrangements are also possible. There is more than one pattern to be observed in any particular reality, and the descriptive writer must choose. But even in this relatively analytical description, the information is organized in a pattern suggested by the observed reality. The arrangement of descriptive writing usually suggests spatial metaphors and can be compared to the motion of a movie or videotape camera (with a long zoom lens for close-ups, as well as medium-, and long-range shots).

The following piece, written by a first-year university student, also starts from a center and expands outward. Presented from the point of view of a very young child, it is written almost as if she carried that camera mounted in her "rusty red wagon". As she moves through her world, she pauses at each important point and uses the zoom lens to bring details into focus. As she shows us these images, the writer acts as narrator, commenting sometimes from the perspective of a young girl immersed in the scene and sometimes from the perspective she has now. As in "Whosoever Will, Let Him Come," there is some sense of motion in time as a secondary organizing principle. The motion from the center outward and from past to present is paralleled by a movement from simplicity to complexity. Thus there is also a thematic principle at work reflecting, reinforcing, and adding symbolic value to the spatial organizing principle.

> I lived, for the first four years of my life, in North Bend, British Columbia. Its setting was significant—an obscure grouping of houses nestled snugly atop the canyon wall at the edge of the muddy brown Fraser River. North Bend was seldom placed on maps because its total area was only a half square mile. However, that little hole of a town did, as it does now, exist in B.C.'s interior

land of dust and trees, blazing heat, and cruel winters. While I lived there that little hole was the world.

My world's focal point was my big white-with-pink-trim wooden house. From there I strayed in only two directions, forming a tightly closed triangular world. Slightly northwest of my house, on a small but pronounced hill, rested by best friend's yellow stucco home. It had a grey porch with majestic beams that supported the porch roof. I always stood and gazed at that house thinking it was the grand home of a great king. Yet I knew that, in reality, my friend's father was not a king. He did not even dress as a king.

The other point in my triangular world was directly west of my house. I remember it as the square pink general store at the end of the dusty dirt road. I used to go there often to buy a jaw breaker or maybe an orange popsicle to slurp on because of the scorching heat. Sometimes I would go back to my house and find my rusty red wagon abandoned beside my homemade wooden swing set, but usually my wagon was my source of transportation. It took me to my focus points, or perhaps I took it! I travelled to and from the three places, but I never found it necessary to visit any of the area in between them. There was nothing there except a few houses with neatly kept gardens.

What was beyond was, however, important because it seemed to threaten the static simplicity I had created in my world. Tall, thick-trunked, hanging-branched evergreens grew in an impenetrable mass not far behind my house. Their size and shape made them seem ominous and tough and frightening. Their existence fathered dreams of bears and wolves and other vicious animals attacking anyone who dared to walk into the forest.

Another feature outside my world also scared me. Small muddy-white cement homes, big enough to shelter perhaps three adults if they were standing upright, stood just by the edge of the canyon wall east of my house in a dusty, gravelly area. People of reddish-brown skin lived in these homes. I saw the houses only once, but the fear they instilled is with me even today. These houses were not right. They were not like my comfortable big house. Something about them was wrong. Therefore, both the mighty trees and the meagre homes I dismissed as not belonging to my world—I still knew they were there.

I realized, too, that the world might be a little bigger and more complex when I rode the cable for the first time. The cable was much like a basket box hanging from a tow line over the Fraser River. The box, like an article of clothing on a clothesline, was swung to the other side. The other side was a busy place. Cars whizzed by on the highway. Large stores, much bigger than my little pink store, were side by side along the shoulder of the street. I was troubled by the idea that my world was linked to this other world by a cable. That constituted a connection and I found it hard to see the relationship, for my world seemed not as complicated.

I feared aspects of North Bend that I could not easily understand fitting into my triangular setting. Perhaps the trees, the Indian homes and the buzzing little village across the river would have been less ominous had I not first of all created a simple setting. Yet I, as a child, wanted things to be simple, and I therefore resisted anything that seemed complex. North Bend was a town that I loved within my boundaries and feared in its entirety.

Susan-Ann Green

Note how the writer uses the "triangle" of her home, her friend's house, and the general store to help readers structure and visualize the details she presents. Note also how she selects certain points to emphasize while quickly passing over or even ignoring others. The assignment called on students to describe a place where they had grown up in such a way as to give strangers a sense of it. That became her principle of selection, and she did not need to attempt an objectively complete, physical description of North Bend.

It is also interesting how the writer uses sentence structure to reinforce perspective. When she writes most directly from the child's point of view, she uses childish sentence structures. Toward the end of the fourth paragraph, for example, she unnecessarily repeats *ands* as a child might. In other places, especially in the fifth and sixth paragraphs, she uses short, choppy sentences which contrast sharply with her normally complex style. She makes some use of comparison (e.g., "The box, like an article of clothing on a clothesline, was swung to the other side.") For the most part, however, she relies on the simple presentation of vivid detail and the contrasts produced by the juxtaposition of those details.

Such descriptions, given their assigned purpose, have much in common with literary descriptions. They aim not at a scientifically accurate description (which would demand an even-handed emphasis and an objective "completeness"); they aim rather to set mood, to give a sense of place. Such descriptions succeed best when readers are *shown* rather than *told about* whatever is being described.

With these points in mind, consider the following excerpt from a piece written by another student in the same class for whom English is a second language.

> Thirty years ago, my parents left China during the beginning of the Communist revolution. They settled in a small town near Saskatoon, Saskatchewan, which had a meagre population of two hundred. My father owned a store which had a market of clients living within a radius of one mile. The opportunities which exist in cities beckoned too many families and consequently, the store's business suffered. The increasing drainage of people soon reduced the town's population to a mere fifty. In 1968, we moved to Vancouver, where my present life began.
>
> I dislike living in the typical slum neighbourhood of run-down houses, weed-covered lawns, and littered street curbs. On hot summer nights, it is not uncommon to hear the man and woman living on the second floor of the apartment adjacent to our home sobbing hysterically, screaming obscenities and threatening each other—with the rest of the boarders who live on either side of the couple joining in the slanderous match. The neighbor living across

the street in his shabby, moss-covered house did little better. Two years ago, the police raided the house, arresting a girl on grounds of illegal possession of drugs while her father sat in a chair staring out his porch throughout the episode. It is very saddening to have such scenes blight an otherwise good day.

We are not a close family. We seldom show physical affection towards one another. Instead, we are a group of individuals who struggle to solve their problems privately. The inability to voice my conflicts has made my past life difficult, lonely and fiercely independent.

Dovey Wong

Objectively, the description is again incomplete—only one of the three paragraphs speaks directly to the assignment—but the passage fulfills its assigned purpose effectively. We get not only a sense of the neighborhood, but also a sense of the circumstances which are beyond the control of the writer and her family. We are told, moreover, about the internal nature of the family, which helps shape the response to the neighborhood. It is this context which makes poignant sense of the egocentric final sentence of the second paragraph.

A description is always a report of perceptions. But one makes observations for a wide variety of reasons. A scientist, a salesperson, and a novelist may write descriptions of the same piece of laboratory equipment; however, their selections of information and words will vary as radically as their purposes (and the purposes of their readers). The general principle is this: good description is based on the selection and accurate verbal representation of information that is relevant to the purposes that writing will serve. One need only contrast the descriptive styles of William Faulkner and Ernest Hemingway—or Albert Einstein and Karl Marx—or Pablo Neruda and George Eliot—or Jane Austen and Joan Baez—to realize that more specific rules about "good" description are either oversimplifications or applicable only to certain particular types of description.

ADDITIONAL READING

Harrington, John. *The Rhetoric of Film.* New York: Holt, Rinehart and Winston, 1973. Uses an analysis of film techniques to approach rhetorical principles that can be applied to written composition.

Primeau, Ronald. *The Rhetoric of Television.* New York: Longman, 1979. Uses an analysis of television to approach rhetorical principles that can be applied to written composition.

EXERCISE

1. Write a description of a place where you lived as a child. Write it in such a way as to give a stranger a sense of what it would be like to grow up there.

2. Write a description of a job you held, giving readers a sense of what it would be like to work at that job.

3. Select an emotion, and write a description of a person or place which evokes that emotion in readers.

4. Write a technical description of a piece of scientific apparatus which would allow a scientist, who wished to replicate an experiment in which that apparatus was used, to reconstruct it. (*Note*: Do not write instructions, just a description.)

5. Read an article in your area of special interest and write a 200-word abstract.

COMPARISON/CONTRAST

A distinction is a difference that makes a difference.
Gregory Bateson

There can be no distinction without motive . . .
G. Spencer Brown

SIMILARITIES AND DIFFERENCES

To think is to make distinctions. Perhaps *the* most basic mental act is to perceive similarities and differences. The rhetorical equivalent is comparison/contrast.

Effective description is often based on juxtaposition. The writer juxtaposes two or more images, and readers make the appropriate comparisons and contrasts. "Two years ago," reports Dovey Wong (page 233) "the police raided the house, arresting a girl on grounds of illegal possession of drugs while her father sat in a chair staring out his porch throughout the episode." Two images: the girl being arrested; the father just sitting and staring. The juxtaposition is poignant in part because of the images, and in part because of a contrast between the father's reaction and readers' expectations about how a father should react to his daughter's arrest. As in most literature, there is an implicit contrast between *what is* and *what could or should be.*

Explanation, likewise, is often based on comparison and contrast. In explanation, the writer goes beyond simple juxtaposition, however, and points out the similarities and differences. An explanation does not simply show; it tells. To *explain* is to *make plain* what readers might miss. You abstract similarities and differences for readers and try to make certain readers notice the distinctions that matter.

The following short essay is one black person's response to the way the word *black* is used in English.

THE ENGLISH LANGUAGE IS MY ENEMY!

A superficial examination of *Roget's Thesaurus of the English Language* reveals the following facts: the word WHITENESS has 134 synonyms; 44 of which are favorable and pleasing to contemplate, i.e., purity, cleanness, immaculateness, bright, shining, ivory, fair, blonde, stainless, clean, clear, chaste, unblemished, unsullied, innocent, honorable, upright, just, straight-forward, fair, genuine, trustworthy. Only ten synonyms for WHITENESS appear to me to have negative implications— and these only in the mildest sense: gloss over, whitewash, gray, wan, pale, ashen, etc.

The word BLACKNESS has 120 synonyms, 60 of which are distinctly unfavorable, and none of them even mildly positive. Among the offenders were such words as: blot, blotch, smut, smudge, sully, begrime, soot, becloud, obscure, dingy, murky, low-toned, threatening, frowning, foreboding, forbidden, sinister, baneful, dismal, thundery, evil, wicked, malignant, deadly, unclean, dirty, unwashed, foul, etc. . . . not to mention 20 synonyms directly related to race, such as: Negro, Negress, nigger, darky, blackamoor, etc.

When you consider the fact that *thinking* itself is sub-vocal speech—in other words, one must use *words* in order to think at all—you will appreciate the enormous heritage of racial prejudgment that lies in wait for any child born into the English language. Any teacher, good or bad, white or black, Jew or Gentile, who uses the English language as a medium of communication is forced, willy-nilly, to teach the Negro child 60 ways to despise himself, and the white child 60 ways to aid and abet him in the crime.

Who speaks to me in my Mother Tongue damns me indeed! . . . the English language—in which I cannot conceive myself as a black man without, at the same time, debasing myself . . . [is] my enemy, with which to survive at all I must continually be at war.

Ossie Davis, 1967

Recently the idea that thinking is always subvocal speech has been called into question, but that does not undermine Davis' main point. If you like, you can test Davis' response by going to the thesaurus yourself. Divide a sheet of paper into four columns for words (a) with good connotations, (b) with bad connotations, (c) with neutral connotations, and (d) words you do not know well enough to classify. Then copy on to that sheet all the synonyms for BLACK and WHITE from an unabridged thesaurus.

Of course, Ossie Davis presumably did not set out to write a comparison/contrast essay; he set out to make a point about the "racial prejudgment" inherent in the connotations of certain English words. Outside of composition courses, few people sit down with the intention of writing comparison/contrast essays. The comparison/contrast essay *as such* is an exercise. It is a useful exercise because it embodies the essence of a very basic thought process. Master this pattern of arrangement as an exercise, and it will be available to you later when you want to use it. This is the general principle behind practicing various patterns of arrangement, such as those described in the rest of this and subsequent chapters.

Comparison/contrast—the perception and representation of similarities and differences—is, moreover, implicit in all the patterns of arrangement discussed in this chapter. Classification and division, discussed in the next section, must be based on noting similarities among all that goes into each class and making distinctions between that and what does not. The main purpose of definition is to make a distinction between whatever is being defined and everything else. Analogies and examples are not only based on perceived similarities but also are usually designed to help readers perceive similarities and make distinctions.

TWO FORMATS

The conceptual process that underlies comparison/contrast can be represented by a grid.

	Subject A	Subject B
Characteristic 1:		
Characteristic 2:		
Characteristic 3:		
Characteristic 4:		
Characteristic 5:		
Characteristic 6:		
. . .		
Characteristic N:		

The number of characteristics you choose to include depends, of course, on your subjects and your purposes. It is also possible to do comparison/contrast among three or more subjects, but two is most common. In any event, you can generate your material by filling in a grid like the one diagrammed.

There are basically two ways to organize that material into a comparison/contrast essay. Ossie Davis uses the divided or "half-and-half" format. He makes all his points about *whiteness*; then he makes all his points about *blackness* (and then he moves to a higher level of generalization). The essential structure is this:

Introduction
Subject A (*whiteness*)
Subject B (*blackness*)
Conclusion

This is the easier comparison/contrast structure to compose and, since Ossie Davis' point is relatively simple, there is no reason to do anything more complicated.

If the substance is more complex, readers may need more help—or they may miss some of the points. Then one uses the alternating characteristics format. The essential structure is this:

Introduction
Characteristic 1
  Subject A
  Subject B
Characteristic 2
  Subject A
  Subject B
Characteristic 3
  Subject A
  Subject B
. . . etc.
Conclusion

The alternating characteristics format is a bit more work for writers. It is also safer in two ways. First, it forces writers to be more rigorous (you are not likely to leave out a point, as you might in an extended half-and-half comparison/contrast). And second, readers are not likely to miss any of your points. In academic contexts, if the comparison/contrast is extended, the alternating characteristics format is, therefore, generally preferred.

The following paper is a short piece of literary criticism that was written originally in the half-and-half format and then rewritten, using the same material, in the alternating characteristics format.

"LOOK WHAT THEY'VE DONE TO MY SONG, MA"

The 1962 New Canadian Library edition of Susanna Moodie's *Roughing it in the Bush* omits certain portions of the original 1852 London edition. The most significant of these omissions harm the reader's sense of the evolution of Moodie's response to the Canadian landscape and of her poetic style.

The nature poems and songs in the first half of the original edition document Moodie's Wordsworthean response to nature, reflected in her choice of language and imagery:

The mighty river, as it onward rushes
To pour its floods in ocean's dread abyss
Checks at thy feet its fierce impetuous gushes,

And gently fawns thy rocky base to kiss.
Stern eagle of the crag! thy hold should be
The mountain home of heaven-born liberty!

Here Moodie's verse is imitative, her rhyme is obtrusive, and her imagery is clichéd. She has written this poem from a decidedly European perspective—that of a recent Canadian immigrant trying to relate to the Canadian landscape, the Canadian experience, in terms of her English experience. In fact when Moodie wrote this poem, she had not yet set on foot on Canadian soil; she was still on the ship that brought her from England. How Moodie's naive expectations of life in the Canadian backwoods are to be rudely fulfilled.

The nature poems and songs in the second half of the original text, on the other hand, indicate that Moodie has become more realistically aware of and more adjusted to the Canadian landscape, and that she has found a more appropriate imagery to describe that landscape.

Come, launch the light canoe;
  The breeze is fresh and strong;
The summer skies are blue,
  And 'tis joy to float along,
    Away o'er the waters,
    The bright-glancing waters,
    The many-voiced waters,
As they dance in light and song.

Here Moodie's style is much more simple and direct, and her language is less flowery and clichéd. The attitude toward nature revealed in her verse is more realistic, more loving. Moodie has now come to terms with the Canadian landscape; she can appreciate the Canadian landscape for what it is and without contrasting it to her beloved England.

In terms of the apprenticeship theme of the text, then, the omission of Moodie's nature poems and songs from the 1962 edition of *Roughing It in the Bush* harms the reader's sense of the structure, style and emphasis of the original text. The poems and songs of the original edition document Moodie's role as a precursor to contemporary descriptions of the effect of the Canadian geography and climate on the Canadian imagination, and document Moodie's concern for finding an appropriate language to describe that landscape. Look what they—the Canadian writers—have done with her song.

Mishelle Panagopoulos

Here Mishelle writes first about the earlier poems that were omitted from the 1962 edition and then makes her contrast. In the following version, Mishelle begins with the same introductory paragraph and then tries the alternating characteristics format.

"LOOK WHAT THEY'VE DONE TO MY SONG, MA"

The 1962 New Canadian Library edition of Susanna Moodie's *Roughing It in the Bush* omits certain portions of the original 1852 London edition. The most significant of these omissions harm the reader's sense of the evolution of Moodie's response to the Canadian landscape and of her poetic style.

Moodie's response to the Canadian landscape, for example, changes in the course of the text. Her early poems indicate that she has written from a decidedly European perspective—that of a Canadian immigrant trying to relate the Canadian landscape, the Canadian experience, in terms of her English experience:

Queen of the West!—upon thy rocky throne,
In solitary grandeur sternly placed;
In awful majesty thou sitt'st alone,
By Nature's master-hand supremely graced.
The world has not thy counterpart, thy dower,
Eternal beauty, strength, and matchless power!

How Moodie's romantic and naive expectations of life in the Canadian backwoods are to be rudely fulfilled.

The later poems, on the other hand, indicate that Moodie has become more realistically aware of, more adjusted to the Canadian landscape:

Come launch the light canoe;
The breeze is fresh and strong:
The summer skies are blue,
And 'tis joy to float along,
Away o'er the waters,
The bright-glancing waters,
The many-voiced waters,
As they dance in light and song.

Moodie has now come to terms with the Canadian landscape—she can appreciate the Canadian landscape for what it is and without comparing it to her beloved England.

Secondly, Moodie's poetic style evolves in the course of the text. The nature poems and songs in the first half of the original edition document Moodie's Wordsworthean response to nature, reflected in her choice of language and imagery: "Stern eagle of the crag! thy hold should be/ The mountain home of heaven-born liberty!" Here Moodie's verse is imitative, her rhyme is obtrusive, and her imagery is clichéd.

The nature poems and songs in the second half of the original edition, on the other hand, indicate that Moodie has found a more appropriate language and imagery to describe the Canadian landscape. Her style is much more simple and direct, and her language is less flowery and clichéd:

When the snows of winter are melting fast,
  And the sap begins to rise,
And the biting breath of the frozen blast
  Yields to the spring's soft sighs,
    Then away to the wood
    For the maple, good,
Shall unlock its honied store.

In terms of the apprenticeship theme of the text, then, the omission of Moodie's nature poems and songs from the 1962 edition of *Roughing It in the Bush* harms the reader's sense of the structure, style and emphasis of the original text. The poems and songs of the original edition document Moodie's role as a precursor to contemporary descriptions of the effect of the Canadian geography and climate on the Canadian imagination, and document Moodie's concern for finding an appropriate language to describe that landscape. Look what they—the Canadian writers—have done to her song.

Mishelle Panagopoulos

Mishelle's first version was easier to write and seems to have a more unified effect. The second version requires more transitions. On the other hand, switching to the alternating characteristics format led Mishelle to change one quotation and to add another—both of which support her point more strongly than anything in the first version. The alternating characteristics format, since it tends to make writers (and readers) more aware of missing comparisons or weak support, often does generate better evidence and a tighter argument.

The point is not that one or the other format makes for a better comparison/contrast essay, but rather to demonstrate the effects of each. Which you should use will depend on what you are trying to accomplish. The following two essays were both written by the same advanced composition student. In the first he used the half-and-half format. In the second he used the alternating characteristics format.

The Borough of Ealing is a suburban town some eight miles west of the centre of London, England. In the 1930's, when I was a boy, it had a small population of perhaps 75,000 , which was thinly spread over its eight or ten square miles.

In the peaceful 1930's, Ealing was a dormitory suburb that had no industries. It was a very green and pleasant place, which was the domain of both a minority of working class folk, who occupied neatly kept row houses, and a majority of professional upper middleclass: civil servants, solicitors, architects and businessmen who resided in large detached mansions. These gentry, complete in bowler hats, all used the convenient and frequent Underground to travel to and from their offices in 'the West End' or the City of London itself.

Ealing, in fact, was so 'green' a suburb that it was known as 'The Queen of the Suburbs.' The streets were bordered by leafy English plane trees, and in the parks were many large horsechestnut trees, which were especially magnificent when in flower. The citizens of Ealing took joy and the borough council pride in their chestnut trees, and this pride was represented by three chestnut trees 'florissant' emblazoned on the Borough Coat of Arms.

Ealing possessed several parks; there were also two 'Commons.'[1] These contributed even more greenery, especially the two largest parks: Walpole Park and Lamas Park, which joined to make a green tract through the very centre of the town.

Ealing had few historical connections; however, Sir Robert Walpole, the 18th century statesman, chose Ealing for his suburban London home and built a large residence. This mansion, which was decorated with the advice of Robert Adam, the renowned 18th century architect, still survives complete with its gardens and grounds. The mansion itself is now in use as the Borough Library, and the gardens and grounds have become Walpole Park.

Ealing had a school system that was dominated by the English system of class. It was, therefore, divided into public, private and sectarian schools. Those who were Protestant and working class went to free government-run elementary and secondary schools, and could go to a technical college. The middle or upper class attended the fee-charging Dustin House private elementary and secondary school or Upper and Lower Bishop Latimer House School in neighbouring Hammersmith. From these schools they could graduate to University or the professions. Those who were Catholic, if they were working class, went to Catholic elementary and secondary schools. If upper class, they attended the fee-charging Preparatory School of St. Benedict and went on to the high fee-charging St. Benedict's Abbey School itself. There was also a similar St. Augustine's School for Girls.

The Abbey School, run by Benedictine monks, maintained high standards and was considered to impart the best education in the west of London; each year it had a large number of successful entrants in the University Entrance Exams and the competitive Civil Service Exam. Because of these successes, it attracted and accepted a sizeable number of non-Catholic students.

Ealing, then, was a pleasant place to live with its parks and good schools, but it had no glamour—no professional soccer team, rugby team or cricket eleven. The centre of town was a large collection of good 'shops.' There were two large department stores and no fewer than five genteel 'tea shops'; there were also two large hotels.[2] There was a choice of three cinemas: two large and ornate. The third, less ornate and dilapidated, was known unofficially as 'The Big House.' There was no live theatre in Ealing because the world's most famous actors could be seen in 'The West End,' which was only a half hour away on 'The Underground.' However, there were the Ealing Film Studios, which gained some fame for turning out the popular trite series of 'Ealing Comedies.'[3]

[1] Unenclosed and uncultivated public land.

[2] Public houses with restaurants.

[3] "Is there a doctor in the house," etc.

After the 1939-45 war, Ealing suffered a population explosion and today has ballooned to a mixed half a million. Nearly all the large detached mansions have been demolished and replaced by concrete tenement blocks; the few that remain have been renovated and divided up into flats. The town still remains a dormitory suburb that has no industries although it is no longer the domain of the professional upper class. The tenement blocks are populated by nearly half a million newcomers, a mix of Blacks, Asians and a minority of white working class. The upper class has chosen to move out to 'greener' places. The working class folk and their children, who have remained, together with the newcomers, find employment in industries that have mushroomed in surrounding areas, such as Heathrow Airport or the new high-rise office blocks in Brentford.

St. Benedict's Abbey School maintains its large number of successes in University and Civil Service Exams and, although it charges even higher fees, has become multiracial. More than half the student body is Hindu, Muslim or other non-Christian. This is evidence that parents, no matter what their religious beliefs may be, are willing to pay to send their children to the school that offers the best education.

Those who return to Ealing will no longer find it green and pleasant; instead it is now congested, polluted and dirty. The genteel tea shops in the centre of town have closed and the plane trees have been uprooted to widen the streets. They have been replaced by copper beech trees in concrete tubs.

Anthony Clarke

Delete the last three paragraphs, and this becomes a description not essentially different from Susan-Ann Green's description of North Bend (pages 230-231). Those three paragraphs create the contrast between Ealing as it was in the 1930s and Ealing as it is now. The effect is to re-create in readers some feelings the writer felt when revisiting his boyhood home. The description itself is rather "objective," but the feelings are evoked by the contrasts.

In the next piece, the same writer uses comparison/contrast to serve a very different purpose. An alternating characteristics format of comparison/contrast is embedded in an extended persuasion. The goal is to win sports fans over to ballet by demonstrating similarities between athletes and dancers.

DANCERS SHOULD BE REGARDED AS ATHLETES, AND AN OPERA HOUSE IS AS IMPORTANT AS A SPORTS ARENA

Dear Achilles:

It seems from the article published in last Saturday's edition of "The Sportsman" that you, as a sports fan, have some controversial views about dancers and ballet. You wrote ". . . that ballet is nothing but a bunch of girls running around on their tippy toes and fairys jumping about in white long-johns." You also argue that you cannot see any value in ballet training because ". . . dancers, especially males, are effete, and ballet performances are unnecessary and a waste of time, and do not deserve government subvention." Furthermore, you maintain "... that the money dance companies do receive from government sources should be cut and the money saved should be applied to amateur sport and better sports training facilities for youth which would assist their physical development and promote fitness." Finally, you conclude by advocating that "Sports arenas are more important than opera houses."

I must agree with you that you have raised points that many of your readers who have never seen a ballet performance may readily accept. However, you are a sportsman who always makes a fair summary of a game, and you are always ready to commend the opposing team for good play. So I am asking you to allow that there have to be two sides to any point of view, just as captains of opposing teams will take opposing sides on the fairness of a referee's ruling. Although I support the arts, I also enjoy watching fine athletes. With this in mind, can I first focus on your argument that there is no value in ballet training. I can sympathize with this point of view because, at first, it may appear that ballet training has nothing whatsoever in common with athletic sports or sports training programs which fall under your field of expertise. Your second argument, that the government should cut the money they give to dance and apply it to more sports training facilities for youth, is motivated no doubt, by your ongoing concern for the well-being and physical fitness of youth, and this point of view can also be understood.

The opposite point of view to yours would be that dancers and ballet companies deserve support by the government just as much as amateur sport and sport training facilities for youth. These, of course, are my views, but I do hope to persuade you that dancers and ballet companies deserve this different appraisal. This is because there happen to be quite a few similarities between dancers and athletes, some of which I would like to demonstrate. Indeed, the whole dance spectrum has many facets that resemble sport. To begin with, a ballet company has its own supporters, just like any hockey team or baseball team. For example, the National Ballet of Canada is now playing a six week season in Toronto to mostly full houses, that means 21,000 people a week—a total of some 125,000. This is more, in fact, than will see the Toronto Maple Leafs in the same period.

Can I appeal to your fairmindedness by first discussing the Olympic Games, the goal of the top athletes and sports fans in the world? There are some sports that I would like to single out in the games, and these are the ones on which you are considered an authority and will, perhaps, be covering in Moscow next summer: track and field, soccer and gymnastics. I know you will also be in Lake Placid for the Winter Olympics to cover hockey and skating.

Before any athlete is selected for the games, you might agree that his body will have been prepared by a training program that will have commenced as far back as childhood. This proves that athletes and dancers begin with one basic thing in common; they both have to be trained very early in life. In fact, a dancer begins serious training at the age of eight or nine years. Obviously, athletic training and exercises have to be very specialized and specific to the particular sport in question. So does dance training, for example, "contemporary" or "modern" dancers will concentrate on exercises that develop different strengths than classical ballet dancers require.

It was necessary to discuss the Olympics in order to demonstrate some of the facets of dance which are common to sports. Can we, now, suggest that, perhaps, you may wish to re-examine your views that dancers are weak and soft? Dancers have dedicated their lives to training their bodies which have to have almost perfect physical proportions. Ballerinas train for at least four or five hours a day, doing strenuous exercises to sharpen their technique, in addition to performing. They are often called upon to dance allegro variations, that is, dance full out for two minutes, which is equivalent to the 400 metre dash. The male dancer must be able to do the same, and *also* perform high turning jumps and be capable of supporting the ballerina in high overhead lifts. This requires stamina to burn and great strength in both legs and arms.

All athletes and dancers fear a common enemy, which is injury. Injury can result from a body contact or an accidental fall, however serious. Incapacitating injury can also result from a pulled muscle or snapped tendon or a strain. This kind of injury can often be avoided by stretching exercises in early training programs. These will lengthen the muscles, create greater elasticity in the tendons, and develop greater suppleness in the body. They can also be used to "warm up" the body prior to competitions. Most athletic coaches today have learnt about the value of the stretching exercises that dancers are trained with, and with the Iron Curtain coaches leading the way, they are incorporating more and more of such exercises into their training programs. Today, athletes rigorously warm up before competitions with stretching exercises just as dancers have been doing before performances, for the last few hundred years.

Many sports fans are not aware of the extent that athletes have borrowed exercises from the ballet curriculum. "Methods," such as "Cecchetti" or "Bournonville" or "Russian" build up leg muscles. They also improve coordination and develop a better ability to balance, and generally, strengthen all the body and back muscles. The Russian Olympic Hockey Team, for example, do floor exercises based upon ballet specifically to improve balance, to create suppleness, and to strengthen the legs. Perhaps this is why they regularly beat us at our own National game!

Some North American college football coaches order their players to attend a ballet class once a week in the College Dance Department to improve their footwork, balance and jumping. You will agree that gymnasts, whether performing on the parallel bars or executing their floor routines, exhibit the highest degree of balance and grace. Their floor routines are, when analyzed, just a combination of dance and gymnastic tumbling.

The skaters of the American Olympic Team train in Colorado Springs, where, in addition to several indoor ice rinks, there are also ballet studios and resident ballet teachers. Like the Russian Olympic skaters, some of whom have had training at the Bolshoi Ballet School itself, the American skaters regard ballet exercises as an important part of their training.

All this brings me to your final point. I agree with you that it is important that a city should have a good sports arena and training facilities for youth. In

Greece, where the Olympics began, the Grecian cities all had their arenas. However, in addition to their devotion to sport, the Greeks were also fond of dance and the theatre. The Greek democracies recognized that athletics were but one form of recreation and exercise, so they built amphitheatres to present dance and drama that were popular in those days.

Unfortunately, in our time, neither the athlete nor the dancer can exist without government support, especially when it comes to building sports arenas and opera houses. We can agree that both have their followers, and I put it to you that they should, therefore, both receive a fair share of the funds available.

I hope that this letter has made you change your mind a little and persuaded you that dancers should be regarded as athletes. Perhaps I can look forward to seeing you at the ballet one evening soon!

Yours sincerely,

Terpsichore

Anthony Clarke

The central strategy here is to win sports fans over by demonstrating similarities between the sports in which they already believe and the dance which they misconceive. The body of the paper is an extended comparison. The writer first demonstrates that he has some understanding of his readers and then works his way through a series of comparisons to a plea for sports fans to understand his position. The persuasive framework is Rogerian (see pages 339-350), not antagonistic.

Comparison/contrast can be put to a variety of expressive, explanatory, and persuasive uses. Occasionally, especially in expressive writing, it stands on its own. More typically, it provides a basis on which writers can build explanations and persuasions.

EXERCISE

1. Write a short comparison/contrast essay using the half-and-half pattern. Rewrite it using the alternating characteristics pattern. How does the effect vary?

2. Reading in your area of special interest, find several passages that use comparison/contrast. For what purposes is it used?

3. Find two or more writings on the same subject written for distinct purposes—for example, a journalist, a novelist, and an historian narrating the same event. Write a comparison/contrast of the two approaches.

4. Do a comparison/contrast of several pieces of literature with similar subjects—for example, D. H. Lawrence's *Sons and Lovers* and Agnes

Smedley's *Daughter of Earth* (both about growing up among coal miners) or the creation myths of the Hopis, Christians, and Taoists.

5. Compare and contrast two (or more) writers who have something important in common—for example, two nineteenth century English Romantic poets or two gothic novelists (perhaps Mary Shelley and Bram Stoker).

6. Compare and contrast several advertisements for similar products (perhaps aimed at distinct audiences).

7. Compare and contrast two analyses of the same war written by historians who sympathized with opposing sides—for example, a Canadian and a U.S. historian on the War of 1812.

CLASSIFICATION AND DIVISION

[P]erception takes whatever it perceives as a thing of a certain sort. All thinking from the lowest to the highest—whatever else it may be—is sorting. . . . [M]eanings, from the very beginning have a primordial generality and abstractness . . . . We begin with the general abstract everything, split it, as the world makes us, into sorts and then arrive at concrete particulars . . . .

I. A. Richards

Language is thus a way of experiencing the universe, of conceptualizing color, time, space, action, causality, and so on. All people do not see the world in the same way. Through language we divide and organize experience in different ways. Writing is one of many ways of experiencing reality, and an important one at that.

Frank D'Angelo

CATEGORIZING

Classification is the act of grouping, of putting your subject into a large category or class. Division is the act of breaking your subject down into smaller parts or aspects. Both involve the same thought process: making distinctions that establish boundaries on the continuum of experience. (The word *classification* is occasionally used loosely to include both.)

The color spectrum is a useful analogy for thinking about classification and division. The human eye is sensible to a certain continuum of light rays, from what we call ultraviolet to what we call infrared. When you look at a rainbow, you probably see red, orange, yellow, green, blue and purple. In other words, you divide the spectrum into six colors.

Actually, the human eye is capable of discriminating about 7,500,000 colors; the human mind, however, is not capable of dealing with 7,500,000 distinct colors, so it groups them. Our culture happens, for most ordinary purposes, to classify those 7,500,000 colors into six groups. Some cultures have only two or three distinct color words; others have more.

The important point—and one which is very hard to accept—is that most of the schema we use to classify and divide our experiences are not "natural" and do not exist materially in the world; instead, they are concepts that we use to organize our experiences. We cannot perceive, think, feel, or communicate without such schema, and one of the important functions of writing (especially academic writing) is to create and justify our schema. Classification and division are, therefore, very basic and important patterns of arrangement. Often it is very useful to put your subject into larger contexts by classifying it, and you must almost always divide your subject in order to write about it.

Real-world phenomena exist in overwhelming numbers and complexity. The ordinary human mind can handle approximately seven items (give or take two) in short-term memory. This is most apparent when we have to remember numbers. If you try to memorize the series "85490341," you will find it helpful to think of it as "854-903-41." Telephone numbers, credit card numbers, student identification numbers, and so forth, are usually so grouped.

The underlying thought process is crucially important. When Janice Carroll writes, "A major fault that runs consistently through my essays is the problem of fully developing themes and ideas" (page 18), she is classifying. She has taken a number of flaws in a number of essays and generalized a single class that englobes them all. She has reduced a number of flaws to a single problem and thus made an important step toward solving it.

The movement from "I don't know how to use commas properly" to "I misuse commas with coordinating conjunctions and with restrictive clauses" is division (because use of commas has been divided into a number of specific rules so that the two problematic rules can be selected out). Here division is used to identify a vague problem more specifically, and thus an important step is made toward solving it.

CHOOSING A SALIENT FEATURE

A classificatory schema is a mental construct, a thought structure we use to organize our perceptions. Different people will, for distinct purposes, use very different schema to categorize the same set of phenomena. Classificatory schema constrain us to emphasize certain features, deemphasize others, and ignore the rest. In this sense, they are like maps: just as we have various maps of the same terrain (e.g., road maps, hiking maps, nautical maps, aerial maps, geological maps), so we can have various schema. As a writer, you should be aware of this and choose schema that are relevant to your purposes (just as you would choose a nautical map for sailing, an aerial map for flying, and a geological map for prospecting). You should remember that any subject about which you are writing can be categorized in many distinct ways; then you should choose the way or ways that are appropriate.

There are, for instance, almost two hundred countries in the world, too many for most of us to think about individually. So we classify them. To do so, we must choose a *salient feature*. If the salient feature is *location* (by continent), then Canada, the United States, and Mexico go in one class; Japan, China, Thailand, and Vietnam in another. If the salient feature is *population*, then Canada goes with Thailand and Vietnam, Japan with the United States and Mexico, and China in a class by itself. If the salient feature is *size*, however, then China goes with Canada, the United States, and Mexico.

The point is that classificatory schema are not "natural" or neutral: they are purposive. The choice of schema can have important implications. When you construct a classificatory schema for a piece of writing, you should be conscious of the salient feature on which it is based, and you should think about the implications of using that particular schema.

Classificatory schema are not totally arbitrary; they are based on real features of the phenomena being categorized. In Chapter 0, for example, writing was classified as a craft (page 8). Two paragraphs were devoted to trying to convince you to perceive writing neither as a skill, nor as an art, but as a craft. You might wonder why anyone would make a big deal out of such a distinction. The answer is that classifications carry hidden assumptions. If writing is a skill, like typing or swimming, then one can presumably master it through training in a series of subskills—and most of the theory in this text is superfluous. If writing is an art, like sculpture, then technique, though important, is secondary—and one would do better to try to inspire than to teach it. Only if writing is a craft, like silversmithing or furniture-making, does the mixture of theory and technique in this book make sense. The classification in and of itself may not matter, but the unexamined assumptions it brings with it do matter. Depending on whether they perceive writing as a skill, craft, or art, people take radically distinct approaches to learning or teaching it. And, if we can agree on the distinctions among the three terms, then the correct classification of writing is an empirical question to be answered by examining the nature of the writing process.

The person choosing the salient feature on which to base a particular categorization does sometimes have considerable leeway. How much leeway varies from case to case. The following lists of synonyms for "masculinity" and "femininity" were selected from *Roget's International Thesaurus* (3rd edition):

> MASCULINITY: *manliness, manhood, mannishness, gentlemanliness, virility, potency, sexual power, manly vigor, manhood, homo, sire, fellow, chap, guy, bloke, gent, don, sahib, he-man, full-blooded, viripotent, ultramasculine, he-manish, two-fisted, broadshouldered, hairy-chested, uneffeminate, hoyden.*
>
> FEMININITY: *womanliness, muliebrity, ladylikeness, matronliness, effeminacy, effeminateness, androgyny, sissiness, prissiness, milksopism, homo-sexuality, womankind, woman, calico, the distaff, the sex, the opposite sex, the fair sex, softer sex, weaker sex, "the lesser man," womanbody, weaker vessel, milady, gentlewoman, dame, dowager, squaw, girl, hen, biddy, petticoat, skirt, broad, curve, fem, frail, moll, "a rag a bone and a hank of hair," "God's second mistake," "one of Nature's agreeable blunders," secrets, "a necessary evil," "the female of the human species and not a different kind of animal," mollycoddle, old wife, henhussy, mother's darling, mamma's boy, muff, chicken, goody-goody, pantywaist, cream puff, powder puff, ladyfinger, lily, weak sister, softy, demasculinize, womanly, unmanly, womanish, chichi.*

Perhaps the first question this listing ought to bring to mind is one of validity. Why did the editors of the thesaurus choose to classify under "femininity" words like "homosexuality," "demasculinize," "goody-goody," and "cream puff"? Why are there quotations under "femininity," but no comparable quotations under "masculinity"? In other words, what were the salient features by which the editors created this listing?

Using Ossie Davis' "The English Language is My Enemy!" as your model (see pages 235-238), consider how you would categorize these words. You will probably find that the synonyms for masculinity/femininity do not fit so neatly and easily into good/bad as did the synonyms for black/white; but you should be able to categorize them. What features of the traditional images of masculinity and femininity are implicit in the connotations of the words listed? What stereotypes (if any) of men and women are built into the English language?

Note how the preceding two questions provide a purpose that guides your categorization, leading you to select certain features as salient. The features are real: the words do have those connotations. But the words could be grouped in other ways (e.g., calico, petticoat, skirt, and pantywaist could be grouped as having to do with clothing; hen, biddy, henhussy, and chicken as having to do with poultry).

Like comparison/contrast, classification and division are patterns of arrangement that can serve various purposes and often are parts of larger writings. Classification, in particular, is often used to provide a context for the actual subject. Here, for instance, is a classificatory paragraph excerpted from a student's essay about the journal as a literary form.

> The memoir, autobiography, diary and journal may be grouped together as literature of personal revelation. In each form, the interest for the reader lies, to a large extent, in the self-portrayal of the author. Memoirs usually give some prominence to personalities and activities other than the writer's own, and sometimes convey an historical event described from a personal viewpoint. Autobiographies are narratives of an author's life with stress upon introspection, or upon the significance of their life against a wider background. Diaries and journals recount personal impressions while they are still fresh in the mind of the author and often provide reappraisals in the light of later experience. "What they lose in artistic shape and coherence, they [diaries and journals] gain in frankness and immediacy, many of the most famous having been kept with little if any thought of subsequent publication."[1] Although the two terms are identical in primary meaning, the journal has gained a slight differentiation of being a more reflective or detached record than the diary.
>
> Dianne Longson

[1]Joseph T. Shipley, ed., *Dictionary of World Literary Terms*, p. 23.

Here the journal is classified, along with three other forms, under the heading, "literature of personal revelation." That heading itself suggests a larger schema:

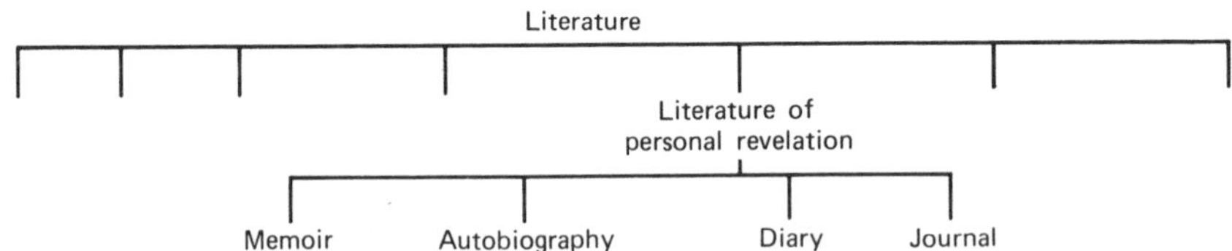

This classificatory paragraph serves to locate the subject of the writing so that readers will know where it fits into a larger body of knowledge. The paragraph is developed by a comparison/contrast among the four forms. The first two sentences establish a basic similarity; the rest of the paragraph makes distinctions. The final emphasis falls on the most problematic distinction, between the diary and the journal.

DIVISION AND PARTITION

Almost every piece of writing utilizes division to at least some degree. The subject matter must be divided into its parts or aspects, and those parts or aspects must be arranged in some order. Ordinarily, it is useful to make this division explicit for readers (see pages 137-147 on frameworks and especially pages 137-142 on openings).

This *partition* (to use the classical term) is virtually inevitable because of the nature of the medium: in ordinary written verbal communication, one cannot say simultaneously all that one wants to say—not even in the sense that one sometimes can with a picture, or a gesture, or a tone of voice. Written words come one after another in a line, as do sentences, paragraphs, and larger units of language. Although poets (and other verbal artists) may transcend these lineal limitations of verbal communication through the use of metaphor and other forms of comparison, writing ordinarily involves making one point first, another second, another third, and so forth. The subject must be somehow divided and ordered if it is to be communicated in expository prose. Indeed, it must be divided and ordered if it is to be thought about in certain ways that we call "rational" or "logical." This constraint is sometimes a boon and produces very useful analyses; it can also be a problem that creates contradictions. As I write these words, I am struggling with one version of this problem: on the one hand, if I want to help people learn, I should discuss classification, division, comparison/contrast, definition, analogy, and exemplification as simply as possible; on the other hand, an important "part" of what I am saying is that you should see these patterns of arrangement as variants of one basic thought process. I could write this chapter most simply (and make it most easy for you to read) if I treated these six patterns as totally distinct; but I think that any real understanding of these patterns must include the realization that classification and division are opposite sides of the same coin, that analogy is a form of comparison/contrast, and so forth.

Division, in other words, is both a useful and a dangerous pattern: the real phenomenon you are discussing may be distorted or oversimplified in the process of partition. Using division can lead you inadvertently to imply that the whole is equal to the sum of its parts, that nothing essential gets lost in the process of discussing each part separately. You may not see the forest for the trees, not see the ecosystem because you are concentrating on the mosquitos. Nonetheless, we cannot ordinarily write without using division.

Obviously, division is more easily applied to some subjects than to others. Consider this metaphor: you can take an automobile engine apart, study each part, and put it back together again without losing anything; but do not try to perform the same operation on someone's pet dog. Students who complain when an English teacher makes them "dissect" poems are objecting precisely because once they get the "parts" analyzed they cannot get the poem together again. (The solution, incidentally, is not to stop analyzing poems but to learn how to get them back together again.) When you use division, therefore, be careful to compensate for any mechanistic errors that may sneak into your analysis and distort what you are trying to communicate.

Although the philosophical implications are complex, the practical applications often are not. Any pattern of arrangement you are using will suggest how to divide your subject matter; by careful use of framing paragraphs, transitions, and qualifiers, you can avoid mechanistic errors.

Academic writers, in particular, often use thesis sentences to divide and order their papers. How well this technique works depends in large part on how specific the division is. One student, for instance, began an essay on anger like this:

> Anger has both positive and negative points.

The positive point to be made about that sentence is that it does serve to divide and order the paper. The negative point is that it is vague and, therefore, less helpful to readers than it might be—virtually any phenomenon has both positive and negative aspects.

The following thesis sentences, used by students from the same class, perform the same function somewhat more specifically:

> This paper analyzes and compares two marital typologies—monogamy and group marriage—with an attempt to convince you of the potential strengths of the latter and the possible weaknesses of the former.

> Kissinger's personal characteristics, his ideas, and his previous experiences were major factors influencing his strategy to end the war. These factors immediately narrowed his range of options and forced him to make the particular choices he did during his five years at the White House.

The first is much more formal (aside from the second-person pronoun, *you*) than the second, but both serve to divide the subject and allow the reader to anticipate the overall shape of the essay. Both, incidentally, also suggest a secondary division between explanation (presumably "factual") and conclusion (more opinionated). Generally, the more specifically you can help your reader anticipate how you are going to divide and order your material, the more coherent and readable your writing will be.

Remember that *any* subject can be divided in various ways. The real world is continuous—as Thoreau said, pick up anything and you will find it attached to the rest of the universe. The divisions we make are the product of an interaction between our minds and that real world. These divisions, although they may correspond with certain features of the phenomenon, do not exist "in" objective reality. As a writer (and a thinker), you are responsible for choosing those divisions that are most useful to your purposes and most appropriate to your audience.

ADDITIONAL READING

Berthoff, Ann. *Forming/thinking/writing.* Rochelle Park, N.J.: Hayden, 1978. See pages 50-62 on "Listing and Classifying: Purposes and Presuppositions" for a practical discussion of the implications of classification.

EXERCISE

1. Do an "audience analysis" that classifies and divides the probable readers of something you intend to write.

2. Do an analysis of the types of writing that are common in your area of special interest. Classify writing in that area, relative to writing in general. Distinguish (divide) the various types of writing within the area. Do this classification and division in terms of both function (i.e., rhetorical context) and form (i.e., patterns of arrangement, format, conventions, etc.)

3. Write an essay analyzing a dispute that turns on how to categorize people (e.g., "Should principals be allowed to join a teachers' union?" "Can apartheid be justified in South Africa?" "Do girls have a right to play on Little League baseball teams?" "Should Haitian 'boat people' be allowed into the United States as political refugees?" Remember your primary purpose is to *explain* the dispute as an issue that turns on how people are categorized. If you want to use that explanation as a basis for asserting your opinion, do so. But be certain your essay includes the assigned analysis.

4. It is asserted in Chapter 0 that writing should be classified as a craft, not as a skill or an art. That classification is asserted in order to make a point about how writing ought to be learned. Find another example where classification is used to set up an argument, and write a short analysis.

DEFINITION

". . . and that shows that there are three hundred and sixty-four days when you might get un-birthday presents—"

"Certainly," said Alice.

"And only one for birthday presents, you know. There's glory for you!"

"I don't know what you mean by 'glory,'" Alice said.

Humpty Dumpty smiled contemptuously. "Of course you don't—till I tell you. I meant 'there's a nice knock-down argument for you!'"

"But 'glory' doesn't mean 'a nice knock-down argument,'" Alice objected.

"When I use a word," Humpty Dumpty said in rather a scornful tone, "it means just what I choose it to mean—neither more nor less."

"The question is," said Alice, "whether you can make words mean so many different things."

"The question is," said Humpty Dumpty, "which is to be master—that's all."

Lewis Carroll

The master's right of giving names goes so far that it is permissible to look on language itself as the expression of the power of the masters. They say: "This is that and that." Finally sealing every object and every event with a sound, they thereby at the same time take possession of it.

Friedrich Nietzsche

WHAT IS A DEFINITION?

Definition is a particularly important form. It embodies in one rhetorical form both sides of the thought structure with which this chapter is concerned: to define a concept you must both put it in a category (*classify* it, show what it is *similar* to) and also indicate how it is distinct from all else in that category (in-*divide*-ualize it). Defining your terms is often a good way to make sure you know (and can articulate) what you think you know. Definition of the central concept is often a good way to begin a writing. Indeed, in certain types of writings, definition of key terms is mandatory.

The word *define* comes from the Latin, *finire*, "to limit or end," which itself comes from *finis*, "boundary." To define is to establish limits, to make distinctions, to draw out-lines, to articulate boundaries.

To define "yellow," for example, we classify it as a color and then create two boundaries on the spectrum, which distinguish it from orange, on the one hand, and green, on the other. We put it in a class ("color") and distinguish it from all other members of the class. The function of a definition is to allow someone to distinguish the defined concept from all else, and such a definition of "yellow" does so.

Note that this definition exists in our minds, not in the spectrum (see page 249). It is a concept we use to perceive, think, feel, and communicate about color. People from other human cultures divide the spectrum differently. Although they certainly perceive the wavelengths of light we call "yellow," in a significant sense they do not "see yellow" if they have not defined or conceptualized it.

We say definition is an abstract form of description because a definition is a description of an abstract concept. You can describe the yellow color of a particular schoolbus. To see that bus *as yellow*, however, you must preconsciously juxtapose it with your concept of yellow (see pages 210-212). You see the bus in terms of your concept of yellow, and your definition of yellow describes that concept. To see it as a schoolbus, moreover, you must preconsciously juxtapose it with your concept of schoolbus, and your definition of schoolbus describes that concept.

Ordinarily, of course, when we want a definition, we do not become introspective and examine our concepts. We turn to a dictionary. Consequently, some people think definitions *come from* dictionaries. Indeed, the aura of absolute authority that surrounds "the dictionary," might lead you to suspect that the makers of dictionaries received their definitions from some omniscient deity.

In reality, however, a dictionary definition of a word is a generalized description of the way a certain class of people use that word—that class usually being those who the dictionary makers define as "literate." A dictionary definition is, therefore, a sociological "fact" about how certain people use the word; it can, therefore, be judged as true or false.

Dictionary makers examine texts by noted authors, political leaders, and other such people. They isolate sentences using the word to be defined and then compose a definition (or set of definitions) that covers all those uses. This is easier if one is defining "desk" than if one is defining "pretty" or "tragedy." But the process remains the same. A dictionary definition is an abstracted and generalized description of how a certain word is actually used by certain people at a certain time in history.

To get a sense of how this dictionary-making process works, you could ask a group of people to complete a sentence, such as "A *man* is a person who . . ." or "Being a *man* means . . . ." (You may, of course, substitute any other word you are interested in defining.) After you have a sufficient number of responses, try to categorize and generalize them. If you are using the term *man*, you will probably get a definition (or set of competing definitions) of *masculinity* rather than "A *man* is an adult male *Homo sapiens*." That is all right: *man* is an interesting word to define these days precisely because our definition of masculinity seems to be in the process of changing.

Here is what happened when a group of seventh and eighth graders from mid-Michigan were asked to complete such a sentence in 1973.

BEING A *MAN* IS . . .

The girls' answers:

. . . being able to do more things than a woman.
. . . not much.
. . . being strong.
. . . to act like a man.
. . . accepting responsibility. (2)
. . . being mature and brave. (2)
. . . being able to be independent and responsible.
. . . liking girls. (2)
. . . being a good friend to a girl.
. . . being a male chauvinist pig. (2)
. . . taking care of a family.
. . . understanding your daughters' and sons' problems.
. . . a lot, being strong and brave.
. . . accepting responsibility when you have a family. But I was not dumb enough to be born a male!

The boys' answers:

. . . being loyal to your country.
. . . best.
. . . being a hard worker.
. . . being a neat dude.
. . . being responsible, grown up acting, and not being a baby.
. . . growing up and being on your own, having a job and being able to go when you want to, and be responsible for something.
. . . better than being a woman.
. . . great.

... being a girl's friend.
... to be old enough to judge yourself.
... not any fun.
... not often.
... caring and supporting a family.
... super cool.
... strength, power, leadership, judgment.
... having pride.
... having authority.
... accepting responsibilities such as taking authority, having a job, and going to school.
... super tough.

These responses embody a somewhat contradictory sense of manhood. Although there are certainly similarities, there seem to be some distinctions between the way the girls conceptualize it and the way the boys do. If one were to do a sampling in another place (or in 1983), moreover, one might well get significantly different responses. These distinctions are real because the social concept of masculinity is changing. A good definition would reflect (and possibly even make some sense of) the distinctions and contradictions. (Compare the list of synonyms for "masculinity" and "femininity" on page 251 and Ossie Davis' essay on "blackness" and "whiteness," pages 235-236.)

The seventh and eighth graders were responding to a word. Words matter because they name concepts, and concepts matter because they influence our perceptions. Definitions matter because they describe concepts. In and of themselves, of course, words do not matter: "Sticks and stones will break my bones, but names will never harm me." But the words name concepts, and the concepts influence people's perceptions; and those perceptions may lead people to pick up "sticks and stones." So words do matter. It is not "*just* semantics."

A language, of course, reflects the culture that shaped it historically. One would expect the English language to contain words and phrases which express the attitudes that English-speaking people have had. It would not make much sense to blame the language for cultural stereotypes; after all, the language was created by people (and certain types of people—e.g., English teachers and employers—have had more influence than others).

Now that the language exists, however, it does help to define the perceptions and attitudes of the people who learn and use it. The English language did not cause cultural stereotypes, but it does help to perpetuate them. It is one of the social factors that affect the development of an individual's ideas. In this sense and to this degree, our language defines us. As we go on to work with the formal processes of logical definition, it is important to remember that definition is a social process with which we live all the time. Formal definition is simply a verbal representation of that process.

FORMAL DEFINITION

The standard formula for definition is to give the *class* to which a term belongs and then show how it is *distinct* from all other members of that class.

DEFINITION	=	CLASS	+	DISTINCTIONS
A chair is		a piece of furniture		that has a back and is used for seating one person.

By putting *chair* in the class *furniture*, we distinguish it from most of the rest of the universe and reduce the task of defining it to manageable proportions. Had we said merely *a chair is a type of object*, completing the definition would be significantly more difficult. The phrase *used for seating* distinguishes chairs from most other furniture (bookshelves, television stands, dressers, china closets, etc.). *Has a back* rules out stools. *For one person* rules out couches and loveseats.

Thus we have a definition that can be used as a tool; one can go through the world armed with this definition and distinguish chairs from everything else, including other types of seats. This definition is not true or false—except in the sense that it matches fairly closely the way most English-speaking people do indeed use the word *chair*. Insofar as it does not match this usage (or perhaps even insofar as we decide this usage ought to change), we will have to revise our definition.

Yet all of this is not very interesting so long as we are defining *chair*. You probably already know what a chair is and are perfectly capable of distinguishing one from a stool, couch, or loveseat. But what if we define a term you are not so sure about, or a term whose definition is debatable, or a term that we wish to use in an unusual sense for some special reason? Suppose we define *tragedy* or *communism*.

DEFINITION	=	CLASS	+	DISTINCTIONS
A tragedy		is an imitation of an action		that is serious, complete and of a certain magnitude; in language embellished with each kind of artistic ornament, the several kinds being found in separate parts of the play; in the form

			of action, not of narrative; through pity and fear effecting the proper purgation of these and similar emotions.
Communism	is	a type of society	in which the workers control the means of production and goods are distributed according to need.

The definition of tragedy is Aristotle's, and it worked quite well for the tragic drama of classical Greece. Since then, however, a great deal of literature has been produced that many critics consider tragic, some of which is not drama and much of which would not meet Aristotle's other criteria. Considerable effort has been expended, therefore, on deciding which literary works should be considered tragedies (e.g., Is Milton's *Samson Agonistes* a tragedy? Is Dreiser's *An American Tragedy?* Is Miller's *Death of a Salesman?*) and on trying to redefine the term. The problem has been seen as how to broaden the term enough to include all of what the critic would consider tragedy without broadening it so much as to make any text with an unhappy ending a "tragedy."

The definition of communism is Marx's. If we accept it, none of the "Communist" countries in the world today would qualify, and many of them might not even qualify as "moving toward" communism. Indeed, if you hear such a definition of communism today, it is likely to be in the context of a discussion about whether the Soviet Union is really a communist country.

EFFECTIVE DEFINITIONS

In addition to the basic formula, there are certain rules we can state about *formal* logical definitions. (These rules do not necessarily apply in informal contexts.)

1. *In order to function effectively a formal logical definition should not contain* any synonyms *or* derivatives *of the word being defined.*

Do *not* say: A beautiful man is one who is unusually attractive.

Communism is a form of government in which the Communist Party runs the country.

Humor is a disposition caused by being exposed to something funny.

Synonyms can be useful for expanding formal definitions or for giving informal definitions; but from a logical point of view they are tautological (i.e., circular reasoning). Although it might be useful to a person learning English who happened to know the word *attractive* but not the word *beautiful*, the first definition essentially says merely that *beautiful* is a stronger synonym for *attractive*.

The second definition will not help a person who does not know what the words *communist* or *communism* mean. On the other hand, one might well want to use that definition in a statement like, "According to Marx, communism is a type of society in which the workers control the means of production and goods are distributed according to need; but in many so-called 'communist' countries, communism seems to be merely a form of government in which the Communist Party runs the country." Thus, although the latter definition is not a logical formal definition, it may still be a useful and meaningful statement (which we should probably classify as an ironic definition).

2. *A formal logical definition should not contain words that are ambiguous, figurative, or obscure.*

Do *not* say: An immature person is one who is very sensitive.

To be ironic is to speak with a forked tongue.

A net is any reticulated fabric, decussated at regular intervals, with interstices at the intersections.

There are several problems with the first definition, one of which is that it begins to make sense only if the ambiguous word *sensitive* is construed in only one of several possible ways. The second definition is an insightful cross-cultural metaphor, which may possibly have broadened or sharpened your sense of the word *ironic*, if you already know what that word means. But it probably was not of much use if you did not understand the word to begin with. And the third definition, one of Samuel Johnson's most famous ironic definitions, would not be useful to people who did not know what *net* signified because such people would be highly unlikely to know half the other words in the definition.

3. *A formal logical definition should use the same parts of speech as the term you are defining. (Avoid using "is when" or "is where.")*

Do *not* say: Swimming is when you propel yourself through the water with parts of your body.

Women's liberation means they give women the right to crash men's clubs.

Definitions like these are not always wrong, but they tend to be. The first one needs merely syntactical revision: "Swimming is the act of propelling . . ." etc. In the second one, however, the writer has given an example rather than a formal definition (and an inaccurate example at that).

4. *A formal logical definition should be positive.*

Do *not* say: A whale is a big animal that lives in the ocean and is not a fish.

When one defines terms negatively, one tends to be imprecise. Precision, in this case, means saying "is a mammal" rather than "is not a fish."

5. *Generally, try to keep formal logical definitions as tight and precise as possible.*

The underlying principle here is the same as the general stylistic principle which calls for tight construction of most sentences.

Consider, for example, the following definition from a student's paper:

> Boredom is that state in which an individual is, to different degrees, uninterested in his present situation or the events at hand.

Must boredom be individual? Could not a group (e.g., an audience) be bored? Must that which bores be present or at hand? Could one not be bored by the actions of a governmental body thousands of kilometers away? Is there any point in stipulating "to different degrees"? Would one not assume that such a state could be experienced to different degrees unless the writer stated otherwise? In short, gobbledygook removed, does this definition not reduce itself to the following: "Boredom is the state of being uninterested"? Having reduced it to that, are we not in a better position to consider just how useful a logical definition it is? (Of course, the student who wrote it may well have written it in gobbledygook precisely to make it sound more impressive—not an unjustifiable response to a situation in which one is being judged, but not a useful way to reach the clearest possible definition of the term either.)

Another student wrote,

> Child abuse shall be defined in this essay as intentional bodily assault, sexual molestation or neglect causing bodily harm to any child under seventeen years of age.

The style here is quite formal, but it is not gobbledygook; and the definition is quite precise.

This last definition came from a causal explanation, the primary purpose of which was not to define child abuse, but to explain why it occurs. It was written by a young woman who was willing to admit that she was an abused child, and she wrote the paper in order to deepen her own understanding of what had happened to her. Writers often use formal definitions in this way. Such definitions are called *stipulative definitions*, because the writer is saying, in effect, "For the purposes of this paper, I *stipulate* that child abuse will mean . . . ." A stipulative definition is often a one-sentence, formal logical definition set into a larger paper written for another purpose.

EXTENDING DEFINITIONS

Other pieces of writing are centrally and primarily "definition papers," sometimes called *extended definitions*. Such a paper almost always contains a precise formal logical definition, but it also goes beyond that definition in an attempt to give a fuller sense of an important concept. The techniques used for expanding definitions are also useful as definitions in less formal contexts; for example, if your husband looks up from the book he is reading and asks what a word means, you might respond most usefully and simply with a synonym or an example.

1. *Definitions can be expanded by synonyms.*

One student, who was expanding her definition of anger as "the natural reflexive result of frustration—our reaction to having a goal blocked," turned to her thesaurus (often a dangerous turn, but one which she utilized effectively) and produced the following paragraphs (the middle paragraphs of a twelve-paragraph essay).

> Anger is sometimes hidden even from ourselves because it hides behind resentment, aggression, frustration, hate, fury, indignation, outrage, wrath, antagonism, crossness, hostility, bitterness, destructiveness, spite, rancor, ferocity, scorn, disdain, enmity, malevolence, and defiance. Actually, no matter how it is described, it still all means we are simply angry.
>
> Our vocabulary has become very rich in describing other people who are angry. We call people mad, bitter, frustrated, griped, fed up, sore, excited, seething, annoyed, troubled, antagonistic, or antagonized, exasperated, vexed, indignant, furious, provoked, hurt, irked, irritated, sick, cross, hostile, ferocious, savage, deadly, dangerous, and on the offensive. A lot of words, but they often mean the same thing—angry.
>
> What happens as a result of anger is behavior which prevents communication. This kind of behavior, which is communication-shattering, is described as, to hate, wound, damage, annihilate, despise, scorn, disdain, loathe, vilify, curse, despoil, ruin, demolish, abhor, abominate, desolate, ridicule, tease, kid, take out spite on, rail at, scold, bawl out, humble, irritate, beat up, take for a ride, ostracize, fight, beat, vanquish, compete with, brutalize, crush, offend or bully. We are angry—face the fact!
>
> Janice Moulton

An entire essay written in this way would probably not work very well. But these three paragraphs came in the context of a longer writing, one point of which was that we too often try to deny and disguise our anger when we would be better off if we accepted it and tried to direct it effectively (at least when our goals are just and righteous). Note also that the synonyms were used to expand, not to state the definition.

In another essay, this same student illustrates two other techniques for expanding definitions.

2. *Definitions can be expanded by examples and analogies.*

A logical definition is logically sufficient, but often we do not fully comprehend a concept until it is concretized. Thus Janice writes,

> In the New Testament in the Book of Hebrews, it says that "to have faith is to be sure of the things we hope for, to be certain of the things we cannot see." Faith is what won man's approval to God in ancient times. Faith lets us believe that God created the universe. Faith made Abel sacrifice something better than Cain. Faith made Noah hear God's warning. Faith made Abraham become a father way past his age. . . .

(Note, incidently, Janice's effective use of parallel structure in both this and the preceding example.)

3. *Definitions can be expanded by comparison and/or contrast.*

Janice, defining "faith" suggests that it is very similar to trust, except that trust is based on good reasons or evidence. Another student in the same course extended a definition of "magic" by contrasting it with scientific rationalism.

As you might have guessed, definitions can be clarified and sharpened by using any of the other basic rhetorical patterns discussed in this chapter. They may also be expanded using the patterns discussed in Chapter 5, which can help establish the significance of a concept.

4. *Definitions can be expanded by narration, process-analysis, causal analysis, or logical progression.* (See Chapter 5.)

You can tell a story that brings out the implications of a term or concept. You can explain how it might be used, why it came to exist, or what purposes it serves. You can relate it to processes or functions, to past and future.

One very common way to expand a definition is to give the etymology of the term. Thus a student defining "political modernization" wrote, "The Greek word *polis* is the root of the word 'political' and originally referred to the Greek city-state; [it has come to refer to] any organization of human beings in groups." In an article I wrote recently about error, I noted the derivation from the Latin *errare*, to wander, and went on to argue that, "just as wandering can be defined only in terms of a destination, so errors should be defined only in terms of goals," The etymology and history of a word often tells us a great deal about the concept it represents (and about the people who formed that concept). Does it suggest anything to you that, according to the *Oxford English Dictionary*, the word *man* once referred to any adult and the word *girl* to any child? (See pages 173-174.)

Definitions can be expanded by discussing why's and wherefore's. A definition of water might be expanded by noting that it can be created by burning hydrogen in oxygen. It might also be expanded by listing the multitude of functions water has in an industrialized society. Kenneth Burke expands his definition of rhetoric by saying that rhetoric

> is rooted in an essential function of language itself, a function that is wholly realistic and is continually born anew: the use of language as a symbolic means of inducing cooperation in beings that by nature respond to symbols.

In the same section of *A Rhetoric of Motives*, he points out that rhetoric is an ingredient in all socialization processes, that the manipulation of people's beliefs for political ends has been "a most characteristic concern of rhetoric, and [is] the use of words by human agents to form attitudes or to induce actions in other human agents."

ESSENTIAL AND OPERATIONAL DEFINITIONS

The potential to expand definitions by talking about function suggests a very important distinction between two types of definitions: the essential and the operational. An essential definition defines something in terms of what it *is* (essence); an operational definition in terms of what it *does* (function). An essential definition of a human being might be "an erect, bipedal, giant mammal relatively unspecialized in body form." An operational definition of a human being might be "a social mammal that survives and produces by means of cooperation, typically uses tools and symbolic language, and whose nature is shaped more significantly by socialization than by heredity." Note that both definitions use the same class (mammal) and that there is no contradiction between them. Which type of definition you should use in any given case depends to some extent on the concept you are defining but more importantly on your purpose.

Typically, in modern Western culture, philosophy has been concerned with *essences*, with determining the "inner nature"of phenomena, with that which remains the same as more superficial "outer" characteristics change. Western philosophers have assumed that what we *are* determines what we *do*; that is why we reserve the phrase *essential definition* for definitions based on what something is, on its "inner" nature. More recently, certain philosophies (e.g., existentialism) have argued that what we do determines what we are—in effect, asking for an operational definition. Operational definitions have been more common in the sciences and technologies—generally in fields that are process-oriented and concerned with results.

To bring this discussion down to earth, consider the lowly screwdriver. We could define a screwdriver as a tool with a handle, a shaft, and a tip shaped to fit the head of a screw. For certain purposes that would be an effective definition (e.g., if you were sending someone to a hardware store to buy one). Now imagine that you are cross-country skiing and the screws have come out of your bindings somewhere in the wilderness. An operational—even tautological—definition would be more useful (e.g., a screwdriver is anything that might turn a screw) because such a definition might help you realize that a coin can be a screwdriver. Certainly if you were trying to invent a new type of screwdriver an operational definition would be superior. Again, the choice of an appropriate form is determined by purpose.

THE IMPORTANCE OF DEFINITION

Sometimes definitions are important because they are necessary preliminaries to the main point of a piece of writing. Often definitions are important because defining can be a form of hidden persuasion. Consider two social scientists arguing about whether apes can learn to use language: that is a very real question, but the answer (on one level at least) depends on your definition of language, and the scientist who gets to define language is likely to win the argument. That is why debators have a slogan, "Define your terms," and often devote considerable time to debating those definitions.

How much poverty is there in the world? That, too, is a very real question; but it cannot be answered until *poverty* is defined. Is *Lady Chatterley's Lover* pornographic? Is *Ulysses*? That depends on your definition of pornographic. (Both of these novels have, incidentally, been classified as pornographic by agencies of various governments, including the government of the United States.) Whether a person goes to prison often depends on a definition: in the United States in the 1950s court cases turned on the definitions of *subversive* and *freedom of speech*; in the 1960s on the definition of *conspiracy*.

As a writer you are concerned with definition as a rhetorical form; always remember, however, that rhetorical form corresponds with a mental activity and relates significantly to events in the real world.

ADDITIONAL READING

Berthoff, Ann. *Forming/thinking/writing.* Rochelle Park, N.J.: Hayden, 1978. See pages 94-110 on "Defining."

Burke, Kenneth. "Definition of Man" and "Terministic Screens." In *Language as Symbolic Action.* Berkeley, Calif.: University of California, 1966. See pages 3-22 and 44-57. Here Burke argues that human beings are symbol-using and cultural animals and discusses the senses in which our terms define us.

EXERCISE

1. Choose a term that names a socially significant group of people (e.g., "politician," "student," "jock," "gear," "parent," "feminist," "Vietnam veteran," "secretary"). Select a particular group of people and ask them to complete a sentence beginning, "Being a ______________ means . . . ." Write a short paper analyzing what that term means to those people (see pages 258-259).

2. Choose a term that is important in your area of special interest. Construct two definitions, one essential and one operational. Check the derivation of the term in a historical or etymological dictionary (e.g., *The Oxford Dictionary of English Etymology*). Think of some synonyms and examples. Make up several analogies. Contrast the term with some similar terms. Think about how the term is used and why it is useful. Write an extended definition of the term for readers who are not familiar with your area of special interest.

3. Choose a technical term from this textbook (e.g., "heuristic," readability," "framework," "*persona*"). Write an extended operational definition aimed at high school composition students.

4. Choose a term referring to a particular type of literary writing (e.g., "satire," "haiku," "epic," "gothic fiction," "Harlequin romance," "proletarian novel," "medieval English lyric"). Write an extended definition aimed at students in a university introduction to literature course.

5. Choose a current slang term. Write an essay that defines the term *and* explains how the term defines its users. Consider both how the term influences the perceptions of those who use it and how its use may label them.

ANALOGY AND EXEMPLIFICATION

All slang is metaphor, and all metaphor is poetry.
G. K. Chesterton

While it is true that argument by analogy always rests on shaky ground, it is possible for someone to become so niggling in his attitude toward all analogy that he is liable to strain at a gnat and swallow a camel. Perhaps we can avoid this carping habit by remembering that an analogy never proves anything; at best, it persuades someone on the grounds of probability
Edward Corbett

The earth—our mother—and I are of one mind.
Native American chieftain

TO CLARIFY, EMPHASIZE, AND CONVINCE

Analogies and examples are often considered secondary support techniques—not valid as proof, but powerful as ways to emphasize, clarify, or concretize a point. In addition to supporting a point with deductive logic or empirical proof, writers often make analogies and give examples to help readers understand or to increase emotional impact.

Analogy is based on the logic of comparison. The word comes from the Greek *analogos*, originally a mathematical term, meaning "proportion" or "equality of ratios." When you make an analogy, you point out a similarity. You compare two situations and argue, implicitly or explicitly, that what is true for the first is also true for the second. Usually, you are comparing your subject with something more familiar or concrete.

In Chapter 1, I used the analogy of "mike fright" to explain the difficulty writers often have getting started:

> Writers do not have the advantage of immediate feedback. Writing is, in this respect, very much like speaking into a radio microphone without the presence of a studio audience; and writer's block is very much like *mike fright*. When feedback is delayed, it is hard to continue verbalizing. But delayed feedback is in the very nature of writing: you write a sentence; then, before receiving any

> indication of whether that sentence has been understood, you have to write the next.

Writer's block is compared with mike fright; and on the basis of that comparison, what we know to be true for mike fright is asserted to be true also for writing. The analogy was intended to clarify and explain—and thus to convince you that a certain amount of difficulty generating words is to be expected when you are writing. If the analogy worked, it persuaded you to worry a little less about that difficulty.

This book is filled with examples—the last paragraph was an example (of analogy). The most important examples are the selections from the writings of students—because there is presumably a similarity between their level of writing ability and yours. Here is an example that was quoted in the preface.

> The principle applies equally to the biological ecosystem and to the ecosystem of ideas. The Boy Scout who twenty years ago memorized the rule that one should always bury cans and other non-burnable garbage has had the environmental context shift out from under him. Most North American backpacking areas are so crowded these days that people would be burying cans faster than the earth could decompose them. Although the higher level value of preserving for other hikers an undamaged natural environment has remained the same, the specific rule has now been inverted—now a good Scout carries out her or his unburnable garbage. What this example illustrates is the tendency to memorize low-level rules instead of understanding higher-level principles. This tendency leads to inappropriate behavior when the context shifts.

The example is more concrete and of a lower level of generality than the proposition it illustrates. It was intended to help readers understand an abstract idea about the relationship between rules and principles.

Unlike an analogy, which asserts a similarity between two distinct and parallel ideas, an example fits within and under the idea it illustrates. An example, as Aristotle says, is the rhetorical equivalent of inductive reasoning. Like empirical proof, its logic moves from the particular to the general: the example of the Boy Scout (a particular) supports the proposition about rules and principles (a generality).

In a piece of writing, it is usually impossible to present enough examples to constitute statistically reliable proof. But the example represents that proof. When you present an example, you imply that it *exemplifies*, that is typical, that it could be multiplied by enough examples to constitute empirical proof.

An analogy, like an enthymeme (see pages 330-331), is the rhetorical equivalent of deductive reasoning. If the comparison is valid, then what is true for the analog is also true for the subject. The logical syllogism would look like this:

> Writer's block is equivalent to mike fright.
>
> Mike fright results from delayed feedback.
>
> Therefore, writer's block results from delayed feedback.

Note that an analogy does not assert that the two terms are identical, just that they are similar in this context. The two terms are compared in respect to one or more salient features, and the analogy is valid only if the similar features are actually salient in the conclusion.

The power of analogies and examples is particularly apparent when they are used in refutations. In the following passage, Martin Luther King refutes the argument that peaceful demonstrations should be banned because they may precipitate a violent response:

> In your statement you assert that our actions, even though peaceful, must be condemned because they precipitate violence. But is this a logical assertion? Isn't this like condemning a robbed man because his possession of money precipitated the evil act of robbery? Isn't this like condemning Socrates because his unswerving commitment to truth and his philosophical inquiries precipitated the act by the misguided populace in which they made him drink hemlock? Isn't this like condemning Jesus because his unique God-consciousness and never-ceasing devotion to God's will precipitated the evil act of crucifixion? We must come to see that, as the federal courts have consistently affirmed, it is wrong to urge an individual to cease his efforts to gain his basic constitutional rights because the quest may precipitate violence. Society must protect the robbed and punish the robber.

King uses three analogies, each phrased as a rhetorical question. He arranges them in order of increasing power—how many Christians would blame Jesus for precipitating his own crucifixion? He makes a brief appeal to authority (the federal courts), and he closes with an implicit assertion that an injunction preventing peaceful demonstrations against racism is equivalent to a decision to protect thieves and punish their victims. (He also makes good use of repetitive sentence structure; see pages 195-196.)

Sometimes even a single counterexample can devastate an argument. For millions of North Americans, according to public opinion polls, a single near-disaster at the Three Mile Island nuclear generator plant refuted volumes of statistics and expert testimony about the safety of such plants.

In some cases, a single counterexample is a logically valid refutation (especially if the original proposition contained absolutes like "all" or "never"). In other cases, the counterexample does not disprove, but only challenges the probability of original proposition. (Compare Antony's funeral speech in *Julius Caesar*, reprinted on pages 332-336 below.)

Perhaps the most effective counterexamples are created when you turn your opponents' statements against them and, as the saying goes, hoist them on their own petards. Here are some counterexamples used by Professor Joe Williams, who was refuting some of the simplistic generalizations that composition textbooks offer writing students. In every case, as indicated by the italics, the very reputable authors violate their own rules.

From *Simple & Direct* by Jacques Barzun:

> In conclusion, I recommend using *that* [not *which*] with defining clauses except when stylistic reasons interpose [p. 68].
>
> Next is a typical situation *which* a practiced writer corrects for style virtually by simple reflex. . . (p. 69).

From *The Elements of Style* by William Strunk, Jr., and E. B. White

> Express coordinate ideas in similar form. The principle, that of parallel construction, requires that expressions similar in context and function be outwardly similar [p. 20].
>
> *That, which. That* is the defining or restrictive pronoun, *which* the non-defining or non-restrictive [p. 47].

In "Death of a Pig," however, E. B. White writes,

> . . . the premature expiration of a pig is, I soon discovered, a departure *which* the community marks solemnly on its calendar, a sorrow in which it feels fully involved. I have written this account *in penitence and in grief*, as a man who failed to raise his pig, *and to explain* my deviation from the classic course of so many raised pigs. The grave in the woods is unmarked, but Fred can direct the mourner to it *unerringly and with immense good will*, and I know he and I shall often revisit it. (Italics added.)

From *Barnet & Stubbs Practical Guide to Writing*:

> Negative constructions are often wordy and sometimes pretentious
>
> 1. wordy Housing for married students is not unworthy of consideration.
>   concise Housing for married students is worthy of consideration (p. 216).
>
> • • •
>
> The following example from a syndicated column is *not untypical* [p. 216].

Professor Williams' point was that rules are overgeneralized and imprecise, that they may be generally valid but even their advocates do not always follow them. Faulty parallelism *is* a stylistic problem, but E. B.

White demonstrates in "Death of a Pig" that it is not always necessary (or even desirable) to represent coordinate ideas in similar form. A counter-example, even though it may not be a logically airtight refutation, can persuasively deflate an authoritative statement, especially if that statement is overgeneralized. (See pages 330-331.)

ANALOGY AS A HIDDEN PERSUADER

Analogies are much more common than is ordinarily thought, in part because many analogies are covert. We cannot think, or even perceive, without making comparisons. Whenever we attach familiar words to a new concept, we have the beginning of an analogy. Since the words carry connotations associated with the old concept, the very use of those words suggests an analogy between the old and new concepts. Any perception of similarity is an incipient analogy, and we cannot learn anything new without perceiving it as somehow similar to something we already understand.

In Chapter 1, I cited experts who refer to an "incubation" stage in the creative process. To incubate is to maintain something under conditions favorable for development, as when a hen sits on an egg. The very use of that word suggests an analogy between the biological creation of a new organism and the psychological creation of a new idea.

There is no problem with that analogy: it is apt. It is, moreover, made explicit a few pages later when Gertrude Stein's analogy between writing and having a baby is quoted in full. The question, however, is this: when you read the word, "incubation," did you stop to think critically about the implicit analogy it suggested? Presumably not. There are so many analogies implicit in the language we use that one simply cannot stop to think critically about them all.

For any subject, however, there are certain key analogies or *root metaphors* (see pages 117-118) that function as "hidden persuaders" and covertly persuade us to perceive that subject in certain ways. Insofar as they are accepted uncritically, these covert comparisons are as much a form of "subliminal seduction" as any advertising technique. They subliminally seduce us into perceiving in the ways they suggest.

The problem is not necessarily the analogy—which is often valid—but the covert and uncritical way it operates. Here are three short paragraphs from a newspaper feature article about sexually titillating magazines and advertisements:

> There is too much show and tell about sex these days. It is time the pendulum swung the other way.

> I would like to be able to chat with my neighbor at the supermarket checkout without the magazines on display shouting: "Lookee here. All you wanted to know about orgasms and more, more." Or be able to buy a tube of toothpaste at the corner drugstore without a blatant Playboy model intruding on the transaction.
>
> • • •
>
> Granted there was too much puritanism at one time (that seems a very long time ago) and change often swings too far before a balance is obtained. Still, I look for the romance and find it missing when a sexpot coos me into buying a certain laxative.

People reading this ten-paragraph article in their afternoon newspapers probably did not stop to think about the commonplace analogy: social change is like a pendulum. To what extent is that analogy valid? A pendulum, as the writer suggests, swings regularly and predictably between two extremes before stopping in the center. Is that how social change works (and, if so, is there no such thing as progress)? Prior to the "puritanism" mentioned (note another implicit analogy), was there really a libertine period essentially comparable to the present in its tolerance for soft-core pornography?

There is no need to be overly picky. After all, this is a casual and commonplace analogy. And an analogy is only an assertion of similarity: it does not assert that the two terms (in this case, social change and a pendulum) are identical, just that they are similar in respect to certain salient features. But if the writer and readers of this article really want to do something about soft-core pornography in supermarkets and laxative advertisements, it matters whether they understand how and why it got to be there. Certainly, there is some similarity between social change and a pendulum, but is there enough to make it a valid analogy in this rhetorical context?

Let us bring the issue closer to home. I. A. Richards thinks that you will have a clearer understanding of writing if you think of the composing process by analogy to a plant growing. Gertrude Stein suggests the analogy of a baby forming in a womb. Some contemporary rhetoricians, myself included, have used the analogy of an evolving ecosystem. What all these analogies have in common is this: they are consistent with Richards' assertion that language processes should be understood *organically*, by analogy "with some patterns of Biology." How will this set of analogies help you understand the writing process?

Richards says that we can avoid "some traditional mistakes" by using organic analogies in place of certain standard "bad analogies." He attacks the analogy that asserts "language is a dress which thought puts on" because it implies that thinking is complete before writing starts. He attacks analogies that assert meaning is "a can that has been filled or a lump of clay that has been moulded" because they imply too rigid a relationship between "form and content." These analogies are "bad" because they can lead you to take an overly rigid approach to the composing process (thus interfering with your creative process) and to underestimate the importance of rhetorical contexts (thus interfering with your communicative process). It is these potential effects that make the analogies "bad."

As a writer, you need to know that analogy, like exemplification, is an important technique you can use to clarify your explanations and convince your readers. To be honest, you should also understand the broader implications of the key analogies or root metaphors you use. This chapter began with the thesis that we compose our perceptions (and that readers recompose writers' expressions) by juxtaposing sensory input with mental concepts. Verbal analogies epitomize that process. They embody all the advantages (and all the potential flaws) of the human mode of perception and communication. That is why analogy is such a powerful rhetorical form.

ADDITIONAL READING

Barthes, Roland. *Mythologies.* Selected and translated from the French by Annette Lavers. New York: Hill and Wang, 1972. Fascinating analysis of cultural analogies. See especially "The Romans in Films," "Wine and Milk," "The Brain of Einstein," and "MYTH TODAY."

Bateson, Gregory. "Pathologies of Epistemology," "The Roots of Ecological Crisis," and "Ecology and Flexibility in Urban Civilization." All reprinted in *Steps to an Ecology of Mind.* New York: Ballantine, 1972. Bateson argues that certain standard cultural analogies lead us to behave in ways which create our ecological problems.

Kuhn, Thomas. *The Structure of Scientific Revolutions.* 2nd ed. Chicago: University of Chicago, 1970. If you are going to write (or do) science, you should read this book. Among other things, Kuhn demonstrates how symbolic generalizations, analogies, and methodological values help shape scientific knowledge and influence which "facts" will be discovered. Even if you are not involved with science, science is a good example of knowledge, so Kuhn's insights are analogously relevant for anyone concerned with knowledge.

Richards, I. A. *The Philosophy of Rhetoric.* London: Oxford, 1936. Richards' discussion of the sorts of analogies that may validly be used to understand language processes is found in the first chapter.

EXERCISE

1. Write an analysis of a conflict that occurred when two or more people perceived the same event differently because their perceptions were based on different analogies. Intercultural or intergenerational communications are good places to look for appropriate subjects. Be certain you are writing about a difference of perception, not just a difference of opinion (i.e., about a situation in which people "see" an event differently, not just one in which they make different value judgments about the event.)

2. In *The Art of Loving*, Erich Fromm argues that the analogy implicit in the phrase, "falling in love" constrains us toward impractical expectations by implying that love is easy, that all one need do is wait for the right person and then "fall." He tries to convince readers to perceive the "problem of love" *as* one of how to love rather than *as* finding the right person. He tries to persuade readers to approach love *as an art* rather than *as an experience*. He uses a series of analogies in an attempt to change the root metaphor that shapes many people's approach to love. Here is an excerpt:

> *Our whole culture is based on the appetite for buying, on the idea of a mutually favorable exchange. . . . [We look] at people in a similar way. For a man an attractive girl [sic]—and for the woman an attractive man—are the prizes they are after. . . . What specifically makes a person attractive depends on the fashion of the time, physically as well as mentally. . . . At any rate, the sense of falling in love develops usually only with regard to such human commodities as are within reach of one's own possibilities of exchange. I am out for a bargain. . . . Two persons thus fall in love when they feel they have found the best object available on the market, considering their own exchange values. Often, as in buying real estate, the hidden potentialities which can be developed play a considerable role in this bargain. In a culture in which the marketing orientation prevails, and in which material success is the outstanding value, there is little reason to be surprised that human love relations follow the same pattern of exchange which governs the commodity and the labor market.*

Write a short essay in which you use concrete examples to argue for or against this extended analogy (or in which you evaluate the extent of its validity). Read Fromm's short opening chapter, "Is Love An Art?" and write an analysis of his use of both analogy and exemplification as persuasive techniques.

3. Thomas Kuhn argues that the members of a scientific discipline share a set of "preferred or permissible analogies and metaphors" (e.g., "the molecules of a gas behave like tiny elastic billiard balls in random motion"). These "standard analogies," he asserts, constrain the perceptions of the scientists and "help to determine what will be accepted as an explanation." He also asserts that there were standard examples, to which those scientists were exposed as students, that function similarly. Select a standard analogy or example from your own field of special interest, and write an analysis of how it influences the perceptions of people in that field.

4. What analogies do you ordinarily use when thinking about writing? Can you remember how you acquired them? Write a short analysis of these analogies and their influence on your understanding and attitudes.

5. Pick any subject of particular interest to you and analyze the way in which standard analogies and examples influence people's perception of the subject. (Controversial social issues often make good subjects to analyze because people who take distinct positions usually use radically different analogies and examples.)

The accelerated motion of a falling body, the cycle of a storm, the gradations of a sunrise, the stages of a cholera epidemic, the ripening of crops—in all such instances we find the material of progressive form.

Kenneth Burke

Narration (What happened? When did it happen?) is related to process (How did it happen? How does it work?); to cause and effect (Why did it happen? What caused or produced it? What are the results or consequences?); to syllogistic progression (If certain things happen, then what must follow?).

Frank D'Angelo

How you broke open what sheathed you
until this moment

Adrienne Rich

What does not change
Is the will to change

Charles Olson

CHAPTER 5

PROGRESSIVE PATTERNS

This chapter is about a group of rhetorical forms used to write about *change*. Abstracted from narration, they are called the diachronic or *progressive patterns of arrangement*.

Narration is concerned with *what* happened. Process-analysis explains *how* it happens (in general). Causal analysis explains *why*. The distinctions among the three forms are equivalent to the distinctions among the three questions: What? How? Why?

Like the synchronic patterns discussed in Chapter 4, the progressive patterns are founded on the nature of human perception and thought. In all our perceiving, thinking, feeling, and communicating, we make connections among events separated in time. We *see that* one event follows another. We *see that* a certain process leads to certain results. We *see that* one event is causally related to another. When you look at this textbook, for instance, you do not just see it; you see that it arose out of past actions and has future potentials. You see that it was written, printed, and bound. You see that it may help you to develop your writing abilities.

With the possible exception of dolphins, human beings are the only organisms on this planet that can communicate about events widely separated in time. Only human language has markers to indicate past and future. Only human language can communicate *if-then* propositions. (A dog's growl, for instance, can communicate, "I am about to attack"; but a dog cannot communicate, "I will attack next week.") A sophisticated ability to make connections among events separated in time is quintessentially human.

As in Chapter 4, we are concerned with these patterns primarily as patterns of arrangement for written composition. But, like all such forms, they can be used to generate material as well as to arrange it. By narrating what happened in a particular instance, generalizing that account into a process-analysis of how it happens in general, and explaining why it happens, you are generating material as well as organizing it.

The first section of this chapter is about narration. It is a relatively short section because you are probably already relatively good at narration. The second section is about process-analysis. It distinguishes between lineal processes, which you probably can already write about fairly well, and more complex processes, about which you most likely have more to learn. The third section is about causal analysis. It, too, distinguishes ways to write about various types of causation. Again, the emphasis is on the most complex type.

If you did the assignments in Chapter 0, you have already narrated (an account of what you did while producing a particular piece of writing) and generalized that narrative into a process-analysis. When you tried to figure out why certain weaknesses recur in your writings, you did a causal analysis. This chapter should help you develop a more sophisticated ability to use these patterns.

NARRATION

We can perceive widely varying intentions in different narratives such as fictional story, a factual report of events, a scientific account of a sequence . . . , and a narrative contained within an advertisement . . . . It is no difficult matter to find narrative . . . which has as its dominant function calculated persuasion or highly didactic explanation.

James Britton et al.

Time is 'counted movement' said Aristotle, and it was precisely the impossibility of counting the repeated instants of movement in time which led Zeno of Elea to pose the famous paradoxes.

Anthony Wilden

TELLING WHAT HAPPENED

Narratives are sometimes called *accounts*; writers of narratives are said to *recount* events. In Latinate languages, the very word for story derives from the Latin, *computare*, to count (e.g., Spanish, *cuento*; French, *conte*). This is a clue to the structure of narrative, which in a sense *counts* (or accounts for) the moments of time. In this sense, narration is the description of change: when the element of time is added to description, we have narration.

Elementary narratives start at the beginning and account for each significant moment until the end. More sophisticated narratives may start in the middle (or even at the end) and "flashback" to earlier moments. In any case, the underlying movement of narrative is progression through time. The essential order is chronological (from the Greek, *chronos* + *logos*; hence "following the logic of time").

If you tell some friends what happened on a television show they did not see, you are narrating. If you begin a literature paper by summarizing the plot of a novel, you are narrating (as was the author of the novel). If you recount something outrageous your boss did at work yesterday, or something bizarre that happened when your younger sister tried to join a Little League baseball team, or something funny that happened the first time you drove a tractor, . . . you are narrating.

As in description, so in narration the key task of the writer is selection. You must discover what happened—perhaps by searching your memory, perhaps by researching—and you must select significant events to be *re*-presented verbally. Arrangement is relatively easy because it is essentially chronological. Explicit analysis is usually minimal because narration is generally most effective if you follow the rule, "Show, don't tell"; recreate the events, do not tell about them.

The nature of the selection, of course, varies with the writers' purposes. A technical reporter, a newsreporter, and a novelist may watch the same rocket launching, but their reports will be as distinct as their purposes.

THE PURPOSES OF NARRATION

Many narratives serve expressive purposes. The purpose of a personal narrative, for example, may be to express and share an emotion (e.g., your outrage at what your boss did). If readers understand what happened, feel the emotion and respond empathetically, the narrative has succeeded.

Expressive narratives may be directed toward readers to whom the experience is foreign. Until I read D. H. Lawrence's *Sons and Lovers* and Agnes Smedley's *Daughter of Earth*, I had only the vaguest inkling of what it would have been like to grow up in a mining town in the early years of this century. One function of such narratives is to allow readers vicariously to share experiences foreign to them.

Expressive narratives may also be directed toward readers who have had similar experiences. The function of the narrative may then create a sense of community. A personal narrative—originally written, perhaps, as self-expression because the writer needed to articulate and clarify an experience—can come to serve this function if other people identify with it. Much of the recently published literature of oppressed groups (women's literature, Black, Chicano, Puerto Rican, and Quebecois literature) takes the form of personal narrative and serves this function. The power of such narratives comes from readers' recognition of the social validity of the personal experiences. (See the quotation from Hans Guth on page 202.) Indeed, a purely personal narrative that touches no social nerve is rarely published.

Such narratives, which express the shared experience of a group, also embody shared values. By expressing those shared values, they create a sense of community. That is the function of mythology in human societies. Any narratives that serve this function are, in the best sense of the word, *mythical*—whether they are stories about ordinary people or imaginary beings. (From this point of view, the literal truth or falsity of such a myth is quite beside the point; the myth is essentially true if it embodies the right values.)

The parable of the Good Samaritan is such a myth. The story is generally familiar, even to those who have not read the Bible. Almost everyone can identify with the conflict between selfishness and charity. And our culture upholds the latter as an ideal (and the former as "realism").

Frontier stories (e.g., "westerns") serve similar functions. Only on the most superficial levels are "westerns" about nineteenth-century cowboys (whom they depict with incredible inaccuracy). Science fiction, likewise, for all its intergalactic travel, is essentially a commentary on contemporary society. Both are really about the society that reads them.

In this sense, expressive narratives can become persuasive. By telling stories that embody certain values, they may serve also to persuade readers to maintain or adopt those values. Even a narrative television commercial which has been impressed on the popular imagination is a "myth" in this sense. In addition to telling a story which is expressive enough to hold viewers' attention, and in addition to persuading them to purchase the advertiser's product, it also persuades them to maintain or adopt values it embodies (e.g., about the appropriate roles of men and women). As with any myth, each telling of such a narrative may have only slight persuasive power. But the repeated telling of that story, together with other stories embodying similar values, and in a social context which constrains people toward those values, can be powerfully persuasive.

Similarly, that story about your employer's outrageous behavior may be part of an attempt to convince fellow workers to unionize. Its moral may be left unstated, but the reiteration of that moral over time, through similar stories, may have a cumulative persuasive effect—at least if other workers recognize it as typical.

Narratives can also serve as examples in explanatory writings. That story about your younger sister's trying to join a Little League team may illustrate how perfectly ordinary people can behave bizarrely when their stereotypes are challenged.

Samuel Taylor Coleridge's "Prefatory Note to Kubla Khan" is a narrative that served and still serves a variety of purposes.

> The following fragment is here published at the request of a poet of great and deserved celebrity, and, as far as the Author's own opinions are concerned, rather as a psychological curiosity, than on the ground of any supposed *poetic* merits.
>
> In the summer of the year 1797, the Author, then in ill health, had retired to a lonely farm-house between Porlock and Linton, on the Exmoor confines of Somerset and Devonshire. In consequence of a slight indisposition, an anodyne had been prescribed, from the effects of which he fell asleep in his chair at the moment that he was reading the following sentence, or words of the same substance, in "Purchas's Pilgrimage": "Here the Khan Kubla commanded a palace to be built, and a stately garden thereunto. And thus ten miles of fertile ground were inclosed with a wall." The Author continued for about three hours in a profound sleep, at least of the external senses, during which time he has the most vivid confidence, that he could not have composed less than from two to three hundred lines; if that indeed can be called composition in which all the images rose up before him as *things*, with a parallel production of the correspondent expressions, without any sensation or consciousness of effort. On awaking he appeared to himself to have a distinct recollection of the whole, and taking his pen, ink, and paper, instantly and eagerly wrote down the lines that are here preserved. At this moment he was unfortunately called out by a person on business from Porlock, and detained by him above an hour, and on his return to his room, found, to his no small surprise and mortification, that though he still retained some vague and dim recollection of the general purport of the vision, yet, with the exception of some eight or ten scattered lines and images, all the rest had passed away like the images on the surface of a stream into which a stone has been cast, but alas! without the after restoration of the latter!

Coleridge recounts, in chronological order, the significant events which led to the creation and loss of several hundred lines of poetry. Some literary critics have accepted the account as accurate; others have doubted it to one degree or another. At any event, its original purpose was persuasive: it served, among other arguments, to justify the publication of a wonderfully rich but incomplete poem. In a sense, it has also since become part of the poem (with which it is usually published). And, among those who study the creative process, it has also become a standard illustration (i.e., a "myth") of the importance of unconscious processes in human creation. Thus the narrative serves persuasive, expressive, and explanatory purposes.

Another statement by Coleridge summarizes the same information in a single sentence fragment:

> This fragment with a good deal more, not recoverable, composed in a sort of Reverie brought on by two grains of Opium, taken to check a dysentery, at a Farm House between Porlock and Linton, a quarter of a mile from Culbone Church, in the fall of the year 1797.

This version, probably earlier, lacks narrative form. It also lacks significant details and could not serve the persuasive, expressive, or explanatory purposes of the preface. Certainly, it could not stand as a myth representing the interaction of conscious and unconscious processes in human creation (see pages 30-32).

A narrative should not attempt to recount everything that happened. It need only include those events that are significant. And it is only in terms of purposes that writers can distinguish significant from insignificant events.

This is especially true for narratives that serve persuasive or explanatory purposes. Expressive narratives often stand on their own and are often read, as with novels, for the sheer pleasure of the story. Even in our efficient age, they are permitted to be quite lengthy. Narratives that serve persuasive or explanatory purposes, however, are likely to be subordinate parts of larger writings and are usually expected to be subordinated efficiently to their purposes.

The following expressive writing, by a first-year university student, is primarily narrative.

> Christmas in Mesachie Lake was always something special. Typical of small towns, Mesachie had community spirit but it seemed to double at Christmas time. Every year we had a Christmas pageant in the town hall on Christmas Eve. The hall was always decorated with holly and ivy, streamers, and pictures of Santa Claus. But the best trimming was the huge Christmas tree. Each year the men would go and get a big bushy evergreen tree and decorate it with lights, Christmas tree ornaments, silver icicles, and, of course, candy canes. The whole hall would smell deliciously of fresh pine.
>
> The main feature of the pageant was "the Nativity Scene," which was the effort of all the mothers. The kids who could sing were in the choir and the ones who couldn't composed the scene. I remember one year I was the angel in the nativity scene. I was dressed in white robes and I had to stand high on a tier so that it seemed as if I was in the sky. As a result of the height and the warmth of my robes, I got dizzy and I almost fell off.
>
> After the pageant Santa Claus would arrive. The pianist would play "Here Comes Santa Claus" and everyone would sing along as he walked through the

audience and up onto the stage. He would call each little kid to come and receive his present and sit on his knee. To me he was rather awesome; I always knew he was just a man dressed up, but he was so big and he "Ho, Ho, Ho"-ed so loudly he scared me.

Cathy Traer

The style of this excerpt could be tightened and the details further concretized, but it gives a good sense of Mesachie Lake as a small town—so small that "each little kid" can be called up onto the stage to receive a present and sit on Santa's knee. Like the Christmas pageant itself, the writing embodies the values of the community in both what it shows and what it excludes. One gets some sense of the mixture of secular and Christian values in the Christmas celebration and of the division of labor between men and women in the community, all from the uncritical perspective of a young girl. One gets no mention of the Chinese and East Indian residents, who, although they lived in Mesachie Lake, were not perceived as part of this community. (Indeed, I know they were not at the Christmas pageant only because I asked the writer.)

In the next example, the contrast are more explicit. On one level, it is a character sketch. On another, it expresses the writer's feelings. On yet another, it presents an image with which many women workers can identify.

SEXUAL INITIATION AT $1.35 AN HOUR

The Lamas Restaurant was bleak, even at the noon hour when it was filled to capacity with hungry workers from the surrrounding area. I am still not certain why anybody ate there at all. There was a loneliness about the place, and time passed slowly within its boundaries. Working there was like serving a prison sentence or being confined to hospital for a very long time. My shift lasted from eleven o'clock in the morning until eight o'clock in the evening, six days a week. Mr. Lamas preferred that I take all my meals in the restaurant and avoid walking the neighbourhood streets. He was afraid I might bring shame upon his establishment.

Lamas did all the cooking while his wife and I waited table. The only other staff member was an ancient Greek, who washed the dishes and scrubbed the floors. Toothless, humorless, nameless, he hobbled through the kitchen, cursing his life and coddling his dishes and brooms. When he cornered me in the basement with a wet mop in his hand, Lamas fired him and threw him off the premises. For the remainder of the summer, in addition to my waitress duties, I washed the dishes and scrubbed the floors. Lamas said it would be a lesson to me, but I knew that it really meant one fewer salary he had to pay out.

Lamas ran his meagre business as if he were putting on a show. Everything was said and done for the benefit of the customers. He treated them like rubes, paying fools whom he delighted in deceiving. Before them, he was magnanimous. As he stepped behind the kitchen door, his warmth would vanish. Only his wife and I would see the cruel stupidity that characterized the man.

The husband and wife gave no sense of being a couple or a partnership. She slept upstairs in her husband's bed at night and worked in his restaurant all day. He controlled—no, he hoarded—food, money and hardware. She used to steal special treats for us while he was out on business; like slaves, we would furtively gobble, and laugh at the mysterious motivation of Lamas and all tyrants.

It was Lamas who gave me my first lecture on sex education. He would not allow me to fraternize with the customers. It was simply forbidden. He treated me to a pathetic pantomime in which he illustrated the appropriate behaviour for a waitress to adopt toward her clientele. Pressed for a deeper explanation, he led me to the cash register and revealed the truth about men and women.

"Human beings," whispered Lamas, "are evil. They carry poisonous juices inside themselves. These juices can only be released through sex. Even I have these juices. When I need to get rid of them, I go to the street and find a woman. If you want to clean out your own poison, go to another neighbourhood. Never, never give it to a customer. You will infect the business. The business will become poisoned. Do you understand?"

I understood. The sickness of Lamas' philosophy had permeated the space around him. Life itself was a disease to be flushed out periodically into foreign territory. The restaurant, which he held sacred and struggled to protect from evil, embodied health. Its somberness, its sterility, reflected the imprisoned spirit of its confused owner.

Ginny Fortin

This piece was written to re-create one person's experience of working in a particular restaurant. Aside from the analogy in the fourth paragraph ("*like slaves*, we would furtively gobble, and laugh at the mysterious motivation of Lamas *and all tyrants*"), there is little in the text itself to suggest generalization. And yet, like good literature, it does suggest a contrast between *what is* (or was) and *what should be*. And insofar as readers are reminded of similar experiences, it serves to create a sense of community.

When you think of narratives, you probably think of the sort of material represented by these last two examples. But any writing that reports what happened in a particular instance or set of instances is narration. Consider the following as narrative.

The method by which I wrote my first paper for this English course is typical of my writing process for most creative essays.

My first step was to consider briefly each of the topic choices as they were assigned, weighing the potential of each. Through the course of that day and the next, I thought of the topics from time to time. By the night after they had been assigned, I had a few ideas; and after re-examining them, I settled on one and mentally formed a rough draft of how I would describe my summer job. I was now ready to begin my second step: the actual writing.

Upon thinking of a thesis sentence, I began writing quickly. As I wrote, I was mentally a few sentences ahead of what I was actually writing, but I did not follow a concrete outline. As I wrote, I didn't pay a great deal of attention to spelling mistakes or punctuation. If I was at a loss for an appropriate word or phrase, I would pause briefly; but if I failed to think of the word, I would temporarily insert a synonym or a phrase which would convey the same meaning and continue writing. I wrote rapidly until I reached my concluding paragraph, at which point I stopped and re-read my essay, not for the sake of making corrections but rather to obtain an overall picture of what I had written. I then proceeded with the conclusion.

After having completed step two, I then progressed to the third stage in which I re-read the essay in order to correct any punctuation and spelling mistakes. With the aid of a thesaurus, I substituted appropriate words for those I was not satisfied with. Once this operation was finished, I waited one or two days before I commenced with the final stage.

This stage entails re-reading the paper to see if it flows smoothly and if what I had written made sense. Waiting a day or so increases my objectivity for this task. After making any further appropriate corrections or revisions, I copied the essay out neatly and the grueling process ground to a halt.

Fiona Barnett

Aside from the first sentence (and, perhaps, the beginning of the last paragraph), this is narration: it reports a particular happening in chronological order. Its first function was to make the writer articulate, and thus become more aware of, how she writes. In a writing class or workshop, a narrative of this kind could be shared, and sharing usually leads to a sense of "community" as members of the group realize that they are not alone in their difficulties. This particular narrative should perhaps have been more fully articulated: *How* did Fiona think of a thesis sentence? Aside from corrections, what sorts of revisions did she make? Those details could help readers understand just what Fiona did—and probably lead to some insights about why her writing came out as it did. Here, as so often, the quality of a narration results from the quality of detail, and what is left out can be as important as what is selected for inclusion.

ADDITIONAL READING

Burke, Kenneth. "Lexicon Rhetoricae." In *Counter-Statement*, rpt., Berkeley, Calif.: University of California, 1968. A sophisticated discussion of the meaning of form with frequent examples from literary narratives.

Macrorie, Ken. *Telling Writing*. New York: Hayden, 1970. See especially the chapters on "telling facts" and dialogue.

EXERCISE

1. Tell a story, or string together a series of incidents, that will give readers a sense of a place (e.g., where you grew up), a person (e.g., your mother), or an activity (e.g., a job you once had).

2. Select one of your important values or beliefs. Think of an event you witnessed that epitomizes that value or belief. Narrate the event in such a way that it communicates the value or belief, but do not actually state your point in the writing. See if readers get the point.

3. Write up a recent frustrating experience as (a) an expression of your feelings addressed to a good friend, (b) an attempt to get someone in authority to do something about the situation, and (c) an illustration of a principle for a university class in psychology or sociology. How does the narrative change as your purpose changes?

4. Narrate everything that happened the last time you wrote something. Start from when you decided (or were assigned) to write. End when the piece of writing was ready for its readers. Share this narrative with other writers.

5. Select a contemporary popular narrative (e.g., a hit song, a best-selling novel, a television commercial). Analyze it as a "myth" which embodies and reinforces cultural values. Write a conclusion to this analysis that discusses the implications for writers and readers.

PROCESS-ANALYSIS

Like narration, process suggests ongoing movement and continuous action. The emphasis in a process theme, however, is on the how, *rather than the* what.

Frank D'Angelo

Syllogistic progression is the form of a perfectly conducted argument, advancing step by step. It is the form of a mystery story, where everything falls together, as in a story of ratiocination by Poe. It is the form of a demonstration in Euclid. To go from A *to* E *through stages* B, C, *and* D *is to obtain such a form.*

Kenneth Burke

LINEAL PROCESSES

To move from narration to process-analysis is to move to a higher level of generality, from *what happened in a particular instance* to *how it happens in general.* A process-analysis can be an explanation of how something happens. It can also be instructions about how to make something happen.

Process-analysis as you are familiar with it from school assignments probably meant writing compositions like, "How to Change a Flat Tire," "Baking Banana Bread," "The Life Cycle of the Butterfly," "Supply and Demand: How They Affect Prices," and so on. Such processes, at least as typically treated in school essays, are simple; their analysis is elementary.

The general pattern is "*first* this, *then* that, . . . and *finally* the other"; the transitions are similar to those used in narrative writings.

First you take the spare tire, jack and tire-iron out of the trunk, *then* you loosen the lug-nuts, . . . *finally* you let the car down off the jack, tighten the lug-nuts and put everything back in the trunk.

First there is the egg, *then* the caterpillar, . . . *finally* the female butterfly lays her eggs and the cycle begins again.

The process may be described as a *straight* line, which ends at the last step or phase. Or it may be described as a *circle*, which begins anew at the last step or stage. But whether the line of development is straight or curved, the process may be accurately described step by step or phase by phase. Because it can be represented by a line, such a process is called lineal.

The following recipe, like virtually all recipes, describes a lineal process. If followed step by step, it produces a lemon meringue pie.

Easy Lemon Meringue Pie

To make a quick and easy lemon meringue pie, here is what you do. First obtain the following ingredients:

1½ cups graham cracker crumbs
2 tablespoons sugar (preferably brown)
¼ cup butter or margarine
3 eggs
14 ounces condensed (not evaporated) milk
⅓ cup lemon juice (approximately 3 lemons) and grated rind from one lemon
6 tablespoons white sugar

Begin with the crust. Preheat oven to approximately 190°C (375°F). Mix graham cracker crumbs with 2 tablespoons of sugar (preferably brown) in a 9-inch pie plate. (Note: if you cannot obtain graham cracker crumbs any other way, you can crumble graham crackers, in a blender or by hand.) Melt butter or margarine and mix thoroughly with crumb-and-sugar mixture. Press against bottom and sides of pie plate with back of spoon. Bake for seven minutes. Set aside to cool. Leave oven on.

As an alternative, of course, you could just buy a graham cracker crust. That is needlessly expensive: most of the price represents packaging and marketing costs. It is also wasteful, especially because it usually involves throwing away a light aluminum pie plate—and making aluminum is a high-energy process. It also does not taste nearly as good.

Next make the filling. Separate the egg yolks from the egg whites. Put the whites aside. Mix the yolks with the condensed milk and lemon rind. Beat in lemon juice until filling sets. Pour into crust.

Next make the meringue. Meringue sets up best if everything is clean and at room temperature (20°C) or slightly warmer. In a ceramic bowl, beat the egg whites until frothy. After they are frothy, slowly add 6 tablespoons of white sugar while continuing to beat rapidly. After the meringue holds stiff peaks when you lift the beater, spread over pie. Be certain to seal the edges.

Bake for 15 minutes at 190°C (375°F) or until meringue browns. Cool. Enjoy.

Some recipes are difficult to follow, but that has more to do with subtlety or number of steps than with intrinsic complexity. In this recipe, for example, the filling may not set if the lemon juice is not measured precisely, and the meringue may not stiffen if there is yolk in the egg whites. Nonetheless, the process itself is lineal and may be accurately presented in this step-by-step format. In the end, the test is in the pie: if the typical reader can follow the instructions and produce a tasty lemon meringue pie, the writing was successful.

This recipe also represents an ideal of process-analysis: *whenever you can do so without distorting your subject, present process-analyses in this lineal, step-by-step (or phase-by-phase) format.* The lineal structure is easiest for readers to follow.

However, not all processes are lineal. Many processes are grossly distorted when reduced to lineal representations. The process by which we understand the meanings of a poem, for example, is usually distorted if so reduced. The multiplicity of connotations and the simultaneity of their expression is usually part of what makes a poem poetic.

Nonetheless, in literary criticism and especially in teaching people how to read poems, we often do reduce the poem's multiple meanings to a series of lineal representations. Since reading a poem is a *supralineal* process, such literary critical, and pedagogical representations distort the poem. The distortion is usually intentional, and the unstated assumption is that people will go back to the poem, that they will reread it in light of what they have learned from critic or teacher, and that the rereading will restore the unity of the poem by recreating the simultaneity and multiplicity of meanings. Without this assumption, the distortion would not be justifiable.

SUPRALINEAL PROCESSES

A supralineal process is one in which the various aspects or subprocesses cannot properly be considered as steps or phases because they intertwine, interact, occur simultaneously on various levels, and ebb and flow instead of following discretely one after another. We can treat such a process *as if* it were lineal by focusing on the subprocess or aspect that predominates at any given point in time. To do so is a distortion, although under some circumstances a justifiable distortion. How should we then verbally represent supralineal processes? When and to what extent are we justified in presenting them as if they were lineal? What are our other options?

In a sense the very problem derives from the nature of verbal communication: when we speak or write, listen or read, the words themselves are arranged linearly, one after another. It is the potential of a single word to carry more than one connotation and what I. A. Richards called "the interanimation of words" which allow us to communicate supralineal meanings. Only because a single word can have multiple connotations and because the meanings it represents are partially determined by its contexts is there even the potential to represent supralineal meanings. (It is the special function of poetry to represent the most complex of such meanings, and so we often resort to poetic language when we need to communicate these meanings even in other types of writings.)

When we say, "the writing process has three stages: prewriting, drafting, and revising," we are representing the writing process as lineal. Although a distortion, this statement is justifiable in certain contexts. When it was originally put forth, for instance, it served to focus writing teachers' attention on an aspect of the writing process that had been neglected for more than a century: the means by which writers invent or generate material for their writings. Even now, it can be a useful oversimplification for guiding immature or inexperienced writers.

Many processes, of course, are lineal and may be so represented without distortion. This is especially true of mechanistic and inorganic processes, such as those that predominate in certain areas of the hard sciences and in their applications in engineering. As we start to deal with living systems, processes become less and less lineal. By the time we get to what we consider quintessentially human, whether we are concerned with aesthetics or psychology, we are almost always involved with supralineal processes. Social and ecological processes are even more typically supralineal. If we try to analyze these processes by analogy to "How to Change a Flat Tire," we often distort them and sometimes end up in a mess.

The writing process is an apt example. It is a quintessentially human creative (psychological) and communicative (social) process. Empirical studies of experienced writers clearly show that lineal representations seriously distort what writers actually do when they write. A more accurate representation was suggested in Chapter 1 (page 86).

> *Writing consists of two contradictory subprocesses: on the one hand, we must generate or discover material; on the other, we must select and order that material. The first subprocess usually predominates in the early phases, the second in the late phases of writing. Both are typically active during drafting . . . .*

Within the framework provided by a statement like this (and with appropriate reiteration to keep the framework in readers' minds), one can go on to discuss first the generation of material and second the selection and ordering of that material. The principle is this: *within a framework which asserts that the process is supralineal and which makes readers aware of the distortion, one can justifiably discuss various aspects of that process in a lineal order.* Or to use Richards' term, it is the interanimation of the framework with the parts of the writing that communicates the supralineal meanings.

Part One of this textbook is a process-analysis of a complicated supralineal process: writing. The subject—how to write—is not reducible to a lineal representation without dangerous distortions. Consequently, this text is itself an attempt to resolve the problem we are considering: how to verbally represent a supralineal process.

Here is an example of a student's attempt to write an analysis of a supralineal process.

MY SUPRA-LINEAL WRITING PROCESS TOLD IN A LINEAL WAY

My writing process, from initial assignment to final completion, roughly follows three basic stages. I name these stages with the acknowledgement that the thinking process involved in writing does not follow neat, orderly stages of development, but rather that thought processes are haphazard and that, consequently, writing is a supra-lineal process. Naming stages allows me to simplify a normally complex process in reality. The stages are procrastination, thought and actual writing.

When I have been given an assignment, the majority of my time (from assignment to completion) is spent procrastinating; I never do today what I can do tomorrow. I generally avoid thinking about the project and do nothing towards its completion.

But when the due-date of any particular essay creeps uncomfortably close, small beads of sweat form above my brow and I enter my thought stage: I consider just what I should do. Generally, no writing is attempted. If the assignment is a research essay, I choose a topic (if I have a choice), gather relevant books and begin reading. If the assignment is like the first essay of this class, I merely think about how I should tackle the essay because I already have the knowledge and no research is necessary. This thought stage prepares me for the third stage, actual writing.

My actual writing stage is the most complicated and confusing of all the stages. Procrastination, thinking, reading, agony, and writing all play roles in this stage—with no particular order. And since this stage is generally inspired by due-date proximity, it is further confused by the hastiness with which I must write.

I seldom know exactly what my essay will say until I begin writing. I must write to clarify my ideas; my thoughts are too fleeting to possibly organize and write an essay in my head, so I must capture those elusive ideas and ground them on paper. Once I have written many ideas down, my thesis-statement or controlling idea begins to show itself. With such a controlling idea, the purpose of my paper becomes clear and further reading, thinking and writing that I do becomes focussed; the essay begins to become organized.

Yet, even with such an organizer as a controlling idea, my writing process is far from the accepted methodology for writing essays. For example, I constantly revise as I write, not after I have finished. Also, I generally write the body of the essay first; and as I mentioned previously, I seldom come up with a controlling idea until I have written much of this body. After I have the controlling idea and have finished the body of the essay, I write the introduction, making it suit the body. Then comes a conclusion, a title, and a rewrite. Because I procrastinate so much, I have little time for the actual writing and therefore revise only once. I do this revision as I am making the good draft. Consequently, though, my final draft is seldom as polished as it could be.

Despite my haphazard ways of completing an essay, the essay does get finished. This lineal process-analysis can capture only some of the complexities of my supra-lineal writing process.

Brad Lloyd

Brad makes good use of the framework—title, opening, and ending—to state explicitly that his writing process is supralineal, that he is "naming stages" only "to simplify a normally complex process." Since clarity often demands that the aspects of a process be discussed individually, using the framework to emphasize the actual complexity of the process is a very important technique.

Brad also emphasizes the supralineal complexity in the body of his process-analysis. About his "actual writing stage" he states, "Procrastination, thinking, reading, agony and writing all play roles in this stage—with no particular order." In his penultimate paragraph, he makes use of readers' contextual knowledge when he contrasts his process with "the accepted methodology" (see page 9). Referring to contexts of various sorts is another important technique for communicating the supralineal nature of a process.

It is worth noting that Brad's process-analysis is characterized by a certain degree of guilt, manifested first on the level of word choice. It starts with "haphazard," something of a snarl-word for what is actually a *recursive* process. We call recursive any process that regularly loops back upon itself, repeating procedures that were initiated in earlier phases, as when Brad returns to thinking and reading after he has already begun "actual writing."

"Procrastination" is also a snarl-word, which may or may not be appropriate. Insofar as Brad's first stage is essentially stalling and results in his not having enough time to revise adequately, the connotations of "procrastination" are correct. Insofar as this may actually be an incubation stage (see page 30), it may be more functional than Brad realizes.

At any event, there is order to this process. It just is not the lineal order of "the accepted methodology." It moves from thinking to unstructured writing, finds a center of gravity (i.e., a controlling idea), and then is organized; the body is finished, and an introduction, title, and ending are written (in that order); the essay is polished and recopied. Revision recurs throughout this process. Although the "actual writing" starts too late and structural revision is probably slighted, the process is not haphazard. Like most writers' creative processes, it just has an order distinctly different from "the accepted methodology."

A careful investigation would probably reveal, moreover, that Brad emphasizes distinct types of revision during different phases. Good writers, although they may do any type of revision at any point, in the early phases of revision want to get meanings right and to develop an appropriate strategy for the rhetorical context in which they imagine the writing will be read. In the later phases, they tend to emphasize revision for style and correctness.

THE GENETIC FALLACY

There is a certain similarity between progression in time and logical progression. That is because logic *is* the structure that underlies certain thought processes, which do progress in time. The similarity is emphasized when the logical structure is represented in *if-then* statements.

If we plant in June, *then* we should have fresh corn in September.

If Socrates is human, *then* he is mortal.

If whales are warm-blooded and nurse their young, *then* they must be mammals.

In the first case, there is actually a progression in time, from June to September; but the logical progression is actually from general to particular. The unstated generalization is, "Corn takes three months to grow." The thought process moves from that generalization through the particular instance to a particular conclusion.

In the second case, the unstated generalization is, "All human beings are mortal." If Socrates is a particular instance of human being, it follows that he must be mortal. In the third case, the unstated generalization is the definition of mammal, which includes being warm-blooded and nursing young.

The term *logical progression** represents the way logical structures reflect thought processes, which do progress in time. Fully stated, the progression includes one or more thinkers and could be written as follows:

> If you admit that all human beings are mortal and I demonstrate that Socrates is human, then you must logically admit that Socrates is mortal.

Thus stated, it clearly represents a thought process.

It also suggests a causal connection:

> *Because* you are a logical person who admits that all human beings are mortal and *because* I will demonstrate that Socrates is human, you will admit that Socrates is mortal.

A logical progression thus can be a causal explanation of why someone believes (or should believe) something.

Since premises come first and, in a sense, *cause* conclusions, however, we sometimes fall from process-analysis into *the genetic fallacy*. This fallacy occurs when someone argues that whatever came first *must* be the explanation of whatever comes later. For example, although it usually comes first when one is learning to write, penmanship is not the basis of good writing.

Perhaps the best-known example of the genetic fallacy is the psychoanalytic assertion that people's adult dispositions are determined by

*Although usually treated under the heading of argumentation, logical progression can be properly classified as one of the progressive patterns of arrangement and could have been a section in this chapter. Formal logic will not be treated in detail here, however, in part because there are many good textbooks devoted entirely to formal logic and in part because we lack sufficient evidence to indicate that formal training in logic significantly improves thinking in ways that lead to improved writing.

childhood traumas. That assertion may be true, or somewhat true—certainly childhood experiences have some influence on one's adult character. But the degree of influence remains to be proven empirically. It is illogical to presume that, *just because* they came first, early childhood experiences *must be* the explanation for later development.

A particular version of the genetic fallacy, "the intentional fallacy," was criticized by the school of literary criticism that was dominant in North America during the mid-twentieth century. The critics of that school asserted that it is fallacious to determine the meaning of a literary text by asking its author what she or he *intended* it to mean. The author was motivated to write the text by her or his intentions. Those intentions were, in a sense, the seed from which the text grew. But we cannot deduce the meaning of the finished text from those intentions.

The meaning, and even the wording, of a literary text is influenced by a variety of factors. Since we know that essential parts of the human creative process are unconscious, we know that the author was not fully aware of how and why the text took the form it did. We also know that writers work in social contexts, and that they choose words, images, and even concepts from among—or in reaction against—those available at the time. Furthermore, we know that some of the meaning of a literary text results from what readers bring to it, that the meaning of the text emerges in the interaction between text and reader (which also occurs in a social context).

Given these complexities, we must move carefully from process-analysis to causal explanation. And the more complex the process, the more carefully we must move.

ADDITIONAL READING

Burke, Kenneth. "Poetics in Particular; Language in General." In *Language as Symbolic Action*. Berkeley: University of California, 1966. Burke here uses Poe's essay on "The Philosophy of Composition" to discuss the common tendency to treat principles, which logically come first, as if they actually occurred first in time.

Wimsatt, W. K., and Monroe C. Beardsley. "The Intentional Fallacy" and "The Affective Fallacy." In *The Verbal Icon*. Lexington: University of Kentucky, 1954. Also available in various anthologies, such as Hazard Adams, ed., *Critical Theory Since Plato*. New York: Harcourt Brace Jovanovich, 1971.

EXERCISE

1. Do a process-analysis of your own writing process. (See pages 8-15 and Exercise 4 on page 289.)

2. Consider the process-analyses you have written in the past. If you had a choice, what type of processes did you choose to write about.? Did you represent the processes as lineal? To what extent was this representation accurate?

3. Select any supralineal process (e.g., the interaction around your family's dinner table, the process by which someone gets to be a political leader in the United States, Canada, New Zealand, Australia, or Great Britain). Be sure to select a process you know well. Analyze it carefully. Write a process-analysis that accurately represents the process.

4. Try to write an analysis of the mental processes of a person reading a complex poem.

5. In the science section of a newspaper or newsmagazine, find a summary of a process-analysis originally presented as a scientific paper or article. Obtain the original. Compare and contrast the two versions.

6. Find an instance in which a lineal process-analysis led to a social or ecological blunder because a choice was made or a policy chosen on the basis of a simplistic analysis. Write a critique.

7. Find an example of the genetic fallacy. Write a critique.

8. Read Wimsatt and Beardsley's argument against "the intentional fallacy" (in *The Verbal Icon*). To what extent are they making a valid and useful point. To what extent, if any, might it be useful to know an author's intentions.

9. Study a textbook of formal logic, preferably one oriented toward writers' needs (e.g., Howard Kahane's *Logic & Contemporary Rhetoric*). What can you learn from it that might help you as a writer.

10. Revise the process-analysis you wrote about your writing (see pages 8-9 and Exercise 1 above) to help readers avoid perceiving that process as more lineal than it actually is.

CAUSATION

Now whether it be
Beastly oblivion, or some craven scruple
Of thinking too precisely on the event—
A thought which, quarter'd, hath but one part wisdom
And ever three parts coward,—I do not know
Why yet I live to say "this thing's to do,"
Sith I have cause, and will, and strength, and means
to do't.

William Shakespeare (1601), *Hamlet:* IV/4

. . . [I]t is very remarkable how often a symptom is determined in several ways, is 'overdetermined.'

Sigmund Freud (1895)

We are especially arbitrary in picking out the cause from among the whole group, or context, of conditions—of prior and subsequent events which hang together.

I. A. Richards (1936)

Some brain researchers estimate that more than 80% of the neurons (nerve cells) in the human brain act to inhibit other cells, suppressing muscular response or preventing them from transmitting information to other cells.

Monte Buchsbaum (1978)

CORRELATION AND THE TYPES OF CAUSATION

Scientists make a useful distinction between causation and correlation. A *correlation* has been established when it has been demonstrated that two events regularly occur in conjunction with each other. The demonstration of a correlation does not necessarily mean there is a causal connection between the events. ("Almost every morning, my father makes a pot of coffee and then takes a shower." The correlation is close to 100%, but it seems highly unlikely that the shower is caused by the making of the coffee.)

Scientific reports are often reports of correlations. A correlation is much easier to demonstrate than a causal relationship: if events occur in conjunction more frequently than can be explained by chance, there is a correlation. Scientists (or for that matter, literary critics) often demonstrate a correlation first and only second attempt a causal analysis to explain that correlation. The correlation between smoking cigarettes and contracting lung cancer, for example, was demonstrated long before any causal relationship was scientifically established. The parallels between Dickens' *Dombey and Son* and Lawrence's "A Rockinghorse Winner" are more easily established than Dickens' influence on Lawrence's story.

A common fallacy confuses correlation with causation. It is easy to jump to the conclusion that because two events regularly occur one after the other, the first must be causing the second. But a correlation is actually no more than grounds for suspicion that a causal relationship may exist. Even if a causal relationship is discovered, the first event may not have caused the second: it is possible, for instance, that both events result from a third factor not originally considered. ("In order to help himself wake up, my father takes a shower and drinks coffee.")

We are concerned with causation whenever we ask, "*Why* did such-and-such happen?" In human affairs, the question of causation becomes a question of motivation, "*Why* did so-and-so do such-and-such?" We are also concerned with causation when we ask about meanings. The question, "Why does this text have this meaning?" is essentially "Why is a reader justified in taking this meaning from the text?" or "How are readers constrained to see this meaning in the text?" Thus the question of causation is a very broad, important, and quintessentially human question.

Distinct types of societies seem to rely on distinct types of causal analysis. This may be difficult to accept because we all tend, ethnocentrically, to consider the ways of thinking that predominate in our own cultures to be "obvious" and "natural." Nonetheless, historical and cross-cultural studies indicate that there are at least four basic types of causal analysis, any one of which may be predominant in a given culture or subculture.

Non-industrial societies tend to rely primarily (not exclusively) on explanation by analogy or on explanation by authority. Explanation by authority takes this form: "Why should I obey the Queen?" "Because God said so." (The authority, of course, need not be personified; it may take a form like, "Because that is the nature of the universe.")

Explanation by authority is often a special case of explanation by analogy. If asked, "Why should I obey the Queen?" someone in Elizabethan England might have replied, "Because the universe is arranged in a Great Chain of Being with God on top, then the angels, the Queen, the aristocrats, the freemen, the serfs, the animals, and so on; just as the angels should obey God and the animals should obey people, so ordinary people should obey the Queen and the aristocrats." This type of explanation has predominated in most human societies for most of the time human beings have been on this planet. It operates by establishing analogical parallels (sometimes called *myths*). These parallels may, for instance, be between past and present or between the behavior of gods and the behavior of people. But there is no attempt to demonstrate a cause-effect relationship, say, between God's authority over the angels and the Queen's authority over her subjects. (People in such cultures are not unaware that physical actions produce physical reactions, but another form of explanation is primary.)

A third type of explanation, cause-effect reasoning, comes into its own in industrial societies. (For reasons which we will leave to the historians, classical Greece and ancient Rome seem to have had tendencies in this direction also). A dramatic negative demonstration of the correlation between cause-effect reasoning and industrialization may be found at present in many Third World countries that are trying to industrialize quickly: the people have difficulty thinking along the lines required to run imported machinery (for example, the kind of cause-effect reasoning required to repair a broken machine).

A fourth type of causal analysis explains events in terms of constraints. Although used increasingly widely in some fields (e.g., computer science, linguistics, psychology, biology, and system theory), it is not very well known or broadly generalized. It is very useful for explaining complex events and choices. As we move from an age dominated by machines to an age dominated by computers, and as our social systems grow ever more complexly interrelated, this type of causal analysis will probably gain primacy. Causal analysis by constraints is as useful as it is unfamiliar. It will, therefore, be explained at some length below after the varieties of cause-effect patterns have been discussed.

CAUSE-EFFECT PATTERNS

If you learned a structure for writing about causation from a previous writing textbook or composition course, it was almost undoubtedly "cause to effect." That is because this is a relatively simple structure and also because mechanical cause-effect reasoning predominates in industrial societies. It is the type of reasoning that gave rise to machines and that best explains their internal workings. But it is not always adequate for writing about other kinds of subject matter.

Philosophers sometimes call cause-effect thinking "the billiard ball model of the universe" because events are explained in much the same way as motion on the billiard table. The physical analogy is apt because this type of cause-effect reasoning became dominant first in physics, where it is called *action-reaction* (i.e., Newton's third law of motion). Cause-effect reasoning was so effective in physics (especially in mechanics) that it has since been applied in the other sciences. In psychology, for example, it becomes *stimulus-response*.

The terms "cause" and "effect" are labels we attach to events to represent our explanations of *why* those events happen. One billiard ball ("the cause") strikes another ("the effect"). But if the second ball strikes something, it becomes a cause and the reaction of that something becomes the effect. Likewise, the motion of the first ball was itself caused when it was struck by the billiard cue, and the motion of the cue was caused by a person.

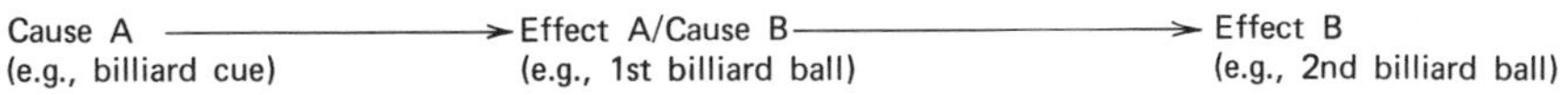

Cause A (e.g., billiard cue) → Effect A/Cause B (e.g., 1st billiard ball) → Effect B (e.g., 2nd billiard ball)

FIGURE 5.1 Simple Linear Cause-Effect

The result of cause-effect reasoning is a causal chain. There is an old nursery rhyme that epitomizes the causal chain:

For want of a nail the shoe was lost,
For want of a shoe the horse was lost,
For want of a horse the rider was lost,
For want of a rider the battle was lost,
For want of a battle the kingdom was lost,
And all for the want of a horseshoe nail.

A causal chain can branch, for example, if the second billiard ball strikes two or three others. And naturally, if the chain is broken at any point—for example, if the billiard cue misses the first ball—all subsequent effects disappear. These possibilities may complicate an explanation somewhat.

In an industrialized culture, the most common response to the question, "Why?" is a causal chain. "Why were you late to class?" "Because it takes nine minutes to walk here from my previous class, and the instructor didn't let us out until three minutes ago." A *full* explanation would be more complex—"Why couldn't you interrupt or leave before you were 'let out?'"—but the causal chain is accepted as a *sufficient* explanation in most social contexts.

Causal chains flow from cause to effect. But explanations based on them can flow in either direction. One may reason from *effect to cause*. In human terms, this involves explaining, though not necessarily justifying, the means in terms of the ends. ("I couldn't interrupt or leave before my instructor let us out because I was afraid that might affect my grade.") In terms of Burke's Pentad (pages 67-71), we would say the *act* is explained by the *purpose* (i.e., by the purpose-act ratio).

Thus the anticipated effect explains the act. In an essay about mugging, for instance, a writer might argue that such crimes are common because they so often go unpunished. The anticipated effect (lack of punishment) is offered as an explanation of the crime, even though the mugging occurs first and the lack of punishment later.

As this example suggests, explanations often must be multiple. The anticipated lack of punishment would not by itself explain a mugging. There must be at least one other anticipated effect, such as financial gain or the pleasure of being in a position of relative power. And, as so often, these further explanations raise further questions: Why does the mugger desire financial gain or power? Why is the mugger morally willing to steal in this situation? Writers using cause-effect reasoning must be careful not to oversimplify by leaving out important parts of an explanation.

In some cases of multiple causation, the effect can occur even when only some of the factors are present. In other cases, all factors are necessary. Consider, for instance, the following problem-example.

> *A student is studying late on the last night of finals week because he has three examinations on the last day. He runs out of cigarettes. Tired and groggy, he goes downstairs to buy some more. He cuts across an alley to an all-night store. A car with one headlight and bad brakes comes down the alley. The driver had taken his last examination that day and had been celebrating. He tries to stop quickly, but cannot. The police form, which must be filled out, asks, "What was the cause of the accident?"*

Remove almost any single element from the story and the accident probably does not occur—for example, if the student did not smoke cigarettes or if examinations had been scheduled so that no one had more than one test on any given day. That raises questions like why people smoke cigarettes and why universities are structured as they are. But the police, of course, are not looking for a full explanation. All the police form requires is, "Defective vehicle and intoxicated driver." That is a sufficient explanation for police purposes.

Whether it be single or multiple, this type of cause-effect reasoning is linear. An event is explained in terms of other events that occur before or afterwards. Causes and effects are assumed to be proportional with each other (which is the definition of "linear"). The connections among events are often diagrammed as lines (which is the definition of "lineal").

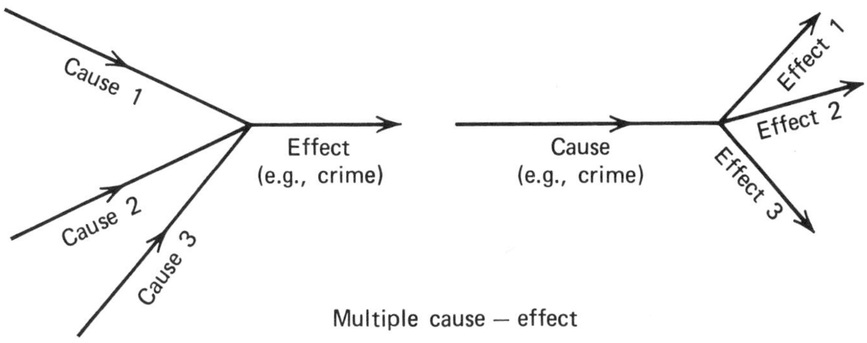

FIGURE 5.2 Multiple Cause-Effect

As this drawing suggests, linear cause-effect patterns are comparable to lineal processes. Indeed, lineal processes are most accurately explained by cause-effect reasoning.

Just as processes can be cyclical (see pages 290-291), so cause-effect chains can be circular. When the cause-effect pattern is circular, as in an on-going cycle, distinguishing cause from effect can be problematic (or irrelevant). The classic example is, "Which came first—the chicken or the egg?" To avoid errors, one must take this additional complexity into account. Consider the following two cases.

Hudson's Bay Company records from certain areas of northern Canada demonstrate a cyclical relationship between the lynx population and the snowshoe hare population. The cycle typically runs four years, during which the lynx population rises to a peak and abruptly drops off to near extinction. Meanwhile the snowshoe hare population slowly declines and then starts to rise rapidly. The explanation is as follows: as there get to be more and more lynx in this simple ecosystem, they eat more hares until there are so few hares that the lynx have little to eat and most of them die off; this allows a rapid rise in the hare population, which allows the lynx population to grow again until the system once more reaches its limit. This sort of oscillation, incidentally, is typical of simple—not of complex—ecosystems.

Scientists (and therapists) investigating couple relationships among human beings have often discovered cyclical patterns. Imagine a stereotypical married couple in which he tends to criticize and she tends to withdraw. The correlation is undenied. But her explanation is that she withdraws because *he criticizes her (or to use the sexist snarl-word, because he nags her). And his explanation is that he criticizes her because she is so withdrawn that he has to do something aggressive to get any response whatsoever. In other words, both agree about the ongoing causal chain, but each blames the other; each says, "My undesirable behavior is an* effect*; yours is the* cause*.*

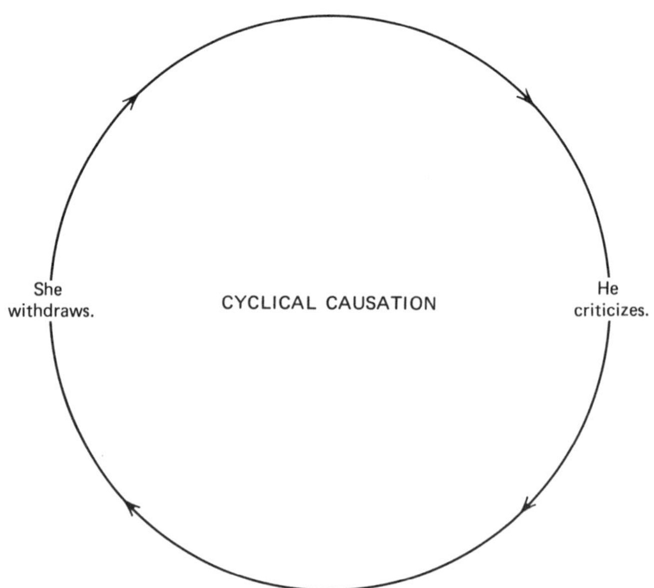

FIGURE 5.3 Cyclical Causation

From an ecological, therapeutic, or just a logical perspective, the cause-effect distinction tends to break down when a causal chain is cyclical. Either we must say that each event is *both cause and effect* or we must say that the distinction is not relevant. Even if we wish to assign blame, when a cycle has been ongoing long enough, the appropriate question changes from "Who started it?" to "Who is keeping it going?" An investigation aimed at finding out whether, many years ago, he criticized before the first time she withdrew, or *vice versa*, is probably futile and almost certainly irrelevant. Indeed, such couples spend a lot of time arguing about who started it—which allows each to blame the other and also allows the cycle to continue.

The futility of trying to impose cause-effect distinctions onto ongoing cycles has interesting implications in practical situations. One standard example of a cyclical relationship is the escalating international arms race: the U.S. government, in effect, says "We must increase our military strength *because* the Soviet Union is increasing its military strength"; the U.S.S.R. government, in effect, says "We must increase our military strength *because* the United States is increasing its military strength." Each government claims that its armaments are defensive, that it is increasing its military might only in reaction to the threat from the other; and, for a variety of reasons, the cycle continues (and continues to escalate).

What you need to remember is that the distinction between "cause" and "effect" is difficult to make in cyclical systems. Fortunately, it is often also unimportant, because events are shaped not so much by initial conditions as by the structure of the ongoing process. To cite Hippocrates, the ancient physician whose medical texts sometimes approach the literary, "All parts of the organism form a circle. Therefore every part is both beginning and end."

CAUSES AND CONTEXTS

There are certain types of situations which are at a level of complexity such that any sort of cause-effect analysis (even multiple or cyclical) oversimplifies them. To use a cause-effect pattern when you are writing about such situations will distort them and may lead you into errors. Fortunately, there is an ancient rhetorical pattern that is admirably suited for verbally representing just these types of situations.

Look again at the nursery rhyme cited on page 303. The moral is quite clear: be painstakingly careful about every detail. The rhyme fulfills its rhetorical purpose—to convince little children that extreme carefulness is a virtue. But it is not very informative about why kingdoms fall (nor, for that matter, is it seriously intended to be). Just as no straw ever broke a camel's back unless the camel was overloaded to begin with, so no kingdom ever fell for want of a horseshoe nail unless it was already in dreadful peril. Although it might have been the immediate cause, "*all* for the want of a horseshoe nail" is hardly an adequate answer to, "Why was the kingdom lost?" Pushing this nursery rhyme beyond its intended purpose suggests the limitations of "the billiard ball model."

To make the point another way, let us return to the billiard table. Suppose we take up the same billiard cue and make the identical stroke—but strike a person instead of a billiard ball. We are no longer dealing with merely physical motion. To predict or explain subsequent events, we must analyze a person's interpretive response to a symbolic action. And such human "reactions" cannot be explained adequately by analogy to physical motion.

The nature of the response will depend on how the person who is struck interprets the event. And that we cannot predict without knowing a lot of *contextual* information. Is this person an acquaintance, a friend, a stranger, an enemy? Are we in a billiard parlor, a bar, a friend's gameroom? What memories and interpretations does this person have of comparable events? What analogies come into her or his mind? Is this person presently sober, slightly intoxicated, drunk, or stimulated?

Of course, we could call all these contexts "causes." We could say, for example, "Since we were in a bar and the person was a drunken stranger who had recently been poked by a police officer's nightstick (which reminded him of the times he used to be poked by his father as a child), his response to being struck by a billiard cue was to throw a punch." But such a causal analysis is an explanation on a distinct level of complexity from one based on the momentum and direction of the billiard cue. So long as we stay on the billiard table, the effect is basically explained by the immediate prior cause, that is, by the stroke of the billiard cue (or "the want of a horseshoe nail"). That is because on the billiard table we are concerned with the mechanical transfer of physical energy. As soon as we become involved with meaning (that is, with the transfer and interpretation of information), various contextual constraints become more important than the immediate physical "cause" for explaining the event.

Consider the following example.

Konrad Lorenz, the Nobel-prize winning ethologist, was crouching in the tall grass outside his country house, moving about in figure-eights, glancing regularly over his shoulders and quacking con-

stantly. He looked up to see a group of tourists standing at the garden fence, staring horrified in his direction.

From the tourists' perspective, Lorenz' behavior was inexplicable (if not insane*). However, hidden in the tall grass was a line of ducklings; Lorenz had substituted himself for their mother, and he was at that moment congratulating himself "on the obedience and exactitude with which my ducklings came waddling after me." The tourists could not explain the event because they could not see the ducklings *and* because they did not know Lorenz was an ethologist doing an experiment. Even if they had seen the ducklings, they still might have judged Lorenz insane if they did not understand the scientific context.

It is tempting to treat contextual constraints as if they were just another set of causes and then to explain such situations as if we were dealing with multiple cause-effect. Sometimes that can be done without distorting meanings. Other times, especially when the matters are psychological, social, aesthetic, or ecological, such analyses oversimplify actual events and lead toward erroneous conclusions.

In the example of the student struck by the automobile, all of the factors mentioned in the narrative function on the same level. But suppose we wish to get at a deeper explanation. We might argue, for example, that the incident occurred because the city in which it happened lacked an inexpensive and efficient system of public transport, which the second student could have used instead of driving while drunk. This is another level of explanation. It does not contradict the level called for by the police form. The *immediate* causes still include bad brakes and slowed reflexes. (See page 304.)

Suppose we then ask what motivated the first student to smoke despite clear evidence that tobacco fumes are harmful to his health. Perhaps he smoked cigarettes because (1) they were available, (2) he could afford them, (3) having been raised by a father who smoked, he associated cigarettes with masculinity and maturity, (4) having been exposed to advertising, he associated cigarettes with sensuality and independence, and because (5) nicotine physiologically reduces tension in mammals who are habituated to it. How does this information mix with bad brakes, slowed reflexes, and the absence of an inexpensive, efficient public transport system?

*Perhaps this parenthesis is unnecessary. After all, we usually use the word *insane* precisely when we have failed to explain an action.

The point is that a *full* causal analysis of any such event is complex and involves many levels of explanation. For the police, this is no problem. Given their practical purposes, they can ignore all but one level. Writers, if their rhetorical purposes are similarly simple, can sometimes do the same. But what if your purposes are such that a simplistic explanation will not do?

HIERARCHY AND CONSTRAINTS

Historians try to deal with such complexities by creating a distinction between *immediate* and *basic* causation. Thus World War I may be explained by writing,

> The largest war the world had yet seen was immediately precipitated by the assassination of Archduke Francis Ferdinand of Austria-Hungary by a Serbian nationalist in 1914. There were, however, many factors that had led toward war. Prominent causes were the imperialistic, territorial and economic rivalries that had been intensifying from the late 19th century, particularly among Germany, France, Great Britain, Russia, and Austria-Hungary. Of equal importance was the rampant spirit of nationalism, especially unsettling in the empire of Austria-Hungary and perhaps also in France.
>
> *The New Columbia Encyclopedia*

This distinction creates a *hierarchy* with two levels. The "basic causes" create a *basis* for the event; the immediate causes spark the event. The assassination of Archduke Ferdinand could no more have caused a war by itself than a straw could break the back of a lightly loaded camel. If asked whether World War I was caused by the assassination of the Archduke or by "imperialistic territorial and economic rivalries," one should answer, "Both," and then go on to explain the relationship between the two levels of explanation. That is the reason for using the term *hierarchy*; it suggests that the relationship between the levels of explanation has been made clear.

There are not necessarily only two levels of explanation. Just as a poem may have more than two levels of meaning, so a causal analysis may require more than two levels of explanation. The writing process is again a good example. A writer's choices are accurately explained only by a complex hierarchy of causation.

In Part One of this textbook, writers' choices are explained in terms of a three-level hierarchy: meaning, rhetorical context, and language. On each level, there are a variety of factors that guide choices. Consciously or unconsciously, good writers choose and arrange words within these constraints. Logically, meaning is the highest level: the words should represent the writers' meanings. After this level of constraint is met, rhetorical context is logically the next concern: the words should achieve the writers' purposes with their intended audiences on the intended occasions. Then the level of language: the words should create the desired *persona*, have the intended connotations, and so forth. As we move down the hierarchy, the writers' choices narrow.

Of course, the writing process itself is psychological, not logical. This hierarchy should not be confused with a process-analysis. Writers do not choose words by moving logically down this hierarchy. But the hierarchy does logically explain their choices and is, therefore, useful for someone learning to write better.

The hierarchy does not, moreover, force a writer to choose a particular word. In any given situation, a writer is free to choose any word that meets all relevant criteria (i.e., that does not violate any constraints on any of the three levels).

Suppose, for example, we want to explain a writer's choice of the last word of the following sentence:

By 1910, Kansas City was definitely __________.

To simplify the example, instead of starting with all the words in the English language, let us imagine that the writer has brainstormed and come up with the following possibilities: *metropolitan, citified, urban, suburban, oppidan, civic.* But the most basic constraint—that the word match the intended meaning—rules out *suburban* and *civic.* Then the writer is constrained not to choose *oppidan* because most of the intended readers would not know the word. The writer happens not to remember how to spell *metropolitan* (and does not want to make a bad impression with a misspelling). *Citified* does not "sound" quite right because it has slightly negative connotations, and the writer does not want to create a judgmental *persona.* Thus, by a process of elimination, the sentence becomes

By 1910, Kansas City was definitely urban.

This sort of analysis is called *explanation by constraints.*Its advantage is flexibility. Cause-effect reasoning is rigid. If a particular cause or combination of causes is present, then a particular effect must follow. Explanation by constraints allows for individual differences. Various events are possible, as long as they meet all the constraints present in the situation. Our writer is free to choose any word that meets the constraints present in that writing situation.

Explanation by constraints is formally negative. That is, it explains an event by explaining why other possible events did not occur. The writer's choice of a particular word is explained by listing the constraints that ruled out other words. In a sense the question is changed from *why?* to *why not?*

Because it is formally negative, explanation by constraints is equivalent to what classical rhetoricians called argument by *reductio ad absurdum*. In this type of argument, one begins by stating all the possibilities. One then eliminates possibilities one by one until only a single possibility remains.

> *Any of the six people in the house could have committed the murder. The husband was too frail to lift the murder weapon. The gardener, the maid, the cook and the valet were playing poker together at the time of the crime. Therefore, the butler did it.*

Indeed, this is how Hercules Poirot (Agatha Christie's fictional detective) says he solves mysteries: he begins by considering all possibilities, however improbable; he gathers information which eliminates possibilities; having ruled out the impossible, he then accepts the remaining possibility, however improbable. A perfect example of explanation by constraints.

Explanation by constraints is more difficult to do than cause-effect reasoning. Since simpler patterns are to be preferred, all else being equal, explanation by constraints should be used only when cause-effect reasoning is inadequate. For better and for worse, this means you usually should use explanation by a *hierarchy of constraints* when you want to give a reasonably full explanation of almost any human, ecological, or aesthetic event.

USING EXPLANATION BY CONSTRAINTS

Explanation by constraints is becoming increasingly common in various disciplines, from biology to psychology, from linguistics to computer science. Often it is used to explain decision-making processes. Sometimes it is used simply to make an argument more forceful, as in the following excerpt.

> . . . However, the critics were not aware of the fact that Garibaldi Lifts was severely restricted in its choice of location. Due to a series of geographic, legal and economic constraints, the Olympic Run lift system was an impossibility! If one is to understand the lift company's choice of location, therefore, it is first necessary to examine the constraints that affected their decision. Only then is it possible to see that the Alpine lift system was the best alternative solution.

> . . . Through government financing, plans are underway for the construction of a town site on the Olympic Run side of Whistler. . . . If Garibaldi Lifts Limited were to begin construction on an Olympic Run lift in the summer of 1978, . . . they would not only restrict the location of the town site, but also possibly jeopardize its success. This, in itself, was reason enough for Garibaldi Lifts to consider an alternative location for a 1978 lift. There were, however, two other constraints that eliminated the Olympic Run lift as a possibility.
>
> While it was possible for the lift company to cut a two hundred foot wide line up the Olympic Run side to accommodate a lift system, it was not legally possible for them to cut any new trails in the surrounding terrain. . . .
>
> The final constraint that forced Garibaldi Lifts to seek a new lift location is perhaps the most surprising. . . . Garibaldi Lifts is a subsidiary of Power Corporation in Toronto. Power Corporation is also the parent company of Grouse Mountain Resorts Limited. . . . Grouse is feeling the pinch of two extremely poor winters on top of a six million dollar loan for a new "Skyride." Power Corporation, and indirectly Garibaldi Lifts, has therefore been footing the bill for Grouse's misfortunes. . . . The Olympic Run lift, unlike the Alpine system, demanded a lengthy chairlift (some 2500 feet as opposed to 1000), additional manpower requirements (to handle parking and ticket sales), and finally, additional facilities (ticket office and base station). All of these added up to a high cost in comparison to an Alpine chairlift. The economics of the system, therefore, dictated that an Olympic Run lift was an impossibility and an Alpine chairlift a solution.
>
> If one examines the constraints placed on Garibaldi Lifts through geographical, legal, and economic limitations, it becomes clearly obvious why the Alpine region of Whistler was selected over the Olympic Run side for the construction of a new chairlift. . . . What it will do is provide a quicker access to the top of the mountain, reduce crowds in the Alpine region, and lastly, make more terrain accessible to Whistler skiers. . . .
>
> Andrew Crosse

Note that any one of the three factors is logically sufficient to explain the decision. Given the strength of the opposition to the decision from several special-interest groups, however, Andrew chose to use all three. Note also that there is a "positive" explanation which justifies the Alpine lift, but that Andrew relegates it to one sentence in his final paragraph. In other words, there was an alternative strategy available to him—he could have emphasized the positive benefits of the Alpine lift and avoided detailed discussion of the Olympic lift—but he chose the fuller and more basic explanation. Thus we have here a case in which cause-effect explanation would have been adequate, but explanation by constraints was more effective.

Freud used the word *overdetermination* to describe cases where there is more determination present than is needed to explain the event. Freud used the word first in speaking of psychological symptoms. Later he applied it to dream symbolism—which suggests why the concept is also usefully applied to literary criticism.

Richards took up the word in explaining his "context theorem of meaning." This theorem, he said, "regards all discourse—outside the technicalities of science—as over-determined, as having multiplicity of meaning." He added that it restrains the "One and Only One True Meaning Superstition." Thus it was, in part, his literary critical background that led him to assert,

> *we are especially arbitrary in picking out the cause from among the whole group, or context, of conditions—of prior and subsequent events which hang together.*

When using cause-effect reasoning to write analysis, writers tend to stop when they have provided sufficient "cause" to explain the event. They have answered the question implicit in the cause-effect pattern—the poem, incident, decision, or whatever has been "explained." The writing has formally achieved closure (see pages 130-131) and feels complete. So the writer stops.

But the most interesting and important levels of explanation may not have been reached. If the event is "overdetermined," the closure may be premature. One of the greatest virtues of the constraints format is that it encourages writers to delve more deeply and readers to consider more fully. The following paper is an analysis of why people eat popcorn in movie theaters. On the most immediate level, the explanation is obvious (and boring). But by delving more deeply, the writer comes up with an interesting and significant theory.

POPCORN GOES TO THE MOVIES

People go to the movies for various reasons. They like to enjoy themselves, learn something new, edify themselves, etc. In short, they are in search of illusions, dreams, entertainment, magic. Having equipped themselves with a box of popcorn and a cup of Seven-Up, and having occupied their comfortable seats, they are ready to be amused. Popcorn and Seven-Up only heighten and add to their enjoyment of a movie.

The factors which influence this widespread and unique ritual seem quite obvious. One of them is simply the fact that popcorn tastes good. Going to a movie is, therefore, a perfect occasion for buying a box of it. Another constraint is the traditional association of popcorn with movie-going. For some people movie-going is just inseparable from popcorn-eating. At the movies, the odor of popcorn and the fizzing of Seven-Up and Coke mixes with their joyful expectations of something new and enjoyable that will start unreeling before their eyes in a few moments. It has, therefore, become a habit to eat popcorn at the movies. This habit is also reinforced by parents who are quick to oblige their little ones with a bucket of popcorn. For others who are also being initiated into movie-going, this atmosphere at the movies can be contagious, and the odor of popcorn so attractive that they quickly line up to get their own box of epicurean pleasure.

These are the factors that lend themselves easily to the apparent and superficial explanation of the eating habits at the movies. There are, however, several other factors which also influence popcorn consumption at the movies. Since people usually go to the movies after a week of hard work, they are feeling relaxed and free. Their thoughts are not only tuned to the atmosphere at the cinema, but are also motivated by the steep admission price. The four or five dollars should entitle them to get their money's worth of entertainment and for a few cents more also a box of popcorn. Complete enjoyment, of course, means not only a "good" movie, but lots of popcorn along with it. In this narrow sense, money also functions as a constraint. If they are going to spend money, they might just as well spend it in a proper way.

Eating and watching a movie could, however, be considered two actions which are quite incompatible. Usually a movie should demand a certain degree of commitment to its message and, of course, its artistic qualities. It seems that, by drinking and eating while watching it, the viewers interfere with the communication between the movie and themselves. Consequently, these eating habits point to the most important constraint: the attitude of viewers towards movies in general.

This attitude is quite simple. An average movie-goer pays his four dollars, buys his popcorn and a drink, sits in the back row and waits to be entertained. Indeed, the very use of the word "cinema" and the word "movie" seems to point at the underlying difference in approach to the cinematic art. While "movie" is a popular word denoting something entertaining, "cinema" implies something more serious. What with the influence of television and the impact of Hollywood's movie industry, films have in a sense degenerated into movies: pure entertainment. As people go to the movies mostly to enjoy themselves, the pleasure of eating becomes extremely compatible with watching a movie. Like sitting in front of a TV set, for some people watching a movie is not complete if they are not gorging on popcorn while Dudley Moore is falling in love with Bo Derek. Ironically, it is not so much the attitude towards food in general that constrains the eating habits of some movie-goers, but primarily their attitude towards movie-theaters as places of entertainment.

This attitude has been promoted largely by the consumerist nature of North American society. Not only does this society dispose of diapers and paper cups, but also of works of art: films. The prevailing getting-your-money's worth mentality of this society functions as a kind of underlying constraint. This mentality can be seen in the attitude of movie-goers. Parallel with the change in the social significance of the movies, the public has also changed its attitude towards them. The movie-theater, an enchanting place of entertainment, edification, and even an occasional catharsis, has, therefore, degenerated into a supermarket of amusement and a feast of popcorn.

To summarize, the constraints that influence the eating habits of some movie-goers are the following:

Constraint 1: popcorn tastes good
Constraint 2: association of popcorn with movie-going
Constraint 3: atmosphere at the movies
Constraint 4: money
Constraint 5: attitude towards movies
Constraint 6: consumer society

Although each of the constraints separately determines popcorn eating at the movies, no one can singly explain the complex pattern of motivation. Only by demonstrating how and why these factors mutually constrain popcorn eaters can an adequate explanation of the habit be provided. In terms of these constraints, movies are viewed as an integral part of the North American consumer society, which sheds additional light on this facet of the North American way of life. However, if you happen to agree with the quotation of Orson Welles—"All the good movies have already been made"—it might not be unreasonable to contend that some people chew richly buttered popcorn and chase it down with a huge cup of Coke because they are inclined to agree with Mr. Welles.

Branka Ozbolt

In a sense, this essay could have ended after the second paragraph. Had it been written in a cause-effect format, perhaps for an ordinary freshman composition class, it might well have. The second paragraph contains sufficient causation to explain the widespread eating of popcorn in movie theaters. But the interesting part of the essay—the writer's theory that the popcorn-eating is a symptom of a consumer society—would have been lost. The constraints format encourages writers to generate meanings beyond the obvious minimum.

Note also that there is some indication of hierarchy. The most basic, encompassing constraint is the consumer society, which promotes the attitudes toward both films and money. These attitudes then allow and encourage the association of popcorn with movies. The association of popcorn with movies and the good taste of the popcorn lead some people to buy it, thus creating an atmosphere that encourages other people. It is important in a constraints analysis, especially in the introduction or conclusion, to indicate what the relationships are among the various constraints. Only then has one demonstrated a *hierarchy of constraints.*

You should remember, moreover, that, in some instances, no single factor is an adequate explanation. A writer's word choice, for example, can usually be explained adequately only in terms of a number of overlapping constraints. This is also often the case when a number of individuals are noticed acting in remarkably similar ways. You must then explain what about the context constrains individuals toward that particular sort of behavior. The following paper attempts to explain why some—but not all—people get depressed and disoriented when they move into an old age home. The explanation is not simple because individuals vary and similar behavior may be motivated by different factors in different individuals.

JUST FILED AWAY. . .

An elderly person who has just moved into a nursing home is often depressed, disoriented and dissatisfied with this change in his life. Because of certain constraints, the senior citizen may decide to run away from the home, refuse to get up and eat in the morning, or even commit suicide. The reasons for his depression and his inability to adapt to the new surroundings are complex.

Constraint 1: Although a nursing home is generally viewed as a place which offers adequate to excellent care and opportunities for the resident, some people find it difficult to adjust to the home. When he enters a home, the new resident is astounded by how different the surroundings are from his apartment or son's home (for example). The nursing home could also be as far away as five hundred miles from his family or friends. The nursing home can be impersonal in decor and furniture. The colours of the walls are often quite dull. There may also be many wings to the home, making it difficult for the new resident to find his way from his room to the dining-hall. Although he may not be ill, he is confronted by nurses in white uniforms many times during the day. The lounge, t.v. room, and identical bedrooms combine to give the home an institutional atmosphere.

Constraint 2: The daily routine of the home can also make the resident feel as if he is just another patient in the home—even if the nurses are kind and caring. (And often the nurses are too busy to give a resident the type of emotional support or attention that he may need.) Although independence is encouraged in most "good" homes, a resident may feel that he is no longer in control of his life. In fact, he must wake up at a precise hour and have his meals in the dining hall at a certain hour. He must also eat what the particular menu for that day might be. In addition to this, he must exercise in the exercise room at 11:00 a.m. He is given/allowed only one bath on a certain day once a week. Also, if he leaves the home for an afternoon of shopping downtown, he must notify the nursing station. If he does not notify them of his return, they will search for him and perhaps call the police for assistance.

Constraint 3: Other residents in the home can also contribute to the dissatisfaction of life in a home. Because most residents and their families can afford only double rooms, a resident must usually share his room with someone else. Often personality-clashes arise because one might be tidy or messy, loud or quiet. They may even end up fist-fighting with one another or spreading malicious gossip about each other.

Constraint 4: Often a new resident has trouble adjusting to the home because he is too introverted or confused about his new surroundings to participate in the craftroom activities, excursions, and card games with the other residents. At times, other residents do not welcome a new resident into their "clique."

Constraint 5: The feelings of alienation are compounded by the fact that children and family often do not visit, phone, or write. When a resident is not invited for Christmas by his family, he can feel quite depressed and lonely. At these holiday times, he is most vulnerable to depression and the consequent actions of withdrawing from the routine of the home, running away, or attempting suicide.

Constraint 6: Society is to blame for the frustrating, serious, demoralizing condition of the senior citizen in a nursing home. Once someone who is used to being independent enters a home, he soon feels useless and depressed. He feels as if he has been "filed" away by the rest of society. The nursing home is viewed by society as a suitable place to leave the aged, for they no longer play a productive role in society. Yet society, on the whole, does not realize that this attitude only makes a resident feel ignored, unwanted and forgotten.

These six constraints—(1) the impersonal environment, (2) the daily routine, (3) the other residents, (4) his own inability to adapt to a new situation, (5) family and friends who do not call, and (6) an uncaring society—all contribute to the confusion and depression a resident may feel when he enters a nursing home. Society is ultimately to blame for the depression and uselessness felt by a new resident of a nursing home. Although this constraint is most out of the resident's control, it is responsible in the long-run for his condition in the nursing home. The negative attitudes towards aging and the aged must change for the new resident's condition to improve within a nursing home.

Claudia Moryn

In this case, social attitudes toward the elderly are presented as the basic, encompassing constraint at the top of the hierarchy, the factor that should be changed to allow the other constraints to be modified.

One of the important qualities of the constraints format is that it allows writers to explain causation flexibly. If you say that someone is *constrained toward* some action, you avoid the deterministic implication that he or she has no free will. You are able to discuss causation without implying a rigid determinism, without suggesting that *either* people have free will *or* their actions are biologically and socially predetermined. The constraints format allows writers clearly to assume that people have *both* a significant degree of free will *and* are constrained in various ways on various levels.

Each constraint is then said to *underdetermine* the event. For instance, a person's preconceptions and the perceptual context *underdetermine* what that person will perceive. Only the combination of sensory stimuli, preconceptions, and perceptual context can explain the perception.

Perhaps the most basic and important example of explanation by constraints is the theory of evolution. That theory is important here because, essentially, it is a theory about *change*, and causal analysis aims to explain change. As a theory about change, the theory of evolution is applicable, by analogy, to virtually any subject that might be treated using the progressive patterns of arrangement discussed in this chapter. It is especially relevant to linguistics, which is concerned with the "survival" of words, and to rhetoric, which is concerned with the "survival" of verbal messages.

In biology, the theory of evolution begins with the assumption that any organism could evolve and that, all else being equal, only chance explains the existing plants and animals. But many existing species do not seem very probable—some seem downright strange. Darwin's explanation was that all else is not equal, that environmental constraints prevented other variants from surviving.

Thus an organism that is fit to survive in one ecosystem may be unfit in another. In an environment with few predators and little food, an organism that is small, slow, and efficient might be more fit than an organism that is strong, fast, and expends a great deal of energy. The biologists' term for a set of ecological constraints is niche. To survive an organism must fit into a niche in the environment.

Like any explanation by constraints, the theory of evolution is formally negative. As Konrad Lorenz writes, "In nature we find . . . everything which is not *so* inexpedient as to endanger the existence of the species." In other words, the theory of evolution explains not so much "the survival of the fittest" as the extinction of the less fit. Similarly, a piece of writing does not need to be perfect; it need only be good enough to meet all the semantic, rhetorical, and linguistic constraints imposed by its context. Consequently, there is not one right way to write (although there are many wrong ways).

In a situation defined by linear cause-effect relations, there is no freedom or flexibility; events are determined; actions are forced. In most social, ecological, and aesthetic contexts, however, choices are constrained, not forced. Which type of reasoning and which pattern of arrangement is best for a particular piece of writing will depend on the subject and the purpose of the piece. As a writer, you should learn how to use both patterns because the wrong choice can lead you either to oversimplify or to overly complicate your explanations.

ADDITIONAL READING

Bateson, Gregory. *Steps to an Ecology of Mind.* New York: Ballantine, 1972. See "Cybernetic Explanation," "Conscious Purpose Versus Nature," and "The Roots of Ecological Crisis."

Coe, Richard. "Rhetoric 2001." *Freshman English News,* 3:1 (Spring 1974).

D'Angelo, Frank. *Process and Thought in Composition.* 2nd ed. Cambridge, Mass.: Winthrop, 1980. See Chapter Seven, pages 225-237, on cause and effect.

EXERCISE

1. Choose a novel or play that you understand well. Select one character. Write an analysis of the constraints within which that character acts. (For example, what are the constraints which lead Hamlet not to avenge his father's murder sooner than he does?)

2. Read several samples of a particular type of writing (e.g., scientific research reports, Harlequin romances, literary critical articles interpreting a single text and published in a particular journal, advertisements in a particular magazine.) Analyze the constraints that explain any consistencies of style, structure, or substance.

3. Write an analysis of the readers of a particular piece of writing you intend to do, showing how they constrain the choices you will make.

4. Choose any topic in your area of special interest. Write two short explanations, one using cause-effect reasoning, the other explanation by constraints. Compare and contrast the results.

5. Choose any situation in which large numbers of individuals act similarly (e.g., a disco, a classroom). Write an analysis of the constraints that explains the similarity within this group.

6. Choose a situation in which you acted strangely. Do a causal analysis of your unusual behavior.

Rhetoric may be defined as the faculty of observing in any given case the available means of persuasion.

Aristotle

For rhetoric as such is . . . rooted in an essential function of language itself, . . . the use of language as a symbolic means of inducing cooperation in beings that by nature respond to symbols.

Kenneth Burke

The art of writing well is the art of making up one's mind. It is the art of establishing clarity where there was confusion, of working out one's conclusions and commitments. Ideally, at least, it is not the skill of presenting a preconceived point of view to advantage. Nor is it skill in filling in a preconceived pattern—say, one of three ways of writing an argumentative theme.

Hans Guth

CHAPTER 6
PERSUASION

Human society is founded on cooperation. Perhaps the most basic function of language is to induce and facilitate that cooperation. If the members of a particular human society share certain beliefs and attitudes that enable them to work together toward shared goals, we may say that they have been *persuaded* and that much of the persuasion was linguistic.

We all use language, both directly and indirectly, to induce people to adopt attitudes and perform actions. Whereas Chapter 5 focused on verbally representing and explaining change, this chapter will focus on *inducing* change. Persuasion—like representation and explanation—is a basic *purpose* of discourse. All of the patterns of arrangement discussed in the preceding two chapters—description, comparison/contrast, classification and division, definition, analogy and exemplification, narration, process-analysis, causal analysis and logical progression—may be used in the service of that primal purpose, persuasion.

Rhetoric began in the fifth century B.C.E. as a theory of persuasion. This chapter will begin with a discussion of some of the insights of classical and traditional rhetoric. Various types of appeals will be discussed and the format of a classical persuasion will be presented. A modern format—Rogerian persuasion—which is appropriate to distinct sorts of persuasive contexts, will be presented also. The chapter will conclude with a short section on constructive criticism and consensus (both of which can be important to writing students and writers, and both of which are essentially persuasive techniques).

As you read this chapter, you should try to master several distinct persuasive strategies and formats. You should work on your ability to evaluate rhetorical contexts (see Chapter 2), so you can select the appropriate strategy and format for each particular persuasion. Specifically, you should learn how to do both classical and Rogerian persuasions. You should also learn how to give constructive criticism (i.e., how to persuade people to accept your criticisms). This chapter contains a number of formulas for constructing persuasions. As you practice using those formulas, however, remember that the formulas are just guidelines. If you master the underlying principles of persuasion, you will be able to modify the formulas to match the requirements of particular situations.

TRADITIONAL ARGUMENT

Mere knowledge of the truth will not give you the art of persuasion.

Plato (Socrates speaking in the *Phaedrus*)

Of the modes of persuasion furnished by the spoken word there are three kinds. The first kind depends on the personal character of the speaker; the second on putting the audience into a certain frame of mind; the third on the proof, or apparent proof, provided by the words of the speech itself.

Aristotle

. . . [I]n order to persuade, there are two things which must be carefully studied by the orator. The first is to excite some desire or passion in the hearers; the second is to satisfy their judgment that there is a connexion between the action to which he would persuade them and the gratification of the desire or passion he excites.

George Campbell

THREE TYPES OF APPEAL

According to Aristotle, there are basically three ways to appeal to people and thus to induce them to agree with you. The first type of appeal is based on *persona* (see pages 159-160), on the image of yourself that is projected by your speech or writing: an audience that perceives you as wise, knowledgeable, and trustworthy is more likely to be persuaded by you. The second type of appeal is based on the emotional nature of the audience: the emotions aroused in an audience will affect its judgment and thus the ease with which it is persuaded. The third type of appeal is based on the speech or writing itself: if you present what at least *seems* to be a logical case, that should help persuade.

In certain contexts—for example, writing for university courses—you are concerned mainly with the third type of appeal. Since your primary interest is in reaching truth, you should confine yourself to logical and empirical argumentation. But any complete discussion of persuasion should include all three types of appeal.

The first type of appeal is called *ethical* because it turns on the ethical judgment readers make about the character of the writer. Readers who trust you may be persuaded even by unsupported assertions. That trust may be based on the *persona* you project or on readers' previous knowledge of you. Thus a recognized authority, such as a certified expert or a leader who is perceived as having been right often in the past, may be able to persuade people without providing much detailed argumentation. On the other hand, those who are perceived as having been wrong often in the past may fail to persuade even when they have good evidence and make a logical case.

Aristotle argues that the ethical appeal is based on your ability to project yourself (1) as a sensible person who knows the subject, (2) as a good and forthright person who would not lie to your readers, and (3) as an unselfish and benevolent person who has their best interests at heart. On a trivial level, this might mean that poor spelling could convince some readers that you are not intelligent, a minor inconsistency that you are being dishonest, and a few unfortunate word choices that you do not understand them. On the most exalted level, this means that effective persuasion is honest, truthful, and loving. According to the classical rhetoricians, the place to emphasize the ethical appeal is generally toward the beginning of a speech or writing.

The second type of appeal is *emotional*. Given the rationalistic biases of our culture, we tend to feel there is something wrong with appealing to emotions. And, in certain contexts, judgment may be warped by emotional appeals, as Adolf Hitler so devastatingly demonstrated. But it is not degrading to appeal to someone's love of freedom or unselfish caring about other people. It is not necessarily improper to supplement statistics on malnutrition with a vivid description of one starving child. As Scottish rhetorician George Campbell asserted, "So far . . . is it from being an unfair method of persuasion to move the passions, that there is no persuasion without moving them."

As human beings, we always choose our ultimate goals passionately (be those passions large or small, loving or selfish). We must and should set our ultimate aims on the basis of what we disparagingly call "emotions"; it is the means to those ends that should be chosen rationally. Thus it is as proper to use emotional appeals to motivate people as it is improper (though not necessarily ineffective) to continue using emotional appeals when the focus shifts from ends to means. In part for this reason, according to the classical rhetoricians, the place to emphasize the emotional appeal is generally toward the end of a speech or writing, when you hope that your readers have been convinced and now need to be motivated to do something about it.

The third type of appeal is *logical*. Aristotle reminds us that it is not logic, but apparent logic, which persuades. To an honest writer, however, this distinction ordinarily makes little difference, except as a reminder that the logic *must be made apparent* to readers. Still, since even the best of writers may have occasion to lie—perhaps to protect innocent people from violence—you should remember that it is *the appearance of logic* which persuades.

Any and all of these three basic types of appeal may be used or abused. The ethical appeal, despite its name, is often abused for unethical purposes, notably in commercial advertising and political propaganda (e.g., when a celebrity who has no relevant expertise endorses a product or candidate). History is replete with cases in which logical arguments were used to abuse and oppress "illogical" peoples. And emotional appeals have an obvious potential for abuse.

Aristotle's classification of appeals into three types can help you both to invent and to analyze persuasive discourse. But moral judgements about whether you *should* use any particular appeal depend, at least to some degree, on how it is used, to what ends, and in what contexts. Certain generalizations are possible; but, in the end, persuasive strategies can be evaluated morally only in real contexts.

EVALUATE THE RHETORICAL CONTEXT

Persuasive writing is oriented toward its readers. It aims to induce them to act in a certain way or, at least, to adopt certain attitudes (an attitude being, as Burke asserts, "an incipient act"). More than other types of writing, persuasion is purposive. More than other types of writing, it is properly judged by its effects on readers. More than other types of writing, therefore, persuasion must be adapted to its rhetorical contexts.

The first section of Chapter 2 (especially pages 111-119) is particularly relevant to persuasive writing. To achieve your persuasive purposes, you should carefully evaluate your intended readers and the circumstances in which they will be reading your writing. In addition to knowing what you mean to communicate, you will generally find it useful to know explicitly what you want your readers to believe and do after they have finished reading. An explicit statement of rhetorical context (page 113) is especially useful when you want to write persuasively. An awareness of your readers' knowledge, attitudes, beliefs, and vested interests and of any distinctions between primary and secondary audiences (pages 114-115) is particularly important.

You might well use the Pentad to analyze your readers and decide how best to motivate them. Certainly, you should ask what frameworks or root metaphors your readers have for your subject. And you certainly want to be writing reader-based prose that appeals to a mutual purpose, is focused according to readers' needs, and is organized to facilitate readers' discovery processes. (See Table 2.2 and pages 116-119.)

LOGICAL PROGRESSION

The simplest format for persuasion is to make a statement and support it, either logically or empirically. The epitome of deductive logical argument is found in philosophy. The philosopher says, "Here is my thesis; here are my premises. Grant me that my premises are true, and I will demonstrate that my thesis can be logically deduced from them, thereby proving my thesis." The epitome of empirical argument is found in science. The scientist says, "Here is my hypothesis; here are the results of my empirical investigations. Grant me the validity of my experimental design, and my statistical calculations demonstrate that my hypothesis of confirmed to a statistical probability of $\frac{X}{100}$." This type of argument assumes a rational audience: readers who will be persuaded by proof and who need not be induced by other sorts of appeals.

The conventions of academic and professional discourse generally demand that writers assume—or at least pretend to assume—an ideal audience of rational readers. Of course, real academics, scientists, and professionals are human beings and, therefore, are less than perfectly rational.* Nonetheless, overt ethical or emotional appeals are not permitted in this sort of discourse. The persuasive *persona* the writer must project is one of disinterested and dispassionate objectivity.

The basic structure is *statement plus proof*. The statement comes first, even though it is logically the conclusion of the proof, so readers may know what they are judging as they follow the argument. The basic structure may be put in context. It may, for example, be preceded by an introduction explaining why the particular statement matters, that is, why it is important enough to be proven. It may also be followed by a discussion of implications. The proof may be deductive (the statement

*Scientific studies of scientists clearly demonstrate that extrinsic factors have a great deal to do with whether a scientific article actually convinces its readers. Some of these factors have to do with format, both of the experiment and of the article reporting it. Some of these factors have to do with status—of the experimenters and of the journal that published the article. And, of course, even the most objective and academic writing ultimately has some persuasive purpose—if only to enhance the reputation of the writer (i.e., to persuade readers to respect the writer) and to persuade granting institutions to give financial support for further research.

may be deduced logically from a more general principle). Or it may be inductive (the statement may be proven by generalizing from empirical particulars). In any case, the underlying structure remains statement plus proof.

In the following example, the authors are putting forth the first axiom of their theory of communication, and they are eager to persuade readers to accept it. The passage begins by deducing its thesis statement from an even more basic assumption. Represented as a logical syllogism, the first three sentences look like this:

All behavior communicates.

One cannot *not* behave (i.e., even doing "nothing" is behavior).

Therefore one cannot *not* communicate.

Having reached its thesis statement in the final clause of the third sentence, the passage goes on to support it inductively and with examples.

> First of all, there is a property of behavior that could hardly be more basic and is, therefore, often overlooked: behavior has no opposite. In other words, there is no such thing as nonbehavior or, to put it even more simply: one cannot *not* behave. Now, if it is accepted that all behavior in an interactional situation has message value, i.e., is communication, it follows that no matter how one may try, one cannot *not* communicate. Activity or inactivity, words or silence all have message value: they influence others and these others, in turn, cannot *not* respond to these communications and are thus themselves communicating. It should be clearly understood that the mere absence of talking or of taking notice of each other is no exception to what has just been asserted. The man at a crowded lunch counter who looks straight ahead, or the airplane passenger who sits with his eyes closed, are both communicating that they do not want to speak with anybody or be spoken to, and their neighbors usually "get the message" and respond appropriately by leaving them alone. This, obviously, is just as much an interchange as an animated discussion.
>
> Paul Watzlawick, Janet Beavin, and Don Jackson

Even in this one paragraph, the writers try to "prove" their point twice. The deductive proof is somewhat unusual in that it is completely stated. *Both* premises and the conclusion are made explicit (although not in the standard order of formal logic), and the more general premise is actually framed by, "if it is accepted that . . . , then it follows that . . . ."

More typically in persuasive writing, it is not necessary or even desirable to state both premises. Thus one writes,

If Socrates is human, he is mortal.

The major premise ("All human beings are mortal") will be obvious to readers. Similarly, one writes,

> Corn takes three months to grow, so the corn planted in June should mature in September.

The minor premise ("September is three months after June") is so obvious that it is not stated.

In these two cases, one leaves a premise unstated because readers will fill it in. Thus the readers participate in the reasoning process, and that participation has the psychological effect of making the writing more persuasive, even though the underlying logic has not changed. To have stated the obvious premises, on the other hand, would have seemed condescending and made the writing less persuasive. Watzlawick, Beavin, and Jackson state both premises because they are not sure that readers will fill in the missing premise, which is "often overlooked."

In another sort of case, one might write,

> Men have the right to vote in all democratic countries; therefore, women should have the right to vote in those countries, too.

Here the major premise, that "in democratic countries, women have equal rights (i.e., the same rights as men)," is only probable; indeed, historically, it would have been judged improbable until fairly recently. Even as a legal fact, it is only probable in the United States (because it is dependent on the Supreme Court's interpretation of the Fourteenth Amendment, not enshrined in the Constitution). The mere probability of the major premise is reflected by the *should* in the conclusion.

If a premise is left unstated or if a premise is only probable, then we do not have a formally proper and logical syllogism. What we have instead is an *enthymeme*: a syllogism that is either incomplete or based on a merely probable premise. ("If we plant in June, we *should* have fresh corn in September; then again, corn worms might kill the plants in August.")

Aristotle says that an enthymeme is the equivalent in verbal persuasion of a syllogism in formal logic. Generally, he is correct. Writers often must deal with subjects where the premises can be known only probably. Where definite knowledge is possible, persuasion is often inappropriate. And writers often leave premises unstated, either because the premises are so obvious that readers would feel "talked down to" or because the premises might be rejected if stated overtly.

Just as an enthymeme is the rhetorical equivalent of deductive logic, so an example is the rhetorical equivalent of empirical proof. Note that Watzlawick, Beavin, and Jackson supported their thesis statement with examples, not with statistically valid empirical evidence. (It is, at any event, extremely difficult to provide empirical proof for a negative statement—for example, that Zeus, Jehovah, or Allah does not exist or that "one cannot *not* communicate.") Well-chosen examples can, however, establish the probability of a statement in readers' minds—so long as the readers do not think of counterexamples. (See pages 271-273.)

Essentially, then, a logical argument consists of a statement plus proof. The proof which supports the statement may be either deductive (syllogism or enthymeme) or inductive and empirical (statistics or examples). The format may vary, but this is the essential structure.

THE ARRANGEMENT OF A CLASSICAL PERSUASION

Classical rhetoric offers a standard format for arranging persuasions. Although this format has not been widely studied in modern times, analyses of many modern speeches and writings show that it is still used and still works. That is because the six parts of a classical persuasion represent six basic functions of persuasive discourse. Although the format was (and is) more a guideline than a hard-and-fast formula, it remains one very effective way to structure a persuasive speech or writing.

The format is as follows:

INTRODUCTION. The Latin term is *exordium*, which is related to the English *exhort* and means "beginning a web," as in weaving. Here one makes contact with the audience, indicates one's subject (and perhaps even one's thesis), and tries to dispose the audience favorably to what one is going to say. Here is the place for ethical appeal.

NARRATION. The facts are set forth and the issue defined. In a legal case, this might mean literally *narrating* the events which judge and jury will have to evaluate (hence the term, *narration*). In a funeral oration, it might mean telling the story of the dead person's life. In a political context, it might mean describing the present situation and stating the alternative courses of action. Aristotle, at least, makes clear that this is not usually a "neutral" statement of facts: ethical and emotional appeals, he asserts, should be implicit here.

PARTITION. One states one's thesis (if it has not been made obvious earlier) and indicates how the rest of the discourse will be organized (i.e., indicates the *parts* of the argument to follow and their order), thus preparing the audience for what will follow. (See pages 137-142, on frameworks and their function.) Here one names the various proofs and refutations that will follow.

PROOFS. Called *confirmatio* in Latin, this part is devoted to confirming the thesis statement. Here one offers arguments in support of one's thesis, proves that the defendant could not possibly have committed the crime, demonstrates that the deceased lived an exemplary life, argues for a particular course of action. Often this is the bulk of the speech or writing.

REFUTATION. Other viewpoints are criticized and their flaws demonstrated. One pokes holes in the prosecution's case, attacks evil people who spread false rumors about the deceased, demonstrates the disadvantages of the alternatives suggested by others.

CONCLUSION. This may be a summary of proofs and refutations. It may also be a renewal of ethical and, especially, emotional appeals.

Even though the classical rhetoricians emphasized the need to be flexible, it will be worth your while to practice this format rigorously. After you have mastered it, you can change the order, combine or eliminate parts, so long as the functions are accomplished. If the opposing case is strong and has already been argued, it may be best to put the refutation before the proofs—or even to begin with the refutation. If the narration of events will serve as an introduction, there may be no need for a separate *exordium*. If the facts are well known, there may be no need for a full narration. It is even possible to imagine situations in which the proofs might be left out (e.g., a defense attorney might say no more than, "Your honor, the prosecution has failed to make a case, my client is innocent until proven guilty, so I move that all charges be immediately dismissed.")

Consider in these terms the speech Shakespeare writes for Antony to deliver at Caesar's funeral (*Julius Caesar*, Act III, Scene 2). It is something less than formal discourse because it is much interrupted and because Antony seems to improvise in response to his audience. The rhetorical context, moreover, demands that the refutation come before the proofs. And Antony wisely leaves his thesis unstated, thereby allowing the audience to state it as their own. Nonetheless, Antony's speech performs all the functions of a classical persuasion and includes Aristotle's three types of appeals. Despite his denial of rhetorical abilities ("I am no orator, as Brutus is;/But, as you know me all, a plain blunt man . . ."), Antony deftly improvises on the classical structure. Aristotle and Cicero would have been proud.

Ant. Friends, Romans, countrymen, lend me your ears;
I come to bury Caesar, not to praise him.
The evil that men do lives after them;
The good is oft interred with their bones;

So let it be with Caesar. The noble Brutus
Hath told you Caesar was ambitious:
If it were so, it was a grievous fault,
And grievously hath Caesar answer'd it.
Here, under leave of Brutus and the rest—
For Brutus is an honourable man;
So are they all, all honourable men—
Come I to speak in Caesar's funeral.
He was my friend, faithful and just to me:
But Brutus says he was ambitious;
And Brutus is an honourable man.
He hath brought many captives home to Rome,
Whose ransoms did the general coffers fill:
Did this in Caesar seem ambitious?
When that the poor have cried, Caesar hath wept:
Ambition should be made of sterner stuff:
Yet Brutus says he was ambitious;
And Brutus is an honourable man.
You all did see that on the Lupercal
I thrice presented him a kingly crown,
Which he did thrice refuse: was this ambition?
Yet Brutus says he was ambitious;
And, sure, he is an honourable man.
I speak not to disprove what Brutus spoke,
But here I am to speak what I do know.
You all did love him once, not without cause:
What cause withholds you then, to mourn for him?
O judgement! thou art fled to brutish beasts,
And men have lost their reason. Bear with me;
My heart is in the coffin there with Caesar,
And I must pause till it come back to me.

First Citizen. Methinks there is much reason in his sayings.

Sec. Cit. If thou consider rightly of the matter, Caesar has had great wrong.

Third Cit. Has he, masters?
I fear there will a worse come in his place.

Fourth Cit. Mark'd ye his words? He would not take the crown;
Therefore 'tis certain he was not ambitious.

First Cit. If it be found so, some will dear abide it.

Sec. Cit. Poor soul! his eyes are red as fire with weeping.

Third Cit. There's not a nobler man in Rome than Antony.

Fourth Cit. Now mark him, he begins again to speak.

Ant. But yesterday the word of Caesar might
Have stood against the world; now lies he there,
And none so poor to do him reverence.
O masters, if I were disposed to stir
Your hearts and minds to mutiny and rage,

I should do Brutus wrong, and Cassius wrong,
Who, you all know, are honourable men:
I will not do them wrong; I rather choose
To wrong the dead, to wrong myself and you,
Than I will wrong such honourable men.
But here's a parchment with the seal of Caesar;
I found it in his closet, 'tis his will:
Let but the commons hear this testament—
Which, pardon me, I do not mean to read—
And they would go and kiss dead Caesar's wounds
And dip their napkins in his sacred blood,
Yea, beg a hair of him for memory,
And, dying, mention it within their wills,
Bequeathing it as a rich legacy
Unto their issue.

Fourth Cit. We'll hear the will: read it, Mark Antony.

All. The will, the will! we will hear Caesar's will.

Ant. Have patience, gentle friends, I must not read it;
It is not meet you know how Caesar loved you.
You are not wood, you are not stones, but men;
And, being men, hearing the will of Caesar,
It will inflame you, it will make you mad:
'Tis good you know not that you are his heirs;
For, if you should, O, what would come of it!

Fourth cit. Read the will; we'll hear it, Antony;
You shall read us the will, Caesar's will.

Ant. Will you be patient? will you stay awhile?
I have o'ershot myself to tell you of it:
I fear I wrong the honourable men
Whose daggers have stabb'd Caesar; I do fear it.

Fourth Cit. They were traitors: honourable men!

All. The will! the testament!

Sec. Cit. They were villains, murderers: the will! read the will.

Ant. You will compel me, then, to read the will?
Then make a ring about the corpse of Caesar,
And let me show you him that made the will.
Shall I descend? and will you give me leave?

Several Cit. Come down.

Sec. Cit. Descend.

Third Cit. You shall have leave. [*Antony comes down.*]

Fourth Cit. A ring; stand round.

First Cit. Stand from the hearse, stand from the body.

Sec. Cit. Room for Antony, most noble Antony.

Ant. Nay, press not so upon me; stand far off.

Several Cit. Stand back; room; bear back.

Ant. If you have tears, prepare to shed them now.

You all do know this mantle: I remember
The first time ever Caesar put it on;
'Twas on a summer's evening, in his tent,
That day he overcame the Nervii:
Look, in this place ran Cassius' dagger through:
See what a rent the envious Casca made:
Through this the well-beloved Brutus stabb'd;
And as he pluck'd his cursed steel away,
Mark how the blood of Caesar follow'd it,
As rushing out of doors, to be resolved
If Brutus so unkindly knock'd, or no;
For Brutus, as you know, was Caesar's angel:
Judge, O you gods, how dearly Caesar loved him!
This was the most unkindest cut of all;
For when the noble Caesar saw him stab,
Ingratitude, more strong than traitors' arms,
Quite vanquish'd him: then burst his mighty heart;
And, in his mantle muffling up his face,
Even at the base of Pompey's statua,
Which all the while ran blood, great Caesar fell.
O, what a fall was there, my countrymen!
Then I, and you, and all of us fell down,
Whilst bloody treason flourish'd over us.
O, now you weep; and, I perceive, you feel
The dint of pity: these are gracious drops.
Kind souls, what, weep you when you but behold
Our Caesar's vesture wounded? Look you here,
Here is himself, marr'd, as you see, with traitors.
First Cit. O piteous spectacle!
Sec. Cit. O noble Caesar!
Third Cit. O woful day!
Fourth Cit. O traitors, villains!
First Cit. O most bloody sight!
Sec. Cit. We will be revenged.
All. Revenge! About! Seek! Burn! Fire! Kill! Slay!
Let not a traitor live!
Ant. Stay, countrymen.
First Cit. Peace there! hear the noble Antony.
Sec. Cit. We'll hear him, we'll follow him, we'll die with him.
Ant. Good friends, sweet friends, let me not stir you up
To such a sudden flow of mutiny.
They that have done this deed are honourable:
What private griefs they have, alas, I know not,
That made them do it: they are wise and honourable,
And will, no doubt, with reasons answer you.
I come not, friends, to steal away your hearts:

I am no orator, as Brutus is;
But, as you know me all, a plain blunt man,
That love my friend; and that they know full well
That gave me public leave to speak of him:
For I have neither wit, nor words, nor worth,
Action, nor utterance, nor the power of speech,
To stir men's blood: I only speak right on;
I tell you that which you yourselves do know;
Show you sweet Caesar's wounds, poor poor dumb mouths,
And bid them speak for me: but were I Brutus,
And Brutus Antony, there were an Antony
Would ruffle up your spirits and put a tongue
In every wound of Caesar that should move
The stones of Rome to rise and mutiny.
All. We'll mutiny.
First Cit. We'll burn the house of Brutus.
Third Cit. Away, then! come, seek the conspirators.
Ant. Yet hear me, countrymen; yet hear me speak.
All. Peace, ho! Hear Antony. Most noble Antony!
Ant. Why, friends, you go to do you know not what:
Wherein hath Caesar thus deserved your loves?
Alas, you know not: I must tell you, then:
You have forgot the will I told you of.
All. Most true. The will! Let's stay and hear the will.
Ant. Here is the will, and under Caesar's seal.
To every Roman citizen he gives,
To every several man, seventy five drachmas.
Sec. Cit. Most noble Caesar! We'll revenge his death.
Third Cit. O royal Caesar!
Ant. Hear me with patience.
All. Peace, ho!
Ant. Moreover, he hath left you all his walks,
His private arbours and new-planted orchards,
On this side Tiber; he hath left them you,
And to your heirs for ever, common pleasures,
To walk abroad, and recreate yourselves.
Here was a Caesar! when comes such another?

Antony addresses a hostile audience, which has just been convinced by Brutus that Caesar had to be killed because he was ambitious to become dictator of Rome. Brutus' speech has succeeded largely because of ethical appeal, for all Rome knows that Brutus is honorable. So Antony moves quickly from an *exordium*, in which he calls for attention and ironically denies his own rhetorical purpose, to careful refutation. He skips the narration of facts, for those are well known. He offers no partition, for to announce his line of argument would cause his audience to refuse to listen. He begins with his weakest refutation ("He was my friend, faithful and just to me") and works toward his strongest ("I thrice presented him a kingly crown,/ Which he did thrice refuse: was this ambition?"). Only after the logic of these refutations has taken effect does Antony move to an emotional appeal ("You all did love him once,—not without cause:/ What cause withholds you, then, to mourn for him?")

Throughout the speech, Antony's ethical appeal turns on his feigned reluctance to speak against Brutus or to stir the citizens to remember their love for Caesar. His main proof of Caesar's love for them—and thus that they ought to love Caesar—is Caesar's will. Yet he stalls. He moves to the narration, using the details of the assassination for their emotional appeal. He renews his ethical appeal by presenting himself as a plain speaker, not a clever orator "as Brutus is." Only after he has won the crowd does he present his strongest argument, using it to move his audience from belief to action.

The format of classical persuasion, like Aristotle's three types of appeal, has stood the test of time and changing contexts. It may be used to organize a written persuasion in the late-twentieth century quite as effectively as it was used to organize spoken persuasions more than two millennia ago. Flexible though it is, however, it is not always the most effective format. The next section of this chapter will present an alternative format as well as criteria for deciding which format to use in which rhetorical contexts.

ADDITIONAL READING

The Rhetoric of Aristotle. Lane Cooper, translator. Englewood Cliffs, N.J.: Prentice-Hall, 1932. See Book I, Chapter 2 (Pages 7-16) for Aristotle's discussion of the three types of appeal and of enthymeme. See Book III, Chapters 13-19 (pages 220-241) for his discussion of the arrangement of argument.

Readings in Classical Rhetoric. Thomas Benson and Michael Prosser, editors. Bloomington, Ind.: Indiana University, 1972. See pages 193-213 for advice on arrangement from Cicero, Quintilian, and the author of the *Rhetorica ad Herennium.*

Corbett, Edward P. J. *Classical Rhetoric for the Modern Student.* 2nd Ed. New York: Oxford, 1971. See pages 50-107 and 303-338.

Kahane, Howard. *Logic & Contemporary Rhetoric:* The Use of Reason in Everyday Life, 3rd ed. Belmont, Calif.: Wadsworth, 1980. An extended discussion of logical argument with an emphasis on helping readers to detect logical fallacies in contemporary discourse.

EXERCISE

1. Choose an appropriate topic, thesis, and rhetorical context, and write a persuasion that follows the classical format as outlined in this section.

2. Select several short, published persuasions from recent newspapers, magazines, and journals. Analyze each in terms of ethical, emotional, and logical appeals.

3. Select a short, published persuasion written some years ago (perhaps a newspaper editorial from the day you were born). Judging by the writer's persuasive strategy, construct a statement of rhetorical context (see pages 112-115) as the writer probably saw it.

4. Select a persuasive writing that you did at least a year ago. Create a statement of rhetorical context for it, and consider how well it was adapted to that context.

5. Consider the substance of the passage from Watzlawick, Beavin, and Jackson presented in this section. What implications does its main point—"one cannot *not* communicate"—have for writers?

6. Read the following excerpts from Aristotle's *Rhetoric*:

   Book I: Chapters 1, 2, 9, and 10
   Book II: Chapters 1, 19, 20, and 25
   Book III: Chapters 1, 7, 12, 13, 14, 16, 17, and 19

Write a short essay evaluating the relevance of Aristotle's advice to North American writers in the late-twentieth century.

7. Compare and contrast Antony's funeral speech in *Julius Caesar* with the speech by Brutus that precedes it. Why do you think Shakespeare wrote Brutus' speech in prose and Antony's in verse? Is Antony correct when he calls himself a "plain blunt man" and Brutus an "orator"? How is Brutus' speech structured to fit its rhetorical context?

ROGERIAN PERSUASION

The old Rhetoric was an offspring of dispute; it was the theory of the battle of words and has always been itself dominated by the combative impulse. Perhaps what it has most to teach us is the narrowing and blinding influence of that preoccupation, that debaters' interest.

I. A. Richards

You persuade a man only insofar as you can talk his language . . . , identifying *your ways with his. . . . True, the rhetorician may have to change an audience's opinion in one respect; but he can succeed only insofar as he yields to that audience's opinions in other respects.*

Kenneth Burke

[T]he object in a debate is to induce the opponent to admit stimuli which he had not admitted before, in short to enlarge his vision. To do this, some feel, it is best to show him not the limits outside of which he is wrong, but, on the contrary, the limits inside of which he is right. They are, of course, the same limits! But putting it one way is likely to emphasize the threat to the image, while putting it the other way is likely to dilute the threat.

Anatol Rapoport

ANTAGONISTIC AND NON-ANTAGONISTIC RHETORICAL CONTEXTS

Traditional advice about persuasion generally presumes an antagonistic rhetorical context—essentially a speaker or writer to represent each side of the issue and an audience to judge who is right. The word *antagonistic* comes from the Greek *agonia*, meaning a "contest," such as a wrestling match, in which athletes contend for a prize; and that is essentially the sort of context rhetoricians have traditionally assumed when discussing persuasion.

The epitome of this type of antagonistic context is found in an English or North American courtroom. There is an issue: Is the defendant guilty as charged? There are representatives of both viewpoints: the prosecuting and defense attorneys. There is an audience to decide who is right: the judge and jury. There is a complete separation of functions: no one represents more than one point of view; and those who will pass judgment are, at least in principle, neutral (i.e., they represent no point of view). Everyone would be shocked if the defense attorney were to announce, "Your Honor, after hearing the prosecution's case, I am convinced of my clients' guilt, so I will say nothing in their defense," because attorneys are supposed to represent, not to judge.

The key point is the separation of functions: *the opponents who are arguing with each other are not trying to convince each other.* The prosecutor does not expect to convince the defense attorney, just the judge and jury. Debating politicians, similarly, are not trying to change each other's minds; they argue with each other in order to convince the voters. Antony's speech was designed to convince the citizens of Rome (and the audience in Shakespeare's theatre), not Brutus.

Similarly, when a writer produces an article that takes a position on a controversial issue, perhaps responding to a previous article in the same publication, that writer is usually trying to convince the general readership. The writer may argue overtly against the author of a previous article, but the persuasion is ordinarily aimed at other readers who are, in effect, a third party judging the debate.

Under these circumstances, the appropriate strategy is antagonistic: represent your position as strongly as you can. Depending on the nature of the issue, opponents and audience, this strategy may include criticizing, refuting, or even ridiculing opposing viewpoints and their representatives.

If, on the other hand, you are arguing with somebody *and trying to convince that same person*, the rhetorical context is radically different and demands a distinct persuasive strategy. Suppose you are writing a private letter to the author of that article you disagree with. Suppose that your rhetorical purpose is to change that author's mind, perhaps even to convince that author to print a retraction of the view expressed in the original article. Under this sort of circumstance, where the "opponent" and the audience are the same person, the antagonistic strategy is often entirely ineffective.

To present your case strongly is to strongly attack the position with which your reader or readers identify. When attacked, people feel threatened. When people feel threatened, they get defensive and "stick to their guns." So if your purpose is to persuade people to change, the last thing you want is for them to feel defensive.

People do sometimes manage not to take arguments personally. They manage not to react defensively even though their beliefs and/or statements are being criticized. And even if they do react defensively at first, people often manage to hear the argument and may well change later, after the threat is gone—often without even remembering when and by whom they were persuaded.

But to use a persuasive strategy that threatens your readers is not the best way to achieve your persuasive purposes. In a three-way situation, you can attack your opponent's position with impunity because that will not threaten your readers (after all, it is not *their* position being attacked) except insofar as they identify with your opponent. A two-way situation, however, usually calls for a less aggressive strategy.

If you have enough power, of course, you can threaten all you like and still get people to do and say what you want. But then what you have done is forced them, not persuaded them. (And it should not be forgotten that a combination of force and persuasion is often quite effective—as in typical North American child-rearing practices.)

But there is an apparent contradiction in all of this. You are attempting persuasion because you disagree with your readers. You want to explain why your position is correct. But to present your position strongly is to attack theirs, which is not a good way to encourage them to change. How then can you state your case persuasively without threatening your readers?

THE ROGERIAN WAY

There is a form of persuasion, identified with the humanistic psychologist Carl Rogers, that is especially appropriate to rhetorical contexts where you should avoid threatening those who hold opposing views. It is especially appropriate to conflicts that seem to be antagonistic but really are not because you actually share significant common ground with your "opponents." Although it can be used manipulatively to win arguments, Rogerian persuasion basically aims at achieving consensus around a correct position. The objective is truth, not victory.

In Rogerian persuasion, you begin by convincing your "opponents" that you understand their position. You do so by restating their position so fairly that they recognize your restatement as an accurate representation of their position. What is more, you next validate their position by explaining the senses or contexts in which you see that position as correct.

This may seem an odd way to begin to persuade them to change their minds. But note what you have done. You have demonstrated that you are a fair-minded person who can understand your readers—and who cares enough to try to. You have indicated that, at least in some sense or some context, you can see some validity in their position. Although you disagree, you do not think they are totally stupid. In a situation where they probably expected to be attacked, they feel understood and valued.

In other words, you have done exactly what Aristotle says to do when he discusses emotional and ethical appeals: you have put your readers "in the right frame of mind" and convinced them that you are at least somewhat empathetic, fair-minded, and sensible. You have not done so in quite the way Aristotle had in mind, but that is because you are dealing with a sort of rhetorical context with which the classical rhetoricians did not much concern themselves.

The logical appeal comes next, now that your readers have been prepared to consider it. You make a fair statement of your own position, trying to avoid exaggerated claims and biased language. Then you explain in which contexts you believe your position is valid. (Presumably, at least one of these contexts, in your opinion, closely resembles the actual context.)

Finally, instead of restating your case, you explain how your readers would benefit by adopting your position (or at least some aspects of it). In other words, you explicitly state what in Chapter 2 was called the *mutual purpose* you share with your readers (see pages 116-117).

The ideal format of a written Rogerian persuasion looks something like this.

INTRODUCTION. Here, of course, you are trying to introduce the matter in such a way that your readers will read on. That may be difficult because most people try to avoid reading material with which they radically disagree. Try presenting it as a *problem* rather than as an *issue*.

FAIR STATEMENT OF THE OPPOSING POSITION. The goal here is to convince your readers that you understand their perspective by stating their position in a way they will recognize as fair and accurate.

STATEMENT OF CONTEXTS IN WHICH THAT POSITION MAY BE VALID. Here you are trying to convince your readers that you understand how they could hold their position by suggesting that in certain contexts it has some validity.

FAIR STATEMENT OF YOUR OWN POSITION. Although you want to state your position convincingly, you also want to maintain your image as fair-minded. Your immediate goal is to get your readers to reciprocate, to understand your position as fairly and thoroughly as you have understood theirs.

STATEMENT OF CONTEXTS IN WHICH YOUR POSITION IS VALID. Here you are trying to induce your readers to look at the problem from new perspectives and hence to see it in contexts they may previously have ignored.

STATEMENT OF HOW READERS WOULD BENEFIT BY ADOPTING AT LEAST ELEMENTS OF YOUR POSITION. Here you are appealing to your readers' self-interests, at least in the broader, long-term sense. You are trying to transform your position from a *threat* to a *promise*.

Rogerian persuasion is especially appropriate for dealing with touchy subjects or hostile readers. Broadly conceived, it is an application of the ancient ethical principle, "Do unto others as you would have others do unto you"; in other words, demonstrate that you have considered and understood their position as carefully as you want them to consider yours. The Rogerian combination of ethical and emotional appeals minimizes the threat that is usually implicit in any change and thus allows the logical appeal to be more rationally considered. That, not the precise format, is what makes it Rogerian and humanistic.

Rogerian persuasion is particularly appropriate for touchy subjects. The following essay, for instance, attempts to persuade middle-aged couples with teenage children to choose abortion if the mother accidentally becomes pregnant again. Note how carefully the writer approaches the issue.

For middle-aged couples with grown children, an unexpected pregnancy is often a traumatic discovery. This kind of news raises an important issue that must be considered slowly and thoughtfully. Such couples must ask themselves: "Are we, at this point in our lives, physically and emotionally prepared to deal with the responsibilities and demands of a new-born child?"

For some couples, the thought of abortion is totally unacceptable because it is considered the unjustified destruction of an innocent human life. Other individuals frown on abortion because they feel a child is a cherished gift created through the mutual expression of love. To such couples, destroying their child would be like destroying the love they share for one another.

In addition to these emotional views, there are also a few practical reasons supporting a middle-aged couple's decision to spurn abortion. Because they have had experience raising children, these couples might be more knowledgeable and more understanding of a child's needs than those parents who have not had any previous child-raising experience. Also, most couples approaching middle age have managed to achieve some degree of financial stability in their lives. In this way, a child may have innumerable opportunities to experience the finer things in life. I'm not suggesting that money is a prerequisite to a happy childhood, but in some cases it does enable parents to give their child a fuller, more enlightening education.

Despite the advantages of late parenthood, we must not ignore some of the serious disadvantages. A child is a heavy responsibility that alters one's lifestyle considerably. Before having another child, there are many questions the expectant parents should ask themselves: "Can we face raising another child right now? Are our temperaments as easy-going as they used to be? Can we deal with a baby crying out for her bottle at four o'clock in the morning?" People often look forward to a calm, relaxing household in middle age, but an infant is a demanding creature, who constantly needs to be fed, bathed, or diapered. If one is looking for a peaceful, uncomplicated lifestyle, a baby is certainly not the answer.

Some couples enjoy the freedom they experience once their children have all left home; they are able to come and go as they please. A baby, however, is a heavy responsibility, who needs a great deal of attention. The old cliché that a baby ties a couple down is not a falsehood—a couple must be prepared to sacrifice their social life in favour of caring for their child.

Sometimes a couple finds themselves swamped with diapers while all their friends are involved in exciting careers and enjoyable recreational activities. Even if a couple arranges to have their baby cared for, they often find they no longer have much in common with their old friends. A middle-aged couple with a new-born child is often a rather small minority. To their friends, whose children have all grown away from home, listening to cute little stories about Junior is no longer an interesting topic of conversation. The couple often finds themselves alienated from their old way of life as they try, often with considerable difficulty, to adapt to their new roles as parents of a new-born child.

These are just a few of the issues that should be taken into consideration when one is contemplating abortion, but in my opinion, the most important factor is the health of both the mother and her child. It has been shown that incidences of fetal damage increase considerably as the mother enters her forties. After a woman has passed the child-bearing age, the odds that both she and her child will suffer no serious damage decrease significantly. A couple in this age bracket must ask themselves: "Should we carry this pregnancy to term knowing there is a good chance our child may be physically or mentally handicapped? Is it fair to our child to take that risk?"

I feel that, although a decision to abort a child may be almost unbearable, it is the right decision for a middle-aged couple with grown children. Even if they are able to re-adjust their entire lifestyle to accommodate a new-born child, the risks seem much too severe. It seems rather senseless to bring yet another life into this over-crowded and polluted world, especially if that life does not have a strong guarantee of surviving as a healthy, completely normal child.

Wendi LeSage

The success of a Rogerian persuasion depends first and foremost on how well the writer understands the readers. If readers are to feel understood, they must recognize their own opinions and reasons in the first part of the essay.

Word choice is also crucial. An inappropriate purr-word or snarl-word (see page 172), a bit of overstatement at the wrong spot, or an awkward transition can ruin the effect. Wendi generally succeeds on this count, though there is an occasional slip. The transition into the third paragraph, for instance, uses the word *emotional* in a way that could be read as a snarl-word. Later in that paragraph, the assertion that financial stability may allow a middle-aged couple to give their child "*innumerable* opportunities to experience the finer things in life" is enough of an overstatement that Wendi immediately adds a sentence to clarify her meaning. Substituting a more accurate word for "innumerable" would have been better.

Generally, however, this piece is effective. It follows the Rogerian format rather closely, except that Wendi saves her most powerful argument (the next-to-last paragraph) to build up to her final pitch, somewhat as Antony saves Caesar's will for his final point. Since this variation makes the piece more effective, it is all to the good.

The following paper, which tries to create awareness of how the North American meat industry affects the world food shortage and to convince people to help solve that problem by eating less meat, also modifies the Rogerian format while maintaining an essentially Rogerian approach. The writer wrote the paper with the idea that it would be distributed through community organizations in conjunction with specific related events.

THOUGHT FOR FOOD

As population grows and land resources become depleted, the job of feeding the world becomes more difficult. We are all familiar with this problem but do not believe we can help solve it on a personal basis. An attitude of apathy is easy for an affluent society to adopt since malnutrition and starvation on a large scale do not affect it and because most of us still are not aware of how our dietary and agricultural practices contribute to the world food shortage. The following will help to make clear the role we play in this.

The average North American family probably feels deprived if it does not eat steak, roast beef, hamburger or some other form of meat at least once a day. Given this overall concentration of meat in the North American diet, it might be interesting to look at some of the reasons behind it. Most important, meat is a compact source of the protein all humans need to perform body metabolism. Protein comprises eighteen to twenty percent of body weight, providing a framework of tendons, muscles, hormones, enzymes and the like.[1]

[1]Francis Lappé, *Diet for a Small Planet* (New York: Ballantine, 1971), p. 34. All further references appear parenthetically in the text.

In its continual breakdown and buildup of tissues, the body requires daily replacement of protein; and meat, being one of the most concentrated sources of protein, easily fulfills this function. Thus meat contains the life-giving protein which is basic to our body chemistry. Meat is also a readily accessible source of protein which tastes good and is quick and easy to prepare. Granted, not all families can afford T-bone or sirloin steak, but most can buy some form of meat which will sustain the body's daily requirement. And it takes little time and planning to prepare a meal with meat as the main course; from shopping at the local grocery store to putting the chops, steak or hamburger in the frypan or oven, it takes only one to two hours. This is important in our busy society where most working people do not have the time for elaborate preparation and planning of meals.

Social and cultural background also contribute to our meat bias. We like to pride ourselves that we are among the most affluent and well-fed countries in the world; and the nutritional value of meat seems to be at the heart of this. Families that eat steak for dinner have come to regard it as a social status symbol and a key to good health. Starvation and malnutrition do not conjure up images of American or Canadian children suffering from kwashiorkor. Because we are among the few countries lucky enough to have meat as a staple, it is an important cultural symbol. In addition, most of us like meat and have been conditioned to enjoy its flavor better than that of any other source of protein. Compared to vegetables, legumes or grains, meat seems definitely more palatable to us. Clearly then, the socio-cultural as well as the nutritional and convenience value of meat contributes to its popularity in the North American diet.

But how does all this affect the world food shortage? The problem is this: our meat industry uses scarce rich agricultural land to grow grain for cattle—high quality grain that could be eaten directly by humans. This includes land and grain of the starving countries, producing a situation where their land is used to make money for a few instead of food for many. In a world where the majority are starving, this practice of land usage is inefficient and wasteful. Besides wasting land to grow grain for cattle, the ratio of protein we feed a cow to protein we recover in humanly edible meat is twenty to one. This means it takes twenty pounds of protein fed to a cow to obtain one pound of protein for humans (p. 6). Bearing this in mind, I would like to suggest the more rational use of agricultural land and the food it produces by looking at the alternatives to meat as the sole source of protein in our diets. It is possible to obtain the same high quality protein by the right combination of vegetables, grains, fish and dairy products in conjunction with a smaller intake of meat. As individuals, we can be part of the solution to feeding the world's hungry and malnourished by reducing the amount of meat we eat and thereby releasing grain for human consumption instead of feed for cattle.

Still and all, considering the favorable qualities previously mentioned, it would be absurd to think of substituting some other source of protein for meat. Furthermore, there are yet other contexts in which our traditional diet would be equally valid: for instance, in the eighteenth century when cattle were fed grass instead of grain. We did not have to worry about how our livestock were raised because it was not on humanly edible substances; starvation then was due to natural causes like crop failures. Then too, overpopulation was not the problem that it is today; there were proportionately fewer mouths to feed. Also, since marginal or agriculturally poor land cannot grow food for people, grazing cattle on it would be another good reason to continue raising livestock for our meat industry. Cattle could eat the grass which grows here on otherwise idle land. This would seem doubly efficient since we would not be feeding cattle humanly edible grain and because this land could not be used for anything else. Although it is possible to grow cattle this way and it is being done to some extent today, most livestock are "finished off" for market on feeds of high quality grain (p. 11). It has become economically unfeasible for farmers to graze cattle on grass for long periods of time; on grain they can fatten up and can be sold sooner for more money because it is the fat content which determines the grade of meat: choice has sixty-three percent more fat than standard grade (p. 11). Obviously, the sooner cattle fatten, the sooner they are sold, and the greater the rate of turnover, the greater the profits. There are the reasons we have to begin to look at alternative ways to obtain protein in our diets.

A varied diet of vegetables, grains, fish, fruit and dairy products, supplemented with meat, can supply sufficient protein while at the same time surpassing meat in provision of other basic nutrients. Non-meat protein sources contain vitamins, minerals and roughage not found in meat; and for quality and quantity of protein, these foods are superior. Soybean, for example, contains forty percent protein, haddock and cod are almost completely protein. It is true that these sources do not contain the highly concentrated protein of meat, but the necessity of eating a variety of vegetables, dairy products, grains and fruits will actually result in better nutrition. This new approach to our diets—eating more plant products and less meat—not only increases nutrition, but it also offers high quality protein, equivalent to or better than most. And, contrary to popular rumor, these foods are no higher in calorie content than the equivalent diets of meat. However, there is the disadvantage that it takes more time and trouble to prepare and plan vegetable/grain-centered diets. Part of this is because we are not yet accustomed to the ways of preparing these kinds of foods. But, with experience, it will become just as convenient and easy to prepare as meat because we will get used to our favorite recipes and follow them just as unconsciously as we now do those for meat. Too, new types of food combinations will add interest to our diets while at the same time contributing to a solution for the world's food problem. It would be unrealistic to expect a change overnight in something so deeply rooted as our cultural eating habits, but it is a goal worth striving for when health and nutrition are at its center.

June Wood

Note that the third paragraph explains the social and cultural context of the opposed position rather than the context in which that position would be valid. That context is stated in the fifth paragraph in juxtaposition with the contexts in which the writer's position is considered valid. Given the nature of the audience, the material, and the persuasive purpose, that modification seems appropriate. To assert in the third paragraph that the valid context for the readers is the eighteenth century would probably create an ironic effect hardly in keeping with the spirit of Rogerian persuasion.

There are a few problems with this piece. There is, for instance, some ambiguity because the generalizations are about meat, but the detailed support is only about beef. There are a couple of awkward constructions. The tone of the opening paragraph may be slightly condescending, and its final sentence is rather formal. Basically, however, the piece works because June approaches her readers gently and firmly. She has a lot of information to offer, and she adopts a strategy that is likely to keep her readers open to considering that information.

The format of Rogerian persuasion, like any other rhetorical format, should be treated as a guideline. When you are first learning it, you will probably do well to follow it explicitly. Once you have mastered it, however, you should adapt it to suit your purposes and your readers.

The traditional and Rogerian approaches to persuasion are quite distinct (although the classical notions of ethical and emotional appeals do provide a link between the two). You will do well to learn both and to use each where appropriate. There is also a larger lesson to be learned from the juxtaposition of these two approaches: the rhetorical forms you use to give shape to your ideas are very important. If you do not believe that, try doing a traditional and a Rogerian version of the same argument.

ADDITIONAL READING

Young, Richard, Alton Becker, and Kenneth Pike. *Rhetoric: Discovery and Change*. New York: Harcourt, Brace & World, 1970. See Chapter Twelve, pages 273-283, on Rogerian persuasion.

EXERCISE

1. Choose an appropriate thesis, imagine an appropriate rhetorical context, and write a Rogerian persuasion that follows the Rogerian format.

2. Carl Rogers' original use of the principles behind Rogerian persuasion was in oral communication. The basic rule was this: no one may speak without first summarizing what the last speaker said accurately enough to satisfy that speaker. Next time you have an argumentative discussion, try following this rule. How does it affect the discussion?

What does this exercise teach you that might be useful when you are writing Rogerian persuasion?

3. In *A Rhetoric of Motives*, Kenneth Burke asserts that

> *you persuade a man only insofar as you can talk his language by speech, gesture, tonality, order, image, attitude, idea,*—*identifying your ways with his.*

Explain how both Rogerian and traditional persuasive strategies encourage such identification.

4. The following paper was addressed to parents of pupils in a school that had just instituted sex education classes for seventh-graders. It makes some tactical errors, but it is generally a well-structured Rogerian persuasion. Evaluate its effectiveness and make suggestions about how it might be improved.

SHOULD WE HAVE SEX EDUCATION CLASSES IN THE SEVENTH GRADE?

Many parents of children in this school have expressed their disapproval of our recent decision to implement sex education classes in the seventh grade. A number of you feel that the material presented in these classes could—and should—be discussed only in the home. As concerned parents many of you feel that some of the children simply are not ready to learn the facts of life. In many instances, you are correct. Even at the seventh grade level, many children are not mature enough to be told about sex. It is something they may not be concerned with personally for a good many years.

We can sympathize with the difficulties faced by today's parents. It is indeed frightening to consider that there is a need to educate children about the "facts of life" at such an early age. For many of you, it is also upsetting that the people imparting this information are relative strangers. In addition, because the information is being relayed in a classroom situation, many of you feel that sex will become the number one topic of conversation outside the classroom as well. We can certainly see why you would prefer to have something as personal as sex discussed in the home rather than in the school. We can agree with you that the ideal situation for children to learn about sex is in the home, with clear and concise information being given. However, it is almost impossible to ensure that every child is being informed about sex in this manner.

If sex education is the responsibility of the school, the material is presented clearly. The teachers lose a great deal of emotional bias which is felt by a parent protecting his or her child from the realities of life. Questions which many parents would feel uncomfortable dealing with are dealt with much more easily in the classroom. Topics such as homosexuality, on which many parents have very biased opinions, are discussed openly. Many of you question the wisdom of presenting such advanced topics in the classroom. However, unless your children do not watch television or look at newspapers, it is very unlikely that we are telling them about anything they do not already worry and wonder about. It has also been our experience that when all children are equally informed about sex, the clandestine street-corner discussions usually disappear, and the topic of sex loses its allure. It is these secret teaching sessions that promote sexual ignorance, and sexual ignorance can only lead to tragedy.

CRITICISM AND CONSENSUS

[H]ow easily the combative impulse can put us in mental blinders and make us take another man's words in the ways in which we can put him down with least trouble.

I. A. Richards

Real communication occurs . . . when we listen with understanding. What does this mean? It means to see the expressed idea and attitude from the other person's point of view, to sense how it feels to him, to achieve his frame of reference in regard to the thing he is talking about.

Carl Rogers

CONSTRUCTIVE CRITICISM

The ability to give and take criticism constructively is very important to you as a writer for two reasons. First, writing constructive criticism—say, a formal critique of a colleague's project proposal or an evaluation of a subordinate's performance—is one of the more sensitive tasks you may face as a writer. Second, the processes of writing and of learning to write better both require you to take constructive criticism from editors, collaborators, instructors, and so forth.

Constructive criticism is a type of persuasion, closely related to Rogerian persuasion. It aims not merely to be correct (thereby allowing the criticizer to feel righteous), but to persuade the criticized person or people to construct changes.

Constructive criticism is especially important in a writing workshop, class, or group. Writers need feedback to improve. Positive feedback ("That's a terrific paper you wrote!") makes writers feel good and encourages them to keep writing. In the long run, positive feedback can lead to growth: if a writer tries something different and is praised for it, she or he will probably try it again—thus positive feedback can reinforce positive changes writers may make. But it is negative feedback ("I don't understand that sentence" or "That paper would work better with stronger transitions") which induces change and directs improvement.

However useful it may be, criticism is threatening. Constructive criticism is much like Rogerian persuasion in its attempts to minimize threat. One way to achieve a reassuring context is to praise before criticizing. The praise should be genuine and specific: hardly anyone is taken in by the formula, "This is basically a good paper, but . . . ." There is almost always something good about any piece of writing; by demonstrating your ability to find it and describe it, you earn your right to criticize. Another way to achieve a reassuring context is by self-criticism: "I can see what's wrong here because I often do (or used to do) the same thing myself."

The threatening nature of criticism can also be reduced if you make it clear that you are criticizing a particular action (or set of actions), not the person or people who did it. Criticism is most threatening (and least constructive) when it is not clear what can be done about it. If someone tells me, "Your paper is terrible," I do not know what to do (aside from feeling bad), so I respond defensively. If someone tells me, "This paper doesn't work as it stands, but if you do such-and-such and such-and-such it could be really effective," I can respond constructively.

There is a formula for constructive criticism that helps keep the criticism specific, makes it clear that a particular action (not a person) is being criticized, and forces the criticizer to indicate what can be done about the criticism. It goes like this:

> When you __________, I feel/think ____________________, so I wish you would __________ .

> *When you* hand me a sloppy manuscript, *I feel* insulted because I don't think you care enough about your work or my time, *so I wish you would* take the trouble to make the manuscript easier to read.

> *When you* use words like *chick, spic,* and *gyp, I feel* angry and stop listening to what you're saying, *so I wish you would* avoid sexist and racist language. (*Note: Gyp* is a derogatory term derived from *gypsy* and meaning "cheat.")

> *When you* tell me my writing is "incoherent, ungrammatical, and confused," *I feel* stupid, discouraged, and angry, *so I wish you would* make more specific and constructive criticisms instead.

It is important that the first slot in the formula be filled with a specific criticism. (Do *not* say, "When you punctuate so unconventionally . . . ." Do say, "When you use comma-splices . . . .") The second slot should contain a response, not a judgment. (Do *not* say, ". . . I think you must be a bigot, ..." Do say, ". . . I feel angry and stop listening to what you're saying . . . .") The third slot should contain a specific and constructive suggestion. (Do *not* say, ". . . so I wish you would start making some sense." Do say, ". . . so I wish you would organize more carefully and supply your readers with a framework and clear transitions.")

When using this formula for constructive criticism, there are two things you can do to help it work effectively. The first is to make certain that the person you wish to criticize is prepared to receive criticism. If you have any doubt, ask. Say, "I have a criticism of your writing. Can we discuss it now?"

The second is to consider the other person's vested interest in receiving your criticism. What does the other person have to gain from your criticism? The third slot in the criticism contains your desire; your purpose in making the criticism is to encourage the other person to do what you are suggesting there. Just as you try to establish a mutual purpose with your readers, just as you end a Rogerian persuasion by appealing to your readers' interests, so you can end a constructive criticism by indicating what the other person could gain by adopting your suggestion.

The distinction between antagonistic and constructive criticism is parallel to the distinction between traditional and Rogerian persuasion. Antagonistic criticism plays to an audience. Its goal is to demonstrate the superiority of the criticizer and the inferiority of those criticized. It does not so much induce change as pass judgment. Constructive criticism is addressed to those criticized. Its goal is to minimize threat and induce change.

Both types of criticism have their uses. For example, newspaper columnists typically write antagonistic criticisms of politicians that aim at getting the newspaper's readers to pass judgment (and perhaps decide not to vote for those politicians). Sometimes, however, newspaper columnists write constructive criticisms that seem to assume that the politicians in question will be among the newspaper's readers and that aim at persuading the politicians to change. The material may be the same, but the tone and the form of the presentation shift distinctly.

When you criticize, you should be clear about your purposes and use the appropriate kind of criticism. When you are criticized, you should try to grasp what is constructive in that criticism instead of just reacting defensively.

ON ACHIEVING CONSENSUS

When a piece of writing is being written or edited by more than one person, there must be a consensus about what is to be communicated and how. Achieving consensus is in certain ways similar to making constructive criticisms and Rogerian persuasions. The process of reaching consensus is a process of clarifying and improving both the substance and the form of the writing.

The camel, it has been suggested, is a horse designed by a committee. A group writing can be equally ungainly if it is not founded on consensus. Consensus means that everybody (or almost everybody) is in essential agreement. It is achieved by extended discussion. Consensus is not majority rule and is not achieved by voting. Indeed, the need for voting and other such procedures indicates the absence of a consensus. When the goal is a clear and effective piece of writing, extend the discussion until all issues are resolved. The early majority may not be right, and an unconvinced minority may not cooperate whole-heartedly.

Here are some instructions for achieving consensus.

1. Keep the group's purpose always in view. Remember that the goal is not for any individual member's suggestion to "win," but to make decisions which will best achieve the group's purpose. Avoid egotism and arguing for your own position just because you identify with it.
2. View the differences of opinion as helpful rather than as hindrances. Attempt to involve everyone in the decision-making process because more information and more perspectives usually produce better decisions, and more involvement usually produces more commitment to follow through on those decisions.
3. Avoid conflict-reducing techniques such as majority rule, averaging, compromises, and trade-offs. When the discussion locks, seek alternative solutions that synthesize the best of all the individual suggestions or offer a whole new approach. Avoid "changing your mind" only in order to reach agreement and avoid conflict.

Clearly making decisions by consensus is more difficult and time-consuming than making decisions by majority-rule. Making decisions by consensus, moreover, is possible only when the group shares a common purpose. When conditions are right, however, consensus can produce better decisions.

ADDITIONAL READING

Lyons, Gracie. *Constructive Criticism*. Oakland, Calif.: Inkwords Press, 1976.

EXERCISE

1. Apply the formula for constructive criticism to your analysis of *your own* writing weaknesses. (See Chapter 0, pages 18-25.) Does it help you focus your own goals?

2. Select some newspaper editorials that make antagonistic criticisms. Practice transforming them into constructive criticisms.

3. Select some constructive journalistic criticisms from newspapers widely read by political leaders (e.g., *The New York Times*, the *Washington Post*, the *Wall Street Journal*, the *Toronto Globe & Mail*). Choose the same politicians and the same issues and contrast the views of the different papers.

4. In your writing group, workshop, or class, devote the last five minutes to criticizing the way criticisms were made during the preceding meeting. Try to put the emphasis on self-criticism (i.e., rather than criticizing others, try to say first, "I did such-and-such, but it would have been better if I had done this-and-that instead.")

5. Do a group writing, and try to make decisions by consensus.

... [A]ll structures in words are partly rhetorical, and ... the notion of a scientific or philosophical verbal structure free of rhetorical elements is an illusion.

Northrup Frye

People in literary studies generally pride themselves on their liberality. Teachers give A's to diverse interpretations. Editors accept works with opposing conclusions. But while freedom is permitted in content, formal conformity is rigidly demanded.

Keith Fort

The act of writing is complicated, but in the tidal conflict between the artist's freedom and the craftsman's discipline there is a consistent pattern of work which can be identified and passed on to the student writer.

The student writer and his teacher, however, must first understand what every writer knows: there are no absolute laws of composition. . . . The only test a writer applies to a page is the craftsman's question, "Does it work?"

Donald Murray

CHAPTER 7
SPECIALIZED FORMS

An accomplished writer, who has mastered the general principles of composition, should be able to figure out how to imitate almost any specialized type of writing. The mark of a writer, considered as a generalist, is the ability to adapt to various sorts of writing tasks and various kinds of rhetorical contexts. The general principles discussed in this textbook can be adapted to almost any writing task. If you expect to be doing a lot of writing of any particular type, it makes sense to analyze that kind of writing and figure out exactly how the general principles apply to it.

The purpose of this chapter is twofold: first, to help you develop an analytical ability that will contribute to your versatility as a writer and, second, to help you learn how to do any special kinds of writing you may need or wish to master. Since this textbook will be used mainly by advanced students, there will also be specific discussion of certain specialized writing tasks that are particularly useful to university students and graduates: term papers, business letters, résumés, proposals, and professional publications.

As you read this chapter, you should be thinking about the particular types of writing that are or will be important to you. If you are, say, a third-year university student, how does the general advice about term papers apply in your major? What sort of résumé and letter will you have to write to get a job in your field? What types of writing does a person have to do in your chosen profession? What types of writing will you need or want to do outside your job?

If you can take the general principles of composition and learn to apply them to particular writing tasks, then you will have mastered what this book is trying to teach. You will be no longer a writing student, but a writer. You will not be finished learning—writing itself is a learning process and a writer can always improve—but you will be a writer.

This chapter begins with a heuristic for analyzing any particular type of writing. It goes on to discuss certain specialized forms. As you learn those specialized forms, try to see how they relate to the general principles of composition on which the heuristic is based. Then see if you can apply the heuristic to a type of writing task that is of special importance to you. If you can do that, you have taken a big step toward being able to teach yourself how to do whatever types of writing you may wish to do.

In the end, reaching real readers—delivery—is the final stage of the composing process. That is where the composing merges into the communicative process. Some writing may be just for yourself or just a school exercise. But you should write for real readers too. Reader response is the ultimate criterion by which writing can be judged. Just knowing that what you are writing may be published can change how you relate to it and how you work on it. You should experience that difference, if only by writing a letter to the editor of a community or campus newspaper. The last section of this chapter is about publication.

A HEURISTIC FOR ANALYZING WRITING TASKS

The common ingredient that I find in all of the writing I admire—excluding for now novels, plays and poems—is something that I shall reluctantly call the rhetorical stance, a stance which depends on discovering and maintaining in any writing situation a proper balance among the three elements that are at work in any communicative effort: the available arguments about the subject itself, the interests and peculiarities of the audience, and the voice, the implied character, of the speaker.

Wayne Booth

Clearly, the structure of anything limits the uses to which it may be put.

James Kinneavy

THE APPROACH

What follows is a procedure by which you can investigate and analyze almost any particular type of writing. The goal of the analysis is to describe the assumptions and structures which typify a particular type of writing. Although the writings you analyze probably will not be literary, the analysis itself is, in effect, a kind of literary criticism. Literary critics have done this sort of analysis of literary texts for millennia, as rhetoricians have done it with persuasive texts and philosophers with certain types of logical texts. A writer does this sort of analysis in order to learn how to produce a specific type of writing.

The approach is two-pronged, involving both library and empirical research. Since there is little point in starting from scratch if other people have already attempted the very task you are undertaking, you should search the library for style sheets or manuals about the particular type of writing.

Style sheets are often published by professional organizations. The Modern Language Association (MLA), for example, publishes the style sheet generally used by North American literary critics. The main function of a style sheet is to assure that all the writers in a particular profession or organization use a standardized format and style. You may learn, for example, that it is usual in your field to begin journal articles with a statement of the problem being investigated and a review of previous studies. You may be told that your manuscript should have a left-hand margin of 1½ inches (4 cm). If there is a style sheet for the type of writing you are trying to master, you should obtain it and follow it. If you are a student, your professors will probably expect you to follow the style sheet that is standard in their field.

Manuals often give more substantive advice. The following excerpt is a student's summary of what she learned about the structure and style of news articles by consulting several journalism manuals.

> The news story is strictly governed by a prescribed format which can be visualized as an inverted pyramid: the most important facts are placed at the beginning, with the less important following. This enables the reader to get the "gist" of the story by scanning the first paragraph. It also makes it easier for the copy editor to shorten a story—he starts "cutting" from the bottom, knowing he is eliminating the least important facts.
>
> The beginning of a story is called its "lead." The lead can run from a few words to two or more graphs, and how its information is presented can make or break the story. The readers read the lead before anything else, apart from the headline, and if they don't like it, they won't continue. The lead sets the tone for the story and contains the most important information. The traditional "5W's and H" (who? what? where? why? when? and how?) are usually contained in the lead. (See page 64.)
>
> Following the lead is the body of the story. The body elaborates on the facts presented in the lead, as well as introducing new ones. This information is presented in the shortest possible space. "Tight," concise writing is important in news stories for two reasons: one, because it makes it easier for the reporter to keep his audience interested; and two, because as far as publishers are concerned, space is money.[1]
>
> Short words and compact phrases are the keys to good, "tight" journalistic writing. The reporter is taught to substitute "suddenly" for "all of a sudden"; to write "soon" instead of "in the near future"; and that "now" is preferable to "at the present time."[2] Newspaper-writing style manuals contain long lists of similar words and phrases with their more succinct equivalents. [See pages 177-179.]
>
> Fiona Barnett
>
> ---
>
> [1]William Burrows, *On Reporting the News* (New York: New York University Press, 1977), p. 65.
>
> [2]Ibid., p. 34.

Since writing can hardly be separated from thinking, any descriptions or analyses of the sort of thinking required in the field are also likely to be helpful. The structure and style of a piece of writing often follow from the structure of the thinking processes which underlie it. If you are trying to figure out how to do research reports in sociology, an article by a philosopher of science analyzing the logic of contemporary sociology may be most useful. In academic and professional writing, it is often particularly important to understand just what "objectivity" means in the particular field and what you must *do* to achieve it (see pages 221-223 on objectivity and 266-267 on *operational* definitions).

Thus far you have been doing secondary research, collecting other people's opinions. The second prong of the approach involves empirical, primary research. This means you collect and analyze a sampling of successful writing of the particular type. Style sheets and manuals are often incomplete or dated, and the experts who wrote them were not always totally correct to begin with. Whether you are trying to learn how to write literary criticism, political analysis, financial reports, magazine feature stories, or poems, you should double-check whatever you learn from your secondary sources to be sure it matches the empirical evidence.

ANALYZING A SAMPLE

You begin by choosing some examples of successful writing. In an academic or professional field, articles published in the most reputable journals are good choices. Thus, if you are trying to learn how to write scholarly literary criticism, you might select ten articles from recent issues of *PMLA, American Literature, College English, Victorian Studies,* and *Modern Drama.* If, on the other hand, you are trying to learn how to write popular film reviews, you might turn to *Newsweek, Cosmopolitan, Maclean's, McCall's,* and *Variety.*

As you read the pieces of writing you have selected, you will be doing an unusual type of reading. Although you will be paying some attention to what the writers are saying, your focus will be on how they approach their subject matter, which sorts of material they choose to include, how they structure it, what they seem to assume about their rhetorical contexts, and what sort of *persona* and style they adopt.

Here is a list of questions, derived from the principles of composition discussed in previous chapters of this textbook, to guide your analysis.

1. What sort of material is usually treated? Do the writers seem to share approaches, methods, or techniques for handling that material? Does there seem to be a shared heuristic (see pages 63-73) that some or all of the writers use to generate their material? Could you invent such a heuristic for this type of writing?

2. How are these writings focused? Do they treat fully all aspects of a narrow subject? Are they focused around a problem?
3. Is there a standard format or typical structure for the whole writing or any part of it? How do the writings begin? How do they end? How long are the paragraphs and how are they typically structured? What is the relationship among levels of generality (see pages 95-99) within typical paragraphs and for whole pieces of writing?
4. How long are most of the writings in your sample? How long and difficult are the words and sentences? What is the level of readability (see pages 121-124)?
5. Are there certain key terms or analogies that recur? Are there "buzz words" or a standard jargon?
6. Who reads this type of writing? Either from analyzing the writing or from outside knowledge, can you describe the readers? What assumptions do the writers seem to make about the knowledge, attitudes, beliefs, and vested interests of the readers?
7. Where is this type of writing usually published? Is it likely to be read casually or seriously, for entertainment or for use? If the writings must be accepted by an editor, what can you surmise about the editor's motives and criteria?
8. Is there a common *persona* (see pages 159-160) that the writers adopt? Can you detect shared values (e.g., a common definition of objectivity, or belief in the value of knowledge, democracy, marriage, or whatever)? Do the writers take a particular stance (as indicated, perhaps, by avoidance of the pronouns, *I* and *you*)? How formal is the writing in word choice and usage (e.g., does it use slang or contractions)?
9. What basic purposes does the writing serve? Is it primarily expressive, explanatory, persuasive or literary? Are distinct purposes emphasized in different parts of the writings?
10. Which of the basic patterns of arrangement does the writing use regularly? (See Chapters 4 and 5.) Does it rely mostly on description and/or narration? Does it use the more analytical patterns? Does it tend to use different patterns in different parts?

By answering these questions (and others which may arise as you analyze your sample and review your secondary sources), you should reach an understanding of the particular type of writing that concerns you. You should then try to write out your answers as a set of contraints (see pages 307-320) within which a writer must work to produce this type of writing. In particular, you should try to create a heuristic that will help generate the material, an outline of any common format or structure, and an analysis of the rhetorical context (purpose, audience, and occasion). By doing these things, you will produce your own writer's manual and be well on your way toward teaching yourself to do the particular type of writing successfully and efficiently.

The constraints within which a writer must work are often quite specific. After analyzing storybooks for very young children, a writing student reports the following constraints.

> These books must not be too long because the young child has a short attention span. Forty-eight pages is usually cited as the maximum length for picture books (with a maximum of five hundred words per book). Sentence length must also be monitored. Most sentences have a maximum of eight words. Any longer than this and the child will lose the sense of the words. There are usually no paragraphs, and seldom are there more than eight or ten lines per page. The actual text occupies only half of the book, and it is attractively alternated with pictures.

Here are some other generalizations excerpted from the same paper.

> To be successful, the story must deal with the needs and common experiences of the wee tots. For this reason, many children's writers use tiny children as their central characters. Kids will identify with other kids who share their problems and interests.
>
> • • •
>
> These stories are meant to be read aloud, and this means that narration is emphasized. The style of writing is very informal, precisely because the writer uses language in an attempt to create a story-telling atmosphere. There is limited description because the vivid illustrations usually fulfill this function.
>
> • • •
>
> The plot consists of a very simple progression: one central idea is presented and carried clearly throughout the story. . . . Picture stories start with an inciting incident, which grabs the young reader's attention and then leads to further action within the story. . . . Frequently the plot is circular: by the end of the story the character and conditions have often returned to their original condition. Most of the action usually occurs in the middle of the book.
>
> The ending must be satisfying and pleasant for the youngster. . . . By the end of the book, the tiny tot has usually had an adventure, learned to accomplish something, overcome a fear, or learned a lesson. . . .
>
> • • •
>
> The picture books are quite short; therefore, the characters are never fully developed. Although they are uncomplicated and flat, they must still arouse interest and excitement. Maggie Scraggles is a stereotyped witch, but her

magical actions make her lively, and this holds the attention. Character names are important because they snag the child's attention.

• • •

Most picture stories have an element of humour in them, whether is is presented in the comic illustrations or within the story. The humour is always obvious and direct; this is no place for adult wit or complex word plays. In these books, laughter is initiated by the juxtaposition of incompatible elements or by the reversal of common expectations.

• • •

The writer must always be conscious of the sound of his words because the story will be read aloud. Often key words or phrases (for example, "everybody said no!") are repeated throughout the story. This repetition will create pleasing, friendly landmarks for a child. Kids react strongly to the colors, shapes, sizes, sounds, and smells of their world, and they will respond to such elements within a story. A children's writer should strive to use textural, rhythmic and onomatopoeic words.

Mishelle Panagopoulos

To generalizations like these, Mishelle added many concrete examples from storybooks she had examined. She began her paper with a discussion of purpose, audience, and occasion. She ended it with a revision-heuristic, a set of questions that a writer or editor could use to evaluate and revise the draft of a story. Her advice is very specific. In a paper of approximately 2500 words, she produced an excellent little manual for storybook writers.

Virtually any type of writing you may wish to master can be analyzed similarly. The following essay is a structural analysis of a particular brand of popular romance.

A HARLEQUIN ROMANCE: THE FINAL FRONTIER

Rowena, the shy, but unusually intelligent, librarian, could not look away. She stood still, spellbound by the glints in the publisher's dark, flashing eyes. He winked and grinned his approval. He came down the steps toward her, triumphantly brandishing a paperback. Suddenly, she found herself running, running away from a fate she knew she could never escape!

Bookstores, newstands, and libraries everywhere are filled with a distinct brand of paperback love story bearing the emblem "Harlequin Romance." Once opened, these stories transport the reader to an exotic land where true love predictably conquers all. In a larger sense, these stories possibly represent the biggest money-makers in the publishing industry.

What are Harlequin Romances? Some people call them "junky novels." Others call them "a form of relaxation," while others prefer the term "escape."

In order to understand more fully just what Harlequin Romances are and the reasons behind their phenomenal success, one should first investigate the range of characters, settings, and narrative sequences typical in this genre.

The principal characters of a Harlequin Romance conform to four easily recognizable stereotypes: the heroine, the hero, the side characters, and the friendly adviser.

The heroine: The heroine is usually young and attractive, possessing high intelligence and even higher morals. During the course of the story, she is revealed to have some special ability which elevates her from the more ordinary characters. The following charts her special ability as it occurs with a variety of roles:

ROLE	"ABILITY"
governess	—She has the ability to get along with vicious, hateful brats. Generosity, fairness, and honesty are her virtues.
secretary	—She whips the office into better shape than it has ever been before. Organization, tidiness, and a keen eye for business are her special traits.
journalist	—She usually possesses a superior writing ability accompanied with a remarkable intuition for scoops.
doctor or nurse	—She is unappreciated and overworked, but she always has the time to care for people. She is generous in spirit and loving in heart.

The hero: The hero is usually older, more sophisticated and sexually experienced than the heroine. He is either bored with an all-too-wearisome world or a bitter cynic, more hurt by an uncaring world than he will ever let on. He is introduced to the reader with a description of his lean, weathered good looks, his stubborn jaw, and his intense, steely eyes. At the beginning, he is ruggedly independent, but as the story progresses, he, first grudgingly, then wholeheartedly, admits his need for the heroine.

Side characters: These characters play an important role in the story by providing most of the conflicts. They are more colorful in personality and action than the hero and heroine but lack the strong moral values of the latter. The side characters are as follows:

The "other woman": This woman is beautiful, sophisticated, and very much a woman of the world. Secure in her claim for the hero, she is rather condescending to the heroine.

The "other man": There are two distinct types of the "other man." The first is older and lecherous, forever drooling after Harlequin heroines. The second is young and klutzy, but is sweet.

The friendly adviser to the hero and/or heroine: This is usually a friend who acts as a fairy godmother. The adviser knows that the hero and heroine are meant for each other and is determined to remedy Fate's procrastination.

The exotic Harlequin settings provide the perfect backdrop for the characters. Whether it is the beach, a ranch in the back country of Australia, or a castle amid the moors, the surroundings are guaranteed to provide the romance and mystique necessary for the reader's escape to the world of Harlequin.

Though not as exotic as the scenery, the storylines maintain the Harlequin tradition or formula. Twelve different stories come out each month, but there seems to be a common structure to the narrative sequence that identifies them as Harlequins. This common structure can be depicted in this way:

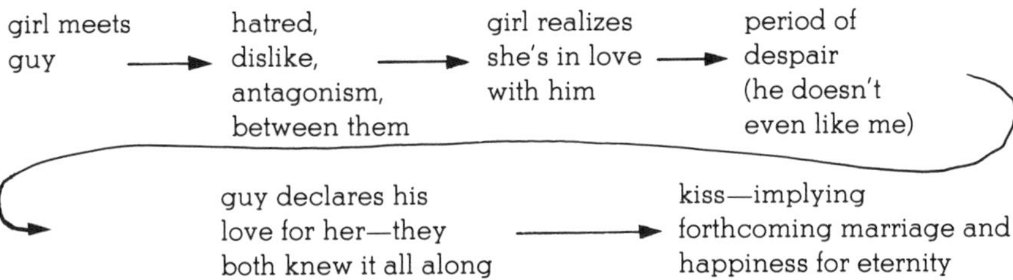
girl meets guy
hatred, dislike, antagonism, between them
girl realizes she's in love with him
period of despair (he doesn't even like me)
guy declares his love for her—they both knew it all along
kiss—implying forthcoming marriage and happiness for eternity

With this one formula, hundreds of variations can be generated. For many readers, the entertainment that the book provides lies in guessing which variation the author will use. I asked one woman why she reads Harlequin Romances and she replied, "I know that the girl is going to get the guy. I read them to find out *how* she's going to get him."

However, these books can hardly be called intellectual exercises. Even their advertisements acknowledge this by emphasizing their relaxing qualities. These books offer more than just escape and relaxation. They are fantasies where traditional values, attitudes, and roles are re-evaluated and tested against the picture of modern society. Life is rewritten and changed. The stereotypes and predictability of these novels, which some "discriminating" readers describe as disgusting, give meaning and a sense of order to this otherwise chaotic world where roles and values are hopelessly ambiguous. Perhaps Harlequin Romance readers are looking for stability in an unstable world.

Margaret Coe*

In this short essay, Margaret captures the essence of the Harlequin Romance. She analyzes the basic structure of character and plot. She discusses social function and rhetorical context. To write a Harlequin, you would need to know also about language (length, level of readability, etc.) But Margaret demonstrates that even certain types of fiction can be analyzed and imitated.

*No relation to the author of this textbook.

The rest of this chapter is devoted to certain types of writing tasks that are likely to be useful to most of the people who will read this textbook. Learn how to do your own analysis, however, and you can apply the basic principles of composition to virtually any type of writing you want to master.

EXERCISE

1. Make a list of the various types of writing that are done in your area of special interest. Using the procedures discussed above, analyze one such type of writing. Write a short manual based on your results. (If possible, work together with others from your field, and do the manual as a group writing project.)

2. Using specific examples from one particular type of writing, explain James Kinneavy's assertion that "the structure of anything limits the uses to which it may be put." Demonstrate and discuss the extent to which the structure of that type of writing constrains writers. Does the structure limit their choice of material? Does it constrain them toward certain approaches? In other words, does the form constrain the substance? If so, does it do so in ways that are helpful?

TERM PAPERS

Although . . . study involves a lot of hard thinking, it is, in a sense, a receptive process. We study in order to understand. But there comes a time in a college course when one is expected to demonstrate his understanding . . . .

Leon Dickinson

Research is a way of learning, important in formal study, which we can use for the rest of our lives: we can research the voting records of congressmen, recipes, genealogy, precedents in zoning for the neighborhood, or types of schooling for information of the PTA. Research is a method. The research paper is a particular embodiment of the general method.

Donald Hall

Writing a research paper, then, is not just stringing together statements from books and magazines. It is completely reorganizing and reworking the source material into an original composition.

James McCrimmon

WHY STUDENTS WRITE

Students are asked to write various kinds of papers in university courses. Some of those papers require research, some require critical thinking, and some require both. Some are basically reports, in which students present information they have found, selected and organized into a meaningful pattern. Some are critical or "opinion" papers, in which students must analyze, evaluate, and draw conclusions. Some are critical research papers, in which students use research findings to validate critical judgments and support conclusions.

To understand term papers, consider their rhetorical purposes, audience, and occasion. Students write papers mainly as exercise: the papers serve primarily to help students develop, practice, and demonstrate certain abilities. Most term papers are primarily explanatory, but the reader usually does not need the explanation. The audience is usually a single reader, an expert who presumably knows more about the subject than the writer does. The occasion is evaluative: students receive grades or comments indicating how well they have learned and what they need to continue working on.

Term papers help students develop independence. Even a simple research report requires students to find, select, and organize information. This may be the same sort of information that the instructor has presented in class, but the students must discover it themselves. Thus they learn how to acquire that sort of information without depending on the instructor to give it to them.

A critical paper requires students to make inferences and draw their own conclusions. They use the concepts and methods of interpretation that were taught in the course, but they apply those concepts and methods to new material. Thus they learn to think critically instead of depending on the instructor to interpret for them.

An objective examination can measure how well students have learned the material the instructor gave them. A term paper can be used to develop and evaluate their abilities to acquire information and think critically on their own—which is what education and graduation are ultimately about. It is in this rhetorical context that term papers make sense.

To understand the structure and style of term papers, one must realize that they are modeled after the kinds of papers professionals and academics write for publication in journals, presentation at conferences, and other such occasions. In professional contexts, these papers serve to keep members of the profession up to date on new research results and their implications, new or modified theories, innovative procedures, and so forth. The intended readers are specialists in the same field, who can be presumed to share certain concepts, knowledge, and methodological values. The format and language of the papers reflect the formality of the professional occasions and the specialized purposes and knowledge of the audiences.

There are two basic processes involved in preparing such papers, and any given paper may require either or both. One is research: finding information. The other is critical thinking: analyzing, evaluating, and drawing conclusions.

There is a place for the pure research report, which simply presents information for others to think about. There is a place for the pure critical paper, which generalizes and draws conclusions from generally accepted information. Indeed, in some fields there is a division of labor between those who find information and those who build theories with it. Nonetheless, most academic papers involve some combination of research and critical thinking, although they are sometimes segregated into distinct parts of the paper.

Research is divided into two types. When you investigate a subject directly yourself, you are doing *primary research*. If you do an experiment, that is primary research. If you read and reread a literary text to find details which support an interpretation, that is primary research.

When you consult the reports and analyses of other investigators, you are doing *secondary research*. If you read a report about an experiment someone else did, that is secondary research. If you read someone else's interpretation of a literary text, that is secondary research. When university professors ask for "a research paper," they are asking for one based on secondary research.

However you get your information, when you analyze it, evaluate it, and draw conclusions from it, you are doing critical thinking. In what is sometimes called an "opinion" paper, you support your conclusions with your own observations (i.e., primary research, however informal) and with general knowledge (i.e., information and theories that you may presume your readers share). In a critical research paper, you support your conclusions with secondary research (i.e., with information reported by other investigators and with the critical judgments of experts). In other words, you use your secondary research findings as the basis and support for your conclusions, but the paper is built around your own thesis statement.

When you do a research paper, the bulk of the research may come before the bulk of the critical thinking. You may start with a question, use that to focus your research, and draw your conclusions afterwards. You may, on the other hand, start with an hypothesis, and then do research to confirm (or disconfirm) it. Most likely, the research and thinking will proceed side by side: thinking critically will raise questions that research will start to answer, thus setting off more thinking, and so forth.

However you work, the research findings are ultimately and logically subordinate to the critical thinking process they serve. A pure research report makes no sense in isolation: research findings are meaningless unless somebody interprets and generalizes them, thereby building a theory or solving a problem. We will, therefore, consider critical papers first and research papers afterwards.

THE CRITICAL PAPER

A critical paper begins with a critical problem. This may be a contradiction between a general theory and some particular instance. It may be a contradiction between someone else's opinion and your own. Or it may simply be some event or thing that has not yet been successfully explained. (See pages 51-54.)

Perhaps your theory tells you that all wars are based on economic conflicts, but your newspaper tells you about a war being fought over religious differences. You must then reinterpret the particular instance or modify your theory. Perhaps you read a sociologist who asserts that human nature is genetically determined, but you believe that human behavior is primarily the result of socialization. You must then present evidence and arguments for your opinion. Perhaps you notice in the novels of George Eliot a recurring image which your English professor tells you has never been analyzed. You must then provide an explanation for the recurrence, probably by discovering a symbolic significance that is consistent with the main themes of the novels.

A critical term paper for a university course usually takes a concept or method that has been taught in the course and applies it to new material. Although your effort is focused on explaining that material, you are more importantly developing and demonstrating your ability to use the concepts and methods of the discipline. Through readings, lectures, demonstrations, class discussions, and guided experiences, you have learned certain concepts and ways to approach certain types of material. On tests, you have shown that you understand those concepts and methods well enough to define and exemplify them, and even to apply them in limited ways. A term paper is your opportunity to develop your ability to think critically about and independently utilize the concepts and approaches you have been learning.

Suppose you take an anthropology course in which you study and analyze the kinship structures of various societies. Do you understand the concept and method well enough to apply it to societies you did not study? Suppose you take an English course in which you study and interpret five of Shakespeare's tragedies. Could you, on your own, interpret one you did not study? Writing a critical paper is a good way to find out. To write it, you must go beyond passive understanding and actively use what you have learned in the course.

A critical paper is basically an explanation. There is an element of persuasion in its attempt to convince readers that the explanation is valid. And the paper almost inevitably reports information in support of its analysis. Research, primary and/or secondary, may be used to validate the explanation. Research may also aid the writer's discovery process, especially when it includes a review of previous analyses and explanations of the same or similar material. But the paper's primary function is to present the writer's interpretation and conclusions. The dominant purpose is explanation.

Although a critical paper may use any of the patterns of arrangement discussed in Chapters 4 and 5, it is likely to emphasize the more analytical ones. Although large sections of the paper may be narration, description, comparison/contrast, and exemplification, these patterns are likely to be subordinated to definition, classification and division, process-analysis and, especially, causal explanation. In the end, a critical paper usually answers a *why?* "Why does such-and-such happen?" "Why is thus-and-such a correct interpretation of this poem?"

A critical paper often explains research results. In a sense, the "Conclusions" section at the end of a scientific article is a short critical paper. The "Results" section answers *what?* or *how?* But ultimately we want to know *why?* (Or perhaps even *so what?*)

A critical paper may pull together research findings from a number of investigations and suggest a single, consistent interpretation. Or it may pull together a number of interpretations and suggest one general theory that encompasses them all.

One reader may, for example, point out that snow (frozen water) is a symbol of spiritual paralysis in James Joyce's "The Dead." Other readers may find other symbols. To interpret the story, however, a literary critic must show how the symbols cluster—how snow is associated with darkness and fire with light—and then, by weight of evidence, show that the many clusters can be explained by a theme that contrasts paralysis (spiritual death) with motion (resurrection). Then this interpretation can be linked with interpretations of other stories in the collection to reach a more general theory of the meaning of Joyce's *Dubliners.* Only then do we understand why the recurrent symbol patterns exist in that text.

In practice, critical analysis and explanation often come after the research, to make sense of the findings (and suggest promising directions for future research). But an "opinion" paper can become a critical research paper if its empirical assumptions are researched and its interpretations supported with expert testimony—if one asks "How do I know this is true?" and "What do the recognized authorities say about this?" What matters is the logical relationship among levels of generality, between information and explanation.

THE RESEARCHED PAPER

Students often consider research papers onerous assignments—necessary (or perhaps unnecessary) evils involving a lot of drudgery, such as note cards, precisely formated footnotes, bibliographies, and so forth. Only when the purposes of research papers are made clear do the complicated paraphernalia that accompany them become meaningful.

Research answers empirical questions, such as the following.

What percentage of paragraphs in published modern prose begin with topic sentences?

How do experienced writers work?

How has the symbolism of the lighthouse in Virginia Woolf's *To the Lighthouse* been interpreted by critical authorities?

Is there any historical connection between the word *niggardly* and the racial epithet *nigger*? Between *Gypsy* and *gyp*? Between *Welsh* and *welsh*?

Is there any correlation between diet and juvenile delinquency?

What happens to the divorce rate among contemporary North American married couples as the husband's earnings increase? As the wife's earnings increase?

What is the correlation between scores on scholastic aptitude tests and school grades? Between scores and father's professional status?

What is the correlation between the state of the economy and the length of fashionable women's skirts?

What at present is the authoritative explanation among geophysicists of the aurora borealis?

Each of these questions can, in principle, be answered by empirical investigation.

Depending on the nature of the question, the research may have to be conducted in the library, the laboratory, or the world. It may be very difficult and expensive to discover the required information. In the case of an historical question, like the relationship between *Welsh* and *welsh*, the information needed to provide an empirical answer may be irretrievably lost. And pure research generally demonstrates only correlations, not causal relationships (see pages 300-301). Nonetheless, all of the above are *research questions*, and every reasonable attempt should be made to answer them empirically rather than speculatively.

There are two other types of questions that, in principle, cannot be answered by research alone. The first type tends to go beyond correlation and to inquire about causal and meaningful relationships. For example:

Does the way experienced writers work explain the relatively high quality of their writing?

What are the correct interpretations of the symbolism of the lighthouse in Virginia Woolf's *To the Lighthouse*?

Are dietary inadequacies among the factors that contribute to juvenile delinquency?

To what extent do economic factors affect the stability of contemporary North American marriages? The length of fashionable women's skirts?

Although research findings can provide an informed basis for answering such questions, the answers depend on interpretation and critical judgment. That is why Aristotle said that the answers to such questions are never definite, but only probable. Even physical explanations, such as the causes of the aurora borealis, sometimes change when scientists reinterpret old research results in the light of new theories.

The second type of question that cannot be answered by research alone is ethical (or aesthetic). These questions have to do with relationships among means and ends, with effects (and affects). They are characterized by the word *should* and value-laden terms, like "fair" or "great."

> Should modern writers begin paragraphs with topic sentences?
>
> Is *To the Lighthouse* a great work of literature?
>
> Should we stop using *gyp*? If so, should we substitute *cheat*?
>
> Should we restrict juvenile delinquents to two quarts of milk per day?
>
> To what extent should married couples be discouraged from separating?
>
> Is it fair to use scholastic aptitude tests scores when determining university admissions?
>
> If the aurora borealis becomes endangered by pollution, what is the maximum amount of money that ought to be spent to protect it?

At best, research can provide information about the effectiveness of means; it cannot, by itself, be the basis for choosing ends. At best, it might describe how *To the Lighthouse* affects readers; it cannot, by itself, be used to define "great work of literature."

If research reports are onerous, it is because they require a lot of painstaking work and do not answer the questions that ultimately matter. Research alone cannot guarantee you a correct interpretation of *To the Lighthouse*, let alone a judgment as to its greatness. What research can do, however, is provide an informed basis for interpretations, judgments, and decisions.

Scientists and scholars often justify their research precisely on the grounds that it is, in a sense, "purposeless." Insofar as their choices of research questions are constrained by personal or social values, the availability of funding, or other extrinsic factors, they say it is less than objective.

To many students, however, it is this very "purposelessness" that makes research a drudgery. A research report separates information gathering from interpretation, judgment, and decision making. It confines the researcher to the lower levels of generality. These separations can make research seem like meaningless drudgery.

But research is not meaningless to someone who needs the information. Research is not meaningless to the lawyer who later uses it to get a client acquitted. Research is not meaningless to the television journalist who later uses it to expose the lies being told by a national leader. Research is not meaningless to the scholar who later uses it as evidence to resolve a critical issue or to reach the definitive interpretation of a text. Research is not meaningless to the teacher who later uses it to teach more successfully. Research is not meaningless to the scientist who later builds an explanatory theory based on it.

The separation of information gathering from decision making is, moreover, increasingly real in North America, as elsewhere in the developed world. As decision making becomes more centralized, the people who make the basic decisions are often very far away from where those decisions will be implemented. There is a division of labor between those who discover and provide the information and those who make the basic decisions. Under these circumstances, report writing becomes very important—otherwise the decision makers have no basis for making realistic decisions. Independent research reports, which will be utilized by people other than those who did the work of preparing them, are becoming common and necessary.

A research report, nonetheless, remains ultimately without significance until it is used to develop theoretical explanations, define implications, or make decisions. From an educational perspective, the writing of a research report is not as useful as the writing of a critical research paper, which combines the research report with the critical paper and develops the implications of the research. Although certain courses of study, even in the university, put considerable emphasis on research reports—often because those courses are training people for subordinate roles in industry, public service, or academia—typical university "research papers" are critical research papers. They are usually based on library research and designed to develop both research and critical thinking abilities.

There is a standard procedure for writing research papers. It is modeled after processes developed by scholars for major library-research projects, such as theses and dissertations, scientific and scholarly books. The research papers students write to practice this standard procedure are much shorter; therefore, students are often tempted to take short cuts. But one of the points of an undergraduate research paper, especially in a writing course, is to master the procedure.

If one remembers both the educational purposes for writing research papers and the academic models on which they are based, then the standard procedure should make sense. What follows is, I hope, a relatively intelligent version of this procedure.

1. FINDING A TOPIC. Finding a topic for a research paper is much like discovering a topic for any writing. In the real world, a piece of writing often begins because a question has presented itself and you lack the information to answer it reliably. For the student, however, the topic more often has to be discovered. Since a research paper is often a somewhat lengthy project involving considerable drudgery, you should find a topic that will sustain your interest, either because you find it intrinsically interesting or because it is a matter of some importance.

You could start with a critical problem, with a contradiction that has come to your attention during the course for which you are writing the paper. Perhaps there is a question that arose in a class discussion but was never answered. Perhaps an interpretation was put forth with which you disagree. Perhaps two or more assertions were made which seem to contradict each other. Perhaps a few particulars seem to contradict a general theory. Any such contradiction could be a starting point for a research paper. The advantage of starting with such a critical problem is that your research efforts are clearly focused right from the beginning.

Another good starting point could be an "opinion" paper you have already written—or even just an opinion that you have not written out. Opinions usually have a basis in beliefs about reality. Finding out if those beliefs are true and if you can prove them might make a good and interesting research project.

Let us imagine that you have written an opinion paper about marriage (or that you will draft one as a starting point for this research project). Perhaps you attempted to persuade readers that the structure of the traditional Western marriage is superior to any of the alternatives that have been tried. In asserting that opinion, you have inevitably made a number of empirical assumptions, probably based on your own experiences and observations. Investigating, if necessary correcting, and proving those assumptions could produce a good, critical research paper. All you have to do is go through the paper, stop at each factual statement or implicit assumption, and ask, "How do I know this is true? How can I prove it? What do the recognized authorities say?" That might lead to a list of questions like these.

Is the traditional Western marriage really like my image of it?

Am I really aware of all the alternatives that have been tried? How did they work out?

What are the social functions of marriage in modern Western societies? What is marriage expected to do for the individuals involved?

What alternatives are possible within the structure of modern Western societies? How well would they fulfill the social and personal functions of marriage?

Go to the library, find the answers to the questions you have discovered, insert them at appropriate places in your paper, revise as necessary, add footnotes and bibliography—and you have turned an "opinion" paper into a research paper.

If neither of these methods produces a topic, choose some rather general area and do some introductory reading. Go to the library, find some materials related to the area you picked, and read until you discover a more focused topic that interests you. There is no need to take notes during such introductory reading. Just read quickly and broadly, getting a general background for your paper and watching for a critical problem or researchable question. Since what you want at this stage is an overview, useful sources might include (1) review articles that summarize major books and articles on the topic, (2) a general textbook that includes the topic, (3) a good encyclopedia, and (4) the *Book Review Digest*.

Whichever method you use, you want to focus your topic as soon as possible. Not too soon, because you need to have some background in order to focus on a good research topic, and you do not want to be stuck with a dull topic or one which is excessively difficult to research. But on the other hand, not too late, because research can be a time-consuming process, and you want to focus soon enough to leave yourself plenty of time for the rest of the project.

You also want to make sure that the topic you choose can be researched. Are the empirical questions substantial enough? Will the information you need be available when you need it? Does your university library have enough material on the topic, or will you have to resort to interlibrary loans?

2. FINDING INFORMATION. If you do not know your way around a library very well, you will probably head straight for the card catalog. Inexperienced university students turn to the card catalog as automatically as high school students turn to the encyclopedia. The card catalog is useful; it will lead you to books on your topic. But much of the information you want will probably be located in journal articles, and those are not listed in the card catalog. You can, moreover, often get a better overview by reviewing ten or fifteen articles than by reading the same number of pages in a single book.

Ask a librarian. Most university libraries have research librarians with graduate degrees in library science. They are experts on finding information in libraries, and one of their functions is to help people find information. If you know, even roughly, what you are looking for, a research librarian may save you a lot of time.

More and more university libraries also offer guided tours. Such tours are devoted primarily to telling people how to find information in the library. You may have been bored by such an orientation tour at some time when you did not have a research project to do. But you may well want to take one now if it is available.

If you are new at library research, perhaps the most important advice is to look at indexes and bibliographies as well as at the card catalog. You may be familiar with *The Readers' Guide to Periodical Literature*, which lists articles published in over a hundred U.S. magazines since 1900. This is an index of *popular* magazines, however; much of what it lists will not be considered sufficiently reliable for the sort of research done at the university level. The *Social Sciences and Humanities Index* lists more scholarly sources. The *Essay and General Literature Index* is a good place to look for articles that were published in collections rather than in journals. There are also restricted indexes on such subjects as agriculture, art, education, industrial arts, and Catholic publications. Both *The New York Times* and the *London Times* publish annual indexes.

Bibliographies are lists of books and articles on given subjects. Some bibliographies cover rather broad fields. Many of them are published annually by major scholarly journals or professional organizations. Your main problem is to find the bibliography or bibliographies that will cover your topic. In some fields, especially the sciences, bibliographies have been computerized, and you can do a computer search on your topic. Ask a librarian how.

There are also works like *A World Bibliography of Bibliographies*. Your best bet, however, would be to ask a research librarian or a professor who specializes in the field which bibliography includes your topic. Any active scholar or scientist should be aware of the standard bibliographies in her or his field.

In English language literary studies, for example, the standard bibliography is published annually in *PMLA* by the Modern Language Association. There are also journals that publish annual bibliographies for particular literary periods and for the literatures of various countries or regions. If you were looking for critical articles about some works of English literature, these would be the bibliographies in which to look.

In addition to indexes and bibliographies, you can sometimes find listings like *Psychological Abstracts* and *Abstracts of English Studies*.

Like bibliographies, these give the title, author, and facts of publication for articles on certain general topics. As their titles imply, moreover, they also include abstracts, that is, very brief summaries of each article. By reading the abstracts, you can save yourself the trouble of having to check articles which, judging by title alone, you might have thought relevant to your research. Two other important resources, which many researchers overlook, are the *Book Review Digest* and *Dissertation Abstracts*.

The card catalog, indexes, bibliographies, abstracts, and other reference works should provide enough sources for you to begin your research. You will ordinarily discover other sources as you work: the books and articles you read will refer to others (either in the texts themselves, in footnotes, or possibly in selected bibliographies). Eliminating the less important references may become more of a problem than finding enough information to answer your research questions.

Each time you find a potentially useful reference, copy it onto a bibliography card. Such a card is usually 3″ X 5″ or 4″ X 6″. On it you should copy all the information you might need later for your footnotes or bibliography: full name(s) of the author(s), full title, and the facts of publication (e.g., for a book, publisher, date, and place of publication). Add whatever information you may need to locate the reference, usually a library call number. You may also wish to write yourself a brief note indicating what can be found in this source. Some researchers also code their cards for reasons which will be discussed below.

Put only one reference on each card. What you are assembling is a *working bibliography*. As you work with it, you will be discarding items that turn out not to contain useful information. You will be adding new items as you find them. And you will want to keep the bibliography alphabetized. If the bibliography is on cards, with only one item to a

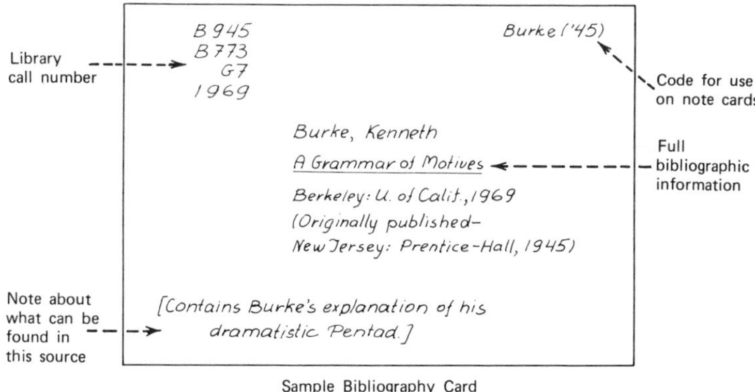

Sample Bibliography Card

card, it will be easy to add and discard items while maintaining alphabetical order. If you try to keep the bibliography in a notebook, it will get very messy and probably need to be recopied several times.

3. COLLECTING INFORMATION. After you have done your background reading and found at least the beginnings of your working bibliography, you begin a period of intensive reading. At this point you have enough sense of what information you are seeking so that you can start taking notes.

Your intensive reading should be critical reading. You are now collecting the evidence on which your paper will be based. You want that evidence to be valid. Beware of unsupported or sweeping generalizations. Watch out for statistics that are slanted or that leave out relevant information (e.g., "50% of all voters surveyed" sounds impressive, but what if only twenty voters were surveyed?) Take note of any conflicting assertions, whether within one source or among several sources. Be sensitive to apparent biases.

Take notes on cards, usually 4″ X 6″ or 5″ X 7″. Put only one bit of information on each card. You will be collecting information in the order in which you happen to discover it. Later, you will want to reorder that information to reflect your understanding of the subject and support your thesis statement. That can be done efficiently only if each item is on a separate card.

The first thing to put on each note card is the exact source of the information. Typically, that might be the author's last name and the year of publication. The rest of what you will need is already on the bibliography card, which you can easily locate because it is filed alphabetically by the author's last name. If the author's name is inordinately long or if you are using several sources written by the same author, you may wish to invent a code. You might, for example, refer to Edward P. J. Corbett's *Classical Rhetoric for the Modern Student* as "Cor (65)"—the first three letters of the author's name plus the last two numbers of the year of publication. If you do invent such a code, be sure to copy it on the bibliography card.

The second thing to put on each note card is the information you are noting. This may be an exact quotation (in which case be sure to put it in quotation marks). Or it may be a paraphrase, the author's information rephrased in your words. Either way it will have to be footnoted, but you will need to distinguish exact quotations from paraphrases when you are writing your paper. Under the quote or paraphrase write the page number(s) you will need for your footnote.

If the quotation or paraphrase is very long, you may also wish to title

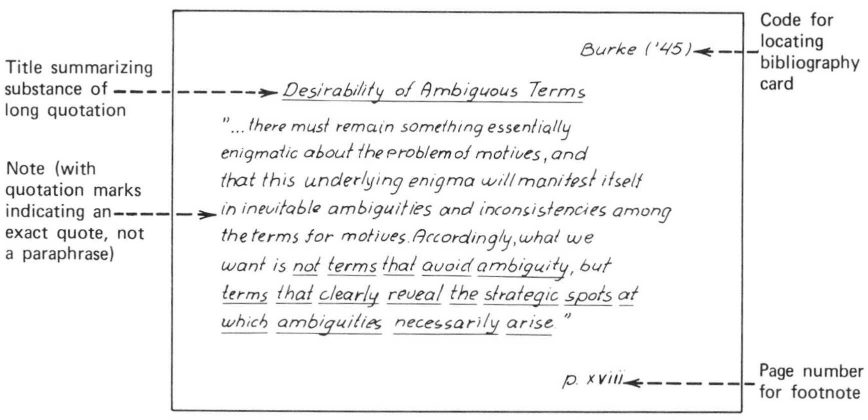

Code for locating bibliography card
Burke ('45)
Title summarizing substance of long quotation
Desirability of Ambiguous Terms
"... there must remain something essentially enigmatic about the problem of motives, and that this underlying enigma will manifest itself in inevitable ambiguities and inconsistencies among the terms for motives. Accordingly, what we want is not terms that avoid ambiguity, but terms that clearly reveal the strategic spots at which ambiguities necessarily arise."
Note (with quotation marks indicating an exact quote, not a paraphrase)
p. xviii
Page number for footnote

Sample Note Card

it with a short phrase that will allow you later to identify its content at a glance.

4. ORGANIZING YOUR INFORMATION. Having collected a mass of information in whatever order you happened to find it, you now must rearrange it into a meaningful pattern. This is done by sorting the note cards into smaller piles which constitute subtopics and may become sections of your paper.

If you have a pretty good idea of what you are going to say, the sorting is relatively easy. If you can write out a tentative thesis statement and outline for your paper, you can sort the note cards into piles that correspond to the major divisions of your outline. You may even be able to subdivide each pile, perhaps even assigning each note card to a particular line on the outline. Or you may leave the subdividing until you are ready to draft that section of the paper.

On the other hand, you may not yet know what the main point of the paper will be or how it will be organized. In that case, you might try to sort the cards into piles without having any predetermined divisions in mind. Just look for related bits of information. The sorting process could well organize the paper for you.

Or it may be that you have a pretty clear sense of one section of the paper. For example, you may have decided that the paper will include (and probably will begin with) a chronological review of previous positions on the issue. If so, pull out the cards related to that one section. Go ahead and draft that section, hoping that the rest of the paper will become clearer as you work. If it does, you will be able to start on a second section of the paper. This is the system I most commonly use, and it works rather well. I sometimes feel a little guilty about not knowing how the parts will hang together until I have drafted most of the paper. But what I finally end up writing is often a lot better than what I would have thought I wanted to say if I had been forced to come up with a thesis statement and outline immediately after collecting all my information. It is how you interrelate your information that makes or breaks a research paper.

5. SUPPLEMENTING YOUR INFORMATION. As you organize, you will often realize that you do not have all the information you need. When you sort your note cards, for example, you may realize that you have very little supporting evidence for one of the points you wish to make. Or you may realize that, to be complete, the paper will need to include a whole section you had not originally planned. Fortunately, you have been managing your time efficiently (of course!) So you still have time to go back to the library to collect this additional information.

Supplementary research of this sort does not take much time. It is usually directed by very specific questions. You know what information you need and can go straight to it. Nonetheless, it is hard to do while the library is closed the night before the paper is due. It is even hard to do the day before the paper is due if a book you need happens to be checked out. So it is important to work well ahead of your deadline.

6. DRAFTING THE PAPER. You draft a research paper pretty much the way you draft any other paper. Some people work from memory, write out their own interpretations and opinions, and then insert supporting evidence from their note cards. Other people work from the note cards, building their own assertions from the evidence. Which way you work does not much matter, so long as the evidence, interpretations, and opinions all come together in the end.

It is important to work quotations and other evidence into the paper smoothly. In part, this depends on the skillful use of transition words and phrases. In part, it is a matter of making good stylistic choices about when to use direct quotations, indirect quotations, and paraphrases. Short quotations should be woven into your own sentences in such a way that nothing more than the quotation marks interrupts the flow of the writing (i.e., indirect quotation). If a quotation does not fit smoothly, try paraphrasing all or part of it.

In certain fields there are standard formats for research papers. Those formats make it easier for readers to anticipate and absorb information. If such a format is available, you should usually use it. It will help you to organize and draft the paper, and it will help readers to understand it. Even when there is no standard format, it remains your responsibility to frame and integrate your information into a meaningful and readable whole. A research paper is not a list of findings; it is the coherent communication of a meaningful pattern of information. Readers must be able to perceive structure.

7. DOCUMENTING YOUR EVIDENCE. Most people's least favorite part of writing a research paper is adding the footnotes and list of references. Even as a typing chore, it can be rather painful. The details of doing it properly can also get quite complicated. This is especially true in the humanities (most of the sciences use a highly rationalized system of notes).

To help preserve your sanity, remember the purpose of documentation. In writing a research paper you have used a great deal of evidence for which you cannot personally vouch. By the time it appears in your paper, this is second-hand information (or even further removed from the original source). Your readers have a right to know where it came from. They may wish to go back to the original source in order to verify your accuracy or to evaluate the information in its original context. You should also give credit where credit is due: if you took an idea or phrase from someone else's work, that person deserves credit.

A real research paper (as opposed to one done primarily as a school exercise) is usually part of a larger, on-going search for knowledge. It is important that readers, who may be participating in the continuation of that search, be able to go to your sources. Otherwise they will work from your second-hand evidence, which will be third-hand by the time it appears in their writings. As other people work from their papers, it will become fourth-hand, fifth-hand, and so forth. An inquiry which gets further and further from its first-hand evidence is more and more likely to make errors. Thus documentation is important because it allows readers the option of verifying and reevaluating your evidence, it gives credit where credit is due, and it helps keep other researchers in touch with the original sources.

The format of documentation can get confusing. That is in part because it varies considerably from discipline to discipline. What varies, however, is only the arrangement of information. The information itself is determined by the purposes documentation serves. Readers need enough information so that they can readily find and refer to your sources. Essentially that means they need *author, title, and facts of publication.*

Giving the full names of all authors and full titles allows readers to identify your sources precisely. Giving the facts of publication allows readers to locate the volume in which the information appears. And, of course, for each citation, you must indicate the page(s) on which the particular information or quotation can be located. Your readers do not want to look through the entire volume.

The facts of publication for a book include the date and place of publication and, in almost all systems, also the name of the publisher. You should also indicate which edition you used (if you did not use the first) and the names of any translators or editors. If you are referring to an article, the facts of publication include the name of the periodical, the volume number, and the issue number and/or date.

Depending on which system is used in your discipline, you may have to give some or all of this information twice. Generally, it appears in a complete form at the end of the paper as a *list of references* or *bibliography*. In some fields, such as literary criticism, this *may* be optional.

All or part of the same information also appears as a footnote each time you make a reference. The term *footnote* came into being because the citation was a *note* at the *foot* of the page. Nowadays, the note may be found at the foot of the page, at the end of the paper, or parenthetically in the text itself.

In many fields, especially in the sciences, the note is foreshortened. It appears in parentheses in the text, usually at the end of a clause or sentence. It consists of a code, which allows readers to locate the item in the list of references (usually an author's surname and the year of publication, and the page number of the citation). Readers who want the rest of the bibliographic information must turn to the back of the paper.

In other fields, again literary criticism is an example, all the documenting information is supposed to appear in a note the first time each source is cited. This means that the bibliography is largely a duplication of information from the footnotes (slightly rearranged). In short papers, therefore, it is sometimes permissible to omit the bibliography. Some journals, in fact, are reluctant to publish bibliographies. Students, however, are often required to include bibliographies, if only to practice the format.

Since the format of documentation varies so considerably from field to field, you need to locate instructions for the particular discipline in which you are writing. Most professional organizations publish style sheets describing the standard format for manuscripts and documentation in that field. Most journals indicate which style sheet they wish contributors to follow. These style sheets should be available in your library or university bookstore. If not, they are available from the professional organizations. When you have chosen an academic or professional specialization, you should acquire your own copy of the appropriate style sheet. Keep it with your dictionary, grammar handbook, and other reference works.

What is most important is that you include all the documenting information readers may need. To make things easy for your readers, you should also use the standard format. At first that may seem like drudgery, but in the long run a standard format facilitates the communication of this sort of information. In this, as in all writing, a clear sense of purpose, audience, and occasion will enable you to make sense of what you are doing.

What follows is a short critical research paper on a specialized subject. The topic was chosen precisely because you probably know little or nothing about it: you most probably have not read Milton's *Samson Agonistes* and very likely have not read Aristotle's *Poetics* either. As you read the following paper, notice how it gives you the information you need about those two texts without going into a long summary of either. The writer is presuming that most readers are somewhat familiar with both, but is writing nonetheless in such a way that you can understand the paper even if you are not.

Notice also the second, fourth, and sixth footnotes. The second footnote demonstrates the standard way to avoid repeated notes to the main text about which you are writing. The fourth footnote demonstrates the usual way of avoiding excessive repetition of what has been well established by previous research. The writer could have gone on for pages showing the parallels between *Samson Agonistes* and various classical Greek tragedies. Instead, one long footnote sends readers who might doubt those parallels to previous research which establishes them. The sixth footnote, similarly, demonstrates the usual way of avoiding excessive summaries of previous research on the topic: refer the readers to a published summary of that research.

Notice also the structure of the paper. The title and introductory paragraphs explain the critical problem. The last two sentences of the second paragraph state the writer's thesis and, by partition (see page 331), summarize the substance of the body of the paper. The body consists of five paragraphs that discuss the five critical elements mentioned in the partition sentence. The concluding paragraph restates the thesis more strongly, generalizes it with a comparison to another play, and suggests its implications.

Finally, notice that this is basically a critical paper. Most of the quotations and footnotes provide expert testimony in support of the writer's judgments. Although thoroughly researched, this paper is organized around the writer's thesis.

Since the paper is short and the footnote form provides complete bibliographic information, that information is not repeated in a list of references at the end.

IS *SAMSON AGONISTES* A TRAGEDY?

John Milton consciously imitated Classical Greek tragedy when he composed *Samson Agonistes*. Even without Milton's explicit introductory essay, no knowledgeable critic would fail to notice that *Samson Agonistes* "agrees with classical theory and practice" in its plot and structure, in how it uses the chorus, in the ways it limits the scope of the action and confines itself to a single place and day, and in making *hubris* [excessive pride] "the ultimate cause of the tragedy."[1] Equally apparent is the intent of Milton's closing lines—

His servants he with new acquist
Of true experience from this great event
With peace and consolation hath dismist
And calm of mind, all passion spent[2]

—to conform to Aristotle's definition of the purpose of tragedy as "through pity and fear effecting the proper purgation of these emotions."[3] The parallels with Aeschylus' *Prometheus Bound* and Sophocles' *Oedipus at Colonus* are clear, and indebtedness to other Classical tragedies can be argued.[4]

Since 1751, however, when Samuel Johnson charged that *Samson Agonistes* "must be allowed to want a middle, since nothing passes between the first act and the last that either hastens or delays the death of Samson,"[5] there has been considerable debate about whether *Samson Agonistes* is essentially tragic.[6] Milton clearly modeled his drama upon Classical Greek tragedy. He clearly intended it to meet Aristotle's definition. He used the forms prescribed by Classical theory and practice. Because of his Puritan religious beliefs, however, he filled those forms in ways that undercut their tragic impact. There are five critical elements in Milton's drama that are qualitatively distinct from their equivalents in Classical Greek tragedy: the hero's weakness, the reversal of fortune, the catastrophe, the clear causal relation of each event to the catastrophe, and the evocation of pity and fear.

According to Aristotle, the error or frailty that brings about the hero's downfall should be a weakness, not a vice.[7] As Milton's drama opens, we see Sam-

---

[1]P. H. Epps, "Two Notes on English Classicism," *Studies in Philology* 13 (1916), p. 196.

[2]*Samson Agonistes*, 11. 1755-1758. Future citations will be indicated by parenthetical line numbers.

[3]*Poetics*, tr. S. H. Butcher, rpd. in J. H. Smith and E. W. Parks, eds., *The Great Critics*, 3rd ed. (New York: Norton, 1951), p. 34.

[4]See William Brewer, "Two Athenian Models for *Samson Agonistes*," *PMLA* 42 (1927), p. 913; Paul F. Baum, "*Samson Agonistes* Again," *PMLA* 36 (1921), p. 363; C. M. Bowra, *Inspiration and Poetry* (Folcroft, PA.: 1955). p. 114 ff.; and P. W. Timberlake, "Milton and Euripides," *The Parrot Presentation Volume* (New Jersey: Princeton, 1935).

[5]*The Rambler* 3: 139 (July 16, 1751).

[6]For a review of the critical literature, see Michael F. Krouse, *Milton's Samson and the Christian Tradition* (New Jersey: Princeton, 1949), pp. 3-21.

[7]Aristotle, p. 41.

son fallen to the "lowest pitch of abject fortune" (l. 169), having been betrayed by Delila, captured and blinded by the Philistines. In an apparent parallel to the most common weakness of the heroes of Greek tragedy, Milton portrays Samson as having been "swoll'n with pride" (l. 532) prior to his downfall and now as on the brink of despair. In a Judeo-Christian context, however, pride and the despair that follows from it are serious sins; a true believer should know that the glory is God's and that whatever occurs is God's will. Thus Samson's misfortune is not "unmerited," as Aristotle would have it.[8] It is lack of "virtue" (l. 174) that cast him down, not fate, error or frailty. He himself realizes he was "the prime cause" (l. 234) of his own misfortune. From a Protestant point of view, he has taken the first step toward a restoration of faith in God, but his full responsibility for his own misfortune is not compatible with the Greek conception.

Aristotle states, moreover, that the reversal of fortune in a tragedy "should be not bad to good, but . . . from good to bad."[9] It is true that in *Oedipus at Colonus*, the hero is at the beginning persecuted and miserable, but in the end he dies mystically illuminated, having achieved sainthood and transcended misery through death. But *Oedipus at Colonus* is extremely atypical, and the play ends with an awareness of misery pending for Oedipus' family and city. Samson, by contrast, repents his sins, regains his faith, revenges himself on his enemies, and is reunited with God. *Samson Agonistes* presents a "steady psychological progression from despair through heroic conflict upwards to exultation and the final assumption of beatitude."[10] Samson "becomes a knight of God, a saint, distinguished by his faith and obedience."[11]

Samson's pulling down of the Philistine temple is catastrophic for the Philistines and their god, Dagon, but hardly for himself. True, Samson dies along with his enemies, but the blinded Samson has five times announced his preference to be dead (ll. 548-50, 575-76, 590-98, 629-30, 1262-63). He has been "restored to harmony with God's will,"[12] and his act "is the vindication of Jehovah . . . over Dagon."[13] Even his father admits there is little cause for lamentation (ll. 1708-9).

Another objection to classifying Milton's drama as a tragedy has its roots in Johnson's charge that "the action does not precipitate the catastrophe."[14]

---

[8]Aristotle, p. 41.

[9]Aristotle, p. 47.

[10]Una Mary Ellis-Fermor, *The Frontiers of Drama* (London: Methuen, 1945), p. 32.

[11]George Wesley Whiting, *Milton and This Pendant World* (Austin: University of Texas, 1958), p. 208.

[12]Whiting, p. 216.

[13]J. W. Tupper, "The Dramatic Structure of *Samson Agonistes*," *PMLA* 35 (1920), p. 377.

[14]Cited by A. S. P. Woodhouse, "Tragic Effect in *Samson Agonistes*," rpt. in A. E. Barker, *Milton: Modern Essays in Criticism* (New York: Oxford, 1965), p. 460.

Johnson's point, which does not lack supporters,[15] is that *Samson Agonistes* lacks unity of action because the events of the play do not all function as causes or motives for the catastrophe, as they should according to Classical theory. The scenes with Delila and with the Philistine captain, Harapha, could be deleted without undercutting the main action of the play. The scene with Delila allows Samson to "demonstrate by Delila's powerlessness to reassert her sway the completeness of [his] repentence";[16] it does not bring about that repentence or bring him closer to his revenge. The scene with Harapha likewise allows Samson to demonstrate his regeneration; it does not move him closer to either God or revenge.

The strongest objection to accepting *Samson Agonistes* as a tragedy is that Milton fails to meet Aristotle's central criterion, that the tragic incident and the play as a whole should evoke pity and fear. As C. M. Bowra points out, "Samson's fault is stressed so strongly that we hardly pity him, and if we feel any fear it is for the Philistines."[17] Where Oedipus' misfortune was excessive and his death mysterious, Samson's misfortune is just and his death happy. Samson sacrifices himself to expiate both his own sin and Israel's sins. *Samson Agonistes* is "concerned essentially with the fallen Samson's recovery of friendship with God"[18] and restoration to "harmony with God's will."[19] There is no reason why this conclusion should evoke pity or fear.

Samson Agonistes falls into the same category of religious drama as Thomas Eliot's *Murder in the Cathedral*,[20] which is also heavily indebted to Greek forms. It is a religious drama that portrays a hero's passage through temptation. The hero avoids sin, rises above human frailty, and achieves union with God. The hero's death, like Christ's, is an expiatory sacrifice, an offering made for the salvation of his people. Whatever else this type of drama may be, it is not tragic—neither in the Greek, nor in any other sense. To read it as a tragedy is to miss its essense.

---

[15]See, for example, E. C. Knowlton, "Causality in *Samson Agonistes*," *Modern Language Notes* 37 (1922) and J. W. Tupper, *op. cit.*

[16]Woodhouse, p. 453.

[17]*Inspiration and Poetry* (Folcroft, Pa.: Folcroft, 1955), p. 128.

[18]Miriam Clare, *Samson Agonistes: A Study in Contrast* (New York: Pageant, 1964), p. 33.

[19]Whiting, p. 216.

[20]K. Fell, "From Myth to Martyrdom: Towards a View of *Samson Agonistes*," *English Studies* 34 (1953), p. 152.

ADDITIONAL READING

Turabian, Kate L. *A Manual for Writers of Term Papers, Theses and Dissertations*, 4th ed. Chicago: University of Chicago, 1973. A durable, widely used and accepted general manual.

D'Angelo, Frank. *Process and Thought in Composition*. 2nd ed. Cambridge, Mass.: Winthrop, 1980. See Chapter 15, "The Research Paper," for a useful comparison/contrast of deductive and inductive approaches to writing research papers.

EXERCISE

1. Think of three topics for "opinion" papers on general subjects that interest you. A good way to discover such topics is to think of subjects you wish you knew more about. State each topic as a question. To what extent could empirical information and expert opinion help you develop an informed answer to each question? Choose one topic, do the research, and write the paper. To what extent did the research influence your opinion?

2. Think of three topics for long critical papers (2000 to 10,000 words) in your area of special interest or specialization. Could you write these papers without doing research? To what extent could each involve a significant research component? What type of research would be involved? How much would it improve the quality and validity of the paper?

3. Write a critical research paper by investigating and documenting all the empirical assumptions in an "opinion" paper you wrote earlier.

4. Obtain a professional style sheet, preferably one you are likely to use. Examine it. Compare and contrast it with other style sheets, perhaps those obtained by other members of your writing class or group. Try to suggest functional explanations for the requirements of your style sheet.

5. List the most important standard bibliographic sources in your field of special interest or specialization. Locate each in a library, and make sure you know how to use it.

6. Compile a *selected* and *annotated* bibliography on a topic of interest to you and of use to others. "Selected" means you should list only those sources you consider most useful. "Annotated" means you should write one or several sentences telling what can be found in each source. Distribute this bibliography to some people who might find it useful.

7. Write an abstract of a long paper you wrote recently. Confine yourself to a maximum of 200 words.

8. What kinds of research *reports* are written in your area of special interest or specialization? What are their functions in that field? What uses do they make of primary research (e.g., polls, experiments, textual analyses)? What uses do they make of library research? What is the relationship between the two kinds of research—primary and secondary—in each type of report?

9. Practice the standard procedure for writing a long research paper. Choose a topic. Do some preliminary reading, and compile a working bibliography. Collect information on note cards. Organize the note cards, and construct a rough outline. Draft the paper. Add documentation. Write an abstract. Submit the paper together with a brief evaluation of the procedure by which you wrote it.

WRITING ABOUT LITERATURE

"The business of a poet," said Imlac, "is to examine not the individual, but the species. . . . He must write as the interpreter of nature, and the legislator of mankind, and consider himself as presiding over the thoughts and manners of future generations."

Samuel Johnson

Tradition . . . involves a perception, not only of the past, but of its presence. . . . A sense, that is, of its relevance now—of the extent to which the past is entering into the content of the present creating and forming the present into what it is.

T.S. Eliot

Like the literature in the class, the form of the essay conditions thought patterns and, particularly, attitude towards authority.

Keith Fort

THE SUBJECT IS LITERATURE

Because distinct types of material call for distinct approaches, the nature of a term paper varies somewhat from discipline to discipline. If you are a university student, you need to know the particular forms that are used for writing in your major field. These are also the forms that you will use after graduation if you work and write as a professional in that field.

Here we will take literary criticism as an example, in part because advanced composition students are often asked to write about literature. If you are specializing in some other area, you should do a parallel analysis of writing about that subject matter (see pages 359-367 on analyzing specialized writing tasks). Begin by obtaining the appropriate style sheet. Try to obtain also a bibliography of basic research sources, a glossary of key terms, and one or two of the better manuals. Any professor in your field ought to be able to suggest titles. For the study of literature, you might choose the following:

MLA Handbook for Writers of Research Papers, Theses, and Dissertations. New York: Modern Language Association, 1977.

An expanded version of *The MLA Style Sheet*, designed for students and published by the major North American organization of literary critics, this is the definitive arbiter on matters of format, footnote and bibliographic forms, abbreviations, and the other "conventions governing the written presentation of research."

Altick, Richard D. and Andrew Wright. *Selective Bibliography for the Study of English & American Literature*. 6th ed. New York: Macmillan, 1978.

An extensive and well-categorized list of useful resources for students of literature.

Abrams, M. H. *A Glossary of Literary Terms*, 3rd ed. New York: Holt, Rinehart and Winston, 1971.

Brief discussions of important literary critical terms and concepts, arranged alphabetically and written by a major literary critical theorist.

Dickinson, Leon T. *A Guide to Literary Study*. New York: Holt, Rinehart and Winston, 1959.

One of the better manuals on writing literary criticism.

The discussion that follows is based in part on secondary sources like these, in part on an analysis of a selection of articles from major literary critical journals, and in part on an analysis of high-quality student papers.

Generally, one's purpose in writing about literature is to explain the meaning and significance of the literary text(s)—in a word, *interpretation*. If you are a student, another purpose of the writing is to develop and demonstrate your ability to handle, independently, the material of the course. You must choose a topic and an approach that allow you to fulfill these purposes.

First, you must decide which literary text(s) you will write about. You must write about something that falls within the scope of the course or journal for which you are writing—but you must also be able to say something about it that has not been said before (in class discussions and assigned readings, or in previous publications). You could choose a text that was not discussed. You could choose one or more texts that were discussed, but take a distinctive approach or focus on some undiscussed aspect. Or you could juxtapose a text that was discussed with one that was not, perhaps even with material from outside the scope of the course. If your paper is for a Shakespeare course, in which you discussed the major tragedies, you could write about *Titus Andronicus* or one of the other minor tragedies. If *King Lear* was discussed in class, you might find a topic by comparing and contrasting it with *Titus Andronicus*—or with Sophocle's *Oedipus at Colonus* (another play about an old king who has given up his throne).

Literary critical articles and term papers usually focus rather narrowly on critical problems. The "problem" may be simply some aspect of a text that has never been explicated. Perhaps while reading D. H. Lawrence's *Sons and Lovers*, you notice many metaphors using images of clothing. If no critic has yet explained this pattern and its relationship to the major themes of the novel (check the library), you have found a potential topic.

The appropriate structure and style for a literary critical paper follow from its rhetorical purpose, audience, and occasion. The primary purpose is *explanatory*. The primary audience is well-educated and somewhat specialized: you may not presume that your readers have recently read the text(s) you are discussing, but you should presume a general familiarity with major texts and critical concepts. The occasion—whether a term paper, a presentation at a scholarly conference, or an article to be published in an academic journal—is professional and relatively formal.

The *persona* you project, therefore, should be that of one professional writing to others. You want your readers to perceive you as a careful and accurate interpreter of literature. To create this voice, your style should be rather formal. You should rely primarily on logical appeal to convince them of the validity of your interpretation.

You should not explain too much. Do not give long plot summaries (unless you are dealing with an obscure, minor text). But it is appropriate to remind readers briefly about a text they may not have read recently and to give specific details where they are relevant as evidence for your interpretation. Similarly, you should presume familiarity with basic critical terms and concepts. But it is appropriate to define terms that come out of a special school of literary criticism or terms that you are using in a special way.

The basic structure of a literary critical paper is thesis statement and support. The thesis statement is usually near the beginning, perhaps the last sentence of the introductory section. Readers will be able to evaluate the supporting evidence more efficiently if they know what you are trying to prove. The introductory section also usually indicates what the critical problem is, so readers can understand what the implications of the paper are and why its thesis matters. Indicating the critical problem and putting the thesis in context often includes giving a brief summary of what previous critics have said on the subject. It may also include giving a brief summary of any historical material or theories that will be used in the interpretation.

The body of the paper is usually the interpretation itself, the detailed explanation of meanings and significances. Citations from interpretations by previous critics and historical or theoretical material may be used here, often with more detail than in the introductory section. But such citations are subordinated: they are presented as evidence in support of the points *you* are making. The same is true for any details you give about the literary text(s) you are interpreting. Although your topic probably should be researched, at least to make certain that you are not duplicating previously published work, this is primarily a critical paper.

The conclusion summarizes and may develop implications. It is often brief. In the interests of clarity, it usually reiterates the thesis statement and main supporting arguments. It may also answer the question *so what?* Since a literary critical paper typically includes a carefully detailed analysis and runs only 2000 to 8000 words, it is often confined to a rather narrow subject. Thus it may be necessary to indicate the relationship between that narrow topic and some more significant critical problem. An interpretation of the images of clothing in D. H. Lawrence's *Sons and Lovers* matters only if it helps us to understand the meaning and significance of that text or of Lawrence's work or of some other body of literary discourse.

The structure of a literary critical paper, therefore, might typically look something like this.

> *Introduction.* A statement of the literary critical problem that the paper will solve (or help solve). A summary of such previous criticism, historical or theoretical material as may be relevant to readers' understanding of the paper, and its implications. A thesis statement and, perhaps, some of the main lines of argument that will be offered to support it.
>
> *Body.* A detailed explanation of meanings and significances, supported by details from the text(s) you are interpreting and, perhaps by relevant citations from previous criticism, historical or theoretical material.
>
> *Conclusion.* Reiteration of the thesis statement and, perhaps, of the main supporting arguments. An indication of how the paper contributes to some broader critical task or has other significant implications (unless these implications or contributions are obvious).

The paper should have a title that clearly indicates its subject. It may also be accompanied by an abstract (i.e., a 100 to 200 word summary of itself), notes, and/or a bibliography. Relevant background material, which does not belong in the paper itself because it probably interests only a few readers, may be inserted as an appendix, just before the endnotes and bibliography.

CRITICAL CONCEPTS

The members of any specialized discipline share certain concepts that characterize their ways of handling their material. Their concepts are represented by certain key terms, a professional jargon. To an outsider, this jargon often seems like unnecessary mystification designed to prevent ordinary people from understanding what the specialists are saying to each other. Sometimes, unfortunately, jargon does become excessive and does serve this elitist function. Properly, however, jargon is just a kind of shorthand that saves specialists from having to clutter their work with explanations of concepts already familiar to other members of the discipline. Learning the jargon of a discipline, therefore, is often a good way to acquire key concepts.

Here are some key terms from literary criticism that you can use to help yourself interpret literary texts.

Allegory. A literary device in which the characters, themes, and events of a narrative parallel another set of people, ideas, and events.

Ambiguity. The use of a single term that simultaneously represents multiple meanings.

Archetype. A narrative structure, character-type, or symbolic image that recurs in a wide variety of literary (and nonliterary) texts and that is purportedly a reflection of the basic structure of the human mind and human experience.

Characterization. The process by which a literary text, through dialogue, description, and action, creates the image of a personality. A character may be *flat* if built around a single idea, quality, or motive. A character may be *round* if complex and subtly represented.

Convention. A customary device, widely accepted by readers of a particular period or type of literature.

Genre. A category into which literary works can be placed according to their form—for example, drama, poetry, fiction, essay, biography.

Imagery. Mental images created by figurative language, especially metaphors and other comparisons.

Irony. A literary device in which a statement or structure ostensibly has one meaning but actually has another.

Metaphor. A comparison asserted as a statement of identity—for example, "War *is* hell!" (An overt comparison, by contrast, is a *simile*—

for example, "War is *like* hell.") A metaphor has two parts: the *tenor*, which names the subject, and the *vehicle*, which names the comparison.

Meter. A regular pattern of stresses (i.e., accented syllables)—what we feel as rhythm.

Myth. A narrative that embodies the values of a culture.

Onomatopoeia. A literary device in which the sound of a word echoes the sense.

Structure. A stable relationship among the parts, themes, or other aspects of a work—for example, the five-act structure of Elizabethan drama or the recurring opposition between loyalty to the clan and loyalty to the state in classical Greek drama.

Symbol. Anything that represents something else, but especially a single thing (often concrete) that represents something more complex or abstract, as a cross can represent the crucifixion of Christ and hence Christian faith, as a hammer and sickle can represent a worker-peasant alliance and hence the socialist revolution in the Soviet Union.

Theme. A recurring concept, conflict, or motif.

These are some of the most common and important terms used by literary critics. There are many others, including those that name more specific archetypes, character types, conventions, genres, literary devices, meters, types of symbols, structures, and themes.

The terms and concepts specialists use indicate how they approach, analyze, and interpret their material. Behind the shared terms and concepts are shared values. *Ambiguity* and *irony* are important terms because of the belief that literature typically represents multiple meanings and that one of the critic's important tasks is to explicate those meanings. *Archetype* became an important term when certain critics asserted their belief that literature reflects the basic structure of the human mind and experience. An examination of key terms and concepts can reveal the beliefs and values that a group of specalists share and use to approach their material.

APPROACHES AND TECHNIQUES

In addition to deciding what literary text(s) to write about, you must also decide how to approach them. If you are a student, the main purpose of writing about literature is to develop and test your ability to use literary critical techniques—to read literature critically on your own. When you write about literature, there are four possible angles of approach. You can focus (1) on the text itself, or (2) on the relationship between the text and the world it represents, or (3) the text and its author, or (4) the text and its readers. You can emphasize one of these angles of approach or use some combination to interpret the meanings and significance of the text(s). (See the figure below for an overview of these four approaches.)

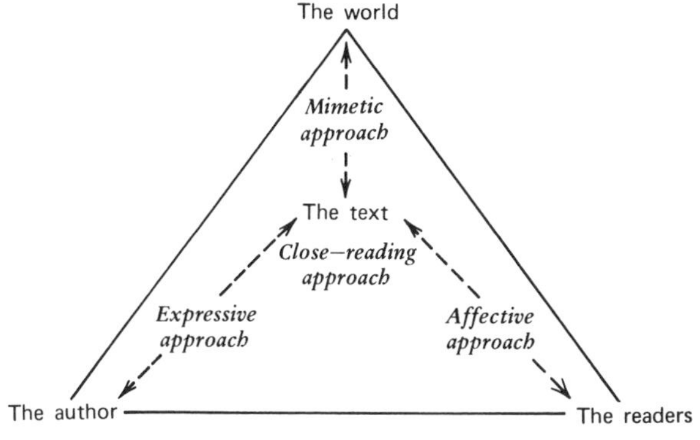

FOUR APPROACHES TO LITERATURE

THE CLOSE-READING APPROACH. From the 1940s into the 1980s, the most common approach in North America has been to concentrate on the literary text itself. The most common technique used by those who write for literary critical journals has been to isolate and analyze some aspect of a literary text (or group of texts). Most typically, this aspect is a recurring symbol. The critic goes through the text(s) and notes (perhaps on note cards) every instance of the symbolic image. This may mean going through all of Margaret Atwood's poems looking for mention of wild animals. Having by this sort of "selective filtration" isolated all the animal images in the poems, the critic then looks for any connotation or symbolic significance that they have in common.

This technique can be applied to any aspect of any literary text that can be isolated in this way, not just to images. After the pattern is identified and explained, it is usually (but not always) used to support some more general interpretation. An analysis of symbolism, style, or allegory, for example, is usually used to support conclusions about character, structure, or theme. Analysis of character or structure is usually used to support thematic conclusions.

A similar and common technique is to focus on one small part of a text, perhaps a stanza from a poem, a scene from a play, or a minor character from a novel. The part is analyzed and then, usually, related back to the whole text. If you read and discussed Ernest Hemingway's *For Whom the Bell Tolls* in a course, you might try to write a paper about El Sordo. The point of the paper would be to analyze this minor character and explain his function in relation to the main characters and themes of the novel.

Both of these techniques are part of a method in which the literary text itself is the object of critical analysis. The focus is on the work of art itself, not on the text as a communication from author to readers about the world. The ultimate criteria are aesthetic, having to do with unity, complexity, and other such qualities within the scope of the work.

THE MIMETIC APPROACH. A second way to approach literature is as a representation of reality. This approach goes back at least as far as Plato and is behind Aristotle's assertion that tragic drama is "an imitation of the real actions of men." To consider literature as a representation of reality raises the question of truth: is it an *accurate* representation? Obviously, a poem or novel cannot be true in the same sense that a newspaper article may be. We call novels fiction precisely because they are literally false. But we do demand verisimilitude: we do want literature to "ring true."

To consider literature in relation to the reality it represents, we must know something not only about the literature, but also about the reality. Particularly with literary works from other historical periods or foreign cultures, this can be a problem. A literary text may easily be misinterpreted by readers who are ignorant of the reality it represents. It is easy to misread Amos Tutuola's *The Palm-Wine Drinkard* if one does not know anything about West African society and culture. It is easy to misread Chaucer's *Canterbury Tales* if one does not know anything about fourteenth-century England.

From this approach to literature follows a kind of paper that tries to place the literary text in context. Often this means doing historical research. To better understand *Henry IV, Part One*, you study the politics of Elizabethan period. Only then do you realize the full significance of various conflicts within the play, for example, about the proper education of a prince, the division of the kingdom, and so on. Indeed, the notes that often accompany a Shakespearean text are the result of this kind of historical criticism, and without them most readers would miss much of the significance (and most of the puns).

Other, more controversial, methods fall within this approach to literature. They are controversial because they are based on controversial theories about reality. At least three theories from the social sciences are widely used in literary criticism: psychoanalytical criticism, archetypal criticism, and marxist criticism, based on the insights of Freud, Jung, and Marx, respectively.

To write a literary critical paper based on a theory from the social sciences, you juxtapose the theory's insights about reality with the representation of that same reality in the literary text. You might, for example, apply Freudian psychological theory to *Henry IV, Part One*. If that juxtaposition leads you to a new understanding of Prince Hal's character and his relationship with his father, then you have the substance of a paper. Similarly, you might apply marxist theory to the same play and try to understand its major themes in terms of Elizabeth class conflict. If marxist theories about the conflict between the established feudal nobility and the rising merchant capitalists lead you to a new understanding of the thematic conflict within the play between honor and pragmatism, then you have the substance of a paper.

There are two difficulties with this approach. First, you must know the social science—whether that be the history of Elizabethan politics or the theories of Freud, Jung, or Marx. If your social science is half-baked, your interpretation of the literary text will be half-baked also. Second, if you depend on a theory, your insights into the literature will be, at best, no better than the theory. If Freud is wrong about human nature or if his theory is not applicable to Elizabethan England, you are likely to be wrong about Hal's relationship with his father. If Marx is wrong about the interrelationship of class conflict and the development of ideas and values, you are likely to be wrong about the significance of the conflict between honor and pragmatism in the play.

Despite these dangers, the mimetic approach is fruitful. A paper based on this approach should do the following.

1. State the literary critical problem you intend to solve.
2. Give a *brief* summary of the historical material or the relevant aspects of the theory you are using.
3. Analyze the literary text (or some aspect of it), supporting your analysis with particulars from both the text and the historical or theoretical material.
4. Show how the insights produced by that analysis resolve the literary critical problem and lead to a valid interpretation of the literary text.

Remember your purpose is to interpret the literature, so your primary focus must be on the literature. The historical or theoretical material is just being used to help you achieve your literary critical purpose, so it must be appropriately subordinated. (There is another sort of paper in which literary material is used to support or exemplify a psychological or social theory. But such a paper would be written for a social science course or journal.)

THE EXPRESSIVE APPROACH. A third way to approach a literary text is as an expression of the author. The focus here is on the relationship between author and text. This sort of criticism explores the various factors that influenced the author. It is essentially causal explanation (see pages 300-320). It tries to explain the text by explaining the creative process that produced it.

The most common sort of paper within this approach argues that one literary text influenced the production of another. Thus a critic might argue that D. H. Lawrence's "The Rocking-Horse Winner" was influenced by Charles Dickens' *Dombey and Son*. The main technique is to compare the two texts and demonstrate similarities too numerous and remarkable to be explained as coincidences. Secondarily, the critic tries to prove that the author of the second text was (or at least could have been) familiar with the first text. Once the influence has been demonstrated, the critic may use it to argue that the second text should be interpreted in a certain way—for example, that "The Rocking-Horse Winner" should be read as a social parable (like *Dombey and Son*) rather than just as a character study.

One can also consider other factors that influenced an author's creative process. These may include nonliterary texts, the author's personal life, the social context, and so forth. To write about the influence of the author's personal life is to bring in biography and psychology. To write about the influence of the social context is to bring in other social sciences. This produces the same kinds of difficulties (and the same advantages) here as it does within the mimetic approach.

Again, it is important to remember that your purpose is to interpret the literature. Literary critics, as such, are concerned with influences only insofar as understanding the relationship between author and text aids their interpretation of the literature. If you use this approach, therefore, you should try to demonstrate not just the influence, but also its implications for interpreting the text. (See pages 240-241 for an example of a literary critical essay that uses an expressive approach.)

THE AFFECTIVE APPROACH. A fourth way to approach literature is to consider how it affects readers. This approach was dominant as long ago as Ancient Roman times and has increased steadily in North America over the past two decades. To some extent, it resembles the close-reading approach, but the text is analyzed in order to explain why and how it affects readers. The focus is on the relationship between text and readers.

However much attention it may pay to the text, in the end this approach analyzes the reading process. It is a rhetorical criticism in the sense that it tries to explain how the author influences readers' responses to the text and/or to the realities represented in the text. It may confine itself to explaining readers' responses: aesthetic pleasure, emotions, ideas, and so forth. It may also become instruction in how one ought to read particular types of literary texts. It may become an analysis of the social functions of literature, that is, of how literary texts influence readers to perceive reality in particular ways.

Aristotle was taking an affective approach when he asserted that tragedy, by presenting a certain kind of hero in a certain type of situation, first arouses pity and fear and then purges us of those same emotions. Aristotle's analysis of the structure of tragic drama is (1) an explanation of why it affects us as it does, (2) instruction in both how to interpret and how to write tragic drama, and (3) a justification of tragic drama as having a positive social function (i.e., purging us of harmful emotions).

One common technique used in this approach to literature is classification. The point of the classification is to aid interpretation. The assumption is that distinct types of texts should be read in distinct ways. Thus proper classification leads to correct interpretation. From this assumption follows another: that readers actually do read various types of texts in distinct ways. Thus misclassification can cause them to read the wrong way and thus to misinterpret the text.

These assumptions are quite consistent with modern reading theory and are confirmed by certain striking examples. For some decades after its publication, James Joyce's *Dubliners* was classified as a collection of naturalistic short stories. Since naturalistic fiction generally makes little use of symbolism, even astute literary critics consistently overlooked the extraordinarily rich symbolism of the text. And since *Dubliners* is unified primarily by symbols that run consistently from one story to the next, it was widely read as fifteen stories when it should have been read as a unified whole.

Literary texts are commonly classified according to the nature of the text itself. Thus literature may be divided into three or four genres—poetry, drama, fiction, and (sometimes) essays—and each of these may be variously subdivided. But texts can also be classified by other criteria such as who wrote them (e.g., Chicano literature), when and/or where they were written (e.g., nineteenth-century Irish literature), who reads them (e.g., popular literature), their social functions (e.g., proletarian literature), or what they are about (e.g., detective stories).

Within an affective approach, classification aids in interpretation. If you are writing a paper for a course in which you read Milton's *Samson Agonistes*, which is usually classified as a tragedy, you might devote most of the paper to explaining why you disagree with that classification. but you should also show that *Samson Agonistes* is likely to be misread if it is perceived as a tragedy; and, if possible, you should try to suggest a more accurate classification. (See pages 386-388.)

An increasingly common method used in this approach to literature analyzes certain kinds of "structures." Superficially, this technique resembles the textual analysis of the close-reading approach. The analysis of "structures" often begins with the very same images, metaphors, characters, and so forth. And the structuralist critic who starts with Margaret Atwood's animal images behaves very much as a close reader would: the critic isolates those images and tries to figure out what they represent, what their significance is. The structuralist critic also tries to relate those images to what seem very much like thematic conflicts. Thus if 'wolves' signify 'nature' in Atwood's poems and if they usually occur in opposition to other images that signify 'civilization,' then the critic calls 'nature/civilization' a "structure." The critic looks for other images in the poems that represent the same structure and tries to analyze the structure more precisely.

What makes structuralism a kind of affective approach is this: the structures embodied in the text also exist in human minds and cultures. They are the concepts we use to compose our perceptions (see pages 210-211). Thus a work of literature embodies a way of perceiving. The text affects readers by evoking similar structures in their minds and also by influencing them to accept its structures, to see things its way. Atwood's poems influence readers to perceive certain events as a certain kind of opposition between nature and civilization.

Just as Part Two of this textbook began with a section on "Seeing and Writing," so structuralists might introduce their discussion of literature with "Reading and Seeing." Indeed, Part Two of this textbook has been largely a discussion of structures you can use in your writing—for example, various structures for representing causality. A structuralist approach to literature reverses the process: it starts with written text and looks for the structures. Thus the core of the method is sometimes described as de-composition.

If you analyze a specialized type of writing as the first section of this chapter suggests, you will be looking for the various kinds of structures which underlie that type of writing. You will be doing so in order to figure out how your writings can affect readers in similar ways. "The Harlequin Romance: A Final Frontier" (pages 364-366) is an example of this sort of structuralist analysis.

A literary critic would take the analysis of Harlequin romances further by asking what values are embodied in the opposition between the heroine and the "other woman," the hero and the "other man." A literary critic might also ask how those values relate to the readers and their world. Because they are concerned with interpreting meanings, literary critics must ultimately explain not only how the text is structured, but also why.

What follows is a shortened version of a paper about one aspect of *Dracula*. Like many interpretative papers, including those you may write, it does not fall neatly into a single critical category. Indeed, it includes elements of all four basic approaches. The five-paragraph introductory section states the critical problem, indicates how it will be approached, and discusses the sources the author used to create his tale (an *expressive approach*). Note that the discussion of sources is not included for its own sake, but used to suggest an interpretation. The body of the paper is predominantly textual analysis (*close-reading approach*). The results of that analysis, however, are discussed in terms of archetypes and in relation to characteristics of Victorian England (*mimetic approach*). The three-paragraph conclusion summarizes the interpretation and also brings out its implications by juxtaposing it both with the literary tradition and with the realities of Victorian England. Both the last paragraph of the introduction and the second half of the conclusion suggest a relationship between the structures and values embodied by *Dracula*, on the one hand, and how *Dracula* affects readers, on the other hand (*affective approach*). Although the bulk of the paper is devoted to close-reading and mimetic techniques, its implications have more to do with how *Dracula* was created and how it affects readers. Note how all four approaches can be used together in one paper and how they can serve each other.

IT TAKES CAPITAL TO DEFEAT DRACULA

"Thank God!...we are well supplied with money....Judge Moneybag will settle this case I think!"

Jonathan Harker's journal
15 October, Varna[1]

Though that seems a strange exclamation to find just before the climatic chase in *Dracula*, it is only one of a dozen similar assertions that can be found in Bram Stoker's gothic novel. That they seem strange is an indication of the meanings we usually overlook when reading monster stories.

Like every monster, Dracula is, of course, monstrous. If we are to understand a monster story, however, we must overlook the inevitable monstrousness of the monster and inquire about values. What values are destroyed with the monster and by what opposing values?

Stoker based his tale on two sources. He adopted the folk image of the vampire and attached it to a fifteenth century nobleman renowned for his cruelty. The connection is not difficult because the vampire of folklore is a symbolic image of the lord of the manor, who sucked the serfs' lifeblood metaphorically. The historical Dracula was a genuinely perverse count, who tortured and killed upwards of a hundred thousand people.[2]

---

[1]Bram Stoker, *Dracula* (1897; rpt. New York: Signet, 1965), p. 339. Further citations will be indicated by parenthetical page numbers.

[2]Raymond T. McNally and Radu Florescu, *In Search of Dracula: A True History of Dracula and Vampire Legends* (New York, Galahad, 1972), pp. 34-81.

But Stoker represents Dracula as having been brave, patriotic, intelligent and as heroic in his defense of his nation against the Turks as Stoker's heroes are in their defense of England against the vampire (pp. 307-8). According to Stoker, his perversion began with the black magic he used to avoid his natural death, a sin against both Christianity and rationality. Dracula is represented as a dangerous force from the past seeking to restore the medieval order (and a perverted version of the medieval order at that). Dracula's evilness is precisely that of an anachronism, Un-Dead centuries after his time.

If we are to be frightened, the image of the monster must match our own psychological structures. Archetypally, *Dracula* portrays the old battle of chaos against order. The impulsive, emotional forces of the blood and the body rise in revolt against the rational, socialized brain. The savage seeks to overthrow the civilized, emotion to undermine thought. Sexually, the vampire is metaphorically a rapist, who not only invades the bodies of his victims but takes permanent control and uses them for his own purposes. But what are the particular values with which Stoker fills these structures?

Within the imagery of the book, it is the identification of blood/brain with feminine/masculine that gives the first major indication of what is really at stake. Stoker places near the beginning of Mina's diary an apparently irrelevant attack on the "New Woman" (pp. 99-100). He associates all those who are vulnerable to the vampire with women. The lunatic, Renfield, is compared to a woman (p. 181); and when a male wolf is responsive to Dracula, his keeper says, "You can't trust wolves no more, nor women" (p. 145).

All the "irrational"—lunatics, children, workers and, of course, women—are Dracula's victims and dupes. His conquerers are wealthy, rational men. Chief among them is Van Helsing, a doctor and lawyer, a scientist of iron nerve and icy temper, with indomitable resolution and self-command, clean-shaven, well-balanced, poised, a specialist in the brain with thought-power so strong that his broad forehead is said to actually repel the sensuality of his own red hair (pp. 121, 170, 188, 190, 194). He is aided by four younger men, who supply money, courage, connections and youthful vigor, and by Mina, who has "a man's brain" and "a woman's heart" (p. 241, repeated p. 344). She is temperamentally closer to Dracula than the men are, their link with him as well as their vulnerability (p. 319)—and she also does the typing.

Dracula is associated with wild animals—bats, wolves, owls, rats, moths and foxes. He is himself part beast, having hair in the palm of his hand (and on his face). He moves in night and fog, storm and thunder. In him, the blood rules the brain; his eyes (windows to his brain and "soul") are red. He is aided by gypsies, lunatics, women and wolves, by all beings whose minds do not willfully rule their actions in the "light" of rationality.

In terms of its own archetypes and metaphors, these are the values embodied in the conflict between Dracula and his opponents. Western "civilization" defends itself against eastern "superstition," bourgeois order against medieval "disorder," knowledge and culture against animal impulses. But the book is permeated by anomalies, like the attack on feminism, that indicate more precisely which values are being defended and against what.

Perhaps the most striking anomaly for the modern reader is the significance of money in the tale. Workingmen regularly must be bribed before they will give any information. Mina writes of "the wonderful power of money! What can it not do when properly applied" (p. 360). Even Dracula, his very existence at stake, pauses to grasp a handful of money to pay his passage out of England (p. 312).

The book is permeated with similarly strange anomalies, each one apparently insignificant in itself. Important aids in Dracula's defeat turn out to be shorthand (which he cannot read), the telegraph, records of many kinds (including business accounts, diaries, newspaper reports and even phonograph records) and Mina's portable typewriter. What the men defend is characterized by punctuality (p. 13), and by statements like "my duty is imperative" or "there was business to be done" (p. 15). Duty, orderliness, punctuality, service, business ethics, the precision of modern technology and record-keeping techniques, and the privileges of money—it is precisely these qualities that Stoker ascribes to his heroes and thus associates with the archetypal life-forces.

Dracula is a celebration of a particular type of rationality. Insofar as Stoker's heroes have careers, they are businessmen, lawyers and doctors. Thus they represent the economic rationality of modern business and industry, the political rationality of the law, and the intellectual rationality of science. They share the usual bias of this mode of rationality against anything that cannot be counted, measured, predicted or scheduled. They are stern with "hysterical servant-women" (and with lunatics); they are condescending with workers and foreigners. Van Helsing lists science, the potential for coordinated action, and unselfish devotion as their strengths.

Always they are more concerned with hard "facts" than with tonalities. It is Jonathan's collation of business records that enables the heroes to trace Dracula (p. 231); but is was also his duty-bound repression of his intuitions that enabled the vampire to reach England in the first place—although the latter fact is, significantly, deemphasized in the book (as are all connections between the heroes' "rationality" and their difficulties). When the lunatic, Renfield, does everything *but explicitly state* that he is allied with the vampire, Dr. Seward meets his desperate entreaties with the suggestion that he "try to behave more discreetly" (p. 252). It is this particular blindness on the part of Seward, who "reasons well" according to Van Helsing (p. 196) and who already knew that Renfield was some sort of "index" to Dracula's comings and goings (p. 231), which allows Dracula to infect Mina.

Dracula, who embodies the other side of this opposition, has a strong sense of self, retains (as Van Helsing notes) certain child-like qualities, has a wonderful connection with animals, can be both extremely imaginative and extremely patient, is capable of great impulsiveness and strong feelings, and (in his female cohorts—despite its great importance in the life of the historical Dracula, Stoker does not allow more than a hint of homosexuality) is voluptuously sensual. Indeed, Dracula has all the qualities of a Romantic hero, including a streak of cruelty and strong associations with death.

What Stoker portrays as brain/blood, what he associates with life/death, order/chaos, medieval/modern and masculine/feminine is also what the Romantics dichotomized as reason/imagination. Stoker uses the structures of the gothic novel, made popular by the Romantics, to attack the imagination and the erotic. In *Frankenstein*, Mary Shelley exposed the dangers and limitations of extreme scientific rationality. Stoker uses the same literary form to make the opposite point.

Both the Romantics and anti-Romantics like Stoker accept reason/imagination as a defining structure. The values that triumph in *Dracula* are also the values that triumphed in the society which produced and read the book. The Romantics looked to the past and the pastoral; they celebrated feeling, experience and imagination. *Dracula* asserts that the modern, "masculine" rationality should rule. And the Industrial Revolution, based in the cities and founded on just that sort of scientific rationality, had shaped Victorian England.

It would be excessive and inaccurate to see *Dracula* as nothing more than a piece of propaganda. When its values are considered, however, it becomes clear that *Dracula* embodies some of the same values that were dominant in Victorian England (and that remain dominant, although less so, in Western industrialized societies today).

ADDITIONAL READING

Dickinson, Leon T. *A Guide to Literary Study*. New York: Holt, Rinehart and Winston, 1959.

McGuire, Richard L. *Passionate Attention: An Introduction to Literary Study*. New York: Norton, 1973.

MLA Handbook for Writers of Research Papers, Theses, and Dissertations. New York: Modern Language Association, 1977.

EXERCISE

1. Write a literary critical paper, relying primarily on *one* of the four angles of approach discussed in this section. If possible, work with three or more other people who are taking other angles of approach to the same text. Compare and contrast your results. Could you combine the various papers into one coherent interpretation of that literary text?

2. Choose a short literary text and write an interpretation. Go to the library and find out how a number of critics (preferably using a variety of approaches) have interpreted that same text. Rewrite your interpretation as a critical research paper, incorporating the insights of the critics you have read. How has the research changed your paper?

LETTERS, RÉSUMÉS, AND PROPOSALS

The writing of a business letter as a college assignment serves a double purpose: to acquaint students with the conventional forms of business correspondence and to provide a practical application of the principles of effective composition. . . . The conventions of business correspondence . . . are easily learned. The effectiveness of any letter you write will depend, as it does in any composition, on what you have to say and how you say it.

J. McCrimmon, S. Miller, W. Salmon

BUSINESS LETTERS

The word *business* comes from *busy*. The first principle of writing a business letter is to presume your reader is busy. You almost always have a specific purpose for writing, so come quickly to the point. Be clear and concise. Provide your reader with enough information to make whatever decision needs to be made. In closing, be certain your reader knows precisely what you want and what you are willing to do.

There is a standard format for a business letter, and you should follow it. A business letter is generally an attempt to persuade somebody to do something. Following the standard format establishes you as someone to be dealt with seriously. The *persona* it projects is of someone who knows how business is properly handled. The standard format, since it puts information where the reader expects it, also allows the reader to respond efficiently. Using the proper format is persuasive: it increases the chances that you will get the response you want.

The format is as follows.

1. YOUR ADDRESS AND THE DATE. You want a response, so your reader needs to know your address. Your letter may be opened by a secretary and the envelope, with its return address, discarded.

Correct format is somewhat variable. Traditionally, your address and the date belong at the top of the letter with their left-hand border exactly centered on the page. If you are writing on letterhead stationery with a printed address, of course, you need not repeat the address.

Your letter should be dated for the record, whether for your files or for those of your reader. The date may be used to refer to your letter in future correspondence ("In response to your letter of 21 December, I . . . .") The date is placed immediately below your address. On letterhead stationery with a printed address, the date is set with its left-hand border exactly centered on the page. The date may be written in either of two forms: month-day-year ("December 21, 1981") or day-month-year ("21 December 1981"). Note the comma in the first form.

2. YOUR READER'S ADDRESS. Obviously your reader knows her or his own address. Nonetheless, it goes on the letter for three reasons: (1) as a signifier of formality, (2) for your records (assuming you file a copy), and (3) so your secretary (if you have one) knows how to address the envelope. Your reader's address is placed against the regular left-hand margin of the letter.

3. THE SALUTATION. Ordinarily, the salutation is the word *Dear*, the title and surname of the person you are addressing, and a colon.

Dear Professor Suzuki:
Dear Ms. Espinosa:
Dear President Reagan:

4. THE LEAD. The lead is a short paragraph that makes clear why you are writing. Your letter may be opened by a clerk or secretary whose task is to classify it so that it goes to the proper person or it may be grouped with similar letters (e.g., other applications for the same job). Even if the letter is opened by the person who will read and respond to it, your lead paragraph should tell that person what you want. Business people often receive much correspondence and do not appreciate rambling letters that take their time coming to the point.

5. THE BODY. Here you give your reader information and reasons. In a letter of complaint, for instance, this may be a summary of what has happened and your grounds for expecting the person reading the letter to do something about it. In a job application, this may be a summary of the qualities that you think qualify you for the particular position.

For readability, the paragraphs should be short and the style clear, concise, and specific. Although your ultimate purpose is persuasive, individual paragraphs and the tone of the letter are more often explanatory. Paragraphing is generally indicated by skipping lines between paragraphs, not by indenting.

6. THE CONCLUSION. Here you indicate precisely what you want and/or are willing to do. In a job application, for instance, what you want immediately is to be considered and perhaps interviewed. So you might conclude,

> I will be happy to provide any additional information or references you may need. I can be available for an interview at your convenience. Thank you for whatever consideration you are able to give me.

7. THE COMPLIMENTARY CLOSE AND SIGNATURE. Business letters are signed with a complimentary close, a handwritten signature, and your name typed. The complimentary close is an adverbial phrase that indicates the formality of your relationship with your reader. Some complimentary closes, in descending order of formality, are as follows: "Respectfully," "Very truly yours," "Yours truly," "Sincerely yours," "Cordially," "Warmly." "Respectfully" is so formal and "Warmly" so informal that they are infrequently used. "Cordially" is normally reserved for someone with whom you have both a business and a personal relationship.

The handwritten signature is the legal signature. Your name is typed below it for clarity because not everyone's handwritten signature is legible.

The complimentary close and signature go directly below your address and the date, with their left-hand border exactly centered on the page. Skip a line between the conclusion and the complimentary close and three lines between the complimentary close and your typed name.

8. ADDENDA. There are three types of codes that are often added to business letters. If the letter is typed by someone other than the writer, the typist puts both the writer's and his or her own initials below the signature at the left-hand margin (e.g., "RMC: vm"). If anything is enclosed with the letter which might become separated, that is indicated in the same place (e.g., "Enc: résumé"). And if copies of the letter are being sent to anyone, that too is indicated (e.g., "cc: Better Business Bureau"). This is a polite way of informing your reader who will be seeing the letter and is also useful for your files.

Business letters are generally written to people you do not know personally. The letter itself must establish your *persona*. Neatness counts. So does following the standard format. And the tone you use is very important.

2001 Corax Place
Syracuse, NY 13210
30 May 1981

Ms. Alicia Ponce
Director of Personnel
Social Research Institute
1910 Guaraguao Court
Austin, TX 78703

Dear Ms. Ponce:

I write in response to your notice, posted at my university's placement office, that the Social Research Institute has an opening for a writer/editor. I believe I would be particularly well suited to fill that position.

I have just completed work on an M.A. in English with a special emphasis on writing and rhetoric. As an undergraduate, I minored in English while majoring in sociology. Consequently, I have the combination of writing abilities and social science background needed by a writer working at the Social Research Institute.

In the year between completing my bachelor's degree and starting graduate school, I worked as a researcher and writer for a project investigating literacy standards in upstate New York. I was responsible for writing one section of the final report, which I can make available to you as a sample of my writing.

In the course of my own studies, I have read several reports produced by the Social Research Institute. I am familiar with the type of work done at the Institute. I believe I could function effectively and happily as a writer and editor at the Institute. Having close relatives there, I know Austin fairly well, and I would be quite happy to live there.

I will be in Austin the second week of July and would welcome a chance to meet you for an interview at that time. Meanwhile I will be pleased to send you any further information you may require. My résumé is enclosed. Thank you for whatever consideration you are able to give me.

Very truly yours,

Christopher Spiros

enc: résumé

Since the person to whom you are writing is probably busy, try to confine your letter to one or two pages. One page is best. A long letter may be set aside to be dealt with later, or it may be skimmed instead of being read carefully. If there is a lot of information you must communicate, summarize it in the letter and include an enclosure with the details.

RÉSUMÉS

A résumé or vita is a set of notes—but unlike the notes you might take in a university class, these are about yourself and for someone else. The word *vita* is Latin for "life"; the word *résumé* is from Old French, meaning "summary." By whichever name, it is a summary of the relevant aspects of your life. Called a résumé in the business world and a vita (or curriculum vitae) in academia, it is usually submitted with any letter of application for employment.

Résumés are sometimes compared with outlines. They do have something in common with outlines, especially their schematic format. But to understand the purpose and function of your résumé, it is better to think of it as a formalized set of notes about yourself that you supply to a potential employer. Your résumé provides more information than you can fit into a one- or two-page application letter. It is easy to skim and is arranged so that the employer can locate particular information easily. It saves the employer from having to take notes on your letter or during an interview which may follow.

Your résumé should include some or all of the following types of information: personal data and career goals, education, work experience, related activities and interests, and (in academia) names of references. Generally, you may order this information in whatever way will be most impressive.

Personal data should include your name, address, and telephone number (both home and office if you have both). You might also include, if relevant, citizenship, date of birth, state of health, height, and weight. At the beginning of your career, it is often customary to state your goals.

You should summarize your education in reverse chronological order, beginning with the educational institution most recently attended. Give the name of each institution, dates of attendance or graduation, degree granted (if any), and course or program taken. You may also indicate any special courses, activities, or honors—but be brief.

Your employment history should also be in reverse chronological order, but you may wish to separate short-term or part-time work (and perhaps summarize it at the end). Jobs not relevant to your career goals may be similarly treated. If not obvious from the job title, the duties you performed should be stated briefly. Also give the dates of employment, name, location of the employer.

Especially in the earlier phases of your career, employers are often influenced by indications of your interest and talent. The following information might be included: membership in professional associations, publications, elective positions you have held, volunteer work, campus activities, sports, hobbies, and so forth. Choose information that might show something about you that could influence someone to hire you.

If your letter of application and résumé interest an employer, she or he will probably wish to obtain references from people who know you and your abilities. Generally, three types of references are used: employment (e.g., a former employer), academic (e.g., a professor with whom you worked or from whom you took several courses), and personal (e.g., a member of the clergy who knows you).

Résumés may be arranged and laid out on the page in various ways. Categories should be indicated by headings. Your résumé should be neither so long nor so imposing that it puts employers off: try to confine yourself to one or two pages, and do not squeeze too much print onto a page.

Generally, you make up one résumé, have it printed or photocopied, and use it with all your letters of application. The letter then repeats information that is especially relevant to the particular job and supplements it as necessary. The résumé, therefore, can be a brief summary. If you are applying for two radically different types of positions—say, academic and business—you might want to make up two distinct résumés. But it is excessive to type a new résumé for each job application.

CHRISTOPHER P. SPIROS

PERSONAL:

2001 Corax Place	Born: 4 January 1957
Syracuse, NY 13210	Health: Excellent
(315) 555-1776	Citizenship: U.S.A.

CAREER GOALS:

To work as a writer or teacher of writing, preferably in a context related to the social sciences.

EDUCATION:

M.A.: Peripatetic University (1981)
Program in Writing and Rhetoric

Thesis: "Comparison/Contrast: A Study of the Composing Processes of Sociology Students and Professional Sociologists"

B.S.: Academy College (1978)
Magna Cum Laude; Phi Beta Kappa
Editor-in-Chief, student newspaper (1977-78)
Major: Sociology. Minor: English.

EMPLOYMENT:

1978-79: Writer and Researcher. Syracuse School Board.
Worked on a project investigating literacy standards in upstate New York. Had special responsibility for the historical section, summarizing 18th and 19th century standards.

Summer 1977: Research Assistant. Syracuse School Board.
Worked on a pilot project and proposal for investigating literacy standards in upstate New York.

Summers 1974-76: Camp Counselor. Johnny Appleseed Camp.
Had primary responsibility for a group of 12-15 preteen boys each summer. Also supervised the camp's mimeographed newspaper in 1975 and 1976.

REFERENCES: Professional, academic, and personal references available on request.

PROPOSALS

The ability to write an effective proposal is increasingly important and valuable. Both approval and funding for a great many sorts of projects depend on responses to written proposals.

A professor proposes a new course, a scientist seeks funding for research, a writer wants an advance against royalties on a book not yet written, a data processing company offers its services to a major corporation, a community organization tries to raise money for a preventative medicine center, a would-be publisher wants investors for a new magazine, a multinational corporation competes for a government contract—in each of these cases a proposal must be written. Indeed, almost any project that requires approval or funding from a bureaucracy, whether corporate or public, also requires a written proposal. And, while a well-written proposal may not get a faulty project off the ground, a poorly written proposal can put an end to an otherwise viable project.

The underlying structure of a proposal is essentially *problem-solution*. Writing it involves application of the progressive patterns of arrangement, discussed in Chapter 5: you have to explain *why* the problem exists and *how* your project will resolve it. Remember that any problem exists in a pattern of causation and in a context. Your solution must either change the causation so that the problematic event no longer occurs or change the context so that the event is no longer a problem. To explain how your project will work, you have to write a process-analyis. To convince readers that your project will solve the problem, you usually have to do causal explanation.

Writing a proposal is a persuasive task. Assuming you know what you want, the first and most important thing to think about is your audience. In some cases—for instance if you are seeking funding for a community project—the very first thing may be to find your audience: Who approves and funds projects of the sort you are proposing? Answering this question means doing research, either by asking people likely to know or by using the library. You may want to consult sources like the *Annual Register of Grant Support, The Catalog of Federal Domestic Assistance* (U.S.), or *The Foundation Directory*. In other cases—for instance if you are competing for a government contract—it may be clear who your audience is.

Once you have identified your audience, you need to know how to approach it. What will motivate these people to approve or fund your project? Often the best way to find out is to ask them, either in person or through a letter of inquiry. First find out whom you should contact. Then plan your communication. If you are writing, follow proper business-letter format. Begin by stating why your particular readers should be concerned with your project. Briefly explain the project. If you want funding, indicate roughly how much. Ask for advice about whether and how to submit a proposal.

The general format for the proposal itself is as follows.

Cover letter. This is similar to the letter of inquiry in substance. Its main purpose is to motivate your audience to read the proposal carefully. It accompanies the proposal proper.

Introduction. Introduce yourself (or your organization). Who are you? What are your goals? What have you accomplished in the past? What is your expertise? Who has supported you in the past? Keep this section brief, if necessary by putting supporting information into the addenda section. You want to establish credibility, but you also want to get on to the substance of the proposal.

Problem. Describe the problem you propose to solve. Be specific. Cite authorities. Use statistics and examples. Give enough of a causal explanation of the problem so that your proposed solution will make sense to your readers. Make clear how your (or your organization's) expertise and resources relate to the problem.

Goals. Explain specifically what you want to accomplish. Make clear how your project relates to similar existing projects. If possible, keep your goals concrete and measurable. If this is not possible, explain why.

Procedure. Explain how you will achieve your goals. This is often the most crucial part of a proposal. Here you lay out your strategy. The quality of that strategy serves to convince readers of your competence. In the two previous sections, you described the problem and your proposed solution; here you explain how you propose to get from problem to solution.

Assessment. Here you are dealing with accountability. How will you—and the people who approve or fund your project—know if you have achieved your goals? What verification procedures will you use? Explain how you will evaluate your project, both while it is in process and after it has been completed.

Personnel. Who will carry out the project? What is their competence? Include résumés if relevant (or indicate that they can be found among the addenda).

Budget. This is especially important if you are seeking funding, but it also serves to establish your credibility. List all anticipated expenses, as well as any potential income.

Conclusion. Give a summary and explain the broader or more long-term implications of your project. Here is your chance to renew your appeal and also to reestablish the importance of your project by demonstrating its implications.

Addenda. This section is for detailed support that was too cumbersome to include elsewhere. It may include résumés, letters of support, a bibliography, a history of the problem, a history of your organization, documents, newspaper clippings, and so forth.

Remember, this is a general format for writing a proposal. Use it as a guideline; do not follow it slavishly. If you did the assignment at the end of Chapter 0, for instance, you have already written a proposal—a proposal for improving your writing abilities. Although you may not have followed the general format as listed here, you probably included everything except the cover letter, personnel, budget, and addenda. Writing a proposal, like most rhetorical tasks, involves your adapting general principles to a particular situation.

ADDITIONAL READING

All About Letters. A booklet produced by the U.S. Postal Service in cooperation with the National Council of Teachers of English.

Guide to Resume Writing. Toronto: University and College Placement Association, 1978. A brief pamphlet that demonstrates seven potential formats for resumes so that you can use the one that will show you in the best light.

Grantsmanship: Money and How to Get It. New Jersey: Academic Media, 1973. A succinct introduction and brief list of additional sources.

Story, Jill. "You Deserve a Grant Today: Cracking the Funding Game." *Ms.* (April 1980), pages 91-94.

EXERCISE

1. Think about your employment goals—either short-term or long-term—and prepare a résumé for yourself. Do not make anything up, but do present yourself in the best possible light.

2. Write a business letter, preferably a real one. Perhaps there is a problem that might be resolved if it were properly brought to the attention of the right person. Mail the letter. Wait for a response. Reconsider how you wrote the letter in light of the response.

3. Use the format for writing a proposal to do the final assignment of Chapter 0. That is, write a proposal for how you will improve your writing abilities.

4. What kinds of proposals are normally written in your field of specialization? Is there any standard format? Write such a proposal.

PUBLICATION

'Tis pleasant, sure, to see one's name in print . . . .
George Gordon Byron

PRESENTING A PAPER

As a student, professional or academic, you may have to read a paper aloud to a group of your peers. Professionals and academics often present papers at conferences, conventions, symposia, and other such meetings. Students who take seminars are usually required to make formal presentations, which are modeled after professional papers. Moreover, it is increasingly common for graduate students, and occasionally even undergraduates, to present papers at professional meetings, in part because such presentations improve their chances of finding employment later.

These presentations—whether to a university seminar or a professional meeting—serve two purposes. First, the paper informs your peers—other students or members of your profession—of the results of your work. In a professional context, this allows members of the profession to be informed about research findings, theoretical or practical work that is still to recent or too incomplete to have been published. In a seminar, this allows other students to benefit from your detailed investigation of some particular aspect of the subject.

Second, the presentation is an opportunity for you to receive feedback on your work in progress. A professional or academic will ordinarily revise the presentation, in part on the basis of criticism received after the reading, and then submit it to a professional journal. A student will usually use the seminar presentation as a base from which to write the term paper for the same course. In short, such a presentation should be seen not only as an opportunity to communicate, but also as part of the writing process. It enables you not only to improve the substance of your paper, but also to adjust it to suit the rhetorical context of your particular audience. In a writing class or group, the main function of such a presentation is to help you develop your sense of rhetorical context.

Since the principles behind seminar presentations are based on the delivery of professional papers, the following discussion will emphasize the latter. One major difference between the two contexts, however, is this: before you can read a professional paper, it must be accepted. You should be aware that papers for scholarly conferences often must be submitted as much as a year in advance. Submission may mean sending no more than a title (or title and abstract). Or it may mean submitting a draft of the entire paper. Different organizations have different procedures. Investigate well in advance.

A professional paper is typically twenty minutes long. For the average speaker, this means about eight typewritten pages (rule of thumb: allow two-and-a-half minutes per page, assuming normal margins and an elite typeface). Confining yourself to the time limit is important. In some organizations or seminars, the person chairing the session will cut you off at the time limit; if you realize while reading that you are going to exceed your time, you may have to choose between not finishing or making extemporaneous cuts. Should the chair or professor let you exceed your time limit, the time allotted to other speakers or for questions and discussion will be reduced. Since part of the point of presenting a professional or seminar paper is to get feedback, this makes little sense.

Although the paper will be read, think of it as a speech, perhaps even as a performance. Your purpose is to communicate with listeners, not to read words. It may help to mark pauses and to underline words or phrases you wish to emphasize.

You should read the paper aloud beforehand, perhaps to a mirror, tape recorder, and your husband (or wife, mother, father—or anyone else who can be induced to listen). Beware of a tendency to read more quickly than usual. And be conservative: you may make an extemporaneous introduction or additions when you present the paper; allow time for such remarks. If the original paper is only seven or eight pages long, your performance can be more flexible.

Give listeners as much of a framework as possible, perhaps even a brief summary at both beginning and ending. If there are any handouts which will follow the reading (e.g., a bibliography), announce that, so people will not take unnecessary notes when they could be listening more intently. If the paper has already been accepted for publication, announce that too.

At a professional meeting, there are often many papers being read simultaneously (in different rooms). You want to get the best, not necessarily the biggest, audience for yours. Use a title that accurately indicates what you will be talking about. Try to make clear early in the paper what your subject is and what sort of listeners you are addressing. Thus if you are dealing with a highly specialized and technical subject, people can leave and you will not be talking to a room filled with people, only 10% of whom can understand you and only 20% of whom would even want to.

Read at the speed of normal speech, not faster, so listeners can absorb your words. Try to maintain some eye contact with the audience. You may wish to make brief digressions from your written paper if you notice signs of confusion or misunderstanding.

If, as is usual at professional meetings, several papers are being read at the same session, listen to the others. If you can make any connection or draw any parallels between your paper and the others, you may wish to do so, either before your paper or during any discussion period afterwards. At any event, you do not want to project yourself as an inconsiderate person or to distract listeners from another person's paper. Your *persona* is communicated in all your gestures and comments.

Typically, there is a question-and-discussion period after each paper or at the end of the session. Listen carefully: be sure you understand any question or comment directed to you. If necessary, ask the chairperson or the questioner for clarification. If you are not certain you understood or that everyone in the audience could hear the question, repeat it.

Both at professional meetings and in seminars, people often have vested interests, professional and otherwise. Try to listen for any implications that go beyond the content of the question or comment. You may wish to ignore or to respond to such implications, or even to refer the question to the person at whom the implication is actually aimed. Whatever response you choose, it is useful to be aware of such implications.

Remember that you have two purposes: (1) to present yourself and what you want to say as effectively as possible, and (2) to get feedback on your work. Orient your presentation toward achieving these goals. Presenting a professional or seminar paper can be a gratifying experience and also a way to keep your work in touch with professional realities. If you are going to submit your paper for publication—and you may be asked to at the meeting itself—or use it as a term paper, try to revise it as soon as possible, while questions, suggestions, and criticisms are still fresh in your mind.

PUBLICATION

Writers sometimes can reach their readers easily, for instance, by putting a letter into a stamped, addressed envelope or by handing a report to the person who requested it. Other times, reaching readers can be one of the hardest parts of writing.

Where and how to get your writing published is properly the subject for a whole book. Indeed, there are many such books, some of them highly specialized. There are, for example, several books listing just journals that publish scholarly literary criticism. There are other books about how to sell your writing to commercial magazines and book publishers. There are even magazines about how to sell your writing to magazines. Here the subject will, of necessity, be discussed only briefly.

The first point to be made is this: publication is important. Knowing that a piece of your writing may be published can change your whole way of relating to it. Most, if not all, of the writing you have done probably has been either for exercise or personal. Either you have done it (as at school) to exercise your abilities. Or it has been for your own eyes only. Or it has been addressed to people you knew, people who probably would not judge you by how you wrote.

Writing for publication is a distinct sort of experience, different from the other writing you probably have done. You should find out what it feels like. It will probably change your composing process—for one thing, you are likely to find yourself motivated to put a lot more time into revision (as most professional writers do). And seeing your words in print makes you read them in a whole different way: usually with pride and sometimes with chagrin (especially if you did not put that extra time into revision).

The experience is worth having. Considering all the writing you have been doing if you are using this book, you should try to get at least one piece into print. If nothing else, try a letter to the editor of a community or campus newspaper.

Assuming you can write fairly competently, the key to publishing is finding the right medium. To do that, ask yourself two questions. What do I want to say? To whom do I want to say it? The trick is to find a publication that prints the sort of material you want to write and that is read by the people you want to communicate with. This is often not very difficult because the people who have an interest in what you want to write probably read publications which carry that sort of material. Occasionally, there is no such publication—in which case you may want to start your own.

You can begin at either end. Define your audience, and find out what they read (perhaps by talking to some of them, perhaps by checking marketing surveys). Or go to the library, get a list of publications in the general area, and look at them. If you wish to publish a piece of adademic literary criticism, for instance, check the *MLA Directory of Periodicals*, which both indicates the sorts of material each journal publishes and explains how to submit your manuscript.

Once you have located some publications that might suit your purposes, you will need to analyze them. What sorts of articles do they print? To analyze a particular publication, ask the same questions you would ask about a specialized type of writing (see pages 361-362).

1. What is the purpose of this publication? Who reads it? On what occasions?
2. What sorts of material are usually treated? How are the writings focused? Do the writers seem to share approaches, methods, or techniques for handling the material? How long are the writings? What is the level of readability (see pages 121-125)? Is there a standard format or typical structure? How long are the paragraphs and how are they typically structured. What is the relationship among levels of generality (see pages 95-99) within typical paragraphs and for whole pieces of writing?
3. Is there a common *persona* most of the writers adopt? Are there key terms or analogies that recur? Are there "buzz words" or a standard jargon? Can you detect shared values? How formal is the writing in word choice and usage?
4. Can you create a heuristic that will structure your material to meet the apparent requirements of this publication?

See if you can find any statements by the publisher, editor, or advertising manager that can answer some of these questions. Look at the publication itself. Look at the advertisements too: they often indicate a lot about the readers and their interests.

After you have analyzed some publications, think again about what you want to write. Unless you are going to prostitute yourself by writing whatever you can get paid for, you must ask yourself if what you want to write can be adapted to the apparent requirements of one of these publications. To reach the readers you want to reach, you may have to compromise. But if you compromise too much, you will no longer be communicating what you want to communicate.

Once you have located a likely publication, write and/or revise the piece. Prepare and submit the manuscript properly. Then wait. You should receive at least a postcard acknowledging receipt of the manuscript fairly promptly. A decision may take longer. Certain academic publications can take over a year to make a decision. On rare occasion, your manuscript may be lost, so be sure you have a copy. And be prepared for rejection slips—most writers have collected more rejections than acceptances, even writers who publish regularly. If you have done your analysis well, however, you have zeroed in on the right publications for what you have written; that should reduce the number of rejections and help you find a publisher more quickly.

At any event, do it. Reaching real readers—delivery—is the final stage of the composing process, the fruition. And, to paraphrase George Gordon Byron, 'tis pleasant sure to see one's work in print.

EXERCISE

1. Write a paper to be read aloud. Think about any differences this makes in the way you write. Practice reading the paper aloud to a tape recorder. Listen to the recording and then revise the paper. If possible, read the paper to a real audience, preferably one like the readers for whom you wrote it.

2. Find out how to submit a paper to a professional conference in your area of special interest. If you have an appropriate paper (or conception for a paper), submit it.

3. Find out how to get funding to travel to a professional meeting in your field. If you have submitted a paper, try to get that funding.

4. Write a letter to the editor of a newspaper. Mail it.

5. Select three magazines that print articles on the same subjects for similar readers (e.g., three North American travel magazines or three professional journals read by high school English teachers). Analyze those periodicals to determine what sorts of writings they publish.

6. With several particular periodicals in mind, write an article for publication. Investigate the proper procedure for submitting a manuscript to such periodicals. Prepare and submit the manuscript properly. If you receive a rejection slip, try again. Remember that writing it is more than half the fun. Also remember that getting it published and read is part of the fun too.

NAME INDEX

SUBJECT INDEX

Page numbers in *italics* indicate a primary discussion or a definition of the topic.

REVISION SYMBOLS

Ab	Incorrect or inappropriate abbreviation
Agr	Faulty agreement, either between subject and verb or between pronoun and antecedent
Amb	Ambiguous; can be read more than one way
Apos	Misuse or absence of apostrophe
Awk	Hard to read because awkwardly constructed
Bib	Inappropriate bibliographical form
Cap	Error in capitalization
Choppy	Choppy style caused by excessively short sentences or repetitive sentence structures
Coh	Passage hard to understand because it lacks transitions or other coherency cues
Cs	Comma splice
D	Inappropriate diction
Dev	Inadequate development
Det	Inadequate detail
Dm	Dangling modifier
Emph	Inappropriate emphasis or lack of clear emphasis
Fn	Inappropriate footnote form
Format	Inappropriate format
Frag	Nonfunctional sentence fragment
Gr	Grammatical error
Id	Faulty idiom
Ital	Italics (underlining) needed or misused
Lc	Use lower case letters
Logic	Faulty logic
Num	Error in use or form of numbers
¶	Start new paragraph
N¶	Do not start new paragraph
Pass	Ineffective use of passive voice
Pn	Punctuation error (see below for specific symbols)
Q	Error in use or format of quotation
Red	Excessive redundancy (substantive)
Ref	Faulty pronoun reference
Rep	Excessive repetition (of words or phrases)
R-o	Run-on sentence
Source?	Source of this concept or quotation should be indicated
Sp	Misspelling
Tense	Error in verb tense
T/shift	Inappropriate or inaccurate shift in verb tense
Title	Inadequate or ineffective title
Trans	Inadequate or faulty transition
Trite	Trite concept or word choice
Unity	Passage hard to understand because unity among concepts is not clear
Usage	Error in usage
Vague	Passage hard to understand because vague
Wo	Inappropriate or ineffective word order
Wordy	Excessive verbiage
WW	Word choice does not seem to reflect meaning
?	Reader cannot understand (perhaps because illegible)
//ism	Faulty parallelism
~	Transpose (tr.)
#	Insert space
⁀	Delete space
^,	Insert comma

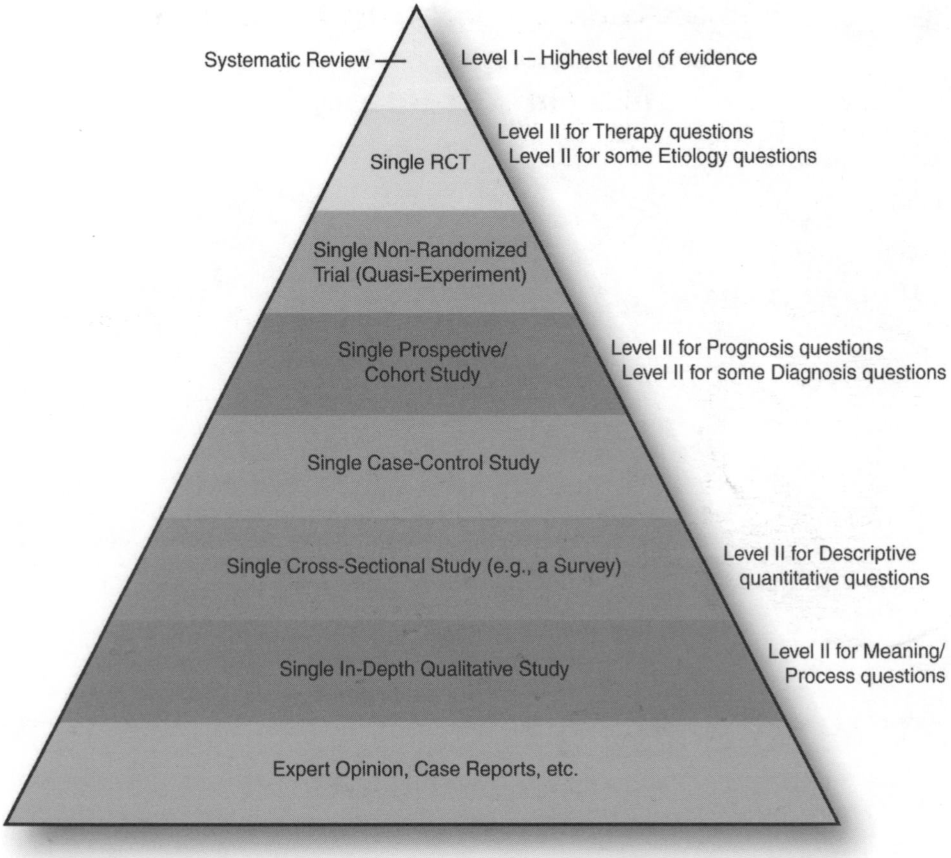

Systematic Review
Level I – Highest level of evidence

Single RCT
Level II for Therapy questions
Level II for some Etiology questions

Single Non-Randomized Trial (Quasi-Experiment)

Single Prospective/ Cohort Study
Level II for Prognosis questions
Level II for some Diagnosis questions

Single Case-Control Study

Single Cross-Sectional Study (e.g., a Survey)
Level II for Descriptive quantitative questions

Single In-Depth Qualitative Study
Level II for Meaning/ Process questions

Expert Opinion, Case Reports, etc.

FIGURE 2.1 ● Evidence hierarchy: levels of evidence.

To

Our Families—Husbands, Children, Grandchildren

Husbands: Alan and Chuck

Children: Alex, Alaine, Lauren, Norah and Curt, Lisa

Grandchildren: Julia and Maren

REVIEWERS

Susan E. Bernheiel, EdD, MSN, CNE
Professor of Nursing
Mercy College of Northwest Ohio
Toledo, Ohio

Elizabeth W. Black, MSN, RN
Assistant Professor, Nursing
Gwynedd-Mercy College
Gwynedd Valley, Pennsylvania

Diane M. Breckenridge, PhD, MSN, RN
Associate Professor
School of Nursing
La Salle University
Philadelphia, Pennsylvania

Colleen Carmody-Payne, EdD, MS, RN
Assistant Professor
Center for Professional and International Studies
Keuka College
Penn Yan, New York

Barbara Cheyney, MS, BSN, RN-BC
Adjunct Faculty
Seattle Pacific University
Seattle, Washington

Christine Coughlin, EdD, RN
Associate Professor
School of Nursing
Adelphi University
Garden City, New York

Darlene Del Prato, PhD, RN
Assistant Professor
State University of New York Institute of Technology
Utica, New York

Cheryl Hettman, PhD, RN
Chairperson and Associate Professor
California University of Pennsylvania
California, Pennsylvania

Patrick E. Kenny, EdD, RN-BC, ACRN, APRN-PMH, NE-BC
Assistant Professor of Nursing
DeSales University
Center Valley, Pennsylvania

Kereen Forster Mullenbach, PhD, MBA, MSN, RN
Assistant Professor
Radford University
Radford, Virginia

Judee E. Onyskiw, PhD, MN, BScN, RN
Faculty, and Research and Scholarship Advisor
Grant MacEwan University
Edmonton, Alberta

Sabita Persaud, PhD, RN
Assistant Professor
Bowie State University
Bowie, Maryland

Rosemarie DiMauro Satyshur, PhD, RN
Assistant Professor
School of Nursing
University of Maryland
Baltimore, Maryland

Linda J. Scheetz, EdD, RN, FAEN
Associate Professor
Department of Nursing
SUNY New Paltz
New Paltz, New York

Denise Schilling, PT, PhD
Associate Professor/Chair
Department of Physical Therapy Education
Western University of Health Sciences
Pomona, California

Suzanne Sutherland, PhD, RN
Professor of Nursing
California State University Sacramento
Sacramento, California

Linda Thompson, DSN, MSN, RN
Professor of Nursing
School of Nursing
Austin Peay State University
Clarksville, Tennessee

Sharon L. Van Sell, EdD, RN, PAHM
Professor
College of Nursing
Texas Woman's University
Dallas, Texas

Pamela B. Webber, PhD, APRN, BC, FNP
Professor of Nursing
School of Nursing
Shenandoah University
Winchester, Virginia

Jeana Wilcox, PhD, RN, CNS, CNE
Associate Professor and Associate Dean of Undergraduate Programs
Graceland University
Independence, Missouri

USER'S GUIDE

Learning Objectives focus student's attention on critical content

LEARNING OBJECTIVES

On completing this chapter, you will be able to:

- Discuss the rationale for an emergent design in qualitative research, and describe qualitative design features
- Identify the major research traditions for qualitative research and describe the domain of inquiry of each
- Describe the main features of ethnographic, phenomenologic, and grounded theory studies
- Discuss the goals and methods of various types of research with an ideological perspective
- Define new terms in the chapter

Key New Terms alert students to important terminology

KEY TERMS

Basic social process (BSP)
Bracketing
Case study
Constant comparison
Core variable
Critical ethnography
Critical theory
Descriptive phenomenology
Descriptive qualitative study
Emergent design
Ethnonursing research
Feminist research
Hermeneutics
Interpretive phenomenology
Narrative analysis
Participant observation
Participatory action research (PAR)

Example of qualitative comparisons:
Baum and colleagues (2012) explored the experiences of 30 Israeli mothers of very-low-birth-weight babies when the babies were still in neonatal hospitalization. The researchers discovered that there were three patterns with regard to attribution of blame for not carrying to full term: those who blamed themselves, those who blamed others, and those who believed that premature delivery was fortunate because it saved their baby's life.

Examples help students apply content to real-life research

Tip boxes describe what is found in actual research articles

TIP: Experimental designs can be depicted graphically using symbols to represent features of the design. In these diagrams, the convention is that R stands for randomization to treatment groups, X represents receipt of the intervention, and O is the measurement of outcomes. So, for example, a pretest–posttest design would be depicted as follows:

$$R\,O_1\,X\,O_2$$
$$R\,O_1\,O_2$$

Space does not permit us to present these diagrams for all designs, but many are shown in the supplement to this chapter on thePoint.

How-to-tell Tip boxes explain confusing issues in actual research articles

HOW-TO-TELL TIP: How can you tell if a phenomenological study is descriptive or interpretive? Phenomenologists often use terms that can help you make this determination. In a descriptive phenomenological study such terms may be bracketing, description, essence, and Husserl. The names of Colaizzi, Van Kaam, or Giorgi may appear in the methods section. In an interpretive phenomenological study, key terms can include being-in-the-world, hermeneutics, understanding, and Heidegger. The names van Manen, Benner, or Diekelmann may appear in the method section. These names are discussed in Chapter 16 on qualitative data analysis.

Critiquing Guidelines boxes lead students through key issues in a research article

BOX 14.1 Guidelines for Critiquing Qualitative Designs

1. Is the research tradition for the qualitative study identified? If none was identified, can one be inferred? If more than one was identified, is this justifiable or does it suggest "method slurring"?
2. Is the research question congruent with a qualitative approach and with the specific research tradition (i.e., is the domain of inquiry for the study congruent with the domain encompassed by the tradition)? Are the data sources, research methods, and analytic approach congruent with the research tradition?
3. How well is the research design described? Are design decisions explained and justified? Does it appear that the researcher made all design decisions up-front, or did the design emerge during data collection, allowing researchers to capitalize on early information?
4. Is the design appropriate, given the research question? Does the design lend itself to a thorough, in-depth, intensive examination of the phenomenon of interest? What design elements might have strengthened the study (e.g., a longitudinal perspective rather than a cross-sectional one)?
5. Was there evidence of reflexivity in the design?
6. Was the study undertaken with an ideological perspective? If so, is there evidence that ideological methods and goals were achieved? (e.g., was there evidence of full collaboration between researchers and participants? Did the research have the power to be transformative, or is there evidence that a transformative process occurred?)

RESEARCH EXAMPLES WITH CRITICAL THINKING EXERCISES

This section presents examples of different types of qualitative studies. Read these summaries and then answer the critical thinking questions, referring to the full research report if necessary.

EXAMPLE 1 ● A Grounded Theory Study

Study: Preserving the self: The process of decision-making about hereditary breast cancer and ovarian cancer risk reduction (Howard et al., 2011).

Statement of Purpose: The purpose of the study was to understand how women make decisions about strategies to reduce the risk of hereditary breast and ovarian cancer (HBOC), such as cancer screening and risk-reducing surgeries.

Research Examples highlight critical points made in the chapter and sharpen critical thinking skills

CRITICAL THINKING EXERCISES

Visit thePoint website for a discussion of all questions.

1. Answer the relevant questions from Box 14.1 on page 00 regarding this study.
2. Also consider the following targeted questions:
   a. Was this study cross-sectional or longitudinal?
   b. Could this study have been undertaken as an ethnography? A phenomenological inquiry?
3. If the results of this study are trustworthy, in what ways do you think the findings could be used in clinical practice?

Critical Thinking Exercises provide opportunities to practice critiquing actual research articles

Summary Points review chapter content to ensure success

SUMMARY POINTS

- Qualitative research involves an **emergent design**—a design that emerges in the field as the study unfolds.
- Although qualitative design is elastic and flexible, qualitative researchers plan for broad contingencies that can pose decision opportunities for study design in the field.
- Ethnography focuses on the culture of a group of people and relies on extensive field work that usually includes **participant observation** and in-depth interviews with **key informants**. Ethnographers strive to acquire an **emic** (insider's) perspective of a culture rather than an **etic** (outsider's) perspective.
- Nurses sometimes refer to their ethnographic studies as **ethnonursing research.** Most ethnographers study cultures other than their own; ***autoethnographies*** are ethnographies of a group or culture to which the researcher belongs.
- Phenomenologists seek to discover the *essence* and *meaning* of a phenomenon as it is experienced by people, mainly through in-depth interviews with people who have had the relevant experience.
- In **descriptive phenomenology**, which seeks to describe lived experiences, researchers strive to **bracket** out preconceived views and to *intuit* the essence of the phenomenon by remaining open to meanings attributed to it by those who have experienced it.
- **Interpretive phenomenology (hermeneutics)** focuses on interpreting the meaning of experiences, rather than just describing them.
- **Grounded theory** researchers try to account for people's actions by focusing on the main concern that their behavior is designed to resolve. The manner in which people resolve this main concern is the **core variable.** The goal of grounded theory is to discover this main concern and the **basic social process (BSP)** that explains how people resolve it.
- Grounded theory uses **constant comparison**: categories elicited from the data are constantly compared with data obtained earlier.
- A controversy in grounded theory concerns whether to follow the original Glaser and Strauss procedures or to use procedures adapted by Strauss and Corbin; Glaser has argued that the latter approach does not result in *grounded theories* but rather in *conceptual descriptions*. More recently, Charmaz's **constructivist grounded theory** has emerged,

Special icons alert students to important content found on thePoint and in the accompanying Study Guide

NEW! INTERACTIVE CRITICAL THINKING ACTIVITY

This new interactive activity brings the content from the text to an easy-to-use tool that enables students to apply new skills that they learn in each chapter. Students are guided through appraisals of real research examples and then ushered through a series of questions that challenge them to think about the quality of evidence from the study. Responses can be printed or e-mailed directly to instructors for homework or testing.

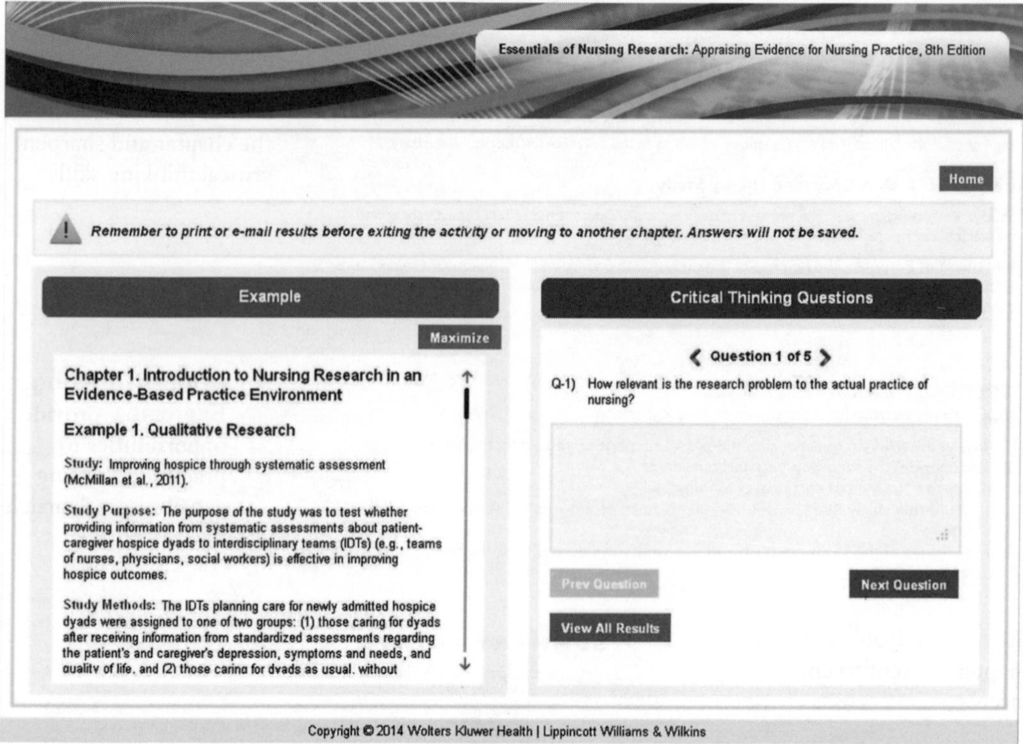

Essentials of Nursing Research: Appraising Evidence for Nursing Practice, 8th Edition
Home
Remember to print or e-mail results before exiting the activity or moving to another chapter. Answers will not be saved.
Example
Maximize
Chapter 1. Introduction to Nursing Research in an Evidence-Based Practice Environment
Example 1. Qualitative Research
Study: Improving hospice through systematic assessment (McMillan et al., 2011).
Study Purpose: The purpose of the study was to test whether providing information from systematic assessments about patient-caregiver hospice dyads to interdisciplinary teams (IDTs) (e.g., teams of nurses, physicians, social workers) is effective in improving hospice outcomes.
Study Methods: The IDTs planning care for newly admitted hospice dyads were assigned to one of two groups: (1) those caring for dyads after receiving information from standardized assessments regarding the patient's and caregiver's depression, symptoms and needs, and quality of life, and (2) those caring for dyads as usual, without
Critical Thinking Questions
Question 1 of 5
Q-1) How relevant is the research problem to the actual practice of nursing?
Prev Question
Next Question
View All Results
Copyright © 2014 Wolters Kluwer Health | Lippincott Williams & Wilkins

PREFACE

This publication marks the eighth time we have worked on this textbook, its accompanying ***Study Guide for Essentials of Nursing Research***, and student learning ancillaries and instructor teaching materials available on the**Point**. This integrated learning–teaching package is designed to teach students how to read and critique research reports and to appreciate the application of research findings to nursing practice.

We continue to enjoy immensely our job of developing a suite of educational tools that convey the important innovations in research methodology while providing updates on nurse researchers' use of new methods.

We are confident that we have introduced numerous improvements to both the content and organization of the text—but at the same time, we have retained many features that have made this book a classic throughout the world. We think that this book and its student resources on the**Point**, along with the additional activities provided in its accompanying print Study Guide, will make it easier and more satisfying for nurses to pursue a professional pathway that incorporates thoughtful appraisals of evidence.

Legacy of *Essentials of Nursing Research*

This edition, like its predecessors, is focused on the art—and science—of research critiques. It offers guidance to students who are learning to appraise research reports and use research findings in practice.

Among the basic principles that helped to shape this and earlier editions of this book are:

1. An assumption that competence in doing and appraising research is critical to the nursing profession
2. A conviction that research inquiry is intellectually and professionally rewarding to nurses
3. An unswerving belief that learning about research methods need be neither intimidating nor dull

Consistent with these principles, we have tried to present research fundamentals in a way that both facilitates understanding and arouses curiosity and interest.

New to This Edition

New Organization of Qualitative and Quantitative Materials

In previous editions we made efforts to balance material on qualitative and quantitative research methods, to ensure that each would be given similar emphasis. This balance may have been obscured, however, by intermingling content on both approaches within chapters. In this edition, we blended material on qualitative and quantitative research only in early chapters—for example, in the chapters on evidence-based practice (EBP) and research ethics. Then, we devoted an entire section of the book (Part III) to quantitative research methods and another section (Part IV) to methods for qualitative inquiry. We think this new organization offers greater continuity of ideas and hope it will better meet the needs of students and faculty.

Streamlining—and New Online Content

We have condensed and revised the content of the book to make it more manageable for use in a one-semester course. For this edition, we are offering online Chapter Supplements (e.g., details about the history of nursing research) on thePoint website so that instructors can choose which supplementary material to assign to students. A list of all Chapter Supplements available online at thePoint are included on page xviii.

New Chapter on Mixed Methods Research

We have added a new chapter on mixed methods research, which involves the blending of qualitative and quantitative data in a single inquiry. This new chapter represents a formal recognition of the surge of interest in mixed methods research among nurse researchers in the past decade.

Increased Emphasis on Evidence-Based Practice

To an even greater extent than in the past, in this edition we emphasize that research is a crucial enterprise for building an evidence base for nursing practice. In particular, we have devoted more attention in this edition to the issue of asking well-worded questions for EBP and to searching for such evidence.

New Interactive Critical Thinking Activity

This new interactive activity brings the content from the text to an easy-to-use tool that enables students to apply new skills that they learn in each chapter. Students are guided through appraisals of real research examples and then ushered through a series of questions that challenge them to think about the quality of evidence from the study. Responses can be printed or e-mailed directly to instructors for homework or testing.

Enhanced Assistance for Instructors

One of the biggest improvements in this edition is the assistance we provide for teaching research methods to students—many of whom may be anxious about the course content and may also question its relevance to their nursing practice. We offer numerous suggestions in the Instructor's Manual on thePoint website on how to make learning about—and teaching—research methods more rewarding.

Organization of the Text

The content of this edition is organized into five main parts.

- **Part I—Overview of Nursing Research and Evidence-Based Practice** introduces fundamental concepts in nursing research. Chapter 1 summarizes the background of nursing research, discusses the philosophical underpinnings of qualitative research versus quantitative research, and describes major purposes of nursing research. Chapter 2 offers guidance on using research to build an evidence-based practice. Chapter 3 introduces readers to key research terms, and presents an overview of steps in the research process for both qualitative and quantitative studies. Chapter 4 focuses on research journal articles, explaining what they are and how to read them. Chapter 5 discusses ethics in nursing studies.
- **Part II—Preliminary Research Steps** further sets the stage for learning about the research process by considering aspects of a study's conceptualization. Chapter 6 focuses on the development of research questions and the formulation of research hypotheses. Chapter 7 discusses how to retrieve research evidence and the role of research literature reviews. Chapter 8 presents information about theoretical and conceptual frameworks.
- **Part III—Quantitative Research** presents material on the design and conduct of quantitative nursing studies. Chapter 9 describes fundamental design principles and discusses many specific aspects of quantitative research design. Chapter 10 introduces the topics of sampling and data collection in quantitative studies. Chapter 11 describes the concept of *measurement* and criteria for assessing data quality in quantitative studies. Chapter 12 reviews methods of quantitative analysis. The chapter assumes no prior instruction in statistics and focuses primarily on helping readers to understand why

statistics are needed, what tests might be appropriate in a given situation, and what statistical information in a research article means. Chapter 13 discusses ways of appraising rigor in quantitative studies, and approaches to interpreting statistical results.

- **Part IV—Qualitative Research** presents content relating to the design and conduct of qualitative nursing studies. Chapter 14 addresses the various research traditions that have contributed to the growth of constructivist inquiry and qualitative research. Chapter 15 describes sampling and data collection in qualitative research, and how these differ from approaches used in quantitative studies. Chapter 16 discusses qualitative analysis, with an emphasis on ethnographic, phenomenologic, and grounded theory studies. Chapter 17 elaborates on criteria for appraising trustworthiness and integrity in qualitative studies.
- **Part V—Special Topics in Research** discusses topics that are of increasing importance in research. The emphasis of Chapter 18 is on mixed methods research, but the chapter also discusses other special types of research such as surveys and outcomes research. Finally, Chapter 19 describes systematic reviews, including how to understand and appraise both meta-analyses and metasyntheses.

Integrated Learning Solution: *Our Text, Study Guide, and Student and Faculty Resources on* thePoint

Key Features of the Text

We have retained many of the key features that were successfully used in previous editions to assist consumers of nursing research:

- **Clear, "User-Friendly" Style**. Our writing style is designed to be easily digestible and nonintimidating. Concepts are introduced carefully and systematically, difficult ideas are presented clearly, and readers are assumed to have no prior knowledge of technical terms.
- **Critiquing Guidelines**. Each chapter includes guidelines for conducting a critique of various aspects of a research article. The guidelines provide a list of questions that walk students through a study, drawing attention to aspects of the study that are amenable to appraisal by research consumers. *Electronic versions of the guidelines are available on* thePoint.
- **Research Examples**. Each chapter concludes with summaries of one or two actual research examples designed to highlight critical points made in the chapter. In addition, these research examples are used to stimulate students' thinking about interesting areas of research inquiry. We have chosen many international examples to communicate to students that nursing research is growing in importance worldwide.
- **Critical Thinking Exercises**. Each of the Research Examples is followed by critical thinking exercises designed to help hone the student's skill in critiquing key aspects of research articles. Additional Critical Thinking Exercises in each chapter pertain to the full-length research articles in Appendices A and B of the book.
- **Tips for Consumers**. The textbook is filled with practical guidance and "tips" on how to translate the abstract notions of research methods into more concrete applications. In these tips, we have paid special attention to helping students *read* research reports, which are often daunting to those without specialized research training.
- **Graphics.** Colorful graphics, in the form of supportive tables, figures, and examples, reinforce the text and offer visual stimulation.
- **Chapter Objectives.** Learning objectives are identified in the chapter opener to focus students' attention on critical content.
- **Key Terms**. Each chapter includes a list of new terms, and we have made the list less daunting by including only *key* new terms. New terms are defined in context (and bolded) when used for the first time in the text. A *glossary* at the end of the book provides additional support for those needing to look up the meaning of a methodologic term.

- **Bulleted Summary Points**. A succinct list of summary points that focus on salient chapter content is provided at the end of each chapter.
- **Full-Length Research Articles**. The appendices in the textbook include **four full-length studies**—two quantitative, one qualitative, and one mixed methods—that students can read, analyze, and critique.
- **Critiquing Supports.**
  - Some of the **Critical Thinking Exercises** at the end of each chapter focus on the full-length articles in Appendix A (a quantitative study) and Appendix B (a qualitative study). *Students can get immediate feedback about their grasp of the material by visiting* thePoint *to find our "answers" (our expert thoughts about each question in these exercises).*
  - This edition also includes **full critiques of the two full-length studies** in Appendix C (a quantitative study) and Appendix D (a mixed methods study). Students can use our critiques as models for a comprehensive research critique.

Key Features of the Study Guide

Study Guide for Essentials of Nursing Research, 8e augments the text and provides students with **application exercises** for each text chapter.

- **Critiquing opportunities** abound in the *Study Guide,* **which includes eight research articles in their entirety**. The studies represent a range of nursing topics and types of study, including:
  - A randomized controlled trial
  - A correlational/mixed methods study
  - An evaluation of an evidence-based practice project
  - A grounded theory study
  - A phenomenologic study
  - An ethnography
  - A meta-analysis
  - A metasynthesis (meta-ethnography)
- The **Application Exercises** in each chapter are based on these eight studies and guide students in reading, understanding, and critiquing them.
- Answers to the set of "Questions of Fact" in each chapter are presented in Appendix I of the *Study Guide*, so that students can receive immediate feedback about their responses.
- **Although critiquing skills are emphasized in the Study Guide**, other activities support students in learning fundamental research terms and principles including:
  - Fill-in-the-blank exercises
  - Matching exercises
  - Study questions
- Answers to questions for which there is an objective answer are provided in Appendix I.

***Student Resources Available on* thePoint**

- **Interactive Critical Thinking Activity** brings the Critical Thinking Exercises from the textbook (except those pertaining to the studies in Appendices A and B) to an interactive tool. The new format makes it easy for students to respond to the series of targeted questions about the Research Examples. Responses can be printed or e-mailed directly to instructors for homework or testing.
- **19 Full Journal Articles** (one corresponding to each chapter) are provided for additional critiquing opportunities. Several of these are the full journal articles for studies used as the end-of-chapter Research Examples. All journal articles that appear on thePoint website are identified in the text with the Point icon.

- **Hundreds of Student Review Questions** to assist students in self-testing. This review program provides a rationale for both correct and incorrect answers, helping students to identify areas of strength and areas needing further study.
- **Internet Resources with relevant and useful websites** related to chapter content can be "clicked" on directly without having to retype the URL and risk a typographical error.
- **Chapter Supplements** to further students' exploration of specific topics. A full list of the Supplements appears on page xviii.
- **Critiquing Guidelines** from the text are available in MSWord for your convenience.
- **Answers to the Critical Thinking Exercises** for Appendixes A and B of the textbook offer suggestions for possible responses.
- **An e-book available at no additional cost with the purchase of your text!**

***The Instructor's Resources Available on* thePoint**

- **Instructor's Manual** includes a chapter corresponding to every chapter in the textbook and contains the following:
  - **Statement of Intent.** Discover the authors' goal for each chapter.
  - **Special Class Projects.** Find numerous ideas for interesting and meaningful class projects. Check out the Icebreakers and activities relating to the Great Cookie Experiment with accompanying SPSS data files.
  - **Test Questions and Answers.** Application questions, short answer questions, and essay questions are specifically designed to test students' ability to comprehend research reports.
  - **Answers to the Interactive Critical Thinking Activity.** Suggested answers to the questions in the new Interactive Critical Thinking Activity are available to instructors. Students can either print or e-mail their responses directly to the instructor for testing or as a homework assignment.
  - **Self-Test PowerPoint Slides.** For each chapter, a series of 5 "test questions" relating to key concepts in the chapter are followed immediately by answers to the questions. The aim of these slides is not to evaluate student performance, but to offer an opportunity for students to obtain quick feedback about whether they have grasped important concepts. All the questions are "application" type questions, to enhance the likelihood that students will see the relevance of the concepts to clinical practice. We hope instructors will use the slides to clarify any misunderstandings and, importantly, to reward students with immediate positive feedback about newly acquired skills.
- **PowerPoint Presentations** offer the traditional summaries of key points in each chapter for use in class presentations. These slides are available in a format that permits easy adaptation and also include audience response questions that can be used on their own or are compatible with i-clicker and other audience response programs and devices.
- **Test Generator Questions** offer hundreds of multiple choice questions to aid instructors in assessing their students' understanding of the chapter content.
- **Image Bank** includes figures from the text and Chapter Supplements that you can include in your own class presentations.
- **Chapter Supplements** include additional information that instructors can use to further their students' understanding and knowledge of a specific topic.

It is our hope and expectation that the content, style, and organization of this eighth edition of *Essentials of Nursing Research* will be helpful to those students desiring to become skillful and thoughtful readers of nursing studies and to those wishing to enhance their clinical performance based on research findings. We also hope that all of the resources that we offer will help to develop an enthusiasm for the kinds of discoveries and knowledge that research can produce.

ACKNOWLEDGMENTS

Denise F. Polit, PhD, FAAN

Cheryl Tatano Beck, DNSc, CNM, FAAN

This eighth edition, like the previous seven editions, depended on the contribution of many generous people. Many faculty and students who used the text have made invaluable suggestions for its improvement, and to all of you we are very grateful. Suggestions were made to us both directly in personal interactions (mostly at the University of Connecticut and Griffith University in Australia) and via e-mail correspondence. In addition to all those who assisted us during the past three decades with the earlier editions, there are some who deserve special mention for this new work.

We would like to acknowledge the comments of the reviewers of the seventh edition of *Essentials*, whose anonymous feedback influenced our revisions. Several of the comments triggered several important changes, including the reorganization of the content, and for this we are indebted.

Other individuals made specific contributions. Although it would be impossible to mention all, we note with thanks the nurse researchers who shared their work with us as we developed examples, including work that in some cases was not yet published. We also extend our warm thanks to those who helped to turn the manuscript into a finished product. The staff at Lippincott Williams & Wilkins has been of tremendous assistance in the support they have given us over the years. We are indebted to Christina Burns and Helen Kogut and all the others behind the scenes for their fine contributions.

Finally, we thank our family, our loved ones, and our friends, who provided ongoing support and encouragement throughout this endeavor and who were tolerant when we worked long into the night, over weekends, and during holidays to get this eighth edition finished.

CONTENTS

CHAPTER SUPPLEMENTS AVAILABLE ON thePoint

part 1

Overview of Nursing Research and Its Role in Evidence-Based Practice

chapter 1

Introduction to Nursing Research in an Evidence-Based Practice Environment

LEARNING OBJECTIVES

On completing this chapter, you will be able to:

- Describe why research is important in nursing and discuss the need for evidence-based practice
- Describe broad historical trends and future directions in nursing research
- Describe alternative sources of knowledge for nursing practice
- Describe major characteristics of the positivist and constructivist paradigms, and discuss similarities and differences between the traditional scientific method (quantitative research) and constructivist methods (qualitative research)
- Identify several purposes of qualitative and quantitative research
- Define new terms in the chapter

KEY TERMS

Assumption
Cause-probing research
Clinical nursing research
Constructivist paradigm
Empirical evidence
Evidence-based practice
Generalizability
Paradigm
Positivist paradigm
Qualitative research
Quantitative research
Research methods
Scientific method
Systematic review

NURSING RESEARCH IN PERSPECTIVE

We know that many of you readers are not taking this course because you plan to become nurse researchers. Yet, we are also confident that many of you *will* participate in research-related activities during your careers, and virtually all of you will be expected to be research-savvy at a basic level. Although you may not yet appreciate the relevance of research to a career in nursing, we hope that you will come to see the value of nursing research during this course, and will be inspired by the efforts of the thousands of nurse researchers now working worldwide to develop better methods of patient care. You are embarking on a lifelong journey in which research will play an increasingly important role. We hope to prepare you to enjoy the voyage.

What Is Nursing Research?

You have already done a lot of research. When you use the Internet to find the "best deal" on a backpack you want, or on an airfare to visit a friend, you start with a question (Where can I get the best deal?), collect the information, and then come to a conclusion. This "everyday research" has much in common with formal research—but, of course, there are important differences, too.

As a formal enterprise, **research** is *systematic* inquiry that uses disciplined methods to answer questions and solve problems. The ultimate goal of formal research is to gain knowledge that would be useful for many people. **Nursing research** is systematic inquiry designed to develop trustworthy evidence about issues of importance to nurses and their clients. In this book, we emphasize **clinical nursing research**, that is, research designed to guide nursing practice. Clinical nursing research typically begins with questions stemming from practice problems—problems you may have already encountered.

Example of nursing research questions:

- Does a 6-month program of aerobic exercise result in improvements in executive function, global cognition, and quality of life in community-dwelling elders with mild or moderate Alzheimer's disease (Yu et al., 2012)?
- What are the experiences of people who suffer from facial lipoatrophy with regard to the reconstructive treatments they receive (Gagnon, 2012)?

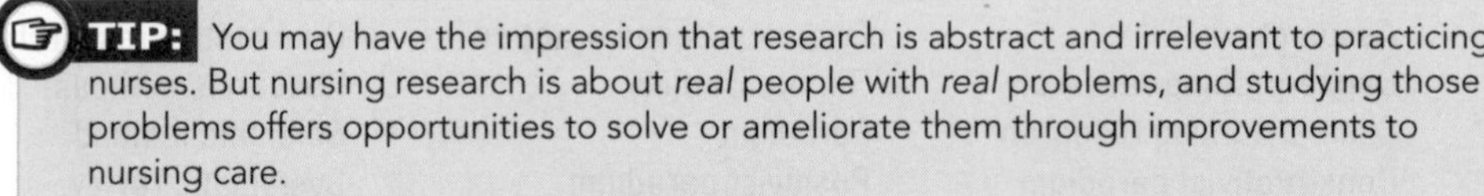

TIP: You may have the impression that research is abstract and irrelevant to practicing nurses. But nursing research is about *real* people with *real* problems, and studying those problems offers opportunities to solve or ameliorate them through improvements to nursing care.

The Importance of Research to Evidence-Based Nursing

Nursing has experienced profound changes in the past few decades. Nurses are increasingly expected to understand and undertake research, and to base their practice on evidence from research—that is, to adopt an **evidence-based practice (EBP)**. EBP, broadly defined, is the use of the best evidence in making patient care decisions, and such evidence typically comes from research conducted by nurses and other health care professionals. Nurse leaders recognize the need to base specific nursing decisions on evidence indicating that the decisions are clinically appropriate, cost-effective, and result in positive client outcomes.

In the United States and elsewhere, research plays an important role in terms of nursing credentialing and status. The American Nurses Credentialing Center—an arm of the American Nurses Association—has developed a Magnet Recognition Program to recognize health care organizations that provide high-quality nursing care. To achieve Magnet status, practice environments must demonstrate a sustained commitment to EBP and nursing research. Changes to nursing practice are happening every day because of EBP efforts.

Example of evidence-based practice:
Many clinical practice changes reflect the impact of research. For example, "kangaroo care," the holding of diaper-clad preterm infants skin-to-skin, chest-to-chest by parents, is now widely practiced in neonatal intensive care units (NICUs), but in the early 1990s only a minority of NICUs offered kangaroo care options. The adoption of this practice reflects good evidence that early skin-to-skin contact has clinical benefits, and no negative side effects. Some of this evidence came from rigorous studies by nurse researchers (e.g., Cong et al., 2009, 2011; Ludington-Hoe et al., 2006).

Roles of Nurses in Research

In the current EBP environment, every nurse is likely to engage in one or more activities along a continuum of research participation. At one end of the continuum are users (*consumers) of nursing research*—nurses who read research reports to keep up-to-date on findings that may affect their practice. EBP depends on well-informed nursing research consumers.

At the other end of the continuum are the *producers of nursing research*: nurses who actively design and undertake studies. At one time, most nurse researchers were academics who taught in schools of nursing, but research is increasingly being conducted by practicing nurses who want to find what works best for their clients.

Between these two end points on the continuum lie a variety of research activities in which nurses engage. Even if you never conduct a study, you may (1) help to develop an idea for a clinical study; (2) assist researchers by collecting research information; (3) offer advice to clients about participating in a study; (4) solve a clinical problem by searching for research evidence; or (5) discuss the implications of a new study in a **journal club** in your practice setting, which involves meetings to discuss research articles. In all the possible research-related activities, nurses who have some research skills are better able than those without them to make a contribution to nursing and to EBP. That means that, at some level, *you* will be contributing to the advancement of nursing.

Nursing Research: Past and Present

Most people would agree that research in nursing began with Florence Nightingale in the mid-19th century. Based on her skillful analysis of factors affecting soldier mortality and morbidity during the Crimean War, she was successful in bringing about some changes in nursing care and in public health. For many years after Nightingale's work, however, research was absent from the nursing literature. Studies began to appear in the early 1900s, but most concerned nurses' education.

Forces combined in the 1950s to put nursing research on an accelerating upswing in the United States. An increase in the number of nurses with advanced skills and degrees, an increase in the availability of research funding, and the establishment of the journal *Nursing Research* helped to propel nursing research in the mid-20th century. During the 1960s, practice-oriented research began to emerge, and research-oriented journals started publication in several countries. During the 1970s, there was a decided change in emphasis in nursing research from areas such as teaching and nurses themselves to improvements in client care. Nurses also began to pay attention to the utilization of research findings in nursing practice.

The 1980s brought nursing research to a new level of development. Of particular importance in the United States was the establishment in 1986 of the National Center for Nursing Research (NCNR) at the National Institutes of Health (NIH). The purpose of NCNR was to promote and financially support research projects and training relating to patient care. Nursing research was strengthened and given more visibility when NCNR was promoted to full institute status within the NIH: in 1993, the *National Institute of Nursing Research* (NINR) was established. The birth and expansion of NINR helped put nursing research more into the mainstream of research activities enjoyed by other health disciplines. Funding opportunities expanded in other countries as well.

The 1990s witnessed the birth of several more journals for nurse researchers, and specialty journals increasingly came to publish research articles. International cooperation around the issue of EBP in nursing also began to develop in the 1990s. For example, Sigma Theta Tau International sponsored the first international research utilization conference, in cooperation with the faculty of the University of Toronto, in 1998.

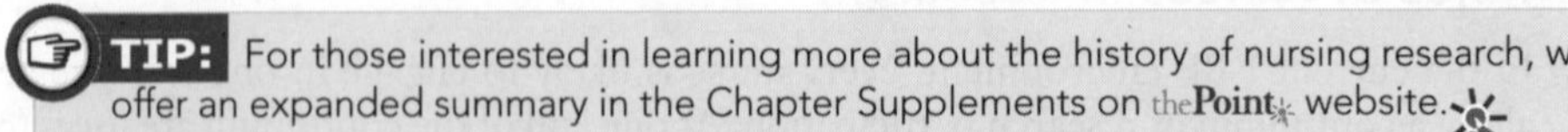
TIP: For those interested in learning more about the history of nursing research, we offer an expanded summary in the Chapter Supplements on thePoint website.

Future Directions for Nursing Research

Nursing research continues to develop at a rapid pace and will undoubtedly flourish in the 21st century. In 1986, NCNR had a budget of $16 million, whereas NINR funding in fiscal year 2011 was about $150 million. Among the trends foreseen for the near future are the following:

- *Continued focus on EBP*. Concerted efforts to use research findings in practice are sure to continue, and nurses at all levels will be encouraged to engage in evidence-based patient care. This means that improvements will be needed in the quality of nursing studies, and in nurses' skills in locating, understanding, critiquing, and using relevant study results.
- *Stronger evidence through confirmatory strategies*. Practicing nurses rarely adopt an innovation on the basis of poorly designed or isolated studies. Strong research designs are essential, and confirmation is usually needed through deliberate *replication* (i.e., repeating) of studies with different clients and in different clinical settings to ensure that the findings are robust.
- *Greater emphasis on systematic reviews*. **Systematic reviews** are a cornerstone of EBP and have assumed increasing importance in all health disciplines. Systematic reviews rigorously integrate research information on a topic so that conclusions about the state of evidence can be reached.
- *Expanded local research in health care settings*. Small studies designed to solve local problems will likely increase. This trend will be reinforced as more hospitals apply for (and are recertified for) Magnet status in the United States and in other countries.
- *Expanded dissemination of research findings*. The Internet has had a big impact on the dissemination of research information, which in turn helps to promote EBP. Through technological advances, information about innovations and research findings can be communicated more widely and more quickly than ever before.

- *Increased focus on cultural issues and health disparities*. The issue of health disparities has emerged as a central concern in nursing and other health disciplines, and this in turn has raised consciousness about the cultural sensitivity of health interventions. There is growing awareness that research must be sensitive to the health beliefs, behaviors, epidemiology, and values of culturally and linguistically diverse populations.

What are nurse researchers likely to be studying in the future? Although there is tremendous diversity in research interests, research priorities have been articulated by NINR, Sigma Theta Tau International, and other nursing organizations. As but one example, NINR's 2010 budget request identified three broad areas of research emphasis: promoting health and preventing disease; symptom management, self-management, and caregiving; and end-of-life research (NINR website: http://ninr.nih.gov/ninr/).

TIP: All websites cited in this chapter, plus additional websites with useful content relating to the foundations of nursing research, are in the Internet Resources on thePoint website. This will allow you to simply use the "Control/Click" feature to go directly to the website, without having to type in the URL and risk a typographical error. Websites corresponding to the content of most chapters of the book are also in the Internet Resources on thePoint website.

Sources of Evidence for Nursing Practice

Nurses make clinical decisions based on a large repertoire of knowledge. As a nursing student, you are gaining skills on how to practice nursing from your instructors, textbooks, and clinical placements. When you become a registered nurse (RN), you will continue to learn from other nurses and health care professionals. Because evidence is constantly evolving, learning about best-practice nursing will persist throughout your career.

Some of what you have learned thus far is based on systematic research, but much of it is not. What *are* the sources of evidence for nursing practice? Where does knowledge for practice come from? Until fairly recently, knowledge primarily was handed down from one generation to the next based on clinical experience, trial and error, tradition, and expert opinion. These alternative sources of knowledge are different from research-based information.

Tradition and Authority

Within nursing, certain beliefs are accepted as truths—and certain practices are accepted as effective—simply based on custom. Tradition may, however, undermine effective problem solving. There is growing concern that many nursing actions are based on tradition, custom, and "unit culture" rather than on sound evidence. Another common source of knowledge is an authority, a person with specialized expertise. Reliance on authorities (such as nursing faculty or textbook authors) is unavoidable. Like tradition, however, authorities as a source of information have limitations. Authorities are not infallible—particularly if their expertise is based primarily on personal experience; yet, their knowledge is often unchallenged.

Example of "myths" in nursing textbooks:
A recent study suggests that nursing textbooks may contain many "myths." In their analysis of 23 widely used undergraduate psychiatric nursing textbooks, Holman and colleagues (2010) found that all books contained at least one unsupported assumption (myth) about loss and grief—i.e., assumptions not supported by current research evidence. And, many evidence-based findings about grief and loss failed to be included in the textbooks.

TIP: The consequences of not using research-based evidence can be devastating. For example, from 1956 through the 1980s, Dr. Benjamin Spock published several editions of *Baby and Child Care*, a parental guide that sold over 19 million copies worldwide. As an authority figure, he wrote the following advice: "I think it is preferable to accustom a baby to sleeping on his stomach from the beginning if he is willing." (Spock, 1979, p. 164). Research has clearly demonstrated that this sleeping position is associated with heighted risk of sudden infant death syndrome (SIDS). In their systematic review of evidence, Gilbert and colleagues (2005) wrote, "Advice to put infants to sleep on the front for nearly half a century was contrary to evidence from 1970 that this was likely to be harmful" (p. 874). They estimated that if medical advice had been guided by research evidence, more than 60,000 infant deaths might have been prevented.

Clinical Experience and Trial and Error

Clinical experience is a functional source of knowledge. Yet, personal experience has limitations as a source of evidence for practice because each nurse's experience is too narrow to be generally useful, and personal experiences are often colored by biases. Trial and error, a related source, involves trying alternatives successively until a solution to a problem is found. Trial and error can be practical, but the method tends to be haphazard and solutions may be idiosyncratic.

Assembled Information

In making clinical decisions, health care professionals also rely on information that has been assembled for various purposes. For example, local, national, and international *benchmarking data* provide information on such issues as the rates of using various procedures (e.g., rates of cesarean deliveries) or rates of clinical problems (e.g., nosocomial infections). *Quality improvement and risk data*, such as medication error reports, can be used to assess practices and determine the need for practice changes. Such sources offer some information that can be used in practice, but provide no mechanism to actually guide improvements.

Disciplined Research

Disciplined research is considered the best method of acquiring reliable knowledge that humans have developed. Evidence-based health care compels nurses to base their clinical practice to the extent possible on rigorous research-based findings rather than on tradition, authority, intuition, or personal experience—although nursing will always remain a rich blend of art and science.

PARADIGMS AND METHODS FOR NURSING RESEARCH

The questions that nurse researchers ask, and the methods they use to answer their questions, spring from a researcher's view of how the world "works." In research parlance, a **paradigm** is a world view, a general perspective on the world's complexities. Disciplined inquiry in nursing has been conducted mainly within two broad paradigms. This section describes the two paradigms and outlines the research methods associated with them.

The Positivist Paradigm

The paradigm that dominated nursing research for decades is called *positivism*. Positivism is rooted in 19th century thought, guided by such philosophers as Newton and Locke.

TABLE 1.1 Major Assumptions of the Positivist and Constructivist Paradigms

Type of Assumption	Positivist Paradigm	Constructivist Paradigm
The nature of reality	Reality exists; there is a real world driven by real natural causes	Reality is multiple and subjective, mentally constructed by individuals
Relationship between researcher and those being researched	The researcher is independent from those being researched	The researcher interacts with those being researched; findings are the creation of the interactive process
The role of values in the inquiry	Values and biases are to be held in check; objectivity is sought	Subjectivity and values are inevitable and desirable
Best methods for obtaining evidence	• Deductive processes→ hypotheses testing • Emphasis on discrete, specific concepts • Focus on the objective and quantifiable • Corroboration of researchers' predictions • Fixed, prespecified design • Controls over context • Measured, quantitative information • Statistical analysis • Seeks generalizations	• Inductive processes→ hypothesis generation • Emphasis on the whole • Focus on the subjective and nonquantifiable • Emerging insight grounded in participants' experiences • Flexible, emergent design • Context-bound, contextualized • Narrative information • Qualitative analysis • Seeks in-depth understanding

Positivism is a reflection of a broader cultural movement (*modernism*) that emphasizes the rational and the scientific.

As shown in Table 1.1, a fundamental assumption of positivists is that there is a reality *out there* that can be studied and known. (An **assumption** is a principle that is believed to be true without verification). Adherents of positivism assume that nature is ordered and regular, and that a reality exists independent of human observation. In other words, the world is assumed not to be merely a creation of the human mind. The related assumption of *determinism* refers to the positivists' belief that phenomena are not haphazard, but rather have antecedent causes. If a person has a stroke, the scientist in a positivist tradition assumes that there must be one or more reasons that can be potentially identified. Within the **positivist paradigm**, much research activity is aimed at understanding the underlying causes of natural phenomena.

TIP: In this chapter, we often mention *phenomena.* What are phenomena? In a research context, *phenomena* are those things in which researchers are interested—such as a health event (e.g., a patient fall), a health outcome (e.g., pain), or a health experience (e.g., living with chronic pain).

Because of their belief in objective reality, positivists prize objectivity. Their approach involves the use of orderly, disciplined procedures with tight controls over the research situation to test hunches about the nature of phenomena being studied and relationships among them.

Strict positivist thinking has been challenged and undermined, and few researchers adhere to the tenets of pure positivism. Postpositivists still believe in reality and seek to understand it, but they recognize the impossibility of total objectivity. Yet, they see objectivity as a goal and strive to be as neutral and unbiased as possible. Postpositivists also appreciate the barriers to knowing reality with certainty, and therefore seek *probabilistic* evidence—i.e., learning what the true state of a phenomenon *probably* is, with a high degree of likelihood. This modified positivist position remains a dominant force in nursing research. For the sake of simplicity, we refer to it as positivism.

The Constructivist Paradigm

The **constructivist paradigm** (sometimes called the *naturalistic paradigm*) began as a countermovement to positivism with writers such as Weber and Kant. The constructivist paradigm is a major alternative system for conducting research in nursing. Table 1.1 compares four major assumptions of the positivist and constructivist paradigms.

For the naturalistic inquirer, reality is not a fixed entity but rather a construction of the people participating in the research; reality exists within a context, and many constructions are possible. Naturalists take the position of relativism: if there are multiple interpretations of reality that exist in people's minds, then there is no process by which the ultimate truth or falsity of the constructions can be determined.

The constructivist paradigm assumes that knowledge is maximized when the distance between the inquirer and participants in the study is minimized. The voices and interpretations of those under study are crucial to understanding the phenomenon of interest, and subjective interactions are the best way to access them. Findings from a constructivist inquiry are the product of the interaction between the inquirer and the participants.

Paradigms and Methods: Quantitative and Qualitative Research

Research methods are the techniques researchers use to structure a study and to gather and analyze relevant information. The two paradigms correspond to different methods of developing evidence. A key methodologic distinction is between **quantitative research**, which is most closely allied with positivism, and **qualitative research**, which is associated with constructivist inquiry—although positivists sometimes undertake qualitative studies, and constructivist researchers sometimes collect quantitative information. This section gives an overview of the methods linked to the two alternative paradigms.

The Scientific Method and Quantitative Research

The traditional, positivist **scientific method** involves using a set of orderly procedures to gather information. Quantitative researchers typically move in a systematic fashion from the definition of a problem to the solution of the problem. By *systematic*, we mean that investigators progress through a series of steps, according to a prespecified plan. Quantitative researchers use objective methods designed to control the research situation with the goal of minimizing *bias* and maximizing validity.

Quantitative researchers gather **empirical evidence**—evidence that is rooted in objective reality and gathered directly or indirectly through the senses rather than through personal beliefs or hunches. Evidence for a quantitative study is gathered systematically, using formal instruments to collect needed information. Usually (but not always) the information is **quantitative**—that is, numeric information that results from some type of formal measurement and that is analyzed statistically. Quantitative researchers strive to go beyond the specifics of a research situation; the ability to generalize research findings to individuals other than those who took part in the study (referred to as **generalizability**) is an important goal.

The traditional scientific method has been used productively by nurse researchers studying a wide range of questions. Yet, there are important limitations. For example, quantitative researchers must deal with problems of *measurement*. To study a phenomenon, scientists must measure it, that is, attach numeric values that express quantity. For example, if the phenomenon of interest were patient stress, researchers would want to assess if stress is high or low, or higher under certain conditions or for some people. Physiologic phenomena like blood pressure and temperature can be measured with accuracy and precision, but the same cannot be said of most psychological phenomena, such as stress or resilience.

Another issue is that nursing research focuses on human beings, who are inherently complicated and diverse. The traditional scientific method typically focuses on a relatively small aspect of human experiences (e.g., weight gain, depression) in a single study. Complexities tend to be controlled and, if possible, eliminated rather than studied directly, and this narrowness of focus can sometimes obscure insights. Relatedly, quantitative research within the positivist paradigm has sometimes been accused of a narrowness and inflexibility of vision that does not capture the full breadth of human experience.

TIP: Students often find quantitative studies more intimidating and difficult to read and understand than qualitative ones. Try not to worry too much about the jargon at first—remember that each study has a *story* to tell, and grasping the main point of the story is what is initially important.

Constructivist Methods and Qualitative Research

Researchers in constructivist traditions emphasize the inherent complexity of humans, their ability to shape and create their own experiences, and the idea that truth is a composite of realities. Consequently, constructivist studies are heavily focused on understanding the human experience as it is lived, through the careful collection and analysis of **qualitative** materials that are narrative and subjective.

Researchers who reject the traditional scientific method believe that a major limitation is that it is *reductionist*—that is, it reduces human experience to only the few concepts under investigation, and those concepts are defined in advance by the researcher rather than emerging from the experiences of those under study. Constructivist researchers tend to emphasize the dynamic, holistic, and individual aspects of human life and try to capture those aspects in their entirety, within the context of those who are experiencing them.

Flexible, evolving procedures are used to capitalize on findings that emerge during the study, which typically take place in naturalistic settings. The collection of information and its analysis typically progress concurrently. As researchers sift through information, insights are gained, new questions emerge, and further evidence is sought to confirm the insights. Through an inductive process (going from specifics to the general), researchers integrate information to develop a theory or description that illuminates the phenomena under observation.

Constructivist studies yield rich, in-depth information that can potentially clarify the varied dimensions of a complicated phenomenon. Findings from qualitative research are typically grounded in the real-life experiences of people with first-hand knowledge of a phenomenon. Nevertheless, the approach has several limitations. Human beings are used directly as the instrument through which information is gathered, and humans are highly intelligent—but fallible—tools. The subjectivity that enriches the analytic insights of skillful researchers can yield trivial "findings" among less competent ones.

Another potential limitation involves the subjectivity of constructivist inquiry, which sometimes raises concerns about the idiosyncratic nature of the conclusions. Would two constructivist researchers studying the same phenomenon in similar settings arrive at similar conclusions? The situation is further complicated by the fact that most constructivist studies involve a small group of participants. Thus, the generalizability of findings from constructivist inquiries is an issue of potential concern.

 **TIP:** Researchers often do *not* discuss or even mention the underlying paradigm of their studies in their reports. The paradigm provides the context, without being explicitly referenced.

Multiple Paradigms and Nursing Research

Paradigms are lenses that help to sharpen researchers' focus on phenomena of interest, not blinders that limit intellectual curiosity. We think that the emergence of alternative paradigms for studying nursing problems is a healthy and desirable trend that can maximize the breadth of new evidence for practice. Nursing knowledge would be thin if it were not for the rich array of methods available in the two paradigms—methods that are often complementary in their strengths and limitations.

We have emphasized differences between the two paradigms and associated methods so that distinctions would be easy to understand. It is equally important, however, to note that these two paradigms have many features in common, some of which are mentioned here:

- *Ultimate goals*. The ultimate aim of disciplined research, regardless of paradigm, is to answer questions and solve problems. Both quantitative and qualitative researchers seek to capture the truth with regard to an aspect of the world in which they are interested.
- *External evidence*. Although the word *empiricism* has come to be allied with the classic scientific method, researchers in both traditions gather and analyze evidence empirically, that is, through their senses.
- *Reliance on human cooperation*. Evidence for nursing research comes primarily from humans, and so human cooperation is essential in both qualitative and quantitative research. To understand people's characteristics and experiences, researchers must persuade them to participate in the study *and* to speak candidly.
- *Ethical constraints*. Research with human beings is guided by ethical principles that sometimes interfere with research goals. Ethical dilemmas often confront researchers, regardless of paradigms or methods.
- *Fallibility*. Virtually all studies have limitations. Every research question can be addressed in different ways, and inevitably there are tradeoffs. Financial constraints are often an issue, but limitations exist even in well-funded research. This means that *no single study can ever definitively answer a research question*. The fallibility of any single study makes it important to understand and critique researchers' methods when evaluating evidence quality.

Thus, despite philosophic and methodologic differences, researchers using the traditional scientific method or constructivist methods often share basic goals and face many similar constraints and challenges. The selection of an appropriate method depends on researchers' philosophy and world view, but also on the research question. If a researcher asks, "What are the effects of cryotherapy on nausea and oral mucositis in patients undergoing chemotherapy?" the researcher needs to examine effects through the careful quantitative assessment of patients. On the other hand, if a researcher asks, "What is the process by which parents learn to cope with the death of a child?" the researcher would be hard pressed to quantify such a process. Personal world views of researchers help to shape their questions.

In reading about the alternative paradigms, you likely were more attracted to one of the two paradigms—the one that corresponds most closely to your view of the world. It is important, however, to learn about and respect both approaches to disciplined inquiry, and to recognize their respective strengths and limitations. In this textbook, we describe methods associated with both qualitative and quantitative research in an effort to help you become *methodologically bilingual.*

HOW-TO-TELL TIP: How can you tell if a study is qualitative or quantitative? As you progress through this book, you should be able to identify most studies as qualitative versus quantitative based simply on the study's title, or based on terms in the summary at the beginning of an article. At this point, though, it may be easiest to distinguish the two types of studies based on how many numbers appear in the article, especially in tables. Qualitative studies may have no tables with quantitative information, or only one numeric table describing participants' characteristics (e.g., the percentage who were male or female). Quantitative studies typically have several tables with numbers and statistical information. Qualitative studies often have "word tables" or diagrams and figures illustrating processes inferred from the narrative information gathered.

THE PURPOSES OF NURSING RESEARCH

Why do nurses do research? The general purpose is to answer questions or solve problems of relevance to nursing. Beyond this broad description, several different systems have been devised to classify different goals. We describe two such classification systems—not because it is important for you to categorize a study as having one purpose or the other, but rather because this will help us to illustrate the broad range of questions that have intrigued nurses, and to further show differences between qualitative and quantitative inquiry.

TIP: Sometimes a distinction is made between basic and applied research. *Basic research* is appropriate for discovering general principles of human behavior and biophysiologic processes; *applied research* is designed to indicate how these principles can be used to solve problems in nursing practice.

Research to Achieve Varying Levels of Explanation

One way to classify research purposes concerns the extent to which studies are designed to provide explanations. A fundamental distinction that is especially relevant in quantitative research is between studies whose primary goal is to *describe* phenomena, and those that are **cause probing**—that is, studies designed to illuminate the underlying causes of phenomena.

Using a descriptive/explanatory framework, the specific purposes of nursing research include identification, description, exploration, prediction/control, and explanation. When researchers state their study purpose, they often use these terms (e.g., The purpose of this study was to *explore*....). For each purpose, various types of questions are addressed—some more amenable to qualitative than to quantitative inquiry, and vice versa.

Identification and Description

Qualitative researchers sometimes study phenomena about which little is known. In some cases, so little is known that the phenomenon has yet to be clearly identified or named or

TABLE 1.2 Purposes on the Descriptive–Explanatory Continuum, and Types of Research Questions

Purpose	Types of Questions: Quantitative Research	Types of Questions: Qualitative Research
Identification		What is this phenomenon? What is its name?
Description	How prevalent is the phenomenon? How often does the phenomenon occur?	What are the dimensions or characteristics of the phenomenon? What is important about the phenomenon?
Exploration	What factors are related to the phenomenon? What are the antecedents of the phenomenon?	What is the full nature of the phenomenon? What is really going on here? What is the process by which the phenomenon evolves?
Prediction and Control	If phenomenon X occurs, will phenomenon Y follow? Can the phenomenon be prevented or controlled?	
Explanation	What is the underlying cause of the phenomenon? Does the theory explain the phenomenon?	Why does the phenomenon exist? What does the phenomenon mean? How did the phenomenon occur?

has been inadequately defined. The in-depth, probing nature of qualitative research is well suited to answering such questions as, "What is this phenomenon?" and "What is its name?" (Table 1.2). In quantitative research, by contrast, researchers begin with a phenomenon that has been previously studied or defined.

Qualitative example of identification:
Rosedale (2009) studied the experiences of women after breast cancer treatment. She identified, through in-depth conversations with 13 women, descriptions of intense loneliness that she identified as *survivor loneliness*.

Description of phenomena is an important purpose of research. In descriptive studies, researchers count, delineate, and classify. Nurse researchers have described a wide variety of phenomena, such as patients' stress, health beliefs, and so on. Quantitative description focuses on the prevalence, size, and measurable aspects of phenomena. Qualitative researchers describe the nature, dimensions, and salience of phenomena, as shown in Table 1.2.

Quantitative example of description:
Covelli and colleagues (2012) described the prevalence of biologic measures of hypertension risk (e.g., elevated salivary cortisol, cardiovascular reactivity) among African American adolescents.

Exploration

Exploratory research begins with a phenomenon of interest; but rather than simply describing it, exploratory researchers examine the nature of the phenomenon, the manner in which it is manifested, and other factors to which it is related—including factors that might be *causing* it. For example, a *descriptive* quantitative study of patients' preoperative stress might document the degree of stress that patients experience. An *exploratory* study might ask: What factors increase or lower a patient's stress? Is a patient's stress related to nurses' behaviors or to the patient's age? Qualitative methods can be used to explore the nature of little understood phenomena and to shed light on the ways in which a phenomenon is expressed.

Qualitative example of exploration:

Overgaard and colleagues (2012) explored the illness experiences and vocational adjustments of patients with acute heart failure who had surgical implantation of a left ventricular assist device.

Explanation

Explanatory research seeks to understand the underlying causes or full nature of a phenomenon. In quantitative research, *theories* or prior findings are used deductively to generate hypothesized explanations that are then tested. Qualitative researchers search for explanations about how or why a phenomenon exists or what a phenomenon means as a basis for *developing* a theory that is grounded in rich, in-depth, experiential evidence.

Quantitative example of explanation:

Liu et al. (2012) tested a theoretical model to explain family caregiving of older Chinese people with dementia. The model purported to explain how caregiving appraisal, coping, perceived social support, and familism influence the impact of caregiving stressors on the psychological health of caregivers.

Prediction and Control

Many phenomena defy explanation, yet often it is possible to predict or control them based on research evidence. For example, research has shown that the incidence of Down syndrome in infants increases with maternal age. We can predict that a woman aged 40 years is at higher risk of bearing a child with Down syndrome than a woman aged 25 years. We can partially control the outcome by educating women about the risks and offering amniocentesis to women older than 35 years of age. The ability to predict and control in this example does not rely on an explanation of what *causes* older women to be at a higher risk. In many quantitative studies, prediction and control are key goals. Although explanatory studies are powerful, studies whose purpose is prediction and control are also critical to EBP.

Quantitative example of prediction:

Lilja and colleagues (2012) conducted a study to assess whether depressive mood in women at childbirth predicted their mood and quality of their relationship with their infant and partner at 12 months postpartum.

Research Purposes Linked to EBP

Another system for classifying studies has emerged in efforts to communicate EBP-related purposes (e.g., DiCenso et al., 2005; Guyatt et al., 2008; Melnyk & Fineout-Overholt, 2011). Table 1.3 identifies some of the questions relevant for each EBP purpose, and offers an actual nursing research example. In this classification scheme, the various purposes can best be addressed with quantitative research, except the last category (meaning/process), which requires qualitative research.

TABLE 1.3 Research Purposes Linked to EBP, and Key Research Questions

EBP Purpose	Key Research Question	Nursing Research Example
Therapy/ Intervention	What therapy or intervention will result in better health outcomes or prevent an adverse health outcome?	Hendrix and colleagues (2012) tested the effectiveness of an individualized caregiver intervention on caregivers' psychological well-being and cancer patients' physical symptoms.
Diagnosis/ Assessment	What test or assessment procedure will yield accurate diagnoses or assessments of critical patient conditions and outcomes?	Paulson-Conger and colleagues (2011) evaluated two methods of assessing pain in nonverbal critical care patients.
Prognosis	Does exposure to a disease or health problem increase the risk of subsequent adverse consequences?	Jalowiec and colleagues (2012) studied the prognosis of heart transplant recipients who had a sex-mismatched heart, compared to those with a sex-matched heart.
Etiology/ Cause/Harm	What factors cause or contribute to the risk of a health problem or disease?	Bowie and co-researchers (2012) studied whether parents' methods of regulating their children's emotions were associated with children's levels of anxiety and depression.
Meaning/ Process	What is the meaning of life experiences, and what is the process by which they unfold?	Wilkes and colleagues (2012) studied the meaning of impending fatherhood among prospective adolescent fathers.

Therapy, Treatment, or Intervention

Studies with a therapy purpose seek to identify effective treatments for ameliorating or preventing health problems. Such studies range from evaluations of highly specific treatments (e.g., comparing two types of cooling blankets for febrile patients) to complex multicomponent interventions designed to effect behavioral changes (e.g., nurse-led smoking cessation interventions). Intervention research plays a critical role in EBP.

Diagnosis and Assessment

Many nursing studies concern the rigorous development and evaluation of formal instruments to screen, diagnose, and assess patients and to measure clinical outcomes. High-quality instruments with documented accuracy are essential both for clinical practice and for research.

Prognosis

Studies of prognosis examine the consequences of a disease or health problem, explore factors that can modify the prognosis, and examine when (and for which types of people) the consequences are most likely. Such studies facilitate the development of long-term care plans for patients. They also provide valuable information for guiding patients to make beneficial lifestyle choices or to be vigilant for key symptoms.

Etiology (Causation) and Harm

It is difficult to prevent harm or treat health problems if we do not know what causes them. For example, there would be no smoking cessation programs if research had not provided firm evidence that smoking cigarettes causes or contributes to a range of health problems. Thus, determining the factors and exposures that affect or cause illness, mortality, or morbidity is an important purpose of many studies.

Meaning and Processes

Many health care activities (e.g., motivating people to comply with treatments, providing sensitive advice to patients, designing appealing interventions) can greatly benefit from understanding the clients' perspectives. Research that offers evidence about what health and illness mean to clients, what barriers they face to positive health practices, and what processes they experience in a transition through a health care crisis are important to evidence-based nursing practice.

TIP: Most of these EBP-related purposes (except *diagnosis* and *meaning*) involve *cause-probing* research. For example, research on interventions focuses on whether an intervention *causes* improvements in key outcomes. Prognosis research asks if a disease or health condition *causes* subsequent adverse consequences. Etiology research seeks explanations about the underlying *causes* of health problems.

ASSISTANCE FOR CONSUMERS OF NURSING RESEARCH

We hope that this book will help you develop skills that will allow you to read, appraise, and use nursing studies—and to appreciate nursing research. In each chapter, we present information relating to methods used by nurse researchers and provide guidance in several ways. First, we offer tips on what you can expect to find in actual research articles, identified by the icon. There are also special "how-to-tell" tips (identified with the icon) that help with some potentially confusing issues in research articles. Second, we include guidelines for critiquing various aspects of a study. The guiding questions in Box 1.1 are designed to assist you in using the information in this chapter in a preliminary assessment of a research article. And third, we offer opportunities to apply your new skills. The critical thinking activities at the end of each chapter guide you through appraisals of real research examples (some of which are presented in their entirety in the appendix) of both qualitative and quantitative studies. These activities also challenge you to think about how the findings from these studies could be used in nursing practice. Answers to many of these questions are available on thePoint website. The full journal article for studies identified with are also available on thePoint website.

BOX 1.1 Questions for a Preliminary Overview of a Research Report

1. How relevant is the research problem to the actual practice of nursing?
2. Is the research quantitative or qualitative?
3. What is the underlying purpose (or purposes) of the study—identification, description, exploration, explanation, or prediction/control? Does the purpose correspond to an EBP focus such as therapy/treatment, diagnosis, prognosis, etiology/harm, or meaning?
4. What might be some clinical implications of this research? To what type of people and settings is the research most relevant? If the findings are accurate, how might *I* use the results of this study?

RESEARCH EXAMPLES WITH CRITICAL THINKING EXERCISES

We conclude with a brief description of a quantitative and a qualitative nursing study.

Examples 1 and 2 below are also featured in our *Interactive Critical Thinking Activity* on thePoint website where you can easily record, print, and e-mail your responses to the related questions.

EXAMPLE 1 ● Quantitative Research

Study: Improving hospice through systematic assessment (McMillan et al., 2011).

Study Purpose: The purpose of the study was to test whether providing information from systematic assessments about patient-caregiver hospice dyads to interdisciplinary teams (IDTs) (e.g., teams of nurses, physicians, social workers) is effective in improving hospice outcomes.

Study Methods: The IDTs planning care for newly admitted hospice dyads were assigned to one of two groups: (1) those caring for dyads after receiving information from standardized assessments regarding the patient's and caregiver's depression, symptoms and needs, and quality of life, and (2) those caring for dyads as usual, without routinely receiving assessment information. There were 338 dyads in the special group, and 371 in the usual care group. For all dyads, information regarding depression, quality of life, and symptom distress was obtained on admission, and then 1 week after the first two IDT meetings in which the dyads were discussed.

Key Findings: The researchers found that patients in the special intervention group had lower levels of depression than those in the usual care group at the end of the study. Quality of life improved over time in both the intervention and usual care groups.

Conclusions: McMillan and colleagues concluded that the IDT's knowledge regarding patient and caregiver depression assessments may have improved the care the team provided because depression is not normally a focus of hospice staff.

CRITICAL THINKING EXERCISES

1. Answer the relevant questions from Box 1.1 on page 15 regarding this study.
2. Also consider the following targeted questions:
   a. Why do you think quality of life improved over time in both the intervention and usual-care groups?
   b. Could this study have been undertaken as a qualitative study? Why or why not?

EXAMPLE 2 ● Qualitative Research

Study: Experiences of self-blame and stigmatization for self-infliction among individuals living with chronic obstructive pulmonary disease (COPD) (Halding et al., 2011).

Study Purpose: The purpose of this study was to understand how patients with COPD experience daily life in a society with strong messages about tobacco control.

Study Methods: Eighteen men and women with COPD were recruited from two Norwegian pulmonary rehabilitation units. Patients participated in two in-depth interviews, each lasting 40 to 90 minutes. Most interviews were conducted in the patients' homes. The interviews, which were audiotaped and then transcribed, focused on what the patients' day-to-day experiences with COPD were like.

Key Findings: Participants spontaneously brought up the topics of smoking, blame, and guilt. The overarching theme that emerged in the analysis of the interviews was *Exiled in the world of the healthy*. The participants experienced feelings of disgrace, self-blame, and lack of support from their social network and health care professionals, reflecting perceptions that COPD is self-inflicted.

Conclusions: The researchers noted the challenge of how to combine health advice on smoking cessation with nonblaming psychosocial support throughout the course of COPD.

CRITICAL THINKING EXERCISES

1. Answer the relevant questions from Box 1.1 on page 15 regarding this study.
2. Also consider the following targeted questions, which may assist you in assessing aspects of the study's merit:
   a. Why do you think that the researchers audiotaped and transcribed their in-depth interviews with study participants?
   b. Do you think it would have been appropriate for the researchers to conduct this study using quantitative research methods? Why or why not?

EXAMPLE 3 ● Quantitative Research in Appendix A

- Read the abstract and the introduction from Howell and colleagues' (2007) study ("Anxiety, anger, and blood pressure in children") in Appendix A on pages 395–402.

CRITICAL THINKING EXERCISES

1. Answer the relevant questions from Box 1.1 on page 15 regarding this study.
2. Also consider the following targeted questions:
   a. Could this study have been undertaken as a qualitative study? Why or why not?
   b. Who helped to pay for this research? (This information appears at the end of the report.)

EXAMPLE 4 ● Qualitative Research in Appendix B

- Read the abstract and the introduction from Beck and Watson's (2010) study ("Subsequent childbirth after a previous traumatic birth") in Appendix B on pages 403–412.

CRITICAL THINKING EXERCISES

1. Answer the relevant questions from Box 1.1 on page 15 regarding this study.
2. Also consider the following targeted questions:
   a. What gap in the existing research was the study designed to fill?
   b. Was Beck and Watson's study conducted within the positivist paradigm or the constructivist paradigm? Provide a rationale for your choice.

WANT TO KNOW MORE? A wide variety of resources to enhance your learning and understanding of this chapter are available on thePoint.

- Interactive Critical Thinking Activity
- Chapter Supplement on The History of Nursing Research
- Answers to the Critical Thinking Exercises for Examples 3 and 4
- Student Review Questions
- Full-text online
- Internet Resources with useful websites for Chapter 1

Additional study aids including eight journal articles and related questions are also available in *Study Guide for Essentials of Nursing Research, 8e.*

SUMMARY POINTS

- **Nursing research** is systematic inquiry to develop evidence on problems of importance to nurses.
- Nurses in various settings are adopting an **evidence-based practice (EBP)** that incorporates research findings into their decisions and interactions with clients.
- Knowledge of nursing research enhances the professional practice of all nurses—including both *consumers of research* (who read and evaluate studies) and *producers of research* (who design and undertake studies).
- Nursing research began with Florence Nightingale but developed slowly until its rapid acceleration in the 1950s. Since the 1980s, the focus has been on **clinical nursing research**—that is, on problems relating to clinical practice.
- The NINR, established at the U.S. NIH in 1993, affirms the stature of nursing research in the United States.
- Future emphases of nursing research are likely to include EBP projects, **replications** of research, research integration through **systematic reviews**, expanded dissemination efforts, and increased focus on health disparities.
- Disciplined research stands in contrast to other knowledge sources for nursing practice, such as tradition, authority, personal experience, and trial and error.
- Disciplined inquiry in nursing is conducted mainly within two broad **paradigms**—world views with underlying **assumptions** about reality: the positivist paradigm and the constructivist paradigm.
- In the **positivist paradigm**, it is assumed that there is an objective reality and that natural phenomena are regular and orderly. The related assumption of *determinism* refers to the belief that phenomena result from prior causes and are not haphazard.
- In the **constructivist paradigm**, it is assumed that reality is not a fixed entity but is rather a construction of human minds—and thus "truth" is a composite of multiple constructions of reality.
- **Quantitative research** (associated with positivism) involves the collection and analysis of numeric information. Quantitative research is typically conducted within the traditional **scientific method**, which is systematic and controlled. Quantitative researchers base their findings on **empirical evidence** (evidence collected by way of the human senses) and strive for **generalizability** beyond a single setting or situation.
- Constructivist researchers emphasize understanding human experience as it is lived through the collection and analysis of subjective, narrative materials using flexible procedures; this paradigm is associated with **qualitative research.**
- A fundamental distinction that is especially relevant in quantitative research is between studies whose primary intent is to *describe* phenomena and those that are **cause probing**—i.e., designed to illuminate underlying causes of phenomena. Specific purposes on the description/explanation continuum include identification, description, exploration, prediction/control, and explanation.
- Many nursing studies can also be classified in terms of a key EBP aim: therapy/treatment/intervention; diagnosis and assessment; prognosis; etiology and harm; and meaning and process.

REFERENCES FOR CHAPTER 1

Bowie, B., Carrere, S., Cooke, C., Valdivia, G., McAllister, B., & Doohan, E. (2012). The role of culture in parents' socialization of children's emotional development. *Western Journal of Nursing Research*, PubMed ID 20500623.

Cong, X., Ludington-Hoe, S., McCain, G., & Fu, P. (2009). Kangaroo care modifies preterm infant heart rate variability in response to heel stick pain. *Early Human Development, 85*, 561–567.

Cong, X., Ludington-Hoe, S., & Walsh, S. (2011). Randomized crossover trial of kangaroo care to reduce biobehavioral pain responses in preterm infants. *Biological Research for Nursing, 13*, 204–216.

Covelli, M. M., Wood, C., & Yarandi, H. (2012). Biologic measures as epidemiological indicators of risk for the development of hypertension in an African American adolescent population. *Journal of Cardiovascular Nursing, 27*, 476–484.

DiCenso, A., Guyatt, G., & Ciliska, D. (2005). *Evidence-based nursing: A guide to clinical practice*. St. Louis, MO: Elsevier Mosby.

Gagnon, M. (2012). Understanding the experience of reconstructive treatments from the perspective of people who suffer from facial lipoatrophy: A qualitative study. *International Journal of Nursing Studies* 2012;49(5):539–548.

Gilbert, R., Salanti, G., Harden, M., & See, S. (2005). Infant sleeping position and the sudden infant death syndrome: Systematic review of observational studies and historical review of recommendations from 1940 to 2002. *International Journal of Epidemiology, 34*, 874–887.

Guyatt, G., Rennie, D., Meade, M., & Cook, D. (2008). *Users' guide to the medical literature: Essentials of evidence-based clinical practice* (2nd ed.). New York: McGraw Hill.

Halding, A., Heggad, K., & Wahl, A. (2011). Experiences of self-blame and stigmatisation for self-infliction among individuals living with COPD. *Scandinavian Journal of Caring Sciences, 25*, 100–107.

Hendrix, C., Landerman, R., & Abernathy, A. (2012). Effects of an individualized caregiver training intervention on self-efficacy of cancer caregivers. *Western Journal of Nursing Research*, PubMed ID 21949091.

Holman, E., Perisho, J., Edwards, A., & Mlakar, N. (2010). The myths of coping with loss in undergraduate psychiatric nursing books. *Research in Nursing & Health, 33*, 486–499.

Jalowiec, A., Grady, K., & White-Williams, C. (2012). First-year clinical outcomes in sex-mismatched heart transplant recipients. *Journal of Cardiovascular Nursing, 27*, 519–527.

Lilja, G., Edhborg, M., & Nissen, E. (2012). Depressive mood in women at childbirth predicts their mood and relationship with infant and partner during the first year postpartum. *Scandinavian Journal of Caring Science, 26*(2), 245–253.

Liu, Y., Insel, K., Reed, P., & Crist, J. (2012). Family caregiving of older Chinese people with dementia: Testing a model. *Nursing Research, 61*, 39–50.

Ludington-Hoe, S., Johnson, M., Morgan, K., Lewis, T., Gutman, J., Wilson, P., et al. (2006). Neurophysiologic assessment of neonatal sleep organization: Preliminary results of a randomized, controlled trial of skin contact with preterm infants. *Pediatrics, 117*, 909–923.

McMillan, S., Small, B., & Haley, W. (2011). Improving hospice through systematic assessment. *Cancer Nursing, 34*, 89–97.

Melnyk, B. M., & Fineout-Overhold, E. (2011). *Evidence-based practice in nursing and healthcare: A guide to best practice* (2nd ed.). Philadelphia, PA: Lippincott Williams & Wilkins.

Overgaard, D., Kjeldgaard, H., & Egerod, I. (2012). Life in transition: A qualitative study of the illness experience and vocational adjustment of patients with left ventricular assist device. *Journal of Cardiovascular Nursing*, PubMed ID 21912269.

Paulson-Conger, M., Leske, J., Maidl, C., Hanson, A., & Dziadulewicz, L. (2011). Comparison of two pain assessment tools in nonverbal critical care patients. *Pain Management Nursing*, 12, 218–224.

Rosedale, M. (2009). Survivor loneliness of women following breast cancer. *Oncology Nursing Forum, 36*, 175–183.

Spock, B. (1979). *Baby and child care*. New York: Dutton Publishing.

Wilkes, L., Mannix, J., & Jackson, D. (2012). "I am going to be a dad": Experiences and expectations of adolescent and young adult expectant fathers. *Journal of Clinical Nursing, 21*, 180–188.

Yu, F., Nelson, N., Savik, K., Wyman, J., Dyksen, M., & Bronas, U. (2012). Affecting cognition and quality of life via aerobic exercise in Alzheimer's disease. *Western Journal of Nursing Research*, PubMed ID 21911546.

chapter

2 Fundamentals of Evidence-Based Nursing Practice

LEARNING OBJECTIVES

On completing this chapter, you will be able to:

- Distinguish research utilization (RU) and evidence-based practice (EBP), and discuss their current status within nursing
- Identify several resources available to facilitate EBP in nursing practice
- Identify several models for implementing EBP
- Discuss the five major steps in undertaking an EBP effort for individual nurses
- Identify the components of a well-worded clinical question and be able to frame such a question
- Discuss broad strategies for undertaking an EBP project at the organizational level
- Define new terms in the chapter

KEY TERMS

Clinical practice guideline
Cochrane Collaboration
Evidence hierarchy
Evidence-based practice
Implementation potential
Meta-analysis
Metasynthesis
Pilot test
Research utilization
Systematic review

Learning about research methods provides a foundation for evidence-based nursing practice (EBP). The emphasis in EBP is on identifying the best available research evidence and *integrating* it with other factors in making clinical decisions. Advocates of EBP do not minimize the importance of clinical expertise. Rather, they argue that evidence-based decision making should integrate best research evidence with clinical expertise, patient preferences, and local circumstances. EBP involves efforts to personalize evidence to fit a specific patient's needs and a particular clinical situation.

This book will help you to develop methodologic skills for reading research articles and evaluating research evidence. Before we elaborate on methodologic techniques, we discuss key aspects of EBP to further help you understand the key role that research now plays in nursing.

BACKGROUND OF EVIDENCE-BASED NURSING PRACTICE

This section provides a context for understanding EBP. Part of this context involves a closely related concept, research utilization.

Research Utilization

Research utilization (RU) is the use of findings from disciplined research in a practical application that is unrelated to the original research. In RU, the emphasis is on translating research findings into real-world applications. The starting point in RU is new evidence or a research-based innovation.

EBP is broader than RU because it integrates research findings with other factors. Whereas RU begins with the research itself (how can I put this innovation to good use in my clinical setting?), EBP starts with a clinical question (what does the evidence say is the best approach to solving this problem?).

The Research Utilization Continuum

RU begins with the emergence of new knowledge. Research is conducted and, over time, evidence on a topic accumulates. In turn, the evidence works its way into use—to varying degrees and at differing rates.

People who study the diffusion of ideas acknowledge a continuum in terms of the specificity of the use to which research findings are put. At one end of the continuum are clearly identifiable attempts to base specific actions on research findings (e.g., placing infants on their backs for sleeping to minimize the risk of sudden infant death syndrome). Yet, research findings can be used more diffusely, in a way that reflects cumulative awareness or understanding. Thus, a nurse may read a qualitative study describing *courage* among people with chronic illnesses as a dynamic process that includes efforts to accept reality and to develop problem-solving skills. The study may make the nurse more observant and sensitive in working with patients with chronic illnesses, but it may not lead to formal changes in clinical actions. The RU continuum suggests roles for both qualitative and quantitative research.

The History of Research Utilization in Nursing Practice

During the 1980s, RU emerged as an important buzz word, and several changes in nursing education and research were prompted by the desire to develop a knowledge base for nursing practice. In education, nursing schools began to include courses on research methods so that students would become skillful research consumers. In the research arena, there was a shift in focus toward clinical nursing problems.

At the same time, there were growing concerns about how infrequently research findings were actually used in delivering nursing care. Some of these concerns were based on studies that found that practicing nurses were unaware of or ignored important research findings. Recognition of the gap between research and practice led to formal attempts to bridge the gap. The best-known of several early RU projects is the *Conduct and Utilization of Research in Nursing (CURN) Project*, which was awarded to the Michigan Nurses' Association by the Division of Nursing in the 1970s. CURN aimed to increase nurses' use of research findings by disseminating research findings, facilitating organizational changes, and encouraging collaborative clinical research. CURN project staff saw RU as an organizational process requiring commitment by organizations that employ nurses (Horsley, Crane, & Bingle, 1978). The CURN project team concluded that RU by practicing nurses was feasible, but only if the research is relevant to practice and if the results are broadly disseminated.

During the 1980s and 1990s, many RU projects were undertaken. These projects involved attempts to change nursing practices based on research findings, and to evaluate the effects of the changes. Although studies continued to document a gap between research and practice, the findings suggested some improvements in nurses' utilization of research. During the 1990s, however, the call for RU began to be superseded by the push for EBP.

Evidence-Based Practice in Nursing

The EBP movement has had both advocates and critics. Supporters argue that EBP offers a solution for improving health care quality in a cost-constrained environment. In their view, a rational approach is needed to provide the best possible care to the most people, in the most cost-effective manner. Advocates also note that EBP provides a good framework for lifelong learning that is essential in an era of rapid clinical advances and the information explosion. Critics worry that EBP advantages are exaggerated and that clinical judgments and patient inputs are being devalued. They are also concerned that insufficient attention is being paid to qualitative research. Although there is a need for close scrutiny of how the EBP journey unfolds, health care professionals will likely follow an EBP path in the years ahead.

Overview of the Evidence-Based Practice Movement

One keystone of the EBP movement is the Cochrane Collaboration, which was founded in the United Kingdom based on work by British epidemiologist Archie Cochrane. Cochrane published an influential book in the 1970s that drew attention to the dearth of solid evidence about the effects of health care. He called for efforts to make research summaries about interventions available to health care providers. This eventually led to the development of the Cochrane Center in Oxford in 1993, and the international **Cochrane Collaboration**, with centers now established in locations throughout the world. Its aim is to help providers make good health care decisions by preparing and disseminating systematic reviews of the effects of health care interventions.

At about the same time that the Cochrane Collaboration began, a group from McMaster Medical School in Canada developed a clinical learning strategy called *evidence-based medicine*. The evidence-based medicine movement, pioneered by Dr. David Sackett, has broadened to the use of best evidence by *all* health care practitioners. EBP has been considered a major paradigm shift in health care education and practice. With EBP, skillful clinicians can no longer rely on a repository of memorized information, but rather must be adept in accessing, evaluating, and using new research evidence.

Types of Evidence and Evidence Hierarchies

There is no consensus about what constitutes usable evidence for EBP, but there is general agreement that findings from rigorous research are paramount. Yet, there is some debate about what constitutes "*rigorous*" research and what qualifies as "*best*" evidence.

Early in the EBP movement, there was a strong bias toward reliance on evidence from a type of study called a *randomized controlled trial* (RCT). This bias reflected the Cochrane Collaboration's initial focus on evidence about the effectiveness of therapies, rather than about broader health care questions. RCTs are especially well suited for drawing conclusions about the effects of health care interventions (see Chapter 9). The bias in ranking research approaches in terms of questions about effective therapies led to some resistance to EBP by nurses who felt that evidence from qualitative and non-RCT studies would be ignored.

Positions about the contribution of various types of evidence are less rigid than previously. Nevertheless, there are many published **evidence hierarchies** that purport to rank evidence sources according to the strength of the evidence they provide. We offer a modified evidence hierarchy that looks similar to others that are available in material on EBP, but ours illustrates that the ranking of evidence-producing strategies depends on the type of question being asked.

Figure 2.1 shows that systematic reviews are at the pinnacle of the hierarchy (level I), because the strongest evidence comes from careful syntheses of multiple studies. The next highest level (level II) depends on the nature of inquiry. For Therapy questions regarding the efficacy of a therapy or intervention (what works best for improving health outcomes?),

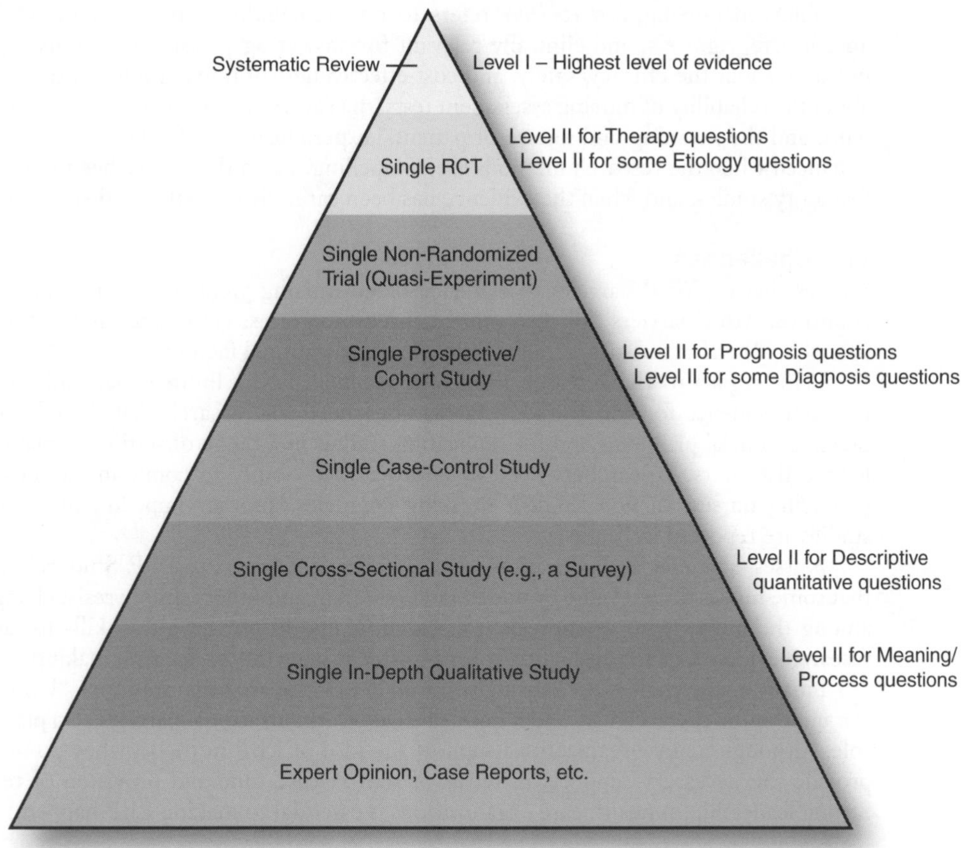

FIGURE 2.1 ● Evidence hierarchy: levels of evidence.

individual RCTs constitute level II evidence (systematic reviews of multiple RCTs are level I). Going down the "rungs" of the evidence hierarchy for Therapy questions results in less reliable evidence—for example, level III evidence comes from a type of study called quasi-experiment. In-depth qualitative studies are near the bottom, in terms of evidence regarding intervention effectiveness. (Terms in Fig. 2.1 will be discussed in later chapters.)

For a Prognosis question, by contrast, level II evidence comes from a single prospective cohort study, and level III is from a type of study called case-control (level I evidence is from a systematic review of cohort studies). Thus, contrary to what is often implied in discussions of evidence hierarchies, multiple hierarchies are a reality. If one is interested in best evidence for questions about Meaning, an RCT would be a poor source of evidence, for example. We have tried to portray the notion of multiple hierarchies in Figure 2.1, with information on the right indicating the type of *individual study* that would offer the best evidence (level II) for different questions. In all cases, appropriate systematic reviews are at the pinnacle. Information about different hierarchies for different types of cause-probing questions is addressed in Chapter 9.

Of course, *within* any level in an evidence hierarchy, evidence quality can vary considerably. For example, an individual RCT could be well designed, yielding strong level II evidence for Therapy questions, or it could be so flawed that the evidence would be weak.

Thus, in nursing, *best evidence* refers to research findings that are methodologically appropriate, rigorous, and clinically relevant for answering pressing questions—questions not only about the efficacy, safety, and cost effectiveness of nursing interventions, but also about the reliability of nursing assessment tests, the causes and consequences of health problems, and the meaning and nature of patients' experiences. Confidence in the evidence is enhanced when the research methods are compelling, when there have been multiple confirmatory studies, and when the evidence has been carefully evaluated and synthesized.

EBP Challenges

Studies that explored barriers to evidence-based nursing yielded similar results in many countries. Most barriers fall into one of three categories: (1) quality and nature of the research, (2) characteristics of nurses, and (3) organizational factors.

With regard to the research itself, one problem is the limited availability of strong research evidence for some practice areas. The need for research that directly addresses pressing clinical problems and for replicating studies in a range of settings remains a challenge. Also, nurse researchers need to improve their ability to communicate evidence to practicing nurses. In non-English speaking countries, another impediment is that most studies are reported in English.

Nurses' attitudes and education are also potential barriers to EBP. Studies have found that some nurses do not value or understand research, and others simply resist change. And, among the nurses who *do* appreciate research, many do not have the skills for accessing research evidence or for evaluating it for possible use in clinical decision making.

Finally, many challenges to using research in practice are organizational. "Unit culture" can undermine research use, and administrative or organizational barriers also play a major role. Although many organizations support the idea of EBP in theory, they do not always provide the necessary supports in terms of staff release time and provision of resources. Strong leadership in health care organizations is essential to making EBP happen.

RESOURCES FOR EVIDENCE-BASED PRACTICE

In this section we describe some of the resources that are available to support EBP and to address some of the challenges.

Preappraised Evidence

Research evidence comes in various forms, the most basic of which is from individual studies. *Primary studies* published in journals are not preappraised for quality and use in practice.

Preprocessed (preappraised) evidence is evidence that has been selected from primary studies and evaluated for use by clinicians. DiCenso and colleagues (2005) have described a hierarchy of preprocessed evidence. On the first rung above primary studies are synopses of single studies, followed by systematic reviews, and then synopses of systematic reviews. Clinical practice guidelines are at the top of the hierarchy. At each successive step in the hierarchy, there is greater ease in applying the evidence to clinical practice.

Synopses of systematic reviews and of single studies are available in evidence-based abstract journals. For example, *Evidence-Based Nursing*, published quarterly, presents critical summaries of studies and systematic reviews from hundreds of journals. The summaries include commentaries on the clinical implications of each reviewed study. Another journal-based resource is the "evidence digest" feature in each issue of *Worldviews on Evidence-Based Nursing*. In the remainder of this section, we focus on two important types of preappraised evidence: systematic reviews and clinical practice guidelines.

Systematic Reviews

EBP relies on meticulous integration of all key evidence on a topic so that well-grounded conclusions can be drawn about EBP questions. A systematic review is not just a literature review. A systematic review is in itself a methodical, scholarly inquiry that follows many of the same steps as those for other studies.

Systematic reviews can take various forms. One form is a narrative (qualitative) integration that merges and synthesizes findings, much like a rigorous literature review. For integrating evidence from quantitative studies, narrative reviews increasingly are being replaced by a type of systematic review known as a meta-analysis.

Meta-analysis is a technique for integrating quantitative research findings statistically. In essence, meta-analysis treats the findings from a study as one piece of information. The findings from multiple studies on the same topic are combined and then all of the information is analyzed statistically in a manner similar to that in a usual study. Thus, instead of study participants being the *unit of analysis* (the most basic entity on which the analysis focuses), individual studies are the unit of analysis in a meta-analysis. Meta-analysis provides an objective method of integrating a body of findings and of observing patterns that might not have been detected.

Example of a meta-analysis:
Nam and colleagues (2012) conducted a meta-analysis to analyze evidence on the effectiveness of culturally tailored diabetes education interventions in ethnic minorities with Type 2 diabetes. Integrating results from 12 intervention studies, the researchers concluded that such interventions are effective for improving glycemic control among ethnic minorities. (This study appears in its entirety in *Study Guide for Essentials of Nursing Research, 8e*).

For qualitative studies, integration may take the form of a **metasynthesis**. A metasynthesis, however, is distinct from a quantitative meta-analysis: a metasynthesis is less about reducing information and more about interpreting it.

Example of a metasynthesis:
Duggleby and colleagues (2012) undertook a metasynthesis of studies exploring the hope experience of older persons with chronic illness. Their metasynthesis of 20 qualitative studies identified five main themes that captured important concepts that emerged in the 20 studies.

Fortunately, systematic reviews are increasingly available. Such reviews are published in professional journals that can be accessed using standard literature search procedures (see Chapter 7), and are also available in databases that are dedicated to such reviews. In particular, the Cochrane Database of Systematic Reviews (CDSR) contains thousands of systematic reviews relating to health care interventions.

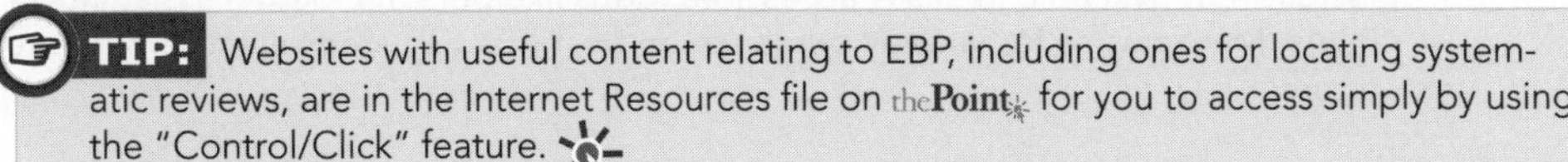
TIP: Websites with useful content relating to EBP, including ones for locating systematic reviews, are in the Internet Resources file on thePoint for you to access simply by using the "Control/Click" feature.

Clinical Practice Guidelines

Evidence-based **clinical practice guidelines** distill a body of evidence into a usable form. Unlike systematic reviews, clinical practice guidelines (which often are *based* on systematic reviews) give specific recommendations for evidence-based decision making. Guideline development typically involves the consensus of a group of researchers, experts, and clinicians. The use or adaptation of a clinical practice guideline is often an ideal focus for an EBP project.

Example of a nursing clinical practice guideline:
In 2009, the Registered Nurses Association of Ontario issued an evidence-based practice guideline on the care and management of ostomies. Developed by an interdisciplinary panel under the leadership of Kathryn Kozell, the guideline provides nurses with an evidence-based summary of strategies to assess and manage people with various types of ostomy.

Finding clinical practice guidelines can be challenging, because there is no single guideline repository. A standard search in bibliographic databases such as MEDLINE (see Chapter 7) will yield many references—but could yield a mixture of citations to not only the actual guidelines, but also to commentaries, implementation studies, and so on.

A recommended approach is to search in guideline databases, or through specialty organizations that have sponsored guideline development. A few of the many possible sources deserve mention. In the United States, nursing and health care guidelines are maintained by the National Guideline Clearinghouse (www.guideline.gov). In Canada, the Registered Nurses Association of Ontario (RNAO) (www.rnao.org/bestpractices) maintains information about clinical practice guidelines. Two sources in the United Kingdom are the Translating Research into Practice (TRIP) database and the National Institute for Clinical Excellence (NICE).

There are many topics for which practice guidelines have not yet been developed, but the opposite problem is also true: sometimes there are multiple guidelines on the same topic. Worse yet, because of differences in the rigor of guideline development and interpretation of evidence, different guidelines sometimes offer different or even conflicting recommendations (Lewis, 2001). Thus, those who wish to adopt clinical practice guidelines should appraise them to identify ones that are based on the strongest evidence, have been meticulously developed, are user-friendly, and are appropriate for local use or adaptation.

Several appraisal instruments are available to evaluate clinical practice guidelines, but one with broad support is the Appraisal of Guidelines Research and Evaluation (AGREE) Instrument (AGREE Collaboration, 2001; www.agreecollaboration.org). The AGREE instrument has ratings for 23 dimensions within six domains (e.g., scope and purpose, rigor of development, presentation). As examples, a dimension in the Scope and Purpose domain is: "The patients to whom the guideline is meant to apply are specifically described"; and one in the Rigor of Development domain is: "The guideline has been externally reviewed by experts prior to its publication." The AGREE tool should be applied to a guideline by a team of two to four appraisers.

 **TIP:** Clinical decision support tools based on research evidence are becoming increasingly available in easily accessible forms like personal digital assistants or PDAs. Mechanisms for speedy guidance on best practice are likely to proliferate in the future.

Models of the EBP Process

EBP models offer frameworks for designing and implementing EBP projects in practice settings. Some models focus on the use of research from the perspective of individual clinicians (e.g., the Stetler Model, one of the oldest models that originated as an RU model), but most focus on institutional EBP efforts (e.g., the Iowa Model). The many worthy EBP models are too numerous to list comprehensively, but include the following:

- ACE Star Model of Knowledge Transformation (Academic Center for EBP, 2009)
- Advancing Research and Clinical Practice Through Close Collaboration (ARCC) Model (Melnyk & Fineout-Overholt, 2011)
- Clinical Nurse Scholar Model (Schultz, 2005)
- Diffusion of Innovations Theory (Rogers, 2003)
- Iowa Model of Evidence-Based Practice to Promote Quality Care (Titler et al., 2001)
- Johns Hopkins Nursing EBP Model (Newhouse et al., 2005)
- Model for Change to Evidence-Based Practice (Rosswurm & Larabee, 1999)
- Promoting Action on Research Implementation in Health Services (PARiHS) Model, (Rycroft-Malone et al., 2002)
- Stetler Model of Research Utilization (Stetler, 2001)

For those wishing to follow a formal EBP model, the cited references should be consulted. Several are also nicely synthesized by Melnyk and Fineout-Overholt (2011). Each model offers different perspectives on how to translate research findings into practice, but several steps and procedures are similar across the models. We provide an overview of key activities and processes in EBP efforts, based on a distillation of common elements from the various models, in a subsequent section of this chapter. We rely especially heavily on the Iowa Model, a diagram for which is shown in Figure 2.2.

TIP: The most prominent of the EBP models have been the PARiHS model, the Stetler Model, the Johns Hopkins model, and the Iowa Model. Gawlinski and Rutledge (2008) offer suggestions for selecting an EBP model.

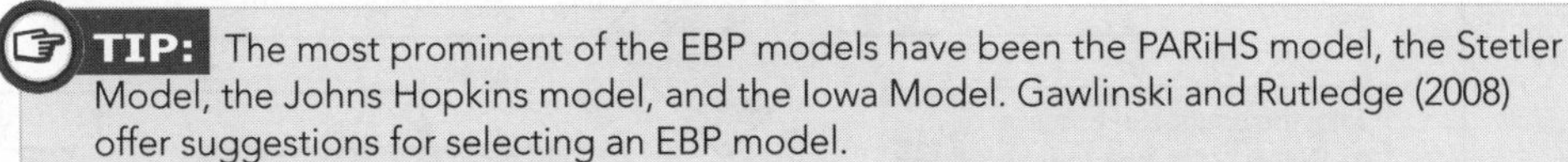

EBP IN INDIVIDUAL NURSING PRACTICE

This and the following section provide an overview of how research can be put to use in clinical settings. We first discuss strategies and steps for individual clinicians and then describe activities used by organizations or teams of nurses.

Clinical Scenarios and the Need for Evidence

Individual nurses make many decisions and are called upon to provide health care advice, and so they have ample opportunity to put research into practice. Here are four clinical scenarios that provide examples of such opportunities:

- Clinical Scenario 1. You work on an intensive care unit and notice that *Clostridium difficile* infection has become more prevalent among surgical patients in your hospital. You want to know if there is a reliable screening tool for assessing the risk of infection so that preventive measures could be initiated in a more timely and effective manner.
- Clinical Scenario 2. You work in an allergy clinic and notice how difficult it is for many children to undergo allergy scratch tests. You wonder if an interactive distraction intervention would help reduce children's pain when they are being tested for allergens.
- Clinical Scenario 3. You work in a rehabilitation hospital and one of your elderly patients, who had total hip replacement, tells you she is planning a long airplane trip.

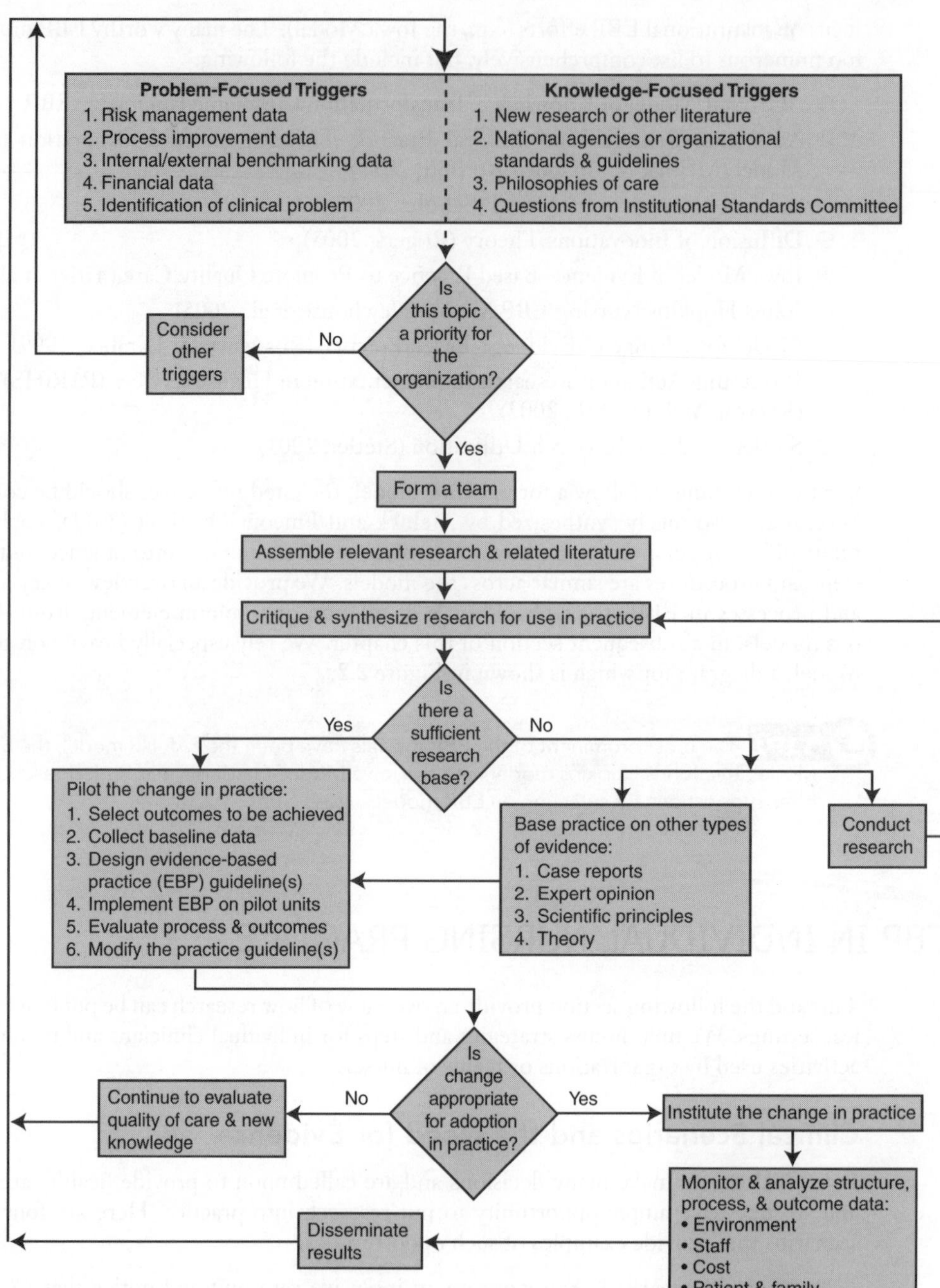

FIGURE 2.2 ● Iowa model of evidence-based practice to promote quality care. (Adapted from Titler, M. G., Kleiber, C., Steelman, V., Rakel, B., Budreau, G., Everett, L., et al. (2001). The Iowa Model of Evidence-Based Practice to Promote Quality Care. *Critical Care Nursing Clinics of North America*, *13*, 497–509.)

You know that a long plane ride will increase her risk of deep vein thrombosis and wonder if compression stockings are an effective in-flight treatment. You decide to look for the best possible evidence to answer this question.

- Clinical Scenario 4. You are caring for a hospitalized cardiac patient who tells you that he has sleep apnea. He confides in you that he is reluctant to undergo continuous positive airway pressure (CPAP) treatment because he worries it will hinder intimacy with his wife. You wonder if there is any evidence about what it is like to undergo CPAP treatment so that you can better understand how to address your patient's concerns.

In these and thousands of other clinical situations, research evidence can be put to good use to improve nursing care. Some situations might lead to unit-wide or institution-wide scrutiny of current practices, but in other situations individual nurses can personally examine evidence to help address specific problems.

For individual EBP efforts, the major steps in EBP include the following:

1. Asking clinical questions that are answerable with research evidence
2. Searching for and collecting evidence that addresses the question
3. Appraising and synthesizing the evidence
4. Integrating the evidence with your own clinical expertise, patient preferences, and local context
5. Assessing the effectiveness of the decision, intervention, or advice

Asking Clinical Questions: PIO and PICO

A crucial first step in EBP involves asking relevant clinical questions that reflect uncertainties in clinical practice. Some EBP writers distinguish between background and foreground questions. *Background questions* are foundational questions about a clinical issue, for example, what is cancer cachexia (progressive body wasting), and what is its pathophysiology? Answers to such questions are typically found in textbooks. *Foreground questions*, by contrast, are those that can be answered based on current best research evidence on diagnosing, assessing, or treating patients, or on understanding the meaning or prognosis of their health problems. For example, we may wonder, is a fish oil-enhanced nutritional supplement effective in stabilizing weight in patients with advanced cancer? The answer to such a question may provide guidance on how best to address the needs of patients with cachexia.

Most guidelines for EBP use the acronyms PIO or PICO to help practitioners develop well-worded questions that facilitate a search for evidence. In the most basic PIO form, the clinical question is worded to identify three components:

1. P: the *population* or *patients* (What are the characteristics of the patients or people?)
2. I: the *intervention*, *influence*, or *exposure* (What are the interventions or therapies of interest? or, What are the potentially harmful influences/exposures of concern?)
3. O: the *outcomes* (What are the outcomes or consequences in which we are interested?)

Applying this scheme to our question about cachexia, our *population* (P) is cancer patients with cachexia; the *intervention* (I) is fish oil-enhanced nutritional supplements; and the *outcome* (O) is weight stabilization. As another example, in the second clinical scenario about scratch tests cited earlier, the population is children being tested for allergies; the intervention is interactive distraction; and the outcome is pain.

For questions that can best be answered with qualitative information (e.g., about the meaning of an experience or health problem), two components are most relevant:

1. The *population* (What are the characteristics of the patients or clients?
2. The *situation* (What conditions, experiences, or circumstances are we interested in understanding?)

For example, suppose our question was, What is it like to suffer from cachexia? In this case, the question calls for rich qualitative information; the *population* is patients with advanced cancer and the *situation* is the experience of cachexia.

In addition to the basic PIO components, other components are sometimes important in an evidence search. In particular, a comparison (C) component may be needed, when the intervention or influence of interest is contrasted with a specific alternative. For example, we might be interested in learning whether fish oil-enhanced supplements (I) are better than melatonin (C) in stabilizing weight (O) in cancer patients (P). When a *specific* comparison is of interest, a PICO question is required, but if we were interested in uncovering evidence about *all* alternatives to the intervention of primary interest, then PIO components are sufficient. (By contrast, when asking questions to undertake an actual *study*, the "C" must always be specified).

TIP: Other components may be relevant, such as a time frame or "T" (for PICOT questions) or a setting or "S" (for PICOS questions).

Table 2.1 offers templates for asking well-worded clinical questions for different types of foreground questions. The right hand column includes questions with an explicit comparison (PICO), while the middle column does not have a comparison (PIO). The questions are categorized in a manner similar to that discussed in Chapter 1 (EBP Purposes), as featured in Table 1.3 on page 14. One exception is that we have added Description as a category. Note that although there are some differences in components across question types, there is always a P component.

TIP: It is crucial to practice asking clinical questions—it is the starting point for evidence-based nursing. Take some time to fill in the blanks in Table 2.1 for each question category. Do not be too self-critical at this point. Your comfort in developing questions will increase over time. Chapter 2 of *Study Guide for Essentials of Nursing Research, 8e* offers additional opportunities for you to practice asking well-worded questions.

Finding Research Evidence

By wording clinical queries as PIO or PICO questions, you should be able to search the research literature for the information you need. Using the templates in Table 2.1, the information you insert into the blanks constitutes *key words* that can be used in an electronic search.

For an individual EBP endeavor, the best place to begin is by searching for evidence in a systematic review, clinical practice guideline, or other preprocessed sources because this approach leads to a quicker answer—and, if your methodologic skills are limited, potentially a superior answer as well. Researchers who prepare reviews and clinical guidelines typically are well trained in research methods and use rigorous standards in evaluating the evidence. Moreover, preprocessed evidence is often prepared by a team, which means that the conclusions are cross-checked and fairly objective. Thus, when preprocessed evidence is available to answer a clinical question, you may not need to look any farther—unless the review is outdated. When preprocessed evidence cannot be located or is old, you will need to look for best evidence in primary studies, using strategies we describe in Chapter 7.

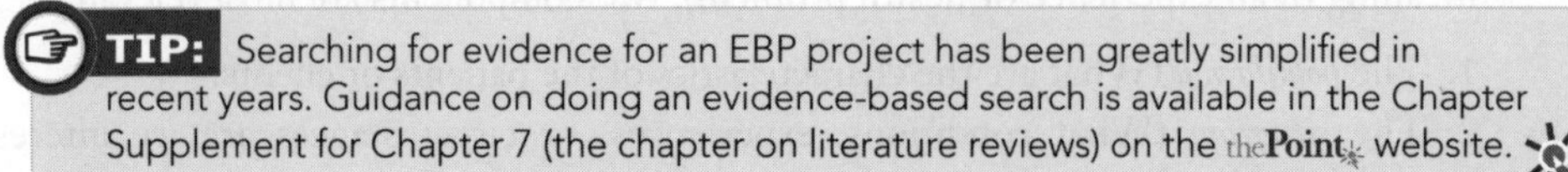
TIP: Searching for evidence for an EBP project has been greatly simplified in recent years. Guidance on doing an evidence-based search is available in the Chapter Supplement for Chapter 7 (the chapter on literature reviews) on the thePoint website.

TABLE 2.1 Question Templates for Selected Clinical Foreground Questions: PIO and PICO

Type of Question	PIO Question Template (Questions Without an Explicit Comparison)	PICO Question Template (Questions With an Explicit Comparison)
Therapy/treatment/ intervention	In ______ (**P**opulation), what is the effect of ______ (**I**ntervention) on ______ (**O**utcome)?	In ______ (**P**opulation), what is the effect of ______ (**I**ntervention), in comparison to ______ (**C**omparative/alternative intervention), on ______ (**O**utcome)?
Diagnosis/assessment	For ______ (**P**opulation), does ______ (**I**dentifying tool/procedure) yield accurate and appropriate diagnostic/assessment information about ______ (**O**utcome)?	For ______ (**P**opulation), does ______ (**I**dentifying tool/procedure) yield more accurate or more appropriate diagnostic/assessment information than ______ (**C**omparative tool/procedure) about ______ (**O**utcome)?
Prognosis	For ______ (**P**opulation), does ______ (**E**xposure to disease or condition) increase the risk of ______ (**O**utcome)?	For ______ (**P**opulation), does ______ (**E**xposure to disease or condition), relative to ______ (**C**omparative disease or condition) increase the risk of ______ (**O**utcome)?
Etiology/harm	In ______ (Population), does ______ (**I**nfluence, exposure, or characteristic) increase the risk of ______ (**O**utcome)?	Does ______ (**I**nfluence, exposure, or characteristic) increase the risk of ______ (**O**utcome) compared to ______ (**C**omparative influence, exposure or condition) in ______ (**P**opulation)?
Description (prevalence/incidence)	In ______ (**P**opulation), how prevalent is ______ (**O**utcome)?	*Explicit comparisons are not typical, except to compare different populations*
Meaning or process	What is it like for ______ (**P**opulation) to experience ______ (condition, illness, circumstance)? **OR** What is the process by which ______ (**P**opulation) cope with, adapt to, or live with ______ (condition, illness, circumstance)?	*Explicit comparisons are not typical in these types of questions*

Appraising the Evidence for EBP

Evidence should be appraised before clinical action is taken. The critical appraisal of evidence for the purposes of EBP may involve several types of assessments (Box 2.1), but often focuses primarily on evidence quality.

BOX 2.1 Questions for Appraising the Evidence

1. What is the quality of the evidence—i.e., how rigorous and reliable is it?
2. What *is* the evidence—what is the magnitude of effects?
3. How precise is the estimate of effects?
4. What evidence is there of any side effects/side benefits?
5. What is the financial cost of applying (and not applying) the evidence?
6. Is the evidence relevant to my particular clinical situation?

Evidence Quality

The overriding appraisal issue is the extent to which the findings are valid. That is, were the study methods sufficiently rigorous that the evidence can be believed? Ideally, you would find preappraised evidence, but a goal of this book is to help you evaluate research evidence yourself. If there are several primary studies and no existing systematic review, you would need to draw conclusions about the body of evidence taken as a whole. Clearly, you would want to put most weight on the most rigorous studies.

Magnitude of Effects

You would also need to assess whether study findings are clinically important. This criterion considers not whether the results are "real," but how powerful the effects are. For example, consider clinical scenario 3 cited earlier, which suggests this question: Does the use of compression stockings lower the risk of flight-related deep vein thrombosis for high-risk patients? In our search, we found a relevant systematic review in the nursing literature—a meta-analysis of nine RCTs (Hsieh & Lee, 2005)—and another in the Cochrane database (Clarke et al., 2006). The conclusion of these reviews, based on reliable evidence, was that compression stockings are effective and the magnitude of the risk-reducing effect is fairly substantial. Thus, advice about using compression stockings may be appropriate, pending an appraisal of other factors. The magnitude of effects can be quantified in various ways, and several are described later in this book.

Precision of Estimates

Another consideration, relevant when the evidence is quantitative, is how precise the estimate of effect is. This level of appraisal requires some statistical sophistication and so we postpone our discussion of *confidence intervals* to Chapter 12. Suffice it to say that research results provide only an *estimate* of effects and it may be useful to understand not only the exact estimate, but also the range within which the actual effect probably lies.

Peripheral Effects

Even if the evidence is judged to be valid and the magnitude of effects is sizeable, peripheral benefits and costs may be important in guiding decisions. In framing your clinical question, you would have identified the outcomes (O) in which you were interested—for example, weight stabilization for an intervention to address cancer cachexia. Research on this topic, however, would likely have considered other outcomes that need to be taken into account—for example, quality of life, comfort, and side effects.

Financial Costs

Another issue concerns the costs of applying the evidence. Costs sometimes may be small or nonexistent. For example, in clinical scenario 4 concerning the experience of CPAP treatment, nursing action would be cost-neutral because the evidence would be used to reassure and inform patients. When interventions and assessment protocols are costly, however, the resources needed to put best evidence into practice need to be estimated and factored into any decision. Of course, although the cost of a clinical decision needs to be considered, the cost of *not* taking action is equally important.

Clinical Relevance

Finally, it is important to appraise the evidence in terms of its relevance for the clinical situation at hand—that is, for *your* patient in a specific clinical setting. Best practice evidence can most readily be applied to an individual patient in your care if he or she is sufficiently similar to people in the study or studies under review. Would your patient have qualified for participation in the study—or would some factor (e.g., age, illness severity, comorbidities) have disqualified him or her? DiCenso and colleagues (2005), who advised clinicians to ask whether there is a compelling reason to conclude that results may *not* be applicable in their clinical situation, have written some useful tips on applying evidence to individual patients.

Actions Based on Evidence Appraisals

Appraisals of the evidence may lead you to different courses of action. You may reach this point on your EBP quest and conclude that the evidence base is not sufficiently sound, or that the likely effect is too small, or that the cost of applying the evidence is too high. The evidence appraisal may suggest that "usual care" is the best strategy. If, however, the initial appraisal of evidence suggests a promising clinical action, then you can proceed to the next step.

Integrating Evidence in EBP

Research evidence needs to be integrated with other types of information, including your own clinical expertise and knowledge of your clinical setting. You may be aware of factors that would make implementation of the evidence, no matter how sound and how promising, inadvisable. Patient preferences and values are also important. A discussion with the patient may reveal strong negative attitudes toward a potentially beneficial course of action, or possible impediments (e.g., lack of health insurance).

One final issue is the desirability of integrating evidence from qualitative research. Qualitative research can provide rich insights about how patients experience a problem, or about barriers to complying with a treatment. A potentially beneficial intervention may fail to achieve desired outcomes if it is not implemented with sensitivity to the patients' perspectives. As Morse (2005) so aptly noted, evidence from an RCT may tell us whether a pill is effective, but qualitative research can help you understand why patients may not swallow the pill.

Implementing the Evidence and Evaluating Outcomes

After the first four steps of the EBP process have been completed, you can use the integrated information to make an evidence-based decision or to provide evidence-based advice. Although the steps in the process, as just described, may seem complicated, in reality the process can be quite efficient—*if* there is adequate evidence, and especially if it has been skillfully preprocessed. EBP is most challenging when findings from research are contradictory, inconclusive, or "thin"—that is, when better quality evidence is needed.

One last step in an individual EBP effort concerns evaluation. Part of the evaluation process involves following up to determine if your actions achieved the desired outcome. Another part, however, concerns an evaluation of how well you are performing EBP. Sackett and colleagues (2000) offer self-evaluation questions that relate to the previous EBP steps, such as asking answerable questions (Am I asking any clinical questions at all? Am I asking well-worded questions?), and finding external evidence (Do I know the best sources of current evidence? Am I efficient in my searching?). A self-appraisal may lead to the conclusion that at least some of the clinical questions of interest to you are best addressed as a group effort.

EBP IN AN ORGANIZATIONAL CONTEXT

For some clinical scenarios, individual nurses may be able to implement EBP strategies on their own (e.g., giving advice about compression stockings). Many situations, however, require decision making by an organization, or by a team of nurses working to solve a recurrent problem. This section describes some additional issues that are relevant to institutional efforts at EBP—efforts designed to result in a formal policy or protocol affecting the practice of many nurses.

Many of the steps in organizational EBP projects are similar to the ones described in the previous section. For example, gathering and appraising evidence are key activities in both, as shown in the Iowa Model in Figure 2.2 on page 28 (Assemble relevant research; critique and synthesize research). Additional issues are relevant at the organizational level, however, including the selection of a problem, an assessment of whether the topic is a priority for the organization, deciding whether the evidence is sufficiently sound to implement on a trial basis, and deciding, based on the trial, whether the innovation should be adopted into practice. We briefly discuss some of these topics.

Selecting a Problem for an Institutional EBP Project

Some EBP projects originate in deliberations among clinicians who have encountered a recurrent problem and seek a resolution. Others, however, are "top-down" efforts in which administrators take steps to stimulate the use of research evidence among clinicians. This latter approach is increasingly likely to occur in United States hospitals as part of the Magnet recognition process.

Several models of EBP, such as the Iowa Model, have distinguished two types of stimulus ("triggers") for an EBP endeavor: (1) *problem-focused triggers*—the identification of a clinical practice problem in need of solution, or (2) *knowledge-focused triggers*—readings in the research literature. Problem-focused triggers may arise in the course of clinical practice (as in the case of the clinical scenarios described earlier) or in the context of quality-assessment or quality-improvement efforts. The problem-identification approach is likely to be clinically relevant and to have staff support if the problem is one that numerous nurses have encountered.

A second catalyst for an EBP project is the research literature—knowledge-focused triggers, which is the origin akin to RU. The catalyst might be a new clinical guideline or a research article discussed in a journal club. With knowledge-focused triggers, the clinical relevance and applicability of the research might need to be assessed. The central issue is whether a problem of significance to nurses in that particular setting will be solved by making a change or introducing an innovation. Using concepts from Rogers' Diffusion of Innovations Model, Titler and Everett (2001) offer suggestions for selecting interventions to test.

Appraising Implementation Potential

With either type of trigger, an important issue concerns the feasibility of undertaking an EBP project in a particular organizational setting. In the Iowa Model (Fig. 2.2), the first major decision point involves determining whether the topic is a priority for the organization considering practice changes. Titler and colleagues (2001) advised considering the following issues before finalizing a topic for EBP: the topic's fit with the organization's strategic plan; the magnitude of the problem; the number of people invested in the problem; support of nurse leaders and of those in other disciplines; costs; and possible barriers to change.

Some EBP models recommend a formal assessment of organizational "fit," often called **implementation potential** (or, *environmental readiness*). In determining the implementation potential of an innovation in a particular setting, several issues should be considered, particularly the transferability of the innovation (i.e., the extent to which the innovation might be appropriate in new settings), the feasibility of implementing it, and its cost-benefit ratio.

TIP: For those interested in learning more about assessments of implementation potential, we offer an expanded summary in the Chapter Supplements on thePoint website.

If the implementation assessment suggests that there might be problems in testing the innovation in that particular practice setting, then the team can either identify a new problem and begin the process anew or consider adopting a plan to improve the implementation potential (e.g., seeking external resources if costs are prohibitive).

Evidence Appraisals and Subsequent Actions

In the Iowa Model, the second major decision relies on the synthesis and appraisal of research evidence. The crux of the decision concerns whether the research base is sufficient to justify an evidence-based change—for example, whether an existing clinical practice guideline is of sufficiently high quality that it can be used or adapted, or whether the research evidence is sufficiently rigorous to recommend a practice innovation.

Assessments about the adequacy of the evidence can lead to different action paths. If the research evidence is weak or inconclusive, the team could assemble nonresearch evidence (e.g., through consultation with experts or client surveys) to determine the benefit of a practice change. Another option is to conduct an original study to address the practice question, thereby gathering new evidence. This course of action may be impractical, and would result in years of delay.

If, on the other hand, there is a solid research base or a high-quality clinical practice guideline, then the team would develop plans for moving forward with implementing a practice innovation. A key activity usually involves developing or adapting a local evidence-based clinical practice protocol or guideline. Strategies for developing clinical practice guidelines are suggested in DiCenso et al. (2005) and Melnyk and Fineout-Overholt (2011). Whether a guideline is developed "from scratch" or adapted from an existing one, independent peer review is advisable to ensure that the guidelines are clear, comprehensive, and congruent with best existing evidence.

Implementing and Evaluating the Innovation

Once the EBP product has been developed, the next step is to **pilot test** it (give it a trial run) and evaluate the outcome. Building on the Iowa Model, this phase of the project likely would involve the following activities:

1. Developing an evaluation plan (e.g., identifying outcomes to be achieved, determining how many clients to include, deciding when and how often to measure outcomes).
2. Measuring client outcomes prior to implementing the innovation, so that there is a comparison against which the outcomes of the innovation can be assessed.

3. Training relevant staff in the use of the new guideline and, if necessary, "marketing" the innovation to users.
4. Trying the guideline out on one or more units or with a group of clients.
5. Evaluating the pilot project, in terms of both process (e.g., how was the innovation received, what problems were encountered?) and outcomes (e.g., how were client outcomes affected, what were the costs?).

A fairly informal evaluation may be adequate, but formal efforts are often appropriate and provide opportunities for dissemination to others at conferences or in professional journals.

TIP: Every nurse can play a role in using research evidence. Here are some strategies:

- *Read widely and critically*. Professionally accountable nurses keep abreast of important developments and read journals relating to their specialty, including research reports in them.
- *Attend professional conferences*. Studies with clinical relevance are presented at many nursing conferences. Conference attendees get opportunities to meet researchers and to explore practice implications.
- *Become involved in a journal club*. Many hospitals sponsor journal clubs that review studies with potential relevance to practice. Online journal clubs that acknowledge time constraints and the inability of nurses from all shifts to come together at one time are increasingly common.
- *Pursue and participate in EBP projects*. Several studies have found that nurses who are involved in research-related activities (e.g., an EBP project or data collection activities) develop more positive attitudes toward research and better research skills.

RESEARCH EXAMPLES WITH CRITICAL THINKING EXERCISES

Example 1 below is also featured in our *Interactive Critical Thinking Activity* on thePoint website where you can easily record, print, and e-mail your responses to the related questions.

EXAMPLE 1 ● Research Translation Project

Hundreds of projects to translate research evidence into nursing practice are underway worldwide. Those that have been described in the nursing literature offer good information about planning and implementing such an endeavor. In this section we summarize such a project.

Study: Care of the patient with enteral tube feeding: An evidence-based protocol (Kenny & Goodman, 2010)

Purpose: The TriService Nursing Research Program sought to create a culture of incorporating best evidence into nursing practices in military hospitals throughout the United States. Kenny and Goodman's article described a protocol development and testing project that was implemented at a large military medical center under that initiative. The project's purpose was to understand the evidence for managing enteral tube feedings in adult patients, to develop and implement an evidence-based protocol, and to evaluate its effects. A secondary aim was to educate the nursing staff about the EBP process.

Framework: The project used the Iowa Model as its guiding framework. The team's decision to select enteral feedings was based on a sentinel event.

(continues on page 37)

Protocol Development: When the project began, nursing practice relating to enteral feedings in the medical center was based on tradition, and varied from nurse to nurse. The topic had support from clinical nursing staff and administrators, and fit with organizational priorities. The project team included nurses, a physician, a clinical nurse specialist, and a nutrition care specialist. The team met for about 6 months to review evidence and develop a protocol. The work began with a thorough review and evaluation of existing evidence on managing enteral tube feedings. The evidence was not especially strong, but the team identified many practices with sufficient research support to craft a set of recommendations. The team developed relevant educational materials (e.g., one-page *Nursing Cliff Notes*, tabletop education in acrylic sign holders), and offered inservice sessions on each ward to explain the new protocol.

Evaluation: Project outcomes were assessed at three levels: patient, nursing, and organization. Patient outcomes were assessed using anecdotal reports of tube clogging incidents. Nursing outcomes included knowledge of the evidence base (measured before and after protocol implementation), and process measures to examine compliance with the new protocol. The organizational outcome was actions by executives demonstrating support of the EBP model.

Findings and Conclusions: Anecdotal data supported a tentative conclusion of better patient outcomes (e.g., a decrease in clogged tubes). There was a significant increase in staff knowledge and implementation of evidence-based processes. The authors concluded that "The project has infused the creation of a culture of value for EBP from the level of the clinical staff nurse to the nursing executive level" (p. S29).

CRITICAL THINKING EXERCISES

1. Of the EBP-focused research purposes (Table 1.3, p. 14), which purpose was the central focus of this project?
2. Using the template in Table 2.1 on page 31, phrase a clinical question that the EBP team might have asked when they were searching for evidence for their project. The questions might be about tube placement, tube management, prevention of aspiration, and so on.
3. Would you say that this project had a knowledge-focused or problem-focused trigger?

EXAMPLE 2 ● Quantitative Research in Appendix A

- Read the abstract and the introduction from the Howell and colleagues' (2007) study ("Anxiety, anger, and blood pressure in children") in Appendix A on pages 395–402.

CRITICAL THINKING EXERCISES

1. Identify one or more clinical foreground questions that, if posed, would be addressed by this study. Which PIO or PICO components do your questions capture?
2. How, if at all, might evidence from this study be used in an EBP project (individual or organizational)?

EXAMPLE 3 ● Qualitative Research in Appendix B

- Read the abstract and the introduction from Beck and Watson's (2010) study ("Subsequent childbirth after a previous traumatic birth") in Appendix B on pages 403–412.

CRITICAL THINKING EXERCISES

1. Identify one or more clinical foreground questions that, if posed, would be addressed by this study. Which PIO or PICO components do your questions capture?
2. How, if at all, might evidence from this study be used in an EBP project (individual or organizational)?

WANT TO KNOW MORE? A wide variety of resources to enhance your learning and understanding of this chapter are available on thePoint.

- Interactive Critical Thinking Activity
- Chapter Supplement on Assessing Implementation Potential for EBP Projects
- Answers to the Critical Thinking Exercises for Examples 2 and 3
- Student Review Questions
- Full-text online
- Internet Resources with useful websites for Chapter 2

Additional study aids including eight journal articles and related questions are also available in *Study Guide for Essentials of Nursing Research, 8e.*

SUMMARY POINTS

- **Evidence-based practice (EBP)** is the conscientious use of current best evidence in making clinical decisions about patient care; it is a clinical problem-solving strategy that de-emphasizes decision making based on custom and emphasizes the integration of research evidence with clinical expertise and patient preferences.
- **Research utilization (RU)** and EBP are overlapping concepts that concern efforts to use research as a basis for clinical decisions, but RU *starts* with a research-based innovation that gets evaluated for possible use in practice.
- Nurse researchers have undertaken several major utilization projects, such as the *Conduct and Utilization of Research in Nursing* or *CURN* project.
- Two underpinnings of the EBP movement are the **Cochrane Collaboration** (which is based on the work of British epidemiologist Archie Cochrane), and the clinical learning strategy developed at the McMaster Medical School called *evidence-based medicine*.
- EBP involves evaluating evidence to determine *best evidence*; often an **evidence hierarchy** is used to rank study findings according to the strength of evidence provided, but different hierarchies are appropriate for different types of questions. In all evidence hierarchies, however, *systematic reviews* are at the pinnacle.
- **Systematic reviews** are rigorous integrations of research evidence from multiple studies on a topic. Systematic reviews can involve either narrative approaches to integration (including **metasynthesis** of qualitative studies), or quantitative methods (**meta-analysis**) that integrate findings statistically.
- Evidence-based **clinical practice guidelines** combine an appraisal of research evidence with specific recommendations for clinical decisions.
- Many models of EBP have been developed, including models that provide a framework for individual clinicians (e.g., the *Stetler model*) and others for organizations or teams of clinicians (e.g., the *Iowa Model*).
- Individual nurses have opportunities to put research into practice. The five basic steps for individual EBP are: (1) asking an answerable clinical question; (2) searching for relevant research-based evidence; (3) appraising and synthesizing the evidence; (4) integrating evidence with other factors; and (5) assessing effectiveness.

- One scheme for asking well-worded clinical questions involves four primary components, an acronym for which is PICO: Population (P), Intervention or influence (I), Comparison (C), and Outcome (O). When there is no explicit comparison, the acronym is PIO.
- An appraisal of the evidence involves such considerations as the validity of study findings; their clinical importance; the magnitude and precision of effects; associated costs and risks; and utility in a particular clinical situation.
- EBP in an organizational context involves many of the same steps as individual EBP efforts, but is more formalized and must take organizational factors into account.
- *Triggers* for an organizational project include both pressing clinical problems (*problem-focused*) and existing knowledge (*knowledge-focused*).
- Before an EBP-based guideline or protocol can be tested, there should be an assessment of its **implementation potential**, which includes the issues of transferability, feasibility, and the cost–benefit ratio of implementing a new practice in a clinical setting.
- Once an evidence-based protocol or guideline has been developed and deemed worthy of implementation, the EBP team can move forward with a **pilot test** of the innovation and an assessment of the outcomes prior to widespread adoption.

REFERENCES FOR CHAPTER 2

Academic Center for Evidence-Based Practice (2009). ACE Star Model of Knowledge Transformation. Retrieved October 8, 2009, from http://www.acestar.uthscsa.edu

AGREE Collaboration (2001). *Appraisal of guidelines for research and evaluation: AGREE instrument*. Retrieved July, 2012, from www.agreecollaboration.org

Clarke, M., Hopewell, S., Juszczak, E., Eisinga, A., & Kjeldstrom, M. (2006). Compression stockings for preventing deep vein thrombosis in airline passengers. *Cochrane Database of Systematic Reviews*, CD004002.

DiCenso, A., Guyatt, G., & Ciliska, D. (2005). *Evidence-based nursing: A guide to clinical practice*. St. Louis, MO: Elsevier Mosby.

Duggleby, W., Hicks, D., Nekolaichuk, C., Holtslander, L. Williams, A., Chambers, T., et al. (2012). Hope, older adults, and chronic illness: A metasynthesis of qualitative research. *Journal of Advanced Nursing, 68*(6), 1211–1223.

Gawlinksi, A., & Rutledge, D. (2008). Selecting a model for evidence-based practice changes. *AACN Advanced Critical Care, 19*, 291–300.

Horsley, J. A., Crane, J., & Bingle, J. D. (1978). Research utilization as an organizational process. *Journal of Nursing Administration, 8*, 4–6.

Hsieh, H. F., & Lee, F. P. (2005). Graduated compression stockings as prophylaxis for flight-related venous thrombosis: Systematic literature review. *Journal of Advanced Nursing, 51*, 83–98.

Kenny, D. J., & Goodman, P. (2010). Care of the patient with enteral tube feeding: An evidence-based practice protocol. *Nursing Research, 59*, S22–S31.

Lewis, S. (2001). Further disquiet on the guidelines front. *Canadian Medical Association Journal, 154*, 180–181.

Melnyk, B. M., & Fineout-Overhold, E. (2011). *Evidence-based practice in nursing and healthcare: A guide to best practice* (2nd ed.). Philadelphia, PA: Lippincott Williams & Wilkins.

Morse, J. (2005). Beyond the clinical trial: Expanding criteria for evidence. *Qualitative Health Research, 15*, 3–4.

Nam, S., Janson, S., Stotts, N., Chesla, C., & Kroon. L. (2012). Effect of culturally tailored diabetes education in ethnic minorities with Type 2 diabetes: A meta-analysis. *Journal of Cardiovascular Nursing 27*, 505–518.

Newhouse, R., Dearholt, S., Poe, S., Pugh, L. C., & White, K. M. (2005). Evidence-based practice: A practical approach to implementation. *Journal of Nursing Administration, 35*, 35–40.

Rogers, E. M. (2003). *Diffusion of innovations* (5th ed.). New York: Free Press.

Rosswurm, M. A., & Larrabee, J. H. (1999). A model for change to evidence-based practice. *Image: The Journal of Nursing Scholarship, 31*, 317–322.

Rycroft-Malone, J., Seers, K., Titchen, A., Harvey, G., Kitson, A., & McCormack, B. (2002). Getting evidence into practice: Ingredients for change. *Nursing Standard, 16*, 38–43.

Sackett, D. L., Straus, S. E., Richardson, W. S., Rosenberg, W., & Haynes, R. B. (2000). *Evidence-based medicine: How to practice and teach EBM* (2nd ed.). Edinburgh, UK: Churchill Livingstone.

Schultz, A. (2005). Clinical scholars at the bedside. An EBP mentorship model for how nurses work today. Nursing Knowledge International, Sigma Theta Tau International, retrieved April 6, 2011, from http://www.nursingknowledge.org

Stetler, C. B. (2001). Updating the Stetler model of research utilization to facilitate evidence-based practice. *Nursing Outlook, 49*, 272–279.

Titler, M. G., & Everett, L. Q. (2001). Translating research into practice. Considerations for critical care investigators. *Critical Care Nursing Clinics of North America, 13*, 587–604.

Titler, M. G., Kleiber, C., Steelman, V., Rakel, B., Budreau, G., Everett, L., et al. (2001). The Iowa model of evidence-based practice to promote quality care. *Critical Care Nursing Clinics of North America, 13*, 497–509.

chapter

3 Key Concepts and Steps in Qualitative and Quantitative Research

LEARNING OBJECTIVES

On completing this chapter, you will be able to:

- Define new terms presented in the chapter, and distinguish terms associated with quantitative and qualitative research
- Distinguish experimental and nonexperimental research
- Identify the three main disciplinary traditions for qualitative nursing research
- Describe the flow and sequence of activities in quantitative and qualitative research, and discuss why they differ

KEY TERMS

Cause-and-effect (causal) relationship
Clinical trial
Concept
Conceptual definition
Construct
Data
Dependent variable
Emergent design
Ethnography
Experimental research
Gaining entrée
Grounded theory
Hypothesis
Independent variable
Informant
Intervention protocol
Literature review
Nonexperimental research
Observational research
Operational definition
Outcome variable
Phenomenology
Qualitative data
Quantitative data
Relationship
Research design
Sample
Saturation
Statistical analysis
Study participant
Subject
Theme
Variable

THE BUILDING BLOCKS OF RESEARCH

Research, like any discipline, has its own language—its own *jargon*—and that jargon can sometimes be intimidating. We readily admit that the jargon is abundant and is sometimes confusing. A lot of research jargon used in nursing research has its roots in the social sciences, but sometimes different terms for the same concepts are used in medical research. Also, some terms are used by both qualitative and quantitative researchers, but others are used mainly by one or the other group. Please bear with us as we cover key terms that you will need to understand to read other chapters of this book.

The Faces and Places of Research

When researchers answer a question through disciplined research—regardless of whether it is qualitative or quantitative—they are doing a **study** (or an *investigation*). Studies with

TABLE 3.1 Key Terms in Quantitative and Qualitative Research

Concept	Quantitative Term	Qualitative Term
Person contributing information	Subject Study participant —	— Study participant Informant, key informant
Person undertaking the study	Researcher Investigator	Researcher Investigator
That which is being investigated	— Concepts Constructs Variables	Phenomena Concepts — —
Information gathered	Data (numerical values)	Data (narrative descriptions)
Connections between concepts	Relationships (cause-and-effect, associative)	Patterns of association
Logical reasoning processes	Deductive reasoning	Inductive reasoning

humans involve two sets of people: those who do the research and those who provide the information. In a quantitative study, the people being studied are called **subjects** or **study participants**, as shown in Table 3.1. In a qualitative study, the people cooperating in the study are called study participants or **informants**. The person who conducts the research is the *researcher* or *investigator*. Studies are often undertaken by a research team rather than by a single researcher.

HOW-TO-TELL TIP: How can you tell if an article appearing in a nursing journal is a *study*? In journals that specialize in research (e.g., the journal *Nursing Research*), most articles are original research reports, but in specialty journals there is usually a mix of research and nonresearch articles. Sometimes you can tell by the title, but sometimes you cannot. You can tell, however, by looking at the major headings of an article. If there is no heading called "Method" or "Research Design" (the section that describes what a researcher *did*) and no heading called "Findings" or "Results" (the section that describes what a researcher *learned*), then it is probably not a study.

Research can be undertaken in a variety of *settings* (the types of place where information is gathered), for example, hospitals, homes, or other community settings. A *site* is the specific location for the research—it could be an entire community (e.g., a Haitian neighborhood in Miami) or an institution (e.g., a clinic in Seattle). Researchers sometimes do *multisite studies* because the use of multiple sites offers a larger and often more diverse sample of participants.

Concepts, Constructs, and Theories

Research involves real-world problems, but studies are conceptualized in abstract terms. For example, *pain*, *fatigue*, and *resilience* are all abstractions of particular aspects of human behavior and characteristics. These abstractions are called *phenomena* (especially in qualitative studies) or **concepts**.

Researchers sometimes use the term **construct**, which also refers to an abstraction, but often one that is deliberately invented (or constructed). For example, *self-care* in Orem's model of health maintenance is a construct. The terms *construct* and *concept* are sometimes used interchangeably, but by convention a construct often refers to a slightly more complex abstraction than a concept.

A **theory** is an explanation of some aspect of reality. In a theory, concepts are knitted together into a coherent system to describe or explain some aspect of the world. Theories play a role in both qualitative and quantitative research. In a quantitative study, researchers often start with a theory and, using deductive reasoning, make predictions about how phenomena would behave in the real world *if the theory were true*. The specific predictions are then tested in a study, and the results are used to support or challenge the theory. In qualitative studies, theory often is the *product* of the research: The investigators use information from study participants inductively to develop a theory rooted in the participants' experiences.

TIP: The reasoning process of *deduction* is associated with quantitative research, and *induction* is associated with qualitative research. See the Chapter Supplement located on thePoint website for a full discussion of these terms.

Variables

In quantitative studies, concepts are usually called **variables**. A variable, as the name implies, is something that varies. Weight, anxiety, and fatigue are all variables—they vary from one person to another. Most human characteristics are variables. If everyone weighed 150 pounds, weight would not be a variable, it would be a *constant*. But it is precisely because people and conditions *do* vary that most research is conducted. Quantitative researchers seek to understand how or why things vary, and to learn how differences in one variable relate to differences in another. For example, in lung cancer research, lung cancer is a variable because not everybody has this disease. Researchers have studied factors that might be linked to lung cancer, such as cigarette smoking. Smoking is also a variable because not everyone smokes. A variable, then, is any quality of a person, group, or situation that varies or takes on different values. Variables are the central building blocks of quantitative studies.

TIP: Every study focuses on one or more phenomena, concepts, or variables, but these terms per se are not necessarily used in research reports. For example, a report might say: "The purpose of this study is to examine the effect of nurses' workload on hand hygiene compliance." Although the researcher did not explicitly label anything a variable, the variables under study are *workload* and *hand hygiene compliance.* Key concepts or variables are often indicated in the study title.

Variables are often inherent human characteristics, such as age or weight, but sometimes researchers *create* a variable. For example, if a researcher tests the effectiveness of patient-controlled analgesia compared to intramuscular analgesia in relieving pain after surgery, some patients would be given one type of analgesia and some would receive the other. In the context of this study, the method of pain management is a variable because different patients are given different analgesics.

Some variables take on a wide range of values than can be represented on a continuum (e.g., a person's age or weight). Other variables take on only a few values; sometimes such variables convey quantitative information (e.g., number of children) but others simply involve placing people into categories (e.g., male, female, or blood type A, B, AB, or O).

Dependent and Independent Variables

As noted in Chapter 1, many studies seek to understand causes of phenomena. Does a nursing intervention *cause* improvements in patient outcomes? Does smoking *cause* lung cancer? The presumed cause is the **independent variable**, and the presumed effect is the **dependent** or **outcome variable**. In terms of the PICO scheme discussed in Chapter 2, the dependent variable corresponds to the "O" (outcome). The independent variable corresponds to the "I" (the intervention, influence, or exposure), plus the "C" (the comparison).

TIP: In searching for evidence, a nurse might want to learn about the effects of an intervention or influence, compared to *any* alternative, on a designated outcome. In a study, however, researchers must always specify what the comparative intervention or influence (the "C") is.

Variation in the dependent variable is presumed to *depend on* variation in the independent variable. For example, researchers investigate the extent to which lung cancer (the dependent variable) depends on smoking (the independent variable). Or, investigators might examine the extent to which patients' pain (the dependent variable) depends on different nursing actions (the independent variable). The dependent variable is the outcome that researchers want to understand, explain, or predict.

The terms *independent variable* and *dependent variable* also can be used to indicate *direction of influence* rather than cause and effect. For example, suppose we compared levels of depression among men and women diagnosed with pancreatic cancer and found men to be more depressed. We could not conclude that depression was *caused* by gender. Yet the direction of influence clearly runs from gender to depression: it makes no sense to suggest that patients' depression influenced their gender. Although it may not make sense to infer a cause-and-effect connection, it is appropriate to consider depression as the outcome variable and gender as the independent variable.

TIP: Few research reports explicitly label variables as dependent and independent. Moreover, variables (especially independent variables) are sometimes not fully spelled out. Take the following research question: What is the effect of exercise on heart rate? In this example, heart rate is the dependent variable. Exercise, however, is not in itself a variable. Rather, exercise versus something else (e.g., no exercise) is a variable; "something else" is implied rather than stated in the research question.

Many outcomes have multiple causes or influences. If we were studying factors that influence people's body mass index, the independent variables might be height, physical activity, and diet. And, two or more outcome variables may be of interest. For example, a researcher may compare two alternative dietary interventions in terms of participants' weight, lipid profile, and self esteem. It is common to design studies with multiple independent and dependent variables.

Variables are not *inherently* dependent or independent. A dependent variable in one study could be an independent variable in another. For example, a study might examine the effect of an exercise intervention (the independent variable) on osteoporosis (the dependent variable) to answer a therapy question. Another study might investigate the effect of osteoporosis (the independent variable) on bone fracture incidence (the dependent variable) to address a prognosis question. In short, whether a variable is independent or dependent is a function of the role that it plays in a particular study.

Example of independent and dependent variables:
Research question (Etiology/Harm question): Is low cognitive functioning associated with reduced instrumental activities of daily living (e.g., medication management, driving) in people with heart failure (Alosco et al., 2012)?

Independent variable: Level of cognitive functioning

Dependent variables: Instrumental activities of daily living

Conceptual and Operational Definitions

The concepts of interest to researchers are abstractions of observable phenomena, and researchers' world view shapes how those concepts are defined. A **conceptual definition** is the abstract or theoretical meaning of a concept. Researchers need to conceptually define even seemingly straightforward terms. A classic example is the concept of *caring*. Morse and colleagues (1990) examined how researchers and theorists defined *caring*, and identified five categories of conceptual definitions: as a human trait; a moral imperative; an affect; an interpersonal relationship; and a therapeutic intervention. Researchers undertaking studies of caring need to clarify which conceptual definition they have adopted.

In qualitative studies, conceptual definitions of key phenomena may be a major end product, reflecting an intent to have the meaning of concepts defined by those being studied. In quantitative studies, however, researchers must define concepts at the outset, because they must decide how the variables will be observed and measured. An **operational definition** indicates what the researchers specifically must do to measure the concept and collect needed information.

Variables differ in the ease with which they can be operationalized. The variable weight, for example, is easy to define and measure. We might operationally define weight as the amount that a person weighs in pounds, to the nearest full pound. This definition designates that weight will be measured using one measuring system (pounds) rather than another (grams). We could also specify that weight will be measured using a digital scale with subjects fully undressed after 10 hours of fasting. This operational definition clearly indicates what the variable *weight* means.

Few variables are operationalized as easily as weight, however. Most variables can be measured several ways, and researchers must choose a method that best captures the variables as they conceptualize them. Take, for example, *anxiety*, which can be defined in terms of both physiologic and psychological functioning. For researchers emphasizing physiologic aspects of anxiety, the operational definition might involve a measure such as pulse rate. If, on the other hand, anxiety is conceptualized as a psychological state, the operational definition might be scores on a paper-and-pencil test such as the State Anxiety Scale. Readers of research articles may not agree with how researchers conceptualized and operationalized variables, but definitional precision is important in communicating what concepts mean within the context of the study.

Example of conceptual and operational definitions:
Fogg and colleagues (2011) developed a scale to measure people's beliefs and intentions about HIV screening. The scale relied on constructs from a theory called the Theory of Planned Behavior (see Chapter 8). The article provided examples of both conceptual and operational definitions of key constructs. For example, "Subjective norm" was conceptually defined as "The overall perception of social pressure to perform or not perform the behavior" and a scale item used to measure this construct was "The people in my life whose opinions I value are regularly tested for HIV" (p. 76).

BOX 3.1 Example of Quantitative Data

Question: Thinking about the past week, how depressed would you say you have been on a scale from 0 to 10, where 0 means "not at all" and 10 means "the most possible"?

Data: 9 (Subject 1)
0 (Subject 2)
4 (Subject 3)

Data

Research **data** (singular, datum) are the pieces of information gathered in a study. In quantitative studies, researchers identify and define their variables, and then collect relevant data from subjects. The actual *values* of the study variables constitute the data. Quantitative researchers collect primarily **quantitative data**—information in numeric form. For example, if we conducted a quantitative study in which a key variable was *depression*, we would need to measure how depressed participants were. We might ask, "Thinking about the past week, how depressed would you say you have been on a scale from 0 to 10, where 0 means 'not at all' and 10 means 'the most possible'?" Box 3.1 presents quantitative data from three fictitious respondents. The subjects provided a number along the 0 to 10 continuum corresponding to their degree of depression—9 for subject 1 (a high level of depression), 0 for subject 2 (no depression), and 4 for subject 3 (little depression). The numeric values for all subjects, collectively, would comprise the data on depression.

In qualitative studies, researchers collect primarily **qualitative data**, that is, narrative descriptions. Narrative data can be obtained by conversing with participants, by making notes about their behavior in naturalistic settings, or by obtaining narrative records, such as diaries. Suppose we were studying depression qualitatively. Box 3.2 presents qualitative data for three participants responding conversationally to the question, "Tell me about how you've been feeling lately—have you felt sad or depressed at all, or have you generally been in good spirits?" Here, the data consist of rich narrative descriptions of participants' emotional state.

BOX 3.2 Example of Qualitative Data

Question: Tell me about how you've been feeling lately—have you felt sad or depressed at all, or have you generally been in good spirits?

Data: "Well, Actually, I've been pretty depressed lately, to tell you the truth. I wake up each morning and I can't seem to think of anything to look forward to. I mope around the house all day, kind of in despair. I just can't seem to shake the blues and I've begun to think I need to go see a shrink." (Participant 1)

"I can't remember ever feeling better in my life. I just got promoted to a new job that makes me feel like I can really get ahead in my company. And I've just gotten engaged to a really great guy who is very special." (Participant 2)

"I've had a few ups and downs the past week but basically things are on a pretty even keel. I don't have too many complaints." (Participant 3)

Relationships

Researchers usually study phenomena in relation to other phenomena—they examine relationships. A **relationship** is a bond or connection between two or more phenomena; for example, researchers repeatedly have found that there is a *relationship* between cigarette smoking and lung cancer. Qualitative and quantitative studies examine relationships in different ways.

In quantitative studies, researchers are interested in the relationship between independent variables and outcomes. Variation in the outcome variable is presumed to be systematically related to variation in the independent variable. Relationships are often explicitly expressed in quantitative terms, such as *more than*, *less than*, and so on. For example, consider a person's weight as our dependent variable. What variables are related to (associated with) a person's weight? Some possibilities include height, caloric intake, and exercise. For each of these independent variables, we can make a prediction about its relationship to the outcome variable:

Height: Taller people will weigh more than shorter people.
Caloric intake: People with higher caloric intake will be heavier than those with lower caloric intake.
Exercise: The lower the amount of exercise, the greater will be the person's weight.

Each statement expresses a predicted relationship between weight (the outcome) and a measurable independent variable. Most quantitative research is conducted to assess whether relationships exist among variables and to measure how strong the relationship is.

TIP: Relationships are expressed in two basic forms. First, relationships can be expressed as "if more of Variable X, then more of (or less of) Variable Y." For example, there is a relationship between height and weight: With greater height, there tends to be greater weight, i.e., taller people tend to weigh more than shorter people. The second form involves relationships expressed as group differences. For example, there is a relationship between gender and height: men tend to be taller than women.

Variables can be related to one another in different ways. One type of relationship is a **cause-and-effect** (or **causal**) **relationship**. Within the positivist paradigm, natural phenomena are assumed to have antecedent causes that are discoverable. In our example about a person's weight, we might speculate that there is a causal relationship between caloric intake and weight: all else being equal, eating more calories causes weight gain. As noted in Chapter 1, many quantitative studies are *cause-probing*—they seek to illuminate the causes of phenomena.

Example of a study of causal relationships:
Chuang and co-researchers (2012) studied whether a structured relaxation program caused lower stress in hospitalized pregnant women with preterm labor.

Not all relationships between variables can be interpreted as cause-and-effect. There is a relationship, for example, between a person's pulmonary artery and tympanic temperatures: people with high readings on one tend to have high readings on the other. We cannot say, however, that pulmonary artery temperature *caused* tympanic temperature, nor that tympanic temperature *caused* pulmonary artery temperature, despite the relationship that exists between the two variables. This type of relationship is sometimes referred to as an *associative* (or *functional*) *relationship* rather than a causal one.

Example of a study of associative relationships:
Kelly and colleagues (2012) studied the relationship between social support networks and adherence to antiretroviral therapy among HIV-infected substance abusers.

Qualitative researchers are not concerned with quantifying relationships, nor in testing and confirming causal relationships. Rather, qualitative researchers may seek patterns of association as a way of illuminating the underlying meaning and dimensionality of phenomena of interest. Patterns of interconnected concepts are identified as a means of understanding the whole.

Example of a qualitative study of patterns:
Stålkrantz and colleagues (2012) studied everyday life for the spouses of patients with untreated obstructive sleep apnea syndrome. They found that the spouses differed on two key dimensions: social adjustment (circumstances limited or unchanged) and new feelings (against the partner or supporting the partner).

MAJOR CLASSES OF QUANTITATIVE AND QUALITATIVE RESEARCH

Researchers usually work within a paradigm that is consistent with their world view, and that gives rise to the types of question that excite their curiosity. In this section, we briefly describe broad categories of quantitative and qualitative research.

Quantitative Research: Experimental and Nonexperimental Studies

A basic distinction in quantitative studies is the difference between experimental and nonexperimental research. In **experimental research**, researchers actively introduce an intervention or treatment—most often, to address therapy questions. In **nonexperimental research**, on the other hand, researchers are bystanders—they collect data without introducing treatments or making changes (most often, to address etiology, prognosis, or diagnosis questions). For example, if a researcher gave bran flakes to one group of subjects and prune juice to another to evaluate which method facilitated elimination more effectively, the study would be experimental because the researcher intervened in the normal course of things. If, on the other hand, a researcher compared elimination patterns of two groups whose regular eating patterns differed, the study would be nonexperimental because there is no intervention. In medical and epidemiological research, experimental studies usually are called **clinical trials**, and nonexperimental inquiries are called **observational studies**.

TIP: There are many different strategies and designs for experimental and nonexperimental research, as we discuss in Chapter 9. On the evidence hierarchy shown in Figure 2.1 on page 23, the two rungs below systematic reviews (Randomized Controlled Trials and quasi-experiments) involve interventions and are experimental. The four rungs below that are nonexperimental.

Experimental studies are explicitly designed to test causal relationships—to test whether an intervention *caused* changes in the outcome variable. Sometimes nonexperimental studies also explore causal relationships, but causal inferences in nonexperimental research are tricky and less conclusive, for reasons explained in a later chapter.

Example of experimental research:
Yang and colleagues (2011) tested the effectiveness of a home-based walking intervention in improving symptom and mood distress in women following surgery for breast cancer. Some study participants received the moderate-intensity intervention while others did not.

In this example, the researchers intervened by designating that some patients would receive the special walking intervention, and that others would not be given this opportunity. In other words, the researcher *controlled* the independent variable, which in this case was the walking intervention.

Example of nonexperimental research:
Enderlin and co-researchers (2012) compared sleep quality and daytime sleepiness in women with nonmetastatic breast cancer versus those without cancer. The two groups differed with regard to several sleep outcomes, such as sleep onset latency and insomnia severity.

In this nonexperimental study to address a prognosis question, the researchers did not intervene in any way. They were interested in a similar population as in the previous example (women with breast cancer), but their intent was to explore existing relationships rather than to test a potential solution to a problem.

Qualitative Research: Disciplinary Traditions

The majority of qualitative studies can best be described as **qualitative descriptive research**. Many qualitative studies, however, are rooted in research traditions that originated in anthropology, sociology, and psychology. Three such traditions, prominent in qualitative nursing research, are briefly described here. Chapter 14 provides a fuller discussion of these and other traditions, and the methods associated with them.

The **grounded theory** tradition seeks to describe and understand the key social psychological processes that occur in a social setting. Grounded theory was developed in the 1960s by two sociologists, Glaser and Strauss (1967). The focus of most grounded theory studies is on a developing social experience—the social and psychological phases that characterize a particular event or episode. A major component of grounded theory is the discovery of a *core variable* that is central in explaining what is going on in that social scene. Grounded theory researchers strive to generate explanations of phenomena that are grounded in reality.

Example of a grounded theory study:
Neill and colleagues (2012) studied how families manage acute childhood illnesses at home, and the role that felt or enacted criticism play in parents' help-seeking behaviors.

Phenomenology, rooted in a philosophical tradition developed by Husserl and Heidegger, is concerned with the lived experiences of humans. Phenomenology is an approach to thinking about what life experiences of people are like and what they mean.

The phenomenological researcher asks the questions: What is the *essence* of this phenomenon as experienced by these people? Or, What is the meaning of the phenomenon to those who experience it?

Example of a phenomenological study:
McCloud and colleagues (2012) studied the lived experience of undergoing vitreoretinal day surgery in an Australian public hospital.

Ethnography, the primary research tradition in anthropology, provides a framework for studying the patterns, lifeways, and experiences of a defined cultural group in a holistic fashion. Ethnographers typically engage in extensive *fieldwork*, often participating to the extent possible in the life of the culture under study. Ethnographers strive to learn from members of a cultural group, to understand their world view, and to describe their customs and norms.

Example of an ethnographic study:
Emilsdóttir and Gústafsdóttir (2011) conducted extensive ethnographic fieldwork in a nursing home in Iceland to examine nurses' care of the dying elderly.

Major Steps in a Quantitative Study

In quantitative studies, researchers move from the beginning point of a study (posing a question) to the end point (obtaining an answer) in a reasonably linear sequence of steps that is broadly similar across studies (see Fig. 3.1). This section describes that flow, and the next section describes how qualitative studies differ.

Phase 1: The Conceptual Phase

The early steps in a quantitative study typically involve activities with a strong conceptual element. During this phase, researchers call on such skills as creativity, deductive reasoning, and a grounding in existing research evidence on the topic of interest.

Step 1: Formulating and Delimiting the Problem

Quantitative researchers begin by identifying an interesting, significant research problem and formulating good **research questions**. In developing their questions, nurse researchers must attend to substantive issues (Is this problem important?); theoretical issues (Is there a conceptual context to enrich understanding of this problem?); clinical issues (Will study findings be useful in clinical practice?); methodologic issues (How can this question be answered to yield high-quality evidence?); and ethical issues (Can this question be addressed in an ethical manner?).

Step 2: Reviewing the Related Literature

Quantitative research is conducted within the context of previous knowledge. Quantitative researchers typically strive to understand what is already known about a topic by undertaking a thorough **literature review** before any data are collected.

Step 3: Undertaking Clinical Fieldwork

Researchers embarking on a clinical study often benefit from spending time in relevant clinical settings (in the *field*), discussing the topic with clinicians and observing

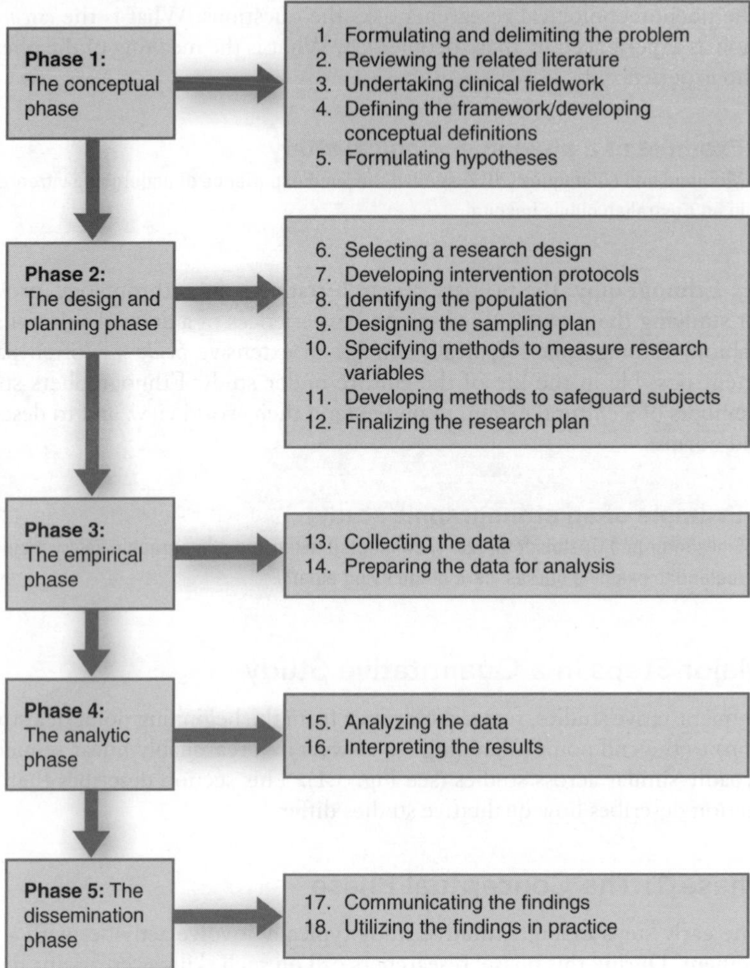

Phase 1:
The conceptual phase
1. Formulating and delimiting the problem
2. Reviewing the related literature
3. Undertaking clinical fieldwork
4. Defining the framework/developing conceptual definitions
5. Formulating hypotheses
Phase 2:
The design and planning phase
6. Selecting a research design
7. Developing intervention protocols
8. Identifying the population
9. Designing the sampling plan
10. Specifying methods to measure research variables
11. Developing methods to safeguard subjects
12. Finalizing the research plan
Phase 3:
The empirical phase
13. Collecting the data
14. Preparing the data for analysis
Phase 4:
The analytic phase
15. Analyzing the data
16. Interpreting the results
Phase 5: The dissemination phase
17. Communicating the findings
18. Utilizing the findings in practice

FIGURE 3.1 ● Flow of steps in a quantitative study.

current practices. Such clinical fieldwork can provide insights into clinicians' and clients' perspectives.

Step 4: Defining the Framework and Developing Conceptual Definitions

When quantitative research is performed within the context of a theoretical framework, the findings may have broader significance and utility. Even when the research question is not embedded in a theory, researchers should have a conceptual rationale and a clear vision of the concepts under study.

Step 5: Formulating Hypotheses

Hypotheses state researchers' deductively derived expectations about relationships between study variables. Hypotheses are predictions of the relationships researchers expect to observe in the study data. The research question identifies the concepts of interest and asks how the concepts might be related; a hypothesis is the predicted answer. Most quantitative studies are designed to test hypotheses through statistical analysis.

Phase 2: The Design and Planning Phase

In the second major phase of a quantitative study, researchers make decisions about the methods and procedures to be used to address the research question. Researchers typically have flexibility in designing a study, and make many methodologic decisions that have crucial implications for the integrity and generalizability of the study findings.

Step 6: Selecting a Research Design

The **research design** is the overall plan for obtaining answers to the research questions and for handling challenges that can undermine the study evidence. Quantitative research designs tend to be highly structured and controlled, with the goal of minimizing bias. Research designs also indicate other aspects of the research—for example, how often data will be collected, what types of comparisons will be made, and where the study will take place. The research design is the architectural backbone of the study.

Step 7: Developing Protocols for the Intervention

In experimental research, researchers create the independent variable, which means that participants are exposed to different treatments. An **intervention protocol** for the study must be developed, specifying exactly what the intervention will entail (e.g., who would administer it, how frequently and over how long a period the treatment would last, and so on) *and* what the alternative condition would be. In nonexperimental research, this step is not necessary.

Step 8: Identifying the Population

Quantitative researchers need to know what characteristics the study participants should possess, and clarify the group to whom study results can be generalized—that is, they must identify the population to be studied. A **population** is *all* the individuals or objects with common, defining characteristics (the "P" component in PICO questions).

Step 9: Designing the Sampling Plan

Researchers typically collect data from a **sample**, which is a subset of the population. Using samples is more practical than collecting data from an entire population, but the risk is that the sample might not adequately reflect the population's traits. The researcher's *sampling plan* specifies how the sample will be selected and how many subjects there will be.

Step 10: Specifying Methods to Measure Variables

Quantitative researchers must find methods to measure the research variables accurately. A variety of quantitative data collection approaches exist; the primary methods are *self-reports* (e.g., interviews and questionnaires), *observations* (e.g., watching and recording people's behavior), and *biophysiologic measurements*. The task of measuring research variables and developing a *data collection plan* is complex and challenging.

Step 11: Developing Methods to Safeguard Human/Animal Rights

Most nursing research involves human subjects, although some involve animals. In either case, procedures need to be developed to ensure that the study adheres to ethical principles.

Step 12: Reviewing and Finalizing the Research Plan

Before collecting data, researchers often perform a number of "tests" to ensure that procedures will work smoothly. For example, they may evaluate the *readability* of written materials to see if participants with low reading skills can comprehend them. Researchers usually have their research plan critiqued by reviewers to obtain clinical or methodologic feedback before implementing it. Researchers seeking financial support submit a *proposal* to a funding source, and reviewers usually suggest improvements.

Phase 3: The Empirical Phase

The third phase of quantitative studies involves collecting the research data. This phase is often the most time-consuming part of the study. Data collection may require months of work.

Step 13: Collecting the Data

The actual collection of data in a quantitative study often proceeds according to a pre-established plan. The plan typically spells out procedures for training data collection staff; for actually collecting data (e.g., where and when the data will be gathered); and for recording information.

Step 14: Preparing the Data for Analysis

Data collected in a quantitative study must be prepared for analysis. For example, one preliminary step is *coding*, which involves translating verbal data into numeric form (e.g., coding gender information as "1" for females and "2" for males). Another step may involve transferring the data from written documents onto computer files for analysis.

Phase 4: The Analytic Phase

Quantitative data gathered in the empirical phase must be subjected to analysis and interpretation, which occurs in the fourth major phase of a project.

Step 15: Analyzing the Data

To answer research questions and test hypotheses, researchers analyze their data in an orderly fashion. Quantitative data are analyzed through **statistical analyses**, which include some simple procedures (e.g., computing an average) as well as more complex, sophisticated methods.

Step 16: Interpreting the Results

Interpretation involves making sense of study results and examining their implications. Researchers attempt to explain the findings in light of prior evidence, theory, and clinical experience—and in light of the adequacy of the methods they used in the study.

Phase 5: The Dissemination Phase

In the analytic phase, researchers come full circle: the questions posed at the outset are answered. The researchers' job is not completed, however, until the study results are disseminated.

Step 17: Communicating the Findings

A study cannot contribute evidence to nursing practice if the results are not communicated. Another—and often final—task of a research project is the preparation of a *research report* that can be shared with others. We discuss research reports in the next chapter.

Step 18: Putting the Evidence into Practice

Ideally, the concluding step of a high-quality study is to plan for its use in practice settings. Although nurse researchers may not themselves be able to implement a plan for using research findings, they can contribute to the process by developing recommendations on how the evidence could be used in practice, by ensuring that adequate information has been provided for a meta-analysis, and by pursuing opportunities to disseminate the findings to practicing nurses.

ACTIVITIES IN A QUALITATIVE STUDY

Quantitative research involves a fairly linear progression of tasks—researchers plan the steps to be taken and then follow those steps as faithfully as possible. In qualitative studies, by contrast, the progression is closer to a circle than to a straight line. Qualitative researchers are continually examining and interpreting data and making decisions about how to proceed based on what has already been discovered (Fig. 3.2).

Because qualitative researchers have a flexible approach to collecting and analyzing data, we cannot show the flow of activities precisely—the flow varies from one study to another, and researchers themselves do not know in advance exactly how the study will unfold. We try to provide a sense of how qualitative studies are conducted by describing some major activities and indicating how and when they might be performed.

Conceptualizing and Planning a Qualitative Study

Identifying the Research Problem

Qualitative researchers usually begin with a broad topic, often focusing on an aspect about which little is known. Qualitative researchers often proceed with a fairly broad initial

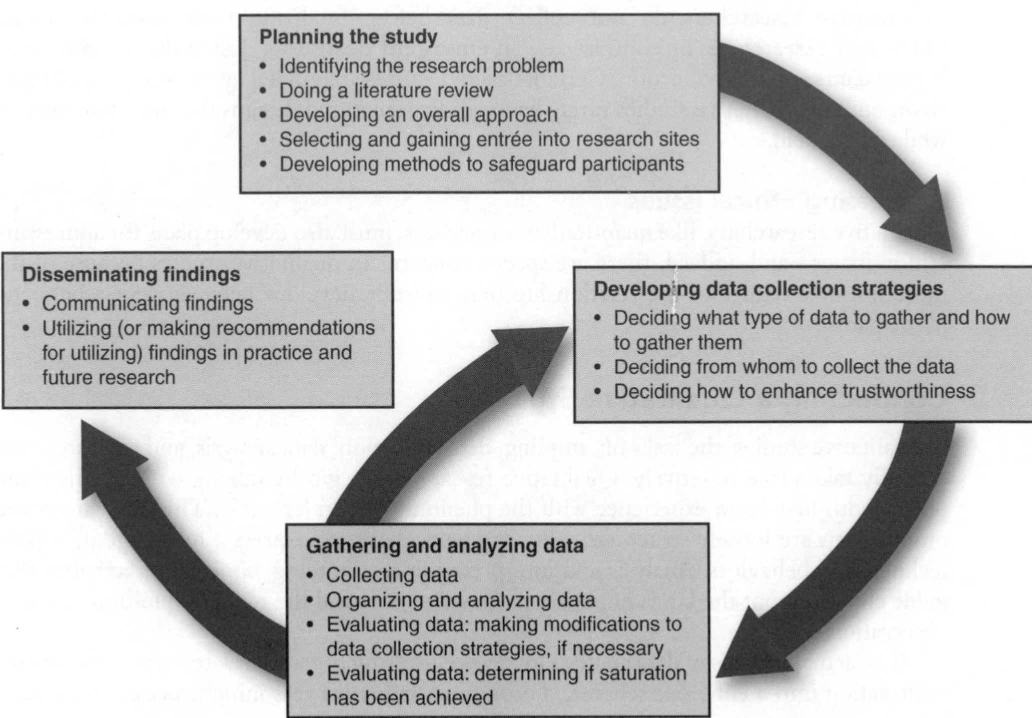

Planning the study
• Identifying the research problem
• Doing a literature review
• Developing an overall approach
• Selecting and gaining entrée into research sites
• Developing methods to safeguard participants
Developing data collection strategies
• Deciding what type of data to gather and how to gather them
• Deciding from whom to collect the data
• Deciding how to enhance trustworthiness
Gathering and analyzing data
• Collecting data
• Organizing and analyzing data
• Evaluating data: making modifications to data collection strategies, if necessary
• Evaluating data: determining if saturation has been achieved
Disseminating findings
• Communicating findings
• Utilizing (or making recommendations for utilizing) findings in practice and future research

FIGURE 3.2 ● Flow of activities in a qualitative study.

question that allows the focus to be sharpened and delineated more clearly once the study is underway.

Doing a Literature Review

Not all qualitative researchers agree about the value of doing an upfront literature review. Some believe that researchers should not consult the literature before collecting data. They worry that prior studies might influence the conceptualization of the phenomenon under study, which they believe should be elucidated based on participants' viewpoints rather than on prior findings. Others believe that researchers should conduct at least a brief literature review at the outset. In any case, qualitative researchers typically find a relatively small body of relevant previous work because of the type of questions they ask.

Selecting and Gaining Entrée Into Research Sites

Before going into the field, qualitative researchers must identify an appropriate site. For example, if the topic is the health beliefs of the urban poor, an inner-city neighborhood with a concentration of low-income residents must be identified. In some cases, researchers may have access to the selected site, but in others they need to **gain entrée** into it. Gaining entrée typically involves negotiations with **gatekeepers** who have the authority to permit entry into their world.

 **TIP:** The process of gaining entrée is usually associated with doing fieldwork in qualitative studies, but quantitative researchers often need to gain entrée into sites for collecting data as well.

Developing an Overall Approach

Quantitative researchers do not collect data before finalizing their research design. Qualitative researchers, by contrast, use an **emergent design**—a design that emerges during the course of data collection. Certain design features are guided by the study's qualitative tradition, but qualitative studies rarely have rigidly structured designs that prohibit changes while in the field.

Addressing Ethical Issues

Qualitative researchers, like quantitative researchers, must also develop plans for addressing ethical issues—and, indeed, there are special concerns in qualitative studies because of the more intimate nature of the relationship that typically develops between researchers and participants.

Conducting a Qualitative Study

In qualitative studies, the tasks of sampling, data collection, data analysis, and interpretation typically take place iteratively. Qualitative researchers begin by talking with or observing people with first-hand experience with the phenomenon under study. The discussions and observations are loosely structured, allowing participants to express a full range of beliefs, feelings, and behaviors. Analysis and interpretation are ongoing, concurrent activities that guide choices about the kinds of people to question next and the types of question to ask or observations to make.

The actual process of data analysis involves clustering together related types of narrative information into a coherent scheme. Through an inductive reasoning process, researchers begin to identify **themes** and categories, which are used to build a rich description or theory of the phenomenon. The kinds of data gathered become increasingly purposeful as the theory emerges. Concept development and verification shape sampling choices—as conceptualizations develop, the researcher seeks participants who can confirm and enrich theoretical understandings, as well as participants who can potentially challenge them and lead to further insights.

Quantitative researchers decide in advance how many subjects to include in the study, but qualitative researchers' sampling decisions are guided by the data. Many qualitative researchers use the principle of **saturation**, which occurs when themes and categories in the data become repetitive and redundant, such that no new information can be gleaned by further data collection.

Quantitative researchers seek to collect high-quality data by measuring their variables with instruments that have been demonstrated to be accurate and valid. Qualitative researchers, by contrast, *are* the main data collection instrument and must take steps to demonstrate the *trustworthiness* of the data. The central feature of these efforts is to confirm that the findings accurately reflect the experiences and viewpoints of participants, rather than researchers' perceptions. One confirmatory activity, for example, involves going back to participants, sharing preliminary interpretations with them, and asking them to evaluate whether the researcher's thematic analysis is consistent with their experiences.

Qualitative nursing researchers also strive to share their findings at conferences and in journal articles. Qualitative studies help to shape nurses' perceptions of a problem or situation, their conceptualizations of potential solutions, and their understanding of patients' concerns and experiences.

GENERAL QUESTIONS IN REVIEWING A STUDY

Box 3.3 presents some further suggestions for performing a preliminary overview of a research report, drawing on concepts explained in this chapter. These guidelines supplement those presented in Box 1.1, Chapter 1 on page 15.

BOX 3.3 Additional Questions for a Preliminary Review of a Study

1. What is the study all about? What are the main phenomena, concepts, or constructs under investigation?
2. If the study is quantitative, what are the independent and dependent variables?
3. Did the researchers examine relationships or patterns of association among variables or concepts? Does the report imply the possibility of a causal relationship?
4. Are key concepts defined, both conceptually and operationally?
5. What type of study does it appear to be, in terms of types described in this chapter—experimental or nonexperimental/observational, grounded theory, phenomenology, or ethnography?
6. Does the report provide information to suggest how long the study took to complete?

RESEARCH EXAMPLES WITH CRITICAL THINKING EXERCISES

In this section, we illustrate the progression of activities and discuss the time schedule of two studies (one quantitative and the other qualitative) conducted by the second author of this book.

Examples 1 and 2 below are also featured in our *Interactive Critical Thinking Activity* on thePoint website where you can easily record, print, and e-mail your responses to the related questions.

EXAMPLE 1 ● Project Schedule for a Quantitative Study

Study: Further validation of the Postpartum Depression Screening Scale (PDSS) (Beck & Gable, 2001)

Study Purpose: Beck and Gable undertook a study to assess the PDSS, an instrument designed for use by clinicians and researchers to screen mothers for postpartum depression. The scale is currently in wide use throughout the world.

Study Methods: This study required nearly 3 years to complete. Key activities and methodological decisions included the following:

Phase 1. Conceptual Phase: 1 Month. This phase was short, because much of the conceptual work had been done in a prior study, in which Beck and Gable actually developed the scale. The literature had already been reviewed, so they only needed to update it. The framework and conceptual definitions that had been used in the first study were used in the new study.

Phase 2. Design and Planning Phase: 6 Months. The second phase was time-consuming. It included developing the research design for the study, gaining entrée into the hospital from which subjects were recruited, and obtaining approval from the hospital's human subjects review committee. During this period, Beck met with statistical consultants and with Gable, an instrument development specialist, numerous times to finalize the study design.

Phase 3. Empirical Phase: 11 Months. Data collection took almost a year to complete. The design called for administering the PDSS to 150 mothers who were 6 weeks postpartum, and then scheduling them for a psychiatric diagnostic interview to evaluate if they were suffering from postpartum depression. Women were recruited into the study during prepared childbirth classes. Recruitment began 4 months before data collection, and then the researchers gathered their data 6 weeks after delivery. The nurse psychotherapist, who had her own practice, was able to come to the hospital only 1 day a week to conduct the diagnostic interviews; this contributed to the time required to achieve the desired sample size.

Phase 4. Analytic Phase: 3 Months. Statistical tests were performed to determine a cut-off score on the PDSS above which mothers would be identified as having screened positive for postpartum depression. Data analysis also was undertaken to determine the accuracy of the PDSS in predicting diagnosed postpartum depression. The scale was found to be highly accurate. During this phase, Beck met with Gable and other statisticians to interpret results.

Phase 5. Dissemination Phase: 18 Months. The researchers prepared and submitted their report to the journal *Nursing Research* for possible publication. It was accepted within 4 months, but it was "in press" (awaiting publication) for 14 months before being published. During this period, the authors presented their findings at regional and international conferences. The researchers also prepared a summary report for the agency that funded the research.

CRITICAL THINKING EXERCISES

1. Answer the relevant questions from Box 3.3 on page 55 regarding this study.
2. Also consider the following targeted questions:
   a. Who do you think is the *population* for this study?
   b. Would you describe the method of data collection as *self-report* or *observation*?
   c. How would you evaluate Beck and Gable's dissemination plan?

   d. Do you think an appropriate amount of time was allocated to the various phases and steps in this study?
   e. Would it have been appropriate for the researchers to address the research question using qualitative research methods? Why or why not?
3. If the results of this study are valid and generalizable, in what ways do you think the findings could be used in clinical practice?

EXAMPLE 2 ● Project Schedule for a Qualitative Study

Study: The Arm: There is no escaping the reality for mothers of children with obstetric brachial plexus injuries (OBPIs) (Beck, 2009).

Study Purpose: The purpose of this study was to understand the experience of mothers' caring for their children with OBPIs.

Study Methods: The total time required to complete this study was nearly 4 years. Beck's key activities included the following:

Phase 1. Conceptual Phase: 3 Months. One of the participants in Beck's earlier study on traumatic childbirth was a member of the Board of Directors of the United Brachial Plexus Network (UBPN). This mother had experienced a traumatic birth due to shoulder dystocia, which resulted in her infant suffering an OBPI. Every 2 years the UBPN holds a camp for families of children with OBPIs, and the camps include educational sessions for parents. Beck was invited to present her findings on traumatic childbirth at the camp in 2005. At camp Beck discussed with some UBPN Board members the possibility of conducting research on mothers' experiences caring for their children with OBPIs. She obtained their enthusiastic support.

Phase 2. Design and Planning Phase: 3 Months. Beck selected a phenomenological approach for this research in the fall of 2005. She corresponded by email with the UBPN Board of Directors to obtain formal approval to post a recruitment notice on the organization's website www.ubpn.org. Once the basic design was finalized, Beck obtained approval from the human subjects review committee at her university.

Phase 3. Empirical/Analytic Phases: 30 months. Data were collected from October 2005 to December 2007. During this period, 11 women participated in the study via the Internet by sending Beck stories of their experiences of caring for their children with OBPIs. In 2007 Beck was invited to present her research findings about the anniversary of birth trauma at the UPBN camp in Auburn, WA. Beck interviewed 12 mothers individually at the camp, for a total of 23 study participants. For an additional 4 months Beck analyzed the mothers' stories. Six themes emerged from data analysis: (1) In an instant: dreams shattered, (2) The arm: No escaping the reality, (3) Tormented: Agonizing worries and questions, (4) Therapy and surgeries: Consuming mothers' lives, (5) Anger: Simmering pot inside, and (6) So much to bear: enduring heartbreak.

Phase 4. Dissemination Phase: 10 Months. A manuscript describing this study was submitted to the journal *Nursing Research* on September 9, 2008. On December 2, 2008 Beck received a letter from the journal's editor indicating that reviewers recommended she revise and resubmit the paper. On January 6, 2009, Beck submitted a revised manuscript that incorporated the reviewers' recommendations. On February 23, 2009, Beck was notified that the paper had been accepted for publication, and the article was published in the July/August issue. Beck has presented the findings at national conferences. Also, Beck was interviewed regarding her findings, and parts of this interview were featured in UBPN's DVD entitled: "Newborn injuries: The untold story: Preventing the tragedy of unnecessary birth trauma." The DVD has been aired on Public Broadcasting System television stations and is on the UBPN website.

CRITICAL THINKING EXERCISES

1. Answer the questions from Box 3.3 on page 55 regarding this study.
2. Also consider the following targeted questions:
   a. Given the study purpose, was a phenomonological approach appropriate for this study?
   b. Do you think an appropriate amount of time was allocated to the various phases and steps in this study?

c. How would you evaluate the Beck dissemination plan?
d. Would it have been appropriate for Beck to address the research question using quantitative research methods? Why or why not?

EXAMPLE 3 ● Quantitative Research in Appendix A

- Read the abstract and the introduction from Howell and colleagues' (2007) study ("Anxiety, anger, and blood pressure in children") in Appendix A on pages 395–402.

CRITICAL THINKING EXERCISES

1. Answer the relevant questions in Box 3.3 on page 55.
2. Also consider the following targeted questions:
   a. Could any of the variables in this study be considered *constructs*?
   b. Did this report present any actual *data* from the study participants?
   c. Would it have been possible for the researchers to use an experimental design for this study?

EXAMPLE 4 ● Qualitative Research in Appendix B

- Read the abstract and the introduction from Beck and Watson's (2010) study ("Subsequent childbirth after a previous traumatic birth") in Appendix B on pages 403–412.

CRITICAL THINKING EXERCISES

1. Answer the relevant questions in Box 3.3 on page 55.
2. Also consider the following targeted questions, which may further sharpen your critical thinking skills and assist you in assessing aspects of the study's merit:
   a. Find an example of actual *data* in this study. (You will need to look at the "Results" section of this study.)
   b. How long did it take Beck and Watson to collect the data for this study? (You will find this information in the "Procedure" section.)
   c. How much time elapsed between when the paper was accepted for publication and when it was actually published? (You will find relevant information at the end of the paper.)

WANT TO KNOW MORE? **A wide variety of resources to enhance your learning and understanding of this chapter are available on thePoint.**

- Interactive Critical Thinking Activity
- Chapter Supplement on Deductive and Inductive Reasoning
- Answers to the Critical Thinking Exercises for Examples 3 and 4
- Student Review Questions
- Full-text online
- Internet Resources with useful websites for Chapter 3

Additional study aids including eight journal articles and related questions are also available in *Study Guide for Essentials of Nursing Research, 8e.*

SUMMARY POINTS

- The people who provide information to the researchers in a **study** are referred to as **subjects** or **study participants** in quantitative research, or study participants or **informants** in qualitative research; collectively they comprise the **sample.**
- The *site* is the location for the research; researchers sometimes engage in *multisite studies.*
- Researchers investigate **concepts** and *phenomena* (or **constructs**), which are abstractions inferred from people's behavior or characteristics.
- Concepts are the building blocks of **theories**, which are systematic explanations of some aspect of the real world.
- In quantitative studies, concepts are called variables. A **variable** is a characteristic or quality that takes on different values (i.e., varies from one person or object to another).
- The **dependent** (or **outcome**) **variable** is the behavior, characteristic, or outcome the researcher is interested in explaining, predicting, or affecting (the "O" in the PICO scheme). The **independent variable** is the presumed cause of or influence on the dependent variable. The independent variable corresponds to the "I" and the "C" components in the PICO scheme.
- A **conceptual definition** describes the abstract or theoretical meaning of a concept being studied. An **operational definition** specifies how the variable will be measured.
- **Data**—the information collected during the course of a study—may take the form of narrative information (**qualitative data**) or numeric values (**quantitative data**).
- A **relationship** is a bond or connection (or pattern of association) between variables. Quantitative researchers study the relationship between the independent variables and outcome variables.
- When the independent variable causes or affects the outcome, the relationship is a **cause-and-effect** (or **causal**) **relationship**. In an *associative relationship*, variables are related in a noncausal way.
- A key distinction in quantitative studies is between **experimental research**, in which researchers actively intervene to test an intervention or therapy, and **nonexperimental** (or **observational) research**, in which researchers collect data about existing phenomena without intervening.
- Qualitative research often is rooted in research traditions that originate in other disciplines. Three such traditions are grounded theory, phenomenology, and ethnography.
- **Grounded theory** seeks to describe and understand key social psychological processes that occur in a social setting.
- **Phenomenology** focuses on the lived experiences of humans and is an approach to gaining insight into what the life experiences of people are like and what they mean.
- **Ethnography** provides a framework for studying the meanings, patterns, and lifeways of a culture in a holistic fashion.
- In a quantitative study, researchers usually progress in a linear fashion from asking research questions to answering them. The main phases in a quantitative study are the conceptual, planning, empirical, analytic, and dissemination phases.
- The *conceptual phase* involves (1) defining the problem to be studied; (2) doing a **literature review**; (3) engaging in **clinical fieldwork** for clinical studies; (4) developing a framework and conceptual definitions; and (5) formulating **hypotheses** to be tested.

- The *planning phase* entails (6) selecting a **research design**; (7) developing **intervention protocols** if the study is experimental; (8) specifying the **population**; (9) developing a plan to select a **sample**; (10) specifying a **data collection plan** and methods to measure the research variables; (11) developing strategies to safeguard subjects' rights; and (12) finalizing the research plan.
- The *empirical phase* involves (13) collecting data and (14) preparing data for analysis (e.g., *coding* data).
- The *analytic phase* involves (15) analyzing data through **statistical analysis** and (16) interpreting the results.
- The *dissemination phase* entails (17) communicating the findings and (18) efforts to promote the use of the study evidence in nursing practice.
- The flow of activities in a qualitative study is more flexible and less linear. Qualitative studies typically involve an **emergent design** that evolves during data collection.
- Qualitative researchers begin with a broad question regarding a phenomenon of interest, often focusing on a little-studied aspect. In the early phase of a qualitative study, researchers select a site and seek to **gain entrée** into it, which typically involves enlisting the cooperation of **gatekeepers** within the site.
- Once in the field, researchers select informants, collect data, and then analyze and interpret them in an iterative fashion; experiences during data collection help in an ongoing fashion to shape the design of the study.
- Early analysis in qualitative research leads to refinements in sampling and data collection, until **saturation** (redundancy of information) is achieved. Analysis typically involves a search for critical **themes**.
- Both qualitative and quantitative researchers disseminate their findings, most often by publishing their research reports in professional journals.

REFERENCES FOR CHAPTER 3

Alosco, M., Spitznagel, M., Cohen, R., Sweet, S., Colbert, L., Josephson, R., et al. (2012). Cognitive impairment is independently associated with reduced instrumental activities of daily living in persons with heart failure. *Journal of Cardiovascular Nursing, 27*, 44–50.

Beck, C. T. (2009). The arm: There is no escaping the reality for mothers of children with obstetric brachial plexus injuries. *Nursing Research, 58*, 237–245.

Beck, C. T., & Gable, R. K. (2001). Further validation of the Postpartum Depression Screening Scale. *Nursing Research, 50*, 155–164.

Chuang, L. L., Lin, L., Cheng, C., Wu, S., & Chang, C. (2012). Effects of a relaxation training programme on immediate and prolonged stress responses in women with preterm labour. *Journal of Advanced Nursing, 68*, 170–180.

Emilsdóttir, A., & Gústafsdóttir, M. (2011). End of life in an Icelandic nursing home: An ethnographic study. *International Journal of Palliative Nursing, 17*, 405–411.

Enderlin, C., Coleman, E., Cole, C., Richards, K., Kennedy, R., Goodwin, J., et al. (2012). Subjective sleep quality, objective sleep characteristics, insomnia symptom severity, and daytime sleepiness in women aged 50 and older with nonmetastatic breast cancer. *Oncology Nursing Forum, 38*, E314–E325.

Fogg, C., Mawn, B., & Powell, F. (2011). Development of the Fogg Intent-to-screen for HIV Questionnaire. *Research in Nursing & Health, 34*, 73–84.

Glaser, B. G., & Strauss, A. (1967). *The discovery of grounded theory*. New York: Aldine de Gruyter.

Kelly, P., Ramaswamy, M., Li, X., Litwin, A., Berg, K., & Arnsten, J. (2012). Social networks of substance users with HIV infection. *Western Journal of Nursing Research, 34*, 621–634.

McCloud, C., Harrington, A., & King, L. (2012). Understanding people's experience of vitreo-retinal day surgery. *Journal of Advanced Nursing, 68*, 94–103.

Morse, J. M., Solberg, S., Neander, W., Bottorff, J., & Johnson, J. (1990). Concepts of caring and caring as a concept. *Advances in Nursing Science, 13*, 1–14.

Neill, S., Cowley, S., & Williams, C. (2012). The role of felt or enacted criticism in understanding parents' help seeking in acute childhood illness at home: A grounded theory study. *International Journal of Nursing Studies*,.

Stålkrantz, A., Brostrom, A., Wiberg, J., Svnborg, E., & Malm, D. (2012). Everyday life for the spouses of patients with untreated OSA syndrome. *Scandinavian Journal of Caring Sciences, 26*(2), 324–332.

Yang, C., Tsai, J., Huang, Y., & Lin, C. (2011). Effects of a home-based walking program on perceived symptom and mood status in postoperative breast cancer women receiving adjuvant chemotherapy. *Journal of Advanced Nursing, 67*, 158–168.

chapter

4 Reading and Critiquing Research Articles

LEARNING OBJECTIVES

On completing this chapter, you will be able to:

- Identify and describe the major sections in a research journal article
- Characterize the style used in quantitative and qualitative research reports
- Read a research article and broadly grasp its "story"
- Describe aspects of a research critique
- Understand the many challenges researchers face and identify some tools for addressing methodologic challenges
- Define new terms in the chapter

KEY TERMS

Abstract	Inference	Research control
Bias	Journal article	Scientific merit
Blinding	Level of significance	Statistical significance
Confounding variable	*p*	Statistical test
Credibility	Placebo	Transferability
Critique	Randomness	Triangulation
Findings	Reflexivity	Trustworthiness
IMRAD format	Reliability	Validity

Evidence from nursing studies is communicated through research reports that describe what was studied, how it was studied, and what was found. Research reports are often daunting to readers without research training. This chapter aims to make research reports more accessible, and also provides some guidance regarding critiques of research reports.

TYPES OF RESEARCH REPORTS

Nurses are most likely to encounter research evidence in journals or at professional conferences. Research **journal articles** are descriptions of studies published in professional journals. Competition for journal space is keen, and so the typical research article is brief—generally only 15 to 20 double-spaced pages. This means that researchers must condense a lot of information about the study into a short report.

Usually, manuscripts are reviewed by two or more *peer reviewers* (other researchers) who make recommendations about whether to accept or reject the manuscript, or to suggest revisions. Reviews are usually *"blind"*—reviewers are not told researchers' names, and authors are not told reviewers' names. As a result of peer review, consumers have some assurance that journal articles have been critiqued by other nurse researchers. Nevertheless, publication does not mean that findings can be uncritically accepted. Research method courses help nurses to evaluate the quality of evidence reported in journal articles.

At conferences, research findings are presented as oral presentations or poster sessions. *Oral presentations* follow a format similar to that used in journal articles, which we discuss next. The presenter is typically allotted 10 to 20 minutes to describe key features of the study. In *poster sessions*, many researchers simultaneously present visual displays summarizing their studies, and conference attendees walk around the room looking at these displays.

Conferences also offer an opportunity for dialogue between attendees. Attendees can ask questions to help them better understand what the findings mean; moreover, they can offer the researchers suggestions relating to clinical implications of the study. Thus, professional conferences are a valuable forum for clinical audiences.

THE CONTENT OF RESEARCH JOURNAL ARTICLES

Many research articles follow a conventional organization called the **IMRAD format**. This format organizes content into four main sections—**I**ntroduction, **M**ethod, **R**esults, and **D**iscussion. The paper is preceded by a title and an abstract, and concludes with references.

The Title and Abstract

Research reports have a title that succinctly conveys key information. In qualitative studies, the title normally includes the central phenomenon and group under investigation. In quantitative studies, the title communicates key variables and the population (in other words, the PICO components described in Chapter 2).

The **abstract** is a brief description of the study placed at the beginning of the article. The abstract answers questions like the following: What were the research questions? What methods were used to address those questions? What were the findings? What are the implications for nursing practice? Readers can review an abstract to judge whether to read the full report.

Some journals have moved from having traditional abstracts—single paragraphs summarizing the study's main features—to slightly longer, structured abstracts with headings. For example, *Nursing Research* suggests the following abstract heading: Background, Objectives, Method, Results, and Conclusions. Beck and Watson's (2010) qualitative study in Appendix B of this book exemplifies this longer abstract style, whereas the abstract in Appendix A (Howell et al., 2007) illustrates the traditional one-paragraph format.

The Introduction

The introduction to a research article acquaints readers with the research problem and its context. This section usually describes the following:

- The central phenomena, concepts, or variables under study
- The study purpose and the research questions or hypotheses
- A review of the related literature

- The theoretical or conceptual framework
- The significance of and need for the study.

Thus, the introduction sets the stage for presenting what the researcher did and what was learned.

Example of an introductory paragraph:

As the aging population increases, the demand grows for technologies to enhance quality of life and ameliorate physical decline.…Yet few practitioners and researchers have asked older persons their opinions of technological devices…, including traditional technologies like canes and walkers.…Our purpose was to elaborate on what it was like for 40 older homebound women…to negotiate reliance on a cane or walker as a walking device (Porter et al., 2011, p. 534).

In this paragraph, the researchers described the concepts of interest (experiences of relying on canes and walkers among older persons), the need for the study (the fact that little is known about the experience directly from elders), and the study purpose.

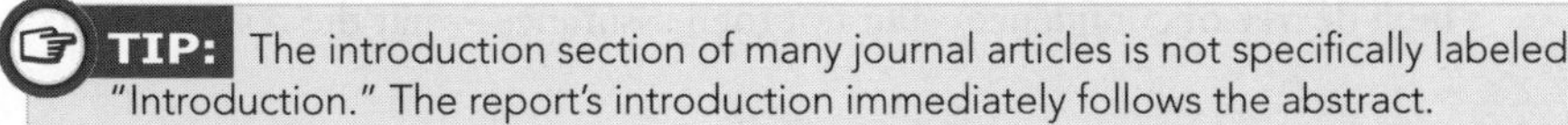

TIP: The introduction section of many journal articles is not specifically labeled "Introduction." The report's introduction immediately follows the abstract.

The Method Section

The method section describes the methods used to answer the research questions. In a quantitative study, the method section usually describes the following, which may be presented in labeled subsections:

- The research design
- The sampling plan
- Methods of measuring variables and collecting data
- Study procedures, including procedures to protect human rights
- Data analysis methods

Qualitative researchers discuss many of the same issues, but with different emphases. For example, a qualitative researchers often provide more information about the study setting and context than quantitative researchers, and less information on sampling and data collection. Increasingly, reports of qualitative studies describe the researchers' efforts to enhance the integrity of the study.

The Results Section

The results section presents the **findings** that were obtained by analyzing the study data. The text presents a narrative summary of key findings, often accompanied by more detailed tables. Virtually all results sections contain basic descriptive information, including a description of the participants (e.g., average age, percent male and female).

In quantitative studies, the results section also reports the following information relating to any statistical tests performed:

- *The names of statistical tests used.* Researchers use **statistical tests** to test their hypotheses and assess the probability that the results are accurate. For example, if the researcher finds that the average birth weight of drug-exposed infants in the sample is lower than the birth weight of infants not exposed to drugs, how probable is it that the same would be true for other infants not in the sample? A statistical test helps answer the question, Is the relationship between prenatal drug exposure and infant birth weight *real*, and would it likely be observed with a new sample from the same population? Statistical tests are based on common principles; you do not have to know the names of all statistical tests to comprehend the findings.

- *The value of the calculated statistic*. Computers are used to calculate a numeric value for the particular statistical test used. The value allows researchers to reach conclusions about their hypotheses. The *actual* value of the statistic, however, is not inherently meaningful and need not concern you.
- *The significance*. A critical piece of information is whether the statistical tests were significant (not to be confused with clinically important). If a researcher reports that the results are **statistically significant,** it means the findings are probably true and replicable with a new sample. Research reports also indicate the **level of significance,** which is an index of how *probable* it is that the findings are reliable. For example, if a report indicates that a finding was significant at the .05 level, this means that only 5 times out of 100 (5/100 = .05) would the obtained result be spurious. In other words, 95 times out of 100, similar results would be obtained with a new sample. Readers can thus have a high degree of confidence—but not total assurance—that the results are accurate.

Example from the results section of a quantitative study:

Li and colleagues (2011) tested the effectiveness of implementing sleep care guidelines for improving sleep quality among patients in a surgical ICU. Half the patients were in a usual care group, and the other half were cared for by nurses who followed guidelines for noise and light reduction. Here is a sentence adapted from the reported results: Sleep interruptions from care-related activities ($t = 5.28$, $p < .001$) were significantly lower in the special intervention group than in the usual care control group.

In this example, the researchers stated that sleep interruptions were *significantly* lower among those cared for by nurses who followed sleep care guidelines. The group differences in sleep interruptions were not likely to have been haphazard, and would probably be replicated with a new sample of patients. This finding is highly reliable: less than one time in 1,000 ($p < .001$) could a difference of the magnitude obtained occur as a fluke. Note that to comprehend this finding, you do not need to understand what a t statistic is, nor do you need to concern yourself with the actual value of the statistic, 5.28.

TIP: Be alert to *p* values (probabilities) when reading statistical results. If a *p* value is >.05 (e.g., $p = .08$), the results are *not* statistically significant, by convention. Also, be aware that results are *more* reliable if the *p* value is *smaller*. For example, there is a higher probability that the results are accurate when $p = .01$ (1 in 100 chance of a spurious result) than when $p = .05$ (5 in 100 chances of a spurious result). Researchers either report an exact probability (e.g., $p = .03$) or a probability below conventional threshholds (e.g., $p < .05$).

In qualitative reports, researchers often organize findings according to the major themes, processes, or categories that were identified in the data. The results section of qualitative reports sometimes has several subsections, the headings of which correspond to the researcher's labels for the themes. Excerpts from the *raw data* (the actual words of participants) are presented to support and provide a rich description of the thematic analysis. The results section of qualitative studies may also present the researcher's emerging theory about the phenomenon under study.

Example from the results section of a qualitative study:
Murdoch and Franck (2012) conducted a phenomenological study of mothers' experiences caring for infants at home after neonatal unit discharge. Six themes formed the mothers' experiences, one of which was *apprehension*. Here is an excerpt illustrating that theme: "Obviously when she did come home it was obviously a big shock from coming from this big support network, in terms of the nurses and doctors around you, to suddenly not having anything at all" (p. 2014).

The Discussion Section

In the discussion, the researcher presents conclusions about the meaning and implications of the findings, i.e., what the results mean, why things turned out the way they did, how the findings fit with other evidence, and how the results can be used in practice. The discussion in both qualitative and quantitative reports may include the following elements:

- An interpretation of the results
- Clinical and research implications
- Study limitations and ramifications for the believability of the results

Researchers are in the best position to point out deficiencies in their studies. A discussion section that presents the researcher's grasp of study limitations demonstrates to readers that the authors were aware of the limitations and probably took them into account in interpreting the findings.

References

Research articles conclude with a list of the books and articles that were referenced. If you are interested in pursuing additional reading on a topic, the reference list of a recent study is an excellent place to begin.

THE STYLE OF RESEARCH JOURNAL ARTICLES

Research reports tell a story. However, the style in which many research journal articles are written—especially reports of quantitative studies—makes it difficult for some readers to figure out or become interested in the story.

Why Are Research Articles So Hard to Read?

To unaccustomed audiences, research reports may seem stuffy and bewildering. Four factors contribute to this impression:

1. *Compactness.* Journal space is limited, so authors compress a lot of information into a short space. Interesting, personalized aspects of the investigation cannot be reported, and, in qualitative studies, only a handful of supporting quotes can be included.
2. *Jargon.* The authors of research articles use research terms that may seem esoteric.
3. *Objectivity.* Quantitative researchers tend to avoid any impression of subjectivity, and so they tell their research stories in a way that makes them sound impersonal. Most quantitative research articles are written in the passive voice, which tends to make the articles less inviting and lively. Qualitative reports, by contrast, are often written in a more conversational style.

4. *Statistical information.* In quantitative reports, numbers and statistical symbols may intimidate readers who do not have statistical training.

A goal of this textbook is to assist you in understanding the content of research reports and in overcoming anxieties about jargon and statistical information.

 **HOW-TO-TELL TIP:** How can you tell if the voice is active or passive? In the active voice, the article would say what the researchers *did* (e.g., "We used a mercury sphygmomanometer to measure blood pressure"). In the passive voice, the article indicates what *was done*, without indicating who did it, although it is implied that the researchers were the agents ("e.g., a mercury sphygmomanometer *was used* to measure blood pressure").

Tips on Reading Research Articles

As you progress through this book, you will acquire skills for evaluating research articles, but the skills involved in critical appraisal take time to develop. The first step is to comprehend research articles. Your first few attempts to read a research article might be overwhelming, and you may wonder whether being able to understand them, let alone appraise them, is a realistic goal. Here are some hints on digesting research reports.

- Grow accustomed to the style of research articles by reading them frequently, even though you may not yet understand all the technical points.
- Read from a report that has been photocopied (or downloaded and printed) so that you can highlight or underline portions, and write questions or notes in the margins.
- Read journal articles slowly. It may be useful to skim the article first to get the major points and then read the article more carefully a second time.
- On the second reading, train yourself to become an *active* reader. Reading actively means that you constantly monitor yourself to verify that you understand what you are reading. If you have difficulty, you can ask someone for help. In most cases, that "someone" will be your instructor, but also consider contacting the researchers themselves.
- Keep this textbook with you as a reference when you read articles so that you can look up unfamiliar terms in the glossary or the index.
- Try not to get bogged down in (or scared away by) statistical information. Try to grasp the gist of the story without letting symbols and numbers frustrate you.
- Until you become accustomed to the style and jargon of research articles, you may want to "translate" them. You can do this by translating jargon into more familiar words, by recasting the report into an active voice, and by summarizing findings with words rather than numbers. As an example, Box 4.1 presents a summary of a fictitious study about the psychological consequences of having an abortion, written in a style that is typical for a journal article. Terms that can be looked up in the glossary of this book are underlined, and marginal notes indicate the type of information being communicated. Box 4.2 on page 68 presents a "translation" of this summary into more digestible language.

CRITIQUING RESEARCH REPORTS

A critical reading of a research article involves a careful appraisal of the researcher's major conceptual and methodologic decisions. You may find it difficult to criticize these decisions at this point, but your skills will improve as you progress through this book.

BOX 4.1 Summary of a Fictitious Study for Translation

Purpose of the study	The potentially negative sequelae of having an abortion on the psychological adjustment of adolescents have not been adequately studied. The present study sought to examine whether alternative pregnancy resolution decisions have different long-term effects on the psychological functioning of young women.	**Need for the study**
Research design	Three groups of low-income pregnant teenagers attending an inner-city clinic were the subjects in this study: those who delivered and kept the baby; those who delivered and relinquished the baby for adoption; and those who had an abortion. The sample included 25 subjects in each group.	**Study population** **Research sample**
Research instruments	The study instruments included a self-administered questionnaire and a battery of psychological tests measuring depression, anxiety, and psychosomatic symptoms. The instruments were administered upon entry into the study (when the subjects first came to the clinic) and then 1 year after termination of the pregnancy.	
Data analysis procedure	The data were analyzed using analysis of variance (ANOVA). The ANOVA tests indicated that the three groups did not differ significantly in terms of depression, anxiety, or psychosomatic symptoms at the initial testing ($p = .36$). At the post-test, however, the abortion group had significantly higher scores on the depression scale, and these girls were significantly more likely than the two delivery groups to report severe tension headaches (both $p < .01$). There were no significant differences on any of the dependent variables for the two delivery groups.	**Results**
Implications	The results of this study suggest that young women who elect to have an abortion may experience a number of long-term negative consequences. It would appear that appropriate efforts should be made to follow up abortion patients to determine their need for suitable treatment.	**Interpretation**

What Is a Research Critique?

A research **critique** is an objective assessment of a study's strengths and limitations. Critiques usually conclude with the reviewer's summary of the study's merits, recommendations regarding the value of the evidence, and suggestions about improving the study or the report.

Research critiques of individual studies are prepared for various reasons, and they vary in scope. Peer reviewers who are asked to prepare a written critique for a journal considering publication of a manuscript may evaluate the strengths and weaknesses in terms of substantive issues (Was the research problem significant to nursing?); theoretical issues (Were the conceptual underpinnings sound?); methodologic decisions (Were the methods rigorous, yielding believable evidence?); interpretive (Did the researcher reach defensible conclusions?); ethics (Were participants' rights protected?); and style (Is the report clear, grammatical, and well organized?). In short, peer reviewers do a comprehensive review to provide feedback to the researchers and to journal editors about the merit of both the study and the report, and typically offer suggestions for revisions.

Students taking a research methods course also may be asked to critique a study. Such critiques are usually expected to be comprehensive, encompassing the various dimensions just described. The purpose of such a thorough critique is to cultivate critical thinking and to induce students to apply newly acquired skills in research methods.

BOX 4.2 Translated Version of Fictitious Research Study

As researchers, we wondered whether young women who had an abortion had any emotional problems in the long run. It seemed to us that not enough research had been done to know whether any psychological harm resulted from an abortion.

We decided to study this question ourselves by comparing the experiences of three types of teenagers who became pregnant—first, girls who delivered and kept their babies; second, those who delivered the babies but gave them up for adoption; and third, those who elected to have an abortion. All teenagers that we recruited were poor, and all were patients at an inner-city clinic. Altogether, we studied 75girls—25 in each of the three groups. We evaluated the teenagers' emotional states by asking them to fill out a questionnaire and to take several psychological tests. These tests allowed us to assess things such as the girls' degree of depression and anxiety and whether they had any complaints of a psychosomatic nature. We asked them to fill out the forms twice: once when they came into the clinic, and then again a year after the abortion or the delivery.

We learned that the three groups of teenagers looked pretty much alike in terms of their emotional states when they first filled out the forms. Yet, when we compared how the three groups looked a year later, we found that the teenagers who had abortions were more depressed and were more likely to say they had severe tension headaches than teenagers in the other two groups. The teenagers who kept their babies and those who gave their babies up for adoption looked pretty similar 1 year after their babies were born, at least in terms of depression, anxiety, and psychosomatic complaints.

Thus, it seems that we might be right in having some concerns about the emotional effects of having an abortion. Nurses should be aware of these long-term emotional effects, and it even may be advisable to institute some type of follow-up procedure to find out if these young women need additional help.

Note, however, that critiques designed to inform evidence-based nursing practice are seldom comprehensive. For example, it is of little consequence to evidence-based practice (EBP) that a research article is ungrammatical. A critique of the clinical utility of a study focuses on whether the evidence is accurate, believable, and clinically relevant. These narrower critiques focus more squarely on appraising the research methods and the findings themselves.

Critiquing Support in This Textbook

We provide several types of support for research critiques. First, detailed critiquing suggestions relating to chapter content are included at the end of most chapters. Second, it is always illuminating to have a good model, so we prepared comprehensive critiques of two studies, one quantitative, the other qualitative. The two studies in their entirety and the critiques are in Appendixes C and D.

Third, we offer an abbreviated set of key critiquing guidelines for quantitative and qualitative reports in this chapter, in Tables 4.1 and 4.2, respectively. These guidelines are appropriate for a more focused critique designed to assess evidence quality. The questions in the guidelines concern the rigor with which the researchers dealt with critical research challenges, some of which are outlined in the next section.

TIP: For those undertaking a comprehensive critique, such as the ones included in Appendixes C and D, we offer more inclusive critiquing guidelines in the Chapter Supplement on thePoint website.

The second column of Tables 4.1 and 4.2 lists some key critiquing questions, and the third column cross-references the more detailed guidelines in the various chapters of the book.

(Text continued on page 71)

TABLE 4.1 Guide to a Focused Critique of Evidence Quality in a Quantitative Research Report

Aspect of the Report	Critiquing Questions	Detailed Critiquing Guidelines
Method Research design	• Was the most rigorous possible design used, given the purpose of the research? • Were appropriate comparisons made to enhance interpretability of the findings? • Was the number of data collection points appropriate? • Did the design minimize biases and threats to the internal, construct, and external validity of the study (e.g., was blinding used, was attrition minimized)?	Box 9.1, page 170
Population and sample	• Was the population identified and described? Was the sample described in sufficient detail? • Was the best possible sampling design used to enhance the sample's representativeness? Were sample biases minimized? • Was the sample size adequate? Was a power analysis used to estimate sample size needs?	Box 10.1, page 183
Data collection and measurement	• Were key variables operationalized using the best possible method (e.g., interviews, observations, and so on)? • Are the specific instruments adequately described and were they good choices, given the study purpose and study population? • Does the report provide evidence that the data collection methods yielded data that were high on reliability and validity?	Box 10.2, pages 193–94 Box 11.1, page 209
Procedures	• If there was an intervention, is it adequately described, and was it properly implemented? Did most participants allocated to the intervention group actually receive it? Was there evidence of intervention fidelity? • Were data collected in a manner that minimized bias? Was the staff who collected data appropriately trained?	Box 9.1, page 170 Box 10.2, pages 193–94
Results Data analysis	• Were appropriate statistical methods used? • Was the most powerful analytic method used? (e.g., did the analysis control for confounding variables)? • Were Type I and Type II errors avoided or minimized?	Box 12.1, page 243
Findings	• Was information about statistical significance presented? • Was information about effect size and precision of estimates (confidence intervals) presented?	Box 13.1, page 261
Summary assessment	• Despite any limitations, do the study findings appear to be valid—do you have confidence in the *truth* value of the results? • Does the study contribute any meaningful evidence that can be used in nursing practice or that is useful to the nursing discipline?	

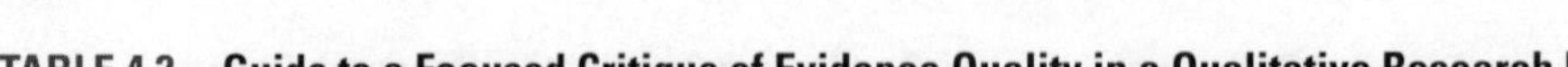

TABLE 4.2 Guide to a Focused Critique of Evidence Quality in a Qualitative Research Report

Aspect of the Report	Critiquing Questions	Detailed Critiquing Guidelines
Method Research design and research tradition	• Is the identified research tradition (if any) congruent with the methods used to collect and analyze data? • Was an adequate amount of time spent in the field or with study participants? • Was there evidence of reflexivity in the design?	Box 14.1, page 278
Sample and setting	• Was the group or population of interest adequately described? Were the setting and sample described in sufficient detail? • Was the best possible method of sampling used to enhance information richness and address the needs of the study? • Was the sample size adequate? Was saturation achieved?	Box 15.1, page 289
Data collection	• Were the methods of gathering data appropriate? Were data gathered through two or more methods to achieve triangulation? • Did the researcher ask the right questions or make the right observations? • Was there a sufficient amount of data? Were they of sufficient depth and richness?	Box 15.3, page 296
Procedures	• Do data collection and recording procedures appear appropriate? • Were data collected in a manner that minimized bias? Were the people who collected data appropriately trained?	Box 15.3, page 296
Enhancement of trustworthiness	• Did the researchers use strategies to enhance the trustworthiness/integrity of the study, and were those strategies adequate? • Do the researchers' clinical, substantive, or methodologic qualifications and experience enhance confidence in the findings and their interpretation?	Box 17.1, page 334
Results Data analysis	• Was the data analysis strategy compatible with the research tradition and with the nature and type of data gathered? • Did the analysis yield an appropriate "product" (e.g., a theory, taxonomy, thematic pattern, etc.)? • Did the analytic procedures suggest the possibility of biases?	Box 16.2, page 316
Findings	• Were the findings effectively summarized, with good use of excerpts and supporting arguments? • Do the themes adequately capture the meaning of the data? Does it appear that the researcher satisfactorily conceptualized the themes or patterns in the data? • Did the analysis yield an insightful, provocative, authentic, and meaningful picture of the phenomenon under investigation?	Box 16.2, page 316
Summary assessment	• Do the study findings appear to be trustworthy—do you have confidence in the *truth* value of the results? • Does the study contribute any meaningful evidence that can be used in nursing practice or that is useful to the nursing discipline?	

We know that most of the critiquing questions are too difficult for you to answer at this point, but your methodologic and critiquing skills will develop as you progress through this book.

The wording of questions in these guidelines calls for a yes or no answer (although it may well be that the answer sometimes will be, "Yes, *but*..."). In all cases, the desirable answer is *yes*, that is, a *no* suggests a possible limitation and a *yes* suggests a strength. Therefore, the more *yeses* a study gets, the stronger it is likely to be. Cumulatively, then, these guidelines can suggest a global assessment: a report with 10 *yeses* is likely to be superior to one with only two. However, these guidelines are not intended to yield a formal quality "score."

We acknowledge that our critiquing guidelines have some shortcomings. In particular, they are generic even though critiquing cannot use a one-size-fits-all list of questions. Important critiquing questions that are relevant to certain studies (e.g., those that have a Therapy purpose) do not fit into a set of general questions for all quantitative studies. Thus, you need to use some judgment about whether the guidelines are sufficiently comprehensive for the type of study you are critiquing. We also note that there are questions in these guidelines for which there are no totally objective answers. Even experts sometimes disagree about methodologic strategies.

TIP: An important thing to remember is that it is appropriate to assume the posture of a skeptic when you are critiquing research reports. Just as a careful clinician seeks research evidence that certain practices are or are not effective, you as a reviewer should demand evidence that the researchers' methodologic decisions were sound.

Critiquing With Key Research Challenges in Mind

In critiquing a study, it is useful to be aware of the challenges that confront researchers. For example, they face ethical challenges (e.g., Can the study achieve its goals without infringing on human rights?); practical challenges (Will I be able to recruit enough study participants?); and methodologic challenges (Will the adopted methods yield results that can be trusted and applied to other settings?). Most of this book provides guidance relating to the last question, and this section highlights key methodologic challenges as a way of introducing important terms and concepts that are relevant in a critique. Keep in mind that the worth of a study's evidence for nursing practice relies on how well researchers deal with these challenges.

Inference

Inference is an integral part of doing and critiquing research. An **inference** is a conclusion drawn from the study evidence using logical reasoning and taking into account the methods used to generate that evidence.

Inference is necessary because researchers use proxies that "stand in" for things that are fundamentally of interest. A sample of participants is a proxy for an entire population. A study site is a proxy for all relevant sites in which the phenomena of interest could unfold. A measuring scale yields proxy information about constructs that can only be captured through approximations. A control group that does not receive an intervention is a proxy for what would happen to the *same* people if they simultaneously received *and* did not receive an intervention.

Researchers face the challenge of using methods that yield good and persuasive evidence in support of inferences that they wish to make. Readers must draw their own inferences based on a critique of methodologic decisions.

Reliability, Validity, and Trustworthiness

Researchers want their inferences to correspond to the *truth*. Research cannot contribute evidence to guide clinical practice if the findings are inaccurate, biased, or fail to represent the experiences of the target group

Quantitative researchers use several criteria to assess the quality of a study, sometimes referred to as its **scientific merit**. Two especially important criteria are reliability and validity. **Reliability** refers to the accuracy and consistency of information obtained in a study. The term is most often associated with the methods used to measure variables. For example, if a thermometer measured Alan's temperature as 98.1°F one minute and as 102.5°F the next minute, the thermometer would be unreliable. The concept of reliability is also important in interpreting statistical analyses. *Statistical reliability* refers to the probability that the same results would be obtained with a new sample of subjects—that is, that the results are an accurate reflection of a wider group than just the particular people who participated in the study.

Validity is a more complex concept that broadly concerns the *soundness* of the study's evidence. Like reliability, validity is an important criterion for evaluating methods to measure variables. In this context, the validity question is whether the methods are really measuring the concepts that they purport to measure. Is a paper-and-pencil measure of depression *really* measuring depression? Or is it measuring something else, such as loneliness or stress? Researchers strive for solid conceptual definitions of research variables and valid methods to operationalize them.

Another aspect of validity concerns the quality of evidence about the relationship between the independent variable and the dependent variable. Did a nursing intervention *really* bring about improvements in patients' outcomes—or were other confounding factors responsible for patients' progress? Researchers make numerous methodologic decisions that can influence this type of study validity.

Qualitative researchers use different criteria (and different terminology) in evaluating a study's quality. In general, qualitative researchers discuss methods of enhancing the **trustworthiness** of the study's data and findings (Lincoln & Guba, 1985). Trustworthiness encompasses several different dimensions—credibility, transferability, confirmability, dependability, and authenticity—which are described in Chapter 17.

Credibility is an especially important aspect of trustworthiness. Credibility is achieved to the extent that the research methods inspire confidence that the results and interpretations are truthful and accurate. Credibility in a qualitative study can be enhanced through various approaches, but one strategy merits early discussion because it has implications for the design of all studies, including quantitative ones. **Triangulation** is the use of multiple sources or referents to draw conclusions about what constitutes the truth. In a quantitative study, this might mean having two ways to measure a dependent variable, to assess whether predicted effects are consistent. In a qualitative study, triangulation might involve efforts to understand the complexity of a phenomenon by using multiple data collection methods to converge on the truth (e.g., having in-depth discussions with participants, as well as watching their behavior in natural settings). Nurse researchers are also beginning to triangulate across paradigms—that is, to integrate both qualitative and quantitative data in a single study to offset the shortcomings of each approach and enhance the validity of the conclusions.

Example of triangulation:

Carlsson and colleagues (2012) conducted a study to describe the accuracy of discharge information for patients with eating difficulties after stroke. They triangulated information from hospital records, interviews with nurses, and observations of patients' eating.

Nurse researchers need to design their studies in such a way that threats to the reliability, validity, and trustworthiness of their studies are minimized, and users of research must evaluate the extent to which they were successful.

> **TIP:** In reading and critiquing research articles, it is appropriate to have a "show me" attitude—that is, to expect researchers to build and present a solid case for the merit of their inferences. They do this by providing evidence that the findings are reliable and valid or trustworthy.

Bias

Bias can threaten a study's validity and trustworthiness. A **bias** is an influence that results in an error in an inference or estimate. Biases can affect the quality of evidence in both qualitative and quantitative studies. Bias can result from various factors, including study participants' lack of candor or desire to please, researchers' preconceptions, or faulty methods of collecting data.

Bias can never be avoided totally because the potential for its occurrence is so pervasive. Some bias is haphazard and affects only small segments of the data. As an example of such *random bias*, a few study participants might provide inaccurate information because they were tired at the time of data collection. *Systematic bias* results when the bias is consistent or uniform. For example, if a spring scale consistently measured people's weight as being 2 pounds heavier than their true weight, there would be systematic bias in the data on weight. Rigorous research methods aim to eliminate or minimize bias.

Researchers adopt a variety of strategies to address bias. Triangulation is one such approach, the idea being that multiple sources of information or points of view help to counterbalance biases and offer avenues to identify them. In quantitative research, methods to combat bias often entail research control.

Research Control

One of the central features of quantitative studies is that they typically involve efforts to control aspects of the research. **Research control** usually involves holding constant influences on the outcome variable so that the true relationship between the independent and outcome variables can be understood. In other words, research control attempts to eliminate contaminating factors that might cloud the relationship between the variables that are of central interest.

Contaminating factors, often called **confounding** (or *extraneous*) **variables**, can best be illustrated with an example. Suppose we were studying whether urinary incontinence (UI) leads to depression. Prior evidence suggests that this is the case, but previous studies have not clarified whether it is UI per se or other factors that contribute to risk of depression. The question is whether UI itself (the independent variable) contributes to higher levels of depression, or whether there are other factors that can account for the relationship between UI and depression. We need to design a study so as to control other determinants of the outcome—determinants that are also related to the independent variable, UI.

One confounding variable here is age. Levels of depression tend to be higher in older people; and, people with UI tend to be older than those without this problem. In other words, perhaps age is the *real* cause of higher depression in people with UI. If age is not controlled, than any observed relationship between UI and depression could be caused by UI, or by age.

Three possible explanations might be portrayed schematically as follows:

1. UI→depression
2. Age→UI→depression
3. 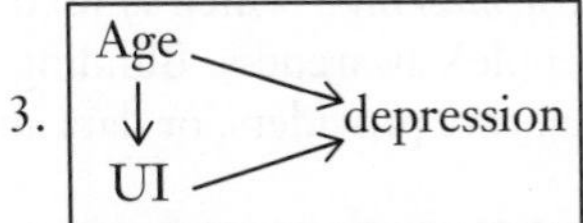

The arrows here symbolize a causal mechanism or an influence. In model 1, UI directly affects depression, independently of any other factors. In model 2, UI is a *mediating variable*—the effect of age on depression is *mediated* by UI. According to this representation, age affects depression *through* the effect that age has on UI. In model 3, both age and UI have separate effects on depression, and age also increases the risk of UI. Some research is specifically designed to test paths of mediation and multiple causation, but in the present example age is extraneous to the research question. We want to design a study so that the first explanation can be tested. Age must be controlled if our goal is to explore the validity of model 1, which posits that, no matter what a person's age, having UI makes a person more vulnerable to depression.

How can we impose such control? There are a number of ways, as we discuss in Chapter 9, but the general principle underlying each alternative is that the confounding variables must be *held constant*. The confounding variable must somehow be handled so that, in the context of the study, the confounding variable is not related to the independent variable or the outcome. As an example, let us say we wanted to compare the average scores on a depression scale for those with and without UI. We would want to design a study in such a way that the ages of those in the UI and non-UI groups are comparable, even though, in general, the groups are not comparable in terms of age.

By exercising control over age in this example, we would be taking a step toward explaining the relationship between variables. The world is complex, and many variables are interrelated in complicated ways. When studying a problem within the positivist paradigm, researchers usually analyze a couple of relationships at a time. Modest quantitative studies can contribute evidence, but the value of the evidence is often related to how well researchers control confounding influences.

Research rooted in the constructivist paradigm does not impose controls. With their emphasis on holism and individual human experience, qualitative researchers typically believe that imposing controls removes some of the meaning of reality.

Bias Reduction: Randomness and Blinding

For quantitative researchers, a powerful tool for eliminating bias involves **randomness**—having certain features of the study established by chance rather than by design or researcher preference. When people are selected *at random* to participate in a study, for example, each person in the initial pool has an equal chance of being selected. This in turn means that there are no systematic biases in the make-up of the sample. Men and women have an equal chance of being selected, for example. Similarly, if participants are allocated *at random* to groups that will be compared (e.g., a special intervention and "usual care" group), then there can be no systematic biases in the groups' composition. Randomness is a compelling method of controlling confounding variables and reducing bias.

Example of randomness:

Lindseth and colleagues (2012) studied the effect of alternative diets on sleep outcomes. Their sample of 44 healthy adults was randomly assigned to different orderings of four diets—a normal diet, high-protein diet, high-fat diet, and high-carbohydrate diet. Sleep efficiency and other measures of sleep were monitored under the different diets.

Another bias-reducing strategy is called **blinding** (or *masking*), which is used in some quantitative studies to prevent biases stemming from people's awareness. Blinding involves concealing information from participants, data collectors, care providers, or data analysts to enhance objectivity. For example, if study participants are aware of whether they are getting an experimental drug or a sham drug (a **placebo**), then their outcomes could be influenced by their expectations of the new drug's efficacy. Blinding involves disguising or withholding information about participants' status in the study (e.g., whether they are in a certain group), or about the study hypotheses.

Qualitative researchers do not consider randomness or blinding desirable tools for understanding phenomena. A researcher's judgment is viewed as an indispensable vehicle for uncovering the complexities of the phenomena of interest.

Reflexivity

Qualitative researchers are also interested in discovering the truth about human experience. Qualitative researchers often rely on reflexivity to guard against personal bias. **Reflexivity** is the process of reflecting critically on the self, and of analyzing and making note of personal values that could affect data collection and interpretation. Qualitative researchers are trained to explore these issues, to be reflective about decisions made during the inquiry, and to record their thoughts in personal diaries and memos.

Example of reflexivity:

Frisvold and colleagues (2012) explored nurses' perceptions of having participated in a stress-reduction course a year earlier. The researchers used reflexive journaling and reflexive tape recording: "the investigator's reactions to certain observations were immediately documented to identify personal bias and preconceived notions that may affect the analysis of data" (p. 271).

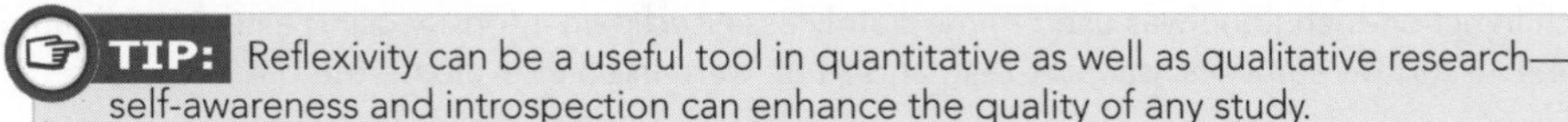

TIP: Reflexivity can be a useful tool in quantitative as well as qualitative research—self-awareness and introspection can enhance the quality of any study.

Generalizability and Transferability

Nurses increasingly rely on evidence from disciplined research as a guide in their clinical practice. EBP is based on the assumption that study findings are not unique to the people, places, or circumstances of the original research.

As noted in Chapter 1, *generalizability* is the criterion used in quantitative studies to assess the extent to which the findings can be applied to other groups and settings. How do researchers enhance the generalizability of a study? First and foremost, they must design studies strong in reliability and validity. There is little point in wondering whether results are generalizable if they are not accurate or valid. In selecting participants, researchers must also give thought to the types of people to whom results might be generalized—and then select subjects in such a way that a representative sample is obtained. If a study is intended to have implications for male and female patients, then men and women should be included as participants.

Qualitative researchers do not specifically aim for generalizability, but they do want to generate knowledge that might be useful in other situations. Lincoln and Guba (1985), in their influential book on naturalistic inquiry, discuss the concept of **transferability**, the extent to which qualitative findings can be transferred to other settings, as another aspect of trustworthiness. An important mechanism for promoting transferability is the amount of rich descriptive information qualitative researchers provide about the contexts of their studies.

RESEARCH EXAMPLES WITH CRITICAL THINKING EXERCISES

Abstracts for a quantitative and a qualitative nursing study are presented below, followed by some questions to guide critical thinking.

Examples 1 and 2 below are also featured in our *Interactive Critical Thinking Activity* on thePoint website where you can easily record, print, and e-mail your responses to the related questions.

EXAMPLE 1 ● Quantitative Research

Study: Effect on pain of changing the needle prior to administering medicine intramuscularly (Ağac & Günes, 2011, p. 563)

Aim: This paper is the report of a study to determine whether changing the needle before administering an intramuscular injection could reduce pain, and to investigate gender differences in pain perception.

Background: A skilled injection technique can make the patient's experience less painful and avoid unnecessary complications, and the use of separate needles to draw up and administer medication ensures that the tip of the needle is sharp and free from medication residue.

Method: A randomized controlled trial was carried out between January 2009 and May 2009 with 100 patients receiving diclofenac sodium intramuscularly in an emergency and traffic hospital in Izmir, Turkey. The primary outcome was pain intensity measured on a numerical rating scale. Each patient received two injections by the same investigator using two different techniques. The two techniques were randomly allocated and the patients were blinded to the injection technique being administered. After each injection, another investigator who had no prior knowledge of which injection technique was used immediately assessed pain intensity using a numerical rating scale. Descriptive statistics, paired t-test, and t-test were used to evaluate the data.

Findings: Findings demonstrated that changing the needle prior to intramuscular medication administration significantly reduced pain intensity. A statistical difference in pain intensity was observed between the two injection techniques.

Conclusions: The results supported the hypothesis that changing the needle prior to administering the medicine significantly reduced pain intensity.

CRITICAL THINKING EXERCISES

1. "Translate" the abstract into a summary that is more consumer friendly. Underline any technical terms and look them up in the glossary.
2. Also consider the following targeted questions:
   a. What were the independent and dependent variables in this study?
   b. Is this study experimental or nonexperimental?
   c. How, if at all, was *randomness* used in this study?
   d. How, if at all, was *blinding* used in this study?
3. If the results of this study are valid and generalizable, in what ways do you think the findings could be used in clinical practice?

EXAMPLE 2 ● Qualitative Research

Study: "How should I touch you?": A qualitative study of attitudes on intimate touch in nursing care (O'Lynn & Krauscheid, 2011, p. 24)

Objective: Although touch is essential to nursing practice, few studies have investigated patients' preferences for how nurses should perform tasks involving touch, especially intimate touch involving private and sometimes anxiety-provoking areas of patients' bodies. Some studies suggest that patients have more concerns about intimate touch from male than female nurses. This study sought to elicit the attitudes of laypersons on intimate touch provided by nurses in general and male nurses in particular.

Methods: A maximum-variation sample of 24 adults was selected and semi-structured interviews were conducted in four focus groups. Interviews were recorded and transcribed; thematic analysis was performed.

Results: Four themes emerged from the interviews: "Communicate with me," "Give me choices," "Ask me about gender," and "Touch me professionally, not too fast and not too slow." Participants said they want to contribute to decisions about whether intimate touch is necessary, and when it is, they want information from and rapport with their nurses. Participants varied in their responses to questions on the nurse's gender. They said they want a firm but not rough touch and for nurses to ensure their privacy.

Conclusion: These findings suggest that nurses and other clinicians who provide intimate care should be more aware of patients' attitudes on touch. Further research on the patient's perspective is warranted.

CRITICAL THINKING EXERCISES

1. "Translate" the abstract into a summary that is more consumer friendly. Underline any technical terms and look them up in the glossary.
2. Also consider the following targeted questions:
   a. On which qualitative research tradition, if any, was this study based?
   b. Is this study experimental or nonexperimental?
   c. How, if at all, was *randomness* used in this study?
   d. Is there any indication in the abstract that *triangulation* was used? What about *Reflexivity*?
3. If the results of this study are trustworthy and transferable, what might be some of the uses to which the findings could be put in clinical practice?
4. Compare the headings used in the two abstracts in Examples 1 and 2. Which do you prefer?

EXAMPLE 3 ● Quantitative Research in Appendix A

- Read the abstract for Howell and colleagues' (2007) study ("Anxiety, anger, and blood pressure in children") in Appendix A on pages 395–402.

CRITICAL THINKING EXERCISES

1. "Translate" the abstract into a summary that is more consumer friendly. Underline any technical terms and look them up in the glossary.
2. Also consider the following targeted questions:
   a. Where does the introduction to this article begin and end?
   b. How, if at all, was *randomness* used in this study?
   c. How, if at all, was *blinding* used?
   d. Comment on the possible generalizability of the study findings.

EXAMPLE 4 ● Qualitative Research in Appendix B

- Read the abstract for Beck and Watson's (2010) study ("Subsequent childbirth after a previous traumatic birth") in Appendix B on pages 403–412.

CRITICAL THINKING EXERCISES

1. "Translate" the abstract into a summary that is more consumer-friendly. Underline any technical terms and look them up in the glossary.
2. Also consider the following targeted questions, which may assist you in assessing aspects of the study's merit:
   a. Where does the introduction to this article begin and end?
   b. How, if at all, was *randomness* used in this study?
   c. Is there any indication in the abstract that *triangulation* was used? What about *Reflexivity*?
   d. Comment on the possible transferability of the study findings.

WANT TO KNOW MORE? A wide variety of resources to enhance your learning and understanding of this chapter are available on thePoint.

- Interactive Critical Thinking Activity
- Chapter Supplement on Critiquing Guidelines for Quantitative and Qualitative Research Reports
- Answers to the Critical Thinking Exercises for Examples 3 and 4
- Student Review Questions
- Full-text online

Additional study aids including eight journal articles and related questions are also available in *Study Guide for Essentials of Nursing Research, 8e.*

SUMMARY POINTS

- Both qualitative and quantitative researchers disseminate their findings, most often by publishing reports of their research as **journal articles**, which concisely communicate what the researcher did and what was found.
- Journal articles often consist of an **abstract** (a synopsis of the study) and four major sections that often follow the **IMRAD format**: an **I**ntroduction (the research problem and its context); **M**ethod section (the strategies used to answer research questions); **R**esults (study findings); **and D**iscussion (interpretation of the findings).
- Research reports are often difficult to read because they are dense, concise, and contain jargon. Quantitative research reports may be intimidating at first because, compared to qualitative reports, they are more impersonal and report on statistical tests.
- **Statistical tests** are used to test hypotheses and to evaluate the reliability of the findings. Findings that are **statistically significant** have a high probability of being "real."
- A goal of this book is to help students to prepare a research **critique**, which is a critical appraisal of the strengths and limitations of a study, often to assess the worth of the evidence for nursing practice.
- Researchers face numerous challenges, the solutions to which must be considered in critiquing a study because they affect the inferences that can be made.
- An **inference** is a conclusion drawn from the study evidence, taking into account the methods used to generate that evidence. Researchers strive to have their inferences correspond to the *truth*.
- **Reliability** (a key challenge in quantitative research) refers to the accuracy and consistency of information obtained in a study. **Validity** is a more complex concept that broadly concerns the *soundness* of the study's evidence—that is, whether the findings are cogent, convincing, and well grounded.
- **Trustworthiness** in qualitative research encompasses several different dimensions, including credibility, dependability, confirmability, transferability and authenticity.
- **Credibility** is achieved to the extent that the methods engender confidence in the truth of the data and in the researchers' interpretations. **Triangulation**, the use of multiple

sources or referents to draw conclusions about what constitutes the truth, is one approach to enhancing credibility.

- A **bias** is an influence that produces a distortion in the study results. In quantitative studies, research control is an approach to addressing bias. **Research control** is used to *hold constant* outside influences on the dependent variable so that the relationship between the independent and dependent variables can be better understood.
- Researchers seek to control **confounding** (or *extraneous*) **variables**—variables that are extraneous to the purpose of a specific study.
- For quantitative researchers, **randomness**—having certain features of the study established by chance rather than by design or personal preference—is a powerful tool to eliminate bias.
- **Blinding** (or *masking*) is sometimes used to avoid biases stemming from participants' or research agents' awareness of study hypotheses or research status.
- **Reflexivity**, the process of reflecting critically on the self and of scrutinizing personal values that could affect data collection and interpretation, is an important tool in qualitative research.
- **Generalizability** in a quantitative study concerns the extent to which the findings can be applied to other groups and settings.
- A similar concept in qualitative studies is **transferability**, the extent to which qualitative findings can be transferred to other settings. One mechanism for promoting transferability is a rich and thorough description of the research context so that others can make inferences about contextual similarities.

REFERENCES FOR CHAPTER 4

Ağac, E., & Günes, U. (2011). Effect on pain of changing the needle prior to administering medicine intramuscularly. *Journal of Advanced Nursing, 67*, 563–568.

Carlsson, E., Ehnfors, M., Aldh, A., & Ehrenberg, A. (2012). Accuracy and continuity in discharge information for patients with eating difficulties after stroke. *Journal of Clinical Nursing, 21*, 21–31.

Frisvold, M., Lindquist, R., & McAlpine, C. (2012). Living life in the balance at midlife: Lessons learned from mindfulness. *Western Journal of Nursing Research, 34*(2), 265–278.

Li, S., Wang, T., Vivienne Wu, S., Liang, S., & Tung, H. (2011). Efficacy of controlling night-time noise and activities to improve paitents' sleep quality in a surgical intensive care unit. *Journal of Clinical Nursing, 20*, 396–407.

Lincoln, Y. S., & Guba, E. G. (1985). *Naturalistic inquiry*. Newbury Park, CA: Sage.

Lindseth, G., Lindseth, P., & Thompson, M. (2012). Nutritional effects on sleep. *Western Journal of Nursing Research*, PubMed ID 21816963.

Murdoch, M., & Franck, L. (2012). Gaining confidence and perspective: A phenomenological study of mothers' lived experiences caring for infants at home after neonatal unit discharge. *Journal of Advanced Nursing, 68*, 2008–2020.

O'Lynn, C., & Krautscheid, L. (2011). "How should I touch you?": A qualitative study of attitudes on intimate touch in nursing care. *American Journal of Nursing, 111*, 24–31.

Porter, E., Benson, J., & Matsuda, S. (2011). Older homebound women: Negotiating reliance on a cane of walker. Qualitative Health Research, 21, 534–548.

chapter

5 Ethics in Research

LEARNING OBJECTIVES

On completing this chapter, you will be able to:

- Discuss the historical background that led to the creation of various codes of ethics
- Understand the potential for ethical dilemmas stemming from conflicts between ethics and research demands
- Identify the three primary ethical principles articulated in the *Belmont Report* and the important dimensions encompassed by each
- Identify procedures for adhering to ethical principles and protecting study participants
- Given sufficient information, evaluate the ethical dimensions of a research report
- Define new terms in the chapter

KEY TERMS

Anonymity	Confidentiality	Minimal risk
Assent	Debriefing	Process consent
Belmont Report	Ethical dilemma	Research misconduct
Beneficence	Full disclosure	Risk/benefit assessment
Certificate of confidentiality	Implied consent	Stipend
Code of ethics	Informed consent	Vulnerable population
Consent form	Institutional Review Board (IRB)	

This chapter discusses some of the major ethical principles relevant to health care research. It also describes procedures that researchers can use to address these principles.

ETHICS AND RESEARCH

In any research with human beings or animals, researchers must address ethical issues. Ethical concerns are especially prominent in nursing research because the line between what constitutes the expected practice of nursing and the collection of research data sometimes gets blurred.

Historical Background

We might like to think that violations of moral principles among researchers occurred centuries ago rather than recently, but this is not the case. The Nazi medical experiments of the

1930s and 1940s are the most famous example of recent disregard for ethical conduct. The Nazi program of research involved using prisoners of war and racial "enemies" in experiments designed to test human endurance and reactions to untested drugs. The studies were unethical not only because they exposed people to harm and even death, but because subjects could not refuse participation. Similar wartime experiments that raised ethical concerns were conducted in Japan and Australia.

There are more recent examples. For instance, between 1932 and 1972, the Tuskegee Syphilis Study, sponsored by the U.S. Public Health Service, investigated the effects of syphilis among 400 poor African-American men. Medical treatment was deliberately withheld to study the course of the untreated disease. Similarly, Dr. Herbert Green in Auckland, New Zealand, studied women with cervical cancer in the 1980s; patients with carcinoma *in situ* were not given treatment so that researchers could study the natural progression of the disease.

In Willowbrook, an institution for the mentally retarded on Staten Island, children were deliberately infected with the hepatitis virus during the 1960s. It was revealed in 1993 that U.S. federal agencies had sponsored radiation experiments since the 1940s on hundreds of people, many of them prisoners or elderly hospital patients. And, in 2010 it was revealed that a United States doctor who worked on the Tuskegee study inoculated prisoners in Guatemala with syphilis in the 1940s. Other examples of studies with ethical transgressions have emerged to give ethical concerns the high visibility they have today.

Codes of Ethics

In response to human rights violations, various **codes of ethics** have been developed. One of the first international set of ethical standards was the Nuremberg Code, developed in 1949 in response to the Nazi atrocities. Several other international standards have subsequently been developed, including the Declaration of Helsinki, which was adopted in 1964 by the World Medical Association and most recently revised in 2008.

Most disciplines, such as medicine and psychology, have established their own code of ethics. Nurses also have developed ethical guidelines. In the United States, the American Nurses Association (ANA) issued *Ethical Guidelines in the Conduct, Dissemination, and Implementation of Nursing Research* in 1995 (Silva, 1995). ANA (2001) also published a revised *Code of Ethics for Nurses with Interpretive Statements*, a document that covers ethical issues for practicing nurses primarily but also includes principles that apply to nurse researchers. In Canada, the Canadian Nurses Association published its *Ethical Research Guidelines for Registered Nurses* in 2002. And, the International Council of Nurses (ICN) has developed the *ICN Code of Ethics for Nurses*, which was most recently updated in 2006.

TIP: There are many useful websites devoted to ethical principles, some of which are listed in the Internet Resources on thePoint website, for you. to click on directly.

Government Regulations for Protecting Study Participants

Governments throughout the world fund research and establish rules for adhering to ethical principles. In the United States, an important code of ethics was adopted by the National Commission for the Protection of Human Subjects of Biomedical and Behavioral Research. The commission issued a report in 1978, known as the ***Belmont Report***, which provided a model for many guidelines adopted by disciplinary organizations in the

United States. The Belmont Report also served as the basis for regulations affecting research sponsored by the U.S. government, including studies supported by the National Institute of Nursing Research (NINR). The United States ethical regulations have been codified at Title 45 Part 46 of the Code of Federal Regulations, and were revised most recently in 2005.

Ethical Dilemmas in Conducting Research

Research that violates ethical principles typically occurs out of a researcher's conviction that knowledge is potentially life-saving or beneficial in the long run. There are research problems in which participants' rights and study demands are put in direct conflict, posing **ethical dilemmas** for researchers. Here are examples of research problems in which the desire for rigor conflicts with ethical considerations:

1. *Research question*: Are nurses equally empathic in their treatment of ICU patients from different ethnic backgrounds?

   Ethical dilemma: Ethics require that participants be informed of their role in a study. Yet if the researcher tells participating nurses that their degree of empathy in treating different patients will be scrutinized, will their behavior be "normal?" If the nurses' usual behavior is altered because of the presence of research observers, then the findings will not be valid.
2. *Research question*: What are the coping mechanisms of parents whose children have a terminal illness?

   Ethical dilemma: To answer this question, the researcher may need to probe into parents' psychological state at a vulnerable time; such probing could be painful, and yet knowledge of the parents' coping mechanisms might help to design more effective ways of addressing parents' grief and stress.
3. *Research question*: Does a new medication prolong life in patients with cancer?

   Ethical dilemma: The best way to test the effectiveness of an intervention is to administer it to some people but withhold it from others to see if the groups have different outcomes. Yet, if the intervention is untested (e.g., a new drug), the group receiving the intervention may be exposed to harmful side effects. On the other hand, the group *not* receiving the drug may be denied a beneficial treatment.
4. *Research question*: What is the process by which adult children adapt to the day-to-day stresses of caring for a parent with Alzheimer's disease?

   Ethical dilemma: In a qualitative study, which would be appropriate for this question, participants may get so closely involved with the researcher that they become willing to share "secrets." Interviews can become confessions. In this example, suppose a woman admitted to physically abusing her mother—how can the researcher report such information to authorities without breaking a pledge of confidentiality? And, if the researcher divulges the information to authorities, how can a pledge of confidentiality be given in good faith to other participants?

As these examples suggest, researchers are sometimes in a bind. Their goal is develop high-quality evidence for practice, but they must also adhere to rules for protecting human rights. Another type of dilemma may arise if nurse researchers face conflict-of-interest situations, in which their expected behavior as nurses conflicts with standard research behavior (e.g., deviating from a research protocol to assist a patient). It is precisely because of such dilemmas that codes of ethics have been developed to guide researchers' efforts.

ETHICAL PRINCIPLES FOR PROTECTING STUDY PARTICIPANTS

The *Belmont Report* articulated three primary ethical principles on which standards of ethical research conduct are based: beneficence, respect for human dignity, and justice. We briefly discuss these principles and then describe methods researchers use to comply with them.

Beneficence

A fundamental ethical principle in research is that of **beneficence**, the duty to minimize harm and maximize benefits. Human research should produce benefits for participants themselves or—a situation that is more common—for other individuals or society as a whole.

The Right to Freedom From Harm and Discomfort

Researchers have an obligation to prevent or minimize harm in studies with humans. Participants must not be subjected to unnecessary risks of harm or discomfort, and their participation in research must be essential to achieving societally important aims. In research with humans, *harm* and *discomfort* can be physical (e.g., injury), emotional (e.g., stress), social (e.g., loss of social support), or financial (e.g., loss of wages). Ethical researchers must use strategies to minimize all types of harms and discomforts, even ones that are temporary.

Protecting human beings from physical harm is often straightforward, but it is not as easy to address the psychological aspects of study participation, which can be subtle. For example, participants may be asked questions about their personal views, weaknesses, or fears. Such queries might lead people to reveal deeply personal information. The need for sensitivity may be greater in qualitative studies, which often involve in-depth exploration into highly personal areas. The point is not that researchers should refrain from asking questions but rather that they need to be aware of the nature of the intrusion on people's psyches.

The Right to Protection From Exploitation

Involvement in a study should not place participants at a disadvantage. Participants need to be assured that their participation, or information they provide, will not be used against them in any way. For example, people describing their economic situation should not risk loss of public health benefits; people reporting drug abuse should not fear exposure to criminal authorities.

Study participants enter into a special relationship with researchers, and this relationship should not be exploited. Exploitation may be overt and malicious (e.g., sexual exploitation), but it might also be more subtle (e.g., getting people to complete a 1-year follow-up interview, without having warned them of this possibility at the outset). Because nurse researchers may have a nurse–patient (in addition to a researcher–participant) relationship, special care may be needed to avoid exploiting that bond. Patients' consent to participate in a study may result from their understanding of the researcher's role as *nurse*, not as *researcher*.

In qualitative research, the risk of exploitation may become high because the psychological distance between investigators and participants typically declines as the study progresses. The emergence of a pseudo-therapeutic relationship is not uncommon, which could create additional risks that exploitation could inadvertently occur. On the other hand, qualitative researchers typically are in a better position than quantitative researchers to *do good*, rather than just to avoid doing harm, because of the close relationships they often develop with participants.

Example of therapeutic research experiences:
Participants in Beck's (2005) studies on birth trauma and posttraumatic stress disorder (PTSD) expressed a range of benefits they derived from e-mail exchanges with Beck. Here is what one informant voluntarily shared: "You thanked me for everything in your e-mail, and I want to THANK YOU for caring. For me, it means a lot that you have taken an interest in this subject and are taking the time and effort to find out more about PTSD. For someone to even acknowledge this condition means a lot for someone who has suffered from it" (p. 417).

Respect for Human Dignity

Respect for human dignity is the second ethical principle articulated in the *Belmont Report*. This principle includes the right to self-determination and the right to full disclosure.

The Right to Self-Determination

The principle of *self-determination* means that prospective participants have the right to decide voluntarily whether to participate in a study, without risking penalty or prejudicial treatment. It also means that people have the right to ask questions, to refuse to give information, and to withdraw from the study.

A person's right to self-determination includes freedom from coercion. *Coercion* involves explicit or implicit threats of penalty from failing to participate in a study or excessive rewards from agreeing to participate. The issue of coercion requires careful thought when researchers are in a position of authority or influence over potential participants, as might be the case in a nurse–patient relationship. The issue of coercion may require scrutiny in other situations as well. For example, a generous monetary incentive (or **stipend**) offered to encourage the participation of a low-income group (e.g., the homeless) might be considered mildly coercive because such incentives may place undue pressure on prospective participants.

The Right to Full Disclosure

Respect for human dignity encompasses people's right to make informed, voluntary decisions about study participation, which requires full disclosure. **Full disclosure** means that the researcher has fully described the study, the person's right to refuse participation, and possible risks and benefits. The right to self-determination and the right to full disclosure are the two major elements on which informed consent—discussed later in this chapter—is based.

Achieving full disclosure is not always straightforward because it can sometimes create two types of bias: biases affecting the accuracy of the data and biases from sample recruitment problems. Suppose we were testing the hypothesis that high school students with a high absentee rate are more likely to be substance abusers than students with good attendance. If we approached potential participants and fully explained the study's purpose, some students might refuse to participate, and nonparticipation likely would be biased; students who are substance abusers—the group of primary interest—might be least likely to participate. Moreover, by knowing the study purpose, those who participate might not give candid responses. In such a situation, full disclosure could undermine the study.

In such situations, researchers sometimes use *covert data collection* or *concealment*—collecting data without participants' knowledge and thus without their consent. This might happen if a researcher wanted to observe people's behavior and was concerned that doing so openly would change the behavior of interest. Researchers might choose to obtain needed information through concealed methods, such as by videotaping with hidden equipment or observing while pretending to be engaged in other activities.

A more controversial technique is the use of deception. *Deception* can involve deliberately withholding information about the study, or providing participants with false information. For example, in studying high school students' use of drugs we might describe the research as a study of students' health practices, which is a mild form of misinformation.

Deception and concealment are problematic ethically because they interfere with people's right to make truly informed decisions about personal costs and benefits of participation. Some people think that deception is never justified, but others believe that if the study involves minimal risk yet offers great benefits to society, then deception may be justified.

Full disclosure has emerged as a concern in connection with data collected over the Internet (e.g., analyzing the content of messages posted to chat rooms). The issue is whether such messages can be used as data without the authors' consent. Some researchers believe that anything posted electronically is in the public domain, but others feel that the same ethical standards must apply in cyberspace research and that researchers must carefully protect the rights of individuals who are participants in "virtual" communities.

Justice

The third broad principle articulated in the *Belmont Report* concerns justice, which includes participants' right to fair treatment and their right to privacy.

The Right to Fair Treatment

One aspect of justice concerns the equitable distribution of benefits and burdens of research. The selection of participants should be based on research requirements and not on people's vulnerabilities. Historically, subject selection has been a key ethical concern, with many researchers selecting groups deemed to have lower social standing (e.g., poor people, prisoners, the mentally disabled) as study participants. The principle of justice imposes particular obligations toward individuals who are unable to protect their own interests (e.g., dying patients) to ensure that they are not exploited for the advancement of knowledge.

Distributive justice also imposes duties to not discriminate against those who may benefit from advances in research. During the early 1990s, there was evidence that women and minorities were being *ex*cluded from many clinical studies in the United States. This led to the promulgation of regulations requiring that researchers who seek funding from the National Institutes of Health (NIH) (including NINR) include women and minorities as study participants.

The right to fair treatment encompasses other obligations. For example, researchers must treat people who decline to participate in a study or who withdraw from it in a nonprejudicial manner; they must honor all agreements made with participants; they must show respect for the beliefs and lifestyles of people from different backgrounds; and they must treat participants courteously and tactfully at all times.

The Right to Privacy

Virtually all research with humans involves intruding into personal lives. Researchers should ensure that their research is not more intrusive than it needs to be and that privacy is maintained. Participants have the right to expect that any data they provide will be kept in strict confidence.

Privacy issues have become even more salient in the U.S. health care community since the passage of the Health Insurance Portability and Accountability Act of 1996 (HIPAA), which articulates federal standards to protect patients' medical records and health information. For health care providers who transmit health information electronically, compliance with HIPAA regulations (the Privacy Rule) has been required since 2003.

TIP: Here are two websites that offer information about the implications of HIPAA for research: http://privacyruleandresearch.nih.gov/ and www.hhs.gov/ocr/hipaa/guidelines/research.pdf. See the Internet Resources on thePoint website.

PROCEDURES FOR PROTECTING STUDY PARTICIPANTS

Now that you are familiar with ethical principles for conducting research, you need to understand the procedures researchers use to adhere to them. It is these procedures that should be evaluated in critiquing the ethical aspects of a study.

TIP: Information about ethical considerations is usually presented in the method section of a research report, often in a subsection labeled Procedures.

Risk/Benefit Assessments

One strategy that researchers use to protect participants is to conduct a **risk/benefit assessment**. Such an assessment is designed to evaluate whether the benefits of participating in a study are in line with the costs, be they financial, physical, emotional, or social—i.e., whether the *risk/benefit ratio* is acceptable. Box 5.1 summarizes major costs and benefits of research participation.

BOX 5.1 Potential Benefits and Risks of Research to Participants

Major Potential Benefits to Participants

- Access to a potentially beneficial intervention that might otherwise be unavailable
- Comfort in being able to discuss their situation or problem with a friendly, objective person
- Increased knowledge about themselves or their conditions, either through opportunity for self-reflection or through direct interaction with researchers
- Escape from normal routine, excitement of being part of a study
- Satisfaction that information they provide may help others with similar problems
- Direct monetary or material gains through stipends or other incentives

Major Potential Risks to Participants

- Physical harm, including unanticipated side effects
- Physical discomfort, fatigue, or boredom
- Emotional distress resulting from self-disclosure, fear of the unknown or repercussions, discomfort with strangers, and embarrassment at the type of questions being asked
- Social risks, such as the risk of stigma, adverse effects on personal relationships, or loss of status
- Loss of privacy
- Loss of time
- Monetary costs (e.g., for transportation, child care, time lost from work)

The risk/benefit ratio should also be considered in terms of whether risks to participants are commensurate with benefits to society and to nursing. The degree of risk by participants should never exceed the potential humanitarian benefits of the knowledge to be gained. Thus, the selection of a significant topic that has the potential to improve patient care is the first step in ensuring that research is ethical.

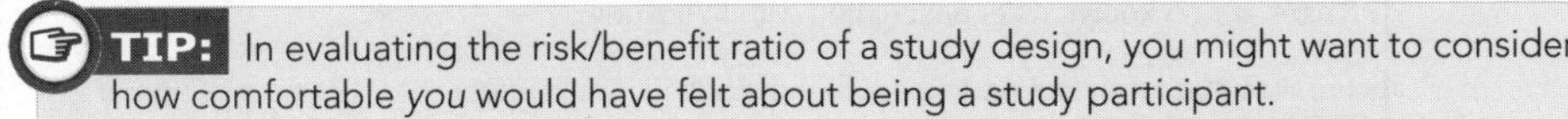

TIP: In evaluating the risk/benefit ratio of a study design, you might want to consider how comfortable *you* would have felt about being a study participant.

In some cases, the risks may be negligible. **Minimal risk** is a risk expected to be no greater than those ordinarily encountered in daily life or during routine tests or procedures. When the risks are not minimal, researchers must proceed with caution, taking every step possible to reduce risks and maximize benefits.

In quantitative studies, most details of the study are spelled out in advance, and so a reasonably accurate risk/benefit assessment can be developed. Qualitative studies, however, usually evolve as data are gathered, and so assessing all risks at the outset may be more difficult. Qualitative researchers must remain sensitive to potential risks throughout the study.

Informed Consent

An important procedure for safeguarding participants involves obtaining their informed consent. **Informed consent** means that participants have adequate information about the study, comprehend the information, and have the power of free choice, enabling them to consent to or decline participation voluntarily.

Researchers usually document informed consent by having participants sign a **consent form**, an example of which is shown in Figure 5.1. This form includes information about the study purpose, specific expectations regarding participation (e.g., how much time will be required), the voluntary nature of participation, and potential costs and benefits.

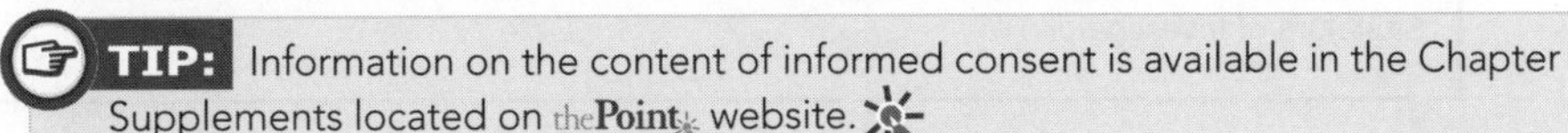

TIP: Information on the content of informed consent is available in the Chapter Supplements located on thePoint website.

Example of informed consent:

Zhang and coresearchers (2012) tested the effectiveness of preoperative education on postoperative anxiety symptoms and complications for patients undergoing coronary artery bypass grafting. Written informed consent was obtained from all participants. Six patients who were otherwise eligible for the study were excluded because they were unable to give written consent.

Researchers may not obtain written informed consent when data collection is through self-administered questionnaires. Researchers often assume **implied consent** (i.e., the return of a completed questionnaire reflects the person's voluntary consent to participate). This assumption may not always be warranted, however (e.g., if patients believe that their care might be affected by failure to cooperate).

In some qualitative studies, especially those requiring repeated contact with participants, it is difficult to obtain meaningful informed consent at the outset. Because the design emerges during data collection and analysis, researchers may not know the exact nature of the data to be collected, what the risks and benefits will be, or how much time will be required. Thus, in a qualitative study, consent may be an ongoing process, called **process consent**, in which consent is continuously renegotiated.

I understand that I am being asked to participate in a research study at Saint Francis Hospital and Medical Center. This research study will evaluate: What it is like being a mother of multiples during the first year of the infants' lives. If I agree to participate in the study, I will be interviewed for approximately 30 to 60 minutes about my experience as a mother of multiple infants. The interview will be tape-recorded and take place in a private office at St. Francis Hospital. No identifying information will be included when the interview is transcribed. I understand I will receive $25.00 for participating in the study. There are no known risks associated with this study.

I realize that I may not participate in the study if I am younger than 18 years of age or I cannot speak English.

I realize that the knowledge gained from this study may help either me or other mothers of multiple infants in the future.

I realize that my participation in this study is entirely voluntary, and I may withdraw from the study at any time I wish. If I decide to discontinue my participation in this study, I will continue to be treated in the usual and customary fashion.

I understand that all study data will be kept confidential. However, this information may be used in nursing publications or presentations.

I understand that if I sustain injuries from my participation in this research project, I will not be automatically compensated by Saint Francis Hosptal and Medical Center.

If I need to, I can contact Dr. Cheryl Beck, University of Connecticut, School of Nursing, any time during the study.

The study has been explained to me. I have read and understand this consent form, all of my questions have been answered, and I agree to participate. I understand that I will be given a copy of this signed consent form.

Signature of Participant	Date
Signature of Witness	Date
Signature of Investigator	Date

FIGURE 5.1 ● Example of an informed consent form.

Example of process consent:
Beech and coresearchers (2012) conducted a longitudinal grounded theory study of the process of restoring a sense of wellness following colorectal cancer. In-depth interviews were conducted with 12 patients at four points in time for 1 year following surgery. Written informed consent was completed at the first interview and process consent was used at later interviews by confirming participant agreement at each contact.

Confidentiality Procedures

Study participants have the right to expect that any data they provide will be kept in strict confidence. Participants' right to privacy is protected through confidentiality procedures.

Anonymity

Anonymity, the most secure means of protecting confidentiality, occurs when the researcher cannot link participants to their data. For example, if questionnaires were distributed to a group of nursing home residents and were returned without any identifying information, responses would be anonymous.

Example of anonymity:
Farrell and Belza (2012) conducted a study to examine whether older patients are comfortable discussing sexuality and sexual health with nurses. The researchers distributed anonymous questionnaires to elders in fitness classes and in retirement communities. Respondents returned the questionnaires in a secure drop box or by mail using preaddressed stamped envelopes.

Confidentiality in the Absence of Anonymity

When anonymity is impossible, appropriate confidentiality procedures need to be implemented. A promise of **confidentiality** is a pledge that any information participants provide will not be publicly reported in a manner that identifies them and will not be made accessible to others.

Researchers may develop elaborate confidentiality procedures. These include securing confidentiality assurances from everyone with access to research data; maintaining identifying information in locked files; substituting *identification (ID) numbers* for participants' names on records and files, to prevent an accidental breach of confidentiality; and reporting only aggregate data for groups of participants, or taking steps to disguise a person's identity in a research report.

Confidentiality is especially salient in qualitative studies because of their in-depth nature, yet anonymity is rarely possible. Another challenge that many qualitative researchers face is adequately disguising participants in their reports to avoid a breach of confidentiality. Because the number of respondents is small and because rich descriptive information is presented, qualitative researchers need to take extra precautions to safeguard participants' identity.

TIP: As a means of enhancing individual and institutional privacy, research articles frequently avoid giving information about the locale of the study. For example, a report might say that data were collected in a 200-bed, private nursing home, without mentioning its name or location.

Confidentiality sometimes creates tension between researchers and legal authorities, especially if participants are involved in criminal activity like substance abuse. To avoid the risk of forced disclosure of sensitive information (e.g., through a court order), researchers in the United States can apply for a **Certificate of Confidentiality** from the NIH. The certificate allows researchers to refuse to disclose information on study participants in any civil, criminal, administrative, or legislative proceeding.

Example of confidentiality procedures:
Mallory and Hesson-McInnis (2012) tested an HIV prevention intervention with incarcerated and other high-risk women. To enhance confidentiality, data were collected using computer-assisted self-interviewing. A federal Certificate of Confidentiality was obtained.

Debriefings and Referrals

Researchers should show their respect for participants during the interactions they have with them. For example, researchers should be polite and tactful, and should make evident their acceptance of cultural, linguistic, and lifestyle diversity.

There are also more formal strategies for communicating respect and concern for participants' well-being. For example, it is sometimes advisable to offer **debriefing** sessions following data collection so that participants can ask questions or air complaints. Debriefing is especially important when the data collection has been stressful or when ethical guidelines had to be "bent" (e.g., if any deception was used).

Researchers can also demonstrate their interest in participants by offering to share study findings with them after the data have been analyzed. Finally, researchers may need to assist participants by making referrals to appropriate health, social, or psychological services.

Example of referrals:
Wong and colleagues (2011) studied depression among Chinese women who experienced intimate partner violence. The interviewers were nonjudgmental and supportive during the interviews and, if deemed necessary, asked participants if they needed referral to community resources or a call to the police.

Treatment of Vulnerable Groups

Adherence to ethical standards is often straightforward. The rights of special vulnerable groups, however, may need extra protections. **Vulnerable populations** may be incapable of giving fully informed consent (e.g., developmentally delayed people) or may be at high risk of unintended side effects (e.g., pregnant women). You should pay particular attention to the ethical dimensions of a study when people who are vulnerable are involved. Among the groups that should be considered as being vulnerable are the following:

- *Children*. Legally and ethically, children do not have the competence to give informed consent and so the consent of children's parents or guardians should be obtained. However, it is appropriate—especially if the child is at least 7 years of age—to obtain the child's assent as well. **Assent** refers to the child's affirmative agreement to participate.
- *Mentally or emotionally disabled people*. Individuals whose disability makes it impossible for them to make informed decisions (e.g., people affected by cognitive impairment, coma, and so on) also cannot legally provide informed consent. In such cases, researchers should obtain the written consent of a legal guardian.
- *Severely ill or physically disabled people*. For patients who are very ill or undergoing certain treatments (e.g., mechanical ventilation), it might be necessary to assess their ability to make reasoned decisions about study participation. For certain disabilities, special consent procedures may be required. For example, with people who cannot read or who have a physical impairment preventing them from writing, alternative procedures for documenting informed consent (e.g., videotaping) should be used.
- *The terminally ill*. Terminally ill people can seldom expect to benefit personally from research, and thus the risk/benefit ratio needs to be carefully assessed.
- *Institutionalized people*. Nurses often conduct studies with hospitalized or institutionalized people who might feel that their care would be jeopardized by failure to cooperate. Inmates of prisons and correctional facilities may similarly feel constrained in their ability to give free consent. Researchers studying institutionalized groups need to emphasize the voluntary nature of participation.

- *Pregnant women*. The U.S. government has issued additional requirements governing research with pregnant women and fetuses. These requirements reflect a desire to safeguard both the pregnant woman, who may be at heightened physical or psychological risk, and the fetus, who cannot give informed consent. The regulations stipulate that a pregnant woman cannot be involved in a study unless risks are minimal.

Example of research with a vulnerable group:
Baggott and colleagues (2012) studied how symptoms clustered in a sample of 131 pediatric oncology patients aged 10 to 18, children and adolescents. Parents or guardians of the patients, if they were younger than 18, signed written informed consent forms. All children provided consent or assent.

External Reviews and the Protection of Human Rights

Researchers may not be objective in developing procedures to protect participants' rights. Biases may arise from their commitment to an area of knowledge and their desire to conduct a rigorous study. Because of the risk of a biased evaluation, the ethical dimensions of a study are usually subjected to external review.

Most hospitals, universities, and other institutions where research is conducted have established formal committees for reviewing research plans. These committees are sometimes called *human subjects committees* or (in Canada) *Research Ethics Boards*. In the United States, the committee is often called an **Institutional Review Board (IRB)**. Before undertaking a study, researchers must submit research plans to the IRB, and must also undergo formal IRB training. An IRB can approve the proposed plans, require modifications, or disapprove them.

Example of IRB approval:
Dickson and Flynn (2012) explored nurses' clinical reasoning regarding safe practices of medication administration. The procedures and protocols for the study were approved by the university IRB where the researchers worked, as well as by the hospital ethics review boards of the 10 hospitals where the data were collected.

OTHER ETHICAL ISSUES

In discussing research ethics, we have given primary consideration to protecting human study participants. Two other ethical issues also deserve mention: the treatment of animals in research and research misconduct.

Ethical Issues in Using Animals in Research

Some nurse researchers who focus on biophysiologic phenomena use animals as their subjects. Ethical considerations are clearly different for animals and humans; for example, *informed consent* is not relevant for animals. In the United States, the Public Health Service has issued a policy statement on the humane care and use of animals. The guidelines articulate principles for the proper care and treatment of animals used in research, covering such issues as the transport of research animals, pain and distress in animal subjects, the use of appropriate anesthesia, and euthanizing animals under certain conditions during or after the study.

Holtzclaw and Hanneman (2002), in discussing the use of animals in nursing research, noted several important considerations. For example, there must be a compelling reason to use an animal model—not simply convenience or novelty. Also, the study procedures should be humane, well planned, and well funded. Animal studies are not necessarily less costly than those with human participants, and they require serious scientific consideration to justify their use.

Example of research with animals:
Akase and colleagues (2011) studied skin changes induced by ultraviolet radiation using an animal model (mice). Animal care included careful attention to temperature, humidity, and lighting. All animals were handled in accordance with ethical guidelines, and the procedures were reviewed by animal ethics committees at two universities.

Research Misconduct

Ethics in research involves not only the protection of the rights of human and animal subjects, but also protection of the public trust. **Research misconduct** has received increasing attention in recent years as incidents of researcher fraud and misrepresentation have come to light.

Research misconduct, as defined by a U.S. Public Health Service regulation, is fabrication, falsification, or plagiarism in proposing, conducting, or reviewing research, or in reporting results. *Fabrication* involves making up data or study results. *Falsification* involves manipulating research materials or processes; it also involves changing or omitting data, or distorting results. *Plagiarism* involves the appropriation of someone's ideas, results, or words without giving due credit. Although the official definition focuses on only these three types of misconduct, there is widespread agreement that research misconduct covers many other issues including improprieties of authorship, conflicts of interest, inappropriate financial arrangements, failure to comply with governmental regulations, and unauthorized use of confidential information.

Example of research misconduct:
In 2008, the U.S. Office of Research Integrity ruled that a nurse in Missouri engaged in scientific misconduct in research supported by the National Cancer Institute. The nurse falsified and fabricated data that were reported to the National Surgical Adjuvant Breast and Bowel Project (NIH Notice Number NOT-OD-08-096).

CRITIQUING THE ETHICAL ASPECTS OF A STUDY

Guidelines for critiquing the ethical aspects of a study are presented in Box 5.2. Members of an IRB or human subjects committee are provided with sufficient information to answer all these questions, but research articles do not always include detailed information about ethics because of space constraints in journals. Thus, it may be difficult to critique researchers' adherence to ethical guidelines. Nevertheless, we offer a few suggestions for considering ethical issues.

Many research reports do acknowledge that the study procedures were reviewed by an IRB or human subjects committee. When a report mentions a formal review, it is usually safe to assume that a panel of concerned people thoroughly reviewed ethical issues raised by the study.

BOX 5.2 Guidelines for Critiquing the Ethical Aspects of a Study

1. Was the study approved and monitored by an Institutional Review Board, Research Ethics Board, or other similar ethics review committee?
2. Were study participants subjected to any physical harm, discomfort, or psychological distress? Did the researchers take appropriate steps to remove or prevent harm?
3. Did the benefits to participants outweigh any potential risks or actual discomfort they experienced? Did the benefits to society outweigh the costs to participants?
4. Was any type of coercion or undue influence used to recruit participants? Did they have the right to refuse to participate or to withdraw without penalty?
5. Were participants deceived in any way? Were they fully aware of participating in a study and did they understand the purpose and nature of the research?
6. Were appropriate informed consent procedures used with all participants? If not, were the reasons valid and justifiable?
7. Were adequate steps taken to safeguard participants' privacy? How was confidentiality maintained? Was a Certificate of Confidentiality obtained—and, if not, should one have been obtained?
8. Were vulnerable groups involved in the research? If yes, were special precautions instituted because of their vulnerable status?
9. Were groups omitted from the inquiry without a justifiable rationale, such as women (or men), or minorities?

You can also come to some conclusions based on a description of the study methods. There may be sufficient information to judge, for example, whether study participants were subjected to harm or discomfort. Reports do not always state whether informed consent was secured, but you should be alert to situations in which the data could not have been gathered as described if participation were purely voluntary (e.g., if data were gathered unobtrusively).

In thinking about the ethical aspects of a study, you should also consider who the study participants were. For example, if the study involves vulnerable groups, there should be more information about protective procedures. You might also need to attend to who the study participants were *not*. For example, there has been considerable concern about the omission of certain groups (e.g., minorities) from clinical research.

RESEARCH EXAMPLES WITH CRITICAL THINKING EXERCISES

Brief summaries of a quantitative and a qualitative nursing study are presented below, followed by some questions to guide critical thinking about the ethical aspects of these studies.

Examples 1 and 2 below are also featured in our *Interactive Critical Thinking Activity* on thePoint website where you can easily record, print, and e-mail your responses to the related questions.

EXAMPLE 1 ● Quantitative Research

Study: Parenting and feeding behaviors associated with school-aged African American and white children (Polfuss & Frenn, 2012)

Study Purpose: The purpose of the study was to examine the relationship between parenting and feeding behaviors on the one hand and children's body mass index on the other hand in families of African American and white children aged 9 to 15.

(continues on page 94)

Research Methods: A total of 176 parent/child dyads were recruited into the study. Parents completed questionnaires about their own parenting behavior, their perceptions and concerns about childhood obesity, and their feeding practices. The children also completed a questionnaire, and both parents and children were measured for height and weight.

Ethics-Related Procedures: The families were recruited through flyers and personal contact at several locations (e.g., clinics, boys and girls clubs). To be eligible, participants had to be alert and oriented, able to speak and read English, and willing to be measured for height and weight. Parents were asked to complete written informed consent forms, and children were asked to give their verbal assent. Data were collected in private areas, and parent and child questionnaires were completed independently. A research assistant was available to help children with reading the questionnaires or to answer any questions. All participants (parents and children) were offered a $10 gift certificate to a local department store. The entire consent and data collection process took 30 minutes. IRBs of a children's hospital and a university granted approval for this study.

Key Findings: Parents who were concerned about their children's weight exhibited greater authoritarian (controlling) parenting and feeding behavior.

CRITICAL THINKING EXERCISES

1. Answer the relevant questions from Box 5.2 on page 93 regarding this study.
2. Also consider the following targeted questions:
   a. Could the data for this study have been collected anonymously?
   b. Comment on the appropriateness of the participant stipend in this study.
3. If the results of this study are valid and generalizable, in what ways do you think the findings could be used in clinical practice?

EXAMPLE 2 ● Qualitative Research

Study: "Grief interrupted: The experience of loss among incarcerated women" (Harner et al., 2011)

Study Purpose: The purpose of the study was to explore the experiences of grief among incarcerated women following the loss of a loved one.

Study Methods: The researchers used phenomenological methods in this study. They recruited 15 incarcerated women who had experienced the loss of a loved one during their confinement. In-depth interviews about the women's experience of loss lasted 1 to 2 hours.

Ethics-Related Procedures: The researchers recruited women by posting flyers in the prison's dayroom. The flyers were written at the 4.5 grade level. Because the first author was a nurse practitioner at the prison, the researchers used several strategies to "diffuse any perceived coercion" (p. 457), such as not posting flyers near the health services unit and not offering any monetary or work-release incentives to participate. Written informed consent was obtained, but because of high rates of illiteracy, the informed consent document was read aloud to all potential participants. During the consent process, and during the interviews, the women were given opportunities to ask questions. They were informed that participation would have no effect on sentence length, sentence structure, parole, or access to health services. They were also told they could end the interview at any time without fear of reprisals. Furthermore, they were told that the researcher was a mandated reporter and would report any indication of suicidal or homicidal ideation. Participants were not required to give their names to the research team. During the interview, efforts were made to create a welcoming and nonthreatening environment. The research team received approval for the study from a university IRB and from the Department of Corrections Research Division.

Key Findings: The researchers revealed four themes, which they referred to as existential lifeworlds: Temporality: frozen in time; Spatiality: no place, no space to grieve; Corporeality: buried emotions; and Relationality: never alone, yet feeling so lonely.

CRITICAL THINKING EXERCISES

1. Answer the relevant questions from Box 5.2 on page 93 regarding this study.
2. Also consider the following targeted questions:
   a. The reseachers did not offer any stipend—was this ethically appropriate?
   b. Might the researchers have benefited from obtaining a Certificate of Confidentiality for this research?
3. If the results of this study are trustworthy and transferable, in what ways do you think the findings could be used in clinical practice?

EXAMPLE 3 ● Quantitative Study in Appendix A

- Read the method section from Howell and colleagues' (2007) study ("Anxiety, anger, and blood pressure in children") in Appendix A on page 395–402.

CRITICAL THINKING EXERCISES

1. Answer relevant questions from Box 5.2 on page 93 regarding this study.
2. Also consider the following targeted questions:
   a. Where was information about ethical issues located in this report?
   b. What additional information regarding the ethical aspects of their study could the researchers have included in this article?
   c. If you had a school-aged sibling or child of your own, how would you feel about him or her participating in the study?

EXAMPLE 4 ● Qualitative Study in Appendix B

- Read the method section from Beck and Watson's (2010) study ("Subsequent childbirth after a previous traumatic birth") in Appendix B on page 403–412.

CRITICAL THINKING EXERCISES

1. Answer the relevant questions from Box 5.2 on page 93 regarding this study.
2. Also consider the following targeted questions:
   a. Where was information about the ethical aspects of this study located in the report?
   b. What additional information regarding the ethical aspects of Beck and Watson's study could the researchers have included in this article?

WANT TO KNOW MORE? A wide variety of resources to enhance your learning and understanding of this chapter are available on thePoint.

- Interactive Critical Thinking Activity
- Chapter Supplement on Elements of Informed Consent
- Answers to the Critical Thinking Exercises for Examples 3 and 4
- Student Review Questions
- Full-text online
- Internet Resources with useful websites for Chapter 5

Additional study aids including eight journal articles and related questions are also available in *Study Guide for Essentials of Nursing Research, 8e.*

SUMMARY POINTS

- Because research has not always been conducted ethically, and because of genuine **ethical dilemmas** that researchers face in designing studies that are both ethical and rigorous, **codes of ethics** have been developed to guide researchers.
- Three major ethical principles from the *Belmont Report* are incorporated into many guidelines: beneficence, respect for human dignity, and justice.
- **Beneficence** involves the performance of some good and the protection of participants from physical and psychological harm and exploitation.
- Respect for human dignity involves the participants' right to self-determination, which includes participants' right to participate in a study voluntarily.
- **Full disclosure** means that researchers have fully described to prospective participants their rights and the costs and benefits of the study. When full disclosure poses the risk of biased results, researchers sometimes use *concealment* (the collection of information without participants' knowledge or consent) or *deception* (either withholding information from participants or providing false information).
- Justice includes the right to fair treatment and the right to privacy. In the United States, privacy has become a major issue because of the Privacy Rule regulations that resulted from the Health Insurance Portability and Accountability Act (HIPAA).
- Procedures have been developed to safeguard study participants' rights, including the performance of a risk/benefit assessment, the implementation of informed consent procedures, and taking steps to safeguard participants' confidentiality.
- In a **risk/benefit assessment**, the potential benefits of the study to individual participants and to society are weighed against the costs to individuals.
- **Informed consent** procedures, which provide prospective participants with information needed to make a reasoned decision about participation, normally involve signing a **consent form** to document voluntary and informed participation.
- In qualitative studies, consent may need to be continually renegotiated with participants as the study evolves, through **process consent** procedures.
- Privacy can be maintained through **anonymity** (wherein not even researchers know participants' identities) or through formal **confidentiality procedures** that safeguard the information participants provide.
- Some United States researchers obtain a **Certificate of Confidentiality** that protects them against the forced disclosure of confidential information through a court order.
- Researchers sometimes offer **debriefing** sessions after data collection to provide participants with more information or an opportunity to air complaints.
- **Vulnerable populations** require additional protection. These people may be vulnerable because they are not able to make an informed decision about study participation (e.g., children); because of diminished autonomy (e.g., prisoners); or because their circumstances heighten the risk of harm (e.g., pregnant women, the terminally ill).
- External review of the ethical aspects of a study by a human subjects committee or **Institutional Review Board (IRB)** is highly desirable and is often required by universities and organizations from which participants are recruited.
- Ethical conduct in research involves not only protecting the rights of human and animal subjects, but also efforts to maintain high standards of integrity and avoid such forms of **research misconduct** as plagiarism, fabrication of results, or falsification of data.

REFERENCES FOR CHAPTER 5

Akase, T., Nagase, T., Huang, L., Ibuki, A., Minematsu, T., & Sanada, S. (2011). Aging-like skin changes induced by ultraviolet irradiation in an animal model of metabolic syndrome. *Biological Research for Nursing, 14*(2), 180–187.

American Nurses' Association. (2001). *Code for nurses with interpretive statements*. Kansas City, MO: Author.

Baggott, C., Cooper, B., Marina, N., Matthay, K., & Maiskowski, C. (2012). Symptom cluster analyses based on symptom occurrence and severity ratings among pediatric oncology patients during myelosuppressive chemotherapy. *Cancer Nursing, 35*, 18–28.

Beck, C. T. (2005). Benefits of participating in internet interviews: Women helping women. *Qualitative Health Research, 15*, 411–422.

Beech, N., Arber, A., & Faithful, S. (2012). Restoring a sense of wellness following colorectal cancer: A grounded theory. *Journal of Advanced Nursing, 68(5)*, 1134–1144.

Canadian Nurses Association. (2002). *Ethical guidelines for nurses in research involving human subjects*. Ottawa, ON: Author.

Dickson, G., & Flynn, L. (2012). Nurses' clinical reasoning: Processes and practices of medication safety. *Qualitative Health Research, 22*, 3–16.

Farrell, J., & Belza, B. (2012). Are older patients comfortable discussing sexual health with nurses? *Nursing Research, 61*, 51–67.

Harner, H., Hentz, P., & Evangelista, M. (2011). Grief interrupted: The experience of loss among incarcerated women. *Qualitative Health Research, 21*, 454–464.

Holtzclaw, B. J., & Hanneman, S. K. (2002). Use of non-human biobehavioral models in critical care nursing research. *Critical Care Nursing Quarterly, 24*(4), 30–40.

Mallory, C., & Hesson-McInnis, M. (2012). Pilot test results of an HIV prevention intervention for high-risk women. *Western Journal of Nursing Research*.

Polfuss, M. L., & Frenn, M. (2012). Parenting and feeding behaviors associated with school-aged African American and white children. *Western Journal of Nursing Research, 34*, 677–696.

Silva, M. C. (1995). *Ethical guidelines in the conduct, dissemination, and implementation of nursing research*. Washington, DC: American Nurses' Association.

Wong, J., Tiwari, A., Fong, D., Humphreys, J., & Bullock, L. (2011). Depression among women experiencing intimate partner violence in a Chinese community. *Nursing Research, 60*, 58–65.

Zhang, C., Jiang, Y., Yin, Q., Chen, F., Ma, L., & Wang, L. (2012). Impact of nurse-initiated preoperative education on postoperative anxiety symptoms and complications after coronary artery bypass grafting. *Journal of Cardiovascular Nursing, 27*, 84–88.

part 2

Preliminary Steps in Research

chapter 6

Research Problems, Research Questions, and Hypotheses

LEARNING OBJECTIVES

On completing this chapter, you will be able to:

- Describe the process of developing and refining a research problem
- Distinguish the functions and forms of statements of purpose and research questions for quantitative and qualitative studies
- Describe the function and characteristics of research hypotheses and distinguish different types of hypotheses (directional vs. nondirectional, research vs. null)
- Critique statements of purpose, research questions, and hypotheses in research reports with respect to their placement, clarity, wording, and significance
- Define new terms in the chapter

KEY TERMS

Directional hypothesis
Hypothesis
Nondirectional hypothesis
Null hypothesis
Problem statement
Research hypothesis
Research problem
Research questions
Statement of purpose

OVERVIEW OF RESEARCH PROBLEMS

Studies to generate new research evidence begin in much the same fashion as an evidence-based practice (EBP) effort—as problems that need to be solved or questions that need to be answered. This chapter discusses the formulation and evaluation of research problems. We begin by clarifying some relevant terms.

TABLE 6.1 Terms Relating to Research Problems, With Examples

Term	Example
Topic	Side effects of chemotherapy
Research problem (Problem statement)	Nausea and vomiting are common side effects among patients on chemotherapy, and interventions to date have been only moderately successful in reducing these effects. New interventions that can reduce or prevent these side effects need to be identified.
Statement of purpose	The purpose of the study is to test an intervention to reduce chemotherapy-induced side effects—specifically, to compare the effectiveness of patient-controlled and nurse-administered antiemetic therapy for controlling nausea and vomiting in patients on chemotherapy.
Research question	What is the relative effectiveness of patient-controlled antiemetic therapy versus nurse-controlled antiemetic therapy with regard to (a) medication consumption and (b) control of nausea and vomiting in patients on chemotherapy?
Hypotheses	Subjects receiving antiemetic therapy by a patient-controlled pump will (1) be less nauseated, (2) vomit less, and (3) consume less medication than subjects receiving nurse-administered therapy.

Basic Terminology

At the most general level, a researcher selects a *topic* on which to focus. Examples of research topics are claustrophobia during MRI tests and pain management for sickle cell disease. Within broad topic areas are many possible research problems. In this section, we illustrate various terms using the topic *side effects of chemotherapy*.

A **research problem** is an enigmatic or troubling condition. The purpose of research is to "solve" the problem—or to contribute to its solution—by gathering relevant data. A **problem statement** articulates the problem and an *argument* that explains the need for a study. Table 6.1 presents a simplified problem statement related to the topic of side effects of chemotherapy.

Many reports include a **statement of purpose** (or purpose statement), which is the researcher's summary of the overall goal. Sometimes the words *aim* or *objective* are used in lieu of purpose, but these alternatives sometimes encompass broader goals (e.g., developing recommendations for changes to nursing practice based on the study evidence).

Research questions are the specific queries researchers want to answer, which guide the types of data to be collected in a study. Researchers who make specific predictions about answers to research questions pose **hypotheses** that are then tested.

These terms are not always consistently defined in research textbooks. Table 6.1 illustrates the interrelationships among terms as we define them.

Research Problems and Paradigms

Some research problems are better suited to qualitative versus quantitative inquiry. Quantitative studies usually involve concepts that are fairly well developed and for which reliable methods of measurement have been (or can be) developed. For example, a quantitative study might be undertaken to assess whether people with chronic illness who continue working past age 62 are less (or more) depressed than those who retire. There are relatively accurate measures of depression that would yield quantitative data about the level of depression in employed and retired chronically ill seniors.

Qualitative studies are often undertaken because a researcher wants to develop a rich and context-bound understanding of a poorly understood phenomenon. Qualitative methods would not be well suited to comparing levels of depression among employed and retired seniors, but they would be ideal for exploring, for example, the *meaning* of depression among chronically ill retirees. In evaluating a research report, one consideration is whether the research problem is suitable for the chosen paradigm and its associated methods.

Sources of Research Problems

Where do ideas for research problems come from? At the most basic level, research topics originate with researchers' interests. Because research is a time-consuming enterprise, curiosity about and interest in a topic are essential to a project's success.

Research reports rarely indicate the source of researchers' inspiration for a study, but a variety of explicit sources can fuel their curiosity, including the following:

- *Clinical experience*. Nurses' everyday experience is a rich source of ideas for research topics.
- *Nursing literature*. Ideas for studies often come from reading the nursing literature.
- *Social issues*. Topics are sometimes suggested by global social or political issues of relevance to the health care community (e.g., health disparities).
- *Theories*. Theories from nursing and other disciplines sometime suggest a research problem.
- *Ideas from external sources*. External sources can sometimes provide the impetus for a study (e.g., a funding agency's research priorities).

Additionally, researchers who have developed a *program of research* may get inspiration for "next steps" from their own findings, or from a discussion of those findings with others.

Example of a problem source for a quantitative study:

Beck (one of this book's authors) developed a strong research program on postpartum depression (PPD). Beck was approached by Dr. Carol Lanni Keefe, a professor in nutritional sciences, who had studied the effect of DHA (docosahexaemoic acid, a fat found in cold-water marine fish) on fetal brain development. Evidence suggested that DHA might play a role in reducing the severity of PPD, and so the two researchers collaborated in a study to test the effects of dietary DHA supplements on the incidence and severity of PPD. Their clinical trial has recently been completed and analyses are underway.

Development and Refinement of Research Problems

Developing a research problem is a creative process. Researchers often begin with interests in a broad topic area, and then develop a more specific researchable problem. For example, suppose a hospital nurse begins to wonder why some patients complain about having to wait for pain medication when certain nurses are assigned to them. The general topic is discrepancy in patient complaints about pain medications administered by different nurses. The nurse might ask, What accounts for this discrepancy? This broad question may lead to other questions, such as, How do the two groups of nurses differ? or What characteristics do the complaining patients share? The nurse may then observe that the ethnic background of the patients and nurses could be a relevant factor. This may direct the nurse to review the literature on nursing behaviors and ethnicity, or it may provoke a discussion of these observations with peers. These efforts may result in several research questions, such as the following:

- What is the essence of patient complaints among patients of different ethnic backgrounds?
- Is the ethnic background of nurses related to the frequency with which they dispense pain medication?
- Is the ethnic background of patients related to the frequency of complaints of having to wait for pain medication?
- Does the number of patient complaints increase (or do nurses' dispensing behaviors change) when the patients are of dissimilar ethnic backgrounds as opposed to when they are of the same ethnic background as the nurse?

These questions stem from the same general problem, yet each would be studied differently; for example, some suggest a qualitative approach, and others suggest a quantitative one. A quantitative researcher might become curious about nurses' dispensing behaviors, based on some evidence in the literature regarding ethnic differences. Both ethnicity and nurses' dispensing behaviors are variables that can be measured reliably. A qualitative researcher would be more interested in understanding the *essence* of patients' complaints, patients' *experience* of frustration, or the *process* by which the problem got resolved. These aspects of the research problem would be difficult to measure quantitatively. Researchers choose a problem to study based on its inherent interest to them, and on its fit with a paradigm of preference.

COMMUNICATING RESEARCH PROBLEMS AND QUESTIONS

Every study needs a problem statement that articulates what is problematic and what is driving the research. Most research reports also present either a statement of purpose, research questions, or hypotheses, and often combinations of these three elements are included.

Many students do not really understand problem statements and may even have trouble identifying them in a research article. A problem statement is presented early in a research article and often begins with the first sentence after the abstract. Research questions, purpose statements, or hypotheses appear later in the introduction.

Problem Statements

A good problem statement is a well-structured declaration of what it is that is problematic, what it is that "needs fixing," or what it is that is poorly understood. Problem statements, especially for quantitative studies, often have most of the following six components:

1. *Problem identification*: What is wrong with the current situation?
2. *Background*: What is the nature of the problem, or the context of the situation, that readers need to understand?
3. *Scope of the problem*: How big a problem is it, and how many people are affected?
4. *Consequences of the problem*: What is the cost of *not* fixing the problem?
5. *Knowledge gaps*: What information about the problem is lacking?
6. *Proposed solution*: How will the new study contribute to the solution of the problem?

BOX 6.1 Draft Problem Statement on Humor and Stress

A diagnosis of cancer is associated with high levels of stress. Sizeable numbers of patients who receive a cancer diagnosis describe feelings of uncertainty, fear, anger, and loss of control. Interpersonal relationships, psychological functioning, and role performance have all been found to suffer following cancer diagnosis and treatment.

A variety of alternative/complementary therapies have been developed in an effort to decrease the harmful effects of cancer-related stress on psychological and physiological functioning, and resources devoted to these therapies (money and staff) have increased in recent years. However, many of these therapies have not been carefully evaluated to assess their efficacy, safety, or cost effectiveness. For example, the use of humor has been recommended as a therapeutic device to improve quality of life, decrease stress, and perhaps improve immune functioning, but the evidence to justify its advocacy is scant.

Let us suppose that our topic was humor as a complementary therapy for reducing stress in hospitalized patients with cancer. One research question (discussed later in this section) might be, "What is the effect of nurses' use of humor on stress and natural killer cell activity in hospitalized cancer patients?" Box 6.1 presents a rough draft of a problem statement for such a study. This problem statement is a reasonable draft, but it could be improved.

Box 6.2 illustrates how the problem statement could be made stronger by adding information about scope (component 3), long-term consequences (component 4), and possible solutions (component 6). This second draft builds a more compelling *argument* for new research: millions of people are affected by cancer, and the disease has adverse consequences not only for patients and their families, but also for society. The revised problem statement also suggests a basis for the new study by describing a possible solution on which the new study might build.

BOX 6.2 Some Possible Improvements to Problem Statement on Humor and Stress

Each year, more than 1 million people are diagnosed with cancer, which remains one of the top causes of death among both men and women (reference citations).* Numerous studies have documented that a diagnosis of cancer is associated with high levels of stress. Sizeable numbers of patients who receive a cancer diagnosis describe feelings of uncertainty, fear, anger, and loss of control (citations). Interpersonal relationships, psychological functioning, and role performance have all been found to suffer following cancer diagnosis and treatment (citations). These stressful outcomes can, in turn, adversely affect health, long-term prognosis, and medical costs among cancer survivors (citations).

A variety of alternative/complementary therapies have been developed in an effort to decrease the harmful effects of cancer-related stress on psychological and physiological functioning, and resources devoted to these therapies (money and staff) have increased in recent years (citations). However, many of these therapies have not been carefully evaluated to determine their efficacy, safety, or cost effectiveness. For example, the use of humor has been recommended as a therapeutic device to improve quality of life, decrease stress, and perhaps improve immune functioning (citations), but the evidence to justify its advocacy is scant. Preliminary findings from a recent small-scale endocrinology study with a healthy sample exposed to a humorous intervention (citation), however, hold promise for further inquiry with immunocompromised populations.

*Reference citations would be inserted to support the statements.

HOW-TO-TELL TIP: How can you tell a problem statement? Problem statements are rarely explicitly labeled and must therefore be ferreted out. The first sentence of a research report is often the starting point of a problem statement. The problem statement is usually interwoven with findings from the research literature. Prior findings provide the evidence backing up assertions in the problem statement and suggest gaps in knowledge. In many articles it is difficult to disentangle the problem statement from the literature review, unless there is a subsection specifically labeled "Literature Review" or something similar.

Problem statements for a qualitative study similarly express the nature of the problem, its context, its scope, and information needed to address it, as in the study in Appendix B on page 403. Qualitative studies embedded in a research tradition often incorporate terms and concepts that foreshadow the tradition in their problem statements. For example, the problem statement in a grounded theory study might mention the need to generate a theory relating to social processes. A problem statement for a phenomenological study might note the need to know more about people's experiences or meanings they attribute to those experiences. An ethnographer might indicate the desire to describe how cultural forces influence people's behavior.

Statements of Purpose

Many researchers articulate their research goals as a statement of purpose. The purpose statement establishes the general direction of the inquiry and captures, usually in one or two sentences, the study's substance. It is usually easy to identify a purpose statement because the word *purpose* is explicitly stated: "The purpose of this study was…"—although sometimes the words *aim*, *goal*, or *objective* are used instead, as in "The aim of this study was to…."

In a quantitative study, a statement of purpose identifies the key study variables and their possible interrelationships, as well as the population of interest (i.e., all the PICO elements).

Example of a statement of purpose from a quantitative study:
The purpose of this study was to investigate the effectiveness of chilled and unchilled baby oil therapy for treating uremic pruritus in hemodialysis patients (Lin et al., 2012).

This purpose statement identifies the population of interest as patients on hemodialysis. The key study variables were the patients' exposure to chilled or unchilled baby oil therapy (the independent variable), and the patients' severity of itchiness (the dependent variable).

In qualitative studies, the statement of purpose indicates the nature of the inquiry, the key concept or phenomenon, and the group, community, or setting under study.

Example of a statement of purpose from a qualitative study:
The purpose of this study was to explore the experiences of Latina mothers who immigrated to the United States without legal documentation, and without their children (Sternberg & Barry, 2011).

This statement indicates that the group under study is Latina mothers, and the central phenomenon is the experience of illegally immigrating to the United States without their children.

In the statement of purpose researchers also communicate the manner in which they sought to solve the problem, or the state of knowledge on the topic, through their choice of verbs. A study whose purpose is to *explore* or *describe* some phenomenon is likely to be an investigation of a little-researched topic, often involving a qualitative approach, such as phenomenology or ethnography. A statement of purpose for a qualitative study—especially a grounded theory study—may also use verbs such as *understand*, *discover*, *develop*, or *generate*. The statements of purpose in qualitative studies often "encode" the tradition of inquiry not only through the researcher's choice of verbs but also through the use of certain terms or "buzz words" associated with those traditions, as follows:

- *Grounded theory*: Processes; social structures; social interactions
- *Phenomenological studies*: Experience; lived experience; meaning; essence
- *Ethnographic studies*: Culture; roles; lifeways; cultural behavior

Quantitative researchers also use verbs to communicate the nature of the inquiry. A statement indicating that the study purpose is to *test* or *evaluate* something (e.g., an intervention) suggests an experimental design, for example. A study whose purpose is to *examine* or *explore* the relationship between two variables is more likely to involve a nonexperimental design. Sometimes the verb is ambiguous: if a purpose statement states that the researcher's intent is to *compare* two things, the comparison could involve alternative treatments (using an experimental design) or two preexisting groups (using a nonexperimental design). In any event, verbs such as *test*, *evaluate*, and *compare* suggest quantifiable variables and designs with scientific controls.

The verbs in a purpose statement should connote objectivity. A statement of purpose indicating that the study goal was to *prove*, *demonstrate*, or *show* something suggests a bias.

Research Questions

Research questions are, in some cases, direct rewordings of statements of purpose, phrased interrogatively rather than declaratively, as in the following example:

- The purpose of this study is to assess the relationship between the dependency level of renal transplant recipients and their rate of recovery.
- What is the relationship between the dependency level of renal transplant recipients and their rate of recovery?

Direct and simple questions invite an answer and help to focus attention on the kinds of data needed to answer them. Some research articles omit a statement of purpose and state only research questions. Other researchers use research questions to clarify or add greater specificity to a global purpose statement.

Research Questions in Quantitative Studies

In Chapter 2, we discussed clinical foreground questions to guide an EBP inquiry. Many of the EBP question templates in Table 2.1 on page 31 could yield questions to guide a research project as well, but *researchers* tend to conceptualize their questions in terms of their *variables*. Take, for example, the first question in Table 2.1: "In (population), what is the effect of (intervention) on (outcome)?" A researcher would be more likely to think of the question in these terms: "In (population), what is the effect of (independent variable) on (dependent variable)?" Thinking in terms of variables helps to guide researchers' decisions about how to operationalize them. Thus, in quantitative studies research questions identify the population (P) under study, the key study variables (I, C, and O components), and relationships among the variables.

TIP: As noted in Chapter 3, the independent variable in a study captures both the I and C components of PICO questions because researchers must be explicit about what the comparison is. Those pursuing an evidence-based practice (EBP) question are often interested in the "I" component in contrast to *any* comparison that has been made by researchers.

Most research questions concern relationships among variables, and thus many quantitative research questions could be articulated using a general question template: "In (population), what is the relationship between (independent variable or IV) and (dependent variable or DV)?" Examples of variations include the following:

- *Treatment, intervention*: In (population), what is the effect of (IV: intervention versus an alternative) on (DV)?
- *Prognosis*: In (population), does (IV: disease or illness versus its absence) affect or increase the risk of (DV)?
- *Etiology/harm*: In (population), does (IV: exposure versus nonexposure) cause or increase risk of (DV)?

Not all research questions are about relationships—some are primarily descriptive. As examples, here are some descriptive questions that could be answered in a quantitative study on nurses' use of humor:

- What is the frequency with which nurses use humor as a complementary therapy with hospitalized cancer patients?
- What are the characteristics of nurses who use humor as a complementary therapy with hospitalized cancer patients?
- Is my *Use of Humor Scale* a reliable and valid measure of nurses' use of humor with patients in clinical settings?

Answers to such questions might, if addressed in a methodologically sound study, be useful in developing effective strategies for reducing stress in patients with cancer.

Example of research questions from a quantitative study:
Ryan-Wenger and Gardner (2012) studied the perspectives of 496 hospitalized children regarding their nursing care. Their research questions included: (1) What nurse behaviors matter most to hospitalized pediatric patients? And (2) What physical or emotional characteristics of the children are related to their perceptions of nurses' behaviors?

In this example, the first question is descriptive, and the second asks about the relationship between independent variables (children's characteristics) and a dependent variable (their perception of nurses' behavior).

Research Questions in Qualitative Studies

Research questions in qualitative studies include the phenomenon and the group of interest. Researchers in the various qualitative traditions vary in their views of what types of question are important. Grounded theory researchers are likely to ask *process* questions, phenomenologists tend to ask *meaning* questions, and ethnographers generally ask *descriptive* questions about cultures. The terms associated with the various traditions, discussed previously in connection with purpose statements, are likely to be incorporated into the research questions.

Example of a research question from a phenomenological study:
What is the lived experience and personal meaning of hereditary breast cancer risk and surveillance? (Underhill & Dickerson, 2011)

Not all qualitative studies are rooted in a specific research tradition. Many researchers use constructivist methods to describe or explore phenomena without focusing on cultures, meaning, or social processes.

Example of a research question from a descriptive qualitative study:
In their descriptive qualitative study, Weng and co-researchers (2012) asked, What is the nature of distress among family caregivers of children with a rare genetic disorder, Russell-Silver Syndrome?

In qualitative studies, research questions sometimes evolve during the study. Researchers begin with a *focus* that defines the broad boundaries of the inquiry, but the boundaries are not cast in stone. Constructivists are often sufficiently flexible that the question can be modified as new information makes it relevant to do so.

TIP: Researchers most often state their purpose or research questions at the end of the introduction or immediately after the review of the literature. Sometimes, a separate section of a research article is devoted to formal statements about the research problem and might be labeled "Purpose," "Statement of Purpose," "Research Questions," or, in quantitatve studies, "Hypotheses."

RESEARCH HYPOTHESES

Some quantitative researchers explicitly state their hypotheses. A hypothesis is a prediction, almost always involving a predicted relationship between two or more variables. Qualitative researchers do not have formal hypotheses, because qualitative researchers want the inquiry to be guided by participants' viewpoints rather than by their own hunches. Thus, our discussion here focuses on hypotheses in quantitative research.

Function of Hypotheses in Quantitative Research

Many research questions are queries about relationships between variables, and hypotheses are predicted answers to these queries. For instance, the research question might ask: Does sexual abuse in childhood affect the development of irritable bowel syndrome in women? The researcher might predict the following: Women (P) who were sexually abused in childhood (I) have a higher incidence of irritable bowel syndrome (O) than women who were not abused (C).

Hypotheses sometimes emerge from a theory. Scientists reason from theories to hypotheses and test those hypotheses in the real world; the soundness of a theory is evaluated through hypothesis testing. For example, the theory of reinforcement posits that behavior that is positively reinforced (rewarded) tends to be learned (repeated). The theory is too abstract to test directly, but predictions based on it can be tested. For instance, we could test the following hypothesis, deduced from reinforcement theory: Pediatric patients who are given a reward (e.g., permission to watch television) for cooperating during nursing procedures tend to be more cooperative than nonrewarded peers. This proposition can be put to a test, and the theory gains support if the hypotheses are supported with real data.

Even in the absence of a theory, well-conceived hypotheses offer direction and suggest explanations. For example, suppose we hypothesized that the incidence of desaturation in low-birth-weight infants undergoing intubation and ventilation would be lower using the closed tracheal suction system (CTSS) than using partially ventilated endotracheal suction (PVETS). Our hypothesis might be based on studies or clinical observations. *The development of predictions forces researchers to think logically and to exercise critical judgment.*

Now let us suppose the preceding hypothesis is not confirmed in a study; that is, we find that rates of desaturation are similar for both the PVETS and CTSS methods. *The failure of data to support a prediction forces researchers to analyze theory or previous research critically, to review study limitations, and to explore alternative explanations for the findings.* The use of hypotheses tends to induce critical thinking and to facilitate interpretation of the data.

To illustrate further the utility of hypotheses, suppose we conducted the study guided only by the question, Is there a relationship between suction method and rates of desaturation? Without a hypothesis, the researcher is seemingly prepared to accept any results. The problem is that it is almost always possible to explain something superficially after the fact, no matter what the findings are. Hypotheses reduce the possibility that spurious results will be misconstrued.

TIP: Some quantitative research articles explicitly state the hypotheses that guided the study, but many do not. The absence of a hypothesis may indicate that researchers have failed to consider critically the existing evidence or theory, or have failed to disclose their hunches.

Characteristics of Testable Hypotheses

Research hypotheses usually state the expected relationship between the independent variable (the presumed cause or influence) and the dependent variable (the presumed outcome or effect) within a population.

Example of a research hypothesis:

Liu and colleagues (2011) studied quality of life in community-dwelling patients with heart failure in Taiwan. They hypothesized that sleep quality and daytime sleepiness were factors influencing the patients' quality of life.

In this example, the population is community-dwelling Taiwanese patients with heart failure. The independent variables are sleep quality and daytime sleepiness, and the outcome variable is the patients' quality of life. The hypothesis predicts that, in the population, sleep quality and daytime sleepiness are related to (affects) quality of life.

Hypotheses that do not make a relational statement are problematic. Take the following example: *Pregnant women who receive prenatal instruction about postpartum experiences are not likely to experience postpartum depression*. This statement expresses no anticipated relationship, and cannot be tested using standard statistical procedures. In our example, how would we decide whether to accept or reject the hypothesis?

To illustrate more concretely, suppose we asked a group of new mothers who had received prenatal instruction the following question: On the whole, how depressed have you been since you gave birth? Would you say (1) extremely depressed, (2) moderately depressed, (3) a little depressed, or (4) not at all depressed? Based on their responses, how could we compare the actual outcome with the predicted outcome? Would *all* the women have to say they were "not at all depressed?" Would the prediction be supported if 51% of the women said they were "not at all depressed" *or* "a little depressed?" It is difficult to test the accuracy of the original prediction.

We could, however, modify the prediction as follows: Pregnant women who receive prenatal instruction are less likely than those who do not to experience postpartum depression. Here, the outcome variable (O) is postpartum depression, and the independent variable is receipt (I) versus nonreceipt (C) of prenatal instruction. The relational aspect of the prediction is embodied in the phrase *less than*. If a hypothesis lacks a phrase such as *more than, less than, different from, related to*, or something similar, it is not readily testable. To test the revised hypothesis, we could ask two groups of women with different prenatal instruction experiences to respond to the question on depression and then compare the groups' responses. The absolute degree of depression of either group would not be at issue.

Hypotheses should be based on justifiable rationales. Hypotheses often follow from previous research findings or are deduced from a theory. When a new area is being investigated, researchers may have to rely on logical reasoning or clinical experience to justify the predictions.

TIP: Hypotheses are typically fairly easy to identify because researchers make statements such as, "The study tested the hypothesis that …" or, "It was predicted that …".

Wording of Hypotheses

Hypotheses can be stated in various ways, as in the following example:

1. Older patients are more likely to fall than younger patients.
2. There is a relationship between a patient's age and the likelihood of falling.
3. The older the patient, the greater the likelihood that she or he will fall.
4. Older patients differ from younger ones with respect to their risk of falling.
5. Younger patients are at lower risk of falling than older patients.
6. The risk of falling increases with the age of the patient.

In all six examples, the hypotheses state the population (patients), the independent variable (age), the outcome variable (falling), and an anticipated relationship between them.

Hypotheses can be either directional or nondirectional. A **directional hypothesis** specifies not only the existence but the expected direction of the relationship between variables. In the six versions of the hypothesis, versions 1, 3, 5, and 6 are directional because they explicitly predict that older patients are more likely to fall than younger ones. A **nondirectional hypothesis** does not stipulate the direction of the relationship (versions 2 and 4). These hypotheses predict that a patient's age and falling are related, but they do not specify whether *older* patients or *younger* ones are predicted to be at greater risk. Note that in all six examples, the hypotheses are worded in the present tense. Researchers make a prediction about a relationship that exists in the population—not just about a relationship for a particular sample of study participants.

TIP: Hypotheses can be either simple hypotheses (with a single independent variable and dependent variable) or complex (multiple independent or dependent variables). Supplementary information about this differentiation is available in the Chapter Supplement on thePoint website.

Another distinction is between research and null hypotheses. **Research hypotheses** are statements of expected relationships between variables. All the hypotheses presented thus far are research hypotheses that indicate actual expectations.

Statistical inference operates on a logic that may be confusing. This logic requires that hypotheses be expressed as an expected *absence* of a relationship. **Null hypotheses** state that there is no relationship between the independent and dependent variables. The null form of the hypothesis in our preceding example would be: "Older patients are just as likely as younger patients to fall." The null hypothesis might be compared with the assumption of innocence in English-based systems of criminal justice: the variables are assumed to be "innocent" of any relationship until they can be shown "guilty" through statistical procedures. The null hypothesis is the formal statement of this assumption of innocence.

Research articles typically state research rather than null hypotheses. In statistical testing, the underlying null hypotheses are assumed, without being stated. If the researcher's *actual* research hypothesis is that no relationship among variables exists, the hypothesis cannot be adequately tested using traditional statistical procedures, as explained in Chapter 13.

> **TIP:** If a researcher uses statistical tests (which is true in most quantitative studies), it means that there are underlying hypotheses—regardless of whether the researcher explicitly stated them—because statistical tests are designed to test hypotheses.

Hypothesis Testing and Proof

Hypotheses are formally tested through statistical analysis. Researchers use statistics to test whether their hypotheses have a high probability of being correct (i.e., has a probability <.05). Statistical analysis does not provide proof, it only supports inferences that a hypothesis is *probably* correct (or not). Hypotheses are never *proved* (or disproved); rather, they are *accepted* or *supported* (or rejected). Findings are always tentative. Hypotheses come to be increasingly supported with evidence from multiple studies.

To illustrate why this is so, suppose we hypothesized that height and weight are related. We predict that, on average, tall people weigh more than short people. Suppose we happened by chance to get a sample of short, heavy people, and tall, thin people. Our results might indicate that there is no relationship between a person's height and weight. Would we be justified in stating that this study *proved* or *demonstrated* that height and weight are unrelated?

As another example, suppose we hypothesized that tall nurses are more effective than short ones. In reality, we would expect no relationship between height and job performance. But suppose that, by chance again, we drew a sample of nurses in which tall nurses received better job evaluations than short ones. Could we conclude definitively that height is related to a nurse's performance? These two examples illustrate the difficulty of using observations from a sample to generalize to a population. Other issues, such as the accuracy of the measures and the effects of uncontrolled variables prevent researchers from concluding that hypotheses are proved.

CRITIQUING RESEARCH PROBLEMS, RESEARCH QUESTIONS, AND HYPOTHESES

In a comprehensive critique of a research article, you would evaluate whether researchers have adequately communicated their research problem. The problem statement, purpose, research questions, and hypotheses set the stage for describing what was done and what was learned. You should not have to dig too deeply to decipher the research problem or to discover the questions.

A critique of the research problem involves multiple dimensions. Substantively, you need to consider whether the problem has significance for nursing. Studies that build on existing evidence in a meaningful way are well-poised to make contributions to evidence-based nursing practice. Also, research problems stemming from established research priorities (see Chapter 1) have a high likelihood of yielding important new evidence for nurses because they reflect expert opinion about areas of needed research.

Another dimension in critiquing the research problem concerns methodologic issues—in particular, whether the research problem is compatible with the chosen research paradigm

BOX 6.3 Guidelines for Critiquing Research Problems, Research Questions, and Hypotheses

1. What is the research problem? Is the problem statement easy to locate and is it clearly stated? Does the problem statement build a cogent and persuasive argument for the new study?
2. Does the problem have significance for nursing? How might the research contribute to nursing practice, administration, education, or policy?
3. Is there a good fit between the research problem and the paradigm within which the research was conducted? Is there a good fit with the qualitative research tradition (if applicable)?
4. Does the report formally present a statement of purpose, research question, and/or hypotheses? Is this information communicated clearly and concisely, and is it placed in a logical and useful location?
5. Are purpose statements or research questions worded appropriately (e.g., are key concepts/ variables identified and the population specified? Are verbs used appropriately to suggest the nature of the inquiry and/or the research tradition?
6. If there are no formal hypotheses, is their absence justified? Are statistical tests used in analyzing the data despite the absence of stated hypotheses?
7. Do hypotheses (if any) flow from a theory or previous research? Is there a justifiable basis for the predictions?
8. Are hypotheses (if any) properly worded? Do they state a predicted relationship between two or more variables? Are they presented as research or as null hypotheses?

and its associated methods. You should also evaluate whether the statement of purpose or research questions have been properly worded and lend themselves to empirical inquiry.

If a research article describing a quantitative study does not state hypotheses, you should consider whether their absence is justified. If there are hypotheses, you should evaluate whether the hypotheses are sensible and consistent with existing evidence or relevant theory. Also, hypotheses are valid guideposts in scientific inquiry only if they are testable. To be testable, hypotheses must predict a relationship between two or more measurable variables.

Specific guidelines for critiquing research problems, research questions, and hypotheses are presented in Box 6.3.

RESEARCH EXAMPLES WITH CRITICAL THINKING EXERCISES

This section describes how the research problem and research questions were communicated in two nursing studies, one quantitative and one qualitative.

Examples 1 and 2 below are also featured in our *Interactive Critical Thinking Activity* on thePoint website where you can easily record, print, and e-mail your responses to the related questions.

EXAMPLE 1 ● Quantitative Research

Study: "Randomized clinical trial testing efficacy of a nurse-coached intervention (NCI) in arthroscopy patients" (Jones, Duffy, & Flanagan, 2011)

Problem Statement (excerpt): "Ambulatory surgical patients experience many symptoms such as pain, nausea and vomiting, fatigue, and unexpected limitations in daily living, isolation, and suffering. Collectively, findings show that patients have many distressing symptoms after ambulatory surgery, and these constitute major problems during recovery for patients and their families.

There is a lack of data about nursing interventions aimed at assisting ambulatory surgical patients with the management of postoperative symptoms at home." (pp. 92–93) (Citations were omitted to streamline the presentation).

Statement of Purpose: "The purpose of this study was to determine the efficacy of a NCI in relieving symptom distress and in improving functional health state" (p. 93).

Hypotheses: Arthroscopy patients who receive the NCI intervention (NCI group) when compared with a similar group who receive usual practice (UP group) will significantly have: (Hypothesis 1) less symptom distress at 72 hours and 1 week postsurgery; and (Hypothesis 2) better functional health status as measured by perceived physical health status and mental health status at 1 week postsurgery.

Intervention: The NCI focused on giving information, interpreting the experience, and validating and clarifying responses and actions related to the surgical experience. The NCI was delivered by telephone, beginning on the first surgical evening and at 24, 48, and 72 hours postarthroscopic surgery.

Study Methods: A sample of 102 arthroscopy patients at an academic medical center was assigned at random to either the NCI group or the UP group. Symptom distress was measured using the Symptom Distress Scale, and functional health was measured using the Medical Outcomes Study Short Form Health Survey (widely referred to as the SF-36). Data were collected from all participants three times: at baseline when patients enrolled in the study, 72 hours postsurgery, and 1 week postsurgery.

Key Findings: Participants in the intervention group had significantly less symptom distress at 72 hours and 1 week postsurgery, and significantly better physical and mental health status scores at 1 week postsurgery than those in the usual practice group.

CRITICAL THINKING EXERCISES

1. Answer the relevant questions from Box 6.3 on page 111 regarding this study.
2. Also consider the following targeted questions:
   a. Where in the research report do you think the researchers would have presented the hypotheses? Where in the report would the results of the hypothesis tests be placed?
   b. The report did not state research questions. What might some research questions be?
   c. Were the hypotheses directional or nondirectional?
3. If the results of this study are valid and generalizable, what are some of the uses to which the findings might be put in clinical practice?

EXAMPLE 2 ● Qualitative Research

Study: Andropause syndrome in men treated for metastatic prostate cancer (Grunfeld et al., 2012)

Problem Statement (excerpt): "Prostate cancer is the most common cancer among men in the United Kingdom, with more than 36,000 new cases per year. The incidence rate has increased threefold in the last 30 years, mainly due to improvements in detection of the disease. Outcomes are good, with a 5-year survival rate of 77% in the United Kingdom. Androgen deprivation therapy (ADT) has become the cornerstone of treatment for men with metastatic prostate cancer… However, treatments are associated with a number of adverse effects. Adverse effects vary according to the type of treatment but include erectile dysfunction, decreased libido, infertility, loss in bone mineral density, gynecomastia, depressed mood, and hot flashes. Collectively, these symptoms in healthy men are referred to as andropause syndrome… Previous studies have neglected to examine the impact of these symptoms or the cognitive and behavioral responses used to reduce the impact of the symptoms." (p. 64). (Citations were omitted to streamline the presentation.)

Statement of Purpose: "The aim of this study was to explore, through in-depth interviews, the experiences and impact of andropause symptoms (particularly hot flashes) among men being treated with ADT for metastatic prostate cancer" (p. 64). (The researchers did not state specific research questions in this article.)

Method: The researchers recruited 21 men who were identified from a clinic database at a large London teaching hospital. The researchers conducted in-depth interviews with the men, mostly in face-to-face interviews at the hospital. Participants were asked several conversational questions, such as, What have been the main effects of your symptoms on your daily life?

Key Findings: Hot flashes and night sweats were among the most frequently mentioned adverse effects of ADT. These symptoms disturbed the men's sleep patterns and led to irritability and fatigue. The men expressed reluctance to disclose their symptoms to others.

CRITICAL THINKING EXERCISES

1. Answer the relevant questions from Box 6.3 on page 111 regarding this study.
2. Also consider the following targeted questions:
   a. Where in the research report do you think the researchers would have presented the statement of purpose?
   b. Does it appear that this study was conducted within one of the three main qualitative traditions? If so, which one?
3. If the results of this study are trustworthy, what are some of the uses to which the findings might be put in clinical practice?

EXAMPLE 3 ● Quantitative Research in Appendix A

- Read the abstract and the introduction from Howell and colleagues' (2007) study ("Anxiety, anger, and blood pressure in children") in Appendix A on page 395–402.

CRITICAL THINKING EXERCISES

1. Answer the relevant questions from Box 6.3 on page 111 regarding this study.
2. Also consider the following targeted questions:
   a. Based on the review of the literature, it would be possible to state several research hypotheses. State one or two.
   b. If your hypothesis in exercise 2.a was a directional hypothesis, state it as a nondirectional hypothesis (or vice versa). Also state it as a null hypothesis.

EXAMPLE 4 ● Qualitative Research in Appendix B

- Read the abstract and introduction from Beck and Watson's (2010) study ("Subsequent childbirth after a previous traumatic birth") in Appendix B on page 403–412.

CRITICAL THINKING EXERCISES

1. Answer the relevant questions from Box 6.3 on page 111 regarding this study.
2. Also consider the following targeted questions:
   a. Do you think that Beck and Watson provided a sufficient rationale for the significance of their research problem?
   b. In their argument for their study, did Beck and Watson say anything about the fourth element of an argument identified in the book—i.e., the consequences of the problem?

WANT TO KNOW MORE? A wide variety of resources to enhance your learning and understanding of this chapter are available on thePoint.

- Interactive Critical Thinking Activity
- Chapter Supplement on Simple and Complex Hypotheses
- Answers to the Critical Thinking Exercises for Examples 3 and 4
- Student Review Questions
- Full-text online

Additional study aids including eight journal articles and related questions are also available in *Study Guide for Essentials of Nursing Research, 8e.*

SUMMARY POINTS

- A **research problem** is a perplexing or troubling situation that a researcher wants to address through disciplined inquiry.
- Researchers usually identify a broad *topic*, narrow the scope of the problem, and then identify research questions consistent with a paradigm of choice.
- Common sources of ideas for nursing research problems are clinical experience, relevant literature, social issues, theory, and external suggestions.
- Researchers communicate their aims in research articles as problem statements, statements of purpose, research questions, or hypotheses.
- The **problem statement** articulates the nature, context, and significance of a problem to be studied and an *argument* explaining the need for the study. Problem statements typically include several components: problem identification; background, scope, and consequences of the problem; knowledge gaps; and possible solutions to the problem.
- A **statement of purpose**, which summarizes the overall study goal, identifies the key concepts (variables) and the study group or population. Purpose statements often communicate, through the choice of verbs and other key terms, aspects of the research design or the research tradition.
- **Research questions** are the specific queries researchers want to answer in addressing the research problem.
- A **hypothesis** states predicted relationships between two or more variables—that is, the anticipated association between independent and dependent variables.
- **Directional hypotheses** predict the direction of a relationship; **nondirectional hypotheses** predict the existence of relationships, not their direction.
- **Research hypotheses** predict the existence of relationships; **null hypotheses**, which express the absence of a relationship, are the hypotheses subjected to statistical testing.
- Hypotheses are never proved or disproved in an ultimate sense—they are accepted or rejected, supported or not supported by the data.

REFERENCES FOR CHAPTER 6

Jones, D., Duffy, M., & Flanagan, J. (2011). Randomized clinical trial testing efficacy of a nurse-coached intervention in arthroscopy patients. *Nursing Research, 60*, 92–99.

Grunfeld, E., Halliday, A., Martin, P., & Drudge-Coates, L. (2012). Andropause syndrome in men treated for metastatic prostate cancer: A qualitative study of the impact of symptoms. *Cancer Nursing, 35*, 63–72.

Lin, T. C., Lai, Y., Guo, S., Liu, C., Tsai, J., Guo, H., (2012). Baby oil therapy for uremic pruritus in haemodialysis patients. *Journal of Clinical Nursing, 21*, 139–148.

Liu, J. C., Hung, H., Shyu, Y., & Tsai, P. (2011). The impact of sleep quality and daytime sleepiness on global quality of life in community-dwelling patients with heart failure. *Journal of Cardiovascular Nursing, 26*, 99–105.

Ryan-Wenger, N., & Gardner, W. (2012). Hospitalized children's perspectives on the quality and equity of their nursing care. *Journal of Nursing Care Quality, 27*, 35–42.

Sternberg, R., & Barry, C. (2011). Transnational mothers crossing the border and bringing their health care needs. *Journal of Nursing Scholarship, 43*, 64–71.

Underhill, M., & Dickerson, S. (2011). Engaging in medical vigilance: Understanding the personal meaning of breast surveillance. *Oncology Nursing Forum, 38*, 686–694.

Weng, H. J., Niu, D., Turale, S., Tsao, L., Shih, F., Yamamoto-Mitani, N., et al. (2012). Family caregiver distress with children having rare genetic disorders. *Journal of Clinical Nursing, 21*, 160–169.

chapter

7 Finding and Reviewing Research Evidence in the Literature

LEARNING OBJECTIVES

On completing this chapter, you will be able to:

- Understand the steps involved in doing a literature review
- Identify bibliographic aids for retrieving nursing research reports, and locate references for a research topic
- Understand the process of screening, abstracting, critiquing, and organizing research evidence
- Evaluate the style, content, and organization of a literature review
- Define new terms in the chapter

KEY TERMS

Bibliographic database
CINAHL database
Keyword
Literature review
MEDLINE® database
Primary source
PubMed
Secondary source

A **literature review** is a written summary of the state of evidence on a research problem. Both consumers and producers of nursing research need to acquire skills for reading, critiquing, and preparing written evidence summaries.

BASIC ISSUES RELATING TO LITERATURE REVIEWS

Before discussing the activities involved in undertaking a research-based literature review, we briefly discuss some general issues. The first concerns the purposes of doing a literature review.

Purposes of Research Literature Reviews

The primary purpose of literature reviews is to integrate research evidence to sum up what is known and what is not known. Literature reviews are sometimes stand-alone documents intended to share the state of evidence with interested readers, but reviews are also used to lay the foundation for new studies. A literature review undertaken for a quantitative study can help to shape research questions, suggest appropriate methods, and point to a conceptual framework. Literature reviews also help researchers to interpret their findings.

In qualitative research, opinions about literature reviews vary. Grounded theory researchers typically begin to collect data before examining the literature. As the grounded theory emerges, researchers then turn to the literature, seeking to relate prior findings to the theory. Phenomenologists, by contrast, often undertake a preliminary literature search at the outset of a study. Ethnographers often familiarize themselves with the literature to help shape their choice of a cultural problem before going into the field.

Regardless of when they perform the review, researchers usually include brief summaries of relevant literature in their introductions. The literature review tells readers about current knowledge on a topic and illuminates the significance of the new study. Literature reviews are often intertwined with the problem statement as part of the argument for the study.

Types of Information to Seek for a Research Review

Findings from prior studies are the most important type of information for a research review. If you are preparing a literature review, you should rely mostly on **primary sources**, which are descriptions of studies written by the researchers who conducted them. **Secondary source** research documents are descriptions of studies prepared by someone else. Literature reviews, then, are secondary sources. Recent reviews may be a good place to start because they offer a quick overview of the literature and a valuable bibliography. If you are doing your own literature review, however, secondary sources should not be considered substitutes for primary sources because secondary sources are not sufficiently detailed and are seldom completely objective.

> **TIP:** For an evidence-based practice (EBP) project, a recent, high-quality systematic review may be sufficient to provide the needed information about the evidence base, although it is usually wise to search for studies published after the review. We provide more explicit guidance on searching for evidence for an EBP query in the Chapter Supplements on thePoint website.

A literature search may yield nonresearch references, including opinion articles, case reports, and clinical anecdotes. Such materials may broaden understanding of a problem, demonstrate a need for research, or describe aspects of clinical practice. These writings, however, usually have limited utility in research reviews because they do not address the central question of written reviews: What is the current state of *evidence* on this research problem?

Major Steps and Strategies in Doing a Literature Review

Conducting a literature review is a little bit like doing a full-fledged study: a reviewer must start with a question, such as an evidence-based practice (EBP) question (Chapter 2) or a question for a new study (Chapter 6). The reviewer then must gather, analyze, and interpret the information, and summarize the "findings" in a written product. Figure 7.1 depicts the literature review process, and shows that there are potential feedback loops, with opportunities to go back to earlier steps in search of more information.

Conducting a literature review is an art and a science. A high-quality review should be unbiased, thorough, and up-to-date. Also, a high-quality review is systematic. Decision rules for including or excluding a study should be explicit because a good review should be reproducible. This means that another diligent reviewer would be able to apply the same decision rules and come to similar conclusions about the state of evidence on the topic.

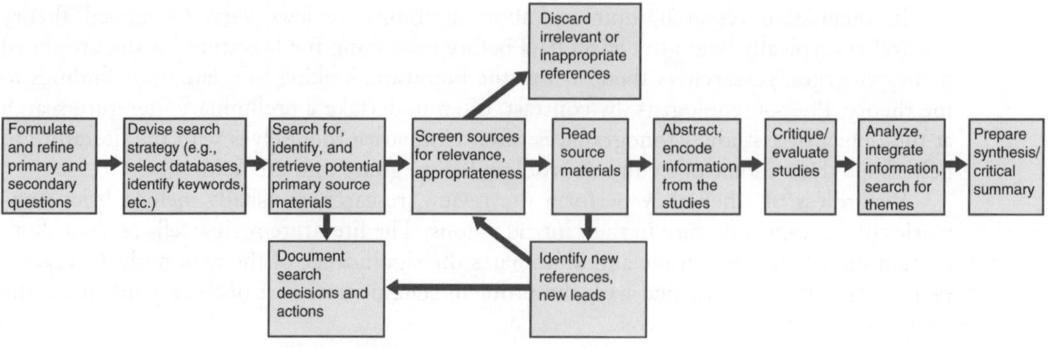

FIGURE 7.1 ● Flow of tasks in a literature review.

TIP: Locating all relevant information on a research question is like being a detective. The literature retrieval tools we discuss in this chapter are helpful, but there inevitably needs to be some digging for, and sifting of, the clues to evidence on a topic. Be prepared for sleuthing!

Doing a literature review is in some ways similar to undertaking a qualitative study. This means that it is useful to have a flexible approach to "data collection" and to think creatively about opportunities for new sources of information. It also means that the analysis of the "data" typically involves a search for important themes.

LOCATING RELEVANT LITERATURE FOR A RESEARCH REVIEW

An early step in a literature review is devising a strategy to locate relevant studies. The ability to locate evidence on a topic is an important skill that requires adaptability—rapid technological changes mean that new methods of searching the literature are introduced continuously. We urge you to consult with librarians or faculty at your institution for updated suggestions.

Developing a Search Strategy

Having good search skills is critically important for EBP and for researchers. A particular important approach is to search for evidence in bibliographic databases, which we discuss next. Another strategy is the *ancestry approach* ("footnote chasing"), in which citations from relevant studies are used to track down earlier research on which the studies are based (the "ancestors"). A third method, called the *descendancy approach*, is to find a pivotal early study and to search forward in citation indexes to find more recent studies ("descendants") that cited the key study.

TIP: You may be tempted to begin a literature search through an Internet search engine, such as Google or Yahoo. Such a search is likely to provide you with a lot of "hits" on your topic, including information about support groups, advocacy organizations, commercial products, and the like. Internet searches are not likely to give you comprehensive bibliographic information on the *research* literature on your topic.

Decisions must also be made about delimiting the search. For example, many reviewers constrain their search to reports written in their own language. You may also want to limit your search to studies conducted within a certain time frame (e.g., within the past 15 years).

Searching Bibliographic Databases

Bibliographic databases are accessed by computer, often through software made available by commercial vendors. These programs are user-friendly, offering menu-driven systems with on-screen support so that minimal instruction is needed to retrieve articles. Your university or hospital library probably has a subscription to these services.

Getting Started With an Electronic Search

Before searching a bibliographic database electronically, you should become familiar with the features of the software you are using to access it. The software has options for restricting or expanding your search, for combining two searches, for saving your search, and so on. Most programs have tutorials, and most also have Help buttons.

An early task in an electronic search is identifying keywords to launch the search (although an *author search* for prominent researchers in a field is also possible). A **keyword** is a word or phrase that captures the key concepts in your question. For quantitative studies, the keywords are usually the independent or dependent variables (i.e., at a minimum, the "I" and "O" of the PICO components), and perhaps the population. For qualitative studies, the keywords are the central phenomenon and the population. If you use the question templates for asking clinical questions in Table 2.1 on page 31, the words you enter in the blanks are likely to be good keywords.

 **TIP:** If you want to identify all research reports on a topic, you need to be flexible and to think broadly about keywords. For example, if you are interested in anorexia nervosa, you might look up *anorexia*, *eating disorders*, and *weight loss*, and perhaps *appetite*, *eating behavior*, *food habits*, *bulimia*, and *body weight changes*.

There are various search approaches for a bibliographic search. All citations in a database have to be coded so they can be retrieved, and databases and programs use their own system of categorizing entries. The indexing systems have specific *subject headings* (subject codes) and a hierarchical organizational structure with subheadings.

You can undertake a *subject* search by entering a subject heading into the search field. You do not have to worry about knowing the subject codes because most software has mapping capabilities. *Mapping* is a feature that allows you to search for topics using your own keywords, rather than the exact subject heading used in the database. The software translates ("maps") your keywords into the most plausible subject heading, and then retrieves citation records that have been coded with that subject heading.

Keyword searches and subject heading searches yield overlapping but nonidentical search results, so it is a good idea to identify relevant subject headings. Subject headings for databases can be accessed in the database's thesaurus or other reference tools.

When you enter a keyword into the search field, the program likely will launch both a subject search, as just described, and a textword search. A *textword search* looks for your keyword in the text fields of the records, that is, in the title and the abstract. Thus, if you searched for *lung cancer* in the MEDLINE® database (which we describe in a subsequent section), the search would retrieve citations coded for the subject code of *lung neoplasms* (the MEDLINE® subject heading used to code entries), and also any entries in which the phrase *lung cancer* appeared, even if it had not been coded for the *lung neoplasm* subject heading.

Although it is beyond the scope of this book to offer extensive guidance on doing an electronic search, we offer a few suggestions. One widely available tool is wildcard characters. A **wildcard character**—which is a symbol, such as "*" or "$," depending on the search program—allows you to search for multiple words with the same root. The wildcard character typically is inserted after a truncated root. For example, if we entered nurs* in the search field for a MEDLINE® search, the software would search for any word that begins with "nurs," such as *nurse*, *nurses*, and *nursing*. This can be efficient, but the use of a wildcard character may turn off mapping and result in a textword search exclusively.

One way to force a textword search is to use quotation marks around a phrase, which yields citations in which the exact phrase appears in text fields. In other words, *lung cancer* and "lung cancer" might yield different results. A thorough search strategy might entail doing a search with and without wildcard characters and with and without quotation marks.

Boolean operators can be used to expand or restrict a search. For example, if you wanted citations on *lung cancer* and *smoking*, you could enter the following: *lung cancer AND smoking*. The Boolean operator AND would restrict the search to citations with both lung cancer and smoking as textwords or subject headings. The Boolean operator "OR" expands a search—if you entered *lung cancer OR smoking*, you would retrieve all references with either term.

Two especially useful electronic databases for nurses are **C**umulative **I**ndex to **N**ursing and **A**llied **H**ealth **L**iterature (CINAHL) and MEDLINE® (**Med**ical Literature On-**Line**), which we discuss in the next sections. Other useful bibliographic databases for nurses include the Cochrane Database of Systematic Reviews, Web of Knowledge, Scopus, and EMBASE (the Excerpta Medica database). The Web of Knowledge database is useful for a descendancy search strategy because of its strong citation indexes.

TIP: If your goal is to conduct a *systematic* review, you will need to establish an explicit formal plan about your search strategy and keywords, as discussed in Chapter 19.

The CINAHL Database

CINAHL is an important electronic database for nurses. It covers references to hundreds of nursing and allied health journals, as well as to books, book chapters, and dissertations. CINAHL contains more than 1 million records.

CINAHL provides information for locating references (i.e., the author, title, journal, year of publication, volume, and page numbers), and abstracts for most citations. Documents identified as potentially useful can often be ordered electronically. We illustrate some basic features of CINAHL, but note that changes are introduced periodically.

A "basic search" in CINAHL involves entering keywords in the search field (more options for expanding and limiting the search are available in the "Advanced Search" mode). You can restrict your search to records with certain features (e.g., only ones with abstracts); to specific publication dates (e.g., only those after 2005); to those published in English; or to those coded as being in a certain subset (e.g., nursing). The basic search screen also allows you to expand the search by clicking the option "Apply related words."

To illustrate with a concrete example, suppose we were interested in research on the effect of music on agitation in people with dementia.

We entered the following terms in the search field, and placed only one limit on the search—only records with abstracts:

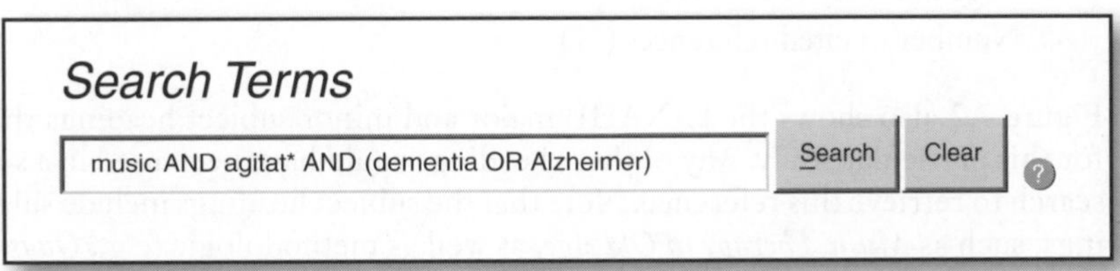

By clicking the "Search" button, we got 47 "hits" (citations). Note that we used two Boolean operators. The use of "AND" ensured that retrieved records had to include all three keywords, and the use of "OR" allowed either dementia or Alzheimer to be the third keyword. Also, we used a wildcard character* in the second keyword. This instructed the computer to search for any word that begins with "agitat" such as agitated or agitation. (Note that a search without the Boolean operators—that is, searching for the keywords music, agitat*, dementia, Alzheimer—yielded nearly 800 records).

By clicking the Search button, the 47 references would be displayed on the monitor, and we could view and print full information for ones that seemed promising. An example of an abridged CINAHL record entry for a report identified through this search is presented in Figure 7.2. The title of the article and author information is displayed, followed by source information. The source indicates the following:

- Name of the journal (*Pain Management Nursing*)
- Year and month of publication (2010 September)

Title:	Effect of music on pain for home-dwelling persons with dementia.
Authors:	Park H.
Affiliation:	College of Nursing, Keimyung University, South Korea, hparknursing@yahoo.co.kr
Source:	Pain Management Nursing (PAIN MANAGE NURS), 2010 Sep; 11(3): 141-7 (37 ref)
Language:	English
Major Subjects:	Music Therapy -- In Old Age; Pain -- Prevention and Control -- In Old Age; Dementia; Community Living; Comfort -- In Old Age
Minor Subjects:	Human; Aged; Pilot Studies; Quasi-Experimental Studies; Clinical Nursing Research; Male; Female; South Korea; Nonprobability Sample; Convenience Sample; Pain Measurement; Home Environment; Effect Size; Prospective Studies; Analysis of Variance; Descriptive Statistics; Patient Attitudes -- Evaluation; Time Factors; Scales
Abstract:	The purpose of this study was to investigate the effect of **music** on pain for home-dwelling persons with **dementia**. A quasiexperimental design was used. Fifteen subjects listened to their preferred **music** for 30 minutes before peak **agitation** time, for 2 days per week, followed by no **music** for 2 weeks. The process was repeated once. The findings of this study showed that mean pain levels after listening to **music** were significantly lower than before listening to the **music** ($t=2.21$, $df=28$; $p < .05$). The findings of this pilot study suggest the importance of **music** intervention to control pain for home-dwelling persons with **dementia**.
Instrumentation:	Mini-Mental Status Examination (MMSE) (Folstein et al) Assessment of Personal **Music** Preference (APMP) Modified Cohen-Mansfield **Agitation** Inventory (M-CMAI) Modified Pain Assessment in the Dementing Elderly (M-PADE)
MEDLINE Info:	*PMID: 20728063 NLM UID: 100890606*
Accession Number:	2010767993

FIGURE 7.2 ● Example of a printout from a Cumulative Index to Nursing and Allied Health Literature search (CINAHL).

- Volume (11)
- Issue (3)
- Page numbers (141–147)
- Number of cited references (37)

Figure 7.2 also shows the CINAHL major and minor subject headings that were coded for this particular study. Any of these headings could have been used in a subject heading search to retrieve this reference. Note that the subject headings include substantive headings, such as *Music Therapy in Old Age*, as well as methodologic (e.g., *Quasi-Experimental Studies*) and sample characteristic headings (e.g., *Male; Female*). The subject names have hyperlinks so that we could expand the search by clicking on them (we could also click on the author's name or on the journal). The abstract for the study is then presented, with the search terms appearing in boldface. Next, the names of any formal instruments are printed under Instrumentation. Each entry shows an accession number that is the unique identifier for each record in the database, as well as other identifying numbers. Based on the abstract, we would then decide whether this reference was pertinent to our inquiry.

The MEDLINE® Database

The MEDLINE® database, developed by the U.S. National Library of Medicine, is the premier source for bibliographic coverage of the biomedical literature. MEDLINE® covers about 5,000 medical, nursing, and health journals and has more than 21 million records. MEDLINE® can be accessed for free on the Internet at the **PubMed** website (http://www.ncbi.nlm.nih.gov/PubMed). PubMed is a lifelong resource regardless of your institution's access to bibliographic databases.

MEDLINE® uses a controlled vocabulary called **MeSH** (Medical Subject Headings) to index articles. MeSH terminology provides a consistent way to retrieve information that may use different terminology for the same concepts. Once you have begun a search, a field on the right side of the screen labeled "Search Details" lets you see how keywords you entered mapped onto MeSH terms, which might lead you to pursue other leads. You can also search for references using the MeSH database directly by clicking on "MeSH database" on the PubMed home page. MeSH subject headings may overlap with, but are not identical to, subject headings in CINAHL.

When we did a PubMed search of MEDLINE® analogous to the one we described earlier for CINAHL, using the same keywords and restrictions, 40 records were retrieved. The list of records in the two PubMed and CINAHL searches overlapped considerably, but new references were found in each search. Both searches, however, retrieved the study by Park—the CINAHL record for which was shown in Figure 7.2. The PubMed record for the same reference is presented in Figure 7.3. (To get MeSH codes, you would need to click on the link for "Publication Types, MeSH terms" that appears after the abstract). As you can see, the MeSH terms in Figure 7.3 are different from the CINAHL subject headings in Figure 7.2.

TIP: After you have found a study that is a good exemplar of what you are looking for, you usually can search for similar studies in the database. In PubMed, for example, after identifying a key study, you could click on "Related Citations" on the right of the screen to locate similar studies. In Cumulative Index to Nursing and Allied Health Literature, you would click on "Find Similar Results."

Pain Manag Nurs. 2010 Sep;11(3):141-7. Epub 2009 Sep 8.

Effect of music on pain for home-dwelling persons with dementia.

Park H. College of Nursing, Florida State University, Tallahassee, FL, USA. hparknursing@yahoo.co.kr

The purpose of this study was to investigate the effect of music on pain for home-dwelling persons with dementia. A quasiexperimental design was used. Fifteen subjects listened to their preferred music for 30 minutes before peak agitation time, for 2 days per week, followed by no music for 2 weeks. The process was repeated once. The findings of this study showed that mean pain levels after listening to music were significantly lower than before listening to the music (t=2.21, df=28; p < .05). The findings of this pilot study suggest the importance of music intervention to control pain for home-dwelling persons with dementia.

PMID: 20728063

MeSH Terms

- Aged, 80 and over
- Analysis of Variance
- Assisted Living Facilities
- Attitude to Health*
- Dementia/complications*
- Dementia/psychology
- Factor Analysis, Statistical
- Female
- Home Care Services*/organization & administration
- Humans
- Male
- Mental Status Schedule
- Music Therapy/methods*
- Nursing Evaluation Research
- Pain/diagnosis
- Pain/etiology
- Pain/prevention & control*
- Pain Measurement
- Pilot Projects
- Severity of Illness Index
- Treatment Outcome

FIGURE 7.3 ● Example of printout from PubMed search.

Screening, Documentation, and Abstracting

After searching for and retrieving references, several important steps remain before a synthesis can begin.

Screening and Gathering References

References that have been identified in the search need to be screened for accessibility (will I be able to retrieve the article?) and relevance. You can usually surmise a reference's relevance by reading the abstract. When you find a relevant article, try to obtain a copy rather than taking notes about its content. Each article should be organized in a manner that permits easy retrieval. We find that alphabetical filing, using the first author's last name, is a good method.

Documentation in Literature Retrieval

Search strategies are often complex, so it is wise to document your search actions and results. You should make note of databases searched, keywords used, limits instituted, studies used to launch a "descendancy" search, and any other information that would help you keep track of what you did. Part of your strategy can be documented by printing your search history from the electronic databases. Documentation will help you to conduct a more efficient search by preventing unintended duplication, and will also help you to assess what else needs to be tried.

Abstracting and Recording Information

Once you have retrieved useful articles, you need a strategy to organize and make sense of the information in the articles. For simple literature reviews, it may be sufficient to make notes about key features of the retrieved studies, and to base your review on these notes. When a literature review is complex or involves a large number of studies, a formal system of recording information from each study may be needed. One mechanism that we recommend for very complex reviews is to code the characteristics of each study and then record codes in a set of matrices, a system that we describe in detail elsewhere (Polit & Beck, 2012).

Example of a Mini Protocol for a Literature Review (Therapy Question)

Citation and Abstract	(copy and paste information from bibliographic database)
Variables:	Intervention (Independent Variable): ______
	Outcome Variable: ______
Framework/Theory:	______
Design Type:	☐ Experimental ☐ Quasi-experimental
	Specific Design: ______
	Control for confounding variables: ______
	Blinding? ☐ No ☐ Yes Who blinded? ______
	Intervention description: ______
	______
	Control group condition: ______
Sample:	Size: ___ Sampling method: ______
	______
	Sample characteristics: ______
Data Sources:	☐ Self-report ☐ Observational ☐ Biophysiologic ☐ Other
	Description of measures: ______
	______
	Data Quality: ______
Key Findings:	______
	______
	______
	______

FIGURE 7.4 ● Example of a mini protocol for a literature review (therapy question).

Another approach is to "copy and paste" each abstract and citation information from the bibliographic database into a word processing document. Then, the bottom of each page could have a "miniprotocol" for recording important information that you want to record consistently across studies. There is no fixed format for such a protocol—you must decide what elements are important to record systematically to help you organize and analyze information. We present an example for a half-page protocol in Figure 7.4, with entries that would be most suitable for Therapy/Intervention questions. Although many of the terms on this protocol are probably not familiar to you at this point, you will learn their meaning in subsequent chapters.

EVALUATING AND ANALYZING THE EVIDENCE

In drawing conclusions about a body of research, reviewers must make judgments about the worth of the studies' evidence. Thus, an important part of doing a literature review is evaluating the body of completed studies and integrating the evidence across studies.

Evaluating Studies for a Review

In reviewing the literature, you typically would not undertake a comprehensive critique of each study, but you would need to evaluate the quality of each study so that you could draw conclusions about the overall evidence and about gaps in the evidence base. Critiques for a literature review tend to focus on methodological aspects, and so the critiquing guidelines in Table 4.1 on page 69 and Table 4.2 on page 70 might be useful.

In literature reviews, methodological features of the studies under review need to be assessed with an eye to answering a broad question: To what extent do the findings reflect the *truth* (the true state of affairs) or, conversely, to what extent do flaws undermine the believability of the evidence? The "truth" is most likely to be discovered when researchers use powerful designs, good sampling plans, high-quality data collection procedures, and appropriate analyses.

Analyzing and Synthesizing Information

Once relevant studies have been retrieved, abstracted, and critiqued, the information has to be analyzed and synthesized. As previously noted, we find the analogy between doing a literature review and doing a qualitative study useful, and this is particularly true with respect to the analysis of the "data" (i.e., the information from the retrieved studies). In both, the focus is on the identification of important *themes*.

A thematic analysis essentially involves detecting patterns and regularities—as well as inconsistencies. A number of different types of themes can be identified in a literature review analysis, three of which are as follows:

- *Substantive themes*: What is the pattern of evidence—what findings predominate? How much evidence is there? How consistent is the body of evidence? What gaps are there in the evidence?
- *Methodologic themes*: What methods have been used to address the question? What strategies have *not* been used? What are major methodologic deficiencies and strengths?
- *Generalizability/transferability themes*: To what types of people or settings does the evidence apply? Do the findings vary for different types of people (e.g., men vs. women) or setting (e.g., urban vs. rural)?

In preparing a review, you would need to determine which themes are most relevant for the purpose at hand. Most often substantive themes are of greatest interest.

PREPARING A WRITTEN LITERATURE REVIEW

Writing literature reviews can be challenging, especially when voluminous information and thematic analyses must be condensed into a small number of pages. We offer a few suggestions, but we acknowledge that skills in writing literature reviews develop over time.

Organizing the Review

Organization is crucial in preparing a written review. When literature on a topic is extensive, it is useful to summarize information in a table. The table could include columns with headings such as Author, Sample Characteristics, Design, and Key Findings. Such a table provides a quick overview that allows you to make sense of a mass of information.

Most writers find an outline helpful. Unless the review is very simple, it is important to have an organizational plan so that the review has a meaningful and understandable flow. Lack of organization is a common weakness in first attempts at writing a research literature review. Although the specifics of the organization differ from topic to topic, the goal is to structure the review to lead logically to a conclusion about the state of evidence on the topic.

After finalizing an organizing structure, you should review your notes or protocols to decide where a particular reference fits in the outline. If some references do not seem to fit anywhere, they may need to be omitted. Remember that the number of references is less important than their relevance.

Writing a Literature Review

It is beyond the scope of this textbook to offer detailed guidance on writing research reviews, but we offer a few comments on their content and style. Additional assistance is provided in books such as those by Fink (2010) and Garrard (2011).

Content of the Written Literature Review

A written research review should provide readers with an objective, well-organized synthesis of current evidence on a topic. A literature review should be neither a series of quotes nor a series of abstracts. The central tasks are to summarize and critically evaluate the evidence to reveal the current state of knowledge on a topic—not simply to describe what researchers have done.

Although key studies may be described in detail, it is not necessary to provide particulars for every reference. Studies with comparable findings often can be summarized together, as illustrated in the third paragraph of Example 1 at the end of this chapter.

Findings should be summarized in your own words. The review should demonstrate that you have considered the cumulative worth of the body of research. Stringing together quotes from articles fails to show that previous research has been assimilated and understood.

The review should be as unbiased as possible. The review should not omit a study because its findings contradict those of other studies or if they conflict with your ideas. Inconsistent results should be analyzed and the supporting evidence evaluated objectively.

A literature review typically concludes with a summary of current evidence on the topic. The summary should recap key findings, assess their credibility, and point out gaps in the evidence. When the literature review is conducted for a new study, the summary should demonstrate the need for the research and clarify the context for any hypotheses.

As you read this book, you will become increasingly proficient in critically evaluating the research literature. We hope you will understand the mechanics of doing a research review once you have completed this chapter, but we do not expect that you will be in a position to write a state-of-the-art review until you have acquired more skills in research methods.

Style of a Research Review

Students preparing research reviews often have trouble writing in an acceptable, tentative style. Hypotheses cannot be proved or disproved by statistical testing, and no question can be definitely answered in a single study. The problem is partly semantic: hypotheses are not proved or verified, they are *supported* by research findings.

TIP: Phrases indicating the tentativeness of research results, such as the following, are appropriate:

- Several studies have *found*...
- Findings thus far *suggest*...
- The results *are consistent* with the conclusion that...
- Results from a landmark study *imply* that ...
- There *appears* to be fairly strong evidence that...

A related stylistic problem concerns the expression of opinions. A literature review should include opinions sparingly, and should explicitly reference the source. Reviewers' own opinions do not belong in a review, with the exception of assessments of study quality.

The left-hand column of Table 7.1 presents several examples of stylistic flaws. The right-hand column offers rewordings that are more acceptable for a research literature review. Many alternative wordings are possible.

TABLE 7.1 Examples of Stylistic Difficulties for Research Literature Reviews

Problematic Style or Wording	Improved Style or Wording
Women who do not participate in childbirth preparation classes manifest a high degree of anxiety during labor.	*Studies have found that* women who participate in childbirth preparation classes *tend to* manifest less anxiety than those who do not (Giblin, 2012; Tucker, 2012; Finnerty, 2013).
Studies have proved that doctors and nurses do not fully understand the psychobiologic dynamics of recovery from a myocardial infarction.	Studies by Fortune (2012) and Crampton (2013) *suggest that many* doctors and nurses do not fully understand the psychobiologic dynamics of recovery from a myocardial infarction.
Attitudes cannot be changed quickly.	Attitudes *have been found to be* relatively stable attributes that do not change quickly (Nicolet, 2011; Carroll, 2012).
It is known that uncertainty engenders stress.	*According to* Dr. A. Cassard (2011), an expert on stress and anxiety, uncertainty is a stressor.

Note: Italicized words in the improved version indicate key alterations.

CRITIQUING RESEARCH LITERATURE REVIEWS

Some nurses never prepare a written research review, and perhaps you will never be required to do one. Most nurses, however, do *read* research reviews (including the literature review sections of research reports) and they should be prepared to evaluate such reviews critically.

It is often difficult to critique a research review if you are not familiar with the topic. You may not be able to judge whether the author has included all relevant literature and has adequately summarized knowledge on that topic. Some aspects of a research review, however, are amenable to evaluation by readers who are not experts on the topic. A few suggestions for critiquing research reviews are presented in Box 7.1. Extra critiquing questions are relevant for systematic reviews, as we discuss in Chapter 19.

BOX 7.1 Guidelines for Critiquing Literature Reviews

1. Does the review seem thorough and up-to-date? Does it include major studies on the topic? Does it include recent research?
2. Does the review rely on appropriate materials (e.g., mainly on research reports, using primary sources)?
3. Is the review merely a summary of existing work, or does it critically appraise and compare key studies? Does the review identify important gaps in the literature?
4. Is the review well organized? Is the development of ideas clear?
5. Does the review use appropriate language, suggesting the tentativeness of prior findings? Is the review objective? Does the author paraphrase, or is there an overreliance on quotes from original sources?
6. If the review is in the introduction for a new study, does the review support the need for the study?
7. If it is a review designed to summarize evidence for clinical practice, does the review draw appropriate conclusions about practice implications?

In assessing a literature review, the overarching question is whether it summarizes the current state of research evidence. If the review is written as part of an original research report, an equally important question is whether the review lays a solid foundation for the new study.

TIP: Literature reviews in the introductions of research articles are unlikely to present a thorough critique of existing studies, but are likely to identify gaps in what has been studied.

RESEARCH EXAMPLES WITH CRITICAL THINKING EXERCISES

The best way to learn about the style, content, and organization of a research literature review is to read reviews that appear in the nursing literature. We present an excerpt from a review for a mixed methods study—one involving the collection and analysis of both qualitative and quantitative data.

Example 1 below is also featured in our *Interactive Critical Thinking Activity* on thePoint website where you can easily record, print, and e-mail your responses to the related questions.

EXAMPLE 1 ● Literature Review from a Mixed Methods Study

Study: "Adherence to leg ulcer lifestyle advice; qualitative and quantitative outcomes associated with a nurse-led intervention" (Van Hecke et al., 2011)

Statement of Purpose: The purpose of this study was to examine changes associated with a nursing intervention to enhance adherence to leg ulcer lifestyle advice.

Literature Review (excerpt): "A venous leg ulcer is a chronic problem that mainly occurs as a consequence of chronic venous insufficiency (Brem et al., 2004). Prevalence in adult populations is estimated at 0.63% to 1.9% in Europe, the UK, the USA, and Australia (Briggs & Closs, 2003)... Venous leg ulcers indicate a lifelong treatment plan (Reichardt, 1999) including compression therapy (Nelson et al., 2000, O'Meara et al., 2009), leg exercises, and leg elevation (Heinen et al., 2004). Nonadherence to leg ulcer treatment frequently occurs. However, few studies report the development and testing of nursing interventions to enhance adherence to leg ulcer treatment.

Several authors report the problem of nonadherence among patients with venous leg ulcers. Jull et al. (2004) found that only 52% of the included patients (n = 129) reported wearing compression stockings daily for the first 6 months after leg ulcer healing. About one fifth (22%) of the patients had not worn compression stockings at all. In the study of Raju et al. (2007), only 37% of the patients with chronic venous disease (including leg ulcers) reported full or partial adherence and 63% did not use compression stockings at all or abandoned them after a trial period in the past... Few studies examined nonadherence to leg exercises and leg elevation. Twenty percent of the patients with venous leg ulcers elevated their legs when sitting and they walked for 1.7 hours per day (Johnson 1995). Heinen et al. (2007b) described less positive results regarding physical activity: 56% of the 150 patients were physically active <2.5 hours per week, 13% of the patients walked for 30 minutes at least 5 days of the week and 35% performed lower leg exercises...

Published research concerning the determinants of nonadherence to leg ulcer treatment is limited. Pain, discomfort and inadequate lifestyle advice by health care professionals are the main reasons for nonadherence, as reported by leg ulcer patients (Van Hecke et al., 2009). Additional reasons for nonadherence are difficulties in applying compression, skin problems, uncomfortable footwear, poor cosmetic appearance of compression bandages, and financial restrictions (Van Hecke et al., 2009).... Heinen et al. (2007a) report that pain, comorbidity, difficulties in finding appropriate footwear, compression bandages, incorrect health beliefs, low self-efficacy, and lack of social support are linked to insufficient activity in leg ulcer patients. The fear that physical activity will cause injury and aggravate pain has also been documented as a reason for nonadherence (Walshe, 1995; Chase et al., 1997; Hyde et al., 1999; Ebbeskog & Ekman, 2001).

Nonadherence has a negative impact on the outcomes of venous leg ulcers. It increases the time to complete healing (Mayberry et al., 1991; Erickson et al., 1995; Moffatt et al., 2009). Recurrence rates also increase when patients do not wear compression stockings (Mayberry et al., 1991; Erickson et al., 1995; Harper et al., 1999; Finlayson et al., 2009; Moffatt etal., 2009). Nonadherence is also associated with increased costs (Korn et al., 2002). Therefore, adherence to leg ulcer treatment is important. The need to improve patient adherence to maximize therapeutic benefits is highlighted in the literature. However, few comprehensive programs to optimize patient adherence to leg ulcer lifestyle advice have been initiated (Van Hecke et al., 2008)."

CRITICAL THINKING EXERCISES

1. Answer the relevant questions from Box 7.1 on page 127 regarding this literature review.
2. Also consider the following targeted questions, which may further sharpen your critical thinking skills and assist you in understanding this study:
   a. In performing the literature review, what keywords might the researchers have used to search for prior studies?
   b. Using the keywords, perform a computerized search to see if you can find a recent relevant study to augment the review.

EXAMPLE 2 ● Quantitative Research in Appendix A

- Read the abstract and the introduction from Howell and colleagues' (2007) study ("Anxiety, anger, and blood pressure in children") in Appendix A on page 395–402.

CRITICAL THINKING EXERCISES

1. Answer the relevant questions from Box 7.1 on page 127 regarding this study.
2. Also consider the following targeted questions:
   a. What do you think the independent variable was in this study? Did the literature review cover findings from prior studies about this variable?
   b. What were the dependent variables in this study? Did the literature review cover findings from prior studies about these variables and their relationship with the independent variable?
   c. In performing the literature review, what keywords might have been used to search for prior studies?

EXAMPLE 3 ● Qualitative Research in Appendix B

- Read the abstract and introduction from Beck and Watson's (2010) study ("Subsequent childbirth after a previous traumatic birth") in Appendix B on page 403–412.

CRITICAL THINKING EXERCISES

1. Answer the relevant questions in Box 7.1 on page 127 regarding this study.
2. Also consider the following targeted questions:
   a. What was the central phenomenon in this study? Was that phenomenon adequately covered in the literature review?
   b. In performing their literature review, what keywords might Beck and Watson have used to search for prior studies?

WANT TO KNOW MORE? A wide variety of resources to enhance your learning and understanding of this chapter are available on thePoint.

- Interactive Critical Thinking Activity
- Chapter Supplement on Finding Evidence for an EBP Inquiry in PubMed
- Answers to the Critical Thinking Exercises for Examples 2 and 3
- Student Review Questions
- Full-text online
- Internet Resources with useful websites for Chapter 7

Additional study aids including eight journal articles and related questions are also available in *Study Guide for Essentials of Nursing Research, 8e.*

SUMMARY POINTS

- A research **literature review** is a written summary of the state of evidence on a research problem.
- The major steps in preparing a written research review include formulating a question, devising a search strategy, searching and retrieving relevant sources, abstracting and encoding information, critiquing studies, analyzing and integrating the information, and preparing a written synthesis.
- Research reviews rely primarily on findings in research reports. Information in nonresearch references (e.g., opinion articles, case reports) may broaden understanding of a problem, but has limited utility in summarizing evidence.
- A **primary source** is the original description of a study prepared by the researcher who conducted it; a **secondary source** is a description of a study by another person. Literature reviews should be based on primary source material.
- Strategies for finding studies on a topic include the use of bibliographic tools, but also include the *ancestry approach* (tracking down earlier studies cited in a reference list of a report) and the *descendancy approach* (using a pivotal study to search forward to subsequent studies that cited it.)
- Key resources for a research literature search are the **bibliographic databases** that can be searched electronically. For nurses, the **CINAHL** and **MEDLINE®** databases are especially useful.
- In searching a bibliographic database, users can do a keyword search that looks for terms in *text fields* of a database record (or that *maps* keywords onto the database's subject codes), or can search according to the *subject heading* codes themselves.
- Retrieved references must be screened for relevance, and then pertinent information can be abstracted and encoded for subsequent analysis. Studies must also be critiqued to assess the strength of evidence in existing research.
- The analysis of information from a literature search essentially involves the identification of important *themes*—regularities and patterns in the information.
- In preparing a written review, it is important to organize materials coherently. Preparation of an outline is recommended. The reviewers' role is to point out what has been studied, how adequate and dependable the studies are, and what gaps exist in the body of research.

REFERENCES FOR CHAPTER 7

Fink, A. (2010). *Conducting research literature reviews: From paper to the Internet* (3rd ed.). Thousand Oaks, CA: Sage.

Garrard, J. (2011). *Health sciences literature review made easy: The matrix method* (3rd ed.). Boston, MA: Jones and Bartlett Publishers.

Polit, D., & Beck, C. (2012). *Nursing research: Generating and appraising evidence for nursing practice* (9th ed.) Philadelphia, PA: Lippincott Williams & Wilkins.

Van Hecke, A., Grypdonck, M., Beele, H., Vanderwee, K., & Defloor, T. (2011). Adherence to leg ulcer lifestyle advice; Qualitative and quantitative outcomes associated with a nurse-led intervention. *Journal of Clinical Nursing, 20*, 429–443.

chapter

8 Theoretical and Conceptual Frameworks

LEARNING OBJECTIVES

On completing this chapter, you will be able to:

- Identify major characteristics of theories, conceptual models, and frameworks
- Identify several conceptual models or theories frequently used by nurse researchers
- Describe how theory and research are linked in quantitative and qualitative studies
- Critique the appropriateness of a theoretical framework—or its absence—in a study
- Define new terms in the chapter

KEY TERMS

Conceptual framework
Conceptual map
Conceptual model
Descriptive theory
Framework
Middle-range theory
Model
Schematic model
Theoretical framework
Theory

High-quality studies typically achieve a high level of *conceptual integration*. This means that the research questions fit the chosen methods, that the questions are consistent with existing evidence, and that there is a plausible conceptual rationale for expected outcomes—including a rationale for any hypotheses or interventions. For example, suppose a research team hypothesized that a nurse-led smoking cessation intervention would reduce smoking among patients with cardiovascular disease. Why would they make this prediction—what is the "theory" about how the intervention might change people's behavior? Is it predicted that the intervention will change patients' knowledge? their attitudes? their motivation? or their sense of control over decision making? The researchers' view of how the intervention would "work" should drive the design of the intervention and the study.

Design decisions cannot be developed in a vacuum—there must be an underlying conceptualization of people's behaviors and characteristics, and how these affect and are affected by internal, interpersonal, and environmental forces. In some studies the underlying conceptualization is fuzzy or unstated, but in good research, a clear and defensible conceptualization is made explicit. This chapter discusses theoretical and conceptual contexts for nursing research problems.

THEORIES, MODELS, AND FRAMEWORKS

Many terms are used in connection with conceptual contexts for research, such as theories, models, frameworks, schemes, and maps. These terms are interrelated but are used differently by different writers. We offer guidance in distinguishing these terms, but our definitions are not universal.

Theories

In nursing education, the term *theory* is used to refer to content covered in classrooms, as opposed to actual nursing practice. In both lay and scientific language, *theory* connotes an *abstraction*.

Classically, **theory** is defined as an abstract generalization that explains how phenomena are interrelated. The traditional definition requires a theory to embody at least two concepts that are systematically related in a manner that the theory claims to explain. As classically defined, theories consist of concepts and a set of propositions that form a logically interrelated system, providing a mechanism for deducing hypotheses from the original propositions. To illustrate, consider *reinforcement theory*, which posits that behavior that is reinforced (i.e., rewarded) tends to be repeated and learned. The proposition is that one concept (reinforcement) affects the other (learning). The proposition lends itself to hypothesis generation. For example, if reinforcement theory is valid, we could deduce that hyperactive children who are rewarded when they engage in quiet play will exhibit less acting-out behaviors than unrewarded children. This prediction, as well as others based on reinforcement theory, could then be tested in a study.

The term *theory* is also used less restrictively to refer to a broad characterization of a phenomenon. A **descriptive theory** accounts for and thoroughly describes a phenomenon. Descriptive theories are inductive, observation-based abstractions that describe or classify characteristics of individuals, groups, or situations by summarizing their commonalities. Such theories are important in qualitative studies.

Both classical and descriptive theories help to make research findings meaningful and interpretable. Theories may guide researchers' understanding not only of the "what" of natural phenomena but also of the "why" of their occurrence. Theories can also help to stimulate research by providing both direction and impetus.

Theories vary in their level of generality. *Grand theories* (or *macrotheories*) claim to explain large segments of human experience. In nursing, there are grand theories that offer explanations for the whole of nursing and that address the nature and mission of nursing practice, as distinct from the discipline of medicine. Parse's Theory of Human Becoming (Parse, 1999), for example, has been called a nursing grand theory. Theories of relevance to researchers are often less abstract than grand theories. **Middle-range theories** attempt to explain such phenomena as stress, comfort, and health promotion. Middle-range theories, compared to grand theories, are more specific and more amenable to empirical testing.

Models

A **conceptual model** deals with abstractions (concepts) that are assembled because of their relevance to a common theme. Conceptual models provide a conceptual perspective regarding interrelated phenomena, but they are more loosely structured than theories and do not link concepts in a logically derived deductive system. A conceptual model broadly presents an understanding of the phenomenon of interest and reflects the assumptions and philosophical views of the model's designer. Like theories, conceptual models can serve as springboards for generating hypotheses.

Some writers use the term **model** to designate a method of representing phenomena with a minimal use of words. Words can convey different meanings to different people; thus, a visual or symbolic representation of a phenomenon can sometimes help to express abstract ideas more clearly. Two types of models that are used in research contexts are schematic models and statistical models. *Statistical models*, not discussed here, are equations that mathematically express relationships among a set of variables. These models are tested using sophisticated statistical methods.

Schematic models (or **conceptual maps**) visually represent relationships among phenomena, and are used in both qualitative and quantitative research. Concepts and linkages between them are depicted graphically through boxes, arrows, or other symbols. As an example of a schematic model, Figure 8.1 shows **Pender's Health Promotion Model**

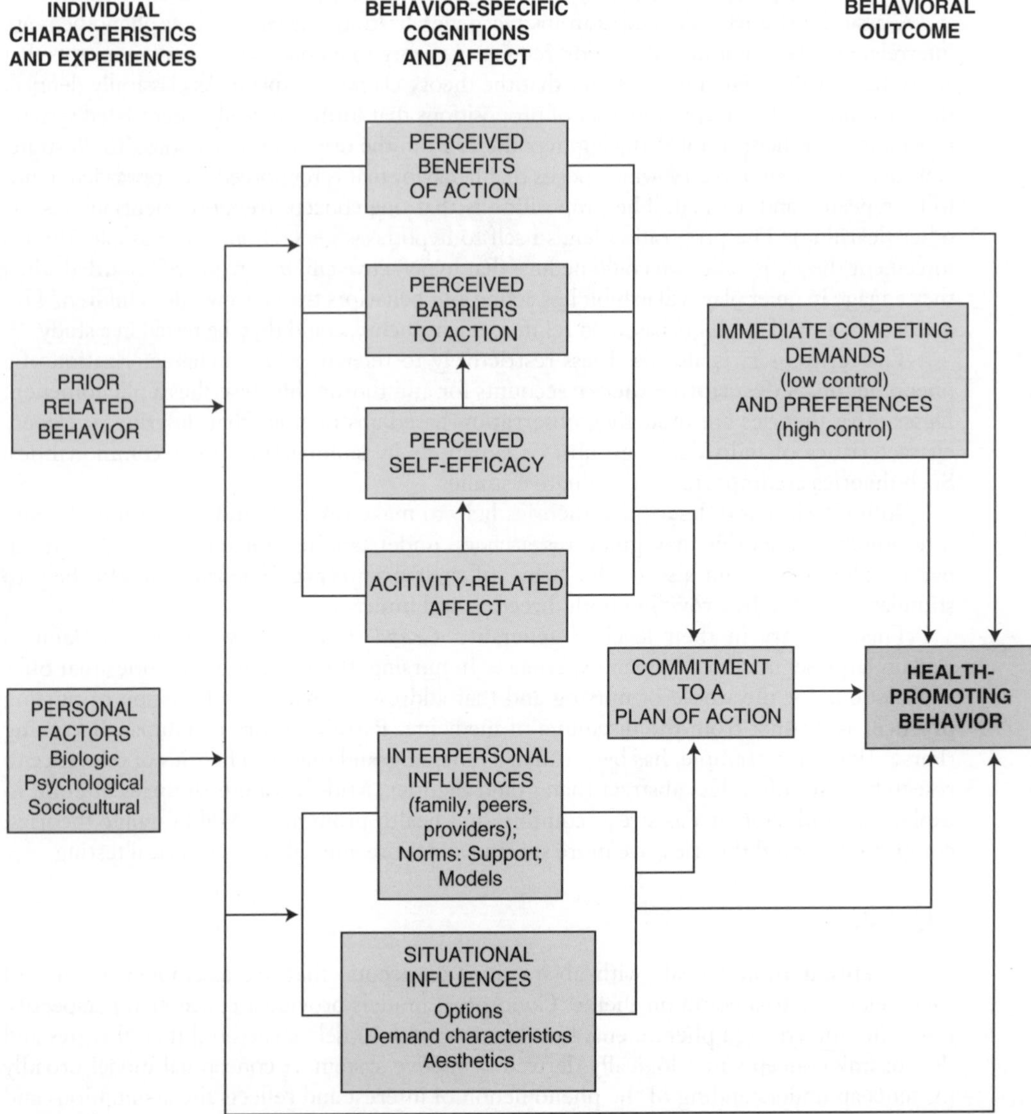

FIGURE 8.1 ● The Health Promotion Model (HPM). (From: The University of Michigan website: http://sitemaker.umich.edu/pender.health.promotion.model/files/chart.gif, retrieved July 25, 2012).

(HPM), which is a model for explaining and predicting the health-promotion component of lifestyle (Pender et al., 2011). Schematic models are appealing as visual summaries of complex ideas.

Frameworks

A **framework** is the conceptual underpinning of a study. Not every study is based on a theory or conceptual model, but every study has a framework. In a study based on a theory, the framework is called the **theoretical framework**; in a study that has its roots in a specified conceptual model, the framework may be called the **conceptual framework**. However, the terms *conceptual framework*, *conceptual model*, and *theoretical framework* are often used interchangeably.

A study's framework is often implicit (i.e., not formally acknowledged or described). World views shape how concepts are defined, but researchers often fail to clarify the conceptual foundations of their variables. Researchers who clarify conceptual definitions of key variables provide important information about the study's framework.

Quantitative researchers are generally more guilty of failing to identify their frameworks than qualitative researchers. In qualitative research, the framework is part of the research tradition in which the study is embedded. For example, ethnographers generally begin within a theory of culture. Grounded theory researchers incorporate sociological principles into their framework and approach. The questions that qualitative researchers ask and the methods they use to address those questions often inherently reflect certain theoretical formulations.

In recent years, *concept analysis* has become an important enterprise among students and nurse scholars. Several methods have been proposed for undertaking a concept analysis and clarifying conceptual definitions (e.g., Walker & Avant, 2010). Efforts to analyze concepts of relevance to nursing should facilitate greater conceptual clarity among nurse researchers.

Example of developing a conceptual definition:

Hodges (2009) did a concept analysis of the concept of *life purpose*. She considered philosophical underpinnings, theoretical frameworks, and research evidence. She proposed this conceptual definition of *life purpose* as it applies to older adults in critical care settings: "The degree to which a person realizes his/her own interpersonal, intrapersonal, and psychological uniqueness on the basis of life experiences that correspond with spiritual values and goals at a specific time in life" (p. 169).

The Nature of Theories and Conceptual Models

Theories, conceptual frameworks, and models are not *discovered*; they are created. Theory building depends not only on observable evidence, but also on a theorist's ingenuity in pulling evidence together and making sense of it. Theory construction is a creative enterprise that can be done by anyone who is insightful, understands existing evidence, and can knit evidence together into a lucid pattern. Because theories are not just "out there" waiting to be discovered, it follows that theories are tentative. A theory cannot be proved—a theory represents a theorist's best efforts to describe and explain phenomena. Through research, theories evolve and are sometimes discarded. This may happen if new evidence undermines a previously accepted theory. Or, a new theory might integrate new observations with an existing theory to yield a more parsimonious explanation of a phenomenon.

Theory and research have a reciprocal relationship. Theories are built inductively from observations, and research is an excellent source for those observations. The theory, in turn, must be tested by subjecting deductions from it (hypotheses) to systematic inquiry. Thus, research plays a dual and continuing role in theory building and testing. Theory guides and generates ideas for research; research assesses the worth of the theory and provides a foundation for new theories.

Example of theory development:
Jean Johnson (1999) developed the middle-range Self-Regulation Theory that explicates relationships between health care experiences, coping, and health outcomes. Here is how she described theory development: "The theory was developed in a cyclic process. Research was conducted using the self-regulation theory of coping with illness. Propositions supported by data were retained, and other propositions were altered when they were not supported. And new theoretical propositions were added when research produced unexpected findings. This cycle has been repeated many times over three decades leading to the present stage of development of the theory" (pp. 435 to 436). Several researchers have developed and tested interventions based on Self-Regulation Theory.

CONCEPTUAL MODELS AND THEORIES USED IN NURSING RESEARCH

Nurse researchers have used both nursing and nonnursing frameworks to provide a conceptual context for their studies. This section briefly discusses several frameworks that have been found useful by nurse researchers.

Conceptual Models of Nursing

Several nurses have formulated conceptual models representing formal explanations of what the nursing discipline is and what the nursing process entails, in the view of the model developer. Four concepts are central to models of nursing (Fawcett, 2005): *human beings*, *environment*, *health*, and *nursing*. The various conceptual models define these concepts differently, link them in diverse ways, and emphasize different relationships among them. Moreover, the models emphasize different processes as being central to nursing. For example, Sister Calista Roy's Adaptation Model identifies adaptation of patients as a critical phenomenon (Roy & Andrews, 1999). Martha Rogers (1994), by contrast, emphasized the centrality of the individual as a unified whole, and her model views nursing as a process in which clients are aided in achieving maximum well-being within their potential.

The conceptual models were not developed primarily as a base for nursing research. Indeed, most models have had more impact on nursing education and clinical practice than on nursing research. Nevertheless, nurse researchers have turned to these conceptual frameworks for inspiration in formulating research questions and hypotheses.

TIP: The Chapter Supplement for Chapter 8 on the thePoint website includes a table of 10 prominent conceptual models in nursing. The table describes the model's key features and identifies a study that claimed the model as its framework.

Let us consider one conceptual model of nursing that has received considerable research attention, **Roy's Adaptation Model**. In this model, humans are viewed as biopsychosocial adaptive systems who cope with environmental change through the process of adaptation (Roy & Andrews, 1999). Within the human system, there are four subsystems: physiologic/physical, self-concept/group identity, role function, and interdependence. These subsystems constitute adaptive modes that provide mechanisms for coping with environmental stimuli and change. Health is viewed as both a state and a process of being and becoming integrated and whole that reflects the mutuality of persons and environment. The goal of nursing, according to this model, is to promote client adaptation; nursing also regulates stimuli affecting adaptation. Nursing interventions usually take the form of increasing, decreasing, modifying, removing, or maintaining internal and external stimuli that affect adaptation. Roy's Adaptation Model has been the basis for several middle-range theories and dozens of studies.

Research example using Roy's adaptation model:
Fawcett and colleagues (2011) used Roy's adaptation model as a basis for their international study of the relationship between a woman's perception of and responses to caesarean birth on the one hand and type of caesarean (planned or unplanned) and prior preparation for caesarean birth on the other.

Middle-Range Theories Developed by Nurses

In addition to conceptual models that describe and characterize the nursing process, nurses have developed middle-range theories and models that focus on more specific phenomena of interest to nurses. Examples of middle-range theories that have been used in research include Beck's (2012) Theory of Postpartum Depression, the Theory of Unpleasant Symptoms (Lenz et al., 1997), Kolcaba's (2003) Comfort Theory, Pender's Health Promotion Model, and Mishel's (1990) Uncertainty in Illness Theory. The latter two are briefly described here.

Nola Pender's (2006) **Health Promotion Model** (HPM) focuses on explaining health-promoting behaviors, using a wellness orientation. According to the revised model (Fig 8.1, p.134), *health promotion* entails activities directed toward developing resources that maintain or enhance a person's well-being. The model embodies a number of propositions that can be used in developing and testing interventions and understanding health behaviors. For example, one HPM proposition is that people commit to engaging in behaviors from which they anticipate deriving valued benefits, and another is that perceived competence or self-efficacy relating to a given behavior increases the likelihood of commitment to action and actual performance of the behavior.

Example using the HPM:
Mohamadian and colleagues (2011) used the HPM as the basis for a study of the determinants of health-related quality of life among Iranian adolescent girls.

Mishel's **Uncertainty in Illness Theory** (Mishel, 1990) focuses on the concept of uncertainty—the inability of a person to determine the meaning of illness-related events. According to this theory, people develop subjective appraisals to assist them in interpreting the experience of illness and treatment. Uncertainty occurs when people are unable to recognize and categorize stimuli. Uncertainty results in the inability to obtain a clear conception of the situation, but a situation appraised as uncertain will mobilize individuals to use their resources to adapt to the situation. Mishel's conceptualization of uncertainty and her Uncertainty in Illness Scale have been used in many nursing studies.

Example using Uncertainty in Illness Theory:
Stewart, Mishel, Lynn, and Terhorst (2010) tested a model of uncertainty and psychological distress in children and adolescents with cancer.

Other Models Used by Nurse Researchers

Many concepts in which nurse researchers are interested are not unique to nursing, and therefore their studies are sometimes linked to frameworks that are not models from the nursing profession. Several of these alternative models have gained special prominence in the development of nursing interventions to promote health-enhancing behaviors and life choices. Five non-nursing theories that have frequently been used in nursing are briefly described in this section.

- **Social Cognitive Theory** (Bandura, 1985, 2001), which is sometimes called *self-efficacy theory*, offers an explanation of human behavior using the concepts of self-efficacy, outcome expectations, and incentives. Self-efficacy concerns people's belief in their own capacity to carry out particular behaviors (e.g., smoking cessation). Self-efficacy expectations determine the behaviors a person chooses to perform, their degree of perseverance, and the quality of the performance. As a research example, Poomsrikaew, Berger, Kim, and Zerwic (2012) examined age and gender differences in social cognitive factors linked to exercise behavior in Thai adults.

TIP: Bandura's self-efficacy is a key construct in several models discussed in this chapter. Self-efficacy has repeatedly been found to affect people's behaviors and to be amenable to change, and so self-efficacy enhancement is often a goal in interventions designed to change people's health-related actions and behaviors.

- In the **Transtheoretical Model** (Prochaska et al., 2002), the core construct is *stages of change*, which conceptualizes a continuum of motivational readiness to change problem behavior. The five stages of change are precontemplation, contemplation, preparation, action, and maintenance. Studies have shown that successful self-changers use different processes at each particular stage, thus suggesting the desirability of interventions that are individualized to the person's stage of readiness for change. For example, Plow, Finlayson, and Cho (2011) studied stages of change for physical activity behavior in a sample of people with multiple sclerosis in relation to their health symptoms, self-efficacy, and behavioral and cognitive processes.
- Becker's **Health Belief Model** (HBM) is a framework for explaining people's health-related behavior, such as health care use and compliance with a medical regimen. According to the model, health-related behavior is influenced by a person's perception of a threat posed by a health problem as well as by the value associated with actions aimed at reducing the threat (Becker, 1976). A revised HBM (RHBM) has incorporated the concept of self-efficacy (Rosenstock et al., 1988). Nurse researchers have used the HBM extensively. For example, Chen and colleagues (2011) used the HBM as a guiding framework in their study of factors affecting parents' decision to vaccinate their children for influenza.
- Ajzen's (2005) **Theory of Planned Behavior** (TPB), which is an extension of another theory called the Theory of Reasoned Action, offers a framework for understanding people's behavior and its psychological determinants. According to the theory, behavior that is volitional is determined by people's intention to perform that behavior. Intentions, in turn, are affected by attitudes toward the behavior, subjective norms

(i.e., perceived social pressure to perform or not perform the behavior), and perceived behavioral control (i.e., anticipated ease or difficulty of engaging in the behavior). Ben Natan and Gorkov (2011), for example, tested the utility of TBP for explaining blood donations among Israelis.

- Lazarus and Folkman's (1984, 2006) **Theory of Stress and Coping** offers an explanation of people's methods of dealing with stress, i.e., environmental and internal demands that tax or exceed a person's resources and endanger his or her well-being. The theory posits that coping strategies are learned and deliberate responses to stressors, and are used to adapt to or change the stressors. According to this model, people's perception of mental and physical health is related to the ways they evaluate and cope with the stresses of living. As a research example, Street and colleagues (2010) studied psychosocial adaptation over time in female partners of men with prostate cancer, and used the Lazarus and Folkman theory for interpreting their findings.

Although the use of theories and models from other disciplines such as psychology (*borrowed theories*) has stirred some controversy, nursing research is likely to continue on its current path of conducting studies within a multidisciplinary perspective. A borrowed theory that is tested and found to be empirically adequate in health-relevant situations of interest to nurses becomes *shared theory*.

TIP: There are websites devoted to many of the theories and models mentioned in this chapter. Several specific websites are listed in the Internet Resources for this chapter on thePoint website.

USING A THEORY OR FRAMEWORK IN RESEARCH

The manner in which theory and conceptual frameworks are used by qualitative and quantitative researchers is elaborated on in this section. In the discussion, the term *theory* is used in its broadest sense to include conceptual models, formal theories, and frameworks.

Theories and Qualitative Research

Theory is almost always present in studies that are embedded in a qualitative research tradition such as ethnography or phenomenology. However, different traditions involve theory in different ways.

Sandelowski (1993) distinguished between *substantive theory* (conceptualizations of a specific phenomenon under study) and theory reflecting a conceptualization of human inquiry. Some qualitative researchers insist on an atheoretical stance vis-a-vis the phenomenon of interest, with the goal of suspending prior conceptualizations (substantive theories) that might bias their inquiry. For example, phenomenologists are committed to theoretical naiveté, and try to hold preconceived views of the phenomenon in check. Nevertheless, phenomenologists are guided by a framework that focuses their inquiry on certain aspects of a person's lifeworld—i.e., lived experiences.

Ethnographers bring a cultural perspective to their studies, and this perspective shapes their fieldwork. Fetterman (2010) has observed that most ethnographers adopt one of two cultural theories: *ideational theories*, which suggest that cultural conditions and adaptation stem from mental activity and ideas, or *materialistic theories*, which view material conditions (e.g., resources, money, production) as the source of cultural developments.

Grounded theory is a general inductive method that is not attached to a particular theoretical perspective. Grounded theorists can use various theoretical perspectives, such as systems theory or social organization theory. A popular theoretical underpinning of grounded theory research is *symbolic interaction* (or *interactionism)*, which has three underlying premises (Blumer, 1986). First, humans act toward things based on the meanings that the things have for them. Second, the meaning of things is derived from the interaction humans have with fellow humans. And third, meanings are handled in, and modified through, an interpretive process.

Example of a grounded theory study:
Thomas (2011) did a grounded theory study within a symbolic interaction framework to explore older adults' experience managing diabetes in the workplace and maintaining employment.

Despite this theoretical perspective, grounded theory researchers, like phenomenologists, try to hold prior substantive theory about the phenomenon in abeyance until their own substantive theory begins to emerge. The goal of grounded theory is to develop a conceptually dense understanding of a phenomenon that is *grounded* in actual observations. The intent is to use the data, grounded in reality, to describe or explain processes as they occur in reality, not as they have been conceptualized previously. Once the theory starts to take shape, grounded theorists use previous literature for comparison with the emerging categories of the theory. Grounded theory researchers, who focus on social or psychological processes, often develop conceptual maps to illustrate how a process unfolds. Figure 8.2 illustrates such a conceptual map for a study of women controlling urinary tract symptoms (Wang et al., 2011); this study is described at the end of this chapter.

In recent years, a growing number of qualitative nurse researchers have adopted a perspective known as *critical theory* as a framework in their research. Critical theory is a paradigm that involves a critique of society and societal processes and structures, as we discuss in Chapter 14.

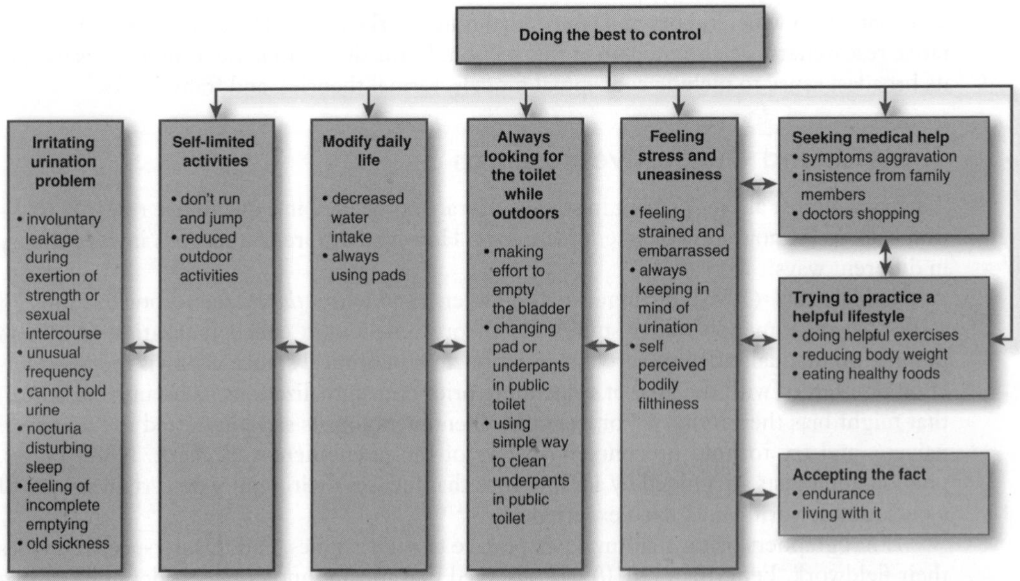

FIGURE 8.2 ● Model for a grounded theory, "Doing the Best to Control." (From: Wang, Y., Chen, S., Jou, H., & Tsao, L. (2011). Doing the best to control: The experience of Taiwanese women with lower urinary tract symptoms. *Nursing Research, 60*, 66–72, Figure 1, with permission.)

Qualitative researchers sometimes use conceptual models of nursing or other formal theories as interpretive frameworks. For example, a number of qualitative nurse researchers acknowledge that the philosophic roots of their studies lie in conceptual models of nursing, such as those developed by Newman (1997), Parse (1999), and Rogers (1994).

Example of using nursing theory in a qualitative study:
Rosa (2011) based her study of the process of transformative nursing practice in caring for patients with a chronic illness in Margaret Newman's (1997) Theory of Health as Expanding Consciousness.

Another strategy that can lead to substantive theory development relies on a systematic review of qualitative studies on a specific topic. In such metasyntheses, qualitative studies are combined to identify their essential elements. The findings from different sources are then used for theory building. Metasyntheses are discussed in Chapter 19.

Theories in Quantitative Research

Quantitative researchers link research to theory or models in various ways. The classic approach is to test hypotheses deduced from an existing theory. For example, a nurse might read about Pender's HPM (Fig. 8.1, p.134) and might reason as follows: If the HPM is valid, then I would expect that patients with osteoporosis who perceive the benefit of a calcium-enriched diet would be more likely to alter their eating patterns than those who perceived no benefits.

In testing a theory, quantitative researchers deduce implications (as in the preceding example) and develop hypotheses, which are predictions about the manner in which variables would be interrelated if the theory were correct. Key variables in the theory would be measured, data would be collected, and the hypotheses would be tested through statistical analysis. The testing process involves a comparison between observed outcomes with those predicted in the hypotheses. Repeated acceptance of hypotheses derived from a theory lends support to the theory.

TIP: When a quantitative study is based on a theory or conceptual model, the research article typically states this fact fairly early—often in the first paragraph, or even in the title. Some studies also have a subsection of the introduction called "Conceptual Framework" or "Theoretical Framework." The report usually includes a brief overview of the theory so that all readers can understand, in a broad way, the conceptual context of the study.

Tests of a theory also take the form of testing theory-based interventions. Theories have implications for influencing people's health-related attitudes or behavior, and hence their health outcomes. If an intervention is developed based on an explicit conceptualization of human behavior, then it likely has a better chance of being effective than if it is developed in a conceptual vacuum. Interventions rarely affect outcomes directly—there are mediating factors that play a role in the causal pathway between the intervention and the outcomes. For example, interventions based on Social Cognitive Theory posit that improvements to a person's self-efficacy will in turn result in positive changes in health behavior.

Example of theory testing in an intervention study:
Wambach and colleagues (2011) developed an educational and counseling intervention designed to promote breast-feeding in adolescent mothers, and designed their intervention elements on the basis of the TPB.

Many researchers who cite a theory or model as their framework are not directly *testing* the theory. One older study found, for example, that when nursing models were used in research, they most often were used to provide an *organizing structure* (Silva, 1986). In such an approach, researchers begin with a broad conceptualization of nursing (or stress, and so on) that is consistent with the model. The researchers *assume* that the model they espouse is valid, and then use its constructs or schemas to provide a broad interpretive context. To our knowledge, Silva's study has not been replicated with a more recent sample of studies. We suspect that, even today, a high percentage of quantitative studies that cite theories as their conceptual frameworks are using them primarily as organizational or interpretive tools, not as tests of the theory.

Quantitative researchers also use another approach to creating a conceptual context, and that involves using findings from prior research to develop an original model, usually presented in a conceptual map. In some cases the model incorporates elements or constructs from a theory, but the research is not a direct test of the theory.

Example using an original conceptual framework:
Chang and Mark (2011) studied whether a hospital's learning climate moderates the relationship between error-producing conditions in the hospital and medication errors. They developed an original framework based on theoretical writings by organizational learning researchers, and on studies of factors affecting patient safety. Their conceptual framework is shown in Figure 8.3.

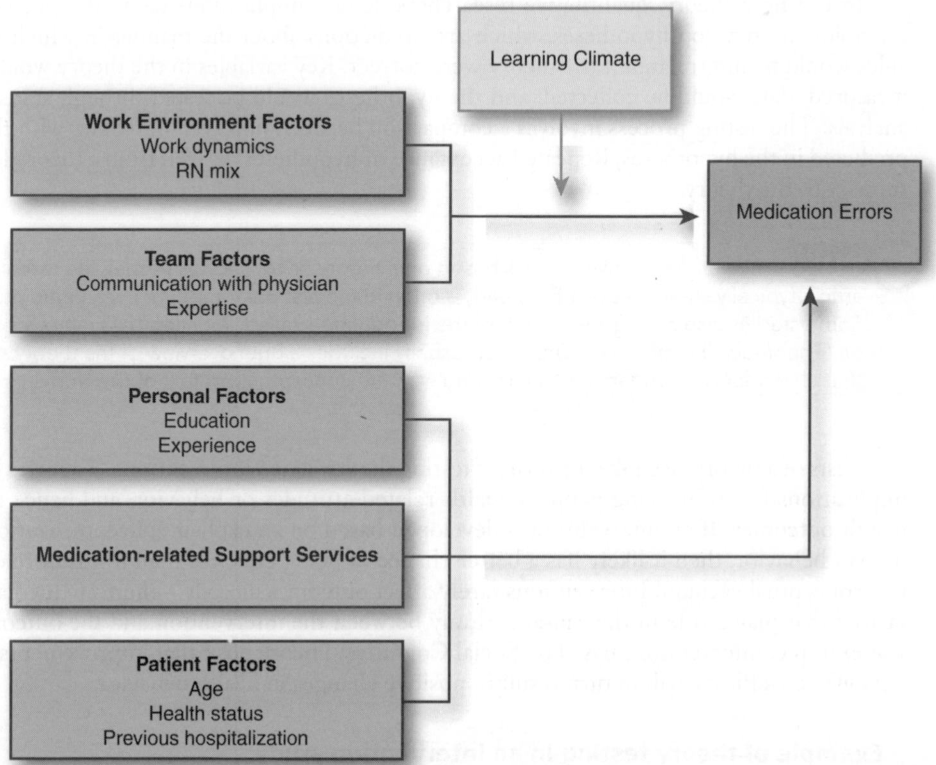

FIGURE 8.3 ● Theoretical framework to explain medication errors. (From: Chang, Y., & Mark, B. (2011). Effects of learning climate and registered nurse staffing on medication errors. *Nursing Research, 60*, 32–39, Figure 1, with permission.)

CRITIQUING FRAMEWORKS IN RESEARCH REPORTS

You will find references to theories and conceptual frameworks in some (but not all) of the studies you read. It is often challenging to critique the theoretical context of a published research report—or its absence—but we offer a few suggestions.

In a qualitative study in which a grounded theory is developed and presented, you may not be given enough information to refute the proposed theory because only evidence supporting the theory is presented. You can, however, assess whether the theory seems logical, whether conceptualizations are truly insightful, and whether the evidence is convincing. In a phenomenological study you should look to see if the researcher discusses the philosophical underpinnings of the study, that is, the philosophy of phenomenology.

Critiquing a theoretical framework in a quantitative report is also difficult, especially because you are not likely to be familiar with the theories and models that might be relevant. Some suggestions for evaluating the conceptual basis of a quantitative study are offered in the following discussion and in Box 8.1.

The first task is to determine whether the study does, in fact, have a conceptual framework. If there is no mention of a theory, model, or framework (and often there is not), you should consider whether this absence diminishes the value of the study. Research often benefits from an explicit conceptual context, but some studies are so pragmatic that the lack of a theory has no effect on its usefulness. For example, research designed to test the optimal frequency of turning patients has a utilitarian goal; a theory might not enhance the value of the findings. If, however, the study involves the test of a hypothesis or a complex intervention, the absence of a formal framework suggests conceptual fuzziness and perhaps interpretive problems.

If the study does have an explicit framework, you can examine its appropriateness. You may not be able to challenge the researcher's use of a particular theory or to recommend an

BOX 8.1 Guidelines for Critiquing Theoretical and Conceptual Frameworks

1. Does the report describe an explicit theoretical or conceptual framework for the study? If not, does the absence of a framework detract from the study's significance or its conceptual integration?
2. Does the report adequately describe the major features of the theory or model so that readers can understand the conceptual basis of the study?
3. Is the theory or model appropriate for the research problem? Does the purported link between the problem and the framework seem contrived?
4. Is the theory or model used as the basis for generating hypotheses, or is it used as an organizational or interpretive framework? Was this appropriate? Do the hypotheses (if any) naturally flow from the framework?
5. Are the concepts defined in a way that is consistent with the theory? If there is an intervention, are intervention components consistent with the theory?
6. Did the framework guide the study methods? For example, was the appropriate research tradition used if the study was qualitative? If quantitative, do the operational definitions correspond to the conceptual definitions?
7. Does the researcher tie the study findings back to the framework at the end of the report? Are the findings interpreted within the context of the framework?

alternative, but you can evaluate the logic of using a particular framework and assess whether the link between the problem and the theory is genuine. Does the researcher present a convincing rationale for the framework used? In quantitative studies, do the hypotheses flow from the theory? Will the findings contribute to theory validation? Does the researcher interpret the findings within the context of the framework? If the answer to such questions is no, you may have grounds for criticizing the study's framework, even though you may not be able to suggest ways to improve the conceptual basis of the study.

TIP: Some studies claim theoretical linkages that are not justified. This is most likely to occur when researchers first formulate the research problem and then later find a theoretical context to fit it. An after-the-fact linkage of theory to a research question is usually problematic because the researcher will not have taken the nuances of the theory into consideration in designing the study. If a research problem is truly linked to a conceptual framework, then the design of the study, the measurement of key constructs, and the analysis and interpretation of data will *flow* from that conceptualization.

RESEARCH EXAMPLES WITH CRITICAL THINKING EXERCISES

This section presents two examples of studies that have a strong theoretical link. Read the summaries and then answer the critical thinking questions, referring to the full research report if necessary.

Examples 1 and 2 below are also featured in our *Interactive Critical Thinking Activity* on thePoint website where you can easily record, print, and e-mail your responses to the related questions.

EXAMPLE 1 ● The Health Promotion Model in a Quantitative Study

Study: "The effects of coping skills training (CST) among teens with asthma" (Srof et al., 2012)

Statement of Purpose: The purpose of the study was to evaluate the effects of a school-based intervention, CST, for teenagers with asthma.

Theoretical Framework: The HPM, shown in Figure 8.1 on page 134, was the guiding framework for the intervention. The authors noted that within the HPM, various behavior-specific cognitions (e.g., perceived barriers to behavior, perceived self-efficacy) influence health-promoting behavior *and* are modifiable through an intervention. In this study, the overall behavior of interest was asthma self-management. The CST Training intervention was a five-session small-group strategy designed to promote problem solving, cognitive–behavior modification, and conflict resolution using strategies to improve self-efficacy and reduce perceived barriers. The researchers hypothesized that participation in CST would result in improved outcomes: asthma self-efficacy, asthma-related quality of life, social support, and peak expiratory flow rate (PEFR).

Method: In this pilot study, 39 teenagers with asthma were randomly assigned to one of two groups—one that participated in the intervention, and the other that did not. The researchers collected data about the outcomes from all participants at two points in time, before the start of the intervention and 6 weeks later.

Key Findings: Teenagers in the treatment group scored significantly higher at the end of the study on self-efficacy, activity-related quality of life, and social support than those in the control group.

Conclusions: The researchers noted that the self-efficacy and social support effects of the intervention were consistent with the HPM model. They recommended that, although the findings were promising, replication of the study and an extension to specifically examine asthma self-management behavior would be useful.

(continues on page 145)

CRITICAL THINKING EXERCISES

1. Answer the relevant questions from Box 8.1 on page 143 regarding this study.
2. Also consider the following targeted questions:
   a. In the model shown in Figure 8.1 on page 134, which factors did the researchers predict that the intervention would affect, according to the abbreviated description in the textbook?
   b. Is there another model or theory that was described in this chapter that could have been used to study the effect of this intervention?
3. If the results of this study are valid and generalizable, in what ways do you think the findings could be used in clinical practice?

EXAMPLE 2 ● A Grounded Theory Study

Study: "Doing the best to control: The experiences of Taiwanese women with lower urinary tract symptoms (LUTS)" (Wang et al., 2011)

Statement of Purpose: The purpose of the study was to generate descriptive theory of the experiences in controlling urinary tract symptoms among Taiwanese women.

Theoretical Framework: A grounded theory approach was chosen because an explicit goal of the study was to develop a substantive theory based on the first-hand experiences of women with LUTS. Grounded theory methods enabled the researchers to explore the "multilayered and interconnected experiences of women living with LUTS" (p. 71).

Method: Data were collected through individual interviews with 16 Taiwanese women with LUTS. Women were recruited to participate through diverse social and medical connections. Each interview lasted between 40 and 90 minutes. The interviewer asked broad questions, such as "Would you talk about what urination symptoms you have now?" "What do you think causes your urination symptoms?" "How have these symptoms affected your life?" Interviewing continued until no new information was revealed—that is, until data saturation occurred. All interviews were audiotaped and transcribed for analysis.

Key Findings: Based on their analysis of the in-depth interviews, Wang and colleagues identified a core category to describe the process of women's finding unique ways to control urination problems: Doing the best to control. A schematic model for the substantive theory is shown in Figure 8.2 on page 140.

CRITICAL THINKING EXERCISES

1. Answer the relevant questions from Box 8.1 on page 143 regarding this study.
2. Also consider the following targeted questions:
   a. In what way was the use of theory different in Wang et al.'s study than in the previous study by Srof and colleagues?
   b. Comment on the utility of the schematic model shown in Figure 8.2 on page 140.
3. If the results of this study are trustworthy, in what ways do you think the findings could be used in clinical practice?

EXAMPLE 3 ● Quantitative Research in Appendix A

- Read the introduction of Howell and colleagues' (2007) study ("Anxiety, anger, and blood pressure in children") in Appendix A on page 395–402.

CRITICAL THINKING EXERCISES

1. Answer relevant questions from Box 8.1 on page 143 regarding this study.
2. Also consider the following targeted questions:
   a. Develop a simple schematic model that captures the hypothesized relationships that were implied in this study.
   b. Would any of the theories or models described in this chapter have provided an appropriate conceptual context for this study?

EXAMPLE 4 ● Qualitative Research in Appendix B

- Read the introduction of Beck and Watson's (2010) study ("Subsequent childbirth after a previous traumatic birth") in Appendix B on page 403–412.

CRITICAL THINKING EXERCISES

1. Answer relevant questions from Box 8.1 on page 143 regarding this study.
2. Also consider the following targeted questions:
   a. Do you think that a schematic model would have helped to present the findings in this report?
   b. Did Beck and Watson present convincing evidence to support their use of the philosophy of phenomenology?

WANT TO KNOW MORE? A wide variety of resources to enhance your learning and understanding of this chapter are available on thePoint.

- Interactive Critical Thinking Activity
- Chapter Supplement on Prominent Conceptual Models of Nursing Used by Nurse Researchers
- Answers to the Critical Thinking Exercises for Examples 3 and 4
- Student Review Questions
- Full-text online
- Internet Resources with useful websites for Chapter 8

Additional study aids including eight journal articles and related questions are also available in *Study Guide for Essentials of Nursing Research, 8e.*

SUMMARY POINTS

- High-quality research requires *conceptual integration*, one aspect of which is having a defensible theoretical rationale for the study. Researchers demonstrate conceptual clarity through the delineation of a theory, model, or framework on which the study is based.
- As classically defined, a **theory** is an abstract generalization that systematically explains relationships among phenomena. **Descriptive theory** thoroughly describes a phenomenon.
- *Grand theories* (or *macrotheories*) attempt to describe large segments of the human experience. **Middle-range theories** are specific to certain phenomena.
- Concepts are also the basic elements of **conceptual models**, but concepts are not linked in a logically ordered, deductive system.
- In research, the overall objective of theories and models is to make findings meaningful, to integrate knowledge into coherent systems, to stimulate new research, and to explain phenomena and relationships among them.
- **Schematic models** (or **conceptual maps**) are graphic representations of phenomena and their interrelationships using symbols or diagrams and a minimal use of words.
- A **framework** is the conceptual underpinning of a study, including an overall rationale and conceptual definitions of key concepts. In qualitative studies, the framework often springs from distinct research traditions.

(continues on page 147)

- Several conceptual models of nursing have been used in nursing research. The concepts central to models of nursing are *human beings*, *environment*, *health*, and *nursing*. An example of a model of nursing used by nurse researchers is Roy's Adaptation Model.
- Nonnursing models used by nurse researchers (e.g., Bandura's Social Cognitive Theory) are referred to as *borrowed theories*; when the appropriateness of borrowed theories for nursing inquiry is confirmed, the theories become *shared theories*.
- In some qualitative research traditions (e.g., phenomenology), the researcher strives to suspend previously held *substantive theories* of the specific phenomena under study, but each tradition has rich theoretical underpinnings.
- Some qualitative researchers seek to develop *grounded theories*, data-driven explanations to account for phenomena under study through inductive processes.
- In the classical use of theory, quantitative researchers test hypotheses deduced from an existing theory. An emerging trend is the testing of theory-based interventions.
- In both qualitative and quantitative studies, researchers sometimes use a theory or model as an organizing framework, or as an interpretive tool.

REFERENCES FOR CHAPTER 8

Ajzen, I. (2005). *Attitudes, personality, and behavior*. (2nd ed.). Milton Keynes: Open University Press/McGraw Hill.

Bandura, A. (1985). *Social foundations of thought and action: A social cognitive theory*. Englewood Cliffs: Prentice Hall.

Bandura, A. (2001). Social cognitive theory: An agentic perspective. *Annual review of psychology, 52*, 1–26.

Beck, C. T. (2012).Exemplar: Teetering on the edge: A second grounded theory modification (pp. 257–284). In P. L. Munhall (Ed.). *Nursing research: A qualitative perspective* (5th ed).Sudbury: Jones & Bartlett Learning.

Becker, M. (1976). *Health Belief Model and personal health behavior*. Thorofare: Slack, Inc.

Ben Natan, M., & Gorkov, L. (2011). Investigating the factors affecting blood donation among Israelis. *International Emergency Nursing, 19*, 37–43.

Blumer, H. (1986). *Symbolic interactionism: Perspective and method*. Berkeley: University of California Press.

Chang, Y., & Mark, B. (2011). Effects of learning climate and registered nurse staffing on medication errors. *Nursing Research, 60*, 32–39.

Chen, M., Wang, R., Schneider, J., Tsai, C., Jiang, D., Hung, M., et al. (2011). Using the Health Belief Model to understand caregiver factors influencing childhood influenza vaccinations. *Journal of Community Health Nursing, 28*, 29–40.

Fawcett, J. (2005). *Contemporary nursing knowledge: Analysis and evaluation of nursing models and theories*. Philadelphia: F.A. Davis Company.

Fawcett, J., Aber, C., Haussler, S., Weiss, M., Myers, S., Hall, J., et al. (2011). Women's perceptions of caesarean birth: A Roy international study. *Nursing Science Quarterly, 24*, 352–362.

Fetterman, D. M. (2010). *Ethnography: Step by step*. (3rd ed.). Newbury Park: Sage.

Hodges, P. J. (2009). The essence of life purpose. *Critical Care Nursing Quarterly, 32*, 163–170.

Johnson, J. E. (1999). Self-Regulation Theory and coping with physical illness. *Research in Nursing & Health, 22*, 435–448.

Kolcaba, K. (2003). *Comfort theory and practice*. New York: Springer Publishing Co.

Lazarus, R. (2006). *Stress and emotion: A new synthesis*. New York: Springer Publishing.

Lazarus, R., & Folkman, S. (1984). *Stress, appraisal, and coping*. New York: Springer Publishing.

Lenz, E. R., Pugh, L. C., Milligan, R. A., Gift, A., & Suppe, F. (1997). The middle-range theory of unpleasant symptoms. *Advances in Nursing Science, 19*, 14–27.

Mishel, M. H. (1990). Reconceptualization of the uncertainty in illness theory. *Image: Journal of Nursing Scholarship, 22*(4), 256–262.

Mohamadian, H., Eftekhar, H., Rahimi, A., Mohamad, H., Shojaiezade, D., & Montazeri, A. (2011). Predicting health-related quality of life by using a health promotion model among Iranian adolescent girls. *Nursing & Health Sciences, 13*, 141–148.

Newman, M. (1997). Evolution of the theory of health as expanding consciousness. *Nursing Science Quarterly, 10*, 22–25.

Parse, R. R. (1999). *Illuminations: The human becoming theory in practice and research*. Sudbury: Jones & Bartlett.

Pender, N. J., Murdaugh, C., & Parsons, M. A. (2011). *Health promotion in nursing practice* (6th ed.). Upper Saddle River: Prentice Hall.

Plow, M., Finlayson, M., & Cho, C. (2011). Correlates of stages of change for physical activity in adults with multiple sclerosis. *Research in Nursing & Health, 34*, 378–388.

Poomsrikaew, O., Berger, B., Kim, M., & Zerwic, J. (2012). Age and gender differences in social cognitive factors and exercise behavior among Thais. *Western Journal of Nursing Research, 34*(2), 245–264.

Prochaska, J. O., Redding, C. A., & Evers, K. E. (2002). The Transtheoretical Model and stages of changes. In F.M. Lewis (Ed.). *Health behavior and health education: Theory, research and practice* (pp. 99–120). San Francisco: Jossey Bass.

Rogers, M. E. (1994). The science of unitary human beings: current perspectives. *Nursing Science Quarterly, 7*, 33–35.

Rosa, K. C. (2011). The process of healing transformations. *Journal of Holistic Nursing, 29*, 292–301.

Rosenstock, I., Stretcher, V., & Becker, M. (1988). Social learning theory and the Health Belief Model. *Health Education Quarterly, 15*, 175–183.

Roy, C., Sr., & Andrews, H. (1999). *The Roy Adaptation Model.* (2nd ed.). Norwalk: Appleton & Lange.

Sandelowski, M. (1993). Theory unmasked: The uses and guises of theory in qualitative research. *Research in Nursing & Health, 16*, 213–218.

Silva, M. C. (1986). Research testing nursing theory: State of the art. *Advances in Nursing Science, 9*, 1–11.

Srof, B., Velsor-Friedrich, B., & Penckofer, S. (2012). The effects of coping skills training among teens with asthma. *Western Journal of Nursing Research*, PubMed ID 21511980.

Stewart, J., Mishel, M., Lynn, M., & Terhorst, L. (2010). Test of a conceptual model of uncertainty in children and adolescents with cancer. *Research in Nursing & Health, 33*, 179–191.

Street, A., Couper, J., Love, A., Bloch, S., Kissane, D., & Street, B. (2010). Psychosocial adaptation in female partners of men with prostate cancer. *European Journal of Cancer Care, 19*, 234–242.

Thomas, E. A. (2011). Diabetes at work: A grounded theory pilot study. *AAOHN Journal, 59*, 213–220.

Walker, L., & Avant, K. (2010). *Strategies for theory construction in nursing* (5th ed.). Upper Saddle River: Prentice-Hall.

Wambach, K., Aronson, L., Breedlove, G., Domian, E., Roijanasrirat, W., & Yeh, H. (2011). A randomized controlled trial of breastfeeding support and education for adolescent mothers. *Western Journal of Nursing Research, 33*, 486–505.

Wang, Y., Chen, S., Jou, H., & Tsao, L. (2011). Doing the best to control: The experience of Taiwanese women with lower urinary tract symptoms. *Nursing Research, 60*, 66–72.

part 3

Quantitative Research

chapter 9

Quantitative Research Design

LEARNING OBJECTIVES

On completing this chapter, you will be able to:

- Discuss key research design decisions for a quantitative study
- Discuss the concepts of causality and counterfactuals, and identify criteria for causal relationships
- Describe and evaluate experimental, quasi-experimental, and nonexperimental designs
- Distinguish between and evaluate cross-sectional and longitudinal designs
- Identify and evaluate alternative methods of controlling confounding variables
- Understand various threats to the validity of quantitative studies
- Evaluate a quantitative study in terms of its overall research design and methods of controlling confounding variables
- Define new terms in the chapter.

KEY TERMS

Attrition
Baseline data
Case–control design
Cohort design
Control (comparison) group
Correlational study
Crossover design
Cross-sectional design
Counterfactual
Experiment
External validity
History threat
Homogeneity
Internal validity
Intervention fidelity
Longitudinal design
Matching
Maturation threat
Mortality threat
Nonequivalent control group design
Nonexperimental study
Posttest-only design
Pretest–posttest design
Prospective design
Quasi-experiment
Random assignment (randomization)
Randomized controlled trial (RCT)
Retrospective design
Selection threat (self-selection)
Time-series design

For quantitative studies, no aspect of a study's methods has a bigger impact on the validity and accuracy of the results than the research design—particularly if the inquiry is *cause probing*. Thus, this chapter has important information about how you can draw appropriate conclusions about the worth of evidence in a quantitative study.

OVERVIEW OF RESEARCH DESIGN ISSUES

The research design of a study spells out the strategies that researchers adopt to answer their questions and test their hypotheses. This section describes some basic design issues.

Key Research Design Features

Table 9.1 describes seven key design features that are typically addressed in the design of a quantitative study. The design decisions that researchers must make include the following:

- *Will there be an intervention?* A basic design issue is whether or not researchers will actively introduce an intervention and test its effects—the distinction between experimental and nonexperimental research.
- *What types of comparisons will be made?* Quantitative researchers often make comparisons to provide a context for interpreting results. Sometimes the *same* people are compared under different conditions or at different points in time (e.g., preoperatively

TABLE 9.1 Key Design Features

Feature	Key Questions	Design Options
Intervention	Will there be an intervention? What specific design will be used?	Experimental (RCT), quasi-experimental, nonexperimental (observational) design
Comparisons	What type of comparisons will be made to illuminate key relationships?	Same participants (at different times or conditions); different participants
Control over confounding variables	How will confounding variables be controlled? Which confounding variables will be controlled?	Randomization, crossover, homogeneity, matching, statistical control
Blinding	From whom will critical information be withheld to avert bias?	Blinding participants, family members, interventionists, other staff, data collectors
Time frames	How often will data be collected? When, relative to other events, will data be collected?	Cross-sectional, longitudinal design
Relative timing	When will information on independent and dependent variables be collected—looking backward or forward?	Retrospective (case control), prospective (cohort)
Location	Where will the study take place?	Setting choice: single site versus multisite

versus postoperatively), but often different people are compared (e.g., those getting versus not getting an intervention).

- *How will confounding variables be controlled?* In quantitative research, efforts typically are made to control factors extraneous to the research question. This chapter discusses techniques for controlling confounding variables.
- *Will blinding be used?* Researchers must decide if information about the study—e.g., who is getting an intervention—will be withheld from data collectors, study participants, or others to minimize the risk of *expectation bias* or *awareness bias*—i.e., the risk that such knowledge could influence study outcomes.
- *How often will data be collected?* Data sometimes are collected from participants at a single point in time (*cross-sectionally*), but other studies involve multiple points of data collection (*longitudinally*).
- *When will "effects" be measured, relative to potential causes?* Some studies collect information about outcomes and then look back *retrospectively* for potential causes. Other studies, however, begin with a potential cause and then see what outcomes ensue, in a *prospective* fashion.
- *Where will the study take place?* Data for quantitative nursing studies are collected in various settings, such as in hospitals or people's homes. Another design decision concerns how many different sites will be involved in the study—a decision that could affect the generalizability of the results.

Many design decisions are independent of the others. For example, both experimental and nonexperimental studies can compare different people or the same people at different times. This chapter describes the implications of design decisions on the study's rigor.

TIP: Information about the research design usually appears early in the method section of a research article.

Causality

Many research questions—and questions for evidence-based practice (EBP)—are about *causes* and *effects*. For example, does turning patients cause reductions in pressure ulcers? Does exercise cause improvements in heart function? Causality is a hotly debated issue, but we all understand the general concept of a **cause**. For example, we understand that failure to sleep *causes* fatigue and that high caloric intake *causes* weight gain. Most phenomena are multiply determined. Weight gain, for example, can reflect high caloric intake *or* other factors. Most causes are not *deterministic*; they only increase the likelihood that an effect will occur. For example, smoking is a cause of lung cancer, but not everyone who smokes develops lung cancer, and not everyone with lung cancer smoked.

While it might be easy to grasp what researchers mean when they talk about a *cause*, what exactly is an **effect**? One way to understand an effect is by conceptualizing a counterfactual (Shadish et al., 2002). A **counterfactual** is what would happen to people if they were exposed to a causal influence and were simultaneously *not* exposed to it. An effect represents the difference between what actually did happen with the exposure and what would have happened without it. A counterfactual clearly can never be realized, but it is a good model to keep in mind in thinking about research design.

Three criteria for establishing causal relationships are attributed to John Stuart Mill.

1. *Temporal*: a cause must precede an effect in time. If we test the hypothesis that smoking causes lung cancer, we need to show that cancer occurred *after* the smoking behavior.
2. *Relationship*: there must be an association between the presumed cause and the effect. In our example, we have to demonstrate an association between smoking behavior and cancer—that is, that a higher percentage of smokers than nonsmokers get lung cancer.
3. *Confounders*: the relationship cannot be explained as being *caused by a third variable*. Suppose that smokers were especially likely to live in urban environments. There would then be a possibility that the relationship between smoking and lung cancer reflects an underlying causal connection between the environment and lung cancer.

Other criteria for causality have been proposed. One important criterion in health research is *biologic plausibility*—evidence from basic physiologic studies that a causal pathway is credible. Researchers investigating casual relationships must provide persuasive evidence regarding these criteria through their research design.

Research Questions and Research Design

Quantitative research is used to address different types of research questions (Chapters 1 and 2), and different designs are appropriate for different questions. In this chapter, we focus primarily on designs for therapy, prognosis, etiology/harm, and description questions (meaning questions require a qualitative approach, and diagnosis questions are discussed in Chapter 11).

Except for description questions, questions that call for a quantitative approach usually concern causal relationships:

- Does a telephone counseling intervention for patients with prostate cancer *cause* improvements in their psychological distress? (therapy question)
- Do birth weights under 1,500 g *cause* developmental delays in children? (prognosis question)
- Does salt *cause* increases in blood pressure? (etiology/harm question)

Some designs are better at revealing cause-and-effect relationships than others. In particular, experimental designs (randomized controlled trials or RCTs) are the best possible designs for illuminating causal relationships—but it is not always possible to use such designs. Table 9.2 summarizes a "hierarchy" of designs for answering different types of causal questions and augments the evidence hierarchy presented in Figure 2.1 on page 23.

TABLE 9.2 Hierarchy of Designs for Different Cause-Probing Research Questions

Type of Question	Hierarchy of Designs
Therapy	RCT/Experimental > Quasi-experimental > Cohort > Case control > Descriptive correlational
Prognosis	Cohort > Case control > Descriptive correlational
Etiology/harm (prevention)	RCT/Experimental > Quasi-experimental > Cohort > Case control > Descriptive correlational

EXPERIMENTAL, QUASI-EXPERIMENTAL, AND NONEXPERIMENTAL DESIGNS

This section describes designs that differ with regard to whether or not there is an intervention.

Experimental Design: Randomized Controlled Trials

Early physical scientists learned that complexities occurring in nature often made it difficult to understand relationships through pure observation. This problem was addressed by isolating phenomena and controlling the conditions under which they occurred. These experimental procedures have been profitably adopted by researchers interested in human physiology and behavior.

Characteristics of True Experiments

A true experimental design or RCT is characterized by the following properties:

- *Intervention*—the experimenter *does* something to some participants by manipulating the independent variable.
- *Control*—the experimenter introduces controls into the study, including devising a good approximation of a counterfactual—usually a control group that does not receive the intervention.
- *Randomization*—the experimenter assigns participants to a control or experimental condition on a random basis.

By introducing an **intervention** or treatment, experimenters consciously vary (manipulate) the independent variable and then observe its effect on the outcome. To illustrate, suppose we were investigating the effect of physical exertion (I) on mood (O) in healthy young adults (P). One experimental design for this research problem is a **pretest–posttest design**, which involves observation of the outcome (mood) at two points in time: before and after the intervention. Participants in the experimental group undergo a physically demanding exercise routine, whereas those in the control group undergo a sedentary activity. This design permits us to examine what changes in mood were *caused* by the exertion because only some people were subjected to it, providing an important comparison. In this example, we met the first criterion of a true experiment by varying physical exertion, the independent variable.

This example also meets the second requirement for experiments, use of a control group. Inferences about causality require a comparison, but not all comparisons yield equally persuasive evidence. For example, if we were to supplement the diet of premature babies (P) with special nutrients (I) for 2 weeks, their weight (O) at the end of 2 weeks would tell us nothing about the intervention's effectiveness. At a minimum, we would need to compare their posttreatment weight with their pretreatment weight to determine whether their weights had increased. But suppose we find an average weight gain of one pound. Does this finding support an inference of a causal connection between the nutritional intervention (the independent variable) and weight gain (the outcome)? No, because infants normally gain weight as they mature. Without a control group—a group that does not receive the supplements (C)—it is impossible to separate the effects of maturation from those of the treatment. The term **control group** refers to a group of participants whose performance on an outcome variable is used to evaluate the performance of the **experimental group** (the group getting the intervention) on the same outcome. A control group used for comparative purposes represents a proxy for the ideal counterfactual.

Experimental designs also involve placing participants in groups at random. Through **randomization** (or *random assignment*), every participant has an equal chance of being included in any group. If people are randomly assigned, there is no systematic bias in the groups with regard to attributes that may affect the dependent variable. *Randomly assigned groups are expected to be comparable, on average, with respect to an infinite number of biologic, psychological, and social traits at the outset of the study*. Group differences on outcomes observed *after* randomization can therefore be inferred as being caused by the treatment.

Random assignment can be accomplished by flipping a coin or pulling names from a hat. Researchers typically either use computers to perform the randomization or rely on a *table of random numbers*, a table displaying hundreds of digits arranged in random order.

TIP: There is a lot of confusion about random assignment versus random sampling. Random assignment is a *signature* of an experimental design (RCT). If subjects are not randomly assigned to intervention groups, then the design is not a true experiment. Random *sampling*, by contrast, refers to a method of selecting people for a study, as we discuss in Chapter 10. Random sampling is *not* a signature of an experimental design. In fact, most RCTs do *not* involve random sampling.

Experimental Designs

The most basic experimental design involves randomizing people to different groups and then measuring the outcome. This design is sometimes called a **posttest-only design**. A more widely used design, discussed previously, is the pretest–posttest design, which involves collecting *pretest data* (also called **baseline data**) on the outcome before the intervention and **posttest** (outcome) **data** after it.

Example of a pretest–posttest design:

Carter and colleagues (2012) evaluated the effectiveness of a brief postanesthesia care unit (PACU) visit on reducing family members' anxiety. Participants were randomly assigned to a PACU visit or usual care. The family members' anxiety was measured before and after the visit, and changes in anxiety levels were used as the outcome variable.

TIP: Experimental designs can be depicted graphically using symbols to represent features of the design. In these diagrams, the convention is that R stands for randomization to treatment groups, X represents receipt of the intervention, and O is the measurement of outcomes. So, for example, a pretest–posttest design would be depicted as follows:

$$\begin{array}{l} R\,O_1\ X\ O_2 \\ R\,O_1\ \ \ \ O_2 \end{array}$$

Space does not permit us to present these diagrams for all designs, but many are shown in the Chapter Supplement on thePoint website.

In a standard design, the people who are randomly assigned to different conditions are different people. For example, if we were testing the effect of music on agitation (O) on patients with dementia (P), we could give some patients music (I) and others no music (C). A **crossover design**, by contrast, involves exposing people to more than one treatment. Such studies are true experiments only if people are randomly assigned to different orderings of treatment. For example, if a crossover design were used to compare the effects of music on patients with dementia, some would be randomly assigned to receive music first followed by a period of no music, and others would receive no music first. In such a study, the three conditions for an experiment have been met: there is intervention, randomization, and control—with *subjects serving as their own control group*.

A crossover design has the advantage of ensuring the highest possible equivalence among the people exposed to different conditions. Such designs are inappropriate for certain research questions, however, because of possible *carryover effects*. When subjects are exposed to two different treatments, they may be influenced in the second condition by their experience in the first. However, when carryover effects are implausible, as when intervention effects are immediate and short-lived, a crossover design is extremely powerful.

Example of a crossover design:
Liaw and colleagues (2012) used a crossover design to test alternative methods of alleviating infant pain during heel-stick procedures. Infants were randomly assigned to a sequence of three treatments (nonnutritive sucking, facilitated tucking, and a control condition).

TIP: Research reports do not always identify the specific experimental design that was used by name; this may have to be inferred from information about the data collection plan (in the case of posttest-only and pretest–posttest designs), or from such statements as: The subjects were used as their own controls (in the case of a crossover design).

Experimental and Control Conditions

In designing experiments, researchers make many decisions about what the experimental and control conditions entail, and these decisions can affect the results. To give a new intervention a fair test, researchers need to design one that is of sufficient intensity and duration that effects on the outcome might reasonably be expected. Researchers describe the intervention in formal *protocols* that stipulate exactly what the treatment is for those in the experimental group.

The control group condition (the counterfactual) must also be carefully conceptualized. Researchers have choices about what to use as the control condition, and the decision affects the interpretation of the findings. Among the possibilities for the control condition are the following:

- No intervention—the control group gets no treatment at all
- "Usual care"—standard or normal procedures used to treat patients
- An alternative treatment (e.g., music versus massage)
- A **placebo** or pseudointervention presumed to have no therapeutic value, which is also called an *attention control condition* (the control group gets attention but not the intervention's active ingredients)
- A lower dose or intensity of treatment, or only parts of the treatment
- *Delayed treatment*, i.e., control group members are *wait-listed* and exposed to the experimental treatment at a later point

Example of a wait-listed control group:
White (2012) tested the effectiveness of an 8-week mindful yoga intervention for reducing stress and enhancing self-esteem in school-aged girls. Girls in the fourth and fifth grade were randomly assigned to the intervention group or a wait-listed control group.

From a methodologic standpoint, the best test is between two conditions that are as different as possible, as when the experimental group gets a strong intervention and the control group gets nothing. Ethically, however, the most appealing option is often the "delay of treatment" design, which is not always feasible. Testing two alternative interventions is also appealing ethically, but the risk is that the results will be inconclusive because it may be difficult to detect differential effects.

Researchers must also consider possibilities for *blinding*. Many nursing interventions do not lend themselves easily to blinding. For example, if the intervention were a smoking cessation program, participants would know whether they were receiving the intervention, and the intervener would know who was in the program. It is usually possible and desirable, however, to blind the participants' group status from the people collecting outcome data.

Example of an experiment with blinding:
Kassab and colleagues (2012) tested the efficacy of 25% oral glucose for pain relief in infants undergoing immunizations. Infants were randomized to receive either the glucose solution or sterile water. Researchers, nurses, parents, and infants were blinded with regard to which solution the infants received.

TIP: The term *double blind* is widely used when more than one group is blinded (e.g., participants and interventionists). However, this term is falling into disfavor because of its ambiguity, in favor of clear specifications about exactly who was blinded and who was not.

Advantages and Disadvantages of Experiments

RCTs are the most powerful designs for testing hypotheses of cause-and-effect relationships. RCTs are the "gold standard" for intervention studies (therapy questions) because they yield the highest-quality evidence about the effects of an intervention. Through randomization to groups, researchers come as close as possible to attaining an "ideal" counterfactual. Experiments offer greater corroboration than other designs that, *if* the independent variable (e.g., diet, drug dosage, counseling) is varied, *then* certain consequences in the outcome variable (e.g., weight loss, recovery of health, coping) may be expected to ensue.

The great strength of experiments, then, lies in the confidence with which causal relationships can be inferred. Through the controls imposed by intervening, comparing, and—especially—randomizing, alternative explanations to causal connections can often be ruled out. It is because of these strengths that meta-analyses of RCTs, which integrate evidence from multiple studies that used an experimental design, are at the pinnacle of evidence hierarchies for questions relating to causes (Figure 2.1, p. 23).

Despite the advantages of experiments, they have some limitations. First, a number of interesting variables simply are not amenable to intervention. A large number of human characteristics, such as disease or health habits, cannot be randomly conferred on people. That is why RCTs are not at the top of the hierarchy for prognosis questions (Table 9.2, p. 152), which concern the long-term consequences of health problems. For example, infants could not be randomly assigned to having cystic fibrosis to see if this disease causes poor psychosocial adjustment.

Second, there are many variables that could technically—but not ethically—be experimentally varied. For example, there have been no RCTs to study the effect of cigarette smoking on lung cancer. Such a study would require us to assign people randomly to a smoking group (people forced to smoke) or a nonsmoking group (people prohibited from smoking). Experimentation with humans will always be subject to such ethical constraints. Thus, although RCTs are technically at the top of the evidence hierarchy for etiology/harm questions (Table 9.2, p. 152), many etiology questions cannot be answered using an experimental design.

In many health care settings, RCTs may not be feasible even for therapy questions because of practical issues. It may, for instance, be impossible to secure the cooperation from administrators or other stakeholders to randomize people to groups.

Another potential problem is the *Hawthorne effect*, a term derived from experiments conducted at the Hawthorne plant of the Western Electric Corporation in which various environmental conditions (e.g., light, working hours) were varied to determine their effect on worker productivity. Regardless of what change was made (i.e., whether the light was made better or worse), productivity increased. Thus, knowledge of being in a study may cause people to change their behavior, thereby obscuring the effect of the research variables. In summary, experimental designs have some limitations that make them difficult to apply to real-world problems; nevertheless, RCTs have a clear superiority for testing causal hypotheses.

HOW-TO-TELL TIP: How can you tell if a study is experimental? Researchers usually indicate in the method section of their reports that they have used an experimental or randomized design (RCT). If such terms are missing, you can conclude that a study is experimental if the article says that the study purpose was to *test or evaluate the effects of* an intervention or treatment, AND if individual participants were put into groups (or exposed to different conditions) at random.

Quasi-Experiments

Quasi-experiments (called *trials without randomization* in the medical literature), also involve an intervention; however, quasi-experimental designs lack randomization, the signature of a true experiment. Some quasi-experiments even lack a control group. The signature of a quasi-experimental design, then, is an intervention in the absence of randomization.

Quasi-Experimental Designs

A frequently used quasi-experimental design is the **nonequivalent control group pretest–posttest design**, which involves comparing two or more groups of people before and after implementing an intervention. As an example, suppose we were studying the effect of introducing a new hospital-wide model of care that involved having a patient care facilitator (PCF) be the primary point person for hospitalized patients (P) during their stay. Our main outcome is patient satisfaction (O). The new system is being implemented throughout the hospital, and so randomization to PCF (I) versus "usual care" (C) is not possible. We opt to collect data in a similar hospital that is not instituting the PCF model. Data on patient satisfaction is collected in both hospitals before the change is made (baseline) and again afterwards.

This quasi-experimental design is identical to the pretest–posttest experimental design discussed in the previous section, *except* participants were not randomized to groups. The quasi-experimental design is weaker because, without randomization, *it cannot be assumed that the experimental and comparison groups are equivalent at the outset*. Quasi-experimental comparisons are much farther from an ideal counterfactual than experimental comparisons. The design is, nevertheless, a strong one because the collection of baseline data allows us to see whether patients in the two hospitals had similar levels of satisfaction before the change was made. If the groups are comparable at baseline, we could be relatively confident inferring that posttest differences in satisfaction was the result of the new model of care. If patient satisfaction is different initially, however, it will be difficult to interpret postintervention differences. Note that in quasi-experiments, the term *comparison group* is sometimes used in lieu of *control group* to refer to the group against which outcomes in the treatment group are evaluated.

Now suppose we had been unable to collect baseline data. Such a design (*nonequivalent control group posttest-only*) has a flaw that is difficult to remedy. We no longer have information about the initial equivalence of the hospitals. If patient satisfaction in the experimental hospital is higher than that in the control hospital at the posttest, can we conclude that the new method of delivering care *caused* improved satisfaction? There could be other explanations for the differences. In particular, patient satisfaction in the two hospitals might have differed initially. Quasi-experiments lack some of the controlling properties of experiments, but the hallmark of strong quasi-experiments is the effort to introduce some controls, such as baseline measurements.

Example of a nonequivalent control group design:
Aitken, Burmeister, Clayton, Dalais, and Gardner (2011) used a nonequivalent control group pretest–posttest design to test the effect of launching clinical nursing rounds in intensive care units on nurses' satisfaction and perceived work environments. Nurses in the hospital that introduced nursing rounds were compared to nurses in a hospital that was similar in workload and staffing characteristics.

In the designs just described, a control group was used but randomization was not, but some quasi-experiments have neither. Suppose that a hospital implemented rapid response teams (RRTs) in its acute care units. We want to learn the effects on patient outcomes (e.g., mortality) and nurse outcomes (e.g., stress). For the purposes of this example, assume no other hospital would be a good comparison, and so the only comparison that can be made is a before–after contrast. If RRTs were implemented in January, we could compare the mortality rate, for example, during the 3 months before RRTs with the mortality rate in the subsequent 3-month period.

This **one-group pretest–posttest design** seems logical, but it has weaknesses. What if one of the 3-month periods is atypical, apart from the RRTs? What about the effect of other changes instituted during the same period? What about the effects of external factors, such as seasonal migration? The design in question offers no way of controlling these factors.

In this example, the design could be modified so that at least some alternative explanations for changes in mortality could be ruled out. For example, the **time-series design** involves collecting data over an extended time period, and introducing the treatment during that period. The present study could be designed with four observations before the RRTs are introduced (e.g., four quarters of mortality data for the prior year) and four observations after it (mortality for the next four quarters). Although a time-series design does not eliminate all the problems of interpreting changes in mortality, the extended time perspective strengthens the ability to attribute change to the intervention.

Example of a time-series design:
Polit and Chaboyer (2012) described a study that used a time-series design. Patient safety data were collected over a 33 month period, and a nursing practice improvement intervention was introduced in the 15th month. Patient harms decreased substantially after the introduction of the intervention.

Advantages and Disadvantages of Quasi-Experiments

It is not always possible to conduct RCTs, and so a strength of quasi-experiments is that they may be practical. Nursing research often occurs in natural settings, where it is difficult to deliver an innovative treatment randomly to some people but not to others. Strong quasi-experimental designs introduce some research control when full experimental rigor is not possible.

Another issue is that people are not always willing to be randomized in clinical trials. Quasi-experimental designs, because they do not involve random assignment, are likely to be acceptable to a broader group of people. This, in turn, has implications for the generalizability of the results—but the problem is that the results are usually less conclusive.

The major disadvantage of quasi-experiments is that causal inferences cannot be made as readily as with RCTs. Alternative explanations for results abound with quasi-experiments. For example, suppose we administered a special diet to a group of frail nursing home residents to assess its impact on weight gain. If we use a nonequivalent control group and then observe a weight gain, we must ask: Is it *plausible* that some other factor caused the gain? Is it *plausible* that pretreatment differences between the intervention and comparison groups resulted in differential gain? Is it *plausible* that there was an average weight gain simply because the most frail died or were transferred to a hospital? If the answer to any of these *rival hypotheses* is yes, then the inferences about the causal effect of the intervention are weakened. With quasi-experiments, there is almost always at least one plausible rival explanation.

HOW-TO-TELL TIP: How can you tell if a study is quasi-experimental? Researchers do not always identify their designs as quasi-experimental. If a study involves an intervention and if the report does not explicitly mention random assignment, it is probably safe to conclude that the design is quasi-experimental.

Nonexperimental Studies

Many research questions—including cause-probing ones—cannot be addressed with an RCT or quasi-experimental design. For example, take this prognosis question: Do birth weights under 1,500 g *cause* developmental delays in children? Clearly, we cannot manipulate birth weight, the independent variable. Babies' weights are not subject to research control, nor are they random. When researchers do not intervene by controlling the independent variable, the study is **nonexperimental**, or, in the medical literature, **observational**.

There are various reasons for doing a nonexperimental study, including situations in which the independent variable inherently cannot be manipulated (prognosis questions) or in which it would be unethical to manipulate the independent variable (some etiology questions). Experimental designs are also not appropriate for descriptive questions.

Types of Nonexperimental/Observational Studies

When researchers study the effect of a *cause* they cannot manipulate, they design **correlational studies** that examine relationships between variables. A **correlation** is an interrelationship or association between two variables, that is, a tendency for variation in one variable to be related to variation in another (e.g., people's height and weight). Correlations can be detected through statistical analyses.

As noted earlier, one criterion for causality is the existence of a relationship between variables, but it is risky to infer causal relationships in correlational research. In RCTs, investigators predict that deliberate variation of the independent variable will result in a change to the outcome variable. In correlational research, investigators do not control the independent variable, which often has already occurred. A famous research dictum is relevant: *correlation does not prove causation*. The mere existence of a relationship between variables is not enough to warrant the conclusion that one variable caused the other, even if the relationship is strong.

Correlational studies are weaker than RCTs for addressing cause-probing questions, but different designs offer varying degrees of supportive evidence. The strongest design for prognosis questions, and for etiology questions when randomization is impossible, is a cohort design (Table 9.2, p. 152). Observational studies with a **cohort design** (sometimes called a **prospective design**) start with a presumed cause and then go forward to the presumed effect. For example, in prospective lung cancer studies, researchers start with a cohort of adults (P) that includes smokers (I) and nonsmokers (C), and then later compare the two groups in terms of lung cancer incidence (O).

Example of a cohort (prospective) design:
Salamonson, Everett, Koch, Andrew, and Davidson (2012) studied the relationship between part-time employment among nursing students and their academic performance. Hours of paid work were measured in their first year of education, and academic performance was measured in their final year.

TIP: All experimental studies are inherently prospective, because the researcher institutes the intervention (manipulates the independent variable) and subsequently examines its effect.

In **retrospective** correlational studies, an effect (outcome) observed in the present is linked to a potential cause occurring in the past. For example, in retrospective lung cancer research, researchers begin with some people who have lung cancer and others who do not, and then look for differences in antecedent behaviors or conditions, such as smoking habits. Such a retrospective study uses a **case–control design**—that is, *cases* with a certain condition, such as lung cancer, are compared to *controls* without it. In designing a case–control study, researchers try to identify controls who are as similar as possible to cases with regard to key confounding variables (e.g., age, gender). To the degree that researchers can demonstrate comparability between cases and controls with regard to confounding traits, causal inferences are enhanced. The difficulty, however, is that the two groups are almost never comparable with respect to *all* potential factors influencing the outcome.

Example of a case-control design:
Cora, Particino, Munafo, and Palomba (2012) conducted a pilot study of health risks among the family caregivers of terminally ill cancer patients. Their sample included 20 caregivers of terminally ill family members, and 20 noncaregivers who were matched to the cases by age and gender. The two groups were compared in terms of cardiovascular risk and emotional distress.

Prospective studies are more costly, but much stronger, than retrospective studies. For one thing, any ambiguity about the temporal sequence of phenomena is resolved in prospective research (i.e., smoking is known to precede the lung cancer). In addition, samples are more likely to be representative of smokers and nonsmokers.

A second broad class of nonexperimental studies is **descriptive research**. The purpose of descriptive studies is to observe, describe, and document aspects of a situation. For example, an investigator may wish to determine the percentage of teenagers who engage in risky behavior (e.g., drug use, unsafe sex)—i.e., the *prevalence* of such behaviors. Or sometimes a study design is **descriptive correlational**, meaning that researchers seek to describe relationships among variables, without attempting to infer causal connections. For example, researchers might be interested in describing the relationship between fatigue and psychological distress in patients with HIV. Because the intent in these situations is not to explain or to understand the underlying causes of the variables of interest, a descriptive nonexperimental design is appropriate.

Example of a descriptive correlational study:
Liou and colleagues (2012) conducted a descriptive correlational study with a sample of more than 15,000 Taiwanese adolescents to examine factors that correlated with self-induced vomiting as a weight-control strategy.

TIP: For descriptive questions, the strongest design is a nonexperimental study that relies on random sampling of participants. Sampling plans are discussed in the next chapter.

Advantages and Disadvantages of Nonexperimental Research

The major disadvantage of nonexperimental studies is that they do not yield persuasive evidence for causal inferences. This is not a problem when the aim is description, but correlational studies are often undertaken with an underlying desire to discover causes. Yet correlational studies are susceptible to faulty interpretation because groups being compared have formed through **self-selection** (also called *selection bias*). A researcher doing a correlational study, unlike an RCT, cannot assume that the groups being compared were similar before the occurrence of the independent variable—the hypothesized cause or "I." Preexisting group differences may be a plausible alternative to the "I" as an explanation for any differences in "O" (outcomes).

As an example of such interpretive problems, suppose we studied differences in depression (O) of cancer patients (P) who do or do not have adequate social support (I). Suppose we found a correlation—that is, we found that patients without social support were more depressed than patients with adequate social support. We could interpret this to mean that people's emotional state is influenced by the adequacy of their social support, as diagrammed in Figure 9.1A. There are, however, alternative interpretations for the finding. Maybe a third variable influences *both* social support and depression, such as whether the patients are married. Having a spouse may affect how depressed the patients feel *and* the quality of their social support, as diagrammed in Figure 9.1B. A third possibility is reversed causality (Figure 9.1C). Depressed cancer patients may find it more difficult to elicit social support

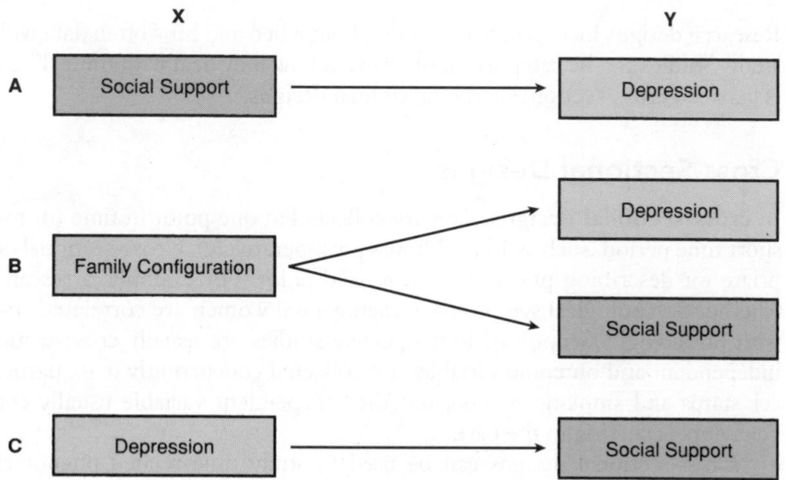

FIGURE 9.1 ● Alternative explanations for correlation between depression and social support in cancer patients.

than patients who are more cheerful. In this interpretation, the person's depression causes the amount of received social support, and not the other way around. The point is that correlational results should be interpreted cautiously.

TIP: Be prepared to think critically when a researcher claims to be studying the "effects" of one variable on another in a nonexperimental study. For example, if a report title were "The Effects of Eating Disorders on Depression," the study would be nonexperimental (i.e., participants were not randomly assigned to an eating disorder). In such a situation, you might ask, Did the eating disorder have an effect on depression—or did depression have an effect on eating patterns? Or, did a third variable (e.g., childhood abuse) have an effect on both?

Despite interpretive problems, nonexperimental studies play a crucial role in nursing because many interesting problems do not lend themselves to randomization or intervention. An example is whether smoking causes lung cancer. Despite the absence of any RCTs with humans, few people doubt that this causal connection exists. Thinking about the criteria for causality discussed earlier, there is ample evidence of a relationship between smoking and lung cancer and, through prospective studies, that smoking precedes lung cancer. Through numerous replications, researchers have been able to control for, and thus rule out, other possible "causes" of lung cancer. The findings have been consistent and coherent, and the criterion of biologic plausibility has been met through basic physiologic research.

Correlational research is often an efficient way to collect large amounts of data about a problem. For example, it would be possible to collect extensive information about people's health problems and eating habits. Researchers could then examine which problems correlate with which eating patterns. By doing this, many relationships could be discovered in a short time. By contrast, an experimenter looks at only a few variables at a time. For example, one RCT might manipulate cholesterol, whereas another might manipulate protein. Nonexperimental work is often necessary before interventions can be justified.

THE TIME DIMENSION IN RESEARCH DESIGN

Research designs incorporate decisions about when and how often data will be collected in a study. Studies can be categorized in terms of how they deal with time. The major distinction is between cross-sectional and longitudinal designs.

Cross-Sectional Designs

In **cross-sectional designs**, data are collected at one point in time (or multiple times in a short time period, such as 1 and 2 hours postoperatively). Cross-sectional designs are appropriate for describing phenomena at a fixed point. For example, a researcher might study whether psychological symptoms in menopausal women are correlated contemporaneously with physiologic symptoms. Retrospective studies are usually cross-sectional: data on the independent and outcome variables are collected concurrently (e.g., participants' lung cancer status and smoking habits), but the independent variable usually concerns events or behaviors occurring in the past.

Cross-sectional designs can be used to study time-related phenomena, but they are less persuasive than longitudinal designs. Suppose we were studying changes in children's health-promotion activities between ages 7 and 10. One way to investigate this would be to interview children at age 7 and then 3 years later at age 10—a longitudinal design. Or, we could question two groups of children, ages 7 and 10, at one point in time and then compare responses—a cross-sectional design. If 10-year-olds engaged in more health-promoting activities than 7-year-olds, it might be inferred that children made healthier choices as they aged. To make this inference, we have to assume that the older children would have responded as the younger ones did had they been questioned 3 years earlier, or, conversely, that 7-year-olds would report more health- promoting activities if they were questioned again 3 years later.

Cross-sectional designs are economical and easy to manage, but they pose problems for inferring changes over time. The amount of social and technological change that characterizes our society makes it questionable to assume that differences in the behaviors or characteristics of different age groups are the result of the passage through time rather than cohort differences. In the previous example, 7- and 10-year-old children may have different attitudes toward health and health promotion, independent of maturation. In such cross-sectional studies, there are often alternative explanations for observed group differences.

Example of a cross-sectional study:
Belanger, and colleagues (2012) examined the relationship between age on the one hand and physical activity preferences on the other in a cross-sectional study of 588 young adult cancer survivors, who were grouped into three age group clusters: 20 to 29, 30 to 39, and 40 to 44.

Longitudinal Designs

Longitudinal designs involve collecting data multiple times over an extended period. Such designs are useful for studying changes over time and for establishing the sequencing of phenomena, which is a criterion for establishing causality. Multiple data collection points can also strengthen causal inferences, such as in a nonequivalent control group design in which collecting pretreatment data offers evidence about the initial comparability of groups.

Longitudinal studies can focus on general, nonclinical populations. For example, the well-known Harvard Nurses' Health Study has followed a sample of thousands of nurses for over 30 years. In nursing research, longitudinal studies are more likely to be *follow-up studies* of a clinical population, undertaken to assess the subsequent status of people with a specified condition or who received a specified intervention. For example, patients who received a smoking cessation intervention could be followed up to assess its long-term effectiveness. To take a nonexperimental example, samples of premature infants might be followed up to assess their subsequent motor development.

Example of a follow-up study:
McCullough and colleagues (2012) did a follow-up study of children with cerebral palsy 2½ years after an initial assessment to examine patterns of health and health behaviors.

In longitudinal studies, the number of data collection points and the time intervals between them depend on the nature of the study. When change or development is rapid, numerous data collection points at relatively short intervals may be required to understand trends. By convention, however, the term *longitudinal* implies multiple data collection points over an extended period of time.

A serious challenge in longitudinal studies is the loss of participants (**attrition**) over time. Attrition is problematic because those who drop out of the study usually differ in important respects from those who continue to participate, resulting in potential biases, the risk of faulty inferences, and concerns about the generalizability of the findings.

TIP: Not all longitudinal studies are prospective, because sometimes the independent variable occurred even before the initial wave of data collection. And not all prospective studies are longitudinal in the classic sense. For example, an experimental study that collects data at 2, 4, and 6 hours after an intervention would be prospective but not longitudinal (i.e., data are not collected over a long time period.)

TECHNIQUES OF RESEARCH CONTROL

A major goal of research design in quantitative studies is to maximize researchers' control over potentially confounding variables. There are two broad categories of confounders that need to be controlled—those that are intrinsic to study participants and those that are external, stemming from the research situation.

Controlling the Study Context

Various external factors, such as the research environment, can affect outcomes. In carefully controlled quantitative research, steps are taken to minimize situational contaminants (i.e., to achieve *constancy of conditions*) so that researchers can be confident that outcomes reflect the influence of the independent variable and not the study context.

Researchers cannot totally control the context in natural settings, but many opportunities exist. For example, researchers can control *when* data are collected. If an investigator were studying fatigue, for example, all data should be collected at the same time of day. Blinding is another means of controlling external sources of bias. By keeping data collectors and others unaware of group allocation or study hypotheses, researchers minimize the risk that other people involved in the study will influence the results.

Most quantitative studies also standardize communications to participants. Formal scripts are often prepared to inform participants about the study purpose, the use that will be made of the data, and so forth. In research involving interventions, researchers develop formal intervention protocols that specify procedures. For example, in an experiment to test the effectiveness of a new medication, care would be needed to ensure that the participants in the intervention group received the same chemical substance and the same dosage, that the substance was administered in the same way, and so forth. Careful researchers pay attention to in *intervention fidelity*—that is, they take steps to monitor that an intervention is faithfully delivered in accordance with its plan and that the intended treatment was actually received. Intervention fidelity helps to avert biases and gives potential benefits a full opportunity to be realized.

Example of attention to intervention fidelity:
Robbins, Pfeiffer, Maier, Ladrig, and Berg-Smith (2012) described their efforts to monitor and enhance intervention fidelity in implementing a motivational interviewing intervention by school nurses to increase physical activity among middle school girls.

Controlling Participant Factors

Control of study participants' characteristics is especially important and challenging. Outcomes in which nurse researchers are interested are affected by dozens of influences and attributes, and most are irrelevant to the research question. For example, suppose we were investigating the effects of a new physical fitness program on the cardiovascular functioning of nursing home residents. In this study, variables such as the participants' age, gender, and smoking history would be confounding variables; each is likely to be related to the outcome variable (cardiovascular functioning), independent of the physical fitness program. In other words, the effects that these variables have on the outcome are extraneous to the study. In this section, we review methods of controlling confounding subject characteristics.

Randomization

Randomization is the most effective method of controlling participants' characteristics. Randomization yields a close approximation to an ideal counterfactual, that is, groups that are equal with respect to confounding variables. A critical advantage of randomization, compared with other methods of control, is that it controls *all* possible sources of extraneous variation, without any conscious decision about which variables need to be controlled. In our example of a physical fitness intervention, random assignment of elders to an intervention or control group would yield groups presumably comparable in terms of age, gender, smoking history, and hundreds of other characteristics that could affect the outcome. Randomization to different treatment orderings in a crossover design is especially powerful: participants serve as their own controls, thereby totally controlling all confounding characteristics.

Homogeneity

When randomization is not feasible, other methods of controlling extraneous subject characteristics and achieving a counterfactual approximation can be used. One alternative is **homogeneity**, in which only people who are similar with respect to confounding variables are included in the study. Confounding variables, in this case, are not allowed to vary. In the physical fitness example, if gender were a confounding variable, we could recruit only men (or women) as participants. If age was considered a confounding influence, participation could be limited to those within a specified age range. Using a homogeneous sample is easy, but one problem is limited generalizability. Indeed, one problem with this approach is that researchers may exclude people who are extremely ill or incapacitated, which means that the findings cannot be generalized to the very people who perhaps are most in need of interventions.

Example of control through homogeneity:
Ngai, Chan, and Ip (2010) studied factors that predicted maternal role competence and satisfaction among mothers in Hong Kong. Several variables were controlled through homogeneity, including ethnicity (all were Chinese), parity (all primiparous), and marital status (all were married).

Matching

A third method of controlling confounding variables is **matching**, which involves consciously forming comparable groups. For example, suppose we began with a group of nursing home residents who agreed to participate in the physical fitness program. A comparison group of nonparticipating residents could be created by matching participants, one by one, on the basis of important confounding variables (e.g., age and gender). This procedure results in groups known to be similar in terms of specific confounding variables. Matching is the technique often used to form comparable groups in case–control designs.

Matching has some drawbacks, however. To match effectively, researchers must know in advance what the relevant confounders are. Also, after two or three variables, it becomes difficult to match. Suppose we wanted to control age, gender, race, and length of nursing home stay. In this situation, if a program participant were an African American woman, aged

80 years, whose length of stay was 5 years, we would have to seek another woman with these same characteristics as a comparison group counterpart. With more than three variables, matching becomes difficult. Thus, matching as a control method is usually used only when more powerful procedures are not feasible.

Example of control through matching:
Yin, Ma, Feng, and Wang (2012) compared levels of anxiety and depression among patients undergoing two types of surgery for congenital heart defects: thoracoscopic closure of defects versus conventional open heart surgery. The two groups were matched by age and sex.

Statistical Control

Researchers can also control confounding variables statistically. You may be unfamiliar at this point with basic statistical procedures, let alone sophisticated techniques such as those referred to here. Therefore, a detailed description of powerful statistical control mechanisms, such as *analysis of covariance*, will not be attempted. You should recognize, however, that nurse researchers are increasingly using powerful statistical techniques to control confounding variables. A brief description of methods of statistical control is presented in Chapter 12.

Example of statistical control:
Grav, Hellzen, Romild, and Stordal (2012) studied the association between social support (both emotional and tangible) and depression in a general adult population in Norway. Both types of support were significantly correlated with depression, even after statistically controlling for age and gender—that is, the effect of support on depression was not because of male–female or age differences in support.

Evaluation of Control Methods

Random assignment is the most effective approach to controlling confounding variables because randomization tends to control individual variation on all possible confounders. Crossover designs are especially powerful, but they cannot be used in many situations because of the possibility of carryover effects. The alternatives described here share two disadvantages. First, researchers must decide in advance which variables to control. To select homogeneous samples, match, or use statistical controls, researchers must identify which variables to control. Second, these methods control only identified characteristics, leaving others uncontrolled.

Although randomization is an excellent tool, it is not always feasible. If the independent variable cannot be manipulated, other techniques should be used. It is better to use matching or statistical control than to ignore the problem of confounding variables.

CHARACTERISTICS OF GOOD DESIGN

A critical question in critiquing a quantitative study is whether the research design yielded valid evidence. Four key questions regarding research design, particularly in cause-probing studies, are as follows:

1. What is the strength of the evidence that a relationship between variables really exists?
2. If a relationship exists, what is the strength of the evidence that the independent variable of interest (e.g., an intervention), rather than other factors, *caused* the outcome?

3. What is the strength of evidence that observed relationships are generalizable across people, settings, and time?
4. What are the theoretical constructs underlying the related variables, and are those constructs adequately captured?

These questions, respectively, correspond to four aspects of a study's **validity**: (1) statistical conclusion validity; (2) internal validity; (3) external validity; and (4) construct validity (Shadish et al., 2002).

Statistical Conclusion Validity

As noted previously, a criterion for establishing causality is showing that there is a relationship between the independent and dependent variable. Statistical tests are used to support inferences about whether such a relationship exists. Design decisions can influence whether statistical tests will actually be able to detect true relationships. Although we cannot discuss all aspects of **statistical conclusion validity**, we can describe a few design issues that can affect it.

One issue concerns **statistical power**, which refers to the capacity to detect true relationships. Statistical power can be achieved in various ways, the most straightforward of which is to use a large enough sample. With small samples, statistical power tends to be low, and the analyses may fail to show that the independent variable and the outcome are related—*even when they are*. Power and sample size are discussed in Chapter 10.

Another aspect of a powerful design concerns how the independent variable is defined. Results are clearer when differences between the groups (treatment conditions) being compared are large. Researchers should maximize group differences on the independent variables (i.e., make the *cause* powerful) so as to maximize differences on the outcome (the effect). If the groups or treatments are not very different, the statistical analysis might not be sufficiently sensitive to detect outcome effects that actually exist. Intervention fidelity can enhance the power of an intervention.

Thus, if you are critiquing a study in which outcomes for the groups being compared were not significantly different, one possibility is that the study had low statistical conclusion validity. The report might give clues about this possibility (e.g., too small a sample or substantial attrition) that should be taken into consideration in interpreting what the results mean.

Internal Validity

Internal validity is the extent to which it can be inferred that the independent variable is truly causing the outcome. RCTs tend to have high internal validity because randomization enables researchers to rule out competing explanations for group differences. With quasi-experiments and correlational studies, there are competing explanations, which are sometimes called **threats to internal validity**. Evidence hierarchies rank study designs mainly in terms of internal validity.

Threats to Internal Validity

Temporal Ambiguity

In a causal relationship, the cause must precede the effect. In RCTs, researchers create the independent variable and then observe performance on an outcome, so establishing a temporal sequence is never a problem. In correlational studies, however—especially ones using a cross-sectional design—it may be unclear whether the independent variable preceded the dependent variable, or vice versa, as illustrated in Figure 9.1 on page 161.

Selection

The **selection threat** reflects biases stemming from preexisting differences between groups. When people are not assigned randomly to groups, the groups being compared may not be equivalent. In such a situation, group differences in the outcome may be caused by extraneous factors rather than by the independent variable. Selection bias is the most challenging threat to the internal validity of studies not using an experimental design (e.g., nonequivalent control group designs, case–control designs), but can be partially addressed using control mechanisms described in the previous section.

History

The **history threat** is the occurrence of events concurrent with the independent variable that can affect the outcome. For example, suppose we were studying the effectiveness of a community-wide program to encourage flu shots among the elderly. Let us also suppose that a national media story about a flu epidemic occurred at about the same time. Our outcome variable, number of flu shots administered, is subject to the influence of at least two forces, and it would be hard to disentangle the two effects. In RCTs, history is not typically a threat because external events are as likely to affect one randomized group as another. The designs most likely to be affected by the history threat are one-group pretest–posttest designs and time-series designs.

Maturation

The **maturation threat** arises from processes occurring as a result of time (e.g., growth, fatigue) rather than the independent variable. For example, if we were studying the effect of an intervention for developmentally delayed children, our design would have to deal with the fact that progress would occur without an intervention. *Maturation* does not refer only to developmental changes but to any change that occurs as a function of time. Phenomena such as wound healing or postoperative recovery occur with little intervention, and so maturation may be a rival explanation for favorable posttreatment outcomes in the absence of a nontreated group. One-group pretest–posttest designs are especially vulnerable to the maturation threat.

Mortality/Attrition

Mortality is the threat that arises from attrition in groups being compared. If different kinds of people remain in the study in one group versus another, then these differences, rather than the independent variable, could account for group differences in outcomes. The most severely ill patients might drop out of an experimental condition because it is too demanding, for example. Attrition bias essentially is a selection bias that occurs after the study unfolds: groups initially equivalent can lose comparability because of subject loss, and differential group composition, rather than the independent variable, could be the "cause" of any group differences on outcomes.

TIP: If attrition is random (i.e., those dropping out of a study are similar to those remaining in it), then there would not be bias. However, attrition is rarely random. In general, the higher the rate of attrition, the greater the risk of bias. Biases are usually of concern if the rate exceeds 10% to 15%.

Internal Validity and Research Design

Quasi-experimental and correlational studies are especially susceptible to threats to internal validity. These threats compete with the independent variable as a cause of the dependent variable. *The aim of a good quantitative research design is to rule out these competing explanations.* The control mechanisms previously described are strategies for improving internal validity—and thus for strengthening the quality of evidence that studies yield.

An experimental design often, but not always, eliminates competing explanations. For example, if constancy of conditions is not maintained for experimental and control groups, history might be a rival explanation for obtained results. Experimental mortality is a particularly salient threat. Because researchers do different things with the groups, members may drop out of the study differentially. This is particularly likely to happen if the intervention is stressful or time-consuming or if the control condition is boring or disappointing. Participants remaining in a study may differ from those who left, nullifying the initial equivalence of the groups.

You should carefully consider possible rival explanations for study results, especially in non-RCT studies. When researchers do not have control over critical confounding variables, caution in drawing conclusions about the evidence is appropriate.

External Validity

External validity concerns inferences about whether relationships found for study participants might hold true for different people, conditions, and settings. External validity has emerged as a major concern in an EBP world in which it is important to generalize evidence from controlled research settings to real-world practice settings.

External validity questions can take several different forms. For example, we may ask whether relationships observed with a study sample can be generalized to a larger population—for example, whether results about rates of postpartum depression in Boston can be generalized to mothers in the United States. Thus, one aspect of a study's external validity concerns its sampling plan. If the sample is representative of the population, the generalizability of results to the population is enhanced. Sampling is discussed in Chapter 10.

Other external validity questions are about generalizing to different types of people, settings, or situations. For example, can findings about a pain-reduction treatment in Canada be generalized to people in the United States? New studies are often needed to answer questions about generalizability, but sometimes external validity can be enhanced by design decisions.

An important concept relevant to external validity is *replication*. Multisite studies are powerful because more confidence in the generalizability of the results can be attained if the results have been replicated in several sites—particularly if the sites differ on important dimensions (e.g., size). Studies involving a diverse sample of participants can test whether study results are replicated for various subgroups—for example, whether an intervention benefits men *and* women. Systematic reviews represent a crucial aid to external validity precisely because they focus on replications across time, space, people, and settings to explore consistencies.

The demands for internal and external validity may conflict. If a researcher exercises tight control to maximize internal validity, the setting may become too artificial to generalize to more naturalistic environments. Compromises are often necessary.

Construct Validity

Research cannot be undertaken without constructs. Researchers conduct a study with specific exemplars of treatments, outcomes, settings, and people, but these are all stand-ins for broad constructs. **Construct validity** involves inferences from the particulars of the study to the higher-order constructs they are intended to represent. If studies contain construct errors, there is a risk that the evidence will be misleading. One aspect of construct validity concerns the degree to which an intervention is a good representation of the underlying construct that was theorized as having the potential to cause beneficial outcomes. Lack of blinding also undermines construct validity: is it an intervention, or *awareness* of the intervention, that resulted in benefits? Another issue concerns whether the measures of the dependent variable are good operationalizations of the constructs for which they are intended. This aspect will be discussed more fully in Chapter 11.

CRITIQUING QUANTITATIVE RESEARCH DESIGNS

A key evaluative question is whether the research design enabled researchers to get good answers to the research question. This question has both substantive and methodologic facets.

Substantively, the issue is whether the researcher selected a design that matches the aims of the research. If the research purpose is descriptive or exploratory, an experimental design is not appropriate. If the researcher is searching to understand the full nature of a phenomenon about which little is known, a structured design that allows little flexibility might block insights (flexible designs are discussed in Chapter 14). We have discussed research control as a bias-reducing strategy, but too much control can introduce bias—for example, when a researcher tightly controls how phenomena under study can be manifested and so obscures their true nature.

Methodologically, the main design issue in quantitative studies is whether the research design provides the most valid, unbiased, and interpretable evidence possible. Indeed, there usually is no other aspect of a quantitative study that affects the quality of evidence as much as research design. Box 9.1 provides questions to assist you in evaluating aspects of research designs; these questions are key to a meaningful critique of a quantitative study.

BOX 9.1 Guidelines for Critiquing Research Design in a Quantitative Study

1. Was the design experimental, quasi-experimental, or nonexperimental? What specific design was used? Was this a cause-probing study? Given the type of question (therapy, prognosis, etc.), was the most rigorous possible design used?
2. What type of comparison was called for in the research design? Was the comparison strategy effective in illuminating key relationships?
3. If the study involved an intervention, were the intervention and control conditions adequately described? Was blinding used, and if so, who was blinded? If not, is there a good rationale for failure to use blinding? Was attention paid to intervention fidelity?
4. If the study was nonexperimental, why did the researcher opt not to intervene? If the study was cause probing, which criteria for inferring causality were potentially compromised? Was a retrospective or prospective design used, and was such a design appropriate?
5. Was the study longitudinal or cross-sectional? Was the number and timing of data collection points appropriate?
6. What steps did the researcher take in designing the study to enhance statistical conclusion validity? Were these steps adequate?
7. What did the researcher do to control confounding external factors and intrinsic participant characteristics, and were the procedures effective? What are the threats to the study's internal validity? Does the design enable the researcher to draw causal inferences about the relationship between the independent variable and the outcome?
8. What are the major limitations of the design used? Are these limitations acknowledged by the researcher and taken into account in interpreting results? What can be said about the study's external validity?

RESEARCH EXAMPLES WITH CRITICAL THINKING EXERCISES

This section presents examples of studies with different research designs. Read these summaries and then answer the critical thinking questions, referring to the full research reports if necessary.

Examples 1 and 2 below are also featured in our *Interactive Critical Thinking Activity* on thePoint website where you can easily record, print, and e-mail your responses to the related questions.

EXAMPLE 1 ● A Randomized Controlled Trial

Study: "Investigation of standard care versus sham Reiki placebo versus actual Reiki therapy to enhance comfort and well-being in a chemotherapy infusion center" (Catlin & Taylor-Ford, 2011).

Statement of Purpose: The purpose of the study was to evaluate the efficacy of Reiki therapy in enhancing comfort and well-being among patients undergoing outpatient chemotherapy. Reiki is a form of energy work that involves laying of hands over a fully clothed person "for the purpose of unblocking energy centers" (p. E213).

Treatment Groups: Three groups of patients were compared: (1) an intervention group that received a Reiki intervention; (2) a placebo group that received a sham Reiki treatment; and (3) a control group that got usual care only.

Method: A sample of 189 participants was randomly assigned to one of the three groups, using a table of random numbers. The sample size was based on an analysis undertaken to ensure adequate statistical power. Patients in the intervention group received a 20-minute Reiki treatment during chemotherapy by an experienced Reiki therapist (an RN). For patients in the placebo group, the therapist pretended to perform a Reiki session. Patients in the control group received standard care. In terms of intervention fidelity, actual sessions were not monitored, but sessions held before the study allowed other Reiki instructors to see that the actual therapist and the sham therapist approached patients in identical ways. All patients completed scales that measured their comfort and well-being, both prior to the treatment and again after the chemotherapy session. Infusion center nurses and patients themselves were blinded as to whether the sham or actual Reiki therapy was being administered. There was no attrition from the study. A comparison of patients in the three study groups at baseline indicated that the three groups were comparable in terms of demographic characteristics (e.g., age, ethnicity) and treatment variables (e.g., round of chemotherapy).

Key Findings: Improvements in both comfort and well-being were observed from baseline to posttest for patients in both the Reiki group and the placebo group, but not for those in the standard care group. The standard care group had significantly lower comfort and well-being scores at the end of the trial than those in the Reiki and placebo groups.

Conclusions: The researchers concluded that the presence of an RN providing one-on-one support during a chemotherapy session helped to improve comfort and well-being, with or without an attempted healing energy field.

CRITICAL THINKING EXERCISES

1. Answer the relevant questions from Box 9.1 on page 170 regarding this study.
2. Also consider the following targeted questions:
   a. Could a crossover design have been used in this study?
   b. Was randomization successful in creating comparable groups?
3. If the results of this study are valid, in what ways do you think the findings could be used in clinical practice?

EXAMPLE 2 ● Quasi-Experimental Design

Study: "Efficacy of controlling nighttime noise and activities to improve patients' sleep quality in a surgical intensive care unit" (Li et al., 2011)

Statement of Purpose: The purpose of the study was to evaluate the effectiveness of implementing a set of sleep care guidelines for improving sleep quality of patients in a surgical intensive care unit (ICU) in a large medical center in Taiwan.

Treatment Groups: The control group of ICU patients received care as usual. Patients in the experimental group were cared for by nurses who followed special sleep care guidelines designed to reduce noise and light between the hours of 11:00 PM to 5:00 AM This entailed making several changes to nursing care, such as changing the time for chest X-rays from midnight to between 7:00 and 10:00 PM, and ensuring that the volume of IV fluid and tube feeding was adequate before 11:00 PM.

Method: A two-phase quasi-experimental design was used. In the first phase (December 2007 to February 2008), a control group of 30 patients got care as usual. In the second phase (March 2008 to May 2008), 30 patients were cared for under the new sleep care guidelines. Nurses received training in the use of the new guidelines, and fidelity to the new protocol was monitored during training. The sample size was based on an analysis designed to yield adequate statistical power. Blinding was not used in this study. Patients responded to a set of questions about sleep quality on the 3rd day after admittance to the ICU. A decibel meter was also used to continuously monitor environmental noise levels. The two groups of patients were similar in terms of such characteristics as age, sex, education, type of surgery, and disease severity. However, patients in the control group were more likely to have had a prior ICU experience that those in the experimental group. Out of the initial total sample of 60 patients, 5 were dropped from the study (2 in the intervention group, 3 in the control group).

Key Findings: Using data from the decibel meter, both the peak sound level and the average noise level were significantly lower after implementing the new guidelines. Patients in the experimental group also reported significantly better sleep quality and sleep efficiency than those in the control group.

Conclusions: The researchers concluded that the sleep care guidelines were effective and that nurses should make efforts to reduce environmental stimuli during nighttime hours.

CRITICAL THINKING EXERCISES

1. Answer the relevant questions from Box 9.1 on page 170 regarding this study.
2. Also consider the following targeted questions:
   a. Is this study prospective or retrospective?
   b. What other quasi-experimental designs could have been used in this study?
3. If the results of this study are valid, in what ways do you think the findings could be used in clinical practice?

EXAMPLE 3 ● Nonexperimental Study in Appendix A

- Read the method section from Howell and colleagues' (2007) study ("Anxiety, anger, and blood pressure in children") in Appendix A on page 395–402.

CRITICAL THINKING EXERCISES

1. Answer the questions in Box 9.1 from page 170 regarding this study.
2. Also consider the following targeted questions:
   a. Could Howell and colleagues have used an experimental or quasi-experimental design to address the research questions?
   b. If the design was retrospective, how could the study have been done prospectively (or vice versa)?

WANT TO KNOW MORE? A wide variety of resources to enhance your learning and understanding of this chapter are available on thePoint.

- Interactive Critical Thinking Activity
- Chapter Supplement on Selected Experimental and Quasi-Experimental Designs
- Answers to the Critical Thinking Exercises for Example 3
- Student Review Questions
- Full-text online
- Internet Resources with useful websites for Chapter 9

Additional study aids including eight journal articles and related questions are also available in *Study Guide for Essentials of Nursing Research, 8e.*

SUMMARY POINTS

- The **research design** is the overall plan for answering research questions. In quantitative studies, the design designates whether there is an intervention, the nature of any comparisons, methods for controlling confounding variables, whether there will be blinding, and the timing and location of data collection.
- Therapy, prognosis, and etiology questions are cause probing, and there is a hierarchy of designs for yielding best evidence for these questions.
- Key criteria for inferring causality include the following: (1) a cause (independent variable) must precede an effect (outcome); (2) there must be a detectable relationship between a cause and an effect; and (3) the relationship between the two does not reflect the influence of a third (confounding) variable.
- A **counterfactual** is what would have happened to the same people simultaneously exposed *and* not exposed to a causal factor. The *effect* is the difference between the two. A good research design for cause-probing questions entails finding a good approximation to the idealized counterfactual.
- **Experiments** (or **randomized controlled trials** [**RCTs**]) involve an intervention (the researcher manipulates the independent variable by introducing an intervention; control (including the use of a **control group** that is not given the intervention and represents the comparative counterfactual); and **randomization** or **random assignment** (with participants allocated to experimental and control groups at random to make the groups comparable at the outset).
- RCTs are considered the gold standard because they come closer than any other design in meeting the criteria for inferring causal relationships.
- **Posttest-only designs** involve collecting data only once—after randomization and the introduction of the treatment; in **pretest–posttest designs**, data are collected both before the intervention (at **baseline**) and after it.
- In **crossover designs**, people are exposed to more than one experimental condition in random order and serve as their own controls. Crossover designs are not appropriate when there is a risk of *carryover effects*.
- The control group can undergo various conditions, including no treatment; an alternative treatment; a **placebo** or pseudointervention; standard treatment ("usual care"); different treatment doses; or a *wait-list* (*delayed treatment*) condition.

- **Quasi-experiments** (*trials without randomization*) involve an intervention but lack a comparison group or randomization. Strong quasi-experimental designs introduce controls to compensate for these missing components.
- **The nonequivalent control-group, pretest–posttest design** involves comparing an intervention group to a **comparison group** that was not created through randomization, and the collection of pretreatment data from both groups to assess initial group equivalence.
- In a **time-series design**, outcome data are collected over a period of time before and after the intervention, usually for a single group.
- **Nonexperimental** (*observational*) **research** includes **descriptive research**—studies that summarize the status of phenomena—and **correlational studies** that examine relationships among variables but involve no intervention.
- In **prospective cohort designs**, researchers begin with a possible cause, and then subsequently collect data about outcomes.
- **Retrospective designs** (**case–control designs**) involve collecting data about an outcome in the present and then looking back in time for possible causes.
- Making causal inferences in correlational studies is risky; a basic research dictum is that *correlation does not prove causation*.
- **Cross-sectional designs** involve the collection of data at one time period, whereas **longitudinal designs** involve data collection at two or more times over an extended period. In nursing, most longitudinal studies are **follow-up studies** of clinical populations.
- Longitudinal studies are typically expensive, time-consuming, and subject to the risk of **attrition** (loss of participants over time) but yield valuable information about time-related phenomena.
- Quantitative researchers strive to control external factors that could affect study outcomes and subject characteristics that are extraneous to the research question.
- Researchers delineate the intervention in formal *protocols* that stipulate exactly what the treatment is. Careful researchers attend to *intervention fidelity*—whether the intervention was properly implemented and actually received as intended.
- Techniques for controlling subject characteristics include **homogeneity** (restricting participants to reduce variability on confounding variables); **matching** (deliberately making groups comparable on some extraneous variables); statistical procedures; and randomization—the most effective method because it controls all possible confounding variables without researchers having to identify them.
- Study **validity** concerns the extent to which appropriate inferences can be made. **Threats to validity** are reasons that an inference could be wrong. A key function of quantitative research design is to rule out validity threats.
- **Statistical conclusion validity** concerns the strength of evidence that a relationship exists between two variables. Threats to statistical conclusion validity include low **statistical power** (the ability to detect true relationships among variables) and factors that undermine a strong treatment.
- **Internal validity** concerns inferences that the outcomes were caused by the independent variable, rather than by extraneous factors. Threats to internal validity include temporal ambiguity (uncertainty about whether the presumed cause preceded the outcome); **selection** (preexisting group differences); **history** (external events that could affect outcomes); **maturation** (changes due to the passage of time); and **mortality** (effects attributable to attrition).
- **External validity** concerns inferences about generalizability—whether findings hold true over variations in people, conditions, and settings.

REFERENCES FOR CHAPTER 9

Aitken, L., Burmeister, E., Clayton, S., Dalais, C., & Gardner, G. (2011). The impact of Nursing Rounds on the practice environment and nursing satisfaction in intensive care. *International Journal of Nursing Studies, 48*, 918–925.

Belanger, L., Plotnikoff, R., Clark, A., & Courneya, K. (2012). A survey of physical activity programming and counseling preferences in young-adult cancer survivors. *Cancer Nursing, 35*, 48–54.

Carter, A., Deselms, J., Ruyle, S., Morrissey-Lucas, M., Kollar, S., Cannon, S., et al. (2012). Postanesthesia care unit visitation decreases family member anxiety. *Journal of Perisanesthesia Nursing, 27*, 3–9.

Catlin, A., & Taylor-Ford, R. (2011). Investigation of standard care versus sham Reiki placebo versus actual Reiki therapy to enhance comfort and well-being in a chemotherapy infusion center. *Oncology Nursing Forum, 38*, E212–E220.

Cora, A., Particino, M., Munafo, M., & Palomba, D. (2012). Health risk factors in caregivers of terminal cancer patients. *Cancer Nursing, 35*, 38–47.

Grav, S., Hellzen, O., Romild, U., & Stordal, E. (2012). Association between social support and depression in the general population. *Journal of Clinical Nursing, 21*, 111–120.

Kassab, M., Sheehy, A., King, M., Fowler, C., & Foureur, M. (2012). A double-blind randomized controlled trial of 25% oral glucose for pain relief in 2-month old infants undergoing immunization. *International Journal of Nursing Studies, 49*(3), 249–256.

Li, S., Wang, T., Wu, S., Liang, S., & Tung, H. (2011). Efficacy of controlling night-time noise and activities to improve patients' sleep quality in a surgical intensive care unit. *Journal of Clinical Nursing, 20*, 396–407.

Liaw, J. J., Yang, L., Katherine-Wang, K., Chen, C., Chang, Y., & Yin, T. (2012). Non-nutritive sucking and facilitated tucking relieve preterm infant pain during heel-stick procedures. *International Journal of Nursing Studies,49*(3), 300–409.

Liou, Y. M., Hsu, Y., Ho, J., Lin, C., Hsu, W., & Liou, T. (2012). Prevalence and correlates of self-induced vomiting as weight control strategy among adolescents in Taiwan. *Journal of Clinical Nursing, 21*, 11–20.

McCullough, N., Parkes, J., Kerr, C., & McDowell. (2012). The health of children and young people with cerebral palsy. *International Journal of Nursing Studies*, PubMed ID 21329925.

Ngai, F., Chan, S., & Ip, W. (2010). Predictors and correlates of maternal role competence and satisfaction. *Nursing Research, 59*, 185–193.

Polit, D., & Chaboyer, W. (2012). Statistical process control in nursing research. *Research in Nursing & Health, 35*, 82–93.

Robbins, L., Pfeiffer, K., Maier, K., Ladrig, S., & Berg-Smith, S. (2012). Treatment fidelity of motivational interviewing delivered by a school nurse to increase girls' physical activity. *Journal of School Nursing, 28*, 70–78.

Salamonson, Y., Everett, B., Koch, J., Andrew, S., & Davidson, P. (2012). The impact of term-time paid work on academic performance in nursing students: A longitudinal study. *International Journal of Nursing Studies,49*(5), 579–585.

Shadish, W. R., Cook, T. D., & Campbell, D. T. (2002). *Experimental and quasi-experimental designs for generalized causal inference*. Boston: Houghton Mifflin Co.

White, L. S. (2012). Reducing stress in school-age girls through mindful yoga. *Journal of Pediatric Health Care, 26*, 45–56.

Yin, Q., Ma, Z., Feng, F., & Wang, L. (2012). Postoperative anxiety and depression in patients undergoing thoracoscopic closure of congenital heart defects. *Journal of Cardiovascular Nursing*, PubMed ID 21926914.

chapter

10 Sampling and Data Collection in Quantitative Studies

LEARNING OBJECTIVES

On completing this chapter, you will be able to:

- Distinguish between nonprobability and probability samples and compare their advantages and disadvantages
- Identify and describe several types of sampling designs in quantitative studies
- Evaluate the appropriateness of the sampling method and sample size used in a study
- Discuss the dimensions along which data collection approaches vary
- Identify phenomena that lend themselves to self-reports, observation, and biophysiologic measurement
- Describe various approaches to collecting self-report data (e.g., interviews vs. questionnaires, composite scales)
- Describe various methods of collecting, sampling, and recording observational data
- Describe the major features and advantages of biophysiologic measures
- Critique a researcher's decisions regarding the data collection plan and its implementation
- Define new terms in the chapter

KEY TERMS

Accessible population
Category system
Checklist
Closed-ended question
Consecutive sampling
Convenience sampling
Eligibility criteria
Interview schedule
Questionnaire
Likert scale
Nonprobability sampling
Nonresponse bias
Observational methods
Open-ended question
Population
Power analysis
Probability sampling
Purposive sampling
Quota sampling
Random sampling
Rating scale
Representative sample
Response alternatives
Response rate
Response set bias
Sample size
Sampling
Sampling bias
Scale
Self-report
Simple random sampling
Strata
Stratified random sampling
Systematic sampling
Target population
Visual analog scale

This chapter covers two important research topics—how quantitative researchers select their study participants and how they collect data from them.

SAMPLING IN QUANTITATIVE RESEARCH

Researchers answer their questions using a sample of participants. In testing the effects of an intervention for pregnant women, nurse researchers reach conclusions without testing it with all pregnant women. Quantitative researchers want samples that allow them to generalize their results to a broader population, and that have adequate power for statistical conculation validity. They develop a **sampling plan** that specifies in advance how participants will be selected and how many to include.

Basic Sampling Concepts

Sampling is a critical part of the design of quantitative research. Let us first consider some terms associated with sampling—terms that are used primarily with quantitative studies.

Populations

A **population** (the "P" in PICO questions) is the entire group of interest. For instance, if a researcher were studying American nurses with doctoral degrees, the population could be defined as all RNs in the United States who have acquired a doctoral-level degree. Other populations might be all patients who had cardiac surgery in St. Peter's Hospital in 2013 or all Australian children under age 10 with cystic fibrosis. Populations are not restricted to people. A population might consist of all hospital records in Memorial Hospital. Whatever the basic unit, the population is an entire aggregate of elements.

Researchers specify characteristics that delimit the population through **eligibility criteria**. For example, consider the population of American nursing students. Does the population include part-time students? Are RNs returning to school for a bachelor's degree included? Researchers establish criteria to determine whether a person qualifies as a member of the population (*inclusion* criteria) or should be excluded (*exclusion* criteria), for example, excluding patients who do not speak English or who are severely ill.

Example of inclusion and exclusion criteria:
Kvitvaer and colleagues (2012) sought to identify a group of symptoms that are highly correlated with unexplained infant crying commonly termed infant colic. Infants were eligible for the study if they were younger than 12 months and had been brought by their parents to a clinic because of excessive crying. Infants were excluded if they had a concurrent or systemic illness and if their parents could not speak English.

Quantitative researchers sample from an accessible population in the hope of generalizing to a target population. The **target population** is the entire population in which a researcher is interested. The **accessible population** is the portion of the target population that is accessible to the researcher. For example, the researcher's target population might be all diabetic patients in the United States, but, in reality, the population that is accessible might be diabetic patients in a particular hospital, from which a sample is selected.

Samples and Sampling

Sampling involves selecting a portion of the population to represent the population. A **sample** is a subset of population elements. In nursing research, the *elements* (basic units) are usually humans. Researchers work with samples rather than populations because it is practical to do so.

Information from samples can, however, lead to erroneous conclusions. In quantitative studies, a key criterion for judging a sample is its representativeness. A **representative sample** is one whose characteristics closely approximate those of the population. Certain sampling plans are less likely to result in biased samples than others. **Sampling bias** is the systematic overrepresentation or underrepresentation of some segment of the population in terms of key characteristics.

Strata

Populations consist of subpopulations, or **strata**. Strata are mutually exclusive segments of a population based on a specific characteristic. For instance, a population consisting of all RNs in the United Kingdom could be divided into two strata based on gender. Or, we could specify three strata based on years of experience (e.g., less than 10 years, 10 to 20 years, or more than 20 years). Strata are often used in sample selection to enhance the sample's representativeness.

 **TIP:** The sampling plan is usually discussed in a report's method section, sometimes in a subsection called "Sample" or "Study participants." Sample characteristics (e.g., average age) are often described at the beginning of the results section.

Sampling Designs in Quantitative Studies

There are two broad classes of sampling designs in quantitative research: probability sampling and nonprobability sampling.

Nonprobability Sampling

In **nonprobability sampling**, researchers select elements by nonrandom methods in which every element usually does not have a chance to be included. Nonprobability sampling is less likely than probability sampling to produce representative samples—and yet, *most* research samples in nursing and other disciplines are nonprobability samples.

Convenience sampling entails selecting the most conveniently available people as participants. A nurse who distributes questionnaires about vitamin use to 100 adults at a church picnic center is sampling by convenience, for example. The problem with convenience sampling is that people who are readily available might be atypical of the population, and so the price of convenience is the risk of bias. Convenience sampling is the weakest form of sampling, but it is also the most commonly used sampling method in many disciplines.

Example of a convenience sample:

Morrison and Ludington-Hoe (2012) studied interruptions to breast-feeding dyads in a community hospital birthing center. A convenience sample of 33 mothers who expressed the intent to breast-feed upon admission to the birth center yielded data on 1,596 interruptions over 360 hours of observation.

In **quota sampling**, researchers identify population strata and figure out how many people are needed from each stratum. By using information about the population, researchers can ensure that diverse segments are properly represented in the sample. As an example, suppose we were interested in studying nursing students' attitudes toward working on an AIDS unit. The accessible population is a nursing school with 500 undergraduates; a sample size of 100 students is desired. With a convenience sample, we could distribute questionnaires to 100 students as they entered classrooms. Suppose, though, that male and female students have

TABLE 10.1 Numbers and Percentages of Students in Strata of a Population, Convenience Sample, and Quota Sample

Strata	Population	Convenience Sample	Quota Sample
Male	100 (20%)	5 (5%)	20 (20%)
Female	400 (80%)	95 (95%)	80 (80%)
Total	500 (100%)	100 (100%)	100 (100%)

different attitudes toward AIDS patients. A convenience sample might result in too many men, or too few. Table 10.1 presents some fictitious data showing the gender distribution for the population and for a convenience sample (columns 2 and 3). The convenience sample seriously underrepresents male students, which in turn means the results will be biased. We can use quota sampling to select participants so that the sample includes an appropriate number of men and women, as shown in the far-right column of Table 10.1.

Procedurally, quota sampling is similar to convenience sampling: participants are a convenience sample from each stratum. Because of this fact, quota sampling shares some of the weaknesses of convenience sampling. For instance, a trip to a dorm might be a convenient way to recruit the 20 needed male students. Yet this approach gives no representation to male students living off campus, who may feel differently about working with AIDS patients. Nevertheless, quota sampling is a big improvement over convenience sampling and does not require sophisticated skills or a lot of effort. Surprisingly, few researchers use this strategy.

Example of a quota sample:

Hung and colleagues (2011) used quota sampling to recruit 859 women from 18 Taiwanese hospitals or clinics into their study of factors predicting postpartum stress. The sample represented births from the 18 facilities proportionately.

Consecutive sampling is a nonprobability sampling method that involves recruiting *all* people from an accessible population over a specific time interval, or for a specified sample size. For example, in a study of ventilated-associated pneumonia in ICU patients, a consecutive sample might consist of all eligible patients who were admitted to an ICU over a 6-month period. Or it might be the first 250 eligible patients admitted to the ICU, if 250 were the targeted sample size. Consecutive sampling is a better approach than sampling by convenience, especially if the sampling period is sufficiently long to deal with potential biases that reflect seasonal fluctuations. Consecutive sampling is often the best possible choice when there is "rolling enrollment" into an accessible population.

Example of a consecutive sample:

Forni and colleagues (2011) conducted a study to evaluate the use of polyurethane foam inside plaster casts to prevent the onset of heel sores. Their intervention group was a consecutive sample of 71 patients requiring lower limb casts in an orthopedic hospital in Italy.

Purposive sampling is based on the belief that researchers' knowledge about the population can be used to hand-pick sample members. Researchers might decide purposely to select people who are judged to be particularly knowledgeable about the issues under study. This method can lead to bias, but can be a useful approach when researchers want a sample of experts.

Example of purposive sampling:
Castro and colleagues (2011) assessed the views of an expert panel of 22 nurses regarding the development of a taxonomy for the domain of clinical nursing research.

HOW-TO-TELL TIP: How can you tell what type of sampling design was used in a quantitative study? If the report does not explicitly mention or describe the sampling design, it is usually safe to assume that a convenience sample was used.

Probability Sampling

Probability sampling involves random selection of elements from a population. Random selection should not be (although it often is) confused with random assignment, which is a signature of a randomized controlled trial (RCT) (Chapter 9). Random *assignment* to different treatment conditions has no bearing on how participants in the RCT were selected in the first place. With **random sampling**, each element in the population has an equal, independent chance of being selected.

Simple random sampling is the most basic probability sampling. In simple random sampling, researchers establish a *sampling frame*, the technical name for the list of population elements. If nursing students at the University of Connecticut were the accessible population, then a student roster would be the sampling frame. Elements in a sampling frame are numbered and then a table of random numbers or an online random sample generator is used to draw a random sample of the desired size. Samples selected in such a fashion are not subject to researcher biases. There is no *guarantee* of a representative sample, but random selection does guarantee that differences between the sample and the population are purely a function of chance. The probability of selecting a markedly atypical sample through random sampling is low, and this probability decreases as the sample size increases.

Example of a simple random sample:
Radzvin (2011) randomly sampled 800 certified registered nurse anesthetists (CRNAs) from the registry of the American Association of Nurse Anesthetists to study moral distress in CRNAs.

In **stratified random sampling**, the population is first divided into two or more strata, from which elements are randomly selected. As with quota sampling, the aim of stratified sampling is to enhance representativeness. Stratification is often based on demographic attributes, such as age or gender. Stratified sampling may not be possible if information on the stratifying variable is unavailable (e.g., student rosters may not include information on age).

Example of stratified random sampling:
Mattila and colleagues (2010) studied patients' perceived access to support from nursing staff. They sent questionnaires to a stratified random sample of patients in a Finnish hospital. The stratifying variable was type of hospital unit—surgical, internal medicine, and gynecologic.

TIP: Many large national studies use *multistage sampling*, in which large units are first randomly sampled (e.g., census tracts, hospitals), then smaller units are randomly selected (e.g., individual people).

Systematic sampling involves the selection of every *k*th case from a list, such as every 10th person on a patient list. Systematic sampling can be used in such a way that an essentially random sample is drawn. First, the size of the population is divided by the size of the desired sample to obtain the **sampling interval**, which is the standard distance between selected cases. For instance, if we needed a sample of 50 from a population of 5,000, our sampling interval would be 100 (5,000/50 = 100). Every 100th case on a sampling frame would be sampled, with the first case selected randomly. If our random number were 73, the people corresponding to numbers 73, 173, 273, and so on would be included in the sample. Systematic sampling done in this manner is essentially the same as simple random sampling, and is often more convenient.

Example of a systematic sample:
Gillespie and colleagues (2009) studied factors that predicted resilience in operating room (OR) nurses. The researchers sent a survey to 1,430 nurses—every other member of the professional association for OR nurses in Australia.

Evaluation of Nonprobability and Probability Sampling

Probability sampling is the only viable method of obtaining representative samples. If all elements in a population have an equal probability of being selected, then the resulting sample is likely to do a good job of representing the population. A further advantage is that probability sampling allows researchers to estimate the magnitude of sampling error. *Sampling error* refers to differences between population values (e.g., the average age of the population) and sample values (e.g., the average age of the sample).

Nonprobability samples are rarely representative of the population. When every element in the population does not have a chance of being selected, it is likely that some segment of it will be underrepresented. When there is sampling bias, there is always a chance that the results could be misleading. Why, then, are nonprobability samples used in most nursing studies? Clearly, the advantages of these sampling designs lie in their ease and economy. Probability sampling, although highly respected, is often impractical. Quantitative researchers using nonprobability samples must be cautious about the inferences drawn from the data, and consumers should be alert to possible sampling biases.

TIP: The quality of the sampling plan is of particular importance when the focus of the research is to obtain descriptive information about prevalence or average values for a population. All national surveys in the United States, such as the National Health Interview Survey, use probability samples. Probability samples are rarely used in randomized controlled trials. For studies whose purpose is primarily quantitative description, data from a probability sample is at the top of the evidence hierarchy for individual studies.

Sample Size in Quantitative Studies

Sample size—the number of study participants—is a major concern in quantitative research. There is no simple formula to determine how large a sample should be, but larger is usually better than smaller. When researchers calculate a percentage or an average based on sample data, the purpose is to estimate a population value, and larger samples have less sampling error.

Researchers can estimate how large their samples should be for testing their research hypotheses through **power analysis**. A simple example can illustrate basic principles of power analysis. Suppose we were testing a new intervention to help people quit smoking;

smokers would be randomized to either an experimental or a control group. How many people should be in the sample? When using power analysis, researchers must estimate how large the group difference will be (e.g., group differences in average daily number of cigarettes smoked after the intervention). This estimate might be based on prior research or on a pilot test. When expected differences are large, a large sample is not needed to reveal group differences statistically but when small differences are predicted, large samples are necessary. For new areas of research, group differences are likely to be small or moderate. In our example, if a small group difference in postintervention smoking were expected, the sample size needed to test group differences in smoking, with standard statistical criteria, would be about 800 smokers (400 per group). If a small-to-moderate difference were expected, the total sample size would need to be about 250 smokers.

The risk of "getting it wrong" (statistical conclusion validity) increases when samples are too small: researchers risk gathering data that will not support their hypotheses *even when those hypotheses are correct*. Large samples are no assurance of accuracy, however. With nonprobability sampling, even a large sample can harbor bias. The famous example illustrating this point is the 1936 United States presidential poll conducted by the magazine *Literary Digest*, which predicted that Alfred M. Landon would defeat Franklin D. Roosevelt by a landslide. A sample of about 2.5 million people was polled, but biases arose because the sample was drawn from telephone directories and automobile registrations during a Depression year when only the well-to-do (who favored Landon) had a car or telephone.

A large sample cannot correct for a faulty sampling design; nevertheless, a large nonprobability sample is better than a small one. When critiquing quantitative studies, you must assess both the sample size and the sample selection method to judge how good the sample was.

TIP: The sampling plan is often one of the weakest aspects of quantitative studies. Most nursing studies use samples of convenience, and many are based on samples that are too small to provide an adequate test of the research hypotheses. Small samples run a high risk of leading researchers to erroneously reject their research hypotheses. Therefore, you should give special scrutiny to the sampling plans of studies that fail to support research hypotheses.

Critiquing Sampling Plans

In coming to conclusions about the quality of evidence that a study yields, the sampling plan merits special scrutiny. If the sample is seriously biased or too small, the findings may be misleading or just plain wrong.

In critiquing a description of a sampling plan, you should consider two issues. The first is whether the researcher has adequately described the sampling strategy. Ideally, research reports should describe the following:

- The type of sampling approach used (e.g., convenience, consecutive, random)
- The population under study and eligibility criteria for sample selection
- The sample size, with a rationale
- A description of the sample's main characteristics (e.g., age, gender, clinical status, and so on)
- The number and characteristics of potential subjects who declined to participate

If the description of the sample is inadequate, you may not be in a position to deal with the second and principal issue, which is whether the researcher made good sampling decisions.

Box 10.1 Guidelines for Critiquing Quantitative Sampling Plans

1. Is the population under study identified? Are eligibility criteria specified? Are the sample selection procedures clearly delineated?
2. What type of sampling design was used? Would an alternative sampling design have been preferable? Was the sampling design one that could be expected to yield a representative sample?
3. Did some factor other than the sampling design (e.g., a low response rate) affect the representativeness of the sample?
4. Are possible sample biases or weaknesses identified?
5. Are key characteristics of the sample described (e.g., mean age, percent female)?
6. Is the sample size sufficiently large to support statistical conclusion validity? Was the sample size justified on the basis of a power analysis or other rationale?
7. Does the sample support inferences about external validity? To whom can the study results reasonably be generalized?

And, if the description is incomplete, it will be difficult to draw conclusions about whether the evidence has relevance in your clinical practice.

We have stressed that a key criterion for assessing the quality of a sampling plan in quantitative research is whether the sample is representative of the population. You will never know for sure, of course, but if the sampling strategy is weak or if the sample size is small, there is reason to suspect some bias.

Even with a rigorous sampling plan, the sample may be biased if not all people invited to participate in a study agree to do so. If certain subgroups in the population refuse to participate, then a biased sample can result, even when probability sampling is used. The research report ideally should provide information about **response rates** (i.e., the number of people participating in a study relative to the number of people sampled), and about possible **nonresponse bias**—differences between participants and those who declined to participate (also sometimes referred to as *response bias)*. In a longitudinal study, attrition bias should be reported.

Your job as reviewer is to come to conclusions about the reasonableness of generalizing the findings from the researcher's sample to the accessible population and from the accessible population to a broader target population. If the sampling plan is seriously flawed, it may be risky to generalize the findings at all without replicating the study with another sample.

Box 10.1 presents some guiding questions for critiquing the sampling plan of a quantitative study.

DATA COLLECTION IN QUANTITATIVE RESEARCH

Phenomena in which researchers are interested must be translated into data that can be analyzed. This section discusses the challenging task of collecting quantitative research data.

Overview of Data Collection and Data Sources

Data collection methods vary along several dimensions. One issue is whether the researcher will collect original data or use existing data. Existing **records**, for example, are an important data source for nurse researchers. A wealth of data gathered for nonresearch purposes in clinical settings can be fruitfully analyzed to answer research questions.

Example of a study using records:
Garten and colleagues (2011) used data from the charts of 127 very low-birth-weight infants to study parental NICU visiting patterns during the first 28 days of life in a German hospital.

If existing data are unsuitable for a research question, researchers must collect new data. In developing their data collection plan, researchers make many important decisions, including the basic type of data to gather. Three types have been used most frequently by nurse researchers: self-reports, observations, and biophysiologic measures. **Self-report** data are participants' responses to questions posed by the researcher, such as in an interview. In nursing studies, self-reports are the most common data collection approach. Direct **observation** of people's behaviors, characteristics, and circumstances is an alternative to self-reports for certain questions. Nurses also use **biophysiologic measures** to assess important clinical variables. In quantitative studies, researchers decide upfront how to operationalize their variables and gather their data. Their data collection plans are almost always "cast in stone" before a single piece of data is collected.

Regardless of type of data collected in a study, data collection methods vary along several dimensions, including structure, quantifiability, and objectivity. Data for quantitative studies tend to be quantifiable and structured, with the same information gathered from all participants in a comparable, prespecified way. Quantitative researchers generally strive for methods that are as objective as possible.

TIP: Most data that are analyzed quantitatively actually begin as qualitative data. If a researcher asked respondents if they have been severely depressed, moderately depressed, somewhat depressed, or not at all depressed in the past week, they answer in words, not numbers. The words are transformed, through *coding*, into quantitative categories.

Self-Reports

A lot of information can be gathered by questioning people. If, for example, we wanted to learn about patients' eating habits, we would likely gather data by asking them relevant questions. The unique ability of humans to communicate verbally on a sophisticated level makes direct questioning an important part of nurse researchers' data collection repertoire.

Structured self-report methods are used when researchers know in advance exactly what they need to know and can frame appropriate questions to obtain the needed information. Structured self-report data are collected with a formal, written document—an *instrument*. The instrument is an **interview schedule** when the questions are asked orally face-to-face or by telephone or a **questionnaire** when respondents complete the instrument themselves.

Question Form and Wording

In a totally structured instrument, respondents are asked to respond to the same questions in the same order. **Closed-ended** (or *fixed-alternative*) **questions** are ones in which the **response alternatives** are prespecified. The alternatives may range from a simple yes or no to complex expressions of opinion. The purpose of such questions is to ensure comparability of responses and to facilitate analysis. Some examples of closed-ended questions are presented in Table 10.2.

Some structured instruments, however, also include **open-ended questions**, which allow participants to respond to questions in their own words (e.g., What led to your decision to stop smoking?). When open-ended questions are included in questionnaires,

TABLE 10.2 Examples of Closed-Ended Questions

Question Type	Example
1. Dichotomous question	Have you ever been pregnant? 1. Yes 2. No
2. Multiple-choice question	How important is it to you to avoid a pregnancy at this time? 1. Extremely important 2. Very important 3. Somewhat important 4. Not important
3. Rank-order question	People value different things in life. Below is a list of things that many people value. Please indicate their order of importance to you by placing a "1" beside the most important, "2" beside the second-most important, and so on. _____ Career achievement/work _____ Family relationships _____ Friendships, social interactions _____ Health _____ Money _____ Religion
4. Forced-choice question	Which statement most closely represents your point of view? 1. What happens to me is my own doing. 2. Sometimes I feel I don't have enough control over my life.
5. Rating question	On a scale from 0 to 10, where 0 means "extremely dissatisfied" and 10 means "extremely satisfied," how satisfied were you with the nursing care you received during your hospitalization? 0 1 2 3 4 5 6 7 8 9 10 Extremely dissatisfied Extremely satisfied

respondents must write out their responses. In interviews, the interviewer writes down responses verbatim.

Good closed-ended questions are more difficult to construct than open-ended ones but easier to analyze. Closed-ended questions are also more efficient: people can complete more closed-ended questions than open-ended ones in a given amount of time. People may be unwilling to compose lengthy written responses to open-ended questions in questionnaires. A major drawback of closed-ended questions is that researchers might omit some potentially important responses. Closed-ended questions also can be superficial. Open-ended questions allow for richer information if the respondents are verbally expressive and cooperative. Finally, some respondents object to choosing from alternatives that do not reflect their opinions precisely.

In drafting (or borrowing) questions for a structured instrument, researchers must carefully monitor the wording of each question for clarity, sensitivity to respondents' psychological state, absence of bias, and (in questionnaires) reading level. Questions must be sequenced in a psychologically meaningful order that encourages cooperation and candor. Developing, pretesting, and refining a self-report instrument can take many months to complete.

Interviews Versus Questionnaires

Researchers using structured self-reports must decide whether to use interviews or self-administered questionnaires. Questionnaires have the following advantages:

- Questionnaires are less costly and are advantageous for geographically dispersed samples. Internet questionnaires are especially economical and are an increasingly important means of gathering self-report data—although response rates to Internet questionnaires tend to be lower than for mailed questionnaires.
- Questionnaires offer the possibility of anonymity, which may be crucial in obtaining information about certain behavior, opinions, or traits.

Example of mailed questionnaires:
Krichbaum and colleagues (2011) developed and tested an instrument to measure *complexity compression* in nurses (being asked to assume new responsibilities in a compressed time frame). They sent questionnaires by mail to a random sample of 1,200 RNs in Minnesota.

The strengths of interviews outweigh those of questionnaires. Among the advantages are the following:

- Response rates tend to be high in face-to-face interviews. Respondents are less likely to refuse to talk to an interviewer than to ignore a questionnaire. Low response rates can lead to bias because respondents are rarely a random subset of the original sample. In the mailed questionnaire study of RNs described earlier (Krichbaum et al., 2011), the response rate was under 20%.
- Many people cannot fill out a questionnaire; examples include young children, the blind, and the very elderly. Interviews are feasible with most people.
- Interviewers can produce additional information through observation of respondents' behavior or living situation, which can be useful in interpreting responses.

Most advantages of face-to-face interviews also apply to telephone interviews. Complicated instruments are not well suited to telephone administration, but for relatively brief instruments, telephone interviews combine relatively low costs with high response rates.

Example of personal interviews:
Wu and co-researchers (2012) explored the relationship between fatigue and physical activity levels in patients with liver cirrhosis. Physical activity was assessed in interviews that involved a 7-day recall of all physical activities and their intensity and duration.

TIP: Even in interview situations, participants are sometimes asked some of their questions in a questionnaire format. Questions that are deeply personal (e.g., about sexuality) or that may require some reflection (e.g., about loneliness) are sometimes easier to answer privately on a form than to express out loud to an interviewer.

Scales

Social-psychological scales are often incorporated into questionnaires or interview schedules. A **scale** is a device that assigns a numeric score to people along a continuum, like a scale for measuring weight. Social-psychological scales quantitatively discriminate among people with different attitudes, perceptions, and psychological traits.

One common scaling technique is the **Likert scale**, which consists of several declarative statements (*items*) that express a viewpoint on a topic. Respondents are asked to indicate

TABLE 10.3 Example of a Likert Scale to Measure Attitudes Toward Condoms

Direction of Scoring*	Item	SA	A	?	D	SD	Person 1 (✓)	Person 2 (X)
		Responses†					Score	
+	1. Using a condom shows you care about your partner.		✓			X	4	1
−	2. My partner would be angry if I talked about using condoms.			X		✓	5	3
−	3. I wouldn't enjoy sex as much if my partner and I used condoms.		X		✓		4	2
+	4. Condoms are a good protection against AIDS and other sexually transmitted diseases.			✓	X		3	2
+	5. My partner would respect me if I insisted on using condoms.	✓				X	5	1
−	6. I would be too embarrassed to ask my partner about using a condom.		X			✓	5	2
	Total score						26	11

*Researchers would not indicate the direction of scoring on a Likert scale administered to participants. The scoring direction is indicated in this table for illustrative purposes only.
†SA, strongly agree; A, agree; ?, uncertain; D, disagree; SD, strongly disagree.

how much they agree or disagree with the statement. Table 10.3 presents an illustrative six-item Likert scale for measuring college students' attitudes toward condom use. In this example, agreement with positively worded statements is assigned a higher score. The first statement is positively worded; agreement indicates a favorable attitude toward condom use. Because there are five response alternatives, a score of 5 would be given for *strongly agree*, 4 for *agree*, and so on. Responses of two hypothetical participants are shown by a check or an X, and their item scores are shown in the right-hand columns. Person 1, who agreed with the first statement, has a score of 4, whereas person 2, who strongly disagreed, got a score of 1. The second statement is negatively worded, and so scoring is reversed—a 1 is assigned for *strongly agree*, and so forth. Item reversals ensure that a high score consistently reflects positive attitudes toward condom use.

A person's total score is the sum of item scores and so these scales are sometimes called *summated rating scales* or *composite scales*. In our example, person 1 has a more positive attitude toward condoms (total score = 26) than person 2 (total score = 11). Summing item scores makes it possible to finely discriminate among people with different opinions. A single Likert item puts people into only five categories. A six-item scale, such as the one in Table 10.3, permits finer gradation—from a minimum possible score of 6 (6 × 1) to a maximum possible score of 30 (6 × 5). Composite scales are often comprised of two or more *subscales* that measure different aspects of a construct. Developing high-quality scales requires a lot of skill and effort.

Example of a Likert scale:
Davidson and colleagues (2011) studied perceptions of cardiovascular risk in patients hospitalized for a percutaneous coronary intervention. They used several existing scales (e.g., the Perceived Stress Scale), and also developed a new Likert scale to measure perceived heart risk.

Another type of scale is the **visual analog scale** (VAS), which can be used to measure subjective experiences, such as pain, fatigue, and dyspnea. The VAS is a straight line, the end anchors of which are labeled as the extreme limits of the sensation or feeling being measured (Fig. 10.1). Participants mark a point on the line corresponding to the amount of sensation experienced. Traditionally, a VAS line is 100 mm in length, which makes it easy to derive a score from 0 to 100 by measuring the distance from one end of the scale to the mark on the line.

Example of a visual analog scale:
Taavoni and colleagues (2011) tested the effect of using birth balls on women's pain in the active phase of labor. Pain was measured using a visual analog scale.

Scales permit researchers to efficiently quantify subtle gradations in the intensity of individual characteristics. Scales can be administered either verbally or in writing and thus can be used with most people. Scales are susceptible to several common problems, however, many of which are referred to as **response set biases**. The most important biases include the following:

- *Social desirability response set bias*—a tendency to misrepresent attitudes or traits by giving answers that are consistent with prevailing social views
- *Extreme response set bias*—a tendency to consistently express extreme attitudes or feelings (e.g., strongly agree), leading to distortions because extreme responses may be unrelated to the trait being measured
- *Acquiescence response set bias*—a tendency to agree with statements regardless of their content by some people (*yea-sayers*). The opposite tendency for other people (*nay-sayers*) to disagree with statements independently of the question content is less common.

Researchers can reduce these biases by developing sensitively worded questions, creating a permissive, nonjudgmental atmosphere, and guaranteeing the confidentiality of responses.

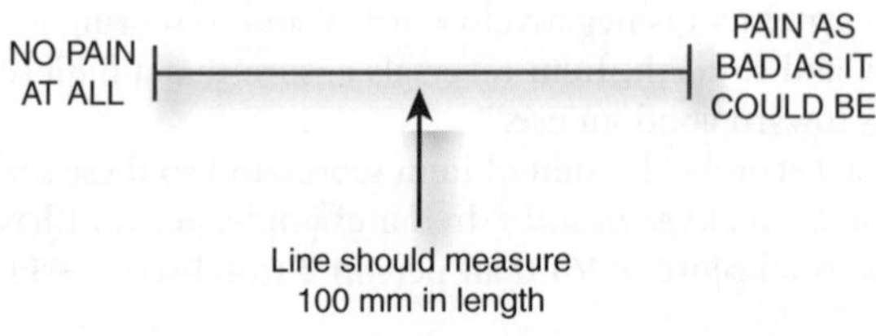

FIGURE 10.1 ● Example of a visual analog scale.

TIP: There are other special types of self-report approaches. *Vignettes*, for example, are brief descriptions of events or situations to which respondents are asked to react. *Q-sorts*, another example, present participants with a set of cards on which statements are written. Participants are asked to sort the cards along a specified dimension, such as most helpful/least helpful. Vignettes and Q-sorts are described in greater detail in the Chapter Supplement on thePoint website.

Evaluation of Self-Report Methods

If researchers want to know how people feel or what they believe, the most direct approach is to ask them. Self-reports frequently yield information that would be difficult or impossible to gather by other means. Behaviors can be *observed*, but only if people are willing to engage in them publicly—and engage in them at the time of data collection.

Despite these advantages, self-reports have some weaknesses. The most serious issue concerns the validity and accuracy of self-reports: How can we be sure that respondents feel or act the way they say they do? How can we trust the information that study participants provide, particularly if the questions ask them about potentially undesirable traits? Investigators usually have no choice but to assume that most respondents have been frank. Yet, we all have a tendency to present ourselves in the best light, and this may conflict with the truth. When reading research reports, you should be alert to potential biases in self-reported data.

Observation

For some research questions, direct observation of people's behavior is an alternative to self-reports, especially in clinical settings. Observational methods can be used to gather such information as the conditions of individuals (e.g., the sleep–wake state of patients); verbal communication (e.g., exchange of information at change-of-shift report); nonverbal communication (e.g., body language); activities (e.g., geriatric patients' self-grooming activities); and environmental conditions (e.g., noise levels in nursing homes).

In observational studies, researchers have flexibility with regard to several important dimensions:

- *Focus of the observation*. The focus can be on broadly defined events (*e.g.*, patient mood swings), or on small, highly specific behaviors (e.g., facial expressions).
- *Concealment*. Researchers do not always tell people they are being observed, because awareness of being observed may cause people to behave atypically. Behavioral distortions due to the known presence of an observer is called *reactivity*.
- *Method of recording observations*. Observations can be made through the human senses and then recorded by paper-and-pencil methods, but they can also be done with sophisticated equipment (e.g., video equipment, audio recording equipment, computers).

Like self-report techniques, observational methods vary in terms of structure and quantifiability. Structured observation involves the use of formal instruments and protocols that dictate what to observe, how long to observe it, and how to record the data. Structured observation is not intended to capture a broad slice of ordinary life, but rather to document specific behaviors, actions, and events. Structured observation requires the formulation of a system for accurately categorizing, recording, and encoding the observations.

TIP: Researchers often use structured observations when participants cannot be asked questions, or cannot be expected to provide reliable answers. Many observational instruments are designed to capture the behaviors of infants, children, or people whose communication skills are impaired.

Categories and Checklists

The most common approach to making structured observations is to use a category system for classifying observed phenomena. A **category system** represents a method of recording in a systematic fashion the behaviors and events of interest that transpire within a setting.

Some category systems are constructed so that *all* observed behaviors within a specified domain (e.g., body positions and movements) can be classified into one and only one category. A contrasting technique is to develop a system in which only particular types of behavior (which may or may not be manifested) are categorized. For example, if we were studying children's aggressive behavior, we might develop such categories as "strikes another child" or "throws objects around the room." In this category system, many behaviors—all that are nonaggressive—would not be classified, and some children may exhibit *no* aggressive actions. Nonexhaustive systems are adequate for many purposes, but one risk is that resulting data might be difficult to interpret. When a large number of behaviors are not categorized, the investigator may have difficulty placing categorized behavior into perspective.

Example of nonexhaustive categories:

Happ and colleagues (2011) undertook a complex observational study of communication between nurses and patients in an intensive care unit. Among many different types of observations made, observers recorded instances of positive and negative nurse behaviors, according to carefully defined criteria. Nurse behaviors that were neutral were not categorized.

Category systems must be accompanied by, explicit operational definitions of the behaviors and characteristics to be observed. Each category must be carefully explained, giving observers clear-cut criteria for assessing the occurrence of the phenomenon. Even with detailed definitions of categories, observers often are faced with making numerous on-the-spot inferences. Virtually all category systems require observer inference, to greater or lesser degree.

Example of moderately low observer inference:

Tsai and colleagues (2011) examined factors that could predict osteoarthritic pain in elders, including nonverbal cues measured through observation. One predictor was motor patterns, which were videotaped in 10-minute sessions in which elders engaged in a set of activities. Observers coded for the presence of five behaviors (e.g., active rubbing of the knee or hip, joint flexion, rigidity) in 30-second intervals.

Category systems are the basis for constructing a **checklist**, which is the instrument observers use to record observations. The checklist is usually formatted with a list of behaviors from the category system on the left, and space for tallying the frequency or duration on the right. The task of the observer using an exhaustive category system is to place *all* observed behaviors in one category for each integral unit of behavior (e.g., a sentence in a conversation, a time interval). With nonexhaustive category systems, categories of behaviors that may or may not be manifested by participants are listed. The observer watches for instances of these behaviors and records their occurrence.

Rating Scales

Another approach to structured observations is to use a **rating scale**, an instrument that requires observers to rate phenomena along a descriptive continuum. The observer may be required to make ratings of behavior at intervals throughout the observation or to summarize an entire event or transaction after observation is completed. Rating scales can be used as an extension of checklists, in which the observer records not only the occurrence of some behavior but also some qualitative aspect of it, such as its intensity. Although this approach yields a lot of information, the disadvantage is that it places an immense burden on observers.

Example of observational ratings:
The NEECHAM Confusion Scale, an observational instrument for recording the presence and severity of acute confusion, has subscales requiring behavioral ratings. For example, one rating in the Processing subscale concerns alertness/responsiveness; ratings are from 0 (responsiveness depressed) to 4 (full attentiveness). Ono and colleagues (2011) used NEECHAM scores as a measure of postoperative delirium in their study that tested the usefulness of bright light therapy after esophagectomy.

Observational Sampling

Researchers must decide when to apply their structured observational systems. Observational sampling methods are a means of obtaining representative examples of the behaviors being observed. One system is **time sampling**, which involves the selection of time periods during which observations will occur. Time frames may be selected systematically (e.g., every 30 seconds at 2-minute intervals) or at random.

With **event sampling**, researchers select integral behaviors or events to observe. Event sampling requires researchers to either have knowledge about the occurrence of events (e.g., nursing shift changes) or be in a position to wait for their occurrence. Event sampling is preferable to time sampling when the events of interest are infrequent and may be missed if time sampling is used. When behaviors and events are relatively frequent, however, time sampling enhances the representativeness of the observed behaviors.

Example of event and time sampling:
In the previously mentioned observational study of nurse–patient communication in the ICU (Happ et al., 2011), events were first sampled (occasions of nurse–patient interaction), and then 3-minute segments of interaction on four separate occasions were videotaped and then coded for a range of outcomes (e.g., making eye contact, communication success).

Evaluation of Observational Methods

Certain research questions are better suited to observation than to self-reports, such as when people cannot adequately describe their own behaviors. This may be the case when people are unaware of their own behavior (e.g., stress-induced behavior), when behaviors are emotionally laden (e.g., grieving), or when people are not capable of reporting their actions (e.g., young children). Observational methods have an intrinsic appeal for directly capturing behaviors. Often, nurses are in a position to watch people's behaviors and may, by training, be especially sensitive observers.

Shortcomings of observational methods include possible ethical problems and reactivity when the observer is conspicuous. One of the most pervasive problems, however, is the vulnerability of observations to bias. A number of factors interfere with objective observations, including the following:

- Emotions, prejudices, and values of the observer may lead to faulty inference.
- Personal views may color what observers see in the direction of what they want to see.
- Anticipation of what is to be observed may affect what is perceived.

Observational biases probably cannot be eliminated, but they can be minimized through careful observer training and assessment.

TIP: As with self-report methods, structured observational methods require thorough pretesting and refinement.

Biophysiologic Measures

Clinical nursing studies involve biophysiologic instruments both for creating independent variables (e.g., a biofeedback intervention) and for measuring dependent variables. Our discussion focuses on the use of biophysiologic measures as dependent (outcome) variables.

Nurse researchers have used biophysiologic measures for a wide variety of purposes. Examples include studies of basic biophysiologic processes, explorations of the ways in which nursing actions and interventions affect physiologic outcomes, product assessments, studies to evaluate the accuracy of biophysiologic information gathered by nurses, and studies of the correlates of physiologic functioning in patients with health problems.

Biophysiologic measures include both *in vivo* and *in vitro* measures. *In vivo* measures are those performed directly within or on living organisms, such as blood pressure, body temperature, and vital capacity measurement. Technological advances continue to improve the ability to measure biophysiologic phenomena more accurately and conveniently. With *in vitro* measures, data are gathered from participants by extracting biophysiologic material from them and subjecting it to analysis by specialized laboratory technicians. *In vitro* measures include chemical measures (e.g., the measurement of hormone levels); microbiologic measures (e.g., bacterial counts and identification); and cytologic or histologic measures (e.g., tissue biopsies).

Example of a study with *in vivo* and *in vitro* measures:
Yamamoto and Nagata (2011) examined the effects of a wrapped warm footbath to induce relaxation in patients with incurable cancer. The researchers measured heart rate variability to assess autonomic and sympathetic activities, and salivary cortisol to assess neuroimmunological parameters.

Biophysiologic measures offer a number of advantages to nurse researchers, including the following:

- Biophysiologic measures are relatively accurate and precise, especially compared to psychological measures, such as self-report measures of anxiety or pain.
- Biophysiologic measures are objective. Two nurses reading from the same spirometer output are likely to record identical tidal volume measurements, and two spirometers are likely to produce the same readouts.
- Patients cannot easily distort measurements of biophysiologic functioning.
- Biophysiologic instrumentation provides valid measures of targeted variables: thermometers can be relied on to measure temperature and not blood volume, and so forth. For nonbiophysiologic measures, there are typically concerns about whether an instrument is really measuring the target concept.

Biophysiologic measures are plentiful, tend to be accurate and valid, and are extremely useful in clinical nursing studies.

Implementing the Data Collection Plan

Researchers must develop and implement a plan for gathering and recording the data. One important decision concerns who will collect the data. Researchers often hire assistants to collect data rather than collect it themselves, especially in large-scale quantitative studies.

From your perspective as a consumer, the critical issue is whether the people collecting data were able to produce valid and accurate data. Adequate training and monitoring of data collectors is essential. Also, blinding of data collectors (withholding information about study hypotheses or group assignments) is a good strategy in most quantitative studies.

Another issue concerns the circumstances under which data were gathered. For example, it may be critical to ensure privacy. In most cases, it is important for researchers to create a nonjudgmental atmosphere in which participants are encouraged to be candid or behave naturally. Again, you as a consumer must ask whether there is anything about the way in which the data were collected that could have created bias or otherwise affected data quality. In evaluating the data collection plan of a study, then, you should critically appraise not only the actual methods chosen but also the procedures used to collect and record the data.

Critiquing Data Collection Methods

The goal of a data collection plan is to produce data that are of exceptional quality. Every decision researchers make about data collection methods and procedures can affect data quality, and hence the overall quality of the study.

It may, however, be difficult to critique data collection methods in studies reported in journals because researchers' descriptions are seldom detailed. Even though space constraints in journals make it impossible for researchers to fully elaborate their methods, however, researchers do have a responsibility to communicate basic information about their approach so that readers can assess the quality of evidence that the study yields.

Degree of structure is important in your assessment of a data collection plan. Researchers' decisions about structure are based on considerations that you can often evaluate, such as the status of knowledge on the topic (in a new area of inquiry, an unstructured approach may be preferred) and the nature of the research question. Another important issue is the *mix* of data collection approaches. Triangulation of methods (e.g., self-report and observation) is often extremely desirable. Finally, it is important to evaluate the actual procedures used to collect and record the data. This means giving consideration to who collected the data, how they were trained, whether formal instruments were adequately pretested, and whether efforts were made to reduce biases. Guidelines for critiquing data collection methods are presented in Box 10.2.

Box 10.2 Guidelines for Critiquing Quantitative Data Collection Plans

1. Given the research question and characteristics of participants, did the researchers use the best method of capturing study phenomena (i.e., self-reports, observation, biophysiologic measures)? Was triangulation of methods used appropriately—that is, were multiple methods sensibly used?
2. Did the researchers make good data collection decisions with regard to structure, quantification, and objectivity?
3. If self-report methods were used, did the researchers make good decisions about the specific methods used to solicit information (e.g., in-person interviews, mailed questionnaires, and so on)? For structured self-reports, was there an appropriate mix of questions and composite scales?
4. Were efforts made to enhance data quality in collecting the self-report data (e.g., were efforts made to reduce or to evaluate response biases? Was the reading level of the instruments appropriate for self-administered questionnaires?)?

(continued)

Box 10.2 Guidelines for Critiquing Quantitative Data Collection Plans *(Continued)*

5. If observational methods were used, did the report adequately describe what the observations entailed? Were risks of observational bias addressed? How much inference was required of the observers, and was this appropriate?
6. Were biophysiologic measures used in the study, and was this appropriate?
7. Did the report provide adequate information about data collection procedures? Were data collectors judiciously chosen and properly trained? Where and under what circumstances were data gathered? Were data gathered in a manner that promoted high-quality responses (e.g., in terms of privacy, efforts to put respondents at ease, etc.)?

RESEARCH EXAMPLES WITH CRITICAL THINKING EXERCISES

In this section, we describe the sampling and data collection plan of a quantitative nursing study, followed by some questions to guide critical thinking.

Example 1 below is also featured in our *Interactive Critical Thinking Activity* on thePoint website where you can easily record, print, and e-mail your responses to the related questions.

EXAMPLE 1 ● Sampling and Data Collection in a Quantitative Study

Study: Family caregivers of hospitalized adults in Israel: A point-prevalence survey and exploration of tasks and motives (Auslander, 2011)

Purpose: The purpose of this study was to examine the prevalence of family inpatient caregiving in acute care hospitals in Israel, to describe characteristics of caregivers and caregiving activities, and to examine the relationship between patient characteristics, caregiver characteristics, motivations for caregiving, and type and amount of caregiving activities.

Design: The researchers collected data in a cross-sectional study of hospitalized patients and family caregivers. The design was descriptive correlational.

Sampling: The sample consisted of adult family caregivers who provided care for patients during their hospitalization in six hospitals in central Israel. On a randomly selected week, a research coordinator gathered hospital record data about all eligible patients in three departments (internal medicine, surgery, and orthopedics) of the six hospitals. To be eligible for inclusion, patients had to be 18 years or older and hospitalized for at least 2 days. Tourists, foreign workers, and prisoners were excluded. A total of 1076 patients were identified in this manner. For each patient, a determination was made (via observations and patient questioning) regarding whether there was a family caregiver. A total of 744 patients had caregivers. All were invited to participate in the study, and 513 did so. Patients whose caregivers did or did not participate in the study were similar in terms of age, sex, ethnicity, residence, and length of stay. The total number in the sample exceeded the sample size that the researchers had estimated would be needed to yield sufficient statistical power.

Data Collection: Background data and some clinical information (e.g., length of hospital stay) were obtained from the patients' charts. Information about the extent of in-hospital caregiving was obtained via observation. For each patient with a caregiver, observers recorded number of hours the caregiver and other family members spent in the hospital, frequency of visits, and whether the caregiver slept in the hospital. The researchers constructed a self-administered caregiver questionnaire that was developed on the basis of in-depth interviews with family caregivers and key informants, and pretested and refined in a pilot study with 200 families. The questionnaire included several composite scales, including one that measured various caregiving tasks and motivation for caregiving. The Motivation scale, for example, consisted of 29 items scored on 5 subscales. Respondents were asked the extent to which they agreed with each statement on a scale from 1 (not at all) to 5 (very much). Examples of items on this scale include: "I get satisfaction from being here" and "The staff expects family members to help."

Key Findings: Patients who lived further from the hospital were less likely to have family caregivers. Caregivers averaged 8 hours a day at the hospital. Their main motivation was the desire to help the patient. Factors that were related to the number of hours spent in caregiving were the patients' age, a caregiving motivation that involved the caregivers' peace of mind, and caregivers' own concerns about being separated from the patient.

CRITICAL THINKING EXERCISES

1. Answer the relevant questions from Boxes 10.1 on page 183 and 10.2 on pages 193-94 regarding this study.
2. Also consider the following targeted questions:
   a. Are there variables in this study that could have been measured through observation, but were not?
   b. Where do you think this study belongs on an evidence hierarchy?
3. If the results of this study are valid and reliable, in what ways do you think the findings could be used in clinical practice?

EXAMPLE 2 ● Sampling and Data Collection in the Study in Appendix A

- Read the method section from Howell and colleagues' (2007) study ("Anxiety, anger, and blood pressure in children") in Appendix A on page 395–402.

CRITICAL THINKING EXERCISES

1. Answer the relevant questions from Boxes 10.1 on page 183 and 10.2 on pages 193-194 regarding this study.
2. Also consider the following targeted questions:
   a. What type of sampling plan might have improved the representativeness of the sample in this study?
   b. Identify some of the major potential sources of bias in the *sample*.
   c. Comment on factors that could have biased the *data* in this study.

WANT TO KNOW MORE? A wide variety of resources to enhance your learning and understanding of this chapter are available on thePoint.

- Interactive Critical Thinking Activity
- Chapter Supplement on Vignettes and Q-Sorts
- Answers to the Critical Thinking Exercises for Example 2
- Student Review Questions
- Full-text online
- Internet Resources with useful websites for Chapter 10

Additional study aids including eight journal articles and related questions are also available in *Study Guide for Essentials of Nursing Research, 8e.*

SUMMARY POINTS

- **Sampling** is the process of selecting elements from a **population**, which is an entire aggregate of cases. An *element* is the basic unit of a population—usually humans in nursing research.
- **Eligibility criteria** (including both *inclusion criteria* and *exclusion criteria*) are used to define population characteristics.
- Researchers usually sample from an **accessible population**; a broader **target population** is the group to which they would like to generalize their results.
- A key criterion in assessing a sample in a quantitative study is its **representativeness**—the extent to which the sample is similar to the population and avoids bias. **Sampling bias** is the systematic overrepresentation or underrepresentation of some segment of the population.
- **Nonprobability sampling** (in which elements are selected by nonrandom methods) includes convenience, quota, consecutive, and purposive sampling. Nonprobability sampling is practical and economical; a major disadvantage is its potential for bias.
- **Convenience sampling** uses the most readily available or convenient group of people.
- **Quota sampling** divides the population into homogeneous **strata** (subpopulations) to ensure representation of the subgroups in the sample; within each stratum, people are sampled by convenience.
- **Consecutive sampling** involves taking *all* of the people from an accessible population who meet the eligibility criteria over a specific time interval, or for a specified sample size.
- In **purposive sampling**, participants are hand-picked to be included in the sample based on the researcher's knowledge about the population.
- **Probability sampling** designs, which involve the random selection of elements from the population, yield more representative samples than nonprobability designs and permit estimates of the magnitude of *sampling error*.
- **Simple random sampling** involves the random selection of elements from a **sampling frame** that enumerates all the elements; **stratified random sampling** divides the population into homogeneous subgroups from which elements are selected at random.
- **Systematic sampling** is the selection of every *k*th case from a list. By dividing the population size by the desired sample size, the researcher establishes the **sampling interval**, which is the standard distance between the selected elements.
- In quantitative studies, researchers can use a **power analysis** to estimate **sample size** needs. Large samples are preferable because they enhance statistical conclusion validity and tend to be more representative, but even large samples do not *guarantee* representativeness.
- Data collection methods vary in terms of structure, quantifiability, and objectivity. The three principal data collection methods for nurse researchers are self-reports, observations, and biophysiologic measures.
- **Self-reports**, which involve directly questioning study participants, are the most widely used method of collecting data for nursing studies.
- Structured self-reports for quantitative studies involve a formal *instrument*—a **questionnaire** or **interview schedule**—that may contain **open-ended questions** (which permit respondents to respond in their own words) and **closed-ended questions** (which offer respondents **response alternatives** from which to choose).

- Questionnaires are less costly than interviews and offer the possibility of anonymity, but interviews yield higher response rates, are suitable for a wider variety of people, and provide richer data than questionnaires.
- Social-psychological **scales** are self-report tools for quantitatively measuring such characteristics as attitudes, needs, and perceptions along a continuum.
- **Likert scales** (or **summated rating scales**) present respondents with a series of *items* worded favorably or unfavorably toward a phenomenon; responses indicating level of agreement or disagreement with each statement are scored and summed into a composite score.
- A **visual analog scale (VAS)** is used to measure subjective experiences (e.g., pain, fatigue) along a 100-mm line designating a bipolar continuum.
- Scales are versatile and powerful but are susceptible to **response set biases**—the tendency of some people to respond to items in characteristic ways, independently of item content.
- **Observational methods** are techniques for acquiring data through the direct observation of phenomena.
- Structured observations dictate what the observer should observe; they often involve **checklists**—tools based on **category systems** for recording the appearance, frequency, or duration of prespecified behaviors or events. Observers may also use **rating scales** to rate phenomena along a dimension of interest (e.g., intensity).
- Structured observations often use a sampling plan (such as **time sampling** or **event sampling**) for selecting the behaviors, events, and conditions to be observed.
- Observational techniques are a versatile and important alternative to self-reports, but observational biases can pose a threat to the validity and accuracy of observational data.
- Data may also be derived from **biophysiologic measures**, which include *in vivo* measurements (those performed within or on living organisms) and *in vitro* measurements (those performed outside the organism's body, such as blood tests). Biophysiologic measures have the advantage of being objective, accurate, and precise.
- In developing a data collection plan, the researcher must decide who will collect the data, how the data collectors will be trained, and what the circumstances for data collection will be.

REFERENCES FOR CHAPTER 10

Auslander, G. K. (2011). Family caregivers of hospitalized adults in Israel: A point-prevalence survey and exploration of tasks and motives. *Research in Nursing & Health, 34*, 204–217.

Castro, K., Bevans, M., Miller-Davis, X., Cusack, G., Loscalzo, F., Matlock, A., et al. (2011). Validating the clinical research nursing domain of practice. *Oncology Nursing Forum, 38*, E72–E80.

Davidson, P., Salamonson, Y., Rolley, J., Everett, B., Fernandez, R., Andrew, S., et al. (2011). Perception of cardiovascular risk following a percutaneous coronary intervention. *International Journal of Nursing Studies, 48*, 973–978.

Forni, C., Loro, L., Tremosini, M., Mini, S., Pignotti, E., Bigoni, O., et al. (2011). Use of polyurethane foam inside plaster casts to prevent the onset of heel sores in the population at risk. *Journal of Clinical Nursing, 20*, 675–680.

Garten, L., Maass, E., Schmalisch, G., & Buhrer, C. (2011). O father, where art thou? Parental NICU visiting patterns during the first 28 days of life of very low-birth-weight infants. *Journal of Perinatal & Neonatal Nursing, 25*, 342–348.

Gillespie, B., Chaboyer, W., & Wallis, M. (2009). The influence of personal characteristics on the resilience of operating room nurses. *International Journal of Nursing Studies, 46*, 968–976.

Happ, M. B., Garrett, K., Thomas, D., Tate, J., George, E., Houze, M., et al. (2011). Nurse-patient communication interactions in the intensive care unit. *American Journal of Critical Care, 20*, e28–e40.

Hung, C., Lin, C., Stocker, J., & Yu, C. (2011). Predictors of postpartum stress. *Journal of Clinical Nursing, 20*, 666–674.

Krichbaum, K., Peden-McAlpine, C., Diemart, C., Koenig, P., Mueller, C., & Savik, K. (2011). Designing a measure of complexity compression in registered nurses. *Western Journal of Nursing Research, 33*, 7–25.

Kvitvaer, B., Miller, J., & Newell, D. (2012). Improving our understanding of the colicky infant. *Journal of Clinical Nursing, 21*, 63–69.

Matilla, E., Kaunonen, M., Aalto, P., Ollikainen, J., & Astedt-Kutki, P. (2010). Support for hospital patients and associated factors. *Scandinavian Journal of Caring Sciences, 24*, 734–745.

Morrison, B., & Ludington-Hoe, S. (2012). Interreuptions to breastfeeding dyads in an LDRP unit. *MCN:American Journal of Maternal/Child Nursing, 37*, 36–41.

Ono, H., Taguchi, T., Kido, Y., Fujino, Y., & Doki, Y. (2011). The usefulness of bright light therapy for patients after oesophagectomy. *Intensive and Critical Care Nursing, 27*, 158–166.

Radzvin, L. C. (2011). Moral distress in certified registered nurse anesthetists. *AANA Journal, 79*, 39–45.

Taavoni, S., Abdolahanian, S., Haghani, H., & Neysani, L. (2011). Effect of birth ball usage in the active phase of labor. *Journal of Midwifery & Women's Health, 56*, 137–140.

Tsai, P., Kuo, Y., Beck, C., Richards, K., Means, K., Pate, B., & Keefe, F. (2011). Nonverbal cues to osteoarthritis knee and/or hip pain in elders. *Research in Nursing & Health, 34*, 218–227.

Wu, L. J., Wu, M., Lien, G., Chen, F., & Tsai, J. (2012). Fatigue and physical activity levels in patients with liver cirrhosis. *Journal of Clinical Nursing, 21*, 129–138.

Yamamoto, K., & Nagata, S. (2011). Physiological and psychological evaluation of the wrapped warm footbath as a complementary nursing therapy to induce relaxation in hospitalized patients with incurable cancer. *Cancer Nursing, 34*, 185–192.

chapter

11 Measurement and Data Quality

LEARNING OBJECTIVES

On completing this chapter, you will be able to:

- Describe the major characteristics of measurement and identify major sources of measurement error
- Describe aspects of reliability and validity, and specify how each aspect can be assessed
- Interpret the meaning of reliability and validity information
- Describe the function and meaning of sensitivity and specificity
- Evaluate the overall quality of a measuring tool used in a study
- Define new terms in the chapter

KEY TERMS

Coefficient alpha
Construct validity
Content validity
Content validity index (CVI)
Criterion-related validity
Cronbach's alpha
Error of measurement
Factor analysis
Internal consistency
Interval measurement
Interrater reliability
Level of measurement
Known-groups technique
Measurement
Nominal measurement
Ordinal measurement
Psychometric assessment
Ratio measurement
Reliability
Reliability coefficient
Sensitivity
Specificity
Test–retest reliability
True score
Validity

An ideal data collection procedure is one that captures a construct accurately, truthfully, and precisely. Few data collection procedures match this ideal perfectly. In this chapter, we discuss criteria for evaluating the quality of data obtained with structured instruments.

MEASUREMENT

Quantitative studies derive data by measuring variables, and so we begin by discussing the concept of measurement.

What is Measurement?

Early American psychologist L. L. Thurstone made a famous statement: "Whatever exists, exists in some amount and can be measured." **Measurement** involves rules for assigning numbers to objects or people to designate the *quantity* of an attribute. Attributes do not have inherent numeric values; humans invent rules to measure them. Attributes are not constant; they vary from day to day or from one person to another. This variability can be expressed numerically to signify *how much* of an attribute is present.

Measurement requires numbers to be assigned according to *rules*. Rules for measuring temperature and weight, for example, are familiar to us. Rules for measuring many variables for nursing studies, however, have to be created. Whether data are collected by observation, self-report, or any other method, researchers specify the criteria according to which numbers are to be assigned.

Advantages of Measurement

Measurement removes guesswork and ambiguity in gathering and communicating information. Consider how handicapped health-care professionals would be without measures of body temperature, blood pressure, and so on. Because measurement has explicit rules, the resulting information tends to be objective; that is, it can be independently verified. Two people measuring the weight of a person using the same scale 5 minutes apart would get identical results. Not all measures are completely objective, but most have mechanisms for minimizing subjectivity.

Measurement also makes it possible to obtain reasonably precise information. Instead of describing Nathan as "tall," we can depict him as being 6 feet 3 inches tall. If necessary, we could achieve greater precision. Such precision allows researchers to make fine distinctions among people with different amounts of an attribute.

Measurement is a language of communication. Numbers are less vague than words and can communicate information clearly. If a researcher reported that the average temperature of a sample of patients was "somewhat high," different readers might have different interpretations, but if the researcher reported an average temperature of 99.6°F, there is no ambiguity.

Levels of Measurement

In this chapter, we discuss how measurements can be evaluated. In the next chapter we consider what researchers *do* with measurements in their analyses. Statistical operations depend on a variable's **level of measurement**. There are four major classes, or levels, of measurement.

Nominal measurement, the lowest level, involves using numbers simply to categorize attributes. Gender and blood type are examples of nominally measured variables. The numbers used in nominal measurement do not have quantitative meaning. If we coded males as 1 and females as 2, the numbers have no quantitative implication—the number 2 does not mean "more than" 1. Nominal measurement provides information only about categorical equivalence and so the numbers cannot be treated mathematically. It makes no sense, for example, to compute a sample's average gender by adding all numeric values and dividing by the number of participants.

Ordinal measurement ranks people based on relative standing on an attribute. For example, consider this ordinal coding scheme for measuring ability to perform activities of daily living (ADL): 1 = completely dependent, 2 = needs another person's assistance, 3 = needs mechanical assistance, and 4 = completely independent. The numbers signify incremental ability to perform ADL independently. Ordinal measurement does not, however, tell us how much greater one level is than another. For example, we do not know if being completely independent is twice as good as needing mechanical assistance. As with nominal measures, the mathematic operations permissible with ordinal-level data are restricted.

Interval measurement occurs when researchers can rank people on an attribute *and* specify the distance between them. Most psychological tests yield interval-levels measures. For example, the Stanford-Binet intelligence test—a standardized IQ test—is an interval measure. A score of 140 on the test is higher than 120, which, in turn, is higher than 100. Moreover, the difference between 140 and 120 is equivalent to the difference between 120 and 100. Interval measures can be averaged, and many statistical procedures require interval data.

Ratio measurement is the highest level. Ratio scales, unlike interval scales, have a meaningful zero and thus provide information about the absolute magnitude of the attribute. The Fahrenheit scale for measuring temperature (interval measurement) has an arbitrary zero point. Zero on the thermometer does not signify the absence of heat; it would be inappropriate to say that 60°F is twice as hot as 30°F. Many physical measures, however, are ratio measures with a real zero. A person's weight, for example, is a ratio measure. It is meaningful to say that someone who weighs 200 pounds is twice as heavy as someone who weighs 100 pounds. Statistical procedures suitable for interval data are also appropriate for ratio-level data.

Example of different measurement levels:
Buck and colleagues (2012) examined the relationship between self-care and health-related quality of life in older adults with heart failure. The study included nominal-level variables (gender, ethnicity), ordinal-level variables (education, NY Heart Association classification), interval-level variables (scores on the Self-care of Heart Failure Index, quality-of-life scores), and ratio-level measures (age, body mass index).

Researchers usually strive to use the highest levels of measurement possible because higher levels yield more information and are amenable to more powerful analyses.

HOW-TO-TELL TIP: How can you tell a variable's measurement level? A variable is *nominal* if the values could be interchanged (e.g., 1 = male, 2 = female OR 1 = female, 2 = male). A variable is usually *ordinal* if there is a quantitative ordering of values AND if there are a small number of values (e.g., excellent, good, fair, poor). A variable is usually considered *interval* if it is measured with a composite scale or test. A variable is *ratio* level if it makes sense to say that one value is twice as much as another (e.g., 100 mg is twice as much as 50 mg).

Errors of Measurement

Researchers work with fallible measures. The procedures used to take measurements and the people themselves are susceptible to influences that can alter the resulting data. We can think of every piece of quantitative data as consisting of two parts: a true component and an error component. This can be written as follows:

$$\text{Obtained score} = \text{True score} \pm \text{Error}$$

The *obtained* (or *observed) score* could be, for example, a patient's heart rate or score on an anxiety scale. The **true score** is the true value that would be obtained if it were possible to have an infallible measure. The true score is hypothetical—it cannot be known because measures are *not* infallible. The final term in the equation is the **error of measurement**. The difference between true and obtained scores is the result of distorting factors. Some errors are random, while others are systematic, representing a source of *bias*. Some common factors contributing to measurement error include

- *Situational contaminants*. Scores can be affected by the conditions under which they are produced. For example, environmental factors (e.g., temperature, lighting, time of day) can introduce measurement error.
- *Response-set biases*. Enduring characteristics of respondents can interfere with accurate measures (see Chapter 10).
- *Transitory personal factors*. Temporary states such as fatigue, hunger, or mood can influence people's motivation or ability to cooperate, act naturally, or do their best.
- *Item sampling*. Errors can reflect the sampling of items used to measure an attribute. For example, a student's score on a 100-item test of research methods will be influenced somewhat by *which* 100 questions are included.

This list is not exhaustive, but it illustrates that data are susceptible to measurement error from a variety of sources.

RELIABILITY

The reliability of a quantitative measure is a major criterion for assessing its quality. **Reliability** is the consistency with which an instrument measures the attribute. If a scale weighed a person at 120 pounds 1 minute and 150 pounds the next, we would consider it unreliable. The less variation an instrument produces in repeated measurements, the higher its reliability.

Reliability also concerns accuracy. An instrument is reliable to the extent that it captures true scores. A reliable instrument maximizes the true score component and minimizes the error component of an obtained score.

Three aspects of reliability are of interest to quantitative researchers: stability, internal consistency, and equivalence.

Stability

The *stability* of an instrument is the degree to which similar results are obtained on separate occasions. The reliability estimate focuses on the instrument's susceptibility to time-related influences, such as participant fatigue. Stability is assessed through **test–retest reliability** procedures. Researchers administer the measure to a sample twice and then compare the scores.

Suppose we were interested in the stability of a self-report self-esteem scale. Self-esteem is a fairly stable attribute, so we would expect a reliable measure of it to yield similar scores on two different days. To check the instrument's stability, we administer the scale 2 weeks apart to a sample of 10 people. Fictitious data for this example are presented in Table 11.1.

The scores on the two tests are not identical but most differences are small. Researchers compute a **reliability coefficient**, a numeric index that quantifies an instrument's reliability, to assess objectively how small the differences are. Reliability coefficients (designated as *r*) range from .00 to 1.00.* The higher the value, the more reliable (stable) is the measuring instrument. In the example shown in Table 11.1, the reliability coefficient is .95, which is high.

---

*Computation procedures for reliability coefficients are not presented in this textbook, but formulas can be found in Polit (2010). Although reliability coefficients can technically be less than .00 (i.e., a negative value), they are almost invariably a number between .00 and 1.00.

TABLE 11.1 Fictitious Data for Test–Retest Reliability of Self-Esteem Scale

Subject Number	Time 1	Time 2	
1	55	57	
2	49	46	
3	78	74	
4	37	35	
5	44	46	
6	50	56	
7	58	55	
8	62	66	
9	48	50	
10	67	63	$r = .95$

TIP: Reliability coefficients higher than .70 are often considered adequate, but coefficients > .80 are far preferable.

Test–retest reliability is easy to compute, but one problem with this approach is that many traits do change over time, regardless of an instrument's stability. Attitudes, mood, and so forth can be changed by experiences between two measurements. Thus, stability indexes are most appropriate for fairly enduring characteristics, like temperament. Even with such traits, test–retest reliability tends to decline as the interval between the two administrations increases.

Example of test–retest reliability:
Hawthorne and colleagues (2011) assessed the stability of scores on the Spiritual Coping Strategies Scale. The 2-week test–retest reliability was .80 for the English version of the scale and .84 for the Spanish version.

Internal Consistency

Composite scales and tests are usually evaluated for internal consistency. Most scales are composed of items that all measure one attribute and nothing else. On a scale to measure nurses' empathy, it would be inappropriate to include an item that measures resilience. An instrument is **internally consistent** to the extent that its items measure the same trait.

Internal consistency reliability is the most widely used reliability approach in nursing research. This approach is the best way to assess an important source of measurement error in scales, the sampling of items. Internal consistency is evaluated by calculating **coefficient alpha** (also called **Cronbach's alpha**). The normal range of values for this reliability index is from .00 to +1.00. The higher the coefficient, the more accurate (internally consistent) the measure.

Example of internal consistency reliability:
Abubakari and co-researchers (2012) evaluated the Illness Perception Questionnaire—Revised (IPQ-R), a scale that has been widely used with adults of European origin, but not evaluated with people from African cultures. In their study of 221 adults of African descent living in London, the internal consistency reliability on the seven subscales ranged from .61 to .90.

Equivalence

Equivalence, in reliability assessment, primarily concerns the degree to which two or more independent observers or coders agree about scoring on an instrument. If there is a high level of agreement, then the assumption is that measurement errors have been minimized.

The degree of error can be assessed through **interrater** (or *interobserver*) **reliability** procedures, which involve having two or more observers or coders make independent observations. An index of agreement is then calculated with these data to evaluate the strength of the relationship between the ratings. When two independent observers score some phenomenon congruently, the scores are likely to be accurate and reliable.

Example of interrater reliability:
Kosits and Jones (2011) studied interruptions experienced by nurses in an emergency department. They developed an observational form to record nurses' tasks and types of interruption experiences. Interrater reliability was assessed and found to be very high (.825).

Interpretation of Reliability Coefficients

Reliability coefficients are important indicators of data accuracy and quality. Unreliable measures reduce statistical power and hence lower statistical conclusion validity. If data fail to support a hypothesis, one possibility is that the instruments were unreliable—not necessarily that predicted relationships do not exist. Knowing an instrument's reliability is critical in interpreting research results, especially if research hypotheses are not supported.

Various things affect an instrument's reliability. For example, reliability is related to sample variability. The more homogeneous the sample (i.e., the more similar the scores), the lower the reliability coefficient will be. Scales are designed to measure differences, and if participants are similar to one another, it is more difficult for the scales to discriminate reliably among them. A depression scale is less reliable with a homeless group than with a general sample. Also, longer scales with more items tend to be more reliable than shorter ones.

Reliability estimates vary according to the procedure used to obtain them. Estimates of reliability computed by different procedures are not identical, and so it is important to consider which aspect of reliability is most important for the attribute being measured.

Example of different reliability estimates:
Pai and colleagues (2012) studied the relationship between sexual self-concept and sexual health behavior intentions among female adolescents in Taiwan. One scale they used was the Sexual Self-Concept Scale, which has three subscales: sexual arousability, sexual agency, and negative sexual affect. The internal consistency reliabilities of the three subscales were .92, .80, and .68, and the test–retest reliabilities were .74, .85, and .51, respectively.

> **TIP:** Many scales contain two or more subscales that tap distinct, but related, concepts (e.g., a measure of independent functioning might include subscales for motor activities, communication, and socializing). Subscale reliability typically is assessed and, if subscale scores are summed for an overall score, the scale's overall reliability would also be assessed.

VALIDITY

The second major criterion for evaluating a quantitative instrument is its **validity**, the degree to which it measures what it is supposed to measure. When researchers develop a scale to measure hopelessness, how can they be sure that the scores validly reflect this construct and not something else, like depression?

Reliability and validity are not independent qualities of an instrument. *A measuring device that is unreliable cannot be valid.* An instrument cannot validly measure an attribute if it is erratic and inaccurate. An instrument can, however, be reliable without being valid. Suppose we had the idea to assess patients' anxiety by measuring the circumference of their wrists. We could obtain highly accurate measurements of wrist circumferences, but such measures would not be valid indicators of anxiety. Thus, an instrument's high reliability provides no evidence of its validity, but low reliability of a measure *is* evidence of low validity.

> **TIP:** Many studies are designed to evaluate the quality of instruments used by clinicians or researchers. In these **psychometric assessments**, information about the instrument's reliability and validity is carefully documented. As may be recalled from Chapter 2, an important evidence-based practice (EBP) question concerns diagnosis and assessment—whether tests yield accurate information for clinicians.

Like reliability, validity has several aspects, one of which is called face validity. *Face validity* refers to whether an instrument looks as though it is measuring the appropriate construct. Although it is good for an instrument to have face validity, three other aspects of validity are of greater importance: content validity, criterion-related validity, and construct validity.

Content Validity

Content validity concerns the degree to which an instrument has an appropriate sample of items for the construct being measured. Researchers designing a new instrument should begin with a thorough conceptualization of the construct, so that the instrument can capture the full content domain. Such a conceptualization usually comes from a thorough literature review, a concept analysis, or findings from a qualitative inquiry.

An instrument's content validity is based on judgment. There are no totally objective methods for ensuring adequate content coverage, but often a panel of experts are asked to evaluate the content validity of new instruments. Researchers can calculate a **content validity index (CVI)** that indicates the extent of expert agreement. We suggest a CVI value of .90 or higher as the standard for establishing excellence in a scale's content validity.

Example of using a content validity index:
Mitchell and colleagues (2012) developed a scale to measure embarrassment as a barrier to colonoscopies. The content validity of their preliminary 26-item scale was assessed by three experts (two on colorectal screening and one on the concept of embarrassment). The scale's CVI was .93.

Criterion-Related Validity

In **criterion-related validity** assessments, researchers examine the relationship between scores on an instrument and an external criterion. The instrument, whatever attribute it is measuring, is said to be valid if its scores correspond strongly with scores on the criterion. A **validity coefficient** is computed by using a mathematic formula that correlates the two scores. The magnitude of the coefficient is an estimate of the instrument's validity. These coefficients (r) range between .00 and 1.00, with higher values indicating greater criterion-related validity. Coefficients of .70 or higher are desirable.

Sometimes, a distinction is made between two types of criterion-related validity. *Predictive validity* is an instrument's ability to differentiate between people's performances on a *future* criterion. When a nursing school correlates students' high school grades with their subsequent grade-point averages, the predictive validity of high school grades for nursing school performance is being evaluated. *Concurrent validity* is an instrument's ability to distinguish among people who differ presently on a criterion. For example, a scale to differentiate between patients in a psychiatric hospital who could or could not be released could be correlated with nurses' contemporaneous behavioral ratings. The difference between predictive and concurrent validity is simply the timing of obtaining measurements on a criterion.

Validation via the criterion-related approach is most often used in applied situations. Criterion-related validity assists decision-makers by giving them some assurance that their decisions will be fair, appropriate, and, in short, valid.

Example of predictive validity:
Grossbach and Kuncel (2011) conducted a meta-analysis of 31 studies that examined the predictive validity of various nursing school admission variables for performance on the NCLEX-RN exam. Admissions tests (SAT and ACT) had good predictive validity, as did grades during baccalaureate degree nursing education.

Construct Validity

As discussed in Chapter 9, **construct validity** is a key criterion for assessing research quality, and construct validity has most often been linked to measurement. Construct validity in measurement concerns these questions: What is this instrument *really* measuring? and Does it validly measure the abstract concept of interest? Construct validation is essentially a hypothesis-testing endeavor, typically linked to theoretical conceptualizations. In validating a measure of death anxiety, we would be less concerned with its relationship to a criterion than with its correspondence to a cogent conceptualization of death anxiety.

Construct validation can be approached in several ways, but it always involves logical analysis and testing relationships predicted on the basis of well-grounded conceptualizations. Constructs are explicated in terms of other abstract concepts; researchers make predictions about the manner in which the target construct will function in relation to other constructs.

One approach to construct validation is the **known-groups technique**. In this procedure, groups that are expected to differ on the target attribute are administered the instrument, and group scores are compared. For instance, in validating a measure of fear of the labor experience, the scores of primiparas and multiparas could be contrasted. On average, women who had never given birth would likely experience more anxiety than women who had already had children; one might question the validity of the instrument if such group differences did not emerge.

A similar method involves examining predicted relationships. Researchers might reason as follows: According to theory, construct X is related to construct Y; scales A and B are measures of constructs X and Y, respectively; scores on the two scales are related to each other, as predicted by the theory; therefore, it is inferred that A and B are valid measures of X and Y. This logical analysis is fallible, but offers supporting evidence.

Another approach to construct validation uses a statistical procedure called **factor analysis**, which is a method for identifying clusters of related items for a scale. Factor analysis identifies and groups together different measures into a unitary scale based on how participants reacted to the items, rather than based on the researcher's preconceptions.

In summary, construct validation employs logical and empirical procedures. Like content validity, construct validity requires judgments about what the instrument is measuring. Construct validity and criterion-related validity share an empirical component, but, in the latter case, there is a pragmatic, objective criterion with which to compare a measure rather than a second measure of an abstract theoretical construct.

Example of construct validation:
Gillespie, Polit and colleagues (2012) developed and tested the Perceived Perioperative Competence Scale. They used factor analysis to identify six distinct subscales, and tested hypotheses about the relationship between perceived competence and nurses' characteristics, such as years of experience.

Interpretation of Validity

An instrument does not possess or lack validity; it is a question of degree. An instrument's validity is not proved or verified, but rather is supported to a greater or lesser extent by evidence.

Strictly speaking, researchers do not validate an instrument but rather an application of it. A measure of anxiety may be valid for presurgical patients but may not be valid for nursing students on the day of a test. Some instruments may be valid for a wide range of uses, but each use requires new supporting evidence. The more evidence that an instrument is measuring what it is supposed to be measuring, the more confidence people will have in its validity.

TIP: In quantitative studies, research reports usually provide validity and reliability information from an earlier study—often a study conducted by the researcher who developed the scale. If sample characteristics in the original study and the new study are similar, the citation provides valuable information about data quality in the new study. Ideally, researchers should also compute new reliability coefficients for the actual research sample.

SENSITIVITY AND SPECIFICITY

Reliability and validity are key criteria for evaluating quantitative instruments, but for screening and diagnostic instruments—be they self-report, observational, or biophysiologic—sensitivity and specificity need to be evaluated.

Sensitivity is the ability of a measure to correctly identify a "case," that is, to correctly screen in or diagnosis a condition. A measure's sensitivity is its rate of yielding *true positives*. **Specificity** is the measure's ability to correctly identify noncases, that is, to screen *out* those without the condition. Specificity is an instrument's rate of yielding *true negatives*. To assess an instrument's sensitivity and specificity, researchers need a highly reliable and valid criterion of "caseness" against which scores on the instrument can be assessed.

To illustrate, suppose we wanted to test the accuracy of adolescents' self-reports about smoking, and we asked 100 teenagers whether they had smoked a cigarette in the previous 24 hours. The "gold standard" for nicotine consumption is cotinine levels in a body fluid, and so let us assume that we did a urinary cotinine assay. Some fictitious data are shown in Table 11.2.

Sensitivity, in this example, is calculated as the proportion of teenagers who said they smoked *and* who had high concentrations of cotinine, divided by all real smokers as indicated by the urine test. Put another way, it is the true positives divided by all *real* positives. In this case, there was underreporting of smoking and so the sensitivity of the self-report was only .50. Specificity is the proportion of teenagers who accurately reported they did not smoke, or the true negatives, divided by all *real* negatives. In our example, specificity is .83. There was much less overreporting of smoking ("faking bad") than underreporting ("faking good"). Sensitivity and specificity are sometimes reported as percentages rather than proportions, simply by multiplying the proportions by 100.

There is, unfortunately, a tradeoff between an instrument's sensitivity and specificity. When the sensitivity of a scale is increased to include more true positives, the number of false negatives increases. Thus, a critical task is to develop the appropriate *cutoff point*, that is, a score value to distinguish cases and noncases. Sophisticated procedures are used to make such a determination. It is difficult to set standards of acceptability for sensitivity and specificity. Both should be as high as possible, but the cutoff points may need to take into account the financial and emotional costs of having tests with false positive versus false negative results.

TABLE 11.2 Fictitious Data to Illustrate Sensitivity and Specificity

	Urinary Cotinine Level		
Self-Reported Smoking	**Positive (Cotinine >200 ng/mL)**	**Negative (Cotinine 200 ng/mL)**	**Total**
Yes, smoked	**A** (True positive) 20	**B** (False positive) 10	A+B 30
No, did not smoke	**C** (False negative) 20	**D** (True negative) 50	C+D 70
TOTAL	A+C ("Real" positives) 40	B+D ("Real" negatives) 60	A+B+C+D 100

Sensitivity = A/(A+C) = .50
Specificity = D/ (B+D) = .83

TIP: In assessing evidence regarding the accuracy of diagnostic or assessment tests (Diagnosis questions, as shown in Table 1.3, p. 14), Level I evidence comes from systematic reviews of diagnostic studies with certain design features. Level II designs for Diagnosis questions are described in the Chapter Supplement on thePoint website.

CRITIQUING DATA QUALITY IN QUANTITATIVE STUDIES

If data are seriously flawed, the study cannot contribute useful evidence. In drawing conclusions about a study and its evidence, it is important to consider whether researchers have collected data that accurately reflect reality. Research consumers must ask: Can I trust the data? Do the data accurately and validly reflect the concepts under study?

Information about data quality should be provided in every quantitative research report. Reliability estimates are easy to communicate and are often reported. Ideally—especially for composite scales—the report should provide reliability coefficients based on data from the study itself, not just from previous research. Interrater or interobserver reliability is especially crucial for assessing data quality in observational studies. The values of the reliability coefficients should be sufficiently high to support confidence in the findings.

Validity is more difficult to document than reliability. At a minimum, researchers should defend their choice of existing measures based on validity information from the developers, and they should cite the relevant publication. If a study used a screening or diagnostic measure, information should also be provided about its sensitivity and specificity. Box 11.1 provides some guidelines for critiquing aspects of data quality of quantitative measures.

BOX 11.1 Guidelines for Critiquing Data Quality in Quantitative Studies

1. Does the report offer evidence of the reliability of measures? Does the evidence come from the research sample itself, or is it based on other studies? If the latter, is it reasonable to conclude that data quality would be similar for the research sample as for the reliability sample (e.g., are sample characteristics similar)?
2. If reliability is reported, which estimation method was used? Was this method appropriate? Should an alternative or additional method of reliability appraisal have been used? Is the reliability sufficiently high?
3. Does the report offer evidence of the validity of the measures? Does the evidence come from the research sample itself, or is it based on other studies? If the latter, is it reasonable to believe that data quality would be similar for the research sample as for the validity sample (e.g., are the sample characteristics similar)?
4. If validity information is reported, which validity approach was used? Was this method appropriate? Does the validity of the instrument appear to be adequate?
5. If there is no reliability or validity information, what conclusion can you reach about the quality of the data in the study?
6. If a diagnostic or screening tool was used, is information provided about its sensitivity and specificity, and were these qualities adequate?
7. Were the research hypotheses supported? If not, might data quality play a role in the failure to confirm the hypotheses?

RESEARCH EXAMPLES WITH CRITICAL THINKING EXERCISES

In this section, we provide details about the development and testing of an instrument, followed by some questions to guide critical thinking.

Example 1 below is also featured in our *Interactive Critical Thinking Activity* on thePoint website where you can easily record, print, and e-mail your responses to the related questions.

EXAMPLE 1 ● Instrument Development and Psychometric Assessment

Studies: Postpartum Depression Screening Scale (PDSS): Development and psychometric testing (Beck & Gable, 2000); Further validation of the PDSS (Beck & Gable, 2001).

Background: Beck had studied postpartum depression (PPD) in several qualitative studies. Based on her in-depth understanding of PPD, she created a scale to screen for PPD, the PDSS. Working with Gable, a psychometrician, Beck developed, refined, and validated the scale, and had it translated into Spanish.

Scale Development: The PDSS is a Likert scale tapping seven dimensions, such as sleeping/eating disturbances and mental confusion. A 56-item pilot form of the PDSS was initially developed. Beck's findings from her research on PPD and her knowledge of the literature were used to specify the domain and draft items.

Content Validity: Content validity was enhanced by using direct quotes from the qualitative studies as scale items (e.g., "I felt like I was losing my mind"). The pilot scale was subjected to content validation, and feedback from experts led to some revisions.

Construct Validity: The PDSS was administered to a sample of 525 new mothers in six states (Beck & Gable, 2000). The PDSS was finalized as a 35-item scale with seven subscales, each with five items. This version of the PDSS was subjected to factor analyses, which involved a validation of Beck's hypotheses about how individual items mapped onto underlying constructs. In a subsequent study, Beck and Gable (2001) administered the PDSS and other depression scales to 150 new mothers and tested hypotheses about how scores on the PDSS would correlate with scores on other scales, and these analyses suggested good construct validity.

Criterion-Related Validity: In the second study, Beck and Gable correlated scores on the PDSS with an expert clinician's diagnosis of PPD for each woman. The validity coefficient was .70.

Internal Consistency: In both studies, Beck and Gable found that the internal consistency reliability of the PDSS subscales was high, ranging from .83 to .94 in the first study and from .80 to .91 in the second study.

Sensitivity and Specificity: In the second validation study, Beck and Gable assessed the scale's sensitivity and specificity at different cutoff points, using the clinician's diagnosis to establish true positives and true negatives for PPD. The clinician diagnosed 46 of the 150 mothers as having major or minor depression. To illustrate tradeoffs in specificity and sensitivity, the researchers found that a cutoff score of 95 on the PDSS yielded a sensitivity of .41 (only 41% of the women actually diagnosed with PPD would be identified) but a specificity of 1.00 (all cases *without* an actual PPD diagnosis would be accurately screened out). At the other extreme, a cutoff score of 45 had a 1.00 sensitivity but only .28 specificity (i.e., 72% false positive), an unacceptable rate of overdiagnosis. Beck and Gable recommended a cutoff score of 60 for major or minor depression, which would accurately screen in 91% of PPD cases, and would mistakenly screen in 28% who do not have PPD. Using this cutoff point, 85% of their sample would have been correctly classified.

Spanish Translation: Beck (Beck & Gable, 2003, 2005) collaborated with translation experts to develop a Spanish version of the PDSS. The alpha reliability coefficient was .95 for the total Spanish scale, and ranged from .76 to.90 for the subscales. (Note: The PDSS has also been translated into Chinese (Li et al., 2011)).

CRITICAL THINKING EXERCISES

1. Answer the relevant questions from Box 11.1 on page 209 regarding this study.
2. Also consider the following targeted questions:
   a. What is the level of measurement of scores on the PDSS?
   b. The researchers determined that there should be seven subscales to the PDSS. Why do you think this might be the case?
   c. Each item on the PDSS is scored on a 5-point scale from 1 to 5. What is the range of possible scores on the scale, and what is the range of possible scores on each subscale?
   d. Comment on the researchers' credentials for undertaking this study together, and on the appropriateness of their overall effort.
3. In what ways do you think the scale could be used in clinical practice?

EXAMPLE 2 ● Measurement and Data Quality in the Study in Appendix A

Read the "Instruments" subsection from Howell and colleagues' (2007) study ("Anxiety, anger, and blood pressure in children") in Appendix A on page 395–402.

CRITICAL THINKING EXERCISES

1. Answer the relevant questions from Box 11.1 on page 209 regarding this study.
2. Also consider the following targeted questions:
   a. What are some potential sources of measurement error in the measurement of trait anger, trait anxiety, and anger expression in this study?
   b. What is the level of measurement of the key variables in this study?

WANT TO KNOW MORE? A wide variety of resources to enhance your learning and understanding of this chapter are available on thePoint.

- Interactive Critical Thinking Activity
- Chapter Supplement on Level II Evidence for Diagnosis Questions
- Answers to the Critical Thinking Exercises for Example 2
- Student Review Questions
- Full-text online
- Internet Resources with useful websites for Chapter 11

Additional study aids including eight journal articles and related questions are also available in *Study Guide for Essentials of Nursing Research, 8e*.

SUMMARY POINTS

- **Measurement** involves the assignment of numbers to objects or people to represent the amount of an attribute, using a set of rules.
- There are four **levels of measurement**: (1) **nominal measurement**—the classification of attributes into mutually exclusive categories; (2) **ordinal measurement**—the ranking of people based on their relative standing on an attribute; (3) **interval measurement**—indicating not only people's rank order but the distance between them; and (4) **ratio measurement**—distinguished from interval measurement by having a rational zero point.
- *Obtained scores* from an instrument consist of a **true score** component (the value that would be obtained for a hypothetical perfect measure of the attribute) and an error component, or **error of measurement**, that represents measurement inaccuracies.
- Sources of measurement error include situational contaminants, response-set biases, item sampling, and transitory personal factors, such as fatigue.
- **Reliability**, a primary criterion for assessing a quantitative instrument, is the degree of consistency or accuracy with which an instrument measures an attribute. The higher the reliability of an instrument, the lower the amount of error in obtained scores.
- There are different methods for assessing an instrument's reliability and for computing a **reliability coefficient**. Reliability coefficients typically range from .00 to 1.00, and should be at least .70 (but preferably > .80) to be considered satisfactory.
- The *stability* aspect of reliability, which concerns the extent to which an instrument yields similar results on two administrations, is evaluated by **test–retest procedures**.
- **Internal consistency** reliability, which refers to the extent to which all the instrument's items are measuring the same attribute, is usually assessed with **Cronbach's alpha**.
- When the reliability assessment focuses on *equivalence* between observers or coders assigning scores, estimates of **interrater** (or *interobserver*) **reliability** are obtained.
- **Validity** is the degree to which an instrument measures what it is supposed to measure.
- **Content validity** concerns the sampling adequacy of the content being measured. Expert ratings on the relevance of items can be used to compute a **content validity index (CVI)**.
- **Criterion-related validity** (which includes both *predictive validity* and *concurrent validity*) focuses on the correlation between an instrument and an outside criterion.
- **Construct validity**, an instrument's adequacy in measuring the targeted construct, involves hypothesis-testing. One construct validation method, the **known-groups technique**, contrasts scores of groups hypothesized to differ on the attribute; another is **factor analysis**, a statistical procedure that identifies items that "go together."
- Sensitivity and specificity are important criteria for screening and diagnostic instruments. **Sensitivity** is the instrument's ability to identify a case correctly (i.e., its rate of yielding true positives). **Specificity** is the instrument's ability to identify noncases correctly (i.e., its rate of yielding true negatives).
- A **psychometric assessment** of a new instrument is undertaken with most scales to gather evidence about validity, reliability, and other assessment criteria.

REFERENCES FOR CHAPTER 11

Abubakari, A., Jones, M., Lauder, W., Kirk, A., Devendra, D., & Anderson, J. (2012). Psychometric properties of the Revised Illness Perception Questionnaire: Factor structure and reliability among African-origin populations with type 2 diabetes. *International Journal of Nursing Studies, 49*(6), 672–681.

Beck, C. T., & Gable, R. K. (2000). Postpartum Depression Screening Scale: Development and psychometric testing. *Nursing Research, 49*, 272–282.

Beck, C. T., & Gable, R. K. (2001). Further validation of the Postpartum Depression Screening Scale. *Nursing Research, 50*, 155–164.

Beck, C. T., & Gable, R. K. (2003). Postpartum Depression Screening Scale: Spanish version. *Nursing Research, 52*, 296–306.

Beck, C. T., & Gable, R. K. (2005). Screening performance of the Postpartum Depression Screening Scale—Spanish version. *Journal of Transcultural Nursing, 16*(4), 331–338.

Buck, H., Lee, C., Moser, D., Albert, N., Lennie, T., Bentley, B., et al. (2012). Relationship between self-care and health-related quality of life in older adults with moderate to advanced heart failure. *Journal of Cardiovascular Nursing, 27*, 8–15.

Gillespie, B., Polit, D., Hamlin, L., & Chaboyer, W. (2012). Developing a model of competence in the operating theater: Psychometric validation of the perceived perioperative competence scale-revised. *International Journal of Nursing Studies, 49*, 90–101.

Grossbach, A., & Kuncel, N. (2011). The predictive validity of nursing admission measures for performance on the National Council Licensure Examination. *Journal of Professional Nursing, 27*, 124–128.

Hawthorne, D., Youngblut, J., & Brooten, D. (2011). Psychometric evaluation of the Spanish and English versions of the Spiritual Coping Strategies Scale. *Journal of Nursing Measurement, 19*, 46–54.

Kosits, L., & Jones, K. (2011). Interruptions experienced by registered nurses working in the emergency department. *Journal of Emergency Nursing, 37*, 3–8.

Li, L., Liu, F., Zhang, H., Wang, L., & Chen, X. (2011). Chinese version of the Postpartum Depression Screening Scale. *Nursing Research, 60*, 231–239.

Mitchell, K., Rawl, S., Champion, V., Jeffries, P., & Welch, J. (2012). Development and psychometric testing of the Colonoscopy Embarrassment Scale. *Western Journal of Nursing Research, 34*(4), 548–564.

Pai, H.C., Lee, S., & Yen, W. (2012). The effect of sexual self-concept on sexual health behaviour intentions. *Journal of Advanced Nursing, 68*, 47–55.

Polit, D. F. (2010). *Statistics and data analysis for nursing research* (2nd ed.). Upper Saddle River, NJ: Pearson.

chapter 12

Statistical Analysis of Quantitative Data

LEARNING OBJECTIVES

On completing this chapter, you will be able to:

- Describe characteristics of frequency distributions, and identify and interpret various descriptive statistics
- Describe the logic and purpose of parameter estimation, and interpret confidence intervals
- Describe the logic and purpose of statistical tests, and interpret *p* values
- Specify the appropriate applications for *t*-tests, analysis of variance, chi-squared tests, and correlation coefficients, and interpret the meaning of the calculated statistics
- Understand the results of simple statistical procedures described in a research report
- Define new terms in the chapter

KEY TERMS

Absolute risk (AR)
Absolute risk reduction (ARR)
Alpha (α)
Analysis of covariance (ANCOVA)
Analysis of variance (ANOVA)
Beta (β)
Central tendency
Chi-squared test
Confidence interval (CI)
Correlation
Correlation coefficient
Correlation matrix
Crosstabulation
d statistic
Degrees of freedom
Descriptive statistics
Effect size
F ratio
Frequency distribution
Hypothesis testing
Inferential statistics
Level of significance
Logistic regression
Mean
Median
Mode
Multiple regression
Multivariate statistics
N
Negative relationship
Negative skew
Nonsignificant result (NS)
Odds ratio (OR)
p value
Pearson's *r*
Positive relationship
Positive skew
Post hoc test
Predictor variable
r
R^2
Range
Repeated measures ANOVA
Risk ratio (RR)
Sampling distribution of the mean
Skewed distribution
Standard deviation
Standard error of the mean (SEM)
Statistical test
Statistically significant
Symmetric distribution
Test statistic
t-test
Type I error
Type II error
Variability

Data collected in a study need to be systematically analyzed. This chapter describes procedures for using statistics to analyze quantitative data.

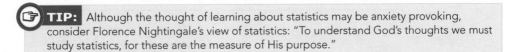

TIP: Although the thought of learning about statistics may be anxiety provoking, consider Florence Nightingale's view of statistics: "To understand God's thoughts we must study statistics, for these are the measure of His purpose."

DESCRIPTIVE STATISTICS

Statistical procedures enable researchers to organize and interpret numeric information. Statistics are either descriptive or inferential. **Descriptive statistics** are used to synthesize and describe data. When indexes such as averages and percentages are calculated with data from a population, they are **parameters**. A descriptive index from a sample is a **statistic**. Most research questions are about parameters; researchers calculate statistics to estimate parameters and use **inferential statistics** to make inferences about the population.

A set of data for a variable can be described in terms of three characteristics: the shape of the distribution of values, central tendency, and variability.

Frequency Distributions

Data that are not organized are overwhelming. Without some structure, even broad trends are hard to discern. Consider the 60 numbers in Table 12.1. Let us assume that these numbers are the scores of 60 preoperative patients on a six-item scale of anxiety. Visual inspection of these numbers provides little insight on patients' anxiety.

Frequency distributions impose order on numeric data. A **frequency distribution** is a systematic arrangement of values from lowest to highest, together with a count or percentage of how many times each value occurred. A frequency distribution for the 60 anxiety scores (Table 12.2, p. 128) makes it easy to see the highest and lowest scores, the most common score, where the scores clustered, and how many patients were in the sample (total sample size is designated as ***N*** in research reports). None of this was apparent before the data were organized.

TABLE 12.1 Patients' Anxiety Scores

22	27	25	19	24	25	23	29	24	20
26	16	20	26	17	22	24	18	26	28
15	24	23	22	21	24	20	25	18	27
24	23	16	25	30	29	27	21	23	24
26	18	30	21	17	25	22	24	29	28
20	25	26	24	23	19	27	28	25	26

TABLE 12.2 Frequency Distribution of Patients' Anxiety Scores

Score	Frequency	Percentage (%)
15	1	1.7
16	2	3.3
17	2	3.3
18	3	5.0
19	2	3.3
20	4	6.7
21	3	5.0
22	4	6.7
23	5	8.3
24	9	15.0
25	7	11.7
26	6	10.0
27	4	6.7
28	3	5.0
29	3	5.0
30	2	3.3
	$N = 60$	100.0%

Frequency data can be displayed graphically in a *frequency polygon* (Fig. 12.1). In such graphs, scores typically are on the horizontal line, with the lowest value on the left, and frequency counts or percentages are on the vertical line. Data distributions can be described by their shapes. **Symmetric distribution** occurs if, when folded over, the two halves of a frequency polygon would be superimposed (Fig. 12.2). In an asymmetric or **skewed distribution**, the peak is off center, and one tail is longer than the other. When the longer tail points to the right, the distribution has a **positive skew**, as in the first graph of Figure 12.3. Personal income is a positively skewed attribute. Most people have moderate incomes, with only a few people with very high incomes at the right end of the distribution. If the longer tail points to the left, the distribution has a **negative skew**, as in the second graph in Figure 12.3. Age at death is negatively skewed: the bulk of people are at the far right end of the distribution, with relatively few people dying at an early age.

Another aspect of a distribution's shape concerns how many peaks it has. A *unimodal distribution* has one peak (graph A of Figure 12.2), whereas a *multimodal distribution* has two or more peaks—that is, two or more values of high frequency. A multimodal distribution with two peaks is *bimodal* (graph B of Figure 12.2).

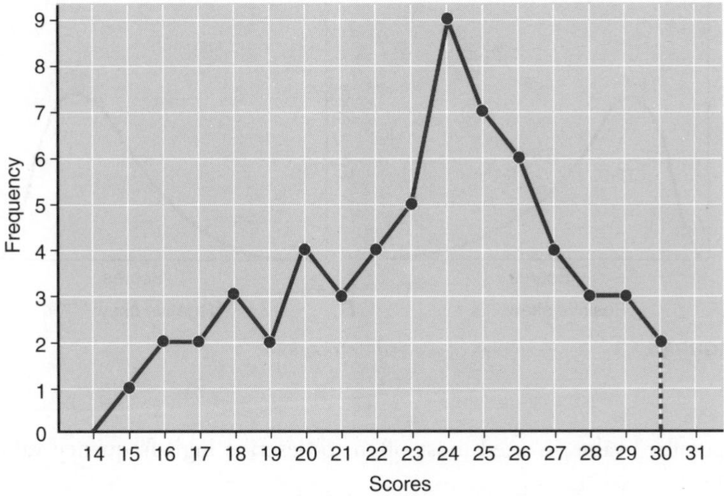

FIGURE 12.1 ● Frequency polygon of patients' anxiety scores.

A special distribution called the **normal distribution** (*a bell-shaped curve*) is symmetric, unimodal, and not very peaked (graph A of Figure 12.2). Many human attributes (e.g., height, intelligence) approximate a normal distribution.

Central Tendency

Frequency distributions help to clarify patterns, but often a pattern is less useful than an overall summary. Researchers usually ask a question such as, "What is the *average* oxygen consumption of myocardial infarction patients during bathing?" Such a question seeks a single number to represent a distribution of values. Indexes of "typicalness" are called measures of **central tendency**. Researchers avoid using the term *average* because there are three indexes of central tendency: the mode, the median, and the mean.

- **Mode**: The mode is the number that occurs most frequently in a distribution. In the following distribution, the mode is 53:

50 51 51 52 53 53 53 53 54 55 56

The value of 53 occurred four times, a higher frequency than for other numbers. The mode of the patients' anxiety scores in Table 12.2 was 24. The mode, which identifies the

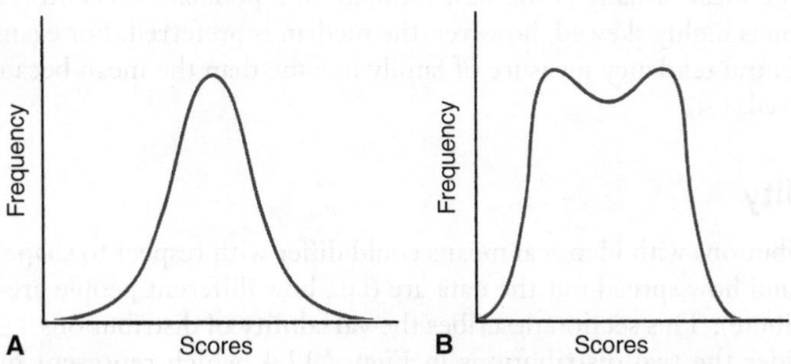

FIGURE 12.2 ● Examples of symmetric distributions.

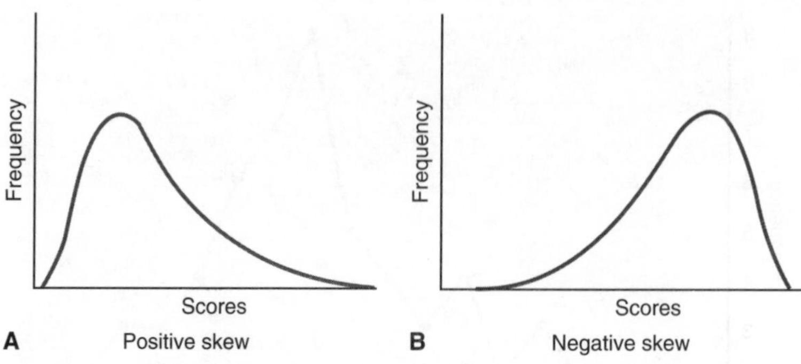

FIGURE 12.3 ● Examples of skewed distributions.

most "popular" value, is used most often to describe high-frequency values for nominal measures.

- **Median**: The median is the point in a distribution that divides scores in half. Consider the following set of values:

2 2 3 3 4 5 6 7 8 9

The value that divides the cases in half is midway between 4 and 5, and thus 4.5 is the median. The median for the anxiety scores in Table 12.2 is 24, the same as the mode. The median does not take into account individual values and so is insensitive to extremes. In the above set of numbers, if the value of 9 were changed to 99, the median would remain 4.5. Because of this property, the median is the preferred index to describe a highly skewed distribution. In research articles, the median may be abbreviated as *Md* or *Mdn*.

- **Mean**: The mean equals the sum of all values divided by the number of participants—what people refer to as the average. The mean of the patients' anxiety scores is 23.4 (1,405 ÷ 60). As another example, here are the weights of eight people:

85 109 120 135 158 177 181 195

In this example, the mean is 145. Unlike the median, the mean is affected by the value of every score. If we exchanged the 195-lb person for one weighing 275 lb, the mean would increase from 145 to 155 lb. In research articles, the mean is often symbolized as *M* or $\bar{X}$ (e.g., $\bar{X} = 145$).

For interval-level or ratio-level measurements, the mean is usually the statistic reported. Of the three indexes, the mean is the most stable: if repeated samples were drawn from a population, the means would fluctuate less than the modes or medians. Because of its stability, the mean usually is the best estimate of a population's central tendency. When a distribution is highly skewed, however, the median is preferred. For example, the median is a better central tendency measure of family income than the mean because income is positively skewed.

Variability

Two distributions with identical means could differ with respect to shape (e.g., how skewed they are) and how spread out the data are (i.e., how different people are from one another on an attribute). This section describes the **variability** of distributions.

Consider the two distributions in Figure 12.4, which represent hypothetical scores for students from two schools on an IQ test. Both distributions have a mean of 100, but

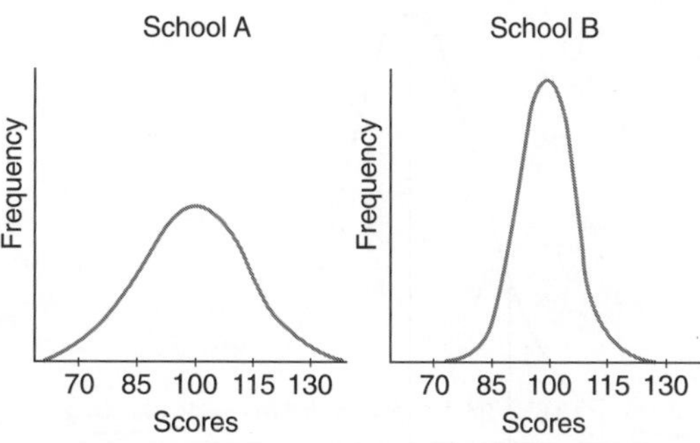

FIGURE 12.4 ● Two distributions of different variability.

the patterns are different. School A has a wide range of scores, with some below 70 and some above 130. In school B, by contrast, there are few low or high scores. School A is more *heterogeneous* (i.e., more varied) than school B, and school B is more *homogeneous* than school A. Researchers compute an index of variability to express the extent to which scores in a distribution differ from one another. Two common indexes are the range and standard deviation.

- **Range**: The range is the highest score minus the lowest score in a distribution. In our anxiety score example, the range is 15 (30–15). In the distributions in Figure 12.4, the range for school A is about 80 (140–60), whereas the range for school B is about 50 (125–75). The chief virtue of the range is ease of computation. Because it is based on only two scores, however, the range is unstable: from sample to sample drawn from a population, the range can fluctuate greatly. The range is used largely as a gross descriptive index.
- **Standard deviation**: The most widely used variability index is the standard deviation. Like the mean, the standard deviation is calculated based on every value in a distribution. The standard deviation summarizes the *average* amount of deviation of values from the mean.* In the anxiety scale example, the standard deviation is 3.725.** In research reports, the standard deviation may be abbreviated as *s* or *SD*.

TIP: Occasionally, *SD*s are shown in relation to the mean without a formal label. For example, the anxiety scores might be shown as $M = 23.4$ (3.7) or $M = 23.4 \pm 3.7$, where 23.4 is the mean and 3.7 is the standard deviation.

A standard deviation (*SD*) is more difficult to interpret than the range. For the *SD* of anxiety scores, you might ask, 3.725 *what?* What does the number mean? We can answer these questions from several angles. First, the *SD* is an index of how variable scores in a distribution are and so if (for example) male and female patients had means of 23 on the anxiety scale, but their *SD*s were 7 and 3, respectively, we would know that females were more homogeneous (i.e., their scores were more similar to one another).

*Formulas for computing the standard deviation, as well as other statistics discussed in this chapter, are not shown in this textbook. The emphasis here is on helping you to understand statistical applications. Polit (2010) can be consulted for computation formulas.

**Another index of variability is the variance which is simply the value of the standard deviation squared. In the example of patients' anxiety scores, the variance is 3.725^2, or 13.88.

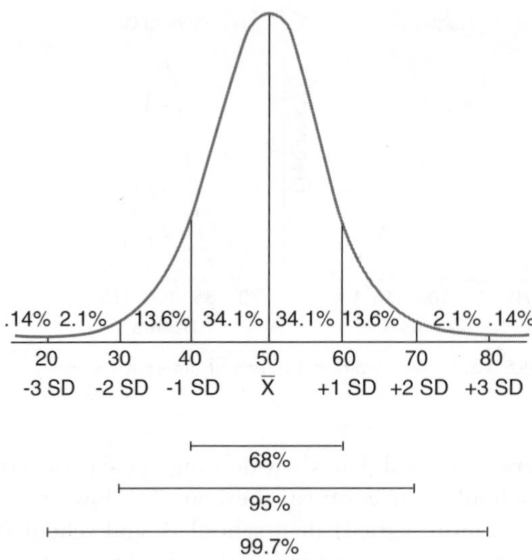

FIGURE 12.5 ● Standard deviations in a normal distribution.

The *SD* represents the *average* of deviations from the mean. The mean tells us the best value for summarizing an entire distribution, and an *SD* tells us how much, on average, the scores deviate from the mean. In the anxiety scale example, scores deviated by an average of just under 4 points. A standard deviation can be interpreted as our degree of error when we use a mean to describe an entire sample.

In normal and near-normal distributions, there are roughly three *SD*s above and below the mean. For a normal distribution with a mean of 50 and an *SD* of 10 (Fig. 12.5), a fixed percentage of cases fall within certain distances from the mean. Sixty-eight percent of all cases fall within 1 *SD* above and below the mean. Thus, nearly 7 of 10 scores are between 40 and 60. In a normal distribution, 95% of the scores fall within 2 *SD*s of the mean. Only a handful of cases—about 2% at each extreme—lie more than 2 *SD*s from the mean. Using this figure, we can see that a person with a score of 70 achieved a higher score than about 98% of the sample.

TIP: Descriptive statistics (percentages, means, standard deviations, and so on) are used for various purposes, but they are most often used to summarize sample characteristics, describe key research variables, and document methodological features (e.g., response rates). They are seldom used to answer research questions—inferential statistics usually are used for this purpose.

Example of descriptive statistics:

Table 12.3 presents descriptive statistics from Padden and colleagues' (2011) study of stress, coping, and well-being in military spouses during deployment separation. The table shows, for three self-report scale scores, the theoretical and actual range of scores, means, and *SD*s. We can see that the scale scores were heterogeneous, with wide ranges. Scores on the Health Survey appear skewed: the mean (69.6) was much higher than the midpoint between the lowest and highest value (42.5), suggesting a negative skew.

TABLE 12.3 Example of Descriptive Statistics: Scores on Selected Scales of Stress, Coping, and Well-Being in Military Spouses During Deployment Separation (N = 105)[a]

	Scale Range	Range of Actual Scores	*M (SD)*
Perceived Stress Scale scores	0–40	1–34	17.5 (6.6)
Jalowiec Coping Scale scores	0–180	48–150	101.1 (19.1)
Rand Health Survey, total scores	0–100	14–99	69.9 (17.9)

[a]Adapted from Padden, D., Connors, R., & Agazia, J. (2011). Stress, coping, and well-being in military spouses during deployment separation. *Western Journal of Nursing Research, 33,* 247–267.

Bivariate Descriptive Statistics

So far, our discussion has focused on *univariate* (one-variable) *descriptive statistics*. A mean or *SD* describe one variable at a time. *Bivariate* (two-variable) *descriptive statistics* describe relationships between two variables.

Crosstabulations

A **crosstabs table** (or *contingency table)* is a two-dimensional frequency distribution in which the frequencies of two variables are **crosstabulated.** Suppose we had data on patients' sex and whether they were nonsmokers, light smokers (less than one pack of cigarettes a day), or heavy smokers (one or more packs a day). The question is whether men smoke more heavily than women, or vice versa (i.e., whether there is a *relationship* between smoking and sex). Fictitious data for this example are shown in Table 12.4. Six **cells** are created by placing one variable (sex) along one dimension and the other variable (smoking status) along the other dimension. After subjects' data are allocated to the appropriate cells, percentages are computed. The crosstab allows us to see at a glance that women were more likely than men

TABLE 12.4 Crosstabs Table for Relationship Between Sex and Smoking Status

	Sex					
	Women		Men		Total	
Smoking Status	***n***	**%**	***n***	**%**	***n***	**%**
Nonsmoker	10	45.4	6	27.3	16	36.4
Light smoker	8	36.4	8	36.4	16	36.4
Heavy smoker	4	18.2	8	36.4	12	27.3
TOTAL	22	100.0	22	100.0	44	100.0

to be nonsmokers (45.4% vs. 27.3%) and less likely to be heavy smokers (18.2% vs. 36.4%). Crosstabs are used with nominal data or ordinal data with few values. In this example, sex is nominal, and smoking, as defined, is ordinal.

Correlation

Relationships between two variables can be described by **correlation** methods. The correlation question is: To what extent are two variables related to each other? For example, to what degree are anxiety scores and blood pressure values related? This question can be answered by calculating a **correlation coefficient**, which describes *intensity* and *direction* of a relationship.

Two variables that are related are height and weight: tall people tend to weigh more than short people. The relationship between height and weight would be a *perfect relationship* if the tallest person in a population was the heaviest, the second tallest person was the second heaviest, and so on. A correlation coefficient indicates how "perfect" a relationship is. Possible values for a correlation coefficient range from –1.00 through .00 to +1.00. If height and weight were perfectly correlated, the correlation coefficient would be 1.00 (the actual correlation coefficient is in the vicinity of .50 to .60 for a general population). Height and weight have a **positive relationship** because greater height tends to be associated with greater weight.

When two variables are unrelated, the correlation coefficient is zero. One might anticipate that women's shoe size is unrelated to their intelligence. Women with large feet are as likely to perform well on IQ tests as those with small feet. The correlation coefficient summarizing such a relationship would be in the vicinity of .00.

Correlation coefficients between .00 and –1.00 express a **negative** (*inverse*) **relationship**. When two variables are inversely related, increments in one variable are associated with decrements in the second. For example, there is a negative correlation between depression and self-esteem. This means that, on average, people with *high* self-esteem tend to be *low* on depression. If the relationship were perfect (i.e., if the person with the highest self-esteem score had the lowest depression score and so on), then the correlation coefficient would be –1.00. In actuality, the relationship between depression and self-esteem is moderate—usually in the vicinity of –.40 or –.50. Note that the higher the *absolute value* of the coefficient (i.e., the value disregarding the sign), the stronger the relationship. A correlation of –.80, for instance, is much stronger than a correlation of +.20.

The most commonly used correlation index is **Pearson's r** (the *product–moment correlation coefficient)*, which is computed with interval or ratio measures. There are no fixed guidelines on what should be interpreted as strong or weak relationships, because it depends on the variables. If we measured patients' body temperature orally and rectally, an r of .70 between the two measurements would be low. For most psychosocial variables (e.g., stress and depression), however, an r of .70 would be high. Perfect correlations (+1.00 and –1.00) are rare.

TIP: Validity coefficients, such as those described in Chapter 11, are usually calculated using Pearson's correlation coefficients.

In research articles, correlation coefficients are sometimes shown in a two-dimensional **correlation matrix**, in which variables are displayed in both rows and columns. To read a correlation matrix, one finds the row for one variable and reads across until the row intersects with the column for another variable, as described in the following example.

Example of a correlation matrix:
Greenslade and Jimmieson (2011) studied the relationship between organizational factors and patient satisfaction. They hypothesized that patient satisfaction is influenced by the setting in which they are treated. Table 12.5, adapted from their report, shows a correlation matrix for some of the variables. This table lists, on the left, four variables: Variable 1: the service climate of the nursing unit in which the patient was cared for, Variable 2: effectiveness of nurses' task performance (e.g., administering medications), Variable 3: effectiveness of nurses' contextual performance (e.g., making special arrangements for patients), and Variable 4: patient satisfaction. The numbers in the top row, from 1 to 4, correspond to the four variables: 1 is service climate, and so on. The correlation matrix shows, in column 1, the correlation coefficient between service climate and all variables. At the intersection of row 1-column 1, we find 1.00, which indicates that service climate scores are perfectly correlated with themselves. The next entry in column 1 is the value of *r* between service climate and task performance. The value of .31 (which can be read as +.31) indicates a modest, positive relationship between these two variables: effective performance tends to be higher in units with a positive service climate. The bottom entry in column 1 shows a positive correlation between service climate and patient satisfaction (.42), indicating greater satisfaction in units with a positive service climate.

Describing Risk

The evidence-based practice (EBP) movement has made decision-making based on research findings an important issue. Several descriptive indexes can be used to facilitate such decision-making. Many of these indexes involve calculating changes in risk—for example, a change in risk after exposure to a potentially beneficial intervention.

In this section, we focus on describing dichotomous outcomes (e.g., had a fall/did not have a fall) in relation to exposure or nonexposure to a beneficial treatment or protective factor. This situation results in a 2 × 2 crosstabs table with four cells. The four cells in the crosstabs table in Table 12.6 are labeled so that various indexes can be explained. *Cell a* is the number with an undesirable outcome (e.g., a fall) in an intervention/protected group; *cell b* is the number with a desirable outcome (e.g., no fall) in an intervention/protected group; and *cells c* and *d* are the two outcome possibilities for a nontreated or unprotected group. We can now explain the meaning and calculation of some indexes of interest to clinicians.

Absolute Risk

Absolute risk can be computed for those exposed to an intervention or protective factor, and for those not exposed. **Absolute risk (AR)** is simply the proportion of people who

TABLE 12.5 Example of a Correlation Matrix: Study of Organizational Factors Affecting Patient Satisfaction (*N* = 172)

Variable	1	2	3	4
1. Service climate in nursing unit	1.00			
2. Effectiveness of nurses' task performance	.31	1.00		
3. Effectiveness of nurses' contextual performance	.22	.52	1.00	
4. Global patient satisfaction	.42	.49	.26	1.00

Adapted from Table 1 of Greenslade, J., & Jimmieson, N. (2011). Organizational factors impacting on patient satisfaction. *International Journal of Nursing Studies, 48*, 1188–1198.

TABLE 12.6 Indexes of Risk and Association in a 2 × 2 Table

Exposure to an Intervention or Protective Factor	Outcome		Total
	Undesirable Outcome	**Desirable Outcome**	
Yes (Exposed)	a	b	a + b
No (Not Exposed)	c	d	c + d
TOTAL	a + c	b + d	a + b + c + d

Absolute Risk, exposed group (AR_E) $= a / (a + b)$

Absolute Risk, non-exposed group (AR_{NE}) $= c / (c + d)$

Absolute Risk Reduction (ARR) $= (c / (c + d)) - (a / (a + b))$ Or $AR_{NE} - AR_E$

Odds Ratio (OR) $= \frac{ad}{bc}$ Or $\frac{a/b}{c/d}$

experienced an undesirable outcome in each group. To illustrate, suppose 200 smokers were randomly assigned to a smoking cessation intervention or to a control group (Table 12.7). The outcome is smoking status 3 months after the intervention. In this example, the absolute risk of continued smoking is .50 in the intervention group and .80 in the control group. Without the intervention, 20% of those in the experimental group would presumably have stopped smoking anyway, but the intervention boosted the rate to 50%.

TABLE 12.7 Hypothetical Data for Smoking Cessation Intervention Example

Exposure to Intervention	Outcome		Total
	Continued Smoking	**Stopped Smoking**	
Yes (Experimental Group)	50	50	100
No (Control Group)	80	20	100
TOTAL	130	70	200

Absolute Risk, exposed group (AR_E) $= 50 / 100 = .50$

Absolute Risk, non-exposed group (AR_{NE}) $= 80 / 100 = .80$

Absolute Risk Reduction (ARR) $= .80 - .50 = .30$

Odds Ratio (OR) $= \frac{(50/50)}{(80/20)} = .25$

Absolute Risk Reduction

The **absolute risk reduction (ARR)** index, a comparison of the two risks, is computed by subtracting the absolute risk for the exposed group from the absolute risk for the unexposed group. This index is the estimated proportion of people who would be spared the undesirable outcome through exposure to an intervention or protective factor. In our example, the value of ARR is .30: 30% of the control group subjects would presumably have stopped smoking if they had received the intervention, over and above the 20% who stopped without it.

Odds Ratio

The odds ratio is a widely reported risk index. The *odds*, in this context, is the proportion of subjects *with* the adverse outcome relative to those *without* it. In our example, the odds of continued smoking for the intervention group is 1.0: 50 (the number who continued smoking) divided by 50 (the number who stopped). The odds for the control group is 80 divided by 20, or 4.0. The **odds ratio (OR)** is the ratio of these two odds—.25 in our example. The estimated odds of continuing to smoke are one-fourth as high for those in the intervention group as for those in the control group. Turned around, we could say that the estimated odds of continued smoking is four times higher among smokers who do not get the intervention as among those who do.

Example of odds ratios:
Matthews and colleagues (2011) examined factors associated with smoking risk among sexual minority women (lesbian, bisexual, transgender). The OR for smoking was, for example, 2.21 among those with any recreational drug use in the prior 6 months. The risk of smoking was also higher among those who frequented lesbian/gay clubs once a week or more (OR = 2.60).

TIP: An index known as the **risk ratio** (RR) is another risk index. The RR (also known as *relative risk*) is the estimated proportion of the original risk of an adverse outcome (in our example, continued smoking) that persists when people are exposed to the intervention. In our example, RR is .625 (.50/.80): the risk of continued smoking is estimated as 62.5% of what it would have been without the intervention.

INTRODUCTION TO INFERENTIAL STATISTICS

Descriptive statistics are useful for summarizing data, but researchers usually do more than describe. **Inferential statistics**, based on the *laws of probability*, provide a means for drawing conclusions about a population, given data from a sample.

Sampling Distributions

When estimating population attributes from a sample, the sample should be representative, and random sampling is the best means to secure such a sample. Inferential statistics are based on the assumption of random sampling from populations—although this assumption is widely violated.

Even with random sampling, however, sample characteristics are seldom identical to those of the population. Suppose we had a population of 50,000 nursing school applicants whose mean score on an entrance exam was 500 with a standard deviation of 100. Assume we do not know these parameters, but must estimate them based on scores from a random sample of 25 applicants. Should we expect a mean of exactly 500 and an *SD* of 100 for the sample? It would be improbable to obtain identical values. Our sample mean might be, for example, 505. If we drew a completely new random sample of 25 applicants and computed the mean, we might obtain a value of 497. Sample statistics fluctuate and are unequal to the parameter because of sampling error. Researchers need a way to assess whether sample statistics are good estimates of population parameters.

To understand the logic of inferential statistics, we must perform a mental exercise. Consider drawing a sample of 25 students from the population of applicants, calculating a mean score, replacing the students, and drawing a new sample. If we drew 5,000 samples, we would have 5,000 means (data points) that we could use to construct a frequency polygon (Fig. 12.6). This distribution is called a ***sampling distribution of the mean***. A sampling distribution is theoretical: in practice no one *actually* draws consecutive samples from a population and plots their means. Statisticians have shown that (1) sampling distributions of means are normally distributed and (2) the mean of a sampling distribution equals the population mean. In our example, the mean of the sampling distribution is 500, the same as the population mean.

Remember that when scores are normally distributed, 68% of the cases fall between +1 *SD* and −1 *SD* from the mean. For a sampling distribution of means, the probability is 68 out of 100 that a randomly drawn sample mean lies between +1 *SD* and −1 *SD* of the population mean. The problem is to determine the *SD* of the sampling distribution—called the **standard error of the mean** (or **SEM**). The word *error* signifies that the sample means contain some error as estimates of the population mean. The smaller the standard error (i.e., the less variable the sample means), the more accurate are the means as estimates of the population value.

Because no one actually constructs a sampling distribution, how can its standard deviation be computed? Statisticians have a formula for estimating the SEM from data from a single sample, using two pieces of information: the *SD* for the sample and sample size. In the present example, the SEM is 20 (Fig. 12.6), which is an estimate of how much sampling error there would be from one sample mean to another in an infinite number of samples of 25 applicants.

We can now estimate the probability of drawing a sample with a certain mean. With a sample size of 25 and a population mean of 500, the chances are 95 out of 100 that a sample mean would fall between 460 and 540—2 *SD*s above and below the mean. Only 5 times

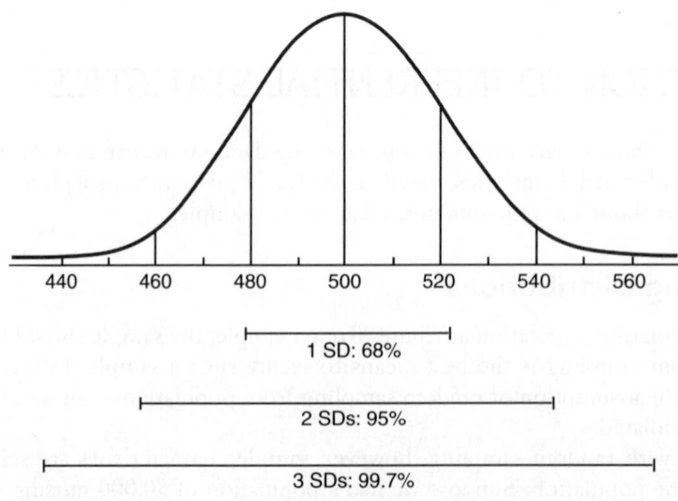

FIGURE 12.6 ● Sampling distribution of a mean.

out of 100 would the mean of a random sample of 25 applicants be greater than 540 or less than 460. In other words, only 5 times out of 100 would we be likely to draw a sample whose mean deviates from the population mean by more than 40 points.

Because the SEM is partly a function of sample size, we need only increase sample size to increase the estimate's accuracy. Suppose we used a sample of 100 applicants to estimate the population mean. With this many students, the SEM would be 10, not 20. The probability would be 95 in 100 that a sample mean would be between 480 and 520. The chances of drawing a sample with a mean very different from that of the population are reduced as sample size increases—large numbers promote the likelihood that extreme values will cancel each other out.

You may wonder why you need to learn about these abstract statistical notions. Consider, though, that we are talking about how likely it is that a researcher's results are accurate. As an intelligent consumer, you need to evaluate critically how believable research evidence is so that you can decide whether to incorporate it into your nursing practice. The concepts underlying the standard error are important in such an evaluation and are related to an issue we stressed in Chapter 10 on sampling: the larger the sample size, the greater is the degree of accuracy.

Parameter Estimation

Statistical inference consists of two techniques: parameter estimation and hypothesis testing. *Parameter estimation* is used to estimate a population parameter—for example, a mean, a proportion, or a mean difference between two groups (e.g., men vs. women). *Point estimation* involves calculating a single statistic to estimate the parameter. To continue with the earlier example, if we calculated the mean entrance exam score for a sample of 25 applicants and found that it was 510, then this would be the point estimate of the population mean.

Point estimates convey no information about the estimate's margin of error. *Interval estimation* of a parameter is useful because it indicates a range of values within which the parameter has a specified probability of lying. With interval estimation, researchers construct a **confidence interval (CI)** around the estimate; the upper and lower limits are called *confidence limits*. The confidence interval around a sample mean establishes a range of values for the population value and the probability of being right—the estimate is made with a certain degree of confidence. By convention, researchers use either a 95% or a 99% confidence interval.

TIP: Confidence intervals (CIs) address a key EBP question for appraising evidence, as presented in Box 2.1 (p. 32): How *precise* is the estimate of effects?

Calculating confidence limits around a mean involves the SEM. As shown in Figure 12.6, 95% of the scores in a normal distribution lie within about 2 *SD*s (more precisely, 1.96 *SD*s) from the mean. In our example, if the point estimate for mean scores is 510 and the *SD* is 100, the SEM for a sample of 25 would be 20. We can build a 95% confidence interval using this formula: $95\%\ \text{CI} = (\bar{X} \pm 1.96 \times \text{SEM})$. That is, the confidence is 95% that the population mean lies between the values equal to 1.96 times the SEM, above and below the sample mean. In our example, we would obtain the following:

$$95\%\ \text{CI} = (510 \pm [1.96 \times 20.0])$$

$$95\%\ \text{CI} = (510 \pm [39.2])$$

$$95\%\ \text{CI} = (470.8 \text{ to } 549.2)$$

The final statement indicates that the confidence is 95% that the population mean is between 470.8 and 549.2.

CIs reflect how much risk researchers are willing to take of being wrong. With a 95% CI, researchers accept the risk that they will be wrong 5 times out of 100. A 99% CI sets the risk at only 1% by allowing a wider range of possible values. The formula is: CI 99% ($\bar{X} \pm 2.58 \times \text{SEM}$). The 2.58 reflects the fact that 99% of all cases in a normal distribution lie within ±2.58 *SD* units from the mean. In our example, the 99% CI is 458.4 to 561.6. The price of having lower risk of being wrong is reduced precision. For a 95% interval, the CI range is about 80 points; for a 99% interval, the range is more than 100 points.

The acceptable risk of error depends on the nature of the problem, but for most studies, a 95% confidence interval is sufficient. CIs are often constructed around risk indexes, such as the OR or RR, and around descriptive indexes like means and percentages.

Example of confidence intervals:
Kottner and colleagues (2011) studied pressure ulcer occurrence in a sample of more than 50,000 German hospital patients. The overall proportion of patients with a pressure ulcer at the trunk was 2.0% (99% CI = 1.8%–2.2%) for staging category 2 and 0.9% (99% CI = 0.8%–1.0%) for staging categories 3 or 4. The narrow CI range resulted from the huge sample size.

Hypothesis Testing

Statistical **hypothesis testing** uses objective criteria for deciding whether research hypotheses should be accepted as true or rejected as false. Suppose we hypothesized that maternity patients exposed to a film on breastfeeding would breastfeed longer than mothers who did not see the film. We find that the mean number of days of breastfeeding is 131.5 for 25 experimental subjects and 125.1 for 25 control subjects. Should we conclude that the hypothesis has been supported? True, group differences are in the predicted direction, but perhaps in another sample, the group means would be nearly identical. Two explanations for the observed outcome are possible: (1) the film is truly effective in encouraging breastfeeding or (2) the difference in this sample was due to chance factors (e.g., differences in the characteristics of the two groups even before the film was shown, reflecting a bias).

The first explanation is the *research hypothesis*, and the second is the *null hypothesis*. The null hypothesis, it may be recalled, states that there is no relationship between the independent and dependent variables. Statistical hypothesis testing is a process of disproof. It cannot be demonstrated directly that the research hypothesis is correct. But it is possible to show, using sampling distributions, that the null hypothesis has a high probability of being incorrect, and such evidence lends support to the research hypothesis. Hypothesis testing helps researchers to make objective decisions about whether results are likely to reflect chance differences or hypothesized effects. The rejection of the null hypothesis is what researchers seek to accomplish through **statistical tests.**

Null hypotheses are accepted or rejected based on sample data, but hypotheses are about population values. The real interest in testing hypotheses, as in all statistical inference, is to use a sample to make inferences about a population.

Type I and Type II Errors

Researchers decide whether to accept or reject the null hypothesis by estimating how probable it is that observed group differences are due to chance. Because information about the population is not available, it cannot be asserted that the null hypothesis is or is not true. Researchers must be content to say that hypotheses are either *probably* true or *probably* false.

The researcher calculates a test statistic and decides that the null hypothesis is:	The actual situation is that the null hypothesis is: True	False
True (Null accepted)	Correct decision	Type II error
False (Null rejected)	Type I error	Correct decision

FIGURE 12.7 ● Outcomes of statistical decision-making.

Researchers can make two types of error: rejecting a true null hypothesis or accepting a false null hypothesis. Figure 12.7 summarizes possible outcomes of researchers' decisions. Researchers make a **Type I error** by rejecting a null hypothesis that is, in fact, true. For instance, if we concluded that the film was effective in promoting breastfeeding when, in fact, group differences were merely due to sampling error, we would be making a Type I error—a false positive conclusion. Or, we might conclude that observed differences in breastfeeding were due to sampling fluctuations, when the film actually *did* have an effect. Acceptance of a false null hypothesis is a **Type II error**—a false negative conclusion.

Level of Significance

Researchers do not know when they have made an error in statistical decision-making. The validity of a null hypothesis could only be known by collecting data from the population, in which case there would be no need for statistical inference.

Researchers control the risk for a Type I error by selecting a **level of significance**, which is the probability of making a Type I error. The two most frequently used levels of significance (referred to as **alpha (α)**) are .05 and .01. With a .05 significance level, we accept the risk that out of 100 samples from a population, a true null hypothesis would be wrongly rejected 5 times. In 95 out of 100 cases, however, a true null hypothesis would be correctly accepted. With a .01 significance level, the risk of a Type I error is lower: In only 1 sample out of 100 would we wrongly reject the null. By convention, the minimal acceptable alpha level is .05.

TIP: Levels of significance are analogous to the CI values described earlier—an alpha of .05 is analogous to the 95% CI, and an alpha of .01 is analogous to the 99% CI.

Researchers would like to reduce the risk of committing both types of error, but unfortunately, lowering the risk of a Type I error increases the risk of a Type II error. The stricter the criterion for rejecting a null hypothesis, the greater the probability of accepting a false null. However, researchers can reduce the risk of a Type II error by increasing their sample size.

The probability of committing a Type II error, called **beta (β)**, can be estimated through *power analysis*, the procedure we mentioned in Chapter 10 with regard to sample size. *Power* is the ability of a statistical test to detect true relationships, and is the complement of beta (that is, power equals 1-β). The standard criterion for an acceptable risk for a Type II error is .20, and thus researchers ideally use a sample size that gives them a minimum power of .80.

TIP: Quantitative researchers should do a power analysis before starting their study, but many do not. If a report indicates that a research hypothesis was not supported by the data, consider whether a Type II error might have occurred because of inadequate sample size.

Tests of Statistical Significance

In hypothesis testing, researchers use study data to compute a **test statistic**. For every test statistic, there is a theoretical sampling distribution, similar to the sampling distribution of means. Hypothesis testing uses theoretical distributions to establish *probable* and *improbable* values for the test statistics, which are used to accept or reject the null hypothesis.

An example from our study of gender bias in nursing research (Polit & Beck, 2009) illustrates the process. We tested the hypothesis that females are over-represented as participants in nursing studies—that is, the average percentage of females in published studies is greater than 50%. We found, using a consecutive sample of 843 studies from eight nursing research journals published over a 2-year period, that the mean percentage of females was 71.0. Using statistical procedures, we tested the hypothesis that the mean of 71.0 is not merely a chance fluctuation from the true population mean of 50.0.

In hypothesis testing, researchers assume that the null hypothesis is true—and then gather evidence to disprove it. Assuming a mean percentage of 50.0 for the entire population of recently published nursing studies, a theoretical sampling distribution can be constructed. For simplicity, let us say that the SEM is 2.0 (in our study, the SEM was actually less than 2.0). This is shown in Figure 12.8. Using a normal distribution, we can determine probable and improbable values of sample means from the population of nursing studies. If, as is assumed in the null hypothesis, the population mean is 50.0 percent, 95% of all sample means would fall between 46.0% and 54.0%, that is, within 2 *SD*s above and below the mean of 50.0%. The obtained sample mean of 71.0% is in the region considered *improbable* if the null hypothesis were correct—in fact, any value greater than 54.0% would be improbable if the true population mean were 50.0%, when alpha = .05. The *improbable* range beyond 2 *SD*s corresponds to only 5% (100% – 95%) of the sampling distribution. In our study, the probability of obtaining a value of 71.0% female by chance alone was less than 1 in 10,000. We rejected the null

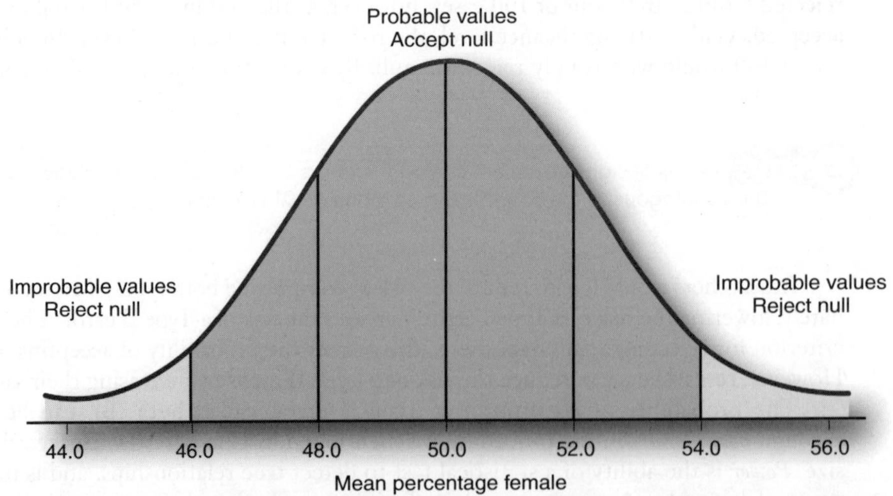

FIGURE 12.8 ● Sampling distribution for hypothesis test example: Percentage female among participants in nursing studies. Based on Polit, D., & Beck, C. (2009). International gender bias in nursing research. *International Journal of Nursing Studies, 46*, 1102–1110.

hypothesis that the mean percentage of female participants in nursing studies was 50.0. We would not be justified in saying that we had *proved* the research hypothesis because the possibility of having made a Type I error remains—but the possibility is, in this case, remote.

Researchers reporting the results of hypothesis tests state whether their findings are **statistically significant**. The word *significant* does not mean important or meaningful. In statistics, the term *significant* means that results are not likely to have been due to chance, at some specified level of probability. A **nonsignificant result (NS)** means that any observed difference or relationship could have been the result of a chance fluctuation.

TIP: It may help to keep in mind that inferential statistics are just a tool to help us evaluate whether study results are likely to be *real* and replicable, or simply spurious.

Overview of Hypothesis Testing Procedures

In the next section, a few statistical tests are discussed. We emphasize applications and interpretations of statistical tests, not computations. Each statistical test can be used with specific kinds of data, but the overall hypothesis-testing process is similar for all tests:

1. *Selecting a test statistic*. Researchers select a test based on such factors as whether certain assumptions are justified, which levels of measurement were used, and, if relevant, how many groups are being compared.
2. *Specifying the level of significance*. An α level of .05 is usually chosen.
3. *Computing a test statistic*. A test statistic is calculated based on the collected data.
4. *Determining degrees of freedom*. The term ***degrees of freedom (df)*** refers to the number of observations free to vary about a parameter. The concept is too complex for elaboration, but computing degrees of freedom is easy.
5. *Comparing the test statistic to a theoretical value*. Theoretical distributions have been developed for all test statistics, and values for these distributions are available for specified degrees of freedom. The computed value of the test statistic is compared to a theoretical value to establish significance or nonsignificance.

When a computer is used for the analysis, as is almost always the case, researchers follow only the first step and then give commands to the computer. The computer calculates the test statistic, degrees of freedom, and the actual probability that the relationship being tested is due to chance. For example, the computer may print that the probability (p) of an experimental group doing better on a measure of postoperative recovery than the control group on the basis of chance alone is .025. This means that fewer than 3 times out of 100 (only 25 times out of 1,000) would a group difference of the size observed occur by chance. The computed ***p* level** (probability) is then compared with the desired alpha. In the present example, if the significance level were .05, the results would be significant because .025 is more stringent than .05. Any computed probability greater than .05 (e.g., .15) indicates a nonsignificant relationship (sometimes abbreviated *NS*), that is, one that could have occurred on the basis of chance in more than 5 out of 100 samples.

TIP: Most tests discussed in this chapter are *parametric tests,* which are ones that focus on population parameters and involve certain assumptions about variables in the analysis, notably the assumption that they are normally distributed in the population. *Nonparametric tests,* by contrast, do not estimate parameters and involve less restrictive assumptions about the distribution's shape.

BIVARIATE STATISTICAL TESTS

Researchers use a variety of statistical tests to make inferences about their hypotheses. Several frequently used bivariate tests are briefly described and illustrated.

t-Tests

Researchers frequently compare two groups of people on an outcome. A parametric test for testing the significance of differences in two group means is called a ***t*-test**.

Suppose we wanted to test the effect of early discharge of maternity patients on perceived maternal competence. We administer a scale of perceived maternal competence at discharge to 20 primiparas who had a vaginal delivery: 10 who remained in the hospital 25 to 48 hours (regular discharge group) and 10 who were discharged 24 hours or less after delivery (early discharge group). Data for this example are presented in Table 12.8. Mean scores for these two groups are 25.0 and 19.0, respectively. Are these differences *real* (i.e., would they exist in the population of early-discharge and later-discharge mothers?), or do group differences reflect chance fluctuations? The 20 scores vary from one mother to another. Some variation reflects individual differences in perceived maternal competence. Some variation might reflect the scale's low reliability, some could result from participants' moods on a particular day, and so forth. The research question is:

TABLE 12.8 Fictitious Data for *t*-Test Example: Scores on a Perceived Maternal Competence Scale

Early-Discharge Mothers	Regular-Discharge Mothers
30	23
27	17
25	22
20	18
24	20
32	26
17	16
18	13
28	21
29	14
Mean = 19.0	Mean = 25.0

***t* = 2.86, *df* = 18, *p* = .011**

Can a significant portion of the variation be attributed to the independent variable—time of hospital discharge? The *t*-test allows us to make inferences about this question objectively.

The formula for calculating the *t* statistic uses group means, variability, and sample size. The computed value of *t* for the data in Table 12.8 is 2.86. Degrees of freedom in this example are equal to the total sample size minus 2 ($df = 20 - 2 = 18$). For an α level of .05, the theoretical cutoff value for *t* with 18 degrees of freedom is 2.10. *This value establishes an upper limit to what is probable if the null hypothesis is true*. Thus, the calculated *t* of 2.86, which is larger than the theoretical value of *t*, is improbable (i.e., statistically significant). We can say that the primiparas discharged early had significantly lower perceived maternal competence than those who were not discharged early. The group difference was sufficiently large that it is unlikely to reflect chance fluctuations. In fewer than 5 out of 100 samples would a difference in means this great be found by chance alone. In fact, the actual *p* value is .011: only in about 1 sample out of 100 would this difference be found by chance.

The situation we just described calls for an *independent groups t-test*: mothers in the two groups were different people, independent of each other. There are situations for which this type of *t*-test is not appropriate. For example, if means for a single group of people measured before and after an intervention were being compared, researchers would use a *paired t-test* (also called a *dependent groups t-test*), which involves a different formula.

Example of *t*-tests:

Karatay and Akkus (2012) tested the effectiveness of a multistimulant home-based program on cognitive function in older adults in Turkey. They used independent group *t*-tests to compare cognitive functioning scores of those in the experimental and control groups, and also used paired *t*-tests to assess differences before and after the program within each group.

As an alternative to *t*-tests, CIs can be constructed around the difference between two means. The results provide information about both statistical significance (i.e., whether the null hypothesis should be rejected) and precision of the estimated difference. In the example in Table 12.8, we can construct CIs around the mean difference of 6.0 in maternal competence scores ($25.0 - 19.0 = 6.0$). For a 95% CI, the confidence limits are 1.6 and 10.4: we can be 95% confident that the true difference between population means for early- and regular-discharge mothers lies between these values.

With CI information, we learn the range in which the mean difference probably lies and we can also see that it is significant at $p < .05$ *because the range does not include 0*. There is a 95% probability that the mean difference is not lower than 1.6, so this means that there is less than a 5% probability that there is no difference at all—thus, the null hypothesis can be rejected.

Analysis of Variance

Analysis of variance (ANOVA) is used to test mean group differences of three or more groups. ANOVA sorts out the variability of an outcome variable into two components: variability due to the independent variable (e.g., experimental group status) and variability due to all other sources (e.g., individual differences, measurement error). Variation *between* groups is contrasted with variation *within* groups to yield an ***F* ratio** statistic.

Suppose we were comparing the effectiveness of interventions to help people stop smoking. One group of smokers receives nurse counseling (group A), a second group is treated by a nicotine patch (group B), and a control group gets no special treatment (group C). The outcome is 1-day cigarette consumption measured 1 month after the intervention.

TABLE 12.9 Fictitious Data for ANOVA Example: Number Of Cigarettes Smoked In 1 Day, Post-Treatment

Group A Nurse Counseling		Group B Nicotine Patch		Group C Untreated Controls	
28	19	0	27	33	35
0	24	31	0	54	0
17	0	26	3	19	43
20	21	30	24	40	39
35	2	24	27	41	36
$Mean_A = 16.6$		$Mean_B = 19.2$		$Mean_C = 34.0$	

$F = 4.98$, $df = 2, 27$, $p = .01$

Thirty smokers who wish to quit smoking are randomly assigned to one of the three groups. The null hypothesis is that the population means for post-treatment cigarette smoking is the same for all three groups, and the research hypothesis is inequality of means. Table 12.9 presents fictitious data for the 30 participants. The mean numbers of post-treatment cigarettes consumed are 16.6, 19.2, and 34.0 for groups A, B, and C, respectively. These means are different, but are they significantly different—or do differences reflect random fluctuations?

An ANOVA applied to these data yields an F ratio of 4.98. For $\alpha = .05$ and $df = 2$ and 27 (2 *df* between groups and 27 *df* within groups), the theoretical F value is 3.35. Because our obtained F-value of 4.98 exceeds 3.35, we reject the null hypothesis that the population means are equal. The *actual* probability, as calculated by a computer, is .014. In only 14 samples out of 1,000 would differences this great be obtained by chance alone.

ANOVA results support the hypothesis that different treatments were associated with different cigarette smoking, but we cannot tell from these results whether treatment A was significantly more effective than treatment B. Statistical analyses known as **post hoc tests** (or ***multiple comparison procedures***) are used to isolate the differences between group means that are responsible for rejecting the overall ANOVA null hypothesis. Note that it is *not* appropriate to use a series of t-tests (group A vs. B, A vs. C, and B vs. C) because this increases the risk of a Type I error.

ANOVA also can be used to test the effect of two independent variables on an outcome variable. Suppose we wanted to assess whether the two smoking cessation interventions (nurse counseling and nicotine patch) were equally effective for men and women. We randomly assign men and women, separately, to the two treatment conditions, without a control condition. Suppose the analysis revealed the following about two *main effects*: On average, people in the nurse-counseling group smoked less than those in the nicotine-patch group (19.0 vs. 25.0), and, overall, women smoked less than men (21.0 vs. 23.0). In addition, there is an *interaction effect*: Female smoking was especially low in the counseling condition (mean = 16.0), whereas male smoking was especially high in that condition (mean = 30.0). By performing a *two-way ANOVA* on these data, it would be possible to test the statistical significance of these differences.

A type of ANOVA known as **repeated measures ANOVA (RM-ANOVA)** can be used when the means being compared are means at different points in time (e.g., mean blood pressure at 2, 4, and 6 hours after surgery). This is analogous to a paired *t*-test, extended to three or more points of data collection. When two or more groups are measured several times, a repeated measures ANOVA provides information about a main effect for time (do the measures change significantly over time, irrespective of group?), a main effect for groups (do the group means differ significantly, irrespective of time?), and an interaction effect (do the groups differ more at certain times?).

Example of an ANOVA:

Lee, Chao, Yiin, Chiang, and Chao (2011) conducted a randomized trial to test the effects of music on preoperative anxiety. Patients were assigned to a headphone music group, a broadcast music group, or a control group with no music. Analysis of variance revealed significant group differences on anxiety ($F = 13.0$, $p < .001$). Post hoc tests revealed that both music groups had significantly lower anxiety than the control group, but anxiety in the two music groups did not differ significantly.

Chi-Squared Test

The **chi-squared (χ^2) test** is used to test hypotheses about the proportion of cases in different categories, as in a crosstabulation. For example, suppose we were studying the effect of nursing instruction on patients' compliance with self-medication. Nurses implement a new instructional strategy with 50 patients, while 50 control group patients get usual care. The research hypothesis is that a higher proportion of people in the treatment than in the control condition will be compliant. Some fictitious data for this example are presented in Table 12.10, which shows that 60% of those in the experimental group were compliant, compared to 40% in the control group. But is this 20 percentage point difference statistically significant—that is, likely to be "real"?

The chi-squared statistic is computed by summing differences between the *observed frequencies* in each cell (such as those in Table 12.10) and the *expected frequencies*—those that would be expected if there were *no* relationship between the variables. The value of the chi-squared statistic here is 4.00, which we can compare with the value from a theoretical chi-squared distribution. In this example, the theoretical value that must be exceeded to establish significance at the .05 level is 3.84. The obtained value of 4.00 is larger than would be expected by chance (the actual $p = .046$). We can conclude that a significantly larger proportion of experimental patients than control patients were compliant.

TABLE 12.10 Observed Frequencies for Chi-Squared Example: Rates of Compliance with Medications

	Group				
Patient Compliance	**Experimental**		**Control**		**Total**
	n	%	*n*	%	*n*
Compliant	30	60.0	20	40.0	50
Noncompliant	20	40.0	30	60.0	50
TOTAL	50	100.0	50	100.0	100

$\chi^2 = 4.0$, $df = 1$, $p = .046$

Example of chi-squared test:
Fukui, Fujita, Tsujimura, and Hayashi (2011) studied factors associated with a home death, versus a hospital death, in home palliative cancer care patients in Japan. They used chi-squared tests to study differences between the two groups on a wide range of variables. For example, a significantly higher proportion of patients who died at home (37%) than who died in the hospital (23%) had a daughter or daughter-in-law as a primary caretaker ($\chi^2 = 12.6$, $df = 1$, $p < .001$).

As with means, it is possible to construct CIs around the difference between two proportions. In our example, the group difference in proportion compliant was .20. The 95% CI in this example is .06 to .34. We can be 95% confident that the true population difference in compliance rates between those exposed to the intervention and those not exposed is between 6% and 34%. This interval does not include 0%, so we can be 95% confident that group differences are "real" in the population.

Correlation Coefficients

Pearson's *r* is both descriptive and inferential. As a descriptive statistic, *r* summarizes the magnitude and direction of a relationship between two variables. As an inferential statistic, *r* tests hypotheses about population correlations; the null hypothesis is that there is no relationship between two variables, that is, that the population $r = .00$.

Suppose we were studying the relationship between patients' self-reported level of stress (higher scores indicate more stress) and the pH level of their saliva. With a sample of 50 patients, we find that $r = -.29$. This value indicates a tendency for people with high stress to have lower pH levels than those with low stress. But we need to ask whether this finding can be generalized to the population. Does the *r* of –.29 reflect a random fluctuation, observed only in this sample, or is the relationship significant? Degrees of freedom for correlation coefficients equal *N* minus 2, which is 48 in this example. The theoretical value for *r* with $df = 48$ and $\alpha = .05$ is .28. Because the absolute value of the calculated *r* is .29, the null hypothesis is rejected. There is a modest but significant relationship between patients' stress level and the acidity of their saliva.

CIs can be constructed around Pearson *r*s. In our example, the 95% CI around the *r* of .29 for stress levels and saliva pH, with a sample of 50 subjects, is .01 and .53. Because the upper confidence limit is less than .00, the correlation in this example was statistically significant at the .05 level (but note that the range of possible values for the population *r* is very large because of the small sample size).

Example of Pearson's *r*:
Suhonen et al. (2012) studied the correlation between patient satisfaction and perceptions of individualized care in a sample of 1,315 surgical patients from five European countries. Pearson correlation coefficients were moderately strong and significant. For example, the *r* between satisfaction and a subscale called "Decisional control over care" was .63, $p < .001$.

TIP: Most tests discussed in this chapter (e.g., *t*-tests, ANOVA, Pearson's *r*) are *parametric tests*, which focus on population parameters. The chi-squared test is nonparametric.

Effect Size Indexes

Effect size indexes are estimates of the magnitude of effects of an "I" component on an "O" component in PICO questions, as described in Chapter 2—an important issue in EBP (see Box 2.1, p. 32). Effect size information can be crucial because, with large samples, even miniscule effects can be statistically significant. *P* values tell you whether results are likely to be *real*, but effect sizes suggest whether they are important. Effect size plays an important role in meta-analyses.

It is beyond our scope to explain effect sizes in detail, but we offer an illustration. A frequently used effect size index is the ***d* statistic**, which summarizes the magnitude of differences in two means, such as the difference between experimental and control group means on an outcome. Thus, *d* can be calculated to estimate effect size when *t*-tests are used. When *d* is zero, it means that there is no effect of the independent variable—the means of the two groups being compared are the same. By convention, a *d* of .20 or less is considered *small*, a *d* of .50 is considered *moderate*, and a *d* of .80 or greater is considered *large*.

Different effect size indexes and interpretive conventions are associated with different situations. For example, the *r* statistic can be interpreted directly as an effect size index, as can the OR. The key point is that they encapsulate information about how powerful the effect of an independent variable is on an outcome.

TIP: Researchers who conduct a power analysis to estimate how big a sample size they need to adequately test their hypotheses (i.e., to avoid a Type II error) must estimate in advance how large the effect size will be—usually based on prior research or a pilot study.

Example of calculated effect size:

Krampe (2012) conducted a pilot study to test the effectiveness of a dance-therapy intervention on balance and mobility in older adults. Although differences between the intervention and control groups were not significant due to the small sample size (*N* = 27), effect size calculations suggested several positive moderate effects. For example, the effect size for backward reach was *d* = .48.

Guide to Bivariate Statistical Tests

The selection of a statistical test depends on several factors, such as number of groups and the levels of measurement of the research variables. To aid you in evaluating the appropriateness of statistical tests used by nurse researchers, Table 12.11 summarizes key features of the bivariate tests mentioned in this chapter.

TIP: Every time a report presents information about statistical tests, such as those described in this section, it means that the researcher was testing hypotheses—whether or not those hypotheses were formally stated in the introduction.

MULTIVARIATE STATISTICAL ANALYSIS

Many nurse researchers now use complex **multivariate statistics** to analyze their data. We use the term *multivariate* to refer to analyses dealing with at least three—but usually

TABLE 12.11 Guide to Major Bivariate Statistical Tests

			Measurement Level	
Name	**Test Statistic**	**Purpose**	**Independent Variable**	**Dependent Variable**
t-test for independent groups	*t*	To test the difference between the means of two independent groups (e.g., experimental vs. control, men vs. women)	Nominal	Interval, Ratio
t-test for paired groups	*t*	To test the difference between the means of a paired group (e.g., pretest vs. posttest for same people)	Nominal	Interval, Ratio
Analysis of variance (ANOVA)	*F*	To test the difference among means of 3+ independent groups or means for 2+ independent variables	Nominal	Interval, Ratio
Repeated measures ANOVA	*F*	To test the difference among means of 3+ related groups, e.g., the same group over time, or to compare 2+ groups over time	Nominal	Interval, Ratio
Pearson's correlation coefficient	*r*	To test the existence of a relationship between two variables	Interval, Ratio	Interval, Ratio
Chi-squared test	χ^2	To test the difference in proportions in 2+ independent groups	Nominal (or ordinal, few categories)	Nominal (or ordinal, few categories)

more—variables simultaneously. The evolution to more sophisticated methods of analysis has resulted in increased rigor in nursing studies, but one unfortunate side effect is that it has become more challenging for those without statistical training to understand research reports.

TIP: Given the introductory nature of this text and the fact that many of you are not proficient with even simple statistical tests, it is not possible to describe in detail the complex analytic tools now used in nursing studies. We present only basic descriptive information about several commonly used multivariate statistics. The Chapter Supplement on thePoint website offers more detail about two of them, multiple regression and analysis of covariance.

Multiple Regression

Correlations enable researchers to make predictions. For example, if the correlation between secondary school grades and nursing school grades were .60, nursing school administrators could make predictions—albeit imperfect ones—about applicants' future performance. Researchers can improve their prediction of an outcome by performing a **multiple regression** in which multiple independent variables are included in the analysis. As an example, we might predict infant birth weight (the outcome) from such variables as mothers' smoking, amount of prenatal care, and gestational period. In multiple regression, outcome variables are interval- or ratio-level variables. Independent variables (also called **predictor variables** in regression) are either interval- or ratio-level variables or dichotomous nominal-level variables, such as male/female.

The coefficient in multiple regression is the **multiple correlation coefficient**, symbolized as R. Unlike the bivariate correlation coefficient r, R does not have negative values. R varies from .00 to 1.00, showing the *strength* of the relationship between several independent variables and an outcome, but not *direction*. Researchers can test whether R is statistically significant (i.e., different from .00). An interesting feature of R is that, when squared, it can be interpreted as the proportion of the variability in the outcome variable that is explained by the predictors. In predicting birth weight, if we achieved an R of .60 ($R^2 = .36$), we could say that the predictors accounted for just over one third (36%) of the variation in birth weights. Two thirds of the variation, however, resulted from factors not identified or measured. Researchers usually report multiple correlation results in terms of R^2 rather than R.

Example of multiple regression analysis:

Buck and colleagues (2012), in their study of older adults with moderate to advanced heart failure, studied the relationship between several demographic, clinical, and psychosocial predictors on the one hand and health-related quality of life (HRQL) on the other. Using multiple regression, they found that the patient's self-care management and their self-care confidence were significant predictors of HRQL ($R^2 = .10$, $p = .008$).

Analysis of Covariance

Analysis of covariance (ANCOVA), which combines features of ANOVA and multiple regression, is used to control confounding variables statistically—that is to "equalize" groups being compared. This approach is valuable in certain situations, for example, when a nonequivalent control group design is used. When control through randomization is lacking, ANCOVA offers the possibility of statistical control.

In ANCOVA, the confounding variables being controlled are called *covariates*. Analysis of covariance tests the significance of differences between group means on an outcome after eliminating the effect of covariates. ANCOVA produces F statistics to test the significance of group differences. ANCOVA is a powerful and useful analytic technique for controlling confounding influences on outcomes.

Example of ANCOVA:

Keough and colleagues (2011) studied differences in self-management behaviors in managing diabetes among youth in early, middle, and late adolescence. The three age groups were compared with regard to problem solving and collaboration with parents, using gender and type of regimen (flexible or conventional) as covariates.

Multivariate Analysis of Variance

Multivariance analysis of variance (MANOVA) is the extension of ANOVA to more than one outcome. MANOVA is used to test the significance of differences between the means of two or more groups on two or more outcome variables, considered simultaneously. For instance, if we wanted to compare the effect of two exercise regimens on both blood pressure and heart rate, then a MANOVA would be appropriate. Covariates can also be included to control confounding variables, in which case, the analysis is a *multivariate analysis of covariance (MANCOVA)*.

Example of MANOVA:
Leiter and colleagues (2011) investigated the anxiolytic effects of myristicin (a major compound found in nutmeg) in male Sprague-Dawley rats. Rats were divided into five groups (two control groups, a myristicin group, and two groups with myristicin plus other compounds). MANOVA was used to test differences in the five groups with respect to a behavioral measure of anxiety and two other outcomes.

Logistic Regression

Logistic regression analyzes the relationships between multiple independent variables and a nominal-level outcome (e.g., compliant vs. noncompliant). It is similar to multiple regression, although it employs a different statistical estimation procedure. Logistic regression transforms the probability of an event occurring (e.g., that a woman will practice breast self-examination or not) into its *odds*. After further transformations, the analysis examines the relationship of the predictor variables to the transformed outcome variable. For each predictor, the logistic regression yields an *odds ratio*, which is the factor by which the odds change for a unit change in the predictors after controlling other predictors. Logistic regression also yields CIs around the ORs.

Example of logistic regression:
Kim and colleagues (2012) used logistic regression to identify various risk factors (e.g., parental education, children's use of computers) for childhood obesity (obese vs. not obese) in a sample of 1,644 Korean children.

Guide to Multivariate Statistical Analyses

In selecting a multivariate analysis, researchers attend to such issues as the number of independent variables, the number of outcome variables, the measurement level of all variables, and the desirability of controlling confounding variables. Table 12.12 is an aid to help you evaluate the appropriateness of multivariate statistics used in many nursing studies.

READING AND UNDERSTANDING STATISTICAL INFORMATION

Statistical findings are communicated in the results section of research reports and are described in the text and in tables (or, less frequently, figures). This section offers assistance in reading and interpreting statistical information.

Tips on Reading Text with Statistical Information

Several types of information are reported in results sections. First, descriptive statistics typically summarize sample characteristics. Information about the participants' background helps readers to draw conclusions about the people to whom the findings can be applied. Second, researchers may provide statistical information for evaluating biases. For example, when a quasi-experimental or case-control design has been used, researchers often test the equivalence of the groups being compared on baseline or background variables, using tests such as *t*-tests.

TABLE 12.12 Guide to Selected Multivariate Analyses

Test Name	Purpose	Measurement Level of Variables[a,b]			Number of Variables[a]		
		IV	**DV**	**Covar**	**IVs**	**DVs**	**Covar**
Multiple regression	To test relationship between 2+ IVs and 1 DV; to predict a DV from 2+ IVs	N, I, R	I, R		2+	1	
Analysis of covariance (ANCOVA)	To test the difference between the means of 2+ groups, while controlling for 1+ covariate	N	I, R	N, I, R	1+	1	1+
Multivariate analysis of variance (MANOVA)	To test the difference between the means of 2+ groups for 2+ DVs simultaneously	N	I, R		1+	2+	
Multivariate analysis of covariance (MANCOVA)	To test the difference between the means of 2+ groups for 2+ DVs simultaneously, while controlling for 1+ covariate	N	I, R	N, I, R	1+	2+	1+
Logistic regression	To test the relationship between 2+ IVs and 1 DV; to predict the probability of an event; to estimate relative risk	N, I, R	N		2+	1	

[a]Variables: IV, independent variables; DV, dependent variable; Covar, covariate.

[b]Measurement levels: N, nominal; I, interval; R, ratio.

The text of research articles usually provides certain information about statistical tests, including (1) which test was used, (2) the value of the calculated statistic, (3) degrees of freedom, and (4) level of statistical significance. Examples of how the results of various statistical tests might be reported in the text are shown below.

1. *t*-test: $t = 1.68$; $df = 160$; $p = .09$
2. Chi-squared: $\chi^2 = 16.65$; $df = 2$; $p < .001$
3. Pearson's *r*: $r = .36$; $df = 100$; $p < .01$
4. ANOVA: $F = 0.18$; $df = 1, 69$, *ns*

Note that the significance level is sometimes reported as the *actual* computed probability that the null hypothesis is correct (example 1), which is the preferred approach. In this case, the observed group mean differences could be found by chance in 9 out of 100 samples. This result is not statistically significant, because the mean difference had an unacceptably high chance of being spurious. The probability level is sometimes reported simply as falling below or above certain thresholds (examples 2 and 3). These results are significant because the probability of obtaining such results by chance is <1 in 100. You must be careful to read the symbol following the *p* value correctly: The symbol < means *less than*—i.e., the results are statistically significant. The symbol > means *greater than*—i.e., the results are not significant. When results do not achieve statistical significance at the desired level, researchers may simply indicate that the results were not significant (*ns*), as in example 4.

Statistical information usually is noted parenthetically in a sentence describing the findings, as in the following example: Patients in the intervention group had a significantly lower rate of infection than those in the control group ($\chi^2 = 5.41$, $df = 1$, $p = .02$). In reading research reports, it is not important to absorb numeric information for the test statistics. For example, the actual value of χ^2 has no inherent interest. What is important is to grasp whether the statistical tests indicate that the research hypotheses were accepted as probably true (as demonstrated by significant results) or rejected as probably false (as demonstrated by nonsignificant results).

Tips on Reading Statistical Tables

The use of tables allows researchers to condense a lot of statistical information, and minimizes redundancy. Consider, for example, putting information from a correlation matrix (Table 12.5, p.22) into the text: "The correlation between service climate and nurses' task performance was .31; the correlation between task performance and patient satisfaction was .49..."

Tables are efficient but they may be daunting, partly because of the absence of standardization. There is no universally accepted method of presenting *t*-test results, for example. Thus, each table may present a new deciphering challenge. Another problem is that some researchers try to include too much information in their tables; we deliberately used tables of relative simplicity as examples in this chapter.

We have a few suggestions for helping you to comprehend statistical tables. First, read the text and the tables simultaneously—the text may help you figure out what the table is communicating. Second, before trying to understand the numbers in a table, try to glean information from the accompanying words. Table titles and footnotes often present critical pieces of information. Table headings should be carefully scrutinized because they indicate what the variables in the analysis are (often listed as row labels in the first column, as in Table 12.3, p. 221) and what statistical information is included (often specified in the top

TABLE 12.13 Effects of Parenting Intervention on Selected Maternal and Infant Outcomes at the 4-Week Follow-Up[a]

Outcome	Intervention Group (*N* = 93) *M*	*SD*	Community Group (*N* = 85) *M*	*SD*	*P*	Mean Difference	95% CI, Mean Difference
Maternal Confidence	61.4	4.7	60.0	4.2	.046	1.4	.03, 2.75
Parenting Sense of Competence	56.3	8.2	53.9	7.0	.045	2.4	.06, 4.73
Postnatal Depression	5.6	4.2	6.1	3.4	.38	−0.5	−.63. 1.66
Maternal Anxiety	2.7	1.7	2.9	1.5	.27	−0.2	−.22,.78

[a]The *p* values are for intervention group versus community group comparisons on each outcome using analysis of covariance (ANCOVA), controlling for the baseline measure of the respective outcome, baby's age, and parity; *F* statistic values were not reported.

Adapted from Hauck, Y., Hall, W., Dhaliwal, S., Bennett, E., & Wells, G. (2012). The effectiveness of an early parenting intervention for mothers with infants with sleep and settling concerns. *Journal of Clinical Nursing, 21*, 52–62.

row as the column headings). Third, you may find it helpful to consult the glossary of symbols on the inside back cover of this book to check the meaning of a statistical symbol. Not all symbols in this glossary were described in this chapter, so it may be necessary to refer to a statistics textbook, such as that of Polit (2010), for further information.

TIP: In tables, probability levels associated with the significance tests are sometimes presented directly (e.g., $p < .05$), as in Table 12.13. Here, the significance of each test is indicated in the third-to-last column, headed "p". However, researchers often indicate significance levels in tables through asterisks placed next to the value of the test statistic. One asterisk usually signifies $p < .05$, two asterisks signify $p < .01$, and three asterisks signify $p < .001$ (but there should be a key at the bottom of the table indicating what the asterisks mean). Thus, a table might show: $t = 3.00$, $p < .01$ *or* $t = 3.00^{**}$. When asterisks are used, the absence of an asterisk would signify a nonsignificant result.

CRITIQUING QUANTITATIVE ANALYSES

It is often difficult to critique statistical analyses. We hope this chapter has helped to demystify statistics, but we also recognize the limited scope of our coverage. It would be unreasonable to expect you to be adept at evaluating statistical analyses, but you can be on the lookout for certain things in reviewing research articles. Some specific guidelines are presented in Box 12.1.

BOX 12.1 Guidelines for Critiquing Statistical Analyses

1. Did the descriptive statistics in the report sufficiently describe the major key variables and background characteristics of the sample? Were appropriate descriptive statistics used—for example, was a mean presented when percentages would have been more informative?
2. Were statistical analyses undertaken to assess threats to the study's validity (e.g., to test for selection bias or attrition bias)?
3. Does the report include any inferential statistics? If inferential statistics were not used, should they have been?
4. Was information provided about both hypothesis testing and parameter estimation (i.e., confidence intervals)? Were effect sizes (or risk indexes) reported? Overall, did the reported statistics provide readers with sufficient information about the evidence the study yielded?
5. Were any multivariate procedures used? If not, should they have been used—for example, would the internal validity of the study be strengthened by statistically controlling confounding variables?
6. Were the selected statistical tests appropriate, given the level of measurement of the variables and the nature of the hypotheses?
7. Were the results of any statistical tests significant? What do the tests tell you about the plausibility of the research hypotheses? Were effects sizeable?
8. Were the results of any statistical tests nonsignificant? Is it plausible that these reflect Type II errors? What factors might have undermined the study's statistical conclusion validity?
9. Was there an appropriate amount of statistical information? Were findings clearly and logically organized? Were tables or figures used judiciously to summarize large amounts of statistical information? Are the tables clearly presented, with good titles and carefully labeled column headings? Is the information presented in the text and the tables redundant?

One aspect of the critique should focus on which analyses were reported in the article. You should assess whether the statistical information adequately describes the sample and reports the results of statistical tests for all hypotheses. Another presentational issue concerns the researcher's judicious use of tables to summarize statistical information.

A thorough critique also addresses whether researchers used the appropriate statistics. Tables 12.11 on page 238 and 12.12 on page 241 provide guidelines for some frequently used statistical tests. The major issues to consider are the number of independent and dependent variables, the levels of measurement of the research variables, and the number of groups (if any) being compared.

If researchers did not use a multivariate technique, you should consider whether the bivariate analysis adequately tests the relationship between the independent and dependent variables. For example, if a *t*-test or ANOVA was used, could the internal validity of the study have been enhanced through the statistical control of confounding variables using ANCOVA? The answer will often be "yes."

Finally, you can be alert to possible exaggerations or subjectivity in the reported results. Researchers should never claim that the data proved, verified, confirmed, or demonstrated that the hypotheses were correct or incorrect. Hypotheses should be described as being *supported* or *not supported*, *accepted* or *rejected.*

The main task for beginning consumers in reading a results section of a research report is to understand the meaning of the statistical tests. What do the quantitative results indicate about the researcher's hypothesis? How believable are the findings? The answer to such questions form the basis for interpreting the research results, a topic discussed in Chapter 13.

RESEARCH EXAMPLES WITH CRITICAL THINKING EXERCISES

In this section, we provide details about analytic portion of a study, followed by some questions to guide critical thinking.

Example 1 below is also featured in our *Interactive Critical Thinking Activity* on thePoint website where you can easily record, print, and e-mail your responses to the related questions.

EXAMPLE 1 ● Descriptive and Bivariate Inferential Statistics

Study: The effectiveness of an early parenting intervention for mothers with infants with sleep and settling concerns (Hauck et al., 2012)

Statement of Purpose: The purpose of this study was to test the effects of a parenting intervention offered at an early parenting center in Australia on maternal well-being and children's sleep and settling behavior.

Methods: A nonequivalent control group before–after design was used. Parents whose 4- to 6-month-old infants exhibited sleep behavior problems were recruited to participate in a Day Stay intervention that emphasized the development of parental confidence and competence relating to infants' sleep patterns. The intervention group ($n = 93$) was compared to a similar community comparison group ($n = 85$) in terms of maternal confidence, competence, depression, and anxiety, and in terms of infants' sleep and settling behaviors. Outcomes were measured for both groups at baseline and again 4 weeks later. Mothers completed self-administered questionnaires about their emotional state, bedtime practices with their infants, and the infants' night waking and settling behavior.

Descriptive Statistics: The researchers presented descriptive statistics (means, *SD*s, and percentages) to describe the characteristics of sample members prior to the intervention. For example, the mean age of the participants was 32.8 (± 4.3) for the intervention group and 32.9 (± 4.0) for the community group. The typical participant was married (94.9%) and had a college degree (63.5%).

Analysis of Bias: Recognizing that the groups might not be equivalent, the researchers assessed their baseline comparability. Using chi-squared tests and *t*-tests, they found the two groups comparable in terms of maternal age, marital status, and educational level. However, mothers in the intervention groups were significantly less likely than those in the community group to be primiparas (54% vs. 79%, respectively), and babies in the intervention group were significantly older (21.5 weeks vs. 20.1 weeks, respectively), both $p < .05$.

Hypothesis Tests: The researchers used paired *t*-tests to test changes over time on all major outcomes for both groups. They found, for example, that maternal confidence increased in both groups from baseline to follow-up, but the change was significant only in the intervention group (from $M = 57.6$ at baseline to $M = 60.5$ four weeks later, $p < .001$). The 95% CI around the mean improvement of 2.9 was 1.9 to 4.1. The researchers also used ANCOVA to test whether posttest scores were significantly different in the two groups. For each outcome, the group means at follow-up were compared after statistically controlling the baseline measure of the outcome, plus the baby's age and mother's parity. The two groups were significantly different on some of the outcomes, but there were no differences on others (see Table 12.13). For example, the two groups differed significantly on maternal confidence and perceived competence, but not on depression or anxiety. Finally, a logistic regression analysis was undertaken to explore factors that might predict whether an infant had a long settling time (>20 minutes). The predictors in the analysis included the baby's age, maternal parity, whether the mother had received the intervention, and whether the infant had needed a long or short time to settle at baseline. The only significant predictor of a long postintervention settling time was a long settling time at baseline. The OR for infants who had a settling time >20 minutes at baseline for predicting a long subsequent settling time was 3.35 (95% CI = 1.47 to 7.62).

CRITICAL THINKING EXERCISES

1. Answer the relevant questions from Box 12.1 on page 243 regarding this study.
2. Also consider the following targeted questions:
   a. Table 12.13 on page 242 shows that the group difference in maternal depression was not statistically significant. State the findings for this outcome in words, including information about the means and *p* value.
   b. Explain what the OR and CI information means regarding the prediction of postintervention settling time.
3. In what ways do you think the findings could be used in clinical practice?

EXAMPLE 2 ● Statistical Analysis in the Study in Appendix A

- Read the "Results" section of Howell and colleagues' (2007) study ("Anxiety, anger, and blood pressure in children") in Appendix A on pages 395–402.

CRITICAL THINKING EXERCISES

1. Answer the relevant questions in Box 12.1 on page 243 regarding this study.
2. Also consider the following targeted questions:
   a. In reporting information about scale scores for boys and girls (Table 1, Appendix A), the researchers stated that "Boys had higher mean anger scores but lower mean anxiety scores than girls." Did the researchers test whether the sex differences were statistically significant? What test was used or would have been used?
   b. Looking at Table 1 of Appendix A, write one or two sentences about the results for diastolic blood pressure, making sure to mention *SD* values.
   c. In Table 2 of Appendix A, which variable was most highly correlated with Systolic blood pressure (SBP) and Diastolic blood pressure (DBP)?

WANT TO KNOW MORE? A wide variety of resources to enhance your learning and understanding of this chapter are available on thePoint.

- Interactive Critical Thinking Activity
- Chapter Supplement on Multiple Regression and Analysis of Covariance
- Answers to the Critical Thinking Exercises for Example 2
- Student Review Questions
- Full-text online
- Internet Resources with useful websites for Chapter 12

Additional study aids including eight journal articles and related questions are also available in *Study Guide for Essentials of Nursing Research, 8e.*

SUMMARY POINTS

- **Descriptive statistics** are used to summarize and describe quantitative data.
- In **frequency distributions**, numeric values are ordered from lowest to highest, together with a count of the number (or percentage) of times each value was obtained.
- Data for a variable can be completely described in terms of the shape of the distribution, central tendency, and variability.
- The shape of a distribution can be **symmetric** or **skewed**, with one tail longer than the other; it can also be unimodal with one peak (i.e., one value of high frequency) or multimodal with more than one peak. A **normal distribution** (bell-shaped curve) is symmetric, unimodal, and not too peaked.
- Measures of **central tendency** represent the average or typical value of a set of scores. The **mode** is the value that occurs most frequently; the **median** is the point above which and below which 50% of the cases fall; and the mean is the arithmetic average of all scores. The **mean** is the most stable measure of central tendency.
- Measures of **variability**—how spread out the data are—include the range and standard deviation. The **range** is the distance between the highest and lowest scores. The **standard** deviation (*SD*) indicates how much, on average, scores deviate from the mean.
- In a normal distribution, 95% of values lie within 2 *SD*s above and below the mean.
- A **crosstabs table** is a two-dimensional frequency distribution in which the frequencies of two nominal- or ordinal-level variables are **cross tabulated.**
- **Correlation coefficients** describe the direction and magnitude of a relationship between two variables, and range from –1.00 (perfect *negative correlation*) through .00 to +1.00 (perfect *positive correlation*). The most frequently used correlation coefficient is **Pearson's *r***, used with interval- or ratio-level variables.
- Statistical indexes that describe the effects of exposure to risk factors or interventions provide useful information for clinical decisions. A widely reported risk index is the **odds ratio (OR)**, which is the ratio of the odds for an exposed vs unexposed group, with the *odds* reflecting the proportion of people with an adverse outcome relative to those without it.
- **Inferential statistics**, based on laws of probability, allow researchers to make inferences about a population based on data from a sample.
- The *sampling distribution of the mean* is a theoretical distribution of the means of an infinite number of same-sized samples drawn from a population. Sampling distributions are the basis for inferential statistics.

- The **standard error of the mean (SEM)**—the standard deviation of this theoretical distribution—indicates the degree of average error of a sample mean; the smaller the SEM, the more accurate are estimates of the population value.
- Statistical inference consists of two types of approach: estimating parameters and testing hypotheses. *Parameter estimation* is used to estimate a population parameter.
- *Point estimation* provides a single value of a population estimate (e.g., a mean). *Interval estimation* provides limits of a range of values—the **confidence interval (CI)**—between which the population value is expected to fall, at a specified probability. Most often the 95% CI is reported, which indicates that there is a 95% probability that the true population value lies between the upper and lower confidence limit.
- **Hypothesis testing** through statistical tests enables researchers to make objective decisions about relationships between variables.
- The *null hypothesis* states that no relationship exists between variables; rejection of the null hypothesis lends support to the research hypothesis. In testing hypotheses, researchers compute a test statistic and then determine whether the statistic falls beyond a critical region on the relevant theoretical distribution. The value of the test statistic indicates whether the null hypothesis is "improbable."
- A **Type I error** occurs if a null hypothesis is wrongly rejected (false positives). A **Type II error** occurs when a null hypothesis is wrongly accepted (false negatives).
- Researchers control the risk of making a Type I error by selecting a **level of significance** (or **alpha** level), which is the probability that such an error will occur. The .05 level (the conventional standard) means that in only 5 out of 100 samples would the null hypothesis be rejected when it should have been accepted.
- The probability of committing a Type II error is **beta** (β). *Power*, the ability of a statistical test to detect true relationships, is the complement of beta (i.e., power equals $1 - \beta$). The standard criterion for an acceptable level of power is .80.
- Results from hypothesis tests are either significant or nonsignificant; **statistically significant** means that the obtained results are not likely to be due to chance fluctuations at a given probability level (***p* value**).
- Two common statistical tests are the ***t*-test** and **analysis of variance (ANOVA)**, both of which can be used to test the significance of the difference between group means; ANOVA is used when there are three or more groups or when there is more than one independent variable. **Repeated measures ANOVA (RM-ANOVA)** is used when data are collected over multiple time periods.
- The **chi-squared test** is used to test hypotheses about differences in proportions.
- Pearson's r can be used to test whether a correlation is significantly different from zero.
- **Effect size** indexes (such as the ***d* statistic**) summarize the strength of the effect of an independent variable (e.g., an intervention) on an outcome variable.
- **Multivariate statistics** are used in nursing research to untangle complex relationships among three or more variables.
- **Multiple regression analysis** is a method for understanding the effect of two or more **predictor** (independent) **variables** on a continuous dependent variable. The square multiple correlation coefficient (**R^2**) is an estimate of the proportion of variability in the outcome variable accounted for by the predictors.
- **Analysis of covariance (ANCOVA)** controls confounding variables (called *covariates*) before testing whether group mean differences are statistically significant.
- Other multivariate procedures used by nurse researchers include **logistic regression** and *multivariate analysis of variance (MANOVA)*.

REFERENCES FOR CHAPTER 12

Buck, H., Lee, C., Moser, D., Albert, N., Lennie, T., Bentley, B., et al. (2012). Relationship between self-care and health-related quality of life in older adults with moderate to advanced heart failure. *Journal of Cardiovascular Nursing, 27*, 8–15.

Fukui, S., Fujita, J., Tsujimura, Y., & Hayashi, Y. (2011). Predictors of home death of home palliative cancer care patients. *International Journal of Nursing Studies, 48*, 1393–1400.

Greenslade, J., & Jimmieson, N. (2011). Organizational factors impacting on patient satisfaction. *International Journal of Nursing Studies, 48*, 1188–1198.

Hauck, Y., Hall, W., Dhaliwal, S., Bennett, E., & Wells, G. (2012). The effectiveness of an early parenting intervention for mothers with infants with sleep and settling concerns. *Journal of Clinical Nursing, 21*, 52–62.

Karatay, G., & Akkus, Y. (2012). Effectiveness of a multistimulant home-based program on cognitive function of older adults. *Western Journal of Nursing Research*, PubMed ID 21685369.

Keough, L., Sullivan-Bolyai, S., Crawford, S., Schilling, L., & Dixon, J. (2011). Self-management of type 1 diabetes across adolescence. *The Diabetes Educator, 37*, 486–500.

Kim, B., Lee, C., Kim, H., Ko, I., Park, C., & Kim, G. (2012). Ecological risk factors of childhood obesity in Korean elementary school children. *Western Journal of Nursing Research*, PubMed ID 22045783.

Kottner, J., Gefen, A., & Lahman, N. (2011). Weight and pressure ulcer occurrence. *International Journal of Nursing Studies, 48*, 1339–1148.

Krampe, J. (2012). Exploring the effects of dance-based therapy on balance and mobility in older adults. *Western Journal of Nursing Research*, PubMed ID 22045782.

Lee, K., Chao, Y., Yiin, J., Chiang, P., & Chao, Y. (2011). Effectiveness of different music-playing devices for reducing pre-operative anxiety. *International Journal of Nursing Studies, 48*, 1180–1187.

Leiter, E., Hitchcock, G., Godwin, S., Johnson, M., Sedgwick, W., Jones, W., et al. (2011). Evaluation of the anxiolytic properties of myristicin, a component of nutmeg, in the male Sprague-Dawley rat. *AANA Journal, 79*, 109–114.

Matthews, A., Hotton, A., DuBois, S., Fingerhut, D., & Kuhns, L. (2011). Demographic, psychosocial, and contextual correlates of tobacco use in sexual minority women. *Research in Nursing and Health, 34*, 141–152.

Padden, D., Connors, R., & Agazia, J. (2011). Stress, coping, and well-being in military spouses during deployment separation. *Western Journal of Nursing Research, 33*, 247–267.

Polit, D. F. (2010). *Statistics and data analysis for nursing research* (2nd ed.). Upper Saddle River, NJ: Pearson Education.

Polit, D., & Beck, C. (2009). International gender bias in nursing research. *International Journal of Nursing Studies, 46*, 1102–1110.

Suhonen, R., Papastavrou, E., Efstanthiou, G., Tsangari, H., Leino-Kilpi, H., Patiraki E., et al. (2012). Patient satisfaction as an outcome of individualized nursing care. *Scandinavian Journal of Caring Sciences,26*(2), 372–380.

chapter

13 Rigor and Interpretation in Quantitative Research

LEARNING OBJECTIVES

On completing this chapter, you will be able to:

- Describe dimensions key aspects for interpreting quantitative research results
- Describe the mindset conducive to a critical interpretation of research results
- Identify approaches to an assessment of the credibility of quantitative results, and undertake such an assessment
- Critique researchers' interpretation of their results in a discussion section of a report
- Define new terms in the chapter

KEY TERMS

CONSORT guidelines
Results

In this chapter, we consider approaches to interpreting researchers' statistical results, which requires consideration of the various theoretical, methodological, and practical decisions that researchers have made in designing and implementing their studies.

INTERPRETATION OF QUANTITATIVE RESULTS

Study **results** from statistical analyses are summarized in the Results section of a research article. Researchers present their *interpretations* of the results in Discussion sections—but researchers are seldom totally objective, and so you should develop your own interpretations.

This chapter offers guidance to help you in interpreting quantitative results and in critiquing Discussion sections of research articles. Another aim of this chapter is to encourage you to think critically about all aspects of a quantitative study. At this point, you are better able to apply the critiquing guidelines in Table 4.1 on page 69 than you were earlier. Results need to be understood and then evaluated within the context of the study aims, its theoretical basis, related research evidence, and the strengths and limitations of the research methods.

Aspects of Interpretation

Interpreting study results involves attending to six different but overlapping considerations, which intersect with the "Questions for Appraising the Evidence" presented in Box 2.1 on page 32:

- The credibility and accuracy of the results
- The precision of the parameter estimates
- The magnitude of effects and importance of the results
- The meaning of the results, especially with regard to causality
- The generalizability of the results
- The implications of the results for nursing practice, theory development, or further research

Before discussing these considerations, we want to remind you about the role of inference in research thinking and interpretation.

Inference and Interpretation

An *inference* is the act of drawing conclusions based on limited information, using logical reasoning. Interpreting research findings involves making a series of inferences. In research, virtually everything is a "stand-in" for something else: A sample is a stand-in for a population, a scale yields scores that are proxies for the magnitude of abstract attributes, and so on.

Figure 13.1 shows that research findings are meant to reflect "truth in the real world"—the findings themselves are "stand-ins" for the true state of affairs. Inferences about the real world are valid, however, to the extent that the researchers have made rigorous methodologic decisions in selecting proxies and have controlled sources of bias. This chapter offers several vantage points for assessing whether study findings really do reflect "truth in the real world."

The Interpretive Mindset

Evidence-based practice (EBP) involves integrating best research evidence into clinical decision-making. EBP encourages clinicians to think critically about clinical practice and to challenge the status quo when it conflicts with "best evidence." Thinking critically and demanding evidence are also part of a research interpreter's job. Just as clinicians should ask, "What *evidence* is there that this intervention or strategy will be beneficial?" so must interpreters ask, "What *evidence* is there that the results are real and true?"

To be a good interpreter of research results, you can profit by starting with a skeptical attitude and a null hypothesis. *The "null hypothesis" in interpretation is that the results are wrong and the evidence is flawed.* The "research hypothesis" is that the evidence reflects the truth. Interpreters decide whether the null hypothesis has merit by critically examining methodologic evidence. The greater the evidence that the researcher's design and methods were sound, the less plausible is the null hypothesis that the evidence is inaccurate.

TIP: In doing a critical interpretation of study results, it is appropriate to adopt a "show me" attitude. You should expect researchers to "show you" that their design is strong, their measurements are reliable and valid, their sample is adequately large and representative, and that their statistical decision-making is sound.

Truth in the Real World ← *Inference* — Study Results

FIGURE 13.1 ● Inferences in interpreting research results.

CREDIBILITY OF QUANTITATIVE RESULTS

One of the most important interpretive tasks is to assess whether the results are *right*. This corresponds to the first question we posed in Box 2.1 on page 32: "What is the quality of the evidence—i.e., how rigorous and reliable is it?" If the results are not judged to be credible, the remaining interpretive issues (the meaning, magnitude, precision, or generalizability, and implications of results) are not likely to be relevant.

A credibility assessment requires a careful analysis of the study's methodologic and conceptual limitations and strengths. To come to a conclusion about whether the results closely approximate "truth in the real world," each aspect of the study—its research design, sampling plan, data collection plan, and analytic approach—must be subjected to critical scrutiny.

There are various ways to approach the issue of credibility, including the use of the critiquing guidelines we have offered throughout this book, and the overall critiquing protocol presented in Table 4.1 on page 69. We share some additional perspectives in this section.

Proxies and Interpretation

Researchers begin with ideas and constructs, and then devise ways to operationalize them. The constructs are linked to the actual strategies and outcomes in a series of approximations, each step of which can be evaluated. The better the proxies, the more credible the results are likely to be. In this section, we illustrate successive proxies using sampling concepts, to highlight the potential for inferential challenges.

When researchers formulate research questions, the population of interest is often abstract. For example, suppose we wanted to test the effectiveness of an intervention to increase physical activity in low-income women. Figure 13.2 shows the series of steps between the abstract population construct (low-income women) and the actual participants. Using data from the actual sample on the far right, the researcher would like to make inferences about the effectiveness of the intervention for a broader group, but each proxy along the way represents a potential problem for achieving the desired inference. In interpreting a study, readers must consider how *plausible* it is that the actual sample reflects the recruited sample, the accessible population, the target population, and the population construct.

Table 13.1 presents a description of a hypothetical scenario in which the researchers moved from the population construct of low-income women to an actual sample of 161 participants. The table identifies some questions that might be asked in drawing inferences about the study results. Answers to these questions would affect the interpretation of whether the intervention *really* is effective with low-income women—or only with cooperative welfare recipients from two neighborhoods of Los Angeles who were recently approved for public assistance.

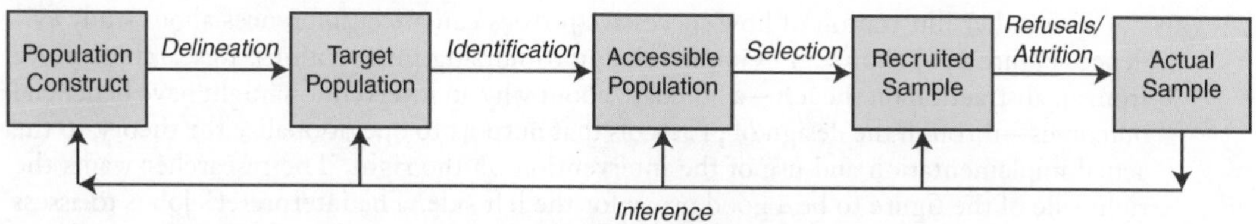

FIGURE 13.2 ● Inferences about populations: from final sample to the population.

TABLE 13.1 Example of Successive Series of Proxies in Sampling

Element	Description	Possible Inferential Challenges
Population construct	Low-income women	
Target population	All women who receive public assistance (cash welfare) in California	* Why only welfare recipients—why not the working poor? * Why not those on disability? * Why California?
Accessible population	All women who receive public assistance in Los Angeles and who speak English or Spanish	* Why Los Angeles? * What about non-English/non-Spanish speakers?
Recruited sample	A consecutive sample of 300 female welfare recipients (English or Spanish speaking) who applied for benefits in January, 2013 at two randomly selected welfare offices in Los Angeles	* Why only new applicants—what about women with long-term receipt? * Why only two offices? Are these representative? * Is January a typical month?
Actual sample	161 women from the recruited sample who fully participated in the study	* Who refused to participate (or was too ill, etc.)? * Who dropped out of the study?

As Figure 13.2 suggests, researchers make methodologic decisions that affect inferences, and these decisions must be carefully scrutinized. However, participant behavior and external circumstances also need to be considered in the interpretation. In our example, 300 women were recruited for the study, but only 161 provided data. The final sample of 161 almost surely would differ in important ways from the 139 who were not in the study, and these differences affect inferences about the study evidence.

Fortunately, researchers are increasingly documenting participant flow in their studies—especially in intervention studies. Guidelines called the Consolidated Standards of Reporting Trials or **CONSORT guidelines** have been adopted by major medical and nursing journals to help readers track study participants. CONSORT flow charts, when available, should be scrutinized in interpreting study results.

Example of a CONSORT flow chart:
Qi and colleagues (2011) tested the effectiveness of a self-efficacy program aimed at preventing osteoporosis among Chinese immigrants. Figure 13.3 shows the progression of study participants through the study, from 111 originally assessed for eligibility to 72 who provided final data. As this figure shows, one person did not meet the inclusion criteria, and another 26 were eliminated because they were a member of a dyad and only one from each dyad was chosen (at random). All of those who enrolled ($N = 83$) did receive the allocated intervention, but 11 participants were lost to follow-up, leaving 72 for the final analysis.

As another illustration of how successive proxies can affect inferences about study evidence, Figure 13.4 shows an example relating to nursing interventions. Researchers move from an abstraction on the left—a "theory" about why an intervention might have beneficial outcomes—through the design of protocols that purport to operationalize the theory, to the actual implementation and use of the intervention on the right. The researcher wants the right side of the figure to be a good proxy for the left side. The interpreter's job is to assess the plausibility that the researcher was successful in the transformation.

Assessed for eligibility (n=111)

Enrollment

Excluded (n=1)
- Not meeting inclusion criteria (n=1)
- Declined to participate (n=0)

Randomized (n=110). Among the 100 participants, 52 of them came in as pairs. Data from one member of 26 dyads were selected randomly to minimize risk of contamination. Total cases for analysis (n=83)

SEOPL* Intervention

Attention Control

Allocation

Allocated to and received intervention (n=42)

Allocated to and received control condition (n=41)

Follow-Up

Lost to follow-up (n=5)

Lost to follow-up (n=6)

Analysis

Analyzed (n=37)

Analyzed (n=35)

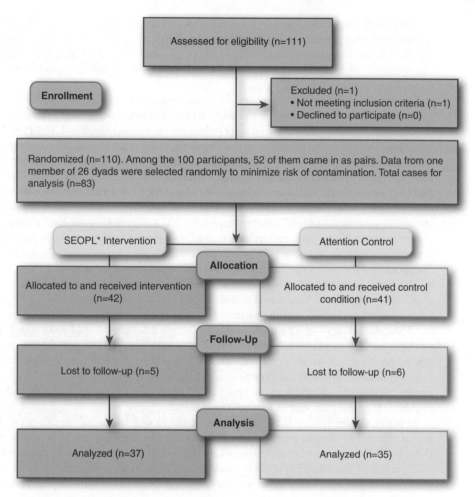

* Self Efficacy-based Osteoporosis Prevention

FIGURE 13.3 ● Consort flow diagram of participant recruitment. (Adapted from Figure 1, Qi, B., Resnick, B., Smeltzer, S., & Bausell, B. (2011). Self-efficacy program to prevent osteoporosis among Chinese immigrants. *Nursing Research, 60,* 393–404.

Credibility and Validity

Inference and validity are inextricably linked. As the research methodology experts Shadish and colleagues (2002) have stated, "We use the term *validity* to refer to the approximate truth of an inference" (p. 34). To be careful interpreters, readers must search for evidence that the desired inferences are, in fact, valid. Part of this process involves considering alternative competing hypotheses about the credibility and meaning of the results.

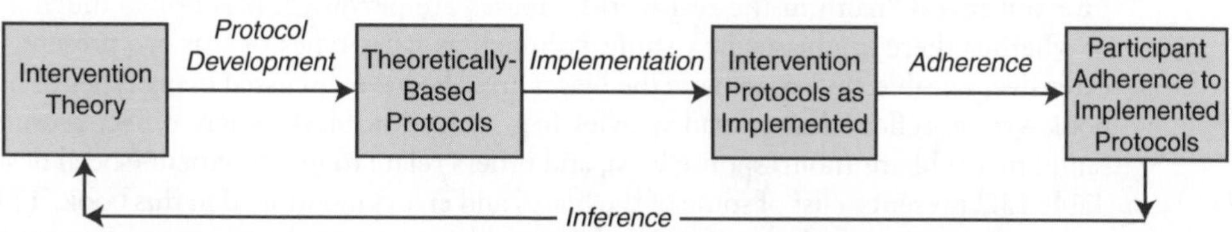

FIGURE 13.4 ● Inferences about interventions: from actual operations to the theory.

In Chapter 9, we discussed four key types of validity that relate to the credibility of study results: statistical conclusion validity, internal validity, external validity, and construct validity. We use our sampling example (Fig. 13.2, p. 251 and Table 13.1, p. 252) to demonstrate the relevance of methodologic decisions to all four types of validity—and hence to inferences about study results.

Construct validity has relevance for measurement (Chapter 11), and also for many aspects of a study. In our example, the population construct is *low-income women*, which led to population eligibility criteria stipulating public assistance recipients in California. Yet, there are alternative operationalizations of the population construct (e.g., California women living below the official poverty level). Construct validity, it may be recalled, involves inferences from the particulars of the study to higher-order constructs. So it is fair to ask, Do the specified eligibility criteria adequately capture the population construct, low-income women?

Statistical conclusion validity—the extent to which correct inferences can be made about the existence of "real" relationships between key variables—is also affected by sampling decisions. To be safe, researchers should do a power analysis at the outset to estimate how large a sample is needed. In our example, let us say we assumed (based on previous research) that the effect size for the exercise intervention would be small-to-moderate, with $d = .40$. For a power of .80, with risk of a Type I error set at .05, we would need a sample of about 200 participants. The actual sample of 161 yields a nearly 30% risk of a Type II error, i.e., wrongly concluding that the intervention was not successful.

External validity—the generalizability of the results—is affected by sampling. To whom would it be safe to generalize the results in this example—to the population construct of low-income women? to all welfare recipients in California? to all new welfare recipients in Los Angeles who speak English or Spanish? Inferences about the extent to which the study results correspond to "truth in the real world" must take sampling decisions and sampling problems (e.g., recruitment difficulties) into account.

Finally, the study's internal validity (the extent to which a causal inference can be made) is also affected by sample composition. In this example, attrition would be a concern. Were those in the intervention group more likely (or less likely) than those in the control group to drop out of the study? If so, any observed differences in outcomes could be caused by individual differences in the groups (for example, differences in motivation), rather than by the intervention itself.

Methodological decisions and the careful implementation of those decisions—whether they be about sampling, intervention design, measurement, research design, or analysis—inevitably affect the rigor of a study. And all of them can affect the four types of validity and hence, the interpretation of the results.

Credibility and Bias

A researcher's job is to translate abstract constructs into plausible and meaningful proxies. Another major job concerns efforts to eliminate, reduce, or control biases—or, as a last resort, to detect and understand them. As a reader of research reports, your job is to be on the lookout for biases, and to consider them in your assessment about the credibility of the results.

Biases are factors that create distortions and that undermine researchers' efforts to capture and reveal "truth in the real world." Biases are pervasive. It is not so much a question of whether there *are* biases in a study, so much as what types of bias are present, and how extensive, sizeable, and systematic the biases are. We have discussed many types of bias in this book—some reflect design inadequacies (e.g., selection bias), others reflect recruitment or sampling problems (nonresponse bias), and others relate to measurement (social desirability). Table 13.2 presents a list of some of the biases and errors mentioned in this book. This table is meant to serve as a reminder of some of the problems to consider in interpreting study results.

TABLE 13.2 Selected List of Major Biases or Errors in Quantitative Studies in Four Research Domains

Research Design	Sampling	Measurement	Analysis
Expectation bias	Sampling error	Social desirability bias	Type I error
Hawthorne effect	Volunteer bias	Acquiescence bias	Type II error
Contamination of treatments	Nonresponse bias	Nay-sayers bias	
Carryover effects		Extreme response set bias	
Noncompliance bias		Recall/memory bias	
Selection bias		Reactivity	
Attrition bias		Observer biases	
History bias			

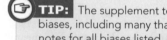

TIP: The supplement to this chapter on thePoint website includes a longer list of biases, including many that were not described in this book. We offer definitions and notes for all biases listed. Different disciplines, and different writers, may use different names for the same or similar biases. The actual names are not important—what is important is to reflect on how different forces can distort the results and affect inferences.

Credibility and Corroboration

Earlier, we noted that research interpreters should seek evidence to disconfirm the "null hypothesis" that the research results of a study are wrong. Some evidence to discredit the null hypothesis comes from the plausibility that proxies were good stand-ins for abstractions. Other evidence involves ruling out biases. Yet another strategy is to seek corroboration for the results.

Corroboration can come from internal and external sources, and the concept of *replication* is an important one in both cases. Interpretations are aided by considering prior research on the topic, for example. Interpreters can examine whether the study results replicate (are congruent with) those of other studies. Consistency across studies tends to discredit the "null hypothesis" of erroneous results.

Researchers may have opportunities for replication themselves. For example, in multisite studies, if the results are similar across sites, this suggests that something "real" is occurring with some regularity. Triangulation can be another form of replication. For example, if the results are similar across different measures of a key outcome, then there can perhaps be greater confidence that the results are "real" and do not reflect some peculiarity of an instrument.

Finally, we are strong advocates of mixed methods studies, a special type of triangulation (see Chapter 18). When findings from the analysis of qualitative data are consistent with the results of statistical analyses, internal corroboration can be especially powerful and persuasive.

OTHER ASPECTS OF INTERPRETATION

If an assessment of the study leads you to accept that the results are probably "real," you have gone a long way in interpreting the study findings. Other interpretive tasks depend on a conclusion that the results appear to be credible.

Precision of the Results

Results from statistical hypothesis tests indicate whether a relationship or group difference is probably real and replicable. A *p* value in hypothesis testing indicates how strong the evidence is that the study's null hypothesis is false—it is not an estimate of any quantity of direct relevance to practicing nurses. A *p* value offers information that is important, but incomplete.

Confidence intervals (CIs), by contrast, communicate information about how precise (or imprecise) the study results are. Dr. David Sackett, a founding father of the EBP movement, had this to say about CIs: "*P* values on their own are…not informative…. By contrast, CIs indicate the strength of evidence about quantities of direct interest, such as treatment benefit. Thus they are of particular relevance to practitioners of evidence-based medicine" (2000, p. 232). It seems likely that nurse researchers will increasingly report CI information in the years ahead because of the value of this information for interpreting study results and assessing their potential utility for nursing practice.

Magnitude of Effects and Importance

Attaining statistical significance does not necessarily mean that the results are meaningful to nurses and clients. Statistical significance indicates that the results are unlikely to be due to chance—not that they are necessarily important. With large samples, even modest relationships are statistically significant. For instance, with a sample of 500, a correlation coefficient of .10 is significant at $p < .05$ level, but a relationship this weak may have little practical value. When assessing the importance of findings, interpreters must attend to actual numeric values and also, if available, to effect sizes. Effect size information is important in addressing the important EBP question (Box 2.1, p. 32): "What *is* the evidence—what is the magnitude of effects?"

The absence of statistically significant results, conversely, does not always mean that the results are unimportant—although because nonsignificant results could reflect a Type II error, the case is more complex. Suppose we compared two procedures for making a clinical assessment (e.g., body temperature) and that we found no statistically significant differences between the two methods. If an effect size analysis suggested a small effect size for the differences *despite a large sample size*, we might be justified in concluding that the two procedures yield equally accurate assessments. If one procedure is more efficient or less painful than the other, nonsignificant findings could be clinically important. Nevertheless, corroboration in replication studies would be needed before firm conclusions could be reached.

Example of contrasting statistical and clinical significance:
Nitz and Josephson (2011) studied whether a balance strategy training program for elders was effective in improving functional mobility and reducing falls. They found statistically significant improvements on several outcomes, but concluded that the improvement was clinically significant for only one of them, 5 sit-to-stands (timed). As the investigators noted, "Statistically significant improvement does not necessarily equate to a meaningful clinical effect" (p. 108).

The Meaning of Quantitative Results

In quantitative studies, statistical results are in the form of test statistic values, *p* levels, effect sizes, and CIs, to which researchers and consumers must attach meaning. Many questions about the meaning of statistical results reflect a desire to interpret causal connections.

Interpreting what results mean is not typically a challenge in descriptive studies. For example, suppose we found that, among patients undergoing electroconvulsive therapy (ECT), the percentage who experience an ECT-induced headache is 59.4% (95% CI = 56.3, 63.1). This result is directly interpretable. But if we found that headache prevalence is significantly lower in a cryotherapy intervention group than among patients given acetaminophen, we would need to interpret what the results mean. In particular, we need to interpret whether it is plausible that cryotherapy *caused* the reduced prevalence of headaches. Clearly, internal validity is a key issue in interpreting the meaning of results with a potential for causal inference—even if the results have previously been deemed to be "real," i.e., statistically significant.

In this section, we discuss the interpretation of various research outcomes within a hypothesis testing context. The emphasis in on the issue of causal interpretations.

Interpreting Hypothesized Results

Interpreting the meaning of statistical results is easiest when hypotheses are supported. Researchers have already considered prior findings, a theoretical framework, and logical reasoning in developing hypotheses. Nevertheless, a few caveats should be kept in mind.

First, it is important to be conservative in drawing conclusions from the results and to avoid the temptation of going beyond the data to explain what results mean. For example, suppose we hypothesized that pregnant women's anxiety level about childbearing is correlated with the number of children they have. The data reveal a significant negative relationship between anxiety levels and parity ($r = -.40$). We interpret this to mean that increased experience with childbirth results in decreased anxiety. Is this conclusion supported by the data? The conclusion appears logical, but in fact, there is nothing in the data that leads directly to this interpretation. An important, indeed critical, research precept is: *correlation does not prove causation.* The finding that two variables are related offers no evidence suggesting which of the two variables—if either—caused the other. In our example, perhaps causality runs in the opposite direction—perhaps a woman's anxiety level influences how many children she bears. Or maybe a third variable, such as the woman's relationship with her husband, influences both anxiety and number of children. As discussed in Chapter 9, inferring causality is especially difficult in studies that have used a nonexperimental design.

Empirical evidence supporting research hypotheses never constitutes *proof* of their veracity. Hypothesis testing is probabilistic. There is always a possibility that observed relationships resulted from chance—that is, a Type I error has occurred. Researchers must be tentative about their results and about interpretations of them. Thus, even when the results are in line with expectations, researchers should draw conclusions with restraint and should give due consideration to limitations identified in assessing the accuracy of the results.

Example of corroboration of a hypothesis:
Houck and colleagues (2011) studied factors associated with self-concept in 145 children with attention deficit hyperactivity disorder (ADHD). They hypothesized that behavior problems in these children would be associated with less favorable self-concept, and they found that internalizing behavior problems were significantly predictive of lower self-concept scores. In their discussion, they stated that "age and internalizing behaviors were found to negatively influence the child's self-concept" (p. 245).

This study is a good example of the challenges of interpreting findings in correlational studies. The researchers' interpretation was that behavior problems were a factor that *influenced* ("caused") low self-concept. This is a conclusion supported by earlier research, yet there is nothing in the data that would rule out the possibility that a child's self-concept *influenced* the child's behavior, or that some other factor influenced both behavior and self-concept. The researchers' interpretation is certainly plausible, but their cross-sectional design makes it difficult to rule out other explanations. A major threat to the internal validity of the inference in this study is temporal ambiguity.

Interpreting Nonsignificant Results

Nonsignificant results pose interpretative challenges because statistical tests are geared toward disconfirmation of the null hypothesis. Failure to reject a null hypothesis can occur for many reasons, and the real reason is usually difficult to discern. The null hypothesis *could* actually be true, for example, accurately reflecting the absence of a relationship among research variables.

On the other hand, the null hypothesis could be false. Retention of a false null hypothesis (a Type II error) can result from a variety of methodologic problems, such as poor internal validity, an anomalous sample, a weak statistical procedure, or unreliable measures. In particular, failure to reject null hypotheses is often a consequence of insufficient power, usually reflecting too small a sample size.

In any event, a retained null hypothesis should not be considered as proof of the *absence* of relationships among variables. *Nonsignificant results provide no evidence of the truth or the falsity of the hypothesis.* Interpreting the meaning of nonsignificant results can, however, be aided by considering such factors as sample size and effect size estimates.

Example of nonsignificant results:
Griffin, Polit, and Byrnes (2007) hypothesized that stereotypes about children (based on children's gender, race, and attractiveness) would influence pediatric nurses' perceptions of children's pain and their pain treatment recommendations. None of the hypotheses was supported—i.e., there was no evidence of stereotyping. The conclusion that stereotyping was absent was bolstered by the fact that the sample was randomly selected and rather large ($N = 334$) and nurses were blinded to the manipulation, i.e., child characteristics. Very small effect sizes offered additional support for the conclusion that stereotyping was absent.

Because statistical procedures are designed to provide support for rejecting null hypotheses, they are not well-suited for testing *actual* research hypotheses about the absence of relationships between variables or about equivalence between groups. Yet sometimes, this is exactly what researchers want to do, especially in clinical situations in which the goal is to test whether one practice is as effective as another. When the actual research hypothesis is null (i.e., a prediction of no group difference or no relationship), stringent additional strategies must be used to provide supporting evidence. In particular, it is imperative to compute effect sizes and CIs as a means of illustrating that the risk of a Type II error was small.

Example of support for a hypothesized nonsignificant result:
Rickard and colleagues (2010) conducted a clinical trial to test whether resite of peripheral intravenous devices (IVDs) based on clinical indications was equivalent to the recommended routine resite every 3 days in terms of IVD complications. Complication rates were 68 per 1,000 IVD days for clinically indicated replacement and 66 per 1,000 IVD days for routine replacement. The large sample ($N = 362$ patients), high p value (.86), and negligible effect size (OR = 1.03) led the researchers to conclude that the evidence supported "the extended use of peripheral IVDs with removal only on clinical indication" (p. 53).

Interpreting Unhypothesized Significant Results

Unhypothesized significant results can occur in two situations. The first involves exploring relationships that were not considered during the design of the study. For example, in examining correlations among research variables, a researcher might notice that two variables that were not central to the research questions were nevertheless significantly correlated—and interesting.

Example of a serendipitous significant finding:
Latendress and Ruiz (2011) studied the relationship between chronic maternal stress and preterm birth. They observed an unexpected finding that maternal use of selective serotonin reuptake inhibitors (SSRIs) was associated with a 12-fold increase in preterm births.

The second situation is more perplexing, and it does not happen often: obtaining results *opposite* to those hypothesized. For instance, a researcher might hypothesize that individualized teaching about AIDS risks is more effective than group instruction, but the results might indicate that the group method was significantly better. Although this might seem embarrassing, research should not be undertaken to corroborate predictions, but rather to arrive at truth. There is no such thing as a study whose results "came out wrong" if they reflect the truth.

When significant findings are opposite to what was hypothesized, it is less likely that the methods are flawed than that the reasoning or theory is problematic. The interpretation of such findings should involve comparisons with other research, a consideration of alternate theories, and a critical scrutiny of the research methods.

Example of significant results contrary to hypothesis:
Strom and colleagues (2011), who studied diabetes self-care in a national sample of more than 50,000 people with type 2 diabetes, hypothesized that rural dwellers would have poorer diabetes self-care than urban dwellers. However, they found the opposite: foot self-checks and daily blood glucose testing were significantly higher among those in rural areas.

Interpreting Mixed Results

Interpretation is often complicated by *mixed results*: some hypotheses are supported, but others are not. Or a hypothesis may be accepted with one measure of the dependent variable, but rejected with a different measure. When only some results run counter to a theory or conceptual scheme, the research methods deserve critical scrutiny. Differences in the validity or reliability of the measures may account for such discrepancies, for example. On the other hand, mixed results may suggest that a theory needs to be qualified. Mixed results sometimes present opportunities to make conceptual advances because efforts to make sense of conflicting evidence may lead to a breakthrough.

Example of mixed results:
Dhruva and colleagues (2012) hypothesized that objective sleep/wake circadian rhythm parameters would be correlated with subjective ratings of sleep disturbance and fatigue in family caregivers of oncology patients. They found significant correlations for some variables (e.g., fatigue and subjective indicators of sleep disturbance), but not for others (e.g., fatigue and objective measures of sleep disturbance). The modest sample ($N = 103$) might have resulted from a Type II error for some of the relationships examined.

In summary, interpreting the meaning of research results is a demanding task, but it offers the possibility of intellectual rewards. Interpreters must play the role of scientific detectives, trying to make pieces of the puzzle fit together so that a coherent picture emerges.

Generalizability of the Results

Researchers typically seek evidence that can be used by others. If a new nursing intervention is found to be successful, perhaps others will want to adopt it. Therefore, an important interpretive question is whether the intervention will "work" or whether the relationships will "hold" in other settings, with other people. Part of the interpretive process involves asking the question, "To what groups, environments, and conditions can the results reasonably be applied?"

In interpreting a study's generalizability, it is useful to consider our earlier discussion about proxies. For which higher-order constructs, which populations, which settings, or which versions of an intervention were the study operations good "stand-ins"?

Implications of the Results

Once you have reached conclusions about the credibility, precision, importance, meaning, and generalizability of the results, you are ready to draw inferences about their implications. You might consider the implications of the findings with respect to future research: What should other researchers in this area do—what is the right "next step"? You are most likely to consider the implications for nursing practice: How should the results be used by nurses in their practice?

Clearly, all of the dimensions of interpretation that we have discussed are critical in evidence-based nursing practice. With regard to generalizability, it may not be enough to ask a broad question about to whom the results could apply—you need to ask, Are these results relevant to *my* particular clinical situation? Of course, if you have reached the conclusion that the results have limited credibility or importance, they may be of little utility to your practice.

CRITIQUING INTERPRETATIONS

Researchers offer an interpretation of their findings and discuss what the findings might imply for nursing in the discussion section of research articles. When critiquing a study, your own interpretation can be contrasted against those of the researchers.

A good discussion section should point out study limitations. Researchers are in the best position to detect and assess sampling deficiencies, practical constraints, data quality problems, and so on, and it is a professional responsibility to alert readers to these difficulties. Also, when researchers acknowledge methodologic shortcomings, readers know that these limitations were considered in interpreting the results. Of course, researchers are unlikely to note all relevant limitations. Your task as reviewer is to develop your own interpretation and assessment of methodologic problems, to challenge conclusions that do not appear to be warranted, and to consider how the study's evidence could have been enhanced.

You should also carefully scrutinize causal interpretations, especially in nonexperimental studies. Sometimes, even the titles of reports suggest a potentially inappropriate causal inference. If the title of a nonexperimental study includes terms like "the effect of...," or "the impact of...," this may signal the need for critical scrutiny of the researcher's inferences.

In addition to comparing your interpretation with that of the researchers, your critique should also draw conclusions about the stated implications of the study. Some researchers make grandiose claims or offer unfounded recommendations on the basis of modest results. Some guidelines for evaluating researchers' interpretation are offered in Box 13.1.

Box 13.1 Guidelines for Critiquing Interpretations/Discussions in Quantitative Research Reports

Interpretation of the Findings

1. Did the researchers discuss any study limitations and their possible effects on the credibility of the results? In discussing limitations, were key threats to the study's validity and biases mentioned? Did the interpretations take limitations into account?
2. What types of evidence were offered in support of the interpretation, and was that evidence persuasive? If results were "mixed," were possible explanations offered? Were results interpreted in light of findings from other studies?
3. Did the researchers make any unjustifiable causal inferences? Were alternative explanations for the findings considered? Were the rationales for rejecting these alternatives convincing?
4. Did the interpretation take into account the precision of the results and/or the magnitude of effects? Did the researchers distinguish between practical and statistical significance?
5. Did the researchers draw any unwarranted conclusions about the generalizability of the results?

Implications of the Findings and Recommendations

6. Did the researchers discuss the study's implications for clinical practice or future nursing research? Did they make specific recommendations?
7. If yes, are the stated implications appropriate, given the study's limitations and the magnitude of the effects—as well as consistent with evidence from other studies? Are there important implications that the report neglected to include?

RESEARCH EXAMPLES WITH CRITICAL THINKING EXERCISES

In this section, we provide details about the interpretive portion of a study, followed by some questions to guide critical thinking.

Example 1 below is also featured in our *Interactive Critical Thinking Activity* on thePoint website where you can easily record, print, and e-mail your responses to the related questions.

EXAMPLE 1 ● Interpretation in a Quantitative Study

Study: An office-based health promotion intervention for overweight and obese uninsured adults: A feasibility study (Buchholz et al., 2012)

Statement of Purpose: The purpose of this study was to assess the feasibility and initial efficacy of a nurse-delivered tailored physical activity intervention for uninsured overweight or obese adults seen at a free clinic.

Method: The researchers used a one-group pretest–posttest design with a convenience sample of 123 adults recruited from two free clinics in a midsized county in Indiana. The health intervention promotion (HIP) was designed as a 30-minute nutrition and physical activity intervention to be incorporated into monthly clinic visits for 6 months. Outcomes, measured at baseline and 6 months later, included body mass index values, physical activity, and self-reported nutrition measures. Adherence, the primary feasibility outcome, was measured by recording attendance at the HIP visits.

Analyses: The researchers used a number of descriptive statistics (means, standard deviations, percentages) to describe their sample and examine rates of adherence. Paired t-tests or chi-squared tests were used to examine changes over time for those who fully adhered to the program (attended all six sessions). The researchers also examined differences between those who fully adhered, and those who only partially adhered to HIP (i.e., attended fewer than six sessions).

Results: A total of 123 people (89% female) agreed to participate, but only 23 (19%) completed all 6 months of the program. About half of the enrollees (49%) completed three or more visits. The body mass index (BMI) of the full adherers declined significantly between baseline and follow-up, from 37.3 to 36.7. The BMI of partial adherers also declined, but the change was not significant. Partial and full adherers were not significantly different in terms of gender, ethnicity, or baseline BMI classification, but full adherers were older (M = 53.4) than partial adherers (M = 45.1).

Discussion: Here are a few excerpts from the Discussion section of this report:

"The strategies used in this study to recruit uninsured people from two free clinics proved effective. The participants were receptive to a nurse-delivered moderate-intensity counseling program to decrease or maintain weight through nutrition and physical activity…The challenge was to retain people in the study through and beyond 3 months. Once a participant missed an appointment (nonadherence), he/she did not return. Repeated attempts were made to find out why these participants did not adhere to the nurse visits. From those we reached, we learned that time and health issues were among the primary reasons for nonadherence. Furthermore, anecdotal staff notes show that conflicting responsibilities because of care of a family member, of other family-related responsibilities, and scheduling difficulties interfered with the ability of some participants to keep appointments with the nurse." (p. 72).

"A program such as this one, with appointments 1 month apart and no intervening contacts, can be problematic when participants miss an appointment…Telephone contacts with patients between visits may provide the additional intervention intensity needed. However, multiple calls often have to be made to make contact, increasing the effort and cost of this strategy…Mobile phone text messaging may offer a nonintrusive, cost-effective way to maintain contact.." (p. 73).

"Throughout this 6-month intervention, participants' step counts remained in the range of 5,000 to 7,500, which has been classified as 'low active.' Likewise, there was little change in fruit and vegetable intake…These findings suggest that additional attention may need to be given to the availability of recreational facilities and grocery stores with adequate produce" (p. 73).

"The main limitation of this pilot study was the lack of a control group with random assignment to group, thereby decreasing the ability to attribute the weight loss to the intervention. Also, the small number of participants who completed all six intervention sessions made it difficult to evaluate the impact of the full intervention on BMI" (p.73).

"This feasibility study demonstrates that a moderate-intensity nurse counseling intervention was modestly effective in decreasing BMI in those participants who were able to fully adhere to the visits…Although this study demonstrates that, for a small percentage of the sample, this intervention was successful in reducing BMI, study results also showed that a large number of participants did not adhere after the 3-month mark, suggesting this time frame needs to be more closely examined in regard to frequency of nurse contact as well as participant loss of interest" (pp. 73–74).

CRITICAL THINKING EXERCISES

1. Answer the relevant questions from Box 13.1 on page 261 regarding this study. (We encourage you to read the report in its entirety, especially the Discussion, to answer these questions).
2. Also consider the following targeted questions:
   a. Comment on the statistical conclusion validity of this study.
   b. Was a CONSORT-type flow-chart included in this report? Should one have been included?
3. What might be some of the uses to which the findings could be put in clinical practice?

EXAMPLE 2 ● Discussion Section in the Study in Appendix A

- Read the "Discussion" section of Howell and colleagues' (2007) study ("Anxiety, anger, and blood pressure in children") in Appendix A on pages 395–402.

CRITICAL THINKING EXERCISES

1. Answer the relevant questions in Box 13.1 on page 261 regarding this study.
2. Also consider the following targeted questions:
   a. Were there any statistically significant correlations that were unanticipated or unhypothesized in this study? Did the researchers discuss them? If yes, do you agree with their interpretation?
   b. Comment on the researchers' recommendations about gender-specific research in the discussion section.

EXAMPLE 3 ● Quantitative Study in Appendix C

- Read McGillion and colleagues' (2008) study (Randomized controlled trial of a psychoeducational program for the self-management of chronic cardiac pain) in Appendix C on pages 413–428 and then address the following suggested activities or questions.

CRITICAL THINKING EXERCISES

1. Before reading our critique, which accompanies the full report, write your own critique or prepare a list of what you think are the study's major strengths and weaknesses. Pay particular attention to validity threats and bias. Then contrast your critique with ours. Remember that you (or your instructor) do not necessarily have to agree with all of the points made in our critique, and you may identify strengths and weaknesses that we overlooked. You may find the broad critiquing guidelines in Table 4.1 on page 69 helpful.
2. Write a short summary of how credible, important, and generalizable you find the study results to be. Your summary should conclude with your interpretation of what the results mean, and what their implications are for nursing practice. Contrast your summary with the discussion section in the report itself.
3. In selecting studies to include in this textbook, we avoided choosing a poor-quality study because we did not wish to embarrass any researchers. In the questions below, we offer some "pretend" scenarios in which the researchers for the study in Appendix C made different methodologic decisions than the ones they in fact did make. Write a paragraph or two critiquing these "pretend" decisions, pointing out how these alternatives would have affected the rigor of the study and the inferences that could be made.
   a. Pretend that the researchers had been unable to randomize subjects to treatments. The design, in other words, would be a nonequivalent control-group quasi-experiment.
   b. Pretend that 130 participants were randomized (this is actually what did happen), but that only 80 participants remained in the study 3 months after randomization.
   c. Pretend that the health-related quality of life measure (the SF-36 scale) and the Seattle Angina Questionnaire (SAQ) were of lower quality—for example, that they had internal consistency reliabilities of .60.

WANT TO KNOW MORE? A wide variety of resources to enhance your learning and understanding of this chapter are available on thePoint.

- Interactive Critical Thinking Activity
- Chapter Supplement on Research Biases
- Answers to the Critical Thinking Exercises for Examples 2 and 3
- Student Review Questions
- Full-text online
- Internet Resources with useful websites for Chapter 13

Additional study aids including eight journal articles and related questions are also available in *Study Guide for Essentials of Nursing Research, 8e.*

SUMMARY POINTS

- The interpretation of quantitative research **results** (the outcomes of the statistical analyses) typically involves consideration of: (1) the credibility of the results, (2) precision of estimates of effects, (3) magnitude of effects, (4) underlying meaning, (5) generalizability, and (6) implications for future research and nursing practice.
- The particulars of the study—especially the methodologic decisions made by researchers—affect the inferences that can be made about the correspondence between study results and "truth in the real world."
- A cautious and even skeptical outlook is appropriate in drawing conclusions about the credibility and meaning of study results.
- An assessment of a study's credibility can involve various approaches, one of which involves an evaluation of the degree of congruence between abstract constructs or idealized methods on the one hand and the proxies actually used on the other.
- Credibility assessments also involve an assessment of study rigor through an analysis of validity threats and biases that could undermine the accuracy of the results.
- Corroboration (replication) of results, through either internal or external sources, is another approach in a credibility assessment.
- Researchers can facilitate interpretations by carefully documenting methodologic decisions and the outcomes of those decisions (e.g., by using the **CONSORT guidelines** to document participant flow).
- In their discussions of study results, researchers should themselves always point out known study limitations, but readers should draw their own conclusions about the rigor of the study and about the plausibility of alternative explanations for the results.

REFERENCES FOR CHAPTER 13

Buchholz, S. W., Wilbur, J., Miskovich, L., & Gerard, P. (2012). An office-based health promotion intervention for overweight and obese uninsured adults: A feasibility study. *Journal of Cardiovascular Nursing, 27*, 68–75.

Dhruva, A., Lee, K., Paul, S., West, C., Dunn, L., Dodd, M., et al. (2012). Sleep-wake circadian activity rhythms and fatigue in family caregivers of oncology patients. *Cancer Nursing, 35*, 70–81.

Griffin, R., Polit, D., & Byrnes, M. (2007). Stereotyping and nurses' treatment of children's pain. *Research in Nursing & Health, 30*, 655–666.

Houck, G., Kendall, J., Miller, A., Morrell, P., & Wiebe, G. (2011). Self-concept in children and adolescents with attention deficit hyperactivity disorder. *Journal of Pediatric Nursing, 26*, 239–247.

Latendresse, G., & Ruiz, R. (2011). Maternal corticotrophin-releasing hormone and the use of selective serotonin reuptake inhibitors independently predict the occurrence of preterm birth. *Journal of Midwifery & Women's Health, 56*, 118–126.

Nitz, J., & Josephson, D. (2011). Enhancing functional balance and mobility among older people living in long-term care facilities. *Geriatric Nursing, 32*, 106–113.

Qi, B., Resnick, B., Smeltzer, S., & Bausell, B. (2011). Self-efficacy program to prevent osteoporosis among Chinese immigrants. *Nursing Research, 60*, 393–404.

Rickard, C., McCann, D., Munñings, J., & McGrail, M. (2010). Routine resite of peripheral intravenous devices every 3 days did not reduce complication compared with clinically indicated resite. *BMC Medicine, 8*, 53–65.

Sackett, D. L., Straus, S.E., Richardson, W.S., Rosenberg, W., & Haynes, R. B. (2000). *Evidence-based medicine: How to practice and teach EBM* (2nd ed.), Edinburgh, UK: Churchill Livingstone.

Shadish, W. R., Cook, T. D., & Campbell, D. T. (2002). *Experimental and quasi-experimental designs for generalized causal inference.* Boston, MA: Houghton Mifflin.

Strom, J., Lynch, C., & Egede, L. (2011). Rural/urban variations in diabetes self-care and quality of care in a national sample of U. S. adults with diabetes. *The Diabetes Educator, 37*, 254–262.

part 4

Qualitative Research

chapter 14

Qualitative Designs and Approaches

LEARNING OBJECTIVES

On completing this chapter, you will be able to:

- Discuss the rationale for an emergent design in qualitative research, and describe qualitative design features
- Identify the major research traditions for qualitative research and describe the domain of inquiry of each
- Describe the main features of ethnographic, phenomenologic, and grounded theory studies
- Discuss the goals and methods of various types of research with an ideological perspective
- Define new terms in the chapter

KEY TERMS

Basic social process (BSP)
Bracketing
Case study
Constant comparison
Constructivist grounded theory
Core variable
Critical ethnography
Critical theory
Descriptive phenomenology
Descriptive qualitative study
Emergent design
Ethnonursing research
Feminist research
Field work
Hermeneutics
Interpretive phenomenology
Narrative analysis
Participant observation
Participatory action research (PAR)
Reflexive journal

Quantitative researchers specify a research design before collecting even one piece of data, and rarely depart from that design once the study is underway: they design and *then* they do. In qualitative research, by contrast, the study design typically evolves during the project: qualitative researchers design *as* they do. Decisions about how best to obtain data, from whom to obtain data, and how long a data collection session should last are made as the study unfolds.

THE DESIGN OF QUALITATIVE STUDIES

Qualitative studies use an **emergent design** that evolves as researchers make ongoing decisions based on what they have already learned. An emergent design in qualitative studies is a reflection of the researchers' desire to have the inquiry based on the realities and viewpoints of those under study—realities and viewpoints that are not known at the outset.

Characteristics of Qualitative Research Design

Qualitative inquiry has been guided by different disciplines, and each has developed methods for addressing questions of interest. Some characteristics of qualitative research design tend to apply across disciplines, however. In general, qualitative design:

- Is flexible and elastic, capable of adjusting to what is being learned during data collection
- Often involves merging together various data collection strategies (i.e., triangulation)
- Tends to be holistic, striving for an understanding of the whole
- Requires researchers to become intensely involved and can necessitate a lengthy period of time
- Benefits from ongoing data analysis to guide subsequent strategies and decisions about when data collection is done.

Although design decisions are not finalized in advance, qualitative researchers typically do advance planning that supports their flexibility. That is, they plan for broad contingencies that may pose decision opportunities once the study has begun. For example, qualitative researchers make advance decisions with regard to their research tradition, the study site, the maximum amount of time available for the study, a broad data collection strategy, and the equipment they will need in the field. Qualitative researchers plan for a variety of circumstances, but decisions about how to deal with them must be resolved when the social context of time, place, and human interactions are better understood.

Qualitative Design Features

Some of the design features discussed in Chapter 9 apply to qualitative studies. However, qualitative design features are often posthoc characterizations of what happened in the field rather than features specifically planned in advance. To contrast qualitative and quantitative research design, we consider the design elements identified in Table 9.1 on page 150.

Intervention, Control, and Blinding

Qualitative research is almost always nonexperimental—although a qualitative substudy may be embedded in an experiment (see Chapter 18). Qualitative researchers do not conceptualize their studies as having independent and dependent variables, and they rarely control any aspect of the people or environment under study. Blinding is rarely used by qualitative researchers. The goal is to develop a rich understanding of a phenomenon as it exists and as it is constructed by individuals within their own context.

Comparisons

Qualitative researchers typically do not plan to make group comparisons because the intent is to thoroughly describe or explain a phenomenon. Yet, patterns emerging in the data sometimes suggest illuminating comparisons. Indeed, as Morse (2004) noted in an editorial in *Qualitative Health Research*, "All description requires comparisons" (p. 1323). In analyzing qualitative data and in determining whether categories are saturated, there is a need to compare "this" to "that."

Example of qualitative comparisons:
Baum and colleagues (2012) explored the experiences of 30 Israeli mothers of very-low-birth-weight babies when the babies were still in neonatal hospitalization. The researchers discovered that there were three patterns with regard to attribution of blame for not carrying to full term: those who blamed themselves, those who blamed others, and those who believed that premature delivery was fortunate because it saved their baby's life.

Research Settings

Qualitative researchers usually collect their data in real-world, naturalistic settings. And, whereas a quantitative researcher usually strives to collect data in one type of setting to maintain constancy of conditions (e.g., conducting all interviews in participants' homes), qualitative researchers may deliberately strive to study phenomena in a variety of natural contexts, especially in ethnographic research.

Example of variation in settings and sites:
Bohman and colleagues (2011) studied the experience of being old and in care-related relationships in a changing South African context. Interviews with elders were supplemented with observations in a variety of community contexts where the care of elders takes place and in participants' homes.

Timeframes

Qualitative research, like quantitative research, can be either cross-sectional, with one data collection point, or longitudinal, with multiple data collection points designed to observe the evolution of a phenomenon. In terms of the retrospective/prospective distinction, most qualitative research is retrospective: an "outcome" or situation occurring in the present may give rise to inquiries into previously occurring factors that led up to or contributed to it.

Examples of a longitudinal qualitative study:
Taylor and colleagues (2011) conducted a longitudinal study over a 12-month period of the experience of surviving colorectal cancer treatment and dealing with fears about recurrence.

Causality and Qualitative Research

In evidence hierarchies that rank evidence in terms of its support of causal inferences (e.g., the one in Figure 2.1 on page 23), qualitative inquiry is often near the base, which has led some to criticize evidence-based practice initiatives. The issue of causality, which has been controversial throughout the history of science, is especially contentious in qualitative research.

Some qualitative researchers think that causality is not an appropriate concept within the constructivist paradigm. For example, Lincoln and Guba (1985) devoted an entire chapter of their book to a critique of causality and argued that it should be replaced with a concept that they called *mutual shaping*. According to their view, "Everything influences everything else, in the here and now" (p. 151).

Others, however, believe that qualitative methods are particularly well suited to understanding causal relationships. For example, Huberman and Miles (1994) argued that qualitative studies "can look directly and longitudinally at the local processes underlying a temporal series of events and states, showing how these led to specific outcomes, and ruling out rival hypotheses" (p. 434).

In attempting to not only describe but also to explain phenomena, qualitative researchers who undertake in-depth studies will inevitably reveal patterns and processes suggesting causal interpretations. These interpretations can be (and often are) subjected to more systematic testing using more controlled methods of inquiry.

QUALITATIVE RESEARCH TRADITIONS

Although some features are shared by many qualitative research designs, there is a wide variety of approaches. One useful taxonomic system is to describe qualitative research according to disciplinary traditions. These traditions vary in their conceptualization of what types of questions are important to ask and in the methods considered appropriate for answering them. Table 14.1 provides an overview of several such traditions, some of which we have previously introduced. This section describes traditions that have been especially prominent in nursing research.

Ethnography

Ethnography is a type of qualitative inquiry that involves the description and interpretation of a culture and cultural behavior. *Culture* refers to the way a group of people live—the patterns of human activity and the symbolic structures (for example, the values and norms) that give such activity significance. Ethnographies typically involve extensive **field work**, which is the process by which the ethnographer comes to understand a culture. Because culture is, in itself, not visible or tangible, it must be inferred from the words, actions, and products of members of a group and then constructed through ethnographic writing.

Ethnographic research sometimes concerns broadly defined cultures (e.g., the Maori culture of New Zealand), in what is sometimes referred to as a *macroethnography*. However, ethnographies sometimes focus on more narrowly defined cultures in a *microethnography* or focused ethnography. Focused ethnographies are fine-grained studies of small units in a group or culture (e.g., the culture of an intensive care unit). An underlying assumption

TABLE 14.1 Overview of Qualitative Research Traditions

Discipline	Domain	Research Tradition	Area of Inquiry
Anthropology	Culture	Ethnography	Holistic view of a culture
Psychology/ Philosophy	Lived experience	Phenomenology	Experiences and meanings of individuals within their lifeworld
		Hermeneutics	Interpretations and meanings of individuals' experiences
Sociology	Social settings	Grounded theory	Social psychological and structural processes within a social setting
History	Past behavior, events, conditions	Historical analysis	Description/interpretation of historical events

of the ethnographer is that every human group eventually evolves a culture that guides the members' view of the world and the way they structure their experiences.

Example of a focused ethnography:
MacKinnon (2011) used an ethnographic approach to explore the work of rural nurses, with specific focus on their safeguarding work to maintain patient safety.

Ethnographers seek to learn from (rather than to study) members of a cultural group—to understand their world view. Ethnographic researchers refer to "emic" and "etic" perspectives. An **emic perspective** refers to the way the members of the culture regard their world—the insiders' view. The emic is the local language, concepts, or means of expression that are used by the members of the group under study to name and characterize their experiences. The **etic perspective**, by contrast, is the outsiders' interpretation of the experiences of that culture—the words and concepts they use to refer to the same phenomena. Ethnographers strive to acquire an emic perspective of a culture and to reveal *tacit knowledge*—information about the culture that is so deeply embedded in cultural experiences that members do not talk about it or may not even be consciously aware of it.

Three broad types of information are usually sought by ethnographers: cultural behavior (what members of the culture do), cultural artifacts (what members make and use), and cultural speech (what they say). Ethnographers rely on a wide variety of data sources, including observations, in-depth interviews, records, and other types of physical evidence (e.g., photographs, diaries). Ethnographers typically use a strategy called **participant observation** in which they make observations of the culture under study while participating in its activities. Ethnographers observe people day after day in their natural environments to observe behavior in a wide array of circumstances. Ethnographers also enlist the help of **key informants** to help them understand and interpret the events and activities being observed.

Ethnographic research is labor-intensive and time-consuming—months and even years of fieldwork may be required to learn about a culture. Ethnography requires a certain level of intimacy with members of the cultural group, and such intimacy can be developed only over time and by working directly with those members as active participants.

The product of ethnographies is a rich and holistic description of the culture under study. Ethnographers also interpret the culture, describing normative behavioral and social patterns. Among health care researchers, ethnography provides access to the health beliefs and health practices of a culture. Ethnographic inquiry can thus help to foster understanding of behaviors affecting health and illness. Leininger coined the phrase **ethnonursing research**, which she defined as "the study and analysis of the local or indigenous people's viewpoints, beliefs, and practices about nursing care behavior and processes of designated cultures" (1985, p. 38).

Example of an ethnonursing study:
Schumacher (2010) explored the meanings, beliefs, and practices of care for rural people in the Dominican Republic. Leininger's theory of culture-care diversity and universality was the conceptual basis for the study, and her four-phase ethnonursing methods were adopted. Interviews were conducted with 29 informants.

Ethnographers are often, but not always, "outsiders" to the culture under study. A type of ethnography that involves self-scrutiny (including scrutiny of groups or cultures to which researchers themselves belong) is called *autoethnography* or *insider research*.

Autoethnography has several advantages, including ease of access and recruitment and the ability to get candid data based on pre-established trust. The drawback is that an "insider" may have biases about certain issues or may be so entrenched in the culture that valuable data are overlooked.

Phenomenology

Phenomenology, rooted in a philosophical tradition developed by Husserl and Heidegger, is an approach to exploring and understanding people's everyday life experiences.

Phenomenologic researchers ask: What is the *essence* of this phenomenon as experienced by these people and what does it *mean?* Phenomenologists assume there is an *essence*—an essential structure—that can be understood, in much the same way that ethnographers assume that cultures exist. Essence is what makes a phenomenon what it is, and without which it would not be what it is. Phenomenologists investigate subjective phenomena in the belief that critical truths about reality are grounded in people's lived experiences. The topics appropriate to phenomenology are ones that are fundamental to the life experiences of humans, such as the meaning of suffering or the quality of life with chronic pain.

Phenomenologists believe that lived experience gives meaning to each person's perception of a particular phenomenon. The goal of phenomenologic inquiry is to understand fully lived experience and the perceptions to which it gives rise. Four aspects of lived experience that are of interest to phenomenologists are *lived space*, or spatiality; *lived body*, or corporeality; *lived time*, or temporality; and *lived human relation*, or relationality.

Phenomenologists view human existence as meaningful and interesting because of people's consciousness of that existence. The phrase *being-in-the-world* (or *embodiment*) is a concept that acknowledges people's physical ties to their world—they think, see, hear, feel, and are conscious through their bodies' interaction with the world.

In phenomenologic studies, the main data source is in-depth conversations. Through these conversations, researchers strive to gain entrance into the informants' world, and to have access to their experiences as lived. Phenomenologic studies usually involve a small number of participants—often 10 or fewer. For some phenomenologic researchers, the inquiry includes not only gathering information from informants but also efforts to experience the phenomenon, through participation, observation, and reflection. Phenomenologists share their insights in rich, vivid reports that describe key *themes*. The results section in a phenomenological report should help readers "see" something in a different way that enriches their understanding of experiences.

Phenomenology has several variants and interpretations. The two main schools of thought are descriptive phenomenology and interpretive phenomenology (hermeneutics).

Descriptive Phenomenology

Descriptive phenomenology was developed first by Husserl, who was primarily interested in the question: *What do we know as persons?* His philosophy emphasized descriptions of human experience. Descriptive phenomenologists insist on the careful portrayal of ordinary conscious experience of everyday life—a depiction of "things" as people experience them. These "things" include hearing, seeing, believing, feeling, remembering, deciding, and evaluating.

Descriptive phenomenologic studies often involve the following four steps: bracketing, intuiting, analyzing, and describing. **Bracketing** refers to the process of identifying and holding in abeyance preconceived beliefs and opinions about the phenomenon under study. Researchers strive to bracket out presuppositions in an effort to confront their data in pure form. Phenomenological researchers (as well as other qualitative researchers) often maintain a **reflexive journal** in their efforts to bracket.

Intuiting, the second step in descriptive phenomenology, occurs when researchers remain open to the meanings attributed to the phenomenon by those who have experienced it. Phenomenologic researchers then proceed to an analysis (i.e., extracting significant statements, categorizing, and making sense of the essential meanings of the phenomenon). Finally, the descriptive phase occurs when researchers come to understand and define the phenomenon.

Example of a descriptive phenomenological study:
Porter and colleagues (2012) used a descriptive phenomenological approach in their longitudinal study of the intentions of elderly homebound women with regard to reaching help quickly.

Interpretive Phenomenology

Heidegger, a student of Husserl, is the founder of **interpretive phenomenology** or hermeneutics. Heidegger's critical question is: *What is being?* He stressed interpreting and understanding—not just describing—human experience. He believed that lived experience is inherently an interpretive process and argued that **hermeneutics** ("understanding") is a basic characteristic of human existence. (The term *hermeneutics* refers to the art and philosophy of interpreting the meaning of an object, such as a *text* or work of art). The goals of interpretive phenomenological research are to enter another's world and to discover the wisdom and understandings found there.

Gadamer, another influential interpretive phenomenologist, described the interpretive process as a circular relationship known as the *hermeneutic circle* where one understands the whole of a text (for example, a transcribed interview) in terms of its parts and the parts in terms of the whole. Researchers continually question the meanings of the text.

In an interpretive phenomenologic study, bracketing does not occur. For Heidegger, it was not possible to bracket one's being-in-the-world. Hermeneutics presupposes prior understanding on the part of the researcher. Interpretive phenomenologists ideally approach each interview text with openness—they must be open to hearing what it is the text is saying.

Interpretive phenomenologists, like descriptive phenomenologists, rely primarily on in-depth interviews with individuals who have experienced the phenomenon of interest, but they may go beyond a traditional approach to gathering and analyzing data. For example, interpretive phenomenologists sometimes augment their understandings of the phenomenon through an analysis of supplementary texts, such as novels, poetry, or other artistic expressions—or they use such materials in their conversations with study participants.

Example of an interpretive phenomenological study:
Vatne and Nåden (2012) used a hermeneutic approach to explore the experiences and reflections of 10 people after suicidal crisis or recently completed suicide attempts.

HOW-TO-TELL TIP: How can you tell if a phenomenological study is descriptive or interpretive? Phenomenologists often use terms that can help you make this determination. In a descriptive phenomenological study such terms may be bracketing, description, essence, and Husserl. The names of Colaizzi, Van Kaam, or Giorgi may appear in the methods section. In an interpretive phenomenological study, key terms can include being-in-the-world, hermeneutics, understanding, and Heidegger. The names van Manen, Benner, or Diekelmann may appear in the method section. These names are discussed in Chapter 16 on qualitative data analysis.

Grounded Theory

Grounded theory has contributed to the development of many middle-range theories of phenomena relevant to nurses. Grounded theory was developed in the 1960s by two sociologists, Glaser and Strauss (1967), whose theoretical roots were in *symbolic interaction*, which focuses on the manner in which people make sense of social interactions.

Grounded theory tries to account for people's actions from the perspective of those involved. Grounded theory researchers seek to understand the actions by first discovering the main concern or problem, and then the behavior that is designed to address it. The manner in which people resolve this main concern is called the **core variable**. One type of core variable is a **basic social process (BSP)**. The goal of grounded theory is to discover the main concern and the basic social process that explains how people resolve it. Grounded theory researchers generate conceptual categories and integrate them into a substantive theory grounded in the data.

Grounded Theory Methods

Grounded theory methods constitute an entire approach to the conduct of field research. A study that truly follows Glaser and Strauss's precepts does not begin with a focused research problem. The problem, and the process used to solve it, emerge from the data and are discovered during the study. In grounded theory research, data collection, data analysis, and sampling of participants occur simultaneously. The grounded theory process is recursive: researchers collect data, categorize them, describe the emerging central phenomenon, and then recycle earlier steps.

A procedure called **constant comparison** is used to develop and refine theoretically relevant concepts and categories. Categories elicited from the data are constantly compared with data obtained earlier so that commonalities and variations can be detected. As data collection proceeds, the inquiry becomes increasingly focused on emerging theoretical concerns.

In-depth interviews and participant observation are common data sources in grounded theory studies, but existing documents and other data may also be used. Typically, a grounded theory study involves interviews with a sample of about 20 to 30 people.

Example of a grounded theory study:

Lundh and colleagues (2012) used grounded theory methods to understand the process of trying to quit smoking from the perspective of patients with COPD. Analysis of data from interviews with 18 patients led to a theoretical model that illuminated factors related to the decision to try to quit smoking, including constructive and destructive strategies.

Alternate Views of Grounded Theory

In 1990, Strauss and Corbin published the first edition of a controversial book, *Basics of qualitative research: Grounded theory procedures and techniques*. The stated purpose of the book was to provide beginning grounded theory researchers with basic procedures involved in building theory at a substantive level.

Glaser, however, disagreed with some procedures advocated by Strauss (his original coauthor) and Corbin (a nurse researcher). Glaser (1992) believed that Strauss and Corbin developed a method that is not grounded theory but rather what he called "full conceptual description." According to Glaser, the purpose of grounded theory is to generate concepts and theories about their relationships that explain, account for, and interpret variation in behavior in the substantive area under study. *Conceptual description*, in contrast, is aimed at describing the full range of behavior of what is occurring in the substantive area.

Nurse researchers have conducted grounded theory studies using both the original Glaser and Strauss and the Strauss and Corbin approaches. They are also using an approach called **constructivist grounded theory** (Charmaz, 2006). Charmaz viewed Glaser and Strauss' grounded theory as being based in the positivist tradition. In Charmaz's approach, the developed grounded theory is viewed as an interpretation. The data collected and analyzed are acknowledged to be constructed from shared experiences and relationships between the researcher and the participants. Data and analyses are viewed as social constructions.

Historical Research

One other qualitative tradition springs from the discipline of history. **Historical research** is the systematic collection and critical evaluation of data relating to past occurrences. Historical research relies primarily on qualitative (narrative) data but can sometimes involve statistical analysis of quantitative data. Nurses use historical research methods to examine a wide range of phenomena in both the recent and more distant past.

Historical research should not be confused with a review of the literature about historical events. Like other types of research, historical inquiry has as its goal discovering *new* knowledge, not summarizing existing knowledge.

Data for historical research are usually in the form of written records: diaries, letters, newspapers, medical or legal documents, and so forth. Nonwritten materials may also be of interest. For example, visual materials, such as photographs and films, are forms of data. In some cases, it is possible to conduct interviews with people who participated in historical events (e.g., nurses who served in recent wars).

Historical research is usually interpretive. Historical researchers try to describe what happened, and also how and why it happened. Relationships between events and ideas, between people and organizations, are explored and interpreted within their historical context and within the context of new viewpoints about what is historically significant.

Example of historical research:
Connolly and Gibson (2011) conducted a historical study of the role nurses played in pediatric tuberculosis care in Virginia from 1900 to 1935. They concluded that although nurses were leaders in designing a template for children's care, they also helped to forge "a system funded by a complicated, poorly coordinated, race- and class-based mix of public and private support" (p. 230). Yet, the researchers also found that these nurses took courageous action and helped invent pediatric nursing.

OTHER TYPES OF QUALITATIVE RESEARCH

Qualitative studies often can be characterized and described in terms of the disciplinary research traditions discussed in the previous section. However, several other important types of qualitative research not associated with a particular discipline also deserve mention.

Case Studies

Case studies are in-depth investigations of a single entity or small number of entities. The entity may be an individual, family, institution, community, or other social unit. Case study researchers attempt to analyze and understand issues that are important to the history, development, or circumstances of the entity under study.

One way to think of a case study is to consider what is at center stage. In most studies, whether qualitative or quantitative, certain phenomena or variables are the core of the inquiry. In a case study, the *case* itself is central. The focus of case studies is typically on understanding *why* an individual thinks, behaves, or develops in a particular manner rather than on *what* his or her status or actions are. Probing research of this type often requires detailed study over a considerable period. Data are often collected that relate not only to the person's present state but also to past experiences and situations relevant to the problem being examined.

The greatest strength of case studies is the depth that is possible when a small number of entities is being investigated. Case study researchers have opportunities to gain an intimate knowledge of a person's feelings, actions (past and present), intentions, and environment. Yet, this same strength is a potential weakness: researchers' familiarity with the person or group may make objectivity more difficult—especially if the data are collected by observational techniques for which the researchers are the main (or only) observers. Another criticism of case studies concerns generalizability: If researchers discover important relationships, it is difficult to know whether the same relationships would occur with others. However, case studies can often play a critical role in challenging generalizations based on other types of research.

Example of a case study:
Moro and colleagues (2011) conducted in-depth case studies of parents' decision-making for life support for extremely premature infants, based on multiple in-depth interviews and data from medical records.

Narrative Analyses

Narrative analysis focuses on *story* as the object of inquiry, to understand how individuals make sense of events in their lives. The underlying premise of narrative research is that people most effectively make sense of their world—and communicate these meanings—by constructing and narrating stories. Individuals construct stories when they wish to understand specific events and situations that require linking an inner world of desire to an external world of observable actions. Analyzing stories opens up *forms* of telling about experience, and is more than just content. Narrative analysts ask, *Why did the story get told that way?*

A number of structural approaches can be used to analyze stories, including ones based on literary analysis and linguistics. Burke's (1969) *pentadic dramatism* is one approach for narrative analysis. For Burke there are five key elements of a story: act, scene, agent, agency, and purpose. The five terms of Burke's pentad are meant to be understood paired together as ratios such as, act: agent, agent: agency, and purpose: agent. The analysis focuses on the internal relationships and tensions of these five terms to each other. Each pairing of terms in the pentad provides a different way of directing the researcher's attention. What drives the narrative analysis is not just the interaction of the pentadic terms but an imbalance between two or more of these terms.

Example of a narrative analysis using Burke's approach:
Beck (2006), one of this book's authors, did a narrative analysis on birth trauma. Eleven mothers sent their stories of traumatic childbirth to Beck. Burke's pentad of terms was used to analyze these narratives. The most problematic ratio imbalance was between act and agency. Frequently, in the mothers' narratives it was the "how" an act was carried out by the labor and delivery staff that led to the women perceiving their childbirth as traumatic.

Descriptive Qualitative Studies

Many qualitative studies claim no particular disciplinary or methodologic roots. The researchers may simply indicate that they have conducted a qualitative study, a naturalistic inquiry, or a *content analysis* of qualitative data (i.e., an analysis of themes and patterns that emerge in the narrative content). Thus, some qualitative studies do not have a formal name or do not fit into the typology we have presented in this chapter. We refer to these as **descriptive qualitative studies**.

Descriptive qualitative studies tend to be eclectic in their designs and methods and are based on the general premises of constructivist inquiry. These studies, which are actually more common in nursing than studies based on a disciplinary tradition, are infrequently discussed in research methods textbooks.

TIP: The Chapter Supplement on thePoint website for this chapter presents additional material relating to descriptive qualitative studies and to studies that nurse researcher Sally Thorne (2008) called interpretive description.

Example of a descriptive qualitative study:
Stewart and colleagues (2012) did a descriptive qualitative study to explore the biopsychosocial burden of chronic hepatitis C and patients' coping and help-seeking. In-depth interviews were conducted with 13 patients, 5 hepatologists, and 2 counselors.

RESEARCH WITH IDEOLOGICAL PERSPECTIVES

Some qualitative researchers conduct inquiries within an ideological framework, typically to draw attention to certain social problems or the needs of certain groups and to bring about change. These approaches represent important investigative avenues.

Critical Theory

Critical theory originated with a group of Marxist-oriented German scholars in the 1920s. Variants of critical theory abound in the social sciences. Essentially, a critical researcher is concerned with a critique of society and with envisioning new possibilities.

Critical social science is typically action oriented. Its aim is to make people aware of contradictions and disparities in their beliefs and social practices, and become inspired to change them. Critical researchers, who reject the idea of an objective, disinterested inquirer, are oriented toward a transformation process. Critical theory calls for inquiries that foster enlightened self-knowledge and social or political change.

The design of research in critical theory often begins with an analysis of certain aspects of the problem. For example, critical researchers might analyze and critique taken-for-granted assumptions that underlie the problem, the language used to depict the situation, and the biases of prior researchers investigating the problem. Critical researchers often triangulate methods, and emphasize multiple perspectives (e.g., alternative racial or social class perspectives) on problems. Critical researchers typically interact with participants in ways that emphasize participants' expertise. Some features that distinguish more traditional qualitative research and critical research are summarized in Table 14.2.

Critical theory has been applied in several disciplines, but has played an especially important role in ethnography. **Critical ethnography** focuses on raising consciousness in the hope of effecting social change. Critical ethnographers address the historical, social, political, and economic dimensions of cultures and their value-laden agendas. Critical ethnographers

TABLE 14.2 Comparison of Traditional Qualitative Research and Critical Research

Issue	Traditional Qualitative Research	Critical Research
Research aims	Understanding, reconstruction of multiple constructions	Critique, transformation, consciousness raising, advocacy
View of knowledge	Transactional/subjective: knowledge is created in interactions between investigator and participants	Transactional/subjective: value-mediated and value-dependent
Methods	Dialectic: truth is arrived at logically through conversations	Dialectic and didactic: dialogue designed to transform naivety and misinformation
Evaluative criteria for inquiry quality	Authenticity, trustworthiness	Historical situatedness of the inquiry, erosion of ignorance, stimulus for change
Researcher's role	Facilitator of multivoice reconstruction	Transformative agent, advocate, activist

attempt to increase the political dimensions of cultural research and undermine oppressive systems. Critical ethnography has been viewed as especially well suited to health promotion research because both are concerned with enabling people to take control over their own situation.

Example of a critical ethnography:
Baumbusch (2011) used a critical ethnographic approach to explore disenfranchised groups in the context of long-term residential care in British Columbia, Canada.

Feminist Research

Feminist research is similar to critical theory research, but the focus is on gender domination and discrimination within patriarchal societies. Similar to critical researchers, feminist researchers seek to establish collaborative and nonexploitative relationships with their informants and to conduct research that is transformative. Feminist investigators seek to understand how gender and a gendered social order have shaped women's lives and their consciousness. The aim is to facilitate change in ways relevant to ending women's unequal social position.

The scope of feminist research ranges from studies of the subjective views of individual women to studies of social movements, structures, and broad policies that affect (and often exclude) women. Feminist research methods typically include in-depth, interactive, and collaborative individual interviews or group interviews that offer the possibility of reciprocally educational encounters. Feminists usually seek to negotiate the meanings of the results with those participating in the study, and to be self-reflective about what they themselves are learning.

Example of feminist research:
Van Daalen-Smith (2011) used feminist theory to explore women's experiences of electroshock, which the women—but not their nurses—believed resulted in damage and devastating loss.

Participatory Action Research

A type of research known as participatory action research is closely allied to both critical research and feminist research. **Participatory action research (PAR)** is based on a recognition that the production of knowledge can be political and used to exert power. Researchers in this approach typically work with groups or communities that are vulnerable to the control or oppression of a dominant group.

PAR is, as the name implies, participatory. Researchers and study participants collaborate in the definition of the problem, the selection of research methods, the analysis of the data, and the use to which findings are put. The aim of PAR is to produce not only knowledge, but also action, empowerment, and consciousness-raising as well. The PAR tradition has as its starting point a concern for the powerlessness of the group under study. Thus, a key objective is to produce an impetus that is directly used to make improvements through education and sociopolitical action.

In PAR, the research methods are designed to facilitate processes of collaboration and dialogue that can motivate, increase self-esteem, and generate community solidarity. Thus, "data-gathering" strategies used are not only the traditional methods of interview and observation (including both qualitative and quantitative approaches), but may also include storytelling, sociodrama, photography, drawing, skits, and other activities designed to encourage people to find creative ways to explore their lives, tell their stories, and recognize their own strengths.

Example of PAR:

Kneipp and colleagues (2011) designed and tested a public health nursing case-management intervention for women with chronic health problems who received public assistance. The community-based intervention had been developed on the basis of PAR.

CRITIQUING QUALITATIVE DESIGNS

Evaluating a qualitative design is often difficult. Qualitative researchers do not always document design decisions and are even less likely to describe the process by which such decisions were made. Researchers often do, however, indicate whether the study was conducted within a specific qualitative tradition. This information can be used to come to some conclusions about the study design. For example, if a report indicated that the researcher conducted 2 months of field work for an ethnographic study, you might well suspect that insufficient time had been spent in the field to obtain a true emic perspective of the culture under study. Ethnographic studies may also be critiqued if their only source of information was from interviews, rather than from a broader range of data sources, particularly participant observations.

In a grounded theory study, you might also be concerned if the researcher relied exclusively on data from interviews; a stronger design might have been obtained by including participant observations. Also, look for evidence about when the data were collected and analyzed. If the researcher collected all the data before analyzing any of it, you might question whether the constant comparative method was used correctly.

In critiquing a phenomenological study, you should first determine if the study is descriptive or interpretive. This will help you to assess how closely the researcher kept to the basic tenets of that qualitative research tradition. For example, in a descriptive phenomenological study, did the researcher bracket? When critiquing a phenomenological study, in

BOX 14.1 Guidelines for Critiquing Qualitative Designs

1. Is the research tradition for the qualitative study identified? If none was identified, can one be inferred? If more than one was identified, is this justifiable or does it suggest "method slurring"?
2. Is the research question congruent with a qualitative approach and with the specific research tradition (i.e., is the domain of inquiry for the study congruent with the domain encompassed by the tradition)? Are the data sources, research methods, and analytic approach congruent with the research tradition?
3. How well is the research design described? Are design decisions explained and justified? Does it appear that the researcher made all design decisions up-front, or did the design emerge during data collection, allowing researchers to capitalize on early information?
4. Is the design appropriate, given the research question? Does the design lend itself to a thorough, in-depth, intensive examination of the phenomenon of interest? What design elements might have strengthened the study (e.g., a longitudinal perspective rather than a cross-sectional one)?
5. Was there evidence of reflexivity in the design?
6. Was the study undertaken with an ideological perspective? If so, is there evidence that ideological methods and goals were achieved? (e.g., was there evidence of full collaboration between researchers and participants? Did the research have the power to be transformative, or is there evidence that a transformative process occurred?)

addition to critiquing the methodology, you should also look at its power in capturing the meaning of the phenomena being studied.

No matter what qualitative design is identified in a study, look to see if the researchers stayed true to a single qualitative tradition throughout the study or if they mixed qualitative traditions ("method slurring"). For example, did the researcher state that grounded theory was used, but then presents results that described *themes* instead of generating a substantive theory?

The guidelines in Box 14.1 are designed to assist you in critiquing the designs of qualitative studies.

RESEARCH EXAMPLES WITH CRITICAL THINKING EXERCISES

This section presents examples of different types of qualitative studies. Read these summaries and then answer the critical thinking questions, referring to the full research report if necessary.

Example 1 below is also featured in our *Interactive Critical Thinking Activity* on thePoint website where you can easily record, print, and e-mail your responses to the related questions.

EXAMPLE 1 ● A Grounded Theory Study

Study: Preserving the self: The process of decision-making about hereditary breast cancer and ovarian cancer risk reduction (Howard et al., 2011).

Statement of Purpose: The purpose of the study was to understand how women make decisions about strategies to reduce the risk of hereditary breast and ovarian cancer (HBOC), such as cancer screening and risk-reducing surgeries.

Method: The researchers used a constructivist grounded theory approach to understanding women's decision-making processes. Participants were recruited through a hereditary cancer program. Women were eligible for the study if they were older than 18 and tested positive for BRCA1/2 mutations in genetic testing. The researchers initially invited all eligible women to participate, but as the study progressed, they used preliminary findings to recruit women who might best refine conceptualizations. Data saturation was achieved with a total of 22 participants. In-depth interviews, lasting 45 to 90 minutes, were audiotaped and subsequently transcribed for analysis. Early interviews covered broad questions about decision-making and changes in decisions over time. Later in the study, the questions became more focused, to explore certain issues in greater depth and to verify emerging findings. Four women, whose decision experiences varied, were interviewed a second time to obtain clarification and feedback about preliminary findings. The analysis of the data was guided by theories of relational autonomy and gender: "Using gender as an analytic tool helped us explore the role of femininity in decision-making in the context of HBOC.... It also enabled us to examine the influence of gendered roles in relation to family, friends, and health professionals on HBOC decision-making" (p. 505).

Key Findings: The women's main concern was making a decision about risk-reducing strategies, and the analysis suggested that the overarching decision-making process entailed *preserving the self*. The process was shaped by various contextual conditions, including characteristics of health services, gendered roles, the nature of the risk-reducing strategies to be considered, and the women's perceptions of their proximity to cancer. These contextual conditions contributed to different decision-making approaches and five distinct decision-making styles: "snap" decision-making, intuitive decision-making, deliberate decision-making, deferred decision-making, and "if-then" decision-making. The researchers concluded that the findings provide insights that could inform the provision of decisional support to BRCA1/2 carriers.

CRITICAL THINKING EXERCISES

1. Answer the relevant questions from Box 14.1 on page 278 regarding this study.
2. Also consider the following targeted questions:
   a. Was this study cross-sectional or longitudinal?
   b. Could this study have been undertaken as an ethnography? A phenomenological inquiry?
3. If the results of this study are trustworthy, in what ways do you think the findings could be used in clinical practice?

EXAMPLE 2 ● Phenomenological Study in Appendix B

- Read the method section from Beck and Watson's (2010) study ("Subsequent childbirth after a previous traumatic birth") in Appendix B on pages 403–412.

CRITICAL THINKING EXERCISES

1. Answer the relevant questions from Box 14.1 on page 278 regarding this study.
2. Also consider the following targeted questions:
   a. Was this study a descriptive or interpretive phenomenology?
   b. Could this study have been conducted as a grounded theory study? As an ethnographic study? Why or why not?
   c. Could this study have been conducted as a feminist inquiry? If yes, what might Beck have done differently?

WANT TO KNOW MORE? A wide variety of resources to enhance your learning and understanding of this chapter are available on thePoint.

- Interactive Critical Thinking Activity
- Chapter Supplement on Qualitative Descriptive Studies
- Answers to the Critical Thinking Exercises for Example 2
- Student Review Questions
- Full-text online
- Internet Resources with useful websites for Chapter 14

Additional study aids including eight journal articles and related questions are also available in *Study Guide for Essentials of Nursing Research, 8e.*

SUMMARY POINTS

- Qualitative research involves an **emergent design**—a design that emerges in the field as the study unfolds.
- Although qualitative design is elastic and flexible, qualitative researchers plan for broad contingencies that can pose decision opportunities for study design in the field.
- Ethnography focuses on the culture of a group of people and relies on extensive **field work** that usually includes **participant observation** and in-depth interviews with **key informants**. Ethnographers strive to acquire an **emic** (insider's) perspective of a culture rather than an **etic** (outsider's) perspective.
- Nurses sometimes refer to their ethnographic studies as **ethnonursing research**. Most ethnographers study cultures other than their own; *autoethnographies* are ethnographies of a group or culture to which the researcher belongs.
- Phenomenologists seek to discover the *essence* and *meaning* of a phenomenon as it is experienced by people, mainly through in-depth interviews with people who have had the relevant experience.
- In **descriptive phenomenology**, which seeks to describe lived experiences, researchers strive to **bracket** out preconceived views and to *intuit* the essence of the phenomenon by remaining open to meanings attributed to it by those who have experienced it.
- **Interpretive phenomenology (hermeneutics)** focuses on interpreting the meaning of experiences, rather than just describing them.
- **Grounded theory** researchers try to account for people's actions by focusing on the main concern that their behavior is designed to resolve. The manner in which people resolve this main concern is the **core variable**. The goal of grounded theory is to discover this main concern and the **basic social process (BSP)** that explains how people resolve it.
- Grounded theory uses **constant comparison**: categories elicited from the data are constantly compared with data obtained earlier.
- A controversy in grounded theory concerns whether to follow the original Glaser and Strauss procedures or to use procedures adapted by Strauss and Corbin; Glaser has argued that the latter approach does not result in *grounded theories* but rather in *conceptual descriptions*. More recently, Charmaz's **constructivist grounded theory** has emerged,

emphasizing interpretive aspects in which the grounded theory is constructed from shared experiences and relationships between the researcher and participants.

- **Case studies** are intensive investigations of a single entity or a small number of entities, such as individuals, groups, families, or communities.
- **Narrative analysis** focuses on *story* in studies in which the purpose is to determine how individuals make sense of events in their lives. Several different structural approaches can be used to analyze narrative data (e.g., Burke's *pentadic dramatism).*
- **Descriptive qualitative studies** are not embedded in a disciplinary tradition. Such studies may be referred to as qualitative studies, naturalistic inquiries, or as qualitative content analyses.
- Research is sometimes conducted within an ideological perspective, and such research tends to rely primarily on qualitative research.
- **Critical theory** is concerned with a critique of existing social structures. Critical researchers conduct studies that involve collaboration with participants and that foster enlightened self-knowledge and transformation. **Critical ethnography** uses the principles of critical theory in the study of cultures.
- **Feminist research**, like critical research, aims at being transformative, but the focus is on how gender domination and discrimination shape women's lives and their consciousness.
- **Participatory action research (PAR)** produces knowledge through close collaboration with groups that are vulnerable to control or oppression by a dominant culture; in PAR research, methods take second place to emergent processes that can motivate people and generate community solidarity.

REFERENCES FOR CHAPTER 14

Baum, N., Weidberg, Z., Osher, Y., & Kohelet, D. (2012). No longer pregnant, not yet a mother: Giving birth prematurely to a very-low-birth-weight baby. *Qualitative Health Research, 22*, 595–606.

Baumbusch, J. (2011). Conducting critical ethnography in long-term residential care. *Journal of Advanced Nursing, 67*, 184–192.

Beck, C. T. (2006). Pentadic cartography: Mapping birth trauma narratives. *Qualitative Health Research,16*, 453–466.

Bohman, D., van Wyck, N., & Ekman, S. (2011). South Africans' experiences of being old and of care and caring in a transitional period. *International Journal of Older People Nursing, 6*, 187–195.

Burke, K. (1969). *A grammer of motives*. Berkley, CA: University of California Press.

Charmaz, K. (2006). *Constructing grounded theory: A practical guide through qualitative analysis*. Thousand Oaks, CA: Sage Publications.

Connolly, C., & Gibson, M. (2011). The "white plague" and color: Children, race, and tuberculosis in Virginia 1900–1935. *Journal of Pediatric Nursing, 26*, 230–238.

Glaser, B. G. (1992). *Emergence versus forcing: Basics of grounded theory analysis*. Mill Valley, CA: Sociology Press.

Glaser, B. G., & Strauss, A. L. (1967). *The discovery of grounded theory: Strategies for qualitative research*. Chicago, IL Aldine.

Howard, A. F., Balneaves, L., Bottorff, J., & Rodney, P. (2011). Preserving the self: The process of decision making about hereditary breast cancer and ovarian cancer risk reduction. *Qualitative Health Research, 21*, 502–519.

Huberman, A. M., & Miles, M. (1994). Data management and analysis methods. In Denzin, N. K., & Lincoln, Y. S. (Eds.), *Handbook of qualitative research*. (1st ed.). Thousand Oaks, CA: Sage.

Kneipp, S., Kairalla, J., Lutz, B., Pereira, D., Hall, A., Flocks, J., et al. (2011). Public health nursing case management for women receiving Temporary Assistance for Needy Families: A randomized controlled trial using community-based participatory research. *American Journal of Public Health, 101*, 1759–68.

Leininger, M. M. (Ed.). (1985). *Qualitative research methods in nursing*. New York: Grune and Stratton.

Lincoln, Y. S., & Guba, E. G. (1985). *Naturalistic inquiry*. Newbury Park, CA: Sage.

Lundh, L., Hylander, I., & Tornkvist, L. (2012). The process of trying to quit smoking from the perspective of patients with chronic obstructive pulmonary disease. *Scandinavian Journal of Caring Sciences*, PubMed ID 22117588.

MacKinnon, K. (2011). Rural nurses' safeguarding work: Reembodying patient safety. *Advances in Nursing Science, 34*, 119–129.

Moro, T., Kavanagh, K., Savage, T., Reyes, M., Kimura, R., & Bhat, R. (2011). Parent decision making for life support for extremely premature infants. *The Journal of Perinatal & Neonatal Nursing, 25*, 52–60.

Morse, J. M. (2004). Qualitative comparison: Appropriateness, equivalence, and fit. *Qualitative Health Research, 14*(10), 1323–1325.

Porter, E., Ganong, L., & Matsuda, S. (2012). Intentions of older homebound women with regard to reaching help quickly. *Western Journal of Nursing Research*, PubMed ID 22146885.

Schumacher, G. (2010). Culture care meanings, beliefs, and practices in rural Dominican Republic. *Journal of Transcultural Nursing, 21*, 93–103.

Stewart, B., Mikocka-Walus, A., Harley, H., & Andrews, J. (2012). Help-seeking and coping with the psychosocial burden of chronic hepatitis C. *International Journal of Nursing Studies, 49*(5), 560–569.

Strauss, A., & Corbin, J. (1998). *Basics of qualitative research: Grounded theory procedures and techniques* (2nd ed.). Thousand Oaks, CA: Sage.

Taylor, C., Richardson, A., & Cowley, B. (2011). Surviving cancer treatment. *European Journal of Oncology Nursing, 15*, 243–249.

Thorne, S. (2008). *Interpretive description*. Walnut Creek, CA: Left Coast Press.

Van Daalen-Smith, C. (2011). Waiting for oblivion: women's experiences with electroshock. *Issues in Mental Health Nursing, 32*, 457–472.

Vatne, M., & Nåden, D. (2012). Finally, it became too much—experiences and reflections in the aftermath of attempted suicide. *Scandinavian Journal of Caring Sciences, 26*(2), 304–312.

chapter

15 Sampling and Data Collection in Qualitative Studies

LEARNING OBJECTIVES

On completing this chapter, you will be able to:

- Describe the logic of sampling for qualitative studies
- Identify and describe several types of sampling in qualitative studies
- Evaluate the appropriateness of the sampling method and sample size used in a qualitative study
- Identify and describe methods of collecting unstructured self-report data
- Identify and describe methods of collecting and recording unstructured observational data
- Critique a qualitative researcher's decisions regarding the data collection plan (general method, informational adequacy, mode of administration)
- Define new terms in the chapter

KEY TERMS

Critical incidents technique
Data saturation
Field notes
Focus group interview
Grand tour question
Key informant
Log
Maximum variation sampling
Photo-elicitation interview
Photovoice
Purposive (purposeful) sampling
Semistructured interview
Snowball sampling
Theoretical sampling
Topic guide
Unstructured interview

This chapter covers two important aspects of qualitative studies—sampling (selecting good study participants) and data collection (gathering the right types and amount of information to address the research question).

SAMPLING IN QUALITATIVE RESEARCH

Qualitative studies almost always use small, nonprobability samples. This does not mean that qualitative researchers are unconcerned with the quality of their samples; rather, they use different considerations in selecting study participants.

The Logic of Qualitative Sampling

Quantitative research is concerned with measuring attributes and identifying relationships in a population, and therefore a representative sample is desirable so that the findings can be generalized. The aim of most qualitative studies is to discover *meaning* and to uncover multiple realities, not to generalize to a target population.

Qualitative researchers ask such sampling questions as: Who would be an *information-rich* data source for my study? Whom should I talk to, or what should I observe, to maximize my understanding of the phenomenon? A first step in qualitative sampling is selecting settings with high potential for information richness.

As the study progresses, new sampling questions emerge, such as the following: Whom can I talk to or observe who would confirm my understandings? Challenge or modify my understandings? Enrich my understandings? As with the overall design, sampling design in qualitative studies is an emergent one that capitalizes on early information to guide subsequent action.

TIP: Like quantitative researchers, qualitative researchers often identify eligibility criteria for their studies. Although they do not specify an explicit population to whom results could be generalized, they do establish the kinds of people who are eligible to participate in their research.

Types of Qualitative Sampling

Qualitative researchers avoid random samples because they are not the best methods for selecting people who will make good informants, that is, people who meet the conceptual needs of the study and are knowledgeable, articulate, reflective, and willing to talk at length with researchers. Qualitative researchers use various nonprobability sampling designs.

Convenience and Snowball Sampling

Qualitative researchers often begin with a convenience sample (also called a *volunteer sample)*. Often, volunteer samples are used when researchers want participants to come forward and identify themselves. For example, if we wanted to study the experiences of people with frequent nightmares, we might recruit them by placing a notice on a bulletin board, in a newspaper, or on the Internet. We would be less interested in obtaining a representative sample of people with nightmares, than in recruiting a diverse group with various nightmare experiences.

Sampling by convenience is efficient, but is not a preferred approach, even in qualitative studies. The aim in qualitative studies is to extract the greatest possible information from a small number of people, and a convenience sample may not provide the most information-rich sources. However, convenience sampling may be an economical way to launch the sampling process.

Example of a convenience sample:

Beal and colleagues (2012) did a narrative analysis of women's early symptom experience of ischemic stroke. The convenience sample of nine women was recruited through fliers distributed at community stroke groups and at hospitals, and an advertisement was placed in a local newspaper.

Qualitative researchers also use **snowball sampling** (or *network sampling*), asking early informants to make referrals for other participants. A weakness of this approach is that the eventual sample might be restricted to a small network of acquaintances. Also, the quality of the referrals may be affected by whether the referring sample member trusted the researcher and truly wanted to cooperate.

Example of a snowball sample:
Cooke and colleagues (2012) studied factors influencing women's decisions to delay childbearing beyond the age of 35. The initial participant referred a further potential participant, and snowball sampling continued until the full sample of 18 women was obtained.

Purposive Sampling

Qualitative sampling may begin with volunteer informants and may be supplemented with new participants through snowballing. Many qualitative studies, however, evolve to a purposive (or *purposeful*) sampling strategy in which researchers deliberately choose the cases or types of cases that will best contribute to the study. Regardless of how initial participants are selected, qualitative researchers often strive to select sample members purposefully based on the information needs that emerge from the early findings.

Within purposive sampling, dozens of strategies have been identified (Patton, 2002), only some of which are mentioned here. Researchers do not necessarily refer to their sampling plans with Patton's labels; his classification shows the kind of diverse strategies qualitative researchers have adopted to meet the conceptual needs of their research:

- **Maximum variation sampling** involves deliberately selecting cases with wide variation on dimensions of interest.
- *Extreme (deviant) case sampling* provides opportunities for learning from the most unusual and extreme informants (e.g., outstanding successes and notable failures).
- *Typical case sampling* involves the selection of participants who illustrate or highlight what is typical or average.
- *Criterion sampling* involves studying cases that meet a predetermined criterion of importance.

Maximum variation sampling is often the sampling mode of choice in qualitative research because it is useful in illuminating the scope of a phenomenon and in identifying important patterns that cut across variations. Other strategies can also be used advantageously, however, depending on the nature of the research question.

Example of maximum variation sampling:
Tierney and colleagues (2011) did an in-depth study of factors that influence physical activity in people with heart failure. Their sample included 22 patients aged between 53 and 82 who were purposively selected to provide variation in gender, age, heart failure duration and severity, and activity levels.

A strategy of sampling confirming and disconfirming cases is another purposive strategy that is used toward the end of data collection. As researchers note trends and patterns in the data, emerging conceptualizations may need to be checked. **Confirming cases** are additional cases that fit researchers' conceptualizations and strengthen credibility. **Disconfirming cases** are new cases that do not fit and serve to challenge researchers' interpretations. These "negative" cases may offer new insights into how the original conceptualization needs to be revised.

TIP: Some qualitative researchers call their sample *purposive* simply because they "purposely" selected people who experienced the phenomenon of interest. Exposure to the phenomenon is, however, an eligibility criterion. If the researcher then recruits *any* person with the desired experience, the sample is selected by convenience, not purposively. Purposive sampling implies an intent to choose *particular* exemplars or *types* of people who can best enhance the researcher's understanding of the phenomenon.

Theoretical Sampling

Theoretical sampling is a method used in grounded theory studies. Theoretical sampling involves decisions about what data to collect next and where to find those data to develop an emerging theory optimally. The basic question in theoretical sampling is: What groups or subgroups should the researcher turn to next? Groups are chosen for their relevance in furthering the emerging conceptualization. These groups are not chosen before the research begins but only as they are needed for their theoretical relevance in developing and refining emerging categories.

Theoretical sampling is not the same as purposeful sampling. The objective of theoretical sampling is to discover categories and their properties and to offer new insights into interrelationships that occur in the substantive theory.

Example of a theoretical sampling:

Porr and colleagues (2012) used theoretical sampling in their grounded theory study that elucidated how public health nurses develop therapeutic relationships with vulnerable, low-income single mothers. After identifying a fundamental pattern of interactional behaviors by interviewing and observing nurses and mothers, the researchers saw that theory construction could be enhanced by interviewing a family physician, two social workers, and other service providers so that they could compare other relationship experiences with the mothers.

Sample Size in Qualitative Research

Sample size in qualitative research is usually determined based on informational needs. A guiding principle is **data saturation**—that is, sampling to the point at which no new information is obtained and redundancy is achieved. The number of participants needed to reach saturation depends on various factors. For example, the broader the scope of the research question, the more participants will likely be needed. Data quality can also affect sample size. If participants are able to reflect on their experiences and communicate effectively, saturation can be achieved with a relatively small sample. Type of sampling strategy may also be relevant: a larger sample is likely to be needed with maximum variation sampling than with typical case sampling.

Example of saturation:

Bertrand (2012) studied nurses' integration of traditional Chinese medicine into their triage process. She thought she had achieved saturation after 15 interviews, but when she conducted the 16th interview, "an operating nurse told me a story I had not heard before" (p. 266). Interviewing continued and saturation was reached at 20 interviews.

TIP: Sample size adequacy in a qualitative study is difficult to evaluate because the main criterion is redundancy of information, which consumers have insufficient information to judge. Some qualitative reports explicitly mention that data saturation was achieved.

Sampling in the Three Main Qualitative Traditions

There are similarities among the main qualitative traditions with regard to sampling: samples are usually small, nonrandom methods are used, and final sampling decisions usually take place during data collection. However, there are some differences as well.

Sampling in Ethnography

Ethnographers may begin with a "big net" approach—that is, they mingle and converse with as many members of the culture as possible. Although they may talk to many group members (usually 25 to 50), ethnographers often rely heavily on a smaller number of **key informants**, who are highly knowledgeable about the culture and who develop special, ongoing relationships with the researcher. Key informants are the researcher's main link to the "inside."

Key informants are chosen purposively, guided by the ethnographer's informed judgments. Developing a pool of potential key informants often depends on ethnographers' ability to construct a relevant framework. For example, an ethnographer might decide to seek out different types of key informants based on their *roles* (e.g., health care practitioners, advocates). Once a pool of potential key informants is identified, key considerations for final selection are their level of knowledge about the culture and how willing they are to collaborate with the ethnographer in revealing and interpreting the culture.

Sampling in ethnography typically involves sampling *things* as well as people. For example, ethnographers make decisions about observing *events* and *activities*, about examining *records* and *artifacts*, and about exploring *places* that provide clues about the culture. Key informants can play an important role in helping ethnographers decide what to sample.

Example of an ethnographic sample:
Lori and Boyle (2011) conducted an ethnographic study exploring cultural childbirth practices, beliefs, and traditions in postconflict Liberia. The researchers engaged in participant observation, which involved participation "in many community activities around the hospital and at out-patient clinics" (p. 457). They also conducted interviews with 56 key informants: 10 postpartum women who had experienced a childbirth complication, 18 family members of women who had died or suffered severe morbidity, and 26 health care workers, indigenous healers, and tribal chiefs in a rural county of Liberia.

Sampling in Phenomenological Studies

Phenomenologists tend to rely on very small samples of participants—typically 10 or fewer. Two principles guide the selection of a sample for a phenomenological study: (1) all participants must have experienced the phenomenon and (2) they must be able to articulate what it is like to have lived that experience. Phenomenological researchers often want to explore diversity of individual experiences and so they may specifically look for people with demographic or other differences who have shared a common experience.

Example of a sample in a phenomenological study:
Roscigno and Swanson (2011) recruited a larger-than-typical purposive sample in their phenomenological study of the experiences of parents from across the United States whose child had a traumatic brain injury. Their sample included 42 parents from 37 families. The goal was to recruit a diverse group of parents and children with varied sociodemographic characteristics.

Interpretive phenomenologists may, in addition to sampling people, sample artistic or literary sources. Experiential descriptions of a phenomenon may be selected from literature, such as poetry, novels, biographies, autobiographies, or diaries. These sources can help increase phenomenologists' understanding of the phenomena under study. Art—including paintings, sculpture, film, photographs, and music—can offer additional insights into lived experience.

Sampling in Grounded Theory Studies

Grounded theory research is typically done with samples of about 20 to 30 people, using theoretical sampling. The goal in a grounded theory study is to select informants who can best contribute to the evolving theory. Sampling, data collection, data analysis, and theory construction occur concurrently, and so study participants are selected serially and contingently (i.e., contingent on the emerging conceptualization). Sampling might evolve as follows:

1. The researcher begins with a general notion of where and with whom to start. The first few cases may be solicited by convenience or through snowballing.
2. In the early part of the study, a strategy such as maximum variation sampling might be used, to gain insights into the range and complexity of the phenomenon.
3. The sample is adjusted in an ongoing fashion. Emerging conceptualizations help to inform the theoretical sampling process.
4. Sampling continues until saturation is achieved.
5. Final sampling may include a search for confirming and disconfirming cases to test, refine, and strengthen the theory.

Example of sampling in a grounded theory study:
Hall and colleagues (2012) conducted a grounded theory study of Canadian health care providers' and pregnant women's approaches to managing birth. They began with purposeful sampling and then used theoretical sampling to further develop categories. The sample included 9 pregnant women, and 56 health care providers including physicians, nurses, midwives, and doulas.

Critiquing Qualitative Sampling Plans

In a qualitative study, the sampling plan can be evaluated in terms of its adequacy and appropriateness (Morse, 1991). *Adequacy* refers to the sufficiency and quality of the data the sample yielded. An adequate sample provides data without "thin" spots. When researchers have truly obtained saturation, informational adequacy has been achieved, and the resulting description or theory is richly textured and complete.

Appropriateness concerns the methods used to select a sample. An appropriate sample results from the selection of participants who can best supply information that meets the study's conceptual requirements. The sampling strategy must yield the fullest possible understanding of the phenomenon of interest. A sampling approach that excludes negative cases or that fails to include people with unusual experiences may not fully address the study's information needs.

Another important issue concerns the potential for transferability of the findings. The transferability of study findings is a direct function of the similarity between the sample of the original study and other people to whom the findings might be applied. Thus, in critiquing a report you should assess whether the researcher provided an adequately *thick description* of the sample and the study context so that someone interested in transferring the findings could make an informed decision. Further guidance in critiquing qualitative sampling decisions is presented in Box 15.1.

TIP: The issue of transferability within the context of broader models of generalizability is discussed in the Chapter Supplement on thePoint website.

DATA COLLECTION IN QUALITATIVE STUDIES

Qualitative researchers typically go into the field knowing the most likely data sources, while not ruling out other possibilities that might come to light as data collection progresses. In-depth interviews are the most common method of collecting qualitative data.

BOX 15.1 Guidelines for Critiquing Qualitative Sampling Plans

1. Is the setting appropriate for addressing the research question, and is it adequately described?
2. What type of sampling strategy was used? Are sampling procedures clearly delineated?
3. Were the eligibility criteria for the study specified? How were participants recruited into the study? Did the recruitment strategy yield information-rich participants?
4. Given the information needs of the study—and, if applicable, its qualitative tradition—was the sampling approach appropriate? Are dimensions of the phenomenon under study adequately represented?
5. Is the sample size adequate and appropriate? Did the researcher indicate that saturation had been achieved? Do the findings suggest a richly textured and comprehensive set of data without any apparent "holes" or thin areas?
6. Are key characteristics of the sample described (e.g., age, gender)? Is a rich description of participants and context provided, allowing for an assessment of the transferability of the findings?

Observation is used in some qualitative studies as well. Physiologic data are rarely collected in a constructivist inquiry.

Table 15.1 compares the types of data and aspects of the data collection process used by researchers in the three main qualitative traditions. Ethnographers typically collect a wide array of data, with observation and interviews being the primary methods. Ethnographers also gather or examine products of the culture under study, such as documents, records, artifacts, photographs, and so on. Phenomenologists and grounded theory researchers rely primarily on in-depth interviews, although participant observation can also play a role in grounded theory studies.

TABLE 15.1 Comparison of Data Collection in Three Qualitative Traditions

Issue	Ethnography	Phenomenology	Grounded Theory
Types of data	Primarily observation and interviews, plus artifacts, documents, photographs, social network diagrams	Primarily in-depth interviews, sometimes diaries or other written or artistic materials	Primarily individual interviews, sometimes group interviews, observation, diaries, documents
Unit of data collection	Cultural system	Individuals	Individuals
Data collection points	Mainly longitudinal	Mainly cross-sectional	Cross-sectional or longitudinal
Length of time for data collection	Typically long, many months or years	Typically moderate	Typically moderate
Salient field issues	Gaining entrée, determining a role, learning how to participate, reactivity, encouraging candor, loss of objectivity, premature exit, reflexivity	Bracketing one's views, building rapport, encouraging candor, listening while preparing what to ask next, keeping "on track," handling emotionality	Building rapport, encouraging candor, listening while preparing what to ask next, keeping "on track," handling emotionality

Qualitative Self-Report Techniques

Qualitative researchers do not have a set of questions that must be asked in a specific order and worded in a given way. Instead, they start with general questions and allow respondents to tell their stories in a naturalistic fashion. Qualitative self-reports, usually obtained through interviews, tend to be conversational. Interviewers encourage respondents to define the important dimensions of a phenomenon and to elaborate on what is relevant to them, rather than relying on investigators' *a priori* notions of relevance.

Types of Qualitative Self-Reports

Several approaches can be used to collect qualitative self-report data. Researchers use completely **unstructured interviews** when they have no preconceived view of the information to be gathered. They aim to learn about respondents' perceptions and experiences without imposing their own views. Researchers begin by asking a **grand tour question** such as, "What happened when you first learned that you had AIDS?" Subsequent questions are guided by initial responses. Ethnographic and phenomenologic studies often rely on unstructured interviews.

Semistructured (or *focused*) **interviews** are used when researchers have a list of topics or broad questions that must be covered in an interview. Interviewers use a written **topic guide** to ensure that all question areas are addressed. The interviewer's function is to encourage participants to talk freely about all the topics on the guide.

Example of a semistructured interview:
Coombs and colleagues (2012) explored how nurses and doctors make the transition from active intervention to palliative and end-of-life care. They collected their data via semistructured interviews with 13 nurses and 13 medical staff. Interviews began with the question, "Could you tell me about what happened around the time of (patient's name) death?" Then a series of probes elicited additional information about end-of-life decisions and the process of care withdrawal.

Focus group interviews involve groups of about 5 to 10 people whose opinions and experiences are solicited simultaneously. The interviewer (or *moderator*) guides the discussion using a topic guide. A group format is efficient and can generate a lot of dialogue, but one problem is that not everyone is comfortable sharing their views or experiences in front of a group. Focus groups have been used by researchers in many qualitative traditions and in qualitative descriptive research.

Example of focus group interviews:
Beck and colleagues (2012) studied nurse assistants' experiences of palliative care in residential care settings in Sweden. Six focus group interviews were conducted with two to six nurse assistants from different residential care units. Examples of questions from the interview guide are: What does palliative care mean to you? What are the major difficulties when providing palliative care?

Personal **diaries** are a standard data source in historical research. It is also possible to generate new data for a study by asking participants to maintain a diary over a specified period. Diaries can be useful in providing an intimate description of a person's everyday life. The diaries may be completely unstructured; for example, individuals who have had an organ transplantation could be asked to spend 15 minutes a day jotting down or audiotaping their thoughts. Frequently, however, people are asked to make diary entries regarding some specific aspect of their lives.

Example of diaries:
Buchwald and colleagues (2012) studied how children aged 11 to 17 handle life when their mother or father was seriously ill and dying. The researchers asked the children to maintain video diaries in daily sessions for 1 month, in which the children were asked to share their feelings, reflections, and the day's events with the camera.

The **critical incidents technique** is a method of gathering information about people's behaviors in specific circumstances. The method focuses on a factual *incident*—an integral episode of human behavior; *critical* means that the incident must have had a discernible impact on some outcome. The technique focuses on incidents about which respondents can testify as expert witnesses. Generally, data on 50 to 100 critical incidents are collected, but this typically involves interviews with a smaller number of people, because each person can often describe multiple incidents.

Example of a critical incident study:
Pavlish and colleagues (2011) used the critical incident technique in a study of nurses' experiences with ethically difficult situations and risk factors for such situations.

Photo elicitation involves an interview stimulated and guided by photographic images. This procedure, most often used in ethnographies and participatory action research (PAR), can help to promote a collaborative discussion. The photographs sometimes are ones that researchers have made of the participants' world, through which researchers can gain insights into a new culture. Photo elicitation can also be used with photos that participants have in their homes. Researchers have also used the technique of asking participants to take photographs themselves and then interpret them, a method sometimes called **photovoice**.

Example of a photovoice study:
Findholt and colleagues (2011), in their PAR study of childhood obesity prevention, used photovoice to engage rural youth in discussions about community assets and barriers that influenced children's physical activity and diets.

Gathering Qualitative Self-Report Data

Researchers gather narrative self-report data to develop a construction of a phenomenon that is consistent with that of participants. This goal requires researchers to overcome communication barriers and to enhance the flow of information. Although qualitative interviews are conversational, the conversations are purposeful ones that require preparation. For example, the wording of questions should reflect the participants' world view and language. In addition to being good questioners, researchers must be good listeners. Only by attending carefully to what respondents are saying can in-depth interviewers develop appropriate follow-up questions.

Unstructured interviews are typically long, sometimes lasting several hours, and so an important issue is how best to record such abundant information. Some researchers take notes during the interview, filling in the details after the interview is completed. This method is, however, risky in terms of data accuracy. Most prefer tape recording the interviews for later transcription. Although some respondents are self-conscious when their conversation is recorded, they typically forget about the presence of recording equipment after a few minutes.

TIP: Although qualitative self-report data are often gathered in face-to-face interviews, they can also be collected in writing. Internet "interviews" are increasingly common.

Evaluation of Qualitative Self-Report Methods

In-depth interviews are an extremely flexible approach to gathering data and, in many research contexts, offer distinct advantages. In clinical situations, for example, it is often appropriate to let people talk freely about their problems and concerns, allowing them to take much of the initiative in directing the flow of conversation. Unstructured self-reports may allow investigators to ascertain what the basic issues or problems are, how sensitive or controversial the topic is, how individuals conceptualize and talk about the problems, and what range of opinions or behaviors exist relevant to the topic. In-depth interviews may also help to elucidate the underlying meaning of a pattern or relationship repeatedly observed in more structured research. On the other hand, qualitative methods are extremely time-consuming and demanding of researchers' skills in gathering, analyzing, and interpreting the resulting data.

Qualitative Observational Methods

Qualitative researchers sometimes collect loosely structured observational data, often as an important supplement to self-report data. The aim of qualitative observation is to understand the behaviors and experiences of people as they occur in naturalistic settings. Skillful unstructured observation permits researchers to see the world as the study participants see it, to develop a rich understanding of the phenomena of interest, and to grasp subtleties of cultural variation.

Unstructured observational data are often gathered in field settings through **participant observation**. Participant observers take part in the functioning of the group under study and strive to observe, ask questions, and record information within the contexts and structures that are relevant to group members. Participant observation is characterized by prolonged periods of social interaction between researchers and participants, in the participants' sociopolitical and cultural milieu. By assuming a participating role, observers often have insights that would have eluded more passive or concealed observers.

TIP: Not all qualitative observational research is *participant* observation (i.e., with observations occurring from *within* the group under study). Some unstructured observations involve watching and recording behaviors without the observers' active participation in activities. Be on the alert for the misuse of the term "participant observation." Some researchers use the term inappropriately to refer to all unstructured observations conducted in the field. A description of what participation actually entailed should be included in reports of participant observational studies.

The Observer-Participant Role in Participant Observation

In participant observation, the role that observers play in the group is important because their social position determines what they are likely to see. The extent of the observers' actual participation in a group is best thought of as a continuum. At one extreme is complete immersion in the setting, with researchers assuming full participant status; at the other extreme is complete separation, with researchers as onlookers. Researchers may in some cases assume a fixed position on this continuum throughout the study, but often researchers' role as participants evolves over the course of the field work. Leininger and McFarland (2006) describe a participant observer's role as evolving through a four-phase sequence:

1. Primarily observation and active listening
2. Primarily observation with limited participation
3. Primarily participation with continued observation
4. Primarily reflection and reconfirmation of findings with informants

In the initial phase, researchers observe and listen to people, allowing everyone to get more comfortable in their interactions. In phase 2, observation is enhanced by a modest degree of participation in the social group. In phase 3, researchers strive to become more active participants, learning by the experience of doing rather than just watching and listening. In phase 4, researchers reflect on the total process of what transpired.

Observers must overcome at least two major hurdles in assuming a satisfactory role vis-à-vis participants. The first is to gain entrée into the social group under study; the second is to establish rapport and trust within that group. Without gaining entrée, the study cannot proceed; but without the trust of the group, the researcher will be restricted to "front stage" knowledge—that is, information distorted by the group's protective facades. The goal of participant observers is to "get backstage"—to learn about the true realities of the group's experiences and behaviors. On the other hand, being a fully participating member does not *necessarily* offer the best perspective for studying a phenomenon—just as being an actor in a play does not offer the most advantageous view of the performance.

Example of participant-observer roles:
Michaelson (2012) conducted a study that focused on nurses' relationships with patients they regard as being difficult. Data were collected by means of participant observation and in-depth interviews over an 18-month period. Michaelson conducted 18 observation sessions, lasting between 3 and 4 hours, of the nurses interacting with patients during home visits. She kept "a balance between being an 'insider' and an 'outsider,' between participation and observation." (p. 92).

Gathering Participant Observation Data

Participant observers typically place few restrictions on the nature of the data collected, but they often have a broad plan for the types of information to be gathered. Among the aspects of an observed activity likely to be considered relevant are the following:

1. *The physical setting—"where" questions.* Where is the activity happening? What are the main features of the setting?
2. *The participants—"who" questions.* Who is present? What are their characteristics and roles? Who is given access to the event? Who is denied access?
3. *Activities—"what" questions.* What is going on? What are participants doing? What methods do they use to communicate?
4. *Frequency and duration—"when" questions.* When did the activity begin and end? Is the activity a recurring one and, if so, how regularly does it recur?
5. *Process—"how" questions.* How is the activity organized? How does it unfold?
6. *Outcomes—"why" questions.* Why is the activity happening, or why is it happening in this manner? What did not happen (especially if it ought to have happened) and why?

Participant observers must decide how to sample events and to select observational locations. They often use a combination of positioning approaches. *Single positioning* means staying in a single location for a period to observe transactions in that location. *Multiple positioning* involves moving around the site to observe behaviors from different locations. *Mobile positioning* involves following a person throughout a given activity or period.

Because participant observers cannot be in more than one place at a time, observation is usually supplemented with information from unstructured interviews. For example, informants may be asked to describe what went on in a meeting the observer was unable to attend, or to describe an event that occurred before the observer entered the field. In such cases, the informant functions as the observer's observer.

Recording Observations

The most common forms of record keeping for participant observation are logs and field notes, but photographs and videotapes may also be used. A **log** (or *field diary)* is a daily record of events and conversations. **Field notes** are broader and more interpretive. Field notes represent the observer's efforts to record information and to synthesize and understand the data.

Field notes can be categorized according to their purpose. *Descriptive notes* (or *observational notes)* are objective descriptions of events and conversations, and the contexts in which they occurred. The goal of participant observers' descriptive notes is thick description.

Reflective notes document researchers' personal experiences, reflections, and progress in the field, and can serve different purposes. *Theoretical notes* document interpretive efforts to attach meaning to observations. *Methodologic notes* are reminders about how subsequent observations should be made. *Personal notes* are comments about the researcher's own feelings during the research process. Box 15.2 presents examples of various types of field notes from Beck's (2002) grounded theory study of mothering twins.

The success of any participant observation study depends on the quality of the logs and field notes. It is clearly essential to record observations as quickly as possible, but participant observers cannot usually record information by openly carrying a clipboard or a tape recorder because this would undermine their role as ordinary participants. Observers must develop skills in making detailed mental notes that can later be written or tape recorded.

Evaluation of Unstructured Observational Methods

Qualitative observational methods, and especially participant observation, can provide a deeper and richer understanding of human behaviors and social situations than is possible with structured methods. Participant observation is valuable for its ability to "get inside" a situation and provide understanding of its complexities. This approach is inherently flexible and thus gives observers the freedom to reconceptualize problems once they are in the field. Participant observation is a good method for answering questions about phenomena that are difficult for insiders themselves to explain because these phenomena are taken for granted.

Like all research methods, however, participant observation faces potential problems. Observer bias is a prominent risk. Observers may lose objectivity in sampling, viewing, and recording observations. Once they begin to participate in a group's activities, the possibility of emotional involvement becomes a concern. Researchers in their member role may fail to attend to scientifically relevant aspects of the situation or may develop a myopic view on issues of importance to the group. Finally, the success of participant observation depends on the observer's observational and interpersonal skills—skills that may be difficult to cultivate.

Critiquing the Collection of Unstructured Data

It is often difficult to critique the decisions that researchers made in collecting qualitative data because details about those decisions are seldom spelled out in research articles. In

BOX 15.2 Example of Field Notes for Unstructured Observations (From a Grounded Theory Study)

Observational Notes: O.L. attended the Mothers of Multiples Support Group again this month, but she looked worn-out today. She wasn't as bubbly as she had been at the March meeting. She explained why she wasn't doing as well this month. She and her husband had just found out that their house has lead-based paint in it. Both twins do have increased lead levels. She and her husband are in the process of buying a new house.

Theoretical Notes: So far, all the mothers have stressed the need for routine in order to survive the first year of caring for twins. Mothers, however, have varying definitions of routine. I.R. had the firmest routine with her twins. B.L. is more flexible with her routine, i.e., the twins are always fed at the same time but aren't put down for naps or bed at night at the same time. Whenever one of the twins wants to go to sleep it is fine with her. B.L. does have a daily routine with regard to housework. For example, when the twins are down in the morning for a nap, she makes their bottles up for the day (14 bottles total).

Methodologic Notes: The first sign-up sheet I passed around at the Mothers of Multiples Support Group for women to sign up to participate in interviews for my grounded theory study only consisted of two columns: one for the mother's name and one for her telephone number. I need to revise this sign-up sheet to include extra columns for the age of the multiples, the town where the mother lives, and older siblings and their ages. My plan is to start interviewing mothers with multiples around 1 year of age so that the moms can reflect back over the process of mothering their infants for the first 12 months of their lives. Right now I have no idea of the ages of the infants of the mothers who signed up to be interviewed.

I will need to call the nurse in charge of this support group to find out the ages.

Personal Notes: Today was an especially challenging interview. The mom had picked the early afternoon for me to come to her home to interview her because that is the time her 2-year-old son would be napping. When I arrived at her house, her 2-year-old ran up to me and said hi. The mom explained that he had taken an earlier nap that day and that he would be up during the interview. Also in the living room with us during our interview were her two twin daughters (3 months old) swinging in the swings and her 2-year-old son. One of the twins was quite cranky for the first half hour of the interview. During the interview, the 2-year-old sat on my lap and looked at the two books I had brought as a little present. If I didn't keep him occupied with the books, he would keep trying to reach for the microphone of the tape recorder.

From Beck, C. T. (2002). Releasing the pause button: Mothering twins during the first year of life. *Qualitative Health Research, 12,* 593–608.

particular, there is often scant information about participant observation. It is not uncommon for a report to simply say that the researcher undertook participant observation, without descriptions of how much time was spent in the field, what exactly was observed, how observations were recorded, and what level of participation was involved. Thus, one aspect of a critique is likely to involve an appraisal of how much information the article provided about the data collection methods used. Even though space constraints in journals make it impossible for researchers to fully elaborate their methods, researchers have a responsibility to communicate basic information about their approach so that readers can assess the quality of evidence that the study yields. Researchers should provide examples of questions asked and types of observations made.

BOX 15.3 Guidelines for Critiquing Data Collection Methods in Qualitative Studies

1. Given the research question and the characteristics of study participants, did the researcher use the best method of capturing study phenomena (i.e., self-reports, observation)? Should supplementary data collection methods have been used to enrich the data available for analysis?
2. If self-report methods were used, did the researcher make good decisions about the specific method used to solicit information (e.g., focus group interviews, critical incident interviews, and so on)? Was the modality of obtaining the data appropriate (e.g., in-person interviews, Internet questioning, etc.)?
3. If a topic guide was used, did the report present examples of specific questions? Were the questions appropriate and comprehensive? Did the wording encourage full and rich responses?
4. Were interviews tape recorded and transcribed? If interviews were not tape recorded, what steps were taken to ensure the accuracy of the data?
5. Were self-report data gathered in a manner that promoted high-quality responses (e.g., in terms of privacy, efforts to put respondents at ease, etc.)? Who collected the data, and were they adequately prepared for the task?
6. If observational methods were used, did the report adequately describe what the observations entailed? What did the researcher actually observe, in what types of setting did the observations occur, and how often and over how long a period were observations made? Were decisions about positioning described? Were risks of observational bias addressed?
7. What role did the researcher assume in terms of being an observer and a participant? Was this role appropriate?
8. How were observational data recorded? Did the recording method maximize data quality?

As we discuss more fully in Chapter 17, triangulation of methods provides important opportunities for qualitative researchers to enhance the integrity of their data. Thus, an important issue to consider in evaluating unstructured data is whether the types and amount of data collected are sufficiently rich to support an in-depth, holistic understanding of the phenomena under study. Box 15.3 provides guidelines for critiquing the collection of unstructured data.

RESEARCH EXAMPLES WITH CRITICAL THINKING EXERCISES

In the following section, we describe the sampling plans and data collection strategies used in a nursing study, followed by some questions to guide critical thinking.

Example 1 below is also featured in our *Interactive Critical Thinking Activity* on thePoint website where you can easily record, print, and e-mail your responses to the related questions.

EXAMPLE 1 ● Sampling and Data Collection in a Qualitative Study

Study: Everyday nursing practice values in the NICU and their reflection on breastfeeding promotion. (Cricco-Lizza, 2011) (A related article by Cricco-Lizza appears in its entirety in the appendix to the accompanying the *Study Guide*).

Method: Cricco-Lizza used ethnographic methods to collect contextually rich and detailed information about NICU nurses, with a particular focus on infant feeding. The research was undertaken over a 14-month period in a level IV NICU in a pediatric hospital in northeastern United States. Data were collected primarily through observations and interviews.

Sampling Strategy: Approximately 250 nurses worked in the NICU; 114 of them participated as general informants. These nurses were observed or informally interviewed during routine NICU activities, and they provided a broad overview of infant feeding on the unit. From these 114 nurses, 18 nurses with a variety of professional experiences and educational backgrounds were purposefully sampled to be key informants. These key informants, who were followed more intensively during the fieldwork, were chosen from different expertise levels (novice to clinical expert) to obtain varied views of the NICU culture with regard to infant feeding.

Data Collection: The researcher observed nurses during the usual course of their activities in the NICU. The researcher focused on the nurses' interactions with babies, families, nurses, and other staff throughout the course of diverse activities. The observational sessions, which lasted for an hour or two, involved sampling of activities on varying days, work shifts, and times of the week. Cricco-Lizza noted that her "role evolved from observation to informal interviewing over the course of 128 participant-observation session" (p. 401). General informants were observed and informally interviewed an average of 3.5 times each over the study period. Cricco-Lizza documented all observational data in detailed field notes immediately after each session. Key informants agreed to formal interviews that lasted about 1 hour each. The researcher asked open-ended questions about breastfeeding and formula feeding, the nature of the nurses' work, and their roles in the NICU. During the formal interviews, the researcher followed up in greater depth on questions that arose during participant observation. Key informants were also observed and informally interviewed a total of 3 to 43 times each, with an average of 13.1 interactions over the study. The repeated contacts during the course of the study "allowed for deeper exploration about everyday practices, values, and breastfeeding in the NICU" (p. 401).

Key Findings: Cricco-Lizza's analysis revealed that uncertainty was a central concern underlying everyday practice values. Three themes described these values: (1) maximizing babies' potentials in the midst of uncertainty, (2) relying on the sisterhood of NICU nurses to deal with uncertainty, and (3) confronting uncertainty through tight control of actions, reliance on technology, and maximal efficiency in use of time.

CRITICAL THINKING EXERCISES

1. Answer the relevant questions from Box 15.1 on page 289 and Box 15.3 on page 296 regarding this study.
2. Also consider the following targeted questions:
   a. Comment on the variation the researcher achieved in type of study participants.
   b. How likely is it that the researcher's presence in the NICU affected the nurses' behaviors?
   c. Comment on the researchers' overall data collection plan in terms of the amount of information gathered and the timing of the data collection.
3. If the results of this study are valid and trustworthy, in what ways do you think the findings could be used in clinical practice?

EXAMPLE 2 ● Sampling and Data Collection in the Study in Appendix B

- Read the method section from Beck and Watson's (2010) study ("Subsequent childbirth after a previous traumatic birth") in Appendix B on pages 403–412.

CRITICAL THINKING EXERCISES

1. Answer the relevant questions from Boxes 15.1 on page 289 and 15.3 on page 296 regarding this study.
2. Also consider the following targeted questions:
   a. Comment on the characteristics of the participants, given the purpose of the study.
   b. Do you think that Beck and Watson should have limited their sample to women from one country only? Provide a rationale for your answer.
   c. Could any of the variables in this study have been captured by observation? Should they have been?
   d. Did Beck and Watson's study involve a "grand tour" question?

WANT TO KNOW MORE? A wide variety of resources to enhance your learning and understanding of this chapter are available on thePoint.

- Interactive Critical Thinking Activity
- Chapter Supplement on Transferability and Generalizability
- Answers to the Critical Thinking Exercises for Example 2
- Student Review Questions
- Full-text online
- Internet Resources with useful websites for Chapter 11

Additional study aids including eight journal articles and related questions are also available in *Study Guide for Essentials of Nursing Research, 8e.*

SUMMARY POINTS

- Qualitative researchers use the conceptual demands of the study to select articulate and reflective informants with certain types of experience in an emergent way, capitalizing on early learning to guide subsequent sampling decisions.
- Qualitative researchers may start with convenience or **snowball** sampling, but usually rely eventually on **purposive sampling** to guide them in selecting data sources that maximize information richness.
- One purposive strategy is **maximum variation sampling**, which entails purposely selecting cases with a wide range of variation. Another important strategy is sampling **confirming cases** and **disconfirming cases**—i.e., selecting cases that enrich and challenge the researchers' conceptualizations. Other types of purposive sampling include *extreme case sampling* (selecting the most unusual or extreme cases), *typical case sampling* (selecting cases that illustrate what is typical), and *criterion sampling* (studying cases that meet a predetermined criterion of importance).
- Samples in qualitative studies are typically small and based on information needs. A guiding principle is **data saturation**, which involves sampling to the point at which no new information is obtained and redundancy is achieved.
- Ethnographers make numerous sampling decisions, including not only *whom* to sample but *what* to sample (e.g., activities, events, documents, artifacts); decision making is often aided by their **key informants** who serve as guides and interpreters of the culture.
- Phenomenologists typically work with a small sample of people (often 10 or fewer) who meet the criterion of having lived the experience under study.
- Grounded theory researchers typically use **theoretical sampling** in which sampling decisions are guided in an ongoing fashion by the emerging theory. Samples of about 20 to 40 people are typical in grounded theory studies.
- In-depth interviews are the most widely used method of collecting data for qualitative studies. Self-reports in qualitative studies include completely **unstructured interviews**, which are conversational discussions on the topic of interest; **semi-structured** (or *focused*) **interviews**, using a broad **topic guide**; **focus group interviews**, which involve discussions with small groups; **diaries**, in which respondents are asked to maintain daily records about some aspects of their lives; the **critical incidents technique**, which involve

probes about the circumstances surrounding an incident that is critical to an outcome of interest; and **photo elicitation** interviews, which are guided and stimulated by photographic images, sometimes using photos that participants themselves take (**photovoice**).

- In qualitative research, self-reports are often supplemented by direct observation in naturalistic settings. One type of unstructured observation is **participant observation**, in which the researcher gains entrée into a social group and participates to varying degrees in its functioning while making in-depth observations of activities and events. Maintaining **logs** of daily events and **field notes** of the observer's experiences and interpretations constitute the major data collection strategies.

REFERENCES FOR CHAPTER 15

Beal, C., Stuifbergen, A., & Volker, D. (2012). A narrative study of women's early symptom experience of ischemic stroke. *Journal of Cardiovascular Nursing, 27*(3), 240–252.

Beck, C. T. (2002). Releasing the pause button: Mothering twins during the first year of life. *Qualitative Health Research, 12*, 593–608.

Beck, I., Tornquist, A., Brostrom, L., & Edberg, A. (2012). Having to focus on doing rather than being: Nurse assistants' experiences of palliative care in municipal residential care settings. *International Journal of Nursing Studies, 49*, 455–464.

Bertrand, S. (2012). Registered nurses integrate traditional Chinese medicine into the triage process. *Qualitative Health Research, 22*, 263–273.

Buchwald, D., Delmar, C., & Schantz-Laursen, B. (2012). How children handle life when their mother or father is seriously ill and dying. *Scandinavian Journal of Caring Sciences, 26*(2), 228–235.

Cooke, A., Mills, T., & Lavender, T. (2012). Advanced maternal age: Delayed childbearing is rarely a conscious choice. *International Journal of Nursing Studies, 49*, 30–39.

Coombs, M., Addington-Hall, J., & Long-Sutehall, T. (2012). Challenges in transition from intervention to end of life care in intensive care. *International Journal of Nursing Studies, 49*(5), 519–527.

Cricco-Lizza, R. (2011). Everyday nursing practice values in the NICU and their reflection on breastfeeding promotion. *Qualitative Health Research, 21*, 399–409.

Findholt, N., Michael, Y., & Davis, M. (2011). Photovoice engages rural youth in childhood obesity prevention. *Public Health Nursing, 28*, 186–192.

Hall, W., Tomkinson, J., & Klein, M. (2012). Canadian care providers' and pregnant women's approaches to managing birth: Minimizing risk while maximizing integrity. *Qualitative Health Research, 22*, 575–586.

Leininger, M. M., & McFarland, M. R. (2006). *Culture care diversity and universality: A worldwide nursing theory*. Boston, MA Jones & Bartlett.

Lori, J., & Boyle, J. (2011). Cultural childbirth practices, beliefs, and traditions in postconflict Liberia. *Health Care for Women International, 32*, 454–473.

Michaelson, J. J. (2012). Emotional distance to so-called difficult patients. *Scandinavian Journal of Caring Sciences, 26*(1), 90–97.

Morse, J. M. (1991). Strategies for sampling. In J. M. Morse (Ed.), *Qualitative nursing research: A contemporary dialogue*. Newbury Park, CA: Sage.

Patton, M. Q. (2002). *Qualitative evaluation and research methods* (3rd ed.). Thousand Oaks, CA: Sage.

Pavlish, C., Brown-Saltzman, K., Hersh, M., Shirk, M., & Nudelman, O. (2011). Early indicators and risk factors for ethical issues in clinical practice. *Journal of Nursing Scholarship, 43*, 13–21.

Porr, C., Drummond, J., & Olson, K. (2012). Establishing therapeutic relationships with vulnerable and potentially stigmatized clients. *Qualitative Health Research, 22*, 384–396.

Roscigno, C., & Swanson, K. (2011). Parents' experiences following children's moderate to severe traumatic brain injury. *Qualitative Health Research, 21*, 1413–1426.

Tierney, S., Elwers, H., Sange, C., Mams, M., Rutter, M., Gibson, M., et al. (2011). What influences physical activity in people with heart failure? *International Journal of Nursing Studies, 48*, 1234–1243.

chapter 16

Analysis of Qualitative Data

LEARNING OBJECTIVES

On completing this chapter, you will be able to:

- Describe activities that qualitative researchers perform to manage and organize their data
- Discuss the procedures used to analyze qualitative data, including both general procedures and those used in ethnographic, phenomenologic, and grounded theory research
- Assess the adequacy of researchers' descriptions of their analytic procedures, and evaluate the suitability of those procedures
- Define new terms in the chapter

KEY TERMS

Axial coding	Content analysis	Open coding
Basic social process (BSP)	Core category	Paradigm case
Category scheme	Domain	Selective coding
Central category	Emergent fit	Substantive coding
Conceptual file	Focused coding	Taxonomy
Constant comparison	Hermeneutic circle	Theme
Constitutive pattern	Level I, II, and III codes	Theoretical coding

Qualitative data are derived from narrative materials, such as transcripts from audiotaped interviews or participant observers' field notes. This chapter describes methods for analyzing such qualitative data.

INTRODUCTION TO QUALITATIVE ANALYSIS

Qualitative data analysis is challenging, for several reasons. First, there are no universal rules for analyzing qualitative data. The absence of standard procedures makes it difficult to explain how to do such analyses.

A second challenge of qualitative analysis is the enormous amount of work required. Qualitative analysts must organize and make sense of hundreds or even thousands of pages of narrative materials. Qualitative researchers typically scrutinize their data carefully and deliberatively, often reading the data over and over in a search for meaning and understanding. Insights and theories cannot emerge until researchers become completely familiar with their data.

A third challenge is that doing qualitative analysis well requires creativity, sensitivity, and strong inductive skills (inducing universals from particulars). A good qualitative analyst must be skillful in discerning patterns and weaving them together into an integrated whole.

Another challenge comes in reducing data for reporting purposes. Quantitative results can often be summarized in a few tables. Qualitative researchers, by contrast, must balance the need to be concise with the need to maintain the richness and evidentiary value of their data.

TIP: Qualitative analyses are more difficult to *do* than quantitative ones, but qualitative findings are easier to understand than quantitative ones because the stories are told in everyday language. Qualitative analyses are often harder to critique than quantitative analyses, however, because readers cannot know firsthand if researchers adequately captured thematic patterns in the data.

QUALITATIVE DATA MANAGEMENT AND ORGANIZATION

Qualitative analysis is supported by several tasks that help to organize and manage the mass of narrative data. A key first step is checking the accuracy of transcribed data. Researchers should begin data analysis with the best-possible quality data, which requires careful training of transcribers, ongoing feedback, and continuous efforts to verify accuracy.

Developing a Category Scheme

Qualitative researchers begin their analysis by developing a method to classify and index their data. Researchers must be able to gain access to parts of the data, without having repeatedly to reread the data set in its entirety. This phase of data analysis is essentially reductionist—data must be converted to smaller, more manageable units that can be retrieved and reviewed.

A widely used procedure is to develop a **category scheme** and then to code data according to the categories. A preliminary category system is sometimes drafted before data collection, but more typically qualitative analysts develop categories based on a scrutiny of actual data. Developing a high-quality category scheme involves a careful reading of the data, with an eye to identifying underlying concepts and clusters of concepts. The nature of the categories may vary in level of detail or specificity, as well as in level of abstraction.

Researchers whose aims are primarily descriptive tend to use categories that are fairly concrete. For example, the category scheme may focus on differentiating various types of actions or events, or different phases in a chronologic unfolding of an experience. In developing a category scheme, related concepts are often grouped together to facilitate the coding process.

Example of a descriptive category scheme:

Elfström and colleagues (2012) explored situations that affect support of a partner's use of continuous positive airway pressure (CPAP) for sleep apnea, using data gathered through the critical incidents technique. The category system of situations negatively affecting partner support included such descriptive categories as *problems with the mask, complicated routines, being fatigued,* and *poor knowledge.*

Studies designed to develop a theory are more likely to involve abstract, conceptual categories. In creating conceptual categories, researchers break the data into segments, closely examine them, and compare them to other segments for similarities and dissimilarities to uncover what the meaning of those phenomena are. This is part of the process referred to as *constant comparison* by grounded theory researchers. The researcher asks questions such as the following about discrete events, incidents, or statements: What is this? What is going on? What else is like this? What is this distinct from?

Important concepts that emerge from examination of the data are then given a label. These names are necessarily abstractions, but the labels are usually sufficiently graphic that the nature of the material to which they refer is clear—and often provocative.

Example of a conceptual category scheme:

Box 16.1 shows the category scheme developed by Beck and Watson (2010) to code data from their interviews on childbirth after a previous traumatic birth (the full study is in Appendix B). The coding scheme includes major thematic categories with subcodes. For example, an excerpt that described a mother interviewing various obstetrical clinicians to determine who would be the best match to care for her would be coded 2J, for "interviewing perspective obstetricians and midwives." (Note that the original coding scheme, as shown in Box 16.1, was refined and made more parsimonious during the analysis. For example, codes 2F, 2J, and 2N, were collapsed into a larger category called "Interactions with obstetrical care providers.")

TIP: A good category scheme is crucial to the analysis of qualitative data. Unfortunately, research reports rarely present the category scheme for readers to critique, but they may provide information that may help you evaluate its adequacy (e.g., researchers may say that the scheme was reviewed by peers or developed and independently verified by other researchers).

Coding Qualitative Data

After a category scheme has been developed, the data are read in their entirety and coded for correspondence to the categories—a task that is seldom straightforward. Researchers may have difficulty deciding the most appropriate code, for example. It sometimes takes several readings of the material to grasp its nuances.

Also, researchers often discover during coding that the initial category system was incomplete. It is common for categories to emerge that were not initially identified. When this happens, it is risky to assume that the category was absent in materials that have already been coded. A concept might not be identified as salient until it has emerged three or four times. In such a case, it would be necessary to reread all previously coded material to check if the new code should be applied.

Another issue is that narrative materials usually are not linear. For example, paragraphs from transcribed interviews may contain elements relating to three or four different categories, embedded in a complex fashion.

Example of a multitopic segment:

Figure 16.1 shows an example of a multitopic segment of an interview from Beck and Watson's (2010) subsequent childbirth after a previous traumatic birth study. The codes in the margin represent codes from the category scheme presented in Box 16.1.

Methods of Organizing Qualitative Data

Before the advent of computer programs for qualitative data management, analysts often developed **conceptual files** for organizing their data. This approach involves creating a physical file for each category, and then cutting out and inserting all of the materials relating

Box 16.1 Beck and Watson's (2010) Coding Scheme for Subsequent Childbirth after a Previous Traumatic Birth

Theme 1. Riding the turbulent wave of panic during pregnancy

A. Fear
B. Panic
C. Anxiety
D. Terror
E. Dread
F. Denial

Theme 2. Strategizing: Attempts to reclaim their body and complete the journey to motherhood

A. Keeping a journal
B. Nurturing self
C. Reading about childbirth process
D. Hiring a doula
E. Hypnobirthing
F. Discussing previous traumatic birth with obstetric health care providers
G. Sharing their fears with partners
H. Writing detailed birth plan
I. Birth art
J. Interviewing prospective obstetricians and midwives
K. Homeopathic remedies
L. Using Internet support group
M. Regaining control
N. Building trust with obstetrical clinicians

Theme 3. Bringing reverence to the birthing process and empowering women

A. Treated with respect during labor and delivery
B. Pain relief taken seriously
C. Mother's wishes listened to
D. Not rushed during labor and delivery
E. Good communication with labor and delivery staff
F. Regaining sense of control
G. Caring health care providers during labor and delivery
H. Mother's body allowed to birth without medical interventions
I. Birth plan honored by labor and delivery staff
J. Feeling empowered

Theme 4. Still elusive: The longed-for healing birth experience

A. Unsuccessful home birth
B. Contrast in way woman was treated emphasized how badly her prior birth was
C. No sense of healing
D. Failed again as a woman

The 9 months of pregnancy after my traumatic delivery in 2003 were 9 of the longest months of my
life! I can honestly say I have never felt so anxious about anything. I had only been diagnosed as
suffering with postpartum PTSD 2 months prior to falling pregnant (accidentally) with my 2nd child 1C
and was only just coming to terms with the fact that the emotions and physical reactions I was
feeling were normal reactions to such an abnormal situation.

The emotions I experienced ranged from sheer terror about the thought of another birth to a 1D
conscious effort to regain my composure and take control of the situation. On a "good day" I would
consider my birth plan and attempt to put various instructions into it that would put me into the 2H
driving seat–control being such an important issue to me following the total lack of control during 2M
my previous birth.

Working in a hospital I was incredibly lucky in that I could speak to my obstetrician on a daily basis.
He recognized that all was not well when I told him about my first birth and he recommended that I 2F
speak with the head of midwifery for a debriefing session. When I did this, she suggested that for
this subsequent pregnancy she would put herself "on call" for my delivery and would attend all my
prenatal appointments. She was true to her word and this made me feel incredibly safe. 2N

I also read Heidi Gordon's book, *Birth and Beyond*, and referred to it like a bible. It helped to feel I 2C
was in full understanding of the birth process. I also spoke with other women to find out if birth 2L
second time around would be easier! My husband and I spoke at length about the birth and my 2G
fears.

FIGURE 16.1 ● Coded excerpt from Beck and Watson's (2010) study.

to that category into the file. Researchers can then retrieve all of the content on a particular topic by reviewing the applicable file folder.

Creating conceptual files is a cumbersome, labor-intensive task. This is particularly true when segments of the narrative materials have multiple codes, such as the excerpt shown in Figure 16.1. In this situation, there would need to be three copies of the second paragraph—one for each file corresponding to the three codes that were used (1D, 2H, 2M). Researchers must also be sensitive to the need to provide enough context that the cut-up material can be understood. Thus, it is often necessary to include material preceding or following the directly relevant materials.

Computer-assisted qualitative data analysis software (CAQDAS) can help to remove some of the work of cutting and pasting pages of narrative material. Dozens of CAQDAS have been developed. These programs permit an entire data set to be entered onto the computer, each portion of an interview or observational record coded, and then portions of the text corresponding to specified codes retrieved for analysis. The software can also be used to examine relationships between codes. Software cannot, however, *do* the coding, and it cannot tell the researcher how to analyze the data.

Computer programs offer many advantages for managing qualitative data, but some people prefer manual methods because they allow researchers to get closer to the data. Others object to having a cognitive process turned into an activity that is technical. Despite concerns, many researchers have switched to computerized data management. Proponents insist that it frees up their time and permits them to pay greater attention to important conceptual issues.

ANALYTIC PROCEDURES

Data *management* in qualitative research is reductionist in nature: It involves converting large masses of data into smaller, more manageable segments. By contrast, qualitative data *analysis* is constructionist: It is an inductive process that involves putting segments together into meaningful conceptual patterns. There are various approaches to qualitative data analysis, but some elements are common to several of them.

A General Analytic Overview

The analysis of qualitative materials usually begins with a search for broad categories or themes. In their review of how the term *theme* is used among qualitative researchers, DeSantis and Ugarriza (2000) offered this definition: "A **theme** is an abstract entity that brings meaning and identity to a current experience and its variant manifestations. As such, a theme captures and unifies the nature or basis of the experience into a meaningful whole" (p. 362).

Themes emerge from the data. They often develop within categories of data (i.e., within categories of the coding scheme used for indexing materials), but may also cut across them. For example, in Beck and Watson's (2010) study (Box 16.1), one theme that emerged was bringing reverence to the birthing process and empowering women; this theme included categories 3A (treated with respect by labor and delivery staff), 3C (mother's wishes listened to), 3E (good communication with labor and delivery staff), and 3I (birth plan honored by labor and delivery staff).

The search for themes involves not only discovering commonalities across participants but also seeking variation. Themes are never universal. Researchers must attend not only to what themes arise but also to how they are patterned. Does the theme apply only to certain types of people or in certain contexts? At certain periods? What are the conditions that precede the observed phenomenon, and what are the apparent consequences of it? In other words, the qualitative analyst must be sensitive to *relationships* within the data.

TIP: Qualitative researchers often use major themes as the subheadings in the results section of their reports. For example, in their analysis of interviews with older Korean women about health behavior, Yang and Yang (2011) identified seven themes that were used to organize their results, including "Being modest and free from greed" and "Staying in harmony with nature."

Researchers' search for themes, regularities, and patterns in the data can sometimes be facilitated by charting devices that enable them to summarize the evolution of behaviors, events, and processes. For example, for qualitative studies that focus on dynamic experiences—such as decision making—it is often useful to develop flow charts or timelines that highlight time sequences, major decision points, and events.

The identification of key themes and categories is seldom a tidy, linear process—iteration is usually necessary. That is, researchers derive themes, go back to the narrative materials with the themes in mind to see if there is a true fit, and then refine the themes. Sometimes apparent insights early in the process have to be abandoned.

Some qualitative researchers use metaphors as an analytic strategy. A **metaphor** is a symbolic comparison, using figurative language to evoke a visual analogy. A metaphor can be a powerfully expressive tool for qualitative analysts, although they can run the risk of "supplanting creative insight with hackneyed cliché masquerading as profundity" (Thorne & Darbyshire, 2005, p. 1111).

Example of a metaphor:

Sun and colleagues (2011) conducted a study of Taiwanese women's journey from a prior pregnancy loss to motherhood. They used the nautical metaphor "sailing against the tide" to capture the essence of the women's journey because "the sea has deep cultural meaning of uncertainty in life for the Taiwanese people" (p. 127).

A further step involves validation. In this phase, the concern is whether the themes accurately represent the perspectives of the participants. Several validation procedures can be used, as we discuss in Chapter 17. If more than one researcher is working on the study, sessions in which the themes are reviewed and specific cases discussed can be productive. Such review cannot ensure thematic validity, but it can minimize idiosyncratic biases.

In validating and refining themes, some researchers introduce **quasi-statistics**—a tabulation of the frequency with which certain themes or insights are supported by the data. The frequencies cannot be interpreted in the same way as frequencies in quantitative studies because of imprecision in enumerating the themes, but, as Becker (1970) pointed out, "Quasi-statistics may allow the investigator to dispose of certain troublesome null hypotheses. A simple frequency count of the number of times a given phenomenon appears may make untenable the null hypothesis that the phenomenon is infrequent" (p. 81).

Example of tabulating data:
Crowe and colleagues (2012) examined how women describe their decisions relating to the use of menopausal hormone therapy following surgical menopause. In their interviews with 30 women, the researchers found three themes that distinguished how the women managed risks associated with hormone therapy: *Waiting for someone to tell me* (13 women), *Life has to go on* (14 women), and *Relying on my body to get me through* (3 women).

TIP: Although relatively few qualitative researchers make formal efforts to quantify features of their data, be alert to quantitative implications when you read a qualitative report. Qualitative researchers routinely use words like "some," "most," or "many" in characterizing participants' experiences and actions, which implies some level of quantification.

In the final analysis stage, researchers strive to weave the thematic pieces together into a cohesive whole. The various themes are integrated to provide an overall structure (such as a theory or full description) to the data. The integration task demands creativity and intellectual rigor if it is to be successful.

Qualitative Content Analysis

In the remainder of this section, we discuss analytic procedures used by ethnographers, phenomenologists, and grounded theory researchers. Qualitative researchers who conduct descriptive qualitative studies may, however, simply say that they performed a content analysis. Qualitative **content analysis** involves analyzing the content of narrative data to identify prominent themes and patterns among the themes. Qualitative content analysis involves breaking down data into smaller *units*, coding and naming the units according to the content they represent, and grouping coded material based on shared concepts.

There are different types of units that can be identified in a text (Krippendorff, 2013). For example, physical units are defined by time, length, or size (not by type of information). Syntactical units are based on grammatical divisions within the data—i.e., words, sentences, paragraphs. Categorical distinctions define units by identifying something they have in common i.e., membership in a category. Thematic distinctions delineate units according to themes. Krippendorff suggested *clustering* as a way to represent the results of content analyses. Clustering is based on similarities among units of analysis and hierarchies that conceptualize the text on different levels of abstraction.

Example of a content analysis:
Ackerson (2012) undertook a content analysis of semistructured interviews with 15 low-income African American women who had a history of sexual trauma to understand their experiences in undergoing gynecological examinations and Pap smear testing. Coding of content was guided by the Interaction Model of Client Health Behavior.

Ethnographic Analysis

Analysis typically begins the moment ethnographers set foot in the field. Ethnographers are continually looking for *patterns* in the behavior and thoughts of participants, comparing one pattern against another, and analyzing many patterns simultaneously. As they analyze the organization and rhythms of everyday life, ethnographers acquire a deeper understanding of the culture being studied. Maps, flowcharts, and organizational charts are also useful tools that help to crystallize and illustrate the data being collected. Matrices (two-dimensional displays) can also help to highlight a comparison graphically, to cross-reference categories, and to discover emerging relationships.

Spradley's (1979) research sequence is often used for ethnographic data analyses. His method assumes that language is the primary means that relates cultural meaning in a culture. The task of ethnographers is to describe cultural symbols and to identify their coding rules. His sequence of 12 steps, which includes both data collection and data analysis, follows:

1. Locating an informant
2. Interviewing an informant
3. Making an ethnographic record
4. Asking descriptive questions
5. Analyzing ethnographic interviews
6. Making a domain analysis
7. Asking structural questions
8. Making a taxonomic analysis
9. Asking contrast questions
10. Making a componential analysis
11. Discovering cultural themes
12. Writing the ethnography

Thus, in Spradley's method there are four levels of data analysis, the first of which is *domain analysis*. **Domains**, which are units of cultural knowledge, are broad categories that encompass smaller categories. During this first level of data analysis, ethnographers identify relational patterns among terms in the domains that are used by members of the culture. The ethnographer focuses on the cultural meaning of terms and symbols (objects and events) used in a culture, and their interrelationships.

In *taxonomic analysis*, the second level of data analysis, ethnographers decide how many domains the data analysis will encompass. Will only one or two domains be analyzed in depth, or will a number of domains be studied less intensively? After making this decision, a **taxonomy**—a system of classifying and organizing terms—is developed to illustrate the internal organization of a domain and the relationship among the subcategories of the domain.

In *componential analysis*, multiple relationships among terms in the domains are examined. The ethnographer analyzes data for similarities and differences among cultural terms in a domain. Finally, in *theme analysis*, cultural themes are uncovered. Domains are connected in cultural themes, which help to provide a holistic view of the culture being studied. The discovery of cultural meaning is the outcome.

Example using Spradley's method:
Bourbonnais and Ducharme (2010) conducted an ethnographic study in a nursing home. They used Spradley's method of ethnographic analysis to explore *screaming* among elders in the nursing home environment as a unique language of communication.

Other approaches to ethnographic analysis have also been developed. For example, in their ethnonursing research method, Leininger and McFarland (2006) provided ethnographers with a four-phase ethnonursing data analysis guide. In the first phase ethnographers collect, describe, and record data. The second phase involves identifying and categorizing descriptors. In phase 3, data are analyzed to discover repetitive patterns in their context. The fourth and final phase involves abstracting major themes and presenting findings.

Example using Leininger's method:
Schumacher (2010) studied culture care meanings, beliefs, and practices in rural areas of the Dominican Republic. Interviews were conducted with 19 general and 10 key informants. Using Leininger's four-phase analytic method, three major cultural themes were identified.

Phenomenological Analysis

Schools of phenomenology have developed different approaches to data analysis. Three frequently used methods for descriptive phenomenology are the methods of Colaizzi (1978), Giorgi (1985), and Van Kaam (1966), all of whom are from the *Duquesne School* of phenomenology, based on Husserl's philosophy. Table 16.1 presents a comparison of these three analytic methods. The basic outcome of all three methods is the description of the essential nature of an experience, often through the identification of essential themes.

Phenomenologists search for common themes emerging from particular instances. There are, however, some important differences among these three approaches. Colaizzi's method, for example, is the only one that calls for a validation of results by querying study participants. Giorgi's view is that it is inappropriate either to return to participants to validate findings or to use external judges to review the analysis. Van Kaam's method requires that intersubjective agreement be reached with other expert judges.

Example of a study using Colaizzi's method:
Doyle and colleagues (2012) explored dietary decision making among patients attending a secondary prevention clinic following myocardial infarction. Transcribed interviews with nine people were analyzed using Colaizzi's method. The analysis identified six recurrent themes, three that facilitated change (fear, determination, and self-control) and three that impeded change (lack of willpower, poor recall of information, and need for support).

Phenomenologists from the *Utrecht School*, such as Van Manen (1997), combine characteristics of descriptive and interpretive phenomenology. Van Manen's approach involves six activities: (1) turning to the nature of the lived experience; (2) exploring the experience as we live it; (3) reflecting on essential themes; (4) describing the phenomenon through the art of writing and rewriting; (5) maintaining a strong relation to the phenomenon; and (6) balancing the research context by considering parts and whole. According to Van Manen,

TABLE 16.1 Comparison of Three Descriptive Phenomenologic Methods

Colaizzi (1978)	Giorgi (1985)	Van Kaam (1966)
1. Read all protocols to acquire a feeling for them.	1. Read the entire set of protocols to get a sense of the whole.	1. List and group preliminarily the descriptive expressions which must be agreed upon by expert judges. Final listing presents percentages of these categories in that particular sample.
2. Review each protocol, and extract significant statements.	2. Discriminate units from participants' description of phenomenon being studied.	2. Reduce the concrete, vague, and overlapping expressions of the participants to more descriptive terms. (Intersubjective agreement among judges needed.)
3. Spell out the meaning of each significant statement (i.e., formulate meanings).	3. Articulate the psychological insight in each of the *meaning units*.	3. Eliminate elements not inherent in the phenomenon being studied or that represent blending of two related phenomena.
4. Organize the formulated meanings into clusters of themes. a. Refer these clusters back to the original protocols to validate them. b. Note discrepancies among or between the various clusters, avoiding the temptation of ignoring data or themes that do not fit.	4. Synthesize all of the transformed meaning units into a consistent statement regarding participants' experiences (referred to as the "structure of the experience"); can be expressed on a specific or general level.	4. Write a hypothetical identification and description of the phenomenon being studied.
5. Integrate results into an exhaustive description of the phenomenon under study.		5. Apply hypothetical description to randomly selected cases from the sample. If necessary, revise the hypothesized description, which must then be tested again on a new sample.
6. Formulate an exhaustive description of the phenomenon under study in as unequivocal a statement of identification as possible.		6. Consider the hypothesized identification as a valid identification and description once preceding operations have been carried out successfully.
7. Ask participants about the findings thus far as a final validating step.		

thematic aspects of experience can be uncovered or isolated from participants' descriptions of the experience by three methods: the holistic, selective, or detailed approach. In the *holistic approach*, researchers view the text as a whole and try to capture its meanings. In the *selective* (or highlighting) *approach*, researchers highlight or pull out statements that seem essential to the experience under study. In the *detailed* (or line-by-line) *approach*, researchers analyze every sentence. Once themes have been identified, they become the objects of reflection and interpretation through follow-up interviews with participants. Through this process, essential themes are discovered.

Example of a study using Van Manen's method:
Haahr and colleagues (2011) studied the experience of living with advanced Parkinson's disease using van Manen's approach. They illustrated with interview excerpts how holistic, selective, and detailed approaches were used to reveal how participants lived with unpredictability.

In addition to identifying themes from participants' descriptions, Van Manen also called for gleaning thematic descriptions from artistic sources. Van Manen urged qualitative researchers to keep in mind that literature, painting, and other art forms can provide rich experiential data that can increase insights into the essential meaning of the experience being studied.

A third school of phenomenology is an interpretive approach called Heideggerian hermeneutics. Central to analyzing data in a hermeneutic study is the notion of the **hermeneutic circle**. The circle signifies a methodological process in which, to reach understanding, there is continual movement between the parts and the whole of the text being analyzed. Gadamer (1975) stressed that, to interpret a text, researchers cannot separate themselves from the meanings of the text and must strive to understand possibilities that the text can reveal.

Diekelmann, Allen, and Tanner (1989) proposed a seven-stage process of data analysis in hermeneutics that involves collaborative effort by a *team* of researchers. The goal of this process is to describe common meanings. Diekelmann and colleagues' stages include the following:

1. All the interviews or texts are read for an overall understanding.
2. Interpretive summaries of each interview are written.
3. A team of researchers analyzes selected transcribed interviews or texts.
4. Any disagreements on interpretation are resolved by going back to the text.
5. Common meanings and shared practices are identified by comparing and contrasting the text.
6. Relationships among themes emerge.
7. A draft of the themes along with exemplars from texts are presented to the team. Responses or suggestions are incorporated into the final draft.

According to Diekelmann and colleagues, the discovery in step 6 of a **constitutive pattern**—a pattern that expresses the relationships among relational themes and is present in all the interviews or texts—is the highest level of hermeneutical analysis. A situation is constitutive when it gives content to a person's self-understanding or to a person's way of being in the world.

Example of a Diekelmann's hermeneutical analysis:
Crotser and Dickerson (2011) described the experiences of women with at-risk relatives who learned of a family potential for cancer through genetic testing. Using team interpretation and Diekelman's seven-step analytic method, they discovered several themes, including *Redefining future possibilities* and *Navigating a twist in the road.*

Benner (1994) offered another analytic approach for hermeneutic phenomenology. Her interpretive analysis consists of three interrelated processes: the search for paradigm cases, thematic analysis, and analysis of exemplars. **Paradigm cases** are "strong instances of concerns or ways of being in the world" (Benner, 1994, p.113). Paradigm cases are used early in the analytic process as a strategy for gaining understanding. Thematic analysis is done to compare and contrast similarities across cases. Lastly, paradigm cases and thematic analysis can be enhanced by *exemplars* that illuminate aspects of a paradigm case or theme. The presentation of paradigm cases and exemplars in research reports allows readers to play a role in consensual validation of the results by deciding whether the cases support the researchers' conclusions.

Example using Benner's hermeneutical analysis:
Tzeng and colleagues (2010) conducted an interpretive phenomenological study of suicide survivors in Taiwan. They used Benner's approach in their analysis. A paradigm case was developed, and the researchers used it to compare and contrast other cases to identify commonalities and differences.

Grounded Theory Analysis

The grounded theory method emerged in the 1960s in connection with research that focused on dying in hospitals by two sociologists, Glaser and Strauss. The two co-originators eventually split and developed divergent schools of thought, which have been called the "Glaserian" and "Straussian" versions of grounded theory. A third analytic approach by Charmaz, constructivist grounded theory, has also emerged.

Glaser and Strauss' Grounded Theory Method

Grounded theory in all three analytic systems uses **constant comparison**, a method that involves comparing elements present in one data source (e.g., in one interview) with those in another. The process continues until the content of all sources has been compared so that commonalities are identified. The concept of fit is an important element in Glaserian grounded theory analysis. **Fit** has to do with how closely the emerging concepts fit with the incidents they are representing—which depends on how thoroughly constant comparison was done.

Coding in the Glaserian approach is used to conceptualize data into categories. Coding helps the researcher to discover the basic problem with which participants must contend. The substance of the topic under study is conceptualized through **substantive codes**, of which there are two types: open and selective. **Open coding**, used in the first stage of constant comparison, captures what is going on in the data. Open codes may be the actual words participants used. Through open coding, data are broken down and their similarities and differences are examined.

There are three levels of open coding that vary in degree of abstraction. **Level I codes** (or *in vivo codes*) are derived directly from the language of the substantive area. They have vivid imagery and "grab." Table 16.2 presents five level I codes and illustrative interview excerpts from Beck's (2002) grounded theory study on mothering twins.

As researchers constantly compare new level I codes with previously identified ones, they condense them into broader **level II codes**. For example, in Table 16.2, Beck's five level I codes were collapsed into a single level II code, "Reaping the Blessings." **Level III codes** (or theoretical constructs) are the most abstract. Collapsing level II codes aids in identifying constructs.

TIP: Additional material relating to Beck's twin study is presented in the Chapter Supplement on thePoint website.

Open coding ends when the core category is discovered, and then selective coding begins. The **core category** (or *core variable*) is a pattern of behavior that is relevant and/or problematic for study participants. In **selective coding**, researchers code only those data that are related to the core category. One kind of core category is a **basic social process**

TABLE 16.2 Collapsing Level I Codes into the Level II Code of *"REAPING THE BLESSINGS"* (Beck, 2002)

Excerpt	Level I Code
I enjoy just watching the twins interact so much. Especially now that they are mobile. They are not walking yet but they are crawling. I will tell you they are already playing. Like one will go around the corner and kind of peek around and they play hide and seek. They crawl after each other.	Enjoying Twins
With twins it's amazing. She was sick and she had a fever. He was the one acting sick. She didn't seem like she was sick at all. He was. We watched him for like 6 to 8 hours. We gave her the medicine and he started calming down. Like WOW! That is so weird. 'Cause you read about it but it's like, Oh come on! It's really neat to see.	Amazing
These days it's really neat 'cause you go to the store or you go out and people are like, "Oh, they are twins, how nice." And I say, "Yeah they are. Look, look at my kids."	Getting Attention
I just feel blessed to have two. I just feel like I am twice as lucky as a mom who has one baby. I mean that's the best part. It's just that instead of having one baby to watch grow and change and develop and become a toddler and school-age child, you have two.	Feeling Blessed
It's very exciting. It's interesting and it's fun to see them and how the twin bond really is. There really is a twin bond. You read about it and you hear about it, but until you experience it, you just don't understand. One time they were both crying and they were fed. They were changed and burped. There was nothing wrong. I couldn't figure out what was wrong. So I said to myself, "I am just going to put them together and close the door." I put them in my bed together, and they patty-caked their hands and put their noses together and just looked at each other and went right to sleep.	Twin Bonding

(BSP) that evolves over time in two or more phases. All BSPs are core categories, but not all core categories have to be BSPs.

Glaser (1978) provided nine criteria to help researchers decide on a core category. Here are a few examples: It must be central, meaning that it is related to many categories; it must recur frequently in the data; it relates meaningfully and easily to other categories; and it has clear and grabbing implications for formal theory.

Theoretical codes provide insights into how substantive codes relate to each other. Theoretical codes help grounded theorists to weave the broken pieces of data back together again. Glaser (1978) proposed 18 families of theoretical codes that researchers can use to conceptualize how substantive codes relate to each other (although he subsequently expanded possibilities in 2005). Four examples of his families of theoretical codes include the following:

- Process: stages, phases, passages, transitions
- Strategy: tactics, techniques, maneuverings
- Cutting point: boundaries, critical junctures, turning points
- The six Cs: causes, contexts, contingencies, consequences, covariances, and conditions

Throughout coding and analysis, grounded theory analysts document their ideas about the data and emerging conceptual scheme in *memos*. Memos encourage researchers to reflect on and describe patterns in the data, relationships between categories, and emergent conceptualizations.

Glaser's grounded theory method is concerned with the *generation* of categories and hypotheses rather than testing them. The product of the typical grounded theory analysis is a theoretical model that endeavors to explain a pattern of behavior that is relevant for study participants. Once the basic problem emerges, the grounded theorist goes on to discover the process these participants experience in coping with or resolving this problem.

Example of Glaser and Strauss grounded theory analysis:
Figure 16.2 presents Beck's (2002) model from a study in which "Releasing the Pause Button" was conceptualized as the core category and process through which mothers of twins progressed as they tried to resume their lives after giving birth. The process involves four phases: Draining Power, Pausing Own Life, Striving to Reset, and Resuming Own Life. Beck used 10 coding families in her theoretical coding for the study. The family *cutting point* offers an illustration. Three months seemed to be a turning point for mothers, when life started to be more manageable. Here is an excerpt from an interview that Beck coded as a cutting point: "Three months came around and the twins sort of slept through the night and it made a huge, huge difference."

Glaser and Strauss cautioned against consulting the literature before a framework is stabilized, but they also saw the benefit of scrutinizing other work. Glaser discussed the evolution of grounded theories through the process of **emergent fit**, to prevent individual substantive theories from being "respected little islands of knowledge" (Glaser, 1978, p. 148). As he noted, generating grounded theory does not necessarily require discovering all new categories or ignoring ones previously identified in the literature. Through constant comparison, researchers can compare concepts emerging from the data with similar concepts from existing theory or research to evaluate which parts have emergent fit with the theory being generated.

Strauss and Corbin's Approach

The Strauss and Corbin (1998) approach to grounded theory analysis differs from the original Glaser and Strauss method with regard to method, processes, and outcomes. Table 16.3 summarizes major analytic differences between these two grounded theory analysis methods.

Glaser (1978) stressed that to generate a grounded theory, the basic problem must emerge from the data—it must be discovered. The theory is, from the very start, grounded

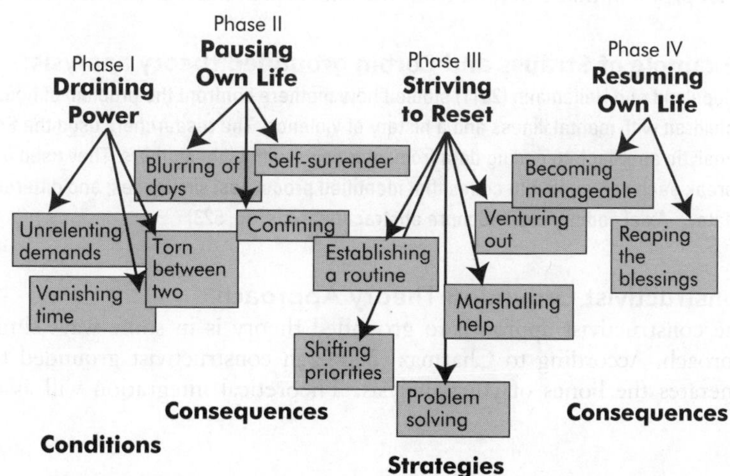

FIGURE 16.2 ● Beck's (2002) grounded theory of mothering twins.

TABLE 16.3 Comparison of Glaser's and Strauss/Corbin's Methods

	Glaser	Strauss & Corbin
Initial data analysis	Breaking down and conceptualizing data involves comparison of incident to incident so patterns emerge	Breaking down and conceptualizing data includes taking apart a single sentence, observation and incident
Types of coding	Open, selective, theoretical	Open, axial, selective
Connections between categories	18 coding families (plus others added subsequently)	Paradigm model (conditions, contexts, action/interactional strategies, and consequences)
Outcome	Emergent theory (discovery)	Conceptual description (verification)

in the data, rather than starting with a preconceived problem. Strauss and Corbin, however, argued that the research itself is only one of four possible sources of a research problem. Research problems can, for example, come from the literature or a researcher's personal and professional experience.

The Strauss and Corbin method involves three types of coding: open, axial, and selective. In **open coding**, data are broken into parts and compared for similarities and differences. In open coding, the researcher focuses on generating categories and their properties and dimensions. In **axial coding**, the analyst systematically develops categories and links them with subcategories. Strauss and Corbin used "axial" to describe this type of coding because coding was viewed as occurring around the axis of a category. What is called the *paradigm* is used to help identify linkages among categories. The basic components of the paradigm include conditions, actions/interactions, and consequences. **Selective coding** is the process in which the findings are integrated and refined. The first step in integrating the findings is to decide on the **central category** (sometimes called the *core category*), which is the main category of the research.

The outcome of the Strauss and Corbin approach is a full conceptual description. The original grounded theory method, by contrast, generates a theory that explains how a basic social problem that emerged from the data is processed in a social setting.

Example of Strauss and Corbin grounded theory analysis:

Copeland and Heilemann (2011) studied how mothers confront the problem of housing their adult children with mental illness and a history of violence. The researchers used the Strauss and Corbin analytic approach to coding data from interviews with eight mothers. They used open coding "to break each sentence into codes that identified processes, similarities, and differences present in the data... Axial coding involved more abstract analysis" (p. 523).

Constructivist Grounded Theory Approach

The constructivist approach to grounded theory is in some ways similar to a Glaserian approach. According to Charmaz (2006), in constructivist grounded theory the "coding generates the bones of your analysis. Theoretical integration will assemble these bones into a working skeleton" (p. 45). Charmaz offered guidelines for different types of coding: word-by-word coding, line-by-line coding, and incident-to-incident coding. Unlike Glaser and Strauss' grounded theory approach in which theory is discovered from data separate from the researcher, Charmaz's position is that researchers construct grounded theories by means of their past and current involvements and interactions with individuals and research practices.

Charmaz distinguished initial coding and **focused coding**. In initial coding, the pieces of data (e.g., words, lines, segments, incidents) are studied so the researcher can learn what the participants view as problematic. In focused coding, the analysis is directed towards identifying the most significant initial codes, which are then theoretically coded. An example of an analysis using the constructivist approach is presented at the end of the chapter.

TIP: Grounded theory researchers often present conceptual maps or models to summarize their results, such as the one in Figure 16.2, especially when the central phenomenon is a dynamic or evolving process.

CRITIQUING QUALITATIVE ANALYSIS

Evaluating a qualitative analysis is not easy to do. Readers do not have access to the information they would need to assess whether researchers exercised good judgment and critical insight in coding the narrative materials, developing a thematic analysis, and integrating materials into a meaningful whole. Researchers are seldom able to include more than a handful of examples of actual data in a journal article. Moreover, the process they used to inductively abstract meaning from the data is difficult to describe and illustrate.

A major focus of a critique of qualitative analyses is whether the researchers have adequately documented the analytic process. The report should provide information about the approach used to analyze the data. For example, a report for a grounded theory study should indicate whether the researchers used the Glaserian, Straussian, or constructivist approach.

Another aspect of a qualitative analysis that can be critiqued is whether the researchers have documented that they have used one approach consistently and have been faithful to the integrity of its procedures. Thus, for example, if researchers say they are using the Glaserian approach to grounded theory analysis, they should not also include elements from the Strauss and Corbin method. An even more serious problem occurs when, as sometimes happens, the researchers "muddle" traditions. For example, researchers who describe their study as a grounded theory study should not present *themes*, because grounded theory analysis does not yield themes. Researchers who attempt to blend elements from two traditions may not have a clear grasp of the analytic precepts of either one. For example, a researcher who claims to have undertaken an ethnography using a grounded theory approach to analysis may not be well informed about the underlying goals and philosophies of these two traditions.

Some further guidelines that may be helpful in evaluating qualitative analyses are presented in Box 16.2.

Box 16.2 Guidelines for Critiquing Qualitative Analyses

1. Was the data analysis approach appropriate for the research design or tradition?
2. Was the category scheme described? If so, does the scheme appear logical and complete?
3. Did the report adequately describe the process by which the actual analysis was performed? Did the report indicate whose approach to data analysis was used (e.g., Glaserian, Straussian, or constructivist in grounded theory studies)?
4. What major themes or processes emerged? Were relevant excerpts from the data provided, and do the themes or categories appear to capture the meaning of the narratives—that is, does it appear that the researcher adequately interpreted the data and conceptualized the themes? Is the analysis parsimonious—could two or more themes be collapsed into a broader and perhaps more useful conceptualization?
5. Was a conceptual map, model, or diagram effectively displayed to communicate important processes?
6. Was the context of the phenomenon adequately described? Did the report give you a clear picture of the social or emotional world of study participants?
7. Did the analysis yield a meaningful and insightful picture of the phenomenon under study? Is the resulting theory or description trivial or obvious?

RESEARCH EXAMPLES WITH CRITICAL THINKING EXERCISES

Example 1 below is also featured in our *Interactive Critical Thinking Activity* on thePoint website where you can easily record, print, and e-mail your responses to the related questions.

EXAMPLE 1 ● A Constructivist Grounded Theory Analysis

Study: Care transition experiences of spousal caregivers: From a geriatric rehabilitation unit (GRU) to home (Byrne et al., 2011). (This study appears in its entirety in the accompanying *Study Guide*).

Statement of Purpose: The purpose of this study was to develop a theory about caregivers' transition processes and experiences during their spouses' return home from a GRU.

Method: This grounded theory study involved in-depth interviews with 18 older adult spousal caregivers. Most of the caregivers were interviewed on three occasions: 48 hours prior to discharge from a 36-bed GRU in a Canadian long-term care hospital, 2 weeks postdischarge, and 1 month postdischarge. In addition to the interviews, which lasted between 35 and 120 minutes, the researchers made observations of interactions between spouses and care recipients.

Analysis: Analysis began with line-by-line coding by the first author. All authors contributed to focused coding, followed by theoretical coding. They used constant comparison throughout the coding and analysis process and provided a good example: "In the early stages of data collection and analysis, we noticed that caregivers continually used the phrase "I don't know," and thus an open code by this name was created... As data collection and analysis proceeded, we engaged in focused coding using the term *knowing/not knowing* to reflect these instances" (p. 1374). The researchers illustrated with an interview excerpt how they came to understand that knowing/not knowing was part of the process of *navigating*. The researchers also noted that "Moving from line-be-line coding to focused coding was not a linear process. As we engaged with the data, we returned to the data collected to explore new ideas and conceptualization of codes" (p. 1375).

Key Findings: The basic problem the caregivers faced was "fluctuating needs," including the physical, emotional, social, and medical needs of their spouses and themselves. The researchers developed a theoretical framework in which *reconciling in response to fluctuating needs* emerged as the basic social process. Reconciling encompassed three subprocesses: navigating, safekeeping, and repositioning. The context that shaped reconciling was a trajectory of prior care transitions and intertwined life events.

CRITICAL THINKING EXERCISES

1. Answer the relevant questions from Box 16.2 on page 316 regarding this study.
2. Also consider the following targeted questions:
   a. Comment on the researcher's decision to use both interview data and observations.
   b. The authors wrote that "To foster theoretical sensitivity, memos focused on actions and processes, and gradually incorporated relevant literature (e.g., theoretical perspectives on transition)" (p. 1375). Comment on this statement.
3. In what ways do you think the findings could be used in clinical practice?

EXAMPLE 2 ● A Phenomenological Analysis in Appendix B

- Read the method and results sections from Beck and Watson's phenomenological study ("Subsequent childbirth after a previous traumatic birth") in Appendix B on pages 403–412.

CRITICAL THINKING EXERCISES

1. Answer the relevant questions from Box 16.2 on page 316 regarding this study.
2. Also consider the following targeted questions:
   a. Comment on the amount of data that had to be analyzed in this study.
   b. Refer to Table 2 in the article, which presents a list of 10 significant statements made by participants. In Colaizzi's approach, the next step is to construct *formulated meanings* (interpretations) from the significant statements. Try to develop your own *formulated meanings* of one or two of these significant statements.

WANT TO KNOW MORE? A wide variety of resources to enhance your learning and understanding of this chapter are available on thePoint.

- Interactive Critical Thinking Activity
- Chapter Supplement on a Glaserian Grounded Theory Study
- Answers to the Critical Thinking Exercises for Example 2
- Student Review Questions
- Full-text online
- Internet Resources with useful websites for Chapter 16

Additional study aids including eight journal articles and related questions are also available in *Study Guide for Essentials of Nursing Research, 8e.*

SUMMARY POINTS

- Qualitative analysis is a challenging, labor-intensive activity, guided by few standardized rules.
- A first step in analyzing qualitative data is to organize and index the materials for easy retrieval, typically by coding the content of the data according to a category scheme.
- Traditionally, researchers have organized their data by developing **conceptual files**, which are physical files in which coded excerpts of data for specific categories are placed. Now, however, computer programs (CAQDAS) are widely used to perform basic indexing functions and to facilitate data analysis.
- The actual analysis of data begins with a search for patterns and **themes**, which involves the discovery not only of commonalities across participants but also of natural variation in the data. Some qualitative analysts use *metaphors* or figurative comparisons to evoke a visual and symbolic analogy.
- Another analytic step involves validation of the thematic analysis. Some researchers use **quasi-statistics**, a tabulation of the frequency with which certain themes or relations are supported by the data. In a final step, analysts try to weave the thematic strands together into an integrated picture of the phenomenon under investigation.
- Researchers whose goal is qualitative description often say they used qualitative **content analysis** as their analytic method.
- In ethnographies, analysis begins as the researcher enters the field. One analytic approach is Spradley's method, which involves four levels of analysis: *domain analysis* (identifying **domains**, or units of cultural knowledge), *taxonomic analysis* (selecting key domains and constructing **taxonomies**), *componential analysis* (comparing and contrasting terms in a domain), and a *theme analysis* (to uncover cultural themes).
- There are numerous approaches to phenomenological analysis, including the descriptive methods of Colaizzi, Giorgi, and Van Kaam, in which the goal is to find common patterns of experiences shared by particular instances.
- In Van Manen's approach, which involves efforts to grasp the essential meaning of the experience being studied, researchers search for themes, using a *holistic approach* (viewing text as a whole), a *selective approach* (pulling out key statements and phrases), or a *detailed approach* (analyzing every sentence).
- Central to analyzing data in a hermeneutic study is the notion of the **hermeneutic circle**, which signifies a process in which there is continual movement between the parts and the whole of the text under analysis.
- Diekelmann's team method of hermeneutic analysis calls for the discovery of a **constitutive pattern** that expresses the relationships among themes. Benner's approach consists of three processes: searching for **paradigm cases**, thematic analysis, and analysis of *exemplars*.
- Grounded theory uses the **constant comparative** method of data analysis, a method that involves comparing elements present in one data source (e.g., in one interview) with those in another. *Fit* has to do with how closely concepts fit with incidents they represent, which is related to how thoroughly constant comparison was done.
- One grounded theory approach is the Glaser and Strauss (Glaserian) method, in which there are two broad types of coding: **substantive coding** (in which the empirical substance of the topic is conceptualized) and **theoretical coding** (in which the relationships among the substantive codes are conceptualized).

- Substantive coding involves **open coding** to capture what is going on in the data and then **selective coding**, in which only variables relating to a core category are coded. The **core category**, a behavior pattern that has relevance for participants, is sometimes a **basic social process (BSP)** that involves an evolutionary process of coping or adaptation.
- In the Glaserian method, open codes begin with **level I (in vivo) codes**, which are collapsed into a higher level of abstraction in **level II codes**. Level II codes are then used to formulate **level III codes**, which are theoretical constructs. Through constant comparison, the researcher compares concepts emerging from the data with similar concepts from existing theory or research to see which parts have **emergent fit** with the theory being generated.
- The Strauss and Corbin grounded theory method has full conceptual description as the outcome. This grounded theory approach involves three types of coding: open (in which categories are generated), **axial coding** (where categories are linked with subcategories), and selective (in which the findings are integrated and refined).
- In Charmaz's constructivist grounded theory, coding can be word-by-word, line-by-line, or incident-by-incident. Initial coding leads to **focused coding**, which is then followed by theoretical coding.

REFERENCES FOR CHAPTER 16

Ackerson, K. (2012). A history of interpersonal trauma and the gynecological exam. *Qualitative Health Research, 22*(5), 679–688.

Beck, C. T. (2002). Releasing the pause button: Mothering twins during the first year of life. *Qualitative Health Research, 12*, 593–608.

Beck, C.T. (2006). Anniversary of birth trauma: Failure to rescue. *Nursing Research, 55*, 381–390.

Becker, H. S. (1970). *Sociological work*. Chicago, IL Aldine.

Benner, P. (1994). The tradition and skill of interpretive phenomenology in studying health, illness, and caring practices. In P. Benner (Ed.), *Interpretive phenomenology* (pp. 99–127). Thousand Oaks, CA: Sage.

Bourbonnais, A., & Ducahrme, F. (2010). The meanings of screams in older people living with dementia in a nursing home. *International Psychogeriatrics, 22*, 1172–1184.

Byrne, K., Orange, J., & Ward-Griffin, C. (2011). Care transition experiences of spousal caregivers: From a geriatric unit to home. *Qualitative Health Research, 21*, 1371–1387.

Charmaz, K. (2006). *Constructing grounded theory: A practical guide to qualitative analysis*. Thousand Oaks, CA: Sage.

Colaizzi, P. (1978). Psychological research as the phenomenologist views it. In R. Valle & M. King (Eds.), *Existential phenomenological alternatives for psychology* (pp. 48–71). New York: Oxford University Press.

Copeland, D., & Heilemann, M. (2011). Choosing "the best of hells": Mothers facing housing dilemmas for their adult children with mental illness and a history of violence. *Qualitative Health Research, 21, 520–533.*

Crotser, C., & Dickerson, S. (2010). Learning about a twist in the road: Perspectives of at-risk relatives learning of potential for cancer. *Oncology Nursing Forum, 37*, 723–733.

Crowe, M., Burrell, B., & Whitehead, L. (2012). Lifestyle risk management: A qualitative analysis of women's descriptions of taking hormone therapy following surgically induced menopause. *Journal of Advanced Nursing, 68*, 1814–1823.

DeSantis, L., & Ugarriza, D. N. (2000). The concept of theme as used in qualitative nursing research. *Western Journal of Nursing Research, 22*, 351–372.

Diekelmann, N. L., Allen, D., & Tanner, C. (1989). *The NLN criteria for appraisal of baccalaureate programs: A critical hermeneutic analysis*. New York: NLN Press.

Doyle, B., Fitzsimons, D., McKeown, P., & McAloon, T. (2012). Understanding dietary decision-making in patients attending a secondary prevention clinic following myocardial infarction. *Journal of Clinical Nursing, 21*, 32–41.

Elfström, M., Karlsson, S., Nilsen, P., Fridlund, B., Svanborg, E., & Broström, A. (2012). Decisive situations affecting partners' support to continuous positive airway pressure-treated patients with obstructive sleep apnea syndrome. *The Journal of Cardiovascular Nursing, 27*(3), 228–239.

Gadamer, H.G. (1975). *Truth and method*. (G. Borden & J. Cumming, trans). London, UK: Sheed & Ward.

Giorgi, A. (1985). *Phenomenology and psychological research*. Pittsburgh, PA: Duquesne University Press.

Glaser, B. G. (1978). *Theoretical sensitivity*. Mill Valley, CA: Sociology Press.

Glaser, B.G. (2005). *The grounded theory perspective III: Theoretical coding*. Mill Valley, CA: Sociology Press.

Glaser, B. G., & Strauss, A. L. (1967). *The discovery of grounded theory: Strategies for qualitative research*. Chicago, IL: Aldine.

Haahr, A., Kirkevold, M., Hall, E., & Ostergaard, K. (2011). Living with advanced Parkinson's disease: A constant struggle with unpredictability. *Journal of Advanced Nursing, 67*, 408–417.

Krippendorff, K. (2013). *Content analysis: An introduction to its methodology* (3rd ed.). Thousand Oaks, CA: Sage.

Leininger, M., & McFarland, M. (2006). *Culture care diversity and universality: A worldwide nursing theory* (2nd ed.). Sudbury, MA: Jones and Bartlett Publishers.

Schumacher, G. (2010). Culture care meanings, beliefs, and practices in rural Dominican Republic. *Journal of Transcultural Nursing, 21*(2), 93–103.

Spradley, J. P. (1979). *The ethnographic interview*. New York: Holt, Rinehart and Winston.

Strauss, A. L., & Corbin, J. M. (1998). *Basics of qualitative research: Techniques and procedures for developing grounded theory* (2nd ed.). Thousand Oaks, CA: Sage.

Sun, H. L., Sinclair, M., Kernohan, G., Chang, T., & Paterson, H. (2011). Sailing against the tide: Taiwanese women's journey from pregnancy loss to motherhood. *MCN: American Journal of Maternal/Child Health, 36*, 127–133.

Thorne, S. & Darbyshire, P. (2005). Land mines in the field: A modest proposal for improving the craft of qualitative health research. *Qualitative Health Research, 15*(8), 1105–1113.

Tzeng, W., Su, P., Chiang, H., Kuan, P., & Lee, J. (2010). A qualitative study of suicide survivors in Taiwan. *Western Journal of Nursing Research, 32*, 185–198.

Van Kaam, A. (1966). *Existential foundations of psychology*. Pittsburgh, PA: Duquesne University Press.

Van Manen, M. (1997). *Researching lived experience* (2nd ed.). London, ON: The Althouse Press.

Yang, J. H., & Yang, B. S. (2011). Alternative view of health behavior: the experience of older Korean women. *Qualitative Health Research, 21*, 324–332.

chapter 17

Trustworthiness and Integrity in Qualitative Research

LEARNING OBJECTIVES

On completing this chapter, you will be able to:

- Discuss some controversies relating to the issue of quality in qualitative research
- Identify the quality criteria proposed in the Lincoln and Guba framework for evaluating quality and integrity in qualitative research
- Discuss strategies for enhancing quality in qualitative research
- Describe different dimensions relating to the interpretation of qualitative results
- Define new terms in the chapter

KEY TERMS

Audit trail
Authenticity
Confirmability
Credibility
Dependability
Disconfirming evidence
Inquiry audit
Member check
Negative case analysis
Peer debriefing
Persistent observation
Prolonged engagement
Researcher credibility
Thick description
Transferability
Triangulation
Trustworthiness

Integrity in qualitative research is a critical issue for both those doing the research and those considering the use of qualitative evidence.

PERSPECTIVES ON QUALITY IN QUALITATIVE RESEARCH

Qualitative researchers agree on the importance of doing high-quality research, yet defining "high quality" has been controversial. It is beyond the scope of this book to explain arguments of the debate in detail, but we offer a brief overview.

Debates about Rigor and Validity

One contentious issue concerns use of the terms *rigor* and *validity*—terms some people shun because they are associated with the positivist paradigm and are viewed as inappropriate goals for constructivist research. For these critics, the concept of rigor is by its nature an empirical analytic term that does not fit into an interpretive paradigm that values insight and creativity.

Others disagree with those opposing the term *validity*. Whittemore and colleagues (2001), for example, argued that validity is an appropriate term in all paradigms, noting that the dictionary definition of validity (the state or quality of being sound, just, and well founded) lends itself equally to qualitative and quantitative research.

The complex debate has given rise to a variety of positions. At one extreme are those who think that validity is an appropriate quality criterion in both qualitative and quantitative studies, although qualitative researchers use different methods to achieve it. At the opposite extreme are those who berate the "absurdity" of validity. A widely adopted stance is what has been called a *parallel perspective*. This position was proposed by Lincoln and Guba (1985), who created standards for the **trustworthiness** of qualitative research that parallel the standards of reliability and validity in quantitative research.

Generic versus Specific Standards

Another controversial issue concerns whether there should be a generic set of quality standards, or whether specific standards are needed for different types of inquiry—for example, for ethnographers and grounded theory researchers. Many writers subscribe to the idea that research conducted within different qualitative traditions must attend to different concerns, and that techniques for enhancing and demonstrating research integrity vary. Thus, different writers have offered standards for specific forms of qualitative inquiry, such as grounded theory, phenomenology, ethnography, and critical research. Some writers believe, however, that there are some quality criteria that are fairly universal within the constructivist paradigm. For example, Whittemore and colleagues (2001) prepared a synthesis of criteria that they viewed as essential to all qualitative inquiry.

Terminology Proliferation and Confusion

The result of these controversies is that there is no common vocabulary for quality criteria in qualitative research. Terms, such as *truth value*, *goodness*, *integrity*, *trustworthiness*, and *rigor*, abound, but each proposed term has been deemed inappropriate by some critics.

With regard to actual *criteria* for evaluating quality in qualitative research, dozens (if not hundreds) have been suggested. Establishing a consensus on what the quality criteria for qualitative inquiry should be, and what they should be named, remains elusive, and it is unlikely that a consensus will be achieved in the near future, if ever.

Given the lack of consensus, and the heated arguments supporting and contesting various frameworks, it is difficult to provide guidance about quality standards. We present information about *criteria* from the Lincoln and Guba framework in the next section. We then describe *strategies* that researchers use to strengthen integrity in qualitative research. These strategies should be viewed as points of departure for considering whether a qualitative study is sufficiently rigorous, trustworthy, insightful, or valid.

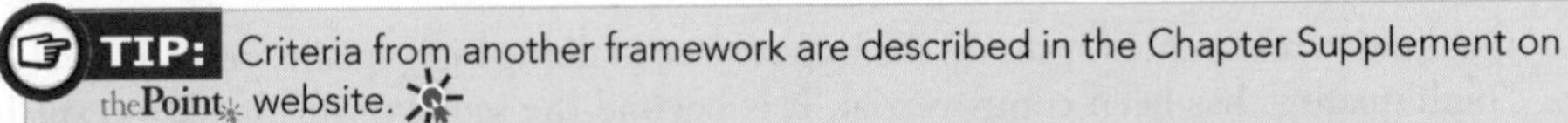

TIP: Criteria from another framework are described in the Chapter Supplement on thePoint website.

LINCOLN AND GUBA'S FRAMEWORK OF QUALITY CRITERIA

Although not without critics, the criteria often viewed as the "gold standard" for qualitative research are those outlined by Lincoln and Guba (1985). These researchers suggested four criteria for developing the *trustworthiness* of a qualitative inquiry: credibility, dependability, confirmability, and transferability. These criteria represent parallels to the positivists' criteria of internal validity, reliability, objectivity, and external validity, respectively. In later writings, responding to criticisms and to their own evolving views, a fifth criterion more distinctively within the constructivist paradigm was added: authenticity (Guba & Lincoln, 1994).

Credibility

Credibility refers to confidence in the truth value of the data and interpretations of them. Qualitative researchers must strive to establish confidence in the truth of the findings for the particular participants and contexts in the research. Lincoln and Guba pointed out that credibility involves two aspects: first, carrying out the study in a way that enhances the believability of the findings, and second, taking steps to *demonstrate* credibility to external readers. Credibility is a crucial criterion in qualitative research that has been proposed in several quality frameworks.

Dependability

Dependability refers to the stability (reliability) of data over time and over conditions. The dependability question is: Would the study findings be repeated if the inquiry were replicated with the same (or similar) participants in the same (or similar) context? Credibility cannot be attained in the absence of dependability, just as validity in quantitative research cannot be achieved in the absence of reliability.

Confirmability

Confirmability refers to objectivity, that is, the potential for congruence between two or more independent people about the data's accuracy, relevance, or meaning. This criterion is concerned with establishing that the data represent the information participants provided, and that the interpretations of those data are not imagined by the inquirer. For this criterion to be achieved, the findings must reflect the participants' voice and the conditions of the inquiry, and not the researcher's biases, motivations, or perspectives.

Transferability

Transferability, analogous to generalizability, is the extent to which qualitative findings can be transferred to or have applicability in other settings or groups. Lincoln and Guba noted that the investigator's responsibility is to provide sufficient descriptive data that consumers can evaluate the applicability of the data to other contexts: "Thus the naturalist cannot specify the external validity of an inquiry; he or she can provide only the thick description necessary to enable someone interested in making a transfer to reach a conclusion about whether transfer can be contemplated as a possibility" (p. 316).

Authenticity

Authenticity refers to the extent to which researchers fairly and faithfully show a range of different realities. Authenticity emerges in a report when it conveys the feeling tone of participants' lives as they are lived. A text has authenticity if it invites readers into a vicarious experience of the lives being described, and enables readers to develop a heightened sensitivity to the issues being depicted. When a text achieves authenticity, readers are better able to understand the lives being portrayed "in the round," with some sense of the mood, feeling, experience, language, and context of those lives.

STRATEGIES TO ENHANCE QUALITY IN QUALITATIVE INQUIRY

The criteria for establishing integrity in a qualitative study are complex and challenging. A variety of strategies have been proposed to address these challenges. This section describes some of them in the hope that they will prompt a careful assessment of steps researchers did or not take to enhance integrity.

We have not organized strategies according to criteria (e.g., strategies researchers use to enhance *credibility*) because many strategies simultaneously address multiple criteria. Instead, we have organized strategies according to different phases of a study—data generation, coding and analysis, and report preparation. Table 17.1 indicates how various quality-enhancement strategies map onto Lincoln and Guba's criteria.

TABLE 17.1 Quality-Enhancement Strategies in Relation to Lincoln and Guba's Quality Criteria for Qualitative Inquiry

Strategy	Credibility	Dependability	Confirmability	Transferability	Authenticity
Throughout the Inquiry					
Reflexivity/reflexive journaling	X				X
Careful documentation, decision trail		X	X		
Data Generation					
Prolonged engagement	X				X
Persistent observation	X				X
Comprehensive field notes	X			X	
Audiotaping and verbatim transcription	X				X
Triangulation (data, method)	X	X			
Saturation of data	X			X	
Member checking	X	X			
Data Coding/Analysis					
Transcription rigor/data cleaning	X				
Intercoder checks; development of a codebook	X		X		
Quasi-statistics	X				

TABLE 17.1 Quality-Enhancement Strategies in Relation to Lincoln and Guba's Quality Criteria for Qualitative Inquiry *(Continued)*

Strategy	Credibility	Dependability	Confirmability	Transferability	Authenticity
Data Coding/Analysis *(Continued)*					
Triangulation (investigator, theory, analysis)	X	X	X		
Stepwise replication		X	X		
Search for disconfirming evidence/ negative case analysis	X				
Peer review/debriefing	X		X		
Inquiry audit		X	X		
Presentation of Findings					
Documentation of quality-enhancement efforts	X			X	
Thick, vivid description				X	X
Impactful, evocative writing					X
Documentation of researcher creden-tials, background	X				
Documentation of reflexivity	X				

Quality-Enhancement Strategies During Data Collection

Qualitative researchers use many strategies to enrich and strengthen their studies, some of which are difficult to discern in a report. For example, intensive listening during an interview, careful probing to obtain rich and comprehensive data, and taking pains to gain participants' trust are all strategies to enhance data quality that cannot easily be communicated in a report. In this section, we focus on some strategies that can be described to readers to increase their confidence in the integrity of the study results.

Prolonged Engagement and Persistent Observation

An important step in establishing integrity in qualitative studies is **prolonged engagement**—the investment of sufficient time collecting data to have an in-depth understanding of the culture, language, or views of the people or group under study, to test for misinformation and distortions, and to ensure saturation of important categories. Prolonged engagement is also essential for building trust and rapport with informants, which in turn makes it more likely that useful and rich information will be obtained.

Example of prolonged engagement:
Salt and Peden (2011) studied decision-making relating to treatment for rheumatoid arthritis in a grounded theory study with 30 women. Data were collected over a 13-month period. The researchers noted that "This prolonged engagement assured that the decision-making process was accurately and fully described" (p. 215).

High-quality data collection in qualitative studies also involves **persistent observation**, which concerns the salience of the data being gathered. Persistent observation refers to the researchers' focus on the characteristics or aspects of a situation that are relevant to the phenomena being studied. As Lincoln and Guba (1985) noted, "If prolonged engagement provides scope, persistent observation provides depth" (p. 304).

Example of persistent observation:
Ward-Griffin and colleagues (2012) conducted a critical ethnography of the management of dementia home care resources in Ontario. They made detailed observations and conducted multiple interviews with persons with dementia, family caregivers, in-home providers, and case managers in nine dementia care networks over a 19-month period.

Reflexivity Strategies

Reflexivity involves awareness that the researcher as an individual brings to the inquiry a unique background, set of values, and a social and professional identity that can affect the research process. Reflexivity involves attending continually to the researcher's effect on the collection, analysis, and interpretation of data.

The most widely used strategy for maintaining reflexivity and delimiting subjectivity is to maintain a reflexive journal or diary. Reflexive notes can be used to record, from the outset of the study and in an ongoing fashion, thoughts about the impact of previous life experiences and previous readings about the phenomenon on the inquiry. Through self-interrogation and reflection, researchers seek to be well positioned to probe deeply and to grasp the experience, process, or culture under study through the lens of participants.

TIP: Researchers sometimes begin a study by being interviewed themselves with regard to the phenomenon under study. Of course, this approach usually only makes sense if the researcher has had experience with that phenomenon.

Data and Method Triangulation

Triangulation refers to the use of multiple referents to draw conclusions about what constitutes truth. The aim of triangulation is to "overcome the intrinsic bias that comes from single-method, single-observer, and single-theory studies" (Denzin, 1989, p. 313). Triangulation can also help to capture a more complete, contextualized picture of the phenomenon under study. Denzin identified four types of triangulation (data triangulation, investigator triangulation, method triangulation, and theory triangulation), and other types have been proposed. Two types are relevant to data collection.

Data triangulation involves the use of multiple data sources for the purpose of validating conclusions. There are three types of data triangulation: time, space, and person. **Time triangulation** involves collecting data on the same phenomenon or about the same people at different points in time. Time triangulation can involve gathering data at different times of the day, or at different times in the year. This concept is similar to test–retest reliability assessment—the point is not to study a phenomenon longitudinally to assess how it changes, but to establish the congruence of the phenomenon across time. **Space triangulation** involves collecting data on the same phenomenon in multiple sites, to test for cross-site consistency. Finally, **person triangulation** involves collecting data from different types or levels of people (e.g., individuals, families, communities), with the aim of validating data through multiple perspectives on the phenomenon.

Example of person and space triangulation:
Miles and colleagues (2011) studied how community responses to HIV play a role in the distress experienced by African Americans with HIV living in the rural south. Data were collected in six communities, and were gathered through focus group and individual interviews with community leaders, service providers, and African Americans with HIV.

Method triangulation involves using multiple methods of data collection about the same phenomenon. In qualitative studies, researchers often use a rich blend of unstructured data collection methods (e.g., interviews, observations, documents) to develop a comprehensive understanding of a phenomenon. Multiple data collection methods provide an opportunity to evaluate the extent to which a consistent and coherent picture of the phenomenon emerges.

Example of method triangulation:
Sloand and colleagues (2012) triangulated multiple data sources in their study of fatherhood and the role of fathers' clubs in promoting child health in Haitian villages. The main data source was personal interviews with 18 fathers from four villages. The researchers triangulated these data with data from interviews with key informants, field notes of meetings with village health agents, and journal entries "to augment the initial analysis findings so that the truest picture could be drawn of fathering in rural Haiti" (p. 490).

Comprehensive and Vivid Recording of Information

In addition to taking steps to record data from interviews accurately (e.g., via careful transcriptions of audiotaped interviews), researchers should prepare field notes that are rich with descriptions of what transpired in the field. Even if interviews are the only source of data, researchers should record descriptions of the participants' demeanor and behaviors during the interactions, and the interview context. Thoroughness in record-keeping helps readers to develop confidence in the data.

Researchers sometimes specifically develop an **audit trail**, that is, a systematic collection of materials and documentation that would allow an independent auditor to come to conclusions about the data. An adequate audit trail might include the following types of records: the raw data (e.g., interview transcripts); methodologic, theoretic, and reflexive notes; instrument development information (e.g., pilot topic guides); and data reconstruction products (e.g., drafts of the final report). Similarly, the maintenance of a *decision trail* that articulates the researcher's decision rules for categorizing data and making analytic inferences is a useful way to enhance the dependability of the study. When researchers can share some decision trail information in their reports, readers can better evaluate the soundness of the decisions and draw conclusions about the trustworthiness of the findings.

Example of an audit trail:
In their ethnographic study of anxiety and agitation in mechanically ventilated patients, Tate and colleagues (2012) maintained careful documentation: "An audit trail of methodologic notes and analytic memos was recorded systematically to detail thoughts and establish dependability" (p. 160).

Member Checking

In a **member check**, researchers give participants feedback about emerging interpretations and then obtain participants' reactions. The argument is that participants should have an opportunity to assess and validate whether the researchers' interpretations are good representations of their realities. Member checking can be carried out as data are being collected (e.g., through deliberate probing to ensure that interviewers have properly interpreted participants' meanings), and more formally after data have been fully analyzed in follow-up interviews or interviews with different participants.

Despite the potential that member checking has for enhancing credibility, it has some potential drawbacks. One issue is that member checks can lead to erroneous conclusions if participants share a common façade or a desire to "cover up." Also, some participants might agree with researchers' interpretations out of politeness or in the belief that researchers are "smarter" or more knowledgeable than they are. Thorne and Darbyshire (2005) cautioned against what they called *adulatory validity*, "a mutual stroking ritual that satisfies the agendas of both researcher and researched" (p. 1110). They pointed out that member checking tends to privilege interpretations that place participants in a charitable light.

Few strategies for enhancing data quality are as controversial as member checking. Nevertheless, it is a strategy that has the potential to enhance credibility if it is done in a manner that encourages candor and critical appraisal by participants.

TIP: Methodologic congruence regarding member checking should be assessed. For example, if Giorgi's phenomenologic methods were used, member checking would not be undertaken, but member checking *is* called for in studies following Colaizzi's approach (see Table 16.1, p. 309).

Example of member checking:
Chen (2012) conducted a descriptive qualitative study of the life experiences of Taiwanese oral cancer patients during the postoperative period. A sample of 13 patients participated in in-depth interviews. The thematic analysis was reviewed by three study participants and by four patients with oral cancer who had not participated in the study to ensure that the results accurately depicted patients' experiences.

Strategies Relating to Coding and Analysis

Excellent qualitative inquiry is likely to involve the simultaneous collection and analysis of data, and so several of the strategies described earlier also contribute to analytic integrity. Member checking, for example, can occur in an ongoing fashion as part of the data collection process, but typically also involves participants' review of preliminary analytic constructions. Some analytic validation procedures, such as the use of quasi-statistics, were described in Chapter 16. In this section, we introduce a few additional quality-enhancement strategies associated with the coding, analysis, and interpretation of qualitative data.

Investigator and Theory Triangulation

During analysis, several types of triangulation are pertinent. **Investigator triangulation** refers to the use of two or more researchers to make data collection, coding, and analytic decisions. The underlying premise is that through collaboration, investigators can reduce the possibility of biased decisions and idiosyncratic interpretations.

Conceptually, investigator triangulation is analogous to inter-rater reliability in quantitative studies, and is a strategy that is often used in coding qualitative data. Some researchers take formal steps to compare two or more independent category schemes or independent coding decisions.

Example of independent coding:
Skär and Söderberg (2012) studied men's complaints about their encounters with the health care system in Sweden. Both researchers independently coded the transcripts of interviews with nine men who had lodged a complaint, using a category system that had been jointly developed after a preliminary review of the data. The authors discussed their coding until consensus was reached.

If investigators bring to the analysis task a complementary blend of skills and expertise, the analysis and interpretation can potentially benefit from divergent perspectives. Blending diverse methodologic, disciplinary, and clinical skills also can contribute to other types of triangulation.

Example of investigator triangulation:
Drach-Zahavy and colleagues (2012) studied psychiatric hospital staff's perceptions of and reactions to aggressive patient behavior. Data from in-depth interviews with 11 health care professionals in an Israeli psychiatric hospital were content analyzed separately by all four researchers. "We then comparatively examined our individual analyses, by both the themes' content and the interpretation of their meanings" (p. 46).

One form of investigator triangulation is called **stepwise replication**, a strategy most often mentioned in connection with Lincoln and Guba's dependability criterion. This technique involves having a research team that can be divided into two groups. These groups deal with data sources separately and conduct, essentially, independent inquiries through which data can be compared.

With **theory triangulation**, researchers use competing theories or hypotheses in the analysis and interpretation of their data. Qualitative researchers who develop alternative hypotheses while still in the field can test the validity of each because the flexible design of qualitative studies provides ongoing opportunities to direct the inquiry. Theory triangulation can help researchers to rule out rival hypotheses and to prevent premature conceptualizations.

Searching for Disconfirming Evidence and Competing Explanations

A powerful verification procedure involves a systematic search for data that will challenge a categorization or explanation that has emerged early in the analysis. The search for **disconfirming evidence** occurs through purposive or theoretical sampling methods. Clearly, this strategy depends on concurrent data collection and data analysis: researchers cannot look for disconfirming data unless they have a sense of what they need to know.

Example of searching for disconfirming evidence:
Enarsson and colleagues (2007) conducted a grounded theory study to examine common approaches among staff toward patients in long-term psychiatric care. The researchers found that all the categories they were discovering were negative in nature. To assess the integrity of their categories, the researchers performed a specific search for data reflecting common staff approaches that related to positive experiences. No such positive episodes could be found either in interviews or observations.

Lincoln and Guba (1985) discussed the related activity of **negative case analysis**. This strategy (sometimes called *deviant case analysis)* is a process by which researchers revise their interpretations by including cases that appear to disconfirm earlier hypotheses. The goal of this procedure is to continuously refine a hypothesis or theory until it accounts for *all* cases.

Example of a negative case analysis:
Ching and colleagues (2012) explored coping among Chinese women afflicted with breast cancer. The researchers explained that they "derived hypotheses when relationships between the codes were identified in one interview and verified or modified in the subsequent interviews, illustrating similar responses, different responses, and negative cases" (p. 251).

Peer Review and Debriefing

Another quality-enhancement strategy involves external validation. **Peer debriefing** involves sessions with peers to review and explore aspects of the inquiry. Peer debriefing exposes researchers to the searching questions of others who are experienced in either the methods of constructivist inquiry, the phenomenon being studied, or both.

In a peer-debriefing session, researchers might present written or oral summaries of the data that have been gathered, categories and themes that are emerging, and researchers' interpretations of the data. In some cases, taped interviews might be played. Among the questions that peer debriefers might address are the following:

- Is there evidence of researcher bias?
- Do the gathered data adequately portray the phenomenon? Have all important themes or categories been identified?
- If there are important omissions, what strategies might remedy this problem?
- Are there any apparent errors of fact or possible errors of interpretation?
- Are there competing interpretations or more parsimonious interpretations?
- Are the themes and interpretations knit together into a cogent, useful, and creative conceptualization of the phenomenon?

Example of peer debriefing:
Van Dover and Pfeiffer (2012) conducted a grounded theory study of the process that patients of parish nurses experience when they receive spiritual care. The two researchers developed codes and categories separately and then reached consensus. An independent researcher then reviewed the analysis when links among theoretical elements were under construction.

Inquiry Audits

A similar, but more formal, approach is to undertake an inquiry audit, a procedure that is a means of enhancing a study's dependability and confirmability. An **inquiry audit** involves a scrutiny of the data and relevant supporting documents by an external reviewer. Such an audit requires careful documentation of all aspects of the inquiry. Once the audit trail materials are assembled, the inquiry auditor proceeds to audit, in a fashion analogous to a financial audit, the trustworthiness of the data and the meanings attached to them. Such audits are a good tool for persuading others that qualitative data are worthy of confidence.

Example of an inquiry audit:
Rotegård and colleagues (2012) studied cancer patients' experiences and perceptions of their personal strengths through their illness and recovery in four focus group interviews with 26 participants. A partial audit was undertaken by having an external researcher review a sample of transcripts and interpretations.

Strategies Relating to Presentation

This section describes some aspects of the qualitative report itself that can help to persuade readers of the high quality of the inquiry.

Thick and Contextualized Description

Thick description refers to a rich, thorough, and vivid description of the research context, the people who participated in the study, and the experiences and processes observed during the inquiry. Transferability cannot occur unless investigators provide sufficient information to permit judgments about contextual similarity. Lucid and textured descriptions, with the judicious inclusion of verbatim quotes from study participants, also contribute to the authenticity of a qualitative study.

TIP: Sandelowski (2004) warned that "...the phrase *thick description* likely ought not to appear in write-ups of qualitative research at all, as it is among those qualitative research words that should be seen but not written" (p. 215).

In high-quality qualitative studies, descriptions typically need to go beyond a faithful rendering of information. Powerful description is evocative and has the capacity for emotional impact. Qualitative researchers should, however, avoid misrepresenting their findings by sharing only the most dramatic or sensational stories. Thorne and Darbyshire (2005) cautioned against what they called *lachrymal validity*, a criterion for evaluating research according to the extent to which the report can wring tears from its readers! At the same time, they observed that the opposite problem with some reports is that they are "bloodless." Bloodless findings are characterized by a tendency of some researchers to "play it safe in writing up the research, reporting the obvious...(and) failing to apply any inductive analytic spin to the sequence, structure, or form of the findings" (p. 1109).

Researcher Credibility

Another aspect of credibility is **researcher credibility**. In qualitative studies, researchers *are* the data collecting instruments—as well as creators of the analytic process—and so their qualifications, experience, and reflexivity are relevant in establishing confidence in the data. Patton (2002) has argued that trustworthiness is enhanced if the report contains information about the researchers, including information about credentials and any personal connections the researchers had to the people, topic, or community under study. For example, it is relevant for a reader of a report on the coping mechanisms of AIDS patients to know that the researcher is HIV positive. Researcher credibility is also enhanced when reports describe the researchers' efforts to be reflexive and to take their own prejudices and perspectives into account.

Example of researcher credibility:
Nilvarangkul and colleagues (2011) did an action study to explore and enhance the health-related quality of life of Laotian migrant workers in Thailand. They included a paragraph describing their qualifications for the research. All four researchers were Thai health care professionals (three were nurses) with a focus on workplace health and safety.

INTERPRETATION OF QUALITATIVE FINDINGS

It is difficult to describe the interpretive process in qualitative studies, but there is considerable agreement that the ability to "make meaning" from qualitative texts depends on researchers' immersion in and closeness to the data. **Incubation** is the process of *living* the data, a process in which researchers must try to understand their meanings, find their essential patterns, and draw well-grounded, insightful conclusions. Another key ingredient in interpretation and meaning-making is researchers' self-awareness and the ability to reflect on their own world view and perspectives—that is, reflexivity. Creativity also plays an important role in uncovering meaning in the data. Researchers need to give themselves sufficient time to achieve the *aha* that comes with making meaning beyond the facts.

For *readers* of qualitative reports, interpretation is hampered by having limited access to the data and no opportunity to "live" the data. Researchers are necessarily selective in the amount and types of information to include in their reports. Nevertheless, you should strive to consider some of the same interpretive dimensions for qualitative studies as for quantitative ones (Chapter 13). In the discussion that follows, we discuss five dimensions.

The Credibility of Qualitative Results

As with quantitative reports, you should consider whether the results of a qualitative inquiry are believable. It is reasonable to expect authors of qualitative reports to provide *evidence* of the credibility of the findings. Because consumers are exposed to only a portion of the data, they must rely on researchers' efforts to corroborate findings through such mechanisms as peer debriefings, member checks, audits, triangulation, and negative cases analysis. They must also rely on researchers' honesty in acknowledging known limitations.

In considering the believability of qualitative results, it makes sense to adopt the posture of a person who needs to be persuaded about the researcher's conceptualization, and to expect the researcher to marshal evidence with which to persuade you. It is also appropriate to consider whether the researcher's conceptualization of the phenomenon is consistent with common experiences and with your own clinical insights.

The Meaning of Qualitative Results

From the point of view of researchers themselves, interpretation and analysis of qualitative data occur virtually simultaneously, in an iterative process. Efforts to validate the qualitative analysis are necessarily efforts to validate interpretations as well. Thus, unlike quantitative analyses, the meaning of the data flows directly from qualitative analysis.

Nevertheless, prudent qualitative researchers hold their interpretations up for closer scrutiny—self-scrutiny as well as review by peers and outside reviewers. Even when researchers have undertaken peer debriefings and other strategies described in this chapter, these procedures do not constitute proof that interpretations are correct. For both qualitative and quantitative researchers, it is important to consider possible alternative explanations for the findings and to take into account methodologic or other limitations that could have affected study results.

TIP: Interpretation in qualitative studies sometimes yields hypotheses that can be tested in more controlled quantitative studies. Qualitative studies are well suited to generating causal hypotheses, but not to testing them in a rigorous fashion.

The Importance of Qualitative Results

Qualitative research is especially productive when it is used to describe and explain poorly understood phenomena. The scantiness of prior research on a topic is not, however, a sufficient barometer for deciding whether the findings can contribute to nursing knowledge. The phenomenon must be one that merits scrutiny.

You should also consider whether the findings themselves are trivial. Perhaps the topic is worthwhile, but you may feel after reading a report that nothing has been learned beyond what is common sense or everyday knowledge—this can happen when the data are too "thin" or when the conceptualization is shallow. Readers, like researchers, want to have an *aha* experience when they read about the lives and concerns of clients and their families. Qualitative researchers often attach catchy labels to their themes and processes, but you should ask yourself whether the labels have really captured an insightful construct.

The Transferability of Qualitative Results

Although qualitative researchers do not strive for generalizability, the possible application of the results to other settings and contexts is important to evidence-based practice. Thus, in interpreting qualitative results, you should consider how transferable the findings are. In what other types of settings and contexts would you expect the phenomena under study to be manifested in a similar fashion? Of course, to make such an assessment, the researchers must have described in sufficient detail the participants and the context in which the data were collected. Because qualitative studies are context bound, it is only through a careful analysis of the key parameters of the study context that the transferability of results can be assessed.

The Implications of Qualitative Results

If the findings are judged to be believable and important, and if you are satisfied with the interpretation of the results, you can begin to consider what the implications of the findings might be. First, you can consider implications for further research: Should a similar study be undertaken in a different setting? Has an important construct been identified that merits the development of a formal measuring instrument? Do the results suggest hypotheses that could be tested through controlled quantitative research? Second, do the findings have implications for nursing practice? For example, could the health-care needs of a subculture (e.g., the homeless) be addressed more effectively as a result of the study? Finally, do the findings shed light on fundamental processes that could play a role in nursing theories?

CRITIQUING INTEGRITY AND INTERPRETATIONS IN QUALITATIVE STUDIES

For qualitative research to be judged trustworthy, investigators must earn the trust of their readers. Many qualitative reports do not provide much information about the researchers' efforts to ensure that their research is strong with respect to the quality criteria described in this chapter. In a world that is very conscious about the quality of research evidence, qualitative researchers need to be proactive in doing high-quality research and persuading others that they were successful.

Clearly, demonstrating integrity to others involves providing a good description of the quality-enhancement activities that were undertaken. Yet some qualitative reports do not address the topic of rigor, integrity, or trustworthiness at all. Others pay lip service to validity concerns, simply noting, for example, that an audit trail was maintained. Just as clinicians seek *evidence* for clinical decisions, research consumers need evidence that findings are believable and true. Researchers should include enough information about their quality-enhancement strategies for readers to draw conclusions about study quality. The research example at the end of this chapter is exemplary in this regard.

Part of the difficulty that qualitative researchers face in demonstrating trustworthiness and authenticity is that page constraints in journals impose conflicting demands. It takes a precious amount of space to present quality-enhancement strategies adequately and convincingly. Using space for such documentation means that there is less space for the thick description of context and rich verbatim accounts that support authenticity and vividness. Qualitative research is often characterized by the need for critical compromises. It is well to keep such compromises in mind in critiquing qualitative research reports.

An important point in thinking about quality in qualitative inquiry is that attention needs to be paid to both "art" and "science," and to interpretation and description. Creativity and insightfulness need to be attained, but not at the expense of soundness. And the quest for soundness cannot sacrifice inspiration and elegant abstractions, or else the results are likely to be "perfectly healthy but dead" (Morse, 2006, p. 6). Good qualitative work is both descriptively accurate and explicit, and interpretively rich and innovative. Some guidelines that may be helpful in evaluating qualitative methods and analyses are presented in Box 17.1.

BOX 17.1 Guidelines for Evaluating Trustworthiness and Integrity in Qualitative Studies

1. Does the report discuss efforts to enhance or evaluate the quality of the data and the overall inquiry? If so, is the description sufficiently detailed and clear? If not, is there other information that allows you to draw inferences about the quality of the data, the analysis, and the interpretations?
2. Which specific techniques (if any) did the researcher use to enhance the trustworthiness and integrity of the inquiry? What quality-enhancement strategies were *not* used? Would additional strategies have strengthened your confidence in the study and its evidence?
3. Has the researcher adequately represented the multiple realities of those being studied? Do the findings seem *authentic*?
4. Given the efforts to enhance data quality, what can you conclude about the study's validity/integrity/rigor/trustworthiness?
5. Did the report discuss any study limitations and their possible effects on the credibility of the results or on interpretations of the data? Were results interpreted in light of findings from other studies?
6. Did the researchers discuss the study's implications for clinical practice or future research? Were the implications well grounded in the study evidence, and in evidence from earlier research?

RESEARCH EXAMPLES WITH CRITICAL THINKING EXERCISES

Example 1 below is also featured in our *Interactive Critical Thinking Activity* on thePoint website where you can easily record, print, and e-mail your responses to the related questions.

EXAMPLE 1 ● Trustworthiness in a Grounded Theory Study

Study: Moving to place: Childhood cancer treatment decision making in single-parent and repartnered family structures (Kelly & Ganong, 2011)

Statement of Purpose: The purpose of this study was to address this overarching question: "How do parents who no longer live together make treatment decisions for their children with cancer?"

Method: The grounded theory study involved in-depth interviews with 15 custodial parents, nonresident parents, and step-parents from eight families that included a child with cancer. The interviews included such grand tour questions as the following: "Please tell me everything you can remember about what it was like for you making the (specific treatment decision)" (p. 351). The audiotaped interviews were transcribed, and analyzed using the Strauss and Corbin approach.

Quality Enhancement Strategies: The researchers' report provided good detail about the efforts the researchers made to enhance the trustworthiness and integrity of their study. They stated that they undertook prolonged engagement with participants, that they triangulated data by gathering information from family members with different perspectives, and that they made efforts to include a diverse sample in terms of family structure and disease experiences. They noted that they reached theoretical saturation with 12 interviews, but conducted three additional interviews to confirm the evolving theory. In these member-check interviews, "parents endorsed the elements of the paradigm model and offered no additional commentary" (p. 351). The first author conducted all the fieldwork, and the second author reviewed her decision trail and ongoing analysis. "Both authors reviewed all the transcripts, category coding decisions, and accompanying memos" (p. 352). They made efforts to maintain objectivity by "thinking comparatively, comparing incident to incident, and staying grounded in the data" (p. 352). At critical points in their analysis, they consulted another grounded theory researcher who had studied parental treatment decision making regarding their conceptualizations. The report also included explicit statements regarding researcher credibility and transferability.

Key Findings: The researchers concluded that "moving to place" was the central psychosocial process by which parents in complex and nontraditional family structures negotiated their involvement in treatment decision making. The process was grounded by a focus on the ill child. Parents used the actions of stepping up, stepping back, being pushed, and stepping away to respond to the need for treatment decision making.

CRITICAL THINKING EXERCISES

1. Answer the relevant questions from Box 17.1 on page 334 regarding this study.
2. Also consider the following targeted questions:
   a. Which quality-enhancement strategy used by Kelly and Ganong gave you the *most* confidence in the integrity and trustworthiness of their study? Why?
   b. Think of an additional type of triangulation that the researchers could have used in their study and describe how this could have been operationalized.
3. In what ways do you think the findings could be used in clinical practice?

EXAMPLE 2 ● Trustworthiness in the Phenomenologic Study in Appendix B

- Read the method and results sections from Beck and Watson's phenomenological study ("Subsequent childbirth after a previous traumatic birth") in Appendix B on pages 403–412.

CRITICAL THINKING EXERCISES

1. Answer the relevant questions from Box 17.1 on page 334 regarding this study.
2. Also consider the following targeted questions:
   a. Suggest one or two ways in which triangulation could have been used in this study.
   b. Which quality-enhancement strategy used by Beck and Watson gave you the *most* confidence in the integrity and trustworthiness of their study? Why?

WANT TO KNOW MORE? A wide variety of resources to enhance your learning and understanding of this chapter are available on thePoint.

- Interactive Critical Thinking Activity
- Chapter Supplement on Whittemore and Colleagues' Framework of Quality Criteria in Qualitative Research
- Answers to the Critical Thinking Exercises for Example 2
- Student Review Questions
- Full-text online
- Internet Resources with useful websites for Chapter 17

Additional study aids including eight journal articles and related questions are also available in *Study Guide for Essentials of Nursing Research, 8e.*

SUMMARY POINTS

- One of several controversies regarding *quality* in qualitative studies involves terminology. Some argue that *rigor* and *validity* are quantitative terms that are not suitable as goals in qualitative inquiry, but others believe these terms are appropriate. Other controversies involve what criteria to use as indicators of integrity and whether there should be generic or study-specific criteria.
- One prominent evaluative framework is that of Lincoln and Guba, who identified five criteria for evaluating **trustworthiness** in qualitative inquiries: credibility, dependability, confirmability, transferability, and authenticity.
- **Credibility**, which refers to confidence in the truth value of the findings, has been viewed as the qualitative equivalent of internal validity. **Dependability**, the stability of data over time and over conditions, is somewhat analogous to reliability in quantitative studies. **Confirmability** refers to the objectivity of the data. **Transferability**, the analog of external validity, is the extent to which findings can be transferred to other settings or groups. **Authenticity** is the extent to which researchers faithfully show a range of different realities and convey the feeling tone of lives as they are lived.
- Strategies for enhancing quality during qualitative data collection include **prolonged engagement**, which strives for adequate scope of data coverage; **persistent observation**, which is aimed at achieving adequate depth; comprehensive recording of information (including maintenance of an **audit trail**); triangulation, and **member checks** (asking study participants to review and react to study data and emerging conceptualizations).

- **Triangulation** is the process of using multiple referents to draw conclusions about what constitutes the truth. This includes **data triangulation** (using multiple data sources to validate conclusions) and **method triangulation** (using multiple methods to collect data about the same phenomenon).
- Strategies for enhancing quality during the coding and analysis of qualitative data include **investigator triangulation** (independent coding and analysis of some of the data by two or more researchers), **theory triangulation** (use of competing theories or hypotheses in the analysis and interpretation of data), **stepwise replication** (dividing the research team into two groups that conduct independent inquiries that can be compared and merged), searching for **disconfirming evidence**, searching for rival explanations and undertaking a **negative case analysis** (revising interpretations to account for cases that appear to disconfirm early conclusions), external validation through **peer debriefings** (exposing the inquiry to the searching questions of peers), and launching an **inquiry audit** (a formal scrutiny of audit trail documents by an independent auditor).
- Strategies that can be used to convince readers of reports of the high quality of qualitative inquiries include using **thick description** to vividly portray contextualized information about study participants and the central phenomenon, and making efforts to be transparent about researcher credentials and reflexivity so that **researcher credibility** can be established.
- Interpretation in qualitative research involves "making meaning"—a process that is difficult to describe or critique. Yet interpretations in qualitative inquiry need to be reviewed in terms of credibility, importance, transferability, and implications.

REFERENCES FOR CHAPTER 17

Chen, S. C. (2012). Life experiences of Taiwanese oral cancer patients during the postoperative period. *Scandinavian Journal of Caring Sciences, 26*(1), 98–103.

Ching, S., Martinson, I., & Wong, T. (2012). Meaning making: psychological adjustment to breast cancer by Chinese women. *Qualitative Health Research, 22*, 250–262.

Denzin, N. K. (1989). *The research act* (3rd ed.). New York: McGraw-Hill.

Drach-Zahavy, A., Goldblatt, H., Granot, M., Hirschmann, S., & Kostintski, H. (2012). Control: Patients' aggression in psychiatric settings. *Qualitative Health Research, 22*, 43–53.

Enarsson, P., Sandman, P-O., & Hellzen, O. (2007). The preservation of order: The use of common approaches among staff toward clients in long-term psychiatric care. *Qualitative Health Research, 17*, 718–729.

Guba, E., & Lincoln, Y. (1994). Competing paradigms in qualitative research. In N. Denzin & Y. Lincoln (Eds.), *Handbook of qualitative research*, (pp. 105–117). Thousand Oaks, CA: Sage.

Kelly, K. P., & Ganong, L. (2011). Moving to place: Childhood cancer treatment decision making in single-parent and repartnered family structures. *Qualitative Health Research, 21*, 349–364.

Lincoln, Y. S., & Guba, E. G. (1985). *Naturalistic inquiry*. Newbury Park, CA: Sage.

Miles, M. S., Isler, M., Banks, B., Sengupta, S., & Corbie-Smith, G. (2011). Silent endurance and profound loneliness: Socioemotional suffering in African Americans living with HIV in the rural south. *Qualitative Health Research, 21*, 489–501.

Morse, J. M. (2006). Insight, inference, evidence, and verification: Creating a legitimate discipline. *International Journal of Qualitative Methods, 5*(1), Article 8. Retrieved August 7, 2012 from http://www.ualberta.ca/ijqm/.

Nilvarangkul, K., McCann, T., Rungreangkulkij, S., & Wongprom, J. (2011). Enhancing a health-related quality of life model for Laotian migrant workers in Thailand. *Qualitative Health Research, 21*, 312–332.

Patton, M. Q. (2002). *Qualitative evaluation and research methods* (3rd ed.). Thousand Oaks, CA: Sage.

Rotegård, A., Fagermoen, M., & Ruland, C. (2012). Cancer patients' experiences of their personal strengths through illness and recovery. *Cancer Nursing, 35*, E8–E17.

Salt, E., & Peden, A. (2011). The complexity of the treatment: The decision-making process among women with rheumatoid arthritis. *Qualitative Health Research, 21*, 214–222.

Sandelowski, M. (2004). Counting cats in Zanzibar. *Research in Nursing & Health, 27*, 215–216.

Skär, L., & Söderberg, S. (2012). Complaints with encounters in healthcare—men's experiences. *Scandinavian Journal of Caring Science, 26*(2), 279–286.

Sloand, E., Gebrian, B., & Astone, N. M. (2012). Fathers' beliefs about parenting and fathers' clubs to promote child health in rural Haiti. *Qualitative Health Research, 22*, 488–498.

Tate, J. A., Dabbs, A., Hoffman, L., Milbrandt, E., & Happ, M. (2012). Anxiety and agitation in mechanically ventilated patients. *Qualitative Health Research, 22*, 157–173.

Thorne, S. & Darbyshire, P. (2005). Land mines in the field: A modest proposal for improving the craft of qualitative health research. *Qualitative Health Research, 15*, 1105–1113.

Van Dover, L., & Pfeiffer, J. (2012). Patients of parish nurses experience renewed spiritual identity: A grounded theory study. *Journal of Advanced Nursing, 68*, 1824–1833.

Ward-Griffin, C., Hall, J., DeForge, R., St-Amant, O., McWilliam, C., Oudshoorn, A., et al. (2012). Dementia home care resources: How are we managing? *Journal of Aging Research, 2012*, 590–724.

Whittemore, R., Chase, S. K., & Mandle, C. L. (2001). Validity in qualitative research. *Qualitative Health Research, 11*, 522–537.

part 5

Special Topics in Research

chapter 18

Mixed Methods and Other Special Types of Research

LEARNING OBJECTIVES

On completing this chapter, you will be able to:

- Identify several advantages of mixed methods research and describe specific applications
- Describe strategies and designs for conducting mixed methods research
- Identify the purposes and some of the distinguishing features of specific types of research (e.g., clinical trials, evaluations, surveys)
- Define new terms in the chapter

KEY TERMS

Clinical trial
Concurrent design
Convergent parallel design
Economic (cost) analysis
Embedded design
Evaluation research
Explanatory design
Exploratory design
Health services research
Impact analysis
Intervention theory
Methodologic research
Mixed methods (MM) research
Nursing intervention research
Outcomes research
Pragmatism
Process analysis
Secondary analysis
Sequential design
Survey research

In this final part of the book, we explain several special types of research. We begin by discussing mixed methods (MM) research that combines qualitative and qualitative approaches.

MIXED METHODS RESEARCH

A growing trend in nursing research is the planned collection and integration of qualitative and quantitative data within single studies or coordinated clusters of studies. This section discusses the rationale for such **mixed methods research** and presents a few applications.

Rationale for Mixed Methods Research

The dichotomy between quantitative and qualitative data represents a key methodologic distinction. Some argue that the paradigms that underpin qualitative and quantitative research are fundamentally incompatible. Most people, however, now believe that many areas of inquiry can be enriched through the judicious triangulation of qualitative and quantitative data. The advantages of an MM design include the following:

- *Complementarity*. Qualitative and quantitative approaches are complementary. By using MM, researchers can possibly avoid the limitations of a single approach.
- *Practicality*. Given the complexity of phenomena, it is practical to use whatever methodological tools are best suited to addressing pressing research questions, and to not have one's hands tied by rigid adherence to a single approach.
- *Incrementality*. Progress on a topic tends to be incremental. Qualitative findings can generate hypotheses to be tested quantitatively, and quantitative findings may need clarification through in-depth probing. It can be productive to build such a feedback loop into the design of a study.
- *Enhanced validity*. When a hypothesis or model is supported by multiple and complementary types of data, researchers can be more confident about their inferences. Triangulation of methods can provide opportunities for testing alternative interpretations of the data and for examining the extent to which the context helped to shape the results.

Perhaps the strongest argument for MM research, however, is that some questions *require* MM. **Pragmatism**, a paradigm often associated with MM research, provides a basis for a position that has been stated as the "dictatorship of the research question" (Tashakkori & Teddlie, 2010, p. 21). Pragmatist researchers consider that it is the research question that should drive the inquiry, and its design and methods. They reject a forced choice between the traditional postpositivists' and constructivists' modes of inquiry.

Purposes and Applications of Mixed Methods Research

In MM research, there is typically an overarching goal, but there are inevitably at least two research questions, each of which requires a different type of approach. For example, MM researchers may simultaneously ask exploratory (qualitative) questions and confirmatory (quantitative) questions. In an MM study, researchers can examine causal *effects* in a quantitative component, but can shed light on causal *mechanisms* in a qualitative component.

Creswell and Plano Clark (2011) identified several types of research situations that are especially well suited to MM research, including the following:

1. The concepts are poorly understood, and qualitative exploration is needed before more formal, structured methods can be used
2. The findings from one approach can be greatly enhanced with a second source of data
3. Neither a qualitative nor a quantitative approach, by itself, is adequate in addressing the complexity of the problem
4. The quantitative results are difficult to interpret, and qualitative data can help to explain them

As this list suggests, mixed methods research can be used in various situations, a few of which are described here.

Developmental Work

When a construct is new, qualitative research can help to capture its full complexity and dimensionality. Nurse researchers sometimes gather qualitative data as the basis for developing formal instruments—that is, for generating and wording the questions on quantitative scales that are subsequently subjected to rigorous testing. Similarly, qualitative research is playing an increasingly important role in the development of promising nursing interventions and in efforts to assess their efficacy.

Example of intervention development:
Zoffman and Kirkevold (2012) described how their grounded theory studies on barriers to empowerment among patients with diabetes led to the development of a problem-solving intervention called Guided Self-Determination (GSD). The intervention was subsequently evaluated in a randomized controlled trial (RCT).

Hypothesis Generation and Testing

In-depth qualitative studies are often fertile with insights into constructs or relationships among them. These insights then can be tested and confirmed with larger samples in quantitative studies. This often happens in the context of discrete mono-method investigations. One problem, however, is that it usually takes years to do a study and publish the results, which means that considerable time may elapse between the qualitative insights and the formal quantitative testing of hypotheses based on those insights. A researcher can undertake a coordinated set of MM studies that has hypothesis generation and testing as an explicit goal.

Example of hypothesis generation and testing:
Elstad and colleagues (2011) undertook a mixed methods study of how individuals with lower urinary tract symptoms (LUTS) use fluid manipulation to self-manage their symptoms. Quantitative data came from a random sample of over 5,000 adults participating in a community health survey. Qualitative data came from in-depth interviews and focus group interviews with 152 of the survey participants who had LUTS. Themes from the qualitative data were used as the basis for hypotheses that were then tested statistically using the quantitative data.

Explication

Qualitative data are sometimes used to explicate the *meaning* of quantitative descriptions or relationships. Quantitative methods can demonstrate that variables are systematically related but may fail to provide insights into *why* they are related. Such explications help to clarify important concepts, corroborate findings from statistical analyses, and give guidance to the interpreting results.

Example of explication with qualitative data:
Smyth and colleagues (2011) studied nursing practices associated with the administration of pro re nata (PRN) analgesics to children postoperatively. They used records data to quantify analgesia practices (e.g., doses, routes, time of day) for 95 children. Then, using in-depth interviews and participant observation, they explored nurses' decisions to administer PRN analgesia.

Theory Building, Testing, and Refinement

An ambitious application of mixed methods research is in the area of theory construction. A theory gains acceptance as it escapes disconfirmation, and the use of multiple methods provides great opportunity for potential disconfirmation of a theory. If the theory can survive these assaults, it can provide a stronger context for the organization of clinical and intellectual work.

Example of theory building:
Gibbons (2009) conducted a theory-validating and theory-synthesizing mixed methods study of *self-neglect.* Qualitative and quantitative data were used to describe characteristics and behaviors of self-neglect among older adults in early stages of the phenomenon and to explain the influence of several variables in the clinical evolution of self-neglect.

Mixed Methods Designs and Strategies

In designing MM studies, researchers make many important decisions. We briefly describe a few.

Design Decisions and Notation

Two critical decisions in MM research concern sequencing and prioritization. There are three options for sequencing components of a mixed methods study: qualitative data are collected first, quantitative data are collected first, or both types are collected simultaneously. When the data are collected at the same time, the design is **concurrent**. The design is **sequential** when the two types of data are not collected at the same time. In well-conceived sequential designs, the analysis and interpretation in one phase informs the collection and analysis of data in the second.

In terms of prioritization, researchers usually decide which approach—qualitative or quantitative—to emphasize. One option is that the two components are given equal, or roughly equal, weight. Usually, however, one approach is given priority. The distinction is sometimes referred to as *equal status* versus *dominant status*.

Janice Morse (1991), a prominent nurse researcher, made an important contribution to the MM literature by proposing a widely used notation system for sequencing and prioritization. In this system, priority is designated by upper case and lower case letters: QUAL/quan designates a mixed methods study in which the dominant approach is qualitative, while QUAN/qual designates the reverse. If neither approach is dominant (i.e., both are equal), the notation stipulates QUAL/QUAN. Sequencing is indicated by the symbols + or →. The arrow designates a sequential approach. For example, QUAN → qual is the notation for a primarily quantitative MM study in which qualitative data collection occurs in phase 2. When both approaches occur concurrently, a plus sign is used (e.g., QUAL + quan). Creswell and Plano Clark (2011) have suggested a modification of Morse's notation to include the use of parentheses, which designate an embedded design structure. The notation QUAN (qual) indicates a design in which the qualitative methods are embedded within a quantitative design.

Specific Mixed Methods Designs

Numerous design typologies have been proposed by different MM methodologists. We illustrate a few basic designs described by Cresswell and Plano Clark (2011).

The purpose of a **convergent parallel design** (also called a *triangulation design*) is to obtain different, but complementary, data about the central phenomenon under study. The goal of this design is to converge on "the truth" about a problem or phenomenon by allowing the limitations of one approach to be offset by the strengths of the other. In this design, qualitative and quantitative data are collected simultaneously, with equal priority (QUAL + QUAN).

Example of a convergent parallel design:
Latter and colleagues (2010) used a QUAL + QUAN triangulation design in their study of the effects of an intervention for nurse prescribers to promote medication compliance among diabetic patients. The quantitative data were derived from structured coding of audiotaped consultations, and the qualitative data came from in-depth interviews with the nurses. The triangulation of approaches "illuminated how the intervention was implemented in practice contexts" (p. 1126).

In an **embedded design**, one type of data is used in a supportive capacity in a study based primarily on the other data type. Either qualitative or quantitative data can be dominant—although qual is often supportive of QUAN in embedded designs. Sequencing is often concurrent. The notation for embedded designs uses parentheses: QUAL(quan) or QUAN(qual).

Example of an embedded design:
Tluczek and colleagues (2011) used a concurrent QUAL (quan) embedded design to study the psychosocial consequences of false-positive newborn screens for cystic fibrosis. The data were collected by means of in-depth interviews with 87 parents of 44 infants. The qualitative data were content analyzed, yielding 13 categories of consequences. Logistic regression was then used to explore parental characteristics that predicted different consequences.

Explanatory designs are sequential designs with quantitative data collected in the first phase, followed by qualitative data collected in the second phase. In explanatory designs, the quantitative strand has priority—that is, the design notation is QUAN → qual. Qualitative data from the second phase are used to build on or explain the quantitative data from the initial phase. This design is especially suitable when the quantitative results are complicated and tricky to interpret.

Example of an explanatory design:
Beery and colleagues (2011) used a QUAN → qual explanatory design to study sports participation decisional conflict in youth with cardiac pacemakers. In phase 1, 35 youth completed the Decisional Conflict Scale. In phase 2, semistructured interviews were conducted with 19 participants. The researchers found that the scale did not capture all decisional conflict and that the qualitative data added enriched perspectives on the youth's struggles with sports participation.

Exploratory designs are also sequential MM designs, but qualitative data are collected first. The design has as its central premise the need for initial in-depth exploration of a concept. Usually, the first phase focuses on detailed exploration of a poorly understood phenomenon, and the second phase is focused on measuring it or classifying it. In an exploratory design, the qualitative phase is typically dominant (QUAL → quan), although in many studies the two strands have equal priority (QUAL → QUAN).

Example of an exploratory design:
Dilles and colleagues (2011) used an exploratory design (QUAL → QUAN) to develop and administer a survey to nurses in Belgian nursing homes. In the first phase, 12 expert nurses convened in small groups to brainstorm barriers that nurses faced with regard to safe medication management in nursing homes. The thematic analysis of these data formed the basis for the survey that was completed by more than 500 nurses and nurse assistants in 20 nursing homes.

Sampling and Data Collection in Mixed Methods Research

Sampling and data collection in MM studies are often a blend of approaches described in earlier chapters. A few special issues for MM studies merit brief discussion.

Mixed methods researchers can combine sampling designs in various creative ways. The quantitative component is likely to rely on a sampling strategy that enhances the researcher's ability to generalize from the sample to a broader population. For the qualitative component, MM researchers usually adopt purposive sampling methods to select information-rich cases who are good informants about the phenomenon of interest. Sample sizes are also likely to be different in the qualitative and quantitative components in ways one might expect—i.e., larger samples for the quantitative component. A unique sampling issue in MM studies concerns whether the same people will be in both the qualitative and quantitative strands. The best strategy depends on the study purpose and the research design, but using overlapping samples can be advantageous. Indeed, a particularly popular strategy is a *nested* approach in which a subset of participants from the quantitative strand is used in the qualitative strand.

Example of nested sampling:
As part of a mixed methods inquiry, Shim and colleagues (2012) conducted a qualitative inquiry focused on the experiences of spousal caregivers of people with dementia. In the quantitative component, 187 caregivers were randomly assigned to a control group or to an intervention designed to increase caregiver preparedness. From the full sample, 21 caregivers were selected for in-depth interviews about their experiences at three points in time.

In terms of data collection, all of the data collection methods discussed previously can be creatively combined and triangulated in MM studies. Thus, possible sources of data include group and individual interviews, psychosocial scales, observations, biophysiological measures, records, diaries, and so on. Mixed methods studies can involve *intramethod mixing* (e.g., structured and unstructured self-reports), and *intermethod mixing* (e.g.,, biophyisologic measures and unstructured observation). A fundamental issue concerns the methods' complementarity—that is, having the limitations of one method be balanced and offset by the strengths of the other.

TIP: One of the greatest challenges in doing mixed methods research concerns how best to analyze the qualitative and quantitative data. The real benefits of MM research cannot be realized if there is no attempt to merge results from the two strands and to develop interpretations and practice recommendations based on integrated understandings. It is, however, beyond the scope of this book to discuss the complex topic of data analysis in MM research.

OTHER SPECIAL TYPES OF RESEARCH

The remainder of this chapter briefly describes types of research that vary by study purpose rather than by research design or tradition.

Intervention Research

In Chapter 9, we discussed RCTs and other experimental and quasi-experimental designs for testing the effects of interventions. In actuality, intervention research is often more complex than a simple experimental–control group comparison of outcomes—indeed, intervention research often relies on mixed methods to develop, refine, test, and understand the intervention.

Different disciplines have developed their own approaches and terminology in connection with intervention efforts. *Clinical trials* are associated with medical research, *evaluation research* is linked to the fields of education and public policy, and nurses are developing their own tradition of intervention research. We briefly describe these three approaches.

Clinical Trials

Clinical trials are designed to assess clinical interventions. Clinical trials undertaken to test an innovative therapy or drug are often designed in a series of phases:

- *Phase I* of the trial is designed to establish safety, tolerance, and dose with a simple design (e.g., before–after with no control group). The focus is on developing the best treatment.
- *Phase II* is a pilot test of treatment effectiveness. Researchers see if the treatment holds promise, look for possible side effects, and identify possible refinements. This phase is designed as a small-scale experiment or a quasi-experiment.
- *Phase III* is a full experimental test of the treatment—an RCT with random assignment to treatment conditions under controlled conditions. The objective is to develop evidence about the treatment's *efficacy*—i.e., whether the innovation is more efficacious than usual care or another alternative. When the term *clinical trial* is used in the nursing literature, it most often is referring to a phase III trial.
- *Phase IV* of clinical trials involves studies of the *effectiveness* of an intervention in the general population. The emphasis in effectiveness studies is on the external validity of an intervention that has demonstrated efficacy under controlled (but artificial) conditions.

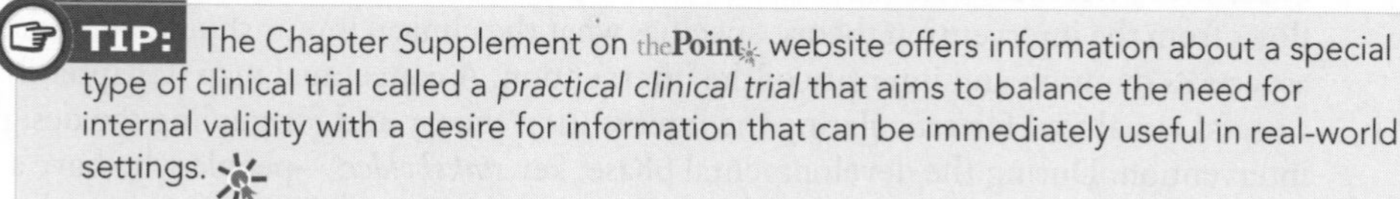
TIP: The Chapter Supplement on thePoint website offers information about a special type of clinical trial called a *practical clinical trial* that aims to balance the need for internal validity with a desire for information that can be immediately useful in real-world settings.

Evaluation Research

Evaluation research focuses on developing useful information about a program or policy—information that decision makers need on whether to adopt, modify, or abandon a program.

Evaluations are undertaken to answer various questions. Questions about program effectiveness rely on experimental or quasi-experimental designs, but other questions do not. Many evaluations are MM studies with distinct components.

For example, a **process analysis** is often undertaken to obtain descriptive information about the process by which a program gets implemented and how it actually functions. A process analysis is designed to address such questions as the following: What exactly *is* the program or intervention and how does it differ from traditional practices? What are the barriers to successful program implementation? How do staff and clients feel about the intervention? Qualitative data play a big role in process analyses.

In an **impact analysis** component of an evaluation, researchers seek to identify the program's *net impacts*, that is, impacts that can be attributed to the program, over and above the effects of usual care. Impact analyses, analogous to phase III clinical trials, use an experimental or strong quasi-experimental design because the aim is to make a causal inference about the benefits of a special program.

Program evaluations may also include an **economic** (or **cost**) **analysis** to assess whether the program's benefits outweigh its monetary costs. Administrators make decisions about resource allocation for health services not only on the basis of whether something "works," but also based on economic viability. Often, cost analyses are done in conjunction with impact analyses—that is, when researchers are also evaluating program efficacy.

Example of an economic analysis:

Hansen and colleagues (2011) examined the effects and total costs associated with the implementation of telemonitoring programs in rural home health agencies.

Nursing Intervention Research

Both clinical trials and evaluations involve *interventions*. However, the term **intervention research** is increasingly being used by nurse researchers to describe a research approach distinguished not so much by research methodology as by a distinctive *process* of planning, developing, testing, and disseminating interventions. Proponents of the process are critical of the simplistic and atheoretical approach that is often used to design and evaluate interventions. The recommended process involves an in-depth understanding of the problem and the people for whom the intervention is being developed; careful, collaborative planning with a diverse team; and the development or adoption of a theory to guide the inquiry.

Similar to clinical trials, nursing intervention research that focuses on the development of a complex intervention involves several phases: (1) basic developmental research, (2) pilot research, (3) efficacy research, and (4) effectiveness research.

Conceptualization, a major focus of the development phase, is supported through collaborative discussions, consultations with experts, critical literature reviews, and in-depth qualitative research to understand the problem. The construct validity of the emerging intervention is enhanced through efforts to develop an **intervention theory** that clearly articulates what must be done to achieve desired outcomes. The intervention design, which flows from the intervention theory, specifies what the clinical inputs should be, and also such aspects as duration and intensity of the intervention. A conceptual map (Chapter 8) is often a useful visual tool for articulating the intervention theory and for guiding the design of the intervention. During the developmental phase, key *stakeholders*—people who have a stake in the intervention—are often identified and "brought on board," which may involve participatory action research. Stakeholders include potential beneficiaries of the intervention and their families, advocates and community leaders, and agents of the intervention.

The second phase of nursing intervention research is a pilot test of the intervention, typically using simple quasi-experimental designs. The central activities during the pilot test are to secure preliminary evidence of the intervention's benefits, to refine the intervention theory and intervention protocols, and to assess the feasibility of a rigorous test. The feasibility assessment should involve an analysis of factors that affected implementation during the pilot (e.g., recruitment, retention, and adherence problems). Qualitative research may be used to gain insight into how the intervention should be refined.

As in a classic clinical trial, the third phase involves a full experimental test of the intervention, and the final phase focuses on effectiveness and utility in real-world clinical settings. This full model of intervention research is, at this point, more of an ideal than an actuality. For example, effectiveness studies in nursing research are rare. A few research teams have begun to implement portions of the model, and efforts are likely to expand.

Example of nursing intervention research:
Van Hecke and colleagues (2011) described the careful and systematic development of a multifaceted nursing intervention to promote adherence to self-care for patients with leg ulcers. Extensive qualitative research and a theoretical perspective on behavior change contributed to the development and validation of the intervention.

Health Services and Outcomes Research

Health services research is the broad interdisciplinary field that studies how organizational structures and processes, health technologies, social factors, and personal behaviors affect access to health care, the cost and quality of health care, and, ultimately, people's health and well-being.

Outcomes research, a subset of health services research, comprises efforts to understand the end results of particular health care practices and to assess the effectiveness of health care services. Outcomes research represents a response to the increasing demand from policy makers and the public to justify care practices in terms of improved patient outcomes and costs.

Many nursing studies evaluate patient outcomes, but efforts to appraise the quality of nursing care—as distinct from care provided by the overall health care system—are less common. A major obstacle is attribution—that is, linking patient outcomes to specific nursing actions, distinct from those of other members of the health care team. It is also often difficult to ascertain a causal connection between outcomes and health care interventions because factors outside the health care system (e.g., patient characteristics) affect outcomes in complex ways.

Donabedian (1987), whose pioneering efforts created a framework for outcomes research, emphasized three factors in appraising quality in health care services: structure, process, and outcomes. The *structure* of care refers to broad organizational and administrative features. Nursing skill mix, for example, is a structural variable that has been found to be related to patient outcomes. *Processes* involve aspects of clinical management, decision making, and clinical interventions. *Outcomes* refer to the specific clinical end results of patient care. There have been several suggested modifications to Donabedian's framework for appraising health care quality, the most noteworthy of which is the Quality Health Outcomes Model developed by the American Academy of Nursing (Mitchell et al., 1998). This model is less linear and more dynamic than Donabedian's original framework and takes client characteristics (e.g., illness severity) and system characteristics into account.

Outcomes research usually concentrates on studying various linkages within such models, rather than on testing the overall model. Some studies have examined the effect of health care structures on various health care processes and outcomes, for example. Most outcomes research in nursing, however, has focused on the process–patient–outcomes nexus. Examples of nursing process variables include nursing actions such as nurses' problem-solving skills, clinical decision making, clinical competence and leadership, and specific activities or interventions (e.g., communication, touch).

Example of outcomes research:
Unruh and Zhang (2012) used 9 years of data from 124 hospitals in Florida to examine the relationship between *changes* in RN staffing and patient safety events.

Survey Research

A **survey** obtains quantitative information about the prevalence, distribution, and interrelations of variables within a population. Political opinion polls, such as those conducted by Gallup, are examples of surveys. Survey data are used primarily in correlational studies, and are most often used to gather information from nonclinical populations (e.g., college students, nurses, community residents).

Surveys obtain information about people's actions, knowledge, intentions, opinions, and attitudes by self-report. Surveys, which yield quantitative data primarily, may be cross-sectional or longitudinal. Any information that can reliably be obtained by direct questioning can be gathered in a survey, although surveys include mostly questions that require brief responses (e.g., yes/no, always/sometimes/never).

Survey data can be collected in several ways, but the most respected method is through personal interviews in which interviewers meet in person with respondents to ask them questions. Personal interviews are expensive because they involve a lot of personnel time, but they yield high-quality data and the refusal rate tends to be low. Telephone interviews are less costly, but when the interviewer is unknown, respondents may be uncooperative on the phone. Self-administered questionnaires (especially those delivered over the Internet) are an economical approach to doing a survey, but are not appropriate for surveying certain populations (e.g., the elderly, children) and tend to yield low response rates.

The greatest advantage of surveys is their flexibility and broadness of scope. Surveys can be used with many populations, can focus on a wide range of topics, and can be used for many purposes. The information obtained in most surveys, however, tends to be relatively superficial: surveys rarely probe deeply into such complexities as contradictions of human behavior and feelings. Survey research is better suited to extensive rather than in-depth analysis.

Example of a survey:
Mealer and colleagues (2012) conducted a survey of intensive care unit (ICU) nurses in the United States. Questionnaires, mailed to a random sample of 3,500 ICU nurses, included measures of resilience, anxiety and depression, and symptoms of psychological distress.

Secondary Analysis

Secondary analysis involves using data gathered in a previous study to address new questions. In most studies, researchers collect far more data than are actually analyzed. Secondary analysis of existing data is efficient and economical because data collection is typically the most time-consuming and expensive part of a study. Nurse researchers have used secondary analysis with both large national data sets and smaller localized sets, and with both qualitative and quantitative data. Outcomes research frequently involves secondary analyses of large clinical datasets.

A number of avenues are available for making use of an existing set of quantitative data. For example, variables and relationships among variables that were previously unanalyzed can be examined (e.g., a dependent variable in the original study could become the independent variable in the secondary analysis). In other cases, a secondary analysis focuses on a particular subgroup of the full original sample (e.g., survey data about health habits from a national sample of adults could be reanalyzed to examine the smoking behavior of rural men).

The use of available data makes it possible to bypass time-consuming and costly steps in the research process, but there are some disadvantages in working with existing data. In particular, secondary analysts may face many "if only" problems: if only an additional question had been asked, or if only a variable had been measured differently. Nevertheless, existing data sets present exciting opportunities for expanding the base of evidence in an economical way.

Example of a quantitative secondary analysis:
Cho and colleagues (2012) studied the effects of informal caregivers on the functioning of older adults in home health care (HHC), using data from a computerized patient care database, the Outcome and Assessment Information Set, from an HHC agency in New York.

Example of a qualitative secondary analysis:
Rush and colleagues (2011) analyzed previously collected qualitative data from 15 community-dwelling older adults who had participated in in-depth interviews focusing on the meaning of *weakness* in the elderly. The researchers used a theory (selective optimization with compensation) as a lens for examining the elders' adaptations made in response to mobility changes.

Methodologic Research

Methodologic research entails investigations of the methods for conducting rigorous research. Methodologic studies address the development, validation, and evaluation of research tools or methods. The growing demands for sound and reliable outcome measures, for rigorous tests of interventions, and for sophisticated procedures for obtaining data have led to an increased interest in methodologic research by nurse researchers.

Many methodologic studies focus on the development of new instruments. Instrument development research often involves complex and sophisticated research methods, including the use of MM designs. Occasionally, researchers use an experimental design to test competing methodologic strategies.

Example of a quantitative methodologic study:
Goshin and Byrne (2012), as part of their longitudinal intervention study of incarcerated women, explored factors that predicted retention in the study following the women's release from prison. Their goal was to learn about variation in retention so they could shed light on possible strategies for retaining such study participants.

In qualitative research, methodologic issues often arise within the context of a substantive study, rather than having a study originate as a methodologic endeavor. In such instances, the researcher typically performs separate analyses designed to highlight a methodologic issue and to generate strategies for solving a methodologic problem.

Example of a qualitative methodologic study:
Cook (2012) conducted an in-depth study to explore what the diagnosis of a viral sexually transmitted infection means to women's lives. They wrote a methodologic paper that focused on the use of online recruitment and email interviewing as an approach to recruiting a diverse, multinational sample of vulnerable women.

Methodologic research may seem less compelling than substantive clinical research, but it is virtually impossible to conduct rigorous and useful research on a substantive topic without adequate research methods.

CRITIQUING STUDIES DESCRIBED IN THIS CHAPTER

It is difficult to provide guidance on critiquing the types of studies described in this chapter, because they are so varied and because many of the fundamental methodologic issues require a critique of the overall design. Guidelines for critiquing design-related issues were presented in previous chapters.

You should, however, consider whether researchers took appropriate advantage of the possibilities of a MM design. Collecting both qualitative and quantitative data is not always necessary or practical, but in critiquing studies, you can consider whether the study would have been strengthened by triangulating different types of data. In studies in which MM were used, you should carefully consider whether the inclusion of both types of data was justified and whether the researcher really made use of both types of data to enhance knowledge on the research topic. Box 18.1 offers a few specific questions for critiquing the types of studies included in this chapter.

BOX 18.1 Guidelines for Critiquing Studies Described in Chapter 18

1. Is the study exclusively qualitative or exclusively quantitative? If so, could the study have been strengthened by incorporating both approaches?
2. If the study used a mixed methods (MM) design, did the inclusion of both approaches contribute to enhanced validity? In what other ways (if any) did the inclusion of both types of data strengthen the study and further the aims of the research?
3. If the study used an MM approach, what was the design—how were the components sequenced, and which had priority? Was this design appropriate?
4. If the study was a clinical trial or intervention study, was adequate attention paid to developing an appropriate intervention? Was there a well-conceived intervention theory that guided the endeavor? Was the intervention adequately pilot tested?
5. If the study was a clinical trial, evaluation, or intervention study, was there an effort to understand how the intervention was implemented (i.e., a process-type analysis)? Were the financial costs and benefits assessed? If not, should they have been?
6. If the study was outcomes research, which segments of the structure–process–outcomes model were examined? Would it have been desirable (and feasible) to expand the study to include other aspects? Do the findings suggest possible improvements to structures or processes that would be beneficial to patient outcomes?
7. If the study was a survey, was the most appropriate method used to collect the data (i.e., in-person interviews, telephone interviews, mail or Internet questionnaires)?
8. If the study was a secondary analysis, to what extent was the chosen dataset appropriate for addressing the research questions? What were the limitations of the dataset, and were these limitations acknowledged and taken into account in interpreting the results?

RESEARCH EXAMPLES WITH CRITICAL THINKING EXERCISES

The nursing literature abounds with studies of the types described in this chapter. Here we describe an important example.

Example 1 below is also featured in our *Interactive Critical Thinking Activity* on thePoint website where you can easily record, print, and e-mail your responses to the related questions.

EXAMPLE 1 ● Clinical Trial, Methodological Research, and Secondary Analysis

Studies: Testing an intervention for preventing osteoporosis in postmenopausal breast cancer survivors (Waltman et al., 2003); The effect of weight training on bone mineral density and bone turnover in postmenopausal breast cancer survivors with bone loss (Waltman et al., 2010); Development of an instrument to measure adherence to strength training in postmenopausal breast cancer survivors (Huberty et al., 2009); Intervention components promoting adherence to strength training exercise in breast cancer survivors with bone loss (McGuire et al., 2011).

Background and Purpose: Dr. Nancy Waltman has, together with an interdisciplinary team of researchers, pursued a program of research focused on bone loss in breast cancer survivors. For over a decade, these researchers conducted exploratory studies and then developed an intervention designed to prevent osteoporosis in women who had been treated for breast cancer. The intervention had components that were based on Bandura's social cognitive theory.

Phase II Clinical Trial: Waltman and colleagues (2003) conducted a pilot test of a 12-month multicomponent intervention for preventing and treating osteoporosis in women who had completed treatment for breast cancer. The intervention involved home-based strength and weight training exercises, a regimen of calcium and vitamin D, and facilitative efforts to promote adherence to the intervention. The intervention was tested with 21 women using a one-group pretest–posttest design. The researchers learned that adherence was high and that the women had significant improvements on several important outcomes, including bone mass density (BMD).

Phase III Clinical Trial: Based on results from the pilot test indicating that the intervention was both feasible and had good potential for effectiveness, Waltman and colleagues (2010) launched a multisite trial using an RCT design. A sample of 223 women was randomly assigned to either a 24-month medication-only control group (risedronate, calcium, vitamin D) or to a 24-month medication plus weight-training group. Both groups had significant improvement over time on some BMD measures (total hip, spine). Women in the exercise group had additional increases in BMD in some locations. In addition to outcome data, the researchers carefully collected process information regarding how much of a "dose" of the intervention participants received.

Methodological Research: A subsample (*N* = 85) of the women participating in the phase III clinical trial also participated in a substudy designed to develop a theory-based instrument for assessing barriers and motivation to engaging in strength- or weight-training exercise among women with measurable bone loss after their treatment for cancer. Items for the 47-item Likert scale were based on Bandura's theory, published research, and interview data from the women regarding why they were or were not adherent to the intervention. The reliability estimates for four subscales of the scale ranged from .70 to .82 (Huberty et al., 2009).

Secondary Analysis: McGuire, Waltman, and Zimmerman (2011) did a secondary analysis using data from the clinical trial to study factors that predicted adherence to the exercise program among the women in the experimental group. Regression analysis was used to predict adherence (percentage of strength-training exercises performed), using demographic variables (e.g., marital status), clinical variables (e.g., comorbidities), and frequency of receipt of intervention components (e.g., feedback) as the predictors. Participants receiving more frequent feedback were significantly more adherent to exercise.

CRITICAL THINKING EXERCISES

1. Answer the relevant questions from Box 18.1 on page 350 regarding this study.
2. Also consider the following targeted questions:
   a. Was the secondary analysis experimental or nonexperimental?
   b. In language associated with evaluation research, could any part of this research be described as a process analysis? Impact analysis? Cost analysis?
   c. Suggest a qualitative component that could have been added to this research and describe its potential utility. Specify how this component would be sequenced and identify the design.
3. If the results of this study are valid, in what ways do you think the findings could be used in clinical practice?

EXAMPLE 2 ● Mixed Methods Study in Appendix D

- Read the report of the mixed methods study by Sawyer and colleagues (2010) in Appendix D on pages 441–466 and then address the following suggested activities.

CRITICAL THINKING EXERCISES

1. Answer Question 3 in Box 18.1 on page 350 regarding this study.
2. The appendix includes our critique of this study. Before reading our critique, either write your own critique or prepare a list of what you think are the major strengths and weaknesses of the study. Pay particular attention to issues relating to the validity and trustworthiness of the study. Then contrast your critique with ours. Remember that you (or your instructor) do not necessarily have to agree with all of the points made in our critique, and that you may identify strengths and weaknesses that we overlooked. You may find the broad critiquing guidelines in Table 4.1 on page 69 and Table 4.2 on page 70 helpful.
3. Suppose that Sawyer and colleagues had only collected qualitative data. Comment on how this might have affected the results and the overall quality of the evidence. Then suppose they had collected all of their data in a structured, quantitative manner. How might this have changed the results and affected the quality of the evidence?

WANT TO KNOW MORE? A wide variety of resources to enhance your learning and understanding of this chapter are available on thePoint.

- Interactive Critical Thinking Activity
- Chapter Supplement on Practical (Pragmatic) Clinical Trials
- Answers to the Critical Thinking Exercises for Example 2
- Student Review Questions
- Full-text online
- Internet Resources with useful websites for Chapter 18

Additional study aids including eight journal articles and related questions are also available in *Study Guide for Essentials of Nursing Research, 8e.*

SUMMARY POINTS

- For many research purposes, MM studies are advantageous. **Mixed methods (MM) research** involves the collection, analysis, and integration of both qualitative and quantitative data within a study or series of studies, often with an overarching goal of achieving both discovery and verification.
- MM research has numerous advantages, including the complementarity of qualitative and quantitative data and the practicality of using methods that best address a question. MM research has many applications, including the development and testing of instruments, theories, and interventions.
- The paradigm most often associated with MM research is **pragmatism**, which has as a major tenet "the dictatorship of the research question."
- Key decisions in designing a MM study involve how to sequence the components and which strand (if either) will be given priority. In terms of sequencing, MM designs are either **concurrent** (both strands occurring in one simultaneous phase) or **sequential** (one strand occurring prior to and informing the second strand).
- Notation for MM research often designates priority—all capital letters for the dominant strand and all lower-case letters for the nondominant strand—and sequence. An arrow is used for sequential designs, and a "+" is used for concurrent designs. Parentheses show an embedded structure. QUAL → quan, for example is a sequential, qualitative-dominant design; QUAN (qual) shows a qualitative strand embedded in a quantitative study.
- Specific MM designs include the **convergent parallel design** (QUAL + QUAN), **embedded design** (e.g., QUAL [quan]), **explanatory design** (e.g., QUAN → qual), and **exploratory design** (e.g., QUAL → quan).
- Sampling in MM studies can involve the same or different people in the different components. *Nesting* is a common sampling approach in which a subsample of the participants in the quantitative strand also participates in the qualitative component.
- Different disciplines have developed different approaches to (and terms for) efforts to evaluate interventions. **Clinical trials**, which are studies designed to assess the effectiveness of clinical interventions, often involve a series of phases. *Phase I* is designed to finalize features of the intervention. *Phase II* involves seeking preliminary evidence of efficacy and opportunities for refinements. *Phase III* is a full experimental test of treatment *efficacy*.

In *Phase IV*, the researcher focuses primarily on generalized *effectiveness* and evidence about costs and benefits.

- **Evaluation research** assesses the effectiveness of a program, policy, or procedure to assist decision makers in choosing a course of action. Evaluations can answer a variety of questions. **Process analyses** describe the process by which a program gets implemented and how it functions in practice. **Impact analyses** test whether an intervention caused any *net impacts* relative to the counterfactual. **Economic (cost) analyses** seek to determine whether the monetary costs of a program are outweighed by benefits.
- **Nursing intervention research** is a term sometimes used to refer to a distinctive *process* of planning, developing, testing, and disseminating interventions. The construct validity of an emerging intervention is enhanced through efforts to develop an **intervention theory** that articulates what must be done to achieve desired outcomes.
- **Outcomes research** (a subset of **health services research**) is undertaken to document the quality and effectiveness of health care and nursing services. A model of health care quality encompasses several broad concepts, including *structure* (e.g., nursing skill mix), *process* (nursing interventions and actions), and *outcomes* (the specific end results of patient care in terms of patient functioning).
- **Survey research** examines people's characteristics, behaviors, intentions, and opinions by asking them to answer questions. Surveys can be administered through personal interviews, telephone interviews, or self-administered questionnaires.
- **Secondary analysis** refers to studies in which researchers analyze previously collected data—either quantitative or qualitative. Secondary analyses are economical, but it is sometimes difficult to identify an appropriate existing dataset.
- In **methodologic research**, the investigator is concerned with the development, validation, and assessment of methodologic tools or strategies.

REFERENCES FOR CHAPTER 18

Beery, T., Smith, C., Kudel, I., & Knailans, T. (2011). Measuring sports participation decisional conflict in youth with cardiac pacemakers and/or ICDs. *Journal of Advanced Nursing, 67*, 821–828.

Cho, E., Kim, E., & Lee, N. (2012). Effects of informal caregivers on function of older adults in home health care. *Western Journal of Nursing Research*, PubMed ID 22068282.

Cook, C. (2012). Email interviewing: Generating data with a vulnerable population. *Journal of Advanced Nursing, 68*(6), 1330–1339.

Creswell, J. W., & Plano Clark, V. L. (2011). *Designing and conducting mixed methods research* (2nd ed.). Thousand Oaks, CA: Sage.

Dilles, T., Elseviers, M., Van Rompaey, B., Van Bortel, L., & Stichele, E. (2011). Barriers for nurses to safe medication management in nursing homes. *Journal of Nursing Scholarship, 32*, 171–180.

Donabedian, A. (1987). Some basic issues in evaluating the quality of health care. In L. T. Rinke (Ed.), *Outcome measures in home care* (Vol. I, pp. 3–28). New York: National League for Nursing.

Elstad, E., Maserejian, N., McKinlay, J., & Tennstedt, S. (2011). Fluid manipulation among individuals with lower urinary tract symptoms: A mixed methods study. *Journal of Clinical Nursing, 20*, 156–165.

Gibbons, S. W. (2009). Theory synthesis for self-neglect: A health and social phenomenon. *Nursing Research, 58*, 194-200.

Goshin, L. S., & Byrne, M. W. (2012). Predictors of post-release research retention and subsequent reenrollment for women recruited while incarcerated. *Research in Nursing & Health, 35*, 94–104.

Hansen, D., Golbeck, A., Noblitt, V., Pinsonneault, J., & Christner, J. (2011). Cost factors in implementing telemonitoring programs in rural home health agencies. *Home Healthcare Nurse, 29*, 375–382.

Huberty, J., Vener, J., Waltman, N., Ott, C., Twiss, J., Gross, G., et al. (2009). Development of an instrument to measure adherence to strength training in postmenopausal breast cancer survivors. *Oncology Nursing Forum, 36*, E266–E273.

Latter, S., Sibley, A., Skinner, T., Cradock, S., Zinken, K., Lussier, M. et al. (2010). The impact of an intervention for nurse prescribers on consultations to promote patient medicine-taking in diabetes. *International Journal of Nursing Studies, 47*, 1126–1138.

McGuire, R., Waltman, N., & Zimmerman, L. (2011). Intervention components promoting adherence to strength training exercise in breast cancer survivors with bone loss. *Western Journal of Nursing Research, 33*, 671–689.

Mealer, M., Jones, J., Newman, J., McFann, K., Rothbaum, B., & Moss, M. (2012). The presence of resilience is associated with a healthier psychological profile in intensive care (ICU) nurses: Results of a national survey. *International Journal of Nursing Studies, 49*, 292–299.

Mitchell, P., Ferketich, S., & Jennings, B. (1998). Quality health outcomes model. *Image: The Journal of Nursing Scholarship, 30*, 43–46.

Morse, J. M. (1991). Approaches to qualitative-quantitative methodological triangulation. *Nursing Research, 40*, 120–123.

Rush, K., Watts, W., & Stanbury, J. (2011). Mobility adaptations of older adults. *Clinical Nursing Research, 20*, 81–100.

Shim, B., Barroso, J., & Davis, L. (2012). A comparative qualitative analysis of stories of spousal caregivers of people with dementia. *International Journal of Nursing Studies, 49*, 220–229.

Smyth, W., Toombes, J., & Usher, K. (2011). Children's postoperative pro re nata (PRN) analgesia: Nurses' administration practices. *Contemporary Nurse, 37*, 160–172.

Tashakkori, A., & Teddlie, C. (2010). *Handbook of mixed methods in social and behavioral research* (2nd ed.). Thousand Oaks, CA: Sage.

Tluczek, A., Orland, K., & Cavanagh, L. (2011). Psychosocial consequences of false-positive newborn screens for cystic fibrosis. *Qualitative Health Research, 21*, 174–186.

Unruh, L., & Zhang, N. (2012). Nurse staffing and patient safety in hospitals: New variable and longitudinal approaches. *Nursing Research, 61*, 3–12.

Van Hecke, A., Verhaeghe, S., Grypdonck, M., Beele, H., Flour, M., & DeFloor, T. (2011). Systematic development and validation of a nursing intervention: The case of lifestyle adherence promotion in patients with leg ulcers. *Journal of Advanced Nursing, 67*, 662–676.

Waltman, N., Twiss, J., Ott, C., Gross, G., Lindsey, A., Moore, T., et al. (2003). Testing an intervention for preventing osteoporosis in postmenopausal breast cancer survivors. *Journal of Nursing Scholarship, 35*, 333–338.

Waltman, N., Twiss, J., Ott, C., Gross, G., Lindsey, A., Moore, T., et al. (2010). The effect of weight training on bone mineral density and bone turnover in postmenopausal breast cancer survivors with bone loss. *Osteoporosis International, 21*, 1361–1369.

Zoffmann, V., & Kirkevold, M. (2012). Realizing empowerment in difficult diabetes care: A guided self-determination intervention. *Qualitative Health Research, 22*, 103–118.

chapter

19 Systematic Reviews: Meta-Analysis and Metasynthesis

LEARNING OBJECTIVES

On completing this chapter, you will be able to:

- Discuss alternative approaches to integrating research evidence, and advantages to using systematic methods of reviewing research
- Describe key decisions and steps in doing a meta-analysis and metasynthesis
- Critique key aspects of a written systematic review
- Define new terms in the chapter

KEY TERMS

Fixed effects model
Forest plot
Frequency effect size
Intensity effect size
Manifest effect size
Meta-analysis
Meta-ethnography
Meta-summary
Metasynthesis
Primary study
Publication bias
Random effects model
Sensitivity analysis
Standardized mean difference
Statistical heterogeneity
Subgroup analysis
Systematic review

In Chapter 7, we described major steps in conducting a literature review. This chapter also discusses reviews of existing evidence but focuses on systematic reviews in the form of **meta-analyses** and **metasyntheses**. Systematic reviews, a cornerstone of evidence-based practice (EBP), are inquiries that follow many of the same rules as those for **primary studies**, i.e., original research investigations. This chapter provides guidance to help you understand and evaluate systematic research integration.

RESEARCH INTEGRATION AND SYNTHESIS

Nurses seeking to adopt EBP must take into account as much of the research evidence as possible, organized and synthesized in a diligent manner. A **systematic review** is a review that methodically integrates research evidence about a specific research question using careful sampling and data collection procedures that are spelled out in advance in a protocol. The review process is disciplined and largely transparent, so that readers of a systematic review can assess the conclusions.

About 20 years ago, systematic reviews usually involved narrative integration, using nonstatistical methods to synthesize research findings. Narrative reviews continue to be published in the nursing literature, but meta-analytic techniques that use statistical integration are being increasingly used. Most reviews in the Cochrane Collaboration, for example, are meta-analyses. Statistical integration, however, is not always appropriate, as we shall see.

Qualitative researchers also are developing techniques to integrate findings across studies. Many terms exist for such endeavors (e.g., meta-study, meta-method, meta-summary, metaethnography, qualitative meta-analysis, formal grounded theory), but the one that appears to be emerging as the leading term among nurse researchers is *metasynthesis*.

The field of research integration is expanding rapidly. This chapter provides a brief introduction to this extremely important and complex topic.

META-ANALYSES

Meta-analyses of randomized controlled trials (RCTs) are at the pinnacle of traditional evidence hierarchies (see Figure 2.1, p. 23). The essence of a meta-analysis is that information from different studies is used to compute a common metric, an *effect size*. Effect sizes are averaged across studies, yielding not only information about the *existence* of a relationship between variables in many studies but also an estimate of its *magnitude* across studies.

Advantages of Meta-Analyses

Meta-analysis offers a simple advantage as an integration method: *objectivity*. It is difficult to draw objective conclusions about a body of evidence using narrative methods when results are disparate, as they often are. Narrative reviewers make subjective decisions about how much weight to give findings from different studies, and so different reviewers may reach different conclusions about the evidence in reviewing the same studies. Meta-analysts also make decisions, but the decisions are explicit and open to scrutiny. The integration itself also is objective because it uses statistical formulas. Readers of a meta-analysis can be confident that another analyst using the same data set and making the same analytic decisions would come to the same conclusions.

Another advantage of meta-analysis concerns *power*, i.e., the probability of detecting a true relationship between variables (Chapter 12). By combining effects across multiple studies, power is increased. Indeed, in a meta-analysis it is possible to conclude, at a given probability, that a relationship is real (e.g., an intervention is effective), even when a series of small studies yielded nonsignificant findings. In a narrative review, 10 nonsignificant findings would almost surely be interpreted as lack of evidence of a true effect, which could be an erroneous conclusion.

Despite these advantages, meta-analysis is not always appropriate. Indiscriminate use has led critics to warn against potential abuses.

Criteria for Using Meta-Analytic Techniques in a Systematic Review

Reviewers need to decide whether it is appropriate to use statistical integration. One basic criterion is that the research question being addressed should be nearly identical across studies. This means that the independent and dependent variables, and the study populations, are sufficiently similar to merit integration. The variables may be operationalized differently, to be sure. A nurse-led intervention to promote weight loss among diabetics could be a 4-week, clinic-based program in one study and a 6-week, home-based intervention in another, for example. However, a study of the effects of a 1-hour lecture to discourage eating "junk food" among overweight adolescents would be a poor candidate to include in this meta-analysis. This is frequently referred to as the "apples and oranges" or "fruit" problem. Meta-analyses should not be about *fruit*—i.e., a broad encompassing category—but rather about specific questions that have been addressed in multiple studies—i.e., "apples," or, even better, "Granny Smith apples."

A second criterion concerns whether there is a sufficient base of knowledge for statistical integration. If there are only a few studies, or if all of the studies are weakly designed and harbor extensive bias, it usually would not make sense to compute an "average" effect.

One final issue concerns the consistency of the evidence. When the same hypothesis has been tested in multiple studies and the results are highly conflicting, meta-analysis is likely not appropriate. As an extreme example, if half the studies testing an intervention found benefits for those in the intervention group, but the other half found benefits for the controls, it would be misleading to compute an average effect. In this situation, it would be better to do an in-depth narrative analysis of *why* the results are conflicting.

Example of inability to conduct a meta-analysis:
Fronteria and Ferrinho (2011) did a systematic review of the literature on nurses' physical health compared to other health workers. They determined that, although there were many relevant studies ($N = 187$), there was too much diversity to undertake a meta-analysis.

Steps in a Meta-Analysis

We begin by describing major steps in a meta-analysis so that you can understand the decisions a meta-analyst makes—decisions that affect the quality of the review and need to be evaluated.

Problem Formulation

A systematic review begins with a problem statement and a research question or hypothesis. As with a primary study, reviewers need to develop research questions that are clearly worded. Questions for a meta-analysis are usually narrow, focusing, for example, on a particular type of intervention and specific outcomes. Key constructs should be conceptually defined—the definitions are critical for deciding whether a primary study qualifies for the synthesis.

Example of research question from a systematic review:
Ndosi and colleagues (2011) conducted a meta-analysis that addressed the following question: Are clinical outcomes of nurse-led care for patients with rheumatoid arthritis (RA) similar to those produced by usual care? In this example, receipt of nurse-led versus usual care was the independent variable; clinical outcomes, such as RA disease activity, functional status, pain, fatigue, and quality of life, were the outcomes. Patients with RA constituted the population.

The Design of a Meta-Analysis

One critical design issue concerns sampling. In a systematic review, the sample consists of the primary studies that have addressed the research question. Reviewers must state exclusion or inclusion criteria, which are often based on substantive, methodologic, and practical considerations. Substantively, the criteria stipulate key variables and the population. For example, if the reviewer is integrating material about the effectiveness of an intervention, which outcomes variables *must* the researchers have studied? With regard to the population, will (for example) certain age groups be excluded? Methodologically, the criteria might specify that only studies that used a randomized experimental design will be included. On practical grounds, the criteria might exclude, for example, reports written in a language other than English. Another decision is whether both published and unpublished reports will be included in the review.

Example of sampling criteria:
McInnes and colleagues (2012) did a meta-analysis that examined evidence on the effectiveness of pressure-redistributing support surfaces in preventing pressure ulcers. Intervention studies (both RCTs and quasi-experiments) that compared "beds, mattresses, mattress overlays, and cushions in any setting, on any clinical population, of any age, with any condition" and that measured the incidence of new pressure ulcers were included. Trials that used subjective measures of the outcome (e.g., skin condition was "worse") were excluded.

A related issue is the quality of the primary studies, a topic that has stirred some controversy. Researchers sometimes use quality as a sampling criterion, either directly or indirectly. Screening out studies of lower quality can occur indirectly if the meta-analyst excludes studies that did not use a randomized design or studies that were not published in a peer-reviewed journal. More directly, each potential primary study can be rated for quality, and excluded if the quality score falls below a certain threshold. Alternatives to handling study quality are discussed in a later section. Suffice it to say, however, that evaluations of study quality are inevitably part of the integration process, and so analysts need to decide how to assess quality and what to do with assessment information.

Another design issue concerns the **statistical heterogeneity** of results in the primary studies. For each study, meta-analysts compute an index to summarize the strength and direction of relationship between an independent variable and a dependent variable. Just as there is inevitably variation *within* studies (not all people in a study have identical scores on the outcome measures), so there is inevitably variation in effects *across* studies. If the results are highly variable (e.g., results are conflicting across studies), a meta-analysis may be inappropriate. But if the results differ modestly, an important design decision concerns exploration of the source of variation. For example, the effects of an intervention might be systematically different for men and women. Researchers often plan for subgroup analyses during the design phase of the project.

The Search for Evidence in the Literature

Reviewers must decide whether their review will cover published and unpublished findings. There is some disagreement about whether reviewers should limit their sample to published studies or should cast as wide a net as possible and include *grey literature*—that is, studies with a more limited distribution, such as dissertations, unpublished reports, and so on. Some people restrict their sample to reports in peer-reviewed journals, arguing that the peer review system is an important, tried-and-true screen for findings worthy of consideration as evidence.

The limitations of excluding nonpublished findings, however, have increasingly been noted. The primary issue concerns **publication bias**—the tendency for published studies to systematically over-represent statistically significant findings (sometimes called the *bias against the null hypothesis*). This bias is widespread: authors often refrain from submitting manuscripts with nonsignificant findings, reviewers and editors tend to reject such reports when they are submitted, and users of evidence tend to ignore the findings if they are published. The exclusion of grey literature in a systematic review can lead to bias, notably the overestimation of effects.

Meta-analysts can use various search strategies to locate grey literature, in addition to the usual methods for a literature review. These include *hand searching* journals known to publish relevant content, contacting key researchers in the field to see if they have done studies that have not (yet) been published, and contacting funders of relevant research.

TIP: There are statistical procedures to detect and correct for publication biases, but opinions vary about their utility. A brief explanation of methods for assessing publication bias is included in the Chapter Supplement on thePoint website.

Example of a search strategy from a systematic review:
Klainin-Yobas and colleagues (2012) did a meta-analysis of the effectiveness of mindfulness-based interventions on depressive symptoms among people with mental disorders. Their search strategy included a search of published and unpublished studies in nine databases, scrutiny of the bibliographies of relevant studies, and a search through journals that commonly publish articles in this domain.

Evaluations of Study Quality

In systematic reviews, the evidence from primary studies needs to be evaluated to assess how much confidence to place in the findings. Rigorous studies should be given more weight than weaker ones in coming to conclusions about a body of evidence. In meta-analyses, evaluations of study quality sometimes involve overall quantitative ratings of evidence quality for each study. Hundreds of rating instruments exist, but the use of an overall scale has been criticized. Quality criteria vary from instrument to instrument, and the result is that study quality can be rated differently with different assessment instruments—or by different raters using the same tool. Also, when an overall scale score is used, there is a lack of transparency to users of the review regarding what the scores mean.

The Cochrane *Handbook* (Higgins & Greene, 2009) recommends a *domain-based evaluation*, that is, a *component approach*, as opposed to a *scale approach*. Individual features are given a separate rating or code for each study. So, for example, a researcher might code for such design elements as whether randomization was used, whether participants were blinded, the extent of attrition from the study, and so on.

Quality assessments of primary studies, whether they are assessments of individual study features or overall ratings, should be done by two or more qualified individuals. If there are disagreements between the raters, there should be a discussion until a consensus has been reached or other raters should be asked to help resolve the difference. Indexes of inter-rater reliability are often calculated to demonstrate to readers that rater agreement on study quality was adequate.

Example of a quality assessment:
Bryanton and Beck (2010) completed a Cochrane review of RCTs testing the effects of structured postnatal education for parents. They used the Cochrane domain approach to capture elements of trial quality. Both reviewers completed assessments, and disagreements were resolved by discussion.

Extraction and Encoding of Data for Analysis

The next step in a meta-analysis is to extract and record relevant information about the findings, methods, and study characteristics of each study in the analysis. The goal is to produce a data set amenable to statistical analysis.

Basic source information about each study must be recorded, such as year of publication and country where data were collected. In terms of methodologic information, sample size is especially critical. Other important attributes include whether participants were randomized to treatments, whether blinding was used, rates of attrition, and the period of follow-up. Characteristics of participants must be encoded as well (e.g., their mean age). Finally, information about findings must be extracted. Reviewers must either calculate effect sizes (discussed in the next section) or must record sufficient statistical information that they can be computed by a program.

As with other decisions, extraction and coding of information should be completed by two or more people, at least for a portion of the studies in the sample. This allows for an assessment of inter-rater agreement, which should be sufficiently high to persuade readers of the review that the recorded information is accurate.

Example of intercoder agreement:
Conn and colleagues (2011), in their meta-analysis of interventions to increase physical activity in healthy adults, coded numerous participant and intervention characteristics. Two thoroughly trained coders independently extracted all data. Codes were then compared to achieve 100% agreement. A third coder verified the extracted effect size information.

Calculation of Effects

Meta-analyses depend on the calculation of an index that encapsulates in a single number the relationship between the independent and outcome variables in each study. Effects are captured differently depending on the level of measurement of variables. The three most common scenarios for meta-analysis involve comparisons of two groups such as an experimental versus a control group on a continuous outcome (e.g., blood pressure), comparisons of two groups on a dichotomous outcome (e.g., stopped smoking vs. continued smoking), or correlations between two continuous variables (e.g., between blood pressure and anxiety scores).

The first scenario, comparison of two group means, is especially common. When the outcomes across studies are on identical scales (e.g., all outcomes are measures of weight in pounds), the effect is captured by simply subtracting the mean for one group from the mean for the other. For example, if the mean post-intervention weight in an intervention group were 182.0 pounds and that for a control group were 194.0 pounds, the effect would be –8.0. More typically, however, outcomes are measured on different scales (e.g., different scales to measure stress). Mean differences across studies cannot in such situations be combined and averaged—researchers need an index that is neutral to the original metric. Cohen's *d*, the effect size index most often used, transforms all effects into standard deviation units (Chapter 12). If *d* were computed to be .50, it means that the group mean for one group was one half a standard deviation higher than the mean for the other group—regardless of the original measurement scale.

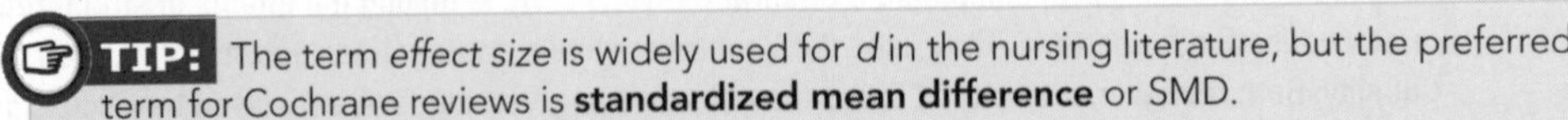
TIP: The term *effect size* is widely used for *d* in the nursing literature, but the preferred term for Cochrane reviews is **standardized mean difference** or SMD.

When the outcomes in the primary studies are dichotomous meta-analysts have a choice of effect index, including the odds ratio (OR) and risk ratio (RR). In nonexperimental studies, a common effect size statistic is Pearson's *r*, which indicates the magnitude and direction of effect.

Data Analysis

After an effect size is computed for each study, as just described, a pooled effect estimate is computed as a *weighted average* of the individual effects. The bigger the weight given to any study, the more that study will contribute to the weighted average. One widely used approach is called the *inverse variance method* which involves using the standard error to calculate a weight. Larger studies, which have smaller standard errors, are given greater weight than smaller ones.

An important decision that meta-analysts make concerns how to deal with the heterogeneity of findings—i.e., differences from one study to another in the magnitude and direction of the effect size. Heterogeneity should be formally tested, and meta-analysts should report their results in their reports.

Visual inspection of heterogeneity usually relies on the construction of **forest plots**, which are often included in meta-analytic reports. A forest plot graphs the effect size for each study, together with the 95% CI around each estimate. Figure 19.1 illustrates forest plots for situations in which there is low heterogeneity (A) and high heterogeneity (B) for five studies.

In panel A, all effect size estimates (here, OR) favor the intervention group; the CI information indicates the intervention effect is statistically significant (does not encompass 1.0, the OR value indicating no difference) for studies 2, 4, and 5. In panel B, by contrast, the results are "all over the map." Two studies favor controls at significant levels (studies 1 and 5) and two favor the treatment group (studies 2 and 4). Meta-analysis is not appropriate for the situation in panel B. Heterogeneity can be evaluated using statistical methods that test the null hypothesis that heterogeneity across studies represents random fluctuations.

Heterogeneity affects not only whether a meta-analysis is appropriate but also which of two statistical models should be used in the analysis. Although this is too complex a topic for this book, suffice it to say that when heterogeneity is low, the researchers may use a *fixed effects model*. When results are more varied, it is better to use a *random effects model*. Some argue that a random effects model is usually more tenable. One solution is to perform a **sensitivity analysis**—which, in general, refers to an effort to test how sensitive the results of an analysis are to changes in the way the analysis was done. In this case, it would involve using *both* statistical models to see how the results are affected. If the results differ, estimates from the random effects model would be preferred.

Many meta-analysts seek to understand the determinants of effect size heterogeneity through formal analyses. Variation across studies could reflect systematic differences with regard to important clinical or methodologic characteristics. For example, in intervention

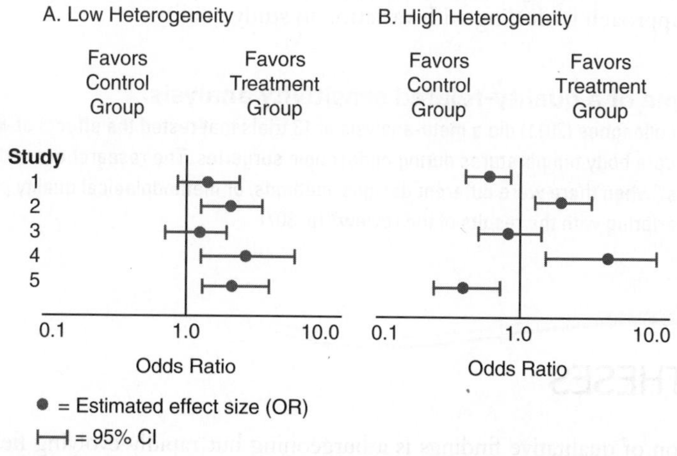

FIGURE 19.1 ● Two forest plots of different heterogeneity.

studies, variation in effects could reflect who the agents were (e.g., nurses vs. others), how long the intervention lasted, and whether or not the intervention was individualized. Or, variation in results could be explained by differences in participant characteristics (e.g., men vs. women).

One strategy for exploring moderating effects on effect size is to do **subgroup analyses**, which involve splitting effect size information into distinct categorical groups—for example, men and women. Effects for studies with all-male (or predominantly male) samples could be compared to those for studies with all or predominantly female samples.

Example of a subgroup analysis:
Hodnett and colleagues (2011) assessed the effects of continuous, one-to-one intrapartum support on birth and labor outcomes. They found positive overall effects for such outcomes as use of analgesia, time in labor, and caesarean birth. Subgroup analyses were conducted to examine whether differences in effects were observed for subgroups defined by the provider's relationship to the hospital and to the women, type of routine practices in the setting, and time of onset of the support.

Another analytic issue concerns study quality. There are four basic strategies for dealing with study quality in a meta-analysis. One, as previously noted, is to establish a quality threshold for study inclusion (e.g., omitting studies with a low score on a quality assessment scale).

Example of excluding low-quality studies:
DeNiet and colleagues (2009) did a meta-analysis of the effects of music-assisted relaxation interventions to improve sleep quality in adults with sleep complaints. They used a nine-item quality assessment list, and only studies with a score of at least five were included in the review.

A second strategy is to undertake sensitivity analyses to determine whether the exclusion of lower-quality studies changes the results of analyses based only on the most rigorous studies. Another approach is to consider quality as the basis for exploring variation in effects. For example, do randomized designs yield different average effect size estimates than quasi-experimental designs? Do effects vary as a function of the study's score on a quality assessment scale? A fourth strategy is to *weight* studies according to quality criteria. Most meta-analyses routinely give more weight to larger studies, but effect sizes can also be weighted by quality scores, thereby placing more weight on the estimates from rigorous studies. A mix of strategies, including appropriate sensitivity analyses, is probably the most prudent approach to dealing with variation in study quality.

Example of a quality-related sensitivity analysis:
Jin and colleagues (2011) did a meta-analysis of 13 trials that tested the effects of warmed irrigation fluid on core body temperatures during endoscopic surgeries. The researchers undertook sensitivity analyses "when there were different designs, methods, or methodological quality problems potentially interfering with the results of the review" (p. 307).

METASYNTHESES

Integration of qualitative findings is a burgeoning but rapidly evolving field for which there are no standard procedures. Indeed, five leading thinkers on qualitative integration noted the "terminological landmines" (p. 1343) that complicate the field, and the challenges of working in "an era of metamadness" (p. 1357) (Thorne, Jensen, Kearney, Noblit, and Sandelowski, 2004).

Metasynthesis Defined

Terminology relating to qualitative integration is diverse and complex. Thorne and colleagues (2004) acknowledged the diversity and used the term metasynthesis as an umbrella term, with metasynthesis broadly representing "a family of methodological approaches to developing new knowledge based on rigorous analysis of existing qualitative research findings" (p. 1343).

Many writers on this topic are fairly clear about what a metasynthesis is *not*. Metasynthesis is not a literature review—i.e., a summary of research findings—nor is it a concept analysis. Schreiber and colleagues (1997) offered a definition that has often been used for what metasynthesis *is*, "...the bringing together and breaking down of findings, examining them, discovering the essential features and, in some way, combining phenomena into a transformed whole" (p. 314). A common view is that metasyntheses are products that are more than the sum of the parts—they offer new insights and interpretations of findings. Most methods of qualitative synthesis involve a transformational process.

Metasynthesis has had its share of controversies, one of which concerns whether to integrate studies based on different research traditions and methods. Some researchers have argued against combining studies from different epistemological perspectives, and have recommended separate analyses using groupings from different traditions. Others, however, advocate combining findings across traditions and methodologies. Which path to follow is likely to depend on several factors, including the focus of the inquiry, its intent vis-à-vis theory development, and the nature of the available evidence at the time the metasynthesis is undertaken.

Steps in a Metasynthesis

Many of the steps in a metasynthesis are similar to ones we described in connection with a meta-analysis, and so some details will not be repeated here. However, we point out some distinctive issues relating to qualitative integration that are relevant in the various steps.

Problem Formulation

In metasynthesis, researchers begin with a research question or focus of investigation, and a key issue concerns the scope of the inquiry. Finfgeld (2003) recommended a strategy that balances breadth and utility. She advised that the scope be broad enough to fully capture the phenomenon of interest, but focused enough to yield findings that are meaningful to clinicians, other researchers, and public policy makers.

Example of a statement of purpose in a metasynthesis:
Finfgeld-Connett and colleagues (2012) stated that the aim of their metasynthesis was "to articulate new insights relating to the most efficient and effective means of helping homeless women with substance abuse problems to enhance their well-being and become more stably housed" (p. 417).

The Design of a Metasynthesis

Like a quantitative systematic review, a metasynthesis requires considerable advance planning. Having a team of at least two researchers to design and implement the study is often advantageous because of the highly subjective nature of interpretive efforts. Just as in a primary study, the design of a qualitative metasynthesis should involve efforts to enhance integrity and rigor, and investigator triangulation is one such strategy.

TIP: Meta-analyses often are undertaken by researchers who did not do one of the primary studies in the review. Metasyntheses, by contrast, are often done by researchers whose area of interest has led them to do both original studies and metasyntheses on the same topic. Prior work in an area offers advantages in terms of researchers' ability to grasp subtle nuances and to think abstractly about a topic, but a disadvantage may be a certain degree of partiality toward one's own work.

Like meta-analysts, metasynthesists must also make upfront sampling decisions. For example, they face the same issue of opting to include only findings from peer-reviewed journals in the analysis. One advantage of including alternative sources, in addition to wanting a more inclusive sample, is that journal articles tend to be constrained by space limitations. Finfgeld (2003) noted that in her metasynthesis on *courage*, she used dissertations even when a peer-reviewed journal article was available from the same study because the dissertation offered richer information. Another sampling decision, as previously noted, involves whether to search for qualitative studies about a phenomenon in multiple traditions. Finally, a researcher may decide to exclude studies in which the reported findings are not adequately supported with direct quotes from participants.

Example of sampling decisions:

Flores and Pellico (2011) conducted a metasynthesis of studies on the postincarceration experiences of women reentering the community. They searched for published and unpublished studies on women's experiences written in the past decade. Relevant studies were drawn from all qualitative traditions. Of the 10 primary studies, 3 were phenomenological, 3 were grounded theory studies, and the others were descriptive qualitative.

The Search for Data in the Literature

It is generally more difficult to find qualitative than quantitative studies using mainstream approaches, such as searching electronic databases. For example, "qualitative" became a MeSH (medical subject heading) term in MEDLINE in 2003, but it is risky to assume that all qualitative studies (e.g., ethnographies) are coded as qualitative.

TIP: Sample sizes in nursing metasyntheses are highly variable, ranging from a very small number—e.g., four primary studies on person-centered nursing in the metasynthesis by McCormack and colleagues (2010)—to nearly 300 in Paterson's (2001) synthesis of qualitative studies on chronic illness. Sample size is likely to vary as a function of scope of the inquiry, the extent of prior research, and type of metasynthesis undertaken. As with primary studies, one guideline for sampling adequacy is whether categories in the metasynthesis are saturated.

Evaluations of Study Quality

Formal evaluations of primary study quality are not as common in metasynthesis as in meta-analysis. Yet, it is often useful for reviewers to perform some type of quality assessment of primary studies, if for no other purpose than to be able to describe the sample of studies in the review. In recent years, nurse researchers have increasingly used the 10-question assessment tool from the Critical Appraisal Skills Programme (CASP) of the Centre for Evidence-Based Medicine in the United Kingdom (http://www.phru.nhs.uk/Pages/PHD/CASP.htm).

Although some reviews exclude low-quality studies from their metasynthesis, not everyone agrees that quality ought to be a criterion for study inclusion. Some have argued that a flawed study does not necessarily invalidate the rich data from those studies. Noblit and Hare (1988), whose ethnographic approach is widely used by nurse researchers, advocated including all relevant studies, but also suggested giving more weight to higher-quality studies. A more systematic application of assessments in a metasynthesis is to use quality information in a sensitivity analysis that explores whether interpretations are altered when low-quality studies are removed.

Example of a sensitivity analysis:
Bridges and colleagues (2010) synthesized studies on the experiences of older people and relatives in acute care settings. Primary studies were appraised using the CASP criteria. A total of 42 primary studies and a previous synthesis were included in the review. A sensitivity analysis revealed that the findings and interpretations were robust to the removal of the nine low-quality studies.

Extraction of Data for Analysis

Information about various features of each study need to be abstracted and coded as part of the project. Just as in quantitative integration, the metasynthesist records features of the data source (e.g., year of publication), characteristics of the sample (e.g., age), and methodologic features (e.g., research tradition). Most important, information about the study findings must be extracted and recorded—typically the key themes, metaphors, or categories from each study.

As Sandelowski and Barroso (2002) noted, however, *finding* the findings is not always easy. Qualitative researchers intermingle data with interpretation and findings from other studies with their own. Noblit and Hare (1988) advised that just as primary study researchers must read and reread their data before they can proceed with a meaningful analysis, metasynthesists must read the primary studies multiple times to fully grasp the categories or metaphors being explicated.

Data Analysis and Interpretation

Strategies for metasynthesis diverge most markedly at the analysis stage. We briefly describe three approaches. Regardless of approach, metasynthesis is a complex interpretive task that involves "carefully peeling away the surface layers of studies to find their hearts and souls in a way that does the least damage to them" (Sandelowski et al., 1997, p. 370).

The Noblit and Hare Approach

Noblit and Hare (1988), whose approach to integration is called **meta-ethnography** argued that integration should be interpretive and not aggregative—i.e., that the synthesis should focus on constructing interpretations rather than descriptions. Their approach for synthesizing qualitative studies includes seven phases that overlap and repeat as the metasynthesis progresses, the first three of which are preanalytic: (1) deciding on the phenomenon, (2) deciding which studies are relevant for the synthesis, and (3) reading and rereading each study. Phase 7 involves writing up the synthesis, but phases 4 through 6 concern the analysis:

- *Phase 4*: Deciding how the studies are related. In this phase, the researcher makes a list of the key metaphors (or themes/concepts) in each study and their relation to each other. Studies can be related in three ways: *reciprocal* (directly comparable), *refutational* (in opposition to each other), or in a *line of argument* rather than either reciprocal or refutational.
- *Phase 5*: Translating the qualitative studies into one another. Noblit and Hare noted that "translations are especially unique syntheses because they protect the particular, respect holism, and enable comparison. An adequate translation maintains the central metaphors and/or concepts of each account in their relation to other key metaphors or concepts in that account" (p. 28).

- *Phase 6*: Synthesizing translations. Here the challenge for the researcher is to make a whole into more than the individual parts imply.

Example of Noblit and Hare's approach:
Schmeid and colleagues (2011) used Noblit and Hare's approach in their meta-ethnography of 31 studies on women's perceptions and experiences of professional breast-feeding support. The meta-synthesis resulted in four categories comprising 20 themes. The synthesis indicated that support for breast-feeding occurred along a continuum from authentic presence at one end to disconnected encounters at the other.

The Paterson, Thorne, Canam, and Jillings Approach

The method developed by Paterson and a team of Canadian colleagues (2001) involves three components: *meta-data* analysis, *meta-method* and meta-theory. A *meta-data* analysis involves the study of the results of reported research in a specific substantive area by analyzing the "processed data." *meta-method* is the study of the methodologic rigor of the studies included in the metasynthesis. Lastly, *meta-theory* refers to the analysis of the theoretical underpinnings on which the studies are grounded. The end product is a metasynthesis that results from bringing back together the findings of these three *meta-study* components.

Example of the Paterson et al. approach:
Bench and Day (2010) used the Paterson framework in their metasynthesis focusing on the specific problems faced by patients and relatives immediately following discharge from a critical care unit to another hospital unit.

The Sandelowski and Barroso Approach

The strategies developed by Sandelowski and Barroso (2007) are likely to inspire metasynthesis in the years ahead. In their multiyear methodologic project, they dichotomized integration efforts based on level of synthesis and interpretation. Primary studies are called summaries if they yield descriptive synopses of the qualitative data, usually with lists and frequencies of themes, without any conceptual reframing. Syntheses, by contrast, are more interpretive and involve conceptual or metaphorical reframing. Sandelowski and Barroso have argued that only findings that are syntheses should be used in a metasynthesis.

Both summaries and syntheses can, however, be used in a **meta-summary**, which can lay a foundation for a metasynthesis. Sandelowski and Barroso provided an example of a meta-summary, using studies of mothering within the context of HIV infection. The first step, extracting findings, resulted in almost 800 complete sentences from 45 reports and represented a comprehensive inventory of findings. The 800 sentences were then reduced to 93 thematic statements or abstracted findings.

The next step involved calculating **manifest effect sizes**, i.e., effect sizes calculated from the manifest content pertaining to mothering in the context of HIV, as represented in the 93 abstracted findings. (Qualitative effect sizes are not to be confused with effects in a meta-analysis). Two types of effect size can be created from the abstracted findings. A **frequency effect size**, which indicates the magnitude of the findings, is the number of reports that contain a given finding, divided by all reports (excluding those with duplicated findings from the same data). For example, Sandelowski and Barroso calculated an overall frequency effect size of 60% for the finding of mothers' struggle about disclosing their HIV status to their children. In other words, 60% of the 45 primary studies had a finding of this nature. Effect size information can be calculated for subgroups of studies—e.g., for published versus unpublished studies, for ones in different research traditions, and so on.

An **intensity effect size** indicates the concentration of findings *within* each report. It is calculated by calculating the number of different findings in a given report, divided by the total number of findings in all reports. As an example, one primary study in Sandelowski and Barroso's meta-summary had 29 out of the 93 total findings, for an intensity effect size of 31%.

Metasyntheses can build upon metasummaries, but require findings that are more interpretive, i.e., from reports that are characterized as syntheses. The purpose of a metasynthesis is not to summarize, but to offer novel interpretations of qualitative findings. Such interpretive integrations require metasynthesists to piece the individual syntheses together to craft a new coherent explanation of a target event or experience.

Example of Sandelowski and Barroso's approach:
Draucker and colleagues (2009) conducted a metasynthesis to identify the essence of healing from sexual violence, as described by adults who experienced it as children or as adults. Meta-summary techniques were used to aggregate findings from 51 reports, and metasynthesis techniques were used to interpret the findings. A total of 11 meta-findings with frequency effect sizes over 15% were abstracted and summarized in a table.

CRITIQUING SYSTEMATIC REVIEWS

Reports for systematic reviews, including meta-analyses and metasyntheses, typically follow a similar format as for a report for a primary study. There is usually an introduction, method section, results section, and discussion, and full citations for the entire sample of studies included in the review (often identified separately from other citations by using asterisks).

The method section is especially important. Readers of the review need to assess the validity of the findings, and so methodologic and statistical strategies, and their rationales, should be adequately described. For example, if reviewers of quantitative studies decided that a meta-analysis was not justified, the rationale for this decision should be made clear. Tables and figures typically play a key role in reports of systematic reviews. For meta-analyses, forest plots are often presented, showing effect size and 95% CI information for each study, as well as for the overall pooled result. There is often a table showing the characteristics of studies included in the review.

Metasynthesis reports are similar to meta-analytic reports, except that the results section contains the new interpretations rather than quantitative findings. When a metasummary has been done, however, the meta-findings would typically be presented in a table. The method section of a metasynthesis report should contain a detailed description of the sampling criteria, the search procedures, and efforts made to enhance the integrity and rigor of the integration.

A thorough discussion section is crucial in systematic reviews. The discussion should include the reviewers' assessment about the strengths and limitations of the body of evidence, suggestions on further research needed to improve the evidence base, and the implications of the review for clinicians. The review should also discuss the consistency of findings across studies and provide an interpretation of why there might be inconsistency.

Like all studies, systematic reviews should be critiqued before the findings are deemed trustworthy and relevant to clinicians. Box 19.1 offers guidelines for evaluating systematic reviews. Although these guidelines are fairly broad, not all questions apply equally well to all types of systematic reviews. In particular, we have distinguished questions about analysis separately for meta-analyses and metasyntheses. The list of questions in Box 19.1 is not necessarily comprehensive. Supplementary questions might be needed for particular types of review.

Box 19.1 Guidelines for Critiquing Systematic Reviews

The Problem

- Did the report clearly state the research problem and/or research questions? Is the scope of the project appropriate? Were concepts, variables, or phenomena adequately defined?
- Was the approach to integration adequately described, and was the approach appropriate?

Search Strategy

- Did the report describe criteria for selecting primary studies, and are the criteria defensible?
- Were the bibliographic databases used by the reviewers identified, and are they appropriate and comprehensive? Were keywords identified, and are they exhaustive?
- Did the reviewers use adequate supplementary efforts to identify relevant studies?

The Sample

- Did the search strategy yield a good and thorough sample of studies?
- If an original report was lacking key information, did reviewers attempt to contact the original researchers for additional information—or did the study have to be excluded?

Quality Appraisal

- Did the reviewers appraise the quality of the primary studies? Did they use a well-defined set of criteria or a well-validated quality appraisal scale?
- Did two or more people do the appraisals, and was interrater agreement reported?
- Was appraisal information used appropriately in selecting studies or analyzing results?

Data Extraction

- Was adequate information extracted about the study design, sample characteristics, and study findings?
- Were steps taken to enhance the integrity of the dataset (e.g., were two or more people used to extract and record information for analysis)?

Data Analysis—General

- Did the reviewers explain their method of pooling and integrating the data?
- Was the analysis of data thorough and credible?
- Were tables, figures, and text used effectively to summarize findings?

Data Analysis—Quantitative

- If a meta-analysis was not performed, was there adequate justification for using narrative integration? If a meta-analysis *was* performed, was this justifiable?
- For meta-analyses, did the report describe how effect sizes were computed? Were procedures for computing effect size estimates appropriate?
- Was heterogeneity of effects assessed? Was the decision to use a random effects model versus a fixed effects model sound? Were appropriate subgroup analyses undertaken—or was the absence of subgroup analyses justified?

Data Analysis—Qualitative

- In a metasynthesis, did the reviewers describe the techniques they used to compare the findings of each study, and did they explain their method of interpreting their data?
- If a meta-summary was done, were appropriate methods used to compute effect sizes? Was information presented effectively?
- In a metasynthesis, did the synthesis achieve a fuller understanding of the phenomenon to advance knowledge? Do the interpretations seem well grounded? Was there a sufficient amount of data included to support the interpretations?

Box 19.1 Guidelines for Critiquing Systematic Reviews *(Continued)*

Conclusions

- Did the reviewers draw reasonable conclusions about the quality, quantity, and consistency of evidence relating to the research question?
- Are limitations of the review/synthesis noted?
- Are implications for nursing practice and further research clearly stated?

Color key

All systematic reviews

Systematic reviews of quantitative studies

Metasyntheses

RESEARCH EXAMPLES WITH CRITICAL THINKING EXERCISES

We conclude this chapter with a description of two systematic reviews. Additionally, a meta-analysis and a metasynthesis appear in their entirety in the *Study Guide* that accompanies this book.

Examples 1 and 2 below are also featured in our *Interactive Critical Thinking Activity* on thePoint website where you can easily record, print, and e-mail your responses to the related questions.

EXAMPLE 1 ● A Meta-Analysis

Study: Use of weaning protocols for reducing duration of mechanical ventilation in critically ill adult patients: Cochrane systematic review and meta-analysis (Blackwood et al., 2011)

Purpose: The purpose of the meta-analytic study was to examine the effects of standardized weaning protocols on the total duration of mechanical ventilation, mortality, adverse events, weaning duration, and length of stay of critically ill adults in intensive care units (ICUs).

Eligibility Criteria: A primary study was included if it examined the effect of using a formal weaning protocol (compared to usual weaning practice) on patient outcomes using an experimental or quasi-experimental design. The population comprised adult patients who were receiving invasive mechanical ventilation with a nasotrachial or orotracheal tube.

Search Strategy: The strategy involved a search of multiple databases, including Medline, Embase, CINAHL, Web of Science, and LILACS. The researchers also searched reference lists of all identified reports and searched registries of ongoing trials. No language restrictions were applied. The search terms included mechanical ventilation; ventilators, mechanical; ventilators, negative pressure; ventilator weaning; and weaning protocol.

Sample: Two authors independently scanned possible studies identified in the search for inclusion in the meta-analysis. The search had retrieved 6,016 citations. Ultimately, only 11 trials met all inclusion criteria. The trials involved a total of 1,971 participants, ranging from 15 to 357 per trial. The studies had been conducted in the United States, Brazil, Italy, Germany, and Australia.

Data Extraction: Using a data extraction form adapted from the Cochrane Anesthesia Review Group, three authors independently extracted data to record study design and sample characteristics, intervention features, and patient outcomes. Disagreements were resolved through consultation with a fourth author.

Quality Assessments: Each study was assessed with regard to its risk of bias, using the Cochrane Collaboration's domain-based evaluation. The researchers coded for six risks (e.g., adequacy of generating the random allocation sequence, blinding of outcome assessors). A table in the report showed how the 11 studies were coded for each bias risk. No studies were eliminated based on quality.

Effect Size Calculation: The outcomes of interest included both dichotomous measures (e.g., mortality) and continuous measures (e.g., duration of mechanical ventilation). For dichotomous outcomes, the OR was used as the effect size index (e.g., the odds of dying in the protocol group relative to the odds of dying in the usual care group). For continuous outcomes, the standardized mean difference (*d*) comparing the two groups was used as the effect size index.

Statistical Analyses: The researchers used a fixed effects model for the meta-analysis. When statistical heterogeneity was detected, however, a random effects model was used. Subgroup analyses were performed to examine whether effect size results varied by the approach to delivering the protocol (professional led vs computer driven) or type of ICU (medical, surgical, neurological). Sensitivity analyses were performed to assess the impact of excluding studies with high risk of bias. Publication bias does not appear to have been formally assessed.

Key Findings: Results were presented in tables and a series of forest plots. Compared to usual care, the mean duration of mechanical ventilation when a formal protocol was used was reduced by 25% (95% CI = 9% to 39%). Duration of weaning itself was reduced by 78%, and length of stay in the ICU was significantly reduced by 10%. There were no significant differences in terms of mortality, adverse events, or length of stay in the hospital. There was significant heterogeneity for total duration of mechanical ventilation, but subgroup analyses could not account for differences among studies. In terms of the sensitivity analysis, the exclusion of six studies with at least one bias risk did not change the observed beneficial effects of the protocol.

Discussion: The researchers concluded that the evidence points to the benefits of using a formal weaning protocol, but noted that the substantial variation among studies and the small number of studies in the meta-analysis make it difficult to understand circumstances under which a standardized protocol is most effective.

CRITICAL THINKING EXERCISES

1. Answer the relevant questions from Box 19.1 on page 368 regarding this study.
2. Comment on the authors' decision to not conduct a publication bias analysis.
3. In what ways do you think the findings could be used in clinical practice?

EXAMPLE 2 ● A Metasynthesis

Study: A systematic review and meta-ethnography of the qualitative literature: Experiences of the menarche (Chang, Hayter, & Wu, 2010)

Purpose: The purpose of the meta-ethnography was to synthesize qualitative studies on women's lived experience of the menarche, and to explore the factors affecting how it is experienced.

Eligibility Criteria: A primary study was included if it used a qualitative approach, was published in English, and described women' experiences of menarche.

Search Strategy: An expert panel guided the review process. The authors searched nine databases (e.g., MEDLINE, CINAHL, EMBASE, Web of Science), using a broad range of keywords, which they listed in a table of their report. An ancestry search was also conducted, using the reference lists of eligible studies.

Sample: The report presented a flow chart showing the researchers' sampling decisions. Of the 2377 studies initially identified by title, 125 abstracts were screened and 22 full papers were examined for eligibility. Some were rejected after full reading or as a result of critical appraisal. In all, 14 papers, mostly of descriptive qualitative studies, were included in the analysis. The combined sample of participants in the primary studies included 483 women, mostly adolescents, from the United States, United Kingdom, and Zimbabwe.

Data Extraction and Analysis: Two reviewers independently assessed and extracted information from the studies. Quality assessment was performed using the CASP critical appraisal criteria. Four studies were deemed to be of insufficient quality and were excluded. Data were extracted using an extraction protocol. Disagreements between reviewers were resolved by consensus. Noblit and Hare's approach was used to analyze, compare, and synthesize study findings.

Key Findings: The five cross-cutting themes were: (1) Preparing for menarche; (2) the response of significant others; (3) the physical experience of menarche; (4) the psychological experience of menarche; and (5) sociocultural perspectives.

Discussion: The reviewers concluded that the menarche experience had a major impact on women. They felt their findings were of particular importance to school nurses, and could provide a framework for interventions aimed at helping adolescents make the transition to womanhood.

CRITICAL THINKING EXERCISES

1. Answer the relevant questions from Box 19.1 on page 368 regarding this study.
2. Also consider the following targeted questions:
   a. Do you think it would have been possible for the researchers to compute frequency and intensity effect sizes with their sample of studies?
   b. Do you think the researchers should have searched for studies written in other languages? Why or why not?
3. In what ways do you think the findings could be used in clinical practice?

WANT TO KNOW MORE? A wide variety of resources to enhance your learning and understanding of this chapter are available on thePoint.

- Interactive Critical Thinking Activity
- Chapter Supplement on Publication Bias in Meta-Analyses
- Student Review Questions
- Full-text online
- Internet Resources with useful websites for Chapter 19

Additional study aids including eight journal articles and related questions are also available in *Study Guide for Essentials of Nursing Research, 8e.*

SUMMARY POINTS

- Evidence-based practice relies on rigorous integration of research evidence on a topic through **systematic reviews** of research findings.
- Systematic reviews often involve statistical integration of findings through **meta-analysis**, a procedure whose advantages include objectivity and enhanced power. Yet, meta-analysis is not appropriate for broad questions or when there is substantial inconsistency of findings.
- The steps in both quantitative and qualitative integration are similar and involve formulating the problem, designing the study (including establishing sampling criteria), searching the literature for a sample of **primary studies**, evaluating study quality, extracting and encoding data for analysis, analyzing the data, and reporting the findings.

- There is no consensus on whether integrations should include the *grey literature*—i.e., unpublished reports; in quantitative studies, a concern is that there is a *bias against the null hypothesis*, a **publication bias** stemming from the underrepresentation of nonsignificant findings in published reports.
- In meta-analysis, findings from primary studies are represented by an **effect size** index that quantifies the magnitude and direction of relationship between the independent and dependent variables. The most common effect size indexes in nursing are *d* (the *standardized mean difference*), the odds ratio, and correlation coefficients.
- Effects from individual studies are pooled to yield an estimate of the population effect size by calculating a weighted average of effects, often using a procedure that gives greater weight to larger studies
- **Statistical heterogeneity** (diversity in effects across studies) is a major issue in meta-analysis, and affects decisions about using a **fixed effects model** (which assumes a single true effect size) or a **random effects model** (which assumes a distribution of effects). Heterogeneity can be examined using a **forest plot**.
- Nonrandom heterogeneity can be explored through **subgroup analyses** (*moderator analyses)*, the purpose of which is to identify clinical or methodologic features systematically related to differences in effects.
- Quality assessments (which may involve formal quantitative ratings of methodologic rigor) are sometimes used to exclude weak studies from reviews, but they can also be used to differentially weight studies or in **sensitivity analyses** to determine if including or excluding weaker studies changes conclusions.
- **Metasyntheses** are more than just summaries of prior qualitative findings; they involve a discovery of essential features of a body of findings and a transformation that yields new interpretations.
- Numerous approaches to metasynthesis (and many terms related to qualitative integration) have been proposed. Metasynthesists grapple with such issues as whether to combine findings from different research traditions and whether to exclude poor-quality studies.
- One approach to qualitative integration, **meta-ethnography** as proposed by Noblit and Hare, involves listing key themes or metaphors across studies and then translating them into each other.
- Paterson and colleagues' metastudy method integrates three components: (1) *meta-data analysis*, the study of results in a specific substantive area through analysis of the "processed data;" (2) *meta-method*, the study of the studies' methodologic rigor, and (3) *meta-theory*, the analysis of the theoretical underpinnings on which the studies are grounded.
- A **meta-summary**, a method developed by Sandelowski and Barroso, involves listing abstracted findings from the primary studies and calculating **manifest effect sizes**. A **frequency effect size** is the percentage of reports that contain a given findings. An **intensity effect size** indicates the percentage of all findings that are contained in any given report.
- In the Sandelowski and Barroso approach, a meta-summary can lay the foundation for a metasynthesis, which can use a variety of qualitative approaches to analysis and interpretations (e.g., constant comparison).

REFERENCES FOR CHAPTER 19

Bench, S., & Day, T. (2010). The user experience of critical care discharge: A meta-synthesis of qualitative research. *International Journal of Nursing Studies, 47*, 487–499.

Blackwood, B., Alderdice, F., Burns, K., Cardwell, C., Lavery, G., & O'Halloran, P. (2011). Use of weaning protocols for reducing duration of mechanical ventilation in critically ill adult patients. *British Medical Journal*, 342c, 7237.

Bridges, J., Flatley, M., & Meyer, J. (2010). Older people's and relatives' experiences in acute care settings: Systematic review and synthesis of qualitative studies. *International Journal of Nursing Studies, 47*, 89–107.

Bryanton, J., & Beck, C. T. (2010). Postnatal parental education for optimizing infant general health and parent-infant relationships. *Cochrane Database of Systematic Reviews, 1*, CD004068.

Chang, Y., Hayter, M., & Wu, S. (2010). A systematic review and meta-ethnography of the qualitative literature: Experiences of the menarche. *Journal of Clinical Nursing, 19*, 447–460.

Conn, V., Hafdahi, A., & Mehr, D. (2011). Interventions to increase physical activity among health adults: Meta-analysis of outcomes. *American Journal of Public Health, 101*, 751–759.

DeNiet, G., Tiemens, B., Lendemeijer, B., & Hutschemaekers, G. (2009). Music-assisted relaxation to improve sleep quality: Meta-analysis. *Journal of Advanced Nursing, 65*, 1356–1364.

Draucker, C., Martsolf, D., Ross, R., Cook, C., Stidham, A., & Mweemba, P. (2009). The essence of healing from sexual violence. *Research in Nursing and Health, 32*, 366–378.

Finfgeld, D. (2003). Metasynthesis: The state of the art—so far. *Qualitative Health Research, 13*, 893–904.

Finfgeld-Connett, D., Bloom, T., & Johnson, E. (2012). Perceived competency and resolution of homelessness among women with substance abuse problems. *Qualitative Health Research, 22*, 416–427.

Flores, J., & Pellico, L. (2011). A meta-synthesis of women's postincarceration experiences. *Journal of Obstetric, Gynecologic, and Neonatal Nursing, 40*, 486–496.

Fronteria, I., & Ferrinho, P. (2011). Do nurses have a different physical health profile? A systematic review of experimental and observational studies on nurses' physical health. *Journal of Clinical Nursing, 20*, 2404–2424.

Higgins, J., & Greene, S. (Eds.). (2009). *Cochrane handbook for systematic reviews of interventions*. Chichester, UK: Wiley-Blackwell.

Hodnett, E., Gates, S., Hofmeyr, G., Sakala, C., & Weston, J. (2011). Continuous support for women during childbirth. *Cochrane Database of Systematic Reviews, (2)*, CD003766.

Jin, Y., Tian, J., Sun, M., & Yang, K. (2011). A systematic review of randomized controlled trials of the effects of warmed irrigation fluid on core body temperature during endoscopic surgeries. *Journal of Clinical Nursing, 20*, 305–316.

Klainin-Yobas, P., Cho, M., & Creedy, D. (2012). Efficacy of mindfulness-based intervention on depressive symptoms among people with mental disorders: A meta-analysis. *International Journal of Nursing Studies, 49*, 109–121.

McCormack, B., Karlsson, B., Dewing, J., & Lerdal, A. (2010). Exploring person-centredness: A qualitative meta-synthesis of four studies. *Scandinavian Journal of Caring Sciences, 24*, 620–634.

McInnes, E., Jammali-Blasi, A., Bell-Syer, S., Dumville, J., & Cullum, N. (2012). Preventing pressure ulcers—are pressure-redistributing support surfaces effective? A Cochrane systematic review and meta-analysis. *International Journal of Nursing Studies, 49*(3), 345–359.

Ndosi, M., Vinall, K., Hale, C., Bird, H., & Hill, J. (2011). The effectiveness of nurse-led care in people with rheumatoid arthritis: A systematic review. *International Journal of Nursing Studies, 48*, 642–654.

Noblit, G., & Hare, R. D. (1988). *Meta-ethnography: Synthesizing qualitative studies*. Newbury Park, CA: Sage.

Paterson, B. (2001). The shifting perspectives model of chronic illness. *Journal of Nursing Scholarship, 33*, 57–62.

Paterson, B. L., Thorne, S. E., Canam, C., & Jillings, C. (2001). *Meta-study of qualitative health research*. Thousand Oaks, CA: Sage.

Sandelowski, M., Docherty, S., & Emden, C. (1997). Qualitative metasynthesis: Issues and techniques. *Research in Nursing and Health, 20*, 365–377.

Sandelowski, M., & Barroso, J. (2002). Finding the findings in qualitative studies. *Journal of Nursing Scholarship, 34*, 213–219.

Sandelowski, M., & Barroso, J. (2007). *Synthesizing qualitative research*. New York: Springer Publishing Company.

Schmeid, V., Beake, S., Sheehan, A., McCourt, C., & Dykes, F. (2011). Women's perceptions and experiences of breastfeeding support: A metasynthesis. *Birth, 38*, 49–60.

Schreiber, R., Crooks, D., & Stern, P. N. (1997). Qualitative meta-analysis. In J. M. Morse (Ed.), *Completing a qualitative project* (pp. 311–326). Thousand Oaks, CA: Sage.

Thorne, S., Jensen, L., Kearney, M., Noblit, G., & Sandelowski, M. (2004). Qualitative metasynthesis: Reflections on methodological orientation and ideological agenda. *Qualitative Health Research, 14*, 1342–1365.

Glossary

Note: A few entries in this glossary were not explained in this book, but are included here because you might come across them in the research literature.

A

Absolute risk (AR) The proportion of people in a group who experienced an undesirable outcome.

Absolute risk reduction (ARR) The difference between the absolute risk in one group (e.g., those exposed to an intervention) and the absolute risk in another group (e.g., those not exposed).

Abstract A brief description of a study, usually located at the beginning of a report.

Accessible population The population available for a study, often a nonrandom subset of the target population.

Acquiescence response set A bias in self-report instruments, especially in psychosocial scales, created when participants characteristically agree with statements ("yea-say"), independent of content.

After-only design An experimental design in which data are collected from participants only after an intervention has been introduced.

Alpha (α) (1) In tests of statistical significance, the significance criterion—the risk the researcher is willing to accept of making a Type I error; (2) in assessments of internal consistency, a reliability coefficient, Cronbach's alpha.

Analysis The organization and synthesis of data so as to answer research questions and test hypotheses.

Analysis of covariance (ANCOVA) A statistical procedure used to test mean differences among groups on an outcome variable, while controlling for one or more covariates.

Analysis of variance (ANOVA) A statistical procedure for testing mean differences among three or more groups by comparing variability between groups to variability within groups, yielding an *F*-ratio statistic.

Ancestry approach In literature searches, using citations from relevant studies to track down earlier research upon which the studies were based (the "ancestors").

Anonymity Protection of participants' confidentiality such that even the researcher cannot link individuals with the data they provided.

Applied research Research designed to find a solution to an immediate practical problem.

Assent The affirmative agreement of members of a vulnerable group (e.g., children) to participate in a study.

Associative relationship An association between two variables that cannot be described as causal.

Assumption A principle that is accepted as being true based on logic or reason, without proof.

Asymmetric distribution A distribution of data values that is skewed, with two halves that are not mirror images of each other.

Attention control group A control group that gets a similar amount of attention to the intervention group, without the "active ingredients" of the treatment.

Attrition The loss of participants over the course of a study, which can create bias by changing the composition of the sample initially drawn.

Audit trail The systematic documentation of material that allows an independent auditor of a qualitative study to draw conclusions about trustworthiness.

Authenticity The extent to which qualitative researchers fairly and faithfully show a range of different realities in the collection, analysis, and interpretation of their data.

Autoethnography An ethnographic study in which a researcher studies his or her own culture or group.

Axial coding The second level of coding in a Strauss and Corbin grounded theory study, involving the process of categorizing and condensing first-level codes by connecting a category and its subcategories.

B

Baseline data Data collected prior to an intervention, including pretreatment measures of the outcomes.

Basic research Research designed to extend the base of knowledge in a discipline for the sake of knowledge production or theory construction, rather than for solving an immediate problem.

Basic social process (BSP) The central social process emerging through analysis of grounded theory data.

Before–after design An experimental design in which data are collected from participants both before and after the introduction of an intervention.

Beneficence An ethical principle that seeks to maximize benefits for study participants, and prevent harm.

Beta (β) (1) In multiple regression, the standardized coefficients indicating the relative weights of the predictor variables in the equation; (2) in statistical testing, the probability of a Type II error.

Bias Any influence that distorts the results of a study and undermines validity.

Bimodal distribution A distribution of data values with two peaks (high frequencies).

Bivariate statistics Statistical analysis of two variables to assess the empirical relationship between them.

Blind review The review of a manuscript or a research proposal such that neither the author nor the reviewer is identified to the other party.

Blinding The process of preventing those involved in a study (participants, intervention agents, or data collectors) from having information that could lead to a bias, e.g., knowledge of which treatment group a participant is in; also called *masking*.

Bracketing In phenomenological inquiries, the process of identifying and holding in abeyance any preconceived beliefs and opinions about the phenomena under study.

C

Carry-over effect The influence that one treatment can have on subsequent treatments, notably in a crossover design.

Case-control design A nonexperimental design that compares "cases" (i.e., people with a specified condition, such as lung cancer) to matched controls (similar people without the condition).

Case study A method involving a thorough, in-depth analysis of an individual, group, or other social unit.

Categorical variable A variable with discrete values (e.g., sex) rather than values along a continuum (e.g., weight).

Category system In studies involving observation, the prespecified plan for recording the behaviors and events under observation; in qualitative studies, a system used to sort and organize the data.

Causal modeling The development and statistical testing of an explanatory model of hypothesized causal relationships among phenomena.

Causal (cause-and-effect) relationship A relationship between two variables wherein the presence or value of one variable (the "cause") determines the presence or value of the other (the "effect").

Cause-probing research Research designed to illuminate the underlying causes of phenomena.

Cell (1) The intersection of a row and column in a table with two or more dimensions; (2) in an experimental design, the representation of an experimental condition in a schematic diagram.

Central (core) category The main category or pattern of behavior in grounded theory analysis using the Strauss and Corbin approach.

Central tendency A statistical index of the "typicalness" of a set of scores, derived from the center of the score distribution; indices of central tendency include the mode, median, and mean.

Chi-square test A statistical test used in various contexts, most often to assess differences in proportions, symbolized as χ^2.

Clinical practice guidelines Practice guidelines that are evidence based, combining a synthesis and appraisal of research evidence with specific recommendations for clinical decisions.

Clinical research Research designed to generate knowledge to guide health care practice.

Clinical trial A study designed to assess the safety, efficacy, and effectiveness of a new clinical intervention, sometimes involving several phases, one of which (Phase III) is a *randomized controlled trial* (RCT) using an experimental design.

Closed-ended question A question that offers respondents a set of mutually exclusive response options.

Cochrane Collaboration An international organization that aims to facilitate well-informed decisions about health care by preparing systematic reviews of the effects of health care interventions.

Code of ethics The fundamental ethical principles established by a discipline or institution to guide researchers' conduct in research with human (or animal) study participants.

Coding The process of transforming raw data into standardized form for data processing and analysis; in quantitative research, the process of attaching numbers to categories; in qualitative research, the process of identifying recurring words, themes, or concepts within the data.

Coefficient alpha (Cronbach's alpha) A reliability index that estimates the internal consistency of a measure comprised of several items or subparts.

Coercion In a research context, the explicit or implicit use of threats (or excessive rewards) to gain people's cooperation in a study.

Cohen's *d* An effect size for comparing two group means, computed by subtracting one mean from the other and dividing by the pooled standard deviation; also called *standardized mean difference (SMD)*.

Cohort design A nonexperimental design in which a defined group of people (a cohort) is followed over time to study outcomes for subsets of the cohorts; also called a *prospective design*.

Comparison group A group of study participants whose scores on an outcome variable are used to evaluate the outcomes of the group of primary interest (e.g., nonsmokers as a comparison group for smokers); term often used in lieu of *control group* when the study design is not a true experiment.

Concealment A tactic involving the unobtrusive collection of research data without participants' knowledge or consent, used to obtain an accurate view of naturalistic behavior when the known presence of an observer would distort the behavior of interest.

Concept An abstraction based on observations of behaviors or characteristics (e.g., fatigue, pain).

Conceptual definition The abstract or theoretical meaning of a concept under study.

Conceptual file A manual method of organizing qualitative data, by creating file folders for each category in the coding scheme and inserting relevant excerpts from the data.

Conceptual map A schematic representation of a theory or conceptual model that graphically represents key concepts and linkages among them.

Conceptual model Interrelated concepts or abstractions assembled together in a rational scheme by virtue of their relevance to a common theme; sometimes called *conceptual framework*.

Concurrent design A study design for a mixed methods study in which the qualitative and quantitative strands of data are collected simultaneously; notated with a plus sign, as in QUAL + QUAN.

Concurrent validity The degree to which scores on an instrument are correlated with scores on an external criterion, measured at the same time.

Confidence interval (CI) The range of values within which a population parameter is estimated to lie, at a specified probability (e.g., 95% CI).

Confidence limit The upper limit (UL) or lower limit (LL) of a confidence interval.

Confidentiality Protection of study participants so that data provided are never publicly divulged.

Confirmability A criterion for integrity in a qualitative inquiry, referring to the objectivity or neutrality of the data and interpretations.

Confounding variable A variable that is extraneous to the research question and that confounds understanding of the relationship between the independent and dependent variables; confounding variables can be controlled in the research design or through statistical procedures.

Consecutive sampling The recruitment of *all* people from an accessible population who meet the eligibility criteria over a specific time interval or for a specified sample size.

Consent form A written agreement signed by a study participant and a researcher concerning the terms and conditions of voluntary participation in a study.

CONSORT guidelines Widely adopted guidelines (Consolidated Standards of Reporting Trials) for reporting information for a randomized controlled trial, including a checklist and flow chart for tracking participants through the trial, from recruitment through data analysis.

Constant comparison A procedure used in a grounded theory analysis wherein newly collected data are compared in an ongoing fashion with data obtained earlier, to refine theoretically relevant categories.

Constitutive pattern In hermeneutic analysis, a pattern that expresses the relationships among relational themes and is present in all the interviews or texts.

Construct An abstraction or concept that is deliberately invented (constructed) by researchers for a scientific purpose (e.g., health locus of control).

Construct validity The validity of inferences from *observed* persons, settings, and interventions in a study to the constructs that these instances might represent; for a measuring instrument, the degree to which it measures the construct under investigation.

Constructivist grounded theory An approach to grounded theory, developed by Charmaz, in which the grounded theory is constructed from shared experiences and relationships between the researcher and study participants and interpretive aspects are emphasized.

Constructivist paradigm An alternative paradigm (also called *naturalistic paradigm)* to the positivist paradigm that holds that there are multiple interpretations of reality, and that the goal of research is to understand how individuals construct reality within their context; associated with qualitative research.

Contamination The inadvertent, undesirable influence of one treatment condition on another treatment condition, as when members of the control group receive the intervention.

Content analysis The process of organizing and integrating narrative, qualitative information according to emerging themes and concepts.

Content validity The degree to which the items in an instrument adequately represent the universe of content for the concept being measured.

Content validity index (CVI) An index of the degree to which an instrument is content valid, based on ratings of a panel of experts; content validity for individual items and the overall scale can be assessed.

Contingency table A two-dimensional table in which the frequencies of two categorical variables are cross-tabulated.

Continuous variable A variable that can take on an infinite range of values along a specified continuum (e.g., height).

Control The process of holding constant confounding influences on the dependent variable (the outcome) under study.

Control group Subjects in an experiment who do not receive the experimental intervention and whose performance provides a baseline against which the effects of an intervention can be measured.

Controlled trial A trial of an intervention that includes a control group, with or without randomization.

Convenience sampling Selection of the most readily available persons as participants in a study.

Convergent parallel design A concurrent, equal-priority mixed methods design in which different but complementary data, qualitative and quantitative, are gathered about a central phenomenon under study; symbolized as QUAL + QUAN; also called a triangulation design.

Core category (variable) In a grounded theory study, the central phenomenon that is used to integrate all categories of the data.

Correlation A bond or association between variables, with variation in one variable systematically related to variation in another.

Correlation coefficient An index summarizing the degree of relationship between variables, ranging from +1.00 (a perfect positive relationship) through 0.0 (no relationship) to –1.00 (a perfect negative relationship).

Correlation matrix A two-dimensional display showing the correlation coefficients between all pairs of a set of variables.

Correlational research Research that explores the interrelationships among variables of interest without researcher intervention.

Cost (economic) analysis An analysis of the relationship between costs and outcomes of alternative nursing or other health care interventions.

Counterbalancing The process of systematically varying the order of presentation of stimuli or treatments to control for ordering effects, especially in a crossover design.

Counterfactual The condition or group used as a basis of comparison in a study, embodying what would have happened *to the same people* exposed to a causal factor if they *simultaneously* were *not* exposed to the causal factor.

Covariate A variable that is statistically controlled (held constant) in ANCOVA, typically a confounding influence on the outcome variable, or a preintervention measure of the outcome.

Credibility A criterion for evaluating integrity and quality in qualitative studies, referring to confidence in the truth of the data; analogous to internal validity in quantitative research.

Criterion-related validity The degree to which scores on an instrument are correlated with an external criterion.

Criterion sampling A purposive sampling approach used by qualitative researchers that involves selecting cases that meet a predetermined criterion of importance.

Critical ethnography An ethnography that focuses on raising consciousness in the group or culture under study in the hope of effecting social change.

Critical incident technique A method of obtaining data from study participants by in-depth exploration of specific incidents and behaviors related to the topic under study.

Critical theory An approach to viewing the world that involves a critique of society, with the goal of envisioning new possibilities and effecting social change.

Cronbach's alpha A widely used reliability index that estimates the internal consistency of a measure composed of several subparts; also called *coefficient alpha*.

Crossover design An experimental design in which one group of subjects is exposed to more than one condition or treatment, in random order.

Cross-sectional design A study design in which data are collected at one point in time; sometimes used to infer change over time when data are collected from different age or developmental groups.

Cross-tabulation A calculation of frequencies for two variables considered simultaneously—e.g., sex (male/female) cross-tabulated with smoking status (smoker/nonsmoker).

Cutoff point The score on a screening or diagnostic instrument used to distinguish *cases* (e.g., people with depression) and *noncases* (people without it).

D

d A widely used effect size index for comparing two group means, computed by subtracting one mean from the other and dividing by the pooled standard deviation; also called *Cohen's d*.

Data The pieces of information obtained in a study (singular is *datum*).

Data analysis The systematic organization and synthesis of research data and, in quantitative studies, the testing of hypotheses using those data.

Data collection protocols The formal guidelines researchers develop to give direction to the collection of data in a standardized fashion.

Data saturation See *saturation*.

Data set The total collection of data on all variables for all study participants.

Data triangulation The use of multiple data sources for the purpose of validating conclusions.

Debriefing Communication with study participants after participation is complete regarding aspects of the study (e.g., explaining the study purpose more fully).

Deception The deliberate withholding of information, or the provision of false information, to study participants, usually to reduce potential biases.

Deductive reasoning The process of developing specific predictions from general principles (see also *inductive reasoning*).

Degrees of freedom (*df*) A statistical concept referring to the number of sample values free to vary (e.g., with a given sample mean, all but one value would be free to vary).

Delayed treatment design A design for an intervention study that involves putting control group members on a waiting list for the intervention until follow-up data are collected; also called a *wait-list design*.

Dependability A criterion for evaluating integrity in qualitative studies, referring to the stability of data over time and over conditions; analogous to reliability in quantitative research.

Dependent variable The variable hypothesized to depend on or be caused by another variable (the *independent variable*); the outcome of interest.

Descendancy approach In literature searches, finding a pivotal early study and searching forward in citation indexes to find more recent studies ("descendants") that cited the key study.

Descriptive research Research that typically has as its main objective the accurate portrayal of people's characteristics or circumstances and/or the frequency with which certain phenomena occur.

Descriptive statistics Statistics used to describe and summarize data (e.g., means, percentages).

Descriptive theory A broad characterization that thoroughly accounts for a phenomenon.

Determinism The belief that phenomena are not haphazard or random, but rather have antecedent causes; an assumption in the positivist paradigm.

Dichotomous variable A variable having only two values or categories (e.g., gender).

Directional hypothesis A hypothesis that makes a specific prediction about the direction of the relationship between two variables.

Disconfirming case A concept used in qualitative research that concerns a case that challenges the researchers' conceptualizations; sometimes used in a sampling strategy.

Domain In ethnographic analysis, a unit or broad category of cultural knowledge.

Double-blind experiment A clinical trial in which neither the participants nor those who administer the treatment know who is in the experimental or control group.

E

Economic analysis An analysis of the relationship between costs and outcomes of alternative health care interventions.

Effect size A statistical expression of the magnitude of the relationship between two variables, or the magnitude of the difference between groups on an attribute of interest; also used in metasummaries of qualitative research to characterize the salience of a theme or category.

Effectiveness study A clinical trial designed to shed light on intervention effectiveness under ordinary conditions, usually with an intervention already found to be efficacious in an efficacy study.

Efficacy study A tightly controlled trial designed to establish the efficacy of an intervention under ideal conditions, using a design that stresses internal validity.

Element The most basic unit of a population for sampling purposes, typically a human being.

Eligibility criteria The criteria designating the specific attributes of the target population, by which people are selected for inclusion in a study.

Embedded design A particular mixed methods design in which one strand is primarily in a supportive role to the other strand; symbolized with brackets, as in QUAL(quan).

Emergent design A design that unfolds in the course of a qualitative study as the researcher makes ongoing design decisions reflecting what has already been learned.

Emic perspective An ethnographic term referring to the way members of a culture themselves view their world; the "insider's view."

Empirical evidence Evidence rooted in objective reality and gathered using one's senses as the basis for generating knowledge.

Error of measurement The deviation between hypothetical true scores and obtained scores of a measured characteristic.

Estimation procedures Statistical procedures that estimate population parameters based on sample statistics.

Ethics A system of moral values that is concerned with the degree to which research procedures adhere to professional, legal, and social obligations to the study participants.

Ethnography A branch of human inquiry, associated with anthropology, that focuses on the culture of a group of people, with an effort to understand the world view and customs of those under study.

Ethnonursing research The study of human cultures, with a focus on a group's beliefs and practices relating to nursing care and related health behaviors.

Etic perspective In ethnography, the "outsider's" view of the experiences of a cultural group.

Evaluation research Research aimed at learning how well a program, practice, or policy is working.

Event sampling A sampling plan that involves the selection of integral behaviors or events to be observed.

Evidence-based practice (EBP) A practice that involves making clinical decisions on the best available evidence, with an emphasis on evidence from disciplined research.

Evidence hierarchy A ranked arrangement of the validity and dependability of evidence based on the rigor of the method that produced it; the traditional evidence hierarchy is appropriate primarily for cause-probing research, especially Therapy questions.

Exclusion criteria The criteria specifying characteristics that a population does *not* have.

Experiment A study in which the researcher controls (manipulates) the independent variable and randomly assigns subjects to different conditions; randomized controlled trials use experimental designs.

Experimental group The study participants who receive the experimental treatment or intervention.

Explanatory design A sequential mixed methods design in which quantitative data are collected in the first phase and qualitative data are collected in the second phase to build on or explain quantitative findings; symbolized as QUAN → qual or quan → QUAL.

Exploratory design A sequential mixed methods design in which qualitative data are collected in the first phase and quantitative data are collected in the second phase based on the initial in-depth exploration; symbolized as QUAL → quan or qual → QUAN.

External validity The degree to which study results can be generalized to settings or samples other than the one studied.

Extraneous variable A variable that confounds the relationship between the independent and dependent variables and that needs to be controlled either in the research design or through statistical procedures; often called *confounding variable*.

Extreme case sampling A qualitative sampling approach that involves the purposeful selection of the most extreme or unusual cases.

Extreme response set A bias in psychosocial scales created when participants select extreme response alternatives (e.g., "strongly agree"), independent of the item's content.

F

***F*-ratio** The statistic obtained in several statistical tests (e.g., ANOVA) in which score variation attributable to different sources (e.g., between groups and within groups) is compared.

Face validity The extent to which an instrument looks as though it is measuring what it purports to measure.

Feminist research Research that seeks to understand, typically through qualitative approaches, how gender and a gendered social order shape women's lives and their consciousness.

Field diary A daily record of events and conversations in the field; also called a log.

Field notes The notes taken by researchers to record the unstructured observations made in the field, and the interpretation of those observations.

Field research Research in which the data are collected "in the field" from individuals in their normal roles, with the aim of understanding the practices, behaviors, and beliefs of individuals or groups as they normally function in real life.

Fieldwork The activities undertaken by qualitative researchers to collect data out in the field, i.e., in natural settings.

Findings The results of the analysis of research data.

Fit An element in Glaserian grounded theory analysis in which the researcher develops categories of a substantive theory that fit the data.

Fixed alternative question A question that offers respondents a set of prespecified response options.

Fixed effects model In meta-analysis, a model in which studies are assumed to be measuring the same overall effect; a pooled effect estimate is calculated under the assumption that observed variation between studies is attributable to chance.

Focus group interview An interview with a group of individuals assembled to answer questions on a given topic.

Focused interview A loosely structured interview in which an interviewer guides the respondent through a set of questions using a topic guide.

Follow-up study A study undertaken to determine the outcomes of individuals with a specified condition or who have received a specified treatment.

Forest plot A graphic representation of effects across studies in a meta-analysis, permitting a visual assessment of heterogeneity.

Framework The conceptual underpinnings of a study—e.g., a *theoretical framework* in theory-based studies, or *conceptual framework* in studies based on a specific conceptual model.

Frequency distribution A systematic array of numeric values from the lowest to the highest, together with a count of the number of times each value was obtained.

Frequency effect size In a metasummary of qualitative studies, the percentage of reports that contain a given thematic finding.

Full disclosure The communication of complete, accurate information to potential study participants.

Functional relationship A relationship between two variables in which it cannot be assumed that one variable caused the other.

Funnel plot In a meta-analysis, a graphical display of some measure of study precision (e.g., sample size) plotted against effect size that can be used to explore the possibility of publication bias.

G

Gaining entrée The process of gaining access to study participants through the cooperation of key actors in the selected community or site.

Generalizability The degree to which the research methods justify the inference that the findings are true for a broader group than study participants; in particular, the inference that the findings can be generalized from the sample to the population.

Grand theory A broad theory aimed at describing large segments of the physical, social, or behavioral world; also called a *macrotheory*.

Grand tour question A broad question asked in an unstructured interview to gain a general overview of a phenomenon, on the basis of which more focused questions are subsequently asked.

Grey literature Unpublished, and thus less readily accessible, research reports.

Grounded theory An approach to collecting and analyzing qualitative data that aims to develop theories about social psychological processes grounded in real-world observations.

H

Hand searching The planned searching of a journal "by hand," to identify all relevant reports that might be missed by electronic searching.

Hawthorne effect The effect on the dependent variable resulting from subjects' awareness that they are participants under study.

Hermeneutic circle In hermeneutics, the methodologic process in which, to reach understanding, there is continual movement between the parts and the whole of the text being analyzed.

Hermeneutics A qualitative research tradition, drawing on interpretive phenomenology, that focuses on the lived experiences of humans, and on how they interpret those experiences.

Heterogeneity The degree to which objects are dissimilar (i.e., characterized by variability) on an attribute.

Historical research Systematic studies designed to discover facts and relationships about past events.

History threat The occurrence of events external to an intervention but concurrent with it, which can affect the dependent variable and threaten the study's internal validity.

Homogeneity (1) In terms of the reliability of an instrument, the degree to which its subparts are internally consistent (i.e., are measuring the same critical attribute). (2) More generally, the degree to which objects are similar (i.e., characterized by low variability).

Hypothesis A statement of predicted relationships between variables or predicted outcomes.

I

Impact analysis An evaluation of the effects of a program or intervention on outcomes of interest, net of other factors influencing those outcomes.

Implementation potential The extent to which an innovation is amenable to implementation in a new setting, an assessment of which is often made in an evidence-based practice project.

Implied consent Consent to participate in a study that a researcher assumes has been given based on participants' actions, such as returning a completed questionnaire.

IMRAD format The organization of a research report into four main sections: the Introduction, Method, Results, and Discussion sections.

Incidence The rate of new cases with a specified condition, determined by dividing the number of new cases over a given period of time by the number at risk of becoming a new case (i.e., free of the condition at the outset of the time period).

Independent variable The variable that is believed to cause or influence the dependent variable; in experimental research, the manipulated (treatment) variable.

Inductive reasoning The process of reasoning from specific observations to more general rules (see also *deductive reasoning*).

Inference In research, a conclusion drawn from the study evidence, taking into account the methods used to generate that evidence.

Inferential statistics Statistics that permit inferences about whether results observed in a sample are likely to occur in the larger population.

Informant An individual who provides information to researchers about a phenomenon under study, usually in qualitative studies.

Informed consent An ethical principle that requires researchers to obtain people's voluntary participation in a study, after informing them of possible risks and benefits.

Inquiry audit An independent scrutiny of qualitative data and relevant supporting documents by an external reviewer, to determine the dependability and confirmability of qualitative data.

Insider research Research on a group or culture—usually in an ethnography—by a member of that group or culture.

Institutional Review Board (IRB) In the United States, a group of people affiliated with an institution who convene to review proposed and ongoing studies with respect to ethical considerations.

Instrument The device used to collect research data (e.g., a questionnaire, test, observation schedule, etc.).

Intensity effect size In a metasummary of qualitative studies, the percentage of all thematic findings that are contained in any given report.

Intention to treat A strategy for analyzing data in an intervention study that includes participants with the group to which they were assigned, whether or not they received or completed the treatment associated with the group.

Interaction effect The effect of two or more independent variables acting in combination (interactively) on an outcome.

Intercoder reliability The degree to which two coders, working independently, agree on coding decisions.

Internal consistency The degree to which the subparts of an instrument are measuring the same attribute or dimension, as a measure of the instrument's reliability.

Internal validity The degree to which it can be inferred that the experimental treatment (independent variable), rather than confounding factors, is responsible for observed effects on the outcome.

Interrater (interobserver) reliability The degree to which two raters or observers, operating independently, assign the same ratings or values for an attribute being measured or observed.

Interval estimation A statistical estimation approach in which the researcher establishes a range of values that are likely, within a given level of confidence, to contain the true population parameter.

Interval measurement A measurement level in which an attribute of a variable is rank ordered on a scale that has equal distances between points on that scale (e.g., Fahrenheit degrees).

Intervention In experimental research (clinical trials), the experimental treatment.

Intervention fidelity The extent to which the implementation of a treatment is faithful to its plan.

Intervention protocol The specification of exactly what the intervention and alternative (control) treatment conditions are, and how they should be administered.

Intervention research Research involving the development, implementation, and testing of an intervention.

Intervention theory The conceptual underpinning of a health care intervention, which articulates the theoretical basis for what must be done to achieve desired outcomes.

Interview A data collection method in which an interviewer asks questions of a respondent, either face-to-face, by telephone, or over the Internet.

Interview schedule The formal instrument that specifies the wording of all questions to be asked of respondents in structured self-report studies.

Intuiting The second step in descriptive phenomenology, which occurs when researchers remain open to the meaning attributed to the phenomenon by those who experienced it.

Inverse relationship A relationship characterized by the tendency of high values on one variable to be associated with low values on the second variable; also called a *negative relationship*.

Inverse variance method In meta-analysis, the use of the inverse of the variance of the effect estimate (one divided by the square of its standard error) as the weight to calculate a weighted average of effects.

Investigator triangulation The use of two or more researchers to analyze and interpret a data set, to enhance validity.

Item A single question on an instrument, or a single statement on a scale.

J

Journal article A report appearing in professional journals such as *Research in Nursing & Health*.

Journal club A group that meets regularly in clinical settings to discuss and critique research articles appearing in journals.

K

Key informant A person knowledgeable about the phenomenon of research interest and who is willing to share information and insights with the researcher (often an ethnographer).

Keyword An important term used to search for references on a topic in a bibliographic database.

Known-groups technique A technique for estimating the construct validity of an instrument through an analysis of the degree to which the instrument separates groups predicted to differ based on known characteristics or theory.

L

Level of measurement A system of classifying measurements according to the nature of the measurement and the type of permissible mathematical operations; the levels are nominal, ordinal, interval, and ratio.

Level of significance The risk of making a Type I error in a statistical analysis, established by the researcher beforehand (e.g., the .05 level).

Likelihood ratio (LR) For a screening or diagnostic instrument, the relative likelihood that a given result is expected in a person with (as opposed to one without) the target attribute; LR indexes summarize the relationship between specificity and sensitivity in a single number.

Likert scale A composite measure of an attribute involving the summation of scores on a set of items that respondents typically rate for their degree of agreement or disagreement.

Literature review A critical summary of research on a topic, often prepared to put a research problem in context or to summarize existing evidence.

Log In participant observation studies, the observer's daily record of events and conversations.

Logical positivism The philosophy underlying the traditional scientific approach; see also *positivist paradigm*.

Logistic regression A multivariate regression procedure that analyzes relationships between one or more independent variables and a categorical dependent variable and yields an odds ratio.

Longitudinal study A study designed to collect data at more than one point in time, in contrast to a cross-sectional study.

M

Macrotheory A broad theory aimed at describing large segments of the physical, social, or behavioral world; also called a *grand theory*.

Manipulation The introduction of an intervention or treatment in an experimental or quasi-experimental study to assess its impact on the dependent (outcome) variable.

MANOVA See *multivariate analysis of variance*.

Masking See *Blinding*

Matching The pairing of participants in one group with those in a comparison group based on their similarity on one or more dimension, to enhance overall group comparability.

Maturation threat A threat to the internal validity of a study that results when changes to the outcome (dependent) variable result from the passage of time.

Maximum variation sampling A sampling approach used by qualitative researchers involving the purposeful selection of cases with a wide range of variation.

Mean A measure of central tendency, computed by summing all scores and dividing by the number of cases.

Measurement The assignment of numbers to objects according to specified rules to characterize quantities of some attribute.

Median A descriptive statistic that is a measure of central tendency, representing the exact middle value in a score distribution; the value above and below which 50% of the scores lie.

Mediating variable A variable that mediates or acts like a "go-between" in a causal chain linking two other variables.

Member check A method of validating the credibility of qualitative data through debriefings and discussions with informants.

MeSH Medical Subject Headings, used to index articles in MEDLINE.

Meta-analysis A technique for quantitatively integrating the results of multiple studies addressing the same or a highly similar research question.

Metasummary A process that lays the foundation for a metasynthesis, involving the development of a list of abstracted findings from primary studies and calculating manifest effect sizes (frequency and intensity effect size).

Metasynthesis The grand narratives or interpretive translations produced from the integration or comparison of findings from qualitative studies.

Method triangulation The use of multiple methods of data collection about the same phenomenon, to enhance validity.

Methodologic research Research designed to develop or refine methods of obtaining, organizing, or analyzing data.

Methods (research) The steps, procedures, and strategies for gathering and analyzing data in a study.

Middle-range theory A theory that focuses on a limited piece of reality or human experience, involving a selected number of concepts (e.g., a theory of stress).

Minimal risk Anticipated risks that are no greater than those ordinarily encountered in daily life or during the performance of routine tests or procedures.

Mixed methods (MM) research Research in which both qualitative and quantitative data are collected and analyzed, to address different but related questions.

Moderator variable A variable that affects (moderates) the relationship between the independent and dependant variables.

Mode A measure of central tendency; the value that occurs most frequently in a distribution of scores.

Model A symbolic representation of concepts or variables and interrelationships among them.

Mortality threat A threat to the internal validity of a study, referring to differential attrition (loss of participants) from different groups.

Multimodal distribution A distribution of values with more than one peak (high frequency).

Multiple comparison procedures Statistical tests, normally applied after an ANOVA indicates statistically significant group differences, that compare different pairs of groups; also called *post hoc tests*.

Multiple correlation coefficient An index that summarizes the degree of relationship between two or more independent variables and a dependent variable; symbolized as *R*.

Multiple regression analysis A statistical procedure for understanding the effects of two or more independent (predictor) variables on a dependent variable.

Multistage sampling A sampling strategy that proceeds through a set of stages from larger to smaller sampling units (e.g., from states, to census tracts, to households).

Multivariate analysis of variance (MANOVA) A statistical procedure used to test the significance of differences between the means of two or more groups on two or more dependent variables, considered simultaneously.

Multivariate statistics Statistical procedures designed to analyze the relationships among three or more variables (e.g., multiple regression, ANCOVA).

N

N The symbol designating the total number of subjects (e.g., "the total *N* was 500").

n The symbol designating the number of subjects in a subgroup or cell of a study (e.g., "each of the four groups had an *n* of 125, for a total *N* of 500").

Narrative analysis A type of qualitative approach that focuses on the story as the object of the inquiry.

Naturalistic paradigm An alternative paradigm (also called *constructivist paradigm)* to the positivist paradigm that holds that there are multiple interpretations of reality, and that the goal of research is to understand how individuals construct reality within their natural context; associated with qualitative research.

Naturalistic setting A setting for the collection of research data that is natural to those being studied (e.g., homes, places of work, and so on).

Negative case analysis The refinement of a theory or description in a qualitative study through the inclusion of cases that appear to disconfirm earlier hypotheses.

Negative relationship A relationship between two variables in which there is a tendency for high values on one variable to be associated with low values on the other (e.g., as stress increases, emotional well-being decreases); also called an *inverse relationship*.

Negative results Results that fail to support the researcher's hypotheses.

Negatively skewed distribution An asymmetric distribution of data values with a disproportionately high number of cases at the upper end; when displayed graphically, the tail points to the left.

Network sampling The sampling of participants based on referrals from others already in the sample; also called *snowball sampling*.

Nominal measurement The lowest level of measurement involving the assignment of characteristics into categories (e.g., males, category 1; females, category 2).

Nondirectional hypothesis A research hypothesis that does not stipulate the expected direction of the relationship between variables.

Nonequivalent control group design A quasi-experimental design involving a comparison group that was not created through random assignment.

Nonexperimental research Studies in which the researcher collects data without introducing an intervention; also called *observational research*.

Nonparametric tests A class of statistical tests that do not involve stringent assumptions about the distribution of variables in the analysis.

Nonprobability sampling The selection of sampling units (e.g., people) from a population using nonrandom procedures (e.g., convenience and quota sampling).

Nonresponse bias A bias that can result when a nonrandom subset of people invited to participate in a study decline to participate.

Nonsignificant result The result of a statistical test indicating that group differences or an observed relationship could have occurred by chance, at a given level of significance; sometimes abbreviated as NS.

Normal distribution A theoretical distribution that is bell shaped and symmetrical: also called a *normal curve* or a *Gaussian distribution*.

Null hypothesis A hypothesis stating no relationship between the variables under study; used primarily in statistical testing as the hypothesis to be rejected.

Number needed to treat (NNT) An estimate of how many people would need to receive an intervention to prevent one undesirable outcome, computed by dividing one by the value of the absolute risk reduction.

Nursing research Systematic inquiry designed to develop knowledge about issues of importance to the nursing profession.

O

Objectivity The extent to which two independent researchers would arrive at similar judgments or conclusions (i.e., judgments not biased by personal values or beliefs).

Observational notes An observer's in-depth descriptions about events and conversations observed in naturalistic settings.

Observational research Studies that do not involve an experimental intervention—i.e., nonexperimental research; also, research in which data are collected through direct observation.

Observed (obtained) score The actual score or numerical value assigned to a person on a measure.

Odds A way of expressing the chance of an event—the probability of an event occurring to the probability that it will not occur, calculated by dividing the number of people who experienced an event by the number for whom it did not occur.

Odds ratio (OR) The ratio of one odds to another odds, e.g., the ratio of the odds of an event in one group to the odds of an event in another group; an odds ratio of 1.0 indicates no difference between groups.

Open-ended question A question in an interview or questionnaire that does not restrict respondents' answers to preestablished response alternatives.

Open coding The first level of coding in a grounded theory study, referring to the basic descriptive coding of the content of narrative materials.

Operational definition The definition of a concept or variable in terms of the procedures by which it is to be measured.

Operationalization The translation of research concepts into measurable phenomena.

Ordinal measurement A measurement level that rank orders phenomena along some dimension.

Outcome variable The dependent variable; a measure that captures the outcome of an intervention.

Outcomes research Research designed to document the effectiveness of health care services and the end results of patient care.

P

***p* value** In statistical testing, the probability that the obtained results are due to chance alone: the probability of a Type I error.

Pair matching See *matching*.

Paradigm A way of looking at natural phenomena that encompasses a set of philosophical assumptions and that guides one's approach to inquiry.

Paradigm case In a hermeneutic analysis following the precepts of Benner, a strong exemplar of the phenomenon under study, often used early in the analysis to gain understanding of the phenomenon.

Parameter A characteristic of a population (e.g., the mean age of all U.S. citizens).

Parametric tests A class of statistical tests that involve assumptions about the distribution of the variables and the estimation of a parameter.

Participant See *study participant.*

Participant observation A method of collecting data through the participation in and observation of a group or culture.

Participatory action research (PAR) A research approach based on the premise that the use and production of knowledge can be political and used to exert power.

Path analysis A regression-based procedure for testing causal models, typically using correlational data.

Pearson's *r* A correlation coefficient designating the magnitude of relationship between two interval- or ratio-level variables; also called *the product–moment correlation*.

Peer debriefing Meetings with peers to review and explore various aspects of a study, used to enhance trustworthiness in a qualitative study.

Peer reviewer A researcher who reviews and critiques a research report or proposal, and who makes a recommendation about publishing or funding the research.

Pentadic dramatism An approach for analyzing narratives, developed by Burke, that focus on five key elements of a story: act (what was done), scene (when and where it was done), agent (who did it), agency (how it was done), and purpose (why it was done).

Per-protocol analysis Analysis of data from a randomized controlled trial that excludes participants who did not obtain the protocol to which they were assigned.

Perfect relationship A correlation between two variables such that the values of one variable can perfectly predict the values of the other; designated as 1.00 or – 1.00.

Persistent observation A qualitative researcher's intense focus on the aspects of a situation that are relevant to the phenomena being studied.

Person triangulation The collection of data from different levels of persons, with the aim of validating data through multiple perspectives on the phenomenon.

Personal interview An in-person, face-to-face interview between an interviewer and a respondent.

Personal notes In field studies, written comments about the observer's own feelings during the research process.

Phenomenon The abstract concept under study; a term sometimes used by qualitative researchers in lieu of the term *variable*.

Phenomenology A qualitative research tradition, with roots in philosophy and psychology, that focuses on the lived experience of humans.

Photo elicitation An interview stimulated and guided by photographic images.

PICO question A well-worded question for evidence-based practice that identifies the population, intervention, comparison, and outcome of interest.

Pilot study A small scale version, or trial run, done in preparation for a major study or to assess feasibility.

Placebo A sham or pseudointervention, often used as a control group condition.

Placebo effect Changes in the dependant variable attributable to the placebo.

Point estimation A statistical procedure that uses information from a sample (a statistic) to estimate the single value that best represents the population parameter.

Population The entire set of individuals or objects having some common characteristics (e.g., all RNs in New York); sometimes called *universe*.

Positive relationship A relationship between two variables in which high values on one variable tend to be associated with high values on the other (e.g., as physical activity increases, pulse rate increases).

Positive results Research results that are consistent with the researcher's hypotheses.

Positively skewed distribution An asymmetric distribution of values with a disproportionately high number of cases at the lower end; when displayed graphically, the tail points to the right.

Positivist paradigm The paradigm underlying the traditional scientific approach, which assumes that there is an orderly reality that can be objectively studied; often associated with quantitative research.

***Post hoc* test** A test for comparing all possible pairs of groups following a significant test of overall group differences (e.g., in an ANOVA).

Poster session A session at a professional conference in which several researchers simultaneously present visual displays summarizing their studies, while conference attendees circulate around the room perusing the displays.

Posttest The collection of data after introducing an intervention.

Posttest-only design An experimental design in which data are collected from participants only after the intervention has been introduced; also called an *after-only design*.

Power The ability of a design or analysis strategy to detect true relationships that exist among variables.

Power analysis A procedure for estimating either the needed sample size for a study or the likelihood of committing a Type II error.

Practical (pragmatic) clinical trial Trials that address practical questions about the benefits, risks, and costs of an intervention as they would unfold in routine clinical practice, using less rigid controls than in typical efficacy trials.

Precision The degree to which an estimated population value (a statistic) clusters closely around the estimate, usually expressed in terms of the width of the confidence interval.

Prediction The use of empirical evidence to make forecasts about how variables will behave with a new group of people.

Predictive validity The degree to which an instrument can predict a criterion observed at a future time.

Pretest (1) The collection of data prior to the experimental intervention; sometimes called baseline data. (2) The trial administration of a newly developed instrument to identify potential weaknesses.

Pretest–posttest design An experimental design in which data are collected from research subjects both before and after introducing an intervention; also called a *before–after design*.

Prevalence The proportion of a population having a particular condition (e.g., fibromyalgia) at a given point in time.

Primary source First-hand reports of facts or findings; in research, the original report prepared by the investigator who conducted the study.

Primary study In a systematic review, an original study whose findings are used as the data in the review.

Priority A key issue in mixed methods research, concerning which strand (qualitative or quantitative) will be given more emphasis; in notation, the dominant strand is in all capital letters, as QUAL or QUAN, and the nondominant strand is in lower case, as qual or quan.

Probability sampling The selection of sampling units (e.g., participants) from a population using random procedures (e.g., simple random sampling).

Probing Eliciting more useful or detailed information from a respondent in an interview than was volunteered in the first reply.

Problem statement An expression of a dilemma or disturbing situation that needs investigation.

Process analysis A descriptive analysis of the process by which a program or intervention gets implemented and used in practice.

Process consent In a qualitative study, an ongoing, transactional process of negotiating consent with participants, allowing them to collaborate in the decision making about their continued participation.

Product moment correlation coefficient (*r*) A correlation coefficient designating the magnitude of relationship between two variables measured on at least an interval scale; also called *Pearson's r*.

Prolonged engagement In qualitative research, the investment of sufficient time during data collection to have an in-depth understanding of the group under study, thereby enhancing credibility.

Proposal A document communicating a research problem, proposed procedures for solving the problem, and, when funding is sought, how much the study will cost.

Prospective design A study design that begins with an examination of a presumed cause (e.g., cigarette smoking) and then goes forward in time to observe presumed effects (e.g., lung cancer): also called a *cohort design*.

Psychometric assessment An evaluation of the quality of an instrument, primarily in terms of its reliability and validity.

Psychometrics The theory underlying principles of measurement and the application of the theory in the development of measuring tools.

Publication bias The tendency for published studies to systematically overrepresent statistically significant findings, reflecting the tendency of researchers, reviewers, and editors to not publish nonsignificant results; also called a *bias against the null hypothesis*.

Purposive (purposeful) sampling A nonprobability sampling method in which the researcher selects participants based on personal judgment about who will be most informative.

Q

Q sort A data collection method in which participants sort statements into piles (usually 9 or 11) according to some bipolar dimension (e.g., most helpful/least helpful).

Qualitative analysis The organization and interpretation of narrative data for the purpose of discovering important underlying themes, categories, and patterns.

Qualitative data Information collected in narrative (nonnumeric) form, such as the dialogue from a transcript of an unstructured interview.

Qualitative research The investigation of phenomena, typically in an in-depth and holistic fashion, through the collection of rich narrative materials using a flexible research design.

Quantitative analysis The manipulation of numeric data through statistical procedures for the purpose of describing phenomena or assessing the magnitude and reliability of relationships among them.

Quantitative data Information collected in a quantified (numeric) form.

Quantitative research The investigation of phenomena that lend themselves to precise measurement and quantification, often involving a rigorous and controlled design.

Quasi-experimental design A design for testing an intervention in which participants are not randomly assigned to treatment conditions; also called a *nonrandomized trial* or a *controlled trial without randomization*.

Quasi-statistics An "accounting" system used to assess the validity of conclusions derived from qualitative analysis.

Questionnaire A document used to gather self-report data via self-administration of questions.

Quota sampling A nonrandom sampling method in which "quotas" for certain subgroups based on sample characteristics are established to increase the representativeness of the sample.

R

r The symbol for a bivariate correlation coefficient, summarizing the magnitude and direction of a relationship between two variables measured on an interval or ratio scale.

R The symbol for the multiple correlation coefficient, indicating the magnitude (but not direction) of the relationship between a dependent variable and multiple independent variables, taken together.

R^2 The squared multiple correlation coefficient, indicating the proportion of variance in the dependent variable explained by a group of independent variables.

Random assignment The assignment of participants to treatment conditions in a random manner (i.e., in a manner determined by chance alone); also called *randomization*.

Random effects model In meta-analysis, a model in which studies are not assumed to be measuring the same overall effect, but rather reflect a distribution of effects; often preferred to a fixed effect model when there is extensive variation of effects across studies.

Random number table A table displaying hundreds of digits (from 0 to 9) in random order; each number is equally likely to follow any other.

Random sampling The selection of a sample such that each member of a population has an equal probability of being included.

Randomization The assignment of subjects to treatment conditions in a random manner (i.e., in a manner determined by chance alone); also called *random assignment*.

Randomized controlled trial (RCT) A full experimental test of an intervention, involving random assignment to treatment groups; often, an RCT is phase III of a full clinical trial.

Randomness An important concept in quantitative research, involving having certain features of the study established by chance rather than by design or personal preference.

Range A measure of variability, computed by subtracting the lowest value from the highest value in a distribution of scores.

Rating scale A scale that requires ratings of an object or concept along a continuum.

Ratio measurement A measurement level with equal distances between scores and a true meaningful zero point (e.g., weight).

Raw data Data in the form in which they were collected, without being coded or analyzed.

Reactivity A measurement distortion arising from the study participant's awareness of being observed, or, more generally, from the effect of the measurement procedure itself.

Readability The ease with which materials (e.g., a questionnaire) can be read by people with varying reading skills, often determined through readability formulas.

Reflexive notes Notes that document a qualitative researcher's personal experiences, reflections, and progress in the field.

Reflexivity In qualitative studies, critical self-reflection about one's own biases, preferences, and preconceptions.

Regression analysis A statistical procedure for predicting values of a dependent variable based on one or more independent variables.

Relationship A bond or a connection between two or more variables.

Relative risk (RR) An estimate of risk of "caseness" in one group compared to another, computed by dividing the absolute risk for one group (e.g., an exposed group) by the absolute risk for another (e.g., the nonexposed); also called the *risk ratio*.

Reliability The degree to which a measurement is free from measurement error--its accuracy and consistency.

Reliability coefficient A quantitative index, usually ranging in value from .00 to 1.00, that provides an estimate of how reliable an instrument is (e.g., Cronbach's alpha).

Repeated-measures ANOVA An analysis of variance used when there are multiple measurements of the dependent variable over time.

Replication The deliberate repetition of research procedures in a second investigation for the purpose of determining if earlier results can be confirmed.

Representative sample A sample whose characteristics are comparable to those of the population from which it is drawn.

Research Systematic inquiry that uses orderly methods to answer questions or solve problems.

Research control See *control*.

Research design The overall plan for addressing a research question, including strategies for enhancing the study's integrity.

Research hypothesis The actual hypothesis a researcher wishes to test (as opposed to the *null hypothesis*), stating the anticipated relationship between two or more variables.

Research methods The techniques used to structure a study and to gather and analyze information in a systematic fashion.

Research misconduct Fabrication, falsification, plagiarism, or other practices that deviate from those that are commonly accepted within the scientific community for conducting or reporting research.

Research problem A disturbing or perplexing condition that can be investigated through disciplined inquiry.

Research question A specific query the researcher wants to answer to address a research problem.

Research report A document (often a journal article) summarizing the main features of a study, including the research question, the methods used to address it, the findings, and the interpretation of the findings.

Research utilization The use of some aspect of a study in an application unrelated to the original research.

Researcher credibility The faith that can be put in a researcher, based on his or her training, qualifications, and experiences.

Respondent In a self-report study, the person responding to questions posed by the researcher.

Response rate The rate of participation in a study, calculated by dividing the number of persons participating by the number of persons sampled.

Response set bias The measurement error resulting from the tendency of some individuals to respond to items in characteristic ways (e.g., always agreeing), independently of item content.

Results The answers to research questions, obtained through an analysis of the collected data.

Retrospective design A study design that begins with the manifestation of the outcome variable in the present (e.g., lung cancer), followed by a search for a presumed cause occurring in the past (e.g., cigarette smoking).

Risk–benefit ratio The relative costs and benefits, to an individual subject and to society at large, of participation in a study; also, the relative costs and benefits of implementing an innovation.

Risk ratio *See* Relative risk

Rival hypothesis An alternative explanation, competing with the researcher's hypothesis, for interpreting the results of a study.

ROC curve *See* Receiver operating characteristic curve

S

Sample The subset of a population selected to participate in a study.

Sampling The process of selecting a portion of the population to represent the entire population.

Sampling bias Distortions that arise when a sample is not representative of the population from which it was drawn.

Sampling distribution A theoretical distribution of a statistic, using the values of the statistic computed from an infinite number of samples as the data points in the distribution.

Sampling error The fluctuation of the value of a statistic from one sample to another drawn from the same population.

Sampling frame A list of all the elements in the population, from which a sample is drawn.

Sampling plan The formal plan specifying a sampling method, a sample size, and procedures for recruiting subjects.

Saturation The collection of qualitative data to the point where a sense of closure is attained because new data yield redundant information.

Scale A composite measure of an attribute, involving the combination of several items that have a logical and empirical relationship to each other, resulting in the assignment of a score to place people on a continuum with respect to the attribute.

Scientific method A set of orderly, systematic, controlled procedures for acquiring dependable, empirical—and typically quantitative—information; the methodologic approach associated with the positivist paradigm.

Scientific merit The degree to which a study is methodologically and conceptually sound.

Screening instrument An instrument used to determine whether potential subjects for a study meet eligibility criteria, or for determining whether a person tests positive for a specified condition.

Secondary analysis A form of research in which the data collected in one study are reanalyzed in another investigation to answer new questions.

Secondary source Second-hand accounts of events or facts; in research, a description of a study prepared by someone other than the original researcher.

Selection threat (self-selection) A threat to a study's internal validity resulting from preexisting differences between groups under study; the differences affect the dependent variable in ways extraneous to the effect of the independent variable.

Selective coding A level of coding in a grounded theory study that involves selecting the core category, systematically integrating relationships between the core category and other categories, and validating those relationships.

Self-determination A person's ability to voluntarily decide whether or not to participate in a study.

Self-report A data collection method that involves a direct verbal report by a person being studied (e.g., by interview or questionnaire).

Semistructured interview An open-ended interview in which the researcher is guided by a list of specific topics to cover.

Sensitivity The ability of a screening instrument to correctly identify a "case," i.e., to correctly diagnose a condition.

Sensitivity analysis An effort to test how sensitive the results of a statistical analysis are to changes in assumptions or in the way the analysis was done (e.g., in a meta-analysis, used to assess whether conclusions are sensitive to the quality of the studies included).

Sequential design A mixed methods design in which one strand of data collection (qualitative or quantitative) occurs prior to the other, informing the second strand; symbolically shown with an arrow, as QUAL → QUAN.

Setting The physical location and conditions in which data collection takes place in a study.

Significance level The probability that an observed relationship could be caused by chance; significance at the 0.5 level indicates the probability that a relationship of the observed magnitude would be found by chance only 5 times out of 100.

Simple random sampling Basic probability sampling involving the selection of sample members from a sampling frame through completely random procedures.

Site The overall location where a study is undertaken.

Skewed distribution The asymmetric distribution of a set of data values around a central point.

Snowball sampling The selection of participants through referrals from earlier participants; also called *network sampling*.

Social desirability response set A bias in self-report instruments created when participants have a tendency to misrepresent their opinions in the direction of answers consistent with prevailing social norms.

Space triangulation The collection of data on the same phenomenon in multiple sites, to enhance the validity of the findings.

Spearman's rank-order correlation (Spearman's rho) A correlation coefficient indicating the magnitude of a relationship between variables measured on the ordinal scale.

Specificity The ability of a screening instrument to correctly identify noncases.

Standard deviation The most frequently used statistic for measuring the degree of variability in a set of scores.

Standard error The standard deviation of a sampling distribution, such as the sampling distribution of the mean.

Standardized mean difference (SMD) In meta-analysis, the effect size for comparing two group means, computed by subtracting one mean from the other and dividing by the pooled standard deviation; also called Cohen's *d*.

Statement of purpose A declarative statement of the overall goals of a study.

Statistic An estimate of a parameter, calculated from sample data.

Statistical analysis The organization and analysis of quantitative data using statistical procedures, including both descriptive and inferential statistics.

Statistical conclusion validity The degree to which inferences about relationships and differences from a statistical analysis of the data are accurate.

Statistical control The use of statistical procedures to control confounding influences on the dependent variable.

Statistical heterogeneity Diversity of effects across primary studies included in a meta-analysis.

Statistical inference The process of inferring attributes about the population based on information from a sample, using laws of probability.

Statistical power The ability of the research design and analytic strategy to detect true relationships among variables.

Statistical significance A term indicating that the results from an analysis of sample data are unlikely to have been caused by chance, at a specified level of probability.

Statistical test An analytic tool that estimates the probability that obtained results from a sample reflect true population values.

Stipend A monetary payment to individuals participating in a study to serve as an incentive for participation and/or to compensate for time and expenses.

Strata Subdivisions of the population according to some characteristic (e.g., males and females); singular is *stratum*.

Stratified random sampling The random selection of study participants from two or more strata of the population independently.

Structured data collection An approach to collecting data from participants, either through self-report or observations, in which categories of information (e.g., response options) are specified in advance.

Study participant An individual who participates and provides information in a study.

Subject An individual who participates and provides data in a study; term used primarily in quantitative research.

Summated rating scale A scale consisting of multiple items that are added together to yield an overall, continuous measure of an attribute (e.g., a Likert scale).

Survey research Nonexperimental research that obtains information about people's activities, beliefs, preferences, and attitudes via direct questioning.

Symmetric distribution A distribution of values with two halves that are mirror images of each other.

Systematic review A rigorous synthesis of research findings on a particular research question, using systematic sampling and data collection procedures and a formal protocol.

Systematic sampling The selection of sample members such that every *kth* (e.g., every 10th) person or element in a sampling frame is chosen.

T

Tacit knowledge Information about a culture that is so deeply embedded that members do not talk about it or may not even be consciously aware of it.

Target population The entire population in which a researcher is interested and to which he or she would like to generalize the study results.

Taxonomy In an ethnographic analysis, a system of classifying and organizing terms and concepts, developed to illuminate a domain's organization and the relationship among the domain's categories.

Test statistic A statistic used to test for the reliability of relationships between variables (e.g., chi-squared, *t*); sampling distributions of test statistics are known for circumstances in which the null hypothesis is true.

Test–retest reliability Assessment of the stability of an instrument by correlating the scores obtained on two administrations.

Theme A recurring regularity emerging from an analysis of qualitative data.

Theoretical sampling In qualitative studies, the selection of sample members based on emerging findings to ensure saturation of important theoretical categories.

Theory An abstract generalization that presents a systematic explanation about relationships among phenomena.

Thick description A rich, thorough description of the context and participants in a qualitative study.

Time sampling In structured observations, the sampling of time periods during which observations will take place.

Time series design A quasi-experimental design involving the collection of data over an extended time period, with multiple data collection points both prior to and after an intervention.

Time triangulation The collection of data on the same phenomenon or about the same people at different points in time, to enhance validity.

Topic guide A list of broad question areas to be covered in a semistructured interview or focus group interview.

Transferability The extent to which qualitative findings can be transferred to other settings or groups; analogous to generalizability.

Treatment The experimental intervention under study; the condition being manipulated.

Treatment group The group receiving the intervention being tested; the experimental group.

Triangulation The use of multiple methods to collect and interpret data about a phenomenon, so as to converge on an accurate representation of reality.

Triangulation design A concurrent, equal-priority mixed methods design in which different, but complementary data, qualitative and quantitative, are gathered about a central phenomenon under study; symbolized as QUAL + QUAN; also called a convergent parallel design.

True score A hypothetical score that would be obtained if a measure were infallible.

Trustworthiness The degree of confidence qualitative researchers have in their data and analyses, assessed using the criteria of credibility, transferability, dependability, confirmability, and authenticity.

***t*-test** A parametric statistical test for analyzing the difference between two group means.

Type I error An error created by rejecting the null hypothesis when it is true (i.e., the researcher concludes that a relationship exists when in fact it does not—a false positive).

Type II error An error created by accepting the null hypothesis when it is false (i.e., the researcher concludes that *no* relationship exists when in fact it does—a false negative).

U

Unimodal distribution A distribution of values with one peak (high frequency).

Unit of analysis The basic unit or focus of a researcher's analysis—typically individual study participants.

Univariate statistics Statistical analysis of a single variable for descriptive purposes (e.g., computing a mean).

Unstructured interview An interview in which the researcher asks respondents questions without having a predetermined plan regarding the content or flow of information to be gathered.

Unstructured observation The collection of descriptive data through direct observation that is not guided by a formal, prespecified plan for observing or recording the information.

V

Validity A quality criterion referring to the degree to which inferences made in a study are accurate and well-founded; in measurement, the degree to which an instrument measures what it is intended to measure.

Variability The degree to which values on a set of scores are dispersed.

Variable An attribute that varies, that is, takes on different values (e.g., body temperature, heart rate).

Variance A measure of variability or dispersion, equal to the standard deviation squared.

Vignette A brief description of an event, person, or situation to which respondents are asked to express their reactions.

Visual analog scale (VAS) A scaling procedure used to measure certain clinical symptoms (e.g., pain, fatigue) by having people indicate on a straight line the intensity of the symptom.

Vulnerable groups Special groups of people whose rights in studies need special protection because of their inability to provide meaningful informed consent or because their circumstances place them at higher-than-average-risk of adverse effects (e.g., children, unconscious patients).

W

Wait-list design An experimental design that involves putting control group members on a waiting list for the intervention; also called a *delayed treatment design.*

Web-based survey The administration of a self-administered questionnaire over the Internet on a dedicated survey website.

Applied Nursing Research 20 (2007) 17–23

Original article

The relationships among anxiety, anger, and blood pressure in children

Carol C. Howell, PhD, APRN-BC[a,*], Marti H. Rice, PhD, RN[b], Myra Carmon, EdD, RN, CPNP[a], Roxanne Pickett Hauber, PhD, CNRN[c]

[a]*Byrdine F. Lewis School of Nursing, Georgia State University, PO Box 4019, Atlanta, Georgia 30302-4019, USA*
[b]*School of Nursing, University of Alabama at Birmingham, Birmingham, Alabama 35294-1210, USA*
[c]*Department of Nursing, University of Tampa, Tampa, FL 33615, USA*

Received 15 July 2005; accepted 23 October 2005

Abstract Relationships between anger and anxiety have been examined in adults but less frequently in children. This investigation explored relationships among trait anxiety, trait anger, anger expression patterns, and blood pressure in children. The participants were 264 third- through sixth-grade children from five elementary schools who completed Jacob's Pediatric Anger and Anxiety Scale and Jacob's Pediatric Anger Expression Scale and had their blood pressure measured. Data were analyzed using descriptive and correlational statistics and hierarchical regression. Results have implications for the way in which anxiety and anger are perceived in children and the importance of teaching children to deal with emotions.

1. Introduction

Hypertension affects over 50 million Americans aged 6 and over and is a recognized risk factor for the development of cardiovascular disease (American Heart Association, 2004). Although few children have hypertension or cardiovascular disease, biological and psychosocial risk factors for the development of hypertension in adulthood are estimated to be present in children by the age of 8 (Solomon & Matthews, 1999). With the large number of individuals with hypertension and the progressive nature of cardiovascular disease, it is important to identify and modify risk factors early in life. Although some risk factors are not modifiable, others, such as anger and anxiety, are more amenable to change. The identification and modification of risk factors at an early age might reduce the incidence of hypertension in adulthood (Ewart & Kolodner 1994; Hauber, Rice, Howell, & Carmon, 1998; Meininger, Liehr, Chan, Smith, & Mueller, 2004).

* Corresponding author. Tel.: +1 404 651 3645 (home); +1 404 255 5453; fax: +1 404 255 1086.
E-mail addresses: chowell@gsu.edu (C.C. Howell), schauf@uab.edu (M.H. Rice), mcarmon@gsu.edu (M. Carmon), rhauber@ut.edu (R.P. Hauber).

0897-1897/$ – see front matter © 2007 Elsevier Inc. All rights reserved.
doi:10.1016/j.apnr.2005.10.006

2. Review of the literature

Trait anger (Johnson, 1989, 1990; Siegel, 1984), patterns of anger expression (Johnson, 1989; Muller, Grunbaum, & Labarthe, 2001; Seigel, 1984), and trait anxiety (Ewert & Kolodner, 1994; Johnson, 1989; Meininger et al., 2004) are psychological factors that have been associated with high blood pressure in adolescents. Biological factors such as sex, height, and weight have also been significantly associated with high blood pressure (Johnson, 1984, 1989; Meininger et al., 2004; Muller et al., 2001). Although the contribution of these factors to the development of hypertension has been investigated in adults and adolescents (Ewart & Kolodner, 1994; Harburg, Gkeuberman, Russell, & Cooper, 1991; Meininger et al., 2004), much less research has been done with children (Hauber et al., 1998). It is the intent of this study to investigate relationships among psychosocial factors, biological factors, and blood pressure in children.

2.1. Psychosocial factors

2.1.1. Trait anger

Trait anger is defined as an emotion that can vary from mild displeasure to rage and reflects a more permanent characteristic than state anger (Speilberger et al., 1985). Anger is thought to lead to an increase in blood pressure through its effect on the sympathetic nervous system (Meininger et al., 2004; Muller et al., 2001; Taylor, Repetti, & Seeman, 1997; Williams & Williams, 1993). Repeated episodes of anger arousal may lead to a chronic state of elevated blood pressure or hypertension (Muller et al., 2001; Williams & Williams, 1993). Researchers have noted an association between anger scores and blood pressure (Hauber et al., 1998; Johnson, 1989, 1990; Siegel, 1984; Siegel & Leitch, 1981).

2.1.2. Anger expression patterns

Anger expression patterns include anger out, which implies that anger is openly expressed. Anger suppression or anger in implies that the anger is denied and held in. Anger reflection control involves a cognitive approach to resolving anger (Speilberger et al., 1985).

Siegel (1984) found that subjects who had higher scores on the Frequent Anger Directed Outward factor also had higher systolic (SBP) and diastolic blood pressure (DBP). In contrast, Johnson (1984, 1989) found significant positive correlations between anger suppression and high blood pressures in male and female adolescents. In one of the few studies with children, Hauber et al. (1998), in a study of 230 third-grade children, found significant inverse relationships between anger suppression and DBP and anger reflection/control for both SBP and DBP. Muller et al. (2001) found that anger expression predicted blood pressure in 167 14-year-olds or after controlling ethnicity, height, weight, percent body fat, and maturity. However, the instrument used in this study did not differentiate between anger in and anger out.

2.1.3. Trait anxiety

Trait anxiety is defined as a subjective feeling of apprehension, tension, and worry, which is thought to be a relatively stable personality characteristic (Speilberger, Edwards, Lushene, Montuori, & Platzek, 1973). Jonas, Franks, and Ingram (1997) suggested that anxiety contributes to the development of hypertension in two ways. Anxiety has been shown to directly stimulate acute autonomic arousal (Russek, King, Russek, & Russek, 1990) and blood pressure reactivity (Krantz & Manuck, 1984; Suls & Wan, 1993; Waked & Jutai, 1990). Responding to stress- or anxiety-provoking experiences with anger has been shown to contribute to cardiovascular disease (Chang, Ford, Meoni, Wang & Klag, 2002; Wascher, 2002). The presence of anxiety has been associated with high-risk health behaviors such as smoking, drinking, low levels of physical activity, and noncompliance with prescribed medical treatments, which in turn have been associated with elevations in blood pressure (Jonas et al., 1997). In addition, Heker, Whalen, Jamner, and Delfino (2002) found that high-anxiety teenagers expressed higher levels of anger when compared with low-anxiety teenagers.

2.2. Biological factors

2.2.1. Gender

Research with children and adolescents has shown a differential association between anger, anger expression, and blood pressure when gender is considered (Hauber et al., 1998; Johnson, 1984, 1989; Muller et al., 2001; Weinrich et al., 2000). In a study with third graders, Hauber et al. (1998) identified a positive correlation between anger reflection/control and SBP in female third graders. In male third graders, however, there was a positive correlation between anger reflection/control and DBP. Starner and Peters (2004) found a significant correlation between anger in and SBP and between anger out and SBP.

2.2.2. Height and weight

Among the factors known to influence blood pressure in children are height and weight. Normative tables published by the National Heart, Lung, and Blood Institute (1996) (Task Force Report of High Blood Pressure in Children and Adolescents) list blood pressure standards based on height, weight, and sex in order to include body size to more accurately classify blood pressure norms. However, a more recent report no longer used weight as a factor for calculating normal blood pressure (National High Blood Pressure Education Program Working Group on High Blood Pressure in Children and Adolescents, 2004). However, the increasing occurrence of hypertension in children has been linked to the increase in weight (Couch & Daniels, 2005; Davis et al., 2005; Wyllie, 2005). Overall, the literature supports height and weight as factors that affect blood pressure (Couch & Daniels, 2005; Markovitz, Matthews, Wing, Kuller, & Meilahn, 1991, Muller et al., 2001; Muller, Wiechmann, Helms, Wulff, & Kolenda, 2000).

3. Purpose

The purpose of this study was to determine the relationships between trait anxiety, trait anger, height, weight, patterns of anger expression, and blood pressure in a group of elementary school children.

4. Research questions

Specific research questions addressed were as follows:

1. What are the bivariate relationships between SBP and DBP and height, weight, and sex, trait anger and patterns of anger expression, and trait anxiety in elementary school children?
2. What is the contribution of height, weight, trait anger, anger expression patterns, and trait anxiety to SBP and DBP in elementary school boys and girls?

5. Method

5.1. Design

A descriptive correlational design was used in this study.

5.2. Sample and setting

A convenience sample of 264 children was recruited from the third through the sixth grades in five public elementary schools serving kindergarten through sixth grade in a large metropolitan city in the southeastern United States. These schools served communities of varying socioeconomic levels in urban and suburban locations.

5.3. Instruments

5.3.1. Trait anger

Trait anger was measured by the Trait Anger subscale of the Jacobs Pediatric Anger Scale (Jacobs & Blumer, 1984) (PANG Forms PPS-1 and PPS-2). The PANG is a 10-item self-report inventory developed for use with children. Reliability coefficients for the PANG range from .77 to .84 (Jacobs & Mehlhaff, 1994). A more recent study found the reliability to be .89 (M. Rice, personal communication, November 2004). Items included in the scale are in a Likert format with responses of 1, *hardly ever*; 2, *sometimes*; and 3, *often*. Scores on the PANG range from 10 to 30 and the higher the score, the greater the trait anger.

5.3.2. Anger expression

The 15-item Jacobs Pediatric Anger Expression Scale (PAES) (Jacobs, Phelps, & Rohrs, 1989) was used to measure patterns of anger expression. The instrument contains three scales that have five items each and measure anger-out, anger suppression, and anger reflection/control. Each item is in the form of declarative statements with choices for responses of 1 for *hardly ever*, 2 for *sometimes*, and 3 for *often*. Possible scores for each scale range from 5 to 15. Alpha coefficients for the entire PAES ranged from .57 to .79 (Jacobs et al., 1989). Coefficients for anger out ranged from .66 to .78, for anger suppression from .57 to .76, and for the anger reflection/control scale from .36 to .62 (Jacobs & Mehlhaff, 1994). A more recent study found reliability measure of internal consistency for anger out to be .85, for anger suppression to be .76, and for anger reflection/control to be .70 (M. Rice, personal communication, November 2004).

5.3.3. Trait anxiety

Measurement of trait anxiety was accomplished through use of the Jacob's Pediatric Anxiety Scale (PANX) (Jacobs & Blumer, 1984), a 10-item self-report inventory designed for use with young children. Item to total correlations range from .37 to .53 with an alpha reliability score of .78 for the total scale. A Likert format with three responses was used with a 1 for *hardly ever*, 2 for *sometimes*, and 3 for *often*. Scale scores are calculated by summing the responses on all items so that scores can range from 10 to 30. The higher the score the greater the anxiety. Alpha coefficients on the scale range from .77 to .84 (Jacobs & Mehlhaff, 1994). A more recent study found the reliability to be .80 (M. Rice, personal communication, November 2004).

5.3.4. Blood pressure

The Hawksley's Random Zero sphygmomanometer (W. A. Braum Company Inc., Copiagne, NY), a conventional mercury sphygmomanometer with calibrations 0 to 300 mmHg, was used to obtain blood pressure. This sphygmomanometer is designed to eliminate error variance due to operator and technique by using a shifting zero device. This allows random halting of the mercury between 0 and 20 mmHg so that the operator cannot automatically assume a value. Mercury values must be subtracted from both systolic and diastolic readings to obtain correct blood pressure. The researchers for the study reported here were trained to use the Hawksley. Independent blood pressures on the same participant were taken until a 100% agreement rate was achieved in order to assure interrater reliability. The suggested protocol for measurement of children, including choice of correct cuff size and use of the first reading for nondiagnostic purposes, was followed (National Heart, Lung, and Blood Institute, 1996). Because blood pressure readings were not obtained for the purpose of diagnosing hypertension but for determining the relationships of blood pressure to anger and anxiety scores, only one blood pressure reading was obtained.

5.3.5. Height and weight

Height and weight were measured by a balanced beam scale and the height rod of the balanced beam scale, respectively.

5.4. Procedures

The human assurance committee of the university and the research committee of the county school district approved the proposal. A letter explaining the project and requesting consent for the child to participate was sent home to each child's legally designated caregiver 1 month prior to data collection at each school. On the day of data collection, children with returned completed forms were requested to sign assent forms. The assent form was read aloud to the children before they were requested to sign the form. After assent forms were signed by the children, the PANG, PAES, and the PANX instruments were administered. All instruments were administered by the same investigator. Directions were read aloud, and then the children responded.

Every child read and completed the scales independently. Special effort was taken to stress to the children that this was not a test and that there were no "right" or "wrong" answers. When the scales were completed, the children walked to an adjoining room where a blood pressure reading was obtained for each child.

6. Results

6.1. Sample characteristics

Of the 264 participants enrolled in the study who indicated gender and ethnicity, 107 were boys, 155 were girls; 189 were Black, 58 were White, and 17 were other ethnicities.

6.2. Scale scores

Table 1 shows scores on the study variables for the entire group and then separately for girls and boys. Boys had

Table 1
Scale scores

Variable	Total		Boys		Girls	
	M	*SD*	*M*	*SD*	*M*	*SD*
Trait anxiety	18.66	4.16	18.13	4.23	19.0	4.11
Trait anger	17.87	4.84	18.72	4.74	17.34	4.84
Anger out	9.00	2.61	9.50	2.62	8.69	2.57
Anger suppression	9.28	2.27	9.30	2.23	9.29	2.31
Anger reflection	9.98	2.42	9.55	2.22	10.32	2.47
Systolic BP	102.58	10.96	104.66	11.03	101.16	10.75
Diastolic BP	63.28	9.83	64.30	8.72	62.55	10.50

higher mean anger scores but lower mean anxiety scores than the girls. The girl participants had higher SBP and DBP readings, lower anger out, lower anger suppression, and higher anger reflection/control scores than the boys.

6.3. Research Question 1: bivariate correlations

Pearson's product–moment correlations were done in order to address Research Question 1. Table 2 shows correlation results for the children as a group and then separately for boys and girls. For the group as a whole, significant although weak correlations were found between anger reflection/control scores and DBP. Significant and moderately strong correlations were found between height and weight and both SBP and DBP. In addition, there was a significant inverse correlation between height and anger/reflection control scores. Moderate to strong correlations between height and weight and both SBP and DBP were noted for boys and girls.

When correlation analyses were restricted to boys and then girls, different results were obtained. Significant although weak correlations were noted in the boys between DBP and trait anger. A moderate significant correlation was noted between weight and DBP, and a significant although weak correlation was noted between height and DBP in the boys. When girls were considered, a significant although weak negative correlation was found between DBP and anger reflection/control scores.

6.4. Research Question 2: hierarchical multiple regression

In order to answer Research Question 2, six separate hierarchical regression analyses were performed. Two regressions were tested with the entire group, for SBP and DBP in turn, followed by two regressions restricted to sample boys and sample girls, again for SBP then DBP. The variables of height, weight, and sex were entered first as a block as these variables were correlated with blood pressure in this study. The next block included the variables of trait anger, anger out, anger reflection control, and anger suppression because links between blood pressure and anger have been widely documented. The anxiety variable was entered last. When SBP was the dependent variable, 24% of the variance was accounted for in the entire group. Only the first block contributed significantly ($p < .001$; $F = 22.58$).

When DBP was the dependent variable, sex, height, and weight together accounted for 12.4% of the variance ($F = 10.21$; $p < .001$). Only the first block contributed significantly to the model.

6.4.1. Gender

In the next two multiple regression equations, the contribution of study variables to SBP and DBP was restricted to the boys in the study group. Thirty percent of the variance in SBP was accounted for by height and weight ($F = 18.05$; $p < .001$). Height and weight also accounted for 8% of the variance in DBP in the boys ($F = 3.90$; $p < .001$). In the last two multiple regression equations, the contribution of study variables to SBP and DBP was restricted to the girls in the study group. Here, the first block, sex, height, and weight, accounted for 18% of the variance in SBP ($F = 14.53$; $p < .001$). Neither the anger variables nor the anxiety variable that was added in the next block contributed significantly to the model. Height and

Table 2
Correlation table for the entire group, boys, and girls

Variable	Trait anger	Anger out	Anger suppression	Anger reflection	Trait anxiety	Height	Weight
SBP							
Entire group	−.02	−.04	−.04	−.08	−.07	.30***	.46***
Boys	−.04	−.03	−.14	−.13	−.02	.45***	.57***
Girls	−.00	−.06	−.04	−.20*	−.13	.27**	.45***
DPB							
Entire group	−.06	−.07	−.04	−.12*	−.04	.21**	.34***
Boys	−.19*	.08	−.07	−.07	−.04	.20	.27**
Girls	−.04	.07	−.10	−.19	−.05	.24**	.37***

* $p \leq .05$.
** $p \leq .01$.
*** $p \leq .001$.

weight accounted for 13% of the variance in DBP (F = 10.09; $p < .001$). Again, neither anger nor anxiety variables made significant contributions to the model.

7. Discussion

In this study, support was found for the relationships of some of the identified psychosocial and biological factors and blood pressure in children. Children in the group as a whole who indicated more use of anger reflection/control had lower DBP readings. This is consistent with earlier research reporting an association between anger reflection/control and lower blood pressures in adults and children (Harburg, Blakelock, Roeper, 1979; Harburg et al., 1991; Hauber et al., 1998; Muller et al., 2001).

There were no significant relationships between trait anxiety and blood pressure. Much of the research linking anxiety to blood pressure has been conducted with adult samples. Anxiety is thought to contribute to hypertension through repeated autonomic arousal (Jonas et al., 1997; Russek et al., 1990), blood pressure reactivity (Suls & Wan, 1993; Waked & Jutai, 1990), or through the association of anxiety and high-risk health behaviors. The findings in the current study are consistent with the work of Johnson (1989) who found that anxiety was not a predictor of blood pressure in a group of older adolescents. Perhaps the young participants in the current study, as well as Johnson's study, had not yet experienced the long-term negative effects of anxiety on blood pressure.

In this study, height and weight were significantly correlated with SBP and DBP for the entire group. In boys, height and weight were significantly correlated with SBP but not with DBP. In girls, height and weight were significantly correlated with both SBP and DBP. As noted earlier, this relationship is widely acknowledged. Blood pressure has been found to vary with the height, weight, sex, age, and fitness of an individual (Task Force Report of High Blood Pressure in Children and Adolescents, National Heart, Lung, & Blood Institute, 1996). Although weight is no longer used as a factor for calculating normal blood pressure (National High Blood Pressure Education Program Working Group on High Blood Pressure in Children and Adolescents, 2004), the results of this research strongly suggest a relationship.

A bivariate correlation between height and anger reflection control was found in this study. This implies that the taller the individual, the less anger reflection control is used. Perhaps taller children feel less inhibited about expressing their anger in more aggressive ways because their size protects them somewhat from reprisal.

Boys had significant correlations between trait anger scores and DBP. Similar findings have been reported between trait anger and higher blood pressure in both adolescents and adults (Markovitz et al., 1991; Siegel & Leitch, 1981). Girls in the present study showed negative correlations between both SBP and DBP and anger reflection/control. Similar findings were obtained in an earlier study with children (Hauber et al., 1998) where an inverse relationship was noted between anger reflection/control and SBP in girls. These findings suggest the importance of gender-specific research in the area of hypertension and cardiovascular disease. In her study of gender and gender-role identity and expression of anger, Thomas (1997) found that gender was an important factor in anger expression. She suggested that masculine sex-role identity was associated with being more anger prone, expressing anger in an outward manner, and being less likely to control anger expression. Female sex role types were less likely to express anger outwardly or to suppress anger and more likely to attempt anger control. Fabes and Eisenberg (1992) found that female preschoolers vented their anger less than their male counterparts. Fuchs and Thelen (1988) suggested that girls were socialized to hide their anger where boys were taught to hide their sadness or any other feeling such as anxiety that could be interpreted as a sign of weakness. Perhaps, even at this young age, anger reflection is a less acceptable choice for males and does not translate into lower blood pressure in male children in this sample. It may be that no particular expression pattern is associated with blood pressure with boys, although the characteristic of trait anger is related.

In the regression models, neither trait anxiety nor any of the other anger expression patterns accounted for any of the variance in blood pressure. Muller et al. (2001) also found that anger variables did not account for any of the variance in blood pressure in a group of 167 adolescents. In their longitudinal study with 541 normotensive middle-aged women, Raikkonen, Matthews, and Kuller (2001) found that baseline levels of anxiety and anger did not predict subsequent hypertension. However, in the 75 women who became hypertensive during this 9-year study, increases in anger and anxiety during follow-up significantly predicted the incidence of hypertension.

When separate analyses were done for boys and girls after controlling for height and weight, no additional variance in SBP or DBP was explained by trait anger, patterns of anger expression, or trait anxiety. These findings were similar to those of Johnson (1990), who identified no overall relationship between anger variables and SBP.

Although neither the anger variables nor anxiety contributed significantly to the regression model in this study, it should be recognized that factors considered in this study are thought to influence blood pressure in adulthood and are risk factors in children for the future development of hypertension. As children with these risk factors move into adulthood, they may develop hypertension due to repeated episodes of anger and anxiety, which continually stimulate the sympathetic–adrenal–medullary system. The end result is damage to cardiovascular health (Muller et al., 2001). It is important to know that these risk factors, if identified as early as childhood, can be modified before hypertension develops (Meininger et al., 2004; Solomon & Matthews, 1999).

8. Limitations

Blood pressure readings and anger instruments were administered only once per subject. Multiple measurements could provide a pattern of blood pressure, and tracking participants for a longer period could aid in the identification of patterns across developmental periods.

9. Implications and recommendations

Because anger and anxiety are associated with hypertension in adults, a longitudinal study would help identify when anger and anxiety begin to contribute to the explanation of hypertension.

Current results indicate that anger reflection/control patterns are associated with lower levels of blood pressure in girls of this age. This finding is consistent with results of an earlier study with 230 third-grade boys and girls (Hauber et al., 1998) and suggests that children may benefit from anger management interventions aimed at anger control strategies. Identification of factors that influence a child's choice of anger expression patterns, the effect on blood pressure, and the contributions of gender would be helpful when designing intervention programs. The school nurse could be involved in identifying and recommending interventions for children who have frequent anger problems in the classroom or whose parents report frequent angry outbursts in the home environment.

Future research should investigate whether these findings remain consistent across younger age groups, different socioeconomic groups, varying regions of the country, and more varied ethnic groups (Rice & Howell, 2006).

This study supports the belief that certain modifiable risk factors for hypertension are present at an early age. It has been recommended that BP should be monitored by the age of 3 for every child during every scheduled physical examination (National High Blood Pressure Education Program Working Group on High Blood Pressure in Children and Adolescents, 2004). It is important to monitor BP across a period of time to determine any elevations or pattern of BP (Cook, Gillman, Rosner, Taylor, & Hennekens, 2000). This type of assessment is most often performed by a nurse (Hauber et al., 1998). According to Moran, Panzarino, Darden, and Reigart (2003) although the rate of BP screening during well-child checkups has increased, it does not meet current recommendations. If the BP reading is normal (less than 90th percentile for sex, age, and height) it should be rechecked at the next scheduled physical exam and the nurse should encourage adequate sleep and an active lifestyle with healthy meals. A prehypertensive reading is the 90th percentile to less than the 95th percentile. This reading should be rechecked in 6 months. In this instance the nurse should counsel the parents and the child about active lifestyle and diet changes and weight reduction if the child is overweight (National High Blood Pressure Education Program Working Group on High Blood Pressure in Children and Adolescents, 2004). If hypertensive (95th–99th percentile with the addition of 5 mmHg) the reading should be checked again on at least two occasions, usually within a few weeks to confirm the diagnosis of hypertension (National High Blood Pressure Education Program Working Group on High Blood Pressure in Children and Adolescents, 2004).

The nurse may also be the first health care professional to recognize unhealthy patterns of anger and anger expression. The nurse may be able to teach healthier means of expressing anger, such as anger reflection control, physical activity, or cognitive behavioral interventions (Rice & Howell, 2006). It is important to intervene in unhealthy lifestyles early rather than later when the disease becomes evident (Meininger et al., 2004; Solomon & Matthews, 1999). Lifestyle changes are more easily accomplished at early ages before behavior patterns become ingrained. If risk factors for cardiovascular disease are reduced early enough, cardiovascular disease will be delayed or avoided altogether. Early anger management training for children holds promise for preventing the translation of anger into medical and behavioral problems.

Acknowledgment

This research was supported by grants from the College of Health Sciences, Georgia State University, Atlanta, Georgia.

References

American Heart Association. (2004). Statistical supplement. Retrieved August 10, 2004, from http://www.americanheart.org.

Chang, P., Ford, D., Meoni, L., Wang, N., & Klag, M. (2002, Apr). Anger in young men and subsequent premature cardiovascular disease. *Archives of Internal Medicine, 162*(8), 901–906.

Cook, N., Gillman, M., Rosner, B., Taylor, J., & Hennekens, C. (2000). Combining annual blood pressure measurements in childhood to improve prediction of young adult blood pressure. *Statistics in Medicine, 19*(19), 2625–2640.

Couch, S., & Daniels, S. (2005). Diet and blood pressure in children. *Current Opinions in Pediatrics, 17*(5), 642–647.

Davis, C., Flickinger, B., Moore, D., Bassali, R., Domel Baxter, S., & Yin, Z. (2005, Aug). Prevalence of cardiovascular risk factors in schoolchildren in a rural Georgia community. *American Journal of Medicine and Science, 330*(2), 53–59.

Ewart, C., & Kolodner, K. (1994). Negative affect, gender and expressive style predict elevated ambulatory blood pressure in adolescents. *Journal of Personality and Social Psychology, 66*(3), 596–605.

Fabes, R., & Eisenberg, N. (1992). Young children's coping with interpersonal anger. *Child Development, 63*, 116–128.

Fuchs, D., & Thelen, M. (1988). Children's expected interpersonal consequences of communicating their affective state and reported likelihood of expression. *Childhood Development, 59*, 1314–1322.

Harburg, E., Blakelock, E., & Roeper, P. (1979). Resentful and reflective coping with arbitrary authority and blood pressure: Detroit. *Psychosomatic Medicine, 41*, 189–202.

Harburg, E., Gleiberman, L., Russell, M., & Cooper, M. (1991). Anger-coping styles and blood pressure in Black and White males: Buffalo, New York. *Psychosomatic Medicine, 41*, 189–202.

Hauber, R., Rice, M., Howell, C., & Carmon, M. (1998). Anger and blood pressure readings in children. *Psychosomatic Medicine, 11*(1), 2–11.

Heker, B., Whalen, C., Jamner, L., & Delfino, R. (2002, June). Anxiety, affect, and activity teenagers: Monitoring daily life with electronic diaries. *Journal of American Academy of Child and Adolescent Psychiatry, 41*(6), 660–670.

Jacobs, G., & Blumer, C. (1984). *The pediatric anger scale*. Vermillion: University of South Dakota, Department of Psychology.

Jacobs, G., & Mehlhaff, C. (1994). *Children's stress and the expression and experience and experience of anger.* Unpublished manuscript, University of South Dakota, Vermillion.

Jacobs, G., Phelps, M., & Rhors, B. (1989). Assessment of anger in children: The pediatric anger scale. *Personality and Individual Differences, 10*, 59–65.

Johnson, E. (1984). *Anger and anxiety as determinants of elevated blood pressure in adolescents: The Tampa study.* Unpublished doctoral dissertation, University of South Florida, Tampa.

Johnson, E. (1989). The role of the experience and expression of anger and anxiety in elevated blood pressure among black and white adolescents. *Journal of the National Medical Association, 81*(5), 573–584.

Johnson, E. (1990). Interrelationships between psychological factors, overweight, and blood pressure in adolescents. *Journal of Adolescent Healthcare, 11*, 310–318.

Jonas, B., Franks, P., & Ingram, D. (1997). Are symptoms of anxiety and depression risk factors for hypertension? *Archives of Family Medicine, 6*, 43–49.

Krantz, D., & Manuck, S. (1984). Acute psychophysiologic reactivity and risk of cardiovascular disease: A review and methodological critique. *Psychological Bulletin, 96*, 535–564.

Markovitz, J. H., Matthews, K., Wing, R. R., Kuller, L. H., & Meilahn, E. N. (1991). Psychological, biological and health behavior predictors of blood pressure changes in middle-aged women. *Journal of Hypertension, 9*, 399–406.

Meinginger, J., Liehr, P., Chan, W., Smith, G., & Muller, W. (2004). Developmental, gender, and ethic group differences in moods and ambulatory blood pressure in adolescents. *Annals of Behavioral Medicine, 28*(1), 10–19.

Moran, C., Panzarino, V., Darden, P., & Reigart, J. (2003). Preventive services: Blood pressure checks at well child visits. *Clinical Pediatrics, 42*(7), 627–634.

Muller, W., Grunbaum, J., & Labarthe, D. (2001, Jul–Aug). Anger expression, body fat, and blood pressure in adolescents: Project HeartBeat. *American Journal of Human Biology, 13*(4), 531–538.

Muller, M., Wiechmann, M., Helms, C., Wulff, C., & Kolenda, K. (2000, May). Nutrient intake with low-fat diets in rehabilitation of patients with coronary heart disease. *Zeitschrift fur Kardiologie, 89*(5), 454–464.

National Heart, Lung, and Blood Institute. National Institutes of Health. (1996). *Update on the task force report on high blood pressure in children and adolescents: A working group report from the National High Blood Pressure Education Program (SDHSS Publication No. NIH 96-3790)*. Washington, DC: U.S. Government Printing Office. Children and Adolescents.

National High Blood Pressure Education Program Working Group on High Blood Pressure in Children and Adolescents. (2004). The fourth report on the diagnosis, evaluation, and treatment of high blood pressure in children and adolescents. *Pediatrics, 114*(2), 555–576.

Raikkonen, K., Matthews, K., & Kuller, L. (2001). Trajectory of psychological risk and incident of hypertension in middle-aged women. *Hypertension, 38*(4), 798–802.

Rice, M., & Howell, C. (2006). Differences in trait anger among children with varying levels of anger expression patterns. *Journal of Child and Adolescent Psychiatric Nursing, 19*(2), 51–61.

Russek, L., King, S., Russek, S., & Russek, H. (1990). The Harvard Mastery of Stress Study 35-year follow-up: Prognostic significance of patterns of psychophysiological arousal and adaptation. *Psychosomatic Medicine. 52*, 271–285.

Siegel, J. (1984). Anger and cardiovascular risk in adolescents. *Health Psychology, 3*, 293–313.

Siegel, J., & Leitch, C. (1981). Behavioral factors and blood pressure in adolescence: The Tacoma study. *American Journal of Epidemiology, 113*, 171–181.

Solomon, K., Matthews, K. (1999, March). *Paper presented at the American Psychosomatic Society Annual Meeting*. Vancouver, British Columbia, Canada.

Speilberger, C., Edwards, C., Lushene, R., Montuori, J., & Platzek, D. (1973). *State-trait anxiety inventory for children*. Palo Alto, CA: Consulting Psychologists Press.

Speilberger, C., Johnson, E., Russell, S., Crane, R., Jacobs, G., & Worden, T. (1985). The experience and expression of anger: Construction and validation of an anger expression scale. In M. Chesney, R. Rosenman, (Eds.), *Anger and hostility in cardiovascular and behavioral disorders* (pp. 5–30). Washington, DC: Hemisphere.

Starner, T., & Peters, R. (2004). Anger expression and blood pressure in adolescents. *Journal of School Nursing, 20*(6), 335–342.

Suls, J., & Wan, C. (1993). The relationship between trait hostility and cardiovascular reactivity: A quantitative review and analysis. *Psychophysiology, 30*, 615–626 http://www.nhlbi.nih.gov/meetings/ish/stamler.htm.

Taylor, S., Repetti, R., & Seeman, T. (1997). Health psychology: What is an unhealthy environment and how does it get under the skin? *Annual Review of Psychology, 48*, 411–447.

Thomas, S. (1997). Women's anger: Relationship of suppression to blood pressure. *Nursing Research, 46*(6), 324–330.

Waked, E., & Jutai, J. (1990). Baseline and reactivity measures of blood pressure and negative affect in borderline hypertension. *Physiological Behavior, 47*, 266–271.

Wascher, R. (2002, April). Stay at home dads and risk of cardiovascular disease. *Jewish World Review* 2002, April.

Weinrich, S., Weinrich, M., Hardin, S., Gleaton, J., Pesut, D., & Garrison, C. (2000). Effects of psychological distress on blood pressure in adolescents. *Holistic Nurse Practitioner, 5*(1), 57–65.

Williams, R., & Williams, V. (1993). *Anger kills*. New York: Harper Collins Publishers.

Wyllie, R. (2005). Obesity in childhood: An overview. *Current Opinions Pediatrics, 17*(5), 632–635.

Nursing Research • July/August 2010 • Vol 59, No 4, 241–249

Subsequent Childbirth After a Previous Traumatic Birth

Cheryl Tatano Beck ▾ Sue Watson

▶ ***Background:*** Nine percent of new mothers in the United States who participated in the Listening to Mothers II Postpartum Survey screened positive for meeting the *Diagnostic and Statistical Manual of Mental Disorders, Fourth Edition* criteria for posttraumatic stress disorder after childbirth. Women who have had a traumatic birth experience report fewer subsequent children and a longer length of time before their second baby. Childbirth-related posttraumatic stress disorder impacts couples' physical relationship, communication, conflict, emotions, and bonding with their children.

▶ ***Objective:*** The purpose of this study was to describe the meaning of women's experiences of a subsequent childbirth after a previous traumatic birth.

▶ ***Methods:*** Phenomenology was the research design used. An international sample of 35 women participated in this Internet study. Women were asked, "Please describe in as much detail as you can remember your subsequent pregnancy, labor, and delivery following your previous traumatic birth." Colaizzi's phenomenological data analysis approach was used to analyze the stories of the 35 women.

▶ ***Results:*** Data analysis yielded four themes: (a) riding the turbulent wave of panic during pregnancy; (b) strategizing: attempts to reclaim their body and complete the journey to motherhood; (c) bringing reverence to the birthing process and empowering women; and (d) still elusive: the longed-for healing birth experience.

▶ ***Discussion:*** Subsequent childbirth after a previous birth trauma has the potential to either heal or retraumatize women. During pregnancy, women need permission and encouragement to grieve their prior traumatic births to help remove the burden of their invisible pain.

▶ ***Key Words:*** phenomenology · posttraumatic stress disorder (PTSD) · subsequent childbirth · traumatic childbirth

In the United States, 9% of new mothers who participated in the Listening to Mothers II Postpartum Follow-Up Survey screened positive for meeting the *Diagnostic and Statistical Manual of Mental Disorders, Fourth Edition* (American Psychiatric Association, 2000) criteria for posttraumatic stress disorder (PTSD) after childbirth (Declercq, Sakala, Corry, & Applebaum, 2008). In this survey, the mothers' voices revealed a troubling pattern of maternity care. A large percentage of women giving birth in the United States experienced hospital care that did not reflect the best evidence for practice nor for women's preferences. The Institute of Medicine (2003) identified childbirth as a national healthcare priority for quality improvement. A maternity care quality chasm still exists (Sakala & Corry, 2007).

Researchers and healthcare professionals at an international meeting on current issues regarding PTSD after childbirth recommended the need for research focusing on women's subjective birth experiences (Ayers, Joseph, McKenzie-McHarg, Slade, & Wijma, 2008). Olde, van der Hart, Kleber, and van Son (2006) called for examining the chronic nature of childbirth-related posttraumatic stress lasting longer than 6 months after birth.

The purpose of the current study was to help fill the knowledge gap of one aspect of the chronicity of birth trauma: women's subjective experiences of the subsequent pregnancy, labor, and delivery after a traumatic childbirth.

Review of Literature

Traumatic childbirth is defined as "an event occurring during the labor and delivery process that involves actual or threatened serious injury or death to the mother or her infant. The birthing woman experiences intense fear, helplessness, loss of control, and horror" (Beck, 2004a, p. 28). For some women, a traumatic birth also involves perceiving their birthing experience as dehumanizing and stripping them of their dignity (Beck, 2004a, 2004b, 2006). After a traumatic childbirth, 2% to 21% of women meet the diagnostic criteria for PTSD (Ayers, 2004; Ayers, Harris, Sawyer, Parfitt, & Ford, 2009), involving the development of three characteristic symptoms stemming from the exposure to the trauma: persistent reexperiencing of the traumatic event, persistent avoiding of reminders of the trauma and a numbing of general responsiveness, and persistent increased arousal (American Psychiatric Association, 2000).

Risk Factors

Risk factors contributing to women perceiving their childbirth as traumatic can be divided into three categories: prenatal factors, nature and circumstances of the delivery,

Cheryl Tatano Beck, DNSc, CNM, FAAN, *is Distinguished Professor, School of Nursing, University of Connecticut, Storrs.*

Sue Watson, *is Chairperson, Trauma and Birth Stress, Auckland, New Zealand.*

and subjective factors during childbirth (van Son, Verkerk, van der Hart, Komproe, & Pop, 2005). Under the prenatal category are factors such as histories of previous traumatic births, prenatal PTSD (Onoye, Goebert, Morland, Matsu, & Wright, 2009), child sexual abuse, and psychiatric counseling. Factors included in the category of nature and circumstances of the delivery include a high level of medical intervention, extremely painful labor and delivery, and delivery type (Ayers et al., 2009). Subjective risk factors during childbirth can include feelings of powerlessness, lack of caring and support from labor and delivery staff, and fear of dying (Thomson & Downe, 2008).

> ***A large percentage of women giving birth in the United States experienced hospital care that did not reflect the best evidence for practice nor for women's preferences.***

Long-Term Impact of Traumatic Childbirth

Researchers are uncovering an unsettling gamut of long-term detrimental effects of traumatic childbirth not only on the mothers themselves but also on their relationships with infants and other family members. Mothers' breastfeeding experiences and the yearly anniversary of their birth trauma can also be negatively impacted.

Impaired mother–infant relationships after traumatic childbirth are being confirmed in the literature. For example, in the study of Ayers, Wright, and Wells (2007) of mothers who experienced birth trauma in the United Kingdom, women described themselves as feeling detached and having feelings of rejection toward their infants. Nicholls and Ayers (2007) reported two different types of mother–infant bonding in couples who shared that PTSD after childbirth affected their relationships with their children; they became anxious/overprotective or avoidant/rejecting. Childbirth-related PTSD also impacted their relationships with their partners, including their physical relationship, communication, conflict, emotions, support, and coping.

Long-term detrimental effects of traumatic childbirth can extend also into women's breastfeeding experiences. In their Internet study, Beck and Watson (2008) explored the impact of birth trauma on the breastfeeding experiences of 52 mothers. For some mothers, their traumatic childbirth led to distressing impediments that curtailed their breastfeeding attempts, such as feeling that their breasts were just one more thing to be violated.

Another aspect of the chronic effect of birth trauma was identified in Beck's (2006) Internet study of the anniversary of traumatic childbirth, an invisible phenomenon that mothers struggled with. Thirty-seven women comprised this international sample of mothers from the United States, New Zealand, Australia, United Kingdom, and Canada. Beck concluded that a failure to rescue occurred for women as the anniversary approached, and all others focused on the celebration of the children's birthdays. This failure to rescue led to unnecessary emotional or physical suffering or both.

Catherall (1998) warned of secondary trauma in families living with trauma survivors. The entire family is vulnerable to becoming secondarily traumatized. The long-term impact of trauma does not result necessarily in PTSD symptoms in family members. Catherall stated that it can have a more insidious effect of a disturbing milieu in the family. The members of the family may be close physically, but their ability to express emotions is limited. True closeness in the family is missing, and their problem solving is impaired. Abrams (1999) identified one of the central clinical characteristics of intergenerational transmission of trauma is the silence that happens in families regarding traumatic experiences. Abrams pleaded that the multigenerational impact of trauma should not be underestimated.

Posttraumatic Growth

Researchers are reporting that traumatic experiences can have positive benefits in a person's life. Posttraumatic growth has been documented in a wide range of people who faced traumatic experiences such as bereaved parents (Engelkemeyer & Marwit, 2008), human immunodeficiency virus caregivers (Cadell, 2007), and homeless women with histories of traumatic experiences (Stump & Smith, 2008). "Posttraumatic growth describes the experience of individuals whose development, at least in some areas, has surpassed what was present before the struggle with the crisis occurred. The individual has not only survived, but has experienced changes that are viewed as important, and that go beyond what was the previous status quo" (Tedeschi & Calhoun, 2004, p. 4). It is not the actual trauma that is responsible for posttraumatic growth but what happens after the trauma. Tedeschi and Calhoun (2004, p. 6) proposed five domains of posttraumatic growth: "greater appreciation of life and changed sense of priorities; warmer, more intimate relationships with others; a greater sense of personal strength; recognition of new possibilities or paths for one's life; and spiritual development."

Childbirth can have an enormous potential to help change how a woman feels about herself and can impact her transition to motherhood (Levy, 2006). Attias and Goodwin (1999, p. 299) noted that a woman who survives a traumatic experience may be able to rebuild her wounded inner self "by having a child, transforming her body from a container of ashes to a container for a new human life." A positive childbirth has the potential to empower a traumatized woman and help her reclaim her life.

One study was located that touched on the positive growth of women after a previous negative birthing experience. In Cheyney's (2008) qualitative study of women in the United States who chose home births after experiencing a negative birth, three integrated conceptual themes emerged from their home birth narratives: knowledge, power, and intimacy. The power of their home births helped heal scars of their past hospital births. Positive growth after birth trauma has yet to be investigated systematically by researchers.

One of the knowledge gaps identified in this literature review focused on an aspect of the long-term effects of birth trauma: mothers' subsequent childbirth. This phenomenological study was designed to answer the research question:

What is the meaning of women's experiences of a subsequent childbirth following a previous traumatic birth?

Methods

Research Design

The term *phenomenology* is derived from the Greek word *phenomenon*, which means "to show itself." The goal of phenomenology is to describe human experiences as they are experienced consciously without theories about their cause and as free as possible from the researchers' unexamined presuppositions about the phenomenon under study. In phenomenology, researchers "borrow" other individuals' experiences to better understand the deeper meaning of the phenomenon (Van Manen, 1984).

The existential phenomenological method developed by Colaizzi (1973, 1978) was used in this Internet study. His method is designed to uncover the fundamental structure of a phenomenon, that is, the essence of an experience. An assumption of phenomenology is that for any phenomenon, there are essential structures that comprise that human experience. Only by examining specific experiences of the phenomenon being studied can their essential structures be uncovered.

Colaizzi's (1973, 1978) method includes features of Husserl's and Heidegger's philosophies. Colaizzi maintains that description is the key to discovering the essence and the meaning of a phenomenon and that phenomenology is presuppositionless (Husserl, 1954). Colaizzi, however, holds a Heideggerian view of reduction, the process of researchers bracketing presuppositions and their natural attitude about the phenomenon being studied. For Colaizzi (1978, p. 58), researchers identify their presuppositions regarding the phenomenon under study not to bracket them off to the side but instead to use them to "interrogate" one's "beliefs, hypotheses, attitudes, and hunches" about the phenomenon to help formulate research questions. Colaizzi agrees with Merleau-Ponty (1956, p. 64) that "the greatest lesson of reduction is the impossibility of a complete reduction." Individual phenomenological reflection about the phenomenon being studied is one approach Colaizzi (1973) offers for assisting researchers to decrease the coloring of their presuppositions and biases on their research activity.

Because the phenomenon of subsequent childbirth after a previous traumatic birth had not been examined systematically before this current study, description of the meaning of women's experiences was the focus of this study. Before the start of the study, the researchers undertook an individual phenomenological reflection. They questioned themselves regarding their presuppositions about the phenomenon of subsequent childbirth after a traumatic birth and how these might influence what and how they conducted their research.

Sample

Thirty-five women participated in the study (Table 1). Saturation of data was achieved easily with this sample size. Their mean age was 33 years (range = 27 to 51 years). All the participants were Caucasian and had two to four children. The length of time since their previous birth trauma to the subsequent birth ranged from 1 to 13 years. Eight of the 35 women (23%) opted for a home birth for their subsequent births. Of these 8 mothers who gave birth at home, 4 lived in Australia, 3 in the United States, and 1 in the United Kingdom. Fourteen mothers (40%) had been diagnosed with PTSD after childbirth.

TABLE 1. Demographic and Obstetric Characteristics

	n	%
Country		
United States	15	43
United Kingdom	8	23
New Zealand	6	17
Australia	5	14
Canada	1	3
Marital status		
Married	34	98
Divorced	1	2
Single	0	0
Education		
High school	3	9
Some college	5	15
College degree	13	38
Graduate	7	19
Missing	7	19
Delivery		
Vaginal	25	72
Cesarean	10	29
Diagnosed PTSD		
Yes	14	40
No	19	55
Missing	2	5
Currently under care of therapist		
Yes	8	23
No	22	63
Missing	5	15

Note. PTSD = posttraumatic stress disorder.

All the birth traumas were self-defined. Women were not asked if they had experienced other traumas before their birth traumas. Therefore, this was not an exclusionary criterion. The most frequently identified traumatic births focused on emergency cesarean deliveries, postpartum hemorrhage, severe preeclampsia, preterm labor, high level of medical interventions (i.e., forceps, vacuum extraction, induction), infant in the neonatal intensive care unit, feeling violated, lack or respectful treatment, unsympathetic, nonsupportive labor and delivery staff, and "emotional torture."

Procedure

Once institutional review board approval was obtained from the university, recruitment began. Data collection continued for 2 years and 2 months. Women were recruited by means of a notice placed on the Web site of Trauma and Birth Stress (TABS; www.tabs.org.nz), a charitable trust located in New Zealand. The mission of TABS is to support women who have experienced traumatic childbirth and PTSD because of their birth trauma. The sample criteria required that the mother had experienced a traumatic childbirth with a previous labor and delivery, that she was willing to articulate her experience, and that she could read and write English. This international representation of participants was a strength of this recruitment method. A disadvantage, however, was that only women who had access to the Internet and who used TABS for support participated in this study.

Women who were interested in participating in this Internet study contacted the first author at her university e-mail address, which was listed on the recruitment notice. An information sheet and directions for the study were sent by attachment to interested mothers. After reading these two documents, women could e-mail the researcher if they had any questions concerning the study.

Women were asked, "Please describe in as much detail as you can remember your subsequent pregnancy, labor, and delivery following your previous traumatic birth." Women sent their descriptions of their experiences as e-mail attachments to the researcher. The sending of their story implied their informed consent. The length of time varied from when a mother first e-mailed about her interest in the study to when she sent her completed story to the researchers. The shortest turnaround time was 2 days whereas the longest was 9 months. If women did not respond within a certain period, the researchers did not recontact them. The women's wish not to follow through on participation in the study was respected. Throughout this procedure, the first author kept a reflexive journal.

Data Analysis

Colaizzi's (1978) method of data analysis was used. The order of his steps is as follows: written protocols, significant statements, formulated meanings, clusters of themes, exhaustive description, and fundamental structure. It should be noted, however, that these steps do overlap. From each participant's description of the phenomenon, significant statements, which are phrases or sentences that directly describe the phenomenon, are extracted (Table 2). For each significant statement, the researcher formulates its meaning. Here, creative insight is called into play. Colaizzi cautioned that in this step of data analysis, the researcher must take a precarious leap from what the participants said to what they mean. Formulated meanings should never sever all connections from the original transcripts. It is in this step of formulating meanings that Colaizzi's connection to Heidegger can be seen. The next step entails organizing all the formulated meanings into clusters of themes. At this point, all the results to date are combined into an exhaustive description. This step is followed by revising the exhaustive description into a more condensed statement of the identification of the fundamental structure of the phenomenon being studied. The fundamental structure can be shared with the participants to validate how well it captured aspects of their experiences. If any participants share new data, they are integrated into the final description of the phenomenon. Member checking was done with one participant who reviewed the themes and

TABLE 2. Example of Extracting Significant Statements

No.	Significant statements
1	One thing that I'd noticed when I was a child was that when my parents got together with other adults, the talk eventually turned to two things: for my father (a Vietnam veteran) and the other men the talk turned to the war and interestingly, to me as a small child, for my mother and the other women the talk always turned to childbirth.
2	It was as if, from a young age, for me, the connections between the two were drawn. A man is tested through war, a women is tested through childbirth.
3	My dad, as abusive as he was, was considered a "good man" because he'd been a good soldier and so, I reasoned forward with a child's intelligence, that all that really mattered for a woman was to be strong and capable in childbirth.
4	And I failed. In the past, with the previous two births (particularly with the one that resulted in PTSD)—that's what it felt like. I failed at being a woman.
5	I don't think that I am alone in feeling. I have a sneaking suspicion that this is pretty universal.
6	Just as a man who "talks" under torture in a POW situation feels as though he's failed, a woman who can't "handle" tortuous situations during childbirth feels like she's failed. It is not true. But it feels true.
7	My dad received two Purple Hearts and a Bronze Star during Vietnam. He, by most standards, would be considered a hero. Where are my Purple Hearts? My Bronze Star? I've fought a war, no less terrifying, no less destroying but there are no accolades. At least that's what it feels like.
8	I am viewed as flawed if not down right strange that I find L & D so terrifying.
9	The medical establishment thinks that I am "mental" and I have no common ground on which to discuss my childbirth experiences with "normal" women.
10	I know, I've tried. And that makes me feel isolated and inferior.

Note. PTSD = posttraumatic stress disorder.

totally agreed with them. In addition, one mother who had not participated in the study but had experienced the phenomenon being studied reviewed the findings and also agreed with them.

Results

The researchers reflected on the written descriptions provided by the 35 women to explicate the phenomenon of their experiences of subsequent childbirth after a previous traumatic birth. These reflections yielded 274 significant statements that were clustered into four themes and finally into the fundamental structure that identified the essence of this phenomenon (Table 3).

Theme 1: Riding the Turbulent Wave of Panic During Pregnancy

Fear, terror, anxiety, panic, dread, and denial were the most frequent terms used to describe the world women lived in during their pregnancy after a previous traumatic birth.

> I remember the exact moment I realized what was happening. I was on my lunch break at work, sitting under a large oak tree, watching cars go by my office, talking with my husband. I suddenly knew... I am pregnant again! I remember the exact angle of the sun, the shading of the objects around me. I remember looking into the sun, at that tree, at the windows to the office thinking, "NO! God PLEASE NO!" I felt my chest at once sink inward on me and take on the weight of a 1000 bricks. I was short of breath, my head seared. All I could think of was "NOOOOOOOOO!"

Another woman described in detail the day she took her pregnancy test.

> I took the test and crumpled over the edge of our bed, sobbing and retching hysterically for hours. I was dizzy. I was nauseous. I was sick. I could not breathe. I thought my chest would implode. I had a terrible migraine. I could not move from the spot where I had crumpled. I could not talk to my husband or see our daughter. I felt torn to pieces, shredded as shards of glass. I spent the next 2 trimesters hanging on for my life with suicidal thoughts but no real desire to carry them out through. I wanted to see my little girl. It was hell on earth.

Some women went into denial during the first trimester of their pregnancy to cope. Throughout her pregnancy, one woman revealed that she "felt numb to my baby." Some women described how they turned their denial of pregnancy into something positive. One multipara explained that after she was in denial for a few months, she then became determined to make things different this next time, and right at the end of her pregnancy she felt empowered by all that she had learned: "After 3 months of ignoring the fact that I was going to have to go through birth again, I decided I would treat my next labor and delivery as a healing and empowering experience."

Other mothers remained in a heightened state of anxiety throughout their pregnancy, and for some this anxiety escalated to panic and terror. Knowing she may have to go through the same "emotional torture" she endured with her previous traumatic birth, one woman shared, "My 9 months of pregnancy were an anxiety filled abyss which was completely marred as an experience due to the terror that was continually in my mind from my experience 8 years earlier." As the delivery date got closer, some mothers reported having panic attacks.

Theme 2: Strategizing: Attempts to Reclaim Their Body and Complete the Journey to Motherhood

"Well, this time; I told myself *things would be different.* I actually started planning for this birth literally while they were stitching me up from the traumatic first birth." During pregnancy women described a number of different strategies they used to help them survive the 9 months of pregnancy while waiting for what they were dreading: labor and delivery (Table 4). Some women spent time nurturing themselves by swimming, walking, going to yoga classes, and spending time outdoors.

Keeping a journal throughout the pregnancy helped mothers because they had somewhere to write things down, especially if they felt that family and friends did not understand just how difficult this pregnancy, subsequent to their prior traumatic delivery, was. Inspirational quotes were placed around the house to read and motivate women.

TABLE 3. Fundamental Structure of the Phenomenon

Subsequent childbirth after a previous traumatic birth far exceeds the confines of the actual labor and delivery. During the 9 months of pregnancy, women ride turbulent waves of panic, terror, and fear that the looming birth could be a repeat of the emotional and/or physical torture they had endured with their previous labor and delivery. Women strategized during pregnancy how they could reclaim their bodies that had been violated and traumatized by their previous childbirth. Women vowed to themselves that things would be different and that this time they would complete their journey to motherhood. Mothers employed strategies to try to bring a reverence to the birthing process and rectify all that had gone so wrong with their prior childbirth. The array of various strategies entailed such actions as hiring doulas for support during labor and delivery, becoming avid readers of childbirth books, writing a detailed birth plan, learning birth hypnosis, interviewing obstetricians and midwives about their philosophy of birth, doing yoga, and drawing birthing art. All these well-designed strategies did not ensure that all women would experience the healing childbirth they desperately longed for. For the mothers whose subsequent childbirth was a healing experience, they reclaimed their bodies, had a strong sense of control, and their birth became an empowering experience. The role of caring supporters was crucial in their labor and delivery. Women were treated with respect, dignity, and compassion. Although their subsequent birth was positive and empowering, women were quick to note that it could never change the past. Still elusive for some women was their longed-for healing subsequent birth.

TABLE 4. Strategies Used to Cope With Pregnancy and Looming Labor and Delivery

- Writing a detailed birth plan
- Mentally preparing for birth
- Learning birth hypnosis
- Doing birth art
- Writing positive affirmations
- Preparing for birthing at home
- Hiring a doula for labor and delivery
- Celebrating upcoming birth
- Avoiding ultrasounds
- Trying not to think about upcoming birth
- Reading books on healthy pregnancy and birth
- Mapping out your pelvis
- Learning birthing positions to open up the pelvis
- Practicing hypnosis for labor
- Researching birth centers and scheduling tours
- Interviewing obstetricians and midwives
- Exercising to help baby get in the correct position
- Using Internet support group
- Hiring a life coach
- Painting previous birth experience
- Creating "what if" sheet with all possible concerns and then solutions for them
- Creating "Yes, if necessary No" sheet for labor of what the mother wanted to happen
- Determining role of supporters during birth
- Researching homeopathic remedies to prepare body for labor and birth
- Developing a tool kit to help cope in labor
- Developing trust with healthcare provider

Figure 1 is an illustration of one mother's poster that she put up in her home.

Women strategized how to ensure that their looming labor and delivery was not another traumatic one. As one multipara explained, "I need to bring a reverence to the process so I won't feel like a piece of meat lost in the system." Attempts were made to put into place a plan that would attempt to rectify all that had gone wrong with the previous childbirth. Some women turned to doulas in hopes of being supported during their subsequent labor and delivery. Hypnobirthing was a plan used by some women to keep the first traumatic birth from being repeated.

Women reported reading avidly to understand the birth process fully. The most frequently cited books were *Rebounding from Childbirth* (Madsen, 1994), *Birthing from Within* (England & Horowitz, 1998), and *Birth and Beyond* (Gordon, 2002). Mothers often engaged in birth art exercises.

> Toward the end of pregnancy I did the birth art exercises out of the book *Birthing from Within*… I began to trust myself. That will stay with me forever. That is more than just what I needed to birth the way I wanted to. That is what I needed to become a real woman.

Opening up to their healthcare providers about their previous traumatic births was helpful for some mothers. Once clinicians knew of their history, they would address the mothers' concerns during each prenatal visit. Also sharing with their partners their fears and insecurities around pregnancy and birth helped women's emotional preparedness.

Theme 3: Bringing Reverence to the Birthing Process and Empowering Women

Three quarters of the women who participated in this Internet study reported that their subsequent labor and delivery was either a "healing experience" or at least "a lot better" than their previous traumatic birth. Women became more confident in themselves as women and as mothers in that they really did know what was best for their babies and themselves. The role of supporters throughout labor and delivery was crucial. What was it that made a subsequent birth a healing experience? In the mothers' own words:

> I was treated with respect, my wishes and those of my husband were listened to. I wasn't made to feel like a piece of meat this time but instead like a woman experiencing one of nature's most wonderful events.
>
> Pain relief was taken seriously. First time around I was ignored. I begged and pleaded for pain relief. Second time it was offered but because I was made to feel in control, I was able to decline.

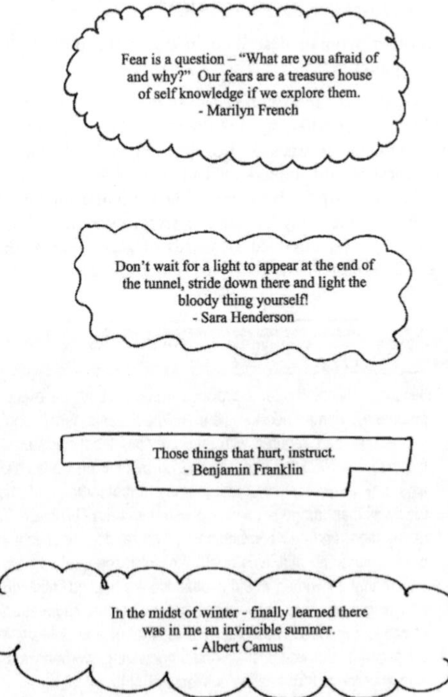

FIGURE 1. A poster of inspirational quotes by one mother.

I wasn't rushed! My baby was allowed to arrive when she was ready. When my first was born, I was told "5 minutes or I get the forceps" by the doctor on call. I pushed so hard that I tore badly.

Communication with labor and delivery staff was so much better the second time. The first time the emergency cord was pulled but no one told me why. I thought my baby was dead and no one would elaborate.

Women reclaimed their bodies, had a strong sense of control, and birth became an empowering experience. Only essential fetal monitoring and minimal medical intervention occurred. Women were allowed to start labor on their own and not be induced. Under gentle supervision of caring and supportive healthcare professionals, women were reassured to just do what their body felt like doing and to follow their body's lead. The number of vaginal examinations was kept at a minimum, and women were permitted to walk around and choose the position they felt best laboring in. One mother described her healing birth:

I pushed my baby into the world and I was shocked. I had never dared to dream for such a perfect delivery. They let me push spontaneously and my baby was delivered into my arms. My husband and I both cried with utter relief that I had given birth exactly how I wanted to and my trauma was healed.

For some women, the birth plan they had prepared during their pregnancy was honored by the labor and delivery staff, which helped them feel like they had some control and were a part of the birth and not just a witness.

Eight women opted for home births after their previous traumatic births, and for six of them, it did end in fulfilling their dream.

It was as healing and empowering as I had always hoped for. I did not want any high tech management. My home birth was the proudest day of my life and the victory was sweeter because I overcame so very much to come to it.

Another mother who had a successful home birth labored mostly in her bedroom under candlelight and music playing. She described it as very peaceful being at home surrounded by all her things. Her dog kept vigil by her side. She shared how it was such a gentle way for her baby to be born.

My baby cried for a minute or two as if telling me his birth story and crawled up my body and found my heart and left breast. My heart swelled with so many emotions—love, joy, happiness, pride, relief, and wonderment.

A couple of women explained that their subsequent birth was healing, but at the same time they mourned what they had missed out with their prior birth. The following quote illustrates this.

Even though it was an enormously healing experience, the expectations I had were unrealistic. What I went through during and after my first delivery cannot be erased from memory. If anything with this second birth being so wonderful, it makes dealing with my first birth harder. It makes it sadder and me angrier as before I had nothing to compare it to. I didn't know how different it could be or how special those first few moments are. I didn't fully understand what I had missed out on. So now 3 years later I find myself grieving again for what we went through, how I was treated and what I missed out on.

Other mothers admitted that although their subsequent births were healing, they could never change the past.

All the positive, empowering births in the world won't ever change what happened with my first baby and me. Our relationship is forever built around his birth experience. The second birth was so wonderful I would go through it all again, but it can never change the past.

Theme 4: Still Elusive: The Longed-for Healing Birth Experience

Sadly, some mothers did not experience the healing subsequent birth they had hoped for. Two women chose to try a home birth after their previous traumatic birth but did not end up with the healing experience they longed for. One mother did deliver at home, but because of postpartum hemorrhage, she was transported by ambulance to the hospital, terrified she would not live to raise her baby. After laboring at home, another multipara who attempted a vaginal birth after cesarean needed to be transported by ambulance for a repeat cesarean birth after she failed to progress.

When the ambulance arrived I felt rescued. I have never been so grateful that hospitals exist. The blue light ambulance journey was terrifying and I was in excruciating pain. By this point I was trying to detach my head from my body, as I had done years earlier when I was being raped.

She went on to vividly describe that as she lay on the operating table:

...with my legs held in the air by 2 strangers while a third mopped the blood between my legs I felt raped all over again. I wanted to die. I had failed as a woman. My privacy had been invaded again. I felt sick.

One multipara shared that although this birth had been a better experience, she would not say it was healing in relation to her first birth that had been so traumatic. "The contrast in the way I was treated just emphasized how bad the first one was. I had no sense of healing until 30 years later when I received counseling for PTSD."

Discussion

Healthcare professionals' failure to rescue women during their previous traumatic childbirth can result in a troubling effect on mothers as they courageously face another pregnancy, labor, and delivery. Subsequent childbirth after a previous birth trauma provides clinicians with not only a golden opportunity but also a professional responsibility to help these traumatized women reclaim their bodies and complete their journey to motherhood.

To help women prepare for a subsequent childbirth after a previous traumatic birth, clinicians first need to identify who these women are. There are instruments available to screen women for posttraumatic stress symptoms due to birth trauma. An essential part of initial prenatal visits should be taking time to discuss with women their previous births. Traumatized women need permission and encouragement to grieve their prior traumatic births to help remove the burden of their invisible pain. Pregnancy is a valuable time for healthcare professionals to help women recognize and deal with unresolved, buried, or traumatic issues. Women should be asked about their hopes and fears for their impending labor and delivery and how they envision this birth. If a woman is exploring the possibility of a home birth, clinicians should question the mother about her previous births. Opting for a home birth may be an indication of a prior traumatic birth (Cheyney, 2008). If women need mental health follow-up during their pregnancy, cognitive behavior therapy and eye movement desensitization reprocessing treatment are two options for PTSD because of birth trauma. Treatment can be given in conjunction with a woman's family members to address secondary effects of PTSD.

Strategies can be employed to help mothers heal and increase their confidence before labor and delivery. Clinicians can share with mothers the Web site for TABS (www.tabs.org.nz), a charitable trust in New Zealand that provides support for women who have suffered through a traumatic birth. Obstetric care providers can suggest to the women some of the numerous strategies that mothers in this study described using during their pregnancies. Women can be encouraged to write down their previous traumatic birth stories. Mothers can share their written stories with their current obstetric care providers so that they understand these women. Some women who participated in this study revealed that birthing artwork definitely helped them prepare for their subsequent labor and delivery after a traumatic childbirth.

Some women in this study touched on one of Tedeschi and Calhoun's (2004) domains of posttraumatic growth, a sense of personal growth. These women revealed feelings of empowerment and of reclaiming their bodies with their subsequent childbirths. Future research needs to be focused specifically on examining the five domains of posttraumatic growth in women who have experienced a subsequent childbirth after a previous birth trauma.

When women are traumatized during childbirth, this can leave a lasting imprint on their lives. If subsequent childbirth has the potential to either heal or retraumatize women, healthcare professionals need to be carefully aware of the consequences their words and actions during labor and delivery can have (Levy, 2006). ■

Accepted for publication January 27, 2010.

To all the courageous women who shared their most personal and powerful stories of their subsequent childbirth after a previous traumatic birth, the authors are forever indebted.

Corresponding author: Cheryl Tatano Beck, DNSc, CNM, FAAN, School of Nursing, University of Connecticut, 231 Glenbrook Road, Storrs, CT 06269-2026 (e-mail: cheryl.beck@uconn.edu).

References

Abrams, M. S. (1999). Intergenerational transmission of trauma: Recent contributions from the literature of family systems approaches to treatment. *American Journal of Psychotherapy, 53*(2), 225–231.

American Psychiatric Association. (2000). *Diagnostic and Statistical Manual of Mental Disorders—text revision.* Washington, DC: Author.

Attias, R., & Goodwin, J. M. (1999). A place to begin: Images of the body in transformation (pp. 287–303). In J. M. Goodwin & R. Attias (Eds.). *Splintered reflections.* New York: Basic Books.

Ayers, S. (2004). Delivery as a traumatic event: Prevalence, risk factors, and treatment for postnatal posttraumatic stress disorder. *Clinical Obstetrics and Gynecology, 47*(3), 552–567.

Ayers, S., Harris, R., Sawyer, A., Parfitt, Y., & Ford, E. (2009). Posttraumatic stress disorder after childbirth: Analysis of symptom presentation and sampling. *Journal of Affective Disorders, 119*(1–3), 200–204.

Ayers, S., Joseph, S., McKenzie-McHarg, K., Slade, P., & Wijma, K. (2008). Post-traumatic stress disorder following childbirth: Current issues and recommendations for future research. *Journal of Psychosomatic Obstetrics and Gynaecology, 29*(4), 240–250.

Ayers, S., Wright, D. B., & Wells, N. (2007). Symptoms of posttraumatic stress disorder in couples after birth: Association with the couple's relationship and parent-baby bond. *Journal of Reproductive and Infant Psychology, 25*(1), 40–50.

Beck, C. T. (2004a). Birth trauma: In the eye of the beholder. *Nursing Research, 53*(1), 28–35.

Beck, C. T. (2004b). Posttraumatic stress disorder due to childbirth: The aftermath. *Nursing Research, 53*(4), 216–224.

Beck, C. T. (2006). The anniversary of birth trauma: Failure to rescue. *Nursing Research, 55*(6), 381–390.

Beck, C. T., & Watson, S. (2008). Impact of birth trauma on breast-feeding: A tale of two pathways. *Nursing Research, 57*(4), 228–236.

Cadell, S. (2007). The sun always comes out after it rains: Understanding posttraumatic growth in HIV caregivers. *Health & Social Work, 32*(3), 169–176.

Catherall, D. R. (1998). Treating traumatized families. In C. R. Figley (Ed.). *Burnout in families: The systematic costs of caring* (pp. 187–215). Boca Raton, FL: CRC Press.

Cheyney, M. J. (2008). Homebirth as systems-challenging praxis: Knowledge, power, and intimacy in the birthplace. *Qualitative Health Research, 18*(2), 254–267.

Colaizzi, P. F. (1973). *Reflection and research in psychology: A phenomenological study of learning.* Dubuque, IA; Kendall/Hunt Publishing Company.

Colaizzi, P. F. (1978). Psychological research as the phenomenologist views it. In R. Valle & M. King (Eds.). *Existential phenomenological alternatives for psychology* (pp. 48–71). New York: Oxford University Press.

Declercq, E. R., Sakala, C., Corry, M. P., & Applebaum, S. (2008). *New mothers speak out: National survey results highlight women's postpartum experience.* New York: Childbirth Connection.

Engelkemeyer, S. M., & Marwit, S. J. (2008). Posttraumatic growth in bereaved parents. *Journal of Traumatic Stress, 21*(3), 344–346.

England, P., & Horowitz, R. (1998). *Birthing from within.* Alburquerque, NM: Partera Press.

Gordon, Y. (2002). *Birth and beyond.* London: Vermilion.

Husserl, E. (1954). *The crisis of European sciences and transcendental phenomenology.* The Hague: Martinus Nijhoff.

Institute of Medicine. (2003). *Board on Health Care Services Committee on identifying priority areas for quality improvements.* Washington, DC: National Academy Press.

Levy, M. (2006). Maternity in the wake of terrorism: Rebirth or retraumatization? *Journal of Prenatal and Perinatal Psychology and Health, 20*(3), 221–249.

Madsen, L. (1994). *Rebounding from childbirth: Toward emotional recovery.* Westport, CT: Bergin & Garvey.

Merleau-Ponty, M. (1956). What is phenomenology? *Crosscurrents,* 6, 59–70.

Nicholls, K., & Ayers, S. (2007). Childbirth-related post-traumatic stress disorder in couples: A qualitative study. *British Journal of Health Psychology, 12*(Pt. 4), 491–509.

Olde, E., van der Hart, O., Kleber, R., & van Son, M. (2006). Posttraumatic stress following childbirth: A review. *Clinical Psychology Review, 26*(1), 1–16.

Onoye, J. M., Goebert, D., Morland, L., Matsu, C., & Wright, T. (2009). PTSD and postpartum mental health in a sample of Caucasian, Asian, and Pacific Islander women. *Archives of Women's Mental Health, 12*(6), 393–400.

Sakala, C., & Corry, M. P. (2007). Listening to Mothers II reveals maternity care quality chasm. *Journal of Midwifery & Women's Health, 52*(3), 183–185.

Stump, M. J., & Smith, J. E. (2008). The relationship between posttraumatic growth and substance use in homeless women with histories of traumatic experience. *American Journal on Addictions, 17*(6), 478–487.

Tedeschi, R. G., & Calhoun, L. G. (2004). Posttraumatic growth: Conceptual foundations and empirical evidence. *Psychological Inquiry, 15*(1), 1–18.

Thomson, G., & Downe, S. (2008). Widening the trauma discourse: The link between childbirth and experiences of abuse. *Journal of Psychosomatic Obstetrics and Gynaecology, 29*(4), 268–273.

Van Manen, M. (1984). Practicing phenomenological writing. *Phenomenology + Pedagogy, 2*(1), 36–69.

Van Son, M., Verkerk, G., van der Hart, O., Komproe, I., & Pop, V. (2005). Prenatal depression, mode of delivery and perinatal dissociation as predictors of postpartum posttraumatic stress: An empirical study. *Clinical Psychology & Psychotherapy, 12*(4), 297–312.

C

Journal of Pain and Symptom Management, 2008, 36(20), 126–140

Original article

Randomized Controlled Trial of a Psychoeducation Program for the Self-Management of Chronic Cardiac Pain

Michael H. McGillion, RN, PhD, Judy Watt-Watson, RN, PhD, Bonnie Stevens, RN, PhD, Sandra M. LeFort, RN, PhD, Peter Coyte, PhD, and Anthony Graham, MD, FRCPC

Lawrence S. Bloomberg Faculty of Nursing (M.H.M., J.W.-W., B.S.) and Faculty of Medicine (B.S., P.C., A.G.), University of Toronto, Toronto; and School of Nursing (S.M.L.), Memorial University of Newfoundland, St. John's, Newfoundland, Canada

Abstract

Cardiac pain arising from chronic stable angina (CSA) is a cardinal symptom of coronary artery disease and has a major negative impact on health-related quality of life (HRQL), including pain, poor general health status, and inability to self-manage. Current secondary prevention approaches lack adequate scope to address CSA as a multidimensional ischemic and persistent pain problem. This trial evaluated the impact of a low-cost six-week angina psychoeducation program, entitled The Chronic Angina Self-Management Program (CASMP), on HRQL, self-efficacy, and resourcefulness to self-manage anginal pain. One hundred thirty participants were randomized to the CASMP or three-month wait-list usual care; 117 completed the study. Measures were taken at baseline and three months. General HRQL was measured using the Medical Outcomes Study 36-Item Short Form and the disease-specific Seattle Angina Questionnaire (SAQ). Self-efficacy and resourcefulness were measured using the Self-Efficacy Scale and the Self-Control Schedule, respectively. The mean age of participants was 68 years, 80% were male. Analysis of variance of change scores yielded significant improvements in treatment group physical functioning [$F = 11.75(1,114)$*,* $P < 0.001$*] and general health [*$F = 10.94(1,114)$*,* $P = 0.001$*] aspects of generic HRQL. Angina frequency [*$F = 5.57(1,115)$*,* $P = 0.02$*], angina stability [*$F = 7.37(1,115)$*,* $P = 0.001$*], and self-efficacy to manage disease [*$F = 8.45(1,115)$*,* $P = 0.004$*] were also significantly improved at three months. The CASMP did not impact resourcefulness. These data indicate that the CASMP was effective for improving physical functioning, general health, anginal pain symptoms, and self-efficacy to manage pain at three months and provide a basis for long-term evaluation of the program.*

This trial was made possible in part by a Canadian Institutes of Health Research Fellowship (No. 452939) and a University of Toronto Centre for the Study of Pain Clinician-Scientist Fellowship.

Portions of the CASMP first appeared in or are derived from the Chronic Disease Self-Management Program Leader's Master Trainer's Guide (1999). Those portions are Copyright 1999, Stanford University.

Address correspondence to: Michael Hugh McGillion, RN, PhD, Lawrence S. Bloomberg Faculty of Nursing, University of Toronto, 155 College Street, Suite 130, Toronto, Ontario M5T 1P8, Canada. E-mail: michael.mcgillion@utoronto.ca

Accepted for publication: September 26, 2007.

0885-3924/08/$–see front matter
doi:10.1016/j.jpainsymman.2007.09.015

Key Words
Chronic stable angina, self-management, randomized controlled trial, health-related quality of life

Introduction

Cardiac pain arising from chronic stable angina (CSA) pectoris is a cardinal symptom of coronary artery disease (CAD), characterized by pain or discomfort in the chest, shoulder, back, arm, or jaw.[1] CSA is a wide-spread clinical problem with a well-documented, major negative impact on health-related quality of life (HRQL), including pain, poor general health status, impaired role functioning, activity restriction, and reduced ability for self-care.[2–14] Limitations in current surveillance systems worldwide have precluded the examination of CSA prevalence in most countries. Available prevalence data estimate CSA prevalence at 6,500,000 (1999–2002) in the United States,[1] and 28/1000 men and 25/1000 women (April 2001–March 2002) in Scotland.[15] With the growing global burden of angina and CAD, nongovernmental organizations in Canada, the United States, and the United Kingdom have stressed the need for developments in secondary prevention strategies.[1,16,17] Current secondary prevention models largely target postacute cardiac event and/or coronary artery bypass patients and, depending on region, can be inaccessible to those with chronic symptoms.[18,19] Consequently, the vast majority of those with CSA and other CAD-related symptoms must manage on their own in the community. Moreover, these models focus predominantly on conventional CAD risk-factor modification to enhance myocardial conditioning and reduce ischemic threshold. However, cumulative basic science and clinical evidence point to the variability of cardiac pain perception for CSA patients, wherein pain can occur in the absence of myocardial ischemia, and conversely, ischemic episodes can be painless.[20–32] Given few alternatives, CSA patients revisit their local emergency departments when uncertain about how to manage their pain.[33,34] There is a critical need for a secondary prevention strategy with adequate scope and complexity to address CSA as a multidimensional ischemic and persistent pain problem, and to help CSA patients learn pain self-management strategies.[33]

Evidence from well-designed randomized controlled trials has demonstrated the effectiveness of psychoeducation for improving the self-management skills, HRQL, self-efficacy, and/or resourcefulness of persons with other chronic pains including arthritis and chronic noncancer pain.[35–37] Psychoeducation interventions are multimodal, self-help treatment packages that use information and cognitive-behavioral strategies to achieve changes in knowledge and behavior for effective disease self-management.[38] To date, the effectiveness of psychoeducation for enhancing CSA self-management is inconclusive.[39] Although a few small trials over the last decade have demonstrated positive effects to some degree related to pain frequency, nitrate use, and stress,[40–43] numerous methodological problems, particularly inadequate power and the lack of a standard intervention approach, have precluded the generalization of findings.[39] Moreover, more recent and robust psychoeducation trial research has been limited to patients with newly diagnosed angina.[44] Therefore, the purpose of this study was to evaluate the effectiveness of a standardized psychoeducation program, entitled the Chronic Angina Self-Management Program (CASMP), for improving the HRQL, self-efficacy, and resourcefulness of CSA patients.

Methods

Study Design

This study was a randomized controlled trial. On completion of demographic and baseline measures, participants were randomly allocated to either 1) the six-week CASMP group or 2) the three-month wait-list control group;

Reprinted with permission.

posttest study outcomes were evaluated at three months from baseline. A short-term follow-up period was chosen for this study as it was the inaugural test of the effectiveness of the CASMP and the basis for a future larger-scale trial, with long-term follow-up. Ethical approval for the study was received from a university in central Canada and three university-affiliated teaching hospitals.

Study Population and Procedure

This study was conducted in central Canada over an 18-month period. The target population was CSA patients living in the community. Participants had a confirmed medical diagnosis of CAD, CSA for at least six months and were able to speak, read, and understand English. Individuals were excluded if they had suffered a myocardial infarction and/or undergone a coronary artery bypass graft in the last six months, had Canadian Cardiovascular Society (CCS) Class IV angina[45] and/or a major cognitive disorder. Participants were recruited from three university-affiliated teaching hospitals with large cardiac outpatient programs, allowing for timely subject referral. Three recruitment strategies found to be effective in prior psychoeducation trials with community-based samples were used.[36,37,46,47] First, clinicians at designated hospital recruitment sites identified eligible patients in the clinic setting. Second, study information was made available in participating clinicians' offices and hospital recruitment site newsletters. Third, the study was advertised in community newspapers.

Participant eligibility was initially assessed by a research assistant (RA) via telephone. Willing participants were then interviewed by the RA on-site to confirm eligibility and obtain informed consent. Demographic and baseline measures were completed on-site and participants were randomly allocated to either the six-week CASMP group, or the three-month wait-list control group. Randomization was centrally controlled using a university-based tamper-proof, computerized randomization service. Those randomized to the six-week intervention group were invited to participate in the next available program, whereas those randomized to usual care were told that they were in the three-month wait-list control group. Usual care consisted of all nursing, medical, and emergency care services as needed; those allocated to the control group did not receive the CASMP during the study period.

Participants were contacted by the RA to schedule posttest data collection at three months from baseline. Assiduous follow-up procedures were used to minimize attrition; participants received up to three telephone calls and a follow-up letter regarding collection of their three-month follow-up data. Participants' completion of all study questionnaires was invigilated by the RA blinded to group allocation. Blinding was preserved by informing participants that their questions would be answered after they completed the questionnaire booklet and that a letter explaining their part in the next phase of the project was forthcoming. Those in the wait-list control group were offered entry into the next available CASMP once posttest measures were completed.

Intervention

The CASMP is a standardized psychoeducation program given in two-hour sessions weekly, over a six-week period. The goal of the CASMP is to improve HRQL by increasing patients' day-to-day angina self-management skills. The CASMP is an adaptation of Lorig et al.'s Chronic Disease Self-Management Program (CDSMP, © 1999 Stanford University).[47–50] In 2004, McGillion et al. conducted a preliminary study to identify CSA patients' specific pain-related concerns and self-management learning needs.[33] With permission, the results of this study were used to adapt the CDSMP to make it directly applicable to CSA. The principal investigator (PI) was certified as a CDSMP "Master Trainer" at the Stanford Patient Education Research Center to ensure that all tenets of the adapted program were in accordance with the standardized CDSMP psychoeducation format.

The program was delivered by a Registered Nurse using a group format (e.g., 8–15 patients) in a comfortable classroom setting. Program sessions were offered both day and evening and participants were encouraged to bring a family member or friend if they wished. A facilitator manual specified the intervention protocol in detail to ensure consistent delivery of the CASMP across sessions. In addition, all sessions were audio taped and a random sample of these tapes (10%) was externally audited to ensure standard intervention delivery.

The CASMP integrates strategies known to enhance self-efficacy including skills mastery, modeling, and self-talk. Designed to maximize discussion and group problem solving, it encourages individual experimentation with various cognitive-behavioral self-management techniques and facilitates mutual support, optimism, and the self-attribution of success. Key pain-related content includes relaxation and stress management, energy conservation, symptom monitoring and management techniques, medication review, seeking emergency assistance, diet, and managing emotional responses to cardiac pain. Fig. 1 provides an overview of all content covered over the six-week course of the program.

Both the content and process components of the CASMP are grounded in Bandura's Self-Efficacy Theory, which states that self-efficacy is critical to improve health-related behaviors and emotional well-being and that one's self-efficacy can be enhanced through performance mastery, modeling, reinterpretation of symptoms, and social persuasion.[51,52] Throughout the program, participants worked in pairs between sessions to help one another to stay motivated, problem solve, and meet their respective self-management goals. A CASMP workbook was also provided for reinforcement of key material from each session.

CASMP Program Overview						
	Week 1	Week 2	Week 3	Week 4	Week 5	Week 6
Overview of Self-management and Chronic Angina	✓					
Making an Action Plan	✓	✓	✓	✓	✓	✓
Relaxation/Cognitive Symptom Management	✓		✓	✓	✓	✓
Feedback/Problem-solving		✓	✓	✓	✓	✓
Common Emotional Responses to Cardiac Pain: Anger/Fear/Frustration		✓				
Staying Active/Fitness		✓	✓			
Better Breathing			✓			
Fatigue/Sleep Management			✓			
Energy Conservation				✓		
Eating for a Healthy Heart				✓		
Monitoring Angina Symptoms and Deciding when to Seek Emergency Help				✓		
Communication				✓		
Angina and Other Common Heart Medications					✓	
Evaluating New/Alternative Treatments					✓	
Cardiac Pain and Depression					✓	
Monitoring Angina Pain Symptoms and Informing the Health Care Team						✓
Communicating with Health Care Professionals About Your Cardiac Pain						✓
Future Self-Management Plans						✓

Fig. 1. CASMP overview.

Measures

Sociodemographic information and angina and related clinical characteristics were obtained via a baseline questionnaire developed for the trial. Braden's evidence-based Self-Help Model of Learned Response to Chronic Illness Experience guided our selection of trial outcomes.[53,54] Braden's model emphasizes human resilience and suggests that people can develop enabling skills to enhance their life quality when faced with the adversities of chronic illness.[53,54] Therefore, the primary outcome was life quality, conceptualized as CSA patients' HRQL. The secondary outcome was enabling skill, reflected by CSA patients' self-efficacy and resourcefulness to self-manage their pain.

Primary Outcome: HRQL. HRQL was measured using the Medical Outcomes Study 36-Item Short Form (SF-36).[55–57] The SF-36 is a comprehensive, well-established, and psychometrically strong instrument designed to capture multiple operational indicators of functional status including behavioral function and dysfunction, distress and well-being, self-evaluations of general health status.[58,59] Eight subscales are used to represent widely measured concepts of overall quality of life: physical functioning (PF), role limitations due to physical problems (RP), social functioning (SF), bodily pain (BP), mental health (MH), role limitations due to emotional problems (RE), vitality (VT), and general health perception (GH).[57] Raw SF-36 data were submitted to QualityMetric Incorporated's 100% accurate online scoring service. Scoring was according to the method of summated ratings where items for each subscale are summed and divided by the range of scores. Raw scores were transformed to a 0–100 scale where higher scores reflect better functioning.[57] We also used norm-based scoring (NBS) where linear T-score transformations were performed to transform all scores to a mean of 50 and standard deviation (SD) of 10.[57,60] We chose the NBS method to allow our SF-36 scores to be readily comparable to current published SF-36 CSA population norms.[57] (Raw SF-36 scores available on request from the first author.) NBS also guards against subscale ceiling and floor effects; scores below 50 can be understood as below average.[57]

Reliability estimates for all eight SF-36 subscales have exceeded 0.70 across divergent patient populations including CSA[58–61] and exceeded 0.8 in this study: PF (0.87), RP (0.86); BP (0.81); RE (0.87); SF (0.83); VT (0.83); MH (0.85); GH (0.83). SF-36 construct, convergent, and discriminant validities have also been well documented.[57–59,62]

Although the SF-36 has discriminated among patient samples with divergent medical, psychiatric, and psychiatric and other serious medical conditions, some evidence suggests that it may inadequately discriminate among those with differing CCS angina functional class.[61] The potential for the SF-36 to be insensitive to changes in angina class necessitated the use of a second disease-specific instrument, the Seattle Angina Questionnaire (SAQ),[61,63] to evaluate HRQL.

The SAQ is a disease-specific measure of HRQL for patients with CAD, consisting of 19 items that quantify five clinically relevant domains of CAD: physical limitation, angina pain stability and frequency, treatment satisfaction, and disease perception.[63] The SAQ is scored by assigning each response an ordinal value and summing across items within each of the five subscales. Subscale scores are transformed (0–100) by subtracting the lowest score, dividing by the range of the scale, and multiplying by 100.[63] Higher scores for each subscale indicate better functioning; no summary score for the five subscales is derived. SAQ reliability, construct validity, and responsiveness to intervention have been demonstrated in a number of studies.[13,14,61,63–65] Internal consistency reliabilities for the SAQ in this study were PL (0.85), AF (0.71), TS (0.73), and DP (0.68).

Secondary Outcomes: Self-Efficacy and Resourcefulness. Self-efficacy to manage angina pain and other symptoms was measured with a modified version of the 11-item "Pain and Other Symptom" scale of Lorig et al.'s Self-Efficacy Scale (SES), originally developed for arthritis intervention studies.[66] This scale assesses people's perceived ability to cope with the consequences of chronic arthritis including pain and related symptoms and functioning[66] via a 10-point graphic rating scale ranging from

10 (very certain) to 100 (very uncertain) for each of its 11 items. A total score for perceived self-efficacy is obtained by summing all items and dividing by the number of items completed; a higher score indicates greater perceived self-efficacy.

SES test-retest stability and construct validity have been reported in large samples.[35,36,67] The SES has also performed consistently with theoretical predictions in a prior psychoeducation trial for chronic pain, having negative correlation with pain (−0.35) and disability (−0.61), and strong positive correlation with role functioning (0.62) and life satisfaction (0.48); internal consistency was 0.90.[37] Permission was received from the SES developer to adapt the SES by replacing the word "arthritis" with "angina." The internal consistency of our adapted version of the SES in this study was 0.94.

Resourcefulness was measured by Rosenbaum's Self-Control Schedule (SCS),[68] designed to assess individual tendencies to use a repertoire of complex cognitive and behavioral skills when negotiating stressful circumstances. Thirty-six items are scored using a six-point Likert scale (−3 to +3) to assess individual tendencies to engage in aspects of self-control behaviors including 1) the use of cognitions and positive self-statements to cope with negative situations, 2) application of problem solving strategies, 3) delay of immediate gratification, and 4) maintenance of a general belief in self when dealing with challenging circumstances.[68] Eleven items are reverse scored, and all items are summed to generate a total score for resourcefulness ranging from −108 to 108; higher scores indicate greater resourcefulness.[68] SCS test-retest stability, internal consistency, and validity are well documented.[37,68–73] The internal consistency for the SCS in this study was 0.80.

All instruments were pilot tested prior to the trial on a sample of six CSA patients (aged 46–68 years) to assess their comprehension of items and response burden; no changes were required.

Sample Size

Sample size estimation was based on achievement of a moderate effect size in our primary outcome of HRQL. Cardiac patients have reported minimum 10-point improvements in SF-36 scales up to four years postinvasive intervention.[7,11] Prior trials suggested that psychoeducation can achieve comparable minimal levels of short-term change in a number of SF-36 scales for patients with chronic pain via the acquisition of disease self-management skills and the self-attribution of success.[35,37] We specified a 10-point difference in SF-36 scores as being clinically important and the sample size was set to test for this difference. Based on Chronic Pain Self-Management Program (CPSMP) trial data,[37] we used an estimated SD of 18; comparable SDs for five SF-36 scales including physical functioning, bodily pain, general health, social functioning, and mental health have been reported among cardiac patients aged 44–84 years.[7] Larger SDs however were reported for two role functioning scales of the SF-36 including role emotional and role physical functioning, thus requiring estimated sample sizes beyond the allowable time frame for this study.[7,57] We therefore expected potentially inadequate power to detect meaningful change in these two SF-36 scales. Allowing for an alpha of 0.05 and 80% power, the required sample for each group was 52. Telephone reminders and flexibility in CASMP program offerings were expected to help minimize attrition. However, to allow for losses to follow-up, the final sample estimate for each group was 65, or 130 in total. The statistics program nQuery Advisor 4.0 was used to compute this sample size estimate.

Data Analysis

Analyses were based on intention-to-treat principles.[74] Equivalence of groups on baseline demographic characteristics and pretest scores was examined using Chi-squared analysis for discrete level data and the Student *t*-test for continuous level data. Change score analyses were conducted to determine the impact of the CASMP on HRQL, self-efficacy, and resourcefulness to manage symptoms. Significant differences in change scores between treatment and control groups were examined via analysis of variance (ANOVA).[75] To guard against Type I error, multivariate analysis of variance (MANOVA) was conducted prior to ANOVA testing on SF-36- and SAQ-related data, due to the multiple subscales involved.[75] We chose a change score approach as opposed to analysis of covariance (ANCOVA) so that observed differences in change scores between treatment and control groups would be accessible to the reader and therefore the magnitude of any intervention effects would be readily apparent.[75,76] For verification, we reanalyzed our data via ANCOVA; the findings supported our change score approach. All data were cleaned and assessed for outliers and departure from normality; assumptions of all parametric analyses were met.

Results

Derivation of the Sample and Attrition

In total, 277 potential participants were assessed for inclusion via telephone during an 18-month period. Of these potential participants, 130 were included and 147 were excluded. Of those excluded, 44% did not meet the inclusion criteria, 30% refused, and 26% missed their initial appointment for consent and completion of baseline questionnaires, despite assiduous follow-up (i.e., three telephone calls and a follow-up letter). Reasons for refusal included: not interested ($n=18$), too busy to participate ($n=15$), transportation problems ($n=6$), and physical limitations precluding travel ($n=5$). Those who did not arrive for enrollment procedures were also counted as refusals when determining acceptance rate. The acceptance rate for enrollment among those eligible was 61%. Of the 130 consenting participants, 66 were randomized to the CASMP, and 64 were randomized to the wait-list control group.

Thirteen participants (treatment group, $n=9$; usual care group, $n=4$) did not complete posttest measures, yielding a 10% loss to follow-up (LTF) rate. Of these, nine participants LTF dropped out of the study without explanation and could not be contacted and four became ineligible to continue due to hospitalization. One hundred seventeen participants (treatment group, $n=57$; usual care group, $n=60$) completed pre- and posttest measures that were used for data analyses (see Fig. 2).

Participant Characteristics and Comparability of Groups

Baseline sociodemographic- and angina-related characteristics of the treatment and control groups are presented in Tables 1 and 2, respectively. The mean age of the sample was 68 (SD 11), living with CSA for 7 (SD 7) years on average. The majority of the sample was male, married or cohabitating, and Caucasian. Individuals of East Indian and Pakistani origin

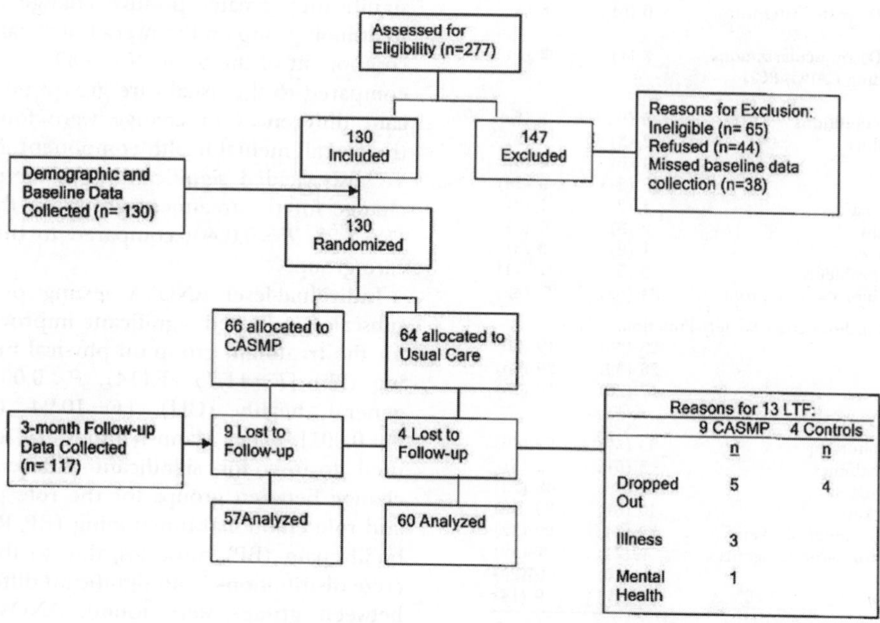

Fig. 2. Trial flow: sample derivation, randomization, data collection, and losses to follow-up.

Table 1
Sociodemographic Characteristics by Group

Characteristic	Treatment ($n = 66$)	Control ($n = 64$)
Demographics	n (%)	n (%)
Mean age (years [SD])	67 (11)	70 (11)
Married/cohabitating	44 (67)	44 (69)
Male	53 (80)	50 (78)
Working full time	16 (24)	15 (23)
Retired	46 (70)	42 (66)
High school	59 (89)	55 (86)
Postsecondary education	42 (64)	44 (69)
Caucasian	48 (73)	54 (84)
Black	3 (5)	0 (0)
Latin American	0 (0)	1 (2)
Asian	2 (3)	1 (2)
East Indian/Pakistani	11 (17)	6 (9)
Middle Eastern	3 (5)	1 (2)
Aboriginal	0 (0)	1 (2)

SD = standard deviation.

constituted the second largest racial group enrolled. Most were either retired or working full time. The majority had completed high school and/or had postsecondary education.

Table 2
Angina and Related Clinical Characteristics by Group

Characteristic	Treatment ($n = 66$)	Control ($n = 64$)
Angina-related history		
Mean (SD) years living with angina	6 (6)	8 (8)
Mean (SD) revascularizations (including CABG, PCI)	2 (1)	2 (1)
Comorbid conditions	n (%)	n (%)
Heart failure	2 (3)	5 (8)
Asthma	4 (6)	2 (3)
Diabetes	18 (27)	9 (14)
Emphysema	1 (2)	1 (2)
Renal failure	2 (3)	1 (2)
Peptic ulcer	1 (2)	3 (5)
Thyroid problems	3 (5)	7 (11)
Other minor medical problem	34 (52)	27 (42)
Canadian Cardiovascular Society Functional Class		
Class I	23 (35)	19 (30)
Class II	26 (39)	29 (45)
Class III	17 (26)	16 (25)
Medications		
Ace inhibitors	33 (50)	29 (46)
Anti-arrhythmics	3 (5)	2 (3)
Anticoagulants	57 (86)	48 (73)
Beta-blockers	40 (61)	38 (59)
Calcium channel blockers	22 (34)	20 (32)
Cholesterol lowering agents	49(74)	38(59)
Diuretics	11(16)	13(20)
Insulins	18 (27)	9 (14)

SD = standard deviation; CABC = coronary artery bypass graft; PCI = percutaneous coronary intervention.

Approximately half had two prior cardiac revascularization procedures, typically either coronary artery bypass grafting or angioplasty. The majority reported having a comorbid condition, typically a minor medical problem or diabetes. The treatment and control groups were not significantly different on any sociodemographic characteristic, comorbid condition, CCS functional class, number of prior revascularizations, or pretest measure. Comparisons were also made on all sociodemographic characteristics and pretest scores between those LTF ($n = 13$) and those who completed ($n = 117$) the study; no significant differences were found. (All baseline scores available on request from the first author.)

Intervention Effects: Between-Group Differences in Change Scores

Primary Outcome: HRQL. Mean change scores by group, group differences in change scores, and results of MANOVA and ANOVA testing for significant differences in change scores between groups for the SF-36 and SAQ are presented in Tables 3 and 4, respectively. Two omnibus MANOVA tests were performed on the SF-36 data as four subscales reflect mental health aspects of HRQL, and four subscales reflect physical health aspects. MANOVA yielded significantly greater positive change for the treatment group on the overall physical health component of the SF-36 ($F = 4.39$, $P = 0.003$), compared to the usual care group; no significant differences in change were found for the overall mental health component. MANOVA also yielded significantly greater positive change for the treatment group on the SAQ ($F = 3.23$, $P = 0.009$), compared to the usual care group.

Individual-level ANOVA testing on SF-36 subscales indicated significant improvements for the treatment group on physical functioning (PF) [$F = 11.75$ (1,114), $P < 0.001$] and general health (GH) [$F = 10.94$ (1,114), $P = 0.001$]. The Mann-Whitney U test was used to test for significant differences in change between groups for the role physical and role emotional functioning (RP, RE) and bodily pain (BP) subscales, due to their discrete distributions;[75] no significant differences between groups were found. ANOVA also yielded significant improvements for the

Table 3
MANOVA and ANOVA Tests for Significant Differences in SF-36 Change Scores between Groups

SF-36 NBS	Change Treatment	Change Control	Difference in Change between Groups	MANOVA		ANOVA	
Range (0–100)	$\Delta(T_2 - T_1)$ M (SD)	$\Delta(T_2 - T_1)$ M (SD)	$(T_\Delta - C_\Delta)$ M (SD)	*F* (df)	*P*	*F* (df)	*P*
Physical health-related items							
PF	5.3 (9.4)	−0.68 (9.3)	5.95 (9.3)	4.39 (4, 110)	0.003[b]	11.75 (1, 114)	<0.001[c]
RP	4.8 (12.7)	3.2 (9.6)	1.66 (11.2)			1.47[a]	ns
BP	4.4 (8.7)	2.1 (9.2)	2.31 (8.95)			1.68[a]	ns
GH	2.27 (7.7)	−1.6 (6.4)	4.33 (7.0)			10.94 (1, 114)	0.001[c]
Mental health-related items							
RE	4.9 (12.2)	3.6 (12.2)	1.31 (12.2)	0.47 (4,108)	ns	1.49[a]	ns
SF	2.1 (10.9)	0.1 (9.5)	2.04 (10.2)			0.28 (1, 114)	ns
VT	2.3 (8.6)	0.3 (7.3)	1.97 (8.0)			1.77 (1, 114)	ns
MH	1.5 (8.8)	0.9 (7.9)	0.58 (8.3)			0.14 (1, 114)	ns

NBS = Norm-based scores; T_1 = Time 1; T_2 = Time 2; T = treatment; C = controls; Δ = mean change; T_Δ = mean change, treatment; C_Δ = mean change, controls; PF = physical functioning; RP = role physical functioning; BP = bodily pain; GH = general health; RE = role emotional functioning; SF = social functioning; VT = vitality; MH = mental health.
Note: SD of mean change scores expected to be large as range of scores not bound by zero.
[a]Mann-Whitney *U* test.
[b]$P < 0.05$.
[c]$P \leq 0.01$.
ns = Nonsignificant ($P > 0.05$).

treatment group on two subscales of the SAQ including angina pain frequency (AF) [$F = 5.57$ (1,115), $P = 0.02$] and stability (AS) [$F = 7.37$ (1,115), $P = 0.001$]. At three months, the CASMP resulted in significantly greater improvements in physical functioning and general health, as measured by the SF-36, and significantly greater improvements in angina pain frequency and stability, as measured by the SAQ, compared to usual care.

Secondary Outcomes: Self-Efficacy and Resourcefulness. Mean change scores by group, group differences in change scores, and results of ANOVA testing for significant differences in change in SES and SCS scores between groups are presented in Table 5. ANOVA yielded significant improvement for the treatment group on the SES [$F = 8.45$ (1,115), $P = 0.004$] compared to controls. No significant group differences in SCS change scores were found. Overall, the CASMP resulted in significantly improved self-efficacy scores at three months, compared to usual care. The CASMP did not impact resourcefulness.

Examination of Intervention Cohort Effects

Because the CASMP was delivered to the treatment group in six small group cohorts of eight to fifteen participants, we examined for

Table 4
MANOVA and ANOVA Tests for Significant Differences in SAQ Change Scores between Groups

SAQ	Change Treatment	Change Control	Difference in Change between Groups	MANOVA		ANOVA	
Range (0–100)	$\Delta(T_2 - T_1)$ M (SD)	$\Delta(T_2 - T_1)$ M (SD)	$(T_\Delta - C_\Delta)$ M (SD)	*F* (df)	*P*	*F* (df)	*P*
AF	11.4 (23.7)	2.2 (18.4)	9.23 (21.2)	3.23 (5,109)	0.009[a]	5.57 (1,115)	0.02[a]
AS	18.0 (35.0)	2.9 (24.4)	15.07 (30.0)			7.37 (1,115)	0.001[b]
DP	9.9 (23.5)	3.3 (19.1)	6.61 (21.4)			2.80 (1,115)	ns
PL	7.1 (16.5)	1.6 (15.1)	5.55 (15.8)			3.54 (1,113)	ns
TS	9.7 (24.6)	4.8 (18.7)	4.82 (21.8)			1.43 (1,115)	ns

SAQ = Seattle Angina Questionnaire; T_1 = Time 1; T_2 = Time 2; T = treatment; C = Controls; Δ = mean change; T_Δ = mean change, treatment; C_Δ = mean change, controls; AF = angina frequency; AS = angina stability; DP = disease perception; PL = physical limitation; TS = treatment satisfaction; SD = standard deviation.
Note: SD of change scores expected to be large as range of scores not bound by zero.
[a]$P < 0.05$.
[b]$P \leq 0.01$.
ns = Nonsignificant ($P > 0.05$).

Table 5
ANOVA Tests for Significant Differences in SES and SCS Change Scores between Groups

	Change Treatment	Change Control	Difference in Change between Groups	ANOVA	
Variable (Range)	$\Delta(T_2 - T_1)$ M (SD)	$\Delta(T_2 - T_1)$ M (SD)	$(T_\Delta - UC_\Delta)$ M (SD)	*F* (df)	*P*
SES (10–100)	8.4 (17.6)	−0.2 (14.4)	8.62 (16.1)	8.45 (1,115)	0.004[a]
SCS (0–100)	4.2 (26.5)	−1.6 (19.2)	5.80 (23.0)	1.60 (1,115)	ns

T_1 = Time 1; T_2 = Time 2; T = treatment; C = Controls; Δ = mean change; T_Δ = mean change; treatment; C_Δ = mean change; controls; SES = Self-Efficacy Scale; SCS = Self-Control Schedule; SD = standard deviation.
Note: SD of change scores expected to be large as range of scores not bound by zero.
[a]$P < 0.01$.
ns = Nonsignificant ($P > 0.05$).

significant associations between intervention cohort and differences found in change scores between treatment and control groups. No significant associations between intervention cohort and group differences in change scores were found.

CASMP Attendance

As a form of process evaluation, an attendance record was kept to track the number of CASMP sessions attended by the treatment group participants. Ninety-three percent of those in the treatment group attended all six program sessions; the remaining 7% attended three or more sessions. The average number of sessions attended overall was 5.8.

Discussion

Statistically reliable short-term improvements in HRQL and self-efficacy were found for those who participated in the CASMP as compared to the control group; specific components of HRQL significantly improved included overall physical functioning and general health (SF-36) and frequency and stability of angina pain symptoms (SAQ). As no prior psychoeducation-based trials for CSA have used the SF-36 or the SAQ, direct comparisons of our HRQL-related results were not possible. However, our findings generally compare favorably with those of trials that have used other means to evaluate HRQL. We found four psychoeducation trials that reported significant improvements in symptoms including duration, frequency, and severity of cardiac pain.[40–43] Two of these trials also found significant improvements in physical functioning with respect to exercise tolerance and general disability.[40,42] Although our findings are consistent with these positive trends, comparisons must be viewed with caution due to heterogeneity of methods including design, interventions, timing of outcome measurement, and instrumentation.[39] Nevertheless, sample characteristics across trials are similar to our sample, suggesting that physical functioning and angina symptoms can improve after participation in psychoeducational interventions that target angina pain symptoms, self-management techniques, and physical activity enhancement. Future angina psychoeducation randomized controlled trials (RCT) using robust methods, and standard reliable and valid measures to evaluate HRQL would allow for more direct comparisons to this trial.

Although focused on a different population, LeFort et al.'s CPSMP trial is the only other known study to have used the SF-36 to evaluate the impact of psychoeducation on a persistent pain problem.[37] Comparable to our study with respect to intervention format, design, and sample size, LeFort et al. found that their CPSMP program significantly improved SF-36 role physical functioning, bodily pain, vitality, and mental health for persons with chronic noncancer pain ($P < 0.003$).[37]

LeFort et al.'s significant improvement in a broader array of SF-36 dimensions than those achieved by our program may be attributable to the nature of respective pain problems addressed and participants' corresponding foci for self-management. Participants in LeFort et al.'s study had a number of chronic pain problems, averaging 6.7 somatic locations for pain per participant. Individuals may therefore have focused on a broader range of goals for pain self-management than our sample, leading to improvements across SF-36 physical and mental health components. Participants in our study however were most concerned with reducing their fear of cardiac pain to enhance their physical capacity. Based on pilot data, our program targeted a common misbelief among CSA patients that sedentary behavior will minimize cardiac pain and risks to personal safety.[33] Accordingly, the vast majority of our treatment group identified their fear of physical activity and subsequent pain as a major contributor to deconditioning, poor overall health, fatigue, and obesity. Enhancement of physical activity was therefore their immediate self-management priority. This concentrated self-management focus may account for our treatment group's narrower, although significant, improvements in SF-36 physical functioning and general health. There is also some evidence to suggest that the SF-36 may inadequately discriminate among those with differing CCS angina functional class.[61] Because our sample included those with CCS Classes I–III angina, some SF-36 subscales may not have been sensitive to improvements in angina-induced disability as a result of our program. Finally, baseline scores on all SF-36 dimensions in this study are below Canadian- and U.S. population-adjusted norms.[57,77] Given the deleterious impact of CSA on HRQL, improvement in multiple SF-36 dimensions may be difficult to achieve for CSA patients in the short term.

Prior work has established that a minimum change of 10 points in SAQ subscales reflects clinically meaningful change for angina patients.[13,63,65] In our study, AS and AF scores changed in a positive direction for the treatment group by a mean 18 (35.0) and 11.4 (23.7) points, respectively, and therefore meet this criterion for clinically meaningful change. This finding is consistent with the positive results of recent studies that have tested multifaceted CSA secondary prevention strategies, with some educational components.[65,78] Spertus et al.[65] and Moore et al.[78] reported similar findings resulting from their intervention strategies, featuring combinations of antianginal drug therapy, regional anesthesia, exercise rehabilitation, education sessions, and/or individual counseling. Greater short-term improvement in frequency and stability of angina pain symptoms in our trial as compared to these studies may be due to the self-efficacy enhancing nature of our standardized intervention format. Our significant improvement in treatment group self-efficacy is consistent with LeFort et al.'s CPSMP trial.[37] and Lorig and Holman's psychoeducation trials for arthritis self-management.[35] Consistent with Bandura' self-efficacy theory, health behavior change by instruction—without addressing self-efficacy—has not shown to be as effective as those interventions that target self-efficacy directly.[79]

Other scores not significantly improved at posttest included SAQ-treatment satisfaction, disease perception and physical limitation, and resourcefulness, as measured by the SCS. As with some SF-36 subscales, a longer-term evaluation period may be required to see significant improvement in these scores for CSA patients. In addition, psychometric properties of the SAQ-physical limitation (PL) scale may account for our lack of a significant finding in this disease-specific HRQL dimension. The SAQ-PL scale was adapted by Spertus et al.[63] from Goldman et al.'s Specific Activity Scale,[80] designed to assess CAD patients' capacity for physical stress. Six of nine total SAQ-PL items examine activities known to increase myocardial oxygen demand including climbing a hill or flight of stairs without stopping, gardening, vacuuming or carrying groceries, walking more than a block at a brisk pace, lifting or moving heavy objects, and participating in strenuous sports.[63] However, as our pilot study suggests, most CSA patients will learn to avoid moderate levels of physical activity due to their fear of pain.[33] Therefore, more strenuous activities captured by the SAQ-PL scale may not be relevant to CSA patients. Notably, Spetrus et al.[65] and Moore et al.[78] also found no significant improvements in SAQ-PL for their chronic angina samples. These data suggest that the responsiveness of the SAQ-PL scale to improvements in mild physical activity for CSA patients, such as walking and household activity, warrants further investigation.

The strengths of our study are the robust methods used to minimize biases and random error including a priori power analysis, centrally controlled randomization, valid and reliable measures, blinding of data collectors, intention-to-treat analyses, and examination for possible intervention cohort effects. In addition, assiduous follow-up procedures and the use of a wait-list control condition guarded against attrition bias, ensuring minimal loss to follow up. Treatment integrity was also maximized using a theoretically sound and standardized intervention protocol, verified by an external auditor via audio recording.

Performance bias cannot be ruled out as it is not possible to blind participants or interveners in a socially based intervention study. Social desirability may also be a possibility due to our use of self-report measures.[81] However, randomization should have equally distributed those prone to socially desirable responses.[74] The risk of sample size bias may be further reduced in a future study by obtaining a larger sample to ensure adequate power for the two SF-36 role functioning scales. Also, our follow-up period was limited to three months after baseline. Therefore, the long-term sustainability of the observed intervention effects is not known. In addition, all CASMP sessions were delivered by a single facilitator. Future studies of this intervention should use multiple facilitators to enhance external validity and include longer-term follow-up. Finally, this study was conducted at a university site in central Canada; the clinical utility and knowledge translation potential of future investigations may be enhanced by examining the effectiveness of the CASMP as an adjunctive component to facets of health care with preexisting infrastructure, such as standard cardiac rehabilitation programs (where applicable), or community health-care programs and facilities.

In conclusion, cumulative evidence supports the deleterious impact of CSA on HRQL. The CASMP was found effective for improving physical functioning, perceived general health, angina pain frequency and stability, and self-efficacy to manage angina at three months posttest. Further research is warranted to determine the capacity of the program to improve other dimensions of generic and disease-specific HRQL, and resourcefulness in the longer term. A subsequent long-term evaluation would also allow for examination of the sustainability of the short-term improvements observed in HRQL and self-efficacy for CSA patients.

Acknowledgments

We are grateful to the participants of this trial who generously gave their time and effort. We also thank Dr. Kate Lorig, Stanford University Patient Education Research Center, for permission to adapt the Chronic Disease Self-Management Program; Dr. Ellen Hodnett who supported this trial at the Randomized Controlled Trials Unit, Faculty of Nursing, University of Toronto; and Kim Boswell, Julie Kim, Linda Belford, Linda Brubacher, Peter Neilson, Marion Ryujin, and Viola Webster, expert clinicians and administrators who supported trial recruitment.

References

1. Gibbons RJ, Chatterjee K, Daley J, et al. ACC/AHA-ASIM guidelines for the management of patients with chronic stable angina: executive summary and recommendations [(A report of the American College of Cardiology/American Heart Association Task Force on practice guidelines (Committee on Management of Patients with Chronic Stable Angina)]. Circulation 1999;99:2829–2848.

2. Lyons RA, Lo SV, Littlepage BNC. Comparative health status of patients with 11 common illnesses in Wales. J Epidemiol Community Health 1994;48: 388–390.

3. Pocock SJ, Henderson RA, Seed P, Treasure T, Hampton J. Quality of life, employment status, and anginal symptoms after coronary artery bypass surgery: three-year follow-up in the randomized intervention treatment of angina (RITA) trial. Circulation 1996;94:135–142.

4. Erixson G, Jerlock M, Dahlberg K. Experiences of living with angina pectoris. Nurs Sci Res Nord Countries 1997;17:34–38.

5. Miklaucich M. Limitations on life: women's lived experiences of angina. J Adv Nurs 1998;28: 1207–1215.

6. Caine N, Sharples LD, Wallwork J. Prospective study of health related quality of life before and after coronary artery bypass grafting: outcome at 5 years. Heart 1999;81:347–351.

7. Brown N, Melville M, Gray D, et al. Quality of life four years after acute myocardial infarction: Short Form 36 scores compared with a normal population. Heart 1999;81:352–358.

8. Gardner K, Chapple A. Barriers to referral in patients with angina: qualitative study. Br Med J 1999; 319:418–421.

9. Wandell PE, Brorsson B, Aberg H. Functioning and well-being of patients with type 2 diabetes or angina pectoris, compared with the general population. Diabetes Metab (Paris) 2000;26:465–471.

10. Brorsson B, Bernstein SJ, Brook RH, Werko L. Quality of life of chronic stable angina patients four years after coronary angioplasty or coronary artery bypass surgery. J Intern Med 2001;249:47–57.

11. Brorsson B, Bernstein SJ, Brook RH, Werko L. Quality of life of patients with chronic stable angina before and 4 years after coronary artery revascularization compared with a normal population. Heart 2002;87:140–145.

12. MacDermott AFN. Living with angina pectoris: a phenomenological study. Eur J Cardiovasc Nurs 2002;1:265–272.

13. Spertus JA, Jones P, McDonell M, Fan V, Fihn SD. Health status predicts long-term outcome in outpatients with coronary disease. Circulation 2002;106:43–49.

14. Spertus JA, Salisbury AC, Jones PG, Conaway DG, Thompson RC. Predictors of quality of life benefit after percutaneous coronary intervention. Circulation 2004;110:3789–3794.

15. Murphy NF, Simpson CR, MacIntyre K, et al. Prevalence, incidence, primary care burden, and medical treatment of angina in Scotland: age, sex and socioeconomic disparities: a population-based study. Heart 2006;92:1047–1054.

16. Heart and Stroke Foundation of Canada. The growing burden of heart disease and stroke in Canada 2003. Ottawa: Heart and Stroke Foundation of Canada, 2003.

17. British Cardiac Society, British Hypertension Society, Diabetes UK, et al. JBS 2: Joint British Societies' guidelines on the prevention of cardiovascular disease in clinical practice. Heart 2005; 91(Suppl V):v1–v52.

18. Naylor CD. Summary, reflections and recommendations. In: Naylor CD, Slaughter PM, eds. Cardiovascular health and services in Ontario: An ICES atlas. Toronto: Institute for Clinical Evaluative Sciences, 1999: 355–377.

19. Stone JA, Arthur HM, Austford L, Blair T. Introduction to cardiac rehabilitation. In: Stone JA, Arthur HM, eds. Canadian guidelines for cardiac rehabilitation and cardiovascular disease prevention, 2nd ed. Winnipeg: Can Assoc Cardiac Rehab, 2004: 2–14.

20. Maseri A, Chierchia S, Davies G, Glazier J. Mechanisms of ischemic cardiac pain and silent myocardial ischemia. Am J Med 1985;79(Suppl 3A):7–11.

21. Malliani A. The elusive link between transient myocardial ischemia and pain. Circulation 1986; 73:201–204.

22. Aronow WS, Epstein S. Usefulness of silent myocardial ischemia detected by ambulatory electrocardiographic monitoring in predicting new coronary events in elderly patients. Am J Cardiol 1988;62: 1295–1296.

23. Langer A, Freeman MR, Armstrong PW. ST segment shift in unstable angina: pathophysiology and association with coronary anatomy and hospital outcome. J Am Coll Cardiol 1989;13:1495–1502.

24. Tzivoni D, Weisz G, Gavish A, et al. Comparison of mortality and myocardial infarction rates in stable angina pectoris with and without ischemic episodes during daily activities. Am J Cardiol 1989;63: 273–276.

25. Deedwania PC, Carbajal EV. Silent ischemia during daily life is an independent predictor of mortality in stable angina. Circulation 1990;81:748–756.

26. Yeung AC, Barry J, Orav J, et al. Effects of asymptomatic ischemia on long-term prognosis in chronic stable coronary disease. Circulation 1991;83: 1598–1604.

27. Sylven C. Mechanisms of pain in angina pectoris: a critical review of the adenosine hypothesis. Cardiovasc Drugs Ther 1993;7:745–759.

28. Bugiardini R, Borghi A, Pozzati A, et al. Relation of severity of symptoms to transient myocardial ischemia and prognosis in unstable angina. J Am Coll Cardiol 1995;25:597–604.

29. Cannon RO. Cardiac pain. In: Gebhart GF, ed, Progress in pain research and management, Vol. 5. Seattle: IASP Press, 1995: 373–389.

30. Malliani A. The conceptualization of cardiac pain as a nonspecific and unreliable alarm system. In: Gebhart GF, ed, Progress in pain research and management, Vol. 5. Seattle: IASP Press, 1995: 63–74.

31. Pepine CJ. Does the brain know when the heart is ischemic? Ann Intern Med 1996;124(11): 1006–1008.

32. Procacci P, Zoppi M, Maresca M. Heart, vascular and haemopathic pain. In: Wall P, Melzack R, eds. Textbook of pain, 4th ed. Toronto: Churchill Livingstone, 1999: 621–659.

33. McGillion MH, Watt-Watson JH, Kim J, Graham A. Learning by heart: a focused groups study to determine the psychoeducational needs of chronic stable angina patients. Can J Cardiovasc Nurs 2004;14:12–22.

34. McGillion M, Watt-Watson J, LeFort S, Stevens B. Positive shifts in the perceived meaning of cardiac pain following a psychoeducation for chronic stable angina. Can J Nurs Res 2007;39: 48–65.

35. Lorig K, Holman HR. Arthritis self-management studies: a twelve year review. Health Educ Q 1993;20:17–28.

36. Lorig K, Mazonson P, Holman HR. Evidence suggesting that health education for self-management in patients with chronic arthritis has maintained health benefits while reducing health care costs. Arthritis Rheum 1993;36:439–446.

37. LeFort S, Gray-Donald K, Rowat KM, Jeans ME. Randomised controlled trial of a community based psychoeducation program for the self-management of chronic pain. Pain 1998;74:297–306.

38. Barlow JH, Shaw KL, Harrison K. Consulting the "experts:" children and parents' perceptions of psychoeducational interventions in the context of juvenile chronic arthritis. Health Educ Res 1999;14:597–610.

39. McGillion MH, Watt-Watson JH, Kim J, Yamada J. A systematic review of psychoeducational interventions for the management of chronic stable angina. J Nurs Manag 2004;12:1–9.

40. Bundy C, Carroll D, Wallace L, Nagle R. Psychological treatment of chronic stable angina pectoris. Psychol Health 1994;10(1):69–77.

41. Payne TJ, Johnson CA, Penzein DB, et al. Chest pain self-management training for patients with coronary artery disease. J Psychosom Res 1994;38: 409–418.

42. Lewin B, Cay E, Todd I, et al. The angina management program: a rehabilitation treatment. Br J Cardiol 1995;2:221–226.

43. Gallacher JEJ, Hopkinson CA, Bennett ML, Burr ML, Elwood PC. Effect of stress management on angina. Psychol Health 1997;12:523–532.

44. Lewin RJP, Furze G, Robinson J, et al. A randomized controlled trial of a self-management plan for patients with newly diagnosed angina. Br J Gen Pract 2002;52:194–201.

45. Campeau L. The Canadian Cardiovascular Society grading of angina pectoris revisited 30 years later. Can J Cardiol 2002;18:371–379.

46. Lorig K, Lubeck D, Kraines RG, Selenznick M, Holman HR. Outcomes of self-help education for patients with arthritis. Arthritis Rheum 1985;28: 680–685.

47. Lorig KR, Sobel DS, Stewart AL, et al. Evidence suggesting that a chronic disease self-management program can improve health status while reducing utilization and costs: a randomized trial. Med Care 1999;37:5–14.

48. Lorig K, Gonzalez V, Laurent D. The chronic disease self-management workshop master trainer's guide 1999. Palo Alto, CA: Stanford Patient Education Research Center, 1999.

49. Lorig KR, Ritter P, Stewart AL, et al. Chronic disease self-management program: two-year health status and health care utilization outcomes. Med Care 2001;39:1217–1223.

50. Lorig KR, Sobel D, Ritter PL, Laurent D, Hobbs M. One-year health status and health care utilization outcomes for a chronic disease self-management program in a managed care setting. Eff Clin Pract 2001;4:256–262.

51. Bandura A. Social foundations of thought and action: A social cognitive theory. Englewood Cliffs: Prentice Hall, 1986.

52. Bandura A. Self-efficacy: The exercise of control. New York: W.H. Freeman, 1977.

53. Braden CJ. A test of the self-help model: learned response to chronic illness experience. Nurs Res 1990;39:42–47.

54. Braden CJ. Research program on learned response to chronic illness experience: self-help model. Holist Nurs Pract 1993;8:38–44.

55. Rand Corporation, Ware J. The Short-Form-36 Health Survey. In: McDowell I, Newell C, eds. Measuring health: A guide to rating scales and questionnaires, 2nd ed. New York: Oxford University Press, 2006: 446–454.

56. Ware JE, Sherbourne CD. The MOS 36-item short-form health survey (SF-36): I Conceptual framework and item selection. Med Care 1992;30: 473–483.

57. Ware JE, Snow KK, Kosinski M, Gandek B. SF-36® health survey: Manual and interpretation guide. Lincoln: QualityMetric Incorporated, 2005.

58. McHorney CA, Ware JE, Rachel Lu JF, Sherborne CD. The MOS 36-item short-form health survey (SF-36): III. Tests of data quality, scaling assumptions, and reliability across divergent patient groups. Med Care 1994;32:40–66.

59. Tsai C, Bayliss MS, Ware JE. SF-36® Health survey annotated bibliography. (1988–1996), 2nd ed. Boston: Health Assessment Lab, New England Medical Center, 1997.

60. Ware JE, Snow KK, Kosinski M, Gandek B. SF-36® health survey: Manual and interpretation guide. Boston, MA: The Health Institute, New England Medical Center, 1993.

61. Dougherty C, Dewhurst T, Nichol P, Spertus J. Comparison of three quality of life instruments in stable angina pectoris: Seattle angina questionnaire, Short Form health survey (SF-36), and quality of life index-cardiac version III. J Clin Epidemiol 1998; 51(7):569–575.

62. McHorney CA, Ware JE, Raczek AE. The MOS 36-item short-form health survey (SF-36): II. Psychometric and clinical tests of validity in measuring physical and mental health constructs. Med Care 1993;31:247–263.

63. Spertus JA, Winder JA, Dewhurst TA, et al. Development and evaluation of the Seattle Angina Questionnaire: a new functional status measure for coronary artery disease. J Am Coll Cardiol 1995;25: 333–341.

64. Seto TB, Taira DA, Berezin R, et al. Percutaneous coronary revascularization in elderly patients: impact on functional status and quality of life. Ann Intern Med 2000;132:955–958.

65. Spertus JA, Dewhurst TA, Dougherty CM, et al. Benefits of an "angina clinic" for patients with coronary artery disease: a demonstration of health status measures as markers of health care quality. Am Heart J 2002;143:145–150.

66. Lorig K, Chastain RL, Ung E, Shoor S, Holman H. Development and evaluation of a scale

to measure perceived self-efficacy in people with arthritis. Arthritis Rheum 1989;32:37–44.

67. Lorig K, Lubeck D, Selenznick M, et al. The beneficial outcomes of the arthritis self-management course are inadequately explained by behaviour change. Arthritis Rheum 1989;31:91–95.

68. Rosenbaum M. A schedule for assessing self-control behaviours: preliminary findings. Behav Ther 1990;11:109–121.

69. Weisenberg M, Wolf Y, Mittwoch T, Mikulincer M. Learned resourcefulness and perceived control of pain: a preliminary examination of construct validity. J Res Pers 1990;24:101–110.

70. Redden EM, Tucker RK, Young L. Psychometric properties of the Rosenbaum schedule for assessing self control. Psychol Rec 1983;33:77–86.

71. Rosenbaum M, Palmon N. Helplessness and resourcefulness in coping with epilepsy. J Consult Clin Psychol 1984;52:244–253.

72. Richards PS. Construct validation of the self-control schedule. J Res Pers 1985;19:208–218.

73. Clanton L, Rude S, Taylor C. Learned resourcefulness as a moderator of burnout in a sample of rehabilitation providers. Rehabil Psychol 1992;37: 131–140.

74. Meinart CL. Clinical trials: Design, conduct and analysis. New York: Oxford University Press, 1986.

75. Norman GR, Streiner DL. Biostatistics: The bare essentials, 2nd ed. Hamilton: BC Decker Inc., 2000.

76. Bonate P. Analysis of pretest-posttest designs. Boca Raton: Chapman & Hall/CRC, 2000.

77. Hopman WM, Towheed T, Anastassiades T, et al. Canadian normative data for the SF-36 health survey. Can Med Assoc J 2000;163:265–271.

78. Moore RK, Groves D, Bateson S, et al. Health related quality of life of patients with refractory angina before and one year after enrolment onto a refractory angina program. Eur J Pain 2005;9:305–310.

79. Marks R, Allegrante JP, Lorig K. A review and synthesis of research evidence for self-efficacy enhancing interventions for reducing chronic disability: implications for health education practice (Part II). Health Promot Pract 2005;6:148–156.

80. Goldman L, Hashimoto B, Cook EF, Loscalzo MS. Comparative reproducibility and validity of systems for assessing cardiovascular functional class: advantages of a new specific activity scale. Circulation 1981;22:1227–1234.

81. Sackett DL. Bias in analytic research. J Chronic Dis 1979;32:51–63.

Critique of McGillion et al.'s (2008) Study "*Randomized Controlled Trial of a Psychoeducation Program for the Self-Management of Chronic Cardiac Pain*"

OVERALL SUMMARY

Overall, this was an extremely well-done study that tested a promising intervention to promote better outcomes among patients with chronic stable angina (CSA). The researchers used a strong research design and implemented stringent strategies to enhance the study's internal validity. They provided evidence that neither selection bias nor attrition bias affected their conclusions. They paid careful attention to such issues as blinding data collectors, reducing attrition, standardizing the intervention, and monitoring intervention fidelity. The instruments they used to measure the outcomes demonstrated strong validity and reliability. The study results indicated significant (and clinically important) improvements for those in the intervention group for many important outcomes. The researchers' power analysis led them to recruit a sample sufficiently large to detect moderate intervention effects, but a larger sample would likely have yielded evidence of even further program benefits—this limitation on statistical power was one that the researchers themselves acknowledged. The researchers provided excellent suggestions for further research on the promising psychoeducation intervention that they studied.

TITLE

The title of this report was excellent. It communicated or implied the research design (a randomized controlled trial or RCT), the independent variable (participation vs. nonparticipation in a special program), the nature of the intervention (psychoeducational program, involving self-management), a dependent variable (self-management of pain), and the study population (patients with chronic pain from cardiac disease). All this information was conveyed succinctly—only 14 words were used. It could be argued that something about health-related quality of life (HRQL) (the primary outcome variable) should have been included in the title, but this would have made the title quite long. The authors did, however, list HRQL as a keyword for indexing purposes.

ABSTRACT

The abstract, written in the traditional abstract style without subheadings, was excellent, summarizing all major features of the study. The abstract presented a summary of the problem, described the intervention, outlined crucial aspects of the research designs and study methods, described the study sample, summarized major findings, and stated the conclusion that the findings warrant further research on the long-term effects of the intervention. Despite its strength, the abstract could perhaps have been shorter without diminishing its informativeness. For example, statistical details (all of the information about the *F* statistics and the actual probability values) were not necessary. Names of the specific instruments that measured the outcomes (e.g., the Medical Outcomes Study 36-Item Short Form) could also have been omitted. People review abstracts to determine whether the full article is of interest, and methodologic details can be excessive to busy readers.

INTRODUCTION

The introduction to this study was short—briefer than is typical, in fact. Yet, the introduction covered a lot of ground in a concise and admirable fashion, thus leaving more space in the article for details about the researchers' methods and findings.

The very first sentence, which stated that cardiac pain from CSA is a cardinal symptom of coronary artery disease, introduced the problem. Later sentences indicated that this clinical problem has not been satisfactorily addressed with secondary prevention strategies. Consequences of the problem were summarized (i.e., that CSA has repercussions for HRQL, including pain, poor general health status, impaired role functioning, reduced ability for self-care, and activity restriction). Ample citations supporting these assertions were provided. Next, the researchers presented information about the prevalence of CSA—that is, about the scope of the problem.

McGillion and colleagues then laid the groundwork for the testing of a new intervention. They noted that existing models of secondary prevention are not necessarily accessible to those managing their chronic symptoms in the community. They identified a potential model of self-management for helping patients with CSA—psychoeducation interventions, which they defined as "multimodal, self-help treatment packages that use information and cognitive-behavioral strategies to achieve changes in knowledge and behavior for effective disease management" (p. 414). They described existing evidence about the utility of such interventions for improving outcomes for patients with other types of chronic pain, but stated that the evidence of the effectiveness of psychoeducation for CSA self-management is inconclusive. They briefly noted some of the methodologic problems with existing studies (e.g., inadequate power, lack of a standardized intervention). McGillion and other colleagues themselves undertook a systematic review of this literature, which they cited, so they were well poised to critique the existing body of work.[1]

The researchers' argument led logically to the undertaking of this study, in that it highlighted the need for a well-designed test of a psychoeducation intervention for CSA patients. Their statement of purpose, placed as the last sentence of the introduction, was: "to

[1] Note that the researchers' presentation of the problem covered all six components we discussed in connection with problem statements in Chapter 6 of the textbook.

evaluate the effectiveness of a standardized psychoeducation program, entitled the Chronic Angina Self-Management Program (CASMP) for improving the HRQL, self-efficacy, and resourcefulness of CSA patients" (p. 414). Although the researchers did not explicitly state a hypothesis, the clear implication is that the researchers expected that patients who participated in the CASMP intervention would have better outcomes than patients who did not. The introduction to this article indicates that the researchers targeted a problem of considerable clinical significance to the health care community.

Overall, the introduction was well written and clearly organized. It concisely communicated the rationale for the study, and interwove supporting literature nicely, rather than having a separate literature review section. One comment about the literature cited, however, is that the majority of studies were fairly old. Of the 81 citations, fully 53 were published before the year 2000 and 16 were published before 1990. Without knowing this literature, we cannot determine whether the researchers were zealous and thorough (and therefore included studies comprehensively, including many older ones) or were not up-to-date in the current literature and therefore relied on older literature. We strongly suspect the former to be the case, but we wonder whether the space devoted to listing older citations in the reference list could have been better used, inasmuch as page constraints for this journal article must have been an issue (see below for some suggested additions to the introduction). On a very positive note, the researchers did a nice job of citing an interdisciplinary mix of studies from medical, nursing, other health care, and psychological journals.

Although the succinctness of the introduction is in many respects laudable, a few additional paragraphs might have better set the stage for readers. Here are some possible supplementary topics that could have strengthened the introduction:

- The authors stated several of the consequences of CSA, but did not document any economic implications (e.g., lost time from work for patients, increased costs from treatment for depression, costs associated with care in emergency departments). Given that psychoeducation programs such as the one tested involve an investment of resources, a more convincing argument for its utility might involve outlining how such an intervention might be cost-effective.
- The theoretical basis of the psychoeducation intervention was not alluded to in the introduction (it is briefly mentioned later in the article). It would be useful to have a brief upfront theoretical rationale for why a psychoeducation intervention might translate into improved psychosocial and physical outcomes.
- Relatedly, the introduction did not articulate a rationale for the researchers' selection of intervention outcomes. Several of the consequences of CSA that were mentioned in the first paragraph (e.g., activity restrictions, impaired role functioning) were apparently not specifically viewed as targets for improvement in this study. Also, certain outcomes stated in the purpose statement (self-efficacy, resourcefulness) were not described earlier as being relevant to either the clinical problem or the intervention model. Perhaps if there had been a better description of the theoretical framework in the introduction, the rationale for selecting these outcomes would have been clearer.
- The purpose statement indicated that the study would be tested on an existing structured intervention, CASMP. The introduction should perhaps have provided readers with a one- to two-sentence description of what prior research had found concerning the effectiveness of this specific intervention.

METHOD

The method section was nicely organized, with numerous subheadings so that readers could easily locate specific elements of the design and methods. The method section included important and useful information about how the researchers designed and implemented their study.

Research Design

McGillion and colleagues' clinical trial involved a very strong research design—a pretest–posttest experimental design that involved random assignment of study participants to an experimental (E) group that received the 6-week CASMP program or a control (C) group that received only "usual care" during the study period. Data were collected from all sample members at baseline and then again 3 months later. The researchers chose an ethically strong control group strategy of wait-listing controls for 3 months so that, after the posttest data were collected, control group members could opt to receive the intervention. One of the shortcomings of such a "delay of treatment" design is that it precludes long-term follow-up. That is, once the Cs are allowed to enroll in the intervention, E–C comparisons no longer provide a valid basis for inferring program effects. The researchers were fully aware of this, and noted that their intent in this research was to seek evidence of short-term (3-month) effects as a basis for launching a larger-scale trial with longer follow-up. (The researchers' rationale for collecting posttest data at 3 months—as opposed to, say, 2 months or 4 months, was not stated). As discussed later in this critique, the research design is one that has the potential for strong internal validity—that is, for permitting inferences about whether the intervention *caused* beneficial outcomes.

Study Population and Procedures

The researchers provided a good description of the study population, recruitment strategies, inclusion and exclusion criteria, methods of screening for eligibility, and procedures for obtaining informed consent. This subsection also did an extraordinarily good job of describing the randomization process and methods the researchers used to eliminate certain biases and validity threats. The researchers used a tightly controlled randomization process to ensure proper allocation to treatment, and used "assiduous follow-up procedures" (p. 415) to minimize attrition, which is the single biggest threat to internal validity in experimental studies. As is always true in interventions wherein both the program participants and the agents know who is in the experimental group, traditional blinding was not possible. Commendably, however, the researchers did take steps to ensure that the research assistant collecting the data was blinded to participants' group status.

The researchers also stated that usual care "consisted of all nursing, medical, and emergency care services as needed" (p. 415) and that Cs did not receive CASMP during the study period. It is noteworthy that the researchers mentioned what *usual care* means—"usual care" is often stated without further elaboration. This section further noted that wait-listed controls were offered entry into the next available CASMP once posttest data were collected. It cannot be ascertained from this article whether there was any possibility of contamination—that is, whether Cs could have been exposed to any part of the intervention during the study period, either through contact with Es being treated at the same hospitals or by the same clinicians, or through more direct contact with intervention agents. Judging from the care the researchers took in implementing the study, contamination likely was not a problem.

Intervention

The CASMP intervention—a psychoeducation program given in 6 weekly sessions of 2 hours in a small classroom-type setting with 8 to 15 patients—was described in this section. The research team had undertaken preliminary research on CSA, and had adapted the CASMP program to increase its relevance to their study population.

The researchers selected an intervention that was standardized, meaning that the independent variable was presumably the same from one session to the next. Moreover, the nurse who delivered the program used a formal facilitator's manual to ensure consistent delivery. It is noteworthy that the researchers made efforts to assess intervention fidelity: all program sessions were audiotaped, and there was an external audit of a random sample of 10% of the tapes. Presumably, these audits provided reassurance to the research team that the intervention was appropriately implemented.

The intervention itself was succinctly but adequately described as an integrated approach using strategies "known to enhance self-efficacy, including skills mastery, modeling, and self-talk." Major strategies included discussion, group problem solving, individual experimentation with self-management techniques, and paired problem solving between sessions to enhance motivation. Figure 1 (p. 416) provided a nice overview of the content covered in the 6 weekly sessions.

In the description of the intervention, the authors noted that both the content and process aspects of CASMP are "grounded in Bandura's Self-Efficacy Theory" (p. 416), which posits that self-efficacy is critical to improving health-related behaviors. Although space constraints likely limited the researchers' ability to include a well-formulated conceptual map linking program components to mediating effects (such as self-efficacy) and to ultimate outcomes, such a map (or a verbal description of the theoretical pathway) would have been useful in understanding some of the researchers' decisions, including their selection of outcome variables.

Measures

The researchers stated that their selection of outcomes was guided by Braden's Self-Help Model of Learned Response to Chronic Illness Experience. According to the authors, this model emphasizes human resilience and that people can develop skills to enhance life quality in the face of chronic illness. The relationship between this model and Bandura's Self-Efficacy Theory, and the link between Braden's model and CASMP is not explicated, and so the conceptual basis of the study remains a bit cloudy. Again, a conceptual map would be useful. The report stated that the primary outcome was HRQL and the secondary outcome was enabling skill (patients' self-efficacy and resourcefulness to manage their pain).

HRQL was measured using the 36-item Medical Outcome Study Short Form (SF-36). The SF-36 has eight subscales used to represent various aspects of health (e.g., physical functioning, bodily pain, vitality), and is a well-respected instrument with strong psychometric properties. The researchers reported that the reliability estimates for the SF-36 in this study (presumably internal consistency estimates as calculated by coefficient alpha) were all above .80, which is excellent. Commendably, because of some evidence that the SF-36 may not adequately discriminate patients with differing angina function, they administered a supplementary scale, the Seattle Angina Questionnaire (SAQ). This scale has five subscales (e.g., pain stability, physical limitation), and in this study the reliabilities ranged from .68 to .85.

The secondary outcome of self-efficacy was measured by an adapted 11-item Self-Efficacy Scale (SES), and resourcefulness was measured by Rosenbaum's 36-item Self Control Schedule (SCS). The known psychometric characteristics of these two scales were good, and the researchers found that internal consistency in this study was .94 for the SES and .80 for the SCS, both very strong.

It is also admirable that the researchers pretested their instrument package with a small sample of patients from the study population. They found that no changes were needed.

Overall, except for some ambiguity about the researchers' rationale for including particular constructs as outcomes (especially resourcefulness) and not including other potential constructs (e.g., ability for self-care, mentioned in the introduction as a documented consequence of CSA), the researchers' data collection plan seems sound and the specific measures they selected had excellent reliability and validity.

Sample Size

The researchers' discussion about their sample size was very good. They assumed a moderate effect size for the effect of the program on their primary outcome, HRQL, and also offered a standard for clinical importance. They provided empirical support from other studies about the viability of their assumption of a moderate effect. Based on their assumption, they projected a need for 52 participants in each study group, to achieve a power of .80 with an alpha of .05. Even though their research plan included methods to keep attrition to a minimum, they built a cushion into their sample size estimates, and therefore sought to enroll 65 participants in each group. This was the total number of patients randomized, with 66 being enrolled in CASMP and 64 put in the wait-list control group.

Data Analysis

The researchers' data analysis strategy was explained in some detail, with information about both analytic strategies and the rationale for analytic decisions.

The first sentence indicated that the intention-to-treat (ITT) principle was used in the analyses, the approach that is considered the gold standard for the analysis of RCT data. Randomization to treatment groups is a critical ingredient in permitting causal inferences to be made about the effect of the intervention on outcomes of interest. Randomization creates groups presumed to be equal in every respect, except that one group gets the intervention and the other does not. Group equivalence is lost, however, whenever there is attrition: people withdrawing from a study cannot be assumed to be a random subset of the original groups. Therefore, the preferred method of analysis is to keep all original participants in the analysis, whether they remained in the study or not. Study dropouts by definition do not provide posttest data, and so researchers using an ITT approach must use some method to estimate (or *impute*) the posttest values for people whose data are missing. ITT yields conservative estimates of program effects because it includes people who may not have actually received the treatment, but it is the only accepted way of preserving randomization and minimizing an important threat to internal validity—the nonequivalence of the groups being compared. In other words, the researchers stated that they adopted the most widely accepted approach to analysis.

It is not clear, however, that ITT *was* used. As indicated in the excellent CONSORT-type flow chart (Figure 2, p. 419), 130 participants were randomized, but 13 dropped out of the study (Nine Es and four Cs). Follow-up data were collected from 117. Judging from the degrees of freedom in Tables 3 through 5 (degrees of freedom can be used to determine how many people were in the analysis), the final analysis was based on the people who actually provided posttest data, not the full sample of 130 who were randomized. Moreover, if the researchers had estimated values for the missing posttest data for the 13 patients who withdrew, they presumably would have explained their method of imputation. In sum, it does not appear that a true ITT was actually used.

The data analysis section provided an excellent explanation of the researchers' primary statistical analyses. The results reported in this paper involved comparisons of the *change scores* for the E versus the C group. That is, for every person, the difference between his or her posttest score and baseline score (for all scale and subscale scores) was used as the dependent variable, so that readers could see directly how much improvement had occurred. The report indicated that an alternative analytic method, ANCOVA, was also used and that the results were totally consistent with that reported. (In ANCOVA, posttest scores, rather than change scores were used as the dependent variables, and baseline scores were used as covariates, so that baseline values would be statistically controlled). Because the researchers had multiple dependent variables—multiple subscale scores for the SF-36, for example—multivariate analysis of variance was used. The tables show results for both ANOVA and MANOVA. The researchers' statistical approach was very strong.

RESULTS

The results section provided useful information about how many people were recruited and what the flow of participants was in this study. Attrition in this study was fairly low, with follow-up data obtained from 90% of the patients randomized.

An excellent early subsection of the results was devoted to analyzing potential biases and threats to internal validity. The researchers presented two tables showing the baseline characteristics of the Es and Cs, and reported that none of the baseline group differences was statistically significant at conventional levels. These tables not only demonstrated the initial comparability of the groups (in terms of demographic and clinical variables), they also communicated vital information about the study population, which is extremely important to readers considering whether the CASMP intervention might be appropriate for their own clients. The researchers also reported their analysis of attrition bias: for all of the demographic and clinical characteristics measured at baseline, people who remained in the study were not significantly different from those who dropped out. (The researchers probably also looked at comparability of the groups in terms of baseline performance on the outcome variables, but these results were not, unfortunately, reported).

The key results were reported in a subsection labeled *Intervention Effects*. The tables summarizing the results were inherently complex, but they were well organized and clear, with good footnotes to help interpret the symbols and abbreviations used. Text was used judiciously to highlight the main findings. The results indicated that improvements were significantly greater for Es than Cs on several important outcome measures. For the SF-36 outcome measure, differences in change scores were significantly better for those who were in the intervention group with regard to physical functioning and general health—but not bodily pain, nor any of the mental health subscales. On the SAQ, significant improvements were observed for both angina frequency and angina stability. In terms of secondary outcomes, the program had significant effects on improving SES scores, but not resourcefulness. One comment is that it would have been desirable to present information about the precision of the change score differences using confidence intervals and (especially) effect size estimates. It is possible, however, that page limitations constrained the researchers' ability to include this information.

The researchers also included very valuable information about cohort effects—results that are seldom noted in RCT reports. When an intervention unfolds over time, as many do, it is useful to see if the intervention effects are consistent over time. Changes in the degree of improvement might occur if, for example, sample characteristics change over time or if the implementation of the program changes over time (for example, improves as a result of early experiences or declines because of waning enthusiasm of the facilitator). McGillion and colleagues noted that there were six cohorts of patients, and that differences in the amount of improvement among the Es in the six cohorts were not significant.

Finally, the researchers provided some information about actual program participation using data from their process evaluation. It is reassuring that the vast majority of patients assigned to the intervention group (93%) actually attended all six sessions. This is a remarkably high rate of participation, and shows a very high "dose" of the treatment for almost all participants. Thus, the report indicated that not only was the *delivery* of the independent variable standardized, its *receipt* was fairly uniform as well.

DISCUSSION

McGillion and colleagues offered a thoughtful discussion of their findings. They began by providing a context, comparing their study findings to findings from other studies of the effects of psychoeducation interventions for CSA patients and patients with slightly different chronic pain problems. They offered some plausible interpretations of differences and similarities in the results. The results of these studies are broadly consistent, in that positive effects on indicators of quality of life were observed in all studies, though on slightly different dimensions (or measures) of HRQL.

The authors also discussed the clinical significance of their findings. That is, in addition to achieving statistically significant program effects, they argued that the amount of improvement demonstrated by the intervention group is sufficiently large to be considered clinically significant.

The authors discussed the strengths of their study, which were considerable. They also noted some possible limitations, which included the following: lack of blinding of participants and intervention agents, which could have led to possible performance bias (i.e., people performing at their best because of their awareness of being in the intervention); the possibility that there was inadequate power to detect group differences for some of the outcomes for which program effects were more modest; the short-term follow-up of participants, making it impossible to draw conclusions about the program's longer-term effects; the use of a single facilitator, which could adversely affect the generalizability of the results; and the setting of the study in a university site, which again has implications for the external validity of the findings. It was admirable and insightful of the investigators to have noted these shortcomings, and they offered suggestions for addressing them in subsequent research.

GENERAL COMMENTS

Presentation

This report was well written and well organized and provided an unusually good amount of detail about the researchers' decisions and their rationales. The primary presentational shortcoming concerned the limited elaboration of the conceptual basis of the study. We suspect that the ambiguity about the linkages between the theories/models and the intervention are not conceptual flaws, but rather communication issues. Given the great care that was taken in the design and execution of the study, the researchers likely had a fully developed conceptualization, but opted to abbreviate their presentation.

Ethical Aspects

The authors did not provide much information about steps they took to ensure that participants were treated ethically—which does not mean that there were ethical transgressions.

For example, no mention was made of having the study approved by a human subject committee (in Canada, a Research Ethics Board). The only relevant information in the report was a statement about obtaining informed consent. There is no indication in the report that the participants were harmed, deceived, or mistreated in any way. And, indeed, their wait-list design is ethically commendable.

Validity Issues

McGillion and colleagues undertook an extremely rigorous study, and they are to be commended for the excellence of their work. They used a powerful research design and made exemplary efforts to reduce or eliminate serious validity threats. Many of the limitations of this excellent study were noted by the authors themselves.

The study was quite strong in terms of internal validity: we can be reasonably confident that the CASMP program had beneficial effects on the participants' perceptions of self-efficacy and on aspects of their quality of life. Participants were carefully randomized, and the authors presented evidence that randomization was successful in creating two groups that were comparable at the outset of the study. Thus, a key threat to internal validity—selection bias—was adequately addressed. There is no reason to suspect that threats such as history, maturation, or testing played a role in influencing the results. The major plausible internal validity threat in experimental designs is mortality—i.e., differential attrition from study groups. Attrition was modestly higher among the Es than the Cs, but overall attrition was low. The authors reported that those who dropped out of the study were not significantly different than those who stayed in the study in terms of baseline characteristics.

In terms of statistical conclusion validity, the fact that the researchers found highly significant group differences for several outcomes indicates that statistical conclusion validity was good—but it was not excellent, as the authors themselves noted. If one looks at Tables 3 through 5, the differences in change scores favored Es over Cs *for every single outcome*, but not always at statistically significant levels. This suggests that, with a larger sample (i.e., greater statistical power), more E–C differences would likely have been statistically significant.

It might be noted however, that the positive and significant intervention effects, while likely "real," might possibly be somewhat inflated, given the fact that an ITT analysis does not appear to have been done (or at least, was not the one reported). People who dropped out of the study might have been patients for whom the CASMP program might not have "worked", for example, because of low motivation, interest, or need. We did a rough calculation that suggests that even with the dropouts included in the analysis, the group differences favoring Es would have continued to be large and almost certainly significant. For example, the first outcome in Table 3 (p. 421) is for the physical functioning subscale of the SF-36. On average, Es improved by 5.3 points on the scale over the 3-month study period, while Cs *deteriorated* by .68 points (mean change = –.68). Based on the degrees of freedom, it appears that the analysis was done with 116 participants (1 + 114 + 1); we will assume that the averages shown are for 57 Es and 59 Cs, for a total of 116. (There is no information about why this number is 116 and not 117, as suggested in Figure 2). The original E group included 66 patients, not 57. So, if we assume conservatively that the average change score for the 9 Es who dropped out of the study was –.68 (i.e., if we imputed the average missing change scores as identical to the average change among the Cs who, like program dropouts, did not get the intervention), and we compute a new average for all 66 Es, the value would

---

[2] Here is how we arrived at the calculation. First, we multiplied .68 × 9 (the number of Es who dropped out) = 6.12. Then, we multiplied the mean of 5.3 × 57 (the number of Es in the analysis) = 302.1. Next, because the change for the C group was negative, we subtracted 6.12 from 302.1 = 295.98. Finally, this overall sum of change scores was divided by the original number of Es (66), to yield the new average of 4.485, which we rounded to 4.5.

drop from 5.3 to 4.5—still considerably better than the –.68 for Cs.[2] In sum, we think that the evidence is persuasive that participation in the program was associated with significant improvement in outcomes.

In terms of construct validity, we have already noted that the researchers could have better communicated information about their conceptualization of the intervention. Performance bias—bias stemming from participants' and researchers' awareness of an innovation, and having the awareness rather than the actual intervention affect outcomes—is another construct validity issue that the authors acknowledged. It seems more plausible to us, however, that the *intervention* itself had beneficial effects on, say, angina frequency and physical functioning, than that *awareness* caused these improvements. This is probably more likely to be the case because the posttest outcomes were measured 6 weeks after the end of program sessions, at which point program awareness likely would have waned.

Finally, external validity in this study is an issue that needs to be addressed in subsequent research. The researchers noted some of the factors limiting the generalizability of the findings (e.g., the use of a single facilitator, and the setting for the intervention in a university site in Canada). Other limiting factors include the relatively small sample, the exclusion of very high-risk patients, and the refusal of about 20% of eligible patients to participate. As is almost invariably true in clinical trials, the viability of the intervention for broader groups of CSA patients depends on replications. It may also depend on the ability of future researchers to demonstrate the cost-effectiveness of psychoeducation interventions for this population.

RESPONSE FROM THE MCGILLION TEAM AND FURTHER COMMENTS:

Dr. McGillion and his team graciously accepted our invitation to review this critique. Many of their comments confirmed that journal page constraints were the reason that some of the additional details or discussion points were absent from their paper. Here, for example, is their comment about conceptual framing (personal communication, June 23, 2008):

> We appreciate the critical importance of a clear conceptual framing that provides the rationale for outcome selection and related measures. Journal style and limitations imposed on length were again factors in why this particular level of detail was left out of the manuscript. The primary outcome for this trial was HRQOL. Secondary outcomes included self-efficacy and resourcefulness. The conceptual framework that guided examination of these outcomes was Braden's Self-Help Model *(references were provided, but are omitted here)*. The effectiveness of the CASMP was tested for improving scores in HRQOL, self-efficacy, and resourcefulness for CSA patients. Braden's Self-Help Model reflects the dynamics of a learned self-management response to chronic illness and was applied in order to link these variables together through the concept of enabling skill. Enabling skill, or one's perceived ability to manage adversity, was the proposed mediating variable by which one learns a self-help capacity, thereby experiencing enhanced life quality.

The authors also commented on our critique of their ITT analysis. This is what they wrote (personal communication, June 23, 2008):

> Regarding intention to treat (ITT) analysis: We do not agree that an analysis conducted according to ITT principles necessarily involves the imputation of posttest values for those participants lost to attrition. Rather, we would argue that ITT is commonly used as an umbrella term for two

> separate issues: a) treatment group [i.e. treatment or control] adherence and b) missing data. We state that we have analyzed our data according to ITT because we analyzed the data according to how participants were randomized–control participants remained in the control group and treatment group's participants remained in the treatment group. When data were missing, they were missing; we did not use any method to impute or estimate missing data. There are several methods to impute or estimate missing data such as 'last observation carried forward', or propensity scores. We felt that the use of such imputation techniques for an intervention study was inappropriate, as they are all means of estimating what missing outcome data 'might' have been.

We respectfully disagree with parts of this comment. The more appropriate term for the type of analysis that these researchers did is a *per protocol* analysis (analyzing people in groups according to the protocol to which they were randomized). This is the analytic approach that virtually all researchers follow. Very few researchers actually do a true ITT analysis that maintains all randomized participants in the analysis.

We do agree with the authors, however, that there is a lot of confusion about ITT in the research literature, and outright disagreement about how to (or even whether to) impute missing values. The "state of the art" at the moment is to use sophisticated statistical procedures to "fill in" missing outcome data, and to then test how different procedures affect the results. (The technical term for this is a *sensitivity analysis*, which we talked about in the textbook in the chapter on meta-analysis).

In the McGillion et al. study, we are reasonably confident that if they had performed a true ITT analysis with imputation of outcome data for dropouts, the conclusions that the intervention had positive effects would have remained the same. Our crude demonstration of "imputation" supports this view. Given the low rate of attrition and the analysis indicating that dropouts were similar to those who remained in the study, it is perhaps understandable that the researchers did not undertake time-consuming and challenging analyses with imputations. The main problem, in our view, is that they used a term that implies a type of analysis they did not pursue.

Despite our disagreement with the authors about this point, the fact remains that this research team took extraordinary steps to ensure the integrity of their study. There is little doubt that their study is extremely high on internal validity—one of the best examples we have seen in the nursing research literature.

D

Differences in Perceptions of the Diagnosis and Treatment of Obstructive Sleep Apnea and Continuous Positive Airway Pressure Therapy Among Adherers and Nonadherers

Amy M. Sawyer • Janet A. Deatrick •
Samuel T. Kuna • Terri E. Weaver

▶ ***Abstract:*** Obstructive sleep apnea (OSA) patients' consistent use of continuous positive airway pressure (CPAP) therapy is critical to realizing improved functional outcomes and reducing untoward health risks associated with OSA. We conducted a mixed methods, concurrent, nested study to explore OSA patients' beliefs and perceptions of the diagnosis and CPAP treatment that differentiate adherent from nonadherent patients prior to and after the first week of treatment, when the pattern of CPAP use is established. Guided by social cognitive theory, themes were derived from 30 interviews conducted postdiagnosis and after 1 week of CPAP use. Directed content analysis, followed by categorization of participants as adherent/nonadherent from objectively measured CPAP use, preceded across-case analysis among 15 participants with severe OSA. Beliefs and perceptions that differed between adherers and nonadherers included OSA risk perception, symptom recognition, self-efficacy, outcome expectations, treatment goals, and treatment facilitators/barriers. Our findings suggest opportunities for developing and testing tailored interventions to promote CPAP use.

▶ ***Key Words:*** Adherence · compliance · content analysis · decision making · health behavior · mixed methods · sleep disorders · social cognitive theory

Obstructive sleep apnea (OSA), characterized by repetitive nocturnal upper airway collapse resulting in intermittent oxyhemoglobin desaturation and sleep fragmentation, contributes to significant disabling sequelae, including daytime sleepiness, impaired cognitive and executive function, mood disturbances, and increased cardiovascular and metabolic morbidity (Al Lawati, Patel, & Ayas, 2009; Harsch et al., 2004; Nieto, et al.

Qualitative Health Research, 2010; 20(7):873–892.

2000; Peppard, Young, Palta, & Skatrud, 2000). The prevalence of OSA, based on minimal diagnostic criteria (apnea/hypopnea index [AHI] of 5 events/hour), has been estimated at 2% in women and 4% in men in the United States (Young et al., 1993). More recently, large U.S.-cohort studies have provided additional evidence of the prevalence of OSA, estimating that approximately one in five adults with a mean body mass index (BMI) of at least 25 kg/m^2 has at least mild OSA, defined as an apnea-hypopnea index (AHI) ≥ 5 events/hour; and one in 15 adults with a mean BMI of at least 25 kg/m^2 has at least moderate OSA (i.e., AHI ≥ 15 events/hour; Young, Peppard, & Gottlieb, 2002). Continuous positive airway pressure (CPAP) therapy is the primary medical treatment for adults with OSA, eliminating repetitive, nocturnal airway closures; normalizing oxygen levels; and effectively improving daytime impairments (Gay, Weaver, Loube, & Iber, 2006; Sullivan, Barthon-Jones, Issa, & Eves, 1981; Weaver & Grunstein, 2008).

Nonadherence to CPAP is recognized as a significant limitation in the effective treatment of OSA, with average adherence rates ranging from 30% to 60% (Engleman, Martin, & Douglas, 1994; Kribbs et al., 1993; Krieger, 1992; Reeves-Hoche, Meck, & Zwillich, 1994; Sanders, Gruendl, & Rogers, 1986; Weaver, Kribbs, et al., 1997). Nonadherent users begin skipping nights of CPAP use during the first week of treatment, and their hourly use of CPAP on days used is significantly shorter than those who apply CPAP consistently (Aloia, Arnedt, Stanchina, & Millman, 2007; Weaver, Kribbs, et al., 1997). Patients who are nonadherent during early treatment generally remain nonadherent over the long term (Aloia, Arnedt, Stanchina, et al., 2007; Krieger, 1992; McArdle et al., 1999; Weaver, Kribbs, et al., 1997). The return of symptoms and other manifestations of OSA with even one night of nonuse underscores the critical nature of adherence to CPAP (Grunstein et al., 1996; Kribbs et al., 1993).

Many studies have explored what factors predict adherence to CPAP (Engleman et al., 1996; Engleman, Martin, et al., 1994; Kribbs et al., 1993; Massie, Hart, Peralez, & Richards, 1999; McArdle et al., 1999; Meurice et al., 1994; Reeves-Hoche et al., 1994; Rosenthal et al., 2000; Schweitzer, Chambers, Birkenmeier, & Walsh, 1997; Sin, Mayers, Man, & Pawluk, 2002). Self-reported side effects of CPAP do not distinguish between adherers and nonadherers to CPAP. Subjective sleepiness, severity of OSA as determined by apnea-hypopnea index, and severity of nocturnal hypoxia are inconsistently identified as correlates, albeit weak, of CPAP adherence (Weaver & Grunstein, 2008). The majority of these studies have focused on physiological variables and patient characteristics as predictors of adherence. Over the past 10 years, studies have identified psychological and social factors and cognitive perceptions, such as self efficacy, risk perception, and outcome expectancies, as determinants of CPAP use (Aloia, Arnedt, Stepnowsky, Hecht, & Borrelli, 2005; Lewis, Seale, Bartle, Watkins, & Ebden, 2004; Russo-Magno, O'Brien, Panciera, & Rounds, 2001; Stepnowsky, Bardwell, Moore, Ancoli-Israel, & Dimsdale, 2002; Stepnowsky, Marler, & Ancoli-Israel, 2002; Wild, Engleman, Douglas, & Espie, 2004). Social and situational variables have also been suggested as influential on CPAP adherence, with those who live alone, who have had a recent life event, and who experienced problems with CPAP on the first night of exposure having lower adherence to CPAP therapy (Lewis et al., 2004). Support group attendance has also been identified as contributing to higher CPAP use in older men (Russo- Magno et al., 2001). Findings of both of these studies suggest that social support is an important factor influencing decisions to use CPAP, yet the sociostructural context of accepting and adhering to CPAP treatment has not been described from the perspective of the patient in the extant literature. Other studies have identified that early experiences with CPAP (i.e., during the first week) are an important influence on patients' perceptions and beliefs about the OSA diagnosis and treatment with CPAP (Aloia, Arnedt, Stepnowsky, et al., 2005; Stepnowsky, Bardwell, et al., 2002).

From the collective published evidence, early experiences with CPAP, combined with patients' perceptions and beliefs about OSA and CPAP and the balance of their sociostructural facilitators/barriers, are critical factors that influence patients' decisions to use CPAP. To date, there are relatively few studies that have systematically examined the influence of disease and treatment perceptions and beliefs on CPAP adherence. Because the first week of CPAP treatment is critically influential on OSA patients' decisions to use CPAP, it is imperative that the contextual experiences and underlying beliefs and perceptions of the diagnosis and treatment be described. There are no published studies that have addressed this significant gap in the scientific literature. Furthermore, no study has directly explored patient perspectives, employing qualitative methodology, both at diagnosis and with treatment, to more fully describe contextual factors that differentiate CPAP adherers and nonadherers. Our study addressed several important questions: (a) What are adult OSA patients' beliefs and perceptions about OSA, the associated risks, and treatment with CPAP prior to treatment use? (b) What are the consequences of these beliefs and perceptions on the use of CPAP? (c) What are the beliefs and perceptions of adults with OSA after 1 week of CPAP use, including perceived benefits of treatment, effect of treatment on health, and perceived ability to adapt to CPAP? and (d) Do differences exist between adherers and nonadherers with regard to their beliefs and perceptions at diagnosis and with treatment use that might, in part, explain differences in CPAP adherence outcomes? To our knowledge, our study findings provide the first published description of beliefs of those who adhere and those who choose not to adhere to CPAP treatment. These findings contribute to understanding patient treatment decisions regarding CPAP use, suggest opportunities for identifying those at risk for nonadherence to CPAP, and contribute toward developing tailored interventions to promote CPAP use.

■ Conceptual Framework

Acceptance and consistent use of CPAP is influenced by a multitude of factors, as is evidenced in previous studies examining predictors of CPAP adherence (Weaver & Grunstein, 2008). It is therefore important to approach the phenomenon of CPAP adherence from a multifactorial perspective that addresses the complex nature of this particular health behavior. The application of social cognitive theory has been widely applied in studies of adoption, initiation, and maintenance of health behaviors (Bandura, 1977, 1992; Schwarzer & Fuchs, 1996). The core determinants of the model include knowledge, perceived self-efficacy, outcome expectations, health goals, and facilitators/barriers. The model posits that health promoting behaviors are primarily influenced by patients' self-efficacy, or their belief in their ability to exercise control over personal health habits, which influences other critical determinants: knowledge, outcome expectations, goals, and perceived facilitators and impediments (Bandura, 2004; see Figure 1). Knowledge of health risks and specific benefits relative to health behaviors is a necessary determinant for health behaviors, but rarely does knowledge alone promote change in behaviors. Outcome expectations, or the expectancies one holds for investing in a particular health behavior, are evaluated by the individual in terms of costs and benefits, including physical, social, and psychological. Individuals who anticipate that the benefits of a health behavior outweigh the costs are more inclined to perceive the health behavior as favorable, and more inclined to set short- and long-term personal goals to guide adoption of that health behavior. This cascade of health behavior determinants does not occur in isolation, but is influenced by barriers and facilitators that derive from personal, social,

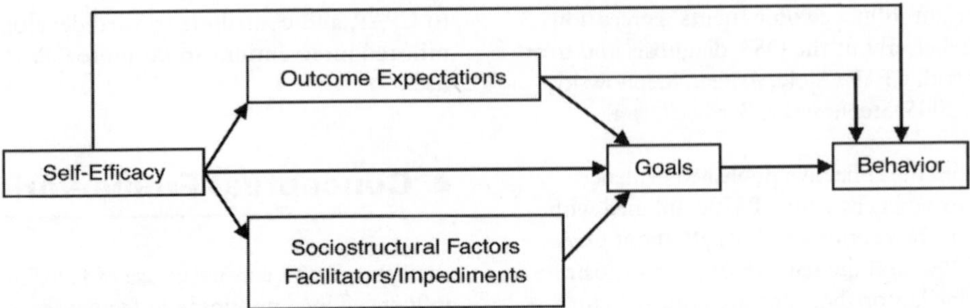

Figure 1. Social cognitive theory health determinants: Pathways of influence of self-efficacy on health behaviors. From Bandura, A. (2004). Health promotion by social cognitive means. *Health Education & Behavior, 31*(2), 146. Copyright 2004 by Sage Publications. Reprinted with permission of the publisher.

and environmental circumstances. As individuals identify facilitators for the health behavior and overcome barriers, their belief in their ability to successfully change or adopt a health behavior (i.e., perceived self-efficacy) increases.

Recognizing that individuals exist within a collective agency or community, the construct of self-efficacy is not confined solely to personal capabilities. Although commonalities in the basic concepts of self-efficacy exist across cultures, the "cultivated identities, values, belief structures, and agentic capabilities are the psychosocial systems through which experiences are filtered" (Bandura, 2002, p. 273). Bandura suggested that the application of social cognitive theory must be situated in context, recognizing that "human behavior is socially situated, richly contextualised, and conditionally expressed" (2002, p. 276). From this conceptual perspective and in a predominantly qualitative research paradigm, we examined patients' perceptions, beliefs, and experiences within their own context to permit an explicit description of salient factors that influenced OSA patients' decisions to use or not use CPAP.

■ Method

DESIGN

Using a concurrent nested, mixed method design, we conducted a longitudinal study extending from initial diagnosis through the first week of home CPAP treatment of newly diagnosed OSA patients. We conducted two individual interviews with participants and collected first-week CPAP adherence data. In contrast to a triangulation design, the concurrent nested study design emphasizes one methodology, and the data are mixed at the analysis phase of the study (Creswell, Plano Clark, Gutmann, & Hanson, 2003). Nesting the less dominant quantitative method within the predominant qualitative method permitted an enriched description of the participants and a more in-depth analysis of the overall phenomenon of interest: CPAP adherence (Creswell et al., 2003).

PARTICIPANTS

Adults with suspected OSA were recruited from a sleep clinic at an urban Veterans Affairs medical center during a 5-month enrollment period. One sleep specialist referred potential participants who were clinically likely to have OSA to the study. Our purposive sampling strategy was to include patients who (a) provided detailed information during their initial clinical visit and were willing to openly discuss their health and health care; (b) had at least moderate OSA (AHI ≥ 15 events/hour; American Academy of Sleep Medicine Task Force, 1999) and were prescribed CPAP treatment; (c) initially accepted CPAP for home

Qualitative Health Research, 2010;20(7):873–892.

use; and (d) were able to speak and understand English. To ensure that participants would be prescribed CPAP treatment based on Veterans Health Administration CPAP prescribing guidelines in place during study enrollment, patients with mild OSA (AHI < 15 events/hour) were excluded. We also excluded participants who had current or historical treatment with CPAP or any other treatment for OSA, a previous diagnosis of OSA, refusal of CPAP treatment by the participant prior to any CPAP exposure (i.e., in-laboratory CPAP titration sleep study), and those who required supplemental oxygen in addition to CPAP and/or bilevel positive airway pressure therapy for treatment of sleep-disordered breathing during their in-laboratory CPAP titration sleep study.

Previous studies have identified that decisions to adhere to CPAP emerge by the second to fourth day of treatment (Aloia, Arnedt, Stanchina, et al., 2007; Weaver, Kribbs, et al., 1997). Therefore, it is possible that patients' beliefs, perceptions, and experiences during the first several experiences with CPAP might significantly influence short- and long-term CPAP adherence patterns. For this reason, we did not include individuals who refused CPAP treatment prior to any CPAP experience, because we sought to describe salient factors preceding and during initial CPAP exposure. The protocol was approved by the research site and the affiliated university's institutional review boards. All participants provided informed consent prior to participating in any study activities.

PROCEDURE

After study enrollment, each participant had two in-laboratory, full-night sleep studies (i.e., polysomnograms). The first sleep study was a diagnostic study and the second sleep study was to determine the therapeutic CPAP pressure necessary to eliminate obstructive sleep apnea events. All sleep studies were performed and scored using standard criteria (American Academy of Sleep Medicine Task Force, 1999; Rechtschaffen & Kales, 1968). The AHI, a measure of disease severity in OSA, was computed from the diagnostic polysomnogram as the number of apneas and/or hypopneas per hour of sleep. The therapeutic CPAP pressure, the pressure required to eliminate hypopneas and apneas, was determined on a manual CPAP titration polysomnogram performed about 1 week (7.9 ± 6.9 days) after the diagnostic polysomnogram.

Semistructured Interviews. Semistructured interviews, conducted by one study investigator, were scheduled with participants at two intervals: within 1 week following diagnosis but prior to the CPAP titration sleep study, and after the first week of CPAP treatment at home (see Figure 2). All interviews were conducted in an informal, private room at the medical center to ensure privacy, participant comfort, and promote open sharing of information (Streubert Speziale & Carpenter, 2003). To minimize attrition, participants were offered the opportunity to participate in interviews at an alternative location or by telephone if transportation difficulties or ambulatory limitations precluded study participation.

Interview guides, consisting of specific questions and probes (i.e., prompts to encourage focus on the particular issue of interest) were used for each interview to ensure that a consistent sequence and set of questions were addressed across participants. A funnel approach was used in the development and execution of the interview guides. This approach begins with broad questions and gradually progresses to focused questions specific to the phenomenon of interest to promote sharing of experiences by the participants (Tashakkori & Teddlie, 1989). The first interview focused on perceptions of the diagnosis, perceived health effects of the diagnosis, pretreatment perceptions of CPAP, and the social and cultural precedents that led to the participant seeking medical care for their sleep problems (see Table 1). The second interview focused on perceived effects of treatment with CPAP, supportive mechanisms or barriers to using CPAP, and how beliefs and perceptions about the diagnosis, associated risks of

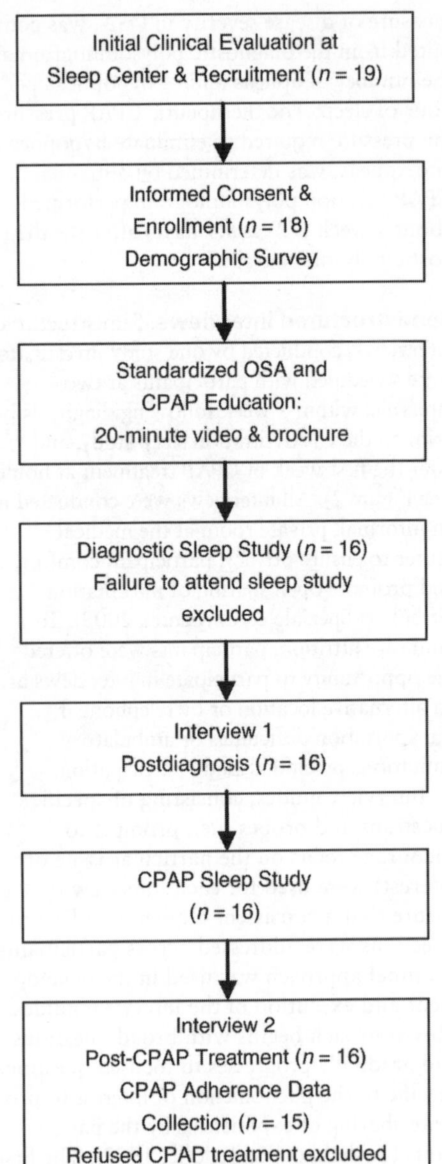

Figure 2. Study design.

the diagnosis, and the treatment experience might have affected CPAP adherence (see Table 2). Interviews were digitally audio-recorded and transcribed to an electronic format by a professional transcriptionist not affiliated with the study. Field notes were maintained by the interviewer before and after each interview to describe the environment of the interview, describe the participant at the time of the interview, and note any aberrations from the planned interview guide that occurred and a description of such aberrations. The field notes not only served as a descriptive context of the interview, but also served as interviewer reflexivity notations (i.e., interviewer biases, suppositions, and presuppositions of the research topic). The purpose of maintaining reflexivity notations was to ensure that interviewer-imposed assumptions did not take precedent over the participant's described experience.

CPAP Adherence. In accordance with the standard of clinical care at the sleep center, all participants were issued the same model CPAP machine (Respironics Rem- Star Pro®) that records on a data card (SmartCardTM) the time each day that the CPAP circuit is pressurized, an objective measurement of daily CPAP mask-on time. CPAP use was defined as periods when the device was applied for more than 20 minutes at effective pressure. One week of CPAP adherence data were uploaded to a personal computer for software analysis (Respironics EncorePro®) at the time of the second semistructured interview. Graphic adherence data were used as probes to discuss specific occurrences of CPAP nonuse. The objectively measured CPAP adherence data were also used to identify adherent ($\geq$ 6hrs/night CPAP use) and nonadherent participants ($<$ 6hrs/night CPAP use). A cut-off point of 6 hours/night was selected a priori to describe adherers and nonadherers to CPAP treatment, as recent evidence suggests that 6 or more hours of CPAP use per night is necessary to improve both functional and objective sleepiness outcomes (Weaver et al., 2007).

ANALYSIS

A sequential analysis was conducted, with qualitative-directed content analysis of interview data followed by quantitative descriptive

Table 1. Postdiagnosis Interview Guide

Concept	Topic/Question
Perceptions and knowledge of diagnosis	How did you know about sleep disorders and the sleep center before coming to your first appointment? Before being told you have OSA,[a] had you heard of OSA? If so, what did you know about OSA? What do you now understand about OSA? After having your sleep study, what are your thoughts about OSA and what it means to you?
Perceived effects of diagnosis	How do you believe OSA affects you in your daily life?
Sociocultural precedents and influences on health, illness/disease, and care seeking	Do you know anyone else who has been diagnosed with OSA? If so, how did that impact you and your interest in coming to the sleep center? Why did you seek care from the sleep center? Is there anyone who influenced you to seek care for this problem? Is there anyone who has helped you understand what OSA is? If so, how did that information impact your desire to receive treatment? What has you experience with a health care system been to this point? Do sleep, sleeping, and/or the sleep environment have any specific meaning(s) to you? To your family? To your spouse/significant other/bed partner?

[a]OSA = Obstructive sleep apnea

analysis of the CPAP adherence data. By sequentially analyzing the data, the priority of the individual as informant was emphasized and the investigators were blinded to CPAP adherence until the final analysis procedure, a mixed methods analysis, was conducted (see Figure 3). By dividing the participants into categories of adherent (i.e., ≥ 6 hrs/night CPAP use) and nonadherent (i.e., < 6 hrs/night CPAP use), we examined across-case consistencies in subthemes and themes to describe the contextualized experience of adhering or not adhering to CPAP treatment.

Each transcript was read in its entirety, highlighting, extracting, and condensing text from individual interviews that addressed individual beliefs, perceptions, and/or experiences during diagnosis and early treatment with CPAP. This process of text analysis brought forward the manifest content of the qualitative data (Graneheim & Lundman, 2004). These responses were separated from the interview text, identified by participant identification number, and entered into an analysis table. Abstraction, or the process of taking condensed, manifest data and interpreting the underlying meaning (i.e., latent meaning), followed as participant responses were then described in a condensed format and interpreted for meaning within a thematic coding process. Trustworthiness was enhanced as the likelihood of investigator bias was minimized by first highlighting relevant text for coding, extracting relevant text from complete interviews transcripts, and then coding the meaning units for theory-driven categories or themes and then for subthemes (Hsieh & Shannon, 2005).

Table 2. One Week Post-CPAP Use Interview Guide

Concept	Topic/Question
Perceived effects and knowledge of treatment with CPAP	Have you been using CPAP[a] for the treatment of your OSA[b]? How would you describe your use of CPAP? Are you experiencing any improvement in the way that you feel since you have started using CPAP? When did you first learn about CPAP? Who first described CPAP to you? What did you think when you first learned about CPAP? First saw CPAP? First used CPAP in the sleep laboratory? What do you see as the most important reason for using CPAP in the short term? In the long term?
Supportive mechanisms or barriers to incorporating CPAP into daily life	How was the first week of CPAP treatment? What kinds of problems are you experiencing using CPAP? What has prevented you from regularly using CPAP? What has been helpful to you in regularly using CPAP?
Sociocultural perspectives of health-related decisions to use or not use CPAP	Do you believe CPAP treatment is a treatment you can [continue to] use? Did this belief change since you first learned about your OSA diagnosis? Since starting CPAP? Do you envision yourself using CPAP during the next 3 months? During the next year? During the next 5 years? Do you have any concerns about the CPAP unit? About your sleep [ability or quality]? About your sleep environment that might affect your CPAP use? How does the diagnosis of OSA and treatment with CPAP affect or been affected by those around you?

[a]CPAP = continuous positive airway pressure.
[b]OSA = obstructive sleep apnea.

The overarching, theory-derived themes were initially determined by applying the broad determinants of health as described in the study's conceptual framework, social cognitive theory (Bandura, 2004). These themes included knowledge, perceived barriers and facilitators, perceived self-efficacy, outcome expectations, and goals. This approach permitted the investigators to examine the applicability of the theoretical framework to the phenomenon of CPAP adherence and elaborate on previous findings suggesting the framework's concepts as measurable predictors of CPAP-related health behaviors (Aloia, Arnedt, Stepnowsky, et al., 2005; Stepnowsky, Bardwell, et al., 2002; Wild et al., 2004). Emergent subthemes were identified as thematic content analysis progressed. The subthemes were then categorized within the overarching conceptual framework themes (see Table 3). We designed the analysis strategy to be consistent with other recent empirical studies of CPAP adherence while permitting a more robust, narrative description of what these theoretically derived variables mean from the perspective of the OSA patient.

Theme definitions were developed by the investigators and reviewed by an expert

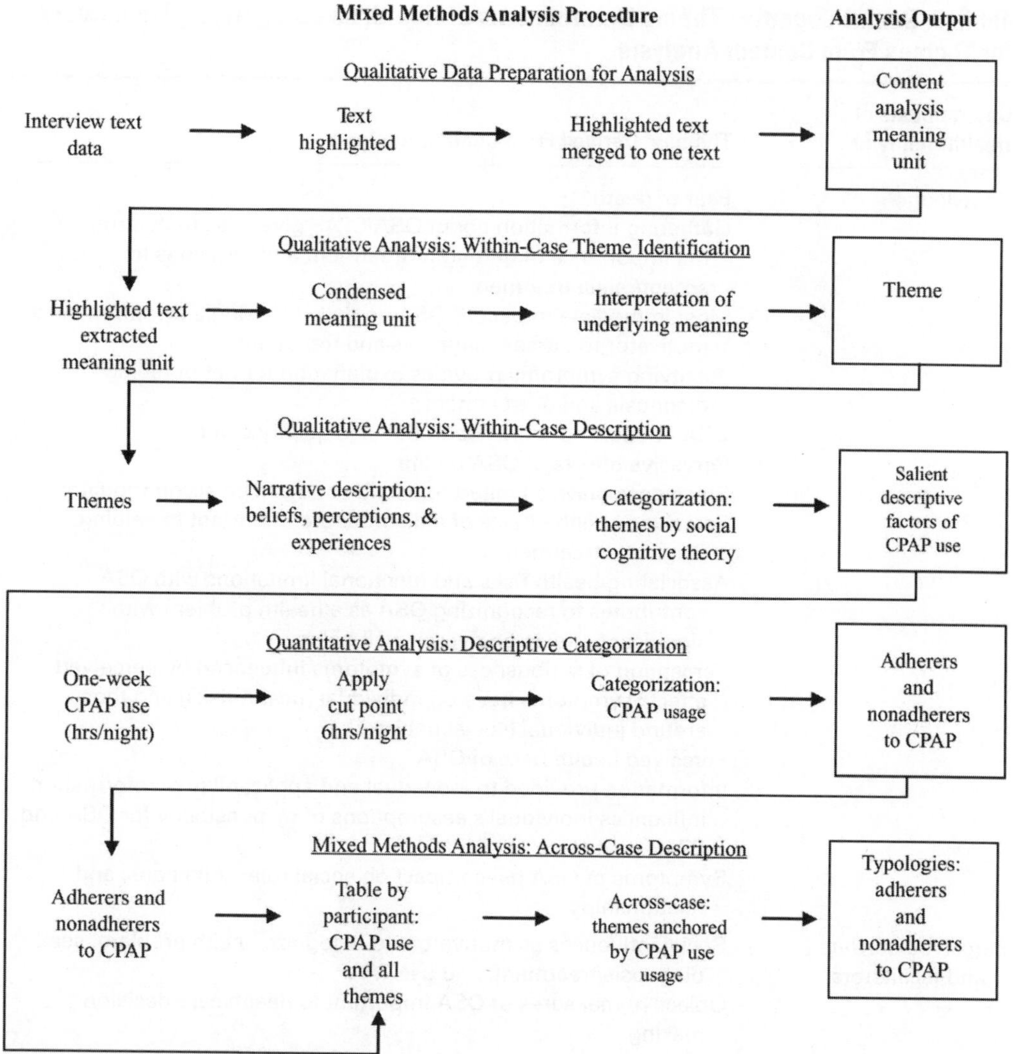

Figure 3. Sequential analysis procedure.

qualitative methodologist and an expert in the research application of theoretical constructs. One study investigator, blinded to CPAP adherence data, coded all interview data for the study. Valid application of the themes was examined by an independent expert coder. Coded interviews were independently recoded by the expert coder to establish validity and reliability of the application of the codes to the interview data. All extracted interview data were eligible for recoding; approximately 15% of the data from each total interview were randomly selected for expert recoding. Agreement of the study coder and the expert coder was 94%, meeting the established criteria of 80% agreement for acceptance of the coded data. When differences in application of codes were identified, code definitions were reviewed by coders, discussion of specific application of the code(s) was held, and

Table 3. Social Cognitive Theory Determinants of Health as Categorizing Framework for Themes From Content Analysis

Determinants of Health Behavior	Themes[a] Derived From Content Analysis
Knowledge	Fear of death
	Gathering information about OSA/CPAP gives rise to determining the importance of getting to treatment and decisions to accept/reject treatment
	Most immediate impact of OSA on daily life [single symptom] as a motivator to pursue diagnosis and treatment
	Justifying symptoms provides explanation for not pursuing diagnosis and/or treatment
	OSA impacts not only health but also quality of life
	Pervasive effects of OSA on life
	Sleepiness plays a limited role in life and can be accommodated
	Perceived health effects of a disorder are important to valuing diagnosis/treatment
	Associating health risks and functional limitations with OSA contributes to recognizing OSA as a health problem with significant effects on overall well-being
	Perception of seriousness of symptoms influenced by perceived effects symptoms have on individual [health risks] and those around individual [social network]
	Perceived health risks of OSA
	Information provided to individual and applicability of information influences individual's assumptions of responsibility for OSA and CPAP treatment
	Symptoms of OSA have impact on social roles, functions, and relationships
Perceived barriers and facilitators	Social influences as motivators to recognize health problem, seek diagnosis/treatment, and use CPAP
	Objective measures of OSA important to health care decision making
	Differences in perception of urgency of treatment between patient and provider influences valuing of diagnosis and treatment by patient
	Social networks contribute to treatment acceptance but not necessarily to treatment use
	Perceived seriousness of symptoms influenced by perceived effects of symptoms on individual [health risks] and those around individual
	Social networks provide support, help problem solve health concerns, and are sources of health-related information commonality of symptoms of OSA promotes perception of normalcy:
	Barrier to seeking diagnosis/treatment

(continued)

Table 3. *(Continued)*

Determinants of Health Behavior	Themes[a] Derived From Content Analysis
	Social influences as motivators to recognize health problem, seek diagnosis and treatment, and use treatment
	Silent symptoms: Fear of what it means if symptoms of OSA are undetectable
	Family and social networks contribute to health beliefs about sleep
	Expectations of health delivery vs. the actual delivery of health care services impact on the importance individual's place on their health and the value they place on their relationship with health care providers
Perceived self-efficacy	Knowledge and information provided to individual and applicability of information influences individual's assumption of responsibility for OSA and CPAP treatment
	Early response to CPAP, consistent or inconsistent with outcome expectations, facilitates or is a barrier to treatment use
	Early experience with CPAP is a source of support or a barrier to belief in own ability to use treatment
	Fitting treatment into life
	Problem-solving difficulties/routinization of CPAP responsibilities contribute to disease management
Outcome expectations	Understanding why symptoms exist and associating specific symptoms with a diagnosis provides hope that treatment will address experienced symptoms and improve overall quality of life
	Expectations of treatment outcomes are facilitators of treatment initiation and use
	Early response to CPAP, consistent or inconsistent with outcome expectations, facilitates or is a barrier to using treatment
Goals	Problem-solving difficulties/routinization of CPAP responsibilities contribute to disease management

[a] Themes derived from participant text data were categorized as a determinant of health behavior from social cognitive theory. Themes are not mutually exclusive. Theme definitions were mutually agreed on by investigators of the study and applied to the directed content analysis procedure by a single investigator acting as the primary coder of text data.

mutual agreement was achieved in all instances of coding differences.

After all interview data were coded for themes, the investigators used the average daily CPAP use during the first week of treatment to separate adherers ($\geq$ 6 hours CPAP use/night) and nonadherers ($<$ 6 hours CPAP use/ night). Descriptive statistics were used in the analysis of 1 week of CPAP adherence data (mean $\pm$ standard deviation [SD]). Across-case analysis of themes and subthemes was then examined from an integrative perspective, using adherent and nonadherent as anchors, or as a unique descriptive qualifier, to identify common perceptions, beliefs, and experiences within the groups of interest. The across-case analysis, including both qualitative and quantitative data sets as complementary within an analysis matrix, gave rise to cases that had common descriptive aspects.

RESULTS

With the recurrence of themes in the content analysis phase, data saturation was reached at 15 participants and the sampling procedure was considered complete. The participants were all veterans, predominantly middleaged (53.9 ± 12.7 years) men (88%; see Table 4). The participants were well educated, with 93% (n = 14) of the sample achieving a high school education or higher. The sample, on average, had severe OSA (AHI 53.5 ± 26.5 events/hr), with an oxygen nadir of 66.4% (± 13.2%). The average CPAP pressure setting was 10.7 ± 1.6 cmH20. Average CPAP use during the first 7 days of CPAP treatment was 4.98 ± 0.5 hours/night. Sorting on CPAP adherence (i.e. ≥ 6hrs/night CPAP use and < 6 hrs/ night CPAP use), there were six adherers and nine nonadherers. The interview prior to CPAP exposure was conducted after the diagnostic polysomnogram, on average at Day 9 (range 2 to 28 days), and the second interview was conducted following at least 1 week of CPAP treatment (average number of days from Day 1 of CPAP use, 18; range 7 to 47 days).

Table 4. Sample Description

Characteristic	Frequency (%) (n = 15)
Gender	
Men	13 (87%)
Women	2 (13%)
Race/ethnicity	
African American	9 (60%)
White	5 (33%)
Other	1 (7%)
Marital status	
Married	7 (47%)
Single	3 (20%)
Divorced	3 (20%)
Widowed	2 (13%)
Highest education	
Middle school	1 (7%)
High school	7 (47%)
2 yr college	4 (27%)
4+ yr college	3 (20%)
Shift work	3 (20%)
Employed	6 (40%)
Retired	6 (40%)
	Mean 6 Standard Deviation
Age, years	53.9 ±12.7
Weight, pounds	248.9 ± 68.7
AHI, events/hour	53.5 ± 26.5
O2 Nadir, %	66.4 ± 13.2
CPAP pressure, cmH_2O	10.7 ± 1.6
1 week CPAP adherence, hours	4.98 ± 0.5

ADHERERS AND NONADHERERS TO CPAP THERAPY

Knowledge and Perceived Health Risks. Knowledge, or the "knowing" an individual has about the health risks and benefits of health behaviors (Bandura, 2004) was a predominant theme in both interviews for all participants. Saturation on nearly every knowledge theme suggests that participants identified that having an understanding of OSA and CPAP is an important part of the experience of being diagnosed with OSA and treated with CPAP. Adherent participants related their knowledge of risks and benefits of CPAP to their own outcome expectations after being diagnosed with OSA. For some participants, knowledge of OSA being simply more than snoring was a first step in recognizing OSA as a syndrome with health implications. One participant described this, saying, "I knew sleep apnea existed, but it just never dawned on me how serious it was in my case. I just didn't pay any attention to it. I just figured I was going to snore for the rest of my life."

For many participants, "putting the whole picture together" after receiving education about OSA and CPAP treatment helped them understand that they not only were experiencing symptoms of OSA on a daily basis, but their overall health and quality of life was impacted by OSA. During the first interview, participants were provided with a summary of their diagnostic sleep study results. The combination of education about the OSA diagnosis and treatment with CPAP, and relating their own diagnosis to their daily health and functioning, was important to adherent participants' formulation of accurate beliefs and perceptions of OSA and CPAP. These beliefs served to motivate or facilitate adherent participants' determination to pursue CPAP after diagnosis:

> I didn't know anything really, how the CPAP worked or anything like that. I just knew that there was a disease called sleep apnea and that a lot of people have it and people don't realize it. I really still didn't know anything about it til after I went through the test [diagnostic polysomnogram]. . . . Five [breathing events] is normal and thirty is severe and I'm doing ninety an hour. You know that literally scared the hell right out of me because all I could think of is I'm going to die in my sleep.
>
> [T]hen when you told me about driving, being tired, I remembered that every time we take off on a long trip, the first hour I got to pull over and rest. So it all came together. So I figured maybe I do have it [OSA].

For many adherent participants, knowledge of health risks associated with OSA was limited to "being sluggish" or "having low energy levels." For some, their perception of OSA was only relative to "falling asleep when I sit down." Participants who "put the whole picture together," relating their diagnosis to their own health status, were motivated to accept CPAP treatment from the outset. For example, one participant said, "It's [OSA] got to take a toll in the long run on a lot of things, like high blood pressure. I'm hoping that it helps me to drop my high blood pressure." These perceptions provided hope for adherent participants that expanded beyond the management of their OSA to other disease and health experiences:

> If I have more energy and I'm not so sluggish—because I go to the local high school track and get in five or six laps, walking around the track—I will have more energy to do those kinds of things that keep you healthy.

Posttreatment, there was less emphasis on knowledge-based themes among adherent participants. This suggested a shift of emphasis among adherers from knowledge of risks and benefits of OSA to perceptions derived from the actual experience of CPAP treatment.

Nonadherent participants' knowledge at diagnosis was not different from adherent participants' knowledge. However, those with knowledge that served as a barrier, rather than a facilitator, to diagnosis were less likely to pursue a diagnostic sleep study in a timely fashion. This was particularly true for those who had inaccurate knowledge and perceptions of OSA, such as OSA being a condition of simple snoring. Even though many acknowledged they probably had OSA, the snoring was the "problem" that defined OSA, not apneic events and resultant untoward health and functional outcomes. As one participant described,

> My brother does it [snores], and he stopped [breathing] all the time in the middle of the night. My father did it, you know, and I do it. I knew I do it so it's been a while, I mean, I don't remember not being a loud snorer. . . . Like I said, my condition is hereditary. I'm sure my oldest son has it and I'm sure my youngest son is going to end up with it. My brother had it and my father had it, you know, my mother probably had it 'cause she's a snorer. I didn't think it was serious of a problem 'cause it's [snoring, stops in breathing] something that I had experienced for so many years.

Furthermore, describing early knowledge of "having to wear a mask" for the treatment of OSA served as a barrier to both seeking diagnosis and treatment for some. This perception was not consistent among only nonadherers though, as many of the participants expressed concerns about the anticipated treatment of their OSA. CPAP adherers and nonadherers described critically important differences in their own ability to reconcile the following: (a) their OSA diagnosis; (b) their experience of symptoms; (c) their goals for treatment use; and (d) their outcome expectations that were met after treatment exposure. These factors, when reconciled by the individual, facilitated overall positive perceptions of the diagnosis and treatment experience.

Goal Setting and Outcome Expectancies. Outcome expectancies are the expected or anticipated costs and benefits for healthful habits/behaviors that support or deter from an individual's investment in the behavior (Bandura, 2004). Among the participants, postdiagnosis outcome expectancies that were consistently met were highly influential on participants' decisions to use CPAP. For example, after being diagnosed with OSA, one participant brought all his experienced symptoms into perspective, relating them to his OSA. With treatment, he was hopeful that these symptoms would resolve. He stated, "It seems like sleep apnea basically causes all those problems. So I figure if I can get this taken care of [by wearing CPAP], basically the problems will subside." Making sense of symptoms in terms of treatment outcome expectancies helped adherers commit to trying CPAP and believing that CPAP was going to be a positive experience. One participant summarized his perception of symptoms and outcome expectations like this: "But without me even trying it I know that what I'm experiencing and how it's affected me, and that I want to get better if I can and so there's nothing going to keep me away from getting a CPAP."

A particularly important perception described by participants was their early response to CPAP as influential on future/continued use of CPAP. These early, first experiences were helpful to formulating realistic and personally important outcome expectancies for CPAP use. One participant described his response to CPAP after wearing it for the first time in the sleep laboratory during his second sleep study (i.e., CPAP sleep study):

> But being like I got relief the first night I was at the hospital. I drove home that morning after they woke me up, I went down, I got breakfast, and I'm driving home, I'm saying to myself, gee, I feel great and I only got from one o'clock to six, you know. I feel so much better and I felt so much better that whole day. I felt so good after that five hours of sleep with the machine on that it sold me.

For adherent participants, having a positive response to CPAP during the sleep study night with CPAP was highly motivating for continued CPAP use at home. Furthermore, this early response set the stage for participants to develop an early commitment to the treatment, even when faced with barriers. Persistent, positive responses to CPAP throughout the early treatment period (i.e., 1 week) reinforced participants' outcome expectancies and helped them formulate a perception of the treatment that was conducive to long-term use.

Goals for improved health and for achieving certain health behaviors are an important part of being successful with any health behavior. According to Bandura (2004), individuals set goals for their personal health, including establishing concrete plans or strategies for achieving those goals. Goal setting among adherent CPAP users focused on "how best to adapt to using CPAP" or identifying "solutions to difficulties with use of CPAP." These goals were established so that adherent CPAP users were able to achieve their outcome expectations. Goal setting was not specifically discussed by adherent participants before using CPAP. With exposure to and experience with CPAP, adherent participants first identified that using CPAP was important and, thereafter, identified "tricks and techniques" to successfully use CPAP. Whether these strategies originated from the participant or were a collaborative effort between participant and a support source, having a plan that addressed how best to adapt to CPAP promoted continued effort directed at using CPAP, as described by one adherent participant:

> I guess the first night I put it on I sort of got a little feeling of claustrophobia, but I pushed it out of my mind, saying to myself, "Don't let this [bother you], this is a machine that is going to help you, you got to wear it," so I just put it in my mind that I was going to wear it.

As this participant described, it was important for him to devise a way that he could use the treatment so that he might realize his overall health goals. Similarly, one participant found that he could not fall asleep with CPAP at full pressure. He emphasized the importance of using CPAP to treat his OSA, but he equated using CPAP to "a tornado blowing through your nose." He recalled being taught about several features on the CPAP machine that might alleviate this sensation. After testing a few tricks on the CPAP machine, he found that he was able to fall asleep on a lower pressure setting while the pressure increased to full pressure setting after he was asleep (i.e., ramp function). By setting an immediate goal to get to sleep while wearing CPAP, he was able to achieve his longer-term goal to wear CPAP each night. The long-term goal of adherent participants was to feel better or sleep better, but the immediate goal was to be able to wear CPAP.

For nonadherers, a negative experience during their CPAP sleep study led them to have an undesirable outlook on CPAP and the overall treatment of OSA. For example, one participant described experiencing no immediate response to CPAP during the CPAP sleep study; therefore, he didn't expect to experience any response to treatment over a more extended period of time:

> I still had the same kind of sleep, I thought. As a matter of fact I thought it took me longer to get to sleep than it did on the first sleep study [without CPAP]. I believe my sleep was still the same type of sleep that I always get, even though, you know, the machine was supposed to make me sleep better. I still woke up in the same condition that I usually wake up in, is what I'm trying to say. I didn't feel any more vigorous or alert or anything after that first night.

Participants' descriptions of their considerations for using CPAP consistently included the question, "What are the down sides of using CPAP?" Combining early negative perceptions of the treatment and early negative experiences with CPAP, nonadherers tended to see the drawbacks of using the treatment as far outweighing any benefits of using the treatment. One participant described both negative perceptions and negative experiences, which caused him to believe that CPAP treatment outcome expectancies were not worth the torment of using the treatment:

> No, I didn't think I couldn't do it from the beginning. I was believing it was gonna do something more than what it did, and it didn't do anything. I'm not getting sleep, I'm still getting up tired. I guess I expected more from it and I didn't get anything, not anything that I could see anyway. No, just a bunch of botheration and I didn't get any sleep.

Among participants who did not adhere, the goal-oriented theme was not present after diagnosis. Nonadherers did not articulate specific goals for attaining treatment and, furthermore, they did not describe strategies to be able to wear CPAP after 1 week of CPAP treatment. For nonadherers, establishing treatment-related goals for use of CPAP was not a priority.

Facilitators of and Barriers to CPAP use. Perceived facilitators and barriers can be personal, social, and/or structural. Although perceived facilitators and barriers are influential on health behaviors, this process is mediated by self-efficacy (Bandura, 2004). Therefore, the existence of a barrier, in and of itself, might not be particularly influential on an individual's behavior if their self-efficacy is high. Consistent with this conceptual perspective, some participants identified barriers that were particularly troublesome when using CPAP, but were vigilant users of CPAP despite these barriers. Conversely, those who described numerous facilitators to using CPAP treatment were not necessarily adherent to CPAP.

Adherent participants were less focused on potential or actual facilitators and barriers to using CPAP over time than nonadherers. When adherent participants discussed facilitators and barriers, their overall descriptions were positive, with facilitators being the focus of their experience after using CPAP for 1 week. No adherent participants emphasized barriers to using CPAP after 1 week of treatment. Furthermore, when faced with barriers, adherent participants described perceptions of the treatment as important and identified a belief in their ability to overcome the barrier. For example, one participant experienced a sensation of not being able to breathe during his second night of

CPAP use at home, but his ability to use CPAP was influenced by his commitment to "needing" the treatment:

> Because it was like I couldn't breathe and even though the machine was on, it was like I was paralyzed, and this happened every time when I tried to go back to sleep. How many times? Three more times that very same night until I was getting really anxious because every time I would try to go to sleep, after a while I would get that anxiety again. Finally, I prayed. I got up and I prayed real hard, asked God to really help me with this and I was right to sleep. Ever since then, I pray every night and have no problems.

As this example demonstrates, barriers and facilitators are not independent determinants of health behavior. Participants described situations and experiences that were labeled as either a facilitator or barrier, but the actual behavioral outcome of getting to diagnosis and using CPAP was not necessarily reflective of such experiences being a barrier or facilitator.

The facilitating experiences described by adherent participants centered on social interactions that provided motivation and facilitation of their CPAP use. Facilitating experiences included descriptions of social support, shared experiences of CPAP use with other CPAP users, and recognition that their own improvement as a result of CPAP treatment was an important influence on social relationships. Social relationships and the ability to be fully engaged in social interactions during their first week of CPAP use was described by several adherent participants as a facilitator to ongoing treatment:

> I see the difference. People see the difference. My wife sees the difference. My kids see the difference. That helps. I think that's 50% of it. People telling you that you have changed and things are getting better and you look a lot better and you a sound a lot better and you act a lot better, because when you have feedback like that you know it's [CPAP] helping.
>
> Our relationship [with spouse] is getting better and better. I think since the sleep machine it's even been more because some things that irritate me, I would speak on and it would cause like a little bit of friction, as it happens in couples. But since I've had the sleep machine, I've been letting the minor things go, things that irritate me or I would complain about before. . . . Communication, our relationship, so we've been able to talk more and enjoy each other even more since then [starting CPAP]. Yeah, I like the machine, I really do, and I like what it's doing.

Adherent participants clearly emphasized the importance of improved social relationships as a result of their CPAP treatment. Many recognized such improvements after a close friend or family member suggested the improvement was obvious.

Nonadherent participants emphasized barriers rather than facilitators to using CPAP after being diagnosed with OSA. However, after using CPAP for 1 week, nonadherers identified few, if any, actual barriers to treatment. Unlike adherent participants, nonadherers did not discuss social interactions as an important part of their post- CPAP treatment experience. Nonadherent participants also identified themselves as single, divorced, or widowed, with the exception of one participant. Nonadherers did not discuss their social networks (i.e., friends, family outside of their residence, coworkers) as important to their experiences of being diagnosed with OSA and starting CPAP treatment.

Perceived Self-Efficacy. Perceived self-efficacy is the belief that one can exercise control over one's own health habits, producing desired effects by one's own health behaviors (Bandura, 2004). This overarching theme was meaningfully described by participants and represented by several subthemes that were important to both adherers and nonadherers in the study. Within these descriptions, participants offered experiences with being diagnosed with OSA and using CPAP that led to their belief in themselves, or lack thereof, to use or not use the treatment.

Adherers in the sample described generally positive perceived self-efficacy regarding future use of CPAP. Adherers had a positive belief in their ability to use CPAP from the outset, which persisted and became increasingly frequent from diagnosis to early CPAP treatment, even if they first doubted their ability to use the treatment. As one participant described, the first thought of wearing a mask during sleep was not appealing, but with a positive first experience with CPAP, the participant was increasingly confident that CPAP was going to be a part of his life:

> I think I seen the masks sitting there and I thought to myself, I hope I don't have to wear one of those things. Then they came in and said, "Now we're going to put the CPAP on you," and I said, "Okay," and they put the CPAP on me and when they came back into the room I felt great when I woke up at six. They had to wake me up at six o'clock because I was sleeping and you know, I think I felt after that, I didn't care what it was if I got that much sleep from one o'clock to six without getting up. I was going to wear or do whatever I had to do to do it [wear CPAP].

Adherent participants also described that they planned to incorporate CPAP into their daily routine, suggesting an underlying positive belief in their ability to accomplish the health behavior of using CPAP. Recognizing that using CPAP would necessitate additional daily "work," adherers had well-defined plans of incorporating the added demands to their daily schedule:

> I have to just add some things that I have to do in order to keep the CPAP machine clean and to make sure that it's dry and each week I have to disinfect it, but once I did it, once I decided I was gonna do it, I just went in the bathroom, did the whole thing, it only took about twenty minutes, twenty-five minutes, and I was all done. And getting up in the morning and doing the daily cleaning, you know, that's not a negative but it's just something I have to make an adjustment to.

Nonadherent participants described having largely negative experiences with CPAP during the first exposure (i.e., CPAP sleep study) or during the early phase of home CPAP use. Few nonadherent participants experienced benefits with treatment and nonadherers described unsuccessful or a lack of problem-solving efforts with CPAP difficulties. These negative experiences were important areas of concern with regard to their perceived ability to use CPAP over the long term (perceived self-efficacy). For example, one participant had such an extremely negative experience during the first week he was exposed to CPAP that he firmly doubted his ability to ever use it:

> I couldn't breathe in [the mask]. This thing, I had to suck in to get a breath out of it. Last night I got a good night's sleep but I woke up, then I was claustrophobic. I felt like I was stuck under a bed someplace and couldn't get out and then I woke up. When I wore it the whole night through I wasn't sleeping so that's one of the reasons [I won't use CPAP], like I didn't sleep with it on; it was too aggravating.

Each participant described getting used to CPAP during the first several nights of treatment. With unsuccessful experiences during this period, participants either identified resources to help improve their experience or made decisions to use CPAP less or not at all. For all participants, early experiences with CPAP contributed to their belief in their own abilities to get used to the therapy.

Individuals who had difficulty fitting CPAP into their lives were challenged to be adherent to the treatment. When CPAP was seen as not fitting into a life routine, participants offered doubts as to their ability to continue to use the treatment. One participant described having a routine of falling asleep with television. With CPAP, she had difficulty watching television and therefore she experienced more difficulty getting to sleep. Although she continued to try to use CPAP, she expressed that using CPAP was generally annoying to her. The complexities presented by using CPAP within the constraints of her normal routine were likely to increasingly influence doubt in her ability to use CPAP.

MARRIED AND UNMARRIED CPAP USERS

With the emerging emphasis placed on social support and social networks by adherers in the study, we explored how the social context of daily life impacted on perceptions of OSA and CPAP treatment by examining married (n = 7) and unmarried (n = 8) participants' responses. Using married and unmarried status from self-reported demographic characteristics as anchors, or as a unique descriptive qualifier, we sorted the subthemes within an analysis matrix to identify common perceptions, beliefs, and experiences within these qualifier groups. We included all participants who identified themselves as married or common-law married as married; all participants who identified themselves as single, divorced, or widowed were included as unmarried.

These groups described different experiences with both diagnosis and CPAP treatment. Married participants offered descriptions of social support resources within immediate proximity that were positive facilitators of seeking diagnosis and starting/staying on treatment. Married participants expressed positive beliefs in their ability to use CPAP with early treatment use, often described in conjunction with a CPAP problem-solving episode that was collaboratively resolved with their partner/spouse. Married participants described overwhelmingly positive early responses and experiences with CPAP treatment. Their outcome expectations were consistent across time. They generally anticipated positive responses to CPAP prior to exposure and experienced positive responses to treatment after 1 week of use. Married participants also identified success in "fitting CPAP into their lives." These participants were able to identify far more benefits from than difficulties with CPAP, benefits that enhanced their ongoing commitment to use of the treatment. Married participants discussed proximate support sources (i.e., spouse, living partner, family members) as important to providing feedback about their response to treatment, trouble-shooting difficulties, and positive reinforcement for persistent use of CPAP.

Unmarried participants commonly identified friends or coworkers as motivating factors (facilitators) to seek diagnosis but less social influence on/facilitation of treatment use after 1 week of CPAP therapy. Without the presence of immediate social support, unmarried participants did not emphasize important social interactions with actual wearing of CPAP. After 1 week of treatment on CPAP, unmarried participants described less confidence in their ability to use CPAP and described less "response" to CPAP than those participants who were married. Unmarried participants described few facilitators of treatment use during the first week of CPAP therapy. Nearly all unmarried participants identified "self-driven" reasons for pursuing treatment, and there was an absence of social sources of support, or "cheerleaders and helpful problem solvers" while using CPAP during the first week.

TYPOLOGIES OF ADHERENT AND NONADHERENT CPAP USERS

Described differences in beliefs, perceptions, and experiences of being diagnosed with OSA and early treatment with CPAP were explicit between adherers and nonadherers. Adherers perceived health and functional risks of untreated OSA, had positive belief in their ability to use CPAP from early in the diagnostic process, had clearly defined outcome expectations, had more facilitators than barriers as they progressed from diagnosis to treatment, and identified important social influences and support sources for both pursuing diagnosis and persisting with CPAP treatment. Nonadherers described not knowing the risks associated with OSA, perceived fewer symptoms of their diagnosis, did not have clearly defined outcome expectations for treatment, identified fewer improvements with CPAP exposure, placed less emphasis on social support and socially derived feedback with early CPAP treatment, and perceived and experienced more barriers to CPAP treatment. As a result of the across-case analysis in which consistencies and differences emerged among adherers and nonadherers in the described experience of being diagnosed with OSA and treated with CPAP, we suggest typologies, or descriptive profiles, of persons with CPAP-treated OSA (see Table 5). The typologies we propose are consistent with previous empirical studies of CPAP adherence, in that predictive relationships between risk perception, outcome expectancies, perceived self-efficacy, and social support with CPAP use have been identified. Our study findings extend the previous findings by illuminating the importance of contextual meaning persons

Table 5. Typologies of Adherent and Nonadherent CPAP Users

Adherent CPAP Users	Nonadherent CPAP Users
Define risks associated with OSA	Unable to define risks associated with OSA
Identify outcome expectations from outset	Describe few outcomes expectations
Have fewer barriers than facilitators	Do not recognize own symptoms
Facilitators less important later with treatment use	Describe barriers as more influential on CPAP use than facilitators
Develop and define goals and reasons for CPAP use	Facilitators of treatment absent or unrecognized
Describe positive belief in ability to use CPAP even with potential or experienced difficulties	Describe low belief in ability to use CPAP
Proximate social influences prominent in decisions to pursue diagnosis and treatment	Describe early negative experiences with CPAP, reinforcing low belief in ability to use CPAP Unable to identify positive responses to CPAP during early treatment

derive from their experiences, beliefs, and perceptions when progressing from diagnosis with OSA to treatment with CPAP. Moreover, the typologies succinctly describe critical differences between these groups of CPAP-treated OSA persons that support the development of patient-centered or -tailored adherence interventions that recognize individual differences.

▪ Discussion

To our knowledge, this is the first study to apply a predominantly qualitative method to describe individuals' beliefs and perceptions of the diagnosis of OSA and treatment with CPAP relative to short-term CPAP adherence. Our findings are consistent with previous, empirical studies with regard to the overall applicability of social cognitive theory to the phenomenon of CPAP adherence. The findings from our study uniquely extend these previous findings by illuminating the importance of the individual experiences, beliefs, and perceptions as influential on decisions to pursue diagnosis and treatment of OSA. The described differences between adherers and nonadherers in our study suggest critical tailored or patient-centered intervention opportunities that might be developed and tested among patients who are newly diagnosed with OSA and anticipate CPAP treatment. The major findings of the study include the following: (a) adults described and assigned meaning to being diagnosed with OSA and treated with CPAP, which in turn influenced their decisions to accept or reject treatment and the extent of CPAP use; and (b) differences in beliefs and perceptions at diagnosis and with CPAP treatment were identified among CPAP adherers and nonadherers and also described in the social context of married and unmarried CPAP users. The described differences between these groups provide data to support the first published typology, or descriptive profile, of CPAP adherers and nonadherers.

Theoretically derived variables, such as the determinants of health behaviors described in social cognitive theory and applied in our study, are operational concepts that help us understand OSA patients' perceptions and beliefs about OSA and CPAP, and can guide interventions to improve adherence to CPAP.

Framed by Bandura's social cognitive theory (1977), differences among adherers and nonadherers to CPAP can be defined across social cognitive theory determinants of health behaviors: (a) knowledge, (b) perceived self-efficacy, (c) outcome expectancies and goals, and (d) facilitators and barriers. As previous studies have demonstrated, psychosocial constructs, such as those consistent with social cognitive theory, provide possibly the most explained variance, to date, among adherers and nonadherers (Aloia, Arnedt, Stepnowsky, et al., 2005; Engleman & Wild, 2003; Stepnowsky, Bardwell, et al., 2002; Weaver et al., 2003). Furthermore, recent intervention studies to promote CPAP adherence have applied similar theoretical constructs with some positive findings (Aloia, Arnedt, Millman, et al., 2007; Richards, Bartlett, Wong, Malouff, & Grunstein, 2007). As our study findings suggest, decisions to use CPAP are individualized and at least in part dependent on the patient's support environment and early experiences with and beliefs about CPAP. Because early commitments to use or not use CPAP predict long-term use (Aloia, Arnedt, Stanchina, et al., 2007; Weaver, Kribbs, et al., 1997), it is critically important to understand and examine opportunities to intervene on factors that influence early commitments to use CPAP. This insight will potentiate the development of patient-centered and -tailored interventions to improve CPAP adherence at the individual level while collectively promoting the health outcomes of the OSA population.

Our study confirms that social cognitive theory is applicable to the unique health behavior of using CPAP treatment. Indeed, the interacting determinants of health as described by Albert Bandura (1977) in relationship to decisions to accept and use CPAP were clearly described by our study participants. This affirmation suggests that any one measured domain within the model (i.e., barriers, facilitators, outcome expectancies) is not likely to identify persons at risk for nonadherence to CPAP. Rather, our study findings support the complex and reciprocating nature of the theoretical model as it applies to this health behavior, and offer clarity to our understanding of CPAP adherence as a multifactorial, iterative decision-making process. It is therefore important to ascertain an understanding of the context of the individual from the initial diagnosis through early treatment use to address the complex nature of the problem of adherence to CPAP and to prospectively identify those likely to be nonadherent to the treatment.

In our study, the experience and perception of symptoms contributed to the participants' motivation to seek diagnosis and treatment and to adhere to CPAP treatment. Although studies that have examined pretreatment symptoms, particularly subjective sleepiness, have produced inconsistent results with regard to subsequent CPAP use, these studies have measured symptoms on quantitative scales that define specific scenarios of "impairment" related to the symptom of interest (i.e., Epworth Sleepiness Scale (Johns, 1993), Functional Outcomes of Sleep Questionnaire (Weaver, Laizner, et al., 1997), Stanford Sleepiness Scale (MacLean, Fekken, Saskin, & Knowles, 1992; Engleman et al., 1996; Hui et al., 2001; Janson, Noges, Svedberg-Randt, & Lindberg, 2000; Kribbs et al., 1993; Lewis et al., 2004; McArdle et al., 1999; Sin et al., 2002; Weaver, Laizner, et al., 1997). Yet, as our study highlights, perceptions of need relative to one's experience of symptoms were highly individual and significantly influenced decisions to pursue both diagnosis and treatment. Consistent with perceptions that influence medicine-taking behavior (Hansen, Holstein, & Hansen, 2009), particular situations necessitated the pursuit of diagnosis and use of the treatment. The experience of symptoms and the impact of symptoms on daily life were highly variable among participants and not readily amenable to discrete categorization. Understanding particular situations is important insight to explaining adherence to CPAP.

Recognizing and acknowledging that perceived symptoms are part of a disease process and logically linked to the diagnosis of OSA was important to the participants of our study, and to their commitment to move forward from diagnosis to treatment, consistent with Engleman and Wild's findings (2003). A recent intervention study to promote CPAP adherence incorporated specific strategies that address "personalization" of OSA symptoms (Aloia, Arnedt, Riggs, Hecht, & Borrelli, 2004; Aloia, Arnedt, Millman, et al., 2007). Results of this randomized controlled trial showed lower CPAP discontinuation rates among those participants who were in the motivational enhancement and education group when compared with "usual care," suggesting the importance of assisting persons diagnosed with OSA to make the connection between the objectively measured disease/diagnosis and their lived experience of the disease (Aloia, Arnedt, Millman, et al., 2007). Personalizing symptoms, recognizing the impact of symptoms on daily function, and identifying the meaning of disease in terms of the perception of one's own health were clearly described by participants in our study. Adherent and nonadherent participants clearly expressed differences in their experiences of having OSA, including the impact of functional impairment on social relationships. From these differing perspectives, participants defined outcome expectations and health risks associated with OSA in different ways, possibly influencing their eventual decision to use or discontinue CPAP.

The described importance of participants' early experiences with CPAP and their initial response to CPAP treatment, both during the CPAP sleep study and during the first week of CPAP use, were influential on participants' interest in continuing to use CPAP. Our study results are consistent with Van de Mortel, Laird, and Jarrett's (2000) findings in which nonadherent, CPAP-treated OSA patients had complaints about their sleep study experience and described "major" problems on the night of their CPAP titration. Similarly, Lewis et al. (2004) found that problems identified on the first night of CPAP use, albeit on autotitrating CPAP, were consistent with lower CPAP use. Not only has the initial experience in terms of difficulties with CPAP been identified as important to subsequent CPAP adherence, but also the patient's response to the first night of CPAP (i.e., degree of sleep improvement) has been correlated with subsequent CPAP adherence (Drake et al., 2003). The importance of promoting a positive initial experience with CPAP and providing anticipatory guidance about outcome expectations is highlighted by our findings.

The significance of social support, both proximate and within the broader social network, was an important facilitator of CPAP use among adherers in our study. Differences between the experiences of married and unmarried individuals with OSA revealed the described importance of an immediate, proximate source of support for CPAP use. Our finding is consistent with previous findings that those CPAP users who lived alone were significantly less likely to use their CPAP than those who lived with someone (Lewis et al., 2004). Not only are immediate sources of support important for continued use of CPAP, but also shared experiences with CPAP from less-immediate social sources. Participants in our study described social relationships as motivators to seek diagnosis, providing positive reinforcement for persisting with treatment use, and a source for sharing tips on managing OSA and CPAP. Studies exploring reasons for nonadherence to antituberculosis drugs have similarly identified the importance of social influences on seeking treatment and using treatment (Naidoo, Dick, & Cooper, 2009). Among CPAP-treated OSA patients, intervention studies that included feedback to participants, positive reinforcement, inclusion of a support person, and assistance with trouble-shooting difficulties resulted in higher CPAP adherence among participants in the intervention groups as compared with placebo or usual-care groups (Aloia et al., 2001; Chervin, Theut, Bassetti, & Aldrich, 1997; Hoy, Vennelle, Kingshott, Engleman, & Douglas, 1999). Confirming the applicability of these intervention strategies, the described experiences of participants in our study provide empirical support for adherence interventions that include a support person, provide

Qualitative Health Research, 2010; 20(7):873–892.

early feedback and positive reinforcement to patients, and assist with trouble-shooting difficulties in the early treatment period.

Barriers to subsequent CPAP use that were identified by participants of our study included the process of having to put a mask on every night, aesthetic issues with mask/headgear use, inconvenience of having to use a machine to sleep, and daily routines that were disrupted by CPAP. Consistent with previous studies (Engleman et al., 1994; Hui et al., 2001; Massie et al., 1999; Sanders et al., 1986), side effects of CPAP were not emphasized by participants as barriers to CPAP use. Although identified barriers did not necessitate nonadherence to CPAP in our study, it was important for individuals who experienced such barriers to identify positive reasons to use CPAP and successfully mitigate barriers, often with the help of others.

This study had several limitations. First, although the sample size of 15 was adequate for a qualitative study, there was limited power to conduct any exploratory quantitative analyses. Although not the objective of this study, quantitative exploration of commonly used measures of subjective sleepiness, functional impairment, and adherence to CPAP correlated with descriptive, quantified typologies of adherent and nonadherent CPAP users would support the findings of the study. Study participants included predominantly male veterans with severe OSA who had relatively high educational preparation. Examining this typology in a larger, more heterogeneous sample of OSA patients is needed. As the relationship of gender, disease severity, symptom perception, and disease- specific literacy with CPAP adherence has not been clearly defined, replicating this study in a more diverse sample and expanding concurrently measured quantitative outcomes would be informative and supportive of typology refinement or expansion. Finally, to reduce the potential confounding effect of clinically delivered psychoeducation, we enrolled participants referred to the study from a single clinical provider with limited participant–provider interaction at the first prediagnostic evaluation. However, participants may have had telephone contact with the sleep center staff, or had unscheduled visits at the sleep center that were not controlled for in any way in our study.

Our mixed methods, exploratory study, employing a predominantly qualitative methodology, achieved saturation of themes regarding the diagnosis of OSA and nightly CPAP use during the first week of treatment. The study results are consistent with previous studies of CPAP, even when adherence, in many previous studies, was defined as four hours/night of use rather than six hours/night of use, as in our study. With recent evidence suggesting better outcomes with longer nightly CPAP use (Stradling & Davies, 2000; Weaver et al., 2007; Zimmerman, Arnedt, Stanchina, Millman, & Aloia, 2006), applying a definition of CPAP adherence of six hours vs. four hours likely contributed to more robust differences in described beliefs and perceptions among adherers and nonadherers. To our knowledge, the results of our study provide the first published, narrative descriptions of CPAP adherers and nonadherers that support an overall composite of characteristics that might be useful in identifying specific subgroups of patients who are most likely to benefit from tailored interventions to lessen the risk for subsequent CPAP nonadherence. To date, studies have provided adherence promotion interventions to unselected groups, possibly minimizing variation of response between intervention and control groups. Future randomized controlled trials testing CPAP adherence interventions delivered to participants who are selected based on their risk for treatment failure because of nonadherence are necessary to evaluate intervention effectiveness.

■ Acknowledgments

We acknowledge the sleep center staff's commitment to the conduct and completion of the study, and the exemplary transcription services provided by Charlene Hunt at Transcribing4You~Homework4You.

■ Declaration of Conflicting Interests

The authors declared a potential conflict of interest (e.g., a financial relationship with the commercial organizations or products discussed in this article) as follows: Dr. Kuna has received contractual support and equipment from Phillips Respironics, Inc. Dr. Weaver has a licensing agreement with Phillips Respironics, Inc., for the Functional Outcomes of Sleep Questionnaire.

■ Funding

The authors disclosed receipt of the following financial support for the research and/authorship of this article: The study was supported by award number F31NR9315 (Sawyer) from the National Institute of Nursing Research. The content is solely the responsibility of the authors and does not necessarily represent the official views of the National Institute of Nursing Research or the National Institutes of Health.

Bios

Amy M. Sawyer, PhD, RN, is a postdoctoral research fellow at the University of Pennsylvania School of Nursing, Philadelphia, Pennsylvania, and a nurse researcher at the Philadelphia Veterans Affairs Medical Center, Philadelphia, Pennsylvania, USA.

Janet A. Deatrick, PhD, RN, FAAN, is an associate professor and associate director, Center for Health Equities Research, at the University of Pennsylvania School of Nursing, Philadelphia, Pennsylvania, USA.

Samuel T. Kuna, MD, is an associate professor of medicine at the University of Pennsylvania School of Medicine and chief, Pulmonary, Critical Care and Sleep Medicine, at the Philadelphia Veterans Affairs Medical Center, Philadelphia, Pennsylvania, USA.

Terri E. Weaver, PhD, RN, FAAN, is the Ellen and Robert Kapito Professor in Nursing Science, chair, Biobehavioral Health Sciences Division, and associate director, Biobehavioral Research Center, at the University of Pennsylvania School of Nursing, Philadelphia, Pennsylvania, USA.

Corresponding Author

Amy M. Sawyer, University of Pennsylvania School of Nursing, Claire

M. Fagin Hall, 307b, 418 Curie Blvd., Philadelphia, PA 19104, USA Email: asawyer@nursing.upenn.edu

REFERENCES

Al Lawati, N. M., Patel, S., & Ayas, N. T. (2009). Epidemiology, risk factors, and consequences of obstructive sleep apnea and short sleep duration. *Progress in Cardiovascular Diseases, 51*, 285–293.

Aloia, M. S., Arnedt, J., Riggs, R. L., Hecht, J., & Borrelli, B. (2004). Clinical management of poor adherence to CPAP: Motivational enhancement. *Behavioral Sleep Medicine, 2*(4), 205–222.

Aloia, M. S., Arnedt, J. T., Millman, R. P., Stanchina, M., Carlisle, C., Hecht, J., et al. (2007). Brief behavioral therapies reduce early positive airway pressure discontinuation rates in sleep apnea syndrome: Preliminary findings. *Behavioral Sleep Medicine, 5*, 89–104.

Aloia, M. S., Arnedt, J. T., Stanchina, M., & Millman, R. P. (2007). How early in treatment is PAP adherence established? Revisiting night-to-night variability. *Behavioral Sleep Medicine, 5*, 229–240.

Aloia, M. S., Arnedt, J. T., Stepnowsky, C., Hecht, J., & Borrelli, B. (2005). Predicting treatment adherence in obstructive sleep apnea using principles of behavior change. *Journal of Clinical Sleep Medicine, 1*(4), 346–353.

Aloia, M. S., Di Dio, L., Ilniczky, N., Perlis, M. L., Greenblatt, D. W., & Giles, D. E. (2001). Improving compliance with nasal CPAP and vigilance in older adults with OAHS. *Sleep and Breathing, 5*(1), 13–21.

American Academy of Sleep Medicine Task Force. (1999). Sleep-related breathing disorders in adults: Recommendations for syndrome definitions and measurement techniques in clinical research. *Sleep, 22*, 667–689.

Bandura, A. (1977). Self-efficacy: Toward a unifying theory of behavioral change. *Psychological Reviews, 84*, 191–215.

Bandura, A. (1992). Exercise of personal agency through the self-efficacy mechanism. In R. Schwarzer (Ed.), *Self-efficacy: Thought control of action* (pp. 3–38). Philadelphia: Hemisphere.

Bandura, A. (2002). Social cognitive theory in cultural context. *Applied psychology: An International Review, 51*(2), 269–290.

Bandura, A. (2004). Health promotion by social cognitive means. *Health Education & Behavior, 31*(2), 143–164.

Chervin, R. D., Theut, S., Bassetti, C., & Aldrich, M. S. (1997). Compliance with nasal CPAP can be improved by simple interventions. *Sleep, 20*, 284–289.

Creswell, J. W., Plano Clark, V. L., Gutmann, M. L., & Hanson, W. (2003). Advanced mixed methods research designs. In A. Tashakkori & C. Teddlie (Eds.), *Handbook of mixed methods in social & behavioral research* (pp. 209–240). Thousand Oaks, CA: Sage.

Drake, C. L., Day, R., Hudgel, D., Stefadu, Y., Parks, M., Syron, M. L., et al. (2003). Sleep during titration predicts continuous positive airway pressure compliance. *Sleep, 26*, 308–311.

Engleman, H. M., Asgari-Jirandeh, N., McLeod, A. L., Ramsay, C. F., Deary, I. J., & Douglas, N. J. (1996). Self-reported use of CPAP and benefits of CPAP therapy. *Chest, 109*, 1470–1476.

Engleman, H. M., Martin, S. E., & Douglas, N. J. (1994). Compliance with CPAP therapy in patients with the sleep apnoea/ hypopnoea syndrome. *Thorax, 49*, 263–266.

Engleman, H. M., & Wild, M. (2003). Improving CPAP use by patients with the sleep apnoea/ hypopnoea syndrome (SAHS). *Sleep Medicine Reviews*, 7(1), 81–99.

Gay, P., Weaver, T., Loube, D., & Iber, C. (2006). Evaluation of positive airway pressure treatment for sleep related breathing disorders in adults. *Sleep, 29*, 381–401.

Graneheim, U. H., & Lundman, B. (2004). Qualitative content analysis in nursing research: Concepts, procedures and measures to achieve trustworthiness. *Nursing Education Today, 24*, 105–112.

Grunstein, R. R., Stewart, D. A., Lloyd, H., Akinci, M., Cheng, N., & Sullivan, C. E. (1996). Acute withdrawal of nasal CPAP in obstructive sleep apnea does not cause a rise in stress hormones. *Sleep, 19*, 774–782.

Hansen, D. L., Holstein, B. E., & Hansen, E. H. (2009). "I'd rather not take it, but · · ·": Young women's perceptions of medicines. *Qualitative Health Research, 19*, 829–839.

Harsch, I., Schahin, S., Radespiel-Troger, M., Weintz, O., Jahrei, H., Fuchs, S., et al. (2004). Continuous positive airway pressure treatment rapidly improves insulin sensitivity in patients with obstructive sleep apnea syndrome. *American Journal of Respiratory & Critical Care Medicine, 169*, 156–162.

Hoy, C. J., Vennelle, M., Kingshott, R. N., Engleman, H. M., & Douglas, N. J. (1999). Can intensive support improve continuous positive airway pressure use in patients with the sleep apnea/hypopnea syndrome? *American Journal of Respiratory & Critical Care Medicine, 159*, 1096–1100.

Hsieh, H., & Shannon, S. (2005). Three approaches to qualitative content analysis. *Qualitative Health Research, 15*,1277–1288.

Hui, D., Choy, D., Li, T., Ko, F., Wong, K., Chan, J., et al. (2001). Determinants of continuous positive airway pressure compliance in a group of Chinese patients with obstructive sleep apnea. *Chest, 120*, 170–176.

Janson, C., Noges, E., Svedberg-Randt, S., & Lindberg, E. (2000). What characterizes patients who are unable to tolerate continuous positive airway pressure (CPAP) treatment? *Respiratory Medicine, 94*, 145–149.

Johns, M. (1993). Daytime sleepiness, snoring, and obstructive sleep apnea. The Epworth Sleepiness Scale. *Chest, 103*, 30–36.

Kribbs, N. B., Pack, A. I., Kline, L. R., Smith, P. L., Schwartz, A. R., Schubert, N. M., et al. (1993). Objective measurement of patterns of nasal CPAP use by patients with obstructive sleep apnea. *American Review of Respiratory Diseases, 147*, 887–895.

Krieger, J. (1992). Long-term compliance with nasal continuous positive airway pressure (CPAP) in obstructive sleep apnea patients and nonapneic snorers. *Sleep, 15*, S42–S46.

Lewis, K., Seale, L., Bartle, I. E., Watkins, A. J., & Ebden, P. (2004). Early predictors of CPAP use for the treatment of obstructive sleep apnea. *Sleep, 27*, 134–138.

MacLean, A. W., Fekken, G. C., Saskin, P., & Knowles, J. B. (1992). Psychometric evaluation of the Stanford Sleepiness Scale. *Journal of Sleep Research 1*, 35–39.

Massie, C., Hart, R., Peralez, K., & Richards, G. (1999). Effects of humidification on nasal symptoms and compliance in sleep apnea patients using continuous positive airway pressure. *Chest, 116*, 403–408.

McArdle, N., Devereux, G., Heidarnejad, H., Engleman, H. M., Mackay, T., & Douglas, N. J. (1999). Long-term use of CPAP therapy for sleep apnea/hypopnea syndrome. *American Journal of Respiratory and Critical Care Medicine, 159*, 1108–1114.

Meurice, J. C., Dore, P., Paquereau, J., Neau, J. P., Ingrand, P., Chavagnat, J. J., et al. (1994). Predictive factors of long-term compliance with nasal continuous positive airway pressure treatment in sleep apnea syndrome. *Chest, 105*, 429–434.

Naidoo, P., Dick, J., & Cooper, D. (2009). Exploring tuberculosis patients' adherence to treatment regimens and prevention programs at a public health site. *Qualitative Health Research 19*, 55–70.

Nieto, F., Young, T., Lind, B., Shahar, E., Samet, J., Redline, S., et al. (2000). Association of sleep-disordered breathing, sleep apnea, and hypertension in a large community-based study. *Journal of the American Medical Association, 283*, 1829–1836.

Peppard, P., Young, T., Palta, M., & Skatrud, J. (2000). Prospective study of the association between sleep-disordered breathing and hypertension. *New England Journal of Medicine, 342*, 1378–1384.

Rechtschaffen, A., & Kales, A. (Eds.). (1968). *A manual of standardized terminology, techniques and scoring system for sleep stages in human subjects.* Los Angeles: BIS/BRI. Reeves-Hoche, M. K., Meck, R., & Zwillich, C. W. (1994). Nasal CPAP: An objective evaluation of patient compliance. *American Journal of Respiratory & Critical Care Medicine, 149*, 149–154.

Richards, D., Bartlett, D. J., Wong, K., Malouff, J., & Grunstein, R. R. (2007). Increased adherence to CPAP with a group cognitive behavioral treatment intervention: A randomized trial. *Sleep, 30*, 635–640.

Rosenthal, L., Gerhardstein, R., Lumley, A., Guido, P., Day, R., Syron, M. L., et al. (2000). CPAP therapy in patients with mild OSA: Implementation and treatment outcome. *Sleep Medicine, 1*, 215–220.

Russo-Magno, P., O'Brien, A., Panciera, T., & Rounds, S. (2001). Compliance with CPAP therapy in older men with obstructive sleep apnea. *Journal of American Geriatric Society, 49*, 1205–1211.

Sanders, M. H., Gruendl, C. A., & Rogers, R. M. (1986). Patient compliance with nasal CPAP therapy for sleep apnea. *Chest, 90*, 330–333.

Schwarzer, R., & Fuchs, R. (1996). Self-efficacy and health behaviours. In M. Conner & P. Norman (Eds.), *Predicting health behaviour: Research and practice with social cognition models* (pp. 163–196). Philadelphia: Open Press.

Schweitzer, P., Chambers, G., Birkenmeier, N., & Walsh, J. (1997). Nasal continuous positive airway pressure (CPAP) compliance at six, twelve, and eighteen months. *Sleep Research, 16*, 186.

Sin, D., Mayers, I., Man, G., & Pawluk, L. (2002). Long-term compliance rates to continuous positive airway pressure in obstructive sleep apnea: A population-based study. *Chest, 121*, 430–435.

Stepnowsky, C., Bardwell, W. A., Moore, P. J., Ancoli-Israel, S., & Dimsdale, J. E. (2002). Psychologic correlates of compliance with continuous positive airway pressure. *Sleep, 25*, 758–762.

Stepnowsky, C., Marler, M. R., & Ancoli-Israel, S. (2002). Determinants of nasal CPAP compliance. *Sleep Medicine,3*, 239–247.

Stradling, J., & Davies, R. (2000). Is more NCPAP better? *Sleep, 23*, S150–S153.

Streubert Speziale, H., & Carpenter, D. (2003). *Qualitative research in nursing* (3rd ed.). Philadelphia: Lippincott Williams & Wilkins.

Sullivan, C., Barthon-Jones, M., Issa, F., & Eves, L. (1981). Reversal of obstructive sleep apnea by continuous positive airway pressure applied through the nares. *Lancet, 1*, 862–865.

Tashakkori, A., & Teddlie, C. (1989). *Mixed methodology: Combining qualitative and quantitative approaches*. London: Sage.

Van de Mortel, T. F., Laird, P., & Jarrett, C. (2000). Client perceptions of the polysomnography experience and compliance with therapy. *Contemporary Nurse, 9*, 161–168.

Weaver, T. E., & Grunstein, R. R. (2008). Adherence to continuous positive airway pressure therapy: The challenges to effective treatment. *Proceedings of the American Thoracic Society, 5*, 173–178.

Weaver, T. E., Kribbs, N. B., Pack, A. I., Kline, L. R., Chugh, D. K., Maislin, G., et al. (1997). Night-to-night variability in CPAP use over first three months of treatment. *Sleep, 20*, 278–283.

Weaver, T. E., Laizner, A. M., Evans, L. K., Maislin, G., Chugh, D. K., Lyon, K., et al. (1997). An instrument to measure functional status outcomes for disorders of excessive sleepiness. *Sleep, 20*, 835–843.

Weaver, T. E., Maislin, G., Dinges, D. F., Bloxham, T., George, C. F. P., Greenberg, H., et al. (2007). Relationship between hours of CPAP use and achieving normal levels of sleepiness and daily functioning. *Sleep, 30*, 711–719.

Weaver, T. E., Maislin, G., Dinges, D. F., Younger, J., Cantor, C., McCloskey, S., et al. (2003). Self-efficacy in sleep apnea: Instrument development and patient perceptions of obstructive sleep apnea risk, treatment benefit, and volition to use continuous positive airway pressure. *Sleep, 26*, 727–732.

Wild, M., Engleman, H. M., Douglas, N. J., & Espie, C. A. (2004). Can psychological factors help us to determine adherence to CPAP? A prospective study. *European Respiratory Journal, 24*, 461–465.

Young, T., Palta, M., Dempsey, J., Skatrud, J., Weber, S., & Badr, S. (1993). The occurrence of sleep-disordered breathing among middle-aged adults. *New England Journal of Medicine, 328*, 1230–1235.

Young, T., Peppard, P., & Gottlieb, D. (2002). Epidemiology of obstructive sleep apnea: A population health perspective. *American Journal of Respiratory & Critical Care Medicine, 165*, 1217–1239.

Zimmerman, M. E., Arnedt, T., Stanchina, M., Millman, R. P., & Aloia, M. S. (2006). Normalization of memory performance and positive airway pressure adherence in memory-impaired patients with obstructive sleep apnea. *Chest, 130*, 1772–1778.

Critique of Sawyer et al.'s Study (2010) "Differences in Perceptions of the Diagnosis and Treatment of Obstructive Sleep Apnea and Continuous Positive Airway Pressure Therapy among Adherers and Nonadherers"

OVERALL SUMMARY

This was a well-written, interesting report of a study on a significant topic. The mixed methods QUAL(quan) approach that was used was ideal for combining rich narrative interview data with objective, quantitative measures of adherence to continuous positive airway pressure (CPAP) treatment. The use of a longitudinal design enabled the researchers to gain insights into changes in patients' perceptions from diagnosis to treatment. The study design and methods were described in commendable detail, and the methods themselves were of exceptionally high quality. The authors provided considerable information about how the trustworthiness of the study was enhanced. The results were nicely elaborated, and the researchers incorporated numerous excerpts from the interviews. This was, overall, an excellent paper describing a very strong study.

TITLE

The title of this report was long, and perhaps a few words could have been omitted (e.g., "differences in" could be removed without affecting readers' understanding of the study). Nevertheless, the title did describe key aspects of the research. The title conveyed the central topic (perceptions about obstructive sleep apnea [OSA] and CPAP therapy). It also communicated the nature of the analysis, which compared perceptions of adherers and nonadherers to CPAP. If this paper had been published in a different journal, it probably would have been desirable to communicate in the title that the study was primarily qualitative, but inasmuch as it was published in *Qualitative Health Research* (QHR), that was not necessary. (However, "qualitative" was not used as a keyword for retrieving this study, either. The keywords included "content analysis" and "mixed methods," but in a search for qualitative studies on OSA or CPAP, this paper might be missed).

ABSTRACT

As required by QHR, the abstract was written as a traditional abstract (no subheadings) of 150 words or fewer. Although brief, the abstract clearly described major aspects of the study so that readers could quickly learn whether the entire paper might be of interest. The first sentence of the abstract described the significance of the topic. The methods were succinctly presented, covering the overall mixed methods design, the longitudinal nature of the study (two rounds of interviews), the sample (15 OSA patients), the basic type of analysis (content analysis), and the focus on comparing adherent and nonadherent patients using objectively measured CPAP use. The use of social cognitive theory to guide the inquiry was noted. Although specific results were not described, the abstract indicated areas in which differences between adherers and nonadherers were observed. Finally, the last sentence suggests some possible applications for the results in terms of developing tailored interventions to promote CPAP use.

INTRODUCTION

The introduction to this study was concise and well organized. It began with a paragraph about OSA as an important chronic health problem, describing its prevalence, its effects, and its primary medical treatment, that is, CPAP. This first paragraph helps readers understand the significance of the topic.

Much of the rest of the introduction discussed adherence to CPAP, which has consistently been found to be low. The researchers nicely set the stage for their study by summarizing evidence about rates of adherence and factors predicting adherence. They also described prior research that affected some of their design decisions, such as studies that have found that early experiences with CPAP—that is, in the first week of use—influence patients' perceptions. The studies cited in the introduction include both older studies and ones written very recently, suggesting that the authors were summarizing state-of-the-art knowledge.

The introduction then further set the stage for the new study by describing knowledge gaps: "To date, there are relatively few studies that have systematically examined the influence of disease and treatment perceptions and beliefs on CPAP adherence (p. 443)." The authors stated their four interrelated research questions, which were well suited to an in-depth qualitative approach.

CONCEPTUAL FRAMEWORK

The article devoted a section to a description of the conceptual framework that underpinned the research. The authors used a conceptual framework that is widely used in health behavior research, Bandura's social cognitive theory. They presented a nice summary of the theory, and included a useful conceptual map (Fig. 1, p. 444). They also noted that Bandura's model is relevant within a qualitative inquiry because of explicit recognition of the role of context: "Bandura suggested that the application of social cognitive theory must be situated in context, recognizing that 'human behavior is socially situated, richly contextualized, and conditionally expressed" (p. 444). One puzzling thing, however, is that both in this section and in the first subsection of the results, considerable attention is paid to the role of *knowledge* in influencing health behaviors. Yet, knowledge is not a component of the theory as depicted in Figure 1.

METHOD

The method section was well organized into four subsections, and was unusually thorough in providing details about how the researchers conducted this study.

Design

Sawyer and colleagues used a mixed methods design to study patients' perceptions and beliefs about OSA and CPAP, and to explore differences among adherers and nonadherers. The researchers used terminology that was slightly different than that used in the textbook, which is not unusual because the field of mixed methods research is relatively new and is evolving. They described their design as a concurrent nested mixed methods design, and provided a citation to a paper by Creswell and Plano-Clark (2003), the two authors whose more recent terminology was used in this textbook. (The 2003 paper was probably a recent publication when the Sawyer et al. study was being planned). Using the terminology presented in the textbook, the design would best be described as an embedded QUAL (quan) design. Had Sawyer and colleagues used Morse's notation system, they might have characterized the study as QUAL + quan, which indicates that the data for the two strands were collected concurrently, and that the qualitative component was dominant.

The design section also noted that the design was longitudinal, with data collected both at initial OSA diagnosis and through the first week of CPAP treatment. Such a longitudinal design is an excellent way to track patients' perceptions and beliefs from diagnosis to the early treatment phase. The decision about *when* to collect the two rounds of data was well supported by earlier research. An excellent graphic (Fig. 2, p. 446) illustrated the study design and the timing of key events in the conduct of the study, such as enrollment and collection of demographic data, receipt of treatment education, conduct of the diagnostic sleep study and the CPAP sleep study, and the two interviews.

Participants

The researchers clearly defined the group of interest and described how participants were recruited into the study. Participants were adults with suspected OSA who were recruited from a Veterans Affairs sleep clinic. To be eligible, patients had to meet various clinical criteria (e.g., had at least moderate OSA, defined as at least 15 apnea or hypopnea events per hour in a sleep study) and practical criteria (had to speak and understand English). Patients were excluded if their responses could have been confounded by prior CPAP experiences, because the researchers were interested in understanding the perceptions and beliefs early in the diagnosis and CPAP treatment transition.

The researchers also excluded individuals who refused CPAP treatment prior to the actual treatment, and Figure 1 suggests that one such person was dropped from the study. That is, 16 patients were interviewed for the pretreatment interview, but only 15 were interviewed a second time, and the analysis was based on responses from 15 patients. (Sample size issues were discussed in a later section).

One comment about this section is that we would have described the sampling approach more as convenience sampling than as purposive sampling. Many qualitative researchers say that their sampling was purposive when they purposefully select people with the characteristic or experience that is the focus of the research. However, we think of these more as eligibility criteria, which need to be identified to ensure that those in the study can provide "expert testimony" about the experience of interest. It would appear that the participants were a convenience sample of those meeting the eligibility criteria, and who were referred by a sleep specialist in one particular clinic. In our view, the term *purposive* connotes conscious and deliberate efforts to sample *particular* exemplars from those who are eligible and who can best meet the conceptual needs of the study. For example, maximum variation sampling is a purposive strategy that involves a deliberate attempt to select participants who not only meet the eligibility criteria but also vary along dimensions thought to be important in understanding the full range of the phenomenon of interest. In this study, the researchers could, for example, have deliberately sampled people with varying degrees of social support, to ensure that this important dimension would have adequate representation. As it turns out, there was variation in social support (marital status) among the study participants, but this does not appear to have been the result of a purposive strategy. With a small sample, and with a goal of looking at differences between adherers and nonadherers, a purposive strategy of sampling patients on dimensions known to differentiate these groups would have increased the likelihood that both groups would be adequately represented.

In terms of the design, the sampling approach for this study would be described as *identical sampling*, a term not mentioned in the textbook. In an identical sample, all study participants provide both qualitative and quantitative data—unlike a nested design, which involves selecting a *subset* of people from the quantitative strand to provide qualitative information.

Procedures

The section on "Procedures" presented considerable information, focusing primarily on data collection. The section began by describing the two sleep studies that all study participants underwent. In both sleep studies, the patient's Apnea–Hypopnea Index (AHI) was computed via a polysomnogram. The initial AHI provided information that helped to determine study eligibility.

Next, the researchers described the major forms of data collection, which included semistructured interviews and instrumentation to assess CPAP adherence objectively. In the subsection on the in-depth interviews, the article specified that the data were collected by a single investigator at two points in time: within a week following OSA diagnosis but before treatment, and then after the first week of treatment. The authors noted that participants were given choices about where the interviews would take place, in an effort to minimize attrition. And, in fact, there was no attrition in this study.

The interview guides were described in admirable detail. Table 1 (p. 447) listed the questions that guided the initial interview, and Table 2 (p. 448) listed questions for the post-treatment interview. These tables were an excellent way to communicate the nature of the interviews to readers, and the text provided even more detail. For example, a rationale for using a topic guide was provided ("to ensure that a consistent sequence and set of questions were addressed across participants" (p. 445)). Consistency was also enhanced by having a single interviewer responsible for conducting all interviews. To maximize data quality, the interviews were digitally recorded and transcribed by a professional transcriptionist.

The interviewer also maintained field notes before and after each interview. Commendably, these field notes were not only descriptive (i.e., describing participants and the interview environments), but also "served as interviewer reflexivity notations (i.e., interviewer biases, suppositions, and presuppositions of the research topic)" (p. 446).

An important feature of this study was that CPAP adherence was not assessed by self-report. Rather, adherence was objectively determined based on quantitative data from the CPAP machine. A standard definition of "CPAP use" was provided, and a criterion of 6 hours or more per night of CPAP use was established for adherence. The researchers provided a convincing rationale for using the 6-hour limit as the cutoff point for adherence versus nonadherence.

One further note is that the researchers might have considered administering a self-efficacy scale during the course of their study, to anchor their discussion of self-efficacy, which is a key construct in their conceptual model. Although many of the major constructs in the model were ones that merited qualitative exploration, self-efficacy is one that perhaps could have been examined from both a qualitative and quantitative perspective, especially in a study that is explicitly mixed methods in design.

Data Analysis

The authors are to be congratulated for their detailed description of their data analysis methods. Not only did they carefully explain data analytic procedures in the text, but they also provided a wonderful flow chart (Figure 3, p. 449) illustrating the sequence of steps they followed. It is extremely rare to find such rich information about data analysis in a qualitative or mixed methods study.

The qualitative data were content analyzed, an approach that is appropriate, given that the study was primarily descriptive. That is, this study was not designed to shed light on the lived experience of the patients (phenomenology), nor on their process of adapting to CPAP treatment (e.g., in a grounded theory study). The purpose was to obtain descriptive information at two points in time about participants' perceptions and beliefs relevant to OSA and CPAP. The researchers explained the procedures used in the content analysis, and provided citations for the approach used.

The data analysis section explained how theory-driven themes were extracted in a manner consistent with the broad conceptualization of health behavior articulated in Bandura's theory. The authors offered specific illustrations in Table 3 (p. 450), which listed broad theoretical determinants of health behavior in the first column, and then relevant themes for each determinant as derived from the content analysis. For example, for the broad construct "Perceived self-efficacy," there were five relevant themes, such as "Fitting treatment into life" and "Problem-solving difficulties."

The section on data analysis also included important information about methods the researchers used to enhance trustworthiness—and these methods were strong. For example, one investigator coded all the interview data. Then, an independent expert recoded a randomly selected 15% of the data from each interview. Overall agreement between the study coder and the expert coder was a high 94%. For any differences of opinion about coding, the discrepancy was resolved by consensus. The theme definitions used in the coding, which were developed by the investigative team, were reviewed by two experts, a qualitative methodologist and an expert in the application of the theoretical constructs.

Importantly, the qualitative data were coded and content analyzed for themes by an investigator who was blinded to whether the participant was classified as adherent or nonadherent based on the quantitative data. Only after coding was complete was the adherence status of participants revealed. At that point, across-case analysis was examined "from an integrative perspective, using adherent and nonadherent as anchors…to identify common perceptions, beliefs, and experiences within the groups of interest." The authors used an excellent device—called a *meta-matrix*, to integrate the qualitative and quantitative data.

RESULTS

The results section began with a description of the study sample, all of whom were military veterans. Table 4 (p. 452) showed basic descriptive statistics on the demographics of the 15 participants, including their gender, race/ethnicity, marital and employment status, educational background, and age. Clinical information (e.g., mean weight, AHI events/hour, and CPAP adherence in terms of hours per night) was also presented. The text stated that the sample included six adherers and nine nonadherers. The introductory paragraph of the results section also noted that data saturation was reached at 15 participants, and that sampling stopped at that point.

Much of the results section was organized according to differences between adherers and nonadherers to CPAP therapy. The differences were nicely organized into major thematic categories, such as "Knowledge and perceived health status," "Goal setting and outcome expectancies," "Facilitators of and barriers to CPAP use," and "Perceived self-efficacy." Key differences between the two groups (and a few areas of overlap) within these major groupings were described and supported with rich excerpts from the interview transcripts.

Social support emerged as an important issue in CPAP adherence, consistent with previous studies. Thus, the researchers performed a useful supplementary analysis in which they examined differences between married and unmarried patients.

The analysis section concluded with a typology (descriptive profiles) of adherent and nonadherent CPAP users, based on an integration of the data across themes. Table 5 (p. 459) nicely summarized their typology.

DISCUSSION

Sawyer and colleagues offered a thoughtful discussion of their findings. Their discussion highlighted ways in which their findings complement and extend the existing body of evidence on CPAP adherence. The discussion nicely wove together findings from the current study and previous studies and discussed the findings within the context of the theoretical framework.

The authors also noted some of the study's limitations. They pointed out, for example, that study participants were all veterans with fairly high levels of education, and thus exploration with a more diverse population of OSA patients would be desirable. The researchers also pointed out that the small sample size of 15 provided limited power for conducting quantitative analyses of numerical data they had at their disposal, such as measures of subjective sleepiness and functional impairment. They noted that with a larger sample, they could have explored correlations between such quantitative measures and the thematic typology.

Although the discussion is reasonably lengthy, relatively little space was devoted to the implications of the study findings. The researchers noted that "The described differences between adherers and nonadherers in our study suggest critical tailored or patient-centered intervention opportunities…" Indeed, they mentioned the opportunity for tailored interventions several times in connection with their discussion of their theoretically derived themes. A bit more elaboration of how the findings could be used in an intervention might have been helpful.

GENERAL COMMENTS

Presentation

This report was clearly written, well organized, and offered an exemplary amount of detail about the research methods. The inclusion of several tables and figures provided readers with explicit and concrete information about aspects of the study that are often ignored or described only briefly. We applaud the authors, and we also applaud the journal, *Qualitative Health Research*, for not having strict page limits.[1] The need for page limits is understandable given the explosion of research that is being undertaken. However, the ability for readers to judge the quality of research evidence is also crucial, and this is sometimes hampered by constraints on researchers' ability to provide thorough information about how the research was conducted.

Ethical Aspects

The authors briefly stated steps they took to ensure ethical treatment of participants in the subsection labeled "Participants." All participants provided informed consent, and the study protocols were approved by the Institutional Review Boards of the affiliated university and the research site.

RESPONSE FROM THE SAWYER TEAM

Dr. Sawyer and her colleagues were asked if they wished to comment on this critique. Dr. Sawyer remarked that she was "in near 100% agreement with the draft critique that you provided" and that there was nothing she felt she needed to rebut. Given the generally positive nature of the critique, Dr. Sawyer noted, "I don't know that I have much in the way of response to offer—however, the suggestion to include a self-efficacy instrument is 'spot on.'"

Her email concluded with the following statement: "My study colleagues and I are very pleased with the published paper in QHR and firmly believe the paper is an excellent teaching resource for mixed methods research in health and disease." We agree.

[1] The QHR guidelines to authors that were is effect in 2010 state the journal's page limit policy as follows: "There is no predetermined word or page limit. Provided they are "tight" and concise, without unnecessary repetition and/or irrelevant data, manuscripts should be as long as they need to be."

INDEX

Note: Page numbers followed by "*f*" indicate figures; those followed by "*t*" indicate tables and those followed by "*b*" indicate boxes. Page numbers in bold denote glossary terms.

D

E

F

N

O

Q

R

T

U

GLOSSARY OF SELECTED STATISTICAL SYMBOLS

This list contains some commonly used symbols in statistics. The list is in approximate alphabetical order, with English and Greek letters intermixed. Nonletter symbols have been placed at the end.

a	Regression constant, the intercept
α	Greek alpha; significance level in hypothesis testing, probability of Type I error; also, a reliability coefficient
b	Regression coefficient, slope of the line
β	Greek beta, probability of a Type II error; also, a standardized regression coefficient (beta weight)
χ^2	Greek chi squared, a test statistic for several nonparametric tests
CI	Confidence interval around estimate of a population parameter
d	An effect size index, a standardized mean difference
df	Degrees of freedom
η^2	Greek eta squared, index of variance accounted for in ANOVA context
f	Frequency (count) for a score value
F	Test statistic used in ANOVA, ANCOVA, and other tests
H_O	Null hypothesis
H_A	Alternative hypothesis; research hypothesis
λ	Greek lambda, a test statistic used in several multivariate analyses (Wilks' lambda)
μ	Greek mu, the population mean
M	Sample mean (alternative symbol for $\bar{X}$)
MS	Mean square, variance estimate in ANOVA
n	Number of cases in a subgroup of the sample
N	Total number of cases or sample members
NNT	Number needed to treat
OR	Odds ratio
p	Probability that observed data are consistent with null hypothesis
r	Pearson's product–moment correlation coefficient for a sample
r_s	Spearman's rank-order correlation coefficient
R	Multiple correlation coefficient
R^2	Coefficient of determination, proportion of variance in *dependent variable* attributable to *independent variables*
R_c	Canonical correlation coefficient
RR	Relative risk
ρ	Greek rho, population correlation coefficient
SD	Sample standard deviation
SEM	Standard error of the mean
σ	Greek sigma (lowercase), population standard deviation
Σ	Greek sigma (uppercase), sum of
SS	Sum of squares
t	Test statistics used in *t*-tests (sometimes called Student's *t*)
U	Test statistic for the Mann-Whitney U-test
$\bar{X}$	Sample mean
x	Deviation score
Y'	Predicted value of Y, dependent variable in regression analysis
z	Standard score in a normal distribution
$\|\ \|$	Absolute value
$\leq$	Less than or equal to
$\geq$	Greater than or equal to
$\neq$	Not equal to